QUANTITATIVE APPROACHES TO MANAGEMENT

QUANTITATIVE APPROACHES TO MANAGEMENT

SEVENTH EDITION

RICHARD I. LEVIN, Ph.D.
DAVID S. RUBIN, Ph.D.
School of Business Administration
University of North Carolina at Chapel Hill

JOEL P. STINSON, Ph.D.
School of Management
Syracuse University

EVERETTE S. GARDNER, Jr., Ph.D.
College of Business
University of Houston

McGraw-Hill Publishing Company

New York   St. Louis   San Francisco   Auckland   Bogotá   Caracas
Hamburg   Lisbon   London   Madrid   Mexico   Milan
Montreal   New Delhi   Oklahoma City   Paris   San Juan
São Paulo   Singapore   Sydney   Tokyo   Toronto

Quantitative
Approaches to
Management

34567890 HDHD 99876543210

P/N 037478-3
PART OF
ISBN 0-07-909187-3

This book was set in Baskerville by Monotype Composition Company.
The editors were Kathleen L. Loy and Ira C. Roberts;
the designer was Betty Binns Graphics;
the production supervisor was Janelle S. Travers.
New drawings were done by Caliber Design Planning, Inc.
Arcata Graphics/Halliday was printer and binder.

Library of Congress Cataloging-in-Publication Data

Quantitative approaches to management.
    Bibliography: p.
    Includes index.
    1. Operations research. 2. Management science.
I. Levin, Richard I.   II. Series.
T57.6.Q36 1989   658.4'03'4   88-13169
P/N 037478-3 (Book)

PHOTO CREDITS

Chapter 1: Fredrik D. Bodin/Stock, Boston; Nancy J. Pierce/
Photo Researchers; © Tom McHugh/Photo, Researchers; H.
Armstrong Roberts; © Barbara Rios/Photo Researchers ■
Chapter 2: Ellis Herwig/Stock, Boston ■ Chapter 3: Fredrik
D. Bodin/Stock, Boston ■ Chapter 4: Nancy J. Pierce/Photo
Researchers ■ Chapter 5: © Tom McHugh/Photo
Researchers ■ Chapter 6: © David Hundley/The Stock
Market ■ Chapter 7: © Jean-Claude Lejeune/Stock, Boston ■
Chapter 8: © Werner H. Müller/Peter Arnold, Inc. ■
Chapter 9: H. Armstrong Roberts ■ Chapter 10: © Donald
Miller/Monkmeyer ■ Chapter 11: © George Ancona/
International Stock Photo ■ Chapter 12: © Jeff Dunn/The
Picture Cube ■ Chapter 13: Wide World Photos ■ Chapter
14: © Barbara Rios/Photo Researchers ■ Chapter 15: ©
Marty Heitner/Taurus Photos ■ Chapter 16: Carol Palmer/
The Picture Cube ■ Chapter 17: © Ray Ellis/Photo
Researchers.

ABOUT THE AUTHORS

RICHARD I. LEVIN has taught quantitative methods for more than 25 years at several universities. His consulting and research interests are in companies with less than $1 billion annual sales. His teaching is concentrated in the MBA program at University of North Carolina.

DAVID S. RUBIN is currently finishing up a five year stint as director of the Ph.D. program in Business Administration at University of North Carolina. He holds a joint appointment in the Department of Operations Research and does research in a number of quantitative topics including vertex generators.

JOEL P. STINSON has taught quantitative methods at Syracuse University for a number of years. He has become a recognized authority in teaching pedagogies for quantitative methods and his imprint can be found on a number of outstanding and widely used teaching aids to quantitative texts.

EVERETTE S. GARDNER, Jr. retired from the U.S. Navy as a commander after a 23-year career. While in the service he received his Ph.D. in Business Administration and went on to manage the largest inventory analysis ever accomplished in the Navy Supply area. He is widely known for his outstanding research contributions in the field of forecasting.

CONTENTS

CHAPTER 7: INVENTORY II   290
Reordering, Backorders, Discounts,
Material Requirements Planning

CHAPTER 8: LINEAR PROGRAMMING I: 340
SOLUTION METHODS
Graphic Method and Using the Computer

CHAPTER 9: LINEAR PROGRAMMING II: 384
THE SIMPLEX METHOD
Maximization and Minimization

■ CHAPTER 10: LINEAR PROGRAMMING III: 422
BUILDING LP MODELS AND INTERPRETING SOLUTIONS
Problem Formulation, Duality, Sensitivity Analysis, Linear Programming Applications

■ CHAPTER 11: SPECIALLY STRUCTURED   482
LINEAR PROGRAMS
Transportation and Assignment Problems

▓ CHAPTER 15: SIMULATION   704

▓ CHAPTER 16: MARKOV ANALYSIS   744

PREFACE

When the first edition of *Quantitative Approaches to Management* (QAM) was published there were only three or four texts available to introduce students of management to the techniques and applications of Management Science/Operations Research. Today, as we publish our seventh edition, there are more than thirty from which to choose. So why do we think our text offers both instructors and students an excellent choice pedagogically and an exceptional value as a teaching-learning aid? There are six reasons:

Freshness: Each edition of *QAM* has introduced new topics, reinforced existing pedagogies with new ones, demonstrated new ways of solving management science/operations research (MS/OR) problems, and strengthened its focus on applying MS/OR successfully. This edition continues that strong tradition with these new features:

■ Computer approaches and solutions to MS/OR problems are now found in many chapters. To help you get experience in using computers to apply the MS/OR methodologies discussed in *QAM*, a disk is a part of every copy of the text; it is located in the back flap of the book and contains all of the standard MS/OR techniques.

■ A real-world successful application of MS/OR is introduced and discussed at the end of each chapter; special attention is paid to the problem environment, the constraints to effective application, and the economic benefit that was finally realized.

■ Each chapter begins with a photographically presented MS/OR opportunity which is discussed in detail and solved later in the chapter; many of these problems come from the authors' own field experiences.

■ The discussion of linear programming and its allied techniques has been significantly expanded; the five-chapter sequence devoted to these topics now represents as comprehensive a treatment as is available in any major textbook.

■ There have been significant additions to the material on heuristic solution methods, forecasting, and the role of the computer in MS/OR.

■ Almost half of the text exercises are new; the total number of exercises has been increased by about 20%.

Teaching Flexibility and Benefits: Our new edition presents a wider set of MS/OR topics than any other textbook available. This makes it easy for instructors to design and teach the course they feel to be appropriate using one textbook. And our expanded set of instructor-focused pedagogical aids makes teaching with this text hassle-free.

Perspective: The team of authors for this edition represents a unique blend of theory and application which spans the entire continuum of MS/OR from research through complex application problems. Our author team for this edition includes the editor of a prestigious journal in the field; a theoretical mathematician who develops new mathematical programming approaches; a professor who has spent twenty years developing and perfecting teaching pedagogy in the field; and someone who probably has as much applied experience in field MS/OR applications as anyone today. Each of these unique individuals brings a different perspective to the book; together they have blended and crafted a teachable, learnable, useable, and very applicable text.

Pedagogical Aids: This edition has an unequaled set of pedagogical aids to promote effective teaching and help ensure effective learning. These include:

■ Over 2,000 margin notes
■ End of chapter quizzes (expanded in this edition)
■ Effective use of color to emphasize important concepts

- Annotated review of equations used in each chapter
- Glossary of terms introduced in each chapter
- Chapter learning objectives
- Instructor's manual
- Student workbook and study guide
- Test bank with worked out answers
- An index of applications

Computer Software: This edition of the text is accompanied by a computer diskette for the IBM PC, free to the student. The software will enable students to become accustomed to using the computer as aid to management decisions. Each problem in the text for which the computer will be appropriate will be marked by one of two symbols: a computer or a computer with a pencil. When the student sees the computer by itself, that will indicate that the entire problem is workable with the models on the disk. If there is a pencil with the computer, that means that a part of the problem can be worked out with the aid of the computer, and part of it requires some pencil work. The Instructor's Manual will carry information about those problems that need both pencil and computer work.

The menu for the software will include: forecasting, inventory models, assignment method, network models, project scheduling, dynamic programs, branch and bound, goal programming, queing models, Markov models. It is menu-driven, and a short instruction sheet will accompany the disk within the text. For those who want additional computer exercises, the Student Workbook and Study Guide will also designate which problems can be used with the computer disk.

Presentation: *QAM* was the first textbook to make it possible for persons with a modest background in mathematics to learn how MS/OR affects our lives. That has been our strategy from the beginning and this edition continues a tradition that has won the approval of a thousand instructors and almost half a million students.

Creating a new edition is never the work of one person, or for that matter four persons. The number of people who leave their mark on this edition is large. As just one example, the manuscript for this edition was subjected to the most extensive review procedure possible. Among those persons who made valuable suggestions are Harvey Adelman; Milton Chen, San Diego State University; Milton Hurwitz, Prescott, Ball, and Turben; Ross Lancer, University of California—San Jose; James McKeown, University of Georgia; Joseph D. Megeath, Metro State University; Warren Smith, University of New Haven; Wayland P. Smith, Western Michigan University; Sidney Sobelman; and Ramaier Sriram, University of Dayton. Special thanks go to Editor Kathleen Loy for her encouragement and help these last couple of years. Ira Roberts must be singled out, too, for the thousand details that he handles so well and which are vital to the finished product.

Finally, we want to thank our adopters who have been generous with their support and their suggestions; most of the latter are incorporated in these pages. You make it fun to write. We hope you enjoy what we've done.

RICHARD I. LEVIN
DAVID S. RUBIN
JOEL P. STINSON
EVERETTE S. GARDNER, JR.

INTRODUCTION

Management Science/ Operations Research (MS/OR) and Its Supporting Information Systems

CHAPTER OBJECTIVES
- INTRODUCE THE PHILOSOPHY OF THE BOOK.
- REVIEW THE STEPS IN THE MS/OR PROCESS.
- PROVIDE A SHORT HISTORY OF MS/OR.
- DISCUSS THE RELATIONSHIP BETWEEN THE MS/OR PRACTITIONER AND THE MANAGER.
- INDICATE SOME OF THE PROBLEMS MS/OR HELPS SOLVE.
- REVIEW THE MS/OR TECHNIQUES TO BE COVERED IN THE BOOK.
- PROVIDE A VERY BRIEF INTRODUCTION TO COMPUTERS AND INFORMATION SYSTEMS.
- EXAMINE DECISION SUPPORT SYSTEMS (DSS) AND EXPERT SYSTEMS.

3

Decision making is what managers do. Some decisions are made largely on the basis of intuitive skills or "feel"; in many situations this is appropriate. Other decision situations, however, reward use of some of the more formal approaches we cover in this book. Still others require both approaches. Successful managers use quantitative approaches when:

1 The problem is complex and involves a number of variables.
2 There are data available which describe the situation.
3 The goals in solving the problem can be specified in quantitative terms.
4 Workable models are currently available for these situations.

1 Management science/operations research: the quantitative approach to management decision making

MS/OR, as it is commonly called, helps managers make better decisions. If you were hired as an MS/OR specialist, you would very likely follow the six steps illustrated in Fig. 1-1 in helping managers make better decisions.

2 The development of scientific management: from industrial engineering to management science/operations research

EARLY EXAMPLES OF
INDUSTRIAL
ENGINEERING
APPROACHES

Industrial engineering was born when the scientific method was applied to management problems, but the date of birth is not certain. Individual instances in which the essence of the scientific method appears to have been used to solve management problems have been found in writings thousands of years old. Moses' father-in-law, Jethro, is credited with a treatise on organization principles in Chapter 18 of the Book of Exodus. The ancient ships of Venice were reconditioned and refitted for sea duty using an extremely ingenious assembly line; each ship was moved (floated) along the assembly line, and a group of skilled workers performed a specific operation at each station in the line. Much more recently (1832), Charles Babbage wrote *On the Economy of Machinery and Manufacturers*, showing much industrial engineering insight.

F. W. TAYLOR

In the late nineteenth century, Frederick W. Taylor converted industrial engineering into a profession; he can, with some justification, be considered the father of scientific management. Taylor's shovel study is an excellent example of the application of the scientific method to a management problem, namely, the productivity of men shoveling ore.

H. L. GANTT

Another man of the early scientific management era was Henry L. Gantt, best known perhaps for his work in scheduling production.

THE EMERGENCE OF
MS/OR

The shift of interest away from the minutiae of management toward broader considerations was actually a transfer of emphasis from industrial engineering to MS/OR, a multidisciplinary approach to complex problems.

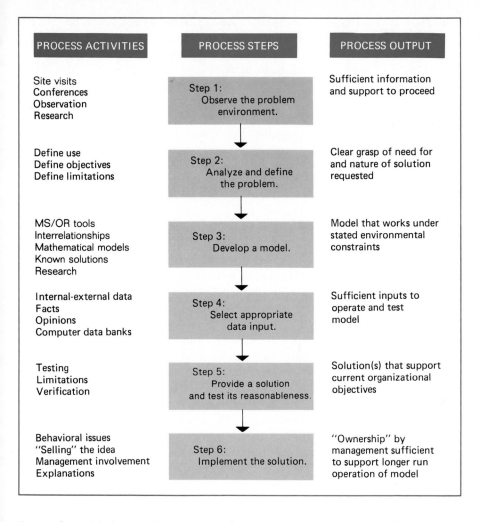

PROCESS ACTIVITIES	PROCESS STEPS	PROCESS OUTPUT
Site visits Conferences Observation Research	Step 1: Observe the problem environment.	Sufficient information and support to proceed
Define use Define objectives Define limitations	Step 2: Analyze and define the problem.	Clear grasp of need for and nature of solution requested
MS/OR tools Interrelationships Mathematical models Known solutions Research	Step 3: Develop a model.	Model that works under stated environmental constraints
Internal-external data Facts Opinions Computer data banks	Step 4: Select appropriate data input.	Sufficient inputs to operate and test model
Testing Limitations Verification	Step 5: Provide a solution and test its reasonableness.	Solution(s) that support current organizational objectives
Behavioral issues "Selling" the idea Management involvement Explanations	Step 6: Implement the solution.	"Ownership" by management sufficient to support longer run operation of model

FIGURE 1-1
Steps in the MS/OR
process.

It can be said that MS/OR emerged as a separate field when (1) industrial engineers became interested in the overall operations of the firm and (2) natural and social scientists became interested in management problems.

3 Early management science/operations research

PRE-WORLD WAR II

Scientists and engineers have been involved with military activities for at least as long as recorded history. One of the best-known instances in ancient history occurred in 212 B.C., when the city of Syracuse employed Archimedes (who was then a man of 75 years) to devise means of breaking the naval siege of the city, which was then under attack by the Romans.

ARCHIMEDES AND THE
SIEGE OF SYRACUSE

The germination of the concept of MS/OR from the military standpoint occurred on both sides of the Atlantic Ocean during World War I. In England in the years 1914–1915, F. W. Lanchester attempted to treat military operations

F. W. LANCHESTER'S
EQUATIONS TESTED

quantitatively. He derived equations relating the outcome of a battle to both the relative numerical strength of the combatants and their relative firepower.

During the period when Lanchester was pioneering military MS/OR in Great Britain, Thomas Alva Edison in America was studying the process of antisubmarine warfare. He collected statistics to be used in analyzing maneuvers whereby surface ships could evade and destroy submarines. He devised a war game to be used for simulating problems of naval maneuver. He even analyzed the merits of "zigzagging" as a merchant ship countermeasure against submarines.

Waiting-line problems were researched as early as 1907. In that year Johannsen published, in an electrical engineer's journal, a paper reporting his findings on waiting times and the number of calls.

In 1917, A. K. Erlang, a Danish mathematician working with the Copenhagen telephone company, published his most important work, "Solutions of Some Problems in the Theory of Probabilities of Significance in Automatic Telephone Exchanges"; it contained his waiting-time formulas which he had developed on the basis of statistical principles. These now well known formulas are of fundamental importance to the theory of telephone traffic.

In the area of inventory control, the well-known economic lot size models have a long genealogy. While it has been reported that G. D. Babcock developed a model stated in the form of a cubic equation, his technique was never published. The first published model on inventory economic lot size is generally attributed to Ford W. Harris, who described his model in 1915.

Probability theory and statistical inference have been a part of management theory for a relatively short time. Walter Shewhart made the earliest recorded applications of statistical inference in 1924, when he introduced the concept of quality control charts. Much of the theory he outlined is still used today.

The utilization of statistical inference and probability theory was aided by the work of H. F. Dodge and H. G. Romig, coworkers with Shewhart at Bell Telephone Laboratories. They developed the technique of sampling inspection in connection with quality control and published statistical sampling tables which, although slowly accepted at first, are now widely used.

Another engineer at Bell Laboratories, T. C. Fry, made additional significant contributions toward the statistical foundations of queuing theory. A series of lectures presented by Fry in 1928 concerning the engineering applications of probability theory became the basis for his important book on the subject.

Of course, Sir Ronald Fisher's work dealing with various modern statistical methods must be included in any survey of the development of MS/OR. At the time it was written, Fisher's work had little direct effect on management thought; but it is the basis for most of the applied statistical theory in use today.

Concern with interindustry input-output theories and measurements (brought about by the Great Depression of the 1930s) stimulated the work of Wassily Leontieff, a Harvard professor, who developed a linear programming model representing the entire U.S. economy. Many military and industrial applications of linear programming models have resulted from these early efforts.

One of the first proponents of business MS/OR in the United States was Horace C. Levinson, an astronomer who began his operations research in the decade 1920–1930. He applied the methods of science to the problems of business—and studied such problems as the relationship between advertising *and* sales, and the relationship between customers' incomes and home locations *and* types of articles purchased.

▮ WORLD WAR II

In 1939, according to one historian, "there was a nucleus of a British operational research organization already in existence,"[1] and its contributions were quickly followed and augmented in various important ways: in improving the early-warning radar system, in antiaircraft gunnery, in antisubmarine warfare, in civilian defense, in the determination of convoy size, and in the conduct of bombing raids upon Germany.[2]

One of the most publicized of Britain's early MS/OR groups was that under the direction of Professor P. M. S. Blackett of the University of Manchester, a Fellow of the Royal Society, Nobel Laureate, and former naval officer. "Blackett's circus," as the group was called, included "three physiologists, two mathematical physicists, one astrophysicist, one Army officer, one surveyor, one general physicist, and two mathematicians."[3] The value of the mixed-team approach was effectively demonstrated over and over again by this group.

Two Americans who were instrumental in the development of MS/OR in the United States during World War II were James B. Conant, then chairman of the National Defense Research Committee, and Vannevar Bush, chairman of the Committee on New Weapons and Equipment, Joint Chiefs of Staff. These men had observed such groups in England in 1940 and in 1942, respectively.[4]

In October 1942, at the request of General Spaatz, Commanding General of the Eighth Air Force, General Arnold (then Chief of Staff) sent a letter to all commanding generals of Air Force commands, recommending that they include in their staffs "operations analysis groups."[5] The first such operations analysis team was assigned to the Eighth Bomber Command, stationed in England.

▮ POST-WORLD WAR II

Operations research activity was considered by American military leaders to be so valuable that such functions were not discontinued at the end of the war. The Army continued its MS/OR functions through the agency of the Operations Research Office (later called the Research Analysis Corporation), in Chevy Chase, Maryland, with Ellis A. Johnson as director. The Navy established the Operations Evaluation Group under the direction of Professor Morse at MIT. The Air Force continued to employ operations analysis groups

---

[1] Florence N. Trefethen, "A History of Operations Research," in Joseph F. McCloskey and Florence N. Trefethen (eds.), *Operations Research for Management* (Baltimore: The Johns Hopkins Press, 1954), vol. 1, pp. 3–35.
[2] Ibid., pp. 5–10.
[3] Ibid., p. 6.
[4] Ibid., p. 12.
[5] Ibid., p. 13.

as a part of the various commands under its Operations Analysis Division. Additionally, the Air Force established Project RAND, administered by the RAND Corporation, for long-range studies of aerial warfare.

It was not until a few of our bolder companies tried MS/OR with considerable success and word began to leak out about its World War II accomplishments that civilian MS/OR began to make any real headway in the United States. Scientists and managers began to learn how to achieve two-way communication.

Two developments during this period deserve a special note. In 1947 George B. Dantzig (about whom we shall have more to say in Chapter 8) developed the simplex solution to the linear programming problem earlier formulated by Leontieff. Since that time, this solution method has become the standard approach to a wide variety of problems. In 1958 the forerunner of most of the material to come in Chapter 12, Networks, was done by the U.S. Navy's Special Projects Office with the help of Booz, Allen, and Hamilton, a well-known consulting company.

4 Management science/operations research today

MS/OR activities have grown rapidly in business, government units, and private institutions. Simultaneously, the scope of the problems addressed by MS/OR practitioners has expanded as well.

ORSA AND TIMS

In the United States in the early 1950s, groups of people interested in these activities organized the Operations Research Society of America (ORSA) and The Institute of Management Sciences (TIMS). Since 1952, ORSA has published the journal *Operations Research;* since 1953, TIMS has published the journal *Management Science.* In the early 1970s, the two societies cooperated to produce *Interfaces,* a quarterly publication of papers and articles concerned with the operational problems of using management science/operations research, and *OR/MS Today,* a bimonthly newsletter for the two organizations.

In England in 1948, people interested in operations research formed the Operational Research Club. Since then, they have changed the name to the Operational Research Society of the United Kingdom. In 1950 the British launched the *Operational Research Quarterly,* a publication which has the distinction of being the first periodical in the field.

DSI

More recently, MS/OR societies have been formed in many developed countries, some with their own journal or bulletin. The most recent American entry into this field was the Decision Sciences Institute, formed in 1971.

You can get a good idea of the variety and scope of MS/OR activities going on today by this list of journals, each of which reports research on and applications of quantitative techniques:

SOME MS/OR
JOURNALS

A.I.E.E. Transactions

C.O.R.S. Journal

Decision Sciences

Industrial Engineering

Journal of Industrial Engineering

Management Science
Mathematical Programming
Mathematics of Operations Research
Naval Research Logistics Quarterly
Networks
Operations Research
Transportation Science

5 The relationship between the MS/OR practitioner and the manager

Earlier, you assumed the role of an MS/OR specialist and reviewed the six steps of the scientific methodology of MS/OR. Figure 1-2 will help you see the relationship between the work of the MS/OR specialist and that of the managerial generalist or decision maker.

6 Applications of management science/ operations research

Here is a *sample* of the applications of the techniques we will introduce in this book:

Accounting and finance
  Forecasting and planning cash flows
  Determining to which customers to extend credit and how much
  Collection systems for delinquent accounts
  Allocation of investment capital among various alternatives in a company
  Managing an investment portfolio
  Improving the effectiveness of cost accounting
  Improving the accuracy of auditing
  Assigning auditing teams effectively
Marketing
  Determining the best product mix, given market demands
  Deciding whether a company should acquire marketing rights to a new
    product
  Allocating advertising among different media
  Finding the best time to introduce a new product
  Assigning salespersons to territories more effectively
  Locating warehouses more effectively to minimize distribution cost
  Evaluating the market strength of a competitor's marketing strategy
  Comparing the marketing attractiveness of various packaging alternatives
  Planning salespersons' travel to minimize the total miles traveled

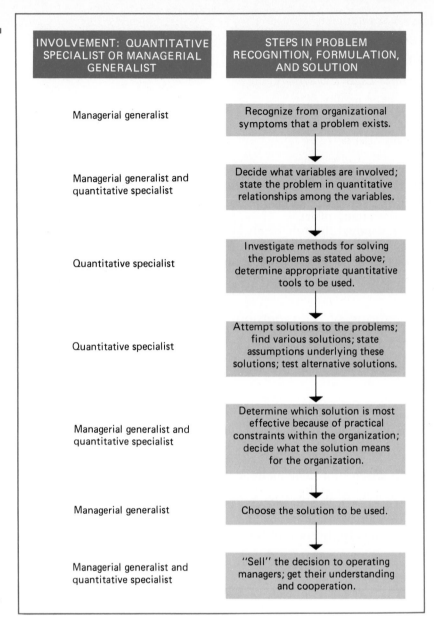

INVOLVEMENT: QUANTITATIVE SPECIALIST OR MANAGERIAL GENERALIST	STEPS IN PROBLEM RECOGNITION, FORMULATION, AND SOLUTION
Managerial generalist	Recognize from organizational symptoms that a problem exists.
Managerial generalist and quantitative specialist	Decide what variables are involved; state the problem in quantitative relationships among the variables.
Quantitative specialist	Investigate methods for solving the problems as stated above; determine appropriate quantitative tools to be used.
Quantitative specialist	Attempt solutions to the problems; find various solutions; state assumptions underlying these solutions; test alternative solutions.
Managerial generalist and quantitative specialist	Determine which solution is most effective because of practical constraints within the organization; decide what the solution means for the organization.
Managerial generalist	Choose the solution to be used.
Managerial generalist and quantitative specialist	"Sell" the decision to operating managers; get their understanding and cooperation.

FIGURE 1-2
Roles for quantitative specialist and managerial generalist.

Production-Operations

    Minimizing the total in-process manufacturing inventory

    Blending coal most economically to meet utility customers' needs

    Moving products through the manufacturing process more effectively

    Smoothing production when demand is highly seasonal

    Mixing animal feeds most economically

    Balancing plant capacity with market demand to increase profitability

Determining whether to make or purchase subassemblies used in production

Balancing an assembly line which has many different operations

Locating a new plant in the most effective place

Allocating an R and D budget most effectively

Improving the quality of a manufacturing operation

Choosing sites for oil and gas exploration most effectively

Determining the best size for a new manufacturing facility

Organizational development/human resources

Hiring new employees at the proper time, given training and retirement constraints

Scheduling training programs for maximum skill development

Assigning employees to operations to make the best use of skills

Coordinating manpower needs with seasonal market demands

Establishing the best size and deployment of a field sales force

Allocating laboratory scientists to research projects in the most effective way

Scheduling operating-room facilities in a hospital to make the most effective use of surgeons and nurses

Staffing emergency rooms in hospitals to offer the best possible care at the lowest possible cost

Minimizing the use of temporary office employees

Determining how hard to negotiate in a bargaining situation

In the rest of the book, you will see many of these applications demonstrated.

7 Advantages and disadvantages of quantitative approaches

The use of quantitative methods to improve decision making has become quite widespread today. In this chapter we have introduced you to a wide number of MS/OR applications in practically every field of organized managerial effort. This remarkable record over the last 40 years or so has not been without its setbacks, however. From time to time, too much has been asked of MS/OR; at other times, practitioners have simply not considered the organizational issues involved in applying models to problems. Still other failures have resulted from managers' lack of knowledge about what to expect from such applications. Here are two short lists of advantages and disadvantages of MS/OR approaches to managerial problems to help you sharpen your own perspective.

Advantages

1 MS/OR quickly shows up gaps in the data required to produce workable solutions to problems.

2 MS/OR allows us to examine a situation, change the conditions under which decisions must be made, and then examine the effect of these changes on the outcome—all without serious damage or excessive cost.

3 MS/OR allows us to find a solution to a complex problem much more quickly than if we had to examine all of the possible combinations of the variables involved.

4 MS/OR lets us model a situation so that future solutions can be done by a computer.

5 By handling problems that are fairly well structured, MS/OR frees management time to work on less structured problems that require a lot of intuition.

Disadvantages

1 MS/OR approaches often have to simplify the problem to handle it; oversimplification often produces answers that are without much value.

2 For problems that must be solved only once, constructing an MS/OR solution is often overly expensive when compared to other less sophisticated solution techniques.

3 Often MS/OR specialists become so enamored of the model they have created that they fail to recognize that it doesn't completely represent the "real world."

4 Sometimes MS/OR practitioners do not counsel decision makers that both quantitative approaches and intuition are required for effective solutions to problems.

5 Many real world problems that warrant MS/OR approaches are so complex that they are difficult to explain to decision makers.

8 Quantitative methods to be discussed

Here is a very brief look at the MS/OR techniques we'll cover in this book:

PROBABILITY
CONCEPTS REVIEW

Probability concepts are reviewed as a background for MS/OR. Methods are indicated for computing and using probabilities. Bayesian statistics develops a powerful method for making decisions when only limited information is available.

FORECASTING

Forecasting is an unavoidable responsibility of management. Faced with uncertainty concerning the future, management looks to past behavior as an indicator of what is to come. Among the topics treated are moving averages, exponential smoothing, trend-adjusted exponential smoothing, trend line fitting, and the decomposition of seasonal data.

DECISION THEORY

Decision theory is concerned with making sensible decisions both under conditions of complete uncertainty about future outcomes and under conditions such that you can make some probability statements about what you think will happen in the future. Methods are presented by which probability theory can be coupled with financial data to generate valuable decision algorithms.

Inventory models make decisions that minimize total inventory costs; these approaches can successfully reduce the total cost of purchasing inventory, carrying inventory, and being out of stock of inventory. Methods useful in dealing with discount evaluation, the joint ordering of items from the same vendor, and making inventory decisions in the absence of complete information are also discussed at some length. Here we also develop a model which suggests that being intentionally "out of stock" of an item may be a sensible alternative.

INVENTORY MODELS

Linear programming is of value when a choice must be made from alternatives too numerous to evaluate with conventional methods. It can be used to determine optimal combinations of the resources of a firm to achieve a given objective or to allocate scarce resources optimally.

LINEAR PROGRAMMING

Special-purpose algorithms are linear programming techniques useful when working with certain specially structured problems. We illustrate the *transportation method* and the *assignment method,* two approaches that are useful when management is confronted with problems concerning the best distribution alternative or the optimum method of assigning operators to machines, accountants to audit teams, and even students to schools. These two methods are included in a larger group of techniques known as *network algorithms.*

SPECIAL-PURPOSE ALGORITHMS

Integer programming, the branch and bound method, dynamic programming, and *goal programming* are methods for choosing among alternatives when answers may have to be found in whole numbers, when the decision confronting management involves many consecutive stages, or when organizational objectives have to be stated in more than simple numerical terms.

INTEGER PROGRAMMING, THE BRANCH AND BOUND METHOD, DYNAMIC PROGRAMMING, GOAL PROGRAMMING

Heuristics are sometimes described as "rules of thumb which work." An example of a commonly used heuristic is "Stand in the shortest line." Although using this rule may not work if everyone in the shortest line requires extra time, in general it's not a bad rule to follow. Many heuristics are very complex, and their formulation involves a great deal of analysis. Heuristics tend to be effective in situations in which some of the more formal, mathematical MS/OR techniques cannot be applied successfully.

HEURISTICS

Simulation is a procedure that studies a problem by creating a model of the process involved in that problem and then, through a series of organized trial-and-error solutions, attempts to determine the best solution to that problem.

SIMULATION

Queuing theory studies random arrivals at a servicing or processing facility of limited capacity. Models allow management to calculate the lengths of future waiting lines, the average time spent in line by a person awaiting service, needed facility additions, and the service level or capacity that minimizes the sum of waiting costs and operating costs.

QUEUING THEORY

Network scheduling enables managers to cope with the complexities involved in large projects; the use of this technique has significantly reduced the time necessary to plan and produce complex products. Techniques covered in this section include PERT (Program Evaluation Review Technique), CPM (Critical Path Method), PERT/Cost, and scheduling with resource limitations.

NETWORK SCHEDULING

Markov analysis permits one to predict changes over time when information about the behavior of a system is known. Although the best-known use of

MARKOV ANALYSIS

this technique is in predicting brand loyalties (the brand behavior of consumers over time), Markov analysis also has considerable use in other areas.

The past, present, and future of MS/OR is the subject of a final chapter. Here we report on current research into the direction that applications seem to be taking, the implications of the further development of these techniques for operating managers, and some of the roadblocks which may limit the effective, continued, profitable use of these techniques.

9 Computers and information systems

The techniques of MS/OR require quite a bit of data for their successful implementation. Each of the quantitative techniques that we introduce in this book requires inputs of data that are:

1 Accurate: The data need to be error-free; they should fairly represent the environment in which we are working toward a solution.

2 Cost-effective: Data cannot cost more to provide than they are worth.

3 Current: Data should reflect environmental conditions of interest to the problem solver, not conditions which no longer exist.

4 Reliable: Data used by one specialist should generate the same result when they are used by another under the same conditions.

5 Usable: Insofar as possible, data should not require further modification before they can be used.

In its simplest form, a management information system can be represented by the schematic in Figure 1-3. Notice that the basic transformation in the management information system process is from *data* to *information*. Raw data enter the system and are transformed into the system's only output, information to support making decisions. It might be a good time to refer to Figure 1-1; there you can see that step 4 of the MS/OR process is the place where quantitative methods and data interact most closely. Without good data, you just can't get the maximum benefit from the quantitative approaches you use to make decisions.

COMPUTERS AS THE BASIS FOR MANAGEMENT INFORMATION SYSTEMS

Given the complexity and scope of managerial decision making today, the need for data is so enormous that most organizations have long since given

FIGURE 1-3
Management
information system
diagram.

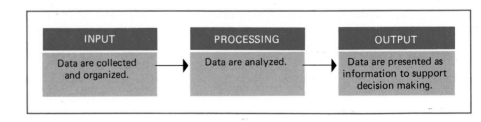

INPUT	PROCESSING	OUTPUT
Data are collected and organized.	Data are analyzed.	Data are presented as information to support decision making.

up trying to provide that data by any other method than the use of computers.
In all but a few cases, the benefit/cost ratio is so overwhelmingly in favor of
using a computer that manual methods can't survive.

Understanding the computer and its use in management information
systems is best approached by first examining the roles of the *human* and the
computer to see what each does, what each does best, and what each does not
do well. Then we can go on to look more closely at the computer as the basis
for a management information system. Figure 1-4 gives a quick picture of
human decision makers and computers, and of the relative strengths and
weaknesses of both. **The critical objective in the design of an effective
management information system as a support for quantitative applications
is to employ the distinct advantages of both components (the human and
the electronic). "Too much computer" and you get mechanistic solutions,
inflexible responses, and narrow decisions. "Too much human" and you
get slow responses, limited use of applicable data, and a narrowed ability
to examine relevant alternatives.**

HOW COMPUTERS WORK (A QUICK REVIEW)

Just about everybody who takes an MS/OR course today has considerable
hands-on computer experience. What was reserved for Ph.D. scientists 20
years ago is now a common experience for first and second graders. Often,

HUMAN DECISION MAKERS	COMPUTERS
Humans have imagination, creative powers, judgment, and common sense.	Computers do only what their programmers tell them to do in the form of instructions.
Human decision makers can learn from their experiences.	Computers can follow rules but cannot learn deductively except in the simplest logic situations.
Human decision makers are not always accurate; sometimes their behavior is inconsistent.	Computers react consistently and give or take electronic problems quite accurately.
Human decision makers can see the "overall" problem (the forest, as it were); they can then see each subproblem as part of an overall scheme.	Computers can be programmed to follow complex, interacting sets of rules; but even when the situation changes, they will continue to follow these rules toward faulty outcomes.
Human decision makers have flexibility (at least most of them do); when the road signs change, they can alter their behavior to optimize under the new situation.	Computers have flexibility only if someone has programmed it in; otherwise they react identically regardless of changed road signs.
Most humans have an enormous memory; they forget a lot, and are not very precise in terms of what they do remember, but they can accommodate a wide variety of information from bits of data to complete complex thinking processes.	Computers never forget; they have an enormous memory in terms of pieces of information, and they are very fast in retrieving this information.

FIGURE 1-4
Computers and human decision makers.

THE RELATIVE ROLES OF HUMANS AND COMPUTERS

INEFFECTIVE TRADE-OFFS

however, we forget what makes the whole thing work so well, so here's a quick review in Figure 1-5.

HARDWARE

▓ HARDWARE

Hardware is the "computer name" we give to all the electronic and mechanical devices which make up a computer.

SOFTWARE

▓ SOFTWARE

Software is a term we use to refer to the instructions we give a computer to perform. A set of instructions which "tells" a computer how to perform a particular task is called a *program.* Any set of programs which enables the computer to perform its functions is called software.

▓ CLASSIFYING MANAGEMENT INFORMATION SYSTEMS IN TERMS OF HOW OR WHERE THE PROCESSING IS DONE

There are at least five ways to classify management information systems in terms of how or where the processing is done:

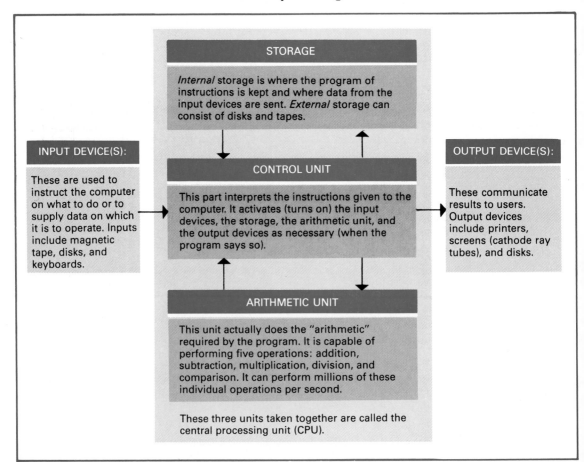

FIGURE 1-5
Computer configuration.

1 Batch processing: In batch processing, the work is done sequentially. Inputs (records, and so forth) are processed through the system in a predetermined order. Because large files are stored on tape, the groups of transactions to be done must be gathered together and then sorted in the same order as the information on the tape prior to processing.

SEQUENTIAL PROCESSING

2 Real-time processing: Rather than starting with the first record to be processed and finishing with the last, a real-time system uses a nonsequential processing method. It provides access to any piece of information and finds that piece of information in the same amount of time as any other piece.

A NONSEQUENTIAL METHOD

3 Online processing: Online processing refers to equipment that operates under control of the central processing unit described in Figure 1-5. You can locate online processing equipment in the same location as the central processing unit or in a remote location. Generally, online processing refers to processing using a terminal (input) that is remote from the central processing unit. Online processing can be used for batch processing or for real-time processing. When it is used for batch processing, it is generally referred to as *remote batch processing,* or *remote job entry.*

WHEN EQUIPMENT OPERATES UNDER CONTROL OF THE CENTRAL PROCESSING UNIT

4 Timesharing: Timesharing refers to an information system that services many clients from one computer; these clients or users are served simultaneously.

SERVICING MANY CLIENTS FROM ONE COMPUTER

5 Distributed data processing: Although this is not a true distinction based on *how* the processing is done, it is a separate category in terms of *where* it's done. In a distributed data processing system, computing capacity is distributed throughout the organization (to functions, departments, and even individuals) based on information need.

DISTRIBUTED DATA PROCESSING

The current level of integration of mainframe computers and microcomputers is so advanced that these distinctions are becoming less and less evident today.

CLASSIFYING MANAGEMENT INFORMATION SYSTEMS IN TERMS OF THE TYPE OF OUTPUT PROVIDED

There are at least two ways to classify management information systems in terms of the format of the output:

1 Management information systems that generate *reports:* These reports can be balance sheets, cash flow statements, accounts receivable statements, inventory status reports, production efficiency reports, or any report on the status of a situation of interest to the decision maker. The reports can be

SYSTEMS CAN PROVIDE REPORTS

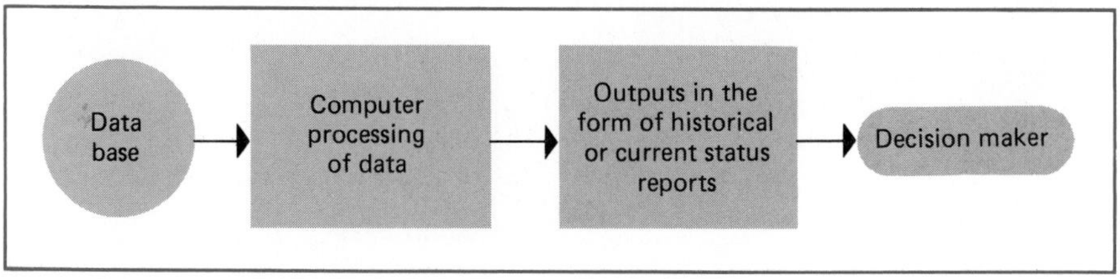

FIGURE 1-6
Report generator management information system.

historical or refer to the current status of the situation. The reports can be generated in a batch system, in a real-time system, from an online system, or on a timesharing system. Figure 1-6 illustrates a report generator management information system.

SYSTEMS CAN ANSWER QUESTIONS ABOUT POSSIBLE ALTERNATIVES

2 Management information systems that answer "what-if" kinds of questions asked by management: These information systems take the information stored in the data base and reply to questions asked by management. These questions are in the form: What would happen if this or that happened? The information system thus uses its stored information, its comparison and calculation capabilities, and a set of programs especially written for this situation to provide management with the consequences of an action they are considering. Figure 1-7 illustrates the configuration of a "what-if" management information system.

10 Decision support systems and expert systems

Although there is no single accepted definition of decision support systems, the significant difference here is that the decision maker's intuition and judgment are able to be used at all stages of the decision process. Decision support systems are designed specifically to support someone who must make decisions; as such, the following characteristics are built into the system:

1 Interactive capability: Decision support systems provide decision makers quick access to data and information which may be used in their decision-making process.

2 Flexibility: Decision support systems can support the decision-making processes of managers in many functional fields (finance, marketing, production-operations) without extensive revision.

3 Model interaction ability: Decision support systems permit the decision maker to interact with a broad range of MS/OR models including manipulation of these models to the demands of very specific decision-making situations.

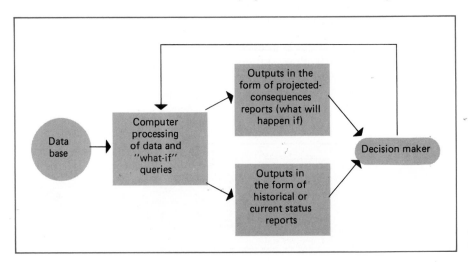

FIGURE 1-7
"What-if"
management
information system.

4 Output flexibility: Decision support systems provide decision makers with a wide variety of output formats, including some "state of the art" graphic abilities to display results of "what if" type questions.

Figure 1-8 illustrates the configuration of a decision support system.

☐ THE FUTURE OF DECISION SUPPORT SYSTEMS

Some scholars in the field of decision support systems claim that these systems are only a dozen years old at this point. Others maintain that true decision support systems only appeared in the mid-1980s. Whatever their date of birth, almost everyone involved with the field of MS/OR agrees that DSSs are developing and changing rapidly, and that the decade to come will see near-revolutionary advances.

A RAPIDLY MOVING DISCIPLINE

Perhaps the most promising development in this area has been the recent emergence of *expert systems*. Here too, there is no single accepted definition of an expert system, but a generally accepted definition is a system that is capable of completely solving a problem with an MS/OR model entirely without human intervention.

EXPERT SYSTEMS

There are a number of these expert systems at work today in the fields of inventory control, production scheduling, personnel assignment, credit granting, and even chess playing. Organizations using expert systems have

WHAT DO EXPERT SYSTEMS DO?

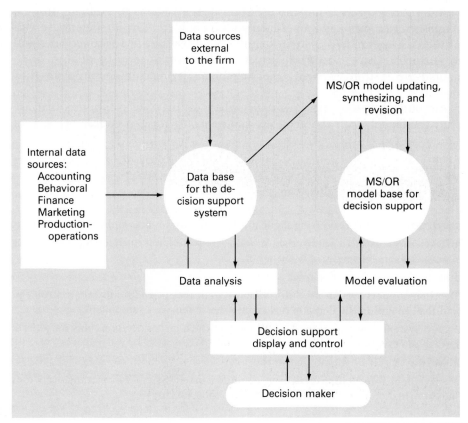

FIGURE 1-8

Configuration of a decision support system.

SOME SUCCESSFUL
APPLICATIONS

FUTURE OF EXPERT
SYSTEMS

MS/OR models programmed to accept and evaluate input data, calibrate those data against objectives also programmed in the system, compute an optimal solution to the problem, and provide output data for the rest of the system.

Most of these expert systems are presently relegated to fairly routine decisions, ones that do not require interpretation, judgment, or intuition. Current expert systems do an effective job of managing inventory systems for large numbers of items, of assigning personnel (and equipment too) to delivery and pick-up routes, of granting or refusing credit to bank and retail store customers, and even of beating some fairly accomplished chess players.

Development in expert systems has moved forward very rapidly in the last few years. Some of these systems can now deal with some ambiguity and make judgments that were impossible earlier. These new "knowledge systems," as they are sometimes called, are presently working in the U.S., Japan, and Western Europe.

In 1986, fewer than a half dozen of these systems existed in business and government. Estimates of the number working successfully today go from 100 to 4,000, and practitioners report that they are increasing at a rate of 50 percent annually.

Much of this success of expert or knowledge systems grew out of the research on artificial intelligence in human decision making conducted in the 1960s and 1970s. Although computers have yet to match human intelligence, or to think like humans, there are a number of applications with significant commercial value.

American Express Company uses knowledge systems to evaluate unusual requests for credit from their 20 million cardholders. The intelligence service of the U.S. uses expert systems to analyze patterns of terrorist activities and to anticipate them, and Ford dealer mechanics will soon be able to use a nationwide computer system to get help on analyzing complex problems they may have with engines.

Although it is too early to predict when we may see computers that are truly intelligent, with the progress made in only the last couple of years, it cannot be too far in the future.

11 Glossary

Batch processing A processing mode in which the work is accomplished sequentially.

Blackett's circus An early British MS/OR group under the leadership of P. M. S. Blackett of the University of Manchester.

DSI Decision Sciences Institute.

Decision support system An information system that provides answers to problems and that integrates the decision maker into the system as a component.

Expert system A system using MS/OR models which makes decisions entirely without human intervention.

Heuristic A rule of thumb that works.

Management information system A computer-based system which transforms data into information useful in the support of decision making.

Management science/operations research The systematic study of a problem involving gathering data, building a mathematical model, experimenting with the model, predicting future operations, and getting the support of management for the use of the model.

MS/OR Management science/operations research.

ORSA Operations Research Society of America.

Sensitivity testing Altering the inputs to a model and watching what happens to the output.

Symbolic model An abstract model, generally using mathematical symbols.

TIMS The Institute of Management Sciences.

12 Exercises

1-1 It appears that some early managerial decision making actually used an MS/OR point of view. To what do you attribute the fact that it has taken about 60 years for MS/OR to come into accepted use in industry?

1-2 Comment on the methodology of pre-World War II MS/OR. How does this work differ from work that was done later?

1-3 What were the significant characteristics of MS/OR applications during World War II? What caused the discipline of MS/OR to take on these characteristics during that period?

1-4 In Section 6 (Applications of MS/OR), eight accounting applications of MS/OR are given. Pick any three of these and (1) determine the relevant variables in the application, (2) comment on what data would be required as inputs to the solution of such a problem, and (3) state what form the output or answer would take.

1-5 In Section 6, nine marketing applications of MS/OR are given. Pick any three of these and (1) determine the relevant variables in the application, (2) comment on what data would be required as inputs to the solution of such a problem, and (3) state what form the output or answer would take.

1-6 Distinguish the role of the human from that of the computer in a well-designed information system.

1-7 Name the five major components of a modern computer system.

1-8 Discuss the following statements: "I can purchase software packages which will solve problems using the quantitative techniques described in this text. Therefore it is not important that I learn the techniques themselves."

1-9 It might be reasonable for a management information system to evolve in stages from a report generator to a "what-if" system and finally to a decision support system. Discuss why you think this could happen.

1-10 What roles does the managerial generalist play in the solution of a problem with MS/OR?

1-11 What is the main objective in designing a management information system which supports quantitative applications?

1-12 Give five applications of expert systems beyond those discussed in the text that you feel would be successful.

13 Chapter concepts quiz

1-1 Skills in qualitative analysis can be obtained by studying a book.   **T F**

1-2 If you were hired as an MS/OR analyst, you would spend all your time observing decision-making environments.   **T F**

1-3 The final step in MS/OR is implementing the solution you have found.   **T F**

1-4 MS/OR activities were more widespread prior to World War II than in the period after it.   **T F**

1-5 There are fewer than five journals in the discipline of MS/OR.   **T F**

1-6 MS/OR applications tend to be found mainly in the area of organizational behavior.   **T F**

1-7 You cannot maximize all the criteria for a good management information system simultaneously.   **T F**

1-8 MS/OR rarely shows up gaps in the data required to produce workable solutions to problems.   **T F**

1-9 MS/OR solutions to problems which must be solved only one time are rarely too expensive to use.   **T F**

1-10 The least time-consuming part of an MS/OR project is often that of testing and refining the model.   **T F**

1-11 All decisions are made either on the basis of feel or by using more formal approaches.   **T F**

1-12 The mathematical techniques of inventory control are among the newest of the operations research tools.   **T F**

1-13 Industrial MS/OR in Great Britain developed in much the same way as it did in the United States.   **T F**

1-14 Simulation is one of the most widely used quantitative techniques.   **T F**

1-15 Computer storage may be either internal or external.   **T F**

Multiple
Choice

1-16 Which of the following is not true?
    a. Modern management information systems must use computers.
    b. Management scientists need to know where their information comes from.
    c. The effectiveness of MS/OR depends upon the effectiveness of the underlying information system.
    d. In its simplest form a management information system consists of three parts.

1-17 Understanding the computer and its use in management information systems is best done by:
    a. Examining the role of the human
    b. Examining the role of the computer
    c. Examining the role of the company
    d. Examining the role of the problem
    e. None of the above

1-18 Which of the following is not a part of a computer?
    a. Control unit
    b. Storage
    c. Input devices

d. Power source
e. Output devices
f. Arithmetic unit

1-19 Hardware refers to which four of the following devices?
  a. The central processing unit
  b. Punched-card readers
  c. The console
  d. Disk drives
  e. Power sources
  f. Roller drives
  g. Magnetic-tape holders

1-20 Expert systems work best on:
  a. Complex decisions
  b. Decisions involving many steps
  c. Fairly routine decisions
  d. Decisions which require judgment

1-21 Software is a term we give to:
  a. The power devices involved in an information system
  b. The nonelectrical part of the computer
  c. The instructions we give a computer to perform
  d. The activities that are performed by a computer operator

1-22 Which of the following is not a characteristic of a decision support system?
  a. Interactive capability
  b. Capacity
  c. Model interaction ability
  d. Flexibility

1-23 When using a qualitative approach to analysis, the manager relies on:
  a. Experience
  b. Intuition
  c. Judgment
  d. All of the above

1-24 A firm's organization chart is a type of model known as:
  a. A scale
  b. An organogram
  c. A technical chain
  d. A dynamic echelon

1-25 In contrast to industrial engineering, the MS/OR approach is:
  a. Multidisciplinary
  b. Scientific
  c. Managerial
  d. More expensive

1-26 A method which combines uncertainty and larger numbers of decision alternatives in solving complex problems is known as:
  a. Queuing theory
  b. Markov analysis
  c. Assignment method
  d. Decision trees

1-27 The electronic and mechanical devices which make up a computer system are known as:
  a. Hardware
  b. Information

c. Programs

d. All of the above

1-28 Artificial intelligence systems:
  a. Cannot deal with ambiguity
  b. Have no commercial application today
  c. Mimic the decision-making power of humans
  d. Are too costly to be practical

1-29 A system which attempts to integrate the decision maker, the data base, and quantitative models is known as:
  a. A "what-if" system
  b. A symbolic system
  c. A heuristic system
  d. A decision support system

1-30 Knowledge processing systems are increasing at the rate of:
  a. 10 percent annually
  b. 30 percent annually
  c. 50 percent annually
  d. 100 percent annually

Fill in the Blanks

1-31 Name the classifications of management information systems in terms of how or where the processing is done:
  a. _____
  b. _____
  c. _____
  d. _____
  e. _____

1-32 Name four of the six attributes of the human decision maker:
  a. _____
  b. _____
  c. _____
  d. _____

1-33 Name four of the six attributes of the computer:
  a. _____
  b. _____
  c. _____
  d. _____

1-34 Name the two classifications of information systems in terms of the type of output provided:
  a. _____
  b. _____

1-35 What two features distinguish a decision support information system from other types of information systems?
  a. _____
     _____

  b. _____
     _____

1-36 List four situations which would cause decision makers to move toward a quantitative approach:

a. _____

_____

b. _____

_____

c. _____

_____

d. _____

_____

1-37 List the outputs of the six steps in the MS/OR process:

a. _____
b. _____
c. _____
d. _____
e. _____
f. _____

1-38 The process of analysis, whether formal or informal, takes on two basic forms which are:

a. _____
b. _____

1-39 Inventory models aid in controlling total inventory costs. Some components of total inventory costs are:

a. _____
b. _____
c. _____

1-40 List three applications of artificial intelligence beyond those in the text that you believe would be feasible. What problems would you foresee?

a. _____
b. _____
c. _____

2

Before deciding whether or not to introduce a new product, it is common practice for the Merryfield Company to conduct a market survey. They use Bayesian probability concepts in order to most effectively combine the survey results with other information including experience and subjective judgment. The better Merryfield can predict the degree of consumer acceptance for their product, the more effective they will be in planning for its production and distribution. Bayesian analysis, along with the other probability concepts presented in this chapter are important tools for management. You will be using these concepts on numerous occasions in later chapters of this text as well as throughout your career in management.

A REVIEW OF PROBABILITY CONCEPTS

CHAPTER OBJECTIVES

- REVIEW THE BASIC IDEAS BEHIND PROBABILITY THEORY.

- PRESENT THE THREE MAJOR CLASSIFICATIONS OF PROBABILITY ACCORDING TO THE SOURCE OF THE INFORMATION.

- DEMONSTRATE HOW TO CALCULATE PROBABILITIES UNDER CONDITIONS OF STATISTICAL INDEPENDENCE.

- DEMONSTRATE HOW TO CALCULATE PROBABILITIES UNDER CONDITIONS OF STATISTICAL DEPENDENCE.

- REVIEW BAYES' THEOREM AND REINFORCE ITS USE WITH EXAMPLES.

- REVIEW PROBABILITY DISTRIBUTIONS AS A CONCEPT.

- DEMONSTRATE THE MEANING OF A RANDOM VARIABLE.

- REVIEW THE MEANING AND USE OF THE MEAN AND THE STANDARD DEVIATION.

- EXAMINE SPECIFICALLY THE BINOMIAL, POISSON, EXPONENTIAL, AND NORMAL DISTRIBUTIONS.

- REINFORCE UNDERSTANDING OF WHEN AND WHERE TO USE EACH OF THESE DISTRIBUTIONS BY THE USE OF EXAMPLES.

- REVIEW THE MEANING AND USE OF THE STANDARD NORMAL PROBABILITY TABLE.

- EXAMINE THE CAVEATS ATTACHED TO THE USE OF ALL THE DISTRIBUTIONS THAT ARE INTRODUCED.

1 Introduction

Much of the material which follows this chapter requires some working knowledge of probability, the kind one would normally get in an introductory college-level statistics course. And most students taking this course will have had one or more such courses. We realize that it is not typical for a text in management science to include a chapter on probability, but we've gone ahead and done so for two reasons:

1 There may be students using this book who for a variety of reasons have *not* had an introductory statistics course; studying this chapter will provide them with everything they need to understand the chapters which follow.

2 Some students who *have* had previous work in statistics may feel a bit rusty or unsure of some of the concepts that were introduced and need a quick, practical look back from time to time.

So for anyone who needs it, here's a self-contained review of probability concepts as a foundation for things to come.

2 Basic probability concepts

PROBABILITY DEFINED

Probability is the chance that something will happen. Probabilities are expressed as fractions (¼, ½, ¾) or as decimals (.25, .50, .75) between 0 and 1. When you assign a probability of 0, you mean that something can *never* happen; when you assign a probability of 1, you mean that something will *always* happen.

EVENTS AND EXPERIMENTS

AN EVENT

In probability theory, an *event* is one or more of the possible outcomes of doing something. If we toss a coin, getting a tail would be an event; getting a head would be still another event. The activity that produces an event is referred to in probability theory as an *experiment*. Using this language, we could ask: In a coin-toss experiment, what is the probability of the event *heads?* In this case, we would answer: ½ or .5.

SAMPLE SPACE

The set of all possible outcomes of an experiment is called the *sample space* for the experiment. In a coin-toss experiment, for example, the sample space is

$$S = \{\text{head, tail}\}$$

If we were drawing cards from a deck, the sample space would have 52 members, one for each card in a standard deck (ace of hearts, king of hearts, and so on).

Mutually exclusive and collectively exhaustive events   Events are *mutually exclusive* if one and only one of them can take place at a time. Consider again the example of the coin toss. We have two possible outcomes, heads and tails. On any single toss, either heads or tails may turn up, but not both. Accordingly, the events *heads* and *tails* on a single toss are said to be *mutually exclusive*.

The crucial question we ask in determining whether events are really mutually exclusive is: Can two or more of these events occur at one time? If we answer yes, the events are *not* mutually exclusive.

When you make a list of the possible events that can result from an experiment and this list includes every possible outcome, you have a *collectively exhaustive* list.

MUTUALLY EXCUSIVE
EVENTS

COLLECTIVELY
EXHAUSTIVE EVENTS

3 Three types of probability

There are three ways of classifying probability. These represent different conceptual approaches to the study of probability theory; in fact, experts disagree over which approach it is proper to use. We will examine these three approaches to probability:

APPROACHES TO
PROBABILITY: THREE
DIFFERENT WAYS

1 The *classical* approach

2 The *relative frequency* approach

3 The *subjective* approach

CLASSICAL PROBABILITY

Classical probability defines the probability that an event will occur as

$$\text{Probability of an event} = \frac{\text{number of outcomes favorable to the occurrence of the event}}{\text{total number of possible outcomes}} \quad (2\text{-}1)$$

In order for Eq. (2-1) to be valid, each of the outcomes must be equally likely. Equation (2-1) may be a somewhat complex way of defining something that is intuitively obvious to us, but we can use it to express our coin-toss example in symbolic form. First, let us illustrate the question: What is the probability of getting heads on one toss?

THE CLASSICAL
APPROACH TO
DEFINING
PROBABILITIES

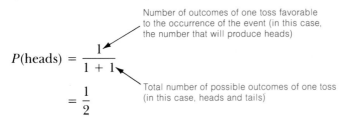

$$P(\text{heads}) = \frac{1}{1 + 1}$$

Number of outcomes of one toss favorable
to the occurrence of the event (in this case,
the number that will produce heads)

Total number of possible outcomes of one toss
(in this case, heads and tails)

$$= \frac{1}{2}$$

Let us try one more example using the definition of classical probability. Suppose the question now is: What is the probability of rolling a 5 on one die? We would calculate the answer this way:

$$P(5) = \cfrac{1}{1 + 1 + 1 + 1 + 1 + 1}$$

Number of outcomes of one roll of the die which will produce a 5

Total number of possible outcomes of one roll of the die (getting a 1, a 2, a 3, a 4, a 5, or a 6)

$$= \frac{1}{6}$$

ASSESSING PROBABILITIES WITHOUT EXPERIMENTS

Classical probability is often called *a priori* probability because—if we keep using these orderly examples of fair coins, unbiased dice, or decks of cards—we can state the answer in advance (a priori) *without ever tossing a coin, rolling a die, or drawing a card*. We do not even have to perform experiments to make probability statements about fair coins, unbiased dice, or decks of cards. Rather, we can make probability statements based on logical reasoning before any experiment takes place.

THE RELATIVE FREQUENCY OF OCCURRENCE

THE RELATIVE FREQUENCY APPROACH TO ASSIGNING PROBABILITIES

This method of defining probability uses the relative frequencies of past occurrences as probabilities. It defines probability as either:

1 The proportion of times that an event occurs in the long run when conditions are stable, or

2 The observed relative frequency of an event in a very large number of trials

USING PAST HISTORY TO ASSIGN PROBABILITIES

To predict the probability that something will happen in the future, we determine how often it happened in the past. Let us look at an example. Suppose that your college admissions office knows from past data that about 50 of its 1,000 entering freshmen usually leave school for academic reasons by the end of the first semester. Using this method, the school would estimate the probability of a freshman leaving school for academic reasons by the end of the first semester as

$$\frac{50}{1,000} \quad \text{or} \quad .05$$

SUBJECTIVE PROBABILITIES

USING PERSONAL FEELINGS TO ASSIGN PROBABILITIES

Subjective probabilities are based on the personal belief or feelings of the person who makes the probability estimate. We can define *subjective probability* as the probability assigned to an event on the basis of whatever evidence is available. This evidence may be data about the relative frequency of occurrence, or it may be nothing more than a good guess. The assignment of subjective probabilities gives us the greatest flexibility of any of the three methods we have discussed. The decision makers can use whatever *evidence* is available and temper this with their own personal feelings about the situations.

FREQUENCY OF OCCURRENCE SUGGESTS USE OF SUBJECTIVE METHOD

Managers generally assign probabilities subjectively when events occur only once or at most a very few times. Suppose it is your responsibility to select a new assistant and you have narrowed the choice down to three persons. All three have an attractive appearance, an apparent high level of energy, high self-confidence, and equally impressive records of past accomplishments. What are the chances that each of these candidates will make a good assistant? Answering this question and choosing one from the three requires you to assign a subjective probability to each person's potential.

4 Probability rules

Most managers who use probabilities are concerned with two situations: (1) when one event *or* another will occur and (2) when two or more events will *all* occur.

We are expressing an interest in the first case when we ask questions like: What is the probability that our water supply will permit the plant to operate today? If we wanted to illustrate the second case, we could ask: What is the probability that our water supply will permit the plant to operate today *and* that plant absenteeism will exceed 5 percent? In the material which follows, we illustrate methods of determining answers to questions similar to these under a variety of conditions.

SITUATIONS IN WHICH PROBABILITIES ARE USEFUL

SOME COMMONLY USED SYMBOLS, DEFINITIONS, AND RULES

Symbol for a marginal probability   In probability theory, symbols are used to simplify the presentation of ideas. For example, the probability of a single event *A* would be expressed symbolically as

MARGINAL PROBABILITY

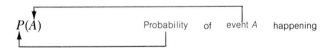

$$P(A) \qquad \text{Probability} \quad \text{of} \quad \text{event } A \quad \text{happening}$$

A *single* probability means that only one event can take place. It is called a *marginal,* or *unconditional, probability.* To illustrate, let us suppose that 10 computer programmers have an equal chance of being promoted to programming supervisor. Any 1 of these programmers could calculate his or her chance of getting the promotion by this formulation:

EXAMPLE OF A MARGINAL PROBABILITY

$$P(\text{promotion}) = \frac{1}{10}$$

$$= .1$$

In this situation, a programmer's chance is 1 in 10 because we are certain that the possible events are mutually exclusive; that is, only one programmer can get promoted to supervisor at a time.

There is a nice diagrammatic way to illustrate this example and other probability concepts. We use a pictorial representation called a *Venn diagram,* after the nineteenth-century English mathematician John Venn. In these diagrams, the entire sample space is represented by a rectangle, and events are represented by parts of the rectangle. If two events *are* mutually exclusive, their parts of the rectangle will not overlap each other, as shown in Figure 2-1*a*. If two events are *not* mutually exclusive, their parts of the rectangle *will* overlap, as in Figure 2-1*b*.

Since probabilities behave a lot like areas, we let the rectangle have an area of 1 (because the probability of *something* happening is 1). Then the probability of an event is the area of *its* part of the rectangle. Figure 2-1*c* illustrates this for the computer programmer example. There the rectangle is divided into 10 parts.

ADDING THE
PROBABILITIES OF
EVENTS THAT ARE
MUTUALLY EXCLUSIVE

The addition rule for mutually exclusive events Often, we are interested in the probability that one thing *or* another will occur. If these two events are mutually exclusive, we can express this probability symbolically, using the addition rule for mutually exclusive events:

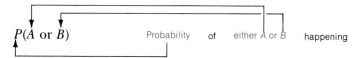

$P(A \text{ or } B)$ Probability   of   either A or B happening

and is calculated by the addition rule as follows:

$$P(A \text{ or } B) = P(A) + P(B) \qquad (2\text{-}2)$$

This addition rule is illustrated by the Venn diagram in Figure 2-2, where we note that the area in the two circles together (denoting the event *A or B*) is the sum of the areas of the two circles.

Let us do one example. These are the experience data for welders in a fabrication shop:

Years of experience	Number	Probability		
0–2	5	$5/50$ = $1/10$ = .1		
3–5	10	$10/50$ = $1/5$ = .2		
6–8	15	$15/50$ = $3/10$ = .3		
More than 8	20	$20/50$ = $2/5$ = .4		
Total	50			

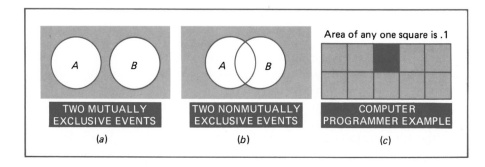

FIGURE 2-1
Venn diagrams
illustrated.

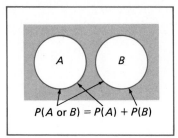

$$P(A \text{ or } B) = P(A) + P(B)$$

FIGURE 2-2
Venn diagram for the
addition rule for mutually
exclusive events.

What is the probability that a welder selected at random will have 6 or more years of experience? Using Eq. (2-2), we can calculate the answer as

$$P(6 \text{ or more}) = P(6 \text{ to } 8) + P(\text{more than } 8)$$
$$= \quad .3 \quad + \quad .4$$
$$= \quad .7$$

The addition rule for events that are not mutually exclusive If two events are not mutually exclusive, it is possible for both events to occur together. In such cases, the addition rule must be modified. Let us use the example of a deck of cards to introduce this idea. What is the probability of drawing either an ace *or* a spade from a deck of cards? Obviously the events *ace* and *spade* can occur together because we could draw the ace of spades; thus ace and spade are *not* mutually exclusive. We must adjust Eq. (2-2) to avoid double counting; specifically, we have to *reduce* the probability of drawing either an ace or a spade by the chance that we could draw them both together. As a result, the correct equation to use for the probability of one or more of two events that are not mutually exclusive is

AVOIDING DOUBLE
COUNTING IN EVENTS
WHICH ARE NOT
MUTUALLY EXCLUSIVE

Probability of A happening   Probability of B happening

$$P(A \text{ or } B) = P(A) + P(B) - P(A \text{ and } B) \qquad (2\text{-}3)$$

Probability of A or B
happening when A and B
are not mutually exclusive

Probability of A and B
happening together

Notice that if A and B are mutually exclusive, then $P(A \text{ and } B) = 0$; so we see that Eq. (2-2) is just a special case of Eq. (2-3).

A Venn diagram illustrating Eq. (2-3) is given in Figure 2-3. There, the event A *or* B is outlined with a heavy line. The event A *and* B is the crosshatched wedge in the middle. If we add the areas of circles A and B, we *double count* the area of the wedge, and so we must subtract it to make sure it is counted only once.

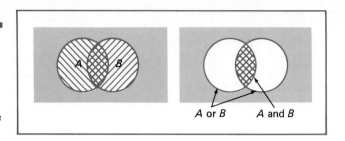

FIGURE 2-3
Venn diagram for the
addition rule for two
not mutually exclusive
events.

The addition rule is illustrated by the following example. The city council of Chapel Hill, North Carolina, is composed of the following 5 persons:

AN EXAMPLE OF
THE ADDITION OF
PROBABILITIES OF
EVENTS WHICH ARE
NOT MUTUALLY
EXCLUSIVE

Person	Sex	Age
1	Male	31
2	Male	33
3	Female	46
4	Female	29
5	Male	41

If the members of the council decide to elect a chairperson by random draw (say, by drawing the names from a hat), what is the probability that the chairperson will be *either* female *or* over 35? To solve this, we can use Eq. (2-3) and set up the solution like this:

$$P(\text{female or over 35}) = P(\text{female}) + P(\text{over 35}) - P(\text{female and over 35})$$

$$= \frac{2}{5} + \frac{2}{5} - \frac{1}{5}$$

$$= \frac{3}{5}$$

$$= .6$$

You can check this quickly by noting that of the 5 council members, 3 would fit the requirement of being *either* female *or* over 35.

5 Probabilities under conditions of statistical independence

STATISTICAL
INDEPENDENCE:
THREE TYPES OF
PROBABILITIES

When events are statistically independent, the occurrence of one event has no effect on the probability of the occurrence of any *other* event. There are three types of probabilities under conditions of statistical independence: (1) marginal, (2) joint, and (3) conditional.

MARGINAL PROBABILITIES UNDER STATISTICAL INDEPENDENCE

35

PROBABILITY
CONCEPTS

MARGINAL
PROBABILITIES UNDER
STATISTICAL
INDEPENDENCE

Marginal probability is the simple probability of the occurrence of an event.

Example 1   In the fair coin example, we have $P(H) = .5$ and $P(T) = .5$; that is, the probability of heads equals .5 and the probability of tails equals .5. This is true for every toss, no matter how many tosses may precede it or what their outcomes may be. Every event (toss) stands alone and is in no way connected with any other event (toss). Thus *each* toss of a coin is a *statistically independent event.*

Example 2   Assume that we have a biased, or unfair, coin which has been altered in such a way that heads occurs .90 of the time and tails .10 of the time. On each individual toss, $P(H) = .90$, and $P(T) = .10$. The outcome of any particular toss is completely unrelated to the outcomes of the tosses which may precede it as well as to the outcomes of any which may follow. The tosses of *this* coin too are therefore statistically independent, even though the coin is biased.

JOINT PROBABILITIES UNDER STATISTICAL INDEPENDENCE

The probability that two or more *independent* events will occur together or in succession is the product of their marginal probabilities. Mathematically, this is defined as

$$P(AB) = P(A) \times P(B) \qquad (2\text{-}4)$$

where $P(AB)$ = probability of events A and B occurring together or in
             succession; this is known as a *joint probability*
      $P(A)$ = marginal probability of event A occurring
      $P(B)$ = marginal probability of event B occurring

In terms of the fair coin example, the probability of heads on two successive tosses is the probability of heads on the first toss (shown as H_1) times the probability of heads on the second toss (shown as H_2). That is, $P(H_1H_2) = P(H_1) \times P(H_2)$. We have shown previously that the events are statistically independent because the probability of any outcome is not affected by any preceding outcome. Therefore the probability of heads on any toss is .5; then $P(H_1H_2) = .5 \times .5 = .25$; thus the probability of heads on two successive tosses is .25 (or ¼, or 25 percent).

Likewise, the probability of getting three heads on three successive tosses is $P(H_1H_2H_3) = .5 \times .5 \times .5 = .125$ (or ⅛, or 12.5 percent).

Assume that we are going to toss an unfair coin which has $P(H) = .9$ and $P(T) = .1$. The events (outcomes) are *independent* because the probabilities of all tosses are exactly the same. That is, the individual tosses are completely separate and in no way affected by any other toss or outcome.

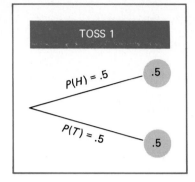

FIGURE 2-4
First toss illustrated.

What is the probability of getting three heads on three successive tosses?

$$P(H_1H_2H_3) = P(H_1) \times P(H_2) \times P(H_3) = .9 \times .9 \times .9 = .729$$

What is the probability of getting three tails on three successive tosses?

$$P(T_1T_2T_3) = P(T_1) \times P(T_2) \times P(T_3) = .1 \times .1 \times .1 = .001$$

Note that these two probabilities do not add up to 1 because $P(H_1H_2H_3)$ and $P(T_1T_2T_3)$ do not constitute a collectively exhaustive list. They *are* mutually exclusive because if one occurs, the other cannot.

As further illustration, we construct a *probability tree* showing the possible outcomes and their respective probabilities of three tosses of a fair coin.

For toss 1 we have two possible outcomes, heads and tails, each with probability of .5. This is shown in Figure 2-4.

Assume that the outcome of toss 1 is heads. We toss again. The second toss has two possible outcomes, heads and tails, each with probability of .5. In Figure 2-5 we add these two branches of the tree.

ILLUSTRATING THE
PROBABILITY OF
OUTCOMES WITH A
PROBABILITY TREE

Next we consider the possibility that the outcome of toss 1 is tails. Then the second toss must stem from the second branch of toss 1. Thus we add two more branches to the tree in Figure 2-6.

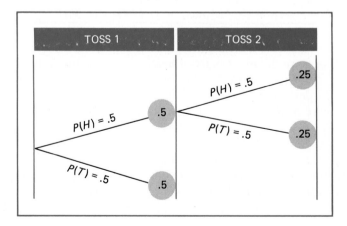

FIGURE 2-5
Partial second toss
illustrated.

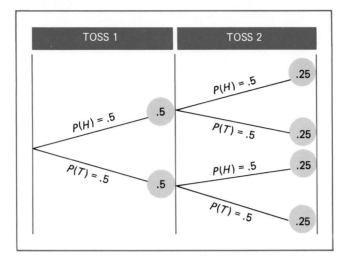

FIGURE 2-6
Two tosses
illustrated.

Notice that on two tosses we have four possible outcomes: H_1H_2, H_1T_2, T_1H_2, T_1T_2. (The subscripts indicate the toss number; for example, T_2 means tails on toss 2.) Thus after two tosses, we may arrive at any one of four possible points. Since we are going to toss three times, we must add more branches to the tree.

Assuming that we have had heads on the first two tosses, we are now ready to begin adding branches for the third toss. As before, the two possible outcomes are heads and tails, each with a probability of .5. The first step is shown in Figure 2-7.

The additional branches are added in exactly the same manner. The completed probability tree is given in Figure 2-8.

ADDING ADDITIONAL
BRANCHES

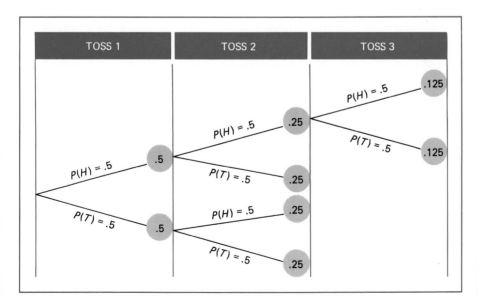

FIGURE 2-7
Partial third toss
illustrated.

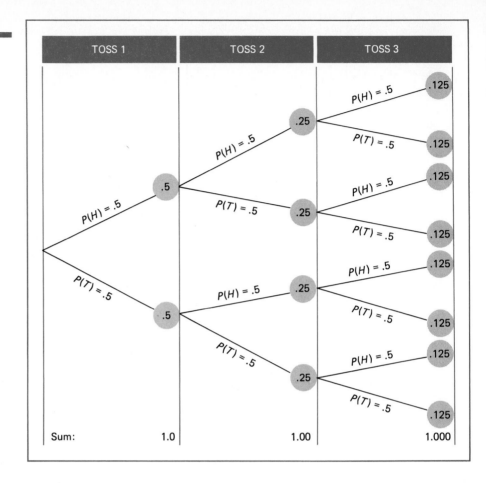

FIGURE 2-8
Completed
probability tree.

Note that both heads and tails have a probability of .5 of occurring no matter how far from the origin (first toss) any particular toss may be. This follows from our definition of *independence;* that is, *no event is affected by the events preceding or following it.*

Suppose we are going to toss a fair coin and want to know the probability that all three tosses will result in heads. Expressing the problem symbolically, we want to know $P(H_1H_2H_3)$. From the mathematical definition of the joint probability of independent events, we know that

$$P(H_1H_2H_3) = P(H_1) \times P(H_2) \times P(H_3) = .5 \times .5 \times .5 = .125$$

READING ANSWERS
DIRECTLY FROM
THE TREE

We could have read this answer from the probability tree by following the branches giving $H_1H_2H_3$.

Here are other brief examples using the probability tree.

Example 1   What is the probability of getting tails, heads, tails *in that order* on three successive tosses of a fair coin? $P(T_1H_2T_3) = P(T_1) \times P(H_2) \times P(T_3)$

= .125. Following the prescribed path on the probability tree will give us the same answer.

Example 2   What is the probability of getting tails, tails, heads *in that order* on three successive tosses of a fair coin? If we follow the branches giving tails on the first toss, tails on the second toss, and heads on the third toss, we arrive at the probability of .125. Thus $P(T_1T_2H_3) = .125$.

It is important to note that the probability of arriving at a given point by a given route is *not* the same as the probability of, say, heads on the third toss. $P(H_1T_2H_3) = .125$, but $P(H_3) = .5$. The first is a case of *joint probability*, that is, the probability of getting heads on the first toss, tails on the second, and heads on the third. The latter, by contrast, is simply the *marginal probability* of getting heads on a particular toss, in this instance toss 3.

Note that the sum of the probabilities of all the possible outcomes for each toss is 1. This is because we have mutually exclusive and collectively exhaustive lists of outcomes. These are given in Table 2-1.

Again referring to the probability tree, consider the following examples.

Example 3   What is the probability of *at least* two heads on three tosses? Recalling that the probabilities of mutually exclusive independent events are additive, we can note the possible ways that at least two heads on three tosses can occur and we can sum their individual probabilities. The outcomes which satisfy the requirement are $H_1H_2H_3$, $H_1H_2T_3$, $H_1T_2H_3$, and $T_1H_2H_3$. Since each of these has an individual probability of .125, the sum is .5. Thus the probability of at least two heads on three tosses is .5.

Example 4   What is the probability of *at least* one tail on three tosses? There is only one case in which no tails occur, namely, $H_1H_2H_3$. Therefore we can simply subtract for the answer:

$$1 - P(H_1H_2H_3) = 1 - .125 = .875$$

The probability of at least one tail occurring in three successive tosses is .875.

TABLE 2-1
Lists of outcomes

Toss 1		Toss 2		Toss 3	
Possible outcomes	**Probability**	**Possible outcomes**	**Probability**	**Possible outcomes**	**Probability**
H_1	.5	H_1H_2	.25	$H_1H_2H_3$	.125
T_1	.5	H_1T_2	.25	$H_1H_2T_3$	.125
	1.0	T_1H_2	.25	$H_1T_2H_3$	.125
		T_1T_2	.25	$H_1T_2T_3$	.125
			1.00	$T_1H_2H_3$	.125
				$T_1H_2T_3$	.125
				$T_1T_2H_3$	.125
				$T_1T_2T_3$	.125
					1.000

Example 5 What is the probability of *at least* one head on two tosses? The possible ways a head may occur are H_1H_2, H_1T_2, T_1H_2. Each of these has a probability of .25. Therefore the probability of at least one head on two tosses is .75. Alternatively, we could consider the case in which no head occurs, namely T_1T_2, and subtract its probability from 1; that is,

$$1 - P(T_1T_2) = 1 - .25 = .75$$

CONDITIONAL PROBABILITIES UNDER STATISTICAL INDEPENDENCE

Thus far we have considered two types of probabilities, *marginal* (or unconditional) *probability* and *joint probability*. Symbolically, marginal probability is $P(A)$ and joint probability is $P(AB)$. There is only one other type of probability, known as *conditional probability*. Symbolically, conditional probability is written $P(B|A)$ and is read

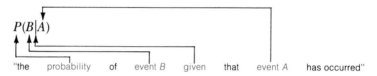

Conditional probability is the probability that a second event (B) will occur *if* a first event (A) has already happened.

For *statistically independent* events, the conditional probability of event B given that event A has occurred is the same as the *unconditional* probability of event B. At first glance this may seem contradictory. However, by definition, independent events are those whose probabilities are *in no way* affected by the occurrence of any other events. In fact, statistical independence is symbolically defined as the condition in which

$$P(B|A) = P(B) \tag{2-5}$$

Example What is the probability that the second toss of a fair coin will result in heads, given that heads occurred on the first toss? Symbolically this is written as $P(H_2|H_1)$. Remember that for two independent events, the results of the first toss have absolutely no effect on the results of the second toss. Since the probabilities of heads and tails are identical for every toss, the probability of heads on the second toss is .5; thus we must say that $P(H_2|H_1) = P(H) = .5$.

For a summary of the three types of probabilities and their mathematical formulas under conditions of statistical independence, see Table 2-2.

TABLE 2-2
Probabilities under
statistical
independence

	Type of probability	Symbol	Formula
1.	Marginal (or unconditional)	$P(A)$	$P(A)$
2.	Joint	$P(AB)$	$P(A) \times P(B)$
3.	Conditional	$P(A|B)$	$P(A)$

6 Probabilities under conditions of statistical dependence

Statistical dependence exists when the probability of some event is *dependent upon* or *affected by* the occurrence of some other event. Just as with independent events, the types of probabilities under statistical dependence are (1) marginal, (2) conditional, and (3) joint.

STATISTICAL
DEPENDENCE DEFINED

MARGINAL PROBABILITIES UNDER STATISTICAL DEPENDENCE

The marginal probability of a statistically dependent event is exactly the same as that of a statistically independent event. This is not difficult to see if we note that a marginal probability is symbolized $P(A)$. *One* and only one probability is involved; a marginal probability refers to only one event.

MARGINAL
PROBABILITY

CONDITIONAL PROBABILITIES UNDER STATISTICAL DEPENDENCE

Conditional and joint probabilities under statistical dependence are somewhat more involved than marginal probabilities. Conditional probabilities will be treated first, because the concept of joint probabilities is best illustrated using conditional probabilities as a basis.

CONDITIONAL
PROBABILITY UNDER
STATISTICAL
DEPENDENCE

Assume that we have one urn containing 10 balls distributed as follows:

3 are blue and dotted

1 is blue and striped

2 are gray and dotted

4 are gray and striped

The probability of drawing any particular ball from this urn is .1, since there are 10 balls, each with equal probability of being drawn. The discussion of the following examples will be facilitated by reference to Table 2-3.

TABLE 2-3
Color and patterns on
10 balls

Event	Probability of event	
1	.1	⎫
2	.1	⎬ Blue and dotted
3	.1	⎭
4	.1	} Blue and striped
5	.1	⎫ Gray and dotted
6	.1	⎭
7	.1	⎫
8	.1	⎪ Gray and striped
9	.1	⎬
10	.1	⎭

EXAMPLES OF
DETERMINING
CONDITIONAL
PROBABILITIES UNDER
STATISTICAL
DEPENDENCE

FOCUSING ON THE
APPROPRIATE
ELEMENTARY EVENT

Example 1 Suppose someone draws a ball from the urn and tells us it is blue. What is the probability that it is dotted? The question then can be expressed symbolically as $P(D|B)$, or: What is the conditional probability that this ball is dotted given that it is blue?

Our question can be expressed diagrammatically as shown in Figure 2-9.

We have been told that the ball drawn is blue. Therefore, to calculate the probability that the ball is dotted, we completely ignore all the gray balls and concern ourselves with the blue only. Diagrammatically, we consider only what is shown in Figure 2-10.

From the statement of the problem, we know that there are 4 blue balls, 3 of which are dotted and 1 of which is striped. Our problem is now broken down to one of finding the simple probabilities of dotted and striped. To do so we divide the number of balls in each category by the total number of blue balls:

$$P(D|B) = \frac{3}{4} = .75$$

$$P(S|B) = \frac{1}{4} = \underline{.25}$$
$$\overline{1.00}$$

In other words, three-fourths of the blue balls are dotted and one-fourth of the blue balls are striped. Thus the probability of dotted, given that the ball is blue, is .75. Likewise, the probability of striped, given that the ball is blue, is .25.

Now that we have calculated the answer, let us observe how our reasoning will enable us to develop the formula for conditional probability under conditions of statistical dependence. We can first assure ourselves that these

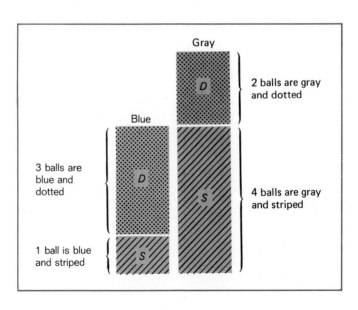

Gray

2 balls are gray
and dotted

Blue

3 balls are
blue and
dotted

4 balls are gray
and striped

1 ball is blue
and striped

FIGURE 2-9
Contents of urn
shown.

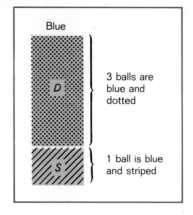

Blue

3 balls are
blue and
dotted

1 ball is blue
and striped

FIGURE 2-10
Probabilities of dotted
and striped, given
blue.

events *are* statistically dependent by observing that the color of the balls
determines the probabilities that they are either striped or dotted; for example,
a gray ball is more likely to be striped than a blue ball. Since color affects the
probability of striped or dotted, these two events are dependent.

To calculate the probability of dotted given blue, $P(D|B)$, we divided the
probability of *blue and dotted* balls (3 out of 10, or .3) by the probability of
blue balls (4 out of 10, or .4). Thus

$$P(D|B) = \frac{P(DB)}{P(B)}$$

or, expressed as a general formula using the letters A and B to represent the
two events,

$$P(A|B) = \frac{P(AB)}{P(B)} \qquad (2\text{-}6)$$

THE GENERAL FORMULA
FOR CONDITIONAL
PROBABILITY UNDER
STATISTICAL
DEPENDENCE

This is the formula for conditional probability under statistical dependence.

Example 2   What is $P(D|G)$? $P(S|G)$?

$$P(D|G) = \frac{P(DG)}{P(G)} = \frac{.2}{.6} = \frac{1}{3}$$

$$P(S|G) = \frac{P(SG)}{P(G)} = \frac{.4}{.6} = \frac{2}{3}$$

The problem is shown diagrammatically in Figure 2-11.

The total probability of gray is .6 (6 out of 10 balls). To determine the
probability that the ball (which we know is gray) will be dotted, divide the
probability of gray and dotted (.2) by the probability of gray (.6), or $.2/.6 = \frac{1}{3}$.
Similarly, to determine the probability that the ball will be striped, divide the
probability of gray and striped (.4) by the probability of gray (.6), or
$.4/.6 = \frac{2}{3}$.

EXAMPLES USING THE
CONDITIONAL
PROBABILITY FORMULA

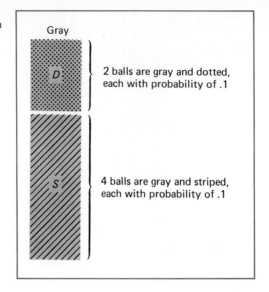

Gray

2 balls are gray and dotted, each with probability of .1

4 balls are gray and striped, each with probability of .1

FIGURE 2-11
Probabilities of dotted and striped, given gray.

Example 3 Calculate $P(B|D)$ and $P(G|D)$.

See Figure 2-12. Having been told that the ball drawn is dotted, we disregard striped entirely and consider only dotted.

Now see Figure 2-13, showing the probabilities of blue and gray, given dotted. Notice that the relative proportions of the two are as .6 is to .4.

$$P(G|D) = \frac{P(GD)}{P(D)} = \frac{.2}{.5} = \quad .4$$

$$P(B|D) = \frac{P(BD)}{P(D)} = \frac{.3}{.5} = \quad .6$$

$$\overline{1.0}$$

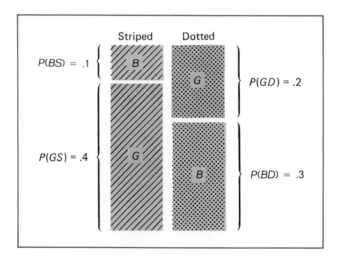

Striped   Dotted

$P(BS) = .1$ B

$P(GD) = .2$ G

$P(GS) = .4$ G

$P(BD) = .3$ B

FIGURE 2-12

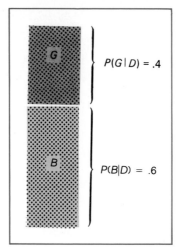

$$P(G|D) = .4$$

$$P(B|D) = .6$$

FIGURE 2-13
Probabilities of blue
and gray,
given dotted.

Example 4 Calculate $P(B|S)$ and $P(G|S)$.

$$P(B|S) = \frac{P(BS)}{P(S)} = \frac{.1}{.5} = .2$$

$$P(G|S) = \frac{P(GS)}{P(S)} = \frac{.4}{.5} = \frac{.8}{1.0}$$

JOINT PROBABILITIES UNDER STATISTICAL DEPENDENCE

We have shown that the formula for conditional probability under statistical dependence is $P(A|B) = P(AB)/P(B)$. If we solve this formula for $P(AB)$—and this can be done simply by cross multiplication—we find that

JOINT PROBABILITIES
UNDER STATISTICAL
DEPENDENCE

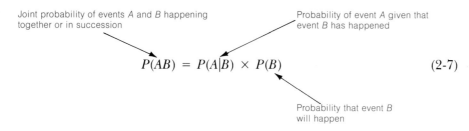

Joint probability of events A and B happening together or in succession

Probability of event A given that event B has happened

$$P(AB) = P(A|B) \times P(B) \tag{2-7}$$

Probability that event B will happen

This is the formula for joint probability under conditions of statistical dependence. It is read "the joint probability of events A and B equals the probability of event A, given that event B has occurred, times the probability of event B." Notice that this formula is *not* $P(AB) = P(A) \times P(B)$, as it would be under conditions of statistical independence.

JOINT PROBABILITIES
UNDER INDEPENDENCE
AND DEPENDENCE
COMPARED

Converting the general formula $P(AB) = P(A|B) \times P(B)$ to terms of blue, gray, dotted, and striped, we have $P(BD) = P(B|D) \times P(D)$, or $P(BD) = .6 \times .5 = .3$, where .6 is the probability of blue given dotted (computed in example 3 above) and .5 is the probability of dotted.

$P(BD) = .3$ can be verified in Table 2-3, where we originally arrived at the probability by inspection. (There are 3 blue and dotted balls among a total of 10 balls.)

The following joint probabilities are computed in the same manner and can also be substantiated by reference to Table 2-3:

$$P(BS) = P(B|S) \times P(S) = .2 \times .5 = .1$$

$$P(GD) = P(G|D) \times P(D) = .4 \times .5 = .2$$

$$P(GS) = P(G|S) \times P(S) = .8 \times .5 = .4$$

▨ COMPUTING MARGINAL PROBABILITIES UNDER STATISTICAL DEPENDENCE

Note that the marginal probability of the event *blue* can be computed by summing the probabilities of the joint events in which blue is contained:

$$P(B) = P(BD) + P(BS) = .3 + .1 = .4$$

AN ALTERNATIVE METHOD TO COMPUTE MARGINAL PROBABILITIES UNDER DEPENDENCE

Similarly, the marginal probability of the event *gray* can be computed by summing the probabilities of the joint events in which gray is contained:

$$P(G) = P(GD) + P(GS) = .2 + .4 = .6$$

Likewise, the marginal probability of the event *dotted* can be computed by summing the probabilities of the joint events in which dotted is contained:

$$P(D) = P(BD) + P(GD) = .3 + .2 = .5$$

And finally, the marginal probability of the event *striped* can be computed by summing the probabilities of the joint events in which striped is contained:

$$P(S) = P(BS) + P(GS) = .1 + .4 = .5$$

The four marginal probabilities $P(B) = .4$, $P(G) = .6$, $P(D) = .5$, and $P(S) = .5$ can be verified by inspection of Table 2-3.

SUMMARY OF PROBABILITIES UNDER DEPENDENCE

We have just considered the three types of probability—*marginal, conditional,* and *joint*—under conditions of statistical dependence. Table 2-4 provides a résumé.

Table 2-5 compares probabilities under dependence with probabilities under independence.

TABLE 2-4
Probabilities under statistical dependence

Type of probability	Symbol	Formula
1. Marginal (or unconditional)	$P(A)$	$P(A)$
2. Joint	$P(AB)$	$P(A|B) \times P(B)$
3. Conditional	$P(A|B)$	$\dfrac{P(AB)}{P(B)}$

Type of probability	Symbol	Formula under statistical independence	Formula under statistical dependence
1. Marginal	$P(A)$	$P(A)$	$P(A)$
2. Joint	$P(AB)$	$P(A) \times P(B)$	$P(A\|B) \times P(B)$
3. Conditional	$P(A\|B)$	$P(A)$	$\dfrac{P(AB)}{P(B)}$

TABLE 2-5
Probabilities under
statistical
independence and
dependence

7 Revising prior estimates of probabilities: Bayes' theorem

When the NFL season opens, the supporters of last year's winner think that their team has a terrific chance to win the title again. But the season goes on, injuries sideline the first-string quarterback, the defensive team's pass defense begins to falter, and the team begins to lose games. Late in the season, the team rooters find they must alter their prior probabilities (their a priori probabilities) of winning.

USING NEW
INFORMATION TO
REVISE A PRIORI
PROBABILITIES

In this example, probabilities were altered after the people involved got additional information. These new probabilities are known as revised, or *posterior*, probabilities. Because probabilities *can* be revised as new information becomes available, probability theory is of consequential value in decision making.

POSTERIOR
PROBABILITIES HAVE
VALUE IN DECISION
MAKING

The origin of the concept of obtaining posterior probabilities with limited information is credited to the Reverend Thomas Bayes (1702–1761), and the basic formula for conditional probability under conditions of statistical dependence,

THE ORIGIN OF
POSTERIOR
PROBABILITIES

$$P(A|B) = \frac{P(AB)}{P(B)} \qquad (2\text{-}6)$$

is called *Bayes' theorem*.

BAYES' THEOREM

CALCULATING POSTERIOR PROBABILITIES

As a first example of revising prior probabilities, assume that we have two types of deformed (biased or weighted) dice in an urn. On half of them, ace (or one dot) comes up 30 percent of the time; $P(\text{ace}) = .3$. On the other half, ace comes up 60 percent of the time; $P(\text{ace}) = .6$. Let us call the former type 1 and the latter type 2. One die is drawn, is rolled once, and comes up ace. What is the probability that it is a type 1 die? Knowing there is the same number of both types, we might answer that the probability is .5; but we can do better. To answer the question more intelligently, we set up Table 2-6.

EXAMPLES OF REVISING
PRIOR PROBABILITIES
USING BAYES'
THEOREM

The sum of the probabilities of the elementary events is 1.0: because there are only two types of dice, the probability of each type is .5. The two types constitute a mutually exclusive and collectively exhaustive list.

Elementary event	Probability of elementary event	P(ace|elementary event)	P(ace, event)
Type 1	.5	.3	$.3 \times .5 = .15$
Type 2	.5	.6	$.6 \times .5 = \underline{.30}$
	1.0		$P(ace) = .45$

TABLE 2-6

The sum of P(ace\|elementary event) does *not* equal 1.0. The figures .3 and .6 simply represent the conditional probabilities of getting an ace, given type 1 and type 2, respectively.

The fourth column is the joint probability that ace and type 1 will occur together, $.3 \times .5 = .15$, and the joint probability that ace and type 2 will occur together, $.6 \times .5 = .30$. The sum of these joint probabilities (.45) is the marginal probability of getting an ace. Note that in each case the joint probability was obtained by using the formula

$$P(AB) = P(A|B) \times P(B) \qquad (2\text{-}7)$$

To find the probability that the die we have drawn is type 1, we use the formula for conditional probability under statistical dependence:

$$P(A|B) = \frac{P(AB)}{P(B)} \qquad (2\text{-}6)$$

Converting to our problem, we have

$$P(\text{type 1}|\text{ace}) = \frac{P(\text{type 1, ace})}{P(\text{ace})}$$

or

$$P(\text{type 1}|\text{ace}) = \frac{.15}{.45} = \frac{1}{3}$$

Thus the probability that we have drawn a type 1 die is ⅓.

Let us compute the probability that the die is type 2:

$$P(\text{type 2}|\text{ace}) = \frac{P(\text{type 2, ace})}{P(\text{ace})} = \frac{.30}{.45} = \frac{2}{3}$$

USING NEW
INFORMATION
EFFECTIVELY

What have we accomplished with the one additional piece of information made available to us? What inferences have we been able to draw from one roll of the die? Before we rolled this die, the best we could say was that there was a .5 chance it was a type 1 die and a .5 chance it was a type 2 die. However, after rolling the die and noticing its behavior, we have been able to revise our prior probability estimate; our new posterior estimate is that there is a higher probability (⅔) that the die we have in our hand is a type 2 than a type 1 (only ⅓).

A PROBLEM WITH THREE OBSERVATIONS

As a more practical problem, consider the case of a manufacturer who has an automatic machine which produces ball bearings. If the machine is correctly set up—that is, properly adjusted—it produces 90 percent acceptable parts. If it is incorrectly set up, it produces 40 percent acceptable parts. Past experience indicates that 70 percent of the setups are correctly done. After a certain setup, the machine produces three acceptable bearings as the first three pieces. What is the revised probability that the setup has been correctly done? See Table 2-7.

We are now ready to compute the revised probability that the machine is correctly set up. We convert the general formula $P(A|B) = P(AB)/P(B)$ to

$$P(\text{correct}|3 \text{ good parts}) = \frac{P(\text{correct, 3 good parts})}{P(3 \text{ good parts})} = \frac{.5103}{.5295} = .9637$$

The posterior probability that the machine is correctly set up is .9637, or 96.37 percent. We have thus revised our original probability of a correct setup from 70 to 96.37 percent, based on three parts produced.

TABLE 2-7
Posterior probabilities
with joint events

Event	P(event)	P(1 good part|event)	P(3 good parts|event)	P(event, 3 good parts)
Correct	.70	.90	.729	.729 × .70 = .5103
Incorrect	.30	.40	.064	.064 × .30 = .0192
	1.00			P(3 good) = .5295

The table headings are interpreted as follows:
P(event) means the individual probabilities of correct and incorrect; that is, P(correct) = .70 (as given in the problem), and P(incorrect) = 1.00 − P(correct) = 1.00 − .70 = .30.

P(1 good part|event) means the probability of a good part, given that the setup is correct or incorrect. These probabilities are given in the problem.

P(3 good parts|event) is the probability of getting 3 good parts on 3 successive tries, given the event, that is, given correct or incorrect. The probabilities are computed as follows:

$$P(3 \text{ good parts}|\text{correct}) = .9 \times .9 \times .9 = .729$$
$$P(3 \text{ good parts}|\text{incorrect}) = .4 \times .4 \times .4 = .064$$

P(event, 3 good parts) is the probability of the joint occurrence of the event (correct or incorrect) and 3 good parts. The probabilities are computed as follows:

$$P(\text{correct, 3 good parts}) = .729 \times .70 = .5103$$
$$P(\text{incorrect, 3 good parts}) = .064 \times .30 = .0192$$

Notice that the last two probabilities conform to the general mathematical formula for joint probabilities under conditions of dependence: $P(AB) = P(A|B) \times P(B)$.

▌POSTERIOR PROBABILITIES WITH
INCONSISTENT OUTCOMES

In each of the problems illustrated to this point, the behavior of the die (or the ball bearings) was consistent; that is, the die came up ace on the only roll, and the automatic machine produced three acceptable ball bearings as the first three pieces. In most situations, the observer would expect a less consistent distribution of outcomes; for example, in the case of the ball bearings, we might observe the first five units of output and find them to be acceptable, unacceptable, acceptable, acceptable, and acceptable. Calculating our *posterior* probability that the machine is correctly set up in this case is really no more difficult than with a set of perfectly consistent outcomes. Using the notation A = acceptable ball bearings and U = unacceptable ball bearings, we have solved this example in Table 2-8.

▌8 The concept of probability distributions

ILLUSTRATING
PROBABILITY
DISTRIBUTIONS WITH A
COIN-TOSS
EXPERIMENT

PRESENTING THE
OUTCOME OF THE COIN-
TOSS EXPERIMENT IN
AN ORGANIZED FORM

The easiest way to think about probability distributions is to go back for a moment to the idea of a fair coin. Suppose we toss the coin twice. Table 2-9 illustrates the possible outcomes from this two-toss experiment.

Now suppose that we are interested in presenting in an organized form the number of *tails* that can possibly result when we toss the coin twice. We can begin by noting in Table 2-9 any outcome which does *not* contain a tail. The only outcome in Table 2-9 which does not contain a tail is the third one: H, H. Then we note those outcomes which contain only *one* tail (the second and fourth outcomes in Table 2-9: T, H, and H, T). Finally we note any outcome which contains *two* tails. The first outcome in Table 2-9—T, T—fits this requirement. Then we rearrange the outcomes first presented in Table 2-9 to emphasize the number of tails contained in each outcome. This we have done in Table 2-10. We must be careful to remember that Table 2-10 is not the *actual* outcome of tossing a fair coin twice; it is the way in which we would expect our two-toss experiment to turn out over time. The right-

TABLE 2-8
Posterior probabilities with inconsistent outcomes

Event	P(event)	P(A|event)	P(AUAAA|event)	P(event, AUAAA)
Correct	.70	.90	$.9 \times .1 \times .9 \times .9 \times .9 = .06561$	$.06561 \times .70 = .045927$
Incorrect	.30	.40	$.4 \times .6 \times .4 \times .4 \times .4 = .01536$	$.01536 \times .30 = \underline{.004608}$
	1.00			$P(AUAAA) = .050535$

$$P(\text{correct setup}|AUAAA) = \frac{P(\text{correct setup}, AUAAA)}{P(AUAAA)}$$
$$= \frac{.045927}{.050535}$$
$$= .9088$$

First toss	Second toss	Number of tails on two tosses	Probability of the four possible outcomes
T	T	2	.5 × .5 = .25
T	H	1	.5 × .5 = .25
H	H	0	.5 × .5 = .25
H	T	1	.5 × .5 = .25
			1.00

TABLE 2-9
Possible outcomes
from two tosses of a
fair coin

hand column in Table 2-10 is called a *probability distribution* because it gives the probabilities we would expect to see associated with each outcome listed in the left-hand column if the experiment were repeated a large number of times. To show a probability distribution in a more formal tabular form, we have slightly rearranged the information in Table 2-10 and have retitled it. The result is Table 2-11: the probability distribution of the possible number of tails from two tosses of a fair coin. It is useful and quite usual for probability distributions to be expressed graphically as well as in tabular form. If we graph the number of tails we might observe in two tosses of our coin against the probability that this number would happen, we get the graphic presentation of a probability distribution shown in Figure 2-14.

A PROBABILITY
DISTRIBUTION

GRAPHIC AND TABULAR
PRESENTATIONS OF
PROBABILITY
DISTRIBUTIONS

Before we consider other aspects of probability distributions, we should note that a probability distribution is a listing of the probabilities associated with all the possible outcomes that *could* result if the experiment were done. Probability distributions can be based on theoretical considerations (the toss of a coin) or on subjective assessments of the likelihood of certain outcomes (the financial manager's personal notions about bond interest rates). Probability distributions can also be based on experience; insurance company actuaries determine premiums for life insurance policies by using experience with death rates to establish the probabilities of death among different age groups.

DIFFERENT BASES FOR
PROBABILITY
DISTRIBUTIONS

▮ DISCRETE AND CONTINUOUS DISTRIBUTIONS

We classify probability distributions as either *discrete* or *continuous*. A *discrete* probability is allowed to take on only a limited number of values; an example of this would be the financial manager's assessment of possible interest rates on the bond issue next week (10½, 10⅝, 10¾, and 10⅞ percent). In the same sense, the probability that you were born in a given month is also discrete (there are only 12 possible values).

DISCRETE PROBABILITY
DISTRIBUTIONS

TABLE 2-10
Possible number of
tails from two tosses
of a fair coin

Number of tails T	Tosses	Probability of this outcome, P(T)
0	(H, H)	.25
1	(T, H) + (H, T)	.50
2	(T, T)	.25

TABLE 2-11
Probability
distribution of
possible number of
tails from two tosses
of a fair coin

Number of tails T	Probability of this outcome, $P(T)$
0	.25
1	.50
2	.25

CONTINUOUS
PROBABILITY
DISTRIBUTIONS

In a *continuous* probability distribution, the variable under consideration is permitted to take on *any* value within a given range. If, for example, we were examining the concentration of fly ash in smokestacks of industrial plants and we measured this concentration by using parts of fly ash per million parts of air, we would expect quite a continuous range of ppm (parts per million). In plants which had installed precipitators, the value of ppm would be quite low; in plants with no smoke-abatement equipment, the value would be very high. It would be quite normal for the variable ppm to take on an enormous number of values; we would call the distribution of this variable (ppm) a *continuous distribution*. In discussing continuous distributions, we associate probabilities only with intervals, rather than with single values of the variable under discussion. Thus we ask questions like, "What is the probability that the concentration of fly ash lies between 15 and 30 ppm?"

9 Random variables

DISCRETE AND
CONTINUOUS RANDOM
VARIABLES

A *random variable* is a variable that takes on different values as a result of the outcomes of a random experiment. A random variable can be either discrete or continuous. If a random variable is allowed to take on only a limited number of values, it is a *discrete random variable*. If, on the other hand, it is allowed to take on any value within a given range, it is known as a *continuous random variable*.

You can think of a random variable as a value or magnitude that changes from occurrence to occurrence in no predictable sequence. A hi-fi components wholesaler has no way of knowing exactly what tomorrow's sales will be. So tomorrow's sales of speakers, for example, is a random variable. The values of a random variable are the numerical values corresponding to each possible

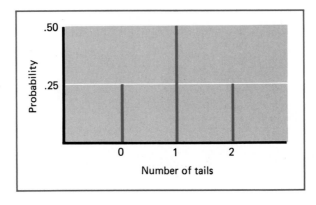

FIGURE 2-14
Probability
distribution of
possible number of
tails from two tosses
of a fair coin.

outcome of the random experiment. In the case of the wholesaler, suppose we know that past daily sales records indicate that the values of the random variable "daily sales of speakers" range from 100 to 115. In this situation the random variable is a discrete random variable.

Table 2-12 illustrates the number of times each sales level has been reached in the last 100 selling days. To the extent that we believe that the experience of the past 100 days has been typical, we can use this historical record to assign a probability to each possible level of sales and thereby find a probability distribution. We have done this in Table 2-12 by normalizing the distribution. *Normalizing* simply means that we took the number of days in the middle column of Table 2-12 and divided each value by 100, the number of days for which the record has been kept.

ASSIGNING
PROBABILITY VALUES
TO EACH POSSIBLE
OUTCOME

NORMALIZING

The probability distribution for the random variable "daily sales of speakers" is illustrated in Figure 2-15. Notice there that the probability distribution for a random variable provides a probability for each possible value and that these probabilities *must sum to 1*. Table 2-12 shows that both these requirements have been met. Remember also that Table 2-12 and Figure 2-15 give us information about the long-run occurrence of daily sales we would expect to see if this experiment were repeated.

PROBABILITY
DISTRIBUTION
PROVIDES
INFORMATION ON
LONG-RUN
OCCURRENCE

THE EXPECTED VALUE OF A RANDOM VARIABLE

Expected value is a fundamental concept in the study of probability distributions. In the last quarter century, this idea has been put to wide use by managers who have to make decisions under conditions of uncertainty.

A KEY CONCEPT

To calculate the *expected value of a discrete random variable*, we multiply each value that the random variable can take on by the probability of occurrence

CALCULATING THE
EXPECTED VALUE OF A
DISCRETE RANDOM
VARIABLE

TABLE 2-12
Probability
distribution of daily
sales of speakers

Number of speakers sold (the random variable)	No. of days this quantity sold (frequency)	Probability that the random variable will take on this value (relative frequency)
100	1	.01
101	2	.02
102	3	.03
103	5	.05
104	6	.06
105	7	.07
106	9	.09
107	10	.10
108	12	.12
109	11	.11
110	9	.09
111	8	.08
112	6	.06
113	5	.05
114	4	.04
115	2	.02
	100	1.00

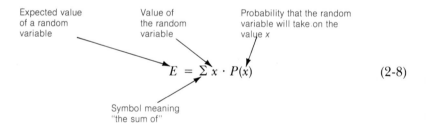

FIGURE 2-15
Probability
distribution for the
discrete random
variable "daily sales
of speakers."

of that value and then sum these products. We have done this in Table 2-13. The total in Table 2-13 tells us that the expected value of the discrete random variable "daily sales of speakers" is 108.02. What does this really mean? It means that over a long period of time, 108.02 is the weighted average daily sales in units. It does *not* imply that tomorrow's sales will be 108.02 speakers.

THE MEANING OF
EXPECTED VALUE

The calculations that we did in Table 2-13 are easily expressed by this equation:

Expected value
of a random
variable

Value of
the random
variable

Probability that the random
variable will take on the
value x

$$E = \sum x \cdot P(x) \qquad\qquad (2\text{-}8)$$

Symbol meaning
"the sum of"

THE EXPECTED VALUE
AS A WEIGHTED
AVERAGE OF
OUTCOMES

REVISING THE
EXPECTED VALUE AS
CONDITIONS CHANGE

USING PATTERNS OF
BEHAVIOR AS THE
BASIS FOR
CALCULATING MORE
DETAILED EXPECTED
VALUES

Management would find it useful to base their decisions on the expected value of daily sales because the expected value is a *weighted average of the outcomes expected in the future.* The expected value weights each possible outcome by the probability associated with its occurrence. In this manner, more common occurrences are given more weight than less common ones. As conditions changed over time, management would recompute the expected value of daily sales and then use this new figure as a basis for decision making. And if management, for example, found through analyzing past sales data that the sales pattern differed for each specific day of the week, their response would be (1) to treat "Monday's sales" as one random variable, "Tuesday's sales" as another random variable, and so forth, and (2) to derive an expected value for sales for *each* day of the week. The availability of data would, of course, determine the extent to which they could employ this more detailed form of analysis.

Possible values of the random variable (1)	Probability that the random variable will take on these values (2)	(1) × (2)
100	.01	1.00
101	.02	2.02
102	.03	3.06
103	.05	5.15
104	.06	6.24
105	.07	7.35
106	.09	9.54
107	.10	10.70
108	.12	12.96
109	.11	11.99
110	.09	9.90
111	.08	8.88
112	.06	6.72
113	.05	5.65
114	.04	4.56
115	.02	2.30
Expected value of the random variable "daily sales of speakers" →		108.02

TABLE 2-13
Calculating the
expected value

TYPES OF PROBABILITY DISTRIBUTIONS

There are many different probability distributions, both discrete and continuous. In the next four sections of the chapter we will look at four which occur very frequently in MS/OR applications:

1 the *binomial* distribution—a discrete distribution describing many processes of interest to management

2 the *Poisson* distribution—a discrete distribution often used to count the number of occurrences of some event in a given time period

3 The *exponential* distribution—a continuous distribution often used to measure the length of time needed to perform some service activity.

4 The *normal* distribution—a continuous distribution used to describe many physical, biological, economic, and managerial phenomena.

10 The binomial distribution

One very widely utilized probability distribution of a discrete random variable is the binomial distribution, which describes many processes of considerable interest to managers. The binomial distribution describes discrete (not continuous) data resulting from an experiment called a *Bernoulli process*. The tossing of a fair coin a fixed number of times is a Bernoulli process, and the outcomes of such tosses can be represented by a binomial probability distribution. The success or failure of college graduates on a job interview aptitude test might also be described by a Bernoulli process. Conversely, the distribution of the dollar amounts in a large number of accounts receivable

BINOMIAL
DISTRIBUTION

EXAMPLES OF A
BERNOULLI PROCESS

held by one company would be better measured on a continuous scale of dollars and therefore would not qualify as a binomial distribution.

USE OF THE BERNOULLI PROCESS

We can use the outcomes of a fixed number of tosses of a fair coin as a good example of a Bernoulli process. We can describe this process as follows:

1 Each trial (toss) has only *two* possible outcomes: heads or tails, yes or no, success or failure.

2 The probability of a success on any trial (toss in this case) remains *fixed* over time. In the case of our fair coin, the probability of heads remains .5 for every toss no matter how many times the coin is tossed.

3 The trials are *statistically independent*; this means that the outcome of one toss in this case has no effect on the outcome of any other toss.

CHARACTERISTIC PROBABILITY

Each Bernoulli process has its own *characteristic probability*. Look at a situation where, historically, four-tenths of all persons recruited by the U.S. Army passed the physical examination. We would say that the characteristic probability here was .4. In this situation we would be warranted in describing our test results as Bernoulli only if we felt certain that the proportion of those passing the test (.4) remained constant over time. The other characteristics of the Bernoulli process would also have to be met. Specifically, each examination would have to have only two outcomes (pass or fail), and the results of all examinations would have to be statistically independent; that is, the outcome of one examination could not affect the outcome of any other examination.

FORMAL SYMBOLS FOR BERNOULLI PROCESSES

SYMBOLS USED IN BERNOULLI PROCESSES

A bit earlier we noted that it was convenient in many cases to represent the probability distribution of a random variable in algebraic form. In the case of a Bernoulli process, the symbol p represents the probability of a success (.4 in the example of our physical examination). The symbol q (where $q = 1 - p$) is used to represent the probability of a failure (in our physical examination example, q would be $1 - .4$, or .6). We use the symbol r to represent a certain number of successes. (If we wanted to know, for example, what the chances were that we would get 11 recruits passing the examination, we would use r to represent 11.) Finally, we use the symbol n to represent the total number of trials. (If, for example, we were examining 14 recruits, n would equal 14.) In each of the situations we shall be discussing, n (the number of trials) is fixed before the experiment is begun.

We can solve problems by using the *binomial formula*:

THE BINOMIAL FORMULA

$$\text{Probability of } r \text{ successes in } n \text{ trials} = \frac{n!}{r!(n-r)!}\, p^r q^{n-r} \qquad (2\text{-}9)$$

This formula probably looks quite complicated, but in fact it can be used quite easily. The symbol ! means *factorial*. As an example, 3! means $3 \times 2 \times$

1, or 6. And 5! means $5 \times 4 \times 3 \times 2 \times 1$, or 120. 0! has been defined to be equal to 1.

1, or 6. And 5! means $5 \times 4 \times 3 \times 2 \times 1$, or 120. 0! has been defined to be equal to 1.

EXAMPLE OF BERNOULLI PROCESSES

Let's illustrate an example using the binomial formula. Some field representatives of the Environmental Protection Agency are doing spot checks of water pollution in streams. Historically, 8 out of 10 such tests produce favorable results, that is, no pollution. The field group is going to perform 6 tests and wants to know the chances of getting exactly 3 favorable results from this group of tests. Let's first define our symbols:

$$p = .8$$
$$q = .2$$
$$r = 3$$
$$n = 6$$

Now we can use the binomial formula to calculate the desired probability:

$$\text{Probability of } r \text{ successes in } n \text{ trials } = \frac{n!}{r!(n-r)!} p^r q^{n-r} \tag{2-9}$$

$$\text{Probability of 3 favorable tests out of 6} = \frac{6 \times 5 \times 4 \times 3 \times 2 \times 1}{(3 \times 2 \times 1)(3 \times 2 \times 1)}(.8^3)(.2^3)$$

$$= \frac{720}{6 \times 6}(.512)(.008)$$

$$= (20)(.512)(.008)$$

$$= .08192$$

Thus we see that there is less than 1 chance in 10 of getting this particular outcome.

ILLUSTRATING THE BINOMIAL DISTRIBUTION GRAPHICALLY

Up to now, we have dealt with the binomial distribution only by using the binomial formula. The binomial distribution, like any other distribution, can be expressed graphically as well as algebraically.

To illustrate the binomial distribution graphically, let's look at a situation where 5 employees are required to operate a chemical process; the process cannot be started until all 5 work stations are manned. Employee records indicate there is a .4 chance of any one employee being late, and we know that they all come to work independently of each other. Management is interested in knowing the probabilities of 0, 1, 2, 3, 4, or 5 employees being late, so that a decision concerning the number of backup personnel can be made. If we want to draw a probability distribution illustrating this situation, we use the binomial formula, with

WATER POLLUTION EXAMPLE OF A BERNOULLI PROCESS

BINOMIAL PROBABILITY EXAMPLE OF LATE ARRIVALS

$$p = .4$$
$$q = .6$$
$$n = 5$$

In defining n in this case, we are interested in the number of employees. The fact that there is a chance that none of them will be late does not alter our choice of $n = 5$.

We would make a separate calculation for each r from 0 through 5.

$$\text{Probability of } r \text{ late arrivals out of } n \text{ employees} = \frac{n!}{r!(n - r)!} p^r q^{n-r} \quad (2\text{-}9)$$

Our calculations for r for 0 and 1 are:

$$P(0) = \frac{5!}{0!(5 - 0)!}(.4^0)(.6^5)$$

$$= \frac{5 \times 4 \times 3 \times 2 \times 1}{(1)(5 \times 4 \times 3 \times 2 \times 1)}(1)(.6^5)$$

$$= \frac{120}{120}(1)(.07776)$$

$$= .07776$$

$$P(1) = \frac{5!}{1!(5 - 1)!}(.4^1)(.6^4)$$

$$= \frac{5 \times 4 \times 3 \times 2 \times 1}{(1)(4 \times 3 \times 2 \times 1)}(.4)(.6^4)$$

$$= \frac{120}{24}(.4)(.1296)$$

$$= .2592$$

Using the same approach, we find that the probabilities for 2, 3, 4, and 5 are .3456, .2304, .0768, and .01024, respectively. The sum of these over all the values of r equals 1.0.

Now if we graph the results of these six different calculations, this binomial distribution will appear as shown in Figure 2-16.

Without doing all the calculations involved, we can illustrate the general appearance of a family of binomial probability distributions. In Figure 2-17, for example, each distribution represents $n = 5$. In each case, the p and q have been changed and are noted beside each distribution. From Figure 2-17, we can make the following generalizations:

1 When p is small (.1), the binomial distribution is skewed to the right.

2 As p increases (to .3, for example), the skewness is less noticeable.

can be corrected. Except as described in this agreement, software and diskettes are distributed "as is" without warranties of any kind, either express or implied, including, but not limited to, implied warranties of merchantability and fitness for a particular purpose or use.

5. Additional rights and benefits may come with the specific software package you have purchased. Consult the support materials that come with this program, or contact the nearest McGraw-Hill Book Company office in your area.

P/N 831412-7

LICENSE AGREEMENT FOR McGRAW-HILL SOFTWARE

This agreement gives you, the customer, certain benefits, rights and obligations. By using the software, you indicate that you have read, understood, and will comply with the terms.

Terms of Agreement:

1. McGraw-Hill licenses and authorizes you to use the software specified below only on a microcomputer located within your own facilities.

2. You will abide by the Copyright Law of the United States. This law provides you with the right to make only one back-up copy. It prohibits you from making any additional copies, except as expressly provided by McGraw-Hill. In the event that the software is protected against copying in such a way that it cannot be duplicated, McGraw-Hill will provide you with one back-up copy at minimal cost or no charge.

3. You will not prepare derivative works based on the software because that is also not permitted under Copyright Law. For example, you cannot prepare an alternative hardware version or format based on the existing software.

4. If you have a problem with the operation of our software or believe it is defective, contact your nearest McGraw-Hill Book Company office about securing a replacement. We cannot, however, offer free replacement of diskettes damaged through normal wear and tear, or lost while in your possession. Nor does McGraw-Hill warrant that the software will satisfy your requirements, that the operation of the software will be uninterrupted or error-free, or that program defects in the software

(Continued on reverse side)

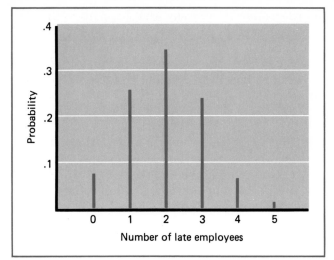

FIGURE 2-16
Binomial probability
distribution of the
number of late
employees.

3 When $p = .5$, the binomial distribution is symmetrical.

4 When p is larger than .5, the distribution is skewed to the left.

5 The probabilities for .3, for example, are the same as those for .7 except that the values of p and q are *reversed*. This is true for any pair of complementary p and q values (.3 and .7), (.4 and .6), and (.2 and .8).

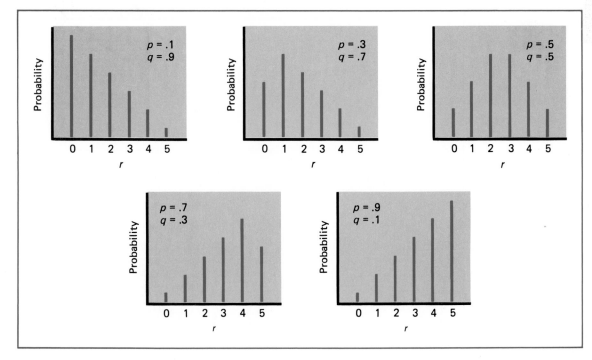

FIGURE 2-17
Group of binomial distributions with constant $n = 5$ and several different p and q values.

Let us examine graphically what happens to the binomial distribution when p stays constant but n is increased. Figure 2-18 illustrates the general shape of a family of binomial distributions with a constant p of .4 and n's from 5 to 30. As n increases, the vertical lines not only become more numerous but also tend to bunch up together to form a *bell shape*. We shall have more to say about this bell shape shortly.

USING THE BINOMIAL TABLES

USING TABLES INSTEAD OF THE BINOMIAL FORMULA TO CALCULATE BINOMIAL PROBABILITIES

From the previous example, it is obvious that it is tedious to calculate probabilities using the binomial formula. Fortunately tables are available which greatly simplify this work. Appendix Table 2 enables us to determine binomial probabilities quickly. Let us illustrate the use of the binomial tables. A large bank hires 15 M.B.A.'s each year and assigns them to the various

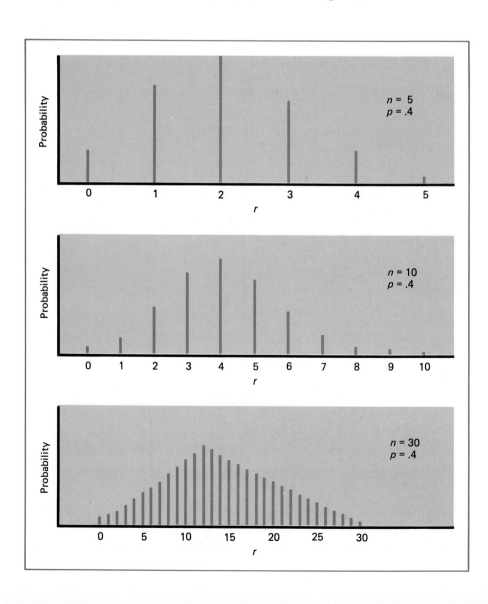

FIGURE 2-18

Group of binomial distributions with $p = .4$ and n's of 5, 10, and 30.

divisions. After a year's experience, the chances that any one M.B.A. will be performing unsatisfactorily have historically been .3. In this year's group, what are the chances that 8 or more will be performing unsatisfactorily after a year? We can begin to answer this question by expressing the elements in this problem using the binomial formula symbols:

$p = .3$ probability that any one M.B.A. will perform unsatisfactorily
$q = .7$ $(1 - p)$
$r = 8$ number of unsatisfactory performers in question
$n = 15$ number of persons in the group

Then, since this situation involves 15 trials, we look in Appendix Table 2 for the $n = 15$ table. Since the probability of unsatisfactory performance for any one person is .3, we look through the $n = 15$ table until we find the column where $p = .30$ (this is denoted as 30). We move down that column to the $r = 8$ row, where we find the value 0500, which can be interpreted as representing a probability of .05; this represents the probability of 8 or more unsatisfactory performances.

If our problem had asked us for the probability of *more than 8* unsatisfactory performances in this group, we would simply have looked up the probability of *9 or more,* in this case .0152. If the problem had asked for the probability of *exactly 8* unsatisfactory performances, we would have subtracted the probability of 9 or more (.0152) from the probability of 8 or more (.05); the answer, .0348, would represent the probability of exactly 8 unsatisfactory performances. And if the problem had asked for the probability of fewer than 8 unsatisfactory performances, we would have subtracted the probability of 8 or more from 1.0 for an answer of .95.

PROBABILITY OF
MORE THAN 8

PROBABILITY OF
EXACTLY 8

PROBABILITY OF
FEWER THAN 8

CARE IN USING THE BERNOULLI PROCESS

When we are using the binomial probability distribution, we must be certain that the three conditions for its use first introduced on page 56 are met. If there is any chance of more than two outcomes, condition 1 is not satisfied. Condition 2 requires that the probability of the outcome of any trial remain fixed over time. In many managerial decisions, this is not really the case. It might be usual to expect that the outcome of a series of trials would have *some* influence on the characteristic probability over time. Even the most carefully maintained machine undergoes some very slight wear each time a part is produced on it. Condition 3 requires that the trials of a Bernoulli process be statistically independent. This condition is also difficult to satisfy in many managerial situations. For example, if you have been making loans in a bank and you have just turned down the last 10 applicants, it may be difficult to evaluate the creditworthiness of the eleventh applicant with complete objectivity; in this case, the trials might not be statistically independent.

11 The Poisson distribution

The Poisson distribution, named after the mathematician and physicist Siméon Poisson (1781–1840), appears frequently in MS/OR literature and finds

THE POISSON
DISTRIBUTION
DESCRIBES A NUMBER
OF SITUATIONS OF
INTEREST TO
MANAGEMENT

a large number of managerial applications. It is used to describe a number of managerial situations including the demand (arrivals) of patients at a health clinic, the distribution of telephone calls going through a central switching system, the arrival of vehicles at a toll booth, the number of accidents at an intersection, and the number of looms waiting for service in a textile mill. All these examples have a common characteristic: they can all be described by a discrete random variable that takes on nonnegative integer (whole number) values (0, 1, 2, 3, 4, 5, and so on). The number of cars arriving at a toll booth on the Petersburg Turnpike during some 10-minute period will be 0, 1, 2, 3, 4, 5, and so on; the number of patients who arrive at a physician's office in a given interval of time will also be 0, 1, 2, 3, 4, 5, and so on.

CHARACTERISTICS OF PROCESSES THAT PRODUCE A POISSON PROBABILITY DISTRIBUTION

Suppose we use the number of patients arriving at a physician's office during the busiest part of the day as an illustration of Poisson probability distribution characteristics:

CHARACTERISTICS OF PROCESSES THAT PRODUCE POISSON PROBABILITY DISTRIBUTIONS

1 The average number of arrivals of patients per 15-minute interval can be estimated from past office data.

2 If we divide the 15-minute interval into smaller intervals of, say, 1 second each, we will see that these statements are true:

a The probability that exactly 1 patient will arrive at the office per second is a very small number and is constant for every 1-second interval.

b The probability that 2 or more patients will arrive within a 1-second interval is so small that we can safely assign a probability of 0 to such events.

c The number of patients who arrive in a 1-second interval is independent of where that 1-second interval is within the larger 15-minute interval.

d The number of patients who arrive in any 1-second interval is not dependent on the number of arrivals in any other 1-second interval.

It is acceptable to generalize from these conditions and to apply them to other processes of interest to management. If these processes meet the same conditions, then it is possible to use a Poisson probability distribution to describe them.

CALCULATING PROBABILITIES WITH THE POISSON DISTRIBUTION

DEFINING X AND x IN POISSON PROBABILITY DISTRIBUTIONS

The Poisson distribution is useful in analyzing certain processes that can be described by a discrete random variable. It is usual for the letter X to represent a Poisson random variable. X can take on integer values (0, 1, 2, 3, 4, 5, and so on); when we refer to *one* of those specific values that X can take, we use a lowercase x. The probability of exactly x occurrences in a Poisson distribution is calculated using this formula:

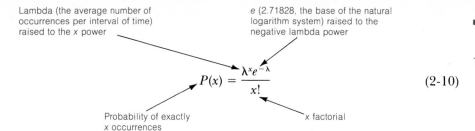

Lambda (the average number of occurrences per interval of time) raised to the x power

e (2.71828, the base of the natural logarithm system) raised to the negative lambda power

$$P(x) = \frac{\lambda^x e^{-\lambda}}{x!} \qquad (2\text{-}10)$$

Probability of exactly x occurrences

x factorial

An example will help us understand the use of this formula. We are considering an emergency room of a small rural hospital where the past records indicate an average of 5 arrivals daily. The demand for emergency room service at this hospital is distributed according to a Poisson distribution. The hospital administrator wants to calculate the probability of exactly 0, 1, 2, 3, 4, and 5 arrivals per day. This calculation is simplified by the use of Appendix Table 4, which frees us from having to calculate e's to negative powers. The appropriate calculations for the probabilities of 0, 1, 2, 3, 4, and 5 requests per day for emergency room service are

$$P(0) = \frac{(5^0)(e^{-5})}{0!}$$

$$= \frac{(1)(.00674)}{1}$$

$$= .00674$$

$$P(1) = \frac{(5^1)(e^{-5})}{1!}$$

$$= \frac{(5)(.00674)}{1}$$

$$= .03370$$

CALCULATION OF THE PROBABILITY OF 0 THROUGH 5 ARRIVALS

$$P(2) = \frac{(5^2)(e^{-5})}{2!}$$

$$= \frac{(25)(.00674)}{2 \times 1}$$

$$= .08425$$

$$P(3) = \frac{(5^3)(e^{-5})}{3!}$$

$$= \frac{(125)(.00674)}{3 \times 2 \times 1}$$

$$= .14042$$

$$P(4) = \frac{(5^4)(e^{-5})}{4!}$$

$$= \frac{(625)(.00674)}{4 \times 3 \times 2 \times 1}$$

$$= .17552$$

$$P(5) = \frac{(5^5)(e^{-5})}{5!}$$

$$= \frac{(3125)(.00674)}{5 \times 4 \times 3 \times 2 \times 1}$$

$$= .17552$$

Notice that the sum of these 6 probabilities = 0.61615. This is less than 1, because it is possible to have more than 5 arrivals on any given day.

We can use the results of these calculations to answer some questions of interest to Rebecca Rubin, the hospital administrator, as she attempts to provide adequate emergency room staff. If she wants to know the probability of more than 3 calls for emergency room service on a given day, she can find

PROBABILITY OF 0, 1, 2, OR 3

this answer by adding together the probabilities of 0, 1, 2, and 3 calls and subtracting the result from 1:

$$P(0) = .00674 \qquad P(\text{more than } 3) = 1 - .26511$$
$$P(1) = .03370 \qquad\qquad\qquad\qquad = .73489$$
$$P(2) = .08425$$
$$P(3) = \underline{.14042}$$
$$.26511$$

Thus Rebecca sees that she will have to be prepared to have more than 3 calls per day slightly less than three-quarters of the time.

Figure 2-19 illustrates graphically the Poisson probability distribution of demand for emergency room services at this hospital.

The distribution illustrated in Figure 2-19 is only for 0 through 5 calls for emergency room service; it would, of course, be possible with additional calculation to produce the required probability values (and thus the graphic distribution) for *any* number of calls.

12 The exponential distribution

The exponential probability distribution is the third of the four probability distributions examined in this chapter. The second, the Poisson distribution, was introduced in the previous section as being used in MS/OR to describe the *distribution of arrivals per unit time* at a service facility. When the number of arrivals per unit time can be described by the Poisson distribution, the *interarrival time* (that is, the time between two successive arrivals) is described by the exponential distribution. Although the Poisson distribution is discrete,

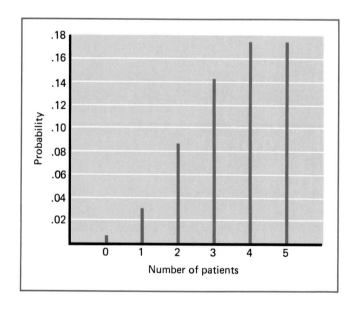

FIGURE 2-19

Poisson probability distribution of demand for emergency room service (0 through 5 calls).

the exponential distribution is continuous, because the interarrival time does not have to be an integer number of time units.

We will often use the exponential distribution to describe the *distribution of time between events*, specifically the random variable that represents the time required for service at a service facility. Examples of this are the time required to handle a bank deposit, the time required to process a motor vehicle license application, the time it takes a physician to complete a medical examination, and the time it took you to register for this course, once you got to the head of the line.

CHARACTERISTICS OF THE EXPONENTIAL DISTRIBUTION

Use of the exponential distribution to describe the distribution of service times at a service facility assumes that the service times are *random*, that is, the time to serve an arrival is independent of how much time has already been spent serving prior arrivals and is independent of the number of arrivals waiting to be serviced.

A second characteristic of the exponential distribution is that the random variable *service times* does not "age"; often we refer to this by saying that the random variable "has no memory." We can illustrate this characteristic with an example. Suppose that service times to handle a certain category of taxpayer complaint at a regional IRS office are best described by an exponential distribution. If a taxpayer has already been in conference with the IRS agent for 5 hours, the probability that the taxpayer's complaint will require, say, another hour to handle, is the same as if he or she had been in conference 2 hours, or 10 hours for that matter.

CALCULATING PROBABILITIES WITH THE EXPONENTIAL DISTRIBUTION

In Figure 2-18, on page 60, we saw a binomial distribution with $n = 30$, and commented about how the vertical lines were becoming more numerous and closer together. With the exponential distribution, and all other *continuous* distributions, we have an infinite number of possible values for the random variable, and the individual vertical lines get replaced by a smooth curve, called the *probability density function*. For the exponential distribution, the probability density function is given by

$$p(t) = \mu e^{-\mu t}, \tag{2-11}$$

where, t = the service time

μ = the mean service rate (units serviced per unit time) (μ is the greek letter *mu*)

e = 1.71828, the base of the natural logarithm system

This *exponential density* is illustrated in Figure 2-20. We will be interested in finding $P(T \leq t)$, the probability that the service time T will be less than or equal to some specific value t. This is equal to the area under the density

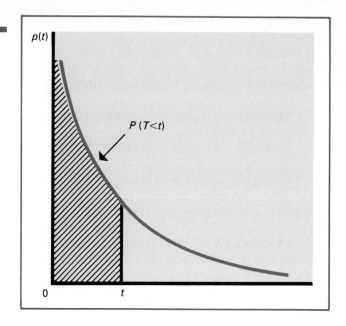

FIGURE 2-20
Exponential
probability
distribution.

function (shown in Figure 2-20) between $T = 0$ and $T = t$, and can be computed using Eq. (2-12):

THE EQUATION FOR
THE EXPONENTIAL
DISTRIBUTION

The probability that the service time T will be less than or equal to t

The $-\mu t$ power

$$P(T \le t) = 1 - e^{-\mu t} \qquad (2\text{-}12)$$

$e = 2.71828$, the base of the natural logarithm system

AN EXAMPLE USING
THE EXPONENTIAL
DISTRIBUTION

Suppose the distribution in Figure 2-20 represents the time it takes for a microcomputer repair facility to repair 1 unit, and suppose the mean repair time has been found to be 3 hours. Thus μ, the mean service *rate*, is $\frac{1}{3}$ unit per hour. What is the probability that service on a faulty microcomputer will be completed in 2 or fewer hours?

Using Eq. (2-12) and Appendix Table 5 (with $\lambda = \mu t$)

$$
\begin{aligned}
P(T \le t) &= 1 - e^{-\mu t} \qquad (2\text{-}12)\\
P(T \le 2) &= 1 - e^{-(1/3)(2)}\\
&= 1 - e^{-2/3}\\
&= 1 - .5134\\
&= .4866, \text{ or almost a 50 percent chance}
\end{aligned}
$$

13 The normal distribution

The fourth probability distribution discussed in this chapter is another important continuous probability distribution: the *normal distribution*. Several mathematicians were instrumental in its development, among them the eighteenth-century mathematician-astronomer Karl Gauss (1777–1855). In honor of his work, the normal probability distribution is often referred to as the *Gaussian* distribution. The normal distribution occupies an important place in management science for two reasons. First, it has properties that make it applicable to a number of managerial situations in which decision makers have to make inferences by drawing samples. Second, the normal distribution comes quite close to fitting the actual observed distribution of many phenomena, including outputs from physical processes and human characteristics (height, weight, intelligence) as well as many other measures of interest to management in the social and natural sciences.

CHARACTERISTICS OF THE NORMAL PROBABILITY DISTRIBUTION

Look now at Figure 2-21, a normal distribution. This diagram indicates several important characteristics of a normal probability distribution and its density function:

1 The curve has a single peak.

2 It is bell-shaped.

3 The mean (average) lies at the center of the distribution; the distribution is symmetrical around a vertical line erected at the mean.

4 The two tails of the normal probability distribution extend indefinitely and never touch the horizontal axis (it is impossible to illustrate this graphically).

Of course, most real world distributions don't extend forever in both directions; but for many distributions the normal distribution is a convenient approximation. As a matter of fact, there is not a single normal curve but rather a whole family of normal curves. Figure 2-22 shows three normal probability distributions, each of which has the same average (mean); each of these three has a different "spread"—that is, the values in curve *A* tend to cluster, or group together very near the mean, and the values in curve *C* tend to spread out far from the mean. The values in curve *B* tend to spread

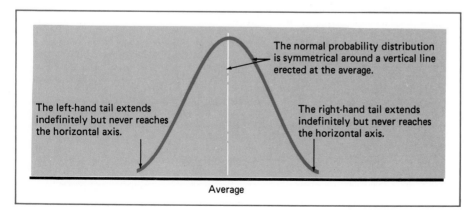

The normal probability distribution is symmetrical around a vertical line erected at the average.

The left-hand tail extends indefinitely but never reaches the horizontal axis.

The right-hand tail extends indefinitely but never reaches the horizontal axis.

Average

FIGURE 2-21
Normal probability distribution.

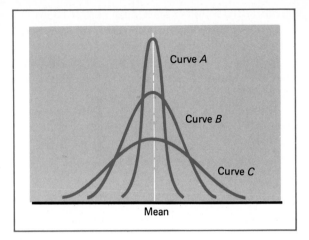

FIGURE 2-22
Three examples of
normal probability
distributions with the
same mean but
different spreads.

NORMAL CURVES WITH
THE SAME MEAN AND
DIFFERENT SPREADS

NORMAL CURVES WITH
THE SAME SPREAD BUT
DIFFERENT MEANS

THE NORMAL CURVE
DESCRIBES MANY SETS
OF DATA

INTERPRETING THE
MEAN OF A
DISTRIBUTION

out more than those in *A* but less than those in *C*. Although the three curves in Figure 2-22 differ in appearance, they are all normal curves.

Now look at the three curves in Figure 2-23. The values in each of these three curves have the same tendency to cluster about their mean, but the means are all different. Each of the three distributions in Figure 2-23 is *also* a normal distribution.

Finally, let us look at the three curves in Figure 2-24; here each distribution has not only a different mean but also a different tendency to spread out from its mean. Each distribution in Figure 2-24 is *also* normal, even though the means and the spreads differ. The nine different normal probability distributions illustrated in Figures 2-22, 2-23, and 2-24 demonstrate that normal curves can describe a large number of groups of data differentiated only by their mean and their tendency to spread. Any normal distribution is defined by two measures: the *mean,* which locates the center, and the *standard deviation,* which measures the spread around the center.

THE MEAN OF A DISTRIBUTION

In our past examples, we have been discussing the *mean,* or *average,* without formally explaining what the mean is and how to calculate it. Most of us

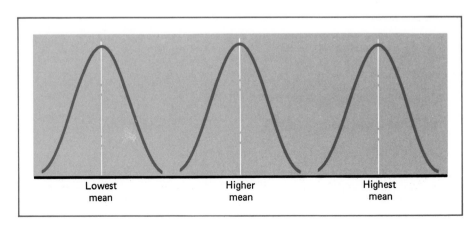

FIGURE 2-23
Three examples of
normal probability
distributions with the
same spread but
different means.

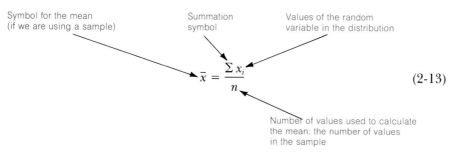

Lowest mean and
most spread

Higher mean
and less spread

Highest mean and
least spread

FIGURE 2-24
Three examples of
normal probability
distributions with
different spreads and
different means.

become familiar with the notion of *average,* and we come to accept it as a measure of something, but of what? The average, or mean, is known as a measure of central tendency, that is, a measure of the center of the data. Take the 30 values in Table 2-14, for example. These represent the daily sales for a used car lot since it was opened last month. We can calculate the *mean* daily sales by dividing the total number of cars sold during the 30-day period by 30:

$$\text{Mean sales per day} = \frac{420}{30}$$

CALCULATING
THE MEAN

$$= 14 \text{ per day}$$

A more formal expression of the calculation of the mean using conventional symbols would be

Symbol for the mean
(if we are using a sample)

Summation
symbol

Values of the random
variable in the distribution

$$\bar{x} = \frac{\Sigma\, x_i}{n}$$

(2-13)

Number of values used to calculate
the mean; the number of values
in the sample

						TABLE 2-14
						Quantity sold

26	20	5	13	18	13
13	19	7	19	9	22
33	5	10	18	9	9
10	18	3	10	10	7
13	17	13	17	17	17

If we are averaging *all* the x_i values (the whole population and not just a sample), the formula becomes

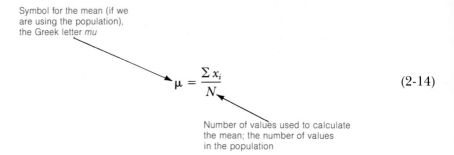

$$\mu = \frac{\Sigma x_i}{N}$$ (2-14)

As you can see, Eqs. (2-13) and (2-14) are the same except for the notation we have used to distinguish between the sample mean and the population mean.

The mean is a very useful measure. In this case, it gives us a reasonable idea of the average daily sale of used cars. We can see from the 30 values in Table 2-14 that the daily sales tend to be around 14.

THE VALUE OF THE
MEAN AS A MEASURE

▌ THE STANDARD DEVIATION

There are several measures of the tendency of data to spread out, or disperse, but we will restrict our attention to the most commonly used statistical measure of the tendency for data to disperse around their own mean. This measure is called the *standard deviation.* Because we can make important management inferences from past data with this measure, we must learn how to calculate it and what it means.

A formal expression of the standard deviation using accepted symbols would be

FORMULA FOR THE
STANDARD DEVIATION

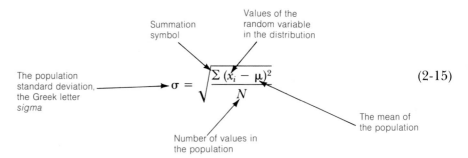

$$\sigma = \sqrt{\frac{\Sigma (x_i - \mu)^2}{N}}$$ (2-15)

With a tiny bit of algebraic manipulation, we can transform Eq. (2-15) into this form:

$$\sigma = \sqrt{\frac{\Sigma x_i^2}{N} - \mu^2}$$ (2-16)

Table 2-15 calculates the standard deviation using *both* equations. Note that the standard deviation is expressed in the *same dimensional units* as the mean.

Observation, x_i	Mean, μ	Deviation, $x_i - \mu$	Deviation^2, $(x_i - \mu)^2$	Observation squared, x_i^2
26	− 14	12	144	676
13	− 14	− 1	1	169
33	− 14	19	361	1089
10	− 14	− 4	16	100
13	− 14	− 1	1	169
5	− 14	− 9	81	25
7	− 14	− 7	49	49
10	− 14	− 4	16	100
3	− 14	− 11	121	9
13	− 14	− 1	1	169
18	− 14	4	16	324
9	− 14	− 5	25	81
9	− 14	− 5	25	81
10	− 14	− 4	16	100
17	− 14	3	9	289
20	− 14	6	36	400
19	− 14	5	25	361
5	− 14	− 9	81	25
18	− 14	4	16	324
17	− 14	3	9	289
13	− 14	− 1	1	169
19	− 14	5	25	361
18	− 14	4	16	324
10	− 14	− 4	16	100
17	− 14	3	9	289
13	− 14	− 1	1	169
22	− 14	8	64	484
9	− 14	− 5	25	81
7	− 14	− 7	49	49
17	− 14	3	9	289
420 ← Σx_i		$\Sigma(x_i - \mu)^2$ → 1264		7144 ← Σx_i^2

(2-15)
$$\sigma = \sqrt{\frac{\Sigma(x_i - \mu)^2}{N}}$$
$$= \sqrt{\frac{1264}{30}}$$
$$= \sqrt{42.13}$$
$$= 6.49$$

← or →

(2-16)
$$\sigma = \sqrt{\frac{\Sigma x_i^2}{N} - \mu^2}$$
$$= \sqrt{\frac{7144}{30} - (14)^2}$$
$$= \sqrt{238.13 - 196}$$
$$= 6.49$$

TABLE 2-15
Calculation of the standard deviation

If the mean is the average distance (in inches) of the hemline of skirts above the knee, then the standard deviation will also be in inches and will indicate the degree of variation of hemlines.

USES OF THE STANDARD DEVIATION

The standard deviation allows us to determine quite accurately where the values in a distribution are located relative to their mean. We can measure with great precision, for example, the percentage of items in a population which fall within specific ranges under a normal distribution. In Figure 2-25 we illustrate three mathematical facts:

1 About 68 percent of the values in the population fall within plus or minus 1 standard deviation from the mean.

2 About 95 percent of the values in the population fall within plus or minus 2 standard deviations from the mean.

3 About 99 percent of the values are in an interval ranging from 3 standard deviations below the mean to 3 standard deviations above the mean.

What does all this mean to the manager of our used car lot? Just this. If the mean of our past daily sales is 14 and if the standard deviation is 6.49 units, then approximately 68 percent of all future sales will fall between 14 plus 6.49 units and 14 minus 6.49 units, or between 20.49 units and 7.51 units. Similarly, about 95 percent of all future sales will fall between 14 + (2 × 6.49) units and 14 − (2 × 6.49) units, or between 26.98 and 1.02 units.

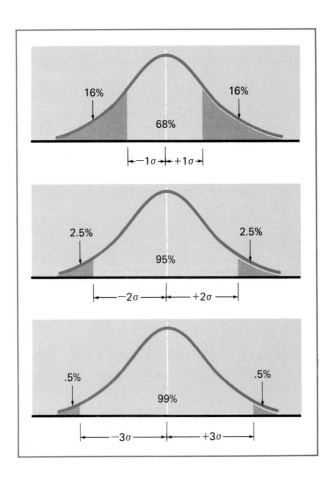

FIGURE 2-25

Approximate areas under intervals of normal curves.

It turns out, however, that very few of the applications we shall make of the normal probability distribution involve intervals of *exactly* 1, 2, or 3 standard deviations (plus and minus) from the mean. What do we do about all those other cases? Unlike the exponential distribution, where we could give a formula, Eq. (2-12), for the area under the probability density function, no such formula exists for the normal distribution. Fortunately, we can refer to statistical tables which have been constructed precisely for these situations. These tables indicate portions of the area under the normal curve that are contained within *any* number of standard deviations (plus and minus) from the mean. No matter what the mean μ and the standard deviation σ are for a normal probability distribution, the *total* area under the normal curve is 1.00, so we may think of areas under the curve as probabilities.

It is neither necessary nor possible to have a different table for every possible normal curve. Instead, we can use a table of areas under the curve of a *standard normal probability distribution*. With this table, we can determine the area, or probability, that a normally distributed random variable with any mean and any standard deviation will lie within certain distances from the mean. These distances are defined in terms of standard deviations.

We can understand the standard normal probability distribution by examining the relationship of the standard deviation to the normal curve. This is shown in Figure 2-26, which illustrates two normal probability distributions, each with a different mean and a different standard deviation. Both area *A* and area *B*, the shaded areas under both curves, contain the *identical* proportion of the total area under the normal curve. Why is this true? Because both these areas are defined as being the area between the mean and 1 standard deviation to the right of the mean. *All* such intervals which contain the same number of standard deviations from the mean will in turn contain the same proportion of the total area under the curve for *any* normal probability distribution. Thus it is possible to use one standard normal probability table, Appendix Table 1.

HOW TO HANDLE
DEVIATIONS OTHER
THAN 1, 2, OR 3

STANDARD NORMAL
PROBABILITY
DISTRIBUTION

EXPLANATION OF THE
STANDARD NORMAL
PROBABLITY
DISTRIBUTION

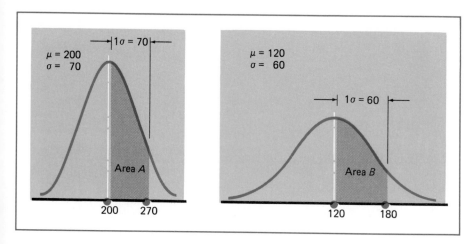

FIGURE 2-26

Two intervals, each 1 standard deviation to the right of the mean.

USING THE STANDARD NORMAL PROBABILITY TABLE

Appendix Table 1 illustrates the area under the normal curve between the left-hand tail and any point to the right of the mean. Notice in this table the location of the column labeled z. The value of z is derived from this equation:

$$z = \frac{x - \mu}{\sigma} \tag{2-17}$$

where x = the value of the random variable with which we are concerned
μ = the mean of the distribution of this random variable
σ = the standard deviation of this distribution
z = the number of standard deviations from x to the mean of this distribution

STANDARD UNITS

Why should we use z instead of "the number of standard deviations"? Because normally distributed random variables take on many *different units* of measure (dollars, parts per million, pounds, time), and since we will use only *one* table, we should talk in terms of *standard units*. This, in fact, really means standard deviations; standard units are given a symbol of z. A glance at Figure 2-27 will show that using z only means that we have changed our scale of measurement on the horizontal axis.

We must work several examples to become comfortable with the use of Appendix Table 1 (The Standard Normal Probability Distribution). As our problem environment, let's consider an accounts receivable auditor examining customer accounts for a client. Past records indicate that the mean amount per account is $5,000 and that this particular random variable has a standard deviation of $1,000.

AN EXAMPLE OF THE
RANDOM VARIABLE
BEING GREATER THAN
THE MEAN

Example 1 What is the probability that an account selected at random will have a balance of *more* than $5,000? In Figure 2-28, we see that half the area under the normal curve is located on either side of the mean of $5,000;

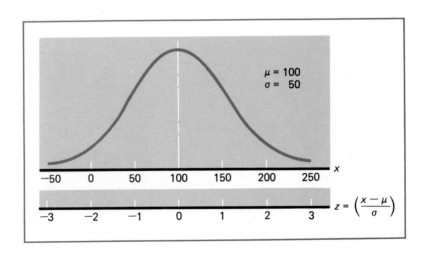

FIGURE 2-27
Normal distribution illustrating relationship of z values and standard deviations.

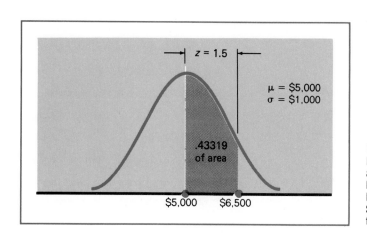

μ = $5,000
σ = $1,000

.5 of area

$5,000

FIGURE 2-28
Distribution of
accounts receivable
balances. The interval
of more than $5,000
is shown in the
shaded area.

therefore we know that the probability that the random variable will take on
a value higher than $5,000 is the shaded half, or .5.

Example 2   What is the probability that an account selected at random will
have a balance *between* $5,000 and $6,500? This situation is shown graphically
in Figure 2-29. The shaded area between the mean ($5,000) and the *x* value
in which we are interested ($6,500) represents this probability. Using Eq.
(2-17) we get a *z* value of

AN EXAMPLE OF THE
RANDOM VARIABLE
BEING BETWEEN THE
MEAN AND A VALUE
LARGER THAN THE
MEAN

$$z = \frac{x - \mu}{\sigma}$$ (2-17)

$$= \frac{\$6,500 - \$5,000}{\$1,000}$$

$$= \frac{\$1,500}{\$1,000}$$

$$= 1.5 \text{ standard deviations}$$

z = 1.5

μ = $5,000
σ = $1,000

.43319
of area

$5,000 $6,500

FIGURE 2-29
Distribution of
accounts receivable
balances. The interval
between $5,000 and
$6,500 is shown in
the shaded area.

If we look up $z = 1.5$ in Appendix Table 1, we find a probability of .93319. Since the area between the left-hand tail of the normal curve and the mean is .5 of the area, we obtain our answer by subtracting .5 from .93319 and get .43319. The chances of randomly getting an account with between $5,000 and $6,500 as a balance are slightly higher than .4.

AN EXAMPLE OF THE RANDOM VARIABLE BEING GREATER THAN A VALUE WHICH IS ABOVE THE MEAN

Example 3 What is the probability that an account drawn at random will have a balance of *more* than $7,000? Now look at Figure 2-30. We are interested in the shaded area to the right of the value $7,000. Using Eq. (2-17), we get a z value as follows:

$$z = \frac{x - \mu}{\sigma} \hspace{3cm} (2\text{-}17)$$

$$= \frac{\$7,000 - \$5,000}{\$1,000}$$

$$= \frac{\$2,000}{\$1,000}$$

$$= 2 \text{ standard deviations}$$

When we look in Appendix Table 1 for a z value of 2.0, we find a probability of .97725. That represents the probability that an account will have a balance of *less* than $7,000. However, we want the probability that the account will have a balance of *more* than $7,000, the shaded area in Figure 2-30. Since the entire area under the normal curve has a value of 1.0, we can find our answer by subtracting .97725 from 1.0; doing this, we get .02275 as our answer.

AN EXAMPLE OF THE RANDOM VARIABLE BEING BETWEEN TWO VALUES THAT ARE BOTH ABOVE THE MEAN

Example 4 Suppose that our auditors want to know the probability that they will select at random an account with a balance between $5,500 and $6,500? This probability is represented by the shaded area in Figure 2-31.

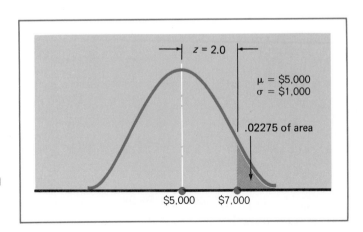

FIGURE 2-30
Distribution of accounts receivable balances. The interval of more than $7,000 is shown in the shaded area.

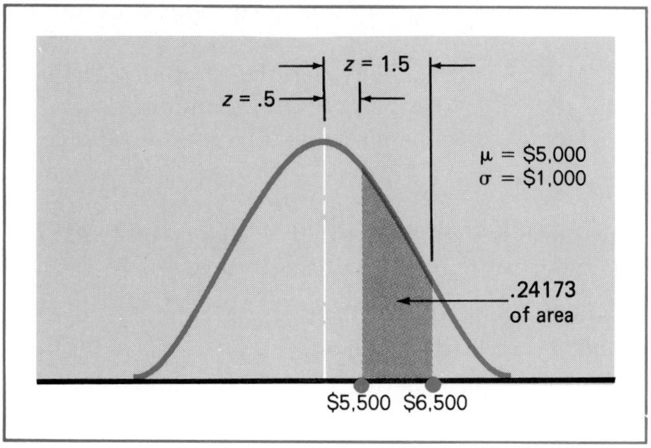

FIGURE 2-31
Distribution of
accounts receivable
balances. The interval
between $5,500 and
$6,500 is shown in
the shaded area.

This time it will take us two steps to find the required probability. First we calculate a z value for the $6,500 value:

$$z = \frac{x - \mu}{\sigma} \qquad \text{(2-17)}$$

$$= \frac{\$6,500 - \$5,000}{\$1,000}$$

$$= \frac{\$1,500}{\$1,000}$$

= 1.5 standard deviations

When we look up a z value of 1.5 in Appendix Table 1, we find a probability value of .93319. This is the probability that the random variable will lie between the left-hand tail and $6,500 (the probability that it will be *less* than $6,500).

In step 2 of this solution, we calculate a z value for the $5,500 value:

$$z = \frac{x - \mu}{\sigma} \qquad \text{(2-17)}$$

$$= \frac{\$5,500 - \$5,000}{\$1,000}$$

$$= \frac{\$500}{\$1,000}$$

= .5 standard deviation

Appendix Table 1 shows a probability of .69146 for this z value; .69146 is the probability that the random variable will be less than $5,500.

To answer our question then, we subtract as follows:

.93319	Probability that the random variable will be less than $6,500
− .69146	Probability that the random variable will be less than $5,500
.24173	Probability that the random variable will lie between $5,500 and $6,500

Thus there is slightly less than 1 chance in 4 that our auditor will select at random an account with a balance between $5,500 and $6,500.

▌ CARE IN USING THE NORMAL PROBABILITY DISTRIBUTION

Somewhat earlier in this chapter, we noted—as one characteristic of the normal probability distribution—that the tails approach, but never touch, the horizontal axis. This implies that there is *some* probability (albeit very small) that the random variable can take on enormous values. In the accounts receivable example on pages 74 to 78, it would be possible for the right-hand tail of a normal curve to assign a very minute probability to an account with a balance of $105,000, for example. An account of this size would lie somewhere about 100 standard deviations to the right of the mean. It would be hard to believe that in a company whose accounts receivable had a mean of $5,000 and a standard deviation of only $1,000, we would find an account with a balance this large. In actual practice, we really do not lose much accuracy by completely ignoring these values far out in the tails of the normal distribution. We must remember, however, that in exchange for the convenience of using this model, we have to accept the fact that it *can* assign impossible values. As a matter of fact, the probability of finding an account with this balance in the distribution we have described begins with over 2,000 zeros to the right of the decimal.

14 Glossary

A priori probability A probability estimate prior to receiving new information.

Bayes' theorem The basic formula for conditional probability under statistical dependence.

Bernoulli process A process in which each trial has only two possible outcomes, where the probability of the outcome of any trial remains fixed over time, and where the trials are statistically independent.

Binomial distribution A discrete distribution of the results of an experiment known as a Bernoulli process.

Classical probability The number of outcomes favorable to the occurrence of an event divided by the total number of possible outcomes.

Collectively exhaustive events The list of events that represents all the possible outcomes of an experiment.

Conditional probability The probability of one event's occurring given that another event has occurred.

Continuous probability distribution A probability distribution in which the variable is permitted to take on any value within a given range.

Continuous random variable A random variable allowed to take on any value within a given range.

Discrete probability distribution. A probability distribution in which the variable is allowed to take on only a limited number of values.

Discrete random variable A random variable allowed to take on only a limited number of values.

Event One or more of the possible outcomes of doing something, or one of the possible outcomes of an experiment.

Expected value A weighted average of the outcomes of an experiment.

Expected value of a random variable A weighted average in which each possible value of the random variable is given its probability as a weight; the long-run average value of the random variable.

Experiment The activity that produces an event.

Exponential distribution A continuous probability distribution used to describe the distribution of service times in a service facility.

Joint probability The probability of two events occurring together or in succession.

Marginal probability The unconditional probability of one event occurring; the probability of a single event.

Mean A measure of central tendency.

Mutually exclusive events Events which cannot happen together.

Normal distribution A distribution of a continuous random variable in which the curve has a single peak, in which it is bell-shaped, in which the mean lies at the center of the distribution and the curve is symmetrical around a vertical line erected at the mean, and in which the two tails extend indefinitely and never touch the horizontal axis.

Poisson distribution A discrete distribution in which the probability of the occurrence of an event within a very small time period is very small, in which the probability that two or more such events will occur within the same small time interval is effectively 0, and in which the probability of the occurrence of the event within one time period is independent of where that time period is.

Posterior probability A probability that has been revised after new information was obtained.

Probability The chance that something will happen.

Probability density function For continuous random variables, the probability that the random variable falls within any given interval is the area under the density function in the interval in question.

Probability distribution A list of the outcomes of an experiment with the probabilities we would expect to see associated with these outcomes.

Random variable A variable that takes on different values as a result of the outcomes of a random experiment.

Relative frequency of occurrence The proportion of times that an event occurs in the long run when conditions are stable, or the observed relative frequency of an event in a very large number of trials.

Sample space The set of all possible outcomes of an experiment.

Standard deviation A measure of the spread of the data around the mean.

Standard normal probability distribution A normal probability distribution in which the values of the random variable are expressed in standard units.

Standard unit The standard deviation of a standard normal probability distribution.

Statistical dependence The condition when the probability of some event is dependent upon or affected by the occurrence of some other event.

Statistical independence The condition when the occurrence of one event has no effect upon the probability of the occurrence of any other event.

Subjective probability A probability based on the personal beliefs of the person who makes the probability estimate.

Venn diagram A pictorial representation of probability concepts in which the sample space is a rectangle and the events in the sample space are portions of that rectangle.

15 Review of equations

Page 29

$$\text{The probability of an event} = \frac{\text{number of outcomes favorable to the occurrence of the event}}{\text{total number of possible outcomes}} \tag{2-1}$$

This is the definition of *classical* probability. In the use of this equation, each of the outcomes must be equally likely.

Page 32

$$P(A \text{ or } B) = P(A) + P(B) \tag{2-2}$$

This is the addition rule for the probability of mutually exclusive events. It refers to the case in which we are interested in the probability that *either* A or B will happen.

Page 33

$$P(A \text{ or } B) = P(A) + P(B) - P(A \text{ and } B) \tag{2-3}$$

This is the correct equation to use to calculate the probability of one or more of two events (A and B) when these events are *not* mutually exclusive.

Page 35

$$P(AB) = P(A) \times P(B) \tag{2-4}$$

This is the probability of two independent events occurring together or in succession, which is known as a *joint* probability. This formula is used under conditions of statistical independence.

Page 40

$$P(A|B) = P(A) \tag{2-5}$$

This is the formula for conditional probability under statistical independence. Since independent events are those whose probabilities are not affected by the occurrence of each other, the probability of *A* given that *B* has happened (under statistical independence) is simply the probability of *A*.

Page 43

$$P(A|B) = \frac{P(AB)}{P(B)}$$

(2-6)

This formula calculates the conditional probability, under statistical dependence, of the event *A* given that *B* has happened.

Page 45

$$P(AB) = P(A|B) \times P(B)$$

(2-7)

With this formula, we can calculate joint probabilities under conditions of statistical dependence. It is read "the joint probability of events *A* and *B* happening together or in succession equals the probability of event *A* given that *B* has happened times the probability of event *B*."

Page 54

$$E = \Sigma x \cdot P(x)$$

(2-8)

This is the expected value of a random variable. Each value that the random variable can take on is multiplied by the probability that it will take on that value, and the resulting products are summed.

Page 56

$$\text{Probability of } r \text{ successes in } n \text{ trials} = \frac{n!}{r!(n-r)!} p^r q^{n-r}$$

(2-9)

This is the binomial formula. In this formula, *p* is the characteristic probability (or probability of success), *q* is $1 - p$, *r* is defined as the number of successes desired, and *n* is the number of trials to be undertaken.

Page 63

$$P(x) = \frac{\lambda^x e^{-\lambda}}{x!}$$

(2-10)

This formula is used to calculate the probability of getting exactly *x* occurrences in a Poisson distribution; λ is the mean of the distribution, *x* is the specific value of the discrete random variable in which we are interested, and *e* is the base of the natural logarithm system.

Page 65

$$p(t) = \mu e^{-\mu t},$$

(2-11)

This formula gives the probability density function for an exponential distribution where μ is the mean service rate in units serviced per unit of time, and $e = 2.71828$ is the base of the natural logarithm system.

Page 66

$$P(T \leq t) = 1 - e^{-\mu t} \tag{2-12}$$

The probability that the random variable T will be less than or equal to any value t in an exponential distribution.

Page 69

$$\bar{x} = \frac{\sum x_i}{n} \tag{2-13}$$

This formula is used to find the mean of a random variable if we are sampling only a few values.

Page 70

$$\mu = \frac{\sum x_i}{N} \tag{2-14}$$

This formula is used to find the mean of a random variable if we are using the entire population (all the values).

Page 70

$$\sigma = \sqrt{\frac{\sum (x_i - \mu)^2}{N}} \tag{2-15}$$

This is the formula for the standard deviation of a population; μ is the mean of the values in the population, x_i represents the value of x for each value in the population, and N is the number of values in the population. The standard deviation is symbolized σ (*sigma*).

Page 70

$$\sigma = \sqrt{\frac{\sum x_i^2}{N} - \mu^2} \tag{2-16}$$

This is just a form of Eq. (2-15) which saves computation time because it allows us to avoid calculating deviations from the mean.

Page 74

$$z = \frac{x - \mu}{\sigma} \tag{2-17}$$

This formula is used to find the number of standard deviations an element lies from its mean (the z value).

2-1 Given the following: $P(A) = .25$; $P(B) = .40$; $P(A \text{ and } B) = .10$, draw a Venn diagram showing these probabilities. From your diagram, determine $P(A \text{ or } B)$. Compute $P(A \text{ or } B)$ using Eq. (2-3). Do your answers agree?

2-2 By very carefully screening applicants, the Bank of Halifax County has been able to limit bad-debt losses on consumer loans to 8 percent. What is the probability that at least four of the five loan applicants that you, as a loan officer trainee, have just approved will repay their loans?

2-3 Of the repair jobs that Bennie's Machine Shop receives, 20 percent are welding jobs and 80 percent are machining jobs.
  a. What is the probability that the next three jobs to come in will be welding jobs?
  b. What is the probability that two of the next three jobs to come in will be machining jobs?

2-4 A building contractor knows that the probability of rain in his region during any given day in August is 30 percent. He has 2 days' work remaining on a job and there are 4 days during which the work can be done without incurring penalty costs. If he gets no work done on rainy days, what is the probability that he will pay a penalty? Assume that rain on any given day is independent of the fact that it did or did not rain on any other day.

2-5 The Mandy Personal Products Company manufactures personal grooming products for men, including a new hair preparation for redheads. Its intention is to distribute the product free to redheaded men and then survey the users' reactions. Research indicates that 46 percent of adults in the general population are male and that 92 percent of the population have a hair color other than red. Mandy feels that it must have at least 1,000 distributions for a valid test. How many persons from the population must it sample before it expects to find 1,000 redheaded men? You may assume that hair color and sex are unrelated.

2-6 An operator on one machine must visually inspect items and remove the defective ones. Three different items are produced simultaneously by the machine and move together down a conveyor past the operator. The process is so designed that it is very difficult for him to remove three items at once. The machine was running normally last week, and production data for that period are given below. What is the probability that the three items appearing on the conveyor at the same time will all be rejects?

	Item A	Item B	Item C
Rejected	18	212	53
Accepted	812	618	777

2-7 From past daily sales at his newsstand, Kurt Phillips has observed the following sales of the *Daily Star* newspaper:

Daily sales	Number of occurrences
43	27
44	32
45	43
46	55
47	52
48	42
49	29
50	16

Compute the probability of selling each of the daily sales figures from 43 to 50 newspapers. What is the expected value of daily sales?

2-8 City Parking Systems, Inc., operates a parking garage in the downtown area. During the rush hour, cars arrive at the garage at the rate of 24 every 60 minutes. Three garage attendants can handle this level of arrivals, but not too much more. What is the probability of more than 4 arrivals in any 10-minute interval, which would require the help of another garage attendant?

2-9 Given the following observations of test scores—87, 63, 74, 92, 94, 78, 73, 88, 83, and 77—compute the mean test score. Using both Eq. (2-15) and Eq. (2-16), compute the standard deviation of the test scores.

2-10 Sarah Shari is the emergency room supervisor at County General Hospital. As a part of her responsibilities, she plans staffing for the facility. An especially busy period is Saturday night after 9 P.M. It is normal for Sarah to schedule three interns to work during that period; from past experience she knows that this level of staffing can handle the usual load of 6 arrivals per hour. However, in the event arrivals rise much above this level, additional professional help would need to be scheduled. Sarah thinks the distribution of arrivals can be described by the Poisson distribution and would like to know what the chances are of 7, 8, or 9 persons arriving in any 1-hour period, since this would make it necessary to provide another attendant.

2-11 The mean output of cold-rolled steel pipe of the Valley Tubing Corporation is 120,000 pounds daily, with a standard deviation of 40,000 pounds. Any output above 185,000 pounds daily would so tax the materials-handling crew as to cause a shutdown of the entire facility. What is the probability of such an event if the output is normally distributed?

2-12 The maintenance manager of the Watson Manufacturing Company has only 4 hours available in which to install a new compressor in the air conditioning unit before the next morning shift begins. The time required to install a compressor is exponentially distributed with a mean time of 2 hours. What is the probability that the installation will be completed before the morning shift begins?

2-13 Alcoholism is an increasing problem among young executives at Carol and Sloam Advertising Agency. The feeling of the managing partner, Richard Best, is that probably 15 percent of the younger executives have a problem serious enough to impair their work effectiveness. Drinking at lunch is considered by Mr. Best to be prima facie evidence that effectiveness is impaired. While out to lunch one day, Best comes across a table at which four of Carol and Sloam's young executives are sitting. What is the probability that two of them are drinking?

2-14 Four small vials (types A, B, C, and D) are produced in sets of four (one of each type) by a machine. They fall in random order down a chute to a conveyor, where they are put in order by an operator. They are then automatically packed. What is the probability that they will come down the conveyor in the proper A, B, C, D order, allowing the operator to take a short rest?

2-15 Suppose you are considering the purchase of stock in IJK Corporation. You feel that if the Dow Jones average rises next year, there is an 85 percent probability that IJK stock will go up. You also feel that there is a 70 percent chance that the Dow Jones average will increase next year. What is the probability that both the Dow Jones average and the price of IJK will rise next year?

2-16 Sylvia Thomas is interested in the potential rise in interest rates in the coming year, as it has a bearing on sales of new homes. She feels that there is a 20 percent probability that both an increase in interest rates and an increase in new-home sales will occur next year and that there is a 30 percent joint probability that interest rates will not rise and new-home sales will increase next year. She thinks there is a 60 percent probability that interest rates will rise. If interest rates do not rise in the following year, what is the probability that new-home sales will increase?

2-17 A child chosen at random in a community school system comes from a low-income family 15 percent of the time. Children from low-income families in the community graduate from college only 20 percent of the time. Children not from low-income families have a 40 percent chance of graduating from college. As an employer of people from this community, you are reviewing applicants and note that the first one had a college degree. What is the probability that that person comes from a low-income family?

2-18 Heidi March has taken 8 cuttings from a plant which won her first prize in last year's county fair. She has set the cuttings in individual pots and hopes they will take root. On the basis of past experience, she knows there is a .7 probability that a given cutting will take root. Use the binomial formula to find the probability that at least 6 of the cuttings take root. Check your answer by using the binomial tables.

2-19 Using the data given in Exercise 2-18, determine from the binomial tables the probability of exactly 0, 1, 2, 3, 4, 5, 6, 7, or 8 cuttings taking root. Then compute the expected value of the number of new plants taking root.

2-20 The likelihood of getting a completely factual financial statement from credit-card applicants in a southeastern department store chain is .9. If the applicant's application is factual, the likelihood of the applicant being a good credit risk is .8. If an application is not factual, the probability of the applicant being a good credit risk is only .3. A spot check of applications that you, as credit manager, have approved is begun, and you are informed that the first applicant turned out to be a good credit risk for the chain. How probable is it that the application was not completely factual?

2-21 Control of the heat in a chemical blending process at University Products Company, Inc., is absolutely essential. Too much or too little heat during the process produces polyvinyl insulation material that is either too brittle or so flimsy that it cannot support the weight of the roofing shingles which are normally laid on top of the insulation. Past processes have produced an output with a mean compression strength of 150 pounds per square inch and a standard deviation of 25 pounds per square inch. Insulation with a compression strength above 220 pounds per square inch or below 105 pounds per square inch is not usable. What portion of a day's run of 50 tons of insulation will be unusable if the heat control of the process stays at the same level of effectiveness?

2-22 A financial analyst computed the return on stockholder's equity for all the companies listed on the New York Stock Exchange. She found that the mean of this distribution was 10 percent, with a standard deviation of 5 percent. She is interested in examining further those companies whose return on stockholders' equity is between 16 and 22 percent. Of the approximately 1,300 companies listed on the exchange, how many are of interest to her?

2-23 Mary Winslow feels that the time to prepare an individual's income tax is exponentially distributed. In the past she has noted that 40 percent of the returns are completed in 2 hours, 60 percent are completed in 4 hours, and 85 percent are completed in 8 hours. Estimate the mean time for completion of a tax return.

2-24 The Singleton Manufacturing Company, Inc., manufactures four fastening products: long fine-thread screws, long coarse-thread screws, short fine-thread screws, and short coarse-thread screws. In the warehouse, there are a number of boxes of mixed screws. You pick up one with 100 screws in it. There are 52 short screws, 83 screws that are either long or fine-thread, and 28 screws that are long but not fine-thread. Determine the probability that a screw picked at random from the box will be:

    a. A short or a fine-thread screw
    b. A long or a coarse-thread screw
    c. A short or a coarse-thread screw

2-25 As a means of increasing worker morale and performance, the management of an assembly shop was considering a plan providing job enrichment (such as self-supervision, team working, and the individual selection of working hours). Two groups of 100 workers were selected at random. The first group worked under existing conditions; the second was placed in a separate room and was allowed to function under the proposed job-enrichment plan. After a year, management compared the performance ratings of all workers and found that in the group operating under existing conditions, for 30 employees the performance ratings improved, for 60 employees the ratings remained the same, and for 10 employees the ratings dropped. Within the group working under the job-enrichment plan, 40 performance ratings improved, 55 remained the same, and 5 dropped. How should management assess the effects of the job-enrichment program on worker morale and performance?

2-26 Suppose you are a wildcat oil-well driller and are considering drilling at a certain site. From past experience, you know there is a 40 percent probability that a well drilled in this area will be profitable, a 40 percent probability that it will break even, and a 20 percent probability that it will be a dry well and will cause you to lose your drilling investment. Before deciding whether to drill, you conduct a scientific study to determine the geological structure. The results of a seismic study will show either no structure, open structure, or closed structure. Experience with a large number of oil wells drilled in the past indicates that of all profitable wells, 60 percent have closed structure, 30 percent have open structure, and 10 percent have no structure. Of all breakeven wells, 30 percent have closed structure, 20 percent have open structure, and 50 percent have no structure. Of all dry wells, 10 percent have closed structure, 40 percent have open structure, and 50 percent have no structure. The seismic study is made, and the results indicate a closed structure. Based upon your experience in drilling in this area and the results of the seismic study, what are your revised probability estimates of a profitable, a breakeven, or a dry well?

2-27 You are the marketing manager of a firm that manufactures paper products purchased on a repeat basis by householders. You want to evaluate a campaign of giveaways designed to increase sales and brand loyalty. You test the special campaign against the regular advertising program in two widely separated cities which have about the same demographic characteristics and the same use rates of your products. The population of each city contains 1,000 regular users. After a 2-month test, these results are revealed: In the regular advertising area, 250 of the users increased their use, 500 decreased their use, and 250 used about the same amount; in the special campaign area, 350 increased their use, 250 decreased their use, and 400 used about the same. How would you assess the effect of the campaign on product usage and on brand loyalty?

2-28 Assume you are a dealer in refrigerators and have hired a new salesman for a two-week trial period. At the end of the two weeks, you must decide either to release him or place him permanently on the payroll. Based upon past experience, you estimate that given your prospective salesman's experience, personality, etc., there is a 20 percent probability he will be a superior salesman, a 70 percent probability he will be an average salesman, and a 10 percent probability he will be an inferior salesman. A superior salesman is one who sells a refrigerator to 40 percent of his customers, an average salesman sells to 30 percent of his customers, and an inferior salesman sells to 20 percent of his customers.

After the two-week period, you note that he has demonstrated refrigerators to a total of 10 customers and has sold refrigerators to 4 of them. Based upon all the information you have, should you retain the man permanently in your employment if your policy is to employ only average or superior salesmen? Assume that the selling of refrigerators is a Bernoulli process.

2-29 The Lane Company sent two advertising brochures to prospective customers to promote sales of two new machines, machine A and machine B. The company estimated that the probability that a customer would buy machine A was 20 percent, and the probability that the customer would buy machine B was 30 percent. The probability that a given customer would buy both was estimated to be 15 percent. After seeing the first brochure, for machine A, the Eaves Company placed an order for one. What is the probability that Eaves will also buy machine B when it receives the second brochure?

2-30 A new diagnostic test to detect gout has been introduced into the Lincoln County Hospital. The manufacturer of the test device has determined that the probability of a false-positive reading (a positive test result for a person who is known not to have gout) is 8 percent. The probability of a false-negative reading (a negative reading for a person who has the disease) is 4 percent. County health authorities estimate that approximately 15 percent of the population in the county have gout. If a test is conducted on a patient from that county and the test result is positive, what is the probability that gout is present?

2-31 The Lincoln County Construction Company is planning to place a bid on a construction contract. After analyzing the work with a technique known as program evaluation and review technique (PERT), it has concluded that the construction project would take 200 days to complete. This estimate carries with it many uncertainties, however. When the uncertainties are taken into consideration, the company feels that the completion time is a random variable, and its distribution approximates a normal distribution having a mean of 200 days and a standard deviation of 40 days. It is company policy to quote in its bid a completion time which has a 95 percent probability of being met, to avoid late-completion penalties which are a provision of the contract. What completion time should it quote in its bid for this contract?

2-32 The Upstate Chemical Company has developed a low-cost spin-stabilized third-stage rocket for injecting satellites into orbit. This rocket is being considered for use in conjunction with the IMP spacecraft for a mission in which a lunar orbit is desired. Upstate has run 10 tests on the rocket and has determined that with a payload of 150 pounds and the weight of the IMP, the velocity increase provided by this rocket would be as follows:

Test number	Velocity added, ft/sec
1	6,820
2	6,790
3	6,840
4	6,810
5	6,830
6	6,770
7	6,830
8	6,790
9	6,810
10	6,790

Assuming the velocity added by this rocket is normally distributed, determine the mean and the standard deviation of the injection velocity for the IMP mission.

2-33 Referring to Exercise 2-32, assume that the project manager for the IMP mission has completed his analysis of the spacecraft's systems. He has found that in order for the mission to succeed, the velocity added by Upstate Chemical's third-stage rocket must be between 6,790 and 6,850 feet per second. What is the probability that the mission will fail because of an incorrect transfer orbit to the moon?

2-34 International Foods, Inc., manufacturer of Zesty, a special Italian tomato sauce, is interested in discovering whether consumers can tell the difference between a competitor's more expensive sauce and its own. Fifteen persons are given a sample of Zesty and then a sample of the competitor's sauce. Then they are each asked to identify the competitor's brand. It is customary to hypothesize that there is no difference in the tastes; if this is so, the chances of a person identifying the competitor's brand are .5. What is the probability that 12 of the 15 persons in the test will identify the competitor's brand if the hypothesis is really true? Use the binomial tables to compute your answer.

2-35 A baker of chocolate chip cookies has noted over the years that if she puts 1000λ chips into a batch of dough which is used to produce 1,000 cookies, then the number of chips per cookie has a Poisson distribution with a mean of λ chips in each cookie. If λ = 7, what is the probability that a randomly chosen cookie has fewer than 5 chocolate chips in it? The baker's ads claim that at least 90 percent of her cookies contain 5 or more chocolate chips. Will 7,000 chips per batch of dough enable her to sustain this claim?

2-36 Rod Raskolnikov works as a toll collector for the New Jersey Turnpike during the "graveyard shift" (midnight to 8:00 A.M.). If the traffic is not too heavy, he passes the time reading mystery stories. During any hour when fewer than 8 cars pass through his toll booth, he can read two chapters of a typical mystery. If 8, 9, or 10 cars pass through, he reads one chapter. However, if more than 10 cars pass through in a given hour, he gets no reading done. How many chapters can Rod expect to read on a given work night if the traffic can be described by a Poisson distribution with an average of 10 cars per hour?

2-37 The Portland Trailblazers and the Philadelphia 76ers are playing in a best-of-seven series. Based upon past performance, you estimate that Portland would have a 40 percent chance of winning a single game against Philadelphia. If the winner is the team which wins four games first, what is the probability that Portland will win in a four-game series? What is the probability that Philadelphia will win in a seven-game series?

2-38 John Silver is the proprietor of Long John's Parrot World, a pet shop that specializes in macaws and other large psittacines. John's protegé, Jim Hawkins, has been learning how to handle the birds by doing miscellaneous tasks for John. One of Jim's jobs is cutting the parrots' nails. This must be done carefully, because the birds could bleed profusely if the nails were cut to the quick. When he first started the job, Jim could trim the nails of 4 birds per hour on average, but he can now do 6 birds per hour on average. Assuming that the time to trim a bird's nails is exponentially distributed, what is the probability that Jim took at most 15 minutes to do one bird when he first started to work at Parrot World? What is that probability now?

2-39 Star slugger Rocky Stallone swings hard and hits lots of home runs when he connects. Unfortunately, he also strikes out 27 times in every 100 at bat. Assuming that his performance in each trip to the plate is independent of all other times at bat, what is the probability that Rocky will strike out at least 5 times in tomorrow's doubleheader if he gets to bat 9 times? What if he has 10 at bats?

2-40 Librarian Polly Cameron estimates that 93 percent of all books that are checked out of the library will be returned on time. She has just checked the cards on 13 randomly selected science fiction books and found out that 5 of them were returned late the last time they were checked out. If the 93 percent figure applies to science fiction books, what is the probability that 5 or more of 13 randomly chosen books will be returned late?

2-41 Occupational Testing Service designs aptitude tests which are given to job applicants in various industries. The tests are designed so that scores on them are normally distributed with mean 100 and standard deviation 20. The personnel office at Newcore Steel Corporation administers OTS's Ferric Metals Assessment Test to all would-be managerial interns, but will hire only those who score at least 145 on the test. What fraction of all applicants does Newcore hire?

2-42 Acme Movers estimates that the time it takes to pack up a typical household for a move is normally distributed with a mean $7.5/n$ hours and standard deviation $6.8/n$ hours, where n is the size of the crew that is sent out to do the job. If Acme wishes 96 percent of all households to be packed up in no more than 8 hours, how large a crew size should be chosen?

17 Chapter concepts quiz

2-1 The set of all possible outcomes of an experiment is called _____ for the experiment. _____ are composed of subsets of this set of all possible outcomes.

2-2 Two events, A and B, are said to be statistically _____ when the probability of one event depends upon or is affected by the occurrence of the other event. In this case, $P(AB) = $ _____ $\times P(B)$.

2-3 Bayes' theorem enables us to calculate _____ probabilities by utilizing additional information and is given mathematically by _____ $= P(AB)/P(B)$. This procedure requires knowing or estimating _____ probabilities as a starting point.

2-4 A list of the possible outcomes of an experiment which includes the probabilities

Fill in the
Blanks

associated with each outcome is called a _____ and may be displayed in either graphic or algebraic form.

2-5 The _____ of a random variable is an average of the values of that random variable weighted by the probabilities of the random variable taking on those values. The _____ of a population is the unweighted average of the values in the population.

2-6 Probabilities based solely on intuition or limited past experiences are _____ probabilities; whereas probabilities based on the observed relative frequency of an event in a large number of trials are _____ probabilities.

2-7 A _____ probability is one which expresses the probability of a single event; a joint probability for A and B gives the probability that _____ (either/both) A _____ (or/and) B occur(s).

2-8 A variable which takes on a limited number of values as a result of the outcome of a random experiment is a _____ random variable; a variable which can take on any value in a given range of possible outcomes of an experiment is a _____ random variable.

2-9 A measure of the dispersion of data about the mean is called the _____.

2-10 The binomial distribution is a discrete probability distribution which gives the probability of r _____ in n trials, where each trial is a _____ with a given characteristic probability.

True-False

2-11 The classical approach to probability theory requires that the total number of possible outcomes be known or calculated and that each of the outcomes be equally likely. **T F**

2-12 For any two statistically independent events, $P(A \text{ or } B) = P(A) + P(B)$. **T F**

2-13 The marginal probability of an event A can be found by summing all the possible joint probabilities which include A as one of the events. **T F**

2-14 Calculating posterior probabilities allows us to update our prior probabilities by making use of additional experimental information. **T F**

2-15 Probability distributions are always based on subjective beliefs about what should happen. **T F**

2-16 Random variables are numerical values corresponding to each possible outcome of an experiment and are between 0 and 1. **T F**

2-17 The expected value of a random variable is a useful basis for managerial decisions because it describes the long-range weighted average of the random variable. **T F**

2-18 Recordings of the number of miles until wearing out for 100 test tires are examples of the values of a continuous random variable. **T F**

2-19 For a discrete random variable which takes on nonnegative values (0, 1, 2, . . .), such as the Poisson random variable, the expected value is always a nonnegative number. **T F**

2-20 The exponential distribution is used to describe the distribution of time between events. **T F**

2-21 The normal random variable may take on any real number as a value. **T F**

2-22 A binomial distribution is uniquely determined by the characteristic probability p of the Bernoulli trials which compose it. **T F**

2-23 The statement, "If we beat their ace pitcher in the first game, then we have an even chance of winning the series," is an example of a conditional probability   **T F**

2-24 In probability theory, an event consists of one possible outcome of doing something.   **T F**

2-25 Posterior probabilities found by employing Bayes' theorem are valid only when there are two elementary events and consistent outcomes.   **T F**

2-26 Two events are mutually exclusive if:
    a. Their probabilities are less than 1.
    b. Their probabilities sum to 1.
    c. Both events cannot occur at the same time.
    d. They contain every possible outcome of an experiment.

Multiple
Choice

2-27 Posterior probabilities for certain events can be equal to prior probabilities for these same events if:
    a. All the prior probabilities are 0.
    b. Never. Posterior probabilities cannot equal prior probabilities.
    c. The events are mutually exclusive and collectively exhaustive.
    d. The joint probability of an event and the sample outcome, when divided by the probability of the outcome, equals the prior probability for the event.

2-28 For any discrete random variable X, $P(y \leqslant X \leqslant z) =$:
    a. $P(X \geqslant y) - P(X \geqslant z + 1)$
    b. $P(X \leqslant z) - P(X \geqslant y)$
    c. $P(X \leqslant z)$
    d. $P(X \geqslant y) - P(X \geqslant y + 1)$

2-29 The symmetry of the normal distribution about its mean guarantees that:
    a. The two tails extend indefinitely in both the positive and the negative direction.
    b. The distribution is bell-shaped.
    c. Ninety-nine percent of the values will be in the range of minus 3 standard deviations to plus 3 standard deviations.
    d. The area below the mean is equal to ½.

2-30 If a service facility's time of service is exponentially distributed, the time of service for a given item taken at random is:
    a. Dependent on the number of items waiting to be serviced
    b. Dependent on the time taken to service the previously completed item
    c. Independent of its mean service time
    d. None of the above

2-31 If A and B are statistically independent:
    a. $P(AB) = P(A) \times P(B)$
    b. $P(A|B) = P(A)$
    c. Both a and b
    d. $P(A \text{ or } B) = P(A) + P(B)$

2-32 The mathematical formula for joint probabilities, $P(AB) = P(A|B) \times P(B)$, holds:
    a. For both statistically dependent and independent events
    b. Only when A and B are statistically dependent
    c. Only when A and B are statistically independent
    d. Only when $P(A) \leqslant .5$

2-33 A manager may find it useful to compute posterior probabilities whenever:
    a. Additional information becomes available at no cost.

b. Limited information makes it necessary to employ subjective probability estimates to describe the state of the system.

c. The cost of doing so is outweighed by the value of the posterior probabilities.

d. All of the above.

2-34 A Bernoulli process has all but which of the following properties:

a. Each trial has only two possible outcomes.

b. The probability of success must equal the probability of failure.

c. The probability of success on any one trial remains the same over time.

d. The outcome of a given trial does not influence the outcome of any other trial.

2-35 Given two normal distributions with the same mean, μ, but different standard deviations σ_1, and σ_2, if $\sigma_1 > \sigma_2$, then:

a. Distribution 1 has a wider spread than distribution 2.

b. $x_1 > x_2$ where x_1 and x_2 are both z standard deviations above the mean of their respective distributions.

c. Both a and b

2-36 Which of the following distributions is discrete?

a. Binomial

b. Exponential

c. Normal

d. All of the above

2-37 The binomial distribution is symmetrical:

a. When $p < .5$

b. When $p = .5$

c. When $p > .5$

d. At any value of p

2-38 Arrivals at a service facility are generally described by the:

a. Normal distribution

b. Binomial distribution

c. Poisson distribution

d. None of the above

2-39 All normal distributions are:

a. Symmetrical

b. Defined by two measures—the mean and standard deviation

c. Bell-shaped

d. All of the above

2-40 Bayes' theorem is used to:

a. Revise probability estimates

b. Compute binomial probabilities

c. Check the validity of using a particular distribution to represent some management problem of interest

d. None of the above

18 Real world MS/OR successes

▮ EXAMPLE: SELLING AT&T COMMUNICATIONS SERVICES

SIMPLE MODELS OFTEN YIELD BIG PAYOFFS

Beginning students often assume that models must be complex to be useful. This is not true. The literature of management science/operations research contains many examples of relatively simple models that yielded enormous payoffs. A good example is given by Charles Stryker[1] of the Management Science Organization at AT&T Long Lines. Using some of the probability concepts in this chapter, Stryker developed a model to determine how sales efforts should be allocated to different classes of business customers. The bottom line: additional revenue of $15 million in the first two years after implementation.

At the time of the study in 1976, about four million business locations were potential customers for AT&T communications services. Several sales tactics were available to stimulate this market, including field contact by Bell account executives, telephone contact, and direct mail. There were four steps in Stryker's analysis of this problem. First, a data base of marketing information was gathered. The data base identified each customer location by a set of characteristics: the Standard Industrial Classification (SIC) of the business, the number of employees, sales volume, and the type and quantity of communications facilities at each location.

SCOPE OF THE SALES
ANALYSIS PROBLEM

The second step was to estimate the probability that a customer with a given set of characteristics would purchase one of various communications services. This was easy. Stryker simply computed the proportions of customers who had purchased services in the past according to AT&T billing data. These proportions were treated as conditional probabilities of sale, given a set of characteristics.

COMPUTING
PROBABILITIES

The third step was to compute sales potential at each customer location. Sales potential is defined as the expected value of revenue (EVR) for a service minus actual revenue currently being billed. EVR is the revenue if the sale is made times the probability of sale.

COMPUTING SALES
POTENTIAL

The last step in the analysis was to assign sales tactics to customers according to sales potential. The data base of customers was sorted by sales potential within a sales region. The highest cost sales tactics (direct field contact) were allocated to the highest potential sales leads in each region. Assignments were made until all field contact sources were exhausted, subject to the limitation that sales potential should exceed the cost of the contact. Remaining leads were assigned the next highest-cost tactics, telephone and mail, subject to the same limitation.

ASSIGNING SALES
TACTICS TO
CUSTOMERS

To ensure that the probability and expected value calculations were reliable, AT&T tested this allocation system in a pilot program to stimulate the sale of a major interstate communications service. Average revenues from customers in the pilot program more than doubled compared to other customers. The allocation system was implemented for all AT&T services in 1976. By the end of 1977, additional revenue generated by the system was estimated at $15 million, a figure certified by auditors in the company's annual financial statements.

IMPLEMENTATION

[1] Charles W. Stryker, "Effective Allocation of Sales Resources," *Interfaces*, vol. 8, no. 4, pp. 1–11, August 1978.

3

The Wolfpack Bottling Company, located in Raleigh, North Carolina experiences highly seasonal sales for its popular Wolfpack Red Soda. In order to minimize overtime in the summer when sales levels are high, Estela Dagum, manager of the bottling plant, schedules winter production levels in excess of winter demand. This allows her to build up inventory during the winter as a buffer against summer demand.

Her scheduling decisions are critical to the company's profitability. If too much is produced in the winter, costs for carrying excess inventory are incurred, especially since warehouse capacity is limited. On the other hand, if scheduled winter production is too low, large costs are incurred during the summer for overtime premium payments. In order to assist her in her scheduling decision, Estela needs accurate and timely forecasts of demand.

Through the use of the forecasting models presented in this chapter, we can assist Estela in her production and sales planning activities.

FORECASTING

CHAPTER OBJECTIVES

- RELATE FORECASTING TO MANAGEMENT AND MS/OR.
- CONTRAST JUDGMENTAL AND QUANTITATIVE APPROACHES TO FORECASTING.
- REVIEW THE ACCURACY MEASURES USED IN FORECASTING.
- DEMONSTRATE EXPONENTIAL SMOOTHING METHODS IN DETAIL.
- DEMONSTRATE THE DECOMPOSITION OF SEASONAL DATA IN DETAIL.

1 Introduction

Virtually all management decisions depend on forecasts. Managers study sales forecasts, for example, to make decisions on working capital needs, the size of the work force, inventory levels, the scheduling of production runs, the location of facilities, the amount of advertising and sales promotion, the need to change prices, and many other problems.

Although forecasts are critically important, they are never as accurate as managers would like. Nevertheless, decisions have to be made every day, and they get made with the best information available, not with perfect forecasts. The real issue in forecasting is not whether the accuracy is perfect, but how to make the best use of the forecasting methodology.

This chapter shows how MS/OR can be used to improve forecasting. Solutions to two practical problems are emphasized throughout the chapter: (1) how to select the best forecasting method for a given situation, and (2) how to evaluate forecast accuracy.

Numerous quantitative forecasting methods have been developed recently. The methods discussed in this chapter were chosen because they have given good results in practice. Some evidence on the practice of forecasting is given in Table 3-1, which is based on a survey of 160 companies. The figures are the percentages of the sample using each of 11 forecasting methods. The methods can be put into three classes: *extrapolation, causal,* and *judgmental.*

Most of the *extrapolation* methods are discussed in detail in this chapter. These methods assume that historical data contain a stable pattern, such as a trend or a seasonal cycle, which will continue in the future. Notice that the use of extrapolation methods declines markedly at forecast horizons beyond

TABLE 3-1
Forecasting in practice: the percentage of companies using each of 11 forecasting methods
(Based on responses from 160 companies)

Method	Forecast horizon		
	Up to 3 months	3 months– 2 years	Over 2 years
Extrapolation:			
1. Moving averages	24	22	5
2. Exponential smoothing	24	17	6
3. Trend line analysis	21	28	21
4. Straight-line projection	13	16	10
5. Classical decomposition	9	13	5
6. Box-Jenkins	5	6	2
Causal:			
7. Causal regression	14	36	28
8. Simulation	4	9	10
Judgmental:			
9. Jury of executive opinion	37	42	38
10. Sales force composite	37	36	8
11. Customer expectations	25	24	12

Source: Adapted from J. T. Mentzer and J. E. Cox, Jr., "Familiarity, Application, and Performance of Sales Forecasting Techniques," *Journal of Forecasting,* vol. 3, pp. 27–36, 1984.

2 years. This makes sense. The patterns of the past cannot be expected to hold indefinitely.

The extrapolation methods are also called *time-series* methods, and the terms are used interchangeably in this book. A time series is a set of data collected at regular intervals, such as every week, every month, or every year.

Moving averages and *exponential smoothing* are related extrapolation methods which use special kinds of averages of the most recent data to forecast. *Trend line analysis* is the comparison of regression models of the rate of growth of the data over time. In the regression model, the dependent variable is sales and the independent variable is some function of time. The *straight-line projection* is similar, except the company does not bother with comparing different regression models—a linear (straight-line) trend is always used.

Classical decomposition assumes that the data are made up of at least three components: seasonality, trend, and randomness. The method attempts to separate these components to simplify the forecasting problem.

Box-Jenkins is a sophisticated statistical technique which attempts to pick an optimal model from a large number of possibilities. The selected model is optimal only in the sense that it gives the smallest errors when used to analyze past history. The details of the Box-Jenkins technique are beyond the scope of this book. Because of its complexity, Box-Jenkins is not popular in practice, as Table 3-1 shows.

The *causal* methods attempt to find a relationship between the variable to be forecast and one or more other variables. For example, with a *causal regression* model, sales might be forecast as a function of advertising and price. This is done statistically with a more complex form of the regression model we will study for time series. The details of causal regression are beyond the scope of this book.

Another causal method, *simulation*, develops a model of a process and then conducts a series of organized trial-and-error experiments to predict the behavior of the process over time. One example of simulation in forecasting is found in the airline industry. Probability distributions of consumer behavior are used to experiment with pricing, scheduling, and overbooking policies in order to forecast revenues. Simulation has many other uses in management science and is discussed in detail in Chapter 15.

The first judgmental method, the *jury of executive opinion,* is anything from a "SWAG" (sophisticated wild guess) by the sales manager to a consensus forecast by the senior executives in a company. The *sales force composite* is the sum of individual forecasts made by a company's salespeople. *Customer expectations* are based on surveys, formal or informal, of planned purchases.

Although this is a book about quantitative approaches to management, it is important to understand the problems of using human judgment to forecast. The next section reviews judgmental forecasting. Then we discuss ways of choosing quantitative models, followed by a detailed look at each model.

2 Judgmental forecasting

There are situations in which human judgment is the only realistic forecasting method. One is when there are few data for building a quantitative model, for example, forecasting sales of a new product. Sometimes the environment changes drastically and historical data are no longer representative, for example, forecasting the sales of energy-related products immediately after the OPEC oil embargo in 1973.

When there are a large number of time series to forecast, a computer-based quantitative model is the only realistic alternative. For example, there are many inventory control systems in which thousands of forecasts are needed each time period. One of the largest computer-based forecasting systems is operated by the U.S. Navy. More than 1.5 million forecasts of the demand for inventory items are generated each quarter.

Between these two extremes, there are no clear-cut rules on when judgment or quantitative models should be favored. In the authors' opinion, when adequate data are available, a quantitative forecast should always be provided to management. Why? Because the quantitative models described in this chapter are cheap and easy to use. Even when management believes that judgment is more appropriate, quantitative forecasts are useful as a bench-mark, or standard, for evaluating the accuracy of judgment.

Furthermore, quantitative analysis may reveal features of the data that could otherwise be overlooked. For example, trends in the data can easily be concealed by seasonal patterns. Quantitative models can be used to adjust the data for seasonality and to give a better picture of trends.

Another reason why judgmental and quantitative forecasts should always be compared, when possible, is that human judgment tends to be *biased*. That is, errors of judgment tend to be systematic rather than random. A huge body of scientific research supports this conclusion.

One type of bias affecting judgmental forecasts is the so-called *gambler's fallacy*. This occurs when people expect that nature will somehow compensate for injustices in the past. A simple example of this fallacy is that a consecutive run of four tails in coin tossing leads many people to predict a head on the next toss. Of course, if someone gets 10 tails consecutively, a good manager will ask to see the coin.

In the business world, executives of companies destined for bankruptcy proceedings usually predict improved earnings until the bitter end. This was the case with Osborne Computer Corporation, one of the early success stories in microcomputing. A series of marketing errors changed Osborne's fortunes in early 1983. In interviews with the press, the chairman, Adam Osborne, predicted improved earnings until the day the company entered receivership.

Another type of bias is often called *conservatism*. As defined here, this is the assumption that the future will look like the past. The forecaster often refuses to accept any evidence of change. A famous example of conservatism is the attitude of Herbert Hoover on the eve of the Great Depression in 1929. A few days after Black Thursday (October 24, 1929) in the stock market, Hoover proclaimed that the "fundamental business . . . of the country is on a sound and prosperous basis."

Numerous studies have found that conservatism causes people to consistently underestimate sales when they are rising and overestimate sales when they are falling. The authors observed this problem in a company in the pharmaceutical industry. One of the company's older products, an aspirin-based analgesic, had experienced a sales decline of 2 to 3 percent per year for more than a decade. This was due to the growth of Tylenol and other nonaspirin products. At the end of every year during this period, the marketing manager forecast that sales would be constant during the next year.

Especially in marketing, it is difficult to separate forecasting from planning, and this leads to bias. The forecast should be an input to the plan, and not the other way around. If forecasting and planning get confused, this will bias the forecasts toward optimism.

What can be done about bias in judgmental forecasting? The first step is to keep records of the accuracy of judgmental forecasts. In the authors' experience, such records are hard to find in most companies. If the track record reveals problems, bias can be reduced by averaging the forecasts from several sources. For example, the sales force composite might be averaged with executive opinion. The average should contain less bias than either forecast alone. Judgmental and quantitative forecasts could also be averaged.

3 Time-series patterns

Quantitative forecasting models assume that the time series follows some pattern which can be extrapolated into the future. A variety of patterns are illustrated in Figure 3-1. The figure can be used as a guide to model selection by comparing the data with the patterns shown.

Four kinds of trends are shown coupled with three kinds of seasonalities. The patterns are often called *forecast profiles* because they show how the forecasts look if they are plotted against time.

The *constant-level* models assume no trend at all in the data. The time series is assumed to have a relatively constant mean. The forecast for any period in the future is a horizontal line. *Linear trend* models forecast a straight-line trend for any period in the future. *Exponential trends* forecast that the amount of growth will increase continuously. At long horizons, these trends become unrealistic. Thus models with a *damped trend* have been developed for longer-range forecasting. The amount of trend extrapolated declines each period in a damped trend model. Eventually, the trend dies out and the forecasts become a horizontal line.

The *additive* seasonal pattern in Figure 3-1 assumes that the seasonal fluctuations are of constant size. The *multiplicative* pattern assumes that the seasonal fluctuations are proportional to the data. As the trend increases, the seasonal fluctuations get larger.

Models for all of the nonseasonal trend patterns in Figure 3-1 are explained in this chapter. In addition, we will explain how to use a multiplicative seasonal pattern with each trend. Additive seasonal patterns are less common in business data and are discussed in the references listed in the bibliography.

4 Evaluating forecast accuracy

There are many ways to measure forecast accuracy. Some possibilities are the mean absolute forecast error, usually called the MAD (for mean absolute

FORECASTING VERSUS PLANNING

AVERAGING FORECASTS TO REDUCE BIAS

FORECAST PROFILES

TREND PATTERNS

SEASONAL PATTERNS

ACCURACY MEASURES MAD, MAPE, AND MSE

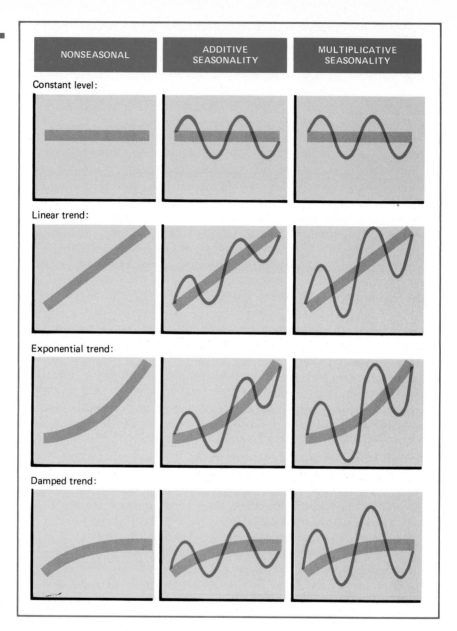

FIGURE 3-1
Time-series patterns.
Adapted from E. S.
Gardner, Jr.,
"Exponential
Smoothing: The State
of the Art," *Journal
of Forecasting*, vol. 4,
1985, pp. 1–38.

deviation), the mean absolute percentage error (MAPE), and the mean square error (MSE).

It is common for two forecasting models to be ranked differently depending on the accuracy measure used. For example, model A may give a smaller MAD but a larger MSE than model B. Why? Because the MAD gives equal weight to each error. The MSE gives more weight to large errors because they are squared.

THE BEST MODEL DEPENDS ON THE MEASURE

It is up to the manager, not the management scientist, to decide which accuracy measure is most appropriate for his or her application. The MSE

WHY MSE IS POPULAR

is most often used in practice. As anyone who has tried to live within a fixed budget will attest, large forecast errors can be extremely disruptive.

Given a preferred accuracy measure, how do we know when our forecasts are good, bad, or indifferent? One way to answer this question is to compare the accuracy of a given model with that of a *benchmark model*. A handy benchmark is the *naive model*, which assumes that the value of the series next period will be the same as it is this period:

MODEL ACCURACY MUST BE COMPARED WITH BENCHMARK ACCURACY

$$F_{t+1} = X_t \qquad (3\text{-}1)$$

THE NAIVE FORECASTING EQUATION

where F is the forecast and X is the observed value. The subscript t is an index for the time period. The current period is t, and the next period is $t + 1$.

The first step in any forecasting problem should be to use the naive model to compute the benchmark accuracy. A model which cannot beat the naive model should be discarded. Checking model accuracy against that of the naive model may seem to be a waste of time, but unless we do so, it is easy to choose an inappropriate forecasting model. One of the authors encountered this problem in a consulting assignment. A company was using a sophisticated exponential smoothing model which predicted a quadratic trend. A quick check showed that this model was a ridiculous choice for the data. The naive model was far more accurate.

DISCARD ANY MODEL WHICH CAN'T BEAT THE NAIVE ONE

To illustrate the accuracy measures and the naive model, we will examine a forecasting problem faced by Spyros Makridakis, the terminal manager at Carrboro International Airport. The airport has been open for a year. Spyros feels that he has enough historical data to forecast the number of passengers embarking. He needs a model to forecast 1 month ahead in order to schedule part-time employment for airport services such as parking, baggage handling, and security.

CARRBORO FORECASTING PROBLEM

Figure 3-2 shows passenger embarkations (in thousands) by month. The forecasting performance of the naive model is shown in Table 3-2. Embarkations are listed in the column under X_t. The first forecast cannot be made until the end of month 1. In month 1, embarkations were 28, which is used as the forecast for month 2. In month 2, embarkations were 27, which is the forecast for month 3, and so on.

The forecast error in each period is

$$e_t = X_t - F_t \qquad (3\text{-}2)$$

THE FORECAST ERROR EQUATION

The last three columns in the table record the absolute error, the absolute percentage error, and the squared error. These are used to compute the mean error measures at the bottom of the table.

Notice that the mean error measures are computed only for the last half of the data. The reason is that the forecasting models described later in the

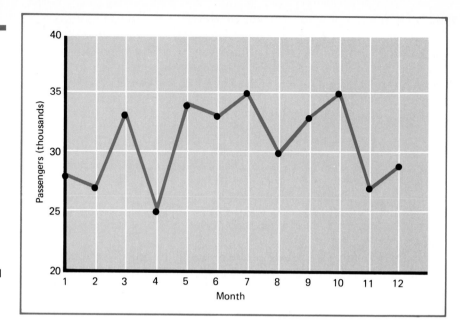

FIGURE 3-2

Carrboro International
Airport passenger
embarkations by
month.

chapter are evaluated by dividing the data into two parts. The first part is used to fit the forecasting model. Fitting consists of running the model through the first part of the data to get "warmed up." We call the fitting data the *warm-up sample*. The second part of the data is used to test the model and is called the *forecasting sample*. Accuracy in the warm-up sample is really irrelevant. Accuracy in the forecasting sample is more important because the pattern of the data often changes over time. The forecasting sample is used to evaluate how well the model tracks such changes. This point will be explained in detail in the next few sections.

WARM-UP SAMPLE
VERSUS FORECASTING
SAMPLE

There are no statistical rules on where to divide the data into warm-up samples and forecasting samples. There may not be enough data to have two samples. A good rule of thumb is to put at least six nonseasonal data points or two complete seasons of seasonal data in the warm-up sample. If there are fewer data than this, there is no need to bother with two samples. In a long time series, it is common practice simply to divide the data in half.

DIVIDING DATA
INTO SAMPLES

Spyros compared his data with the forecast profiles in Figure 3-1 and decided that a constant-level forecast would be appropriate. He decided to use the naive MSE to help evaluate two models which forecast a constant level: the moving average and simple exponential smoothing.

TWO CONSTANT-LEVEL
MODELS

5 Moving averages

TYPES OF MOVING
AVERAGES

Two kinds of moving averages can be used: *unweighted* and *weighted*. With an unweighted moving average, the forecast is the mean of the last N data points. For example, if $N = 3$, the forecasting equation is

THE EQUATION FOR THE
THREE-PERIOD MOVING
AVERAGE

$$F_{t+1} = \frac{X_t + X_{t-1} + X_{t-2}}{3} \tag{3-3}$$

t	Data X_t	Forecast F_t	Error $e_t = X_t - F_t$	Absolute error $\lvert e_t \rvert$	Absolute percentage error $\lvert e_t / X_t \rvert \times 100$	Squared error e_t^2
1	28.0					
2	27.0	28.0	−1.0			
3	33.0	27.0	6.0			
4	25.0	33.0	−8.0			
5	34.0	25.0	9.0			
6	33.0	34.0	−1.0			
7	35.0	33.0	2.0	2.0	5.7%	4.0
8	30.0	35.0	−5.0	5.0	16.7%	25.0
9	33.0	30.0	3.0	3.0	9.1%	9.0
10	35.0	33.0	2.0	2.0	5.7%	4.0
11	27.0	35.0	−8.0	8.0	29.6%	64.0
12	29.0	27.0	2.0	2.0	6.9%	4.0
13		29.0				
Sum (periods 7–12)				22.0	73.7%	110.0

MAD $= 22.0/6 = 3.7$
MAPE $= 73.7\%/6 = 12.3\%$
MSE $= 110.0/6 = 18.3$

TABLE 3-2
A naive forecasting model

Spyros tried a three-period moving average on the passenger embarkation data, as shown in Table 3-3. The forecasts start at the end of period 3, where the forecast for period 4 is

$$F_4 = \frac{X_3 + X_2 + X_1}{3}$$

or

$$F_4 = \frac{28 + 27 + 33}{3} = 29.3$$

At the end of period 4, the oldest observation is dropped and the observation for period 4 is added. The forecast for period 5 is

$$F_5 = \frac{27 + 33 + 25}{3} = 28.3$$

The other forecasts follow in a similar manner. The MSE of the moving average is better than that of the naive benchmark, and this is promising.

But how does Spyros know that a three-period average is best? Why not four, five, or six periods? The only way to decide on the number of periods is by experimentation. Another question is whether the average should be weighted. A generally accepted principle in forecasting is that recent data

DISADVANTAGES: CHOOSING PERIODS AND WEIGHTS

t	Data X_t	Forecast F_t	Error $e_t = X_t - F_t$	Forecast for $t + 1$ $F_{t+1} = (X_t + X_{t-1} + X_{t-2})/3$
1	28.0			
2	27.0			
3	33.0			$F_4 = (28 + 27 + 33)/3 = 29.3$
4	25.0	29.3	−4.3	$F_5 = (27 + 33 + 25)/3 = 28.3$
5	34.0	28.3	5.7	$F_6 = (33 + 25 + 34)/3 = 30.7$
6	33.0	30.7	2.3	$F_7 = (25 + 34 + 33)/3 = 30.7$
7	35.0	30.7	4.3	$F_8 = (34 + 33 + 35)/3 = 34.0$
8	30.0	34.0	−4.0	$F_9 = (33 + 35 + 30)/3 = 32.7$
9	33.0	32.7	0.3	$F_{10} = (35 + 30 + 33)/3 = 32.7$
10	35.0	32.7	2.3	$F_{11} = (30 + 33 + 35)/3 = 32.7$
11	27.0	32.7	−5.7	$F_{12} = (33 + 35 + 27)/3 = 31.7$
12	29.0	31.7	−2.7	$F_{13} = (35 + 27 + 29)/3 = 30.3$
13		30.3		

TABLE 3-3
A three-period moving
average

$$\text{MSE (periods 7–12)} = \frac{4.3^2 + 4.0^2 + 0.3^2 + 2.3^2 + 5.7^2 + 2.7^2}{6} = 13.3$$

contain more information than older data. For example, in the three-period average, Spyros could assign a weight of .5 to the most recent observation, .3 to the second most recent, and .2 to the third. But again, experimentation is the only way to decide what weighting scheme is best.

The need to experiment with both the number of periods and the weights in a moving average is a serious disadvantage. Another disadvantage is the need to store what can be a great deal of historical data. In practice, the most accurate moving average is often found to be 12 periods or more.

For these reasons, Spyros decided not to investigate moving averages any further. Exponential smoothing requires less computation and less data storage.

6 Simple exponential smoothing

Exponential smoothing works like an automatic pilot or a thermostat. If forecast errors are positive ($X_t - F_t$ has a positive sign), the forecasts are increased. If errors are negative ($X_t - F_t$ has a negative sign), the forecasts are reduced. This process of adjustment continues unless the errors reach zero. This usually does not happen but is always the goal. The new forecast is equal to the old forecast plus a fraction of the error. The fraction is α (the Greek letter *alpha*), called the *smoothing parameter*; α lies between 0 and 1. In symbols, the equation is

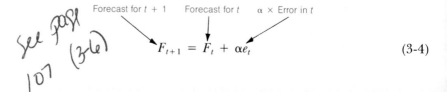

Forecast for $t + 1$ Forecast for t $\alpha \times$ Error in t

$$F_{t+1} = F_t + \alpha e_t \qquad (3\text{-}4)$$

see page (36)
107

Table 3-4 shows what happened when Spyros applied simple exponential smoothing to the passenger data. To get started, one must supply a forecast for period 1 and an α value (more about how to choose these later). After that the model runs automatically.

Spyros decided to use $F_1 = 30$ and $\alpha = .1$. In period 1, the error $e_1 = X_1 - F_1 = 28 - 30 = -2$. The calculations to forecast period 2 are

$$F_2 = F_1 + \alpha e_1$$

$$F_2 = 30.0 + .1(-2.0) = 29.8$$

Because e_1 is negative, the forecast for period 2 goes down.

The error in period 2 is $27 - 29.8 = -2.8$. The next forecast is

$$F_3 = F_2 + \alpha e_2$$

$$F_3 = 29.8 + .1(-2.8) = 29.5$$

Again, the error (e_2) is negative, and the forecast for period 3 goes down.

The error in period 3 is $33 - 29.5 = 3.5$. The next forecast is

$$F_4 = F_3 + \alpha e_3$$

$$F_4 = 29.5 + .1(3.5) = 29.9$$

This time the error is positive, so F_4 increases.

TABLE 3-4
Simple exponential
smoothing, $\alpha = .10$

t	Data X_t	Forecast F_t	Error $e_t = X_t - F_t$	Forecast for $t + 1$ $F_{t+1} = F_t + \alpha e_t$
1	28.0	30.0	-2.0	$F_2 = 30.0 + .1(-2.0) = 29.8$
2	27.0	29.8	-2.8	$F_3 = 29.8 + .1(-2.8) = 29.5$
3	33.0	29.5	3.5	$F_4 = 29.5 + .1(\ 3.5) = 29.9$
4	25.0	29.9	-4.9	$F_5 = 29.9 + .1(-4.9) = 29.4$
5	34.0	29.4	4.6	$F_6 = 29.4 + .1(\ 4.6) = 29.9$
6	33.0	29.9	3.1	$F_7 = 29.9 + .1(\ 3.1) = 30.2$
7	35.0	30.2	4.8	$F_8 = 30.2 + .1(\ 4.8) = 30.7$
8	30.0	30.7	-0.7	$F_9 = 30.7 + .1(-0.7) = 30.6$
9	33.0	30.6	2.4	$F_{10} = 30.6 + .1(\ 2.4) = 30.8$
10	35.0	30.8	4.2	$F_{11} = 30.8 + .1(\ 4.2) = 31.2$
11	27.0	31.2	-4.2	$F_{12} = 31.2 + .1(-4.2) = 30.8$
12	29.0	30.8	-1.8	$F_{13} = 30.8 + .1(-1.8) = 30.6$
13		30.6		

$$\text{MSE (periods 7-12)} = \frac{4.8^2 + 0.7^2 + 2.4^2 + 4.2^2 + 4.2^2 + 1.8^2}{6} = 11.3$$

SIMPLE SMOOTHING
REQUIRES MINIMAL
STORAGE

HOW THE WARM-UP
SAMPLE IS USED

CHOOSING F_1

TESTING α VALUES

MINIMUM AND
MAXIMUM VALUES OF α

The other forecasts follow in a similar manner. Figure 3-3 plots the forecasts versus the data. The plot shows that the forecasts are quite stable, a very desirable outcome.

In this case, the MSE for simple smoothing is an improvement over that of the naive model as well as that of the three-period moving average. Another advantage compared with the moving average is that the data storage requirements for simple exponential smoothing are minimal. Only two data elements have to be stored: the last forecast and α.

The warm-up sample (periods 1 to 6) is used to get the model started—to compute the first forecast (F_1) and to choose α. It would be deceiving to use the warm-up sample to evaluate accuracy as well. Accuracy must be evaluated with different data, the forecasting sample (periods 7 to 12).

If F_1 is not representative of the data, later forecasts will be distorted. A good rule of thumb is to choose F_1 as the mean of the warm-up sample; this is $F_1 = 30$ in this data.

To choose α, a range of trial values must be tested. The "best-fitting" α (.1 in this example) is the one that gives the minimum MSE in the warm-up sample. The minimum MAD or MAPE can also be used as a criterion for α. Although α can be any number between 0 and 1, it is usually adequate to test only nine trial values: .1, .2, ..., .9. The simple smoothing model is not overly sensitive to α values near the optimum.

The minimum value that should be used in practice is $\alpha = .1$. Smaller values result in a very sluggish response to changes in the mean of the time series. The maximum value of α is 1, but there is no need to test this value because $\alpha = 1$ makes simple smoothing equivalent to the naive model. To see this, substitute $\alpha = 1$ into Eq. (3-4). The result is the naive model:

$$F_{t+1} = F_t + (1)e_t = F_t + (X_t - F_t) = X_t$$

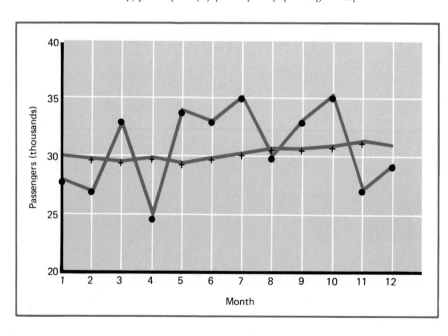

FIGURE 3-3
Forecasts versus data with simple exponential smoothing. (●) Data; (+) forecasts.

There are two factors which interact to determine the best-fitting α. One is the amount of *noise*, or randomness, in the series. The greater the noise, the smaller that particular α should be to avoid overreaction to purely random fluctuations in the time series. The smoothing parameter α is also influenced by the stability of the mean of the time series. If the mean is relatively constant, α should be small. If the mean is changing, α should be large to keep up with the changes.

The value of α also controls the weights assigned to past data. Exponential smoothing is really a weighted moving average in disguise. The weights on past data decline exponentially—hence the name of the model. The weights on past data can be found with a model equivalent to Eq. (3-4) by successively substituting $e_t = X_t - F_t$ for each t:

$$F_{t+1} = \alpha X_t + \alpha(1 - \alpha)X_{t-1} + \alpha(1 - \alpha)^2 X_{t-2} + \alpha(1 - \alpha)^3 X_{t-3}$$
$$+ \alpha(1 - \alpha)^4 X_{t-4} + \cdots + \alpha(1 - \alpha)^k X_{t-k} \qquad (3\text{-}5)$$

EFFECTS OF NOISE ON

EFFECTS OF THE STABILITY OF THE MEAN ON α

THE EQUATION FOR WEIGHTS ON PAST DATA

No one would ever use this form of simple smoothing to forecast, but it is useful for computing the weights assigned to past data. These weights always add up to 1.0. Every data point gets some weight, although the weights for older data quickly become very small. For $\alpha = .1$ in Spyros' passenger data, the weights on the last few data points are

Data	Weight assigned	
$X_{12} = 29$	α	$= .100$
$X_{11} = 27$	$\alpha(1 - \alpha)$	$= .090$
$X_{10} = 35$	$\alpha(1 - \alpha)^2$	$= .081$

A little algebra shows that simple smoothing in Eq. (3-4) is equivalent to another model often seen in practice:

$$F_{t+1} = \alpha X_t + (1 - \alpha)F_t \qquad (3\text{-}6)$$

EQUIVALENT SIMPLE SMOOTHING MODEL

Equation 3-4 should be preferable because it takes less arithmetic. It is true that the error has to be computed before Eq. 3-4 can be used, but the error should always be computed anyhow to evaluate the accuracy of the model.

Empirical studies have shown that simple smoothing is *robust*, meaning that it gives good performance on many different kinds of time series. This is especially true for time series which contain a great deal of noise. The less aggregated the data, the more that noise becomes a problem. For example, the sales of individual products contain more noise than the aggregate sales of the product line.

ROBUSTNESS

Simple smoothing also has an important limitation. The model assumes that any change in the mean of the time series will be slow. If the mean increases suddenly, the forecasts will lag (underestimate) the data. The same thing will happen if there is a trend in the data. Like humans, quantitative models can be biased.

DISADVANTAGE: FORECASTS LAG WHEN THE SERIES CHANGES SUDDENLY

7 Time-series regression

We will discuss two ways to forecast a time series containing a trend. One is fit a trend line to past data and then to project the line into the future. 's is done with a *time-series regression* model discussed in this section. The second approach is to smooth the trend with an expanded version of the simple smoothing model. This is discussed in Sections 8 and 9.

Time-series regression will be illustrated with a forecasting problem facing George E. P. Box, the owner of the Computerland store in Winston-Salem, North Carolina. George's sales (in thousands of dollars) for the last 12 months are plotted in Figure 3-4. Sales have grown by almost 50 percent over the last year. George needs to forecast dollar sales 1 month ahead to help decide how much he needs to borrow from North Carolina National Bank to finance his inventories.

George decided to test a time-series regression model on his sales data. *Regression* in statistics is a term used to describe the process of estimating the relationship between two variables, in this case *time* and *sales*. The relationship is estimated by fitting a straight line through the historical data. In Figure 3-4, we could fit a straight line through all the data. But as with previous models, we will use the first half of the data as a warm-up sample. The straight line in Figure 3-4 is fitted through the first six data points and then projected into the remaining data.

The best-fitting line could be "eyeballed." However, it can be found more precisely, with an equation which yields a line that *minimizes the sum of the squares of the errors* between the estimated points on the line and the actual sales. This is the same idea as that used to justify the MSE as an accuracy

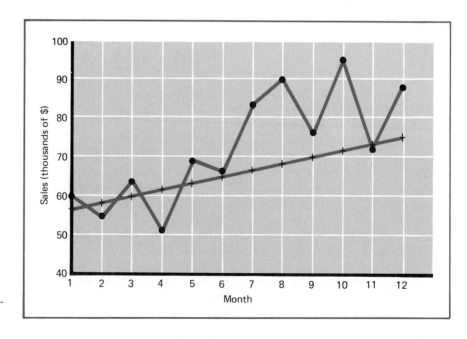

FIGURE 3-4
Dollar sales of Computerland of Winston-Salem for the past year.
(●) Data; (+) regression forecasts.

measure. The farther a point is from the trend line, the more serious the error is. To penalize the large errors, we square them. Since we are searching for the trend line that gives us the minimum sum of the squares of the errors in the warm-up sample, this method of fitting a trend line is often called the *least-squares method.*

The equation for a fitted straight line is

$$F_t = a + bt \qquad (3\text{-}7)$$

where F_t = estimated or forecast value of sales for t
  a = intercept, or the point at which the trend line intercepts the X (sales) axis
  b = slope of the trend line, or the rate of change in sales
  t = time, in this case the months from 1 to 6; any series of numbers can be used for t as long as they are consecutive

Two equations are used to find the slope and intercept of the best-fitting trend line. The slope is always computed first:

$$b = \frac{\sum tX - n\bar{t}\bar{X}}{\sum t^2 - n\bar{t}^2} \qquad (3\text{-}8)$$

where b = slope
  t = time
  X = dependent variable, sales
  $\bar{t}$ = mean of the values of t
  $\bar{X}$ = mean of the values of X

Second, the intercept is calculated as

$$a = \bar{X} - b\bar{t} \qquad (3\text{-}9)$$

where a = intercept
  $\bar{X}$ = mean of the values of X
  b = slope from Eq. (3-8)
  $\bar{t}$ = mean of the values of t

Table 3-5 shows how these equations are used to find the best-fitting trend line for the first 6 months of the data. The trend line equation is calculated as

$$F_t = 54.9 + 1.7t$$

The forecasts are calculated by substituting different values of t into this equation. This is done in Table 3-6, where the data for all 12 months are listed. For month 1, $t = 1$ and the forecast is

$$F_1 = 54.9 + 1.7(1) = 56.6$$

THE LEAST-SQUARES METHOD IS USED TO FIT THE REGRESSION MODEL

STRAIGHT-LINE EQUATION

SLOPE OF THE BEST-FITTING TREND LINE

INTERCEPT OF THE BEST-FITTING TREND LINE

TREND LINE FOR THE FIRST 6 MONTHS OF COMPUTERLAND DATA

t	X	tX	t²
1	60.0	60.0	1
2	55.0	110.0	4
3	64.0	192.0	9
4	51.0	204.0	16
5	69.0	345.0	25
6	66.0	396.0	36
$\sum t = 21$	$\sum X = 365.0$	$\sum tX = 1,307.0$	$\sum t^2 = 91$

$$\bar{t} = \sum t/n \qquad \bar{X} = \sum X/n$$
$$= 21/6 \qquad = 365.0/6$$
$$= 3.5 \qquad = 60.8$$

$$b = \frac{\sum tX - n\bar{t}\bar{X}}{\sum t^2 - n\bar{t}^2} = \frac{1,307.0 - 6(3.5)(60.8)}{91 - 6(3.5)^2} = 1.7$$

$$a = \bar{X} - b\bar{t} = 60.8 - 1.7(3.5) = 54.9$$

$$F_t = a + bt = 54.9 + 1.7t$$

TABLE 3-5
Linear regression
calculations

For month 2, $t = 2$ and the forecast is

$$F_2 = 54.9 + 1.7(2) = 58.3$$

The remaining calculations follow in a similar manner. The MSE for the forecasting sample is 242.6. George also calculates the naive MSE as a benchmark. This is 280.0, so the regression model is an improvement.

ALL REGRESSION
FORECASTS ARE BASED
ON A SINGLE EQUATION

Notice that Table 3-6 is organized differently from the other forecasting tables in the chapter. Before we updated the forecasts at the end of each period. Here we make all the forecasts at once based on a single equation.

A CHANGING TREND
PATTERN

Figure 3-4 shows how the trend line compares with the data. The line looks reasonable for periods 1 to 6. But when we project the trend line, it runs below the data. The trend appears to have changed—the slope has increased, or perhaps the intercept has shifted upward.

One way to deal with the problem of changing slope or intercept is to update the regression equations every time period, that is, to add one more period of data to Table 3-6 after each observation and recompute the values

A DISADVANTAGE:
RECOMPUTING THE
TREND LINE

of a and b. This is tedious, but George should do it if he wants to use regression as a forecasting model. It is not really a fair evaluation to fit the model only once. It should be fitted seven times (at the end of months 6 through 12).

But even if George does refit the model at the end of each month, there is another potential problem in forecasting with any regression model. *In*

A DISADVANTAGE:
EQUAL WEIGHTS ON
THE DATA

regression, equal weight is assigned to all observations. Looking again at Figure 3-4 we see that this is not a good forecasting strategy in these data. Because the data are changing, we should do better if more weight is given to the recent data. This is why exponential smoothing methods for trends were developed; these are explained in the next two sections.

t	Data X_t	Forecast $F_t = a + bt$	Error $e_t = X_t - F_t$
1	60.0	$F_1 = 54.9 + 1.7(1) = 56.6$	3.4
2	55.0	$F_2 = 54.9 + 1.7(2) = 58.3$	−3.3
3	64.0	$F_3 = 54.9 + 1.7(3) = 60.0$	4.0
4	51.0	$F_4 = 54.9 + 1.7(4) = 61.7$	−10.7
5	69.0	$F_5 = 54.9 + 1.7(5) = 63.4$	5.6
6	66.0	$F_6 = 54.9 + 1.7(6) = 65.1$	0.9
7	83.0	$F_7 = 54.9 + 1.7(7) = 66.8$	16.2
8	90.0	$F_8 = 54.9 + 1.7(8) = 68.5$	21.5
9	76.0	$F_9 = 54.9 + 1.7(9) = 70.2$	5.8
10	95.0	$F_{10} = 54.9 + 1.7(10) = 71.9$	23.1
11	72.0	$F_{11} = 54.9 + 1.7(11) = 73.6$	−1.6
12	88.0	$F_{12} = 54.9 + 1.7(12) = 75.3$	12.7
13		$F_{13} = 54.9 + 1.7(13) = 77.0$	

$$\text{MSE (periods 7–12)} = \frac{16.2^2 + 21.5^2 + 5.8^2 + 23.1^2 + 1.6^2 + 12.7^2}{6} = 242.6$$

TABLE 3-6
Linear regression
forecasts

The problem of changing data patterns emphasizes once again the need to divide the data into a warm-up sample and a forecasting sample. How well the model fits the warm-up sample may not be a good indication of how it will forecast later data.

FIT VERSUS
FORECASTING

8 Smoothing linear trends

Simple smoothing continually adjusts the forecasts according to the errors. To start, a forecast for period 1 (F_1) is selected. A fraction of the error in period 1 is added to F_1 to get F_2. A fraction of the error in period 2 is added to F_2 to get F_3, and so on.

CONTINUAL
ADJUSTMENT IN
SIMPLE SMOOTHING

Smoothing a linear trend works the same way except that the errors are used to continually adjust two things: the intercept and the slope of the trend line. The adjustments are made with a sequence of equations repeated each period:

CONTINUAL
ADJUSTMENT IN
LINEAR SMOOTHING

$$\begin{array}{l}\text{Smoothed level} \\ \text{at the end of } t\end{array} = \text{forecast for } t + \alpha_1 \times \text{error in } t$$

$$\begin{array}{l}\text{Smoothed trend} \\ \text{at the end of } t\end{array} = \begin{array}{l}\text{smoothed trend} \\ \text{at the end of } t-1\end{array} + \alpha_2 \times \text{error in } t$$

$$\text{Forecast for } t+1 = \begin{array}{l}\text{smoothed level} \\ \text{at the end of } t\end{array} + \begin{array}{l}\text{smoothed trend} \\ \text{at the end of } t\end{array}$$

The smoothing equations for a linear trend compute a new trend line at the end of each period. The intercept of the new trend line is called the *smoothed level.* This is not quite the same as the regression intercept a. In regression the

SMOOTHED LEVEL
AND TREND

trend line starts at period 1. In smoothing the trend line starts at the current period. The slope of the new trend line is called the *smoothed trend* and is similar to the slope *b* in regression.

To see how this model works, we will put the equations into symbols and then smooth the Computerland sales. The equations are

$$S_t = F_t + \alpha_1 e_t \tag{3-10}$$

$$T_t = T_{t-1} + \alpha_2 e_t \tag{3-11}$$

$$F_{t+1} = S_t + T_t \tag{3-12}$$

where S_t is the smoothed level and T_t is the smoothed trend. There are two smoothing parameters: α_1 for the level and α_2 for the trend. The forecast Eq. (3-12) looks like the regression forecast Eq. (3-7) except that S_t and T_t, not *a* and *bt*, are added together.

The computations for the Computerland sales are shown in Table 3-7. The warm-up sample is again the first six periods. To get started, we do a time-series regression on the warm-up sample. *The intercept and slope of the regression are always used as the initial values of S and T.* The initial values of S and T have the subscript zero. Thus $S_0 = a$, and $T_0 = b$. We will use $\alpha_1 = .10$ and $\alpha_2 = .01$ (how to choose these is explained later).

The values of S_0 and T_0 are recorded in the first row of the table. The forecast for period 1 is computed in the last column of row 0:

$$F_1 = S_0 + T_0 = 54.9 + 1.7 = 56.6$$

The forecast is moved down to the forecast column of row 1. The error in 1 is

$$e_1 = X_1 - F_1 = 60.0 - 56.6 = 3.4$$

Now that the error has been computed, we continue working in row 1 and update the level and trend as of the end of period 1:

$$S_1 = F_1 + \alpha_1 e_1 = 56.6 + .1(3.4) = 56.9$$
$$T_1 = T_0 + \alpha_2 e_1 = 1.7 + .01(3.4) = 1.7$$

The last step in row 1 is to compute the forecast for period 2:

$$F_2 = S_1 + T_1 = 56.9 + 1.7 = 58.6$$

Then F_2 is moved down to the forecast column in row 2.

Let's reflect for a moment on what we have accomplished. The beginning level and trend, S_0 and T_0, are the same thing as *a* and *b* in the regression model. We can project a trend line into the future using these values (as we did in Table 3-6). But at the end of period 1, there is a new trend line. This line can be drawn into the future starting at 56.9, the value of S_1. What we

TABLE 3-7
Exponential smoothing with a linear trend, $\alpha_1 = .10$, $\alpha_2 = .01$

t	Data X_t	Forecast F_t	Error $e_t = X_t - F_t$	Level at the end of t $S_t = F_t + \alpha_1 e_t$	Trend at the end of t $T_t = T_{t-1} + \alpha_2 e_t$	Forecast for t + 1 $F_{t+1} = S_t + T_t$
0				$S_0 = 54.9$	$T_0 = 1.7$	$F_1 = 54.9 + 1.7 = 56.6$
1	60.0	56.6	3.4	$S_1 = 56.6 + .1(3.4) = 56.9$	$T_1 = 1.7 + .01(3.4) = 1.7$	$F_2 = 56.9 + 1.7 = 58.6$
2	55.0	58.6	−3.6	$S_2 = 58.6 + .1(−3.6) = 58.2$	$T_2 = 1.7 + .01(−3.6) = 1.7$	$F_3 = 58.2 + 1.7 = 59.9$
3	64.0	59.9	4.1	$S_3 = 59.9 + .1(4.1) = 60.3$	$T_3 = 1.7 + .01(4.1) = 1.7$	$F_4 = 60.3 + 1.7 = 62.0$
4	51.0	62.0	−11.0	$S_4 = 62.0 + .1(−11.0) = 60.9$	$T_4 = 1.7 + .01(−11.0) = 1.6$	$F_5 = 60.9 + 1.6 = 62.5$
5	69.0	62.5	6.5	$S_5 = 62.5 + .1(6.5) = 63.2$	$T_5 = 1.6 + .01(6.5) = 1.7$	$F_6 = 63.2 + 1.7 = 64.9$
6	66.0	64.9	1.1	$S_6 = 64.9 + .1(1.1) = 65.0$	$T_6 = 1.7 + .01(1.1) = 1.7$	$F_7 = 65.0 + 1.7 = 66.7$
7	83.0	66.7	16.3	$S_7 = 66.7 + .1(16.3) = 68.3$	$T_7 = 1.7 + .01(16.3) = 1.9$	$F_8 = 68.3 + 1.9 = 70.2$
8	90.0	70.2	19.8	$S_8 = 70.2 + .1(19.8) = 72.2$	$T_8 = 1.9 + .01(19.8) = 2.1$	$F_9 = 72.2 + 2.1 = 74.3$
9	76.0	74.3	1.7	$S_9 = 74.3 + .1(1.7) = 74.5$	$T_9 = 2.1 + .01(1.7) = 2.1$	$F_{10} = 74.5 + 2.1 = 76.6$
10	95.0	76.6	18.4	$S_{10} = 76.6 + .1(18.4) = 78.4$	$T_{10} = 2.1 + .01(18.4) = 2.3$	$F_{11} = 78.4 + 2.3 = 80.7$
11	72.0	80.7	−8.7	$S_{11} = 80.7 + .1(−8.7) = 79.8$	$T_{11} = 2.3 + .01(−8.7) = 2.2$	$F_{12} = 79.8 + 2.2 = 82.0$
12	88.0	82.0	6.0	$S_{12} = 82.0 + .1(6.0) = 82.6$	$T_{12} = 2.2 + .01(6.0) = 2.3$	$F_{13} = 82.6 + 2.3 = 84.9$
13		84.9				

$$\text{MSE (periods 7–12)} = \frac{16.3^2 + 19.8^2 + 1.7^2 + 18.4^2 + 8.7^2 + 6.0^2}{6} = 185.1$$

have really done is to adjust the intercept to the end of period 1. The slope of the new trend line is $T_1 = 1.7$. This is what we started with, although it would be slightly different if enough decimal places were used.

The calculations in period 2 are

$$e_2 = X_2 - F_2 = 55.0 - 58.6 = -3.6$$

$$S_2 = F_2 + \alpha_1 e_2 = 58.6 + .1(-3.6) = 58.2$$

$$T_2 = T_1 + \alpha_2 e_2 = 1.7 + .01(-3.6) = 1.7$$

$$F_3 = S_2 + T_2 = 58.2 + 1.7 = 59.9$$

The value of F_3 is moved down to the forecast column in period 3. Again there is a new trend line. This time it starts at 58.2, the value of S_2. The slope of the new line is still approximately 1.7.

The remaining calculations follow in a similar manner. Every period a new trend line is produced. The final trend line starts at 82.6, the value of S_{12}. The final slope is 2.3, an increase from the beginning value of 1.7. The MSE for the forecasting sample is 185.1, an improvement on both the regression results and the naive model.

SMOOTHING PICKS UP A CHANGING TREND

Figure 3-5 illustrates how the smoothing process picks up the change in trend in the last half of the data. Figure 3-5 is the same as Figure 3-4 except that the smoothing forecasts have been added. Notice how the smoothing forecasts rise above the regression forecasts as the change in trend is detected.

FORECASTING MORE THAN ONE STEP AHEAD

So far we have only forecast one period ahead (for $t + 1$). But at any time, forecasts can be made for longer horizons. The *general forecast equation for exponential smoothing of a linear trend* is

$$F_{t+m} = S_t + mT_t \qquad (3\text{-}13)$$

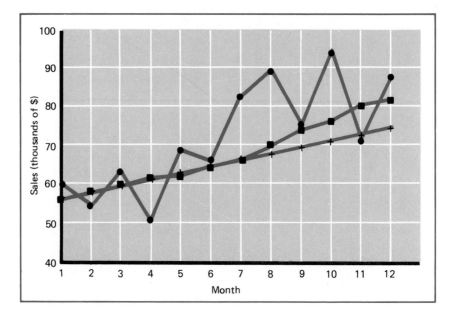

FIGURE 3-5

Comparison of regression and exponential smoothing forecasts. (●) Sales; (+) regression; (■) exponential smoothing.

where m is the number of periods into the future we want to forecast. At the
end of period 12, suppose forecasts are needed for the next two periods. For
one period ahead, $m = 1$ and $t + m = 13$. The equation is

$$F_{13} = S_{12} + (1)T_{12} = 82.6 + (1)2.3 = 84.9$$

This is recorded in row 13 of Table 3-7. For two periods ahead, $m = 2$ and
$t + m = 14$. The equation is

$$F_{14} = S_{12} + (2)T_{12} = 82.6 + (2)2.3 = 87.2$$

The parameters α_1 and α_2 control the rate at which the level and trend
are adjusted. Why do we need two parameters? The reason is that the trend
in any period is usually very small compared with the level. At the end of
period 12, for example, the level is 82.6 and the trend is only 2.3. If we add
the same fraction of the error to both the level and the trend, the forecasts
may be unstable. Thus α_1 for the level is usually greater than α_2 for the
trend. There are some strange time series in which α_1 is smaller than α_2.
However, this is rare.

As in simple smoothing, the best-fitting parameters are found by experimentation in the warm-up sample. In the Computerland data, pairs of α_1,
α_2 were tested until the minimum MSE (at $\alpha_1 = .10$, $\alpha_2 = .01$) was found.
The procedure was to test α_1 in increments of .10. For each α_1 value, a search
was made for the best α_2, starting at .01. For example, at $\alpha_1 = .10$, the MSE
for $\alpha_2 = .01, .02, .03, \ldots, .10$ was computed. This seems tedious, but there
are good computer packages which do efficient searches for the best combination of parameters.

9 Smoothing nonlinear trends

Forecast accuracy can often be improved by using a nonlinear trend. In
Figure 3-1, on page 100, two nonlinear trends are illustrated. The exponential
trend predicts that the amount of growth each period will increase while the
damped trend predicts that the amount of growth will decline. Both nonlinear
trends can be generated by a simple modification to the linear-trend model.
The exponential smoothing model for nonlinear trends is:

Smoothed level at the = forecast for t $+ \alpha_1 \times$ error in t
end of t

Smoothed trend at the = $\phi \times$ smoothed trend $+ \alpha_2 \times$ error in t
end of t at the end of $t-1$

Forecast for $t+1$ = smoothed level at the $+ \phi \times$ smoothed trend
end of t at the end of t

These are the same equations used in Section 8 except that the trend is
multiplied by a new parameter ϕ, called the trend-modification parameter.
The effect of ϕ is to accelerate or decelerate the trend. When ϕ is greater
than one, the model is called an exponential trend since the amount of

growth each period increases. When ϕ is between zero and one, growth decreases and the model is called a damped trend. If $\phi = 1$, the nonlinear model is the same as the linear trend.

To see how the nonlinear model works, let's put the equations into symbols:

$$S_t = F_t + \alpha_1 e_t \qquad (3\text{-}14)$$

$$T_t = \phi T_{t-1} + \alpha_2 e_t \qquad (3\text{-}15)$$

$$F_{t+1} = S_t + \phi T_t \qquad (3\text{-}16)$$

Compare these equations to equations (3-10) through (3-12) for the linear-trend model. Equation (3-14) for S_t is identical to (3-10). Equation (3-15) for T_t is the same as (3-11) except that T_{t-1} is multiplied by ϕ. The forecast equation (3-16) is the same as (3-12) except that T_t is multiplied by ϕ.

FITTING THE
NONLINEAR MODEL

Let's try the nonlinear model with $\phi > 1$, that is, an exponential trend, on the Computerland sales. Computations are shown in Table 3-8. The warm-up sample is the first six periods. To get started, a time series regression is done on the warm-up sample. Like the linear trend, the intercept and slope of the regression are always used as the initial values for S and T. We will use $\alpha_1 = .10$, $\alpha_2 = .01$, and $\phi = 1.1$. These values are selected by a computer search similar to the one for the linear trend. In this case, the search is far more complicated since the best combination of three parameters must be chosen.

S_0 and T_0 are recorded in the first row of the table. The forecast for period 1 is computed in the last column of row 0:

$$F_1 = S_0 + \phi T_0 = 54.9 + 1.1(1.7) = 56.8$$

The forecast is moved down to the forecast column of row 1. The error in 1 is:

$$e_1 = X_1 - F_1 = 60.0 - 56.8 = 3.2$$

Now that the error has been computed we continue working in row 1 and update the level and trend as of the end of period 1:

$$S_1 = F_1 + \alpha_1 e_1 = 56.8 + .1(3.2) = 57.1$$

$$T_1 = \phi T_0 + \alpha_2 e_1 = 1.1(1.7) + .01(3.2) = 1.9$$

The last step in row 1 is to compute the forecast for period 2:

$$F_2 = S_1 + \phi T_1 = 57.1 + 1.1(1.9) = 59.2$$

F_2 is moved down to the forecast column in row 2.

ACCELERATION OF
TREND

Compare the forecast calculations to those for the linear-trend model. Before, we simply added the level and trend to get the new forecast. In the exponential trend, we multiply the trend by ϕ before adding it to the level. Thus, ϕ acts as an accelerator for the trend.

TABLE 3-8
Smoothing a nonlinear trend: $\alpha_1 = .1$, $\alpha_2 = .01$, $\phi = 1.1$

t	Data X_t	Forecast F_t	Error $e_t = X_t - F_t$	Level at the end of t $S_t = F_t + \alpha_1 e_t$	Trend at the end of t $T_t = \phi T_{t-1} + \alpha_2 e_t$	Forecast for t + 1 $F_{t+1} = S_t + \phi T_t$
0				$S_0 =$ 54.9	$T_0 =$ 1.7	$F_1 =$ 54.9 + 1.1(1.7) = 56.8
1	60.0	56.8	3.2	$S_1 =$ 56.8 + .1(3.2) = 57.1	$T_1 =$ 1.1(1.7) + .01(3.2) = 1.9	$F_2 =$ 57.1 + 1.1(1.9) = 59.2
2	55.0	59.2	−4.2	$S_2 =$ 59.2 + .1(−4.2) = 58.8	$T_2 =$ 1.1(1.9) + .01(−4.2) = 2.0	$F_3 =$ 58.8 + 1.1(2.0) = 61.0
3	64.0	61.0	3.0	$S_3 =$ 61.0 + .1(3.0) = 61.3	$T_3 =$ 1.1(2.0) + .01(3.0) = 2.2	$F_4 =$ 61.3 + 1.1(2.2) = 63.7
4	51.0	63.7	−12.7	$S_4 =$ 63.7 + .1(−12.7) = 62.4	$T_4 =$ 1.1(2.2) + .01(−12.7) = 2.3	$F_5 =$ 62.4 + 1.1(2.3) = 64.9
5	69.0	64.9	4.1	$S_5 =$ 64.9 + .1(4.1) = 65.3	$T_5 =$ 1.1(2.3) + .01(4.1) = 2.6	$F_6 =$ 65.3 + 1.1(2.6) = 68.2
6	66.0	68.2	−2.2	$S_6 =$ 68.2 + .1(−2.2) = 68.0	$T_6 =$ 1.1(2.6) + .01(−2.2) = 2.8	$F_7 =$ 68.0 + 1.1(2.8) = 71.1
7	83.0	71.1	11.9	$S_7 =$ 71.1 + .1(11.9) = 72.3	$T_7 =$ 1.1(2.8) + .01(11.9) = 3.2	$F_8 =$ 72.3 + 1.1(3.2) = 75.8
8	90.0	75.8	14.2	$S_8 =$ 75.8 + .1(14.2) = 77.2	$T_8 =$ 1.1(3.2) + .01(14.2) = 3.7	$F_9 =$ 77.2 + 1.1(3.7) = 81.3
9	76.0	81.3	−5.3	$S_9 =$ 81.3 + .1(−5.3) = 80.8	$T_9 =$ 1.1(3.7) + .01(−5.3) = 4.0	$F_{10} =$ 80.8 + 1.1(4.0) = 85.2
10	95.0	85.2	9.8	$S_{10} =$ 85.2 + .1(9.8) = 86.2	$T_{10} =$ 1.1(4.0) + .01(9.8) = 4.5	$F_{11} =$ 86.2 + 1.1(4.5) = 91.2
11	72.0	91.2	−19.2	$S_{11} =$ 91.2 + .1(−19.2) = 89.3	$T_{11} =$ 1.1(4.5) + .01(−19.2) = 4.8	$F_{12} =$ 89.3 + 1.1(4.8) = 94.6
12	88.0	94.6	−6.6	$S_{12} =$ 94.6 + .1(−6.6) = 93.9	$T_{12} =$ 1.1(4.8) + .01(−6.6) = 5.2	$F_{13} =$ 93.9 + 1.1(5.2) = 99.6
13		99.6				

$$\text{MSE (periods 7–12)} = \frac{11.9^2 + 14.2^2 + 5.3^2 + 9.8^2 + 19.2^2 + 6.6^2}{6} = 146.6$$

The calculations in period 2 are:

$$e_2 = X_2 - F_2 = 55.0 - 59.2 = -4.2$$

$$S_2 = F_2 + \alpha_1 e_2 = 59.2 + .1(-4.2) = 58.8$$

$$T_2 = \phi T_1 + \alpha_2 e_2 = 1.1(1.9) + .01(-4.2) = 2.0$$

$$F_3 = S_2 + \phi T_2 = 58.8 + 1.1(2.0) = 61.0$$

F_3 is moved down to the forecast column in period 3. The remaining calculations follow in a similar manner. Every period, a new trend line based on the exponential trend is produced. The final trend line starts at 93.9, the value of S_{12}. The final slope is 5.2, a large increase from the beginning value of 1.7. The MSE for the forecasting sample is 146.6, compared to 185.1 for the linear-trend smoothing model. As shown in Figure 3-6, the exponential trend does a better job at picking up the increased growth in the forecasting sample.

EXPONENTIAL VERSUS LINEAR TREND

FORECASTING MORE THAN ONE STEP AHEAD

To forecast for more than one period in advance, the general forecast equation for exponential smoothing of a nonlinear trend is:

$$F_{t+m} = S_t + \sum_{i=1}^{m} \phi^i T_t \qquad (3\text{-}17)$$

where m is the number of periods into the future that we want to forecast.

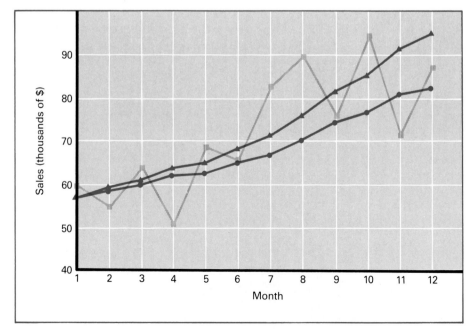

FIGURE 3-6

Comparison of trend-smoothing models. (■) Sales; (●) linear trend; (▲) exponential trend.

Let's compute several forecasts with this equation. At the end of period 12, $m = 1$ and $t + m = 13$. This equation is:

$$F_{13} = S_{12} + \phi^1 T_{12}$$

$$= 93.9 + (1.1)^1 5.2 = 99.6$$

This is recorded in row 13 of the table.

For two periods ahead, $m = 2$ and $t + m = 14$. The equation is:

$$F_{14} = S_{12} + \phi^1 T_{12} + \phi^2 T_{12}$$

$$= 93.9 + (1.1)^1 5.2 + (1.1)^2 5.2 = 105.9$$

For three periods ahead, $m = 3$ and $t + m = 15$. The equation is:

$$F_{15} = S_{12} + \phi^1 T_{12} + \phi^2 T_{12} + \phi^3 T_{12}$$

$$= 93.9 + (1.1)^1 5.2 + (1.1)^2 5.2 + (1.1)^3 5.2$$

$$= 112.8$$

As you may have noticed, a short-cut way to compute each forecast is to add another increment of the modified trend to the previous forecast. For example, F_{14} can be computed as follows:

SHORT-CUT FORECAST COMPUTATIONS

$$F_{14} = F_{13} + \phi^2 T_{12}$$

$$F_{14} = 99.6 + (1.1)^2 5.2 = 105.9$$

Now a short-cut to get F_{15} is:

$$F_{15} = F_{14} + \phi^3 T_{12}$$

$$F_{15} = 105.9 + (1.1)^3 5.2 = 112.8$$

The details of using the damped version of the nonlinear-trend model are similar to the exponential version. The only difference is that the search for the ϕ parameter is made over the range $0 < \phi < 1$. For example, suppose we use the following parameters in the Computerland sales data: $\alpha_1 = .2$, $\alpha_2 = .01$, $\phi = .9$. At the end of period 12, $S_{12} = 81.5$ and $T_{12} = 1.0$. Here are the calculations for forecasting months 13, 14, and 15:

COMPUTING DAMPED FORECASTS

$$F_{13} = S_{12} + \phi^1 T_{12}$$
$$= 81.5 + (0.9)^1 1.0 = 82.4$$

$$F_{14} = S_{12} + \phi^1 T_{12} + \phi^2 T_{12}$$
$$= 81.5 + (0.9)^1 1.0 + (0.9)^2 1.0 = 83.2$$

$$F_{15} = S_{12} + \phi^1 T_{12} + \phi^2 T_{12} + \phi^3 T_{12}$$
$$= 81.5 + (0.9)^1 1.0 + (0.9)^2 1.0 + (0.9)^3 1.0$$
$$= 83.9$$

ASYMPTOTE: LIMIT
ON GROWTH

SELECTING TREND
ALTERNATIVE

DATA MAY BE
TOO LIMITED FOR
FORECASTING TESTS

Notice how the growth declines. From month 13 to 14, growth is .8 units. From month 14 to 15, growth declines to .7 units. If you project the forecasts far enough into the future, eventually growth disappears altogether. The point at which growth stops is called an *asymptote*. In the Computerland sales, the asymptote occurs in month 40, when sales reach a plateau of 90.2 units per month.

If you are concerned with forecasting only one period into the future, selection of a trend alternative is straightforward. Compare the exponential, damped, and linear trends in the forecasting sample and choose the trend which yields the smallest error measure. In Computerland sales, the exponential trend is the best choice (results for the damped trend are worse than the exponential and are not presented here). If you are concerned with longer-range forecasting, you should compare error results at longer forecasting horizons. For example, suppose that you are interested in forecasting three months ahead. Compute the errors in the forecasting sample for three months ahead and choose the model which is best at that horizon.

Often you will not have enough data to conduct long-range forecasting tests and the best trend alternative becomes a matter of judgment. For example, Figure 3-7 shows quarterly circulation data for a computer magazine. Forecasts were made for one through six quarters into the future using three alternative trends (damped, linear, and exponential). All three trends give reasonable fits to past data. But with so little data, long-range forecasting tests are impossible. The exponential trend looks to be too optimistic for this time series, but it is difficult to choose between the linear and damped trends.

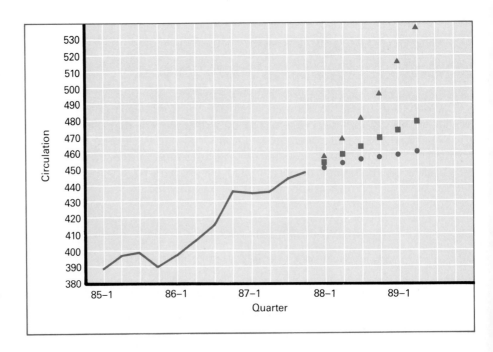

FIGURE 3-7

Trend alternatives. (━) Circulation; (●) damped trend; (■) linear trend; (▲) exponential trend.

10 Decomposition of seasonal data

Seasonal time series contain a pattern which repeats itself, at least approximately, each year. The need to include seasonality in a time series seems obvious, but there are times when it is not used. Two questions should be asked when there is doubt about seasonality. First, *are the peaks and the troughs consistent?* That is, do the high and low points of the pattern occur in about the same periods (weeks, months, or quarters) each year? Second, *is there an explanation for the seasonal pattern?* The most common reasons for seasonality are weather and holidays, although company policy such as annual sales promotions may be a factor. If the answer to either of these questions is no, seasonality should not be used in the forecasts.

QUESTIONS TO VERIFY SEASONALITY

Our approach to forecasting seasonal data is based on the *classical decomposition* method developed by economists in the nineteenth century. Decomposition means separation of the time series into its component parts. A complete decomposition separates the time series into four components: seasonality, trend, cycle, and randomness. The cycle is a long-range pattern related to the growth and decline of industries or the economy as a whole.

COMPLETE DECOMPOSITION

Decomposition in business forecasting is usually not so elaborate. We will start by simply removing the seasonal pattern from the data. The result is called *deseasonalized,* or *seasonally adjusted,* data. Next the deseasonalized data will be forecast with one of the models discussed earlier in the chapter. Finally, the forecasts will be *seasonalized*—the seasonal pattern will be put back.

FORECASTING WITH DESEASONALIZED DATA

The *seasonal* index is an important concept in decomposition. The index is defined as the ratio of the actual value of the time series to the average for the year. There is a unique index for each period of the year. If the data are monthly, there are 12 seasonal indices. If quarterly, there are 4 indices. The index adjusts each data point up or down from the average for the year. The index is used as follows:

SEASONAL INDICES

$$\frac{\text{Actual data}}{\text{Index}} = \text{deseasonalized data}$$

USING THE INDEX TO DESEASONALIZE

Suppose the seasonal index for first-quarter sales is .80. This means that sales in the first quarter are expected to be 80 percent of average sales for the year. Now suppose that actual sales for the first quarter are $5,000. Deseasonalized sales are

$$\frac{\$5,000}{.80} = \$6,250$$

To put the seasonality back, or to seasonalize the sales, we use

Deseasonalized data   Index   Actual data

$$\$6,250 \times .80 = \$5,000$$

USING THE INDEX TO SEASONALIZE

To explain how seasonal indices are computed and used in forecasting, we will analyze the quarterly sales history of Wolfpack Red Soda, a popular soft drink in the Raleigh, North Carolina, area. Estela Dagum, manager of the Wolfpack bottling plant, needs a forecast of sales by quarter for next year. Red Soda is a highly seasonal product, and she will have to start building inventories in advance of the peak quarter in order to meet demand.

Sales (thousands of cases) for the past 16 quarters are plotted in Figure 3-8. The peak is in the summer, the third quarter of the year. The trough occurs in the first quarter. As we have done throughout the chapter, we will divide the data into warm-up and forecasting samples. The first 12 quarters will be used as a warm-up sample. Quarters 13 to 16 will be the forecasting sample. The naive MSE for quarters 13 to 16 will serve as a benchmark.

CHOOSING A WARM-UP
AND A FORECASTING
SAMPLE

Deseasonalized sales are also shown in Figure 3-8. After the seasonal pattern is removed, the sales follow a relatively constant mean, indicating that simple smoothing should be used.

As shown in Tables 3-9 through 3-11, there are nine steps in forecasting seasonal data. Each step is explained below.

Step 1 *Compute a moving average based on the length of seasonality—(4 quarters or 12 months).*

The moving average is computed using the warm-up sample of the first 12 periods. The moving average is not used as a forecast—it is a base figure for computing seasonal indices. The moving average is recorded (centered) next to the third quarter included in the average. Ideally, the average should be placed next to the exact center period. But the exact center is $(1 + 4)/2$, or 2.5. There is no quarter 2.5, so we place the average at quarter 3. It could just as well be placed at quarter 2, but quarter 3 is used as a standard practice.

CENTERING THE
MOVING AVERAGES

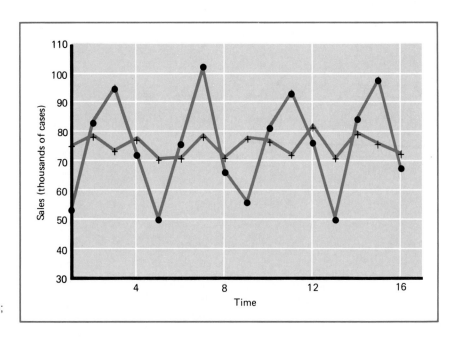

FIGURE 3-8

Sales of Wolfpack
Red Soda. (●) Actual;
(+) deseasonalized.

Notice that there is no moving average for the first two periods nor for the last. This is always the case because of the centering of the averages. If there are N periods of quarterly data, there are $N - 3$ moving averages. If there are N periods of monthly data, there are $N - 11$ moving averages, and centering is on the seventh month.

Step 2 *Divide the actual data by the corresponding moving average.*

In step 2 the ratio of each X_t value to its average is computed. These ratios are approximate seasonal indices. They will be refined in the next few steps.

Step 3 *Average the ratios to eliminate as much randomness as possible.*

The first refinement is in step 3, which computes the mean ratio for each quarter. There are two ratios for each of the first, second, and fourth quarters.

TABLE 3-9
Forecasting seasonal data: steps 1 through 5

		Step 1: Centered moving averages		Step 2: Ratios
t	Qtr.	X_t	4-Qtr. moving average	Ratio = X_t/average
1	1	53		
2	2	83		
3	3	95	(53 + 83 + 95 + 72)/4 = 75.75	95/75.75 = 1.2541
4	4	72	(83 + 95 + 72 + 50)/4 = 75.00	72/75.00 = 0.9600
5	1	50	(95 + 72 + 50 + 75)/4 = 73.00	50/73.00 = 0.6849
6	2	75	(72 + 50 + 75 + 102)/4 = 74.75	75/74.75 = 1.0033
7	3	102	(50 + 75 + 102 + 66)/4 = 73.25	102/73.25 = 1.3925
8	4	66	(75 + 102 + 66 + 55)/4 = 74.50	66/74.50 = 0.8859
9	1	55	(102 + 66 + 55 + 81)/4 = 76.00	55/76.00 = 0.7237
10	2	81	(66 + 55 + 81 + 93)/4 = 73.75	81/73.75 = 1.0983
11	3	93	(55 + 81 + 93 + 76)/4 = 76.25	93/76.25 = 1.2197
12	4	76		

	Step 3: Mean ratios		Step 4: Normalization factor
Qtr.	Mean ratio		Factor = 4/(sum of mean ratios)
1	(0.6849 + 0.7237)/2	= 0.7043	Factor = 4/3.9669 = 1.0083
2	(1.0033 + 1.0983)/2	= 1.0508	
3	(1.2541 + 1.3925 + 1.2197)/3	= 1.2888	
4	(0.9600 + 0.8859)/2	= 0.9230	
	Sum of mean ratios	= 3.9669	

	Step 5: Final seasonal indices		
Qtr.	Mean Ratio	× Factor	= Index
1	0.7043	× 1.0083	= 0.7101
2	1.0508	× 1.0083	= 1.0595
3	1.2888	× 1.0083	= 1.2995
4	0.9230	× 1.0083	= 0.9307
		Sum of indices	= 3.9998

TABLE 3-10
Forecasting seasonal data: steps 6 and 7

Step 6: Deseasonalize data

t	Qtr.	X_t/index	=	Des. X_t
1	1	53/0.7101	=	74.6
2	2	83/1.0595	=	78.3
3	3	95/1.2995	=	73.1
4	4	72/0.9307	=	77.4
5	1	50/0.7101	=	70.4
6	2	75/1.0595	=	70.8
7	3	102/1.2995	=	78.5
8	4	66/0.9307	=	70.9
9	1	55/0.7101	=	77.5
10	2	81/1.0595	=	76.5
11	3	93/1.2995	=	71.6
12	4	76/0.9307	=	81.7
13	1	50/0.7101	=	70.4
14	2	84/1.0595	=	79.3
15	3	98/1.2995	=	75.4
16	4	67/0.9307	=	72.0

Step 7: Forecast deseasonalized data ($\alpha = .10$)

t	Qtr.	Des. X_t	Forecast des. F_t	Error $e_t = X_t - F_t$	F_{t-1}	=	F_t	+	αe_t
1	1	74.6	75.1	−0.5	F_2	=	75.1	+	.1(−0.5) = 75.1
2	2	78.3	75.1	3.2	F_3	=	75.1	+	.1(3.2) = 75.4
3	3	73.1	75.4	−2.3	F_4	=	75.4	+	.1(−2.3) = 75.2
4	4	77.4	75.2	2.2	F_5	=	75.2	+	.1(2.2) = 75.4
5	1	70.4	75.4	−5.0	F_6	=	75.4	+	.1(−5.0) = 74.9
6	2	70.8	74.9	−4.1	F_7	=	74.9	+	.1(−4.1) = 74.5
7	3	78.5	74.5	4.0	F_8	=	74.5	+	.1(4.0) = 74.9
8	4	70.9	74.9	−4.0	F_9	=	74.9	+	.1(−4.0) = 74.5
9	1	77.5	74.5	3.0	F_{10}	=	74.5	+	.1(3.0) = 74.8
10	2	76.5	74.8	1.7	F_{11}	=	74.8	+	.1(1.7) = 75.0
11	3	71.6	75.0	−3.4	F_{12}	=	75.0	+	.1(−3.4) = 74.7
12	4	81.7	74.7	7.0	F_{13}	=	74.7	+	.1(7.0) = 75.4
13	1	70.4	75.4	−5.0	F_{14}	=	75.4	+	.1(−5.0) = 74.9
14	2	79.3	74.9	4.4	F_{15}	=	74.9	+	.1(4.4) = 75.3
15	3	75.4	75.3	0.1	F_{16}	=	75.3	+	.1(0.1) = 75.3
16	4	72.0	75.3	−3.3	F_{17}	=	75.3	+	.1(−3.3) = 75.0
17	1		75.0						

Step 8: Seasonalize forecasts

t	Qtr.	Des. F_t × Index = F_t
13	1	75.4 × 0.7101 = 53.5
14	2	74.9 × 1.0595 = 79.4
15	3	75.3 × 1.2995 = 97.9
16	4	75.3 × 0.9307 = 70.1
17	1	75.0 × 0.7101 = 53.3
18	2	75.0 × 1.0595 = 79.5
19	3	75.0 × 1.2995 = 103.3
20	4	75.0 × 0.9307 = 69.8

Step 9: Compute MSE (forecasting sample)

t	Qtr.	X_t	F_t	$e_t = X_t - F_t$
13	1	50	53.5	−3.5
14	2	84	79.4	4.6
15	3	98	97.9	0.1
16	4	67	70.1	−3.1

$$\text{MSE (periods 13–16)} = \frac{3.5^2 + 4.6^2 + 0.1^2 + 3.1^2}{4} = 10.8$$

TABLE 3-11
Forecasting seasonal
data: steps 8 and 9

For the third quarter, there are three ratios. The odd number is again due to the centering. The mean ratio is computed for each quarter, and the means are summed. The ratios sum to 3.9669. They should sum to 4.0 but almost never do because of noise in the data.

Step 4 *Compute a normalization factor to adjust the mean ratios so they sum to 4 (quarterly data) or 12 (monthly data).*

Step 4 computes a *normalization factor* to get the ratios to sum to a number closer to the length of seasonality. For quarterly data, the ratio is always 4/(sum of mean ratios). For monthly data, it is 12/(sum of mean ratios).

NORMALIZATION

Step 5 *Multiply the mean ratios by the normalization factor to get the final seasonal indices.*

In step 5, the mean ratios are normalized by multiplying the mean ratios by the factor from step 4. The result is the final set of seasonal indices. The sum is 3.9998, which is close enough to 4.0.

THE FINAL INDICES

Step 6 *Deseasonalize the data by dividing by the seasonal index.*

In steps 1 to 5, seasonal indices were computed using only the warm-up sample. In step 6 (Table 3-10), all the data, both warm-up and forecasting sample, are deseasonalized. The reason is that we want to see how well the indices work when projected into the future (the forecasting sample).

DESEASONALIZING
THE DATA

Step 7 *Forecast the deseasonalized data.*

The deseasonalized data can be forecast with any of the models discussed earlier in the chapter. Simple exponential smoothing is used in this case. The first forecast (deseasonalized $F_1 = 75.1$) is the mean of the deseasonalized data in the warm-up sample. The value $\alpha = .1$ is selected by minimizing the MSE for deseasonalized data in the warm-up sample.

Step 8 *Seasonalize the forecasts from step 7 to get the final forecasts.*

The forecasts are seasonalized by multiplying by the seasonal index (Table 3-11). All 16 forecasts could be seasonalized. However, it is only necessary to seasonalize the forecasting sample (periods 13 to 16) plus any future periods needed. The forecasts for periods 17–20 are seasonalized here. Notice that each forecast for periods 17–20 is the product of the deseasonalized forecast for period 17 (75.0) and the appropriate seasonal index. Why? Because simple smoothing projects a constant deseasonalized level for any period in the future. The only change in the forecast is due to the projected seasonal pattern.

Step 9 *Compute the MSE (using seasonalized errors) for the forecasting sample.*

The MSE for the forecasting sample is 10.8. The naive MSE is quite large, 747.3, illustrating how important it is to take seasonality into account in forecasting. The decomposition coupled with simple smoothing does a good job in this data.

Although decomposition is tedious for humans, it is short work for a computer. There are numerous computer packages which follow the decomposition procedures described in this section. There are others which refine the computations with such things as fancier moving averages, adjustments for differences in the number of trading days per period, and adjustments for abnormal data points. However, the basic objective in the more sophisticated programs is the same as the objective in this section—to remove the seasonal pattern from the data so that any trend can be identified and forecast separately.

The decomposition approach to seasonal forecasting has some limitations. One is common to all quantitative models: at least two complete seasons of data are needed to do a decomposition. If there are fewer than two seasons, there are not enough data to compute centered moving averages. All that can be done is to compute the simple average of whatever data are available. In such cases the seasonal indices are the ratio of each data point to the simple average.

Another limitation of decomposition is that equal weight is given to past data in computing the seasonal indices. If the seasonal pattern changes, the forecasts based on a decomposition can be biased. Although this technique is beyond the scope of this book, exponential smoothing can be used to give more weight to recent data in computing seasonal indices. It is interesting that empirical research has shown that smoothing seasonal indices does not appear to improve forecast accuracy. The reason is that seasonal patterns typically contain a great deal of noise. The best smoothing parameter for the seasonal indices is often near 0. Thus there is very little change in the forecasts because of the smoothing.

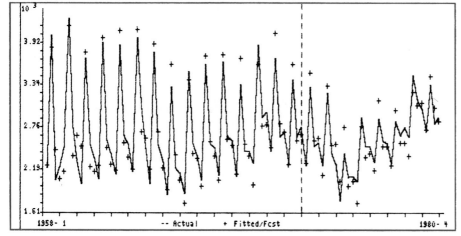

FIGURE 3-9
AUTOCAST forecast
plot.

The final limitation is that decomposition requires storage of the last few seasons of data in order to update the indices. Exponential smoothing requires storage of only the last set of seasonal indices. **A LIMITATION: STORAGE**

Despite these limitations, decomposition is still the simplest way to forecast seasonal data. It also appears to be about as accurate as many more complex approaches. **ADVANTAGES: SIMPLICITY AND ACCURACY**

11 Forecasting with the PC

The forecasting models in this chapter and many others are available in AUTOCAST,[1] an expert forecasting system for the PC based on the principles of exponential smoothing. Using statistical decision rules, AUTOCAST analyzes a time series, selects the best forecasting model, and prepares tables and graphs of the forecasts. You can also override the expert system and select your own forecasting model.

Some AUTOCAST results are illustrated in Figures 3-9 through 3-12, generated using the student version of the program. Figure 3-9 shows quarterly data on the number of sows farrowing (pigs having piglets) in the U.S. Actual data are shown by a connected line while forecasts are shown by plus (+) signs. This is a difficult time series to forecast since the seasonal pattern shrinks drastically and the level of the series shifts several times. The vertical line in the graph separates the warm-up and forecasting samples. Accuracy looks better in the forecasting sample, an impression confirmed by the reports in Figures 3-10 and 3-11.

Figure 3-10 is a summary of model fitting during the warm-up sample, periods 1–60 (shown as Fit: 1–60 at the top of the report). The model has a constant level with smoothed multiplicative seasonality. Smoothing parameters

[1] Everette S. Gardner, Jr., *AUTOCAST: Business Forecasting System*, Houston, Texas, Reason Software, Inc., 1989.

```
        File: SOWS.PRN              Data: Original
        Desc: Sows farrowing: U.S., 1958-1980
        Seas: 4      #Obs: 92      Fit: 1 - 60      Fcst: 61 - 92
        -------------------------------------------------------
        MODEL-FITTING SUMMARY                       Runtime: 00:07

        Model: Constant-level, mul. seas. (min. MSE, 0.001 change)
        Level: 0.580  Seas: 0.420

                                        Your Model        Naive 3
        Mean absolute % error    (MAPE)    5.8751%        5.9757%
        Mean error                        -6.0890         2.8240
        Mean absolute error      (MAD)   153.5445       163.9300
        Root Mean-squared-error  (RMSE)  190.7747       224.0697

        Fit coefficient                    0.2751

        Number of outliers                      3
        Autocorrelation -- lag 1 errors    0.1596
        Regression      -- slope           0.9073%
                        -- intercept     248.6226%
        -------------------------------------------------------
              F9  -  Menu            F10  -  Continue
```

FIGURE 3-10
AUTOCAST model-fitting summary.

for the level and the seasonal component of the model are .580 and .420, respectively. Error comparisons are made to the Naive 3 model (the naive model adjusted for seasonality). The fit coefficient is computed as

FIT COEFFICIENT
DEFINED

$$\text{Fit coefficient} = 1 - \left[\frac{(\text{AUTOCAST MSE})}{\text{Naive 3 MSE}} \right]$$

When the fit coefficient is positive, the AUTOCAST model gives a better fit; when negative, the naive model gives a better fit. The actual fit coefficient is .2751, indicating that the AUTOCAST model is better in the warm-up sample. Comparing fit coefficients is a quick way to evaluate alternative models of a time series.

EVALUATION OF A
FORECASTING MODEL

The report also shows that there were three "outliers" in the warm-up sample. Outliers are unusual data points, out of character with the rest of the time series, and will be adjusted automatically by the program if desired. Autocorrelation is the correlation coefficient between consecutive errors. Ideally, autocorrelation will be zero. If autocorrelation is large, the forecasting model can usually be improved by taking into account the correlation between errors. The actual value is .1596, not statistically significant since there is no asterisk by the number. Finally, the report shows the results of a regression using the values of the time series as the independent variable and the forecasts as the dependent variable. This slope of the regression is another indicator of the quality of the forecasting model. If the slope is 1.0, there is a perfect relationship between forecasts and data.

Now look at Figure 3-11, which gives a similar report for the forecasting sample (periods 61–92). The forecast coefficient is computed like the fit coefficient except that the errors apply to the forecasting sample only. The forecast coefficient is .9185, much higher than in the warm-up sample. Autocorrelation is statistically significant at .4089. The program will automatically adjust the forecasts for autocorrelation if desired.

Figure 3-12 shows another example of AUTOCAST results in forecasting battery sales by the Lenex Corporation. The dotted lines are 95% confidence limits. That is, there is a 95% chance that actual data will fall inside the confidence limits. Confidence limits can be computed for any time series and can be tested by simulation.

FORECAST COEFFICIENT

CONFIDENCE LIMITS

```
File: SOWS.PRN          Data: Original
Desc: Sows farrowing: U.S., 1958-1980
Seas: 4     #Obs: 92    Fit: 1 - 60      Fcst: 61 - 92
-----------------------------------------------------------
SIMULATION SUMMARY (DYNAMIC)

Model: Constant-level, mul. seas. (min. MSE, 0.001 change)
Level: 0.580  Seas: 0.420

                                  Your Model          Naive 3
Mean absolute % error   (MAPE)      5.3274%           14.9521%
Mean Error                         -2.6043           -70.7333
Mean absolute error     (MAD)      135.1294          419.9604
Root Mean-squared-error (RMSE)     160.1342          561.0038

Forecast coefficient                0.9185

Autocorrelation -- lag 1 errors     0.4089%
-----------------------------------------------------------
        F9  -  Menu            F10  -  Continue
```

FIGURE 3-11
AUTOCAST simulation summary.

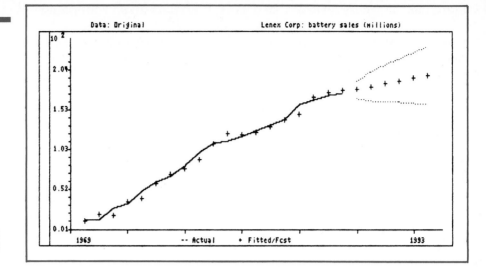

FIGURE 3-12
AUTOCAST forecast
plot with confidence
limits.

12 Glossary

Additive seasonal pattern A type of time series in which the seasonal fluctuations are of constant size, regardless of trend.

Asymptote The limiting value of the forecasts using a damped trend. When sales reach an asymptote, growth disappears.

Benchmark A standard for evaluating accuracy. The naive model is often used as a benchmark.

Bias A tendency for the forecast errors to be systematic rather than random.

Box-Jenkins A sophisticated statistical forecasting method which attempts to fit an optimal model to past history.

Causal method A forecasting method which attempts to find a relationship between the variable to be forecast and one or more other variables.

Classical decomposition A method which attempts to separate a time series into as many as four components: seasonality, trend, cycle, and randomness. In this chapter, only the seasonal component was separated (in the form of seasonal indices).

Conservatism A belief that the future will look like the past regardless of evidence to the contrary. This is one of the major types of bias in judgmental forecasting.

Constant-level model A model which assumes that the time series has a relatively constant mean. The forecast is a horizontal line for any period in the future.

Customer expectations Planned purchases by customers. These are based on surveys, formal or informal.

Damped trend A model used for long-range forecasting in which the amount of trend declines each period.

Decomposition The same as classical decomposition.

Deseasonalize To remove seasonality by dividing each data point by the seasonal index.

Exponential smoothing A weighted moving average technique in which more weight is given to recent data.

Exponential trend model A model in which the amount of growth increases continuously in the future.

Extrapolation A projection of patterns in past data into the future.

Fit To fit a forecasting model is to compute parameters and initial values. See also *Warm-up sample*.

Forecast error The actual data minus the forecast.

Forecasting sample The latter part of the historical data used to measure forecast accuracy. Compare with *Warm-up sample*.

Forecast profile A plot of the forecasts against time. This varies according to the type of trend and the seasonality in the data.

Gambler's fallacy The belief that nature will compensate for past injustices.

Judgmental forecasting Subjective forecasting.

Jury of executive opinion A subjective forecast prepared by one or more executives.

Least-squares method A procedure for fitting a trend line so that the sum of the squares of the errors (the amount that each data point differs from the line) is at a minimum.

Linear exponential smoothing Exponential smoothing adjusted for a linear trend. The model includes two components, smoothed level and trend, and two parameters.

Linear trend A straight-line trend. The amount of change is constant each period.

MAD Mean absolute deviation, or the mean absolute error.

MAPE Mean absolute percentage error.

MSE Mean squared error.

Moving average The unweighted or weighted average of a consecutive number of data points. It can be used as a forecast or simply as a base figure for use in seasonal adjustment of the data.

Multiplicative seasonal pattern A type of time series in which the seasonal fluctuations are proportional in size to the data. As the trend increases, the seasonal fluctuations become larger.

Naive model A forecasting model in which the forecast for the next period is the same as the actual value of the time series this period. The naive model is used as a benchmark.

Noise Randomness in the data. The greater the noise, the more difficult it is to forecast the future data values.

Normalization factor A number used to adjust the seasonal indices so they sum to 4.0 (for quarterly data) or 12.0 (for monthly data).

Regression A process of estimating the statistical relationship between two variables. It is usually done by the least-squares method.

Robust Describes a model which forecasts well on many different types of data.

Sales force composite A sum of the judgmental forecasts made by a company's salespeople.

Seasonal adjustment The same as deseasonalizing.

Seasonal index The average seasonal fluctuation, expressed as a fraction of the average value of the time series for the year.

Seasonalize To put seasonality back into deseasonalized data. This is done by multiplying each deseasonalized data point by its seasonal index.

Simple exponential smoothing A constant-level model in which the new forecast is equal to the last forecast plus a fraction of the error.

Simulation Developing a model of a process and then conducting a series of trial-and-error experiments to predict the behavior of the process over time.

Smoothing parameter A fraction of the error used to adjust the forecasts in exponential smoothing.

Straight-line projection A time-series regression in which the trend is linear.

Time series A set of historical data collected at regular time intervals.

Time-series pattern Same as forecast profile.

Time-series regression A least-squares regression in which the independent variable is some function of time. It is used to predict the average rate of growth in a time series.

Trend-line analysis The comparison of different time-series regression models.

Warm-up sample The first part of historical data used to compute starting values and select model parameters.

13 Review of equations

Page 101

$$F_{t+1} = X_t \tag{3-1}$$

This equation is the naive forecasting model; F_{t+1} is the forecast for the next period, and X_t is the actual value of the time series this period.

Page 101

$$e_t = X_t - F_t \tag{3-2}$$

This equation computes the forecast error e_t for all models in the chapter.

Page 102

$$F_{t+1} = \frac{X_t + X_{t-1} + X_{t-2}}{3} \tag{3-3}$$

This is the three-period moving average model. The forecast, computed at the end of period t, is the average of the last three data points.

Page 104

$$F_{t+1} = F_t + \alpha e_t \tag{3-4}$$

This is the basic equation for simple exponential smoothing. The smoothing parameter is α. The new forecast for period $t + 1$ is equal to the forecast for period t plus a fraction (α) of the error for period t.

Page 107

$$F_{t+1} = \alpha X_t + \alpha(1 - \alpha)X_{t-1} + \alpha(1 - \alpha)^2 X_{t-2}$$
$$+ \alpha(1 - \alpha)^3 X_{t-3} + \alpha(1 - \alpha)^4 X_{t-4} + \cdots + \alpha(1 - \alpha)^k X_{t-k} \qquad (3\text{-}5)$$

This equation is equivalent to Eq. (3-4). It is not used for forecasting. Rather it is used to compute the weights assigned to past data. The weight assigned to a data point k periods in the past is $\alpha(1 - \alpha)^k$.

Page 107

$$F_{t+1} = \alpha X_t + (1 - \alpha)F_t \qquad (3\text{-}6)$$

This equation is an alternative way to do simple exponential smoothing. It is equivalent to Eq. (3-4).

Page 109

$$F_t = a + bt \qquad (3\text{-}7)$$

This is the equation for a fitted straight line. The variable F is the estimated, or forecast, value for period t. The intercept, or point at which the line intercepts the X axis, is a. The slope of the trend line is b. Time is t.

Page 109

$$b = \frac{\sum tX - nt\overline{X}}{\sum t^2 - n\overline{t}^2} \qquad (3\text{-}8)$$

This is the equation for the slope of the best-fitting trend line and is always computed before the intercept. The slope is b, t is time, X is the value of the dependent variable (the time series), $\overline{t}$ is the mean of the values of t, and $\overline{X}$ is the mean of the values of X.

Page 109

$$a = \overline{X} - b\overline{t} \qquad (3\text{-}9)$$

The intercept a of the best fitting trend line is computed with this equation; $\overline{X}$ is the mean of the values of X, b is the slope from Eq. (3-8), and $\overline{t}$ is the mean of the values of t.

Page 112

$$S_t = F_t + \alpha_1 e_t \qquad (3\text{-}10)$$

$$T_t = T_{t-1} + \alpha_2 e_t \qquad (3\text{-}11)$$

$$F_{t+1} = S_t + T_t \qquad (3\text{-}12)$$

These equations perform exponential smoothing of a linear trend; S_t is the smoothed level, and T_t is the smoothed trend. There are two smoothing parameters: α_1 for the level and α_2 for the trend.

Page 114

$$F_{t+m} = S_t + mT_t \tag{3-13}$$

This is the general forecast equation for exponential smoothing of a linear trend, where m is the number of periods into the future we want to forecast.

Page 116

$$S_t = F_t + \alpha_1 e_t \tag{3-14}$$

$$T_t = \phi T_{t-1} + \alpha_2 e_t \tag{3-15}$$

$$F_{t+1} = S_t + \phi T_t \tag{3-16}$$

These equations perform exponential smoothing of a nonlinear trend. S_t is the smoothed level and T_t is the smoothed trend. There are two smoothing parameters: α_1 for the level and α_2 for the trend. There is an additional parameter ϕ for modifying the trend. If $\phi < 1$, the trend is damped. If $\phi > 1$, the trend is exponential.

Page 118

$$F_{t+m} = S_t + \sum_{i=1}^{m} \phi^i T_t \tag{3-17}$$

This is the general forecast equation for exponential smoothing of a nonlinear trend, where m is the number of periods into the future we want to forecast.

14 Exercises*

3-1 Five time series are listed below. Each series has five data points. What is the most accurate simple smoothing parameter for each series? Use $F_1 = 1$ for each series.

    a. 1, 2, 3, 2, 1
    b. 1, 1, 1, 1, 1
    c. 1, 1, 2, 1, 1
    d. 1, 2, 3, 4, 5
    e. 1, 2, 1, 2, 1

3-2 Let's assume you are using simple smoothing with $\alpha = .5$. At the end of period 12, your forecast for period 13 is 50. Actual sales in periods 13 to 18 are constant at 100. Compute the forecasts for periods 14 to 19. If sales always stay at 100, will the forecasts ever be equal to sales? Will the forecasts ever exceed sales?

3-3 The Boyd Manufacturing Company wishes to adopt a simple exponential smoothing model to forecast sales of aluminum ingots. In the past, another type of forecast model called a weighted moving average had been used with some success. Consequently, it was decided as a starting point to select a value for α which closely duplicated the weights of the old method. Calling the most recent period, t, the weighing specifications are:

* See the Preface for an explanation of the computer and pencil symbols.

a. The weight for period t should be about three times the weight for period $t-3$.

b. The weight for period t should be about 8.5 times the weight for period $t-6$.

Select an alpha value which closely duplicates these specifications.

3-4 Two models, A and B, were used to forecast a time series. The results in the forecasting sample (periods 13 to 15) were:

t	Model A error	Model B error
13	10	18
14	8	2
15	6	1

Compare the models using the MAD and MSE criteria. Which is the better model?

3-5 In linear exponential smoothing, what smoothing parameters (α_1 and α_2) result in the same forecasts as:

a. Time series regression?

b. Simple exponential smoothing?

c. The naive model?

3-6 Suppose that a nonlinear-trend model was used to forecast a time series. At the end of period 12, the smoothed level S_t was equal to 100 and the smoothed trend T_t was equal to 10.

a. Compute forecasts for the next four periods using $\phi = 1.2$.

b. Compute forecasts for the next four periods using $\phi = .8$.

3-7 Vicky Ballantyne is the vice president for operations at Cumberland Valley National Bank. She needs a forecast of net deposits each quarter in order to develop the bank's investment plan. Net deposits for the past eight quarters in thousands of dollars were:

Year	Qtr.	Net deposits
1986	1	20.0
	2	16.5
	3	19.9
	4	22.9
1987	1	21.4
	2	24.6
	3	20.7
	4	25.5

Vicky does not believe there is a seasonal pattern in the data.

a. Compute the naive MSE. The warm-up sample is six periods.

b. Apply simple exponential smoothing with $\alpha = .2$. Compute the MSE for the forecasting sample. Does this beat the naive model?

3-8 Forecast the data in Exercise 3-7 with a time-series regression. Use six periods as a warm-up sample. Compute the MSE for the forecasting sample. Does this model improve the forecasts resulting from simple smoothing?

3-9 Forecast the data in Exercise 3-7 with linear exponential smoothing. Use six periods as a warm-up sample and $\alpha_1 = .1$, $\alpha_2 = .05$. Compute the MSE for the forecasting sample. What is the best model for these data?

3-10 Forecast the data in Exercise 3-7 with nonlinear exponential smoothing. Use six periods as a warm-up sample and $\alpha_1 = .1$, $\alpha_2 = .05$, and $\phi = 1.1$. Compute the MSE for the forecasting sample. What is the best model for this data?

3-11 Scott Armstrong, the managing editor of *Your Horoscope* magazine, needs to develop a forecasting system for monthly newsstand sales in order to schedule press runs. Sales in thousands of copies for the first 8 months of 1987 (the first year of publication) were:

Month	Sales
January	50
February	45
March	60
April	52
May	69
June	60
July	47
August	53

Scott does not believe there is a seasonal pattern. Choose a forecasting model and develop forecasts for the remainder of 1987.

3-12 Eric Hoyle is the production manager at Sunbird, Ltd., a company which converts Toyota Corolla sedans into convertibles. Eric needs a sales forecast for the next few years to help decide whether to add new production capacity. Sunbird's sales history (in thousands of conversions) is:

Year	Conversions
1980	9.4
1981	10.7
1982	11.0
1983	15.1
1984	20.6
1985	22.1
1986	25.8
1987	23.0

Choose a forecasting model and develop forecasts for 1988–1990.

3-13 Eddie McKenzie owns the Boiling Springs Trout Farm in Boiling Springs, Pennsylvania. His major customer is the state of Pennsylvania, which buys trout each quarter to restock the Yellow Breeches Creek. The number of trout purchased by the state is seasonal, with the peak quarter in July through September and the trough in January through March. Eddie knows through experience that the seasonal pattern is very stable. He uses the following seasonal indices to analyze trout sales:

Qtr.	Index
1	.50
2	.90
3	1.50
4	1.10

Eddie's sales in thousands of trout for the past 2 years were:

Year	Qtr.	Sales
1986	1	204
	2	379
	3	633
	4	430
1987	1	191
	2	342
	3	650
	4	388

Deseasonalize Eddie's trout sales for 1986 and 1987. Use the seasonal indices given above.

3-14 For the data in Exercise 3-13:
    a. Forecast deseasonalized sales for each quarter of 1988 using simple exponential smoothing with $\alpha = .1$. (Treat all the data as a warm-up sample.)
    b. Seasonalize the forecasts for 1988.

3-15 Cynthia Gardner, sales manager for Georgia Gas Grills, Inc., needs a sales forecast for the next year. She has the following data from the last 2 years (sales are in thousands of grills):

Year	Qtr.	Sales
1986	1	60
	2	91
	3	277
	4	34
1987	1	105
	2	130
	3	522
	4	73

Compute seasonal indices for sales by quarter, using all the data.

3-16 For the data in Exercise 3-15:
    a. Compute the naive MSE. The warm-up sample is six periods.

b. Deseasonalize the data. Use the indices from Exercise 3-15.

c. Apply time-series regression.

d. Seasonalize the forecasts for the last 2 quarters of 1987. Compare the MSE with the naive model.

e. Develop a seasonalized forecast for each quarter of 1988.

 3-17 For the data in Exercise 3-15:

a. Apply exponential smoothing with a linear trend, using $\alpha_1 = .2$ and $\alpha_2 = .1$

b. Seasonalize the forecasts for the last 2 quarters of 1987. Compare the MSE to the naive model.

c. Develop a seasonalized forecast for each quarter of 1988.

d. What is the best model for this data?

3-18 Sergeant Robyn St. John assigns police officers to watches in the Charlotte, North Carolina, police department. Robyn needs a forecast of the number of incoming calls for police assistance. This will help determine the minimum number of officers who should be on duty for each of three watches: midnight to 8 A.M., 8 A.M. to 4 P.M., and 4 P.M. to midnight.

Robyn has kept records of the average number of incoming calls by watch by day of the week. She has decided to develop a separate set of seasonal indices for each day of the week and for holidays. She has determined that calls made on any given day are related only to the same day in the previous week or the same previous holiday.

Here are the numbers of calls for the last four Fridays (a typical month, with no holidays involved). The numbers are in hundreds:

	Watch		
Week	**12 to 8 A.M.**	**8 A.M. to 4 P.M.**	**4 to 12 P.M.**
1	10.1	23.8	62.4
2	8.4	26.7	70.4
3	9.1	21.3	78.5
4	7.6	29.5	65.9

Compute seasonal indices for the number of calls made by watch on Fridays.

3-19 Wanda Wade is an experienced marketing manager who in the past has made the following subjective forecasts of demand for X-33 type engines in hundreds of units:

Year	Qtr.	Forecast	Actual Demand
1986	1	38	34
	2	40	37
	3	43	41
	4	44	45
1987	1	48	46
	2	48	48
	3	50	52
	4	54	53

Compute the mean error, MAD, MAPE, and MSE for her forecasts. Do her forecasts appear to be biased? Use four periods as a warm-up sample.

3-20 Using the data given in Exercise 3-19, determine the MAD, MAPE, and MSE for a naive model. Do Wanda Wade's forecasts seem superior to the naive model? Use four periods as a warmup sample.

3-21 Again using the data from Exercise 3-19, develop a set of forecasts using linear regression. Use the warmup sample of four periods to find the regression coefficients. Does this method produce better forecasts in terms of MAD, MAPE, and MSE?

3-22 Sales of window air conditioners at Cool-n-Nice (in hundreds of units) have been as follows:

Year	Qtr.	Sales
1985	1	6.5
	2	8.2
	3	12.4
	4	5.2
1986	1	7.3
	2	10.4
	3	16.8
	4	7.4
1987	1	8.9
	2	14.6
	3	20.5
	4	9.8

Compute seasonal indices using all the data.

3-23 Using the data and seasonal indices from Exercise 3-22:
   a. Deseasonalize all data.
   b. Develop the least squares regression equation using all data.
   c. Develop seasonalized forecasts for 1988, quarter 1, through 1989, quarter 2.

3-24 Using the data and seasonal indices from Exercise 3-22:
   a. Deseasonalize all data.
   b. Apply exponential smoothing with a linear trend, using $\alpha_1 = .3$ and $\alpha_2 = .2$.
   c. Develop seasonalized forecasts for 1988, quarter 1, through 1989, quarter 2.

15 Chapter concepts quiz

3-1 The _____ forecasting model assumes there will be no change in the time series next period.

3-2 A type of judgmental bias called _____ causes people to consistently underestimate the time series when it is rising and overestimate the time series when it is falling.

3-3 The need to experiment with both the _____ of _____ and _____ in a moving average is a serious disadvantage.

Fill in the Blanks

3-4 The smoothed level in linear exponential smoothing is similar to the _____ in time-series regression.

3-5 In decomposition, if there are N periods of monthly data, there will be _____ moving averages.

3-6 Forecasting methods are classified into three classes called _____, _____, and _____.

3-7 Extrapolation methods are also known as _____.

3-8 The comparison of the rate of growth of the data over time in alternative regression models is called _____.

3-9 The patterns of forecasts plotted against time are often called _____.

3-10 Three measures of forecast accuracy are _____, _____, and _____.

True-False

3-11 In practice, extrapolation methods are commonly used in long forecast horizons. **T F**

3-12 A generally accepted principle in forecasting is that recent data contain more information than older data. **T F**

3-13 The intercept in time-series regression is always computed before the slope. **T F**

3-14 In linear exponential smoothing, α_1 should usually be smaller than α_2. **T F**

3-15 If α in simple smoothing is equal to 1.0, the forecasts are the same as the naive model. **T F**

3-16 If $\phi = 1$, the linear-trend smoothing model is the same as the nonlinear-trend model. **T F**

3-17 The exponential trend is primarily used for long-range forecasting. **T F**

3-18 The damped trend is primarily used for short-range forecasting. **T F**

3-19 Decomposition gives more weight to recent data in computing seasonal indices. **T F**

3-20 Mean seasonal ratios are normalized by dividing by the normalization factor. **T F**

3-21 Extrapolation forecasting methods assume that the historical demand data contain a stable pattern which will continue into the future. **T F**

3-22 Moving averages and exponential smoothing are classified as causal forecasting models. **T F**

3-23 The first step in any forecasting problem should be to use the naive model to compute the benchmark accuracy. **T F**

3-24 The number of periods one should use in a moving average model may be determined by statistical equations. **T F**

3-25 In an exponential smoothing model with $\alpha = .5$, a negative forecast error results in the next period's forecast being lower than the current forecast. **T F**

Multiple Choice

3-26 Which of the following forecasting models assume that the time series has a relatively constant mean?
   a. Unweighted moving average

b. Simple exponential smoothing
c. Linear exponential smoothing with $\alpha_2 = 0$
d. All of the above

3-27 Which of the following models would be most sensitive to large random fluctuations in the data?
   a. Simple exponential smoothing with $\alpha = .1$
   b. Unweighted moving average of 2 periods
   c. Unweighted moving average of 10 periods
   d. Time-series regression

3-28 Judgmental forecasting is most appropriate when:
   a. The time series has a relatively short history.
   b. The data contain a great deal of noise.
   c. The historical data are not representative.
   d. The time series is changing rapidly.

3-29 The MSE in the warm-up sample:
   a. Is usually about the same as in the forecasting sample
   b. Is usually larger than in the forecasting sample
   c. Is usually smaller than in the forecasting sample
   d. May have no relationship to the forecasting sample

3-30 Decomposition has which of the following advantages:
   a. Simplicity
   b. Computational efficiency
   c. Minimal data storage
   d. Responsiveness to changing seasonal patterns

3-31 A time series is a set of data collected at:
   a. Random intervals
   b. Regular intervals
   c. Convenient intervals
   d. All of the above.

3-32 In a time-series regression model, the dependent variable is sales and the independent variable is:
   a. Price
   b. Seasonality
   c. Trend
   d. Some function of time

3-33 The jury of executive opinion is classified as:
   a. Judgmental forecasting
   b. Causal forecasting
   c. Extrapolation forecasting
   d. Computer-based forecasting

3-34 A systematic error in judgment is a:
   a. Conservative error
   b. Compensating error
   c. Bias error
   d. Random error

3-35 A longer-range forecasting model where the extrapolated trend declines each period is the:
   a. Constant-level model
   b. Linear trend model

c. Exponential trend model

d. Damped trend model

3-36 When seasonal fluctuations are proportional to the data, the seasonal pattern is called:

a. Multiplicative

b. Additive

c. Damped

d. Integrated

3-37 The criterion for measuring forecast error which is most commonly used in practice is:

a. Mean absolute deviation

b. Mean standard error

c. Mean absolute percentage error

d. Mean squared error

3-38 In evaluating forecasting models, the data is divided into two parts called:

a. Warm-up and forecasting samples

b. Warm-up and evaluation samples

c. Pre-load and evaluation samples

d. Pre-load and forecasting samples

3-39 In practice it is common to use moving average forecasting models with:

a. Fewer than 6 periods

b. Fewer than 12 periods

c. 6 periods or more

d. 12 periods or more

3-40 In exponential smoothing, the smoothing parameter, α, always lies between:

a. 0 and 100

b. 5 and 500

c. 0 and 1

d. 0 and 1000

16 Real world MS/OR successes

EXAMPLE: FORECASTING INVENTORY DEMANDS IN THE U.S. NAVY

MISSION OF THE SHIPS PARTS CONTROL CENTER

The U.S. Navy Ships Parts Control Center (SPCC) in Mechanicsburg, Pennsylvania, manages parts used to repair shipboard equipment. Parts are purchased from industry and distributed to Navy supply centers and depots for issue to the fleet as demands occur. Procurement and distribution decisions are based on demand forecasts updated on a quarterly basis. In 1987, one of the authors of this text (Gardner[2]) tested alternative forecasting models for SPCC data. Exponential smoothing with a damped trend led to significant improvements in forecast accuracy. The bottom line: a reduction in inventory investment of more than $38 million.

SCOPE OF THE FORECASTING PROBLEM

SPCC manages more than 400,000 different repair parts. Most are stocked so that SPCC can meet wartime demands. Roughly 70,000 parts have

[2] Everette S. Gardner, Jr., "Forecasting for Inventory Control," working paper, College of Business, University of Houston, 1987.

continuing demand under normal operating conditions and must be routinely forecasted. The normal leadtime to procure new parts from industry ranges from four to eight quarters. Thus 70,000 forecasts are updated each quarter and projected four to eight quarters into the future. Prior to Gardner's study, simple exponential smoothing was used. To compute total forecasted demand for eight quarters ahead, the simple smoothing forecast was multiplied by eight.

To test alternative forecasting models, demand history was collected for 5,661 repair parts. The sample included all "Class A" repair parts managed at SPCC, the high value items with the most impact on inventory investment. The demand histories were used as input to a simulation model of SPCC's inventory management system. Nine years of quarterly data were available for each item in the sample. The model simulated forecasting and the resulting procurement and distribution decisions over the nine-year period. Forecasting performance was evaluated by determining the inventory investment needed to meet management's goal for customer service.

Forecast errors have a direct impact on inventory investment and customer service. Additional stock must be carried to compensate for demands that exceed forecasts. If the additional stock is inadequate, emergency procurements must be rushed through. In the meantime, customers suffer delays in receiving parts. Thus, the investment needed to meet a customer service goal for delay time is a good measure of forecasting performance. In general, the more accurate the forecasts, the less investment required.

SPCC's goal for customer service requires that customer requisitions be filled with an average delay of no more than 30 days. This delay time may seem excessive but remember that normal leadtimes to replenish stocks are four to eight quarters. The previous forecasting model, simple exponential smoothing, required $438 million to meet the delay time goal. The damped trend required only $400 million. The reason for the savings is that the demand series contained both trends and sudden shifts in the mean level of demand. Simple smoothing underestimated demand when these problems occurred. The damped trend gave much more responsive forecasts. A linear-trend model was also tested but damping the trend proved to be a better strategy.

Gaining SPCC management's support to implement the damped-trend model was not a problem. The simulation model had been validated many times in the past while evaluating inventory decision rules. Furthermore, the results confirmed management's intuition that trends and sudden shifts in mean demand were degrading forecast accuracy and causing excessive investment levels.

4

Managers of fresh fruit and vegetable markets are faced with the problem of deciding how much produce to stock to meet an uncertain demand. If too much produce is stocked, some of it may go unsold, and because of its perishability, it may have to be thrown away at a loss. On the other hand, if insufficient stock is available to meet the potential demand in the selling period, an opportunity cost of lost profit is incurred. In such cases, the manager is interested in deciding an optimal stocking level—one which results in largest expected profit in the long run. In this chapter, you will gain experience with decision making, using probabilities. These decision-making techniques will allow you to determine optimal courses of action not only for perishable-goods stocking problems, but also for a number of other managerial decision-making applications.

DECISION MAKING USING PROBABILITIES I

Decision Environments, Data Sources, Decision Criteria, Using Experience

CHAPTER OBJECTIVES

- EXAMINE THE DECISION-MAKING PROCESS AS A SERIES OF ORDERLY STEPS.
- REVIEW THE VARIOUS ENVIRONMENTS IN WHICH DECISIONS MUST BE MADE.
- EXAMINE UNCERTAINTY AS A DECISION ENVIRONMENT AND REVIEW METHODS USEFUL FOR MAKING DECISIONS IN THIS ENVIRONMENT.
- EXAMINE RISK AS A DECISION ENVIRONMENT, AND REVIEW METHODS USEFUL FOR MAKING DECISIONS IN THIS ENVIRONMENT.
- INTRODUCE EXPECTED VALUE AS A DECISION CRITERION UNDER CONDITIONS OF RISK.
- REINFORCE UNDERSTANDING OF EXPECTED VALUE WITH EXERCISES INVOLVING MARGINAL ANALYSIS, SALVAGE VALUE, AND CONTINUOUSLY DISTRIBUTED RANDOM VARIABLES.
- ILLUSTRATE METHODS APPROPRIATE FOR SITUATIONS IN WHICH INPUT DATA ARE NOT READILY AVAILABLE TO THE DECISION MAKER.
- SHOW HOW THE EXPERIENCE OF THE DECISION MAKER IS BUILT INTO THE DECISION-MAKING PROCESS.
- INTRODUCE UTILITY AS A DECISION CRITERION, AND DEMONSTRATE THE USE OF THIS APPROACH.

1 Introduction to decision making

Most complex managerial decisions are made with some uncertainty. Managers authorize substantial capital investments with less than complete knowledge about product demand. Government officials make consequential decisions concerning the environment which will affect our lives for years to come, and yet precise knowledge about the future is not available to them. A president of a major power company must decide whether to construct a $5 billion nuclear generating plant in the face of extreme uncertainty about future power demand, government regulation, and environmental impacts. Each of these persons must make decisions under uncertain future conditions; in these and other contexts, the use of some of the probability concepts introduced in Chapter 2 provides decision makers with a rational method for making choices.

Specific tasks and knowledge required by managers before quantitative tools can be used effectively include: specification of organizational goals; knowledge about possible actions, knowledge about possible likelihoods, knowledge about expected payoffs, and specification of the criterion (or criteria) on which choice will be based.

2 Steps in decision making

Decision making generally involves three steps; we shall introduce these by using the example of a record and tape manufacturing company considering several alternative methods of expanding its production to accommodate increasing demand for its products.

STEP 1

The first action a decision maker must take is to list all the viable alternatives that must be considered in the decision. In the case of our record and tape manufacturer, company planners indicate that only three viable options are open to the company:

1 Expand the present plant.
2 Build a new plant.
3 Subcontract out extra production to other record and tape manufacturers.

Company planners agree that they *must* add capacity. If they don't, losses will be so great that doing nothing cannot be considered an alternative.

STEP 2

Having identified all the viable alternatives, the decision maker must now list the future events that may occur. Generally, decision makers can identify most future events that *can* occur; the difficulty is identifying which particular event *will* occur. These future events (not under the control of the decision maker) are called *states of nature* in decision theory. In this listing, we include everything that *can* happen; we also assume that the states of nature are defined in such a way that only one of them can occur. In the case of our record and tape manufacturer, the most significant future events concern demand for the product. These are listed as

1 High demand (resulting from high product acceptance)

2 Moderate demand (resulting from reasonable product acceptance but heavy competitive response)

3 Low demand (resulting from low product acceptance)

4 Failure (no product acceptance)

In defining these states of nature, it would be quite usual for the decision maker to attach a dollar or unit volume value to each of the four possible events to define them more accurately.

STEP 3

The decision maker now constructs a *payoff table*—a table which shows the payoffs (expressed in profits or any other measure of benefit which is appropriate to the situation) which would result from each possible combination of decision alternative and state of nature. Table 4-1 illustrates the 12 possible payoffs in the record and tape company's expansion decision.

CONSTRUCT A
PAYOFF TABLE

3 The different environments in which decisions are made

Decision makers must function in three types of environments. In each of these environments, knowledge about the states of nature differs.

1 *Decision making under conditions of certainty:* In this environment, only one state of nature exists; that is, there is complete certainty about the future. Although this environment sometimes exists, it is usually associated with *very* routine decisions involving fairly inconsequential issues; even here it is usually impossible to guarantee complete certainty about the future.

		Decision maker's alternatives		
		Expand	**Build**	**Subcontract**
States of nature (demand)	High	$500,000	$700,000	$300,000
	Moderate	$250,000	$300,000	$150,000
	Low	−$250,000	−$400,000	−$ 10,000
	Failure	−$450,000	−$800,000	−$100,000

TABLE 4-1
Payoff table for record-tape company expansion decision (payoffs expressed in profits over next 5 years)

2 *Decision making under conditions of uncertainty:* Here more than one state of nature exists, but the decision maker has no knowledge about the various states, not even sufficient knowledge to permit the assignment of probabilities to the states of nature.

3 *Decision making under conditions of risk:* In this situation, more than one state of nature exists, but the decision maker has information which will support the assignment of probability values to each of the possible states.

Under conditions of complete certainty, it is easy to analyze the situation and make good decisions. Since certainty involves only *one* state of nature, the decision maker simply picks the best payoff in that *one* row and chooses the alternative associated with that payoff. In Table 4-1, for example, if John Gwin, the president of the company, knew that demand would be *moderate,* he would choose the alternative "build," since that yields him the highest payoff. Similarly, if he knew that demand would be *low,* he would choose the alternative "subcontract," since even though that generates a loss, it is still his best alternative given that state of nature. Few of us ever enjoy the luxury of having complete information about the future, and thus decision making under conditions of certainty is not of consequential interest to us.

4 The criteria for decision making under uncertainty

In the case of making decisions under conditions of *uncertainty,* John Gwin, the decision maker, knows which states of nature can happen, but he does not have information which would allow him to specify the probability that these states *will* happen. In this situation, there are four criteria John can use to make decisions; we shall examine each of these briefly.

THE MAXIMAX CRITERION

The maximax criterion for decision making under conditions of uncertainty provides John with an *optimistic* criterion. If he wanted to use this criterion, he would select the decision alternative which would maximize his maximum payoff. In our problem illustrated in Table 4-1, John first selects the maximum payoff possible for each decision alternative and then chooses the alternative that provides him with the maximum payoff within this group. Table 4-1 is repeated here as Table 4-2 to illustrate this method. In Table 4-2, John has circled the maximum payoff possible for each of the three decision alternatives. The alternative within this group of three which provides the maximum payoff is "build," with an associated payoff over 5 years of $700,000.

THE MAXIMIN CRITERION

The maximin criterion for decision making under conditions of uncertainty gives a *pessimistic* criterion. To use this method, John tries to maximize his minimum possible payoff; that is, to choose the best of the worst. He begins by first listing the minimum payoff that is possible for each decision alternative; he then selects the alternative within this group of three which results in the

		Decision maker's alternatives		
		Expand	Build	Subcontract
States of nature (demand)	High	$500,000	$700,000	$300,000
	Moderate	$250,000	$300,000	$150,000
	Low	−$250,000	−$400,000	−$ 10,000
	Failure	−$450,000	−$800,000	−$100,000

TABLE 4-2
Payoff table for record-tape company expansion decision (payoffs expressed in profits over next 5 years)

maximum payoff. Table 4-3 repeats Table 4-1. In Table 4-3, John has circled the minimum payoff that is possible for each of the three decision alternatives. The decision alternative within this group of three which provides the maximum payoff is the alternative "subcontract," with an associated payoff of −$100,000 over the next 5 years.

THE MINIMAX REGRET CRITERION

MINIMAX REGRET CRITERION

To introduce this criterion, let us assume that John can step into the future for a minute and look back. Suppose he earlier made a decision to subcontract production of records and tapes (based on the information he had at that time) and it turns out that demand is high. The profit he will make from subcontracting with high demand is $300,000; but had John known demand was going to be high, he would not have subcontracted but would have chosen instead to "build" with a profit of $700,000. The difference between $700,000 (the optimal payoff "had he known") and $300,000 (the payoff he actually realized from subcontracting) is $400,000 and is known as the *regret* resulting from his decision. Let us look at the calculation of one more regret value. Suppose he had chosen alternative "build" and demand turned out to be moderate. In this case there would be *no* regret because, as it turned out, the decision alternative "build" is optimal when demand is moderate, and $300,000 is the maximum payoff possible.

		Decision maker's alternatives		
		Expand	Build	Subcontract
States of nature (demand)	High	$500,000	$700,000	$300,000
	Moderate	$250,000	$300,000	$150,000
	Low	−$250,000	−$400,000	−$ 10,000
	Failure	−$450,000	−$800,000	−$100,000

TABLE 4-3
Payoff table for record-tape company expansion decision (payoffs expressed in profits over next 5 years)

In Table 4-4 we show the regret associated with all 12 combinations of decision alternative and state of nature. These regret values are obtained by subtracting every entry in the payoff table (Table 4-1) from the largest entry in its row. Applying the minimax regret criterion requires John to indicate the maximum regret for each decision alternative; he has done this by circling the maximum regret for the three decision alternatives in Table 4-4. Finally, he chooses the minimum of these three regret values ($350,000, $700,000, and $400,000); in this case, $350,000 is his minimum regret value, and this regret is associated with the decision alternative "expand."

In Chapter 5 we shall have more to say about the application of the minimax criterion in cases where decision making involves an active opponent.

THE CRITERION OF REALISM

THE CRITERION OF
REALISM, A MIDDLE-
GROUND CRITERION

This criterion for decision making under conditions of uncertainty is a middle-ground criterion between maximax and maximin—that is, between optimism and pessimism. This compromise requires the president, John Gwin, to specify a coefficient, or index of optimism, symbolized α (the Greek letter *alpha*), where α is between 0 and 1 in value. When he assigns α a value of 0, John is expressing pessimism about nature; an α of 1 indicates John's optimism about nature. To apply this criterion to his record-tape company expansion decision, John first determines both the maximum and the minimum payoff for each decision alternative. John has done this in Table 4-5. The maximum payoff for each decision alternative is circled in color and the minimum payoff in black. Then for each decision alternative, John computes this value:

$$\text{Measure of realism} = \alpha\,(\text{maximum payoff}) \\ + (1 - \alpha)\,(\text{minimum payoff}) \qquad (4\text{-}1)$$

Suppose in this example that the president of the company feels fairly optimistic and assigns a value of .7 to α. Under these conditions, the measure-of-realism values for the three decision alternatives are

Expand:	.7($500,000) + .3(−$450,000) = $215,000
Build:	.7($700,000) + .3(−$800,000) = $250,000
Subcontract:	.7($300,000) + .3(−$100,000) = $180,000

TABLE 4-4
Regret for each of the
12 combinations of
decision alternative
and state of nature
for record-tape
company

		Decision maker's alternatives		
		Expand	**Build**	**Subcontract**
States of nature (demand)	High	$200,000	0	$400,000
	Moderate	$ 50,000	0	$150,000
	Low	$240,000	$390,000	0
	Failure	$350,000	$700,000	0

		Decision maker's alternatives		
		Expand	Build	Subcontract
States of nature (demand)	High	$500,000	$700,000	$300,000
	Moderate	$250,000	$300,000	$150,000
	Low	−$250,000	−$400,000	−$ 10,000
	Failure	−$450,000	−$800,000	−$100,000

TABLE 4-5

Maximum and minimum payoffs for each decision alternative for record-tape company (color circle = maximum; black circle = minimum)

The application of the realism criterion in this case suggests that John choose the alternative "build." The advantage of using the criterion of realism is that John is able to introduce his own personal feelings of relative optimism or pessimism into the decision process.

5 Decision making under conditions of risk: discrete random variables

When we make decisions under conditions of risk, we need information that will enable us to provide probabilities for the various possible states of nature. This information can be past records or simply the subjective judgment of the decision maker; the source is not important as long as this information enables us to shed some light on which state of nature we feel exists. There are three criteria for decision making under conditions of risk which we shall study; in order, they are *expected value* (often called the *criterion of Bayes*), the *criterion of rationality* (also called the *principle of insufficient reason*), and the *criterion of maximum likelihood.*

THE EXPECTED VALUE CRITERION

This criterion asks the decision maker to calculate the expected value for each decision alternative (the sum of the weighted payoffs for that alternative, where the weights are the probability values assigned by the decision maker to the states of nature that can happen). This rather formidable-sounding notion is really not difficult, and, in fact, we have already used it in Chapter 2. Let us introduce it formally here with the example of Beth Perry, who sells strawberries in a market environment where "tomorrow's sales of strawberries" is a discrete random variable. Later we shall introduce methods that are useful when demand is a continuously distributed random variable.

Beth purchases strawberries for $3 a case and sells them for $8 a case. The rather high markup reflects the perishability of the item and the great risk of stocking it; the product has no value after the first day it is offered for sale. Beth Perry faces the problem of how many to order today for tomorrow's business.

A 90-day observation of past sales gives the information shown in Table 4-6. The probabilities are obtained by normalizing the distribution. Sales were 10 cases on 18 of the 90 days; that is, 18/90 = 2/10 = .20 of the time.

Daily sales	No. days sold	Probability of each number being sold
10	18	.20
11	36	.40
12	27	.30
13	9	.10
	90	1.00

TABLE 4-6
Cases sold during 90 days

This distribution, too, is discrete and random. There are only four possible values for sales volume, and there is no discernible pattern in the sequence in which these four values occur.

TWO KINDS OF COSTS

We assume Beth has no reason to believe that sales volume will behave differently in the future; her problem is to determine how many cases she should buy today for tomorrow's business. If buyers tomorrow call for more cases than the number in stock, Beth's profits suffer by $5 (selling price minus cost) for each sale she cannot make. On the other hand, there are costs which result from the stocking of too many units on any day. Suppose that on a certain day Beth has 13 cases in stock but sells only 10. She makes a profit of $50, $5 per case on 10 cases. But this must be reduced by $9, the cost of the 3 cases not sold and of no value.

Calculating conditional profits One way of illustrating Beth's problem is to construct a table showing the results in dollars of all possible combinations of purchases and sales. The only values for purchases and for sales which have meaning to us are 10, 11, 12, or 13 cases. These were the observed sales magnitudes. There is no reason for her to consider buying fewer than 10 or more than 13 cases.

CONDITIONAL PROFIT TABLE

Table 4-7, called a *conditional profit table,* shows the profit resulting from any possible combination of supply and demand. The profits can be either positive or negative and are conditional in that a certain profit results from taking a specific stocking action (ordering 10, 11, 12, or 13 cases) and having sales of a specific number of cases (10, 11, 12, or 13 cases).

Table 4-7 reflects the losses which occur when stock remains unsold at the end of a day. It does not reflect profit denied Beth because of an out-of-stock condition.

TABLE 4-7
Conditional profit table

Market size, cases	Possible stock action			
	10 cases	11 cases	12 cases	13 cases
10	$50	$47	$44	$41
11	50	55	52	49
12	50	55	60	57
13	50	55	60	65

Notice that the stocking of 10 cases each day will always result in a profit of $50. Even when buyers want 13 cases on some days, Beth can sell only 10.

When Beth stocks 11 cases, her profit will be $55 on days when buyers request 11, 12, or 13 cases. But on days when she has 11 cases in stock and buyers buy only 10 cases, profit drops to $47. The $50 profit on the 10 cases sold must be reduced by $3, the cost of the unsold case.

A stock of 12 cases will increase daily profits to $60, but only on those days when buyers want 12 or 13 cases. When buyers want only 10 cases, profit is reduced to $44; the $50 profit on the sale of 10 cases is reduced by $6, the cost of 2 unsold cases.

The stocking of 13 cases will result in a profit of $65 when there is a market for 13 cases. There will be $5 profit on each case sold, with no unsold cases. When buyers buy fewer than 13 cases, such a stock action results in profits of less than $65. For example, with a stock of 13 cases and sale of only 11 cases, the profit is $49; the profit on 11 cases, $55, is reduced by the cost of 2 unsold cases, $6.

Such a conditional profit table does not tell Beth which number of cases she should stock each day in order to maximize profits. It only shows her what the outcome will be *if* a specific number of cases is stocked and a specific number of cases is sold. Under conditions of risk, she does not know in advance the size of any day's market, but she must still decide which number of cases, stocked consistently, will maximize profits over a long period of time.

Determining expected profits   The next step in determining the best number of cases to stock is to assign probabilities to the possible outcomes or profits. We saw in Table 4-6 that the probabilities of the possible sales are

Cases	Probability
10	.20
11	.40
12	.30
13	.10

Using these probabilities and the information contained in Table 4-7, Beth can now compute the expected profit of each possible stock action.

It was stated earlier that we could compute the expected value of a random variable by *weighting each possible value the variable could take by the probability of its taking on that value.* Using this procedure, Beth can compute the expected daily profit from stocking 10 cases each day, as in Table 4-8.

The figures in column 4 of Table 4-8 are obtained by weighting the conditional profit of each possible sales volume (column 2) by the probability of each conditional profit occurring (column 3). The sum in the last column is the expected daily profit resulting from stocking 10 cases each day. It is not surprising that this expected profit is $50, since we saw in Table 4-7 that

DERIVATION OF ENTRIES FOR THE CONDITIONAL PROFIT TABLE

VALUE OF THE CONDITIONAL PROFIT TABLE

EXPECTED PROFIT

CALCULATING EXPECTED PROFIT FOR THE FOUR DECISION ALTERNATIVES

(1) Market size, cases	(2) Conditional profit		(3) Probability of market size		(4) Expected profit
10	$50	×	.20	=	$10
11	50	×	.40	=	20
12	50	×	.30	=	15
13	50	×	.10	=	5
			1.00		$50

TABLE 4-8

Expected profit from stocking 10 cases

stocking 10 cases each day would always result in a daily profit of $50, regardless of whether buyers wanted 10, 11, 12, or 13 cases.

The same computation for a daily stock of 11 units can be made, as we have done in Table 4-9. This tells us that if Beth stocks 11 cases each day, her expected profit over time will be $53.40 per day. Eighty percent of the time the daily profit will be $55; on these days, buyers ask for 11, 12, or 13 cases. However, column 3 tells us that 20 percent of the time, the market will take only 10 cases, resulting in a profit of only $47. It is this fact that reduces the daily expected profit to $53.40.

For 12 and 13 units, the expected daily profit is computed as shown in Tables 4-10 and 4-11, respectively.

We have now computed the expected profit of each of the four stock actions that are open to Beth. To summarize, these expected profits are as follows:

If 10 cases are stocked each day, expected daily profit is $50.00.
If 11 cases are stocked each day, expected daily profit is $53.40.
If 12 cases are stocked each day, expected daily profit is $53.60.
If 13 cases are stocked each day, expected daily profit is $51.40.

OPTIMAL STOCK ACTION

The optimal stock action is the one that results in the greatest expected profit. It is the action that will result in the largest daily average profits and thus the maximum total profits over a period of time. In this illustration, the proper number to stock each day is 12 cases, since this quantity will give the highest possible average daily profits under the conditions given.

TABLE 4-9

Expected profit from stocking 11 cases

(1) Market size, cases	(2) Conditional profit		(3) Probability of market size		(4) Expected profit
10	$47	×	.20	=	$ 9.40
11	55	×	.40	=	22.00
12	55	×	.30	=	16.50
13	55	×	.10	=	5.50
			1.00		$53.40

(1) Market size, cases	(2) Conditional profit		(3) Probability of market size		(4) Expected profit
10	$44	×	.20	=	$ 8.80
11	52	×	.40	=	20.80
12	60	×	.30	=	18.00
13	60	×	.10	=	6.00
			1.00		$53.60 ← Optimal stock action

TABLE 4-10
Expected profit from
stocking 12 cases

We have not introduced certainty into the problem facing Beth Perry. Rather, we have used her past experience to determine the best stock action open to her. She still does not know how many cases will be requested on any given day. There is no guarantee that she will make a profit of $53.60 tomorrow. However, if she stocks 12 units each day under the conditions given, she will have *average* profits of $53.60 per day. This is the best she can do, because the choice of any one of the other three possible stock actions will result in a lower average daily profit.

INTERPRETATION OF
THIS DECISION
ALTERNATIVE

Expected profit with perfect information Now suppose for a moment that our strawberry retailer, Beth Perry, could remove all uncertainty from her problem by obtaining additional information. Complete and accurate information about the future, referred to as *perfect* information, would remove all uncertainty from the problem. This does not mean that sales would not vary from 10 to 13 cases per day. Sales would still be 10 cases per day 20 percent of the time, 11 cases 40 percent of the time, 12 cases 30 percent of the time, and 13 cases 10 percent of the time. However, with perfect information Beth would know *in advance* how many cases were going to be called for each day.

PERFECT INFORMATION

Under these circumstances, Beth would stock today the exact number of cases buyers will want tomorrow. For sales of 10 cases, she would stock 10 cases and realize a profit of $50. When sales were going to be 11 cases, she would stock exactly 11 cases, thus realizing a profit of $55.

CALCULATING
EXPECTED PROFIT WITH
PERFECT INFORMATION

Table 4-12 shows the conditional profit values that are applicable to Beth's problem if she has perfect information. Given the size of market in advance for a particular day, she chooses the stock action that will maximize her

TABLE 4-11
Expected profit from
stocking 13 cases

(1) Market size, cases	(2) Conditional profit		(3) Probability of market size		(4) Expected profit
10	$41	×	.20	=	$ 8.20
11	49	×	.40	=	19.60
12	57	×	.30	=	17.10
13	65	×	.10	=	6.50
			1.00		$51.40

TABLE 4-12
Conditional profit
table under certainty

Market	Possible stock actions			
size, cases	10 cases	11 cases	12 cases	13 cases
10	$50	—	—	—
11	—	$55	—	—
12	—	—	$60	—
13	—	—	—	$65

profits. This means she buys and stocks so as to avoid *all* losses from obsolete stock as well as *all* opportunity losses which reflect lost profits on unfilled requests for merchandise.

MEANING OF EXPECTED PROFIT WITH PERFECT INFORMATION

She can now compute the expected profit with perfect information. This is shown in Table 4-13. The procedure is the same as that already used. However, you will notice that the conditional profit figures in column 2 of Table 4-13 are the maximum profits possible for each sales volume. For example, when buyers buy 12 cases, Beth will always make a profit of $60 under conditions of certainty because she will have stocked exactly 12 cases. With perfect information, then, she could count on making an average profit of $56.50 a day. This is the *maximum profit* possible.

ALTERNATIVE WAY TO SOLVE THIS PROBLEM

An alternative approach: minimizing expected losses We have just solved Beth Perry's problem by maximizing her expected daily profit. There is another approach to this same problem. We can compute the amounts by which the maximum profit possible ($56.50) will be reduced under various stocking actions; then we can choose that course of action which will *minimize* the expected value of these reductions or *losses*.

TYPES OF LOSSES

Two types of losses are involved: (1) *obsolescence losses* are those caused by stocking too many units; (2) *opportunity losses* are those caused by being out of stock when buyers want to buy.

Table 4-14 is a table of conditional losses for Beth. Each value in the table is conditional on a specific number of cases being stocked and a specific number being requested. The values include *not only* those losses from obsolete inventory when the number of cases stocked exceeds the number buyers desire, *but also* those opportunity losses resulting from lost sales when the market would have been more than the number stocked.

TABLE 4-13
Expected profit with
perfect information

(1) Market size, cases	(2) Conditional profit under certainty		(3) Probability of market size		(4) Expected profit with perfect information
10	$50	×	.20	=	$10.00
11	55	×	.40	=	22.00
12	60	×	.30	=	18.00
13	65	×	.10	=	6.50
			1.00		$56.50

Market size, cases	Possible stock actions			
	10 cases	11 cases	12 cases	13 cases
10	$ 0	$ 3	$6	$9
11	5	0	3	6
12	10	5	0	3
13	15	10	5	0

TABLE 4-14
Conditional loss table

INTERPRETING THE
TABLE OF CONDITIONAL
LOSSES

Neither of these losses is incurred when the number stocked on any day is the same as the number requested. This condition results in the diagonal row of zeros. Dollar figures *above* any zero represent losses arising from obsolete inventory; in each case the number stocked is greater than the number sold. For example, if 13 cases are stocked and only 10 cases are sold, there is a $9 loss resulting from the cost of the 3 cases unsold.

Values *below* the diagonal row of zeros represent opportunity losses resulting from requests that cannot be filled. For example, if only 10 cases are stocked but 13 cases are wanted, there is an opportunity loss of $15. This is represented by the lost profit of $5 per case on the 3 cases requested but not available.

The next step is to assign probabilities to the quantities buyers will be wanting. Table 4-6 gave these probabilities as

Cases	Probability
10	.20
11	.40
12	.30
13	.10

COMPUTING EXPECTED
LOSS

Applying these probabilities to the information in Table 4-14, we can compute the expected "loss" (reduction from maximum profit possible of $56.50) of each possible stock action. We do this by weighting each of the four possible loss figures in each column of Table 4-14 by the probabilities from Table 4-6. For a stock action of 10 cases, the expected loss is computed as in Table 4-15.

TABLE 4-15
Expected loss from
stocking 10 cases

Market size, cases	Conditional loss		Probability of market size		Expected loss
10	$ 0	×	.20	=	$ .00
11	5	×	.40	=	2.00
12	10	×	.30	=	3.00
13	15	×	.10	=	1.50
			1.00		$6.50

Market size, cases	Conditional loss		Probability of market size		Expected loss
10	$ 3	×	.20	=	$ .60
11	0	×	.40	=	.00
12	5	×	.30	=	1.50
13	10	×	.10	=	1.00
			1.00		$3.10

TABLE 4-16
Expected loss from
stocking 11 cases

The conditional losses in Table 4-15 are taken from Table 4-14 for a stock action of 10 cases. The sum in the last column tells us that if 10 cases are stocked each day, over a long period of time the average, or expected, loss will be $6.50 a day. There is no guarantee that *tomorrow*'s loss will be exactly $6.50.

EXPECTED LOSS FOR
THE FOUR DECISION
ALTERNATIVES

Tables 4-16 to 4-18 show the computation of the expected loss resulting from decisions to stock 11, 12, and 13 cases, respectively. The optimal stock action is *the one which will minimize expected losses;* this action calls for the stocking of 12 cases each day, at which point the expected loss is minimized at $2.90.

Beth can approach the optimal stocking action from either point of view, maximizing expected profits *or* minimizing expected losses; both approaches lead to the same conclusion. In Table 4-19, we show that expected profits are *maximized* and expected losses are *minimized* when Beth stocks 12 units daily.

EXPECTED VALUE OF
PERFECT INFORMATION

Expected value of perfect information   Assuming that Beth Perry could obtain a perfect predictor of future demand, what would be the value of such a predictor to her? She would have to compare what such additional information would cost her with the additional profit she would realize as a result of having the information.

Beth can earn average daily profits of $56.50 if she has perfect information about the future (see Table 4-13). Her best expected daily profit without the predictor is only $53.60 (see Tables 4-8 to 4-11). The difference of $2.90 is the maximum amount she would be willing to pay, per day, for a perfect

TABLE 4-17
Expected loss from
stocking 12 cases

Market size, cases	Conditional loss		Probability of market size		Expected loss
10	$6	×	.20	=	$1.20
11	3	×	.40	=	1.20
12	0	×	.30	=	.00
13	5	×	.10	=	.50
			1.00		$2.90 ← Optimal stock action

Market size, cases	Conditional loss		Probability of market size		Expected loss
10	$9	×	.20	=	$1.80
11	6	×	.40	=	2.40
12	3	×	.30	=	.90
13	0	×	.10	=	.00
			1.00		$5.10

TABLE 4-18
Expected loss from
stocking 13 cases

predictor because that is the maximum amount by which she can increase her expected daily profit. This difference is *the expected value of perfect information* (EVPI). There is no sense in paying more than $2.90 for the predictor; to do so would lower the expected daily profit.

Determining what additional information is worth in the decision-making process is a serious problem for managers. In our example, we found that Beth would pay $2.90 a day for a *perfect* predictor. Generalizing from this example, we can say that the expected value of perfect information is equal to the minimum expected loss.

EXPECTED VALUE OF PERFECT INFORMATION EQUALS MINIMUM EXPECTED LOSS

It is not often, however, that one is fortunate enough to be able to secure a *perfect* predictor; thus in most decision-making situations, managers are really attempting to evaluate the worth of information which will enable them to make *better* rather than *perfect* decisions.

Items which have a salvage value   In the previous illustration, we assumed that the product being sold was completely worthless if not sold on the day after delivery, the "selling" day. This assumption that it had no salvage value is, of course, not always realistic. If the product *does* have some salvage value, then this amount must be considered in computing conditional profits for each stock action. Consider the case of fresh blueberries which the retailer orders and receives on the day before the selling day. They cost $5 per case and sell for $8 per case; any remaining unsold at the end of the day can be disposed of at a salvage price of $2 per case. Observation shows that past sales have ranged from 15 to 18 cases per day; there is no reason to believe that sales volume will take on any other value in the future.

EXAMPLE OF DECISION MAKING WITH SALVAGE VALUE

TABLE 4-19
Expected profit and
expected loss

	Stock action			
	10 cases	11 cases	12 cases	13 cases
Expected profit	$50.00	$53.40	$53.60	$51.40
Expected loss	6.50	3.10	2.90	5.10
			↑ Optimal	

Using the same procedures as in Table 4-6, we establish these probabilities for the values sales will take:

Market size	Probability of market size
15	.10
16	.20
17	.40
18	.30
	1.00

The conditional profit table resulting from the above data is Table 4-20. A stock of 15 cases each day will result in daily profits of $45 regardless of whether demand is for 15, 16, 17, or 18 cases. The 15 cases stocked will always be sold, but no more than this can be sold on any day.

A stock of 17 cases each day will result in a profit of $51 on those days when demand is either 17 or 18 cases. So far, the computation of conditional profits is the same as in all our previous examples. However, *any time the number stocked exceeds the demand on the selling day, the computation of conditional profit must take salvage value into consideration.* This happens, for example, when 17 cases are stocked but only 15 cases are sold. Conditional profit in this event is computed as follows:

Profit on the 15 cases sold	$45
Less cost of the 2 cases unsold	− 10
	$35
Plus salvage value of 2 cases	+ 4
Conditional profit	$39

Salvage value can also be considered as a reduction in the cost of unsold cases. In our example, the net cost of each *unsold* case is $3, the original cost of $5 less the salvage value of $2. Thus when 18 cases are stocked but only 16 are sold, the conditional profit is $42; this is $3 per case on the 16 sold less $6, the net cost of the 2 not sold.

TABLE 4-20
Conditional profit
table

Market size, cases	Possible stock actions, cases			
	15	16	17	18
15	$45	$42	$39	$36
16	45	48	45	42
17	45	48	51	48
18	45	48	51	54

The presence of salvage value in an inventory problem does not alter the application of any of the principles discussed earlier in this chapter. It simply means that we must consider its effect on conditional profits and losses. We have just seen that salvage value increases conditional profits because it reduces the losses caused by overstocking.

We proceed just as before in determining the optimal stock action to be taken. The next step is to determine the expected profit of each of the four possible stock actions. This involves weighting the conditional profit figures for each stock action by the probabilities that each will occur and then summing the results for each stock action.

Table 4-21 presents the resulting expected profit figures; the stocking of 17 cases each day is the optimal stock action. Over time, we can realize greater average and total profits by stocking 17 cases each day, even though on some days demand will be for 15, 16, or 18.

In many instances, the salvage value of an unsold item can take on more than one value, depending upon the age of the unsold item; it is not uncommon, for example, for fresh bread to command one price in the supermarket, for "day-old" bread to be sold for a somewhat lower price, and for bread older than 4 days to be nearly worthless. In some instances like this and in more complicated salvage value situations, tabular solutions to the problem become quite complex and cumbersome. In such situations, MS/OR analysts prefer to use more efficient methods rather than the tabular approach. Let's examine one of these now.

Use of marginal analysis In many problems, the use of conditional profit tables and expected profit tables would be difficult because of the number of computations required. Table 4-21 showed 4 possible stock actions and 4 possible sales levels, resulting in a conditional profit table containing 16 possibilities for conditional profits. Suppose there had been 200 possible values for sales volume and an equal number of possible stock actions. There would have been a tremendous number of calculations in determining the conditional and expected profit from each possible combination. The marginal approach avoids this problem of excessive computational work. When an additional unit of an item is bought, two outcomes are possible: the unit will be sold or it will not be sold. The sum of the probabilities of these two events must be 1. For example, if the probability of selling the additional unit is .4, then the probability of not selling it must be .6. The sum? 1.

If we let p represent the probability of selling an additional unit, then $1 - p$ must be the probability of *not* selling it. If the additional unit is sold, we shall realize an increase in our conditional profits as a result of the profit from the additional unit. We shall refer to this as *marginal profit* and designate it MP. In our salvage value illustration, the marginal profit resulting from the sale of an additional unit is $3, selling price less cost.

Reference to Table 4-21 will illustrate this point. If we stock 15 units each day and daily demand is for 15 or more units, our conditional profit is $45 per day. Now we decide to stock 16 units each day. If the sixteenth unit is sold (and this is the case when demand is for 16, 17, or 18 units), our conditional profit is increased to $48 per day. Notice that the increase in

TABLE 4-21
Expected profit table

Market size, cases	Probability of market size	Possible stock actions							
		15 cases		16 cases		17 cases		18 cases	
		Conditional profit	Expected profit	Conditional profit	Expected profit	Conditional profit	Expected profit	Conditional profit	Expected profit
15	.10	$45	$ 4.50	$42	$ 4.20	$39	$ 3.90	$36	$ 3.60
16	.20	45	9.00	48	9.60	45	9.00	42	8.40
17	.40	45	18.00	48	19.20	51	20.40	48	19.20
18	.30	45	13.50	48	14.40	51	15.30	54	16.20
	1.00		$45.00		$47.40		$48.60		$47.40

↑
Optimal action

162

conditional profit does not follow merely from the *stocking* of the sixteenth unit. Under the conditions assumed in the problem, this increase in profit will result *only* when demand is for 16 or more units; this will be the case 90 percent of the time.

We must also consider the effect on profits of stocking an additional unit and *not* selling it. This reduces our conditional profit. The amount of the reduction is referred to as the *marginal loss* (ML) resulting from the stocking of an item which is not sold.

MARGINAL LOSS

Reference again to Table 4-21 will illustrate marginal loss. Assume once more that we decide to stock 16 units. Now assume that the sixteenth unit (the marginal unit) is not sold; only 15 units are sold. The conditional profit is now $42; the $45 conditional profit when 15 units were stocked and 15 were sold is now reduced by $3. This $3 is the cost of the unsold unit ($5) less the salvage value ($2).

Additional units should be stocked so long as the *expected marginal profit* from stocking each of them is greater than the *expected marginal loss* from stocking each. The size of each day's order should be increased up to that point where the expected marginal profit from stocking 1 more unit *if it sells* is just equal to the expected marginal loss from stocking that unit *if it remains unsold.*

RULE FOR STOCKING
ADDITIONAL UNITS

In our illustration, the probability distribution of demand is

Market size	Probability of market size
15	.10
16	.20
17	.40
18	.30
	1.00

This distribution tells us that as we increase our stock, the probability of selling 1 additional unit (this is p) decreases. For example, as we increase our stock from 15 to 16 units, the probability of selling all 16 is .90. This is the probability that demand will be for 16 units or more. Here is the computation:

Probability that demand will be for 16	.20
Probability that demand will be for 17	.40
Probability that demand will be for 18	.30
Probability that demand will be for 16 or more units	.90

PROBABILITY OF
SELLING AN
ADDITIONAL UNIT

With the addition of a seventeenth unit, the probability of selling all 17 units is reduced to .70 (the sum of the probabilities of demand for 17 or 18 units). Finally, the addition of an eighteenth unit carries with it only a .30 probability of our selling all 18 units, because demand will be for 18 units only 30 percent of the time.

The expected marginal profit from stocking and selling an additional unit is the marginal profit of the unit multiplied by the probability that the unit

EXPECTED MARGINAL
PROFIT FROM SELLING
AN ADDITIONAL UNIT

will be sold; that is p(MP). The expected marginal loss from stocking and not selling an additional unit is the marginal loss incurred if the unit is unsold multiplied by the probability that the unit will not be sold; this is $(1 - p)$(ML). From this example we can generalize that the manager in this situation would stock up to the point where

$$p(\text{MP}) = (1 - p)(\text{ML})$$

POINT AT WHICH
EXPECTED PROFIT
FROM AN ADDITIONAL
UNIT EQUALS EXPECTED
LOSS

This equation describes the point at which the expected profit from stocking an additional unit, p(MP), is equal to the expected loss from stocking the unit, $(1 - p)$(ML). So long as p(MP) is larger than $(1 - p)$(ML), additional units should be stocked because the expected profit from such a decision is greater than the expected loss.

In any given problem, there will be only *one* value of p for which the maximizing equation will be true. We must determine that value in order to know the optimal stock action to take. We can do this by taking our maximizing equation and solving it for p in the following manner:

$$p(\text{MP}) = (1 - p)(\text{ML})$$

Multiplying the two terms on the right side of the equation, we get

$$p(\text{MP}) = \text{ML} - p(\text{ML})$$

Collecting terms containing p, we have

$$p(\text{MP}) + p(\text{ML}) = \text{ML}$$

or

$$p(\text{MP} + \text{ML}) = \text{ML}$$

Dividing both sides of the equation by MP + ML gives

Probability for which the
maximizing equation is true
$$p = \frac{\text{ML}}{\text{MP} + \text{ML}} \qquad (4\text{-}2)$$

In Eq. (4-2), p represents *the minimum required probability of selling at least an additional unit to justify the stocking of that additional unit.* Additional units should be stocked so long as the probability of selling at least an additional unit is greater than p.

We can now compute p for our illustration. The marginal profit per unit is \$3 (selling price less cost); the marginal loss per unit is also \$3 (cost of each unit less salvage value); thus

CALCULATION OF
MINIMUM PROBABILITY

$$p = \frac{\text{ML}}{\text{MP} + \text{ML}} \qquad (4\text{-}2)$$

$$= \frac{\$3}{\$3 + \$3} = \frac{\$3}{\$6} = .5$$

This value of .5 for p means that in order to justify the stocking of an additional unit, we must have at least a .5 *cumulative* probability of selling that unit. In order to determine the probability of selling each additional unit we consider stocking, we must compute a series of cumulative probabilities as in Table 4-22.

The cumulative probabilities in the right-hand column of Table 4-22 represent the probabilities that sales will reach or exceed each of the four sales levels. For example, the 1.00 which appears beside the 15-unit sales level means that we are 100 percent certain of selling 15 or more units. This must be true because our problem assumes that one of four sales levels will *always* occur.

The .90 probability value beside the 16-unit sales figure means that we are only 90 percent sure of selling 16 or more units. This can be calculated in two ways. First, we could add the chances of selling 16, 17, and 18 units:

16 units   .20
17 units   .40
18 units   + .30
       .90 = probability of selling 16 or more

Or we could reason that sales of 16 or more units include all possible outcomes except sales of 15 units, which has a probability of .10:

All possible outcomes   1.00
Probability of selling 15   − .10
              .90 = probability of selling 16 or more

The cumulative probability value of .70 assigned to sales of 17 units or more can be established in similar fashion. Sales of 17 or more must mean sales of 17 or of 18 units, so

Probability of selling 17   .40
Probability of selling 18   + .30
           .70 = probability of selling 17 or more

And, of course, the cumulative probability of selling 18 units is still .30 because we have assumed that sales will never exceed 18.

As mentioned previously, the value of p, the cumulative probability, decreases as the level of sales increases. This decrease causes the expected

TABLE 4-22
Cumulative probabilities of sales

Sales, units	Probability of this sales level	Cumulative probability that sales will be at this level or greater
15	.10	1.00
16	.20	.90
17	.40	.70
18	.30	.30

marginal profit to decrease and the expected marginal loss to increase until, at some point, our stocking of an additional unit would not be profitable.

We have said that additional units should be stocked so long as the probability of selling at least an additional unit is greater than p. We can now apply this rule to our probability distribution of sales and determine how many units should be stocked.

EXPECTED PROFIT AND LOSS FOR SIXTEENTH UNIT

This procedure tells us that we should stock a sixteenth unit because the probability of selling 16 or more is .90, a figure clearly greater than our p of .50. This also means that the expected marginal profit from stocking this unit is greater than the expected marginal loss from stocking it. This can be verified as follows:

$$p(\text{MP}) = .90(\$3) = \$2.70 \text{ expected marginal profit}$$

$$(1 - p)(\text{ML}) = .10(\$3) = \$0.30 \text{ expected marginal loss}$$

EXPECTED PROFIT AND LOSS FOR SEVENTEENTH UNIT

A seventeenth unit should be stocked because the probability of selling 17 or more units (.70) is greater than the required p of .50. Such action will result in the following expected marginal profit and expected marginal loss:

$$p(\text{MP}) = .70 \, (\$3) = \$2.10 \text{ expected marginal profit}$$

$$(1 - p)(\text{ML}) = .30(\$3) = \$0.90 \text{ expected marginal loss}$$

OPTIMAL STOCK

Seventeen is the *optimal* number of units to stock because the addition of an eighteenth unit carries with it only a .30 probability that it will be sold; this is less than our required p of .50. The following figures show why the eighteenth unit should not be stocked:

EXPECTED PROFIT AND LOSS FOR EIGHTEENTH UNIT

$$p(\text{MP}) = .30(\$3) = \$0.90 \text{ expected marginal profit}$$

$$(1 - p)(\text{ML}) = .70(\$3) = \$2.10 \text{ expected marginal loss}$$

This tells us that if we stock an eighteenth unit, we will add more to expected loss than we add to expected profit.

Notice that the use of marginal analysis leads us to the same conclusion reached with the use of conditional profit and expected profit tables. Both methods of analysis result in a decision to stock 17 units each period.

In the problem we have just solved, we assumed that "daily sales" was a random variable; accordingly, we proposed a strategy to follow every day without alteration: stock 17 cases. In actual practice, however, we would no doubt find that "daily sales" would take on recognizable patterns depending upon the particular day of the week; this seems to invalidate the concept of a random variable. In retail sales, for example, Saturday is generally recognized as being a higher-volume day than, say, Tuesday. Similarly, Sunday retail sales are typically less than those on Friday. In situations where there are recognizable patterns in daily sales, we can still apply the techniques we have learned. We would compute an optimal stocking rule for each day of the week. For Saturday, for example, we would use as our input data past

DEALING WITH RECOGNIZABLE PATTERNS IN DEMAND

sales experience *for Saturdays only.* Each of the other 6 days could be treated in the same fashion. Essentially this approach represents nothing more than recognition of, and reaction to, discernible patterns in what may first appear to be a completely random environment.

THE CRITERION OF RATIONALITY

In decision-making situations where we have little or no data on past demand, we can apply the *criterion of rationality* (also known as the principle of insufficient reason). This assumption was first introduced by Jacob Bernoulli (1654–1705). This criterion says that in the absence of any strong information to the contrary, you might as well assume that *all states of nature are equally likely.*

CRITERION OF
RATIONALITY

Applying the criterion of rationality to Beth's strawberry problem, we see that since there are four possible states of nature (demand for 10, 11, 12, and 13 cases), she should assign a probability of .25 to each of these states. In Table 4-23, we have repeated the conditional profit table first shown in Table 4-7, added equal probability weights to the four states of nature, and computed the expected value of the four stocking alternatives. Using this criterion, we find that the optimal stocking decision is 12 cases, with an expected profit of $54.

APPLYING CRITERION
OF RATIONALITY TO
PREVIOUS PROBLEM

THE MAXIMUM LIKELIHOOD CRITERION

If Beth wants to use the maximum likelihood criterion, she just selects the state of nature that has the highest probability of occurrence; then, having assumed that this state will occur, she picks the decision alternative which will yield the highest payoff. To demonstrate this criterion, we have repeated in Table 4-24 the information from Table 4-7, adding the probabilities Beth first assigned to the four states of nature. She can see that "demand for 11 cases" with an assigned probability of .40 is the state of nature with the highest probability of occurrence and that the stock action "11 cases" has the highest payoff for the state of nature, $55. In Table 4-24, we have boxed the state of nature "demand for 11 cases" in black and circled the highest-payoff stock action, "11 cases," in color. This decision criterion is rather widely used and will produce valid results when one state of nature is much more probable

MAXIMUM LIKELIHOOD
CRITERION

APPLYING MAXIMUM
LIKELIHOOD CRITERION
TO PREVIOUS PROBLEM

TABLE 4-23
Expected value calculations using the criterion of rationality

Possible demand, cases	Possible stock actions			
	10 cases	**11 cases**	**12 cases**	**13 cases**
10	$50 × .25 = $12.50	$47 × .25 = $11.75	$44 × .25 = $11.00	$41 × .25 = $10.25
11	50 × .25 = 12.50	55 × .25 = 13.75	52 × .25 = 13.00	49 × .25 = 12.25
12	50 × .25 = 12.50	55 × .25 = 13.75	60 × .25 = 15.00	57 × .25 = 14.25
13	50 × .25 = 12.50	55 × .25 = 13.75	60 × .25 = 15.00	65 × .25 = 16.25
	$50.00	$53.00	$54.00	$53.00

Optimal stock action

Possible demand, cases	Probability of this demand	Possible stock action			
		10 cases	11 cases	12 cases	13 cases
10	.20	$50	$47	$44	$41
11	.40	50	(55)	52	49
12	.30	50	55	60	57
13	.10	50	55	60	65

SHORTCOMINGS OF THE
MAXIMUM LIKELIHOOD
CRITERION

than any other, and when the conditional values are not extremely different; however, it is possible to make some serious errors if we use this criterion in a situation where a large number of states of nature exist and each of them has a small, nearly equal probability of occurrence.

6 Using the expected value criterion with continuously distributed random variables

MOVING FROM
DISCRETE TO
CONTINUOUS
EXPECTED VALUE

All the problems we have worked to this point in this chapter have involved *discrete* random variables. Many real situations, however, are concerned with continuously distributed random variables. It is not difficult to apply what we have learned up to this point to situations where the random variable is continuously distributed. Consider Steve Skeebo, a college senior who sells cherry tomatoes every spring. Steve buys them for $9 per crate and resells them for $16 per crate. If a crate is not sold on the first selling day, it is worth $3 as salvage. Steve's examination of past sales records indicates that demand for this particular item is normally distributed, with a mean of 120 crates and a standard deviation of 38 crates. What should Steve's stock be? Steve can use Eq. (4-2) to calculate the minimum required probability of selling at least an additional unit to justify his stocking of that unit with the data he has available to him:

$$p = \frac{ML}{MP + ML} \tag{4-2}$$

$$= \frac{\$6}{\$7 + \$6}$$

$$= \frac{\$6}{\$13}$$

$$= .462$$

MINIMUM REQUIRED
PROBABILITY
ILLUSTRATED ON A
NORMAL DISTRIBUTION

Remember what this probability means. Steve must be .462 sure of selling at least an additional unit before it will pay him to stock that unit. In Figure 4-1, we have illustrated the .462 probability on a normal distribution of past demand. The .462 required probability is the shaded area. Steve should stock

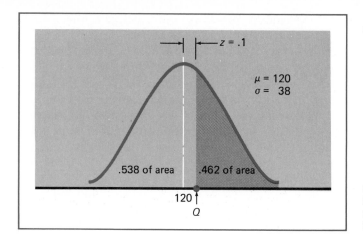

FIGURE 4-1
Continuously
distributed random
variable "past sales."

additional units until he reaches point Q; if he stocks a larger quantity, the probability falls below .462.

Since the shaded area under the normal curve in Figure 4-1 is .462 of the total area under the curve, the open area must be $1.000 - .462$, or .538 of the area under the curve. If we look in Appendix Table 1 (The Standard Normal Probability Distribution) for .538, we see that the appropriate z value is .1. This means that point Q is .1 standard deviation to the right of the mean. Since we know that the standard deviation of the distribution of past demand for this item is 38 crates, point Q is found as follows:

DETERMINING THE
OPTIMAL STOCK USING
THE STANDARD NORMAL
PROBABILITY TABLE

Point Q = mean + .1 standard deviation
        = mean + .1 (38 crates)
        = 120 crates + 3.8 crates
        = 124 crates

The optimal stock for Steve to order is 124 crates.

7   Supplying the numbers

The examples we have solved so far using the normal probability distribution all required one to know both the *mean* and the *standard deviation*. In each of the illustrative examples used, these two values (μ and σ) could be computed from available data. But what about situations where past data are missing or at best incomplete? How does one make use of a probability distribution in these cases? An illustrative example will help to point out how one can often generate the values that are required using an *intuitive* approach.

WHAT ARE THE
ALTERNATIVES WHEN
μ AND σ CANNOT
BE SPECIFIED?

Suppose, for example, that you were contemplating the purchase of a machine which replaces manual labor on an operation. The machine will cost $5,000 per year to operate and will save $4 for each hour it operates. For it to break even, it must operate at least $5,000/$4 = 1,250 hours annually. Now if we are interested in the probability that it will actually run more than 1,250 hours, we must know something about the distribution of running

AN ESTIMATE
OF THE MEAN

times, specifically the *mean* and *standard deviation* of this distribution. But where would we find these figures with no past history of machine operation?

Suppose we went to the supervisor of this operation and asked him to guess the mean running time of the machine. With his close knowledge of the process involved, he would probably be able to give us a "guessed-at" mean: let us say his best estimate here is 1,400 hours. But how would he react if you then asked him to give you the *standard deviation* of the distribution? This term is probably not meaningful to him, and yet, intuitively, he probably has some notion of the dispersion of the distribution of running times. Since most people understand betting odds, let us appeal to him on that basis.

Let us count off an equal distance on each side of his mean, say 200 hours; this gives us an interval from 1,200 to 1,600 hours. Then let us ask him, "What are the odds that the number of hours will lie between 1,200 and 1,600?" If he has had any experience with betting, he should be able to reply. Suppose he says, "I think the odds it will run between 1,200 and 1,600 hours are 5 to 3." We show his answer on a probability distribution in Figure 4-2.

Figure 4-2 indicates exactly what the supervisor replied, that the odds are 5 to 3 the machine will run between 1,200 and 1,600 hours rather than outside those limits. Now what to do? On the distribution in Figure 4-2, we have called the 1,600-hour point Q. We see that the area under the curve to the left of point Q, according to the supervisor's estimates, is $^{13}/_{16}$ of the area under the entire curve, $(3 + 5 + 5)/(3 + 5 + 5 + 3)$. Now see Figure 4-3. Since $^{13}/_{16}$ is approximately .813, let us look in Appendix Table 1 for the value .813. There we find that point Q is .89 standard deviation to the right of the mean.

As the distance from the mean to Q is known to be 200 hours, we see that

$$.89 \text{ standard deviation} = 200 \text{ hr}$$

and thus

$$1 \text{ standard deviation} = 225 \text{ hr}$$

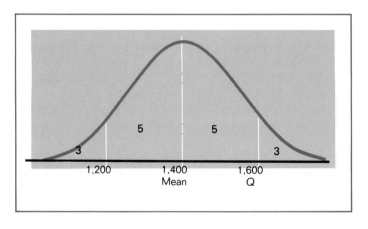

FIGURE 4-2
Supervisor's estimated distribution of running times.

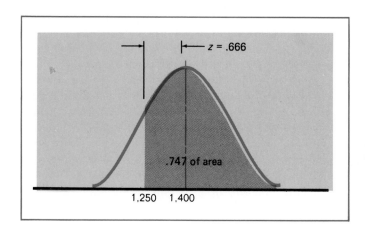

FIGURE 4-3
Supervisor's
estimated distribution
of running times.

Now that we can specify the mean and the standard deviation of the
distribution of running times, we can calculate the probability of the machine's
running less than its breakeven point of 1,250 hours. This situation is shown
in Figure 4-4. From Appendix Table 1 we find that the area between one
tail of the distribution and a point .666 standard deviation past the mean
(1,250 hours) is about .747 of the total area under the curve. Because this is
the probability that the machine will operate *more* than 1,250 hours, the
chance that it will operate fewer than 1,250 hours (its breakeven point) is
$1 - .747$, or .253; it would seem that this is not too risky a situation.

*USING THE ESTIMATED
STANDARD DEVIATION
TO SPECIFY RISK*

In this section, we have illustrated with a hypothetical example how one
can make use of other people's knowledge about a situation without requiring
them to understand the intricacies of various mathematical techniques. Had
we expected the supervisor to comprehend the theory behind our calculations
or even attempted to explain the theory to him, we might never have been
able to benefit from his practical wisdom concerning the situation. In this
case (and for that matter, in most others too) it is wiser to accommodate the

*ASKING FOR
INFORMATION IN
TERMS THAT ARE
RELEVANT*

FIGURE 4-4
Illustration of
probability that
machine will operate
above breakeven
hours.

ideas and knowledge of other people in one's models than to search until you find a situation which will fit a model that has already been developed.

Finally, before we leave this example, we must remember that we *assumed* the distribution of machine operating hours to be a normal distribution. If we had *strong* information to the contrary, we certainly would be wise to heed that information and not to make the assumption we did. However, in the absence of information to the contrary, it would be reasonable to make the assumption we did. In this case as well, the opinion of the supervisor would be quite useful, and his experience would likely allow him to make some intuitive observation about the shape of the distribution.

8 Combining experience and numbers

In the previous example, we saw how the extensive experience of our supervisor was "captured" as a probability distribution and used successfully because we were able to communicate with him in language and terms of reference which he understood. We were able to get workable estimates from him of the *mean* and *standard deviation* of the distribution of operating times for the machine we contemplated purchasing.

There are many situations in which it becomes necessary to combine the extensive experience and intuition of operating personnel with equally valuable statistical evidence. Specifically, this situation might well arise again in the context of the decision whether to purchase a new machine to be used exclusively for the production of a new product. Clearly what is needed here is a reliable estimate of future sales of the new product. But how to get it?

Judgment in this instance is certainly available in the form of the "best estimates" of the sales manager and her staff. So-called hard data in this case might be obtained from a market-research survey of the potential demand for the product. In cases such as this, one must be quite certain not to *discard* judgment simply because it is intuitive and similarly not to *accept* statistical survey results just because they involve numbers; *both* sources of information are subject to estimating errors. The sensible decision maker prefers in most cases to *combine* the two sources of information instead of discarding one or both. Although the underlying mathematical theory is a bit too heady for a text at this level, the procedures by which this combination can be made are easily understood and applied.

Below, we illustrate the sales manager's probability distribution of monthly sales for the new product. She puts the mean sales volume per month at 110 units, and from the same kinds of questions we asked the supervisor in the previous example, we have been able to calculate the sales manager's standard deviation of monthly sales as 10 units. A recently completed market survey indicates potential monthly sales at 70 units with a standard deviation of 7 units.

Now suppose the financial manager, after considering the capital costs involved and the relevant cost-price relationships, has determined that break-even volume on the new product is 80 units a month. At this point, the management of the company can reject the new product on the strength of the assumed greater precision of the market survey, they can accept the new product if they choose to consider the more favorable estimate of mean sales given by the sales manager, or they can choose to combine the two estimates (both the means and the standard deviations) to see what implications the combination of judgment and numbers has for the new-product decision.

Combining estimates like this involves weighting each mean by its *reliability*; that is (without going into the mathematics underlying this operation), we weight each mean by the reciprocal of its variance (the square of its standard deviation), like this:

Estimate source	Mean $\hat{\mu}_i$	Std. deviation $\hat{\sigma}_i$	Variance $\hat{\sigma}_i^2$	Reliability $1/\hat{\sigma}_i^2$
Sales manager	$\hat{\mu}_1 = 110$	$\hat{\sigma}_1 = 10$	$\hat{\sigma}_1^2 = 100$	$1/100$
Market survey	$\hat{\mu}_2 = 70$	$\hat{\sigma}_2 = 7$	$\hat{\sigma}_2^2 = 49$	$1/49$

Combined estimate of mean

$$\hat{\mu} = \frac{\hat{\mu}_1 (1/\hat{\sigma}_1^2) + \hat{\mu}_2 (1/\hat{\sigma}_2^2)}{(1/\hat{\sigma}_1^2) + (1/\hat{\sigma}_2^2)} \qquad (4\text{-}3)$$

where $\hat{\mu}_i$ = the *i*th estimate of the mean

$\hat{\sigma}_i$ = the *i*th estimate of the standard deviation

$\hat{\mu}$ = the combined estimate of the mean

$$\text{Combined estimate of mean sales} = \frac{(110 \times {}^1/_{100}) + (70 \times {}^1/_{49})}{{}^1/_{100} + {}^1/_{49}}$$

$$= 83.17 \text{ units}$$

And the combined standard deviation for the two estimates may be approximated by using a formula many will recognize as being that for the harmonic mean:

COMBINING THE TWO
ESTIMATES OF THE
STANDARD DEVIATION

Combined estimate of standard deviation

$$\sigma = \frac{\sqrt{2}}{\sqrt{(1/\hat{\sigma}_1^2) + (1/\hat{\sigma}_2^2)}} \qquad (4\text{-}4)$$

where $\hat{\sigma}_i$ = the *i*th estimate of the standard deviation

$\hat{\sigma}$ = the combined estimate of the standard deviation

$$\text{Combined standard deviation} = \frac{\sqrt{2}}{\sqrt{{}^1/_{100} + {}^1/_{49}}}$$

$$= 8.11 \text{ units}$$

The best *combined* estimate of the new product's sales results in a mean of slightly higher than 83 units per month and a standard deviation of the distribution around this mean of about 8.11 units. Using these two values, the distribution of sales for the proposed product is illustrated in Figure 4-5.

USING COMBINED
ESTIMATES

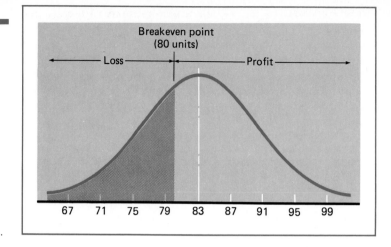

FIGURE 4-5
Estimated monthly
sales in units
(combined estimate).

Because 1 standard deviation for the combined distribution is 8.11 units, we calculate that the breakeven point is $(83 - 80)/8.11$, which is

$$\frac{3}{8.11} \qquad \text{or} \qquad .37 \text{ standard deviation}$$

to the left of the mean of the *combined* distribution (83). From Appendix Table 1, we find that the area under the normal curve from one tail to a point .37 standard deviation past the mean is .64431 of the total area. Thus the portion of the area under the curve representing sales volumes less than the breakeven point (that is, representing potential losses) is calculated as

$$1.0 - .64431 \qquad \text{or} \qquad \text{about} \; .356$$

INTERPRETING
RESULTS

VALUE OF MORE THAN
ONE ESTIMATE

and is shown in Figure 4-5 as the shaded area under the curve. On the strength of our combined estimates of the new product's sales, it then appears that chances for a loss are less than .4, not bad odds at all for a new product.

Let us examine the significance of what we have done. Had we proceeded solely on the strength of the market survey, with its mean of a 70-unit monthly sales volume, chances are that we would *not* have proceeded with the introduction of a product which required 80 units monthly just to break even. On the other hand, had we chosen to disregard the market survey and proceed full speed ahead on the strength of our sales manager's 110-unit monthly estimate, we would have failed to see the chance of failure and thus would have made our new-product decision on incomplete information. We chose to do neither. Instead we combined the considerable experience and "feel" of our sales manager with some valuable quantitative market survey information. Additionally, we looked not only at the *mean* values in each estimate but also at the standard deviations of the estimates. Combining the two means and the two standard deviations, we came to an objective determination of our chances of success with this new product; we chose not to use judgment or quantitative market information alone but to *combine both* to make a better decision.

9 Utility as a decision criterion

Up to this point in the chapter, we have used expected value (expected *profit*, for example) as our decision criterion. This assumed that if the expected profit of alternative A was better than that of alternative B, the decision maker would certainly choose alternative A. Conversely, if the expected loss of alternative C was greater than the expected loss of alternative D, it was assumed that the decision maker would surely choose D as the better course of action.

SHORTCOMINGS OF
EXPECTED VALUE AS A
DECISION CRITERION

There are situations, however, in which the use of expected value as the decision criterion would get one into serious trouble. For example, suppose a businessperson owns a new factory worth, say, $1 million. Suppose further that there is only 1 chance in 1,000 (.001) that it will burn down this year. From these two figures we can compute the expected loss:

$$.001 \times \$1,000,000 = \$1,000 = \text{expected loss}$$

Now suppose an insurance representative comes along and offers to insure the building for, say, $1,250 this year. Strict use of the notion of minimizing expected losses would dictate that the businessperson refuse to insure the building, since the expected loss of insuring, $1,250, is higher than the expected loss of a fire. But if the businessperson felt that a $1 million uninsured loss would mean disaster, the expected value would very probably be discarded as the decision criterion and the insurance would be bought at an extra cost of $250 per year per policy ($1,250 − $1,000). The choice would be *not* to minimize expected loss in this case.

ANOTHER EXAMPLE
IN WHICH EXPECTED
VALUE DOESN'T WORK

Let us look at an example a bit closer, perhaps, to students. Suppose you are the typical struggling graduate student with two children and just enough money to get through the semester and a friend offers to sell you a .9 chance at winning $10 for just $1. You would most likely think of the problem in terms of expected values and reason as follows: Is .9 × $10 greater than $1? Because the expected value of the bet ($9) is 9 times greater than the cost of the bet ($1), you might feel inclined to take your friend up on this offer. Even if you lost, the loss of $1 would not affect your situation materially.

Suppose now that your friend offers to sell you a .9 chance at winning $1,000 for $100. The question you would ponder now is: Is .9 × $1,000 greater than $100? Of course the expected value of the bet ($900) is still 9 times the cost of the bet ($100), but you would more than likely think twice before putting up your money. Why? Even though the pleasure of winning $1,000 would be high, the pain of losing your hard-earned $100 might be more than you cared to experience.

Suppose, finally, that your friend offers to sell you a .9 chance at winning $10,000 for your total assets, which happen to be $1,000. If you use expected value as your decision criterion, you would ask the question: Is .9 × $10,000 greater than $1,000? with the same answer as before, namely, yes. The expected value of the bet ($9,000) is still 9 times greater than the cost of the bet ($1,000), but now you would probably refuse your friend, not because the expected value of the bet is unattractive, but because the thought of losing all your assets is completely unacceptable as an outcome.

In this example, the student changed the decision criterion away from expected value as soon as the thought of losing $1,000 was too painful despite the pleasure to be gained from winning $10,000. At this point, the student was not considering the expected value but was thinking solely of *utility*. In this sense, *utility* refers essentially to the pleasure or displeasure one would derive from certain outcomes. The utility curve of our hypothetical student in Figure 4-6 is linear around the origin ($1 of gain is as *pleasurable* as $1 of loss is *painful* in this region); it turns down rapidly when the potential loss rises to levels near $1,000. Specifically, this utility curve shows us that from the point of view of our hypothetical student, the displeasure from losing $1,000 is greater than the pleasure from winning many times that amount. The shape of one's utility curve is a product of one's psychological makeup, one's expectations about the future, and the particular decision or act being evaluated. A person can well have one utility curve for one type of situation and quite a different one for the next situation.

DIFFERENT UTILITIES

THE UTILITY CURVE

INDIVIDUAL UTILITIES

The utility curves of three different businesspeople faced with the same decision are shown on the graph in Figure 4-7. We have arbitrarily named these individuals Head, Bell, and Lev. The attitudes of these three individuals are readily apparent from analysis of their utility curves. Head is a cautious and conservative businessman; a move to the right of the zero profit point increases his utility only very slightly, whereas a move to the left of the zero profit point decreases his utility rapidly. In terms of numerical values, Head's

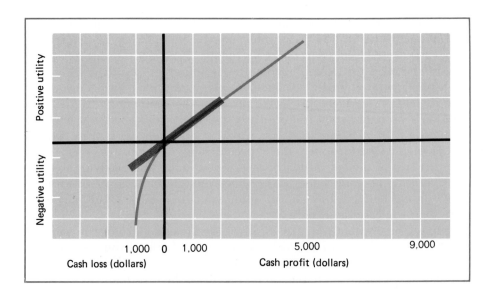

FIGURE 4-6

Utility of various profits and losses.

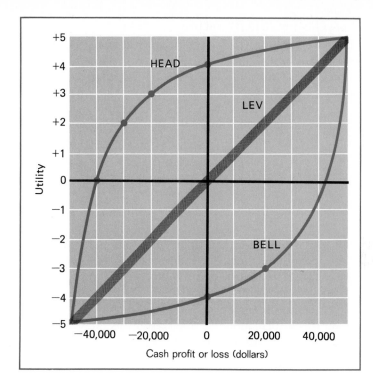

FIGURE 4-7
Utility curves of Head,
Bell, and Lev.

utility curve indicates that going from $0 to $50,000 profit increases his utility by a value of 1 on the vertical scale, while moving into the loss range by only $20,000 decreases his utility by the same value of 1 on the vertical scale. Head will avoid situations where high losses might occur; he is said to be *averse to risk*.

Bell is quite another story. We see from her utility curve that a profit increases her utility by much more than a loss of the same amount decreases it. Specifically, increasing her profits $10,000 (from $40,000 to $50,000) raises her utility from $-\frac{1}{2}$ to $+5$ on the vertical scale, but lowering her profits $10,000 (from $0 to $-$10,000) decreases her utility by only .25, from -4 to -4.25. Bell is a player of long shots; she feels strongly that a large loss would not make things much worse than they are now but, on the contrary, that a big profit would be quite rewarding. She will take large risks to earn even larger gains.

Lev, fairly well off financially, is the kind of businessman who would not suffer too greatly from a $50,000 loss nor increase his wealth significantly from a $50,000 gain. He would get about as much pleasure from making an additional $50,000 as he would pain from losing $50,000. Because Lev's utility curve is linear, he can effectively use *expected value* as his decision criterion, whereas Head and Bell must use *utility*. In summary, whereas Lev will act when the expected value is positive, Head will demand a high expected value for the outcome, while Bell may act when the expected value is negative.

ONLY ONE OF THE
THREE DECISION
MAKERS SHOULD USE
EXPECTED VALUE

▨ CALCULATING UTILITY VALUES

So far we have only talked about utility in general terms. We need to be able to calculate utility values so that we can actually draw one or more of the utility curves illustrated in Figure 4-7 using specific numerical values for the points on the curve.

Let's start by arbitrarily assigning two utility values for the *best* and *worst* possible outcomes. In Figure 4-7, the best outcome shown is $50,000 and the worst outcome shown is −$50,000. Suppose we assign these two outcomes utility values:

$$\text{Utility of } -\$50,000 = 0$$

$$\text{Utility of } \$50,000 = 10$$

Now let's bring in a fourth person (call her Mason) and ask her a few questions to determine her utility preferences; then we shall add a "Mason curve" to the three already in Figure 4-7.

PLOTTING A
UTILITY CURVE

First we will ask Mason her utility for a payoff of, say, $30,000 (we have *already* arbitrarily assigned her a utility of 10 for a payoff of $50,000). To obtain this information, we ask Mason this question: State a probability p at which you are indifferent between a *guaranteed* payoff of $30,000 and a *lottery* (a bet) which has a probability p of getting a payoff of $50,000 and a probability of $1 − p$ of getting a payoff of −$50,000.

Now Mason answers our question, considering her own wealth, her preference for taking risk, and all the other characteristics that make one person's utilities different from another's. How should we interpret her answer to this question? If p is close to 1.0, she is telling us she is averse to risk, since a good *chance* of getting $50,000 is required to make the lottery preferable to $30,000 certain. If, however, p is close to zero, she is saying she prefers to gamble.

After thinking about it for a minute or two, she tells us that at $p = .7$, she is indifferent between the lottery and the $30,000. Good. Now that we have this value of p, we can compute her utility for the $30,000 payoff:

$$\text{Utility of } \$30,000 = p \text{ (utility of } \$50,000) + (1 − p) \text{ (utility of } -\$50,000)$$

and since we have already assigned the values 0 and 10 to the payoffs −$50,000 and $50,000, we can restate Mason's answer like this:

$$\text{Utility of } \$30,000 = .7 \ (10) + .3 \ (0)$$
$$= 7$$

Now suppose we ask her to state her indifference probability for a guaranteed payoff of, say, $10,000 versus the same lottery we used in the previous example (a probability of p of getting a payoff of $50,000 and a probability of $1 − p$ of getting a payoff of −$50,000). This time she responds with an answer of .4.

We interpret her answer like this:

$$\text{Utility of } \$10{,}000 = .4\,(10) + .6\,(0)$$
$$= 4$$

Once more we ask a question. This time we want to know Mason's indifference probability for a guaranteed payoff of $-\$10{,}000$. And this time she responds with .2. We again convert this to a utility value:

$$\text{Utility of } -\$10{,}000 = .2\,(10) + .8\,(0)$$
$$= 2$$

Now if we plot Mason's three answers on the graph in Figure 4-8, we can see that her utility curve (shown in color) is quite different from the other three we had, those of Head, Bell, and Lev. We conclude that Mason is a bit more willing to take risk than Lev. Notice that we have numbered the vertical axis two ways in Figure 4-8, once using the same designation as in Figure 4-7 and the second time using the newer designation 0 to 10. Finally, you should notice that the utility we first assigned to the payoffs $50,000 and $-\$50{,}000$ was purely arbitrary and in no way affected the shape of Mason's utility curve which resulted.

INTERPRETING
MASON'S UTILITY
CURVE

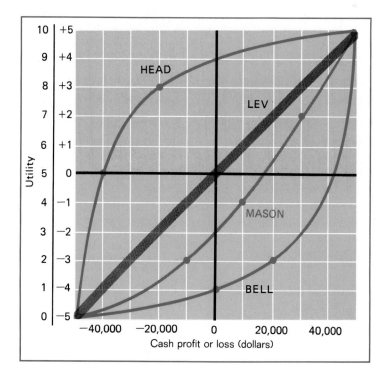

FIGURE 4-8
Utility curve of Mason
shown with three
other utility curves.

10 Glossary

Certainty The decision environment in which only one state of nature exists.

Conditional profit The profit which would result from a given combination of decision alternative and state of nature. Conditional profit is a payoff.

Criterion of rationality The criterion used when all states of nature are assumed equally likely; also known as the *principle of insufficient reason.*

Criterion of realism A middle-ground criterion between maximax and maximin which requires the decision maker to specify a coefficient, or index of optimism.

Cumulative probability The probability of selling a given number or greater.

Decision alternative An alternative choice open to the decision maker.

Expected marginal loss The marginal loss multiplied by the probability of not selling that unit.

Expected marginal profit The marginal profit multiplied by the probability of selling that unit.

Expected profit The sum of the conditional profits for a given decision alternative each weighted by the probability that it will happen.

Expected profit with perfect information The expected value of profit with perfect certainty about the occurrence of the states of nature.

Expected value criterion A criterion which requires the decision maker to calculate the expected value for each decision alternative (the sum of the weighted payoffs for that alternative where the weights are the probability values assigned by the decision maker to the states of nature that can happen).

Expected value of perfect information The difference between expected profit under conditions of risk and expected profit with perfect information.

Marginal loss The loss incurred from stocking a unit which is not sold.

Marginal profit The profit earned from selling one additional unit.

Maximax criterion An optimistic criterion which maximizes the maximum payoff.

Maximin criterion A pessimistic criterion which maximizes the minimum payoff.

Maximum likelihood criterion A criterion which selects that state of nature which has the highest probability of occurring and picks the decision alternative which yields the highest payoff for that state.

Minimax regret criterion A criterion which selects that payoff which minimizes the maximum regret.

Minimum probability The necessary probability of selling at least one additional unit which must exist to justify stocking that unit.

Obsolescence loss The loss occasioned by stocking too many units and having to dispose of unsold units.

Opportunity loss The profit that could have been earned if stock had been sufficient to supply a unit that was demanded.

Payoff The benefit which accrues from a given combination of decision alternative and state of nature.

Payoff table Illustration of the payoffs which would result from each possible combination of decision alternative and state of nature.

Reliability A weight attached to an estimate; the reciprocal of the square of the standard deviation.

Risk The decision environment in which the decision maker has information supporting the assignment of probability values to each of the possible states of nature.

Salvage value The value of an item after the initial selling day.

State of nature A future event not under the control of the decision maker.

Uncertainty The decision environment in which more than one state of nature exists but in which the decision maker cannot assign probabilities to the various states.

Utility The value of a certain outcome or payoff to someone; the pleasure or displeasure that person would derive from that outcome.

11 Review of equations

Page 150

$$\text{Measure of realism} = \alpha\,(\text{Maximum payoff})$$
$$+ (1 - \alpha)\,(\text{Minimum payoff}) \qquad (4\text{-}1)$$

When decision makers would rather not use a completely optimistic or a completely pessimistic decision criterion under conditions of uncertainty, the measure of realism allows them to introduce their personal assessment of optimism (α) and thereby specify a position between a criterion of optimism and a criterion of pessimism.

Page 164

$$p = \frac{ML}{MP + ML} \qquad (4\text{-}2)$$

This formula calculates the p, or probability, which represents the minimum probability of selling at least one additional unit to justify stocking that unit. In this formulation, MP is the marginal profit if the extra unit is sold and ML is the marginal loss if it is not sold.

Page 173

$$\text{Combined estimate of mean} \qquad \hat{\mu} = \frac{\hat{\mu}_1\,(1/\hat{\sigma}_1{}^2) + \hat{\mu}_2\,(1/\hat{\sigma}_2{}^2)}{(1/\hat{\sigma}_1{}^2) + (1/\hat{\sigma}_2{}^2)} \qquad (4\text{-}3)$$

where $\hat{\mu}_i$ = the ith estimate of the mean
  $\hat{\sigma}_i$ = the ith estimate of the standard deviation
  $\hat{\mu}$ = the combined estimate of the mean

This formula enables us to combine two estimates which have different means and different standard deviations. In combining estimates, we weight each estimate by its *reliability* (the reciprocal of the square of its standard deviation).

Page 173

$$\text{Combined estimate of standard deviation} \qquad \hat{\sigma} = \frac{\sqrt{2}}{\sqrt{(1/\hat{\sigma}_1{}^2) + (1/\hat{\sigma}_2{}^2)}} \qquad (4\text{-}4)$$

where $\hat{\sigma}_i$ = the ith estimate of the standard deviation

$\hat{\sigma}$ = the combined estimate of the standard deviation

To get an estimated combined standard deviation from two individual standard deviations, we use this formula. (If we wanted to combine three standard deviations, the formula would become

$$\hat{\sigma} = \frac{\sqrt{3}}{\sqrt{1/\hat{\sigma}_1{}^2 + 1/\hat{\sigma}_2{}^2 + 1/\hat{\sigma}_3{}^2}}$$

and for more than three standard deviations, it would be extended similarly.)

12 Exercises

4-1 Bonnie James is considering the purchase of a delivery truck for distributing auto transmissions to repair shops in Salt Lake City. The manufacturer of the truck has estimated that the truck should have a mean lifetime of 200,000 miles with a standard deviation of 50,000 miles. Bonnie has also asked a business associate who uses the same model truck for his estimate. He feels the truck should have a mean lifetime of 160,000 miles with a standard deviation of 70,000 miles. Determine for Bonnie the combined estimate of mean and standard deviation.

4-2 The Upstate Company is planning to stage a rock concert featuring Ozzie Newburn. They can schedule the concert in one of four arenas, called A, B, C, and D. Each of the arenas has a different seating capacity, and each has a different fixed cost. If Upstate schedules the largest arena and attendance is high, they stand to make the highest profit. However, if attendance is low, they can suffer a loss. The following table gives the conditional profit figures in thousands of dollars for the four arenas and the corresponding possible levels of attendance:

| | Arena scheduled | | | |
Attendance	A	B	C	D
10,000	10,000	8,000	−1,000	−5,000
20,000	10,000	10,000	2,000	−1,000
30,000	10,000	12,000	8,000	9,000
40,000	10,000	12,000	16,000	18,000
50,000	10,000	12,000	16,000	22,000

Using the maximin criterion, which arena should Upstate select for the concert?

4-3 Yogurt Hut, Ltd., sells natural yogurt in a college community. Julie Stoneman, the manager, is filling out the orders for next week's supply of yogurt. She is uncertain what sales will be. Julie has the table below as a historical representation of profits given certain sales and buying-level combinations.

	Actions		
Weekly sales	**Buy 200**	**Buy 300**	**Buy 400**
200	$50	$25	$ 0
300	50	75	50
400	50	75	100

Using the maximax decision criterion, what advice can you give Julie about quantities of yogurt to buy for next week?

4-4 Mutual Funds of the Northeast has $500,000 available for one of four investment alternatives in the stock market: a blue-chip stock offering, a growth-stock offering, a new venture-stock offering, and treasury bills. The investment environment can assume any one of four states, and Mutual has no prior information about what the market will do. Mutual's payoff table looks like this:

Stock market trend	**Type of stock**			
	Blue chip	**Growth**	**Venture**	**Treasury bills**
Boom	$250,000	$375,000	$500,000	$30,000
Moderate growth	75,000	150,000	100,000	30,000
Moderate decline	0	−50,000	−150,000	30,000
Collapse	−300,000	−400,000	−500,000	30,000

Using the minimax regret criterion for decision making, evaluate each alternative and advise Mutual which is preferable.

4-5 The New Era Toy Co., Inc., manufactures children's wooden toys. The company believes that the current trend toward sturdier and simpler toys will continue; thus New Era must decide among three alternative methods of providing for anticipated higher demand for its products. These are completely overhauling the existing plant and installing computerized woodworking machinery, expanding the current plant and adding more machines, or buying a competitor's plant which is available. A fourth alternative would be to limit production to the current plant capacity (do nothing). New Era's payoff table is as follows:

	Alternatives			
Demand	**Overhaul**	**Expand**	**Buy**	**Do nothing**
High	$30,000	$60,000	$50,000	$3,000
Moderate	10,000	20,000	15,000	2,000
Low	−5,000	−10,000	−20,000	−1,000
Failure	−50,000	−70,000	−60,000	−5,000

New Era management has no information on how demand will be likely to shape up.

Using the criterion of realism, with $\alpha = .8$, determine the best choice for New Era under these conditions.

4-6 The Midtown Food Store stocks mangoes during the early summer season. These are flown in from Merritt Island, Florida, each Monday and must be sold within the week following. In the past the store has experienced the following sales of mangoes:

Quantities buyers bought, units	Number of weeks this occurred	Probability of occurrence	Cumulative probability
20	10	.10	1.00
25	30	.30	.90
40	50	.50	.60
60	10	.10	.10

The food store buys mangoes for $2 each and sells them for $4.
  a. If the store stocks 25 every week, what will the expected profit per week be?
  b. What would the expected profit per week be with a 60-unit stock?
  c. What quantity should be bought every week to maximize expected profits?
  d. What is the expected value of perfect information?

4-7 Using the data given in Exercise 4-6, convert the conditional profits to conditional losses and solve for the optimal stocking decision.

4-8 A veterinarian purchases rabies immunization vaccine on Monday of each week. Because of the characteristics of this vaccine, it must be used by Friday or disposed of. The vaccine costs $9 per dose, and the vet charges $16 per dose. In the past, the vet has administered rabies vaccine in the following quantities:

Quantities used per week	Number of weeks this occurred	Probability of occurrence	Cumulative probability
25	15	.3	1.00
40	20	.4	.70
50	10	.2	.30
75	5	.1	.10

Using marginal analysis, determine how many doses the veterinarian should order each week.

4-9 Kentucky Airlines is trying to get more information on the distribution of no-shows (passengers with confirmed reservations for a given flight who do not make the flight). All its flights are with aircraft whose capacity is 200 passengers. It has found from another airline similar to itself that the distribution of no-shows is approximately normal with a mean of 18 and a standard deviation of 7.4. The airline would like to combine this information with figures reflecting its own no-show experience. Therefore, it asked June Baer, a reservations clerk, for her estimate of the no-shows. She responded by saying, "The average number of no-shows is 21; in 3 cases out of 4 the number of no-shows is no more than 8 passengers above or below this average." What is Kentucky Airlines' distribution of no-shows using both sources of information?

4-10 Mary Williams is president of the Ambergate Investment Club. In order to better understand the nature of the club's members, she maintains a file of their utility curves. Jamie Brown has recently joined the club, and so Mary has asked him the following questions:

    a. Utility A gives a guaranteed payoff of $20,000 per year, whereas risky stock B has a probability p of a $30,000 annual payoff or a $1 - p$ probability of losing $30,000 per year. At what probability p would you be indifferent in making a choice between the two investments?

    b. Utility A gives a guaranteed payoff of $10,000 per year compared with the same risky stock B. At what probability p would you be indifferent in choosing between the two investments?

    c. Utility A gives a guaranteed loss of $10,000 per year. At what probability p would you be indifferent in choosing between the two investments?

Jamie has responded to the three questions with probability values of .9, .8, and .4, respectively. Plot Jamie's utility curve assigning a utility of 0 to −$30,000 and a utility of 10 to $30,000. Would you characterize Jamie as being averse to risk?

4-11 Jim Hicks, the general superintendent, asks five of his supervisors to estimate for next year the average operating time of a proposed machine; he also asks each of them to estimate the odds that the machine will operate within +300 and −300 hours of their estimates of the average. For each of the five, calculate the implied standard deviation of the distribution of operating times, based on the following results:

	Estimated average operating hours	Odds that operating hours will be within ±300 hours of the estimated average
Supervisor 1	1,200	5:1
Supervisor 2	1,400	3:5
Supervisor 3	2,000	1:1
Supervisor 4	1,000	4:5
Supervisor 5	1,600	2:3

4-12 The Village of Huron, in anticipation of potential losses due to flu-related sickness among its residents, is faced with three possible decisions: (1) stock 1000 units of type W flu vaccine only, (2) stock 1000 units of type V flu only, or (3) stock 500 units of each type of flu vaccine. Based on the three possible events—light epidemic, moderate epidemic, and heavy epidemic outbreaks—they have determined the following conditional losses in worker-days due to sickness:

	Epidemic level		
Alternative	Light	Moderate	Heavy
Stock W only	100	300	800
Stock V only	80	250	350
Stock V & W	20	200	550

a. Before solving this problem, first attempt to apply *dominance reduction*. A decision alternative may be eliminated from consideration if there exists another alternative with the property that in each state of nature the loss from the first decision alternative is greater than or equal to the loss from the second alternative.

b. Assume that there are no probability estimates for the possible states of nature, and apply the criterion of rationality to find the decision which minimizes expected loss.

4-13 Jim Tilman, a marketing manager, collects three estimates from three different sources about next year's demand for a new product. Calculate the combined mean and standard deviation of the distribution of demand for this product from the following data:

	Estimate of mean sales	Estimate of standard deviation
Salesperson 1	230	60
Salesperson 2	280	50
Salesperson 3	220	60

4-14 From the combined estimates of the mean and standard deviation of sales for the new product in Exercise 4-13, calculate the probability that sales of that product next year will fall below 224 units.

4-15 From the combined estimates of the mean and standard deviation of sales for the new product in Exercise 4-13, calculate the probability that sales of that product next year will be above 300 units.

4-16 Using the data from Exercise 4-13, calculate the probability that sales will fall between 200 and 300 units next year.

4-17 The Captain's Table is a mail-order distributor of fresh lobsters. The company buys these for $4 per pound and sells them for $7.50 per pound. The per-week shipment distribution is as follows:

Shipments per week, pounds	Number of weeks this occurred	Probability of occurrence	Cumulative probability
3,000	5	.05	1.00
5,000	20	.20	.95
8,000	20	.20	.75
12,000	40	.40	.55
18,000	15	.15	.15

The company has been approached by a consulting firm specializing in sales forecasting. The firm has offered to provide The Captain's Table with a sales forecasting model which will increase the distributor's present profit by matching purchases with sales. The cost of buying and running this model will be $7,500 a week. Should the company buy it? (Expected value is already being used to calculate how many lobsters to order each week.)

4-18 The Texas Manufacturing Company is planning to hire two financial planners. Susan Thompson, who is personnel manager of the company, uses four measures to evaluate job applicants. These are personal interview ratings, educational performance, qualification exam scores, and involvement in community activities. All four measures are standardized to a 100-point scale. Susan feels that the most important measure is the personal interview, which is given a weight of 4. The other measures and their corresponding weights are educational performance, with a weight of 3; qualification exam with a weight of 2; and community activities, with a weight of 1. Which two of the following applicants should be given a job offer?

Applicant's name	Personal interview	Educational performance	Qualification exam	Community activities
Steve	75	84	90	80
Celeste	91	88	83	88
Carole	86	93	90	92
Frank	94	90	88	75
Linda	94	84	86	89
Sam	82	70	94	93
Bill	74	89	85	68

4-19 Fred Allen has his own Sno-Cone truck and lives 30 miles from the nearest beach resort. The number of Sno-Cones he sells is highly dependent upon the weather; the most recent forecast indicates a .4 chance of fair weather. If the weather is fair and Fred drives to the beach, he makes $80 per day on average; if he stays home, his profit is $40. If the weather is bad, he makes only $10 at the beach versus $35 at home. Given the latest weather forecast, construct Fred's payoff table and recommend whether he should stay home or drive to the beach. What could Fred afford to pay for a really good forecast of the next day's weather—one which would rarely miss?

4-20 Terry's Pro Shop stocks golf equipment. It is the beginning of the season, and Terry is deciding how many golf bags to stock. She has used past records to formulate the table below, which illustrates demand expectations and conditional profits (losses) given certain stocking actions. Using the principle of maximum likelihood as a decision criterion, how much inventory do you think Terry should stock?

		Conditional profits, stock actions					
Demand	Likelihood	2	4	6	8	10	12
2	.1	$50	$ 20	$ 0	−$ 20	−$ 60	−$100
4	.3	50	100	50	0	20	60
6	.2	50	100	150	120	80	0
8	.2	50	100	150	200	160	120
10	.1	50	100	150	200	250	190
12	.1	50	100	150	200	250	300

4-21 Care, Inc., is a charity meal center which provides indigent families with nourishing food on a daily basis. Each family pays $2 for meals which cost an average of $5 to prepare. If the meals prepared at a given time are not eaten, they go to waste. If more meals are demanded than are fixed, each unfed family is given $6 to buy meals elsewhere. The possible demand for meals ranges from 8 to 12 meals per day. The charity which runs Care, Inc., wants to minimize its expense. If it uses the criterion of rationality, how many meals should it prepare?

4-22 Mr. Wood is approached with an investment opportunity which could result in a profit or loss ranging between −$3,000 and +$3,000. He is quite rich, and losing up to $2,000 will still result in positive utility. In fact, a breakeven situation will result in a rather high level of utility. Plot a utility curve for Mr. Wood.

4-23 Fashion Boutique stocks and sells high fashion clothing for women. For the coming summer season, they plan to order designer swimwear at a cost of $50 per unit. These will be sold for $85 per unit during the summer selling season. At the end of the summer, the swimsuits must be sold at a post-summer sale for $30 per unit, because they will be out of fashion during the following year. Demand during the summer is estimated as:

Demand (units)	Probability
100	.20
200	.30
300	.30
400	.15
500	.05

Develop a table of conditional losses including both opportunity costs of $35 per unit and obsolescence costs of $20 per unit and determine the stocking decision which minimizes expected loss. What is the expected value of perfect information?

4-24 Mrs. Slade is approached by an associate with an investment proposition. The maximum profit that she can realize is $15,000, and the maximum loss possible is $10,000. Mrs. Slade feels that a no-gain or a loss situation carries a low level of utility. Plot a utility curve for her.

4-25 Nicole Spinner has kept records of Friday demand for fresh haddock at her fish market as follows:

Pounds demanded	Probability
20	.10
21	.12
22	.13
23	.12
24	.11
25	.10
26	.09
27	.08
28	.07
29	.05
30	.03

She realizes a profit of 37 cents per pound for all haddock sold. If any haddock is left unsold at the end of the day, she is able to sell it to the Manlius Animal Hospital to be used as catfood. In doing so, she incurs a loss of 27 cents a pound. Using marginal analysis, find Nicole's optimal stocking decision.

4-26 An investor has $10,000 to invest in common stock. His selection is between companies A and B. He feels that for each of the investments he has a .6 probability of doubling his money and a .4 probability of losing half his money. His choices are (1) invest the entire amount in either A or B, (2) invest $5,000 in one company and not invest the other $5,000, (3) invest $5,000 in A and $5,000 in B, or (4) not invest at all. If his utility values for changes in assets are $10,000 = 1; $5,000 = .90; $2,500 = .70; $0 = .40; $-$2,500 = .20; and $-$5,000 = 0; what investment plan should he choose to maximize his expected utility? Assume that the rise or fall of either stock is independent of the other.

4-27 You have undertaken the sponsorship of a racing car and team as part of an advertising campaign. In preparing an expected expense statement for the next race, you have accumulated this information: Complete engines for the race car cost $5,000; complete overhauls cost $2,000; and minor maintenance is essentially a no-cost item, since the crew is already salaried. The team completely "blows" an engine (destroys it) in 20 percent of the races; in 30 percent of the races, the engine needs a complete overhaul after the race; and 50 percent of the time, the engine needs only minor maintenance. Your data also show the following conditional probabilities for qualifying speeds given the kind of engine repair needed after the race:

Qualifying speed before race	Occurrence of "blown" engines, percent	Occurrence of major overhaul, percent	Occurrence of minor maintenance, percent
Over 175 mph	70	60	10
160–175 mph	20	30	30
Below 160 mph	10	10	60

Your driver, Beauford Johnson, has just qualified for the Dixie 600 at 182.375 mph. What is your expected engine expense for the race?

4-28 Benny Weston is famous for his hot sausage sandwiches which he sells each year at the Oklahoma State Fair. For each kilogram of sausage which he stocks and sells, his profit is 65 cents. If he stocks more sausages than he can sell, he can still recover from a complete loss by selling any unsold meat to the Canned Dogfood Company for a net loss of 15 cents per kilogram. He estimates demand in kilograms to be 10% of the total attendance during the week of the fair. This year's attendance is estimated to be as follows:

Attendance	Probability
60,000	.20
80,000	.60
100,000	.20

Construct a table of conditional losses taking into account the opportunity loss due to unmet demand when insufficient stock is available and the obsolescence loss due to overstock. Determine the number of kilograms to stock. What is the expected value of perfect information for fair attendance?

4-29 You own a company that manufactures citizens' band radios. You buy your crystals from two different sources to guarantee the supply. The normal order is

30,000 crystals. One supply source guarantees not more than 1 percent defectives. The other source has had varying rates according to this table:

Percent defective	Probability of this level
.5	.05
2.0	.55
5.0	.40

Your own assembly-line personnel are able to repair defective crystals at a cost of $2 each. The supply source with the guaranteed defective rate charges $1,000 more per order than the other source. Which source provides the lowest cost for your crystal supply?

4-30 Katahdin Farm Supply receives orders for an average of 5,000 pounds of crop dust per week during the potato growing season. The standard deviation of weekly demand is 425 pounds. Crop dust costs $4 a pound and is sold for $10 a pound. The crop dust is a new product which is chemically activated at the factory just prior to shipment. Therefore Katahdin has only a week in which to sell the crop dust at guaranteed full potency. Any crop dust left unsold at the end of a week is considered to have lost half its potency and can only be sold at $2 a pound. Calculate the optimal weekly order for crop dust. Assume that the demand is normally distributed.

4-31 Charlie owns a very old truck which he uses for occasional deliveries both in town and out of town. If he delivers out of town, he can average $200 a trip provided that his truck doesn't break down; if it does, repairs, delay, and towing cut his profit to $20. If he stays in town, he makes $90 a trip, but this is reduced to $60 if his truck breaks down. Compute what the probability of a breakdown would have to be for Charlie to be indifferent about where he delivers.

4-32 An investor is considering two alternatives for which she has $25,000 to invest. The first is commercial property; the second is stocks. Analysis has revealed that the property alternative offers a .5 probability of tripling her investment and a .5 probability of losing 60 percent of the entire amount. The stock alternative has a .3 probability of tripling her investment and a .7 probability of losing 60 percent of the investment. Her choices are (1) invest the entire amount in one or the other, (2) invest half her funds in one or the other and keep half, (3) invest half her money in each alternative, or (4) make no investment. She exhibits these utilities for change in her assets: $50,000 = 1; $25,000 = .8; $17,500 = .6; $0 = .4; −$7,500 = .2; and −$15,000 = 0. What investment plan should this woman follow to maximize her utility? You may assume that the rise or fall of one investment is independent of the other.

4-33 Executive Airlines offers full-service air travel in the northwest including free baggage checking and free meals/drinks. In recent years, some of Executive's market has been taken over by Stark Airlines. Stark Airlines is a no-frills carrier which charges extra for baggage checking and other services. Although Stark does not take reservations for tickets, many passengers are willing to wait in line to fly Stark because of the very low fares. Edmund Wallace, the operations manager for Executive Airlines, is planning to purchase a new aircraft for the route from Tacoma, Washington, to Portland, Oregon, and he is considering either a large SPT 20 aircraft or a smaller aircraft, the SPT 10. Currently, Stark Airlines does not compete on the Tacoma–Portland routing, but there is a possibility they will be granted a license to fly the route. Edmund feels that if he selects the SPT 20 aircraft and Stark's license is not granted, Executive will realize $500,000 profit per year on this route. If Stark is granted a license, the profit using the SPT 20 would drop to about $20,000. If Edmund selects the SPT 10 aircraft, profits on the route are expected to be $280,000 if Stark does not compete; however, profits would drop to $160,000 if Stark competes. Compute the probability of Stark's being granted a license which would result in Edmund's being indifferent to his choice of aircraft.

4-34 Linda Sawyer is in charge of the audit division for the Delaware internal revenue department. In the past year, Linda has observed that 10 percent of the corporate tax returns she has audited result in a payment of $100,000 in additional taxes to the state. In 20 percent of the cases, an audit yields $50,000 additional tax, and in 20 percent of the audits, the state receives an additional $10,000. In the remaining 50 percent of the audits, the tax returns are found to be correct and no additional revenues are received. It costs the state $2,000 to audit a corporate tax return. In the coming year, the state wishes to target for $5 million over and above audit costs to be added to the state's revenues from audited returns. How many returns should Linda plan to audit in order to meet this goal?

4-35 The Suburban Construction Company frequently submits bids for clearing land preparatory to home construction projects. Costs average $500 per lot cleared, and it costs Suburban $40 to make a cost estimate for each lot. From past experience, Suburban has learned that a bid of cost plus 15 percent has a 90 percent chance of being awarded the job. Similarly, bids of cost plus 20 percent, cost plus 25 percent, and cost plus 30 percent have a probability of winning of 80 percent, 40 percent, and 5 percent, respectively. If Suburban wishes to maximize its long-run profit, what bidding policy should it adopt for future jobs?

4-36 The Softskin Cosmetic Company has developed a radically new lipstick. On the basis of a market analysis in a carefully controlled test market, Softskin has determined that there is a 40 percent probability that the new product will be a huge success, with annual sales in the vicinity of 1 million units. Market research also revealed a 45 percent probability that sales would be about 800,000 units per year and a 15 percent probability that sales would be only about 400,000 units per year. If Softskin decides to go into limited production of the new product, its annual fixed costs will be $600,000 and it can produce the new product for a variable cost of $4 per unit. If it goes into large-scale production, annual fixed costs will be $1.5 million but variable costs will be only $3 per unit. The company president is a firm believer in maximizing expected profit. Will he propose limited production or large-scale production? The new product will be sold for $6 per unit.

4-37 The Province of Quebec is planning to issue hunting licenses for moose through a province-wide lottery. They have found that by harvesting some animals during the hunting season, they can increase the number of animals which survive through the winter months because of the limited food supply. Their estimates of moose population (in thousands) conditional upon the number of licenses issued and the severity of the winter are as follows:

Severity of winter	Number of licenses issued				
	5000	6000	7000	8000	9000
Mild	38	36	34	31	25
Moderate	35	33	33	29	22
Severe	28	30	32	27	20
Harsh	22	26	30	25	16

During the years when records have been kept, 20% of the winters have been mild while 30%, 40%, and 10% have been moderate, severe, and harsh, respectively. How many licenses should be issued in order to maximize the expected moose population? How large will the expected springtime moose population be with this decision?

4-38 Daily sales of bread by the Neighborhood Baking Company are normally distributed with a mean of 6,000 loaves and a standard deviation of 900 loaves. It costs the bakery 50 cents to produce a loaf of bread which sells for 95 cents. Any bread unsold at the end of the day is sold to the county jail for 35 cents a loaf. How many loaves should the bakery produce each day to maximize profit?

4-39 An investor is convinced that the price of a share of XYZ stock will rise in the near future. XYZ stock is currently selling for $50 a share. Upon inspecting the latest quotes on the options market, she finds that she can purchase an option to buy XYZ for $48 per share within the next 2 months at a cost of $4 per share. She can also purchase an option to buy the stock within a 4-month period; this option, which costs $8 a share, also allows her to exercise the option at $48 per share. She has estimated that the probability distribution for the price per share is as follows:

Price per share, dollars	Probability of this price	
	2 months	4 months
42	.05	0.00
48	.10	.05
52	.15	.10
56	.20	.15
60	.50	.30
64	0.00	.40

The investor plans to exercise her options just before their expiration if the stock is selling for more than $48 and immediately sell them at the current market price. Of course, if the stock is selling for $48 or less when the options expire, she will lose the entire purchase cost of the options.

The investor is relatively conservative, with the following utility values for changes in her assets:

Change	Utility
+1,200	1.0
+800	.8
+400	.7
0	.6
−400	.1
−800	0.0

The investor is considering one of three alternatives: (1) buy an option for 100 shares which expires in 2 months, (2) buy an option for 100 shares which expires in 4 months, or (3) do not buy at all. Which of the three alternatives will maximize her expected utility?

4-40 You are planning to invest $10,000 in Warner common stock if it has a 60 percent probability of rising to a price of $60 per share within 6 months' time. You ask two knowledgeable brokers the following questions: What is your best estimate of the price of Warner in 6 months? What are the odds that Warner will sell at a price within +$5 or −$5 of your best-estimate price? Their responses are as follows:

Broker	Best estimate	Odds of price in ±$5 range
A	58	2 to 1
B	63	5 to 1

On the basis of the combined assessment of the two brokers, what decision should you make on the proposed purchase of Warner stock?

13 Chapter concepts quiz

Fill in the Blanks

4-1 A _____ is a chart which lists the result of a decision and a state of nature for every possible combination of decision and state of nature. This result would be a _____ if we are seeking to maximize the quantity to arrive at an optimal decision, or a _____ if we are seeking to minimize the quantity.

4-2 When minimizing expected losses, two types of losses are considered. These are obsolescence losses and _____.

4-3 When operating under conditions of uncertainty, the maximax criterion is a(n) _____ criterion because it chooses that decision which has the _____ payoff of all decisions possible.

4-4 The _____ of a given decision alternative is found by weighting the conditional profit associated with each state of nature by the probability that the state of nature will occur, and summing for all states of nature; the _____ is found in the same way by weighting the loss associated with each state of nature.

4-5 The criterion of _____ assumes that in the absence of information to the contrary, each state of nature is equally likely; hence, if there are n possible states of nature, then the probability of any given state of nature occurring is _____.

4-6 In decision theory, the future events, not under the control of the decision maker, which can occur are called _____.

4-7 The criterion of rationality and the criterion of maximum likelihood are examples of decision making under conditions of _____.

4-8 The minimum expected loss is equal to the _____.

4-9 The _____ from stocking and selling an additional unit is the marginal profit of the unit multiplied by the probability that the unit will be sold.

4-10 The pleasure or displeasure some decision maker would derive from some outcome or payoff is called _____.

4-11 A decision maker who is averse to risk welcomes an opportunity to take large gambles. **T F**

4-12 Under the criterion of realism, α is a measure of optimism, since it is the weight assigned to the largest payoff possible for a given decision. **T F**

4-13 The techniques which employ criteria based on expected values are useless when demand has a continuous distribution since such expected values cannot be calculated. **T F**

4-14 The expected profit with perfect information is the weighted sum of the largest profit for each state of nature, where the weights are the probability of occurrence of that state of nature. **T F**

4-15 The conditional profit for a given decision alternative and state of nature is the product of the number of items stocked and the net profit per item (sale price of item − cost of item). **T F**

4-16 The concept of a salvage value only comes into play when stock on hand exceeds demand. **T F**

4-17 Marginal analysis instructs the decision maker to continue to stock more items as long as expected profit is greater than expected loss. **T F**

4-18 It is possible to use estimates for the mean and standard deviation of a distribution of demand, when these are not known, in finding an optimal decision. **T F**

4-19 When two or more separate estimates of the mean and standard deviation are available, a decision maker must choose one in determining the distribution of demand. **T F**

4-20 When combining two estimates in order to develop a combined estimate of a probability distribution, each of the two mean estimates is weighted by its reliability. **T F**

4-21 The most common environment within which decision makers find themselves is decision making under conditions of certainty. **T F**

4-22 If a decision maker makes a decision which later turns out to be optimal, his resulting regret is zero. **T F**

4-23 A conditional profit is the profit resulting from some specific decision alternative and some specific state of nature. **T F**

4-24 Marginal analysis may be used when the random variable of demand is either discrete or continuously distributed. **T F**

4-25 If only one possible state of nature exists, the decision making environment is classified as decision making under conditions of guaranteed uncertainty. **T F**

4-26 When the decision maker possesses information about the probabilities of the possible states of nature, his or her decisions may be made under conditions of:
   a. Uncertainty
   b. Risk
   c. Certainty
   d. Probability

4-27 The expected value of perfect information (EVPI) can be found by:
   a. Subtracting the maximum expected profit under conditions of risk from the expected profit with perfect information

b. Weighting the largest profit for each state of nature by the probability that the state of nature occurs, and summing for all states of nature

c. Calculating the minimum expected loss for all the decisions

d. Both *a* and *c*

4-28 Which of the following statements about marginal analysis is true?
  a. It is useful when the number of decision alternatives and states of nature is large.
  b. It works equally well when we have a continuous or a discrete demand distribution.
  c. It gives the same result as the criteria of maximizing expected profit and minimizing expected loss.
  d. All of the above.

4-29 The maximum likelihood criterion is most useful when:
  a. There are few states of nature and one state is fairly likely to occur.
  b. All states of nature are equally likely.
  c. No estimates of the probability of each state occurring are available.
  d. Both *b* and *c*.

4-30 All of the following are valid decision criteria under conditions of uncertainty except:
  a. Maximax criterion
  b. Maximin criterion
  c. Minimin criterion
  d. Criterion of realism

4-31 In decision theory, it is assumed that:
  a. Only two states of nature can both occur together.
  b. Only one state of nature can occur.
  c. Any number of states of nature can all occur together.
  d. None of the above.

4-32 An optimistic criterion for decision making is:
  a. Maximax
  b. Maximin
  c. Minimax regret
  d. Realism

4-33 The decision maker's personal feelings may influence the decision process when using the criterion of:
  a. Maximax
  b. Maximin
  c. Minimax regret
  d. Realism

4-34 The criterion of rationality is also known as the:
  a. Criterion of maximum likelihood
  b. Expected value criterion
  c. Criterion of Bayes
  d. Principle of insufficient reason

4-35 In the expected value approach, weights are assigned to each state of nature. These weights are given according to:
  a. The probabilities of the states of nature
  b. The relative payoffs for each decision alternative
  c. The decision maker's preferences
  d. All the above

4-36 The values placed in the diagonal row of a conditional loss table showing alternative stock actions are:
   a. Losses due to unsold inventory
   b. Losses due to unmet demand
   c. Always zero because the number stocked equals the number sold
   d. Losses due to ovestocking

4-37 The maximum likelihood criterion can produce poor decisions if:
   a. There are a large number of states of nature.
   b. Each state of nature has a small probability of occurrence.
   c. The states of nature have nearly equal probabilities.
   d. All of the above

4-38 In a decision problem having five possible alternative decisions and seven possible states of nature, the payoff table will include:
   a. 5 elements
   b. 35 elements
   c. 7 elements
   d. 12 elements

4-39 A decision maker using the criterion of realism might select an alpha value of .9 if he is:
   a. An optimist
   b. A pessimist
   c. A maximizer
   d. A minimizer

4-40 The difference between the expected profit under conditions of risk and the expected profit with perfect information is called the:
   a. Expected marginal loss
   b. Optimal decision
   c. Opportunity loss
   d. Expected value of perfect information

14 Real world MS/OR successes

EXAMPLE: DEVELOPING A MERCHANDISING STRATEGY FOR AMOCO OIL COMPANY

THE PROBLEM: SURVIVAL OF AMOCO'S FULL-SERVICE DEALERS

Following the OPEC oil embargo in the early 1970s, profit margins and the demand for gasoline at full-service stations declined. Amoco Oil Company decided to develop a merchandising strategy to help its network of 5,000 independent dealers survive by increasing sales of repair services and tires, batteries, and accessories (TBA). The survival of full-service dealers was important to Amoco since gasoline sales through these outlets totaled $3.5 billion in 1981. Two consultants, James S. Dyer and Richard N. Lund,[1] used utility theory to analyze alternative strategies. As a result, Amoco implemented the "Certicare" guaranteed car repair program. The bottom line: In the first year of a 5-year phased implementation program, full-service dealer sales

[1] James S. Dyer and Richard S. Lund, "Tinker Toys and Christmas Trees: Opening a New Merchandising Package for Amoco Oil Company," *Interfaces*, vol. 12, no. 6, pp. 38–52, December 1982.

improved substantially. The projected increase in profits after full implementation was $10 million.

In brainstorming discussions with marketing people, Dyer and Lund identified numerous potential merchandising strategies. Some examples: guarantee car repairs, promote a single product such as motor oil as a price leader, and integrate the promotion of all Amoco products. To evaluate the strategies, Dyer and Lund analyzed a variety of marketing factors influencing dealer sales. Each factor was assigned a weight of importance and an individual utility value. The total utility for the strategy was the sum of the weights times individual utilities.

THE APPROACH:
WEIGHTED UTILITIES

Weights for marketing factors were assigned using questionnaires given to a group of 72 marketing people. To illustrate, suppose that a customer stops by a station for a 5-quart oil change and that a certain merchandising strategy is assumed to be in effect. The marketing person might estimate that 10% of sales are due to the merchandising strategy, 5% because of the dealer's selling effort, 30% because the customer stopped to purchase other Amoco products, and 55% because of convenience or habit. These percentages were used as weights. A separate set of questionnaires ranked the productiveness of the marketing factors in each strategy relative to Amoco's existing merchandising strategy. Utility values were deduced from the rankings, a process much like the one used to deduce the utility values of profits and losses in this chapter. Finally, the weights and utilities for each factor were combined to calculate an overall utility for each strategy.

DETERMINING
THE WEIGHTS

DETERMINING
UTILITY VALUES

The merchandising strategies, questionnaires, and utility calculations were refined many times as the marketing people gained a better understanding of the problems faced by the dealers. To help visualize the problems, Dyer and Lund constructed a physical model from a set of Tinker Toys. The model used knobs to represent sales events and sticks leading in to the knobs to represent the marketing factors that influence sales.

THE TINKER TOY MODEL

This analytical procedure led to selection of the Certicare program, which guarantees repairs for 90 days or 4,000 miles. Amoco decided to implement Certicare gradually in its 20 major metropolitan markets over a 5-year period. Dyer and Lund's article appeared after the first year of the program, in which Certicare dealers experienced sales increases across the board compared to non-Certicare dealers. After full implementation, Amoco projected additional profits of $10 million.

IMPLEMENTATION

5

Decisions involving the possible purchase of new capital equipment are of vital importance to managers. Although good estimates are often available regarding the mean and standard deviation of the prospective machine's operating time, as well as the minimum weekly hours the machine must be operated in order to break even, there are still many questions which must be answered before undertaking such an important investment. Managers need to know what expected loss might be incurred if the machine fails to operate above its breakeven point. In addition, they need to know the expected profit the machine will generate for the firm at operating levels above its breakeven point.

Information such as this can greatly assist management in coming to an intelligent, cost-effective decision. In this chapter, you will become familiar with a number of quantitative techniques that can assist you in making decisions involving capital investment, replacement strategies, choice among alternatives, and having active opponents.

DECISION MAKING USING PROBABILITIES II

The Normal Distribution and Cost-Volume-Profit Analysis, Combining Money and Probabilities, Replacement Analysis, Decision Trees, Game Theory

CHAPTER OBJECTIVES

- DEMONSTRATE THE USE OF THE NORMAL PROBABILITY DISTRIBUTION IN DECISION MAKING.

- DEMONSTRATE HOW MONETARY VALUE AND PROBABILITY INFORMATION CAN BE COMBINED FOR MORE EFFECTIVE DECISION MAKING.

- SHOW HOW THE VALUE OF ADDITIONAL INFORMATION CAN BE DETERMINED IN SITUATIONS INVOLVING CONTINUOUSLY DISTRIBUTED RANDOM VARIABLES.

- EXAMINE THE USE OF PROBABILITY CONCEPTS IN REPLACEMENT ANALYSIS.

- SHOW HOW COMPLEX DECISIONS CAN BE STRUCTURED WITH DECISION TREES.

- INTRODUCE GAME THEORY AS A MODEL OF DECISION MAKING WITH AN ACTIVE OPPONENT.

1 The normal probability distribution and cost-volume-profit analysis

One of the more useful applications of the probability concepts introduced in Chapter 2 is in analyzing in advance the likely consequences of alternative product, price, or output strategies management is currently considering. *Cost-volume-profit analysis* (often referred to as *breakeven analysis*) allows management to determine in advance (with at least a worthwhile degree of accuracy) the effects that certain contemplated decisions or expected states of nature will have on revenues, costs, and therefore profits. Of the two variables which determine profits (revenues and costs), management has considerably less control over revenues; thus the estimation of revenues is a good example of decision making under conditions of risk, where management can usually specify a *distribution* of revenues. Sales volume is often a random variable, and solutions to cost-volume-profit problems which treat it differently are avoiding some of the real issues in decision making.

COST-VOLUME-PROFIT ANALYSIS

A DISTRIBUTION OF REVENUES CAN USUALLY BE SPECIFIED

SALES VOLUME AS A RANDOM VARIABLE

Let us use as an example a company with these financial data concerning a proposed new product:

Selling price	$7.50
Variable cost/unit	$4.50
Fixed cost/year	$1,500,000

BREAKEVEN POINT

In cost-volume-profit analysis, the *breakeven point* (the point at which total revenue equals total cost) can be expressed algebraically:

$$\text{Breakeven point (in units)} \quad = \frac{\text{Total fixed cost}}{\text{Price/unit} - \text{Variable cost/unit}} \quad (5\text{-}1)$$

where total fixed cost = indirect costs such as rent, interest on debt, property taxes, insurance, executive salaries, depreciation, and other costs which do not vary with volume

price/unit = selling price for the item

variable cost/unit = direct costs per unit which can be charged directly and specifically to the product and which are constant per unit of output over large ranges of volume

Using Eq. (5-1), we can calculate the breakeven point for the new product:

BREAKEVEN POINT CALCULATED

$$\text{Breakeven point (in units)} = \frac{\text{Total fixed cost}}{\text{Price/unit} - \text{Variable cost/unit}} \quad (5\text{-}1)$$

$$= \frac{\$1,500,000}{\$7.50 - \$4.50}$$

$$= \frac{\$1,500,000}{\$3.00}$$

$$= 500,000 \text{ units annually}$$

Now suppose the sales manager estimates that the mean expected sales volume for the new product for the coming year is 600,000 units. When asked about the variability of this estimate, she indicates chances are 2 to 1 that sales will be within 300,000 of the mean she has estimated. Using the same technique first illustrated in Section 6 of Chapter 4, Supplying the Numbers, we illustrate in Figure 5-1 the distribution of sales our sales manager seems to have in mind.

From Figure 5-1 we can see that the area between the left-hand tail of the distribution and the 900,000-unit point is ⅚, or .8333, of the total area under the curve. From Appendix Table 1, we can determine that the 900,000-unit point is about .97 standard deviation to the right of the mean of this distribution. Since

$$.97 \text{ standard deviation} = 300,000 \text{ units}$$

$$1 \text{ standard deviation} = 309,278 \text{ units}$$

1 *What is the probability of at least breaking even?* On the last page we found the breakeven point to be 500,000 units, which is $(600,000 - 500,000)/309,278$ or .323 standard deviation *below* the mean of the distribution of sales. Because the normal distribution is symmetric, the chance of being *at or above some number of standard deviations below the mean* is the same as the chance of being *at or below the same number of standard deviations above the mean.* Hence Appendix Table 1 tells us that there is a .626 chance of at least breaking even, that is, having a sales volume of at least 500,000 units.

2 *What is the probability that profits from the new product would be at least $500,000?* Since the new product's contribution per unit (price − variable cost) is $3, for profits to be at least $500,000, sales will have to be at least $500,000/$3 = 166,667 units above the breakeven point of 500,000 units. Sales of 666,667 units would be $(666,667 - 600,000)/309,278$ or .216 standard deviation *above* the mean of the sales distribution. Again from Appendix Table 1, we can see that the chances are only about .586 that sales would be less than 666,667 units; thus the chance that sales would be no less than that figure (and that profits will be at least $500,000) is $1 - .586 = .414$.

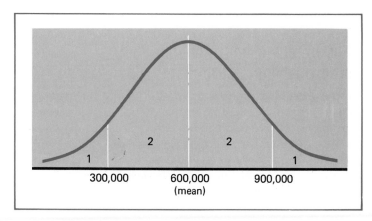

FIGURE 5-1
Sales manager's estimate of distribution.

202

CHAPTER 5

CALCULATING THE
PROBABILITY THAT
LOSSES WILL BE AT
SOME LEVEL

3 *What are the chances that the new product would cause us to lose $250,000 or more?* To lose that much money, sales would have to be at least $250,000/$3 = 83,333 units below the 500,000 unit breakeven point, that is, no higher than 416,667 units. This sales level would be (600,000 − 416,667)/309,278 = .593 standard deviation *below* the mean of the sales distribution. Appendix Table 1 tells us that there is a .723 chance of sales being above this point. Therefore, the chance of sales being no more than 416,667 units (and hence of our losing at least $250,000) is 1 − .723 = .277.

In comparing this new product with other possible uses of company resources, management now has these probability estimates:

a The chance of breaking even on the product is better than .625.
b The chance of making at least $500,000 on this product is .415.
c The chance of losing $250,000 on this product is .277.

CONTRIBUTION OF
PROBABILITY
ESTIMATES TO
THIS DECISION

With these probability estimates, most managements would consider the new product to be an attractive alternative. The contribution that this analysis has made to managerial decision making is simply that it has allowed new-product decisions to be made under market conditions involving risk as to future sales volumes. Whenever questions exist about the levels of future demand, decision analysis of this type will be of considerable use in choosing among alternatives.

In the foregoing example, we have considered sales volume to be the random variable and we used it to answer questions about expected profits accordingly. It is also possible for decision makers to consider fixed costs, variable costs, and price as random variables to test the effect of their variability on profits. When one of these four variables—sales volume, price, variable cost, and fixed cost—is considered a random variable, the analysis is accomplished exactly as we have illustrated it above. However, if all four become random variables *simultaneously,* the statistical calculations are greatly complicated because of the relationships which do exist among the variables. In any case, even though the problem *can* be handled statistically, it is more properly a part of an advanced analysis in this area.

ASSUMPTIONS ABOUT
NORMALITY

Finally, before we leave this topic, we should remember that, once again, we have assumed that the random variable "sales volume" is normally distributed. If we have strong reason to suspect that this is not the case, there are more advanced statistical tests which will confirm or deny our suspicions; however, these are beyond the scope of this text.

2 Combining unit monetary values and probability distributions

PROBABILITY WITHOUT
THE EXPECTED VALUE
OF THE PROFIT OR
LOSS

In the previous examples of the use of the normal probability distribution (our new-product example on pages 172 to 175 and our cost-volume-profit example), we have calculated answers in terms of *probabilities;* in the case of the new product, for example, we determined that the chances of a loss were .356; in the cost-volume-profit example, we calculated three probability values: (1) the probability of at least breaking even, (2) the probability of making at least $500,000 profit, and (3) the probability of losing $250,000 or more.

All these probability values we calculated represent useful information to the decision maker; however, in none of the examples above have we determined the *expected value* of the loss or profit, but only whether we would have a loss or earn a profit.

Both the probability of loss *and* the expected value of that loss are important to the decision maker. Why? Look at the example of Figure 4-5, on page 174; when we discussed this problem, we calculated the probability of loss at .356; this looks like more than a safe bet on a new product. But suppose that if sales turn out to be in the loss area (lower than 80 units a month), we could lose from $100,000 to $1,000,000 a year, depending on the specific sales level within that loss area. In a situation such as this, the decision maker needs to know *not only* what his or her probability of loss is, *but also* what the expected dollar value of that loss is (in this problem the loss area is from 80 units per month all the way down to zero unit sales). Let us look now at a procedure for determining such monetary values.

▓ USING UNIT LOSS AND EXPECTED LOSS

In Figure 5-2, we have illustrated a probability distribution representing management's best estimate of the operating time per year of a proposed new machine. We have assumed that the distribution of operating times will be a normal distribution with a mean of 1,500 hours and a standard deviation of 500 hours. Prior accounting calculations indicate that we would earn a profit on this machine if it operated more than 900 hours annually, that we would break even on this new machine at an operating level of exactly 900 hours a year, and that we would lose $6 per hour for every hour below the breakeven level.

In Figure 5-3 we have repeated the distribution in Figure 5-2 but added our unit loss line (line *AB*), which we shall describe as a line with a slope of $6 (the per-hour loss for each hour of operation below 900). The shaded area in Figure 5-3 represents the probability of the machine operating fewer than 900 hours annually. Using the methods illustrated earlier, this probability can be determined to be about .116. It is at this point that we can employ one of the very useful features of the normal distribution. The availability of Appendix Table 3 (Unit Normal Loss Integral, or UNLI) makes the

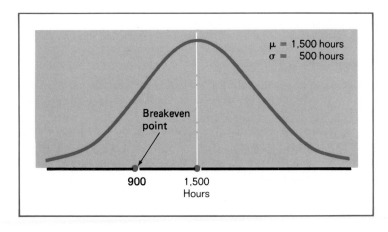

$\mu = 1{,}500$ hours
$\sigma = 500$ hours

Breakeven point

900   1,500
Hours

FIGURE 5-2
Probability distribution of estimated yearly operating hours of proposed new machine.

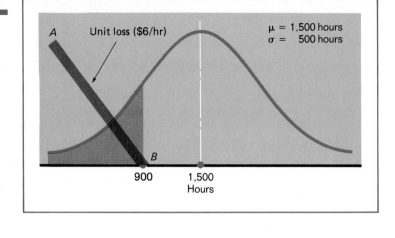

FIGURE 5-3
Distribution of
estimated yearly
operating hours with
unit loss line
illustrated.

CALCULATING THE
EXPECTED LOSS USING
THE UNIT NORMAL
LOSS INTEGRAL

calculation of the expected loss a very straightforward process. The use of Appendix Table 3 permits us to multiply the $6 unit loss times *every one* of the probabilities between 900 hours and the left-hand tail of the distribution in Figure 5-3 and to sum the total of these multiplications.

This problem, illustrated in Figure 5-3, can be solved with these three steps:

1 First determine how many standard deviations there are between the mean (1,500 hours) and the breakeven point (900 hours).

$$\frac{1,500 - 900}{500} = 1.2 \text{ standard deviations}$$

2 Next look up the value which corresponds to 1.2 standard deviations in Appendix Table 3 (UNLI):

$$1.2 \text{ standard deviations} = \text{a table value of } .0561$$

3 Third, to calculate the total expected loss, multiply together the unit loss, the standard deviation of the distribution (in hours), and the value obtained in step 2 from Appendix Table 3:

$$\text{Expected loss} = \$6 \times 500 \times .0561 = \$168.30$$

EXAMINING THE
SIGNIFICANCE OF
THE ANSWER

Now let us examine the significance of the value $168.30. Instead of knowing only that there is a .116 chance of losing money on the purchase of this machine due to the variation in estimated operating hours, we can now state this loss in more definite monetary terms by saying that the expected loss on this purchase is $168.30. But why would a manager authorize the purchase of a machine with an expected loss? Simply because the machine will earn a profit for every hour that it operates *above* 900 hours annually, and since the probability of its operating more than 900 hours is (1.000 −

.116 = .884), this profit is expected to be far larger than the expected loss. All we have done is pinpoint for the manager the total possible extent of the loss because he or she is unable to specify the distribution of operating hours with more precision.

RELATIONSHIP BETWEEN EXPECTED LOSS AND EXPECTED VALUE OF PERFECT INFORMATION

In Chapter 4 we first introduced the idea that there is a maximum price managers should pay for perfect information about the future, and we labeled this value EVPI (the expected value of perfect information). In this example just concluded, let us assume that our manager could buy a perfect predictor, an analysis of the future which would eliminate completely *any* chance of loss; in our example he should be willing to pay up to $168.30 for such "perfect information," but no more. To pay more for perfect information (assuming of course that one can get it in the first place) than the loss which obtains because you lack perfect information is foolish. In our example, the loss we expect to incur with the estimates we have available to us (the estimated mean and standard deviation of the distribution of operating hours) is only $168.30; that is all we would pay to eliminate uncertainty completely (a condition possible only if we had perfect information).

HOW MUCH SHOULD YOU PAY FOR MORE INFORMATION ABOUT THE FUTURE?

Knowing that it is all but impossible to purchase "perfect information" about the future leaves one with the problem of how to evaluate new information in terms of what it costs and what it is worth. Lots of new information is available to decision makers in the form of market surveys, forecasts, interviews, and the like, all of which cost money but may reduce one's uncertainty about the future.

WHAT IS INFORMATION
ABOUT THE FUTURE
WORTH?

Using the same proposed new-machine example from the section just above, let us suppose that a more detailed analysis of past operating hours of similar machines and a concerted survey of other firms using the same type of machine could together give us additional information about the future. Having this new information would not enable us to predict with complete certainty the number of operating hours, but it would enable us to specify the *distribution* of future operating hours more precisely; more specifically, having additional information (if it is any good) should allow us to reduce the *standard deviation* of the estimated distribution of operating hours, that is, to be more sure about the range of hours within which the machine will likely operate.

To illustrate this point, we shall assume that we have been offered a detailed analysis of operating time of similar machines in organizations similar to ours; the asking price of this new information is $50. This new information is of sufficient quality to enable us to specify the distribution of operating times with greater precision (to be more sure about the range within which our proposed machine will operate). Specifically, it will allow us to reduce our estimate of the standard deviation of the distribution of operating hours from 500 to 350 hours. Is the new information worth $50?

Figure 5-4 illustrates the new distribution of estimated operating hours which would be possible if we purchased the detailed analysis. Using the same three-step procedure we employed before, we can compute the expected loss as follows:

1 First, determine how many standard deviations there are between the mean (1,500 hours) and the breakeven point (900 hours):

$$\frac{1,500 - 900}{350} = 1.71 \text{ standard deviations}$$

2 Next, look up the value which corresponds to 1.71 standard deviations in Appendix Table 3:

$$1.71 \text{ standard deviations} = \text{a table value of } .01785$$

3 To calculate the total expected loss, multiply together the unit loss, the new standard deviation of the distribution (in hours), and the value obtained in step 2 from Appendix Table 3:

$$\$6 \times 350 \times .01785 = \$37.49$$

We can see from these results that our expected loss (with the new information) is $37.49. This is a reduction in loss from the previous amount—a saving of

$$\$168.30 - \$37.49 = \$130.81$$

As the new information is being offered to us for $50, we should buy it. In this example, the expenditure of $50 will enable us to reduce our expected loss by $130.81, a handsome return on our investment in new information. Even if the cost of the analysis were to rise substantially, it would pay us to go ahead and purchase the information as long as the cost did not rise above $130.81 and as long as the quality of that new information did not diminish.

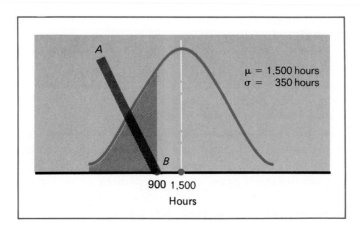

FIGURE 5-4
Distribution of
estimated operating
hours possible with
new information.

Notice that the more certain we are about the future (the smaller the standard deviation is in relation to the mean of the distribution), the less new information is worth to us. If the manager who is estimating the operating hours of our proposed new machine is *almost* positive that it will operate exactly 1,500 hours, the value of new information is almost zero. If the manager is *absolutely* certain that the new machine in our example of Figure 5-3 will operate *exactly* 1,500 hours a year with no chance of this figure being more or less than 1,500, the standard deviation would be zero, and thus the expected loss zero. In numerical terms, with these assumptions added to the problem illustrated in Figure 5-3, expected loss would be

$$\text{Expected loss} = \$6 \times 0 \times 0 \xleftarrow{} \begin{array}{l}\text{As } \sigma \text{ gets smaller, } (1{,}500 - 900)/\sigma \text{ gets larger} \\ \text{and the value of UNLI in Appendix Table 3} \\ \text{decreases to zero.}\end{array}$$
$$= \$0$$

▨ THE EXPECTED VALUE OF SAMPLE INFORMATION (EVSI)

Managers do not really search for "perfect information"; rather, they evaluate the worth to their organizations of additional information. This additional information may be purchased or provided by adding "experts" to the staff. In the case of quality control, additional information is obtained by taking another sample. In any case, however, the managerial decision is always the same, that is, how to evaluate the cost of additional information against the expected benefits that information will provide to the decision process. In more formal terminology, the expected value of this new information is often referred to symbolically as EVSI, an acronym for the *expected value of sample information*. Our example just concluded has illustrated how to compute EVSI and how to compare it with the cost of the new information to determine whether to buy it.

PERFECT INFORMATION
AND SAMPLE
INFORMATION

▨ UNIT MONETARY VALUES AND BOTH SIDES OF THE NORMAL DISTRIBUTION

In each of the two examples just completed of combining unit monetary values and the normal probability distribution, we have concerned ourselves with only one side of the probability distribution. More specifically, we calculated in each case the sum of a set of probability values each of which had been multiplied by a constant, $6 in our example. In these two examples, we limited our analysis to that portion of the probability distribution representing potential loss situations.

USING THE UNIT
NORMAL LOSS
INTEGRAL ON BOTH
SIDES OF THE
DISTRIBUTION

The procedure that we have employed can be used equally well to analyze the entire set of outcomes represented by a normal distribution, both those that are *favorable* (profits) and those that are *not favorable* (losses). We illustrate this procedure now by using a problem similar to the one involving our proposed purchase of a machine. In the case represented by the distribution in Figure 5-5, we estimate the mean of the distribution of operating hours as 1,850 hours and the standard deviation of this distribution as 600 hours. In this particular case, our cost information indicates that we will break even at 1,600 operating hours. Below 1,600 hours we will lose $15 an hour (line

AB), and above 1,600 hours we will earn $11 an hour from the operation of the machine (line *CB*).

The shaded area of the distribution in Figure 5-5 to the left of the breakeven point (1,600 hours) is the loss area. The shaded portion of the distribution to the right of the 1,600-hour value is the profit area. Our task this time is twofold; first we must multiply the $15-per-hour unit loss by each of the probabilities under the normal curve from the 1,600-hour value to the *left*-hand tail and sum these; then we multiply the $11-per-hour unit profit by each of the probabilities under the curve from the 1,600-hour value to the *right*-hand tail and sum these. Knowing the expected loss and the expected profit will allow us to evaluate the "net profit" expected to be earned by the machine simply by subtracting the results in the first step from those in the second.

The procedure is as follows:

(Step 1) Expected loss	**(Step 2)** Expected profit
a. $\dfrac{1,850 - 1,600}{600} = .417$ std. dev.	**a.** $\dfrac{1,850 - 1,600}{600} = .417$ std. dev.
b. Appendix Table 3 value of .417 = .2236	**b.** Appendix Table 3 value of .417 = .2236
	c. Add .417 to .2236:
	.2236 .4170 .6406
c. Expected loss: $15 × 600 × .2236 = $2012.40	(In two-sided cases such as this when the loss or profit line crosses the mean, the procedure is to *add* the z score to the value in the table)*
	d. Expected profit: $11 × 600 × .6406 = $4,227.96

* The derivation of this procedure can be found in R. Schlaifer, *Probability and Statistics for Business Decisions* (New York: McGraw-Hill Book Company, 1959), p. 707.

Subtracting step 1 from step 2 ($4,227.96 − $2,012.40), we get $2,215.56, the expected net profit from the machine purchase given our present information about the future. If the value $2,215.56, when related to the investment required, represents a return felt by management to be adequate, they would purchase the machine.

3 Replacement analysis: items which fail over time

One area to which decision theory concepts can be applied with considerable effectiveness is the replacement of items which fail in use over time. There are many examples of this situation: light bulbs, heating filters, electric motors,

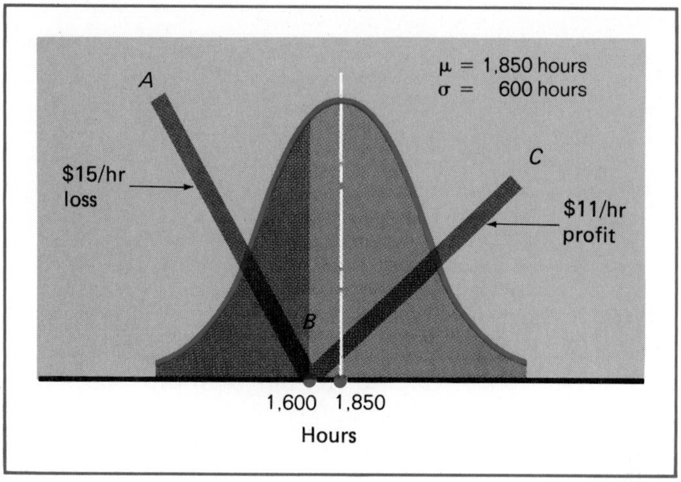

FIGURE 5-5
Estimated distribution
of operating hours
illustrated with unit
loss and unit profit.

and valve washers, to name but a few. Although the exact time of failure of these items cannot be known in advance, it is possible to specify from past information a probability distribution of the lives of the items, that is, to specify the probability of failure for any future time period. With this probability distribution and with appropriate cost information, it is possible to calculate an optimal replacement policy.

In replacing heating filters in a facility, there are basically two alternatives:

1 Replace all the filters at the same time
2 Replace the filters as they become clogged

When all the filters are replaced at one time, the labor cost per filter to accomplish this replacement is only a fraction of what it is when filters are replaced on an individual basis as they become inoperative.

Our problem concerns a large federal agency where cost records indicate that the 1,000 filters in the facility can be replaced for $.25 labor cost each if done on a mass replacement basis. If, however, each filter is replaced as it becomes clogged, the labor cost is $1.75 per filter. Since the filters are bought in large quantities, the cost of the filter itself is $.25 under both replacement alternatives. The past behavior of filters (their life expectancy) is given in Table 5-1. From the information in this table, the average life of the 1,000 filters is computed like this:

PROBLEM
ILLUSTRATING
REPLACEMENT
ANALYSIS APPROACH

$$
\begin{aligned}
.10 \times 1 \text{ month} &= .10 \text{ month} \\
.15 \times 2 \text{ months} &= .30 \text{ month} \\
.25 \times 3 \text{ months} &= .75 \text{ month} \\
.30 \times 4 \text{ months} &= 1.20 \text{ months} \\
.20 \times 5 \text{ months} &= \underline{1.00 \text{ month}} \\
\text{Average life} &= 3.35 \text{ months}
\end{aligned}
$$

	\multicolumn{5}{c}{**Month after replacement**}
	1	**2**	**3**	**4**	**5**
Percent of original filters which have failed *by* the end of that month (cumulative)	10	25	50	80	100
Percent of original filters which fail *in* that month	10	15	25	30	20

TABLE 5-1
Life expectancy of
heating filters

TOTAL COST IF WE
REPLACE AT FAILURE

If we begin any time period with 1,000 filters, we shall be replacing 1,000/3.35 = 299 per month over time if we replace them as they fail; at $2 each ($1.75 labor + $.25 filter) our monthly total replacement cost will be $598 (299 × $2).

Perhaps it would be possible to reduce the cost of this operation by replacing all filters at a fixed interval (say, 4 months). Of course, if we did this, we would still have to replace filters which failed during this interval because we must maintain a constant level of airflow. Calculating the number which would have to be replaced each month is not difficult if we introduce a few symbols:

$$N_0 = \text{original number (1,000)}$$

$$N_1 = \text{number replaced at end of month 1}$$

NOTATION FOR
REPLACEMENT AT
FIXED INTERVAL

$$N_2 = \text{number replaced at end of month 2}$$

$$N_3 = \text{number replaced at end of month 3}$$

$$N_4 = \text{number replaced at end of month 4}$$

$$N_5 = \text{number replaced at end of month 5}$$

$$P_1 = \text{probability of failure during month 1}$$

$$P_2 = \text{probability of failure during month 2}$$

$$P_3 = \text{probability of failure during month 3}$$

$$P_4 = \text{probability of failure during month 4}$$

$$P_5 = \text{probability of failure during month 5}$$

We can now symbolize the number to be replaced in each month as follows:

NUMBER REPLACED
EACH MONTH

$N_1 = N_0 \times P_1$
(The original ones are 1 month old.)

$N_2 = (N_0 \times P_2) + (N_1 \times P_1)$
(The original ones are 2 months old; filters replaced at the end of month 2 are 1 month old.)

$N_3 = (N_0 \times P_3) + (N_1 \times P_2) + (N_2 \times P_1)$
(The original ones are 3 months old; those replaced at the end of month 1 are 2 months old; those replaced at the end of month 2 are 1 month old.)

$N_4 = (N_0 \times P_4) + (N_1 \times P_3) + (N_2 \times P_2) + (N_3 \times P_1)$

(The original ones are 4 months old; those replaced at the end of month 1 are 3 months old; those replaced at the end of month 2 are 2 months old; those replaced at the end of month 3 are 1 month old.)

$N_5 = (N_0 \times P_5) + (N_1 \times P_4) + (N_2 \times P_3) + (N_3 \times P_2) + (N_4 \times P_1)$

(The original ones are 5 months old; those replaced at the end of month 1 are 4 months old; those replaced at the end of month 2 are 3 months old; those replaced at the end of month 3 are 2 months old; those replaced at the end of month 4 are 1 month old.)

And we can calculate the number of filters to be replaced in each month by replacing the symbols with the appropriate numerical values:

$N_1 = 1,000 \times .10$ $= 100$

$N_2 = (1,000 \times .15) + (100 \times .10)$ $= 160$

$N_3 = (1,000 \times .25) + (100 \times .15) + (160 \times .10)$ $= 281$

$N_4 = (1,000 \times .30) + (100 \times .25) + (160 \times .15) + (281 \times .10)$ $= 377$

$N_5 = (1,000 \times .20) + (100 \times .30) + (160 \times .25) + (281 \times .15)$

$+ (377 \times .10) = 350$

The various alternatives open to us can be compared by the use of Table 5-2. From Table 5-2 we see that from the standpoint of total cost, the expense would be least if we replaced all filters at the end of 2 months; those which failed during that period we would replace on an individual basis. The total cost saved by this solution would be $598 (the old method) less $510 (the new method), or about $88 per month.

COMPARISON OF COST
OF ALTERNATIVES

4 Decision trees: graphic displays of the decision-making process

In Chapter 2 we introduced the idea of a probability tree in connection with the study of joint probabilities; we indicated how this "tree" technique could

PROBABILITY TREES
AND DECISION TREES

TABLE 5-2
Labor and material
cost of filter
replacement

Replacement at end of	Cost of replacing 1,000 filters at $.50 each ($.25 labor + $.25 material)	Cost of replacing those which failed at $2 each ($1.75 labor + $.25 material)	Total cost	Cost per month
Month 1	$500	$ 200 (100 × $2)	$ 700	$700
Month 2	500	520 (260 × $2)	1,020	510
Month 3	500	1,082 (541 × $2)	1,582	527
Month 4	500	1,836 (918 × $2)	2,336	584
Month 5	500	2,536 (1268 × $2)	3,036	607

help us analyze the possible outcomes of three successive coin tosses in terms of the probabilities of the various outcomes. When these "trees" contain both probabilities of outcomes *and* conditional monetary values of those outcomes such that expected values can be computed, the common practice is to refer to them as *decision trees.*

DECISION TREE FUNDAMENTALS

Decision trees are usually drawn with standard symbols; in Figure 5-6 we represent the simple decision of making a choice between going to the movies and staying home and watching TV or our VCR. The square node symbolizes a decision point; each alternative is followed by a circular node from which branches on the tree represent the possible outcomes or states of nature which *could* result. In this example, it would be unrealistic to add probability values to the outcomes because we could call up the theater, look in *TV Guide* or look in our cassette library and find out before the fact what the outcome was going to be. Therefore, in this simple case, we would have nearly perfect information. In Figure 5-7, we have presented a decision problem of similar size, but one which allows us to estimate some probability values representing the likelihood of the outcomes. In this problem, we can also introduce some conditional values; then we can compute expected values for the two alternatives and make a choice using that criterion. We have numbered the two state-of-nature nodes in this illustration.

Figure 5-8 repeats the decision tree from Figure 5-7 but adds our estimates of what our $1,000 stock investment would be worth a year from now and what our savings account would be worth under the two conditions of a rising and a falling stock market. We have assumed that the savings account pays 5 percent interest and that the stocks pay no dividends. In our simple investment problem, the expected value of a $1,000 investment in savings

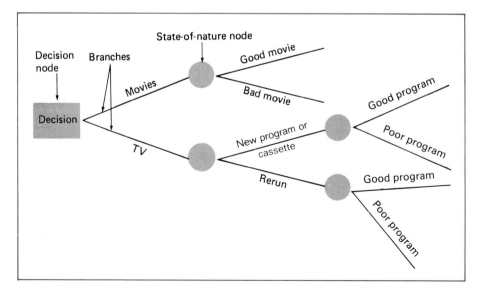

FIGURE 5-6
Simple decision tree.

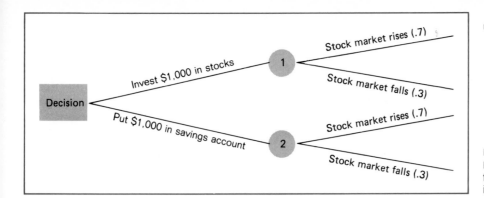

FIGURE 5-7
Use of decision tree
to structure an
investment decision.

(given our assessment) would remain stable (except for interest) regardless of what happened to the stock market. In Figure 5-8 we have shown the expected value of the two state-of-nature nodes, 1 and 2. Since node 1 has the greater expected value, a decision maker using expected value as his or her decision criterion would choose the branch between the decision node and state-of-nature node 1, that is, "invest $1000 in stocks."

ROLLBACK OR
FOLDBACK PROCEDURE

The general process we use in decision tree analysis is to work *backward* through the tree (from right to left), computing the expected value of each state-of-nature node. We then choose the particular branch leaving a *decision* node which leads to the *state-of-nature* node with the highest expected value. This process is known as *rollback* or *foldback*. This example (and the one to come) could have been set up as a payoff table to show the same concepts.

▮ DECISION TREE ILLUSTRATING PLANT INVESTMENT PROBLEM

A MORE COMPLEX
DECISION TREE
PROBLEM

The real managerial value of the decision tree type of analysis is obtained when it is used on more complex kinds of problems, those involving not only

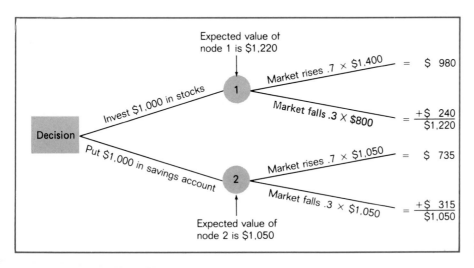

FIGURE 5-8
Use of decision tree
to solve investment
problem.

a greater number of alternatives but also decisions about considerably longer future periods. Consider the following somewhat more complex example.

Stereo Industries, Ltd., must decide to build a large or a small plant to produce a new turntable which is expected to have a market life of 10 years. A large plant will cost $2,800,000 to build and put into operation, while a small plant will cost only $1,400,000 to build and put into operation. The company's best estimate of a discrete distribution of sales over the 10-year period is

PROBABILITY
ESTIMATES

High demand:	Probability = .5
Moderate demand:	Probability = .3
Low demand:	Probability = .2

Cost-volume-profit analysis done by the management at Stereo Industries, Ltd., indicates these conditional outcomes under the various combinations of plant size and market size:

CONDITIONAL VALUES

1 A large plant with high demand would yield $1 million annually in profits.

2 A large plant with moderate demand would yield $600,000 annually in profits.

3 A large plant with low demand would lose $200,000 annually because of production inefficiencies.

4 A small plant with high demand would yield only $250,000 annually in profits, considering the cost of the lost sales because of inability to supply customers.

5 A small plant with moderate demand would yield $450,000 annually in profits because the cost of lost sales would be somewhat lower.

6 A small plant with low demand would yield $550,000 annually because the plant size and the market size would be matched fairly optimally.

INFORMATION ON
THE DECISION TREE

The decision tree in Figure 5-9 illustrates the alternatives graphically. For each of the combinations of plant size and the market size, we have indicated (1) the probability that that outcome will happen, (2) the conditional profit the company would receive if that outcome happened, and (3) the expected value of that outcome. Our decision process is the same as before. We work backward through the tree from right to left (using the rollback approach), computing the expected value of each state-of-nature node. We then choose that particular branch leaving a *decision* node which leads to the *state-of-nature* node with the highest expected value.

▇ CONCLUSIONS AND ASSUMPTIONS
BEHIND THOSE CONCLUSIONS

CHOOSING THE
OPTIMAL ALTERNATIVE

From our decision tree analysis it appears that building a large plant will produce $1,300,000 more profit over the next 10 years ($3,600,000 − $2,300,000 = $1,300,000) and thus, given the information we have, represents the better alternative for that company. We must remember, however, that the assumptions made in this problem include the following:

1 We allowed only *three* discrete levels of demand in our estimates of the future; demand *could* be continuously distributed.

2 We permitted only *two* sizes of plant to be built in response to our estimates of future demand when, in reality, many different sizes could be designed and built.

3 We did *not* allow the small plant to be *expanded* (at an additional cost) in response to either moderate or high demand, or the large plant to be sold.

4 We considered the future as one 10-year period; estimates of demand and benefits could be made for each individual year.

5 We considered the profits received in the tenth year equal to those in the first year; that is, we did not use discounting to place more value on benefits received in the earlier years. In *this* problem, as a matter of interest, the relative merits of the two alternatives would not have been changed by discounting the future benefits.

▉ REMOVING SOME OF THE ASSUMPTIONS IN DECISION TREE ANALYSIS

Each of the assumptions we made in the problem illustrated in Figure 5-9 could be removed if one were willing to draw a larger decision tree and do more arithmetic. For example, if we had wanted to illustrate our decision

HOW TO REMOVE
THE ASSUMPTIONS

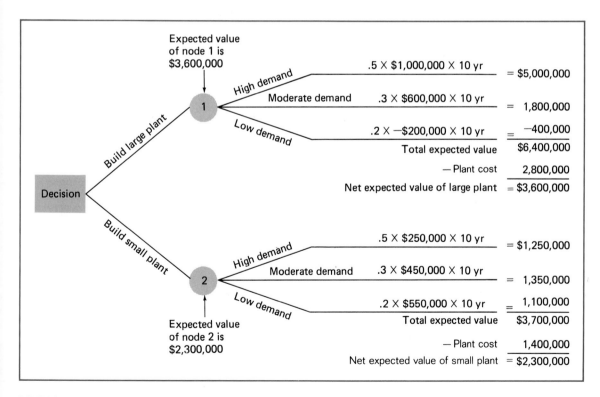

FIGURE 5-9
Decision tree analysis of plant expansion alternatives for Stereo Industries, Ltd.

analysis in two 5-year periods, with three different estimates of demand for *each* of these two periods, the decision tree would have looked like the one in Figure 5-10.

Our process of analysis for the decision tree in Figure 5-10 would involve these steps:

1 Compute the expected value for state-of-nature nodes 3, 4, 5, 6, 7, and 8.

2 Using the probabilities of high, moderate, and low demand for the *first 5 years* and the expected values of nodes 3, 4, and 5, compute the expected value of node 1.

3 Using the probabilities of high, moderate, and low demand for the *first 5 years* and the expected values of nodes 6, 7, and 8, compute the expected value of node 2.

4 Choose the branch leaving the *decision* node which leads to the state-of-nature node (1 or 2) with the higher expected value.

▮ DECISION TREES AND THE EXPECTED VALUE OF NEW INFORMATION

THE VALUE OF WAITING   There are many instances in decision making where the best decision is to wait. Waiting, however, is useless as a strategy unless we spend the time

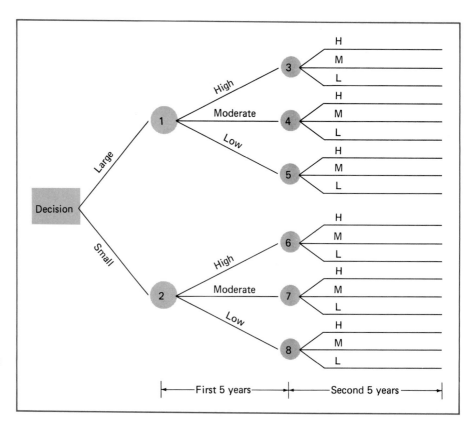

FIGURE 5-10
Illustration of decision tree with estimates of future demand for two separate time periods.

learning about the future; specifically, we need to learn about the risk of future alternatives we may face.

Companies with a new product often decide to build a *pilot plant* before construction of a large commercial facility. In this way, the output of the pilot plant (a much smaller facility) provides the company with information on market acceptance, production yields, design engineering problems, and equipment difficulties. The decision tree in Figure 5-11 illustrates the sequence of decision nodes and state-of-nature nodes involved in deciding whether to build a pilot plant to study process yields before commercial mass production is begun.

PROBABILITY ESTIMATES

In Figure 5-11 management has estimated that a pilot plant (if it is built) has a .8 chance of a high yield and a .2 chance of a low yield. *If* the pilot plant does show a high yield, management assigns a probability of .85 that the commercial plant will also have a high yield. *If* the pilot plant shows a low yield, there is only a .1 chance that the commercial plant will show a high yield. Finally, management's best assessment of a commercial-size plant *without*

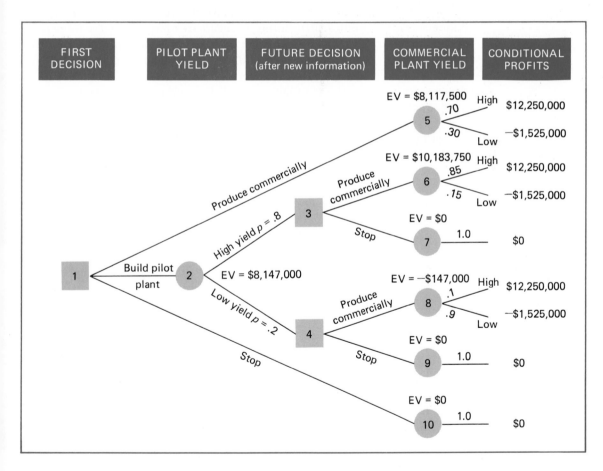

FIGURE 5-11
Decision tree for pilot plant decision.

building a pilot plant first is a .7 chance of high yield. A pilot plant will cost $350,000.

Figure 5-11 shows the expected value (EV) of nodes 5, 6, 7, 8, 9, and 10. Using the rollback procedure, we find that the expected value of node 2 is $8,147,000 (.8 × $10,183,750 + .2 × $0). Our conclusion is that the expected value of the information from the pilot plant is $8,147,000 − $8,117,500 = $29,500. At a cost of $350,000, the pilot plant is not a good idea.

▪ BAYESIAN ANALYSIS AND DECISION TREES

The decision trees in the preceding examples were based on prior probabilities. Posterior probabilities computed with Bayes' theorem are often necessary. To illustrate, we will help Barnes-Wentworth, Inc., an independent Texas oil company, decide whether to buy a geological survey before drilling on a site near Amarillo.

DECISION OUTCOMES

Pamela Barnes, the production manager, expects one of three outcomes if a well is drilled: a dry hole, sour crude, or sweet crude. Whether the crude is sour or sweet depends on the sulfur content. Sour crude has a higher sulfur content, making it more expensive to refine than sweet crude. Numerous other wells drilled in the Amarillo area have been dry 60 percent of the time, sour 20 percent, and sweet 20 percent. Experience indicates that the average loss on a dry well is $50,000. The profit on a sour well is expected to be $200,000. The profit on a sweet well should be $500,000. If Pamela decides not to drill, the company can sell its option on the site to another company for $80,000.

Pamela can buy a geological survey of the site for $25,000. The survey report rates the site as either "favorable" or "unfavorable" and says nothing about whether crude will be sour or sweet. Barnes-Wentworth is a member

RELIABILITY OF SURVEY

of a cartel which issues information on the reliability of geological surveys in south Texas. The cartel estimates that if a dry well has been drilled, then a later survey would be favorable only 10 percent of the time. If the well is sour, a survey would be favorable 40 percent of the time. Finally, if the well is sweet, the survey would be favorable 50 percent of the time.

The decision tree for this problem is shown in Figure 5-12. Let's start the analysis by organizing the unconditional prior probability information available to Pamela:

PRIOR PROBABILITIES: DRILLING WITHOUT A SURVEY

$$P(\text{dry}) = .60$$

$$P(\text{sour}) = .20$$

$$P(\text{sweet}) = .20$$

These probabilities are entered on the branches leaving node 8 (after the decision to drill without a survey).

The conditional probabilities of the type of survey report, given the type of well are:

CONDITIONAL PROBABILITIES: TYPE OF REPORT GIVEN TYPE OF WELL

$$P(\text{favorable} \mid \text{dry}) = .10$$

$$P(\text{unfavorable} \mid \text{dry}) = .90$$

PAMELA BARNES' DRILLING PROBLEM

```
                                                                    DRILLING    EXPECTED   DRILLING     PROBA-
                                                                    DECISION     VALUE     OUTCOME      BILITY      PAYOFF
                                                                    ========    ========   ========     ======      ======
                                                                +-- SELL OPTION ----------------------------------------     $80,000
                                                                :
                                                                :                                  +-- DRY    25.00000%   ($50,000)
                                                                :                                  :
                                                           [3]--+-- DRILL ------$262,500 ---(6)----+-- SOUR   33.33333%   $200,000
                                                                                                   :
                                                                                                   +-- SWEET  41.66667%   $500,000

                                                                +-- SELL OPTION ----------------------------------------     $80,000
                                                                :
                                                                :                                  +-- DRY    71.05263%   ($50,000)
                                                                :                                  :
                                                           [4]--+-- DRILL ------ $61,842 ---(7)----+-- SOUR   15.78947%   $200,000
                                                                                                   :
                                                                                                   +-- SWEET  13.15789%   $500,000

                                                                +-- SELL OPTION ----------------------------------------     $80,000
                                                                :
                                                                :                                  +-- DRY    60.00000%   ($50,000)
                                                                :                                  :
                                                           [5]--+-- DRILL ------$110,000 ---(8)----+-- SOUR   20.00000%   $200,000
                                                                                                   :
                                                                                                   +-- SWEET  20.00000%   $500,000
```

```
                  BUY      EXPECTED   SURVEY    PROBA-
PAYOFF          SURVEY?     VALUE     RESULT    BILITY     PAYOFF
======          =======    =======    ======    ======     ======
                                   +-- FAVORABLE    24%   $262,500 ---[3]
                                   :
               +---YES $123,800 ---(2)
               :                   :
               :                   +-- UNFAVORABLE  76%    $80,000 ---[4]
$123,800 ---[1]
               :
               +---NO -------------------------------------$110,000 ---[5]
```

INPUT DATA AND BAYES' REVISIONS

DRILLING OUTCOME	PRIOR	PROFIT
===	===	===
DRY	60%	($50,000)
SOUR	20%	$200,000
SWEET	20%	$500,000

PROFIT FROM=> $80,000
SELLING OPTION

	SURVEY RESULT PROBABILITIES	
DRILLING OUTCOME	FAVORABLE	UNFAVORABLE
===	===	===
DRY	10%	90%
SOUR	40%	60%
SWEET	50%	50%

JOINT PROBABILITIES	
FAVORABLE	UNFAVORABLE
===	===
6%	54%
8%	12%
10%	10%
24%	76% <=PROBABILITY OF SURVEY RESULTS

$25,000 <=COST OF SURVEY

POSTERIOR PROBABILITIES	
FAVORABLE	UNFAVORABLE
===	===
25.00000%	71.05263%
33.33333%	15.78947%
41.66667%	13.15789%

FIGURE 5-12
Decision tree for drilling problem.

$$P(\text{favorable} \mid \text{sour}) \quad = .40$$

$$P(\text{unfavorable} \mid \text{sour}) \quad = .60$$

$$P(\text{favorable} \mid \text{sweet}) \quad = .50$$

$$P(\text{unfavorable} \mid \text{sweet}) = .50$$

These probabilities cannot be used directly. We need the posterior probabilities of the type of well, given the type of survey report. We also need the probability of a favorable or unfavorable report following node 2. We can compute these probabilities using the same format that we used in our discussion of Bayes' theorem in Chapter 2. Table 5-3 presents the computations.

Notice how the probabilities change depending on the type of report. There is a probability of .25 that Pamela will hit a dry well if she drills after a favorable report. The probability increases to .71 if she drills after an unfavorable report. Without a report, the probability is .60.

WHAT TO DO AT EACH DECISION POINT

The rollback procedure for this tree is identical to that of the preceding examples. At node 3, after a favorable report, the best decision is to drill. At node 4, after an unfavorable report, the best decision is to sell the option on the site. At node 5, without a report, the best decision is to drill.

VALUE OF THE SURVEY INFORMATION

Should Pamela buy the survey? The net expected value with a survey (at node 2) is $123,800 − $25,000 = $98,800. This compares with an expected value of $110,000 from a decision not to buy. Thus Pamela should not buy the survey and should drill on the site. For the purchase of the survey to be a good decision, the cost would have to be less than $13,800; ($123,800 − $110,000).

DECISION TREES ON THE MICROCOMPUTER

You probably noticed that Figure 5-12 (Pamela's decision tree) looks like output from a computer. In fact, we constructed the tree and did the rollback procedure using the Lotus 1-2-3 spreadsheet program on a microcomputer. Similar analysis can be done with other spreadsheet programs and with decision-tree software like "Supertree" and "Arborist." A discussion of how to do this kind of analysis is given by J. Morgan Jones in "Decision Analysis Using Spreadsheets," *The European Journal of Operational Research*, 1985.

TABLE 5-3
Pamela's posterior probabilities

Report	Event	P(event)	P(report|event)	P(report, event)	P(event|report)
Favorable	Dry	.60	.10	.60 × .10 = .06	.06/.24 = .2500
	Sour	.20	.40	.20 × .40 = .08	.08/.24 = .3333
	Sweet	.20	.50	.20 × .50 = .10	.10/.24 = .4167
				P(favorable) = .24	
Unfavorable	Dry	.60	.90	.60 × .90 = .54	.54/.76 = .7105
	Sour	.20	.60	.20 × .60 = .12	.12/.76 = .1579
	Sweet	.20	.50	.20 × .50 = .10	.10/.76 = .1316
				P(unfavorable) = .76	

After seeing these results, Pamela wondered if $500,000 was the appropriate figure to use for the profit on a sweet well. She realized that there were only three reasonable courses of action ("strategies") to take: sell her option, drill without buying the survey first, or buy the survey and drill if the report were favorable but sell her option if the report were unfavorable. She wanted to know how her expected profit and optimal course of action depended on that $500,000 figure. Although such a *sensitivity analysis* is tedious to do by hand, it is quite easy to do in Lotus 1-2-3, and Figure 5-13 shows Pamela what to do as the profit on a sweet well varies from $200,000 to $500,000.

SENSITIVITY ANALYSIS

Although Figure 5-13 does not give the exact breakeven points where Pamela's optimal strategy changes, you can use the breakeven analysis techniques from the beginning of this chapter to see that below $312,000, she should sell her option. Between $312,000 and $388,000, she should buy

```
SENSITIVITY ANALYSIS ON SWEET CRUDE PROFIT
==========================================
STRATEGY 1: SELL OPTION
STRATEGY 2: DRILL WITHOUT SURVEY
STRATEGY 3: TAKE SURVEY AND DRILL
                IF FAVORABLE, SELL
                OPTION OTHERWISE
```

SWEET PROFIT	STRATEGY EXPECTED VALUE 1	2	3	OPTIMAL STRATEGY	EXPECTED VALUE	VALUE OF SURVEY
$200,000	$80,000	$50,000	$68,800	1	$80,000	$13,800
$215,000	$80,000	$53,000	$70,300	1	$80,000	$15,300
$230,000	$80,000	$56,000	$71,800	1	$80,000	$16,800
$245,000	$80,000	$59,000	$73,300	1	$80,000	$18,300
$260,000	$80,000	$62,000	$74,800	1	$80,000	$19,800
$275,000	$80,000	$65,000	$76,300	1	$80,000	$21,300
$290,000	$80,000	$68,000	$77,800	1	$80,000	$22,800
$305,000	$80,000	$71,000	$79,300	1	$80,000	$24,300
$320,000	$80,000	$74,000	$80,800	3	$80,800	$25,800
$335,000	$80,000	$77,000	$82,300	3	$82,300	$27,300
$350,000	$80,000	$80,000	$83,800	3	$83,800	$28,800
$365,000	$80,000	$83,000	$85,300	3	$85,300	$27,300
$380,000	$80,000	$86,000	$86,800	3	$86,800	$25,800
$395,000	$80,000	$89,000	$88,300	2	$89,000	$24,300
$410,000	$80,000	$92,000	$89,800	2	$92,000	$22,800
$425,000	$80,000	$95,000	$91,300	2	$95,000	$21,300
$440,000	$80,000	$98,000	$92,800	2	$98,000	$19,800
$455,000	$80,000	$101,000	$94,300	2	$101,000	$18,300
$470,000	$80,000	$104,000	$95,800	2	$104,000	$16,800
$485,000	$80,000	$107,000	$97,300	2	$107,000	$15,300
$500,000	$80,000	$110,000	$98,800	2	$110,000	$13,800

FIGURE 5-13
Sensitivity analysis on profit from sweet crude.

the survey (given that it costs $25,000). Finally, if the profit from a sweet well exceeds $388,000, she should just go ahead and drill, without buying the $25,000 survey.

The last column in Figure 5-13 gives the maximum amount Pamela should pay for the survey at the different profit levels. These figures will be useful to her if the cost of the survey is negotiable.

We have just seen a sensitivity analysis with respect to a payoff. In a similar fashion, it is possible to see how optimal decisions and profits change when probabilities vary. This is especially important when you are using subjective probability estimates in your decision making, and it can be done in a quite straightforward fashion on a microcomputer. The ability to perform such sensitivity analyses greatly enhances the value of decision trees in helping us to make important decisions.

ADVANTAGES OF THE DECISION TREE APPROACH

The decision tree approach we have illustrated enjoys rather wide use today, and for good reason. It has five distinct advantages:

1 *It structures the decision process,* making the user approach decision making in an orderly, sequential fashion.

2 *It requires the decision maker to examine all possible outcomes,* desirable and undesirable ones alike.

3 *It communicates the decision-making process to others* in a very succinct manner, illustrating each assumption about the future.

4 *It allows a group to discuss alternatives* by focusing on each individual financial figure, probability, and underlying assumption—one at a time.

5 *It can be used with a computer,* so that many different sets of assumptions can be simulated to observe the effect of alterations in these assumptions on the final outcome.

5 Decision making with an active opponent

This section will examine situations where one decision maker competes with or is in conflict with another decision maker. Up to this point, we have faced a non-thinking, non-hostile opponent—states of nature. We can now take a brief look at situations in which our opponent is intelligent and trying to "do us in." These types of competitive situations are found in all sorts of activities, in games, sports, and businesses, and in military strategies. The generic term used to characterize these situations is *games,* that is, general situations of conflict over time.

In games, the participants are competitors; the success of one is usually at the expense of the other. Each participant selects and executes those strategies which he believes will result in his "winning the game." In games, the participants make use of deductive and inductive logic in determining a strategy for winning. The mathematics of the theory of games is of interest to us for this reason.

TWO-PERSON ZERO-SUM GAMES

Our treatment of the theory of games will be limited to *two-person* games, that is, situations of conflict where there are only *two* participants. Many management situations, obviously, involve the participation of many persons and thus are not examples of two-person games. The mathematics for three-person and larger games, however, is too complex to include in a text of this type. Just remember that the basics underlying the generation of optimal or winning strategies in conflict situations must respect the same principles of inductive and deductive logic, regardless of the number of participants.

A two-person game is illustrated in Table 5-4. The players, X and Y, are equal in intelligence and ability. Each has a choice of two strategies. Each knows the outcomes (referred to as *payoffs*) for every possible combination of strategies; these are shown in the body of the table. Note that the game is biased against player Y; but since he is required to play, he will do his best. This is analogous to the business situation in which short-run loss is inevitable; these losses must be minimized by good strategy. The solution to this simple game is easily obtained by analyzing the possible strategies of each player:

1 X wins the game only by playing her strategy M; thus she plays M all the time.

2 Y realizes that X will play strategy M all the time and, in an effort to minimize X's gains, plays his strategy Q.

3 The solution to the game is thus M, Q (strategy M and strategy Q).

4 X wins 2 points (Y loses 2 points) each time the game is played; thus the value of the game to X is 2; the value of the game to Y is -2.

The term *value of the game* used in this sense is the average winnings per play over a long series of plays. Though player Y loses this game, he is still playing his optimal strategy; that is, he is minimizing his losses. If he had used strategy R, his losses would have been 3 points per play.

The simple game in Table 5-4 is a two-person zero-sum game. The term *zero-sum* is used because the sum of gains (X wins 2 points per play on average) exactly equals the sum of losses (Y loses 2 points per play on average).

TABLE 5-4
A two-person game

Player X	Player Y	
	Strategy Q	**Strategy R**
Strategy M	X wins 2 points	X wins 3 points
Strategy N	Y wins 1 point	Y wins 2 points

■ STANDARD LANGUAGE FOR GAMES

If we use the standard language for games, we can express them in a much more concise way than we did in Table 5-4. Here is the same game in abbreviated form:

$$X \begin{array}{c} Y \\ \left[\begin{array}{cc} 2 & 3 \\ -1 & -2 \end{array} \right] \end{array}$$

Now we have expressed the game as a *matrix* (a rectangular array of numbers with rows, →, and columns ↓). This matrix is called a *payoff matrix*. The four individual payoff values (2, 3, −1, and −2) are expressed as numbers. A positive number is a payoff to player X (the player who plays the rows), and a negative number is a payoff to player Y (the player who plays the columns). Here are several payoff matrices with a detailed explanation of the payoff possibilities for each player. In each case the *value of the game* is circled.

Example 1

$$X \begin{array}{c} Y \\ \left[\begin{array}{cc} ② & 4 \\ 1 & -3 \end{array} \right] \end{array}$$

Y sees that his only chance to win, −3, occurs if X plays row 2; he realizes X will never play row 2 for that reason. If X plays row 1, Y must play column 1 to reduce his average loss to 2 points instead of 4. The final strategies are X, 1; Y, 1.

Example 2

$$X \begin{array}{c} Y \\ \left[\begin{array}{ccc} 2 & ⓪ & 4 \\ 1 & -3 & 2 \end{array} \right] \end{array}$$

X observes that Y's only chance to win, −3, occurs if X plays row 2; hence X plays row 1 all the time. To minimize his losses, Y then plays column 2. Neither player wins. Strategies: X, 1; Y, 2.

Example 3

$$X \begin{array}{c} Y \\ \left[\begin{array}{cc} 1 & -3 \\ ② & 4 \\ -1 & 5 \end{array} \right] \end{array}$$

X observes that Y can't win if X plays row 2; hence X plays row 2 all the time. Y then must play column 1 to minimize his losses. The optimal strategies are X, 2; Y, 1.

Example 4

$$X \begin{array}{c} Y \\ \left[\begin{array}{ccc} 3 & 2 & ⊖2 \\ 1 & -3 & -4 \\ 0 & 1 & -3 \end{array} \right] \end{array}$$

Y sees that X can't win if Y plays column 3; he therefore plays that column all the time. To minimize her losses, then, X must play row 1. Strategies: X, 1; Y, 3.

In each of the examples above, there is *one* strategy for player X and *one* strategy for player Y that will eventually be played each time. They may experiment for a while, but in time they will adopt the strategy we have illustrated; this assumes, of course, that each player desires to win (or to minimize his or her losses if winning is impossible). In each of these games, each player has a *pure strategy*, one he or she plays all the time. The payoff obtained when each player plays his or her pure strategy is called a *saddle point;* or expressed a little differently, the saddle point is the *value* of a game in which each player has a pure strategy.

A saddle point can be recognized because it is *both* the smallest numerical value in its row *and* the largest numerical value in its column. Consider for a moment the significance of this. Player Y would rather have as a payoff the smallest numerical value in any row. Player X would rather have as a payoff the largest numerical value in any column. Naturally, when one numerical value satisfies both these conditions (a saddle point), both players will be playing optimally if each chooses that value. Of course, not all two-person games have a saddle point. Examination of the game matrix will reveal whether one is present. When a saddle point is present, complex calculations to determine optimal strategies and game value are unnecessary.

Now let us look at other games, some of which have saddle points. In cases where saddle points exist, they are circled and the strategies and value of the game are shown.

$$\begin{bmatrix} 1 & 0 \\ -4 & 3 \end{bmatrix}$$ No saddle point. (There is no payoff which is *both* the smallest value in its row *and* the largest value in its column.)

$$\begin{bmatrix} 6 & ②\\ -1 & -4 \end{bmatrix}$$ Strategies: X, 1; Y, 2; game value: 2. (The payoff, 2, *is* the smallest value in its row and the largest value in its column.)

$$\begin{bmatrix} -7 & 7 & 8 \\ ㋋-4 & -3 & -2 \end{bmatrix}$$ Strategies: X, 2; Y, 1; game value: −4.

$$\begin{bmatrix} 4 & -2 & 3 \\ 0 & 5 & 6 \end{bmatrix}$$ No saddle point.

$$\begin{bmatrix} 1 & 2 \\ 3 & 4 \\ 5 & -6 \end{bmatrix}$$ No saddle point.

$$\begin{bmatrix} ⓪ & 2 \\ -3 & -6 \\ -4 & -3 \end{bmatrix}$$ Strategies: X, 1; Y, 1; game value: 0.

▌ MIXED STRATEGIES

In cases where there is no saddle point, the players resort to a *mixed strategy;* that is, they each play some combination of their rows (or columns). Our task is to determine what proportion of the time X should play each row and what proportion of the time Y should play each column. Following is a simple two-person, zero-sum game. Because there is no saddle point in this game, there are no pure strategies for the players to use.

$$
\begin{array}{c} Y \\ X \begin{bmatrix} 5 & 1 \\ 3 & 4 \end{bmatrix} \end{array}
$$

There is no payoff which is both the smallest value in its row and the largest value in its column.

PORTION OF TIME ON
EACH ROW AND
COLUMN

Our tasks are to see what portion of the time X should spend on each row and what portion of the time Y should play each column. Suppose we let Q equal the proportion of the time X spends on the first row and $1 - Q$ the proportion of the time she spends on row 2. For player Y, we use the notation P and $1 - P$. We can represent this division of time like this:

$$
\begin{array}{cc} & P \quad\; 1 - P \\ \begin{array}{c} Q \\ 1 - Q \end{array} & \begin{bmatrix} 5 & 1 \\ 3 & 4 \end{bmatrix} \end{array}
$$

This indicates to us that

1 Player X plays the first row Q of the time (Q is a fraction between 0 and 1).

2 Player X plays the second row $1 - Q$ of the time.

3 Player Y plays the first column P of the time (P is a fraction between 0 and 1).

4 Player Y plays the second column $1 - P$ of the time.

SOLVING FOR *P* AND *Q*

Now let us solve for the unknown fractions P and Q. Consider player X first. **Logically, X wants to divide her plays between her rows so that she wins as much when Y is playing column 1 as she does when Y is playing column 2.** Business provides an analogy. A certain firm follows course of action A until B looks more profitable, at which point it switches to B. Later if B become less attractive than A, the firm switches back to A. Of course, Y is assumed to be just as intelligent and will adopt *his* best strategy in return. Table 5-5 represents X's expected winnings from playing row 1 Q of the time and row 2 ($1 - Q$) of the time. To make X's expected winnings when Y plays column 1 equal to X's winnings when Y plays column 2, we let $5Q + 3(1 - Q)$ equal $1Q + 4(1 - Q)$ and solve for the Q which makes the two expectations equal to each other:

$$
5Q + 3(1 - Q) = 1Q + 4(1 - Q)
$$

$$
3 + 2Q = 4 - 3Q
$$

	If Y plays column 1	If Y plays column 2
X plays row 1 Q of the time	X wins 5 points Q of the time	X wins 1 point Q of the time
X plays row 2 $1 - Q$ of the time	X wins 3 points $1 - Q$ of the time	X wins 4 points $1 - Q$ of the time
X's expected winnings	$5Q + 3(1 - Q)$ when Y plays column 1	$1Q + 4(1 - Q)$ when Y plays column 2

TABLE 5-5
X's expected winnings

$$5Q = 1$$
$$Q = \tfrac{1}{5}$$

Therefore,

$$1 - Q = \tfrac{4}{5}$$

Applying the same logic to Y's strategies, we can demonstrate that the unknown fractions P and $1 - P$ are $\tfrac{3}{5}$ and $\tfrac{2}{5}$.

RANDOMNESS IN MIXED STRATEGIES

Of course, when we indicate that each player should play a mixed strategy, we imply that the division of time between the rows (or the columns) must be done *randomly* without any discernible pattern. The player who notices a pattern will adjust his *or* her optimal strategy to take advantage of this disclosed strategy.

SOLVING FOR THE VALUE OF THE GAME

CALCULATING THE VALUE OF A GAME

Now that we have the optimal mixed strategies, we can solve for the value of the game. The original game, with the optimal strategies for each player, is

$$\text{X} \begin{array}{cc} & \text{Y} \\ & \begin{array}{cc} \tfrac{3}{5} & \tfrac{2}{5} \end{array} \\ \begin{array}{c} \tfrac{1}{5} \\ \tfrac{4}{5} \end{array} & \begin{bmatrix} 5 & 1 \\ 3 & 4 \end{bmatrix} \end{array}$$

Looking at the game from player X's point of view, we can reason as follows:

1 During the $\tfrac{3}{5}$ of the time that Y plays column 1, X wins 5 points $\tfrac{1}{5}$ of the time and 3 points $\tfrac{4}{5}$ of the time.

2 During the $\tfrac{2}{5}$ of the time that Y plays column 2, X wins 1 point $\tfrac{1}{5}$ of the time and 4 points $\tfrac{4}{5}$ of the time.

Therefore, X's total expected winnings over time are obtained from statements 1 and 2 above:

$$\underset{1}{} \qquad \underset{2}{}$$

$$\tfrac{3}{5}[5(\tfrac{1}{5}) + 3(\tfrac{4}{5})] + \tfrac{2}{5}[1(\tfrac{1}{5}) + 4(\tfrac{4}{5})]$$

$$\tfrac{3}{5}(\tfrac{5}{5} + \tfrac{12}{5}) + \tfrac{2}{5}(\tfrac{1}{5} + \tfrac{16}{5})$$

$$\tfrac{3}{5}(\tfrac{17}{5}) + \tfrac{2}{5}(\tfrac{17}{5}) = \tfrac{17}{5} = \text{value of the game}$$

This means that player X, if she plays her optimal strategies, can expect to win an average payoff of $3\tfrac{2}{5}$ points for each play of the game. From our earlier observation, we know that X will be the winner of this game, since the value is a positive number. If the value of the game had been a negative number, Y would have been the winner. This, of course, could not be true in this particular game, since the game was slanted in X's favor in that it contained no negative payoffs in the original matrix.

We could have arrived at the same value of the game looking at it from Y's point of view:

1 During the $\tfrac{1}{5}$ of the time that X plays row 1, Y loses 5 points $\tfrac{3}{5}$ of the time and 1 point $\tfrac{2}{5}$ of the time.

2 During the $\tfrac{4}{5}$ of the time that X plays row 2, Y loses 3 points $\tfrac{3}{5}$ of the time and 4 points $\tfrac{2}{5}$ of the time.

Therefore, Y's total expected losses over time are obtained from statements 1 and 2:

$$\underset{1}{} \qquad \underset{2}{}$$

$$\tfrac{1}{5}[5(\tfrac{3}{5}) + 1(\tfrac{2}{5})] + \tfrac{4}{5}[3(\tfrac{3}{5}) + 4(\tfrac{2}{5})]$$

$$\tfrac{1}{5}(\tfrac{15}{5} + \tfrac{2}{5}) + \tfrac{4}{5}(\tfrac{9}{5} + \tfrac{8}{5})$$

$$\tfrac{1}{5}(\tfrac{17}{5}) + \tfrac{4}{5}(\tfrac{17}{5}) = \tfrac{17}{5}$$

Again we see that the value of the game is $3\tfrac{2}{5}$. Since it is a positive value, we know that X wins. The term *value of the game* does not mean that X will win $3\tfrac{2}{5}$ points each time these two opponents play; it does mean that over a long series of plays, if both play their optimal strategies, X's average winnings per play will be $3\tfrac{2}{5}$ points.

▮ FINDING THE GAME VALUE BY USING JOINT PROBABILITIES

If we reproduce the original game matrix and the optimal strategies for the game we have been discussing in this section as follows,

$$\begin{array}{cc} & Y \\ & \begin{array}{cc} \tfrac{3}{5} & \tfrac{2}{5} \end{array} \\ X \begin{array}{c} \tfrac{1}{5} \\ \tfrac{4}{5} \end{array} & \begin{bmatrix} 5 & 1 \\ 3 & 4 \end{bmatrix} \end{array}$$

we can see that each of the players' strategies consists of two probabilities, that is, a $\frac{1}{5}$ probability that player X will play row 1, and a $\frac{4}{5}$ probability that player X will play row 2. Similarly, the probability that player Y will play column 1 is $\frac{3}{5}$, and the probability that Y will play column 2 is $\frac{2}{5}$. Since both players play independently in that neither knows what the other will play for the next move, the probabilities for player X are independent of the probabilities for player Y.

Each of the payoffs in the game (5, 1, 3, and 4) is attained *only* if a particular column and a particular row are played simultaneously. For instance, player X wins 5 points only if she plays row 1 at the same time that player Y plays column 1. The probability that row 1 and column 1 will both be played simultaneously is a joint probability under conditions of statistical independence: $P(\text{row 1, column 1}) = P(\text{row 1}) \times P(\text{column 1})$, or in this case, $\frac{1}{5} \times \frac{3}{5}$, or $\frac{3}{25}$. The probability that 5 will be the payoff after this play of the game is then $\frac{3}{25}$.

Using this same reasoning, we can compute the joint probabilities that each of the payoffs will be obtained:

JOINT PROBABILITIES
OF EACH PAYOFF

Payoff value	Strategies which produce this payoff	Probability of this payoff
5	Row 1, column 1	$\frac{1}{5} \times \frac{3}{5} = \frac{3}{25}$
1	Row 1, column 2	$\frac{1}{5} \times \frac{2}{5} = \frac{2}{25}$
3	Row 2, column 1	$\frac{4}{5} \times \frac{3}{5} = \frac{12}{25}$
4	Row 2, column 2	$\frac{4}{5} \times \frac{2}{5} = \frac{8}{25}$
		1.0

Now we can compute the value of the game by multiplying each of the payoffs by the probability that it will occur:

Payoff		Probability of this payoff	
5	×	$\frac{3}{25}$	= $\frac{15}{25}$
1	×	$\frac{2}{25}$	= $\frac{2}{25}$
3	×	$\frac{12}{25}$	= $\frac{36}{25}$
4	×	$\frac{8}{25}$	= $\frac{32}{25}$
			$\frac{85}{25}$ or $3\frac{2}{5}$ = value of the game

SOLUTION OF GAMES BY DOMINANCE

AVOIDING AN ENTIRE
COLUMN OR ROW

Here are two games in which one player has more than two rows or more than two columns. None of the solution methods we have discussed this far enables us to solve for the optimal strategies and the game value (there is no saddle point). Often it is possible to find an entire row (or column) which one player will avoid when there is another row (or column) which is *always* better for him or her to play. In that case, we say that the avoided row (or column) is dominated by another row (or column).

Example 1

Original game   Resulting 2 × 2 game

Y   Y

$$X \begin{bmatrix} 6 & 4 & -1 & 0 & -3 \\ 3 & 2 & -4 & 2 & -1 \end{bmatrix} \qquad X \begin{bmatrix} -1 & -3 \\ -4 & -1 \end{bmatrix}$$

COLUMNS 1, 2, AND 4 ARE DOMINATED

Player Y will not play columns 1, 2, or 4, since columns 3 or 5 are better for him, regardless of whether opponent X plays row 1 or row 2. Player Y will still *divide* his time between columns 3 and 5 because neither of these is *always* better than the other.

Example 2

Original game   Resulting 2 × 2 game

Y   Y

$$X \begin{bmatrix} 4 & 1 \\ 2 & 3 \\ -1 & 1 \end{bmatrix} \qquad X \begin{bmatrix} 4 & 1 \\ 2 & 3 \end{bmatrix}$$

ROW 3 IS DOMINATED

Player X will not play row 3, since row 1 or row 2 is a better choice than row 3, regardless of which column player Y chooses. Player X will still divide her time between rows 1 and 2, since neither of these is *always* better than the other.

If the resulting game is 2 × 2 size, we can employ any of the solution methods we have already covered; however, you can easily construct games which cannot be reduced to 2 × 2 size.

▋ OTHER KINDS OF GAMES

All the games we have discussed up to this point have been two-person zero-sum games; that is, they have been subject to these two restrictions: (1) only two persons or opposing interests were allowed to be involved, and (2) the payoffs for both players or interests were equal in magnitude but opposite in sign, so that the total outcome to both players or interests was zero (what one opponent gained the other lost). There are several other classifications of games which, although they have not been treated in this basic introduction, are nonetheless part of the ongoing research in this area.

PAYOFFS OTHER THAN ZERO

Nonzero-sum games In these games, the sum of the players' payoffs for some pairs of choices (plays) will be *other* than zero. In other words, both players can win with certain pairs of choices, both players can lose with certain pairs of choices, or one or the other player can win or lose with certain pairs of choices. The players can cooperate to produce the maximum total payoff (it is assumed this would be divided between them) rather than the maximum payoff for one player. A simple finger-matching game where each player holds one hand behind his back and at the count of three reveals a certain number of fingers can be a nonzero-sum game if the payoffs have been set up like this:

Number of fingers displayed		Payoff	
Player 1	**Player 2**	**Player 1**	**Player 2**
Odd	Odd	3	1
Odd	Even	0	5
Even	Odd	−2	2
Even	Even	1	2

Techniques for the solution of nonzero-sum games between two players or opposing interests are available.

N-Person games   Games which involve more than two persons or opposing interests are referred to as *N-person* games. In a two-person zero-sum game, one player's gain is the other player's loss; there is no reason for negotiation or cooperation between two serious opponents. This situation disappears in an *N*-person game. With more than two players, opportunity exists for collusion by some participants against others. Additionally, negotiation among the participants can take place. If the *N*-person game is also nonzero-sum, the participants may be able to cooperate in a way which will maximize the total payoff rather than maximizing the payoff to one participant.

MORE THAN
TWO PERSONS

Negotiability   Games can be further classified according to whether negotiation between or among the players is allowed. In negotiable games, the players are allowed to negotiate among themselves and form coalitions, while in nonnegotiable games, players must make their choices without benefit of negotiation.

WHEN NEGOTIATION
IS ALLOWED

▪ CONSTRAINTS TO THE OPERATIONAL USE OF GAME THEORY

Game theory offers us insights into logical reasoning processes; however, game theory is difficult to use in managerial situations. This lack of operational use doesn't come from our not being able to *solve* games; we have already discussed several methods for doing that. Lack of operational use is perhaps explained with these factors:

LACK OF
OPERATIONAL USE

1 When we move from two-person games to *N*-person games, or when we go from zero-sum games to nonzero-sum games, the theoretical approaches available to us become much weaker. The presence of negotiation, bargaining, coalitions, and even bluffing makes it difficult for theory to work.

2 At the very least, conflict between two businesses rarely involves just the two parties themselves. Government (in multiple forms) is generally a partner to the conflict, and in many situations the presence of a labor union makes it at least a four-party game.

3 The difficulty of specifying payoffs in quantitative terms further complicates the operational use of game theory. Accounting measures the results of certain actions quite well, but is unable to cope analytically with other kinds of consequences.

▌SOME INTERESTING AND PROMISING APPLICATIONS OF GAME THEORY

Martin Shubik of Yale University predicted in 1982 that the next 15 years will see game theory models blossom in every social science. Although this kind of prediction has been made before, such models may be more realistic now than at any previous time.

The Nuclear Regulatory Commission (NRC) safeguards uranium by comparing how much fuel a plant should have with the amount it actually reports—an example of two-person zero-sum game theory. The NRC investigates only if the difference exceeds the expected error in measuring. Theoretically, a smart thief could pilfer very small amounts and still keep the error within measurement limits; the NRC is considering, however, changing its strategy to random investigations. Game theorists say that this random approach (checking when the error is high and when it is low) would keep such thieves on their guard.

The nuclear arms race between the United States and the Soviet Union appears to defy logic. As both countries assess their alternatives, they will both arm themselves to the teeth because the overriding goal is never to fall behind. If the Soviet Union is arming, so must we, says the United States; and if the Soviet Union is falling behind, it's time for us to move ahead. Such strategy means that continued military buildup is the only way to stave off a disastrous situation where your opponent arms while you disarm. Game theory suggests that the only way to change the reaction of both countries is to change the rules of the game, that is, if both countries share reconnaissance data, it may be in their best interests to reject the strategy of arming no matter what your opponent does.

During the Watergate crisis, the U.S. Supreme Court was required to rule on President Nixon's move to keep his tapes secret. New York University political scientists Steven Brams and Douglas Muzzio demonstrated that game theory could be used to analyze the alternatives the Court had. Seen from this point of view, the President had two moves, compliance or defiance; and the Court had two moves, a split or a unanimous decision against the President. The Justices would rather have a split decision, because this would show that verdicts do not have to be unanimous to require compliance. The President's best response to that action, however, would likely be to defy, because he could claim that a narrow decision would not precipitate a constitutional crisis. Conversely, a unanimous decision would likely result in compliance by the President. Game theory suggests that the Justices could anticipate the President's reactions and that they knew they couldn't reach their desired goal with a split decision. A unanimous decision was the only outcome that would let them reach their goal, and that is exactly what happened.

Although we will not go into it in this book, one of the successful applications of game theory is its use in situations involving competitive bidding. In this area we see a great deal of promise for the continued expansion of the technique in managerial decisions.

Other interesting applications of game theory continue to emerge. John Banzhaf of George Washington University Law Center uses game theory to estimate the power of an individual state in the Electoral College. Economists use game theory to explain logical behavior in an auction. And two of the authors of this text have, at one time or another, used it to plan moves in their weekly poker games.

■ DECISION ANALYSIS IN THE FUTURE

The techniques covered in this and the previous chapter will continue to be used in making business decisions because they bring structure and order to decision making in situations where inputs and outputs are not easy to quantify and handle. Whether these approaches become an integral part of *most* decisions is not clear, but will depend on whether we can bridge the gap between management scientists and practicing managers.

To have this happen, managers must continue to become educated in the ideas we have been discussing, and management scientists need to develop a better understanding of the total scope of decision making, that is, the psychological, economic, and social dimensions of a decision beyond quantitative methods. We will discuss methods for bridging this gap in more detail in Chapter 17.

6 Glossary

Breakeven point The point (volume) at which total revenue equals total cost.

Contribution The price per unit less the variable cost per unit.

Cost-volume-profit analysis Sometimes referred to as *breakeven analysis;* the systematic analysis of the relationship of profit to changes in fixed costs, variable costs, and volume.

Decision node A branching point which requires a decision.

Decision tree A graphic display of the decision process indicating decision alternatives, states of nature, probabilities attached to the states of nature, and conditional benefits and losses.

Dominance A situation in which a certain strategy is always better (or always worse) than another strategy.

Expected value of sample information The expected value of new information in a decision process.

Game A generic term given to situations of conflict between two or more parties.

Mixed strategy The optimal reaction of players when there is no saddle point in a game.

Negotiable game A game in which bargaining, coalitions, threats, and so forth, between the players are allowed.

Node A point at which branching takes place in a decision tree.

Nonzero-sum game A game in which payoffs for some pairs of strategies may be other than zero; a game in which both players can win.

Payoff matrix A rectangular array of payoffs for a game situation arranged in rows and columns.

Pure strategy A strategy that a player plays all the time.

Replacement analysis The systematic analysis of alternatives available in situations involving items which fail in use over time.

Rollback Also called *foldback*; a method of using decision trees to find optimal alternatives which involves working from right to left in the tree.

Saddle point The value of the game when both players have a pure strategy that is optimal; the saddle point is the smallest value in its row *and* the largest value in its column.

State-of-nature node A branching point after which more than one state of nature can occur.

Unit normal loss integral A tabular expression of values necessary for the integration of unit benefits or losses into analyses involving the normal probability distribution.

Value of the game The average payoff to the winner over a long series of plays.

Zero-sum game A game in which the total gains of the winner exactly equal the total losses of the loser.

7 Review of equations

Page 200

$$\text{Breakeven point (in units)} = \frac{\text{Total fixed cost}}{\text{Price/unit} - \text{Variable cost/unit}} \tag{5-1}$$

Using this formula solves for the breakeven point (in units), given a level of fixed cost and price and variable cost data.

8 Exercises

5-1 A machine modification which would cost $12,000 per year in additional operating costs is being considered by Frances McKensie, a superintendent. This modification will reduce variable costs by 6 cents per unit. Her supervisor estimates that the mean production level for this machine is about 250,000 units per year. When asked to give odds on production running between 200,000 and 300,000, he indicates that he feels that they would be approximately 3:2. What is the probability that the machine will operate at less than its breakeven point with the modification?

5-2 The ACME Company is contemplating producing a product that would sell for $11 a unit; the per-unit variable cost for this product is $6.60, and the fixed cost per year allocated to this product is $250,000. The sales manager for ACME estimates that annual sales of this product would have a mean of 200,000 with a standard deviation of 85,000 units. Using this information, answer the following questions:

a. What is the expected profit from this product next year?

b. What is the probability that ACME would lose money on this product next year?

5-3 The Acme Company is considering the purchase of a new machine which will be used on the average 3,000 hours per year. The usage time is normally distributed with a standard deviation of 800 hours. If the machine is to break even, it must operate in excess of 2,500 hours per year. For each hour of usage less than the breakeven point, Acme will lose $6. What is Acme's expected loss next year if the machine is purchased?

5-4 The addition of an automatic welding machine to an auto assembly line is estimated to cost $840,000. Savings in labor per car will be about $5. John Gee, the production manager, estimates the average production rate for the line at 200,000 units annually, with 2:1 odds that production will range from 150,000 to 250,000 cars. What is the probability that this assembly line will operate below the breakeven point of the new welding equipment?

5-5 Anne Fulton, marketing vice president for Burrington Textiles, Inc., was looking over a marketing proposal from her assistant, Roger Smythe. Roger suggested spending $125,000 to advertise a new fabric which is unusually stain-resistant. Anne returned the proposal to Roger with this comment: "If you can convince me that there is at least a 60 percent chance that this fabric will make twice as much as your proposal will cost, I'll authorize your proposal." After several days of poring over sales projections, Roger projected sales at 5.5 million yards with a 3:1 chance that the sales would lie between 4.5 and 6.5 million yards. The company would make 5 cents per yard contribution. Can Roger convince his boss?

5-6 The J. L. Beamer Company, Inc., has developed a new apple corer for home canning use and for making applesauce. It is expected to retail for $8.95 and has variable costs of $6.29. The allocated fixed costs are $461,000. Beamer Company market research suggests that annual sales will average 200,000 units; an estimate of the standard deviation of these sales is 40,000 units.

  a. What is the expected profit from this product next year?
  b. What is the probability that the company will lose money on this product next year?
  c. What is the probability that it will make a profit of between $20,000 and $50,000 on this product?
  d. What is the chance it will lose at least $30,000 on this product next year?

5-7 THEIM Machine Company is considering the purchase of a new machine which could generate significant savings by reducing labor costs on a certain operation— conditional, of course, on the machine's operating above the breakeven number of hours annually. The mean annual operating hours are estimated at 1,900, and the standard deviation of the distribution of operating hours has been estimated to be 400 hours. To break even, the machine must operate above 1,175 hours annually; for each operating hour less than the breakeven point, THEIM will lose $5.50. What is THEIM's expected loss next year if the machine is purchased?

5-8 Should THEIM pay $50 for a detailed analysis of future operating times of the machine described in Exercise 5-7 if the analysis will reduce the standard deviation of the distribution of operating hours to 170 hours? What would this new information be worth?

5-9 Suppose the machine THEIM is considering will cost $80,000 installed. THEIM's accountants state that the machine will save $8 for each hour it operates above the breakeven point (1,175 hours annually). Using the data from Exercise 5-7, calculate whether THEIM should purchase the machine if the expected net savings on the $80,000 investment has to be 14 percent.

5-10 The local university laundry is looking at an automatic shirt-pressing machine which will reduce labor cost and bottlenecks in an already overutilized facility. Greta Rogers, the laundry manager, estimates the machine will operate almost two full shifts a year (3,600 hours) with a standard deviation of 300 hours. The breakeven point of the machine is 2,800 hours a year (with current cost information). Below the breakeven point, the university will lose $8 per hour; above the breakeven point, the laundry will earn a net profit of $14 an hour. What is the expected net profit of this machine if it is purchased?

5-11 Mountain Coal Corporation has a new coal extractor on trial and must either return it or buy it this week. At $100,000, this is an expensive machine, but it saves about $27 per operating hour beyond its breakeven point, 1,200 hours annually. Below its breakeven point, however, it loses $8.50 per operating hour. Tom Brandon, mine equipment supervisor, estimates the operating hours to be 2,000 annually with a standard deviation of 500. Mountain Coal has an investment hurdle which demands at least a 10 percent return measured as profit/investment. Should the company invest in this machine?

5-12 Given the following two-person zero-sum games, determine if a saddle point exists. If so, what is the value of the game?

a. $\begin{bmatrix} 7 & -9 \\ 4 & -2 \end{bmatrix}$ b. $\begin{bmatrix} -3 & 4 \\ 6 & -2 \end{bmatrix}$ c. $\begin{bmatrix} 1 & 3 \\ -2 & 4 \end{bmatrix}$

d. $\begin{bmatrix} 4 & 3 \\ -2 & 5 \end{bmatrix}$ e. $\begin{bmatrix} 5 & 3 \\ 2 & 4 \end{bmatrix}$ f. $\begin{bmatrix} 5 & 3 \\ 2 & 1 \end{bmatrix}$

5-13 Players X and Y are playing the following zero-sum game:

$$\begin{bmatrix} 8 & -3 \\ -4 & 2 \end{bmatrix}$$

Determine what percentage of the time X and Y should play either row or column.

5-14 Using the optimal mixed strategies, determine the value of the game given in Exercise 5-13.

5-15 Using joint probabilities, find the value of the game given in Exercise 5-13.

5-16 The University of the Great Northwest is a private university which, like many private educational institutions, depends on the profits from its undergraduate program to support graduate research and teaching activities. The number of graduate students admitted each year is determined by the total "profit" generated by the undergraduate program divided by the "per-student loss" of the graduate program. The provost of the university has calculated that variable costs are $4,000 per undergraduate student, and the university has fixed costs of $10 million annually. Tuition is $5,000 per year. The registrar estimates that the total undergraduate enrollment will average 11,000 students with a standard deviation estimated to be 800.

  a. How much profit will the university show from its undergraduate program next year?
  b. If the university loses $1,800 per graduate student, how many graduate students can the university admit and still break even?

c. How likely is the university to lose money on its undergraduate program next year?

d. If the university wanted to admit 1,500 graduate students next year, how large would the undergraduate program have to be?

5-17 Lycuming Engine Company produces engines for the light aircraft industry. Tight tolerances require the use of computer-controlled milling machines with cutter heads which wear out according to this table:

Hours in use	300	600	900	1,200
Portion of cutter heads which fail before this time (cumulative)	.05	.20	.70	1.00

Anytime a cutter head fails in use, it ruins the camshaft it is working on at that time; the cost of this is $250. The total cost to replace a cutter head is $30, whether the replacement is done when the head fails or during the regular night maintenance period. Should all the cutter heads be replaced after a regular interval? If so, what interval?

5-18 The Midtown Food Market each Thursday advertises a weekly special as a means of attracting shoppers away from its larger competitor, Jumbo Market. If Midtown advertises a produce item when Jumbo also advertises a produce item, Jumbo would gain about 100 of Midtown's shoppers, and if Midtown advertises a meat item in the same week that Jumbo advertises a meat item, Jumbo would gain about 200 of Midtown's shoppers. On the other hand, if Midtown advertises produce when Jumbo is advertising meat, Midtown can gain 150 of Jumbo's shoppers. Similarly, Midtown expects to gain 150 shoppers if it advertises meat while Jumbo is advertising produce. Find the optimal mix of advertising strategies of the two markets. What is the expected value of this strategy over the long run?

5-19 Robert Teer, maintenance engineer for a large construction company, is examining alternatives open to him for the replacement of hydraulic hoses on the firm's 100 front-end loaders; each loader uses six hoses, which—from historical maintenance records—fail at this rate:

Months of use	1	2	3	4	5
Percent requiring replacement by that month	10	15	20	70	100

Robert's supervisor says that the "in-the-field" replacement cost of $80 per hose could be reduced by $40 if all the hoses were replaced at a regular interval during routine maintenance and service. Evaluate the alternatives open to Robert and recommend a course of action.

5-20 Bill Combes is the quarterback for the Clarkson football team. He has been pondering his optimal play strategy for the frequently encountered situation where it is third down with five yards to go for a first down. He feels he has two options (1) call a passing play or (2) call a rushing play. The defense is expected to counter with one of two strategies in such a situation (1) set up a Blue formation and rush the linebackers or (2) set up a Green formation where the linebackers either plug holes in the line or drop back for pass coverage as the play develops. The expected number of yards gained conditional upon the offensive and defensive strategies is as follows:

		Defense	
		Blue	**Green**
Offense	**Pass**	−5	10
	Rush	8	3

Using game theory, find the optimal percentage of the time Bill should call passing and running plays as well as the optimal strategy for the defensive team. If these strategies are followed, what is the value of the game in terms of expected long run yardage gained for third and five situations?

5-21 The Independent Rent-A-Car Agency is considering periodic replacement of tires for its fleet of 500 cars. It is now following a policy of replacing tires as they wear out at a total cost of $80 per tire. The agency feels that it can cut its per-tire replacement cost by $15 by using the periodic replacement method. Evaluate these alternatives and make a recommendation to the agency.

Month after replacement	1	2	3	4	5
Percent of original tires which are worn by that month	10	20	40	70	100

5-22 Given the following two-person zero-sum games, employ dominance whenever possible to reduce the game to a 2 × 2 matrix. For each reduced matrix, determine the optimal strategy for each player and the value of the game.

a. $\begin{bmatrix} 5 & 5 & 3 \\ 3 & 2 & -2 \\ 7 & 4 & 8 \end{bmatrix}$
b. $\begin{bmatrix} 5 & 2 & 7 \\ -5 & 1 & 3 \\ -3 & -1 & 8 \end{bmatrix}$
c. $\begin{bmatrix} 3 & 2 & 7 \\ 3 & 2 & 7 \\ -4 & 3 & 3 \end{bmatrix}$

5-23 Betsy Tipper is considering the purchase of a motel near Waterville. Presently, the motel is operating at a loss, but she feels it can be made profitable if she remodels it and becomes affiliated with a national chain. She has determined from an analysis of similar operations that the mean number of rentals should be about 10 per day, and she anticipates operating over 360 days per year. Further, she feels that the odds are about 3:1 that daily rental will lie between 6 and 14 units. In order to break even, 2,500 units must be rented per year. For each unit rented below the breakeven point, a $35 loss will be incurred, while each unit rented above breakeven will result in a $40 profit.

  a. What is the expected annual loss?
  b. What is the expected annual profit?

5-24 Referring to Exercise 5-23, assume that Betsy learns of an opportunity to hire Williams Survey, Inc., to conduct a marketing analysis of potential demand for her proposed motel operation. The results of this analysis would better pinpoint the demand variation so that the standard deviation of daily demand would be 2.3 rentals per day. The analysis would cost Betsy $1500. Is this worthwile for her to do?

5-25 For the following two-person zero-sum game, find the optimal strategy for each player:

$$\begin{bmatrix} 8 & -3 & 7 \\ 6 & -4 & 5 \\ -2 & 2 & -3 \end{bmatrix}$$

5-26 Using the result obtained in Exercise 5-25, solve for the value of the game.

5-27 Crouse Hospital has recently purchased an expensive piece of equipment for blood testing. The machine has 60 filter units which periodically must be replaced because they become clogged and begin causing erroneous output measurements. When a filter unit fails in service, a diagnostic check within the machine signals the operator, but it cannot isolate the specific filter unit causing the problem. Consequently, considerable time is spent locating the filter needing replacement, and the cost of lost operating time is estimated to be $1,000 for each in-service replacement. If replacements are made for all 60 filter units during a single scheduled down-time, the cost is only $20 per filter unit. The following distribution represents the failure history of the filters:

Hours of operation (in hundreds of hours)	1	2	3	4	5
Percent of original filters which fail by that time	1	3	18	48	100

Determine an effective replacement strategy for these filter units.

5-28 Harry Phelps, owner of Harry's Clothing Cupboard, is considering a move from downtown to a new shopping mall. Because he has been downtown for 20 years and has built up quite a following there, Harry thinks that if he moves there is a 20 percent chance his business will decline by $100,000, a 30 percent chance it will remain stable, and a 50 percent chance it will increase by $175,000 because of the quality of sales promotion done by the mall management. Further, the city is considering a downtown revitalization with a mall in front of Harry's store. He believes there is a 70 percent chance this will pass the city council; if it does, he estimates his business should increase by $200,000. If the mall is not built, Harry thinks his downtown business will decline by about $50,000. Time is of the essence; the mall owners need an answer immediately or he will lose any chance to locate there. Construct a decision tree to help Harry decide on a course of action.

5-29 The investment staff of First Union National Bank is considering four investment alternatives for a client: stocks, bonds, real estate, and savings certificates. These investments will be held for 1 year. Historical stock patterns indicate that there is a 30 percent chance stocks will decline by 10 percent, a 20 percent chance they will remain stable, and a 50 percent chance they will increase in value by 15 percent. The stocks under consideration do not pay dividends. The bonds stand a 30 percent chance of increasing in value by 5 percent and a 70 percent chance of remaining stable, and they yield 10 percent. The real estate parcel being considered has a 10 percent chance of increasing 15 percent in value, a 20 percent chance of increasing

10 percent in value, a 30 percent chance of increasing 5 percent in value, a 20 percent chance of remaining stable, and a 20 percent chance of losing 5 percent of its value. The savings certificates yield 8½ percent with certainty. Use a decision tree to structure the alternatives available to the investment staff, and using the expected value criterion, choose the alternative with the highest expected value.

5-30 The Tarheel Manufacturing Company must decide whether to build a large plant or a small one to process a new product with an expected life of 10 years.

Demand may be high during the first 2 years, but if many users find the product unsatisfactory, demand will be low for the remaining 8 years. High demand during the first 2 years may indicate high demand for the next 8 years. If demand is high during the first 2 years and the company does not expand within the first 2 years, competitive products will be introduced, thus lowering the benefits.

If the company builds a large processing plant, it must keep it for 10 years. If it builds a small plant, the plant can be expanded in 2 years if demand is high or the company can stay in the small plant while making smaller benefits on the small volume of sales.

Estimates of demand are these:

	Probability		
High demand (first 2 years) followed by high demand (next 8 years)	.5	.6	Probability of high demand during first 2 years
High demand (first 2 years) followed by low demand (next 8 years)	.1		
Low demand (first 2 years) followed by continuing low demand (next 8 years)	.4	.4	Probability of low demand during first 2 years
Low demand (first 2 years) followed by high demand (next 8 years)	0		

Financial costs and profits are:

A large plant with high demand would yield $1 million annually in profits.

A large plant with low demand would yield $200,000 annually because of production inefficiencies.

A small plant, not expanded, with a low demand would yield annual profits of $250,000 for 10 years.

A small plant during a 2-year period of high demand would yield $450,000 annually; if high demand continued and if the plant were not expanded, this would drop to $300,000 annually for the next 8 years as a result of competition.

A small plant which was expanded after 2 years to meet high demand would yield $800,000 annually for the next 8 years.

A small plant which was expanded after 2 years would yield $100,000 annually for 8 years if low demand occurred during that period.

A large plant would cost $5 million to build and put into operation.

A small plant would cost $1.5 million to build and put into operation.

Expanding a small plant after 2 years would cost $2.5 million.

Under the conditions stated and with the information furnished, analyze the alternatives to choose the best decision.

5-31 The Mountain Manufacturing Company is planning to produce citizens band radios. One problem it faces is a make-or-buy decision for plug-in intermediate frequency (IF) modules. The company can buy these modules from an electric vendor for $20 a unit. Alternatively, it may produce them at its own plant for variable costs of $12 a unit. If it produces the modules, it will incur annual fixed costs of $25,000 per year. Each citizens band radio produced requires 1.05 of these IF modules (this takes into account defective IF modules). The company foresees annual demand for the citizens band radios to be normally distributed with mean sales of 3,800 units and with a standard deviation of 500 units. What is the probability that the required usage of IF modules will be sufficiently large to justify producing them rather than buying them? If it is company policy to buy components only when there is better than 50 percent probability that usage is 1.8 standard deviations above the make-or-buy breakeven point, what should the decision be on this matter?

5-32 The general manager of the Mountain Manufacturing Company (see Exercise 5-31) would like to deviate from the company policy and produce the IF modules rather than buy them. She has asked you to compute the expected annual cost saving as well as the expected annual loss. What will you tell her?

5-33 A television station has 60 identical plug-in modules in its transmitter. Each of the modules has a life expectancy as follows:

Hours after replacement	100	200	300	400	500
Cumulative percent of modules which fail by this time	10	25	45	70	100

The transmitter has an automatic system which detects a failed module and switches over to a backup. But in order to ensure maximum reliability, the station makes it standard practice to replace any module as soon as it fails. It costs $50 to replace a module which has failed. Alternatively, the company could replace all modules at regular intervals during the early morning hours when the station is off the air. If this is done, it costs only $35 per module. The company is interested in the most cost effective policy in replacing modules. What would you recommend?

5-34 The policy of the Newland Company is not to undertake new business ventures unless annual return on investment has a 70 percent probability of being 15 percent or higher. Company officials are contemplating a new venture, the production of dentures. This venture will require an investment of $400,000. They estimate that a set of dentures will cost $60 in variable costs, and their annual fixed costs are expected to be $125,000. Marketing personnel have analyzed the potential demand for dentures and have found that at a selling price of $130 per set, the expected annual sales would be 4,000 sets; the standard deviation is estimated to be 450 sets. They further determined that at a price of $140 per set, the annual demand would be 3,200 sets with a standard deviation of 300 sets. Should the company proceed with this venture? If so, which of the two selling prices would allow a higher probability of returning 15 percent on the investment annually?

5-35 The Motor City Auto Company is planning to introduce a new automobile which features a radically new pollution control system. The company has two options.

The first option is to build a new plant, anticipating full production in 3 years' time. The second option is to rebuild a small existing pilot plant for limited production for the coming model year. If the results of the limited production show promise at the end of the first year, full-scale production in a newly constructed plant would still be possible 3 years from now. If it is decided to proceed with the pilot plant and later analysis shows that it is unattractive to go into full production, the pilot plant can still be operated by itself at a small profit. The expected annual profits for various alternatives are:

Production facility	Consumer acceptance	Annual profit (millions)
New plant	High	14
New plant	Low	−6
Pilot plant	High	2
Pilot plant	Low	1

Members of Motor City's marketing-research division have estimated that there is a 50 percent probability that consumer acceptance will be high and a 50 percent probability that it will be low. If the pilot plant is put into production, with a correspondingly low-keyed advertising program, they feel that the probabilities are 45 percent for high consumer acceptance and 55 percent for low acceptance. Further, they have estimated that if the pilot plant is built and consumer acceptance is found to be high, there is a 90 percent probability of high acceptance with full production. If consumer acceptance with the pilot models is found to be low, however, there is only a 15 percent probability of high acceptance with full-scale production and advertising. Motor City can rebuild for pilot plant production at a cost of $1 million. What alternative should the company select?

5-36 When the Motor City Auto Company (see Exercise 5-35) announced its plans to produce the new low-pollution automobile with a pilot program, officials of the federal Environmental Protection Agency were pleased. These officials had been pushing Congress for some time to enact stiff new pollution control legislation. They estimated that high consumer acceptance of the new auto would be interpreted as a mandate to Congress, and according to these estimates, there would be a 90 percent probability of passing the new law if acceptance were high. On the other hand, if consumer acceptance were low, there would be only a 20 percent probability that new pollution control laws would be enacted.

By the end of the first year of pilot production, the Motor City sales figures revealed that, alas, consumer acceptance of the new auto was low. Before the company could announce plans not to proceed with construction of the new plant, however, it was informed by friends at the Environmental Protection Agency that Congress had passed the new pollution control law. As a result, Motor City decided to revise its probability estimates based on all the new information and then reevaluate its plans. What decision should it now make?

5-37 The Taub Company is considering whether or not to enter the highly competitive personal computer market with a new design called the PX-20. They have developed prior probabilities and expected ten year's profit figures as follows:

Possible outcome	Probability	Profit with this outcome
Low sales	.20	−2.5 million
Moderate sales	.50	1.3
High sales	.30	7.8

If they decide not to enter the market, they can sell their patents for the product for $1 million. Another alternative open to them is to hire a market survey company to conduct an analysis of potential sales. This would cost $0.25 million. The outcome of the survey would either be favorable or unfavorable. Based on past experience, the market survey company's performance record is:

Eventual outcome	Survey result	Percent of past surveys
Low sales	Favorable	.20
Low sales	Unfavorable	.80
Moderate sales	Favorable	.60
Moderate sales	Unfavorable	.40
High sales	Favorable	.90
High sales	Unfavorable	.10

Develop the decision tree and determine whether or not the survey should be taken. If so, what course of action should be taken with either a favorable or unfavorable market analysis.

9 Chapter concepts quiz

5-1 In cost-volume-profit analysis, costs are divided into two types: those costs which are constant and don't vary with the volume of goods sold, known as _____ _____ costs, and those costs which vary directly with the volume of output, known as _____ costs.

5-2 The _____ is the level of output below which a company operates at a loss and above which it operates at a profit.

5-3 A _____ node is a point on a decision tree which signifies the randomness of the decision process; a _____ node is a point at which the decision maker can exercise some control over the decision-making process.

5-4 The process of working backward through the tree in decision analysis is known as _____.

5-5 A _____ strategy is one which will be pursued for all time; a _____ strategy is one characterized by the proportions of time that each row (or column) is played.

5-6 In game theory, the average payoff per play over a long series of plays is called the _____.

5-7 A situation in which a certain strategy is always better (or always worse) than another strategy is called _____.

5-8 The systematic analysis of alternatives available in situations involving items which fail over time is called _____.

5-9 Since there are only rare cases in practice where perfect information is available, managers are interested in obtaining the _____.

5-10 A tabular expression of values necessary for the integration of unit benefits or losses into analyses involving the normal distribution is the _____.

True-False

5-11 The contribution of a new product is the difference between the total fixed cost and the variable cost per unit. **T F**

5-12 A decision process in which there is a known expected loss cannot also have associated with it an expected profit. **T F**

5-13 The maximum amount that a manager should be willing to pay for complete information about the future is equal to the expected loss of the venture. **T F**

5-14 The unit normal loss integral can always be used to compute expected loss when a decision maker has access to an estimate of the distribution of sales for a product. **T F**

5-15 Replacement analysis can be used to determine the procedure for replacing components which wear out over time such that replacement costs are minimized. **T F**

5-16 In a decision tree representation of a decision process, every branch emanating from a decision node connects that node to a state-of-nature node. **T F**

5-17 In a two-person zero-sum game, a saddle point is the value of the game which results when each player pursues a pure strategy. **T F**

5-18 The expected loss of a certain decision gets smaller as the standard deviation of the distribution of possible outcomes gets smaller. **T F**

5-19 Elimination of dominated rows (or columns) is useful in reducing a large problem to one which can be handled by the available methods of calculating mixed strategies. **T F**

5-20 A saddle point is an entry in the payoff matrix which is the largest in its row and the smallest in its column. **T F**

5-21 Contribution is price per unit minus variable cost per unit. It is independent of volume. **T F**

5-22 Cost-volume-profit analysis is also commonly known as breakeven analysis. **T F**

5-23 One disadvantage of decision trees is that when used over more than a single year's horizon, benefits cannot be discounted to present value. **T F**

5-24 One drawback to the use of game theory in practice is that it is often difficult to express payoffs in quantitative terms. **T F**

5-25 The development of expected values of profit and loss is restricted to those cases where the outcomes can be viewed as having a discrete distribution. **T F**

Multiple Choice

5-26 In a managerial decision environment, the expected value of sample information (EVSI) is just:

a. The cost necessary to produce perfect information about the future.
b. The expected increase in revenue attributed to new information.
c. The reduction in expected loss using the new information.
d. The price per unit of the product in question.

PROBABILISTIC
DECISION MAKING II

5-27 An advantage of decision tree analysis is that:
   a. It handles ill-structured problems easily.
   b. It becomes more efficient to use when the number of possible outcomes increases.
   c. It communicates the decision-making process to others.
   d. All of the above.

5-28 For a game which has no saddle point, how can the value of the game be found?
   a. By using the joint probability of each combination of rows and columns to weight the payoff for that combination and summing over all possible combinations.
   b. By weighting the expected value of the payoff when an opponent plays a given column, by the probability that the opponent will play that column and summing over all columns.
   c. The value of the game cannot be found in this instance.
   d. Both *a* and *b*.

5-29 Games which involve more than two persons or opposing interests are called:
   a. *N*-person games
   b. Negotiable games
   c. Unconstrained games
   d. Conflicting games

5-30 Cost-volume-profit analysis can be used to determine all but which of the following things?
   a. The volume of sales next year.
   b. The probability of sales exceeding the breakeven point.
   c. The probability of making a given profit $X.
   d. The expected loss for the coming year.

5-31 The variables which determine profits are:
   a. Fixed and variable costs
   b. Revenues and costs
   c. Price and sales volume
   d. Price and variable costs

5-32 Which of the following is not considered a fixed cost?
   a. Depreciation
   b. Executive salaries
   c. Insurance
   d. Labor

5-33 The volume of output at which total revenue equals total cost is called the:
   a. Breakeven point
   b. Point of indifference
   c. Plant capacity
   d. Iso-revenue point

5-34 The expected loss of some proposed venture whose outcomes are normally distributed is:
   a. Influenced by the standard deviation of the distribution.
   b. Equal to the expected value of perfect information.

c. Influenced by the location of the breakeven point.
d. All of the above.

5-35 Decision trees are used to analyze decision problems where:
a. Decisions and outcomes are both discrete.
b. Decisions are discrete, but the outcomes are continuous variables.
c. Decisions and outcomes are continuously distributed.
d. Decisions are made under conditions of certainty.

5-36 In game theory, when the sum of one person's gains is equal to the sum of another person's losses, this is known as a:
a. Cumulative game
b. Biased game
c. Matrix game
d. Zero-sum game

5-37 The payoff, when each participant in a game always makes the same decision, is called the:
a. Equilibrium point
b. Saddle point
c. Suboptimal payoff
d. All of the above

5-38 If players in a game are allowed to form coalitions, it is called:
a. An N-person game
b. A negotiable game
c. A non-zero game
d. An unfair game

5-39 A random variable of interest in cost-volume-profit analysis is:
a. Sales volume
b. Price
c. Fixed cost
d. All of the above

5-40 Decision trees can be used in conjunction with:
a. Bayesian analysis
b. Expected value of new information
c. Sensitivity analysis
d. All of the above

10 Real world MS/OR successes

EXAMPLE: PLANNING AMPHIBIOUS ASSAULTS IN THE U.S. MARINE CORPS

PROBLEM: DETERMINE
BEST MIX OF MARINE
HELICOPTERS

The primary mission of the U.S. Marine Corps is to deliver airborne amphibious assaults from Navy ships deep into the coastal regions of the enemy. In 1975, the Marines were planning to buy a light helicopter to augment their fleet for transporting troops. However, the new Marine Commandant stepped in and ordered a complete review of the role and capabilities of all Marine assault helicopters, present and proposed. A study team was assembled to recommend the best helicopter fleet mix. Political and budget pressures were such that the team had only one month to make its recommendations. With the help of two consultants, Richard Thomson and Charles Tiplitz,[1] the team used game theory to analyze this decision problem. The bottom line: cost savings conservatively estimated at $800 million.

The list of options included buying new light helicopters and modifying existing medium and heavy helicopters in various ways, such as by installing more powerful engines to increase lift capacity or adding infra-red suppression to reduce losses from heat-seeking missiles. The helicopter fleet had two roles: an assault role during which troops were delivered to target areas and a logistic role following the assault, during which supplies were delivered. While performing each role, the helicopters were required to operate in several environments defined as combinations of distance to the target area, altitude for pick-up and delivery, and temperature. Altitude and temperature are critical considerations since they affect lift capacity.

To evaluate the options, the study team developed a benefit/cost index: the ratio of payload (number of troops lifted per unit time) to total cost. The payload estimate took into account the capacity, speed, and range of the helicopter. Total cost considered both research and development and annual operating costs. A benefit/cost index was computed for each helicopter performing each role in each environment. The indexes were used as payoffs in a set of two-person, zero-sum games. Player X in each game is the Marine Corps, which selects the aircraft for an amphibious assault, Player Y, the enemy, selects the environment.

The table below illustrates a game under fixed altitude and temperature assumptions and a distance to target ranging from 25 to 100 nautical miles. The highest benefit/cost index is given a payoff value of 100 and the other entry in the column is scaled down proportionately.

		PLAYER Y			
		Distance (nautical miles)			
	Aircraft	**25**	**50**	**75**	**100**
PLAYER	CH-53A	92	99	100	100
X	CH-46-EM	100	100	83	69

Some aircraft and environment strategies were dominated in the games and eliminated from further consideration. In the remaining games, mixed strategies were necessary. Linear equations were solved to find the optimal strategies. The set of solutions for player X determined the best mix of aircraft in the helicopter fleet, a much different mix from that previously planned. To determine the robustness of the mix, sensitivity analysis was conducted by varying costs, life-cycle times, and performance figures. There was no significant change in the optimal mix.

The Commandant of the Marine Corps immediately adopted the study team's recommendations. Compared to original plans, the new mix of helicopters saved $800 million in fulfilling the Marine Corps goal for lift capability in amphibious assaults. This savings figure depends on a variety of assumptions about costs, although the authors used the most conservative assumptions. Actual savings were almost certainly much larger.

[1] Richard Thomson and Charles Tiplitz, "Helicopter Fleet Mix," *Interfaces*, vol. 9, no. 2, part 2, pp. 39–49, 1979.

6

Some of the most important decisions faced by Caroline Boutique, Ltd. involve inventory control. Caroline is fully aware of the fact that poor inventory management can severely cut into the profitability of her enterprise. It is not uncommon for businesses, such as Caroline's, to either succeed or fail because of the manner in which the inventory is managed. Inventory, like cash, is an asset, but inventory cannot be invested in the bank to collect interest. Consequently, for every dollar Caroline spends for her inventory, she must incur inventory carrying costs. She also incurs costs for placing orders for new inventory. If she orders too often, her order costs are high, but then she could order fewer items and save some carrying costs. On the other hand, ordering less often reduces order costs, but increases carrying costs, because more items would have to be ordered each time. Caroline obviously wants to make her inventory decisions in such a way that her total costs are a minimum. The inventory models presented in this chapter can help Caroline make these important decisions.

INVENTORY I
Order Quantity Models

CHAPTER OBJECTIVES

■ EXAMINE THE FUNCTIONS THAT INVENTORY PERFORMS AND ITS IMPORTANCE IN MANAGERIAL SITUATIONS.

■ DEVELOP THE BASIC ECONOMIC ORDER QUANTITY MODEL AND DEMONSTRATE ITS USE.

■ DEVELOP ECONOMIC ORDER QUANTITY MODELS WHICH OPERATE WITHOUT SUCH LIMITING ASSUMPTIONS AS INSTANTANEOUS RECEIPT AND AVAILABILITY OF COMPLETE INFORMATION.

■ DEMONSTRATE HOW THE ECONOMIC ORDER QUANTITY MODEL CAN BE SUCCESSFULLY APPLIED TO PRODUCTION LOT SIZE SITUATIONS.

■ REVIEW THE ASSUMPTIONS BEHIND THE USE OF ECONOMIC ORDER QUANTITY MODELS AND DEMONSTRATE WHEN IT IS APPROPRIATE TO USE EACH OF THE MODELS THAT HAS BEEN DEVELOPED.

For many firms the inventory is the largest current asset. Inventory difficulties can and do contribute to business failures. When a firm does no more than unintentionally run out of an item, results are not pleasant. If the firm is a retail store, the merchant loses the gross margin on the item. If the firm is a manufacturer, the stockout (inability to supply an item from inventory) could, in extreme cases, bring production to a halt. Conversely, if a firm carries *excessive* inventories, the added carrying cost may represent the difference between profit and loss. Skillful inventory management can make a significant contribution to a firm's profit.

1 What functions does inventory perform?

In any organization, inventories add an operating flexibility that would not otherwise exist. In manufacturing, work-in-process inventories are an absolute necessity unless each individual part is to be carried from machine to machine and those machines set up to produce that single part. Patients in a hospital are really inventory for the physician; true, they are there because they are too sick to be at home, but it must be recognized that having them in one location enables the physician to see all his or her patients during "rounds." The many functions inventory performs can be summarized as follows.

SMOOTHING OUT IRREGULARITIES IN SUPPLY

Tobacco is harvested during the late summer months, but the manufacture of tobacco products such as cigarettes and cigars continues throughout the entire year. In cases like this, sufficient raw material must be purchased during the tobacco-producing period to last the entire year; this forces the manufacturer to carry an inventory.

In a simpler sense, because a truck may go 100 miles without passing a gasoline station, its tanks must carry enough fuel to avoid runouts.

BUYING OR PRODUCING IN LOTS OR BATCHES

When the demand for an item will not support its continued production throughout the entire year, it is usually produced in batches or lots on an intermittent basis. During the time when the item is not being produced, sales are made from inventory which is accumulated while the item is being produced. Similarly, a retailer of men's clothing does not purchase a new shirt from the manufacturer each time the store sells one; rather, the retailer chooses to carry in the store an inventory of these shirts so that purchasing can be done in larger quantities, thereby allowing lower costs, less paperwork, and greater customer selection.

ALLOWING ORGANIZATIONS TO COPE WITH PERISHABLE MATERIALS

The packers of frozen lobster tails operate at peak production only a few months each year; they too must store up, or inventory, a supply sufficient to last them through a year's anticipated demand until the next lobster season. The entire production process which deals with freezing fresh fruits and vegetables must also give thoughtful consideration to the rate of inventory accumulation and depletion throughout the peak production and sales periods each year.

STORING LABOR

Although it may be conceptually difficult to think of "inventorying" labor, it is routine practice to do just that. The peak demand for the installation of replacement heating units comes in the fall, just after the old units have been operated for the first time. The manufacturers of heating units store up excess labor by having their workers produce at a designated rate all year long; then, having converted labor into finished heating units, they hold the units in inventory until the point when demand increases rapidly. Even if demand exceeds current productive capacity, a manufacturer can supply the difference out of inventory at that time.

INVENTORY CAN STORE LABOR

2 Inventory decisions

There are two basic inventory decisions managers must make as they attempt to accomplish the functions of inventory just reviewed. These two decisions are made for every item in the inventory:

TWO BASIC DECISIONS IN INVENTORY MANAGEMENT

1 *How much* of an item to order when the inventory of that item is to be replenished
2 *When* to replenish the inventory of that item

Companies use the term *SKU* (stockkeeping unit) instead of referring to *items*. The typical supermarket stocks about 7,000 SKUs of groceries, meats, fruits, vegetables, bakery goods, and nongrocery merchandise.

SKU DEFINED

This chapter and the next will introduce you to the more commonly used inventory models which managers use to make the two decisions enumerated above. This chapter will concentrate on using quantitative models to answer the question: How much to order? Chapter 7 will concentrate on quantitative tools which help managers answer the question: When to order?

3 Selective approach to managing inventory (ABC analysis)

An inventory for a large manufacturing firm or one for a large metropolitan hospital contains even more SKUs than the 7,000 we estimated for the supermarket. In the case of the hospital, these SKUs range from disposable syringes (costing about 26 cents each) to complete hospital beds (costing over $500 each) and a supply of very expensive radioactive isotopes costing much more. The manufacturing firm stocks simple hardware (nuts, bolts, screws, and so forth), where an individual item (say, a wood screw) can cost only pennies. But it also stocks replacement motors for some of its large machinery, where the cost of one motor can be $10,000.

DIFFERENT SKUs HAVE VERY DIFFERENT COSTS

In situations involving such a wide range of costs (and in the case of the protection cost of the radioactive isotopes), it makes no sense to use the same

ABC ANALYSIS

inventory management technique on all the items. Looking after a wood screw with the same care and using the same level of inventory analysis that you would apply to a $10,000 motor is simply poor management. Therefore, it has become quite common to employ one of a family of analyses generally referred to as *ABC analysis*.

ABC analysis classifies the SKUs in an inventory according to their dollar value (this is generally expressed as annual dollar usage). Generally a small portion of the total SKUs in an inventory (say, something near 10 percent) account for a very large proportion of the total dollar value of that inventory (say, 70 percent). These are called *A* items in ABC inventory analysis. These few SKUs should be managed carefully and intensively for two reasons:

1 There are very few of them, and consequently they are "easy" to look after. In the case, for example, of a bakery, one *A*-type SKU (flour) generally accounts for about 60 percent of the total dollar value of the inventory. Thus carefully watching one SKU "watches" 60 percent of the whole inventory.

2 Dollars invested in controlling these *A* items will generate larger returns to the organization. Using a computer system, for example, to control thousands of hardware items whose total value is only several hundred dollars cannot be as valuable to the organization as investing inventory control resources in looking after the major *A*-type inventory SKUs like the large motors we mentioned earlier.

In Figure 6-1, we have illustrated the concept of an ABC approach to inventory management. In this example, the *A* SKUs, while accounting for only 10 percent of the total number of SKUs, account for 70 percent of the dollar value of that inventory. The *B* SKUs account for 30 percent of the total number of SKUs but only 20 percent of the total dollars invested in inventory. Finally, the *C* SKUs account for 60 percent of the total number of SKUs but only 10 percent of the dollars invested in inventory. In this instance, as in most operational situations, a great deal of inventory control effort would be given to managing the *A* SKUs, less to the *B* SKUs, and very little to the *C* SKUs. The techniques to be introduced in this chapter and Chapter 7 are used primarily in the management of *A* and *B* SKUs.

4 Economic order quantity: the basic "how much to buy" model

The economic order quantity (EOQ) model is the oldest and best-known inventory model; its origins date all the way back to 1915. The purpose of using the EOQ model is to find that particular quantity to order which minimizes total inventory costs. Let us look for a moment at these costs.

INVENTORY COSTS

There are two basic inventory costs, *ordering costs* and *carrying costs*.

Ordering costs are basically the costs of getting an item into the firm's inventory. They are incurred each time an order is placed and are expressed

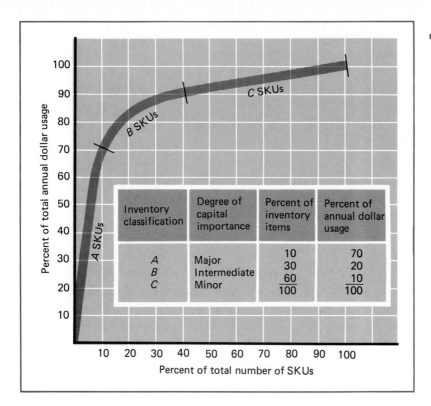

The figure contains the following embedded table:

Inventory classification	Degree of capital importance	Percent of inventory items	Percent of annual dollar usage
A	Major	10	70
B	Intermediate	30	20
C	Minor	60	10
		100	100

FIGURE 6-1
Illustration of *ABC* inventory classification.

as dollar cost per order. Ordering costs start with the requisition sent to the purchasing office, include all costs of issuing the purchase order and of following it up, continue with such steps as receiving the goods and placing them into inventory, and end with the buying firm's paying the supplier. Salaries constitute the major ordering cost; stationery is another ordering cost.

Because we want the *incremental* cost per order, we need cost estimates from the purchasing department, from the receiving warehouse, and from the accounting office covering their operations at two different levels of operation, as shown in Table 6-1. From this table we see that the 2,000 additional orders are estimated to cost us $143,500 ($450,750 − 307,250); the incremental cost per order is $143,500/2,000 = $71.75.

Carrying costs, also referred to as *holding costs,* are basically the costs incurred because a firm owns or maintains inventories. Carrying costs include

CARRYING COSTS

Interest on money invested in inventory.

Obsolescence, a cost incurred when inventories go "out of style."

Storage space cost—this may include heat, lights, or refrigeration.

Stores operation, including record keeping, the taking of physical inventory, and protection.

Taxes, insurance, and *pilferage.*

TABLE 6-1
Ordering costs

Expense category	Annual salary	At 3,000 orders per year		At 5,000 orders per year	
		Number required	Annual cost	Number required	Annual cost
Purchasing department chief	$40,000	1	$ 40,000	1	$ 40,000
Buyers	30,000	3	90,000	5	150,000
Assistant buyers	20,000	2	40,000	3	60,000
Follow-up persons	15,000	1	15,000	2	30,000
Clerks	12,000	3	36,000	4	48,000
Typists	11,000	2	22,000	3	33,000
Supplies	—	—	500	—	500
Receiving clerks	12,000	2	24,000	3	36,000
Receiving supplies	—	—	300	—	500
Accounts payable clerks	13,000	3	39,000	4	52,000
Accounting supplies	—	—	450	—	750
Total expenses			$307,250		$450,750

EXPRESSING CARRYING COSTS

Carrying costs can be expressed as a percentage of the average inventory value (say, 22 percent per year to hold inventory) or as a cost per unit per time period (say, 25 cents per unit per month to hold inventory). Expressing inventory holding costs as a percentage of the value of the product is convenient because, regardless of the price of a product, the same percentage can be applied. Look at an example. If you calculate that it costs you 25 percent of the value of an item to hold it for a year, then inventory carrying costs on a $12 case of floor-cleaning compound would be .25 × $12, or $3 a year. Inventory holding costs on a six-pack of beer which costs the store $1.20 would be .25 × $1.20, or 30 cents per year.

CONCEPT OF AVERAGE INVENTORY

AVERAGE INVENTORY

If a firm buys an item only once for the coming year, if the use of the item is constant, and if the last of the item is used on the last day of the year, then the firm's average inventory equals one-half the amount bought; this is the same as saying one-half the beginning inventory. Figure 6-2 shows average inventory under conditions of constant usage.

The EOQ model is generally applicable when the demand for the SKU has a *constant* or a *nearly constant* rate. Whereas Figure 6-2 shows a demand situation which is perfectly constant, Figure 6-3 illustrates the case we generally find in practice, one where irregularities do occur.

WHICH COSTS ARE MINIMIZED

To minimize inventory costs, management tries to minimize *ordering* costs and *carrying* costs. Having seen how the incremental ordering cost, the carrying cost, and the average inventory are determined, we are now ready to solve for *economic order quantity*. EOQ is that size order which minimizes the total annual cost of ordering and carrying inventory. We are assuming conditions of certainty—annual requirements are known.

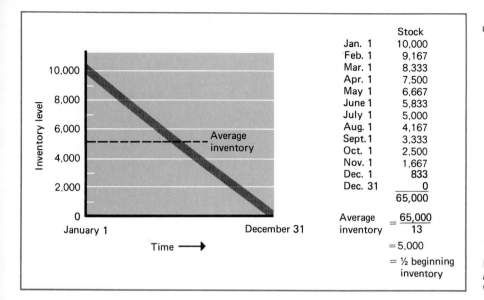

	Stock
Jan. 1	10,000
Feb. 1	9,167
Mar. 1	8,333
Apr. 1	7,500
May 1	6,667
June 1	5,833
July 1	5,000
Aug. 1	4,167
Sept. 1	3,333
Oct. 1	2,500
Nov. 1	1,667
Dec. 1	833
Dec. 31	0
	65,000

$$\frac{\text{Average}}{\text{inventory}} = \frac{65,000}{13}$$

$$= 5,000$$

$$= \text{½ beginning inventory}$$

FIGURE 6-2
Average inventory
with constant usage.

TABULAR SOLUTION FOR EOQ

Caroline, the owner of Caroline's Boutique, Ltd., estimates that she will sell $10,000 worth of a certain decorator table this year. Her accountants have determined that ordering costs amount to $25 per order and that carrying costs amount to 12½ percent of average inventory. Construction of a table such as Table 6-2 is one approach to identifying the EOQ.

SOLVING FOR EOQ
USING A TABLE

Note that as carrying charges decline, ordering costs increase. Note also that *total* costs, the figure we want to minimize, are lowest when carrying

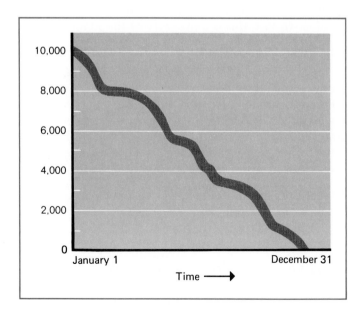

FIGURE 6-3
Inventory with nearly
constant usage.

TABLE 6-2
Identifying the economic order quantity

(1)			No. orders per year → 1	2	3	4	5	10	20
(2)	$10,000/(1)	= $ per order	$10,000	$5,000	$3,333	$2,500	$2,000	$1,000	$500
(3)	(2)/2	= Average inventory	5,000	2,500	1,666	1,250	1,000	500	250
(4)	(3) × 12½%	= Carrying costs	625	313	208	156	125	63	31
(5)	(1) × $25	= Ordering cost	25	50	75	100	125	250	500
(6)	(4) + (5)	= Total cost/year	$ 650	$ 363	$ 283	$ 256	$ 250	$ 313	$531

↑
Optimal

costs are *equal* to ordering costs. This is the point we always need to determine, because it is always the point of lowest total inventory costs for the year. Table 6-2 shows that Caroline should order this particular SKU 5 times during the year.

Note also that the total costs for ordering 4 and 5 times a year (and also 6 if we had calculated it) are nearly the same. The practical significance of this fact and of the fact that the total cost curve is "dish-shaped" is that *approximate* answers in this situation are often very good ones, varying only slightly from ones we might refer to as *optimal* answers. As long as Caroline orders 4 or 5 times a year, her total inventory cost stays near the minimum.

GRAPHIC PRESENTATION OF EOQ

Figure 6-4 graphs the data from Table 6-2. From the minimum point on the total cost curve in this figure, we can see that the optimal number of orders per year is 5. We can also see that at 5 orders a year, the total ordering cost per year equals the total carrying cost per year (the two lines cross at this point). You can notice from Table 6-2 that this is also true in the tabular solution. In fact, this is a property of the EOQ model.

DERIVING EOQ FORMULAS

In the following pages, we shall derive *four* EOQ formulas. Each of these produces the same answer, but in different units. Some inventory systems prefer to consider inventory purchasing in terms of *orders per year;* others would rather deal in terms of the *number of days' supply* to purchase at one time. Too, *the number of dollars per economic order* fits some inventory systems better, while *units per economic order* makes more sense in other situations. The following symbols will be used in our four EOQ formulas:

A = total dollar value of the SKU used per year
R = price of each unit
P = ordering cost per order placed
C = carrying cost expressed as a percentage of average inventory

Optimal number of orders per year   To derive this formula, let

N_o = optimal number of orders per year to minimize
         total inventory costs

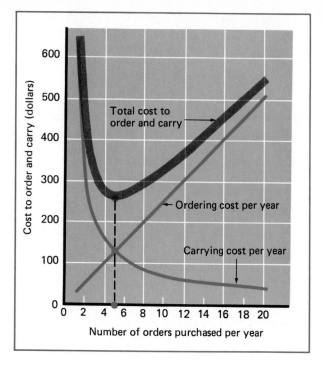

FIGURE 6-4
Identifying the
economic order
quantity.

We have seen that the most economical point for total inventory costs is the point where ordering costs are the same in amount as carrying costs. Thus, we can solve for N_o by letting

$$\text{Total ordering cost/year} = \text{carrying cost/year}$$

$$\text{Total ordering cost/year} = N_o \times P = N_o P$$

$$\text{Carrying cost/year} = \frac{A}{N_o} \times \frac{1}{2} \times C$$

$$\underbrace{\left(\frac{\$\,\text{Used/year}}{\text{No. orders/year}} = \$\,\text{amount per order} \right)}_{} \underbrace{\left(\begin{array}{c} \text{Average} \\ \text{inventory} \\ \text{balance} \\ \text{with} \\ \text{constant} \\ \text{usage} \end{array} \right)}_{} \underbrace{\left(\begin{array}{c} \text{Carrying} \\ \text{cost \%} \end{array} \right)}_{}$$

Equating, we get

$$N_o P = \frac{AC}{2N_o}$$

$$2N_o^2 P = AC$$

$$N_o^2 = \frac{AC}{2P}$$

Optimal number of orders per year $\quad N_o = \sqrt{\frac{AC^*}{2P}} \qquad (6\text{-}1)$

* Derivation of this result by the use of calculus is given in Appendix 7.

Using the formula as derived, we can solve for N_o using the same data seen in Table 6-2 and Figure 6-4:

$$\sqrt{\frac{\$10,000(.125)}{2(\$25)}} = \sqrt{\frac{\$1250}{\$50}} = 5 \text{ orders per year}$$

DERIVING A FORMULA
WHERE EOQ IS DEFINED
IN DAYS' SUPPLY
PER ORDER

Optimal number of days' supply per order   Our second formula tells us how many days' usage Caroline should provide for each time she orders.

Let N_d = optimal number of days' supply per order
Then, since there are 365 calendar days per year,

$$N_d = \frac{365}{N_o} = \frac{365}{\sqrt{AC/2P}}$$

or

Optimal number of
days' supply

$$N_d = 365\sqrt{\frac{2P}{AC}} \qquad (6\text{-}2)$$

Substituting Caroline's data into this formula, we get

$$N_d = 365\sqrt{\frac{2(\$25)}{(\$10,000)(.125)}}$$

$$= 365\sqrt{.04}$$

$$= 73 \text{ days' supply}$$

DERIVING A FORMULA
WHERE EOQ IS DEFINED
IN DOLLARS PER
ORDER

Optimal number of dollars per order   Our third formula indicates how many dollars' worth of an inventory item Caroline should purchase each time she orders.

Let $N_\$$ = optimal number of dollars per order

Then,

$$N_\$ = \frac{A}{N_o} = \frac{A}{\sqrt{AC/2P}}$$

Optimal number of
dollars per order

$$N_\$ = \sqrt{\frac{2AP}{C}} \qquad (6\text{-}3)$$

Substituting our values into *this* formula we get

$$N_\$ = \sqrt{\frac{2(\$10,000)(\$25)}{.125}}$$

$$= \sqrt{4,000,000}$$

$$= \$2,000 \text{ per order}$$

Optimal number of units per order   Another formula can be derived, this one to give us the optimal number of units to order each time an order is placed.

Let N_u = optimal number of units per order

Then,

$$N_u = \frac{N_\$}{R} = \frac{\sqrt{2AP/C}}{R}$$

Optimal number of units per order

$$N_u = \sqrt{\frac{2AP}{R^2C}} \tag{6-4}$$

Suppose Caroline tells us that this year she plans to sell 40 tables; her cost is \$250. You recall that ordering cost per order is \$25 and that carrying cost is 12½ percent. Now, substituting our values into our formula, we get

$$\sqrt{\frac{2(\$10,000)(\$25)}{(\$250)^2(.125)}} = \sqrt{\frac{500,000}{7812.5}} = \sqrt{64}$$

$$= 8 \text{ units/order}$$

COMPARABILITY OF ANSWERS

Application of the four formulas we have derived for Caroline Boutique produced these four answers for her:

Optimal number of orders per year =	5
Optimal number of days' supply to order =	73
Optimal dollars per order =	\$2,000
Optimal number of tables per order =	8

All these answers mean the *same* thing, and Caroline would use the formula that produced the answer in a form most suitable for *her* ordering and inventory system. In any event, she would use only one of the four formulas we have derived.

ASSUMPTIONS WE HAVE MADE

Instead of just handing Caroline one (or all four) of the EOQ formulas we have derived, we ought to be careful to review with her the assumptions under which these formulas work best. First, we assumed that she can estimate annual demand. Second, we assumed that demand was constant or nearly constant. Third, we assumed that when an order arrives, it arrives all at one time. And finally, we assumed that her cost figures for purchasing and carrying were reasonably accurate. If any of these assumptions is wrong, then applying our EOQ formulas will not generate answers useful to her. Fortunately there are ways of coping with situations in which these assumptions are not true; we shall present them later in this chapter.

▍ COST SAVINGS WITH AN EOQ MODEL

HOW MUCH DOES THE EOQ MODEL SAVE?

Before we provided her with an EOQ model, Caroline ordered these decorator tables once a month in an effort to keep her inventory cost down. Now we have suggested that an optimal purchasing policy is for her to order the tables 5 times a year. What is the difference in the two methods? In Table 6-3, we have illustrated the cost difference between these two methods. Using the EOQ model saves her a little over $100 annually on this one SKU.

5 How to eliminate the instantaneous receipt assumption in EOQ models

RECEIPT OF INVENTORY IS NOT ALWAYS SIMULTANEOUS

In the EOQ models presented to this point, we have assumed that all the inventory which is ordered arrives *simultaneously*—that the inventory rises to its maximum level instantaneously. Hence the vertical line to represent the arrival of a new lot of inventory is as shown in Figure 6-5. In many cases, however, this is not a valid assumption because the vendor delivers the order in partial shipments or portions over a period of time. In such cases, inventory is being used while new inventory is still being received and the inventory *does not* build up immediately to its maximum point. Instead it builds up gradually when inventory is received faster than it is being used; then it declines to its lowest level as incoming shipments stop and the use of inventory continues. This concept is illustrated in Figure 6-6.

We can express total ordering and carrying costs as follows. If

$$N_u = \text{optimal lot size in units}$$

TABLE 6-3
Total cost of present and proposed (EOQ) inventory policies for Caroline Boutique

	12 orders/ year	5 orders/ year
Annual cost of the tables	$10,000	$10,000
Cost per order (annual cost/number of orders)	833	2,000
Average inventory (cost/order)/2	417	1,000
Annual carrying cost (.125 × average inventory)	52	125
Annual purchasing cost ($25 × number of orders)	300	125
Total cost per year (annual purchasing cost + annual carrying charge)	352	250

└─ Savings = $102 ─┘

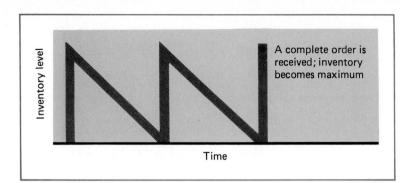

GRAPHIC ILLUSTRATION
OF ASSUMED
INVENTORY BEHAVIOR

FIGURE 6-5
Inventory with
instantaneous receipt.

and

$$x = \text{receipt rate in units received daily}$$

then

$$\frac{N_u}{x} = \text{number of days required to receive entire order}$$

If

$$y = \text{use rate in units used daily}$$

then

$$\frac{N_u}{x} \times y = \text{number of units used during receipt period}$$

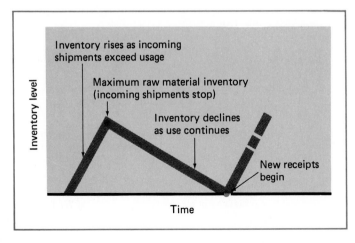

GRAPHIC ILLUSTRATION
OF ACTUAL INVENTORY
BEHAVIOR

FIGURE 6-6
Inventory with receipt
over time.

and

$$N_u - \frac{N_u}{x} \times y = \text{largest inventory which can accumulate}$$

Because the average inventory is half the maximum inventory, the average inventory in this case would be

$$\frac{1}{2}\left(N_u - \frac{N_u}{x} \times y\right) = \frac{1}{2}N_u\left(1 - \frac{y}{x}\right)$$

Let R represent cost per unit, and let C represent carrying costs. If carrying costs equal average inventory in units times cost per unit times carrying costs in percent, we get

$$\text{Carrying costs} = \frac{N_u}{2}\left(1 - \frac{y}{x}\right) \times R \times C$$

$$= \frac{RCN_u}{2}\left(1 - \frac{y}{x}\right)$$

And if annual usage in units is symbolized as U and ordering cost as P,

$$\text{Number of lots per year} = \frac{U}{N_u}$$

and

$$\text{Total ordering cost} = \frac{U}{N_u} \times P$$

From our previous derivations of EOQ models, we realize that total ordering *and* carrying costs are minimum when the cost to order per year equals the cost to carry per year. Thus we equate the two expressions we have already defined and solve for N_u:

$$\frac{UP}{N_u} = \frac{RCN_u}{2}\left(1 - \frac{y}{x}\right)$$

$$RCN_u{}^2\left(1 - \frac{y}{x}\right) = 2UP$$

$$N_u{}^2 = \frac{2UP}{RC(1 - y/x)}$$

Optimal number of units
with instantaneous receipt
assumption eliminated
$$N_u = \sqrt{\frac{2UP^*}{RC(1 - y/x)}} \qquad (6\text{-}5)$$

* Derivation of this result by the use of calculus is given in Appendix 7.

6 Using EOQ models when annual demand cannot be forecast

All the formulas we have derived up to this point have required that annual demand be known. In many situations, however, annual demand simply cannot be predicted with any reliability. Demand per week, for example, may be so erratic that we hesitate to predict annual demand from it; in another situation, we may be dealing with a brand-new product, one with absolutely no previous history. So to predict annual demand is not always possible or prudent. We thus must turn to another approach to EOQ when such is the situation.

Let's go back for a moment to Caroline Boutique and see how it is possible to use EOQ concepts even when annual demand cannot be forecast accurately. Caroline is interested in applying the EOQ model to a new-model rope hammock which she is stocking; however, she can only give us her estimated needs for the next 7 weeks. This short-term demand estimate, the cost of ordering, the cost per hammock, and her carrying cost for this item are all illustrated in Table 6-4. The zero net requirements for the first 3 weeks reflect the fact that some inventory is already on hand.

Caroline can still determine her economic order quantity for this SKU in this situation by using an *iterative* (step-by-step) method. She would begin by computing the carrying costs of the four buying alternatives, enough for 4, 5, 6, or 7 weeks' use.

Number of hammocks bought	Carrying cost
50	(All units used in fourth week) = $ 0
80	30 units held 1 week = $ 3
120	$3 (above) plus 40 units held 2 weeks = $11
160	$11 (above) plus 40 units held 3 weeks = $23

TABLE 6-4
Caroline's estimated requirements for 7 weeks

Week	Net requirements
1	0 ⎫
2	0 ⎬ (Zeros reflect inventory already on hand)
3	0 ⎭
4	50
5	30
6	40
7	40

Inventory item: rope hammock

Unit cost: $20.83

Carrying cost: 25%/year $\left(\$20.83 \times \dfrac{.25}{52} = \$.10/\text{unit per week} \right)$

Ordering cost: $20 per order

Now let us place the carrying costs of the four alternatives beside the ordering costs for the same alternatives:

Number of hammocks bought	Carrying cost	Ordering cost
50	$ 0	$20
80	3	20
120	11	20
160	23	20

As Caroline increases the number purchased at one time, the carrying costs rise until they are greater than the ordering costs. She knows from our past derivations that the optimal EOQ is where the cost to order *equals* the cost to carry; so she should order that number of units which equalizes those two costs. The answer lies somewhere between 120 (ordering cost greater than carrying cost) and 160 (carrying cost greater than ordering cost). An approximate EOQ in this situation can be found by some simple interpolation. She knows that the answer is something more than 120 units and that the extra ones, however many there are, will be carried in stock for 3 weeks. Her real question then is: How many units carried in stock for 3 weeks will cause the carrying charges to rise to $20 so as to equal the ordering costs? The answer is

$$\frac{\$20 - \$11}{\$.10 \times 3 \text{ wk}} = 30 \text{ units}$$

Thus the EOQ is 120 + 30 units = 150. This will cover her requirements through 30 units of the seventh week. Sometime prior to that time, another calculation will have to be made. In this procedure, the EOQ will likely be different each time it is calculated, but it will still be a completely logical outcome as long as the conditions underlying the need for hammocks are themselves changing from order to order. In using this variation of the standard EOQ approach, we must remember that we have assumed the order arrives in the week in which it is needed. More about how to make sure that happens, and what to do if it doesn't, is in the next chapter.

7 Using EOQ models when cost information is not available

In all our consideration of EOQ formulas to this point, we have assumed that the proper use of estimating, accounting, and other cost-finding techniques could produce the appropriate values of *carrying cost* and *ordering cost* our formulas have required. Sometimes, however, organizations have not maintained records which would provide a sufficient accounting information base to generate these two *parameters* (values); in other cases, organizations which have not employed formal inventory theory may wish to do so but may not be willing to wait until they have accumulated inventory cost data, and this is often a considerable period of time. And finally, in certain critical situations (severe overstocking or unusually high numbers of purchase orders being written), an organization may want to take immediate action to *improve* the situation, even though that action might not be optimal in the sense of formal inventory theory.

EOQ BENEFITS CAN BE OBTAINED EVEN WHEN ORDERING AND CARRYING COSTS ARE NOT KNOWN

In situations such as those reviewed above and in many others, it *is* possible to reap many of the benefits of inventory techniques even when ordering cost and carrying cost are not known and cannot be determined. Although it may at first appear that the use of inventory models without cost information is impossible, we will show (with a bit of simple algebra) how this *can* be done to provide management with practical answers to complex inventory situations.

There are two approaches to this problem: (1) we can leave the purchasing workload where it is while we minimize the carrying cost, or (2) we can leave the inventory where it is while we minimize the purchasing workload. Before we develop the models, a caveat is in order. We are *not* reaching an optimal (minimum cost) solution and cannot do so under these circumstances; we *are* minimizing carrying cost for a given number of orders or vice versa.

▌ DEVELOPING A MODEL WHICH WILL MINIMIZE INVENTORY LEVELS WITHOUT INCREASING THE PURCHASING WORKLOAD

Let us begin by repeating Eq. (6-3), which expresses the EOQ in *dollars per order:*

$$N_\$ = \sqrt{\frac{2AP}{C}} \qquad (6\text{-}3)$$

DEVELOPING A MODEL TO MINIMIZE INVENTORY WITHOUT INCREASING PURCHASING WORKLOAD

Now, of the values under the square root sign, organizations generally know or are able to estimate the value of A (the annual dollar use of an item per year). Suppose we separate the right-hand side of Eq. (6-3) into *two* parts, one containing A, the other containing the remaining three terms. Then we have

$$N_\$ = \sqrt{\frac{2P}{C}} \times \sqrt{A}$$

Even though the value 2 is a numerical constant and is therefore not part of our problem of lack of cost data, we have included it with the other two terms (P and C) just to make the following computations a bit easier.

Let us assume the worst possible information condition, that is, that we have no way of knowing or finding the values for P and C; therefore, we substitute X for the entire first part above as follows:

$$N_\$ = X\sqrt{A} \qquad (6\text{-}6)$$

At this point, we can do a bit of simple algebra in several steps as follows:

Step 1   Divide both sides of Eq. (6-6) into *A*:

$$\frac{A}{N_\$} = \frac{A}{X\sqrt{A}}$$

Step 2   Separate the numerator of the *right* side into two parts:

$$\frac{A}{N_\$} = \frac{\sqrt{A} \cdot \sqrt{A}}{X\sqrt{A}}$$

Step 3   Cancel equivalent terms in the numerator and denominator of the right side. This leaves

$$\frac{A}{N_\$} = \frac{\sqrt{A}}{X}$$

Step 4   Solve for *X*:

$$X\frac{A}{N_\$} = \sqrt{A}$$

$$X = \frac{\sqrt{A}}{A/N_\$}$$

Step 5   Because *X* will be a constant for any *single* inventory item, it is useful for purposes of this development to consider *X* as a constant for an *entire inventory* of items; it can therefore be expressed as the ratio of the sums of the numerator and the denominator of the right side:

$$\text{Constant to use for minimizing inventory without increasing purchasing workload} \qquad X = \frac{\Sigma \sqrt{A}}{\Sigma (A/N_\$)} \qquad (6\text{-}7)$$

MINIMIZING CAROLINE'S INVENTORY LEVEL WITHOUT INCREASING HER PURCHASING WORKLOAD

PROBLEM
ILLUSTRATING
INVENTORY
MINIMIZATION
WITHOUT ANY
INCREASE IN
PURCHASING
WORKLOAD

Suppose we have just walked into Caroline Boutique. She has never made any attempt to apply EOQ models, and she has no cost information on purchasing or carrying costs. Her past inventory policy on the five SKUs she stocks was to purchase them quarterly. Table 6-5 illustrates Caroline's inventory situation. What can we do in this situation?

Looking both at Eq. (6-7) and at the information in Table 6-5, we can now solve for *X* in that equation from the information in the table. First, the *numerator* of Eq. (6-7):

$$\Sigma \sqrt{A} = \sqrt{10{,}000} + \sqrt{8{,}000} + \sqrt{5{,}000} + \sqrt{1{,}000} + \sqrt{600}$$
$$= 100.00 + 89.44 + 70.71 + 31.62 + 24.49$$
$$= 316.26$$

TABLE 6-5
Inventory situation at Caroline Boutique

267

INVENTORY I

SKU	Dollar value used annually	No. of times ordered per year	Dollars per order	Average inventory balance
Decorator lamp	$10,000	4	$2,500	$1,250
Rattan chair	8,000	4	2,000	1,000
Rope hammock	5,000	4	1,250	625
Brass chafing dish	1,000	4	250	125
Embroidered place mat	600	4	150	75
		20 = total purchasing workload		$3,075 = average inventory balance

Now the *denominator* of Eq. (6-7):

$$\Sigma \frac{A}{N_\$} = \text{the sum of } \frac{A}{N_\$} \quad \left[\begin{array}{c} \text{As } A/N_\$ \text{ is the number of orders placed for } one \\ \text{inventory item, } \Sigma\,(A/N_\$) \text{ must equal the } total \text{ number} \\ \text{of orders placed.} \end{array} \right]$$
$$= 20$$

Knowing the values for the numerator and denominator of Eq. (6-7), we can now solve for X in that equation as follows:

$$X = \frac{316.26}{20}$$
$$= 15.813$$

From Eq. (6-6) we saw that the optimal dollar value per order for any single inventory item is

$$N_\$ = X\sqrt{A} \tag{6-6}$$

Table 6-6 applies this formula to each of the five SKUs in Caroline's inventory. From the computations represented by this table, we can see that her total

INTERPRETING THE RESULTS

TABLE 6-6
Caroline's inventory: minimum average inventory is achieved without increasing purchasing workload

SKU	A, $ used per year	$\sqrt{A}$	X	$X\sqrt{A}$, $ per order	Average inventory, ($ per order)/2	No. orders per year, A/($ per order)
Decorator lamp	10,000	100.00	15.813	1,581.30	790.65	6.32
Rattan chair	8,000	89.44	15.813	1,414.31	707.16	5.66
Rope hammock	5,000	70.71	15.813	1,118.14	559.07	4.47
Brass chafing dish	1,000	31.62	15.813	500.01	250.01	2.00
Embroidered place mat	600	24.49	15.813	387.26	193.63	1.55
					$2,500.52	20.00

average inventory has been reduced from the $3,075 of Table 6-5 down to $2,500.52, while her total purchasing workload has remained unchanged at 20 orders per year. (The fact that the number of orders per year for several of her SKUs is not an integer is not really relevant. For example, our solution indicates that she should place 6.32 orders per year for lamps; this is nothing more than saying she should order this item every 365/6.32 or 58 calendar days.)

Let us look for a moment at what we have accomplished. Without knowing the value of carrying cost or ordering cost, we have managed to accomplish a significant inventory reduction without increasing purchasing workload. This has been possible because we have used *surrogates,* or substitutes, for carrying cost and ordering cost. Specifically, we have assumed that whatever the true carrying cost might be, carrying a *lower* inventory ($2,500.52) is better than carrying a *higher* inventory ($3,075). Thus we have really let the value of the average inventory serve as a surrogate for carrying cost. Similarly, we have used the total number of purchase orders written per year as a surrogate for ordering cost; this is nothing more complicated than assuming that if Caroline doesn't write any additional orders, her total cost of operating the procurement function probably won't change.

DEVELOPING A MODEL WHICH WILL MINIMIZE THE PURCHASING WORKLOAD WITHOUT INCREASING THE AVERAGE INVENTORY

DEVELOPING A MODEL
TO MINIMIZE
PURCHASING
WORKLOAD WITHOUT
INCREASING AVERAGE
INVENTORY

In the previous section, we were able to minimize the average inventory without increasing the purchasing workload; it is also possible to *minimize the purchasing workload without altering the average level of the inventory.* In situations where temporary shortages of qualified purchasing personnel make exploration of this alternative advantageous, the method to be illustrated represents a very practical alternative. Again we shall assume that information on carrying costs and ordering costs is not available. We begin by first recalling Eq. (6-6).

$$N_\$ = X \sqrt{A} \qquad (6-6)$$

As X is a constant for any single inventory item, it is also a constant for an *entire inventory* of items; thus for the five inventory items of our Caroline Boutique illustration, we can rewrite Eq. (6-6) to

$$\Sigma N_\$ = X \Sigma \sqrt{A}$$

and solving for X we have

Constant to use for minimizing purchasing workload without increasing inventory

$$X = \frac{\Sigma N_\$}{\Sigma \sqrt{A}} \qquad (6-8)$$

PROBLEM
ILLUSTRATING
MINIMIZATION
OF PURCHASING
WORKLOAD WITHOUT
INCREASING AVERAGE
INVENTORY

MINIMIZING CAROLINE'S PURCHASING WORKLOAD WITHOUT INCREASING HER AVERAGE INVENTORY

Let us apply Eq. (6-8) to Caroline's inventory in Table 6-5. The numerator of Eq. (6-8) calls for the sum of the dollars per order; this value can be obtained by summing the "Dollars per order" column of Table 6-5, or more quickly by simply computing twice the average inventory balance:

$$\Sigma N_\$ = 2,500 + 2,000 + 1,250 + 250 + 150$$

$$= 6,150$$

or

$$\Sigma N_\$ = 2 \times 3,075$$
$$= 6,150$$

The denominator of Eq. (6-8) is identical to the numerator of Eq. (6-7) and has previously been computed to be 316.26. Therefore, the required value for X in Eq. (6-8) can now be calculated as

$$X = \frac{\Sigma N_\$}{\Sigma \sqrt{A}} \qquad (6\text{-}8)$$

$$= \frac{6,150}{316.26}$$

$$= 19.446$$

In Eq. (6-6), we saw that the optimal dollar value per order for any single inventory item was

$$N_\$ = X \sqrt{A} \qquad (6\text{-}6)$$

Table 6-7 applies this equation to the inventory situation at Caroline Boutique using the value just calculated for X. The results in Table 6-7 indicate that we have achieved about a 20 percent reduction in purchasing workload (measured in terms of the number of orders processed per year) *without*

INTERPRETING
THE RESULTS

TABLE 6-7
Caroline's inventory: minimizing her purchasing workload without increasing total average inventory

SKU	A, $ used per yr	$\sqrt{A}$	X	$X\sqrt{A}$, $ per order	Average inventory, $ per order/2	No. orders per year, A/$ per order
Decorator lamp	10,000	100.00	19.446	1,944.60	972.30	5.14
Rattan chair	8,000	89.44	19.446	1,739.25	869.62	4.60
Rope hammock	5,000	70.71	19.446	1,375.03	687.51	3.64
Brass chafing dish	1,000	31.62	19.446	614.88	307.44	1.63
Embroidered place mat	600	24.49	19.446	476.23	238.12	1.26
					3,074.99	16.27

increasing her total average inventory above the $3,075 level (there is a slight roundoff error in the calculations, but this is quite normal).

■ CONCLUSION CONCERNING OPTIONS WHEN THERE IS NO COST INFORMATION

RESULTS FROM USING QUANTITATIVE APPROACHES EVEN WHEN COST INFORMATION IS LACKING

We have demonstrated with the preceding two examples how one can still make sensible inventory decisions even in the absence of explicit cost information by using *surrogates* for cost of carrying and cost of ordering. The Caroline Boutique example used an inventory consisting of only five items to simplify the calculations required; in practice, however, the authors have applied, with the use of a computer, the first approach (minimizing the inventory level without increasing the workload) to an actual inventory of over 16,000 different items. The analysis resulted in a reduction of nearly 18 percent in the inventory level in a situation where cost information necessary to support the more traditional EOQ analysis was completely lacking and where it might be several years before such information might be available.

It should be noted that the methods illustrated in this section are capable of providing operational answers to *any* purchasing workload and average inventory condition desired by management; our two illustrations enabled us to determine the following *two* outcomes:

1 Minimum average inventory without increasing purchasing workload
2 Minimum purchasing workload without increasing total average inventory

ALTERNATIVE ANSWERS THAT MAY BE MORE USEFUL

Just as a last couple of examples of flexibility, suppose first that Caroline wanted to find what reduction in total average inventory she could achieve *if she were willing to increase her purchasing workload 20 percent a year* (from 20 to 24 orders, in our simplified example). To do this she would have substituted into Eq. (6-7) as follows:

$$X = \frac{316.26}{24}$$
$$= 13.178$$

MORE FLEXIBILITY WITH THIS MODEL

and used the new value of X in a table just as in Table 6-7.

And finally, if Caroline wanted to determine how much she could reduce her purchasing workload *if she were willing to increase her average inventory by $1,000,* she would have substituted into Eq. (6-8) as follows and used it in a table like Table 6-7:

$$X = \frac{8,150^*}{316.26}$$
$$= 25.770$$

* Remember that *twice* the increase in average inventory has been added here.

8 Applying the EOQ model to production processes

The concept that there is one best pattern of ordering to minimize annual inventory costs can be adapted to the production process. For instance, many companies produce certain items among their product lines in lots or batches instead of manufacturing at a constant rate all year long. This method is generally followed because total annual sales of the finished item are not enough to warrant maintaining a production line for the exclusive manufacture of that item on a yearlong continuous basis.

These firms incur a *setup cost* each time a batch is produced. Setup cost is roughly equivalent to the ordering cost per order already treated in this chapter. It consists of

SETUP COSTS

1 *Engineering* and *labor cost* of setting up the production lines or machines
2 *Paperwork cost* of processing the work order and authorizing production
3 *Ordering cost* to provide raw materials for the batch or order

In addition to these setup costs, the company incurs *carrying costs* on the finished product from the time it is manufactured until it is sold. The carrying charges on finished goods consist of the same items constituting the carrying costs on inventory except that the value of finished goods is higher because of the cost of manufacturing, labor, and overhead. We see, then, that the basic concept of an optimal number of batches or runs—the number to minimize total annual production costs for manufacturing of the intermittent type—is quite similar to the concept we have been using for raw material inventories.

CARRYING COSTS

OPTIMAL PRODUCTION LOT SIZE: PRODUCTION FOR STOCK

One case where an optimal production lot size can be calculated involves finished goods which are to be placed in stock and then sold at a constant rate until some low level is reached; at that time another lot will be produced. Here the procedure for finding the optimal number of runs per year is the same as in the case of inventory control. The symbols used correspond as shown in Table 6-8. If, for instance, (1) a company produces $40,000 worth

PROBLEM ILLUSTRATING OPTIMAL PRODUCTION LOT SIZE

Inventory, Eq. (6-1), optimal no. of orders		Production runs, Eq. (6-9), optimal no. per year	
A	Annual use of item in dollars	A	Annual sales of item in dollars (factory cost)
C	Carrying costs as a percentage of raw materials	C	Carrying costs as a percentage of finished goods
P	Ordering costs per order	S	Setup cost per run
N_o	Optimal no. of orders per year	N_r	Optimal no. of runs per year

TABLE 6-8
Symbols for computing production lot size for stock

COMPARABILITY OF SYMBOLS

of special gears at the factory each year, (2) carrying costs on finished stock are 20 percent per year, and (3) setup cost per production run is $80, then the optimal number of production runs per year for this item would be

$$\text{Optimal number of production runs per year} \quad N_r = \sqrt{\frac{AC}{2S}} \tag{6-9}$$

$$= \sqrt{\frac{\$40{,}000(.20)}{2(\$80)}}$$

$$= \sqrt{\frac{\$8{,}000}{\$160}}$$

$$= \sqrt{50}$$

$$= \text{about 7 runs per year}$$

INTERPRETING
THE RESULTS

In other words, to minimize total annual cost of setting up to produce these gears and of storing them until the gears are sold, the company should manufacture the annual requirement for this item in 7 lots or batches per year. We could, of course, have used other EOQ formulas and derived the answer in terms of optimal number of units per run or in terms of optimal number of months' sales in each run.

OPTIMAL PRODUCTION LOT SIZE: SIMULTANEOUS PRODUCTION AND SALES

Another case in which we can apply the concept of an optimal production lot size is one where the finished goods are being sold while each lot is being produced. In this case, the inventory of finished goods does not build up immediately to its maximum point, as it would in the case of receipt of a complete optimal order of raw materials. Instead, it builds up gradually as goods are produced faster than they are being sold; then it declines to its lowest point as production of a particular batch ceases although sales continue. This concept is illustrated in Figure 6-7.

Table 6-9 shows how the symbols in this situation correspond to those used in calculating inventories. The appropriate formula to use under these conditions is

$$\text{Optimal production lot size with simultaneous production and sales} \quad N_u = \sqrt{\frac{2US}{RC(1 - d/p)}} \tag{6-10}$$

where d is the sales rate in units per day and p is the production rate in units per day. Equation (6-10) corresponds to Eq. (6-5), which was appropriate to use in the case of simultaneous receipt and use of *inventory*.

PROBLEM
ILLUSTRATING
PRODUCTION LOT
SIZE WITHOUT
INSTANTANEOUS
PRODUCTION

To apply Eq. (6-10), consider a Napa Valley, California, company that bottles 5,000 cases of a particular rosé wine annually. The setup cost per run is $90. Factory cost is $5 per case. Carrying costs on finished goods inventory are 20 percent. Production rate is 100 per day, and sales amount to 14 per day. How many cases should be bottled per production run?

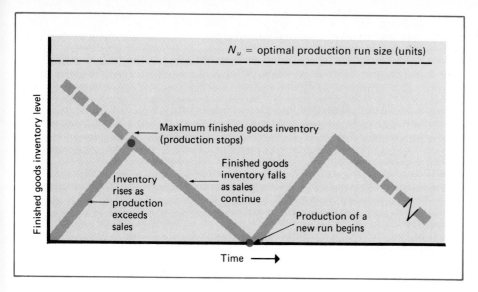

N_u = optimal production run size (units)

Finished goods inventory level

Maximum finished goods inventory
(production stops)

Inventory
rises as
production
exceeds
sales

Finished goods
inventory falls
as sales
continue

Production of a
new run begins

Time

FIGURE 6-7
Finished goods
inventory during
simultaneous
production and sales.

$$N_u = \sqrt{\frac{2US}{RC(1 - d/p)}} \qquad (6\text{-}10)$$

$$= \sqrt{\frac{2(5{,}000)(\$90)}{\$5(.20)(1 - {}^{14}/_{100})}}$$

$$= \sqrt{\frac{\$900{,}000}{\$1(1 - .14)}}$$

$$= \sqrt{1{,}046{,}000}$$

$= 1{,}023$ = number of cases per optimal production run

(From a practical standpoint, the company would probably set up its bottling
line five times a year.)

TABLE 6-9
Symbols for
computing lot size
with simultaneous
sales

COMPARABILITY
OF SYMBOLS

Inventory, Eq. (6-5), optimal units per lot		Production runs, Eq. (6-10), optimal units per run	
U	Annual need in units	U	Annual sales in units
P	Ordering costs per order	S	Setup cost per run
R	Price per unit	R	Factory cost per unit
C	Carrying costs as a percentage of raw materials	C	Carrying costs as a percentage of finished goods
N_u	Optimal no. of units per order	N_u	Optimal no. of units per run
y	Daily use rate of SKU	d	Daily sales rate in units
x	Daily receipt rate of SKU	p	Daily production rate in units

274

CHAPTER 6

USING MODELS OF
PRODUCTION LOT SIZE
WITHOUT COST
INFORMATION:
A CAUTION

▨ USE OF ECONOMIC PRODUCTION LOT SIZE MODELS WHEN COST INFORMATION IS NOT AVAILABLE

Earlier in this chapter, we included a section titled "Using EOQ Models When Cost Information Is Not Available." The concepts brought out there are equally applicable to the production lot size situation when setup costs and carrying costs on finished inventory cannot be determined. One must remember, however, that in the production case, our method would use the total number of setups per year as a surrogate for setup cost; in cases where there is no wide variation in the cost of one setup versus another, this method is perfectly suitable. However, in cases where the setups involved in the manufacture of one part cost $500 and the setups involved in the manufacture of another part cost only $5, one would have to use the results with caution, remembering that reducing the total number of setups by 20 percent per year is not nearly as meaningful if those reduced are of the $5 variety instead of the $500 variety.

▨9 Some conclusions about EOQ models
▨ SENSITIVITY OF EOQ MODELS

SENSITIVITY OF THE
EOQ MODEL TO
CHANGES IN DEMAND

Let us make a few simple tests to see how sensitive the EOQ formula is to increases in annual demand for any item; then we can attempt to set an inventory policy under these conditions. In Table 6-10, using Eq. (6-4), we have calculated EOQ for four different levels of annual demand. What is the significance of these results? In each case, the annual demand rose by a factor of 10, but a quick calculation indicates that the optimal EOQ rose only by 3.16 (the square root of 10). Of course, because the formula involves a square root and because the only value we altered was in the numerator, this should have been obvious before we completed the calculations. The implications of this simple experiment, however, are quite clear. **The size of order, and thus the average inventory held, should rise** *only by the square root of the increase*

TABLE 6-10
Sensitivity of EOQ to
annual demand

SENSITIVITY SHOWN

Annual use, units	EOQ, units per economic lot
1,000	$\sqrt{\dfrac{2(\$2,000)(\$10)}{(\$2)^2(.20)}} = 224$
10,000	$\sqrt{\dfrac{2(\$20,000)(\$10)}{(\$2)^2(.20)}} = 707$
100,000	$\sqrt{\dfrac{2(\$200,000)(\$10)}{(\$2)^2(.20)}} = 2,236$
1,000,000	$\sqrt{\dfrac{2(\$2,000,000)(\$10)}{(\$2)^2(.20)}} = 7,071$

Carrying cost: 20%
Ordering cost: $10
Price per unit: $2

in annual sales of the item. When annual sales are increasing or decreasing, inventory systems which hold a *fixed* percentage of anticipated annual sales in inventory cannot be considered optimal.

INPUT DATA FOR EOQ FORMULAS

Keep in mind that the EOQ formulas are only tools for use in decision making and that the answers derived from them are only as good as the data fed into the formulas. Sloppy cost accounting will not permit optimal use of the kinds of analysis we have been discussing in this chapter.

SELECTIVE USE OF EOQ FORMULAS

As we pointed out earlier, it would be a rare company that uses EOQ formulas for controlling the purchasing of every SKU it carries in its inventory. Most organizations that use EOQ approaches use them for controlling their *A*-type SKUs. Other less technical approaches suffice for the *B* SKUs. To control *C* SKUs, management might just set rule-of-thumb upper and lower inventory limits and leave it at that. In most cases, to do more would "chase pennies with dollars."

EOQ MODELS ARE NOT NORMALLY USED FOR ALL SKUs

IMPORTANCE OF THE EOQ MODELS

EOQ approaches to inventory management are important for a number of reasons:

1 EOQ models are fairly simple to explain (at least the ones we have concentrated on in this chapter).

2 Most EOQ models are not terribly sensitive to changes in the inputs (near-optimal outputs can often be obtained without knowing what the "true" optimal really is).

3 The use of EOQ models in situations where no formal inventory models have been employed generally results in some dramatic savings.

4 EOQ models concentrate on inventory, a current asset of major importance to working capital analysis, and effective financial management.

CAVEATS TO EOQ ANALYSIS

There are a lot of situations where EOQ models can't be used or where they shouldn't be used but are anyhow. These include situations in which

1 The standard EOQ model should not be used even when the conditions of instantaneous receipt of stock are not present.

2 The EOQ model should not be used when price reductions are offered without taking account of such discounts.

3 The standard EOQ model should not be used when demand is not known.

4 EOQ analysis should not be used indiscriminately for all SKUs in an inventory.

5 An EOQ model should not be used with incomplete or inaccurate cost data.

It should be obvious that in any of these instances the actual savings from the use of such techniques may be far less than anticipated. Finally, the likelihood of management disappointment with such results cannot help but reduce the future acceptance of MS/OR approaches to such problems.

10 Glossary

ABC analysis A selective classification and analysis of inventory SKUs according to annual dollar importance.

Average inventory The average balance of inventory on hand; in the case of constant demand, average inventory is half of maximum inventory.

Carrying costs The costs incurred in maintaining an inventory.

EOQ Economic order quantity: that particular quantity which, if ordered each time the inventory is replenished, will minimize the total annual cost of ordering and carrying the inventory.

Instantaneous receipt The condition where the entire quantity of inventory which has been ordered arrives at one time.

Iterative process A step-by-step process.

Optimal production lot size That particular quantity which, if produced in one production run, will minimize the total annual cost of setting up and carrying finished goods inventory.

Ordering costs The costs of getting an item into the inventory; these costs are incurred each time an order is placed.

Purchasing workload The total number of purchase orders written per year; used as a surrogate for total annual ordering cost.

SKU Stockkeeping unit: a specific item in an inventory.

11 Review of equations

Page 257

$$N_o = \sqrt{\frac{AC}{2P}} \tag{6-1}$$

This formula will solve for EOQ in terms of the optimal number of orders per year where P = ordering cost, A = annual usage of the SKU in dollars, and C = carrying cost expressed as a percentage of average inventory. Instantaneous receipt of inventory is assumed.

Page 258

$$N_d = 365 \sqrt{\frac{2P}{AC}} \tag{6-2}$$

Using the same symbols already defined, we can solve for the optimal number of days' supply per order by using this formula. Instantaneous receipt of inventory is assumed.

Page 258

$$N_\$ = \sqrt{\frac{2AP}{C}}$$ 　　　　　　　　(6-3)

This formula will give us the number of dollars per economic order; it uses the same symbols previously defined. This formula, too, assumes instantaneous receipt of inventory.

Page 259

$$N_u = \sqrt{\frac{2AP}{R^2C}}$$ 　　　　　　　　(6-4)

With this formula we can solve for EOQ in terms of the optimal number of units per economic order. The one additional symbol not used in Eq. (6-1) is R, which is the price of each unit. Instantaneous receipt of inventory is assumed.

Page 262

$$N_u = \sqrt{\frac{2UP}{RC(1 - y/x)}}$$ 　　　　　　　　(6-5)

By using this formula, we can remove the assumption of instantaneous receipt of inventory, which was necessary with Eqs. (6-1) through (6-4). In this formulation, P, R, and C are as previously defined; U = the annual demand for the SKU in units; y = daily use rate of the SKU; and x = the daily receipt rate of the SKU.

Page 265

$$N_\$ = X\sqrt{A}$$ 　　　　　　　　(6-6)

This is Eq. (6-3) with X substituting for $\sqrt{2P/C}$. It is a part of the derivation of an equation useful in situations where cost data concerning carrying costs and ordering costs are not available.

Page 266

$$X = \frac{\Sigma \sqrt{A}}{\Sigma A/N_\$}$$ 　　　　　　　　(6-7)

Equation (6-7) is used to minimize inventory level without increasing purchasing workload in situations where cost data for carrying and ordering costs are not available. Average inventory serves as a surrogate for carrying charges, and purchasing workload serves as a surrogate for ordering cost.

Page 268

$$X = \frac{\Sigma N_\$}{\Sigma \sqrt{A}} \tag{6-8}$$

We use this formula when we are interested in minimizing the purchasing workload without increasing the average inventory in situations where cost data for carrying and ordering costs are not available. Average inventory serves as a surrogate for carrying charges, and purchasing workload serves as a surrogate for ordering cost.

Page 272

$$N_r = \sqrt{\frac{AC}{2S}} \tag{6-9}$$

This formula yields the optimal number of production runs per year to minimize the total annual cost of carrying finished inventory and the setup cost of machines. C is defined as it was in previous EOQ formulas; S = the cost per setup in dollars; A = annual sales of the item in dollars of factory cost.

Page 272

$$N_u = \sqrt{\frac{2US}{RC(1 - d/p)}} \tag{6-10}$$

With this formula we can eliminate the assumption of instantaneous maximum inventory of finished goods inherent in Eq. (6-9). Here we allow for simultaneous production and use of inventory. All the symbols used here have been defined previously except d, which equals the sales rate in units per day, and p, which equals the production rate, also in units per day.

12 Exercises*

6-1 Dave Danesh experiences an annual demand of $220,000 for pro quality golf balls at the Arizona Golf Supply Company. It costs Dave $30 to place an order and his carrying cost is 18 percent. How many orders per year should Dave place for the balls?

6-2 Maud Littlefield, owner of Computer Village, needs to determine an optimal ordering policy for Porto-Exec computers. Annual demand for the computers is $28,000 and carrying cost is 23 percent. Maud has estimated order costs to be $48 per order. What are the optimal dollars per order?

6-3 Central University uses $96,000 annually of a particular reagent in the chemistry department labs. The purchasing director of the university estimates the ordering cost at $45 and thinks that the university can hold this type of inventory at an annual storage cost of 22 percent of the purchase price. How many months' supply should the purchasing director order at one time to minimize total annual cost of purchasing and carrying?

* See the Preface for an explanation of the computer and pencil symbols.

6-4 Oklahoma Supply stocks and sells oil drilling parts. The SKUs along with their annual usage, unit costs, and annual dollar volumes are as follows:

SKU	Annual usage	Unit cost	Annual dollars used
1	50	$60,000	$ 3,000,000
2	8000	10	80,000
3	100	2,000	200,000
4	6000	12	72,000
5	150	3,500	525,000
6	4000	25	100,000
7	220	1,800	396,000
8	260	15,400	4,004,000
9	1500	30	45,000
10	2200	18	39,600
11	3500	44	154,000
12	210	1,250	262,500
13	3100	20	62,000
14	4300	35	150,500
15	2500	48	120,000
16	230	2,000	460,000
17	6500	18	117,000
18	2300	15	34,500
19	1900	14	26,600
20	320	500	160,000
			10,008,700

Perform an ABC analysis on Oklahoma Supply's inventory.

6-5 The DeWitt Company is planning to stock a new SKU which is classified as an A inventory item. The company has developed the following information: annual usage is 5,400 units; cost of the SKU is $365; ordering cost is $55 per order; carrying cost is 28 percent per year of inventory value held. Determine the optimal number of units per order.

6-6 Using the information given in Exercise 6-5, find the optimal number of orders per year.

6-7 Cardinal Chemical Company holds its inventory of raw material in special containers, with each container occupying 10 square feet of floor space. There are only 5,000 square feet of storage space available. Each year, Cardinal uses 9,000 containers of raw material, paying $8 per container. If ordering costs for raw material are $40 per order and annual holding costs are 20 percent of the average inventory value, how much is it worth to Cardinal to increase its raw material storage area? How many day's supply of inventory can be stored with the 5,000 square feet storage limitation, assuming Cardinal works a 300-day year?

6-8 The Cardinal Chemical Company of Exercise 6-7 has been advised by its supplier of raw material that perhaps it would be of mutual advantage for the supplier to fill its orders incrementally. This plan would call for the supplier to deliver 50 containers per day, beginning immediately when an order is placed and continuing until the order is filled. Under the plan, would the company realize any savings in annual inventory costs? Assuming a 300-day work year, how many days' supply is there in each order? (Remember to check if the 5,000 square feet of space is adequate).

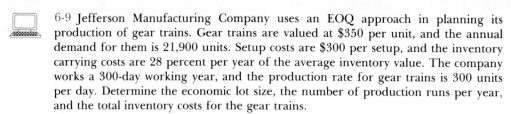

6-9 Jefferson Manufacturing Company uses an EOQ approach in planning its production of gear trains. Gear trains are valued at $350 per unit, and the annual demand for them is 21,900 units. Setup costs are $300 per setup, and the inventory carrying costs are 28 percent per year of the average inventory value. The company works a 300-day working year, and the production rate for gear trains is 300 units per day. Determine the economic lot size, the number of production runs per year, and the total inventory costs for the gear trains.

6-10 The First Flite Golf Ball Company stores its rubber winding material in modular containers, each of which measures 4 feet per side. A total of 3,680 square feet of space is available for keeping these containers on hand. Each year, First Flite uses 14,000 containers of rubber winding material in its manufacturing processes, paying $80 for each container. The company estimates its ordering costs at $30 per order, and holding costs are 25 percent of the average inventory value. Calculate what, if anything, First Flite would be willing to pay to increase its storage area and the size of any projected increase.

6-11 The Carolina Transport Company owns a fleet of tank trucks which haul petroleum products from the port city of Wilmington to various locations in the state. The company is a big purchaser of truck tires, annual use being estimated at 900. These tires cost Carolina Transport $260 each; Carole Sloan, the purchasing manager, estimates their carrying cost at 2 percent a month and their ordering cost at $60. The supplier from whom the company purchases tires has a delivery truck which holds only 12 tires; therefore 12 is the maximum number that can be delivered in a day, since the round-trip haul is over 300 miles. How many times a year should Carolina Transport order tires?

6-12 The Retrieval Systems Company, Inc., is a manufacturer of automatic paging devices used by physicians, lawyers, businesspersons, and others who need to be available on a 24-hour basis. The materials which go into a small "beeper" (paging device) are listed as follows:

SKU	Annual usage	Unit cost	Annual dollars used
H-206	26,000	1.15	29,900
F-213	20,000	.18	3,600
KL-10	14,000	1.70	23,800
J-620	48,000	2.50	120,000
M-110	18,000	.12	2,160
P-118	65,000	.05	3,250
Z-325	70,000	.09	6,300
L-817	34,000	.16	5,440

Perform an ABC analysis on Retrieval Systems' inventory.

6-13 Jerry Wilkes is concerned about his stocking policy for bonding epoxy, which is used on a regular basis in his automotive shop. The manufacturer of the epoxy recommends that the epoxy be used within 90 days of purchase in order to ensure maximum performance. Jerry would like to use EOQ, but still does not want to exceed the recommended shelf life. Each year Jerry purchases $9,800 worth of the epoxy. His order cost is $55 per order, and holding cost is 26 percent. How many days' supply should be ordered according to the EOQ policy? Does this policy cause Jerry to be concerned about shelf life restrictions?

6-14 Yvonne Belyea is planning to order maternity dresses for the Addis Department Store. She has been informed by the dress manufacturer that if maternity dress orders received this month are $3000 or more in value, they will sponsor a one-day visit by Dr. Benjamin Lock, who will come to the store and talk with prospective mothers about child care. Yvonne orders $30,000 worth of maternity dresses per year and her ordering and carrying costs are $30 per order and 28 percent, respectively. If Yvonne places her order according to EOQ, will the dollar value of the order be sufficient to qualify for a visit by Dr. Lock?

6-15 The Benson Company orders electric fans according to the EOQ model with each order being for 1000 fans. Their carrying cost is 32 percent, and their order cost is $58. If the fans are purchased at a price of $120 each, what is the annual dollar value of fans purchased by the company?

6-16 Prior to this year, Mercy Eades has ordered microwave ovens for Eades Restaurant Supply according to EOQ. She places 9.3 orders per year, and her carrying and ordering costs are 30 percent and $46 per order, respectively. Next year, annual demand for microwave ovens is expected to increase by 20 percent. How many orders will Marcy be placing next year?

6-17 In its manufacturing operations, the MANN Company uses a particular subassembly which it orders from a supplier. The company is able to forecast demand for the subassembly for only about 2 months in advance. The subassembly costs $58.60. The MANN Company estimates its inventory holding cost at 2.25 percent per month and its administrative cost of a purchase order at $37.50. There are 100 units on hand, and the table below indicates the demand estimates for the next 9 weeks. Calculate how many subassemblies the company should order if it is now time to place an order.

Week	Estimated demand
1	40
2	50
3	55
4	70
5	80
6	65
7	60
8	50
9	45

6-18 You have been retained as a consultant by a textile company which maintains inventories of 10 items used in its manufacturing process. The company is not able to determine its carrying cost or ordering cost with sufficient reliability to support the use of formal EOQ approaches, but it is nevertheless concerned that it is not managing its inventory as effectively as it might. These data concerning use and purchase of the 10 inventory items are available from last year's records:

Item	Dollars used annually	No. purchase orders placed last year
A	$120,000	5
B	80,000	6
C	50,000	6
D	24,000	4
E	10,500	8
F	5,200	6
G	2,400	7
H	1,100	8
I	900	6
J	300	6

Using the data available, answer these questions:

   a. Without increasing the purchasing workload, what percentage reduction can you make in the average dollar inventory carried?
   b. If the company is willing to increase the purchasing workload by 25 percent, what is the minimum average inventory it can achieve?
   c. If the company is willing to increase its average inventory by 10 percent, what percentage reduction in purchasing workload can it achieve?

6-19 The purchasing agent for Jack Spaniel distillery must each year provide the company with 600 charred oak barrels in which the distillery's fine sour-mash bourbon is aged. The current source of this SKU charges $180 per barrel. The distillery estimates its ordering cost at $85 and figures that it can carry inventory at 2 percent per month of the average balance. The supplier is prepared to ship half of any order immediately and to warehouse the balance at no extra cost to the distillery, shipping this balance as needed. Estimate how many barrels the distillery should order at one time.

 6-20 The Soundresearch Corporation assembles stereo components from subassemblies which are contracted to other firms. The company can forecast needs for only about the next 2 months. The particular subassembly of interest to Soundresearch costs $92.40. Soundresearch estimates its holding cost at 3 percent per month; its purchasing cost is $70. There are currently 120 subassemblies on hand, and the demand estimates for the next 9 weeks are as follows:

Week	Estimated demand
1	45
2	60
3	35
4	70
5	80
6	60
7	70
8	50
9	45

Calculate the number of subassemblies Soundresearch should order if it is now time to place an order.

6-21 You have just been made materials manager of a firm which has been taken over by a large conglomerate. Your new subsidiary has not been particularly well run in terms of inventory management, and as a result, you are unable to obtain precise figures on carrying charges and ordering costs for EOQ models which you would like to apply. By examining last year's records, you find that the seven SKUs used in the manufacturing process had purchase and use records as follows:

SKU	SKU no.	Dollars used/year	No. orders last year
1	112-706	$721,000	6
2	131-J271	461,000	5
3	601-7721	207,000	8
4	66117-I	91,000	3
5	29435706	54,000	4
6	160-7112	26,000	9
7	315-7067	10,000	10

Using the data available, answer these questions:
   a. Without increasing the purchasing workload, what percentage reduction can you make in the average inventory carried?
   b. If you are willing to increase the purchasing workload by 25 percent, what is the minimum average inventory you can achieve?
   c. If you are willing to increase your average inventory by 20 percent, what percentage reduction in purchasing workload can you achieve?

6-22 Monroe Garrett operates an auto parts store. Because of the popularity of a particular car model, Garrett estimates that he sells 5 replacement air filters for it on an average day. These cost him $3 each. Garrett is an astute businessman and feels that every dollar tied up in inventory is a dollar less in his money market account, which draws 8½ percent interest. He figures it takes an order clerk 15 minutes to prepare and call in an order and that the associated paperwork costs 50 cents. An order clerk earns $9 per hour for a 40-hour week. Garrett has unused storage space and therefore calculates only interest cost as his carrying cost. How often should Garrett order this filter? Assume a 365-day year.

6-23 Volper Manufacturing Company makes high-quality hiking and walking boots and shoes. Its heavy winter boot is made with a leather upper, a heavy vinyl sole, a nylon lining, and leather laces. Volper's walking shoe uses a leather upper, a rubber sole, and cloth laces. Materials are ordered every 6 months except the leather for uppers, which is ordered every 3 months. Yearly usage of materials is forecast to be as follows: leather, $200,000; vinyl soles, $40,000; rubber soles, $30,000; nylon lining, $30,000; leather laces, $4,000; cloth laces, $2,000. What minimum average inventory can Volper achieve without adding to its purchasing workload?

6-24 Stylecraft Wood Products Company produces a number of novelty furniture items for specialty shops. An examination of production records indicates this pattern:

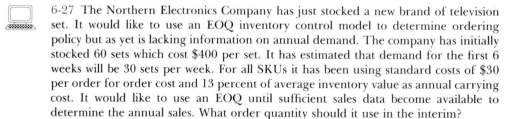

SKU	Value produced/yr	No. of setups used/yr
Fern stand	$80,000	5
Bookshelves	50,000	8
Medicine cabinet	30,000	12
Towel rack	20,000	10
Magazine rack	10,000	9
TV table	5,000	10
Ashtray stand	1,000	6

The company records on cost are very poor; as a result, no one seems to be able to determine either the cost of carrying finished inventory or the cost of setups. The shop supervisor ventured that given the current product mix, the time required for setups does not vary significantly from one product to another. Stylecraft is finding it very difficult to employ trained mechanics able to set up machinery, and it has asked you to calculate whether it would be necessary to increase average inventory in order to reduce the total setup workload next year by 20 percent.

6-25 Company X would like to know what production cost their major competitor, Company Y, has assigned to stock item B. After a bit of investigation, Company X has learned the following about Company Y's production of item B:

Lot size	2,600 units
Setup cost	$135 per setup
Annual demand	30,000 units
Daily demand	100 units
Production rate	200 units per day
Carrying costs	28 percent of average value per year

Company X has further learned that Company Y produces according to an economic lot size model. What is Company Y's cost of producing stock item B?

6-26 The Durham Refrigeration Company maintains an inventory of residential air conditioning units for retail sale. Annual demand for SKU 7980, a window unit, is 6,000 units. Demand is seasonal, however, with sales being rather constant at 300 units a month in the interval from October through April. From May through September, sales have been reasonably constant at 780 units per month. These particular units cost Durham $80 each. It costs Durham $35 to place an order, and inventory carrying costs are 24 percent of inventory value per year. The company has been using an EOQ model to determine order quantities with demand aggregated for an entire year. It is considering using two order policies for this SKU, one policy for the summer season and another for the winter months. How much can costs be reduced if the split policy is adopted?

6-27 The Northern Electronics Company has just stocked a new brand of television set. It would like to use an EOQ inventory control model to determine ordering policy but as yet is lacking information on annual demand. The company has initially stocked 60 sets which cost $400 per set. It has estimated that demand for the first 6 weeks will be 30 sets per week. For all SKUs it has been using standard costs of $30 per order for order cost and 13 percent of average inventory value as annual carrying cost. It would like to use an EOQ until sufficient sales data become available to determine the annual sales. What order quantity should it use in the interim?

6-28 The Jersey Electrical Company is a statewide distributor of electric motors for a number of retail stores. The company has two distribution locations—one in

Freehold and one in Newark. Presently the status of its four inventory items is as follows (identical for each location):

SKU	Value used annually	No. of times ordered/yr	Dollars per order	Average inventory balance
½ horsepower	$60,000	3	20,000	$10,000
1 horsepower	90,000	3	30,000	15,000
2 horsepower	30,000	3	10,000	5,000
6 horsepower	80,000	2	40,000	20,000
		11		$50,000

The Freehold distribution location has limited storage space. Determine an inventory ordering policy which will result in the maximum possible inventory holding cost reductions without increasing the number of orders placed annually.

6-29 The Jersey Electrical Company (see Exercise 6-28) has a very different problem at its Newark location. The clerical staff there is overworked. Determine an inventory ordering policy which will result in the maximum possible cost reductions through a reduction in purchasing workload while maintaining the same average value of inventory.

6-30 The following data are for an inventory item for which the conditions of the EOQ model apply:

$$U = 6,000 \text{ units per year}$$
$$P = \$40 \text{ per order}$$
$$R = \$300 \text{ per unit}$$
$$C = 16 \text{ percent per year}$$

The annual demand of 6,000 units per year is, of course, only an estimate. Demand could be as much as 20 percent above 6,000 units per year or as low as 20 percent below. Assuming you hold to an optimal policy based upon the estimate of 6,000 units per year, compute the sensitivity of the model at the ±20 percent levels. To do this, find the annual costs of holding to an optimal policy at the high and low sales levels and compare them with the costs of using a fixed order quantity (based on the 6,000 sales) at the high and low sales levels.

6-31 For the Freehold location of the Jersey Electrical Company (see Exercise 6-28), assume that management is willing to increase the purchasing workload by about 36 percent per year (15 orders total) if substantial decreases in inventory holding costs can be realized. Determine for them how much inventory costs can be reduced.

13 Chapter concepts quiz

Fill in the Blanks

6-1 In the terminology of ABC analysis, _____ items are those which account for a relatively large proportion of the total dollar value of the inventory; in general, the EOQ model should not be applied to _____ items when the investment in time and labor would be greater than any savings resulting from applying sophisticated inventory techniques.

6-2 Inventory costs can be divided between two basic sources: _____ costs, which are incurred when maintaining an inventory, and _____ costs, which reflect the cost of getting an item into the inventory.

6-3 The purpose of the EOQ inventory model is to determine the _____ which will minimize _____ costs for an inventory item.

6-4 In the notation of the EOQ model, _____ denotes the total dollar value of an inventory item used per year, and _____ denotes the optimal number of orders per year to minimize total inventory costs; thus, A/N_o is the optimal order size in _____ to minimize total inventory costs.

6-5 When applying the EOQ model to production processes, the analogue of the term ordering cost is _____ cost, and the analogue of the economic order quantity is the optimal _____.

6-6 Inventory carrying costs are also referred to as _____ costs.

6-7 With the EOQ model, total costs are at a minimum when annual carrying costs are equal to _____.

6-8 The EOQ model applied to production processes uses a _____ cost instead of ordering costs.

6-9 When demand increases by an amount X in an EOQ application, the optimal order quantity increases by _____.

6-10 Regardless of whether you use an EOQ model with instantaneous receipt of an order or a gradual building of inventory over time, the average inventory is always _____.

True-False   6-11 Inventory techniques such as the EOQ model can most profitably be applied to type C items because of their larger numbers relative to type A and type B items.   **T F**

6-12 The only decision of interest to the manager of an inventory is determining how much to order when an item is to be replenished.   **T F**

6-13 The EOQ is that size order which makes total annual carrying costs equal to total annual ordering costs.   **T F**

6-14 Carrying costs can be expressed in two ways: either as a percentage of average inventory value or as a cost per unit per time period.   **T F**

6-15 Inventory carrying costs include the cost of storage space.   **T F**

6-16 When cost information is not available, EOQ models should not be used because they tend to be more sensitive to cost errors than to demand errors.   **T F**

6-17 For the model which relaxes the instantaneous receipt assumption of the EOQ model, the optimal order quantity is always larger than that of the EOQ model, given identical cost parameters (C, P, R) and that $R \geqslant \$1$.   **T F**

6-18 If annual use increases sixfold and all other cost parameters remain the same, then the EOQ for the new problem will be 6 times that for the original problem.   **T F**

6-19 The use of the EOQ model when cost information is unavailable rests on the assumptions that a lower average inventory results in lower carrying costs and that a smaller total purchasing workload gives lower ordering costs.   **T F**

6-20 The average inventory is equal to half the order quantity under the EOQ model because we assume that all inventory arrives at one time when the inventory level reaches zero and demand is constant.   **T F**

6-21 It is not uncommon to consider labor as an item of inventory.   **T F**

6-22 The curve of total cost for the EOQ model is "dish-shaped." This   **T F** means that even small errors in the estimate of demand can cause large cost increases.

6-23 For the production lot size EOQ model, the maximum level of finished goods inventory is equal to the number of units produced in the production run. **T F**

6-24 A good surrogate of total annual holding cost is the total number of purchase orders written per year. **T F**

6-25 When the price you pay for an inventory item increases, the optimal order quantity will also increase. **T F**

6-26 The EOQ model is based on all the following assumptions except:
  a. Annual demand is known and constant.
  b. Instantaneous receipt of orders occurs exactly when previous inventory is just used up.
  c. Estimates of carrying and ordering costs are accurate.
  d. The ratio of P, ordering cost per order placed, to C, carrying cost as a percentage of average inventory, is a constant for all SKUs considered.

6-27 All of the following may be used to find the EOQ except:
  a. Optimal number of orders per year.
  b. Optimal number of days' supply to order.
  c. Number of orders which minimize ordering costs.
  d. Optimal number of dollars per order.

6-28 Managers usually prefer to express inventory carrying costs as a percentage of average inventory value rather than as a cost per unit per period. This is because the percentage of inventory value is nearly the same for all inventory items independent of their:
  a. Price
  b. Usage rate
  c. Ordering cost
  d. All of the above

6-29 The optimal number of orders per year increases when:
  a. Price increases.
  b. Carrying cost decreases.
  c. Total annual dollar value decreases.
  d. None of the above.

6-30 The EOQ model is of particular importance because:
  a. It is the most realistic model which can be formulated.
  b. It is fairly simple and easy to understand.
  c. No other model can be applied if it cannot be used.
  d. There are only a few assumptions to satisfy, and the needed information is always easy to obtain.

6-31 The decision regarding how much inventory to order has an influence on:
  a. When to order
  b. Inventory carrying costs
  c. Ordering costs
  d. All of the above

6-32 Ordering costs do not include:
  a. Obsolescence
  b. Issuing purchase orders

Multiple Choice

c. Placing goods into inventory

d. None of the above

6-33 In contrast to an EOQ model where all items ordered are received simultaneously, a model where partial shipments are received over a period of time would result in the optimal policy being characterized by a:

a. Larger size of each order.

b. Smaller size of each order.

c. Larger number of orders placed each year.

d. Significant increase in demand.

6-34 Inventory theory is of no value when:

a. Demand is not known.

b. Carrying costs are not known.

c. Ordering costs are not known.

d. None of the above.

6-35 Setup costs do not include:

a. Labor costs of setting up machines.

b. Ordering cost of raw materials.

c. Maintenance cost of the machines.

d. Paperwork cost of processing the work order.

6-36 Variable A is the dollar value of annual demand for an inventory item while U is the number of units demanded per year. Consequently, instead of using the relation

$$N_u = \sqrt{\frac{2AP}{R^2C}},$$ we could use the relation $N_u = \sqrt{\frac{2UP}{RC}}.$ This is because:

a. $A = R \times U$

b. $A = R \times C$

c. $R = A \times U$

d. $R = A \times C$

6-37 Inventories perform the following function:

a. Provide operating flexibility.

b. Smooth out irregularities in demand.

c. Smooth out variations in labor requirements.

d. All of the above.

6-38 The ratio A/N_o is interpreted as:

a. The dollar value ordered per year.

b. The dollar value per order.

c. The number of units ordered per year.

d. The number of units per order.

6-39 The EOQ model applied to the case where the entire order is not instantaneously received is only valid when:

a. The receipt rate x is less than the use rate y.

b. The receipt rate x is greater than the use rate y.

c. The receipt rate x is equal to the use rate y.

d. None of the above. It is valid for any values of x and y.

6-40 In the application of EOQ to minimize inventory level without increasing purchasing workload, average inventory is used as a surrogate for:

a. Purchase cost

b. Annual demand

c. Price per unit of the inventory

d. Carrying costs

EXAMPLE: IMPLEMENTING AN EOQ SYSTEM

In companies that do not use an EOQ system, each inventory item is usually purchased on a fixed time schedule, such as monthly or yearly. It is not difficult to improve on such practices using EOQ principles. A case study that demonstrates the benefits in switching from fixed-time reorders to an EOQ system is given by James W. Prichard and Richard H. Eagle.[1] An anonymous company maintained an inventory of about 15,000 different repair parts, with each item purchased once per year. Prichard and Eagle implemented the EOQ model in this inventory. The bottom line: a 78 percent or $3.8 million reduction in average inventory.

FIXED-TIME PURCHASES REPLACED BY EOQ

Prichard and Eagle found that it was difficult to measure ordering and holding costs in this company. Therefore, they used equation (6-7) to compute X, the constant that minimizes inventory levels without increasing the purchasing workload. Plugging the X constant into the EOQ equation (6-6) for each item reduced average inventory from $4.9 million to $1.1 million. Roughly the same workload of 15,000 purchase orders per year was maintained.

COMPUTING THE X CONSTANT TO MINIMIZE INVENTORY

This was a dramatic reduction in average inventory, but one that was easy to explain to management. Annual sales in the inventory totaled $9.8 million. Only 387 items accounted for $7.8 million in sales. Under the old inventory rules, each item was ordered once per year. This policy meant that the average order size was the same as annual sales and average inventory was half of annual sales. Average inventory was then $7.8 million/2 = $3.9 million. The effect of the EOQ was to reduce the order size for high-value items to an average of one month of stock, with average inventory equal to one-half month of stock. Average order size under the EOQ was then $7.8 million/12 = $650,000. Average inventory was $650,000/2 = $325,000. Thus most of the savings in average inventory came from this small group of high-value items.

ANALYSIS OF HIGH-VALUE ITEMS

One potential problem in using the EOQ to control high-value items was that smaller order sizes caused the purchasing workload to increase. However, this was offset by increasing order sizes for the cheap items in the inventory. For example, about 3,000 items in the inventory had annual sales of less than $12 each. Under old rules, 3,000 purchase orders per year were placed for these items. Under the EOQ, order sizes were increased such that only 750 orders per year were placed. That is, each item was ordered only once every four years.

ANALYSIS OF CHEAP ITEMS

To simplify the new order quantities for the company's purchasing agents, Prichard and Eagle developed a table of rounded EOQ values expressed in months of stock for different ranges of sales. For example, a 48-month supply was recommended for items with annual sales of $12 or less, while a one-month supply was recommended for items with annual sales of $12,000 or more. An analysis showed that using rounded EOQs made little difference in average inventory or total purchasing workload.

IMPLEMENTATION: ROUNDED EOQs

[1] James W. Prichard and Richard H. Eagle, *Modern Inventory Management*, New York: John Wiley, 1965. (This is a *very* old citation, but one of the classics in inventory theory.)

7

Dennis Odle, production vice president of Century Electronics, is faced with a problem not at all uncommon to managers who wish to use an EOQ inventory approach to reduce inventory costs, but who have strong reservations about the assumptions which underlie the basic EOQ model. Specifically, Dennis is concerned about the electric motors used in his company's production of printers for computer systems. The basic EOQ model assumes that once an order is placed to replenish his stock of the motors, both the interval of time he has to wait until the order is delivered and the demand during that interval are exactly known and never vary from one order to the next. Dennis recognizes that these factors are seldom without variation, and if he were to follow the basic EOQ policy, he would risk stocking out of the motors. This would be disruptive to the company's production system, and Dennis feels that the associated costs of disruptions of this kind are about $50 per unit stocked out. Fortunately, Dennis can apply an EOQ approach to his inventory control problem, if he has collected a bit of information regarding the distribution of past demands during the reorder lead time. This information can assist him in determining a cost-effective reorder point which includes both the expected lead-time demand as well as a bit extra, called safety stock. In this chapter, you will learn how to analyze the cost tradeoffs which can enable you to determine the most cost-effective safety stock strategy to follow.

INVENTORY II

Reordering, Backorders, Discounts, Material Requirements Planning

CHAPTER OBJECTIVES

- INTRODUCE THE BASIC REORDER-POINT MODEL FOR DECISION PURPOSES AND REVIEW BOTH FIXED-REORDER-POINT AND FIXED-REVIEW-INTERVAL VERSIONS.

- DEMONSTRATE HOW TO USE A REORDER-POINT MODEL WHEN OUT-OF-STOCK COSTS CANNOT BE FOUND.

- EXTEND THE BASIC REORDER-POINT MODEL TO SITUATIONS INVOLVING DECISION MAKING WITH MULTIPLE SKUS PURCHASED FROM ONE VENDOR.

- INTRODUCE THE BACKORDER MODEL AND DEMONSTRATE ITS USE UNDER SEVERAL ENVIRONMENTAL SITUATIONS.

- SHOW HOW TO EVALUATE QUANTITY DISCOUNTS OFFERED BY VENDORS.

- INTRODUCE MATERIAL REQUIREMENTS PLANNING AS AN ALTERNATIVE TO REORDER-POINT MODELS AND DEMONSTRATE WHEN ITS USE MAY BE MORE EFFECTIVE.

THIS CHAPTER DEALS
WITH THE WHEN-TO-
ORDER DECISION

1 Deciding when to buy: introduction

THE REORDER POINT

Chapter 6 was concerned with the question: How *much* should we buy when it is time to replenish the inventory of an SKU? Among the topics introduced in this chapter are techniques which will help us answer the question: *When* should we replenish the inventory of that SKU? This *when-to-order* point is called the *reorder point*.

LEAD TIME

If you call for home delivery of a pizza and it takes 2 hours for it to arrive, then 2 hours is the *lead time*. If the manager of Caroline Boutique, Ltd., knows that her supplier of brass candlesticks will deliver 30 calendar days after Caroline places an order, then 30 days is the lead time. In larger organizations, it may require some time for the purchasing office to (1) be notified that the inventory has reached the reorder point and (2) initiate purchasing action. If so, then the lead time has to be adjusted to reflect these internal factors.

LEAD TIME DEMAND

Usage of an SKU *during* the lead time is known as *lead time demand*. If Caroline knows that her average daily sale of a particular candlestick is 2, lead time demand for this SKU is calculated as 30 days × 2/day, or 60 candlesticks. When her stock of this SKU gets near 60, Caroline should reorder the item.

STOCKOUTS

If we make the assumption of constant demand and if we assume that lead time is constant, we could represent the reorder situation as in Figure 7-1. But these two assumptions are hardly ever true. Forecast demand of a

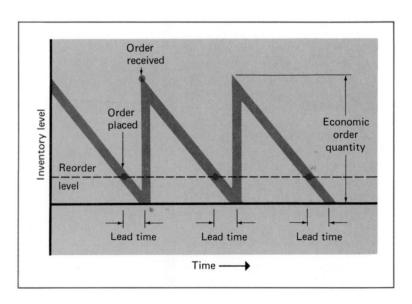

FIGURE 7-1
Inventory level with constant demand and constant lead time.

particular SKU can be affected by unexpected market acceptance, by the weather, or by a strike. The lead time varies too; a supplier may run into problems (strikes, floods, breakdowns), or the transportation company may experience delays.

Variations in the lead time or in demand often cause *stockouts,* the condition that exists when the inventory on hand is not sufficient to cover needs. Figure 7-2 graphically shows a stockout when demand (usage) was normal but receipt of goods ordered (delivery) was later than expected. Figure 7-3 graphically shows a stockout when delivery was on schedule but usage was greater than expected.

Stockouts are undesirable because they can be *quite* expensive. Lost sales and disgruntled customers are examples of *external* costs. Idle machines and employee ill will are examples of *internal* costs. Management's desire to avoid stockouts leads to further consideration of *when* to order and reorder.

◼ SAFETY STOCK

The term *safety stock* refers to extra inventory held as a hedge, or protection, against the possibility of a stockout. It is obvious that a safety stock has two effects on a firm's costs. It will *decrease* the costs of stockouts but *increase* carrying costs. The cost of a stockout multiplied by the number of stockouts prevented by the safety stock gives the cost reduction figure. The value of the safety stock multiplied by the carrying cost percentage gives the cost addition figure. Note that this cost addition is continuing—even permanent—in nature because the safety stock is always a part of total inventory. Note also that because the safety stock does not often decline in quantity, we do not divide it by 2 to get average inventory.

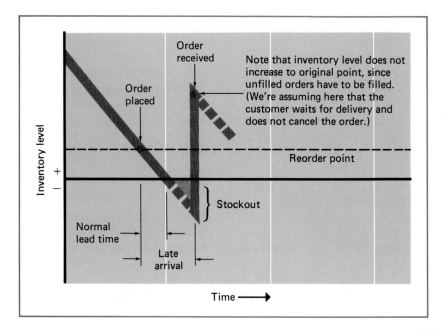

FIGURE 7-2
Inventory level with constant demand and excessively long lead time.

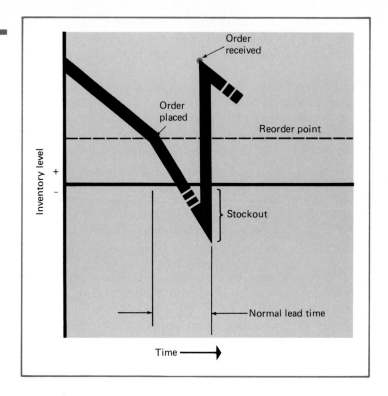

FIGURE 7-3
Inventory level with
excessive demand
and constant lead
time.

2 How to determine the optimal level of safety stock when out-of-stock costs are known

The optimal amount of safety stock to carry is determined in the light of two goals which are somewhat hostile to each other: (1) minimizing the costs of stockouts while also (2) minimizing carrying costs on the safety stock. The decision of how much safety stock to carry is not an easy one. Every approach to this problem has its own limitations. In this section we shall determine an appropriate level for safety stock. Here we will use the *probability* approach, perhaps the most satisfactory approach developed to date. We shall assume a constant lead time; we shall also assume that each lot ordered is delivered all at one time. Under these assumptions, a stockout can be caused *only* by an increase in demand (usage) *after the reorder point has been reached.* Figure
7-4 illustrates this situation. Note that the stockout resulted from increased demand *after the order to replenish inventory had been placed.* If the increase had occurred *before* the reorder point was reached, a purchase order would have been placed at the moment the inventory level fell to the reorder point.

Dennis Odle is the production vice president of Century Electronics Company, a very large manufacturer of printers for computer systems. Each printer uses a fractional horsepower electric motor to drive the roller. Together

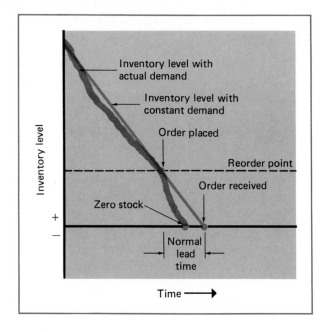

FIGURE 7-4
Inventory level showing the effect of an increase in demand after the order has been placed.

with one of the company cost accountants, Dennis has estimated that the cost of being out of stock for this particular motor is $50 for each unit Century is short. This cost represents the inconvenience, the cost of reprocessing the printers when the motors finally arrive, and the extra storage cost of holding printers without motors.

Using an EOQ model, Dennis has already calculated the economic order quantity of this motor to be 3,600, with an average usage of 50 motors a day. The normal lead time is 6 days. At this point, Dennis would like to know how much safety stock he should carry.

Dennis's first step is to analyze the inventory record card for these motors. By noting the usage during a number of past reorder periods, he can assign a probability to various levels of usage, as shown in Table 7-1.

USING PAST INVENTORY RECORDS TO ESTABLISH PROBABILITY OF STOCKOUTS

If Dennis reorders when the level of stock falls to 300 units, the company will be safe 81 percent of the time (.68 + .06 + .04 + .03), but it will be out

TABLE 7-1

Probabilities of usage during reorder period

Use during reorder period, units	No. times this quantity was used	Use probability	
150	3	$3/100$, or	.03
200	4	$4/100$, or	.04
250	6	$6/100$, or	.06
300	68	$68/100$, or	.68
350	9	$9/100$, or	.09
400	7	$7/100$, or	.07
450	3	$3/100$, or	.03
	100		1.00

of stock of motors 19 percent of the time (.09 + .07 + .03). Dennis should be quite concerned over this figure of 19 percent.

To *reduce* or avoid this shortage, he could carry some *safety stock.* Dennis might consider several levels of safety stock and pick the one which yields the lowest total for (1) cost of stockouts plus (2) carrying costs on the safety stock. Thus he could consider carrying a safety stock of

SPECIFIC RELATIONSHIP BETWEEN SAFETY STOCK AND STOCKOUTS

1 *50 units.* This would cover a usage of 350 during the reorder period; Dennis would be out of stock only when usage was 400 or 450 units; .07 + .03 = .1 of the time.

2 *100 units.* This would cover a usage of 350 or 400 during the reorder period; Dennis would be out of stock only when usage was 450 units; this would be .03 of the time.

3 *150 units.* This would cover usage of 350, 400, or 450 during the reorder period; Dennis should never run out of stock with this amount of safety stock. (Remember that the distribution of usage here is *discrete.*)

MAXIMUM DANGER OF STOCKOUTS IS NEAR THE REORDER POINT

The danger of being out of stock will occur, of course, when stock is nearing the lowest point, the reorder point; thus we will have to take into consideration the number of times Dennis reorders during the year. Suppose one of the EOQ formulas suggested to him that 5 orders per year is optimal. He will, therefore, be in danger of running out of electric motors five times during the year. EOQ thus affects the reorder point.

The costs of being out of stock for the four courses of action (no safety stock, 50 units, 100 units, 150 units) are shown in Table 7-2. If Dennis and the company cost accountant estimate that the cost of carrying one motor in safety stock is $10, then the total annual costs of the four courses of action

TABLE 7-2
Costs of being out of stock

Safety stock	Probability of being out	Number short	Expected annual cost (no. short × probability of being short that many × cost of being out/unit × no. orders/yr)		Total annual stockout costs
0	.09 when use is 350	50	50 × .09 × $50 × 5	$1,125	
	.07 when use is 400	100	100 × .07 × $50 × 5	1,750	
	.03 when use is 450	150	150 × .03 × $50 × 5	1,125	
					$4,000
50	.07 when use is 400	50	50 × .07 × $50 × 5	$ 875	
	.03 when use is 450	100	100 × .03 × $50 × 5	750	
					1,625
100	.03 when use is 450	50	50 × .03 × $50 × 5	$ 375	375
150	0	0		0	0

Safety stock	Cost of being out of stock	Annual carrying costs, no. carried × cost/yr	Total cost/yr, stockout cost + carrying costs
0	$4,000	$ 0	$4,000
50	1,625	50 × $10 = $ 500	2,125
100	375	100 × $10 = $1,000	1,375*
150	0	150 × $10 = $1,500	1,500

* $1,375 is the lowest total cost per year; 100 units as safety stock is the optimal quantity.

TABLE 7-3
Costs of safety stock policies

(stockout cost plus carrying costs on safety stock) would be as shown in Table 7-3. The appropriate safety stock is 100 units.

Adoption of the safety stock policy would change the reorder point. If 100 motors are to be held as safety stock, then the reorder point is determined as follows:

$$\text{Reorder point} = \text{Average daily use} \times \text{Lead time} + \text{Safety stock} \quad (7\text{-}1)$$

In Dennis's situation, the appropriate reorder point would be

$$50 \times 6 + 100 = 400$$

3 Setting safety stock levels when out-of-stock costs are not known

THE SERVICE-LEVEL CONCEPT

In order to use the safety stock model just presented, Dennis was required to furnish an out-of-stock cost per unit. With this value, he was able to determine the relative costs of (1) being out of stock and (2) carrying additional inventory so he could determine the inventory level which minimized the total of these two costs. **In many situations, however, it is extremely difficult, if not impossible, to determine the cost per unit of being out of stock.** In a wholesale or retail firm an item bought for stock is sold at a known markup; here we can assume that the cost per unit of being out of stock is at least equal to the markup you would forgo if there were no unit to sell plus loss of goodwill. If the customer will wait for delivery, then perhaps the loss is limited to slightly diminished goodwill.

In a manufacturing firm, however, the issue is often much more difficult for these reasons:

1 Because component parts purchased for use in manufacturing are not sold individually, their real value to the production process is hard to determine.

2 When being out of stock causes a production bottleneck, the value of this is hard to assess; it might involve one person's being out of work for a few minutes or a shutdown of an entire plant.

USING SERVICE LEVELS WHEN OUT-OF-STOCK COSTS ARE UNKNOWN

3 It is unrealistic to assume that being out of stock 2 units costs twice as much as being out of stock 1 unit; therefore the out-of-stock cost per unit is not a constant.

We can understand, then, why many companies do not attempt to determine the cost per unit of being out of stock. Instead, they adopt what is called a *service-level* policy. Organizations which use this service-level approach simply establish the probability of being out of stock they are willing to "live with"; then they take whatever safety stock action is required to keep the probability of being out of stock at or near this point. For example, a company might adopt a service-level policy of 95 percent on certain items in its inventory; this means that the company wants to be able to supply 95 percent of the requests for those certain items.[1] On what basis is the service level determined? Being in stock 99 percent of the time will obviously cost much more than being in stock only 75 percent of the time. Actually, management must determine what they feel is an acceptable service level; in many cases this is done completely subjectively, although we shall show later in this chapter how we can provide management with the *relative carrying costs* associated with any service level. In other cases, industrial practice really determines what choice a single company might make with respect to service level; certain industries adopt a service-level policy which, although not formally agreed to by all firms in that industry, is often adhered to in practice.

A service-level policy is the usual answer when an accurate determination of the cost of being out of stock is impossible; however, even this approach requires a knowledge of both inventory theory and probability theory. Few real organizations can afford a 100 percent service level because it requires a level of safety stock whose cost is too high relative to the cost of being out of stock. Firms generally choose a service level which appears to them to be a reasonable alternative.

DETERMINING THE SAFETY STOCK REQUIRED FOR ANY DESIRED SERVICE LEVEL

A company is in danger of being out of stock for an item when the inventory of that item is at its lowest level; this occurs during the reorder period while the replenishment inventory is expected to be on its way. For this reason, determination of safety stock policy under a service-level concept depends upon the consumption of the item during the reorder period. For example, if consumption of an item during past reorder periods was quite constant, then a very small safety stock might enable a company to support a very high service level. Let us suppose in this case that use during past reorder periods averaged 100 units and that this use never went over 110 units. Reordering when the stock level falls to 110 units (a safety stock of 10 units) guarantees that we shall never be out of stock (a service level of 100 percent).

---

[1] This 95 percent applies to the reorder period only. The probability of being able to supply a request, in general, during the entire inventory cycle is much better than 95 percent. In fact, it is near 100 percent prior to the reorder period combined with 95 percent during the reorder period.

Now suppose, however, that use of an item during past reorder periods averaged 100 units but had gone as high as 300 units on occasion. In this case, if we want to protect against the highest past recorded usage, we must reorder at 300 units, a safety stock of 200 units. Thus **the pattern of usage during the reorder period determines how large a safety stock is required to support any desired service level.** To provide operational answers for these kinds of inventory problems, we will use some of the concepts about probability distributions we introduced in Chapter 2.

In another one of Century Electronics' products, a liquid cooling device for computers, a small electrically driven pump is used. Dennis Odle has audited past usage records of *lead time demand*. He is able to provide us with the following information about the probability distribution of lead time demand:

$$\mu = 180 \text{ pumps}$$

$$\sigma = 30 \text{ pumps}$$

Dennis also thinks that the distribution of lead time demand is such as to allow the use of the normal distribution to approximate its behavior.

If Dennis wants to maintain a 95 percent service level on this pump, what is the appropriate level of safety stock for him to maintain? We show his situation graphically in Figure 7-5. The shaded area, representing 5 percent of the total area under the curve, is that part of the time he is willing to be out of stock; he is willing to let the probability of being out of stock be 5 percent.

If Dennis reordered at 180 units and carried no safety stock, usage during the reorder period would be above 180 half of the time and he would be out of stock during these periods. Usage, of course, would be under 180 half the time; Dennis would be able to supply pumps during these periods. If he carried no safety stock, then, he would experience a service level of 50 percent.

PATTERN OF USAGE DURING REORDER PERIOD DETERMINES SAFETY STOCK NEEDED FOR ANY SERVICE LEVEL

LEAD TIME DEMAND IS NORMALLY DISTRIBUTED

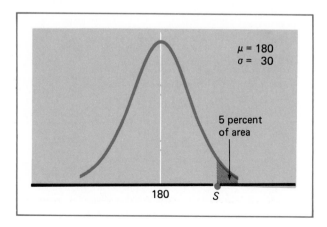

FIGURE 7-5
Distribution of lead time demand.

CALCULATING THE
REQUIRED SAFETY
STOCK FOR THIS
SERVICE LEVEL

Raising the service level to 95 percent will compel Dennis to carry some safety stock. Specifically, he will have to reorder at point S; therefore his safety stock will be $S - 180$. How to find S? This is done exactly as in Chapter 2. We know that the area from point S to the left-hand tail of the curve equals 95 percent of the area under the curve; so we look for the value .95 in Appendix Table 1 and find that point S is 1.64 standard deviations to the right of the mean. As 1 standard deviation is 30 units, 1.64 deviations is 1.64×30, or about 49 units. Thus we have found that if Dennis carries 49 units of safety stock and reorders when the stock level falls to 229 units, he will be able to fill all the orders received during the reorder period about 95 percent of the time. These conclusions are shown in Figure 7-6.

▌ THE COST OF CHANGING THE SERVICE LEVEL

COSTS FOR SEVERAL
SERVICE LEVELS

A simple example will illustrate the relationship between the cost of carrying safety stock and increased service levels. In Table 7-4 we have computed the safety stock required to provide several different service levels for an SKU; then we have computed the costs of carrying these different amounts of safety stock. Notice that the right-hand column in Table 7-4 indicates the approximate cost for a 1 percent increase in the service level; notice also how this cost increases very rapidly relative to the increase in the service level desired. Finally, in Figure 7-7 we have graphed the relationship between carrying cost and increases in the service level for the situation in Table 7-4.

RELATIONSHIP
BETWEEN COST AND
SERVICE LEVEL IS
NOT LINEAR

REASONABLE SERVICE
LEVELS IN PRACTICE

You can quickly see from Figure 7-7 that the relationship between cost and service levels is *not* linear. Because of the enormous cost of raising the service level once it passes about 95 percent, few organizations attempt to achieve service levels above this level unless the SKU is necessary for health and life.

▌ REORDERING AND SAFETY STOCK IN PRACTICE
(TWO STANDARD APPROACHES)

FIXED-REORDER-POINT
SYSTEMS AND FIXED-
REVIEW-INTERVAL
SYSTEMS

The reordering concepts we have discussed are usually applied in practice in one of two ways: (1) a *fixed-reorder-point system* or (2) a *fixed-review-interval system*.

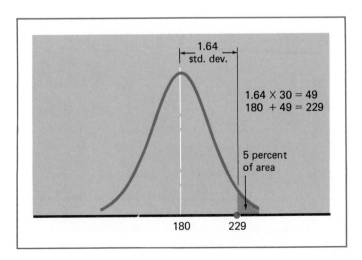

FIGURE 7-6
Determination of
safety stock.

TABLE 7-4
Cost of various service-level policies

Service level desired, %	No. of std. dev. to the right of the mean	No. of units of safety stock required	Cost per year of safety stock	Approximate cost of 1% increase in service level
50	.00	0	$ 0	
60	.25	38	190	$ 19 = ($190 − 0)/10
70	.52	78	390	20 = (390 − 190)/10
80	.84	126	630	24 = (630 − 390)/10
90	1.28	192	960	33 = (960 − 630)/10
95	1.64	246	1,230	54 = (1,230 − 960)/5
96	1.75	262	1,310	80 = (1,310 − 1,230)/1
97	1.88	282	1,410	100 = (1,410 − 1,310)/1
98	2.05	308	1,540	130 = (1,540 − 1,410)/1
99	2.33	350	1,750	210 = (1,750 − 1,540)/1
99.9	3.09	463	2,315	627 = (2,315 − 1,750)/.9

Mean lead time demand = μ = 400
Std. dev. of lead time demand = σ = 150
Cost per year to carry 1 unit of safety stock: $5

1. Fixed-reorder-point system This system operates by setting reorder points on all SKUs under system control, just as we have illustrated. Then when the balance on hand of any SKU reaches its reorder point, an order for the EOQ is placed with the vendor.

2. Fixed-review-interval system This system reviews the inventory status of *every* stockkeeping unit in the system at stipulated intervals, say once every

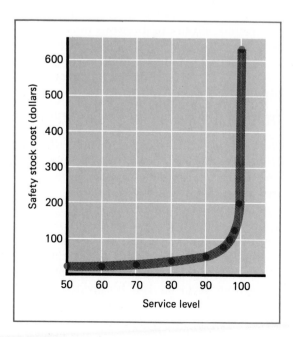

FIGURE 7-7
Cost of raising service level 1 percent at any service level between 50 and 100.

301

2 weeks. Such systems rely on past usage data and forecasting models to forecast use during the *next* 2-week interval; the current stock of every SKU, plus any quantity in transit and expected to arrive in 2 weeks, is compared with the forecast usage during the next review interval; a probability of stocking out during the next 2 weeks is calculated using the methods already illustrated in this chapter. If this probability is above a stipulated level, an order is placed with the vendor for the EOQ. If the probability of running out during the coming review period is not of sufficient magnitude, no ordering action is taken until 2 weeks later, when the inventory status is once again reviewed and new probability values are calculated.

FIXED-REVIEW-
INTERVAL SYSTEMS
GENERALLY REQUIRE
A COMPUTER

Because fixed-review-interval inventory systems depend for their accuracy on good short-run forecasting methods and because they typically control thousands of SKUs, they require computer support to be effective. Fixed-reorder-point systems, on the other hand, can still be managed by hand as long as the number of SKUs is not too great, although it is unusual to find manual systems today.

RELATIONSHIP BETWEEN REORDER POINT AND EOQ

EOQ AND REORDER
POINT RELATED

We have determined the EOQ and the reorder point separately. This is not meant to imply that the two concepts are unrelated. In fact, in the previous section we indicated that a company was more vulnerable to stockouts during the reorder period than at any other time, and here lies the true relationship. **As the EOQ *rises* (more units per lot), the company orders fewer times a year; thus the stock moves to low points fewer times a year and the number of times the company is vulnerable to stockouts diminishes. Conversely, as the EOQ *falls* (fewer units per lot), the company orders more times a year; thus the stock moves to low points more times a year and the company finds itself in a vulnerable position more often.**

Some more sophisticated mathematical models beyond the scope of this text relate EOQ and reorder point so that an optimal combination of the two results. From our previous discussion of the cost of being out of stock, we can realize that such models must depend upon the precise assessment of such a cost (per time out of stock) and thus are open to criticism.

4 Joint ordering: more than one SKU from the same supplier simultaneously

Joint ordering is defined in inventory theory as buying more than one item from the same supplier *at the same time*. The number of items purchased at one time from the same supplier, using a single purchase order or contract, may range from *two* to *hundreds*.

In the previous chapter, we developed EOQ models which indicate the appropriate number of items to purchase when the cost of ordering and the cost of holding are known. In the case of *joint ordering*, however, it is usually profitable to modify slightly the traditional EOQ approach because of the effect joint ordering has on the incremental cost per order.

PARTS OF THE
PURCHASE ORDER

A purchase order can be divided into two parts: (1) the *header,* which contains all the general information concerning the order (including name and address of supplier, shipping information, price discount information, billing information, and other data relevant to all of the items to be purchased on this one order), and (2) the *line items,* each of which contains specific information relevant to one item being purchased, the quantity of this item, unit price, size, finish, color, and stock number.

HEADER AND LINE ITEM COSTS

The *header cost* is that cost incurred in preparing the header portion of the purchase order; the *line item cost* is the cost of adding one additional line item to that order. Thus the purchase of one item from a supplier would cause us to incur a header cost *and* a line item cost, whereas the purchase of additional items from that same supplier on the same purchase order would cause us to incur *only* additional line item costs. Put in another way, the cost of preparing the purchase order for the second item purchased (and for the third and others as well) is a bit less than the cost for the first item because the header cost is part of initiating the purchase order and demands the major portion of executive time *and* paperwork, including clerical costs.

TWO COSTS IN
PREPARING A
PURCHASE ORDER

TRIGGER EOQ AND LINE EOQ

Now, although preparation of the purchase order does *not* represent the entire cost of ordering, it *is* true that the ordering cost for the first item is slightly higher than the ordering cost for each additional item on that same order. Therefore, in ordering more than one item from the same supplier on the same purchase order, we should take account of this difference. But how? In practice, inventory managers who employ joint ordering systems normally compute *two* different EOQs for each item they buy in significant quantities: (1) a *trigger* EOQ and (2) a *line item* EOQ. The trigger EOQ is applied if the item triggered the order—if it reached its reorder point first and thus indicated that an order was required. The line item EOQ is applied to all other items the buyer decides to buy from the same supplier on that same purchase order.

TRIGGER EOQ

LINE ITEM EOQ

From the previous chapter, we know that EOQ is related to the cost of holding and the cost of ordering; we are now considering the effect on EOQ of differing costs of ordering. A lower incremental cost of ordering would dictate that the quantity ordered at one time be less [you can satisfy yourself that this is true by looking at Eq. (6-4) on page 259 and noticing that a lowered value for P in that formula will reduce the value of the entire expression]. We can conclude, therefore, that in operational joint ordering situations, line item EOQs involve lower quantities than trigger EOQs. Now let us apply these concepts to a joint ordering situation.

Jim Brame is the inventory manager of Brame Specialties, Inc., a wholesale distributor of paper products. Table 7-5 shows the five different SKUs Jim orders from National Paper Company, one of his principal suppliers. For each SKU, Jim has indicated its SKU number, description, reorder point, trigger EOQ, and line item EOQ.

PROBLEM
ILLUSTRATING
JOINT ORDERING

Each of the five SKUs comes in cases weighing 100 pounds, and a railroad carload is 80,000 pounds, or 800 cases. National is able to offer substantial discounts if Jim orders a full railroad carload. The problem is represented

TABLE 7-5

SKUs Jim Brame
orders from National
Paper Company

SKU no.	Description	Reorder point	Trigger EOQ	Line item EOQ
1	Paper hand towels (single)	200 cases	300 cases	240 cases
2	Paper kitchen towels	150 cases	250 cases	200 cases
3	Kraft wrapping paper	300 cases	300 cases	240 cases
4	Paper cups	250 cases	350 cases	270 cases
5	Paper hand towels (roll)	50 cases	400 cases	320 cases

TRIGGER SKU

REMAINING FOUR SKUs

graphically in Figure 7-8, where Jim has shown each SKU with its reorder point and its present inventory level. He can see that SKU 1, paper hand towels (single), has reached its reorder point and thus "triggers" the order from National. Ordering the trigger EOQ of that item (300 cases), however, will not fill up the railroad car. *What other items he should order, In what order they should be considered,* and *What quantities of each he should order* are the operational questions of interest to Jim Brame in this situation.

Jim must next determine which of the four remaining SKUs is *closest* to its own reorder point; this is the item that is most likely to need replenishing during the delivery period. A look at items 2, 3, 4, and 5 indicates that items 2, 3, and 4 are *all* 50 units away from their reorder points; this looks like a tie situation. But in practice, the difference between actual inventory and reorder point is never measured in units but in *percent excess.* For example, look at items 2 and 3; inventory of both of these items is 50 units above the reorder point; in the case of item 2, the 50 units represents 33⅓ percent of the reorder point. Using this approach, Jim can see that the present inventory of item 2 gives him considerably more protection than that of item 3 (which is only 16⅔ percent higher than its reorder point). Using the same method

FIGURE 7-8

Reorder point and
present inventory
level for five SKUs
(reorder point is
indicated by the heavy
line and the present
inventory level by the
shaded area).

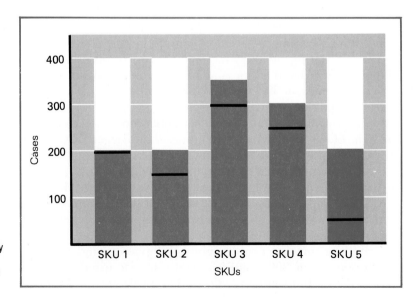

of calculation, Jim can also see that the inventory of SKU 4 is 20 percent higher than its reorder point.

Thus reordering of SKUs 2, 3, and 4 would be considered in the following order: SKU 3 first, SKU 4 second, and SKU 2 last. The inventory of SKU 5 is so far above its reorder point that Jim would order it only if absolutely necessary to fill the railroad car. Jim's solution to this joint ordering problem can be expressed after looking at Table 7-5 and Figure 7-8. He would

APPROPRIATE ACTION

1 First, *order* the trigger EOQ of SKU 1 (300 cases); this leaves 500 cases to fill the railroad car.

2 Next, *order* the line item EOQ of SKU 3 (240 cases); this leaves 260 cases to fill the railroad car.

3 Next, *consider* ordering the line item EOQ of SKU 4 (270 cases); but because this would overfill the railroad car by 10 cases, the order for SKU 4 would have to be reduced to 260 cases.

In the problem above, if Jim were under no pressure to *fill* the railroad car in order to get a substantial discount, chances are he would order only SKU 1 from National at this time. To include quantities of the other items in his order and thus substantially increase his level of inventory would be unprofitable without compensating advantages offered by the supplier.

In some cases, suppliers establish a *minimum dollar value* for orders below which they charge higher unit prices. In cases such as this, the same procedure illustrated above can be employed except that both trigger EOQs and line item EOQs would have to be established in *dollars*.

DOLLARS VERSUS UNITS

5 Reordering with planned stockouts

Up to this point, we have been concerned with methods which *prevent* stockouts. However, in certain situations, management may find it desirable from a cost point of view not only to allow stockouts but to *plan* for them. It is quite common, for example, not to find the sofa you want in the fabric you want at your local furniture store. The manager will, however, order exactly what you want *if you will wait for delivery*.

PLANNING FOR STOCKOUTS MAY BE APPROPRIATE

BACKORDERS

The specific type of stockout we are concerned with here is called a *backorder*. When we speak of an item being backordered, we imply that

BACKORDER ASSUMPTIONS

1 The customer placed an order.

2 The supplier is out of stock in that SKU.

3 The customer does not withdraw the order.

4 The customer waits until the next shipment arrives.

5 The supplier fills the customer's order when the next shipment arrives.

If, however, the customer will *withdraw* the order when the SKU is found to be out of stock, the backorder model we will develop is *not* appropriate.

DEVELOPMENT OF THE BACKORDER MODEL

In Figure 7-9, we have illustrated a typical backorder situation.

COST IN THE BACKORDER MODEL

For our inventory model *with backorders,* we will have the same kind of *carrying costs* we had in EOQ models before; we will also have the same kind of purchasing or *ordering costs.* But, in addition to these two costs, we will have the additional *cost of backordering.* Backordering cost is really composed of two different costs: (1) any cost of handling the backorder (special handling, follow-up, labor) and (2) whatever loss of customer goodwill occurs as a result of having to backorder an SKU. It is common in backorder models to express backorder costs as "how much it costs to have one unit on backorder for a given time period." Of course it is not possible to be precise in calculating this cost, especially when we try to calculate loss of goodwill; but because the EOQ model is not especially sensitive to changes in inputs (look at pages 256 and 274 again), errors in estimates do not prevent us from making reasonably good inventory decisions.

Annual carrying cost in the backorder model   Look at Figure 7-9. During the time t when inventory is available, we have a *maximum* inventory of $N_u - B$ units and a minimum inventory of zero for an average of

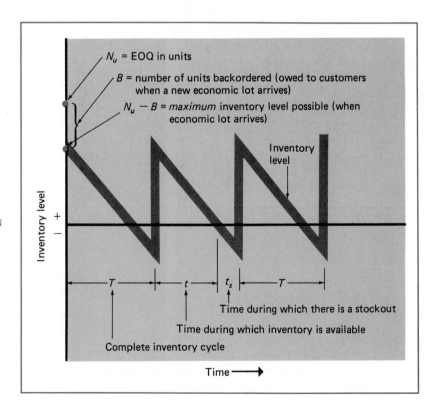

N_u = EOQ in units

B = number of units backordered (owed to customers when a new economic lot arrives)

$N_u - B$ = *maximum* inventory level possible (when economic lot arrives)

Inventory level

Inventory level

Time during which there is a stockout

Time during which inventory is available

Complete inventory cycle

Time ⟶

FIGURE 7-9
Inventory behavior in
backorder situations.

$(N_u - B)/2$. Since we do not carry *any* inventory during time t_s, the average inventory during the complete inventory cycle is

$$\frac{N_u - B}{2} \text{ units}$$

for that portion of the total inventory cycle represented by the fraction t/T, plus 0 units for that portion of the total cycle represented by the fraction t_s/T, which is an average inventory for the total cycle of

$$\text{Average inventory} = \frac{[(N_u - B)/2]t}{T} \text{ units}$$

Let's see whether we can get rid of t and T by expressing them in other terms. Suppose we let d = daily demand; then, since the maximum inventory was $N_u - B$, it will be used up in $(N_u - B)/d$ days. Thus

$$t = \frac{N_u - B}{d}$$

Look now at T. Since N_u units are ordered (and shipped) each inventory cycle, the length of an inventory cycle must be N_u/d days. Thus

$$T = \frac{N_u}{d}$$

Now we substitute our new expressions for t and T into the average inventory equation:

$$\text{Average inventory} = \frac{\left(\dfrac{N_u - B}{2}\right)t}{T}$$

$$= \frac{\left(\dfrac{N_u - B}{2}\right)\left(\dfrac{N_u - B}{d}\right)}{\dfrac{N_u}{d}} \qquad \leftarrow \frac{N_u - B}{d} \text{ substituted for } t \qquad \text{AVERAGE INVENTORY}$$

$$\qquad\qquad\qquad\qquad \leftarrow \frac{N_u}{d} \text{ substituted for } T$$

$$= \frac{(N_u - B)^2}{2N_u} \qquad \leftarrow \text{Expression simplified}$$

And if we let C equal the annual carrying cost expressed in dollars per unit per year, total annual carrying cost becomes

$$\text{Annual carrying cost with backorders} = \frac{(N_u - B)^2}{2N_u} C \qquad\qquad (7\text{-}2)$$

Annual ordering cost in the backorder model   If we let U equal the annual demand in units, then the number of orders per year is the annual demand divided by the units per economic lot, N_u, or

$$\text{Number of orders per year} = \frac{U}{N_u}$$

And if we let P equal the purchasing cost per order, annual ordering cost in the backorder model is

$$\begin{array}{c}\text{Annual ordering cost}\\ \text{with backorders}\end{array} = \frac{UP}{N_u} \qquad (7\text{-}3)$$

Annual backorder cost   In Figure 7-9, we symbolized the maximum number of units backordered, B. To find the average number of units backordered throughout the entire inventory cycle, we can use the same logic we used earlier to find the average inventory.

No units are backordered during the time period t (inventory is available). During the period t_s, the number of units backordered goes from a maximum of B to a minimum of zero; during this period, the average number backordered is $B/2$. The number of units backordered for the complete inventory cycle is then 0 units for that portion of the total inventory cycle represented by the fraction t/T, plus

$$\frac{B}{2} \text{ units}$$

for that portion of the total cycle represented by the fraction t_s/T, which is an average units for the total cycle of

$$\text{Average units backordered} = \frac{(B/2)t_s}{T}$$

Again, we can reason that backorders reach their maximum value B at a daily demand rate of d; therefore, the length of the portion of the inventory cycle in which we *have* backorders is

$$t_s = \frac{B}{d}$$

And we know that the length of an inventory cycle $T = N_u/d$ days; therefore, let's substitute these values for t_s and T into the expression for the average units backordered. Doing this we get

$$\text{Average units backordered} = \frac{\left(\dfrac{B}{2}\right)t_s}{T}$$

$$= \frac{\left(\dfrac{B}{2}\right)\left(\dfrac{B}{d}\right)}{\dfrac{N_u}{d}} \qquad \leftarrow \dfrac{B}{d} \text{ substituted for } t_s$$

$$\leftarrow \dfrac{N_u}{d} \text{ substituted for } T$$

$$= \frac{B^2}{2N_u} \qquad \leftarrow \text{Expression simplified}$$

And if we let V equal the cost to maintain a single unit on backorder status for 1 year (the objective cost of paperwork, and so forth, plus the subjective cost of lost goodwill), the total annual backorder cost is

$$\text{Annual backorder cost} = \frac{B^2 V}{2N_u} \qquad (7\text{-}4)$$

Total annual cost Now we have the three costs that we need (annual carrying cost, annual ordering cost, and annual backorder cost) symbolized in Eqs. (7-2), (7-3), and (7-4), respectively. If we add these three equations together, we get the total annual cost of operating an inventory system in which we allow backorders; it is expressed

$$(7\text{-}2) \qquad + (7\text{-}3) + (7\text{-}4)$$

or

$$\begin{matrix} \text{Total annual cost of an inventory} \\ \text{system that allows backorders} \end{matrix} = \frac{(N_u - B)^2}{2N_u}C + \frac{UP}{N_u} + \frac{B^2 V}{2N_u} \quad (7\text{-}5)$$

TOTAL ANNUAL COST OF THE SYSTEM

USING THE BACKORDER MODEL

Crowell Little is the Ford dealer in Hillsborough, North Carolina. After having the backorder model explained to him, he believes that his situation is one for which the assumptions of this model hold true. Crowell has come up with these estimates:

PROBLEM ILLUSTRATING USE OF THE BACKORDER MODEL

U (annual demand)	400 units
C (annual carrying cost for inventory per unit per year)	$800
P (cost per order)	$100
V (cost to maintain 1 unit on backorder status for 1 year)	$150

With two decision variables, N_u and B, it becomes unwieldy to find the optimal value for both by a trial-and-error method. However, let's make a couple of trial-and-error runs just to see what's involved.

TRIAL-AND-ERROR SOLUTIONS

Crowell would like to use Eq. (7-5) to compute the total annual cost of these two alternatives:

TWO ALTERNATIVES

1 There are 30 cars ordered at a time and 15 backorders per cycle ($N_u = 30$ and $B = 15$)

2 There are 40 cars ordered at a time and 25 backorders per cycle ($N_u = 40$ and $B = 25$)

Here are the calculations for the total cost of operating the inventory system under these two alternatives:

$$\text{Total cost} = \frac{(N_u - B)^2}{2N_u} C + \frac{UP}{N_u} + \frac{B^2 V}{2N_u} \tag{7-5}$$

TOTAL COST OF FIRST
ALTERNATIVE

$$\text{Total cost for alternative 1} = \frac{(30 - 15)^2}{(2)(30)} \$800 + \frac{(400)(\$100)}{30} + \frac{(15)^2(\$150)}{(2)(30)}$$

$$= \$3,000 \qquad + \$1,333 \qquad + \$563$$

$$= \$4,896$$

TOTAL COST OF
SECOND ALTERNATIVE

$$\text{Total cost for alternative 2} = \frac{(40 - 25)^2}{(2)(40)} \$800 + \frac{(400)(\$100)}{40} + \frac{(25)^2(\$150)}{(2)(40)}$$

$$= \$2,250 \qquad + \$1,000 \qquad + \$1,172$$

$$= \$4,422$$

INTERPRETING
THE RESULTS

From these two answers, Crowell knows that alternative 2 (EOQ = 40 cars and backorders = 25 cars) is less expensive than alternative 1 (EOQ = 30 cars and backorders = 15 cars). But what of the other thousands of possibilities? Would one of them be even less expensive?

Obviously, Crowell doesn't have the time to solve this problem using trial-and-error methods; fortunately, this is not necessary. Using mathematical methods beyond the scope of this book, MS/OR analysts have determined that the optimal N_u and B are given by these two equations:

EOQ in units for the
backorder model
$$N_u = \sqrt{\left(\frac{2UP}{C}\right)\left(\frac{C + V}{V}\right)} \tag{7-6}$$

Number of units backordered
when the EOQ arrives
$$B = N_u \left(\frac{C}{C + V}\right) \tag{7-7}$$

In Crowell's situation, these answers turn out to be

$$N_u = \sqrt{\left(\frac{(2)(400)(\$100)}{\$800}\right)\left(\frac{\$800 + \$150}{\$150}\right)}$$

BACKORDER EOQ

$$= \sqrt{(100)(6.333)}$$

$$= 25.166 \text{ cars}$$

Crowell, knowing that EOQs anywhere near the optimum yield about the same cost, would order 25 cars at a time.

$$B = 25.166 \left(\frac{\$800}{\$800 + \$150} \right)$$

$$= (25.166)(.842)$$

$$= 21.19 \text{ cars}$$

Crowell would plan to have 21 cars backordered at the time each shipment of 25 cars, the economic lot, arrived.

Under this optimal alternative, the total annual cost of the inventory system would be obtained by substituting $N_u = 25$ and $B = 21$ into Eq. (7-5) to get

$$\text{Total annual cost} = \frac{(N_u - B)^2}{2N_u} C + \frac{UP}{N_u} + \frac{B^2 V}{2N_u} \qquad (7\text{-}5)$$

$$= \frac{(25 - 21)^2}{(2)(25)} \$800 + \frac{(400)(\$100)}{25} + \frac{(21)^2(\$150)}{(2)(25)}$$

$$= \$256 + \$1{,}600 + \$1{,}323$$

$$= \$3{,}179$$

If Crowell had used the regular EOQ model *without* allowing for backorders, the EOQ would have been 10 cars, with a total annual cost of ordering and carrying of about \$8,000; thus a conscious decision to allow for backorders saved Crowell almost \$5,000 (\$8,000 − \$3,179). If, however, Crowell feels strongly that having this many backordered cars (21) when a new shipment arrives might cost him lost sales and bad customer relations, he should take another look at the value he originally set for V.

COMPARISON WITH
REGULAR EOQ MODEL

SOME SENSITIVITY ANALYSIS
OF THE BACKORDER MODEL

As V (the cost of backorders) increases and C remains constant, $C/(C + V)$ in Eq. (7-7) approaches zero. In this case, B (the number of backorders) also approaches zero. In an operational setting, this means simply that if the cost of backordering becomes quite high (loss of sales, paperwork cost, and loss of goodwill, for example), then Crowell would allow very few cars to be backordered. If no cars are backordered, then Eq. (7-6) should yield an N_u equal to the N_u in the ordinary EOQ equation. Does it? Look at the expression $(C + V)/V$ in Eq. (7-6); as V gets higher, $(C + V)/V$ approaches 1, and Eq. (7-6) becomes an equation for the economic lot size (expressed in units) without backordering.

Now let's hold V (the cost of backordering) constant while we increase C (carrying cost). What happens? As C increases, the expression $C/(C + V)$ in Eq. (7-7) approaches 1, indicating that B, the number of backordered cars, equals N_u, the number of cars per lot. This means simply that the high cost of inventory suggests that Crowell hold no cars in inventory; with no cars in inventory, the entire incoming economic lot is backordered (customers are waiting to claim all the cars in that lot when it arrives).

6 How to evaluate quantity discounts offered by suppliers

Most suppliers offer buyers incentives in the form of lower unit costs for purchases of larger quantities. It is not difficult to analyze such offers once you understand the idea of EOQ. Let us look first at some of the advantages and disadvantages of buying in larger quantities; then we can show how to evaluate discounts offered by suppliers.

ADVANTAGES AND DISADVANTAGES OF QUANTITY BUYING

Buyers who buy in large quantities may well enjoy some of these advantages claimed for the policy:

ADVANTAGES AND DISADVANTAGES OF QUANTITY BUYING

Lower unit prices	Lower ordering costs
Cheaper transportation	Fewer stockouts
Mass display by retailers	Preferential treatment by suppliers

But quantity buying can involve these disadvantages:

Higher carrying costs	Older stock
Lower stock turnover	More capital required
Less flexibility	Heavier deterioration and depreciation

COST COMPARISON APPROACH TO EVALUATING SUPPLIER DISCOUNTS

COST COMPARISON APPROACH TO DISCOUNT EVALUATION

Jim Brame buys a specialty printing paper from National Paper Company. Jim's records indicate that he buys 2,000 rolls of this SKU annually at $20 a roll. His ordering cost is $50 per order, and he estimates his carrying costs at 25 percent of inventory value. Up to this point, National Paper Company has not offered Jim any discount for quantity purchases; therefore Jim has been calculating his EOQ using Eq. (6-4) as follows:

$$N_u = \sqrt{\frac{2AP}{R^2C}} \qquad (6\text{-}4)$$

$$= \sqrt{\frac{2(\$40{,}000)(\$50)}{(\$20)^2(.25)}}$$

$$= \sqrt{40{,}000}$$

$$= 200 \text{ rolls per order}$$

APPROPRIATE EOQ

Jim realized that considering the cost of ordering and holding inventory, ordering in lots of 200 rolls minimized his total inventory cost per year for this SKU.

When Jim got to work this morning, on his desk there was an announcement from National Paper Company initiating a new price policy. Table 7-6 shows

National's new price policy for this particular SKU. Jim saw from National's announcement that he would have to order at least 500 rolls at one time to qualify for the 3 percent discount; he would have to order at least 1,000 rolls at a time to qualify for the larger 6 percent discount. With the 3 percent discount, Jim's EOQ would increase to:

$$\sqrt{\frac{2(\$38{,}800)(\$50)}{(\$19.40)^2(.25)}} = 203 \text{ rolls per order}$$

and with the 6 percent discount, his EOQ would be

$$\sqrt{\frac{2(\$37{,}600)(\$50)}{(\$18.80)^2(.25)}} = 206 \text{ rolls per order}$$

Since each of these EOQs is too small to qualify for the discounts, Jim sees that it would *not* pay him to order more than the minimum quantity which would entitle him to either of these discounts; that is, ordering 600 rolls or 1,100 rolls doesn't reduce price below what it would be if he ordered 500 or 1,000 rolls and only increases his average inventory.

Jim realized that he would have to determine the total cost of the three alternatives open to him: (1) ordering the EOQ of 200 rolls, (2) ordering 500 rolls at a time, or (3) ordering 1,000 rolls at a time. Even without a computer, these calculations are not difficult; Jim set up a table similar to Table 7-7 to organize his calculations. When he finished his calculations, Jim saw that ordering 1,000 rolls at one time would result in the lowest annual cost to him ($40,050). He noticed that this alternative represented a reduction in his total annual cost of $41,000 − $40,050, or $950. Since Jim felt quite secure in his estimate of annual demand of 2,000 rolls for this SKU, he decided to raise his next order to 1,000 rolls. He made a mental note, however, to keep his eye on the demand for this SKU. "After all," he thought, "if the demand begins to fall, making my 1,000-roll order somewhat more risky, I can still save $41,000 − $40,212.50, or $787.50, and only commit myself to 500 rolls at a time."

TOTAL COST OF THE THREE ALTERNATIVES

INTERPRETING THE RESULTS

Why did Jim start his analysis by calculating the EOQs at the discounted price? Suppose that National were to give a 40 percent discount for all orders of 250 or more rolls. With this discount, the EOQ is

$$\sqrt{\frac{2(\$24{,}000)(\$50)}{(\$12)^2(.25)}} = 258 \text{ rolls per order}$$

TABLE 7-6
Prices relative to quantities ordered

Number of rolls ordered	Discount, percent	Price per roll
1–499	0	$20.00
500–999	3	19.40
1,000–1,999	6	18.80

TABLE 7-7
Total annual cost of three purchasing alternatives

	Quantity ordered at one time		
	200 rolls, EOQ	**500 rolls**	**1,000 rolls**
Carrying cost:			
Price	$20.00	$19.40	$18.80
Dollars in one order	200 × $20 = $4,000	500 × $19.40 = $9,700	1,000 × $18.80 = $18,800
Average inventory ($ per order/2)	$4,000/2 = $2,000	$9,700/2 = $4,850	$18,800/2 = $9,400
Annual carrying cost (average inventory × .25)	$2,000 × .25 = $500	$4,850 × .25 = $1,212.50	$9,400 × .25 = $2,350
Purchasing cost:			
Number of orders/yr (2,000/number per order)	2,000/200 = 10	2,000/500 = 4	2,000/1,000 = 2
Annual purchasing cost (number of orders × $50)	10 × $50 = $500	4 × $50 = $200	2 × $50 = $100
Paper cost:			
Cost of paper (2,000 × price per roll)	2,000 × $20 = $40,000	2,000 × $19.40 = $38,800	2,000 × $18.80 = $37,600
Total cost/yr: (Carrying cost + purchasing cost + paper cost)	$ 500.00 500.00 40,000.00 $41,000.00	$ 1,212.50 200.00 38,800.00 $40,212.50	$ 2,350.00 100.00 37,600.00 $40,050.00 (lowest cost)

Since an order of 258 rolls would qualify for the discount, Jim should order 258 rolls at a time.

We can generalize this example as follows: Let's consider the case where a single price reduction, from R to R', is given for orders of more than B units. (The extension to situations with multiple price breaks is straightforward.) Let N_u be the EOQ without the price reduction and N'_u be the EOQ with the reduction. Using Eq. (6-4), we find that

$$N_u = \sqrt{\frac{2AP}{R^2C}} \quad \text{and} \quad N'_u = \sqrt{\frac{2A'P}{(R')^2C}}$$

Since A (the total dollar value of the SKU used per year) and R (the unit price of the SKU) both decrease by the same factor and R^2 appears in the denominator of Eq. (6-4), we see that N'_u is bigger than N_u. This is illustrated in Figure 7-10, where we have shown the total annual costs (carrying cost + ordering cost + material cost) in terms of the number of units per order for both of the unit prices, R and R'. Two additional points to note in Figure 7-10 are that (1) the curve for R' is always below the curve for R (since for any size order the carrying and material costs decrease as the unit price decreases, and ordering cost doesn't depend on the unit price), and (2) the minimum total cost on the R' curve is less than the minimum total cost on the R curve.

To determine how many units should be ordered, we must consider two cases, which depend on the location of B, the minimum number of units purchased to qualify for the price break. In each of these two cases, the applicable total cost curve will consist of two pieces: the R curve for orders of fewer than B units and the R' curve for orders of B or more units.

Case 1: $N'_u \geq B$ (see Figure 7-11). In this case we should order N'_u units at a time.

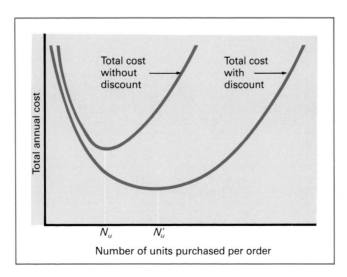

FIGURE 7-10

Total annual costs (carrying, ordering, and material) with and without a price discount.

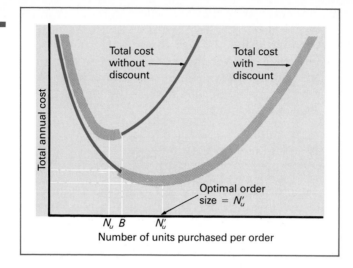

FIGURE 7-11
Optimal order size
with $N'_u \geq B$.

Case 2: $N'_u < B$ (see Figures 7-12 and 7-13). In this case, we must compare the total annual costs for orders of size B and N_u, and order whichever of the two gives the lower total cost.

7 Material requirements planning (MRP)

ORDER-POINT MODELS
ARE LESS EFFECTIVE IN
MANUFACTURING
SITUATIONS

All the approaches to reordering we have discussed so far in this chapter are called *order-point* models. They all generate an order of a fixed size (EOQ) whenever the inventory on hand reaches its order point. In most situations involving the control of inventories of finished goods, they work rather well. However, when you try to apply them to manufacturing situations where you must control the production *and* inventories of components which go

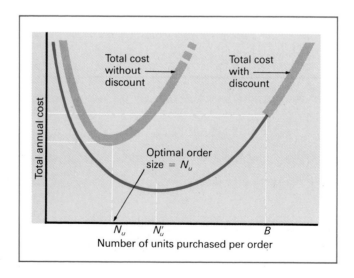

FIGURE 7-12
Optimal order size
with $N'_u < B$ and N_u
better than B.

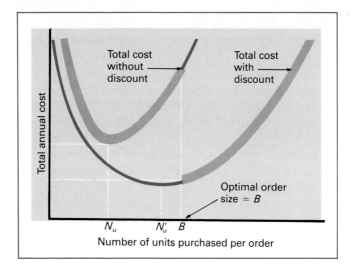

FIGURE 7-13
Optimal order size
with $N'_u < B$ and B
better than N_u.

together to make up finished products, these order-point models are less
effective. One of the more effective approaches to inventory management
under these situations is material requirements planning (MRP), the subject
of this section.

WHY IS A MANUFACTURING SYSTEM DIFFERENT?

In a marketing situation where we are dealing with finished goods, the
purpose of an inventory system is to maintain sufficient inventory to meet
customer demand. Not so in a manufacturing system, where the major
purpose of inventory management is to translate demand for the finished
goods into detailed planning for the components (subassemblies and parts)
which make up the finished product.

DEFINITIONS IN AN MRP SYSTEM

In a manufacturing environment, management uses what is known as a *master*   MRP TERMINOLOGY
production schedule to state the number of finished products that are required
and when the company plans to produce them. Only after a master production
schedule has been decided on can the factory management translate this into
the manufacturing requirements of all the components (when each part will
be manufactured, when these will all be assembled, and so forth). Another
necessary part of an MRP approach is a *bill of materials*. Almost everyone is
familiar with a bill of materials, which is nothing more than a list of the type
and number of each part necessary to manufacture a complete product.
However, in an MRP system, the bill of materials may also show how the
parts go into each other (two A's are fastened together to make one B, and
it takes four B's fastened together to make one C). In cases where the bill of
materials does not contain this "how to put the product together" information,
companies use what is called a "Gozinto" (goes into) chart, which gives the
same information pictorially.

▦ CHARLIE MILLENDER AND THE HI-VOLUME FAN

Charlie is the manager of the Brown Manufacturing Company in Graham, North Carolina. As a part of his new line, Charlie has designed a new low-cost high-volume fan. Its marketing advantages are that it is well made, designed with safety requirements in mind, and attractively finished. Charlie has drawn up a schematic of the bill of materials, shown in Figure 7-14. In this instance, the bill of materials also performs the functions of a Gozinto chart. From this chart we can see not only how many of each component are required to complete one fan, but also in what order they are assembled.

Charlie's master production schedule indicates that 1,000 Hi-volume Fans are scheduled to be assembled during the twenty-fifth week of the current production schedule. Therefore, it will be necessary for each of the four components in Figure 7-14 (leg, motor, switch, and frame) to be completed by the end of the twenty-fourth week of the production schedule. Suppose at this point we look at the motor assembly in a bit more detail as an example of how MRP works. Look at Table 7-8. There we have shown the details of the inventory on hand and the lead time (time to get additional units) for the motor assembly and its three subassemblies. Using a traditional inventory control approach, we would use the information in Table 7-8 to calculate the net new requirement of each component necessary to meet the 1,000-unit assembly schedule for week 25 using the method in Table 7-9.

▦ WEAKNESSES OF THE TRADITIONAL INVENTORY CONTROL APPROACH

The weakness of applying a traditional inventory control approach to Charlie's Hi-volume Fan situation is illustrated in Table 7-9. **There we treated the data exactly as if all four components were completely independent of each other. In fact, however, that is not the case, and the demand for one**

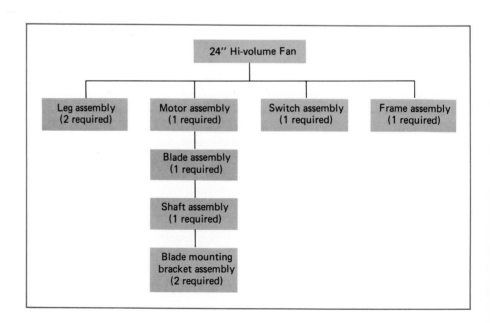

FIGURE 7-14
Bill of materials for
Hi-volume Fan.

Component	On hand	Lead time, in weeks
Motor assembly	100	6
Blade assembly	200	3
Shaft assembly	300	5
Blade mounting bracket assembly	250	2

TABLE 7-8
Inventory and lead time for Hi-volume Fan components

component (blade assemblies, for example) is highly dependent upon the demand for motors. We ignored this fact in Table 7-9 and let the demand for blade assemblies (which we calculated there to be 800) be dependent only upon the demand for completed fans (adjusted of course for the number of blade assemblies on hand). In fact, Charlie doesn't need to schedule production of 800 blade assemblies because with 100 motors already on hand, only 900 more motors need to be scheduled; hence only 700 more blade assemblies need to be scheduled.

The dramatic difference between the traditional inventory control approach to Charlie's problem and an MRP approach to the same problem can be seen by comparing column (4) of Table 7-9 with column (4) of Table 7-10. Although the number of motor assemblies required in both cases is the same, the net new requirements for the other three components have been significantly reduced by applying MRP. This reduction was achieved by acknowledging that demand among the four components is *dependent*, a fact ignored by most of the traditional inventory control approaches.

THE MRP SOLUTION

Component (1)	Number needed to assemble 1,000 fans (2)	Number on hand (3)	Net new requirement (4) = (2) − (3)
Motor assembly	1,000	100	900
Blade assembly	1,000	200	800
Shaft assembly	1,000	300	700
Blade mounting bracket assembly (2 req'd.)	2,000	250	1,750

TABLE 7-9
Calculating net new requirements of components necessary to assemble 1,000 Hi-volume Fans using traditional inventory control approach

Component (1)	Number required to assemble (2)	Number on hand (3)	Net new requirement (4) = (2) − (3)
Motor assembly	1,000 fans = 1,000	100	900
Blade assembly	900 motor assemblies = 900	200	700
Shaft assembly	700 blade assemblies = 700	300	400
Blade mounting bracket assembly (2 req'd.)	400 shaft assemblies = 800	250	550

TABLE 7-10
Calculating net new requirements of components necessary to assemble 1,000 Hi-volume Fans using an MRP approach

CAVEAT TO THE MRP APPROACH

To illustrate the departure of the MRP approach from more traditional inventory control approaches, we have ignored the effect of inventory that has been ordered previously and is scheduled to arrive. Although including this detail in our presentation would have made the "bookkeeping" a bit messier, it would not in any way have altered the concept we have developed.

TIME DIMENSIONS OF AN MRP APPROACH

MRP AND TIME-PHASED SCHEDULES

MRP not only focuses on *how many* of a component to order (or produce), but is also concerned about *when* to order this component. To do this we can use the time information contained in Table 7-8 to calculate a time-phased schedule, which is illustrated in Table 7-11. In each instance, we are working *backward* in time from the scheduled completion date of the Hi-volume Fans (week 25 of the current production schedule), subtracting the lead time of each component from the scheduled time of the component of which it is part. **Again, we are recognizing in doing this that the four components are dependent not only in terms of the quantities of each one required to support each other, but also in terms of the time (lead time) required of each to support the timely ordering of the others.**

THE COMPUTER AND MRP

WHAT DOES THE COMPUTER ADD

Because MRP approaches maintain data on all the components in a manufacturing system, it becomes more practical to use computers to manage this information base. Thus when MRP is used in anything but the simplest manufacturing system, it is implemented with a computer system. It is not necessary for a company to design and program its own MRP system since computer manufacturers offer a variety of existing software packages.

TABLE 7-11

Time-dependent characteristic of MRP illustrated

Step in process	Must be completed by week:
Motor assembly order completed	24
[*Minus*] Lead time for motor assembly	− 6
Begin motor assembly	18
Blade assembly order completed	18
[*Minus*] Lead time for blade assembly	− 3
Begin blade assembly	15
Shaft assembly order completed	15
[*Minus*] Lead time for shaft assembly	− 5
Begin shaft assembly	10
Blade mounting bracket assembly order completed	10
[*Minus*] Lead time for blade mounting bracket assembly	− 2
Begin blade mounting bracket assembly	8

Annual backorder cost The total annual cost of handling backorders generated by the inventory system.

Backorder An item ordered but unable to be delivered for which the customer will wait for delivery without canceling the order.

Backorder cost The cost of handling the backorder (special handling, follow-up, labor) plus whatever loss of goodwill occurs as a result of backordering an item.

Bill of materials Part of a material requirements planning system which details the quantity of each component necessary to complete a finished product and the order of assembly of those individual components.

Discount A reduction from list or regular price given by a supplier in return for the purchase of great quantities of that SKU.

Fixed-reorder-point system An inventory system which sets reorder points for all SKUs under the system control and which initiates an order when the inventory reaches that level.

Fixed-review-interval system An inventory system which reviews the inventory status of every SKU under system control at stipulated intervals.

Header The part of the purchase order containing all the general information concerning the order.

Header cost The cost incurred in preparing the header portion of a purchase order.

Joint ordering The process of purchasing more than one SKU from the same vendor simultaneously.

Lead time The time (usually measured in days) required for inventory to arrive after an order is placed.

Lead time demand The usage of an SKU during the lead time.

Line item Part of the purchase order containing information relevant to one SKU being purchased.

Line item cost The cost incurred in preparing the line item portion of a purchase order for one line item.

Line item EOQ The quantity of an SKU which is to be purchased on a purchase order initiated by some other SKU reaching its reorder point.

Master production schedule A schedule detailing the number of completed products required and when those are scheduled to be produced.

Material requirements planning (MRP) A system which recognizes the dependent nature of individual components in an inventory system and calculates quantities and schedule times accordingly.

Reorder point The inventory level at which it is appropriate to replenish stock.

Safety stock Extra inventory held against the possibility of a stockout.

Service level The percentage of time that all orders arriving during the reorder period can be satisfied; it is computed as one minus the probability (deemed appropriate by a given organization) of being out of stock.

Stockout The condition when available inventory is not sufficient to satisfy demand.

Trigger EOQ The quantity of an SKU which is to be purchased when it reaches its reorder point and initiates the purchasing process.

9 Review of equations

Page 297

Reorder point = average daily use × lead time + safety stock (7-1)

Multiplying average daily use by the lead time in days yields the lead time demand; adding safety stock to this to provide for the variation in lead time demand determines the reorder point.

Page 307

$$\text{Annual carrying cost with backorders} = \frac{(N_u - B)^2}{2N_u} C \qquad (7\text{-}2)$$

Using this formula, we can calculate annual carrying cost in the EOQ model which allows for planned backorders. In this formulation, N_u is the economic lot size in units, B is the quantity backordered during each inventory cycle, and C is the annual carrying cost expressed in dollars per unit per year.

Page 308

$$\text{Annual ordering cost with backorders} = \frac{UP}{N_u} \qquad (7\text{-}3)$$

This formula yields the annual cost of ordering in the EOQ model which allows for backorders. N_u is the same as defined in Eq. (7-2). U is the annual demand for the SKU in units, and P is the cost per purchase order.

Page 309

$$\text{Annual backorder cost} = \frac{B^2 V}{2N_u} \qquad (7\text{-}4)$$

This expression will give us the annual cost of backorders in the EOQ model which allows for planned backorders. N_u and B are the same as defined in Eq. (7-2). V here is the annual cost of a backorder including paperwork cost and any cost attributable to lost sales or lost goodwill.

Page 309

$$\begin{array}{l}\text{Total annual cost of an EOQ inventory} \\ \text{system that allows backorders}\end{array} = \frac{(N_u - B)^2}{2N_u} C + \frac{UP}{N_u} + \frac{B^2 V}{2N_u} \qquad (7\text{-}5)$$

This expression is the sum of the costs introduced in Eqs. (7-2), (7-3), and (7-4). It is the total annual cost of (1) carrying inventory, (2) ordering inventory, and (3) backorders in the system.

$$N_u = \sqrt{\left(\frac{2UP}{C}\right)\left(\frac{C + V}{V}\right)} \qquad (7\text{-}6)$$

Use of this equation solves for the optimal number of units, N_u, per economic lot in an EOQ inventory system which allows for planned backorders.

Page 310

$$B = N_u \left(\frac{C}{C + V}\right) \qquad (7\text{-}7)$$

This equation yields the optimal number of units, B, which are backordered at the time an economic lot arrives.

10 Exercises

7-1 A manufacturer of boilers uses $80,000 worth of valves per year. The administrative cost per purchase is $40, and the carrying charge is 28 percent of the average inventory. The company currently follows an optimal purchasing policy but has been offered a 1.0 percent discount if it purchases four times per year. Should the offer be accepted? If not, what counteroffer should be made?

7-2 The annual demand for teak end tables at Casual Furniture is 200 tables. Carrying cost for the table is $50 per unit held per year, and the cost of placing an order is $30. If the cost of maintaining a backorder per year is $40, determine the optimal order quantity and planned backorder quantity for the tables.

7-3 The Randall Gear Company has experienced a mean use of 250 gears during past reorder periods, with a standard deviation of 50 gears. Assuming a normal distribution of lead time demand, what percentage of the time will stockouts be experienced with a safety stock level of 64 gears?

7-4 In Exercise 7-3, what safety stock would have to be utilized in order to maintain a 95 percent service level?

7-5 The Township Distributing Company has maintained an ordering policy for new inventory of power lawn mowers which allows for an 80 percent service level. Mean demand during the reorder period is 130 lawn mowers, and the standard deviation is 80 mowers. The annual cost of carrying one mower in inventory is $6. The area salespeople have recently told Township's management that they could expect a $500 improvement in profit (based on current figures of cost per lawn mower) if the service level were increased to 99 percent. Is it worthwhile for Township to make this change?

7-6 Assume that you are the purchasing agent for a large retail company which purchases a number of SKUs from the same wholesale supplier. The common shipping unit for these SKUs is cartons, and they are shipped by truck freight. If you are able to order an entire truckload at one time, significant savings result from lower freight rates. A full truckload is 1,600 cartons. Inventory data on SKUs ordered from the same wholesaler are as follows:

SKU	Quantity on hand, cartons	Reorder point, cartons	Trigger EOQ, cartons	Line item EOQ, cartons
A	500	400	450	350
B	350	300	400	300
C	600	600	500	425
D	550	500	600	500
E	105	100	300	200
F	100	75	250	200
G	100	50	350	250
H	200	40	400	300

If you decide to take advantage of the reduced freight rates for a complete truckload, what SKUs should you order and how many cartons of each?

7-7 Radtronics, a manufacturer of microwave ovens, uses $75,000 worth of LED readout circuits annually in its production process. Cost per order is $45, and the carrying charge assessed against this classification of inventory is 25 percent of the average balance per year. Radtronics follows an EOQ purchasing system and to date has not been offered any discounts on these LED circuits. Just yesterday, however, the supplier approached Radtronics and indicated that if the company would buy its circuits four times a year, a discount of 1.5 percent off list price would be given in return. Would you advise Radtronics to accept this offer or to make a counteroffer? If a counteroffer is made, what is the highest price that should be offered to pay for this SKU purchased quarterly for Radtronics not to increase its total cost?

7-8 Sarah Mack sells cloth-bound Bibles at the Monticello Book Store. Annual demand for the Bibles is 400 units, and carrying costs are $10 per unit per year. It costs $35 for Sarah to place orders. She currently uses an EOQ ordering policy, but she is interested in determining what cost savings, if any, can be realized if she allows backorders. Since her store is the only one in Monticello that sells Bibles, she feels that backorder costs would only be $20 per Bible held on backorder per year. Should she allow backorders, and, if so, how many should be allowed and what is the optimal number of Bibles she should purchase per order?

7-9 The purchasing agent for Jack Spaniel Distillery is considering three sources of supply for oak barrels in which the distillery's fine sour-mash bourbon is aged. The first supplier offers any quantity of barrels at $125 each. The second supplier offers barrels in lots of 80 or more at $120. The third supplier offers barrels in lots of 150 or more at $118 each. The distillery uses 1,500 barrels a year at a constant rate. Carrying costs are 20 percent, and it costs the purchasing agent $75 to place an order. From which source should this distillery buy its barrels? What will be the total annual cost of buying the barrels, carrying inventory, and performing the necessary purchasing operations?

7-10 The Barton Company has received an order for 600 desk lamps which need to be shipped 20 weeks from now. The bill of materials for these lamps is as follows:

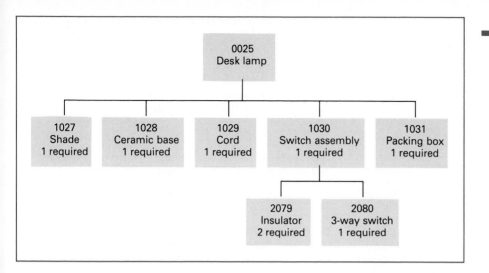

The computer's inventory file currently shows the following levels of inventory for components not already allocated to the production of other firm orders.

Component	On hand	Lead time, weeks	Manufactured or purchased
0025	56	3	Manufactured
1027	23	2	Manufactured
1028	22	3	Manufactured
1029	1000	5	Purchased
1030	87	1	Manufactured
1031	720	1	Manufactured
2079	200	6	Purchased
2080	156	5	Purchased

Determine the net requirements for all the components needed to support delivery of this order.

7-11 For the data above in Exercise 7-10, determine a schedule of order release and production release times for the components.

7-12 Northside General Hospital has instituted an inventory control program for its pharmacy and dispensary; this step has led to a considerable dollar savings in inventory costs. Since a computer was installed, over 90 percent of the hospital's SKUs have been ordered under an EOQ system. The director of supply has computed the cost of carrying inventory at 16 percent per year and the cost of placing an order at $40. The hospital's supplier of surgical thread, which is now one of the optimally ordered SKUs, has just offered a 3 percent discount from list price if the hospital will buy its annual requirement of this item ($9,000) in three equally spaced intervals. Should this offer be acccepted?

7-13 The Wingate Manufacturing Company experiences a mean usage of 160 motor castings during the reorder lead time. The standard deviation of usage during this period is 26 castings. If the usage is normally distributed, what percentage of the time will Wingate experience stockouts if it maintains a safety stock of 24 castings?

7-14 The LeMoyne College bookstore sends its truck to a number of publishing company warehouses in the northeast in late August in order to pick up textbooks for the fall semester. Any unused space in the truck may be used to transport other items sold in the bookstore. These other items are all purchased from Boston College Suppliers at discounted prices when LeMoyne takes on responsibility for the transportation. This year, LeMoyne expects to have available 4,000 cubic feet of unused space in the truck and can consider any of the following items:

SKU	Description	Volume, cubic feet per case	Reorder point	Trigger EOQ	Line item EOQ	Quantity on hand
A	Desk lamp	60	20 cases	24 cases	18 cases	27 cases
B	Waste basket	58	18	22	16	22
C	Pennant	30	14	19	14	14
D	Stuffed dolphin	48	23	25	18	29
E	Sweatshirt	40	20	21	15	29
F	Backpack	56	16	18	13	16
G	Beverage cooler	88	10	14	9	18

How many cases of these various products should be brought back to the bookstore?

7-15 In light of a recent referendum allowing dog racing in their state, a group of investors have decided to build and operate a dog track. The investors have hired a statistician to produce some demand estimates from analyses of other sports operations in the state and similar dog track operations in neighboring states. The statistician reports that attendance can be described by a normal distribution. Additionally, she states that attendance should exceed 22,000 half the time; 80 percent of the time, it should be less than 30,000. If the investors want to plan for a 95 percent service level for their customers, what size track do you recommend they construct?

7-16 Randy Nelson is the purchasing agent for an automobile assembly plant in Midlands, Michigan. He purchases a number of metal fasteners from the same supplier. These are shipped in cartons by rail freight. If Randy orders an entire carload at a time from this supplier (10,000 cartons), he enjoys considerable freight savings. Inventory data on SKUs ordered from this supplier are as follows:

SKU	(Quantities expressed in cartons)			
	Quantity on hand	Reorder point	Trigger EOQ	Line item EOQ
#10 sheet-metal screw	2,000	1,500	4,000	3,000
2" metal rivets	1,200	1,200	2,500	2,000
8/32 × 1½" hex bolts	840	800	1,500	1,000
#4 sheet-metal screws	2,100	1,400	2,500	2,000
5/16" lock washers	1,500	1,000	1,500	1,000
3" pop rivets	800	500	900	600
1" hex head nuts	200	100	300	200
19/32 × 2" hex bolts	3,000	2,800	8,000	5,000
7/16" flat washers	3,000	1,500	4,000	3,000

Suggest for Randy the most favorable carload combination of fasteners to order at this time.

7-17 Village Furniture Company deals in rather expensive upholstered sofas and occasional chairs. The company has analyzed its sales records for a particular style sofa and found that annual sales are 60 units. Cost per purchase order is $50, and the carrying charge is $70 per sofa per year. As a rule, retailers of upholstered furniture expect their customers to wait for delivery of the particular SKU they want, and very little goodwill is lost because of this. Rarely have Village's customers canceled orders for sofas. The cost of processing, paperwork, and accounting for the back-ordered sofas is about $20 a unit per year. What is the EOQ for this particular SKU? When the optimal order arrives, how many customers are waiting for their sofas on average? What is the total annual cost of ordering, carrying, and backordering?

7-18 The Winston Company produces electrical tools. One of its SKUs is electrical pliers; the bill of materials for this item is as follows:

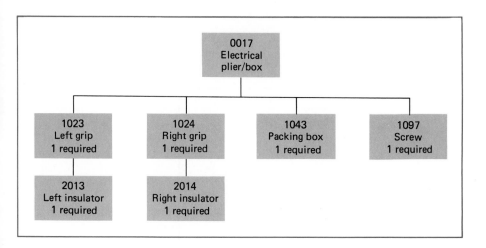

The current levels of inventory on hand and lead time requirements are:

Component	On hand	Lead time, weeks
0017	85	1
1023	91	2
1024	23	2
1043	17	3
1097	14	3
2013	45	4
2014	64	4

Components 0017, 1023, and 1024 are produced by the Winston Company. The remaining components are ordered directly from other manufacturers. If the company has received an order for 825 electrical pliers to be delivered in 10 weeks, determine the net requirement of the components needed.

7-19 Referring to Exercise 7-18, determine the schedule of order release or production release times for the components.

7-20 The Logan Company has determined that the cost of being stocked out of motors is $200 for each unit. The EOQ analysis indicates that the company should reorder 10 times each year. Carrying costs are $20 per motor. Logan is considering dropping the reorder point from 250 to 220. Based on the information in the table below, what would you advise the company to do?

Usage during reorder period	Probability of this usage
200	.10
220	.08
240	.06
260	.04
280	.02

7-21 The following bill of materials describes the assembly of end item A.

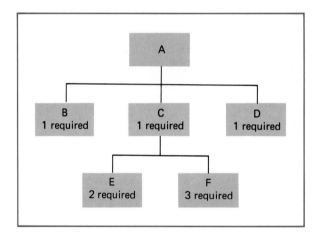

The current inventory levels and lead times for the components are:

Component	On hand	Lead time, weeks
B (produced)	50	3
C (produced)	100	2
D (ordered)	20	1
E (produced)	600	4
F (ordered)	1,200	6

Determine the net new requirements and the order/production schedule for the components if 800 units of end item A are scheduled to be assembled in week 60.

7-22 Given the following data for an SKU used by the Miller Company (assume a 250-day work year), compute the reorder point:

EOQ	100
Average use per day	4 units
Average reorder period	25 days
Cost to store 1 unit per year	$5
Cost of being out of stock per unit per time	$20

Usage during reorder period	Probability of this usage
25	.05
50	.10
75	.15
100	.25
125	.20
150	.15
175	.10

7-23 Mindy Atkinson is planning to place an order for sweaters from the Cascade Woolen Mill. Because of a prior agreement with Cascade, Mindy is required to place orders for no less than $2000. Data regarding the inventory of sweaters being purchased from Cascade are as follows:

SKU	Description	Sweaters on hand	Reorder point	Trigger EOQ	Line item EOQ	Cost, $/sweater
1	V-neck	27	22	20	15	20
2	Ski	51	30	24	18	26
3	Casual	20	20	20	16	18
4	Turtleneck	35	26	24	18	35
5	Buttoned	24	15	12	10	32
6	Vest	19	14	10	8	20
7	Hip-length	30	26	18	14	43
8	Collared	26	18	15	12	35

Which items, and how many of each, should Mindy include in her order?

7-24 Ben's Muffler Repair advertises that it is able to replace a car muffler on the same day a customer brings a car into the shop. If for any reason Ben cannot keep this promise, he pays the customer $100. Ben has found that for LN-70 mufflers, the optimal reorder quantity is 30 mufflers; he orders LN-70 mufflers 10 times a year. As LN-70 mufflers have to be ordered from a manufacturer located a considerable distance away, lead time for his orders is 30 working days, a period of time in which Ben on the average sells 30 LN-70 mufflers. During the past 10 years, 100 orders were placed. There were 10 occasions when Ben sold 32 LN-70s, 5 occasions when he sold 35, and only 1 when he sold 36 during the 30-day order period. On each of the other 84 occasions, he sold 30 or fewer. If it costs Ben $18 a year to hold one LN-70 in safety stock, what should Ben establish as his reorder point for LN-70 mufflers to minimize his costs? At this level of safety stock, how many $100 bills will Ben expect to pay to car owners whose cars require an LN-70 muffler?

7-25 Dave Williams is a management consultant with Systems Enterprise. He has been asked to make recommendations to the city of Marshall regarding the seating capacity of a new athletic stadium which the city is planning to construct. Dave has estimated that attendance at the stadium will be normally distributed with a mean of 6,000 persons. He feels that for about 75 percent of the athletic events, attendance will not exceed 8,000 fans. The city officials would like to accommodate ticket sales at a 95 percent service level. What seating capacity should Dave recommend for the new stadium?

7-26 Computers-For-Fun stocks a very popular computer game called Wonderland. Recently, some of the customers have complained about excessive stockouts at Computers-For-Fun, and Wendy Mills, the store's manager, is considering an increase in safety stock for the games. Wendy has estimated that the demand in the reorder lead time for Wonderland games is normally distributed with a mean of 50 games and a standard deviation of 25 games. She currently places orders for new games, which cost her $10 each, when the stock level drops to 80 games. If holding costs for Wendy are 22 percent, how much will her costs increase if she adopts a service-level policy of 99 percent during the reorder lead time?

7-27 In emergency situations the Breward County Hospital uses a special drug to relieve shock symptoms. Because of its rather remote location and the need to transport this drug from another hospital, the dispensary places the cost of "stocking out" at $200. By use of EOQ analysis, the hospital's industrial engineer has determined that the drug should be ordered 10 times a year. Because the drug must be stored in carefully controlled conditions, the pharmacist estimates the cost of carrying at $25 per dose per year. In an effort to reduce cost, the hospital is considering dropping the reorder point from 105 to 80 doses. On the basis of the information in the table below, what would you advise the hospital to do?

Usage during reorder period	Probability of this usage
75	.10
85	.08
95	.06
105	.04
115	.02

7-28 The Applegate Tool Company has just received an order for 50 units of its special purpose jig for aircraft engine assembly to be delivered in 12 weeks. The bill of materials describing a special purpose jig is as follows:

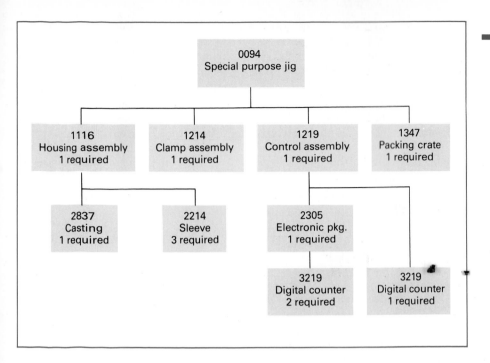

Determine the net requirement of the components if the following data describe current inventory levels not allocated to the production of other products.

Component	On hand	Lead time, weeks
0094	21	3
1116	8	2
1214	12	4
1219	16	3
1347	0	1
2837	16	2
2214	43	1
2305	4	2
3219	20	3

7-29 In reference to Exercise 7-28, determine the schedule of production release times for all needed components.

7-30 The Kwickie Takeout restaurant has a standing offer to its customers that if Kwickie cannot provide any sandwich on its menu, the customer will be paid $5. Kwickie's optimal order for canned hams (from each canned ham, 30 ham sandwiches are made) is 15 hams; the order is placed about 30 times annually. There is a 10-day lead time on ham delivery during which Kwickie sells an average of 15 hams (made up in sandwiches). During the past 10 years, there have been 30 occasions when 17 hams were sold during a reorder period, 15 occasions when 20 hams were sold, and

3 occasions when 25 hams were sold. On all other occasions, there have been 15 or fewer hams sold. If it costs Kwickie $5 per year to hold a ham in cold storage, what should the established reorder point be to minimize costs? At this reorder point, how many $5 offers will Kwickie pay off on?

7-31 Benson Electronics Supply would like to determine the standard deviation of demand for X27 transistors during the reorder lead time. They have fairly good data regarding the mean demand in the reorder lead time; this demand is known to be 140 transistors. They also have records which show that 95 percent of past demands have been met while orders are outstanding. Benson Electronics places an order for X27 transistors when the stock falls below 180 units. From this data, compute the standard deviation of lead time demands.

 7-32 Here are data for disposable water-testing kits stocked by a field unit of the Environmental Protection Agency (optimal N_o = 6 orders/year):

Average daily use	5 kits
Average reorder period	20 days
Cost to store one kit per year	$8
Estimated out-of-stock cost per kit	$30

Usage during reorder period	Probability of this usage
40	.05
60	.15
80	.20
100	.30
120	.20
140	.08
160	.02

What should the field unit's reorder point be for this SKU?

 7-33 Ellen Montgomery is the sales manager of Miller's Truck Sales in Roxboro, North Carolina. Her biggest selling SKU in this year's line is a B-2500 diesel tractor, but the cost of carrying her inventory ($4,000 per truck per year) makes it desirable to keep the inventory on hand to an absolute minimum. To process the rather substantial amount of paperwork involved in ordering a group of trucks currently costs Ellen $200; and she estimates the paperwork, accounting, and goodwill cost of backorders to be $300 per year. Ellen estimates her sales of the B-2500 to be 72 units this year, and her plans are to order 6 units each month. Can you suggest a better ordering strategy for Ellen? What would your plan save her per year if she adopted it?

 7-34 The Doakes Company maintains an inventory of raw materials for production. These materials, as well as their reorder points, trigger EOQs, and line item EOQs are as follows:

Item	Reorder point, kg	Trigger EOQ, kg	Line item EOQ, kg
Rolled steel	1,000	1,500	1,050
Brass	600	900	700
Copper plate	400	800	650
Aluminum	300	600	500
Wrought iron	1,200	2,000	1,600
Copper pipe	200	600	500

All these materials are purchased from Montana Metal Supply, Inc., whose policy is to fill orders only when the total order is at least 4,000 kilograms of metal. At the present time the raw material inventory at the Doakes Company is:

Item	Current inventory, kg
Rolled steel	1,200
Brass	1,200
Copper plate	400
Aluminum	600
Wrought iron	1,200
Copper pipe	250

Which items should Mrs. Doakes order from the metal supplier?

7-35 The Village of Oswego experiences very severe snowstorms during the winter months. In order to keep the roads clear, the maintenance personnel use rock salt. Based upon past experience, the mean winter consumption of rock salt has been found to be 150 tons, and in about 70 percent of the past winter seasons, 200 tons or less have been used. The annual snowfall and consumption of rock salt are nearly normally distributed. Village officials must budget for next year's planned usage of the salt. They know that if sufficient rock salt is not on hand to ensure a 95 percent service level, the good citizens of Oswego will be very irate indeed. How much rock salt should they have on hand for the coming winter? If it costs the village $15 per ton to store unused rock salt through to the next winter, how much should the officials expect to budget for storing their safety stock of rock salt?

7-36 Mrs. Jones, who owns and operates the Village Farm Equipment Company, has been stocking tractors according to an EOQ model. Her holding costs are $1,500 for each tractor held in inventory for a year. The tractors cost her $10,000 each, and she sells them for $12,000. Her annual demand is a fairly predictable 60 units per year. It costs Mrs. Jones $50 to place an order. Recently, Mrs. Jones sent letters to all her customers suggesting that in the future she would like to eliminate her entire inventory of tractors and meet all sales on a backorder basis. According to her proposal, she would wait until there were enough backorders to equal her usual EOQ before placing an order. In this way her ordering costs would be the same as before and holding costs would be eliminated entirely. All cost savings realized with the plan would then be passed on to her customers in the form of price reductions. Mrs. Jones' customers responded overwhelmingly in favor of this plan, since they could anticipate the need for new equipment well in advance. How much price reduction will Mrs. Jones give?

7-37 Kurt and Heidi's Lighting Shop stocks a very popular floor lamp which enjoys an annual demand of about 900 units. The annual holding costs are 26 percent of average inventory value, and the ordering costs are about $30 per order. The floor lamp costs the shop $60 per unit. Kurt and Heidi would like to use a reorder-point model, but cannot realistically assess stockout costs. Therefore, they have decided to set safety stock levels based upon a service-level policy of meeting 90 percent of demand in the reorder lead time. Demand in the reorder lead time has been observed to be normally distributed with a mean of 10 lamps and a standard deviation of 4 lamps. What should they set as their reorder point? What are the annual inventory costs of the floor lamp?

7-38 The Williams Manufacturing Company produces electric motors. The assembly shop orders shafts for these motors from the machine shop, which machines the shafts according to an economic lot size formula. The following data pertain to these shafts:

Carrying cost	$20 per shaft held for a year
Setup cost	$500 per setup
Annual usage	8,000 units per year
Average daily usage	26 units per day
Production rate	100 units per day
Stockout cost	$600 per unit stocked out
Average lead time usage	130 units

The high value of stockout cost reflects the fact that when the shafts are not available in the assembly shop, the assembly line experiences a shutdown. The lead time, or elapsed time between the placement of an order by the assembly shop and the first daily delivery of shafts, is always 5 working days. However, the usage by the assembly shop varies somewhat during these 5 days. The usage levels in excess of average lead time usage and the probabilities of these usage rates are:

Lead time usage, units	Probability
140	.10
150	.06
160	.02
170	.01

Determine an optimal reorder point at which the assembly shop should issue an order to produce an economic lot size of the shafts.

11 Chapter concepts quiz

Fill in the Blanks

7-1 The _____ is the time between the order of inventory and its arrival; _____ is the amount of inventory used during a lead time period.

7-2 Lost sales and disgruntled customers are examples of _____ costs, while idle machines and employee ill will are examples of _____ costs.

7-3 In a _____ system, the inventory level of all SKUs is checked at specified time intervals only; in a _____ system, an order is placed when inventory for any item reaches a prescribed reorder point.

7-4 When stockout costs are unknown, a manager may specify a _____, which is an appropriate probability of being able to avoid a stockout during a lead time.

7-5 Under the situation of joint ordering, the _____ EOQ is the appropriate amount to order of the SKU which initiated the order; the _____ EOQ is the amount to be ordered for all SKUs on the purchase order which did not initiate the order.

7-6 The level of inventory at which a new order needs to be placed for replenishment stock is called the _____.

7-7 Extra inventory held in order to protect against the possibility of a stockout is called _____.

7-8 A purchase order may be divided into two parts: the _____ and the _____.

7-9 If a customer places a demand on an inventory item which is currently out of stock, and he is willing to wait until a new shipment arrives, the stockout is called a _____.

7-10 In manufacturing systems, an inventory control application which focuses upon inventories of the components of a finished product rather than the finished product itself is called _____.

7-11 If demand is constant and known, and stockouts are not permitted, then the reorder point is the same as the lead time demand. **T F** True-False

7-12 Stockouts may occur as a result of variations in the lead time demand and length of the lead time. **T F**

7-13 The average safety stock can be computed by dividing the maximum safety stock level by 2. **T F**

7-14 When stockout costs are known, the size of the EOQ has no influence on determining the optimal safety stock level. **T F**

7-15 Under the service-level approach to finding an appropriate safety stock, the safety stock is that amount of inventory which, together with the expected lead time demand, will be sufficient to cover lead time demand with a probability greater than or equal to the service level. **T F**

7-16 Joint ordering is defined as the situation where two manufacturers jointly order the same item from a given supplier. **T F**

7-17 The trigger EOQ for an item is always less than the line EOQ because the smaller incremental cost of ordering associated with a line item makes it profitable to order more of that item at one time. **T F**

7-18 Because of the additional cost assigned to stocking out of an item in terms of extra paperwork and loss of customer goodwill, it is never optimal to plan for stockouts. **T F**

7-19 If one is to take advantage of discounts offered for ordering in large quantities, it is always optimal from a cost point of view to order the smallest amount necessary to earn a given discount. **T F**

7-20 The advantage of the MRP approach to managing inventory in a manufacturing setting is that it explicitly takes into account the dependence of the demand for various components and subassemblies used in the manufacturing process. **T F**

7-21 After computing the optimal order quantity using the EOQ equation as well as the optimal level of safety stock, the two values are added together in order to determine the appropriate number of units to order. **T F**

7-22 One of the advantages of using a reorder-point inventory model is that stockout costs are easy to determine. **T F**

7-23 If demand in the reorder period is normally distributed, modest increases in service level result in small increases in safety stock because the tail of the distribution has such a small area. **T F**

7-24 The stockout cost is computed independently of the computations used to find the optimal order quantity, because neither has an important bearing on the other. **T F**

7-25 In an MRP environment the master production schedule specifies the number of finished products to produce and when to produce them. **T F**

Multiple Choice

7-26 When using a backorder model, an optimal inventory policy considers:
   a. Backorder costs
   b. Holding costs
   c. Ordering costs
   d. All of the above

7-27 Most companies would place an upper bound on the service level chosen for any item because:
   a. The annual cost of safety stock tends to increase more sharply for larger values of the service level.
   b. Industry standards would make it unfair to competitors to raise the service level beyond a given point.
   c. High service levels place too much emphasis on lost sales and customer satisfaction.
   d. Ordering costs become prohibitive for very high service levels.

7-28 For a stockout to be considered a backorder, it must satisfy all the following requirements except:
   a. The customer does not withdraw his or her order because the item is out of stock.
   b. If the buyer will wait for delivery, the supplier must offer a discount for items that are out of stock.
   c. The supplier fills a customer's order out of the very next shipment of items that arrives.
   d. The maximum inventory level possible is always the difference between the EOQ and the maximum level of the stockout.

7-29 All of the following are advantages of buying in large quantities to earn discounts except:
   a. Lower unit prices
   b. Lower ordering costs

c. Cheaper transportation

d. Lower carrying costs

7-30 Which of the following is an advantage of the MRP approach over the traditional inventory theory approach?

    a. Inventory levels are always less than or the same as the inventory levels under the regular theory when MRP is used.

    b. MRP assists in scheduling the ordering of the various components in a production process.

    c. Neither *a* nor *b*.

    d. Both *a* and *b*.

7-31 Adding to the level of safety stock:

    a. Increases the number of orders placed per year.

    b. Increases annual inventory carrying costs.

    c. Increases the cost of stocking out.

    d. Increases the reorder lead time.

7-32 Stockouts usually occur:

    a. During the reorder lead time.

    b. Before the reorder point is reached.

    c. When demand is lower than normal.

    d. All of the above.

7-33 The expected annual cost of stocking out is influenced by:

    a. The stockout cost per unit.

    b. The number of orders placed per year.

    c. The probability of stocking out.

    d. All of the above.

7-34 By increasing safety stock by 100 units you:

    a. Decrease the reorder point by 50 units.

    b. Increase the reorder point by 50 units.

    c. Increase the reorder point by 100 units.

    d. Increase the lead time demand by 100 units.

7-35 The relationship between safety stock cost and service level is:

    a. Linear

    b. Usually linear

    c. Not linear

    d. Unrelated

7-36 The appropriate inventory system to use when orders for replenishment stock are placed on the first working day each month is:

    a. Fixed-review-interval

    b. Fixed-reorder-point

    c. Fixed-demand-variable

    d. Fixed-recurrent-reorder

7-37 Which of the following is not an order-point model:

    a. EOQ with stockout cost known

    b. EOQ with unknown stockout cost

    c. Backorder model

    d. Material Requirements Planning

7-38 In MRP, the components needed to produce a finished end item product are specified in the:

    a. Master production schedule

    b. Bill of materials

    c. Reorder point

    d. Backorder file

7-39 One reason that stockout costs are difficult to use in order-point inventory applications is because:

    a. Stockout cost per unit is not a constant.

    b. The cost of loss in goodwill is subjective.

    c. All stockouts do not result in lost sales.

    d. All of the above.

7-40 Regardless of whether we use EOQ with either known stockout cost or unknown stockout cost, in order to establish a reorder point, we must know:

    a. The distribution of lead time demand.

    b. Number of orders placed per year.

    c. Holding cost of the safety stock.

    d. All of the above.

12 Real world MS/OR successes

EXAMPLE: MANAGING INVENTORIES WITH HAND-HELD CALCULATORS

The Planters Division of Standard Brands Incorporated is a household name in nut products, producing more than 100 stock-keeping units at three plants in the U.S. In 1980, Donald B. Brout[2] helped Planters implement many of the ideas in this book on forecasting, EOQ models, and safety stocks. The bottom line: a one-time reduction in cash flow of $10 million, followed by a

BENEFITS VERSUS COSTS

continuing increase in annual profits of $3.8 million. The benefit-to-cost ratio was favorable in this application. Brout developed the inventory control system by himself in less than two months. The system was implemented using Hewlett-Packard hand-held calculators at a total equipment cost of $9,000.

FORECASTING AND INVENTORY PROBLEMS

    In late 1979, inventory control at Planters had been decentralized. Manual inventory records were maintained around the country in twelve offices located in or near distribution warehouses, where replenishment orders for finished goods were calculated. Inventory decision rules did not consider the value of the item or the costs of ordering and carrying stock. Forecast errors were large and warehouse managers frequently tried to second-guess the official forecast.

MODELS USED

    Brout's analysis of these problems showed that standard quantitative models would yield substantial savings at Planters. He decided to apply exponential smoothing to forecast demand, the EOQ to compute order quantities, and the service level concept to compute safety stocks. A fixed-reorder-point system was used. Developing computer systems for inventory control usually involves long delays for system and data-base design, programming, procurement of equipment, training, etc. Brout bypassed these delays by setting

EQUIPMENT SELECTION

---

[2] Donald B. Brout, "Scientific Management of Inventory on a Hand-Held Calculator," *Interfaces*, vol. 11, no. 6, pp. 57–69, 1981.

up the models on an HP-41C hand-held calculator. The HP-41C had 320 memory registers. Brout used 219 registers for the program (about 879 keystrokes in length) and another 54 registers for data, leaving 47 registers for later enhancements.

Here is a synopsis of how the calculator program works. To get started, a clerk reads in an inventory record from a magnetic card. Then he or she keys in a transaction, such as a stock receipt or a customer order. The calculator takes it from there, edits the transaction for reasonableness, and updates the record. If the transaction is a receipt, an exponential smoothing model updates estimated leadtime. If the transaction is an order, another smoothing model revises the forecast of leadtime demand. Safety stock is revised by using the standard deviation of forecast errors during leadtime as an estimate of the variability of demand. Given leadtime and safety stock, the reorder point is revised. Finally, the EOQ is revised. An end-of-day routine gives the warehouse manager a report on total inventories, which is phoned in to headquarters.

Using a calculator rather than a computer helped Brout take MS/OR to the manager. Brout demonstrated the program in airplanes and restaurants and the portability and ease of use of the system quickly won management support. Within six months, the system was installed at all twelve warehouses.

At the end of the first year of implementation, finished goods inventory was reduced by 23 percent, the rate of unfilled demand was down by 36 percent, the number of reorders placed declined significantly, and the range of products in stock was generally fresher than in the past. Headquarters management gained more control over the inventory system since they determined the key constants (service level and inventory costs) in the

calculator program. At the time Brout's article appeared, Standard Brands was developing similar calculator-based inventory systems for other major product lines such as Fleischmann's Yeast and Royal Desserts.

8

Oil companies, like most other business enterprises, face myriad decisions: how much crude oil to pump from wells located around the world; how to allocate tankers to transport the crude oil to any of several refineries, where the output volumes of gasoline, kerosene, and other products must be decided; and how and where to ship the final products in order to meet demand.

These decisions are made even more complex because they are constrained. Oil wells all have maximum daily pumping capacities. Tankers are constrained by both payload capacities and transport speeds. Refineries have processing capacities and limits on output for each of their end products. Imagine the benefits if an oil company had a technique to make all of these decisions optimally, enabling them to meet market demands while operating the entire system at least possible cost. Linear programming is such a technique.

Industrial use of linear programming is widespread, because it efficiently solves large real-world problems having thousands of constraints and tens of thousands of decision variables.

This chapter introduces the graphic method for solving linear programming problems. Although this method solves only small problems with two decision variables, getting your feet wet with it will enable you to obtain an intuitive understanding of linear programming. You will also learn much of its technical vocabulary. This will make it easier for you to follow the discussions of computer-based solutions (in the rest of this chapter) and (in Chapter 9) of the simplex method underlying the computer codes used for solving linear programming problems.

LINEAR PROGRAMMING I: SOLUTION METHODS

Graphic Method and Using the Computer

CHAPTER OBJECTIVES

- INTRODUCE LINEAR PROGRAMMING AS AN AID TO DECISION MAKERS.
- REVIEW THE MAJOR REQUIREMENTS FOR A LINEAR PROGRAMMING PROBLEM.
- DEMONSTRATE THE GRAPHIC METHOD FOR SOLVING BOTH MAXIMIZATION AND MINIMIZATION LINEAR PROGRAMMING PROBLEMS.
- INTRODUCE SUCH TECHNICAL ISSUES IN LINEAR PROGRAMMING AS EXTREME POINTS, INFEASIBILITY, REDUNDANCY, AND ALTERNATE OPTIMAL SOLUTIONS, AND DEMONSTRATE THEM WITH THE GRAPHIC METHOD.
- INTRODUCE THE USE OF COMPUTERS TO SOLVE LINEAR PROGRAMS.

341

1 Introduction

APPLICATIONS OF LINEAR PROGRAMMING

All organizations have to make decisions about how to allocate their resources, and there is no organization which operates permanently with unlimited resources; consequently management must continually allocate scarce resources to achieve the organization's goals, whatever they might be. And organizations can have many goals. Here are a few examples:

1 A bank wants to allocate its funds to achieve the highest possible return. It must operate within liquidity limits set by regulatory agencies, and it must maintain sufficient flexibility to meet the loan demands of its customers.

2 An advertising agency wants to achieve the best possible exposure for its client's product at the lowest possible advertising cost. There are a dozen possible magazines in which it can advertise, each one with different advertising rates and differing readership.

3 A furniture manufacturer wants to maximize its profits. It has definite limits on production time available in its three departments as well as commitments of furniture to customers.

4 A food economist in a developing country wants to prepare a high-protein food mixture at the lowest possible cost. There are 10 possible ingredients from which protein can be extracted, and each of these is available in different quantities at different prices.

Each of these organizations is attempting to achieve some *objective* (maximize rate of return, maximize exposure at least cost, maximize profits, minimize cost of food) with *constrained resources* (deposits, client advertising budget, available machine time, ingredients).

Linear programming is a mathematical technique for finding the best uses of an organization's resources. The adjective *linear* is used to describe a relationship between two or more variables, a relationship which is directly and precisely proportional. In a linear relationship between work hours and output, for example, a 10 percent change in the number of productive hours used in some operation will cause a 10 percent change in output. *Programming* refers to the use of certain mathematical techniques to get the best possible solution to a problem involving limited resources.

MAJOR REQUIREMENTS OF A LINEAR PROGRAMMING PROBLEM

Before looking at a linear programming solution, let us consider the major requirements of a linear programming problem in a specific firm. Assume that the firm is a manufacturer of two types of furniture, tables and chairs.

1 The firm must have an *objective* to achieve. The major objective of our manufacturer, we shall assume, is to maximize dollar profits. We recognize that profits are *not* linearly related to sales volume, but the accounting concept of *total contribution is;* you will probably recall from your accounting courses that

$$\text{Total contribution} = \left(\frac{\text{selling price}}{\text{per unit}} - \frac{\text{variable cost}}{\text{per unit}}\right) \times \left(\frac{\text{sales volume}}{\text{in units}}\right)$$

Whenever the term *profit* is used in the context of linear programming, it actually refers to *contribution.*

2 There must be *alternative courses of action,* one of which will achieve the objective. For example, should our firm allocate its manufacturing capacity to tables and chairs in the ratio of 50:50? 25:75? 70:30? Some other ratio?

3 *Resources must be in limited supply.* Our furniture plant has a limited number of machine hours available; consequently, the more hours it schedules for tables, the fewer chairs it can make.

4 *We must be able to express the firm's objective and its limitations as mathematical equations or inequalities, and these must be linear equations or inequalities.* Our furniture maker's objective, dollar profits P, can be expressed in this simple equation:

Profit per table   Profit per chair
↓   ↓
$$P = 8 \text{ (number of tables)} + 6 \text{ (number of chairs)}$$

▌ EQUATIONS AND INEQUALITIES

Although less familiar than the equation, the *inequality* is an important relationship in linear programming. How are the two different? Equations, of course, are represented by the well-known equals sign $=$. They are specific statements expressed in mathematical form. Remember our equation in the preceding paragraph: $P = 8$ (number of tables) $+ 6$ (number of chairs).

Many business problems, however, cannot be expressed in the form of nice, neat equations. Instead of being precise, specifications may provide only that minimum or maximum requirements be met. Here we need *inequalities;* these are another type of relationship expressed in mathematical form. For example, the statement that the total cost of T tables (at a unit cost of $5 per table) and C chairs (at a unit cost of $4 per chair) must not exceed $120 is

INEQUALITIES

$$5T + 4C \leq 120$$

when expressed as an inequality. The sign $\leq$ means "is less than or equal to." In this case any value less than or equal to $120 satisfies the inequality. If this were an equation, the cost of T tables and C chairs would *equal* $120, no more, no less. Hence an equation is much more restrictive than a corresponding inequality.

We might have expressed the cost of T tables and C chairs in still another way. We could have said that the cost of T tables and C chairs *will be at least* $120. The sign $\geq$ means "is greater than or equal to." Any value greater than or equal to $120 would satisfy this inequality.

Most constraints in a linear programming problem are expressed as inequalities. As will be seen, they set upper or lower limits; they do not express exact levels. Thus they permit many possibilities.

2 Graphic method to solve linear programs

VALUE OF THE
GRAPHIC METHOD

It is possible to solve linear programming problems graphically as long as the number of variables (products, for example) is no more than two. Although MS/OR analysts don't use the graphic method (other methods to be introduced later are more efficient), it is a good way to begin to develop an understanding of this useful quantitative technique. We have chosen to introduce you to the graphic method by using the example of a small manufacturer of handcrafted furniture, Dimensions, Ltd., that wants to determine the most profitable combination of products to manufacture given that its resources are limited.

STATEMENT OF THE DIMENSIONS, LTD., PROBLEM

Dimensions, Ltd., makes two products, tables and chairs, which must be processed through assembly and finishing departments. Assembly has 60 hours available; finishing can handle up to 48 hours of work. Manufacturing one table requires 4 hours in assembly and 2 hours in finishing. Each chair requires 2 hours in assembly and 4 hours in finishing.

If profit is $8 per table and $6 per chair, the problem is to determine the best possible combination of tables and chairs to produce and sell in order to realize the maximum profit. There are two limitations (also called *constraints*) in the problem: the time available in assembly and the time available in finishing.

SYMBOLS

Let us use T to represent the number of tables and C to represent the number of chairs. The information needed to solve the problem is summarized in Table 8-1.

FIRST STEP

OBJECTIVE FUNCTION

To begin solving the problem, let us restate the information in mathematical form. In order to do this, we must introduce a new term, *objective function*. This term refers to the expression which shows the relationship of output to profit:

$$8T = \text{total profit from sale of tables}$$

$$6C = \text{total profit from sale of chairs}$$

$$\text{Objective function} = 8T + 6C$$

DEPARTMENT TIME
CONSTRAINTS

Time used in making the two products must certainly not exceed the total time available in the two departments. In other words, the hours required to make 1 table times the number of tables produced—plus the hours required to make 1 chair times the number of chairs produced—must be less than or

	Hours required for 1 unit of product		Total hours available
	Tables	**Chairs**	
Assembly	4	2	60
Finishing	2	4	48
Profit per unit	$8	$6	

TABLE 8-1
Dimensions, Ltd.,
problem information

equal to the time available in each department. Mathematically, this is stated as

Assembly:

$$4T + 2C \leqslant 60$$

Finishing:

$$2T + 4C \leqslant 48$$

The first inequality above states that the hours required to produce 1 table (4 hours) times the number of tables produced (T), plus the hours required to produce 1 chair (2 hours) times the number of chairs produced (C), must be less than or equal to the 60 hours available in assembly. A similar explanation holds for the second inequality. Note that *both* inequalities represent capacity constraints on output and therefore on profit.

In order to obtain meaningful answers, the values calculated for T and C must be positive; they must represent real tables and real chairs. Thus all elements of the solution to a linear programming problem must be greater than or equal to 0 ($T \geqslant 0$, $C \geqslant 0$). These constraints mean that the solution must lie in the quadrant in which all values are positive, the first quadrant. They are called *nonnegativity* constraints. The assembly and finishing constraints are called *structural* constraints.

The problem can now be summarized in a mathematical form:

MATHEMATICAL
SUMMARY OF THE
PROBLEM

Maximize:

$$\text{Profit} = 8T + 6C$$

Subject to the constraints:

$$4T + 2C \leqslant 60$$
$$2T + 4C \leqslant 48$$
$$T \geqslant 0$$
$$C \geqslant 0$$

SECOND STEP

Plot the constraints in the problem on a graph, with tables shown on the horizontal axis and chairs shown on the vertical axis. Figure 8-1 shows the T and C axes.

The inequality $4T + 2C \leq 60$ may be located on the graph by first locating its two terminal points and joining these points by a straight line. The two terminal points for the inequality can be found in the following manner:

1 If we assume that *none* of the time available in assembly is used in making tables (the production of tables is 0), then up to 30 chairs *could* be made. Thus if we let $T = 0$, then $C \leq 30$. If we make the maximum number of chairs, then $C = 30$. Our first point, thus, is (0, 30); this point denotes the production of 0 tables and 30 chairs.

2 In order to find the second point, we assume that none of the time available in assembly is used in making chairs (the production of chairs is 0). Under this assumption we *could* produce up to 15 tables. Thus if we let $C = 0$, then $T \leq 15$. If we make the maximum number of tables, then $T = 15$. Our second point, thus, is (15, 0); this point denotes the production of 15 tables and 0 chairs.

Locating these two points (0, 30) and (15, 0) and joining them results in the straight line shown in Figure 8-2. Now see the same concept shown in Figure 8-3.

Any combination of tables and chairs on line *BC* will use up all the 60 hours available in assembly. For instance, producing 10 tables and 10 chairs [point (10, 10) on the graph] will use up 10(4 hours) + 10(2 hours) = 60 hours.

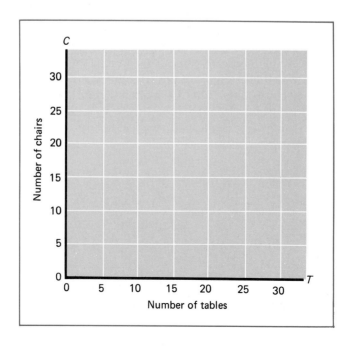

FIGURE 8-1
T and *C* axes.

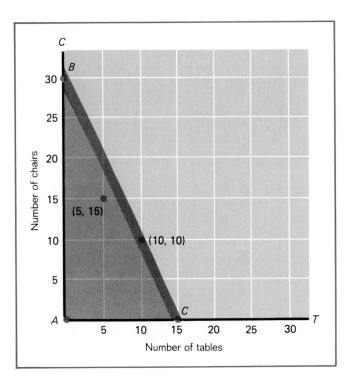

FIGURE 8-2
Graph of equation
$4T + 2C = 60$.

FIGURE 8-3
Capacity constraint
in the assembly
department.

Suppose, however, that the firm can sell only 5 tables and 15 chairs [point (5, 15) on the graph]. This point is not on line *BC*, but this combination *can* be produced without exceeding the 60 hours available: 5(4 hours) + 15(2 hours) = 50 hours, and 50 hours ≤ 60 hours. This point (5, 15), or indeed *any* combination of tables and chairs which lies in the shaded area to the left of line *BC*, can be produced without exceeding the 60 hours available. The shaded area *ABC* is the graphic representation of the inequality $4T + 2C \le 60$ as long as T and C are both greater than or equal to 0.

Here are some illustrations. Each of the combinations of tables and chairs is shown as a point on Figure 8-4.

```
 4 tables and  8 chairs: 4(4)  + 2(8)  = 32 hr required
10 tables and  2 chairs: 4(10) + 2(2)  = 44 hr required
 3 tables and 20 chairs: 4(3)  + 2(20) = 52 hr required
 8 tables and 12 chairs: 4(8)  + 2(12) = 56 hr required
15 tables and 15 chairs: 4(15) + 2(15) = 90 hr required
```

Note that the time requirements of the first four combinations fall within the 60 hours available in assembly. The fifth combination *cannot* be produced because the hours needed exceed the hours available.

GRAPHIC REPRESENTATION OF THE INEQUALITY FOR FINISHING

A similar explanation applies to the graph of the constraint inequality for finishing, that is, $2T + 4C \le 48$. Line *EF* in Figure 8-5 represents all combinations of tables and chairs which will use up exactly 48 hours (2*T* +

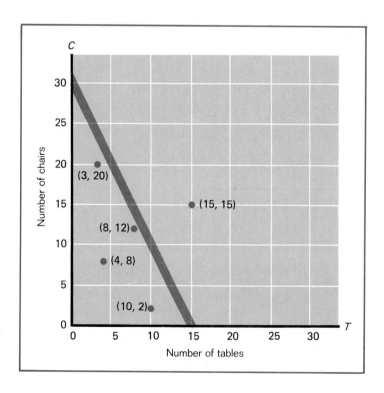

FIGURE 8-4

Graph of equation $4T + 2C = 60$, with various combinations of T and C shown as points.

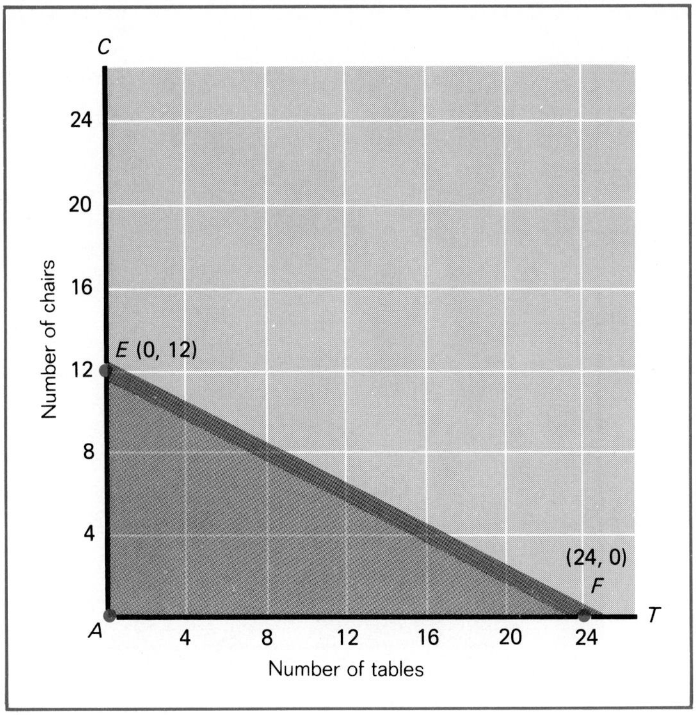

FIGURE 8-5
Capacity constraint in
finishing department.

$4C = 48$). The shaded area AEF contains all possible combinations which do not exceed 48 hours ($2T + 4C \leq 48$) as long as T and C are both greater than or equal to 0; any point, that is, any combination of tables and chairs, falling within the shaded area AEF will satisfy the time restriction in the finishing department. Thus the shaded area AEF is the graphic representation of the inequality $2T + 4C \leq 48$.

In order to complete a table or chair, both departments must be used. This means that the best combination of tables and chairs must fall within the shaded areas of both Figure 8-3 and Figure 8-5; this best combination must not exceed the available time in either assembly or finishing. To find this common area we must plot the two original inequalities (see Figures 8-3 and 8-5) on the same T and C axes (see Figure 8-6).

The area that does not exceed either of the two departmental constraints (the shaded area $AEDC$ in Figure 8-6) contains *all* combinations of tables and chairs satisfying the inequalities

$$4T + 2C \leq 60$$
$$2T + 4C \leq 48$$
$$T \geq 0$$
$$C \geq 0$$

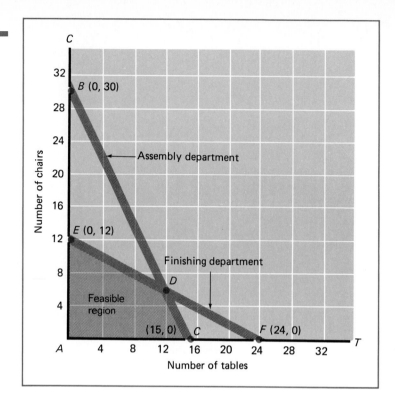

FIGURE 8-6
Graphic
representation of
problem constraints.

Combinations of tables and chairs that fall within *AEDC* are called *feasible solutions,* and *AEDC* is the *feasible region*. Combinations outside *AEDC* are called *infeasible*. Here are some examples:

A FEASIBLE SOLUTION **Example 1** For 10 tables and 5 chairs

Assembly:

$$4T + 2C \leq 60 \text{ hr available}$$
$$4(10) + 2(5) = 50 \text{ hr required}$$

Finishing:

$$2T + 4C \leq 48 \text{ hr available}$$
$$2(10) + 4(5) = 40 \text{ hr required}$$

The time required to make 10 tables and 5 chairs falls within the time available in both departments (see Figure 8-7), and so 10 tables and 5 chairs is a feasible solution.

TWO INFEASIBLE **Example 2** For 11 tables and 10 chairs
COMBINATIONS

Assembly:

$$4T + 2C \leq 60 \text{ hr available}$$
$$4(11) + 2(10) = 64 \text{ hr required}$$

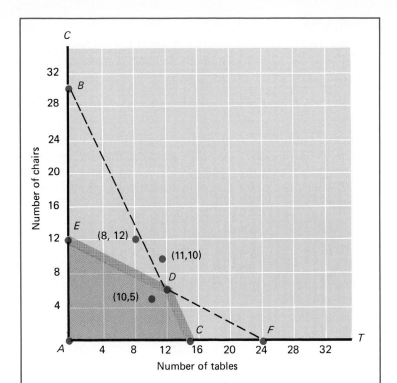

FIGURE 8-7
Feasible region, with
examples 1, 2, and 3
shown.

Finishing:

$$2T + 4C \leq 48 \text{ hr available}$$
$$2(11) + 4(10) = 62 \text{ hr required}$$

Since the time required to make 11 tables and 10 chairs, exceeds the times available in *both* the assembly and finishing departments, this combination is infeasible. It cannot be achieved (see Figure 8-7).

Example 3 For 8 tables and 12 chairs

Assembly:

$$4T + 2C \leq 60 \text{ hr available}$$
$$4(8) + 2(12) = 56 \text{ hr required}$$

Finishing:

$$2T + 4C \leq 48 \text{ hr available}$$
$$2(8) + 4(12) = 64 \text{ hr required}$$

Even though the time required to make 8 tables and 12 chairs falls *within* the time available in assembly, it *exceeds* the time available in the finishing department. As a result, this combination falls outside the area common to both inequalities in Figure 8-7 and therefore is infeasible. **In order to be feasible, a solution must satisfy *all* of the constraints.**

THIRD STEP

Locate point D, because once that point is known, all the points defining the shaded area $AEDC$ will have been delineated precisely. This is true because we already have three points:

LOCATING POINT D

$A\ (0, 0)$ $\qquad$ $E\ (0, 12)$ $\qquad$ $C\ (15, 0)$

How can point D be located? One possibility is to read its location from an accurately drawn graph. Another method, the one we shall be using, is to solve simultaneously the equations of the two lines which intersect to form point D, the only point common to both equations. The equations to be solved are

SOLVING FOR D
ALGEBRAICALLY

$$4T + 2C = 60$$
$$2T + 4C = 48$$

To solve these two equations simultaneously, multiply the first equation by -2:

$$
\begin{aligned}
-2(4T + 2C = 60) = \quad -8T - 4C &= -120 \\
+ \quad\quad 2T + 4C &= \quad\ 48 \\
\hline
-6T \quad\quad &= -72 \\
T &= \quad 12
\end{aligned}
$$
Add the second equation

and now substitute 12 for T in the second equation:

$$
\begin{aligned}
2T + 4C &= 48 \\
2(12) + 4C &= 48 \\
24 + 4C &= 48 \\
4C &= 24 \\
C &= 6
\end{aligned}
$$

Point D, thus, is (12, 6).

FOURTH STEP

Test the four corners of the shaded area to see which yields the greatest dollar profit.

TESTING THE CORNERS
OF THE FEASIBLE
REGION

Point $A\ (0, 0)$: $\qquad$ $8\ (0) + 6\ (0) =\quad\ 0$
Point $E\ (0, 12)$: $\qquad$ $8\ (0) + 6(12) =\quad 72$
Point $C\ (15, 0)$: $\qquad$ $8(15) + 6\ (0) = 120$
Point $D\ (12, 6)$: $\qquad$ $8(12) + 6\ (6) = 132$

The point which yields the greatest profit is point D (\$132).

The concept that the most profitable combination of tables and chairs is found at point D (12, 6) can be seen more clearly by first plotting the objective function $8T + 6C$ (given in the first step) directly on a graph of the feasible region.

To accomplish this, we first let profits equal some minimum dollar figure we know we can attain without violating a constraint. In this case we have elected to let profits equal \$48, a profit easily attainable. Then the objective function is $48 = 8T + 6C$.

We then plot this equation on the graph in Figure 8-8 in the same manner that we originally plotted our constraints (Figure 8-2). First locate two terminal points and then join them with a straight line. When $T = 0$, $C = 8$, and when $C = 0$, $T = 6$.

Figure 8-8 illustrates the feasible region (AEDC) with the profit equation $48 = 8T + 6C$ drawn in. This line (called an *isoprofit* line) represents all the possible combinations of tables and chairs which would yield a total profit of \$48. You might want to check one such combination. For example, point X represents the manufacture of 4 tables and 2⅔ chairs.

$$4(8) + 2⅔(6) = 48$$

Suppose we now graph another isoprofit line representing all combinations of tables and chairs which would produce a \$96 profit:

$$96 = 8T + 6C$$

When $T = 0$, $C = 16$,   and   when $C = 0$, $T = 12$.

Both profit equations ($48 = 8T + 6C$ and $96 = 8T + 6C$) are illustrated on the graph in Figure 8-9. What is the significance of these parallel isoprofit

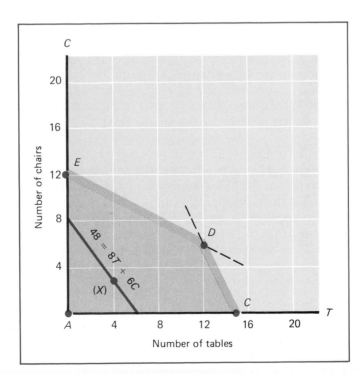

FIGURE 8-8
Objective function
plotted.

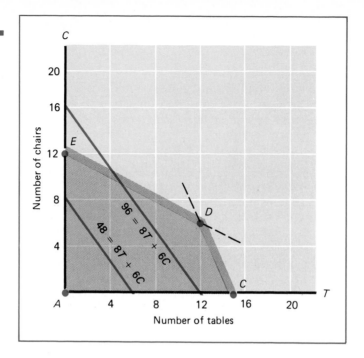

FIGURE 8-9
Two isoprofit
lines plotted.

lines? Simply this: a $48 profit will be generated by manufacturing *any* combination of tables and chairs falling on the line $48 = 8T + 6C$, and a $96 profit will be generated by manufacturing any combination of tables and chairs falling on the line $96 = 8T + 6C$. (Note, however, that we are limited by problem restrictions to those combinations which fall within the feasible region, *AEDC*.)

THE HIGHEST
ISOPROFIT LINE

It is also true that *one* parallel isoprofit line will pass through point *D*. This particular profit line (line 3) is illustrated in Figure 8-10, together with the first two profit lines. Although most of the combinations of tables and chairs on profit line 3 do not fall within the feasible region (*AEDC*), one point does, point *D*.

The second isoprofit line drawn generated more profit than the first one ($96 versus $48). It is obvious, then, that the isoprofit line which can be located *farthest* from the origin (point *A*) will contain *all* the combinations of tables and chairs which will generate the greatest possible profit; and as long as at least *one* point on this maximum profit line is still within the feasible region (*AEDC*), that point represents the *most profitable combination* of products. Point *D* lies on isoprofit line 3 and is still within the feasible region; thus it represents the most profitable combination of tables (12) and chairs (6) for Dimensions to manufacture.

SUMMARY OF GRAPHIC PROCEDURE

1 Restate the problem information (objective function and constraints) in mathematical form (page 344).

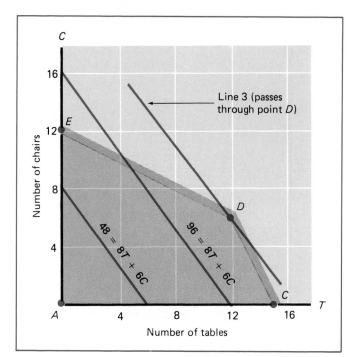

FIGURE 8-10
Three isoprofit
lines plotted.

2 Plot the problem constraints on the graph (page 346).

3 Find the points which define the feasible region (page 352).

4 Plot an isoprofit line and move it parallel to itself so that total profit *increases* until further shifting would move it out of the feasible region (page 352).

GRAPHIC PROCEDURE FOR A MINIMIZATION PROBLEM

The objective in our Dimensions, Ltd., problem was to *maximize profits*. However, we can also consider linear programming problems in which the objective is to be *minimized*. For example, consider a modification of the Dimensions, Ltd., problem. Jeff Smith, the Director of Marketing at Dimensions, has promised customers the firm will make at least 2 tables ($T \geq 2$) and at least 4 chairs ($C \geq 4$). When we add these two new constraints to the problem, the feasible region is now the shaded area *GHID* in Figure 8-11.

Jeff has determined that it costs \$20 per unit to manufacture a table and \$8 per unit to manufacture a chair. In order to see a simple example where the objective function is to be minimized, let's suppose that Jeff wants to minimize the total manufacturing cost of chairs and tables. In order to do this, we have plotted three *iso-objective* lines (in this case, *isocost* lines) in Figure 8-12. These three lines are $20T + 8C = 288$ (passing through point D), $20T + 8C = 180$, and $20T + 8C = 72$ (passing through point H). In this example, it is obvious that the isocost line which can be located *closest* to origin (point A) will contain *all* the combinations of tables and chairs which

TWO NEW
CONSTRAINTS

MINIMIZING
TOTAL COST

ISOCOST LINES

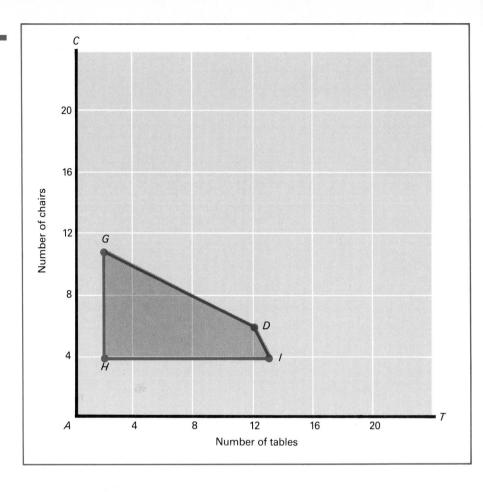

FIGURE 8-11
Graphic
representation of
problem constraints.

will generate the least possible cost; and as long as at least *one* point on this minimum cost line is still within the feasible region (*GHID*), that point represents the *least costly combination* of products. In this case, point *H* represents the least costly combination of tables (2) and chairs (4) for Dimensions to manufacture.

If we compare the way in which we have just solved this minimization problem with the summary of the graphic procedure given on page 354, we see that the first three steps (restate the problem mathematically, plot the problem constraints on the graph, and find the points which define the feasible region) are exactly the same. The only thing which has changed is

RESTATING STEP 4   step 4. Instead of moving an *isoprofit* line parallel to itself so that the total profit *increases*, we move an *isocost* line parallel to itself so that the total cost *decreases*. To cover all cases at once, we restate step 4 as follows:

4 Plot an *iso-objective* line and move it parallel to itself so that the objective *improves* until further shifting would move it out of the feasible region.

3 Some technical issues in linear programming

EXTREME POINTS

From our use of the three isocost lines in Figure 8-12, you saw that point H generated the lowest cost. Similarly, the three isoprofit lines in Figure 8-10 showed you that the highest profit was generated at point D. But now suppose we changed the *profit* for tables and chairs in the original Dimensions, Ltd., problem to \$2 and \$10, respectively, and left the department constraints as they were. We have illustrated four new isoprofit lines in Figure 8-13. What is the result? Now you see that the isoprofit line farthest from the origin passes through only one point which is still in the feasible region, and that is point E. With these two profits, \$2 and \$10, E is the best combination of products.

One more example will help us develop this idea. Look now at Figure 8-14. Here we have changed the profits for tables and chairs to \$12 and \$3,

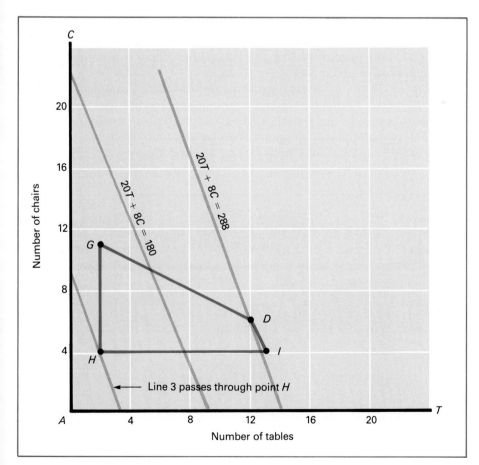

FIGURE 8-12
Three isocost
lines plotted.

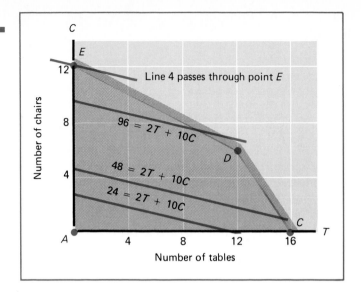

FIGURE 8-13
Four isoprofit lines
plotted for: Profit =
$2T + 10C$.

respectively. What happened? The isoprofit line farthest from the origin
passes through only one point which is still in the feasible region, and that
is point C. With profits of \$12 and \$3, point C now represents the best
combination of products.

AN OPTIMAL SOLUTION
IS FOUND AT AN
EXTREME POINT

We can see from our original problem and the three examples in Figures
8-12, 8-13, and 8-14 that the optimal solution occurred in each case at one of
the corner points of the feasible region; in linear programming language,
we would say the optimal solution occurs at an *extreme point* in the feasible
region. MS/OR analysts have known for some time that if a linear program-

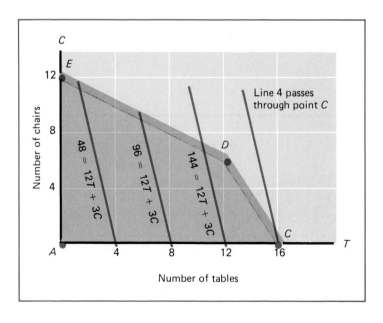

FIGURE 8-14
Four isoprofit lines
plotted for: Profit =
$12T + 3C$.

ming problem has an optimal solution, it is found at at least one of the *extreme points,* or "corners," of the feasible region. This knowledge makes things easier for us; if we are searching for the optimal solution, we have to evaluate only those solutions that are at the extreme points of the feasible region.

Notice that we just said, ". . . if a linear programming problem has an optimal solution. . . ." Is it possible for a linear programming problem to fail to have an optimal solution? The answer is yes. There are two ways in which this can happen, and we shall now discuss both.

▮ INFEASIBILITY

Infeasibility means there is *no* solution which satisfies *all* the constraints. Graphically, infeasibility is the case where there is *no* feasible region which satisfies all constraints. Figure 8-15 shows the problem of Dimensions, Ltd., from earlier in this chapter with two additional constraints: (1) the marketing manager *must* have at least 16 tables, and (2) the marketing manager *must* have at least 12 chairs. From Figure 8-15 we see that no combination of tables and chairs will satisfy both sets of constraints (the original production area, *AEDC,* and the new marketing area). Thus there is no feasible solution to this problem *unless* the Dimensions management make available additional capacity in assembly and finishing. How much? Well, to satisfy the marketing manager's constraints, Dimensions needs 16 tables and 12 chairs; according to the problem data, this will require 88 hours in assembly and 80 in finishing. Unless these additional resources are made available, the marketing constraints cannot be met.

THE CASE WHERE NO
SOLUTION SATISFIES
THE CONSTRAINTS

MORE RESOURCES
WOULD BE REQUIRED

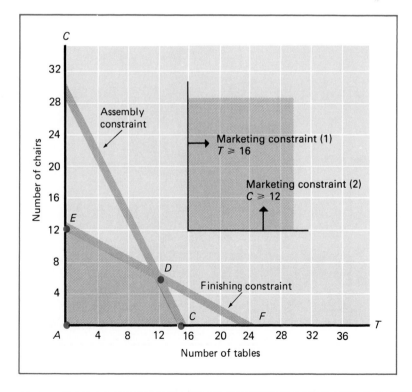

FIGURE 8-15
Production and
marketing constraints
for Dimensions, Ltd.

INCORRECTLY
FORMULATED PROBLEM

ISOPROFIT LINES ARE
NOT CONSTRAINED

MORE CONSTRAINTS
THAN NECESSARY

UNBOUNDEDNESS

A linear programming problem is unbounded if the objective can be made infinitely large without violating any of the constraints in the problem. If we encounter unboundedness in solving real problems, we know that the problem has not been correctly formulated, since *no* situation permits management an infinitely large solution and therefore an infinitely large profit. Figure 8-16 shows the Dimensions, Ltd., problem with only *marketing* constraints. In this formulation of the problem, the feasible region extends indefinitely in both directions. When we begin to draw isoprofit lines through the feasible region, we quickly see that profit can be as high as we want it (isoprofit line 5 can be followed by any number of higher profit lines we desire).

In addition to *infeasibility* and *unboundedness,* there is one more condition in linear programming which we should take note of at this point; we call this *redundancy.*

REDUNDANCY

A constraint which does not affect the feasible region is called a *redundant* constraint. In Figure 8-17 we have shown the Dimensions, Ltd., problem from Figure 8-6, but here a constraint has been added representing the marketing manager's belief that he cannot sell more than 20 chairs. Since the greatest number of chairs that is currently found in the feasible region is 12 (at point *E,*), the marketing manager's *new* constraint is redundant. If chairs satisfy the finishing constraint, they also satisfy the redundant marketing constraint. Thus the marketing constraint can be removed from

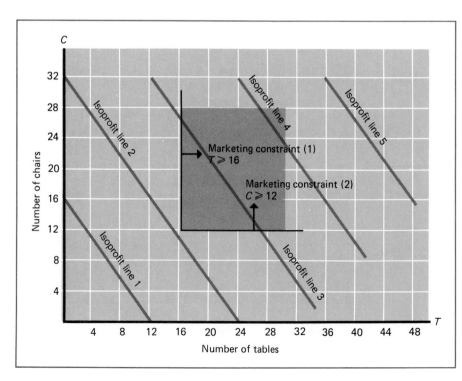

FIGURE 8-16
Unbounded marketing constraints for Dimensions, Ltd.

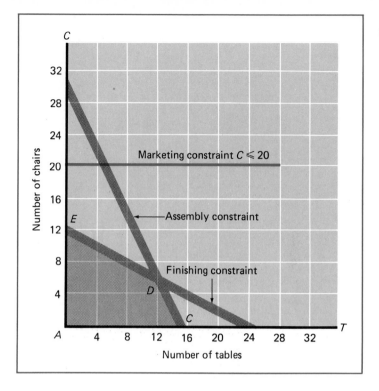

FIGURE 8-17
Dimensions, Ltd.,
problem with market
constraint ($C \leq 20$).

the problem. This saves computation time. In many linear programming problems, redundant constraints are not removed because they are not recognized as being redundant until after the problem is solved. With the use of computers to solve linear programming problems, redundant constraints do not cause any difficulties.

MORE THAN ONE OPTIMAL SOLUTION (ALTERNATIVE OPTIMA)

Look at the Dimensions, Ltd., situation shown in Figure 8-18; here the isoprofit line farthest from the origin coincides with one of the constraint lines, specifically line *ED*. First we need to satisfy ourselves that at least one optimal solution still lies at an extreme point; in this case *each* of the two extreme points, *E* and *D*, is an optimal solution. In addition to these specific points, *any* point on the line *ED* is an optimal solution too. If the profits from tables and chairs are such as to produce this situation, the significance of this to Dimensions is that it has extraordinary flexibility in choosing its product mix, since *any* combination of tables and chairs which lies along line *ED* produces the maximum possible profit for the company.

AN ISOPROFIT LINE
PARALLEL TO A
CONSTRAINT LINE

MANAGERIAL
SIGNIFICANCE OF MORE
THAN ONE OPTIMAL
SOLUTION

4 Using the computer to solve linear programs

The decisions most managers face are much more complex than the one that Dimensions, Ltd., had to make in its choice between tables and chairs. Most

LIMITATIONS OF
GRAPHIC METHOD

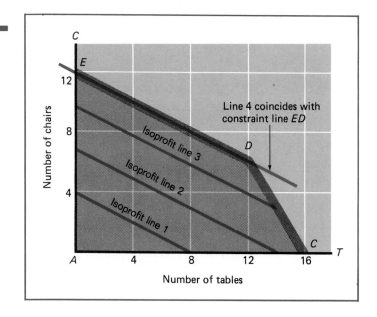

FIGURE 8-18
Isoprofit line which
coincides with a
constraint line.

of these decisions involve not two but many variables. Hence, because the graphic method of linear programming is limited to two variables, we have to look to another procedure—the *simplex method*—which offers an efficient means of solving more complex linear programming problems.

The simplex method of linear programming was developed in 1947 by George Dantzig, then on assignment with the U.S. Air Force. He demonstrated how to find the optimal solution from among the many possible solutions to a linear programming problem.

For over 40 years now, managers have been using the simplex method to solve linear programming problems. As the 6th edition of *Quantitative Approaches to Management* went to press in late 1985, there was much excitement in the MS/OR community over a new method for linear programming developed by Narendra Karmarkar of AT&T Bell Laboratories. Extensive computational testing is still under way to see if this new method will live up to its early promise. However, as you will see in Chapter 10, regardless of the method used to solve linear programming problems, linear programming will continue to be an important analytical tool for managers.

CHARACTERISTICS OF
THE SIMPLEX METHOD

In the simplex method, the computational routine is an *iterative* process. To iterate means to repeat; hence in working toward the optimal solution, the computational routine is repeated over and over, following a standard pattern. Successive solutions are developed in a systematic pattern until the best solution is reached.

Another characteristic of the simplex method is that each new solution yields a value of the objective function at least as good as (and usually better than) the previous solution. This important feature assures us that we are always moving closer to the optimal answer. Finally, the method indicates when the optimal solution has been reached.

If you are interested in the computational details of how the simplex method works, you will find those details in the next chapter. Although it is important to understand how the simplex method works, actually solving linear programs by hand is a tedious (and error-prone) process. Fortunately, there are many excellent computer packages available for linear programming, which can spare you from the drudgery of solving these problems by hand. Among these packages are programs such as MPSX and SAS/OR, which are designed for use on mainframe computers; LINDO and LPSBA, which are free-standing, microcomputer-oriented linear programming codes; and VINO and WHAT'S *BEST!*, which are designed to interface with microcomputer spreadsheet programs such as LOTUS 1-2-3.[1]

HAND SOLUTIONS ARE TEDIOUS

COMPUTER LP PACKAGES

We are going to look at a student-oriented linear programming computer package called LPSBA. This package was developed by our colleague, Professor Alan Neebe of the University of North Carolina at Chapel Hill. The microcomputer version of LPSBA is particularly easy to use. The program prompts you for the problem data and then allows you to display and edit the data you entered, save it for further analysis in the future, and solve your problem. In addition, as we shall see in Chapter 10, LPSBA has the capability to make extensive sensitivity (or *what if*) analyses, in order to see how the problem solution would change if the data in the linear program were changed. As we shall find, this is very powerful tool for managerial decision-making.

LPSBA, A STUDENT-ORIENTED LP PACKAGE

SETTING UP THE PROBLEM

To demonstrate how to use LPSBA, let's use the original Dimensions, Ltd., problem from page 345. Recall that the variables in the problem were T and C, the numbers of tables and chairs that Dimensions should manufacture. The algebraic statement of the problem is:

MATHEMATICAL STATEMENT OF THE PROBLEM

Maximize:

$$\text{Profit} = 8T + 6C$$

Subject to:

$$\begin{aligned} \text{Assembly:} \quad & 4T + 2C \leq 60 \\ \text{Finishing:} \quad & 2T + 4C \leq 48 \\ & \text{All variables} \geq 0 \end{aligned}$$

Before the simplex method can be used to solve a linear program, all the inequality constraints must first be converted to equations. We do this by adding to each of the $\leq$ inequality constraints a variable which measures the *slack time*, that is, the time left over in each department after the tables and chairs are manufactured. These new variables are called *slack variables*, and

USING SLACK VARIABLES TO GENERATE EQUATIONS FROM INEQUALITIES

[1] LINDO and VINO are registered trademarks of LINDO Systems, INC.; LOTUS 1-2-3 is a registered trademark of Lotus Development Corp.; MPSX is a registered trademark of IBM Corporation; SAS/OR is a registered trademark of SAS Institute, Inc.; WHAT'S *BEST!* is a registered trademark of General Optimization, Inc.

the original variables in the problem are called *decision variables* (or *structural variables*). To illustrate this process, let

$$S_A = \text{slack variable (unused time) in assembly}$$

$$S_F = \text{slack variable (unused time) in finishing}$$

S_A is equal to the total amount of time available in assembly (60 hours) less any hours used there in processing tables and chairs. S_F is equal to the total amount of time available in finishing (48 hours) less any hours used there in processing tables and chairs. We can express these two statements in mathematical form by writing equations for the slack variables S_A and S_F as follows:

Assembly:

$$S_A = 60 - 4T - 2C$$

Finishing:

$$S_F = 48 - 2T - 4C$$

EXAMPLES OF
SLACK VARIABLES

By adding the slack variables, we convert the *constraint inequalities* in the problem into *equations*. The slack variable in each department takes on whatever value is required to make the equation relationship hold. Two examples will clarify this point.

Example 1 Assume that in assembly we process 5 tables and 3 chairs:

$$S_A = 60 - 4(5) - 2(3)$$
$$= 34 \text{ hr unused time in assembly}$$

Example 2 Assume that in finishing we process 4 tables and 6 chairs:

$$S_F = 48 - 2(4) - 4(6)$$
$$= 16 \text{ hr unused time in finishing}$$

By adding a slack variable to each inequality, we convert them into these equations:

CONSTRAINT
EQUATIONS

$$4T + 2C + S_A = 60$$
$$2T + 4C + S_F = 48$$

In the simplex method, variables that do not affect an equation are written with a zero coefficient. For example, since S_A and S_F represent unused time which yields no profit, these variables are added to the objective function with zero coefficients. Furthermore, since S_A represents unused time in assembly only, it is added to the equation representing finishing with a zero coefficient. For the same reason $0S_F$ is added to the equation representing the time constraint in assembly. Thus the problem of Dimensions, Ltd., in its final form is

Maximize:

$$\text{Profit} = 8T + 6C + 0S_A + 0S_F$$

Subject to:

$$4T + 2C + S_A + 0S_F = 60$$
$$2T + 4C + 0S_A + S_F = 48$$
$$\text{All variables} \geq 0$$

DATA INPUT FOR LPSBA

Although slack variables must be added in to convert the constraints to equations before the simplex method can be used, you do not have to add these variables in by yourself before you can use LPSBA (or almost any other linear programming package currently available) to solve linear programs. You just tell LPSBA that a constraint is a ≤ inequality, and the program automatically adds in a slack variable before solving the problem. Let's see how to use LPSBA to solve the Dimensions, Ltd., problem. Figure 8-19 shows how to input the data. LPSBA's prompts are shown in lightface; our inputs are shown in boldface and color. We ended our input by asking LPSBA to display the problem formulation. This gives us a chance to see if we have made any input errors. If so, LPSBA gives us the opportunity to correct those mistakes. In Figure 8-20, we see that no input errors were made and we go on to solve the problem, first saving the formulation for future use.

SOLUTION OUTPUT FROM LPSBA

Recall that we said the simplex algorithm is an iterative process, moving from one solution to another, which is at least as good as (and usually better than) the current solution. In fact, what the procedure does is to move from one extreme point (corner) of the feasible region to a neighboring extreme point. The step of moving from one extreme point to another is called a *pivot*. We see from the output shown in Figure 8-21 that the Dimensions, Ltd., problem took 2 pivots to solve. The simplex algorithm started at point A in Figure 8-10 (page 355), where the total profit is $0. It then moved to point E, where the total profit is $72. Then it moved to point D, which it recognized as the optimal solution, with a total profit of $132.

The simplex method divides all the variables (structural and slack) into two sets at each extreme point. The first set is called *nonbasic* or *not in the solution*. These variables are set equal to zero. The method then solves the structural constraints for the remaining variables, which are called *basic* or *in the solution*. LPSBA reports the values of the basic variables in the optimal solution; it does not report the values of the nonbasic variables, since they are all zero. In Figure 8-21, we see once again that the optimal solution to the Dimensions, Ltd., problem is to make 12 tables and 6 chairs. Since this solution uses up all the time available in the assembly and finishing departments, the slack variables for those constraints are zero at the optimal solution. Thus they are both *nonbasic*, and so the column for *basic* slack variables has no entries.

The rest of the output in Figure 8-21 (shadow prices and reduced costs) is used for sensitivity analyses. We will discuss it and additional sensitivity output in Chapter 10.

```
* * * LPSBA/PC * * *        A LINEAR PROGRAMMING CODE      VERSION 12/15/86
        (C) Copyright 1985 by Alan W. Neebe
                             School of Business Administration
                             University of North Carolina
                             Chapel Hill, NC 27514      Tel. (919) 962-3204
                             All Rights Reserved


Enter 0 to send all "printed output" to the printer,
      1 to redirect "printed output" to a disk file: 0

Note: If you wish hardcopy output, make sure the printer is turned online


Enter 1 to key in a new LP problem, 2 to read a problem off disk: 1

Enter problem title (up to 80 characters): Dimensions, Ltd. Original Problem

Enter number of structural variables: 2

Enter number of structural constraints: 2

Enter 1 for a minimization problem, 2 for a maximization problem: 2


Enter variable name  1 (up to 8 characters): TABLES

Enter variable name  2 (up to 8 characters): CHAIRS

Enter objective coefficient for variable TABLES: 8

Enter objective coefficient for variable CHAIRS: 6


Enter 1 if you wish to enter all structural coefficients,
      2 if you wish to enter only the non-zero ones (sparse input): 1


Enter constraint name 1 (up to 8 characters): ASSEMBLY

Enter structural coefficient for constraint ASSEMBLY and variable TABLES: 4

Enter structural coefficient for constraint ASSEMBLY and variable CHAIRS: 2

Enter 1 for a ≤ constraint, 2 for a ≥ constraint, 3 for an = constraint: 1

Enter right-hand-side for constraint ASSEMBLY (must be zero or positive): 60


Enter constraint name 2 (up to 8 characters): FINISHNG

Enter structural coefficient for constraint FINISHNG and variable TABLES: 2

Enter structural coefficient for constraint FINISHNG and variable CHAIRS: 4

Enter 1 for a ≤ constraint, 2 for a ≥ constraint, 3 for an = constraint: 1

Enter right-hand-side for constraint FINISHNG (must be zero or positive): 48


Enter 1 to display problem formulation, 2 to also "print" a hardcopy,
      3 to edit the problem formulation, 4 to continue and solve the problem: 1
```

FIGURE 8-19

Data input with LPSBA.

```
CHECKING THE INPUT, SAVING THE PROBLEM, AND SOLVING IT

* * * LPSBA/PC * * *          A Linear Programming Code     Version 12/15/86

Dimensions, Ltd.: Original Problem

  2 Structural constraints       2 Structural variables
  2 (= Constraints        0 )= Constraints        0 = Constraints

Maximization problem

Objective

 Variable   TABLES    CHAIRS

Obj coeff   8.000     6.000

Constraints

            TABLES    CHAIRS    Relation       RHS

 ASSEMBLY   4.000     2.000      (=        60.000

 FINISHNG   2.000     4.000      (=        48.000


Enter 1 to continue and solve the problem, 2 to edit the problem formulation,
     3 to solve a new problem, 4 to exit: 1


Enter 1 to save the current problem on disk, 2 to continue: 1

Now you must choose a filename to save the problem on disk.

The filename can be up to 8 characters long (with an optional extension),

           can contain only letters and numerals,

           cannot contain any imbedded blanks.

Example: to save the problem "LPPROBLM" on drive B, enter B:LPPROBLM

Enter filename: B:DIMNSION


Enter 1 to display problem solution,
     2 to in addition display first and last simplex tableaux,
     3 to in addition display all simplex tableau,
     4,5,6 same as (1),(2),(3) with a hardcopy "printed": 1
```

FIGURE 8-20
Checking the input, saving the problem, and solving it.

▪ MINIMIZATION PROBLEMS AND GREATER-THAN-OR-EQUAL-TO CONSTRAINTS

Recall Jeff Smith's cost minimization problem from page 355:

Minimize:

$$\text{Cost} = 20T + 8C$$

```
Pivoting      0+ **

Optimal solution obtained after    2 pivots

Maximal objective function value:      132.00000

Basic structural variables        Basic slack and surplus variables
TABLES          12.00000
CHAIRS           6.00000

Shadow prices for constraints     Reduced costs for nonbasic structural vars.
ASSEMBLY         1.66667
FINISHNG          .66667

Enter 1 to display sensitivity analysis, 2 to also "print" a hardcopy,
      3 to edit the current problem and resolve, 4 to solve a new problem,
      5 to exit: 5

LPSBA/PC bids you goodbye
```

FIGURE 8-21
LPSBA's solution to the Dimensions, Ltd., problem.

Subject to:

$$
\begin{array}{ll}
\text{Assembly:} & 4T + 2C \leq 60 \\
\text{Finishing:} & 2T + 4C \leq 48 \\
\text{Minimum number of tables:} & T \quad\;\; \geq 2 \\
\text{Minimum number of chairs:} & C \geq 4 \\
& \text{All variables} \geq 0
\end{array}
$$

SURPLUS VARIABLES
FOR ≥ CONSTRAINTS

In order to convert the last two constraints into equations, we *subtract* from each of them variables which measure the *surplus* numbers of tables and chairs made above and beyond the minimum numbers required. These new variables are another type of slack variable like those we previously used to convert less-than-or-equal-to constraints to equations. The slack variables subtracted from greater-than-or-equal-to constraints to convert them to equations are often referred to as *surplus variables*. To illustrate surplus variables, let

$$S_T = T - 2 = \text{surplus tables}$$

$$S_C = C - 4 = \text{surplus chairs}$$

Thus if 11 tables and 8 chairs are made, the surplus variables are

$$S_T = \;\; 11 - 2 = 9 = \text{surplus tables}$$

$$S_C = \;\;\; 8 - 4 = 4 = \text{surplus chairs}$$

Just as with slack variables, surplus variables do not affect the objective function or the other constraints, so they are added in there with zero coefficients. This gives us Jeff Smith's problem in final form:

Minimize:

$$\text{Cost} = 20T + 8C + 0S_A + 0S_F + 0S_T + 0S_C$$

Subject to:

$$
\begin{aligned}
4T + 2C + \ S_A + 0S_F + 0S_T + 0S_C &= 60 \\
2T + 4C + 0S_A + \ S_F + 0S_T + 0S_C &= 48 \\
T + 0C + 0S_A + 0S_F - \ S_T + 0S_C &= 2 \\
0T + \ C + 0S_A + 0S_F + 0S_T - \ S_C &= 4 \\
\text{All variables} &\geq 0
\end{aligned}
$$

As you have probably already guessed, you do not have to subtract surplus variables yourself before you can use LPSBA (or almost any other linear programming package currently available) to solve a problem with greater-than-or-equal-to constraints. You just tell LPSBA that a constraint is a $\geq$ inequality, and the program automatically subtracts a surplus variable before solving the problem. The names that LPSBA assigns to the slack and surplus variables that it puts into the problem are the same as the names that you specify for the constraints when you enter them.

LPSBA SUBTRACTS SURPLUS VARIABLES AUTOMATICALLY

To input Jeff Smith's problem to LPSBA, we specified 2 structural variables, 4 structural constraints (named ASSEMBLY, FINISHNG, TABLEMIN, and CHAIRMIN), minimization, and entered all the coefficients and types of constraints. This was done in similar fashion to the original Dimensions, Ltd., problem shown in Figure 8-19.

JEFF SMITH'S OPTIMAL SOLUTION

The output for Jeff's problem is in Figure 8-22. Just as in Figure 8-12, we see that the optimal solution is to make 2 tables and 4 chairs, leaving over

$$S_A = 60 - 4(2) - 2(4) = 44 \text{ slack hours in the assembly department}$$
$$S_F = 48 - 2(2) - 4(4) = 28 \text{ slack hours in the finishing department}$$

Notice that these are precisely the values that LPSBA reports for the basic slack and surplus variables. Since only the minimum numbers of tables and

```
Pivoting       0+ **

Optimal solution obtained after    2 pivots

Minimal objective function value:      72.00000

Basic structural variables          Basic slack and surplus variables
TABLES              2.00000         ASSEMBLY           44.00000    Slack
CHAIRS              4.00000         FINISHNG           28.00000    Slack

Shadow prices for constraints       Reduced costs for nonbasic structural vars.
ASSEMBLY            .00000
FINISHNG            .00000
TABLEMIN          20.00000
CHAIRMIN           8.00000
```

FIGURE 8-22
LSPBA's solution to Jeff Smith's problem.

chairs are made in the optimal solution, the two surplus variables are zero, and hence nonbasic.

INFEASIBILITY, UNBOUNDEDNESS, AND ALTERNATIVE OPTIMA

In addition to solving well-posed problems with unique optimal solutions, LPSBA (and other available LP packages) also easily handle infeasible problems, unbounded problems, and problems with alternative optimal solutions. In each case, the package will terminate its solution procedure with a message indicating the condition which has been detected.

In addition, for infeasible problems, most packages will try to provide some information about why the problem is infeasible. For unbounded problems, they will give the last feasible solution examined and indicate a direction in which you could move forever, always staying feasible and improving the objective without any bound. For problems with alternative optimal solutions, they will give one optimal solution, and indicate how to get to other optimal solutions.

5 Glossary

Alternative optima The condition in which a linear programming problem has more than one optimal solution; any of these solutions.

Basic variables Variables which are in the current solution to a linear programming problem.

Constrained resources Organizational resources which are limited in quantity.

Constraint A limit on the availability of resources.

Extreme point A corner of the feasible region.

Feasible region That area containing all the possible solutions to the problem which are feasible, that is, those solutions which satisfy all the constraints in the problem.

Inequality A mathematical expression indicating that minimum or maximum requirements must be met.

Infeasibility The condition when there is no solution which satisfies all the constraints in a problem.

Isocost line A line representing all possible combinations of problem variables which produce the same total cost.

Isoprofit line A line representing all possible combinations of products which will produce a given profit.

Linear programming A mathematical technique for finding the best uses of an organization's resources.

Linear relationship A directly proportional relationship between variables.

Nonbasic variables Variables which are not in the current solution to a linear programming problem.

Nonnegativity constraints Constraints that restrict all the variables to be zero or positive.

Objective A goal of the organization.

Objective function An expression which shows the relationship between the variables in the problem and the firm's goal.

Pivoting The process by which the simplex method goes from one extreme point to another; each *pivot* is an iteration of the method.

Redundancy A constraint which does not affect the feasible region.

Simplex method An iterative procedure for solving linear programming problems.

Slack variables Variables added to less-than-or-equal-to constraints to convert them into equations.

Structural constraints All constraints in a linear problem besides the nonnegativity constraints.

Structural variables Variables present in a linear programming problem before slack and surplus variables are introduced; also called *decision variables*.

Surplus variables Variables subtracted from greater-than-or-equal-to constraints to convert them into equations.

Unboundedness The condition when the objective of a linear programming problem can be made infinitely large without violating any of the constraints.

6 Exercises

8-1 Each weekend in his spare time, Wayne Boggs uses his wood lathe to produce either Jack Rice model baseball bats or Mitch Gedman model bats. He spends 20 hours each weekend in this pursuit. Each Jack Rice bat requires 30 minutes machine time while each Mitch Gedman bat requires 25 minutes of machine time. Next week, Wayne has a firm commitment to deliver 25 Jack Rice bats. Otherwise, he can expect to sell as many bats as he can produce. Jack Rice bats contribute $9 per bat to profit, and Mitch Gedman bats yield a contribution of $8 per bat. How many of each type of bat should Wayne make this weekend in order to maximize profit?

8-2 For Exercise 8-1, draw the isoprofit lines corresponding to profits of $225, $360, $369, and $400. Which of your isoprofit lines result in a feasible but suboptimal solution? Which line is both feasible and optimal? Which is not feasible?

8-3 The Whittier Company needs to produce 40 units of Product A tomorrow. They can produce on either machine X or machine Y or both. Each unit of Product A when processed on machine X takes 30 minutes of time, while a unit processed on machine Y takes 25 minutes. It costs the company $2 per minute and $3 per minute respectively to operate machines X and Y. Tomorrow, machine X has only 10 hours available to produce Product A, while machine Y can be operated as long as desired. Use the graphical method to determine how many hours to schedule on each machine to minimize production costs.

8-4 For Exercise 8-3, draw the isocost lines corresponding to production costs of $2,500, $2,700, $3,000, and $3,500. Which of the isocost lines result in a feasible but suboptimal solution? Which line is both feasible and optimal? Which is not feasible?

8-5 Redikleen Corporation blends solvent from two premixed bases, Donimil and Capilal. Each liter of Donimil costs 80 cents and contains 8 parts kerosene, 10 parts polyvinyl resin, and 6 parts mineral spirits. Capilal costs $1 a liter and contains 6 parts kerosene, 4 parts polyvinyl resin, and 12 parts mineral spirits. Each container of Redikleen solvent must contain at least 24 parts kerosene, 20 parts polyvinyl resin, and 24 parts mineral spirits.

a. Graphically, find the best combination of Donimil and Capilal to meet the requirements for Redikleen solvent at the least cost. What is the cost per liter of the final mix?

b. Use whatever computer package is available to solve this problem.

8-6 Jim Jones manufactures inexpensive set-it-up-yourself furniture for students. He currently makes two products—bookcases and tables. Each bookcase contributes $6 to profit, and each table, $5. Each product passes through two manufacturing points, cutting and finishing. Bookcases take 4 hours a unit in cutting and 4 hours in finishing. Tables require 3 hours a unit in cutting and 5 in finishing. There are currently 40 hours available in cutting and 30 in finishing.

a. Use graphic linear programming to find the product mix that produces the maximum profit for Jim.

b. Use whatever computer package is available to solve this problem.

8-7 Sally Sethness assembles stereo equipment for resale in her shop. She offers two products, turntables and cassette players. She makes a profit of $10 on each turntable and $6 on each cassette. Both must go through two steps in her shop—assembly and bench checking. A turntable takes 12 hours to assemble and 4 hours to bench check. A cassette player takes 4 hours to assemble but 8 hours to bench check. Looking at this month's schedule, Sally sees that she has 60 assembly hours uncommitted and 40 hours of bench-checking time available. Use graphic linear programming to find her best combination of these two products. What is the total profit on the combination you found?

8-8 The Westmoreland Company produces two brands of rabbit food called Diet-Sup and Gro-More. Contribution from Diet-Sup is $1.50 per 7-pound bag while Gro-More yields a contribution of $1.10 per 3-pound bag. Both products are blended from two basic ingredients—a protein source and a carbohydrate source. The products require the following ingredients:

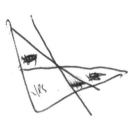

	Protein	Carbohydrate
Diet-Sup (7-lb bag)	4 lb	3 lb
Gro-More (3-lb bag)	2 lb	1 lb

During the coming week, the company wishes to produce the largest profit possible in order to help alleviate a serious shortage of cash. For the week only 700 pounds of protein source and 500 pounds of carbohydrate source are available. How many bags of each product should be produced to maximize profit?

a. Use graphic linear programming to find the answer.

b. Use whatever computer package is available to solve this problem.

8-9 Kimball Draper owns a small perfume shop where she both mixes her own brands and sells other brands. Currently, she is offering two of her own brands, Silent Flower and Mood Swing. Silent Flower makes her $9 an ounce while Mood Swing makes a profit of only $6 an ounce. These two brands are mixed from three essences, E_1, E_2, and E_3. Mixing requirements are:

	E_1	E_2	E_3
Silent Flower	.2 oz	.3 oz	.5 oz
Mood Swing	.1 oz	.1 oz	.8 oz

Kimball checks her essence supply every day. This morning she had 48 ounces of E_1, 30 ounces of E_2, and 60 ounces of E_3. What should she mix today to maximize profits?
    a. Use graphic linear programming to find the answer.
    b. Use whatever computer package is available to solve this problem.

8-10 The Machias Company produces 5,000 electric can openers per week. Their production process is capable of producing 92 percent acceptable units with the remaining 8 percent having electrical defects. Because of warranty costs, they would like to catch most of the defects and repair them before shipping. Their goal is to ship the product with, at most, 2 percent defective. They can do this by employing either experienced inspectors at a weekly cost of $360 per inspector or inexperienced inspectors at $260 per inspector. An experienced inspector can catch 60 defects per week while an inexperienced inspector can find only 50 defects per week. The company feels that it can hire at most 3 experienced inspectors while there is no limit to the availability of inexperienced people. Using the graphical approach, determine how many inspectors of each type should be hired to minimize cost.

8-11 Referring to Exercise 8-10, assume that the $260 per week wage for inexperienced inspectors cannot be lowered because it would violate state minimum wage laws. By how much can the $360 per week wage of experienced inspectors be lowered before there are alternative optimal solutions?

8-12 The Central Fabric Company purchases surplus bolts of fabric from two large
textile mills, A and B. These fabrics are then sold to the public through fabric stores, discount stores, and direct mail. When Central Fabric receives the bolts, it separates them according to the market in which they are sold. Of the fabrics received from textile mill A, 40 percent are sold in fabric stores, 10 percent in discount stores, and 30 percent by direct mail. The fabrics received from textile mill B are 20 percent for fabric stores, 20 percent for discount stores, and 40 percent for direct mail sales. Of the total purchases made from either mill A or mill B, 20 percent of the bolts are unusable and are thrown away. For every 1,000 bolts purchased from mill A, Central Fabric realizes a profit of $8,000; for every 1,000 bolts purchased from mill B, it realizes a profit of $6,000. The sales department forecasts that, at most, 1,600 bolts can be sold through fabric shops, 2,800 through discount stores, and 2,600 through direct mail in the coming year.
    a. Use the graphic method to determine the most profitable numbers of bolts which Central Fabric should purchase from mills A and B.
    b. Use whatever computer package is available to solve this problem.

8-13 The Riverside Auto Company is planning a promotional campaign intended to
bring prospective purchasers of new cars into its showroom. To every prospective buyer who drops by on a given day, Riverside will pay $1. Riverside wants to advertise its "Dollar-a-Look" offer to the public, but in order to hold down costs, it wants to get as many serious buyers as possible without attracting too many freeloaders. It is considering advertising on two television shows. The costs for a commercial on each show, as well as the estimates of drawing power per commercial in terms of serious buyers and freeloaders, are tabulated at the top of the next page.
    There are at most two units of Western and two units of romance movie advertising available. Riverside hopes to keep total costs (advertising plus $1 gifts) at or below $20,000.
    a. Use graphic linear programming to determine the optimal plan for drawing as many serious buyers as possible.
    b. Use whatever computer package is available to solve this problem.

TV show	Cost per ad	Number of serious buyers	Number of freeloaders
Western movie	$ 900	800	4,800
Romance movie	1,000	1,000	3,600

8-14 The Northland Sports Company can manufacture four types of cross-country skis, which are called Tourglide, Slipstream, Lightskim, and Competitor. Production of the skis is constrained by two types of raw materials—fiberglass and a bonding agent. It is also constrained by labor and machine availability. The following table describes the resources used in the production of each pair of the four types of skis:

Type	Fiberglass, lb	Bonding, pints	Labor, hr	Machine time, hr
Tourglide	3.0	1.7	4.3	1.6
Slipstream	2.8	1.6	4.6	1.5
Lightskim	2.5	1.7	4.2	1.7
Competitor	2.3	1.8	5.1	1.9

Each week there are available at most 200 pounds of fiberglass and 130 pints of bonding agent. There are 240 hours of labor time and 160 hours of machine time available per week. What product mix should the company pick if its objective is to maximize the total number of pairs of skis produced?

   a. Formulate the problem as a linear program, but do not solve it.
   b. Use whatever computer package is available to solve this problem.

8-15a. Assuming from Exercise 8-14 that a pair of Tourglide skis contributes $9 to profit while each of the others contributes $12 to profit, reformulate the objective function such that total contribution is maximized.
   b. Reformulate the objective function to provide the objective of using as much of the available machine time as possible.
   c. Reformulate the objective function to ensure that a minimum of labor time is used. What do you think the optimal solution would be if this were the objective function?
   d. Use whatever computer package is available to solve parts a, b, and c.

8-16 The owner of a neighborhood hamburger stand has decided to operate 24 hours a day. On the basis of estimates of trade throughout this period, he feels that he requires at least the following number of employees during the given time periods:

Time period*	Minimum number of employees required
0:01– 4:00	3
4:01– 8:00	5
8:01–12:00	13
12:01–16:00	8
16:01–20:00	19
20:01–24:00	10

*In this notation, 12:00 is noon and 24:00 is midnight.

His employees may report for work at midnight, 4 A.M., 8 A.M., noon, 4 P.M., or 8 P.M. Once employees report in, they must stay continuously for an 8-hour shift.

a. Set up the objective function and constraint equations which would generate a solution to the problem, but do not attempt the solution itself. You should determine the numbers of employees reporting at each of the six possible reporting times if the total overall number of personnel is to be held to a minimum.
b. Use whatever computer package is available to solve this problem.

8-17 The Atlantic States Bus Company is considering the problem of allocating buses on three different express routes for the coming year. The following table represents the number of passengers (in thousands) expected on each route and the income received per passenger.

Route	Numbers	Income per passenger
1	300	$20
2	400	14
3	200	16

Atlantic States has three types of buses (A, B, and C) which can be allocated. The following table shows the number of passengers (in thousands) which can be accommodated in a year's time by a bus allocated to each of the routes; it also shows the maximum number of each type of bus which can be made available for use on all routes.

	Type of bus		
Route	A	B	C
1	18	20	6
2	20	23	8
3	19	21	8
Total buses available	18	7	31

The operating cost (in thousands of dollars) of one bus of type A, B, or C allocated to each of the routes is:

	Type of bus		
Route	A	B	C
1	$18	$18	$18
2	24	22	26
3	20	19	24

Atlantic States estimates that the cost of losing a passenger because of the unavailability of seats is equal to twice the income which would have been received as the fare.

a. Formulate the objective function for the minimum total annual cost solution of this problem, along with the constraint inequalities necessary for its solution. Do not attempt the solution itself.

b. Use whatever computer package is available to solve this problem.

8-18 Shelley Walker plans to add peanuts and soybeans to a mixture of other items and sell the product as a trail mix for hikers and backpackers. If the total weight of peanuts and soybeans is no more than half a pound per pound of mix, she feels she can make a profit on the product. She wishes to advertise that her product is as rich in protein and niacin as her major competitor who produces a more costly trail mix. A pound of peanuts contributes 50 grams of protein and 40 mg. of niacin, while a pound of soybeans contributes 100 grams of protein and 15 mg. of niacin. The other ingredients in the mix have no protein or niacin food value. If her competitor specifies a pound of the more expensive trail mix contains at least 50 grams of protein and 20 mg. of niacin, is there a feasible mix that Shelley can produce which will net her a profit?

a. Show the problem graphically.

b. Use whatever computer package is available to solve this problem.

8-19 For the coming planning period, the Dobbins Company has firm commitments to deliver more products than it has capacity to manufacture. However, it is possible to purchase some of these products from another company, repackage the products, and sell them as Dobbins brand products. The following table lists the three products the company produces, the machine times necessary to produce them, the profit for each product, and the numbers of each which must be delivered in the coming period.

| Product | Machine time, min/unit | | Profit, $/unit | No. needed |
	Machine A	Machine B		
Graphiteen	17	12	122	220
Fibreglow	14	10	138	310
Woodgloss	12	19	154	350

In the coming period Dobbins has only 180 hours of machine A time available for production, and it has 160 hours of machine B time available. Dobbins has been told that it can purchase at most 40 units of Graphiteen and 80 units of Fibreglow, while Woodgloss is in unlimited supply. The profit Dobbins realizes for products purchased from its vendor and resold is only $12, $6, and $8 per unit for the three products, respectively.

a. In order to resolve their make-or-buy decisions for the coming period, formulate the problem as a linear programming problem, but do not solve it.

b. Use whatever computer package is available to solve this problem.

8-20 The Central City Manufacturing Company produces two types of toy model cars, the Stanley Steamer and the Model T. Three machines are required to produce each type; these machines are classified as X, Y, and Z. Each Stanley Steamer requires 7 minutes of process time on machine X, 4 minutes on machine Y, and 10 minutes on machine Z. A Model T requires 4 minutes on X, 15 minutes on Y, and 16 minutes on Z. Each day there are 420 minutes available on machine X, 600 minutes on machine Y, and 840 minutes on machine Z. The variable costs are $10 per unit for the Stanley Steamer and $14 per unit for the Model T. Stanley Steamers sell at a price of $18 per model, whereas Model T's sell for $24 per model. The company's fixed costs are $180 per day. Using the graphic method, determine for the two models the daily production rate which will maximize profit.

8-21 Joe Jelks owns and operates a small store where he sells used construction materials. One day he attended an auction where such materials were going up for bid. Joe decided that he might purchase used concrete blocks which sell in his shop for 50 cents each, or he could buy additional floor planks which bring him a price of $5 each. Upon observing the first few sales, Joe realized that a bid of 25 cents per block should be sufficient to buy as many blocks as he wanted. Also, Joe found that a bid of $4 per plank would enable him to successfully purchase as many planks as he desired. The only limitation to Joe was that all items had to be hauled away by the buyer at the end of the sale, and Joe's pickup truck is limited to a load of 2 tons and a volume of 60 cubic feet. Each concrete block weighs 80 pounds and is .5 cubic foot in volume. Each plank weighs 40 pounds and is 1 cubic foot in volume. How many planks and concrete blocks should Joe have purchased at the auction to maximize his profit? Assume that he could make only a single trip with his pickup truck. Solve the problem with the graphic method.

8-22 Referring to Exercise 8-21, assume Joe missed his guess regarding the amount he would have to bid to successfully outbid the other buyers. Instead of a $4 bid, it took $4.50 to get a plank. The concrete blocks, on the other hand, could be bought for a high bid of only 15 cents as opposed to Joe's original guess of 25 cents. Solve the new problem graphically and determine if Joe should have changed his optimal policy.

8-23 Sue and Al have formed a partnership. They are planning to operate a small lumber mill producing sheets of plywood and pressboard. They have decided to split up the work in such a way that their total profit is maximized. The profit per sheet of plywood is $5, while each sheet of pressboard brings in $8 of profit. If Sue works a full day on plywood, she can produce 12 sheets, whereas Al can produce 10 sheets per day. If they produce only pressboard, Sue can complete 10 sheets and Al can complete 9 sheets in a day's time.
   a. Formulate the objective function and constraints for solving this problem with linear programming. Do not solve the problem.
   b. Use whatever computer package is available to solve this problem.

8-24 The Northwest Lumber Company would like to know what sequence of cuts to make in Douglas fir logs of a certain diameter. One sequence of cuts will produce 7 pieces of 2 × 4 lumber, 3 pieces of 2 × 6, 17 pieces of 1 × 2, 8 pounds of sawdust, and 87 pounds of wood chips. The second sequence produces 8 pieces of 4 × 8, 22 pieces of 1 × 2, 6 pounds of sawdust, and 94 pounds of wood chips. The third alternative in cutting the log produces 9 pieces of 2 × 4, 4 pieces of 2 × 6, 4 pieces of 1 × 2, 9 pounds of sawdust, and 73 pounds of wood chips. The selling price of each size of lumber and the time taken to make each one are given as:

Size	Price	Time to cut, min
1 × 2	$1/piece	1
2 × 4	$4/piece	2
2 × 6	$6/piece	2
4 × 8	$10/piece	3
Sawdust	$0.10/lb	...
Wood chips	$0.07/lb	...

The company has two saws, each of which is in operation 14 hours a day. It would like to know how many logs of each cut sequence should be scheduled each day to maximize its revenue. One restriction, however, is that it has a firm contractual commitment to produce at least 50 pieces of 4 × 8 lumber per day.

    a. Set up the objective function and constraints. Do not solve the problem.

    b. Use whatever computer package is available to solve this problem.

7 Chapter concepts quiz

Fill in the
Blanks

8-1 Linear programming is a technique which attempts to determine how best to allocate _____ in order to achieve some _____.

8-2 Every linear programming problem includes a(n) _____ which relates variables in the problem to the goal of the firm, and _____ which represent the limits on resources available to the firm.

8-3 All the possible solutions which satisfy all the constraints in a problem form the _____. If there are no solutions which satisfy all the constraints, we say that the problem is _____.

8-4 Constraints in a linear program which require all variables to be zero or positive are known as _____ constraints. All the other constraints which result from limited resources are called _____ constraints.

8-5 If there exists a constraint that lies completely outside the feasible region as determined by the other constraints in the problem, we say that this constraint is _____. This type of constraint _____ (does/does not) affect the optimal solution of the problem.

8-6 If two variables always take on values which are in the same proportion, the variables are _____ related.

8-7 A constraint in linear programming must be expressed either as a linear _____ or a linear _____.

8-8 Any two isoprofit or isocost lines for a given linear programming problem are _____ to each other.

8-9 If an optimal solution to a linear programming problem exists, it will lie at _____ of the feasible region.

8-10 Instead of maximizing profit in a linear programming problem, we ensure linearity of the objective function by maximizing _____.

True-False

8-11 Total contribution is used in place of profit in the objective function of a maximization problem because while profit is not linearly related to sales volume, total contribution is.   **T F**

8-12 The requirement of a linear program which makes it "linear" is that the objective function and the constraints be expressible as linear equalities or inequalities.   **T F**

8-13 The graphic method of solving linear programs is useful because of its applicability to problems with many variables.   **T F**

8-14 Total contribution is influenced by volume of sales but not by fixed costs.   **T F**

8-15 Any solution which satisfies at least one of the constraints in a linear **T F**
program is included in the feasible region.

8-16 The intersection of any two constraints is an extreme point which is a **T F**
corner of the feasible region.

8-17 An optimal solution does not necessarily use up all the limited resources **T F**
available.

8-18 The problem of infeasibility in a linear program can only be solved by **T F**
making additional resources available, which in turn changes the constraints
of the problem.

8-19 Unboundedness occurs in a maximization problem when the isoprofit **T F**
lines can be moved as far away from the origin as desired and still touch at
least one point in the feasible region.

8-20 When more than one optimal solution to a problem exists, the firm is **T F**
at a disadvantage since it does not know which of the optimal solutions is
the best.

8-21 An equation is more restrictive than an inequality. **T F**

8-22 Because the constraints to a linear programming problem are always **T F**
linear, we can graph them by locating only two different points on the line.

8-23 An optimal solution to a linear programming problem always occurs **T F**
at the intersection of two constraints.

8-24 If a solution is unbounded, it usually means the constraints were **T F**
incorrectly formulated.

8-25 If there is more than one optimal solution to a linear programming **T F**
problem, there are an infinite number of them.

8-26 Which of the following is not a major requirement of a linear programming   Multiple
problem?   Choice
    a. There must be alternative courses of action among which to decide.
    b. An objective for the firm must exist.
    c. The problem must be of the maximization type.
    d. Resources must be limited.

8-27 All variables in the solution of a linear programming problem are either positive
or zero because of the existence of:
    a. An objective function
    b. Structural constraints
    c. Limited resources
    d. None of the above

8-28 An isoprofit line represents:
    a. An infinite number of solutions all of which yield the same profit.
    b. An infinite number of solutions all of which yield the same costs.
    c. A border of the feasible region.
    d. An infinite number of optimal solutions.

8-29 Which of the following statements is true concerning the optimal solution of a
linear program with two decision variables?
    a. There is only one solution to a linear program.
    b. The optimal solution is either an extreme point or is on a line connecting
       extreme points.

c. All resources must be used up by an optimal solution.

d. All of the above.

8-30 The only difference between solving a maximization or a minimization problem graphically is that in solving a minimization problem:

a. We plot isocost lines and try to find the one which is closest to the origin and still touching the feasible region.

b. There are no nonnegativity constraints.

c. The constraints may be equalities as well as inequalities.

d. The optimal solution is to always set all variables equal to zero.

8-31 It is possible to solve a linear programming problem graphically if there are no more than two:

a. Constraints

b. Inequalities

c. Variables

d. Isoprofit or isocost lines

8-32 Linear programming is a technique for finding the best uses of an organization's:

a. Manpower

b. Money

c. Machinery

d. All of the above

8-33 In linear programming, nonnegativity implies that a variable cannot have:

a. A negative coefficient in the objective function.

b. A negative coefficient in a constraint equation.

c. A negative coefficient in a constraint inequality.

d. None of the above.

In questions 8-34 through 8-38, assume that all coefficients in the linear programs' constraints and objective functions are nonnegative.

8-34 If two ≤ inequalities do not intersect each other in the quadrant of the graph where both variables are positive:

a. The problem is infeasible.

b. One of the constraints is redundant.

c. The solution is unbounded.

d. None of the above.

8-35 If all constraints are ≥ inequalities for a linear programming problem with a maximizing objective function:

a. The problem is infeasible.

b. One of the constraints is redundant.

c. The solution is unbounded.

d. None of the above.

8-36 If a problem has one ≥ constraint and one ≤ constraint and the two do not intersect in the quadrant of the graph where both variables are positive:

a. The problem is infeasible.

b. One of the constraints is redundant.

c. The solution is unbounded.

d. None of the above.

8-37 Suppose you have a linear programming problem with two variables but only one ≤ constraint. If there is only one optimal solution maximizing profits, it would be such that:

a. Both products would be produced.
b. At most, only one product would be produced.
c. Either one or both of the products would be produced.
d. None of the above.

8-38 Suppose we have two $\leq$ constraints, and we substitute the equality condition $=$ in both of them and solve them simultaneously. If our answer has either or both variables taking on a negative value then:
a. One of the constraints is redundant.
b. The optimal solution to the problem is infeasible.
c. The solution is unbounded.
d. None of the above.

8-39 If an isoprofit line yielding the optimal profit lies directly on a constraint line rather than a point on one or more constraints:
a. The solution is unbounded.
b. One of the constraints is redundant.
c. The solution is infeasible.
d. None of the above.

8-40 The problem caused by redundant constraints is that:
a. Two isoprofit lines may not be parallel to each other.
b. The solution is unbounded.
c. The redundant constraint can never be satisfied.
d. None of the above.

8 Real world MS/OR successes

EXAMPLE: MANUFACTURING BIOLOGICAL HEART VALVES

In 1981, American Edwards Laboratories was an innovator in the production of biological heart valves for human implantation. The valves were manufactured using pig hearts purchased from suppliers. Since human heart valves have a different size distribution than the distribution found in pigs, the company had difficulty matching inventories of heart valves with demand. Said S. Hilal and Warren Erikson[2] developed a linear programming model to select the combination of suppliers that would best match the distribution of valve sizes needed for humans. The bottom line: a one-time reduction in inventory of $1.9 million, followed by continuing annual savings of $1.5 million.

THE PROBLEM: MATCHING SUPPLY AND DEMAND

At American Edwards, product availability was of paramount importance and company policy ruled out any attempt to use conventional inventory theory to set safety stocks of heart valves. Instead, the goal was to maintain six to twelve weeks demand in safety stocks at all times. Meeting this goal was difficult because pig heart valves could not be purchased by specific size.

COMPANY POLICY ON INVENTORIES

VALVE SIZES UNKNOWN IN RAW HEARTS

---

[2] Said S. Hilal and Warren Erikson, "Matching Supplies to Save Lives: Linear Programming the Production of Heart Valves," *Interfaces,* vol. 11, no. 6, pp. 48–56, 1981.

Valve sizes were unknown until a batch of raw hearts had been completely processed. The result was that the valve sizes obtained from a batch of hearts often did not match the sizes needed.

Hilal and Erikson's analysis showed that most suppliers provided pig hearts with a relatively stable distribution of valve sizes. These distributions were used in a linear programming model to select the best combination of suppliers. The best way to explain the model is with an example that could

SUPPLIER
INFORMATION

be solved graphically. Suppose the company is buying from two suppliers, A and B, who can supply three valve sizes, 1, 2, and 3. Historical data shows that supplier A's pig hearts contain 30 percent of valve size 1, 50 percent of size 2, and 20 percent of size 3. Supplier B's size distribution is 10 percent, 60 percent, and 30 percent, respectively. Assume also that total purchasing and processing costs for sizes 1, 2, and 3 are $10, $14, and $12, respectively.

OBJECTIVE FUNCTION

The expected value of the cost of a valve from supplier A is .3(10) + .5(14) + .2(12) = $12.40. The expected cost from supplier B is .1(10) + .6(14) + .3(12) = $13. The objective function in the linear program is then:

$$\text{Minimize } 12.4A + 13B$$

where A and B are the numbers of hearts purchased from each supplier. If the demands for the three sizes are 100, 300, and 250 units, the demand constraints are:

$$.3A + .1B \geqslant 100$$
$$.5A + .6B \geqslant 300$$
$$.2A + .3B \geqslant 250$$

The model actually implemented by Hilal and Erikson had more than 20 suppliers and 30 valve sizes and was solved using a linear programming computer package. However, the model structure was the same as in this small example. The objective was to minimize the cost of hearts purchased, given constraints on the number of hearts in each size category.

The linear programming model enabled the company to meet demand by purchasing fewer pig hearts than before. In addition, a great deal of labor was saved in processing hearts. The model was also useful to management in setting prices, scheduling production, and analyzing the design of new heart valves.

9

Each Friday, Lori Barnes, the operations manager of the animal feed division of Allway Farm Products, must determine what ingredients to blend to produce chicken feed during the coming week. Corn, oats, wheat, other vegetable products, and various vitamin and mineral supplements are purchased to use in the feed.

Lori wants to select the least expensive blend of ingredients to produce all of the feed demanded and to satisfy all the nutritional levels specified on the label on each bag of feed. Since the prices of the ingredients vary widely during the year, Lori has found that the profitability of her feed operations depends significantly on her ability to take full advantage of the volatile prices of agricultural commodities by varying the feed blend from week to week.

To solve her problem, Lori uses linear programming. She has already entered the nutritional values of all the candidate ingredients into her computer. Each week, she needs to enter the current prices of the ingredients and the amounts of chicken feed needed. She can then run her linear programming package to find the most cost-effective blend for the coming week.

Lori's feed-blending problem is only one of a large number of applications of linear programming that are successfully used in many industries today. The widespread availability of computer packages based on the simplex method makes linear programming an attractive method for solving many operational problems. In this chapter, you will learn how the simplex method finds optimal solutions to linear programming problems. Your ability to make effective decisions using information derived by the simplex method will be greatly enhanced by the fact that you have developed an understanding of how this important technique works.

LINEAR PROGRAMMING II: THE SIMPLEX METHOD

Maximization and Minimization

CHAPTER OBJECTIVES

- INTRODUCE THE SIMPLEX METHOD OF LINEAR PROGRAMMING.
- EXAMINE IN DETAIL ALL THE STEPS OF THE SIMPLEX METHOD.
- DEFINE AND DISCUSS ALL THE ELEMENTS IN THE SIMPLEX TABLEAU IN TERMS OF THEIR SIGNIFICANCE TO THE PROBLEM STATEMENT AND PROBLEM SOLUTION.
- DEMONSTRATE THE USE OF THE SIMPLEX METHOD ON MINIMIZATION PROBLEMS AND PROBLEMS WITH ALL THREE KINDS OF CONSTRAINTS.
- SHOW HOW THE SIMPLEX METHOD DEALS WITH INFEASIBILITY, UNBOUNDEDNESS, ALTERNATIVE OPTIMA, AND DEGENERACY.

We can envision the use of linear programming as a three stage process:

1 *Problem formulation:* gathering the relevant information, learning what questions need to be answered, and setting the problem up as a linear program.

2 *Problem solution:* finding the optimal solution to this linear program.

3 *Solution interpretation and implementation:* checking that the solution to the linear program is indeed a solution to the original real problem (and if not, we have to go back to stage 1 and refine our formulation), doing appropriate sensitivity analyses, and putting the solution into practice.

Because of the availability of computer LP packages like LPSBA, today's managers can utilize all of the power of linear programming without knowing all of the details of the simplex method. In other words, managers can concentrate on stages 1 and 3. However, they do need to know enough about stage 2 in order to be able to communicate with the technical staff personnel who assist them in their use of techniques such as linear programming. So even if you never actually do solve an LP by hand, you can still profit from the following discussion of how the simplex method works. (The simplex method is also called the simplex *algorithm.* An algorithm is a computational procedure for solving a class of problems.)

We shall use the simplex algorithm to solve the original Dimensions, Ltd., profit maximization problem. For convenience, we repeat here the final form of the problem after the two slack variables were added (from page 365).

Maximize:

$$\text{Profit} = 8T + 6C + 0S_A + 0S_F$$

Subject to:

$$4T + 2C + S_A + 0S_F = 60 \text{ hr}$$
$$2T + 4C + 0S_A + S_F = 48 \text{ hr}$$
$$\text{All variables} \geq 0$$

1 Setting up the initial solution

THE SIMPLEX TABLEAU

To make the equations in the problem easier to handle, they can be put into a tabular form, called the *simplex tableau.*

It will be helpful to describe the simplex tableau and to identify the parts and function of each.

1 See Table 9-1. The two *constraint equations* are shown in the simplex tableau as

	T	C	S_A	S_F
60	4	2	1	0
48	2	4	0	1

TABLE 9-1
Parts of the
simplex tableau

Note first that row 1 (4, 2, 1, 0) represents the coefficients of the equation $4T + 2C + S_A + 0S_F = 60$, and row 2 (2, 4, 0, 1) the coefficients of $2T + 4C + 0S_A + S_F = 48$.

2 Each *variable column* contains all the coefficients of one unknown. For example, under T is written $\frac{4}{2}$, under C is written $\frac{2}{4}$, under S_A is written $\frac{1}{0}$, and under S_F is written $\frac{0}{1}$.

3 The constants (60 and 48) have been placed to the left of the equations. We simply rearrange the terms in the constraint equations to form the simplex tableau.

THE FIRST SOLUTION SHOWN
IN THE SIMPLEX TABLEAU

In the simplex method, we need to establish an initial solution. The simplest starting solution is for Dimensions, Ltd., to make *no* tables or chairs, have all unused time, and earn no profit. This solution is technically feasible but not financially attractive; it is symbolized

$$T = 0 \quad \text{no tables}$$

$$C = 0 \quad \text{no chairs}$$

$$S_A = 60 - 4(0) - 2(0) = 60 \text{ hr unused}$$

$$S_F = 48 - 2(0) - 4(0) = 48 \text{ hr unused}$$

This solution contains only the slack variables S_A and S_F. Substituting the quantities of T, C, S_A, and S_F in the objective function gives the following profit:

$$\begin{aligned} \text{Profit} &= 8T + 6C + 0S_A + 0S_F \\ &= 8(0) + 6(0) + 0(60) + 0(48) \\ &= 0 \end{aligned}$$

ILLUSTRATING THE
FIRST SOLUTION IN THE
SIMPLEX TABLEAU

This first feasible solution is shown in the initial simplex tableau as

Product mix	Quantity	T	C	S_A	S_F
S_A	60	4	2	1	0
S_F	48	2	4	0	1

PRODUCT-MIX AND
QUANTITY COLUMNS

Note that the *product-mix column* contains the variables in the solution. The variables in the first solution are S_A and S_F (the slack variables). In the *quantity column* we find the quantities of the variables that are in the solution:

$$S_A = 60 \text{ hr available in assembly}$$
$$S_F = 48 \text{ hr available in finishing}$$

FIRST SIMPLEX
SOLUTION IS
EQUIVALENT TO A
CORNER POINT IN THE
GRAPHIC SOLUTION

Since the variables T and C do not appear in the mix, they are equal to zero.

Notice that this first solution (no tables and no chairs) is equivalent to point A in the graphic method of Figure 8-6 on page 350.

SUBSTITUTION RATES SHOWN IN THE SIMPLEX TABLEAU

The C_j column in Table 9-1 contains the profit per unit for the variables S_A and S_F. For example, the 0 appearing to the left of the S_A row in Table 9-1 means that profit per unit of S_A is zero.

EXPLAINING THE
ENTRIES IN TABLE 9-1

The last two columns in the initial simplex tableau consist of the coefficients of the slack variables that are added to the constraint inequalities to make them equations.

The fourth and fifth columns consist of the coefficients of the real product variables, T and C. For example, the element 4 in the T column of the table means that if we wanted to make 1 unit of T (to bring 1 table into the solution), we would have to give up 4 hours of S_A in assembly.

Similarly, the element 2 in the C column indicates that the manufacturing of 1 unit of C (bringing 1 chair into the solution) would force us to give up 2 hours of S_A in assembly.

The elements in the fourth and fifth columns thus represent rates of substitution.

The element 1 in the S_A column tells us that to bring in 1 hour of S_A (to make 1 hour of S_A available) we would have to give up 1 of the 60 hours of S_A now in the solution. As there are only 60 hours in assembly available, we must give up 1 of the 60 if we want an hour for some other purpose. This is just like taking 1 hour off the top of a pile and adding another to the bottom.

The 0 in the S_F column immediately under the S_F means that making 1 hour in finishing available for other purposes has *no* effect on S_A, the amount of slack time in assembly.

In our examination of substitution rates, we have treated *two* types of action:

1 The *addition* of real products, T and C, into the production schedule or solution

2 The *withdrawal* of time, S_A and S_F, from the total amount of time available in each of the two departments—withdrawal to make time available for other purposes

PROGRAMMING II

TWO KINDS OF
SUBSTITUTIONS

ADDING TWO MORE ROWS TO THE SIMPLEX TABLEAU

Up to this point, setting up the initial simplex tableau has not involved any computation. We have simply rearranged the problem equations to form the first simplex tableau.

To find the profit for each solution and to determine whether the solution can be improved upon, we need to add two more rows to the initial simplex tableau: a Z_j row and a $C_j - Z_j$ row. This has been done in Table 9-2. The value in the Z_j row under the quantity column represents the total profit from this particular solution: 0, in this case. In this first solution, we have 60 hours of unused time in assembly ($S_A = 60$) and 48 hours of unused time in finishing ($S_F = 48$). The total profit from this solution is found by multiplying the profit per unit of S_A (0) by the quantity of S_A in the solution (60 hours) plus the profit per unit of S_F (0) times the quantity of S_F in the solution (48 hours).

Total profit for the first solution is

Number of unused hours of S_A = 60
Times profit per unit of S_A × $\underline{\ 0\ }$ = 0

$+$

Number of unused hours of S_F = 48
Times profit per unit of S_F × $\underline{\ 0\ }$ = $\underline{0}$
Total profit   0

The four values for Z_j under the variable columns (all 0) are the amounts by which profit would be *reduced* if 1 unit of any of the variables (T, C, S_A, S_F) were added to the mix. For example, if we want to make 1 unit of T, the elements $\binom{4}{2}$ under T tell us we must give up 4 hours of S_A and 2 hours of S_F. But unused time is worth 0 per hour; consequently, there is *no* reduction in profit.

EXPLAINING THE Z_j ROW AND THE $C_j - Z_j$ ROW

THE Z_j ROW

TABLE 9-2
Initial simplex tableau completed (two rows added)

C_j	Product mix	Quantity	8 T	6 C	0 S_A	0 S_F
0	S_A	60	4	2	1	0
0	S_F	48	2	4	0	1
2 rows added $\{$	Z_j	0	0	0	0	0
	$C_j - Z_j$		8	6	0	0

How much profit is lost by adding 1 unit of T to the production schedule or solution?

$$
\begin{array}{lr}
\text{Number of hours of } S_A \text{ given up} = & 4 \\
\text{Times profit per unit of } S_A & \times \underline{0} = 0 \\[6pt]
\text{Number of hours of } S_F \text{ given up} = & 2 \\
\text{Times profit per unit of } S_F & \times \underline{0} = \underline{0} \\[6pt]
\text{Total profit given up} & 0
\end{array}
$$

THE C_j ROW

C_j has been defined as profit per unit; for tables (T), C_j is $8 per unit.

$C_j - Z_j$ is the *net* profit which will result from introducing, that is, adding, 1 unit of a variable to the production schedule or solution. For example, if 1 unit of T adds $8 of profit to the solution *and* if its introduction causes no loss, then $C_j - Z_j$ for $T = 8$.

The calculation of Z_j's for Table 9-2 follows:

COMPUTATION OF Z_j
ROW AND $C_j - Z_j$ ROW

$$
\begin{array}{ll}
Z_j \text{ (total profit)} & = 0(60) + 0(48) = 0 \\
Z_j \text{ for column } T & = 0(\ 4) + 0(\ 2) = 0 \\
Z_j \text{ for column } C & = 0(\ 2) + 0(\ 4) = 0 \\
Z_j \text{ for column } S_A & = 0(\ 1) + 0(\ 0) = 0 \\
Z_j \text{ for column } S_F & = 0(\ 0) + 0(\ 1) = 0
\end{array}
$$

Calculations of *net* profit per unit for each variable follow:

Variable	Profit/unit C_j	−	Profit lost/unit Z_j	=	Net profit/unit $C_j - Z_j$
T	8		0		8
C	6		0		6
S_A	0		0		0
S_F	0		0		0

MEANING OF THE
$C_j - Z_j$ ROW

By examining the numbers in the $C_j - Z_j$ row of Table 9-2, we can see, for example, that total profit can be increased by $8 for each unit of T (tables) added to the mix or by $6 for each unit of C (chairs) added to the mix. Thus a positive number in the $C_j - Z_j$ row ($8 in the case of the T column) indicates that profits will be improved by that amount for each unit of T added. On the other hand, a negative number in the $C_j - Z_j$ row would indicate the amount by which profits would *decrease* if 1 unit of the variable heading that column were added to the solution. Hence the optimal solution is reached when no positive numbers remain in the $C_j - Z_j$ row; that is, no more profit can be made.

2 Developing the second solution

IS IMPROVEMENT
POSSIBLE?

Once the initial simplex tableau is established, the next step is to determine how to improve profits.

We now introduce a computational procedure which will generate the correct second and subsequent tableaus of the problem. In this section we shall limit ourselves to generating the appropriate values for each iteration of the problem; Section 4, "Justification and significance of all elements in the simplex tableau," will demonstrate the logic of the procedures we have followed. The procedure for going from one tableau to the next is called *pivoting*; each iteration is called a *pivot* (first introduced on page 365). The procedure for the second solution (that is, the first pivot) follows.

STEP 1

Determine which variable will add the *most* per unit to profit. The numbers in the $C_j - Z_j$ row tell exactly which product will increase profits most. As stated previously, the presence of positive numbers in the $C_j - Z_j$ row indicates that profit can be improved; the larger the positive number, the greater the improvement possible.

WHICH VARIABLE
WOULD ADD THE MOST
PER-UNIT PROFIT?

We select as the variable to be added to the first solution that variable which contributes the most profit per unit. In Table 9-3, bringing in T (tables) will add \$8 per unit to profit. The T column is the optimal column.

By definition, the *optimal column* (Table 9-3) is that column which has the largest positive value in the $C_j - Z_j$ row, or, stated in another way, that column whose product will contribute the most profit per unit. Inspection of the optimal column tells us that the variable T (tables) should be added to the mix, replacing one of the variables presently in the mix.

STEP 2

The next step is to determine which variable will be replaced. This is done in the following manner: divide 60 and 48 in the quantity column by their corresponding numbers in the optimal column and select the row with the smaller nonnegative ratio as the row to be replaced. In this case, the ratios would be

WHICH VARIABLE WILL
BE REPLACED?

$$S_A \text{ row:} \qquad \frac{60 \text{ hr available}}{4 \text{ hr required/unit}} = \boxed{15} \text{ units of } T$$

$$S_F \text{ row:} \qquad \frac{48 \text{ hr available}}{2 \text{ hr required/unit}} = 24 \text{ units of } T$$

TABLE 9-3
Optimal column in
initial simplex tableau

C_j	Product mix	Quantity	8 T	6 C	0 S_A	0 S_F
0	S_A	60	4	2	1	0
0	S_F	48	2	4	0	1
	Z_j	0	0	0	0	0
	$C_j - Z_j$		8	6	0	0

↑—Optimal column

TABLE 9-4
Replaced row and
intersectional
elements in initial
simplex tableau

C_j	Product mix	Quantity	8 T	6 C	0 S_A	0 S_F	
0	S_A	60	④---2		1	0	← Replaced row
0	S_F	48	②---4		0	1	---Intersectional ---elements
	Z_j	0	0	0	0	0	
	$C_j - Z_j$		8	6	0	0	

Optimal column

HOW MANY UNITS OF THE NEW VARIABLE WILL ENTER THE SOLUTION?

Since the S_A row has the smaller positive value (15 rather than 24), it is called the *replaced row* because it will be replaced in the next solution by 15 units of T. The elements common to both the S_A and S_F rows *and* the optimal column are called *intersectional elements*. Thus the intersectional element of the row to be replaced (S_A row) is 4, and the intersectional element of the S_F row is 2 (see Table 9-4).

STEP 3

DEVELOPING THE SECOND TABLEAU

Having selected the optimal column and the replaced row, we can develop the second simplex solution, an *improved* solution.

The first part of the new tableau to be developed is the T row. The T row appears in place of the replaced row (S_A) in Table 9-5. The T row of the new tableau is computed as follows: divide each number in the replaced row (the S_A row) by the intersectional element (4) of the replaced row:

$$^{60}/_4 = 15 \qquad ^4/_4 = 1 \qquad ^2/_4 = \tfrac{1}{2} \qquad ^1/_4 = \tfrac{1}{4} \qquad ^0/_4 = 0$$

Thus the new T row should be (15, 1, ½, ¼, 0).

THIS SOLUTION IS EQUIVALENT TO ONE OF THE CORNER POINTS OF THE GRAPHIC SOLUTION

In Table 9-5, for the first time, there is a nonzero dollar figure in the C_j column ($8 per unit). Also, S_F and its profit per unit ($0) remain in the new tableau. Notice that making 15 tables (our second solution) is equivalent to point C in the graphic solution in Figure 8-6, page 350.

STEP 4

COMPLETING THE SECOND TABLEAU

To complete the second tableau, we compute new values for the remaining rows. *All* remaining rows of the variables in the tableau are calculated using the formula

TABLE 9-5
Replacing row in
second simplex
tableau

C_j	Product mix	Quantity	8 T	6 C	0 S_A	0 S_F	
8	T	15	1	½	¼	0	← Replacing row
0	S_F						
	Z_j						
	$C_j - Z_j$						

$$\begin{pmatrix} \text{Elements in} \\ \text{old row} \end{pmatrix} - \begin{pmatrix} \text{intersectional} & \text{corresponding} \\ \text{element of} \times \text{elements in} \\ \text{old row} & \text{replacing row} \end{pmatrix} = \begin{pmatrix} \text{Elements in} \\ \text{new row} \end{pmatrix}$$

We use this formula to calculate the new S_F row:

Element in old S_F row	−	$\begin{pmatrix} \text{Intersectional} \\ \text{element of} \\ S_F \text{ row} \end{pmatrix}$	×	$\begin{pmatrix} \text{Corresponding} \\ \text{element in} \\ \text{replacing row} \end{pmatrix}$	=	Element in new S_F row
48	−	(2	×	15)	=	18
2	−	(2	×	1)	=	0
4	−	(2	×	½)	=	3
0	−	(2	×	¼)	=	−½
1	−	(2	×	0)	=	1

The new S_F row as it appears in the second tableau is shown in Table 9-6. The method for computing the Z_j and $C_j - Z_j$ rows (the profit opportunities) has already been demonstrated in developing the initial simplex tableau.

The computation of the Z_j row of the second tableau is as follows:

$$Z_j \text{ (total profit)} = 8(15) + 0(18) \qquad = 120 = \text{total profit of second solution}$$

$$\begin{aligned} Z_j \text{ for } T: & \quad 8(1) \ + 0(0) & = 8 \\ Z_j \text{ for } C: & \quad 8(\tfrac{1}{2}) + 0(3) & = 4 \\ Z_j \text{ for } S_A: & \quad 8(\tfrac{1}{4}) + 0(-\tfrac{1}{2}) & = 2 \\ Z_j \text{ for } S_F: & \quad 8(0) \ + 0(1) & = 0 \end{aligned}$$

Profits given up by introducing 1 unit of these variables

Thus the computations above indicate that introducing a unit of T would lose $8 for us. How can this be?

1 We currently make 15 units of T.
2 Production of 15 tables uses up all the time originally available in assembly.
3 To introduce another T we would have to give up 1 of the current 15 T's.
4 Giving up a table would cost us $8.

TABLE 9-6
Replacing row and new S_F row in second tableau

C_j	Product mix	Quantity	8	6	0	0
			T	C	S_A	S_F
8	T	15	1	½	¼	0
0	S_F	18	0	3	−½	1
	Z_j					
	$C_j - Z_j$					

TABLE 9-7
Second simplex
tableau completed

C_j	Product mix	Quantity	8 T	6 C	0 S_A	0 S_F
8	T	15	1	½	¼	0
0	S_F	18	0	3	-½	1
	Z_j	120	8	4	2	0
	$C_j - Z_j$		0	2	-2	0

THE COMPLETED
SECOND TABLEAU

Using these Z_j values and the C_j values from the problem data, we computed the $C_j - Z_j$ row to complete the second tableau shown in Table 9-7. Certainly the total profit from this second solution ($120) is an improvement over the zero profit in the first solution.

3 Developing the third solution

IS FURTHER
IMPROVEMENT
POSSIBLE?

The presence of a positive number (2) in the C column of the $C_j - Z_j$ row of the second solution (Table 9-7) indicates that further improvement is possible. Therefore, the same process used to develop this solution must be repeated to develop a third solution.

STEP 1

WHICH VARIABLE
WOULD ADD THE MOST
PER-UNIT PROFIT?

A look at the $C_j - Z_j$ row of the second tableau (Table 9-7) shows that C, chairs, contributes a *net* profit of $2 per unit. Thus the optimal column in Table 9-7 is the C column. Chairs will now be added, replacing one of the variables, T or S_F, in the second solution.

STEP 2

WHICH VARIABLE WILL
BE REPLACED AND HOW
MANY UNITS OF THE
NEW VARIABLE WILL
ENTER THE SOLUTION?

The replaced row is found as before by dividing 15 and 18 in the quantity column by their corresponding numbers in the optimal column and selecting the row with the smaller nonnegative ratio as the replaced row. Since $^{15}/_{1/2}$ = 30 (in the T row) and $^{18}/_3$ = 6 (in the S_F row), the S_F row is designated as the replaced row. It will be replaced in the next solution by 6 units of C (chairs). Table 9-8 shows the optimal column, replaced row, and intersectional elements of the second tableau.

TABLE 9-8
Optimal column,
replaced row, and
intersectional
elements of second
tableau

C_j	Product mix	Quantity	8 T	6 C	0 S_A	0 S_F	Intersectional element of T row
8	T	15	1	½	¼	0	
0	S_F	18	0	③	-½	1	← Replaced row (S_F)
	Z_j	120	8	4	2	0	Intersectional element of S_F row
	$C_j - Z_j$		0	2	-2	0	

Optimal column

C_j	Product mix	Quantity	8 T	6 C	0 S_A	0 S_F	
8	T						
6	C	6	0	1	$-\frac{1}{6}$	$\frac{1}{3}$	← Replacing row
	Z_j						
	$C_j - Z_j$						

TABLE 9-9
Replacing row of
third tableau

STEP 3

The replacing row of the third tableau is computed by dividing each number in the replaced row by the intersectional element of the replaced row. Thus the replacing row of the third tableau is $(6, 0, 1, -\frac{1}{6}, \frac{1}{3})$. It assumes the same row position as the replaced row of the second tableau (see Table 9-9).

COMPLETING THE
REPLACING ROW

STEP 4

The new values of the T row are

Element in old T row	−	(Intersectional element of T row	×	Corresponding element of replacing row)	=	Element in new T row
15	−	($\frac{1}{2}$	×	6)	=	12
1	−	($\frac{1}{2}$	×	0)	=	1
$\frac{1}{2}$	−	($\frac{1}{2}$	×	1)	=	0
$\frac{1}{4}$	−	($\frac{1}{2}$	×	$-\frac{1}{6}$)	=	$\frac{1}{3}$
0	−	($\frac{1}{2}$	×	$\frac{1}{3}$)	=	$-\frac{1}{6}$

COMPLETING THE
THIRD TABLEAU

The new T row is $(12, 1, 0, \frac{1}{3}, -\frac{1}{6})$. In Table 9-10 it has been added to the third tableau.

The Z_j's of the third tableau are computed as follows:

Z_j (total profit): $8(12)$ $+ 6(6)$ $= 132 =$ total profit from third

Z_j for T: $8(1)$ $+ 6(0)$ $= 8$ solution

Z_j for C: $8(0)$ $+ 6(1)$ $= 6$

Z_j for S_A: $8(\frac{1}{3})$ $+ 6(-\frac{1}{6}) = \frac{5}{3}$

Z_j for S_F: $8(-\frac{1}{6}) + 6(\frac{1}{3})$ $= \frac{2}{3}$

TABLE 9-10
Replacing row and
new T row in
third tableau

C_j	Product mix	Quantity	8 T	6 C	0 S_A	0 S_F
8	T	12	1	0	$\frac{1}{3}$	$-\frac{1}{6}$
6	C	6	0	1	$-\frac{1}{6}$	$\frac{1}{3}$
	Z_j					
	$C_j - Z_j$					

NO FURTHER
IMPROVEMENT IS
POSSIBLE; THE
OPTIMAL SOLUTION
HAS BEEN REACHED

Using these Z_j values and the C_j values from the problem data, we computed the $C_j - Z_j$ row to complete the third tableau shown in Table 9-11. Certainly, the total profit from this second solution ($132) is an improvement over the $120 profit in the second solution. Since there is no positive $C_j - Z_j$ in Table 9-11, no further improvement is possible; thus the optimal solution has been obtained. It is

$$T = 12 \qquad C = 6 \qquad S_A = 0 \qquad S_F = 0$$

THIS SOLUTION IS
EQUIVALENT TO ONE OF
THE CORNER POINTS
IN THE GRAPHIC
SOLUTION

This solution (12 tables and 6 chairs) is identical to point D in the graphic solution in Figure 8-6 on page 350 and the computer solution on page 368.

Profits will be maximized by making 12 tables and 6 chairs and having no unused time in either department. The variables T and C appear in the product-mix column with their values represented by the corresponding numbers in the quantity column. The variables S_A and S_F do not appear in the product-mix column and therefore are equal to zero.

The Z_j total, $132, represents the profit obtained in the optimal solution.

▋ SUMMARY OF STEPS IN THE SIMPLEX MAXIMIZATION PROCEDURE

In summary form, the steps involved in the simplex procedure for maximization problems are as follows:

THE 11 STEPS IN THE
SIMPLEX METHOD
OF SOLVING A
MAXIMIZING PROBLEM

1 Set up the inequalities describing the problem constraints.

2 Convert the inequalities to equations by adding slack variables.

3 Enter the equations in the simplex tableau.

4 Calculate the Z_j and $C_j - Z_j$ values for this solution.

5 Determine the entering variable (optimal column) by choosing the one with the highest $C_j - Z_j$ value.

6 Determine the row to be replaced by dividing quantity-column values by their corresponding optimal-column values and choosing the smallest nonnegative quotient. (That is, only compute the ratios for rows whose elements in the optimal column are greater than zero; for example, omit ratios like $160/0$ and $15/-5$.)

7 Compute the values for the replacing row.

8 Compute the values for the remaining rows.

TABLE 9-11
Third simplex
tableau completed

| C_j | Product mix | Quantity | 8 | 6 | 0 | 0 |
			T	C	S_A	S_F
8	T	12	1	0	$1/3$	$-1/6$
6	C	6	0	1	$-1/6$	$1/3$
	Z_j	132	8	6	$5/3$	$2/3$
	$C_j - Z_j$		0	0	$-5/3$	$-2/3$

9 Calculate Z_j and $C_j - Z_j$ values for this solution.

10 If there is a positive $C_j - Z_j$ value, return to step 5.

11 If there is no positive $C_j - Z_j$ value, the optimal solution has been obtained.

4 Justification and significance of all elements in the simplex tableau

Up to now, the discussion has centered on the procedures involved in solving a simplex problem. In addition to the solution, however, the simplex method provides us with important information concerning various alternative solutions and the effect of changes in the basic data upon the solutions. Frequently, this information is as valuable and revealing as the answer itself.

In this section we will explain the logic and economic significance of all the elements in the simplex tableau; thus we will give meaning to the procedures learned so far.

In Table 9-12 we have reproduced the second simplex tableau from the preceding section (see Table 9-7) and have numbered each element. Our general interpretation, keyed to each circled number, is as follows.

THE LOGIC OF THE
SIMPLEX METHOD

THE QUANTITY COLUMN (ELEMENTS ①, ②, AND ③)

① In the initial simplex tableau (Table 9-2) we noted that T (tables) made the larger contribution per unit to profit and thus should be added to the second solution. To find the quantity to be added, we proceeded as follows:

EXPLAINING THE THREE
ENTRIES IN THE
QUANTITY COLUMN
OF TABLE 9-12

$$\frac{60 \text{ hr available in assembly}}{4 \text{ hr required/table}} = 15 \text{ tables}$$

We found that 15 was the largest quantity which could be made without violating the time restriction in either department.

TABLE 9-12
Second simplex
tableau with each
element numbered

C_j	Product mix	Quantity	8 T	6 C	0 S_A	0 S_F
			①	⑫	⑯	④ ⑧
8	T	15	1	½	¼	0
			②	⑬	⑰	⑤ ⑨
0	S_F	18	0	3	−½	1
			③	⑭	⑱	⑥ ⑩
	Z_j	120	8	4	2	0
				⑮	⑲	⑦ ⑪
	$C_j - Z_j$		0	2	−2	0

Making 15 tables required all the hours available in assembly (4 hours per unit × 15 units = 60 hours). Thus T replaced S_A in the solution.

② Each of the 15 tables requires 2 hours in finishing. Thus to finish 15 tables requires 30 hours (2 hours per unit × 15 units). Since 48 hours are available and only 30 hours are required, we have 18 hours left in finishing.

③ The 120 represents the total profit from the variables in the product mix: $8T + 6C = 8(15) + 6(0) = 120$ dollars.

■ SUBSTITUTION RATES (ELEMENTS ④, ⑤, ⑧, ⑨, ⑫, ⑬, ⑯, AND ⑰)

④ Since 1 unit of T (1 table) requires 4 hours in assembly, the second solution uses up all the 60 hours in assembly. Therefore, the production of anything else in this department would require that some of the tables be given up. For example, if 1 unit of S_A (1 hour) is made available for other purposes, ¼ table will have to be given up; or stated in another way, every hour of S_A added to the solution reduces the production of T (tables) by ¼ unit.

⑤ Reducing the production of T (tables) by ¼ unit certainly must have an effect on finishing, because *chairs and tables* must be processed through both departments. Because T requires 2 hours per unit in finishing and because adding 1 unit of S_A reduces the production of T (tables) by ¼ unit, ¼ × 2 = ½ hour is freed in finishing.

⑧ Adding 1 unit of S_F has no effect (0) on T. Why? Since assembly is the limiting department (all hours have been used), making available 1 hour of S_F in finishing will have no effect on the production of tables. Since 18 hours are still available in finishing, we can make one of them available without reducing our production of tables.

⑨ Withdrawing 1 unit of S_F: since only 18 hours are available in finishing in the second solution, withdrawing 1 hour would remove 1 of the 18 hours now available.

⑫ Here again we have a one-for-one substitution; that is, each unit of T added to the production schedule replaces 1 unit of T in the solution. From ① we found that 15 was the largest quantity of tables that could be processed in assembly. Thus in order to add another table and at the same time satisfy the time restriction in assembly (60 hours available), we must subtract or give up 1 table in order to make the necessary time available.

⑬ Adding 1 unit of T to the production schedule has no effect on S_F. Why? From ⑫ we found that adding 1 table required giving up 1 table, so that the net change in finishing must be zero $(1 - 1 = 0)$. Since there is no real change in assembly, neither is there any change in finishing. No additional hours are required.

⑯ Adding 1 unit of C (chair) to the program replaces ½ table: a chair requires 2 hours per unit in assembly, and a table requires 4 hours. Now, because assembly is the limiting department (time is exhausted), processing

1 chair would require giving up ¾, or ½ table. Stated another way, processing a chair in assembly takes 2 of the 4 hours required to make a table. Thus for every chair processed in assembly, ½ table must be given up to provide the necessary 2 hours.

⑰ Adding 1 unit of C (chair) replaces 3 units of S_F (3 hours). The problem originally stated that $1C$ required 4 hours in finishing. How can we justify this apparent inconsistency? First note that adding 1 chair replaces ½ table (from ⑯). Second, a table requires 2 hours in finishing. Thus giving up ½ table frees 1 hour in finishing (½ × 2 hours required per unit of T = 1 hour). The 4 hours required to make a chair in finishing minus the 1 hour freed equals 3 hours net change. Processing a chair still requires 4 hours per unit: 3 hours plus the 1 hour freed equals the 4 hours required. The apparent inconsistency therefore disappears when we consider the effect that a change in the number of chairs has on the number of tables which can be produced.

In summary, the eight elements we have discussed represent marginal rates of substitution between the variables in the product mix and the variables heading the column. We found that a positive rate of substitution, for example, ⑯, indicates the decrease in T that occurs if 1 unit of C is added to the program. On the other hand, a negative rate of substitution, for example, ⑤, indicates an increase in S_F, that is, ½ hour freed, that occurs if 1 unit of S_A is added to the program.

THESE EIGHT ELEMENTS
REPRESENT MARGINAL
RATES OF
SUBSTITUTION

▮ THE Z_j ROW (ELEMENTS ⑥, ⑩, ⑭, and ⑱)

We turn now to an explanation of the elements in the Z_j row; these represent the loss of profit that results from the addition of 1 unit of the variable heading the column.

⑥ Adding 1 unit of S_A results in two changes: (1) T is decreased by ¼ unit (see ④); (2) S_F is increased by ½ unit (½ hour freed; see ⑤). How much profit would we lose if these two changes took place? Since profit per unit of T is $8 and T is decreased by ¼ unit, the profit lost from this change would be $8 × ¼ = $2. Because profit per unit of S_F is $0, the increase in S_F by ½ unit results in no gain ($0 × ½ = $0). The *total* profit lost, therefore, is the sum of the two changes, or $2 + $0 = $2.

EXPLAINING THE FOUR
ENTRIES IN THE $C_j - Z_j$
ROW OF TABLE 9-12

The same reasoning process applies to the other elements of the Z_j row. We want to know (1) the changes which occur when 1 unit of the variable heading the column is added, (2) the loss of profit from each change, and (3) the total profit lost, the sum of the losses of each change.

⑩ With the addition of 1 unit of S_F:

Change 1

No change in T (see ⑧)	0	
Profit per unit of T	× $8	
Loss		$0

Change 2

1 unit of S_F given up (see ⑨)	1	
Profit per unit of S_F	× $0	
Loss		0
Total loss		$0

⑭ With the addition of 1 unit of T:

Change 1

1 unit of T given up (see ⑫)	1	
Profit per unit of T	× $8	
Loss		$8

Change 2

No change in S_F (see ⑬)	0	
Profit per unit of S_F	× $0	
Loss		0
Total loss		$8

⑱ With the addition of 1 unit of C:

Change 1

½ unit of T given up (see ⑯)	½	
Profit per unit of T	× $8	
Loss		$4

Change 2

3 units of S_F given up (see ⑰)	3	
Profit per unit of S_F	× $0	
Loss		0
Total loss		$4

▌ THE $C_j - Z_j$ ROW (ELEMENTS ⑲, ⑮, ⑪, AND ⑦)

EXPLAINING THE FOUR
ENTRIES IN THE $C_j - Z_j$
ROW OF TABLE 9-12
Each positive number in the $C_j - Z_j$ row represents the net profit obtainable if 1 unit of the variable heading that column were added to the solution. The following examples help to illustrate this point.

⑲ The positive number 2 represents the net profit if 1 unit of C (1 chair) were added:

Total profit per unit of C	$6
Less total profit per unit lost (see ⑱)	$- \underline{4}$
Net profit	$2

So long as there is a positive dollar figure in the $C_j - Z_j$ row, further improvement in profit can and should be made, because for each unit of C added, we can increase the profit of $120 by $2. Element ② (18 hours) and element ⑰ (3 hours per chair) indicate that $18/3$, or 6, chairs can be added.

⑮ Total profit per unit of T	$8
Total profit per unit lost (see ⑭)	$- \underline{8}$
Net profit	$0

For every unit of T added, total profit will not change. The explanation is that we are already producing as many tables as possible under the time restrictions in assembly. If we add 1 unit of T to the solution, we must give up 1 unit of T. Adding 1 unit of T results in a profit increase of $8, but giving up 1 unit of T results in a profit decrease of $8. Thus nothing is added to total profit.

⑪ Total profit per unit of S_F	$0
Total profit per unit lost (see ⑩)	$- \underline{0}$
Net profit	$0

Each unit of S_F added to the program will not change total profit. Again the explanation is that assembly limits the production of tables to 15. Therefore adding 1 unit of S_F has no effect on T (see ⑧). Total profit, then, cannot be increased by adding any units of S_F.

⑦ Total profit per unit of S_A	$0
Less total profit per unit lost (see ⑥)	$- \underline{2}$
Net loss	$-$2

A negative number (a net loss) in the $C_j - Z_j$ row indicates the decrease in total profit if 1 unit of the variable heading that column were added to the product mix. In this case, each unit of S_A added to the program will decrease total profit by $2. Why? From ④ we found that for every unit of S_A added, $1/4$ table would have to be given up. Profit per unit of S_A is $0, but profit per table is $8. So each S_A added would result in a $2 loss ($8 × $1/4$ = $2).

5 Minimization problems and equal-to and greater-than-or-equal-to constraints

Up to this point, our discussion of the simplex method has been limited to problems having only less-than-or-equal-to constraints and whose objective function was to be maximized. But the procedure can be used to solve more general linear programs involving objective functions that are to be minimized, or equality constraints, or greater-than-or-equal-to constraints. We will use Jeff Smith's cost minimization problem, first discussed on pages 355–356, to illustrate how this is done.

For convenience, we repeat here the form of the problem after the slack variables had been added to the two departments' time constraints and the surplus variables had been subtracted from the two minimum production constraints.

Minimize:

$$\text{Cost} = 20T + 8C + 0S_A + 0S_F + 0S_T + 0S_C$$

Subject to:

$$4T + 2C + S_A + 0S_F + 0S_T + 0S_C = 60$$
$$2T + 4C + 0S_A + S_F + 0S_T + 0S_C = 48$$
$$T + 0C + 0S_A + 0S_F - S_T + 0S_C = 2$$
$$0T + C + 0S_A + 0S_F + 0S_T - S_C = 4$$

$$\text{All variables} \geq 0$$

AN INITIAL SOLUTION WITH ARTIFICIAL VARIABLES

Remember from the Dimensions, Ltd., profit maximization problem that we needed to find an initial solution for starting the simplex algorithm. We started there by making no tables or chairs, letting the slack variables, S_A and S_F, be the initial basic (that is, in-the-solution) variables. Although that solution was ridiculous profitwise, it did nonetheless serve as a starting point or base for improvement.

In this cost minimization problem, we once again need a starting solution. It too will be ridiculous costwise. However, it will be a point of departure in our search for the lowest-cost production plan.

Suppose we decide to let $T = 0$ and $C = 0$ as a first solution; does this solution satisfy all the constraints?

$$4T + 2C + S_A + 0S_F + 0S_T + 0S_C = 60$$
$$0 + 0 + S_A + 0 + 0 + 0 = 60$$
$$S_A = 60$$

The first constraint will be satisfied if we set S_A equal to 60.

$$2T + 4C + 0S_A + S_F + 0S_T + 0S_C = 48$$
$$0 + 0 + 0 + S_F + 0 + 0 = 48$$
$$S_F = 48$$

The second constraint will be satisfied if we set S_F equal to 48.

$$T + 0C + 0S_A + 0S_F - S_T + 0S_C = 2$$
$$0 + 0 + 0 + 0 - S_T + 0 = 2$$

$$-S_T = 2$$

To satisfy the third constraint, we would have to set S_T equal to -2, which is not feasible, since all variables must be nonnegative.

$$0T + C + 0S_A + 0S_F + 0S_T - S_C = 4$$
$$0 + 0 + 0 + 0 + 0 - S_C = 4$$

$$-S_C = 4$$

To satisfy the fourth constraint, we would have to set S_C equal to -4, which is not feasible, since all variables must be nonnegative.

So as it stands now, we cannot start out by setting the structural variables (T and C in this problem) to zero and letting the slacks and surplusses be the variables in the initial solution, because that would be infeasible.

$T = 0$ AND $C = 0$ IS NOT FEASIBLE

We will get around this difficulty by introducing some additional variables into the problem in order to get started. These new variables are called *artificial variables*, because they constitute a trick (or *artifice*) to let us get started. We will change the original third constraint ($T \geqslant 2$) to

$$T + A_T \geqslant 2$$

by adding in the artificial variable A_T. We then convert this to an equation by subtracting the surplus variable S_T:

$$T + A_T - S_F = 2$$

Just what is A_T? It can be thought of as a very expensive substitute table (say \$1000 per unit) which Dimensions, Ltd., could go out and buy instead of producing itself. Because these substitute tables are so expensive, clearly the optimal solution for Jeff will not include any of them. Now if we set $T = 0$ and $C = 0$, we can satisfy the third constraint by setting $A_T = 2$.

EXPENSIVE
ARTIFICIAL TABLES

In a similar fashion, we will introduce another artificial variable (A_C, representing expensive substitute chairs) into the original fourth constraint to get

ARTIFICIAL CHAIRS

$$C + A_C - S_C = 4$$

With $T = 0$ and $C = 0$, we can satisfy this constraint by setting $A_C = 4$. So now all four constraints have been satisfied. In this way, we start out with a solution involving the artificial tables and chairs that is easy to obtain, but the optimal solution will involve only the real tables made by Dimensions, Ltd.

We stated that the artificial variables A_T and A_C would be assigned a very high cost, \$1000 per unit. In many problems, 1000 will not be large enough to prevent the artificial variables from being used in the optimal solution. To avoid having to work with extremely large numbers, we let the letter M represent a very large number; this will simplify the calculations in the simplex method. The final form of Jeff Smith's problem is now

Minimize:

$$\text{Cost} = 20T + 8C + 0S_A + 0S_F + MA_T + MA_C + 0S_T + 0S_C$$

Subject to:

$$4T + 2C + S_A + 0S_F + 0A_T + 0A_C + 0S_T + 0S_C = 60$$

$$2T + 4C + 0S_A + S_F + 0A_T + 0A_C + 0S_T + 0S_C = 48$$

$$T + 0C + 0S_A + 0S_F + A_T + 0A_C - S_T + 0S_C = 2$$

$$0T + C + 0S_A + 0S_F + 0A_T + A_C + 0S_T - S_C = 4$$

$$\text{All variables} \geq 0$$

■ ARTIFICIAL VARIABLES IN GENERAL

Before we apply the simplex method to Jeff Smith's problem, let's look at the general procedure for getting an initial solution. *Although this procedure may seem somewhat formidable, remember that you will only have to use it if you are doing the simplex algorithm by hand. LPSBA and most other commercially available computer codes for linear programming do this procedure automatically, so you won't have to worry about these details.*

Suppose we agree to always set up our linear programming problems so that the *right-hand-side coefficients* (the numbers specifying resource availabilities, minimum requirements, and so forth) are always nonnegative. This is easy to accomplish:

1 If an equality constraint (say $X + 3Y - 2Z = -7$) has a negative right-hand side, just multiply through by -1 to get an equivalent equality constraint with a positive right-hand side ($-X - 3Y + 2Z = 7$).

2 If an inequality constraint (say $2P - Q - 4R + 6S \geq -5$) has a negative right-hand side, just multiply through by -1 to get an equivalent inequality constraint, with the direction of the inequality reversed ($-2P + Q + 4R - 6S \leq 5$).

Once the problem has been put into this form, proceed by

1 Adding slack variables (with objective coefficients of 0) to each less-than-or-equal-to constraint

2 Subtracting surplus variables (with objective coefficients of 0) from each greater-than-or-equal-to constraint

3 Adding artificial variables (with objective coefficients of $+M$ in minimization problems and $-M$ in maximization problems) to all constraints that were originally greater-than-or-equal-to constraints or equal-to constraints.

4 Setting all structural and surplus variables to zero and letting the slack and artificial variables be in the initial solution.

FIRST SIMPLEX TABLEAU FOR JEFF SMITH'S PROBLEM

Now we are ready to use the simplex method to solve Jeff Smith's cost minimization problem. The first simplex tableau is shown in Table 9-13. The entries in the Z_j row were computed exactly as before:

$$Z_{total}: \quad 0(60) + 0(48) + M(\ 2) + M(\ 4) = \quad 6M$$

$$Z_T: \quad 0(\ 4) + 0(\ 2) + M(\ 1) + M(\ 0) = \quad M$$

$$Z_C: \quad 0(\ 2) + 0(\ 4) + M(\ 0) + M(\ 1) = \quad M$$

$$Z_{S_A}: \quad 0(\ 1) + 0(\ 0) + M(\ 0) + M(\ 0) = \quad 0$$

$$Z_{S_F}: \quad 0(\ 0) + 0(\ 1) + M(\ 0) + M(\ 0) = \quad 0$$

$$Z_{A_T}: \quad 0(\ 0) + 0(\ 0) + M(\ 1) + M(\ 0) = \quad M$$

$$Z_{A_C}: \quad 0(\ 0) + 0(\ 0) + M(\ 0) + M(\ 1) = \quad M$$

$$Z_{S_T}: \quad 0(\ 0) + 0(\ 0) + M(-1) + M(\ 0) = \quad -M$$

$$Z_{S_C}: \quad 0(\ 0) + 0(\ 0) + M(\ 0) + M(-1) = \quad -M$$

Note that the total cost of the first solution, $\$6M$, is extremely high. Since the objective is to minimize costs, the optimal column is found by selecting that column which has the most negative value in the $C_j - Z_j$ row (that column whose value will decrease costs most rapidly).

TABLE 9-13
Initial simplex tableau: Jeff Smith's problem

C_j	Product mix	Quantity	20 T	8 C	0 S_A	0 S_F	M A_T	M A_C	0 S_T	0 S_C
0	S_A	60	4	2	1	0	0	0	0	0
0	S_F	48	2	4	0	1	0	0	0	0
M	A_T	2	1	0	0	0	1	0	−1	0
M	A_C	4	0	1	0	0	0	1	0	−1
	Z_j	6M	M	M	0	0	M	M	−M	−M
	$C_j - Z_j$		20 − M	8 − M	0	0	0	0	M	M

Optimal column ↑   Replaced row →

FINDING THE
OPTIMAL COLUMN

How do you find the most negative of a bunch of expressions composed of terms involving M and terms that don't involve M? First you find the expression in which M has the most negative coefficient. If there is only one such expression, then you have found the optimal column. However, if there is a tie (as there is in Table 9-13, where the T column has $C_j - Z_j = 20 - M$ and the C column has $C_j - Z_j = 8 - M$), the tie should be broken by choosing from the tied expressions the one with the most negative term that doesn't involve M. (If, as in our example, the terms not involving M are all nonnegative, then you break the tie by choosing from the tied expressions the one with the least positive term not involving M.) Applying this rule to our example, we see that C is the optimal column.

FINDING THE
REPLACED ROW

Since $^{60}\!/_2 = 30$ (in the S_A row), $^{48}\!/_4 = 12$ (in the S_F row), and $^4\!/_1 = 4$ (in the A_C row), the A_C row is designated as the replaced row. (We did not look at the A_T row in determining the replaced row because our rule specified: find the smallest of the ratios of quantity-column values to the corresponding optimal-column values, considering only those rows in which the optimal-column values were greater than zero.)

COMPUTING
THE NEXT TABLEAU

Now that the optimal column and the replaced row have been determined, we compute the next tableau (shown in Table 9-14) just as before:

1 The replacing row in the next tableau is the replaced row of the current tableau, with each element divided by the intersectional element of the replaced row.

2 The other constraint rows of the next tableau are obtained using the formula:

$$\begin{pmatrix} \text{Elements in} \\ \text{old row} \end{pmatrix} - \begin{pmatrix} \text{intersectional} & & \text{corresponding} \\ \text{element of} & \times & \text{elements in} \\ \text{old row} & & \text{replacing row} \end{pmatrix} = \begin{pmatrix} \text{Elements in} \\ \text{new row} \end{pmatrix}$$

3 The entries in the Z_j row are computed by multiplying each entry in a column by the corresponding entry in the C_j column and then adding up these products.

TABLE 9-14
Second simplex tableau: Jeff Smith's problem

C_j	Product mix	Quantity	20 T	8 C	0 S_A	0 S_F	M A_T	M A_C	0 S_T	0 S_C
0	S_A	52	4	0	1	0	0	-2	0	2
0	S_F	32	2	0	0	1	0	-4	0	4
M	A_T	2	1	0	0	0	1	0	-1	0 ←
8	C	4	0	1	0	0	0	1	0	-1
	Z_j	$2M+32$	M	8	0	0	M	8	$-M$	-8
	$C_j - Z_j$		20-M	0	0	0	0	$-8+M$	M	8

Optimal column ↑   Replaced row

4 The entries in the $C_j - Z_j$ row are obtained by subtracting the entries in the Z_j row from the corresponding entries in the C_j row.

Continuing as before, we find that the optimal column is now the T column and that the A_T row is the replaced row. We perform the second pivot to obtain the third simplex tableau shown in Table 9-15.

Since there are no negative entries in the $C_j - Z_j$ row of the third tableau, we see that the solution there is optimal. Thus to minimize total cost, Dimensions, Ltd., should make two tables and four chairs. The basic slack variables, S_A and S_F, tell us that if they follow this production plan, then there will be 44 hours left over in the assembly department and 28 hours left over in the finishing department. Notice that the artificial variables, A_T and A_C, which enabled us to get started, do not appear in the final solution.

■ SUMMARY OF STEPS IN THE GENERAL SIMPLEX ALGORITHM

In summary form, the steps involved in the general simplex algorithm are as follows:

1 Set up the problem constraints ($\leq$ inequalities, $\geq$ inequalities, and/or equations).

2 Convert any inequalities to equations by adding slack variables to $\leq$ constraints and subtracting surplus variables from $\geq$ constraints.

3 Add artificial variables to all constraints that were originally $\geq$ inequalities or equations. Give the artificial variables objective coefficients of $+M$ in minimization problems and $-M$ in maximization problems.

4 Enter the resulting equations in the simplex tableau.

5 Calculate the Z_j and $C_j - Z_j$ values for this solution.

6 Determine the entering variable (optimal column) by choosing the one with the largest negative $C_j - Z_j$ value in minimization problems and the largest positive $C_j - Z_j$ value in maximization problems.

7 Determine the row to be replaced by dividing quantity-column values by their corresponding optimal-column values and choosing the smallest non-

TABLE 9-15
Third simplex tableau (optimal solution): Jeff Smith's problem

C_j	Product mix	Quantity	20 T	8 C	0 S_A	0 S_F	M A_T	M A_C	0 S_T	0 S_C
0	S_A	44	0	0	1	0	-4	-2	4	2
0	S_F	28	0	0	0	1	-2	-4	2	4
20	T	2	1	0	0	0	1	0	-1	0
8	C	4	0	1	0	0	0	1	0	-1
	Z_j	72	20	8	0	0	20	8	-20	-8
	$C_j - Z_j$		0	0	0	0	$-20 + M$	$-8 + M$	20	8

negative quotient. (That is, only compute the ratios for rows whose elements in the optimal column are greater than zero; for example, omit ratios like 160/0 and 15/−5.)

8 Compute the values for the replacing row.

9 Compute the values for the remaining rows.

10 Calculate the Z_j and $C_j - Z_j$ values for this solution.

11 If there is a negative $C_j - Z_j$ remaining in a minimization problem, or a positive $C_j - Z_j$ remaining in a maximization problem, return to step 6.

12 If there is no negative $C_j - Z_j$ remaining in a minimization problem, or no positive $C_j - Z_j$ remaining in maximization problem, the optimal solution has been obtained.

6 Some technical issues in the simplex method

In Section 3 of Chapter 8, "Some technical issues in linear programming," we introduced—using graphic methods—some problems encountered in solving linear programs. Here we shall consider three of those issues—*infeasibility, unboundedness,* and *alternative optima*. We shall also discuss the problem of *degeneracy*.

INFEASIBILITY

PROBLEM IS
INFEASIBLE IF WE
CAN'T GET ALL
ARTIFICIAL VARIABLES
OUT OF THE SOLUTION

How does the simplex method indicate that a problem is infeasible? **If, when you reach the final solution, one or more artificial variables are still positive, then there is *no* feasible solution to the problem.** Why is this true? Remember that the artificial variables which we introduce into the problem to get started are given *very unfavorable* objective function coefficients, $+M$ in minimization problems, $-M$ in maximization problems. Hence any solution not containing the artificial variables (that is, any *feasible solution* to the original problem) will have a better objective function value than any solution with at least one artificial variable still positive. Thus we see that if the algorithm terminates with an artificial variable still positive, there cannot be any solutions in which all of the artificial variables are zero, and so this shows that the original problem is infeasible.

UNBOUNDEDNESS

WHEN THERE IS NO
CONSTRAINT ON
THE SOLUTION

When we are using the simplex method, how do we recognize unboundedness? Look back for a moment to page 391; there we illustrated how to determine which variable was to be replaced. Our rule was to *select the row with the smaller or smallest nonnegative ratio*. **If there is *no* nonnegative ratio—or if all the ratios are of the form, say, 60/0—then we know the solution is unbounded.** Why is this true? If the ratio *is* negative, this means we "get back" something each time we introduce a unit of the new variable; thus we could conceivably keep introducing that variable forever. If the ratio is of the form 60/0, this can be thought of as meaning that an infinite quantity of the entering variable could be introduced. In either case, these are signals that the solution is

C_j	Product mix	Quantity	8 T	4 C	0 S_A	0 S_F
8	T	12	1	0	1/3	−1/6
4	C	6	0	1	−1/6	1/3 ←
	Z_j	120	8	4	2	0
	$C_j − Z_j$		0	0	−2	0

Optimal column ———┘ ↑ Replaced row

TABLE 9-16
Final simplex tableau
(optimal solution):
illustrating alternative
optima

unbounded, and that generally means we have incorrectly formulated the
problem.

ALTERNATIVE OPTIMA

Suppose we changed the profit margins of the tables and chairs in the original
Dimensions, Ltd., problem to $8 per table and $4 per chair. Then the final
tableau for this problem would be the tableau shown in Table 9-16. We still
have the same optimal solution as before (12 tables and 6 chairs), but the
optimal profit has been decreased from $132 to $120 (because each of the 6
chairs now contributes $2 less profit).

The solution in Table 9-16 is optimal because there are no positive entries
in the $C_j − Z_j$ row. However, notice that even though S_F is not in the solution,
its entry in the $C_j − Z_j$ row is zero. Suppose we bring S_F into the solution (so
its column is the optimal column). Then the C row is the replaced row, and
the next tableau is given in Table 9-17.

There are no negative entries in the $C_j − Z_j$ row in Table 9-17, so it, too,
gives an optimal solution to the problem. Making 15 tables and no chairs
(which uses up all 60 available hours in assembly but leaves 18 slack hours
in finishing) also produces the optimal profit of $120. What's the general
rule?

ZERO $C_j − Z_j$ VALUES
IN OPTIMAL TABLEAU
INDICATE ALTERNATIVE
OPTIMAL SOLUTIONS

**Whenever a non-basic variable (that is, a variable which is not in the
solution) has a zero entry in the $C_j − Z_j$ row of an optimal tableau, then
bringing that variable into the solution will produce a solution which is
also optimal.**

TABLE 9-17
Simplex tableau
showing a second
optimal solution

C_j	Product mix	Quantity	8 T	4 C	0 S_A	0 S_F
8	T	15	1	1/2	1/4	0
0	S_F	18	0	3	−1/2	1
	Z_j	120	8	4	2	0
	$C_j − Z_j$		0	0	−2	0

This is the way in which the simplex algorithm indicates the presence of alternative optimal solutions.

DEGENERACY

Degeneracy refers to a condition sometimes encountered in solving a linear programming problem. It sounds much worse than it actually is, and there are simple procedures which, if used properly, will make the issue a fairly minor one.

To demonstrate what degeneracy is, let us consider the following product-mix problem involving two products and three departments:

Maximize:

$$5X_1 + 8X_2$$

Subject to:

$$4X_1 + 6X_2 \leqslant 24$$
$$2X_1 + X_2 \leqslant 18$$
$$3X_1 + 9X_2 \leqslant 36$$
$$X_1, X_2 \geqslant 0$$

The first two simplex tableaus for this problem are illustrated in Table 9-18. In the first tableau, the values in the $C_j - Z_j$ row indicate that X_2 is the variable which will enter the mix in the second solution. However, when we compute the ratios to determine the replaced row ($24/6 = 4$ in the S_1 row, $18/1 = 18$ in the S_2 row, and $36/9 = 4$ in the S_3 row), we find that we have

TIES IN RATIOS DETERMINING REPLACED ROW

a tie between the first and third rows. To get the second tableau, we arbitrarily broke the tie and chose the third row as the row to be replaced.

Look at the second tableau in Table 9-18. Notice that S_1 *has the value 0, even though it is one of the variables in the solution.* Whenever a variable in the solution has the value 0, that variable and the solution are said to be *degenerate*. And whenever there is a tie in the ratios determining the row to be replaced, the next tableau will give a degenerate solution. (Check for yourself that the second tableau would also have been degenerate if we had chosen the first row of the first tableau as the row to be replaced.)

In the second tableau in Table 9-18, we see that the optimal column is the X_1 column and that the first row (the row with the degeneracy) is to be replaced (since the ratios are $0/2 = 0$ in the S_1 row, $14/(5/3) = 42/5$ in the S_2 row, and $4/(1/3) = 12$ in the X_2 row). The third tableau (shown in Table 9-19) turns out to be optimal for our problem. However, notice that the

OBJECTIVE FUNCTION VALUE DOESN'T CHANGE

objective function value in the third tableau ($32) is exactly the same as the objective function value in the second tableau. In fact, *whenever the simplex algorithm pivots in a degenerate row, the objective function value doesn't change in the next tableau.* And that is the reason why we worry about degeneracy.

Whenever we pivot in a nondegenerate row (a row corresponding to a variable in the solution, but with a strictly positive value), the objective function value increases in the next tableau (or decreases if we are solving a minimization

The First Tableau

C_j	Product mix	Quantity	5 X_1	8 X_2	0 S_1	0 S_2	0 S_3
0	S_1	24	4	6	1	0	0
0	S_2	18	2	1	0	1	0
0	S_3	36	3	9	0	0	1
	Z_j	0	0	0	0	0	0
	$C_j - Z_j$		5	8	0	0	0

↑———— Optimal column

The Second Tableau (after X_2 replaced S_3 in the solution)

C_j	Product mix	Quantity	5 X_1	8 X_2	0 S_1	0 S_2	0 S_3
0	S_1	0	2	0	1	0	$-2/3$
0	S_2	14	$5/3$	0	0	1	$-1/9$
8	X_2	4	$1/3$	1	0	0	$1/9$
	Z_j	32	$8/3$	8	0	0	$8/9$
	$C_j - Z$		$7/3$	0	0	0	$-8/9$

↑———Optimal column

TABLE 9-18
Problem illustrating
degeneracy

problem). And if the objective function value always increases, we can't ever repeat a tableau that we have already seen. However, if the problem is degenerate, we could *theoretically* have a sequence of tableaus, all with the same objective function value, that takes us back to a tableau we have already seen. In this case, the simplex algorithm would have *cycled* and would now continue to repeat that cycle forever, *never finding the optimal solution to that problem.*

CYCLING

Although degenerate problems don't always cycle (our example in Tables 9-18 and 9-19 didn't), the fact that they can means that there *are* linear programming problems that our simplex algorithm won't be able to solve. Examples which do exhibit cycling have been constructed, but real life problems almost never cycle. Furthermore, there are rules for breaking ties (like the one we encountered in Table 9-18) which will guarantee that cycling won't occur. However, these rules are beyond the scope of this book, and since cycling occurs so exceedingly rarely, we simply won't worry about it.

Although we have presented all the details of the simplex algorithm so that you can have an appreciation for how it works, we remind you once

C_j	Product mix	Quantity	5 X_1	8 X_2	0 S_1	0 S_2	0 S_3
5	X_1	0	1	0	1/2	0	−1/3
0	S_2	14	0	0	−5/6	1	4/9
8	X_2	4	0	1	−1/6	0	2/9
	Z_j	32	5	8	7/6	0	1/9
	$C_j − Z_j$		0	0	−7/6	0	−1/9

TABLE 9-19
Problem illustrating degeneracy: optimal solution

again that for all but the most trivial problems you will be utilizing a computer to solve linear programs.

7 Glossary

Algorithm A computational procedure for solving a class of problems. The *simplex algorithm* is used to solve linear programming problems.

Artificial variable A computational device used in linear programming to achieve an initial solution to the problem.

C_j column A column in the simplex tableau which contains the profit or cost per unit for the variable in the solution.

$C_j − Z_j$ row The row containing the net benefit or loss occasioned by bringing one unit of a variable into the solution of a linear programming problem.

Degeneracy A condition resulting from a tie in the ratios determining the replaced row, which produces a basic variable with a zero value. If degeneracy is present, it is *theoretically possible* for the simplex algorithm to cycle and never find an optimal solution. In practice, cycling rarely occurs.

Intersectional elements Elements which are common to both the optimal column and the rows representing variables in the solution.

Iterative process A step-by-step process following a standard pattern.

Optimal column That column in any solution to a maximizing problem which has the largest positive value in the $C_j − Z_j$ row or which has the largest negative value in a minimizing problem.

Pivoting The process of going from one simplex tableau to the next.

Product-mix column The column containing all the variables in a solution in the simplex tableau.

Quantity column The column in a simplex tableau indicating the quantities of the variables that are in a solution.

Reduced costs The entries of the $C_j − Z_j$ row.

Replaced row A row in the simplex tableau which is replaced by the variable entering the new solution.

Right-hand-side coefficients The numbers on the right-hand side of problem constraints, representing available quantities of resources, minimum production levels, and so forth.

Simplex tableau A tabular format for organizing the data of a linear programming problem and performing the computations of the simplex algorithm.

Variable column The column of entries under a heading variable in the simplex tableau.

Z_j **row** The row containing the opportunity costs of bringing one unit of a variable into the solution of a linear programming problem.

8 Exercises

9-1 The Stevens Fertilizer Company markets two types of fertilizer which are manufactured in two departments. Type A contributes $3 per ton, and type B contributes $4 per ton.

| | Hours per ton | | Maximum hours |
Department	Type A	Type B	worked per week
1	2	3	40
2	3	3	~~75~~ 45

Set up a linear programming problem to determine how much of the two fertilizers to make in order to maximize profits. Use the simplex algorithm to solve your problem.

9-2 In step 1 of the simplex method, we decide which new variable is to be introduced in the product mix in the very next tableau. This is done by picking the variable which will add the most per unit to profit in a maximization problem. When you solved Exercise 9-1, you went from your initial, or first, tableau to the second by selecting variable B (associated with type B fertilizer) to be introduced. Starting with your initial tableau, make a pivot to the second tableau, but instead of selecting variable B to enter, select variable A (associated with type A fertilizer). On the basis of your results, what can you conclude about step 1 of the simplex procedure?

9-3 In step 2 of the simplex method, we decide which old variable is to be replaced in the product mix in the very next tableau. This is done by selecting the row with the smallest nonnegative ratio. When you solved Exercise 9-1, you went from your second tableau to the third by selecting variable B to be replaced by variable A; because of the two variables in the solution, B and S_2, the row for B had the smaller ratio. Let's explore what happens if you violate the procedure of step 2. Starting with your second tableau, bring in variable A, but instead of replacing B, replace variable S_2. On the basis of your results, what can you conclude about the role of step 2 in making sure none of the constraints to a linear programming problem is violated?

9-4 Lisa's Craft Shoppe manufactures two products in two departments. Product X_1 contributes $6 and takes 6 hours in department 1 and 6 hours in department 2. Product X_2 contributes $14 and takes 8 hours in department 1 and 12 hours in department 2. Department 1 has a capacity of 38 hours, and department 2 has a capacity of 42 hours. Indicate the maximum production level in units and the maximum dollar contribution production level, and show the dollar contribution difference between the two.

9-5 Becky Grines is planning to produce and sell a new flea powder for dogs which will contain these chemicals: alzene, bartomel, and cathorene. She can use any blend of the chemicals so long as the amount of alzene is no less than 3 parts by weight to 2 parts of bartomel and cathorene combined. In addition, the weight of bartomel in the blend must be equal to or greater than the weight of cathorene. Costs of the three chemicals are $20 per pound for alzene, $15 per pound for bartomel, and $10 per pound for cathorene. Define the objective function and constraints so that it can be solved with linear programming. Show how the problem would appear after augmenting with required slack, surplus, and artificial variables.

9-6 The Statewide Trucking Company needs to haul 20 tons of fertilizer from Masena to Pottsdam. They can use either or both of two types of trucks—model M or model P. Each model M truck is capable of hauling a load of 10 tons at a cost of $300 for the trip. Each model P truck can haul 5 tons at a cost of $100 for the trip. Because of prior commitments, only two model P trucks can be made available for the scheduled haul. Use the simplex method to determine how many of each type of truck should be scheduled to haul the 20 tons at minimal cost.

9-7 Solve the following linear programming problem using the simplex method:

Objective, minimize: $\qquad Z = 2X + 7Y - 3W$

Subject to: $\qquad\qquad\qquad 3X + 2W = 9$
$$2X + 3Y \geqslant 4$$
$$X + Y \geqslant 1$$
$$X, Y, W \geqslant 0$$

9-8 Solve the following problem using the simplex method:

Maximize: $\qquad 15X_1 + 10X_2$

Subject to: $\qquad\qquad 5X_2 \leqslant 25$
$$2X_1 + 1X_2 \geqslant 4$$
$$X_1, X_2 \geqslant 0$$

What conclusions can you reach about this problem?

9-9 Solve the following problem using the simplex method:

Maximize: $\qquad 3A + 4B$

Subject to: $\qquad 2A + 3B \leqslant 6$
$$1A + 2B = 20$$
$$A, B \geqslant 0$$

What conclusions can you draw about this problem?

9-10 The following is a tableau for a maximization problem:

C_i	Product mix	Quantity	8 X_1	6 X_2	0 S_1	0 S_2	0 S_3
8	X_1	4 units/day	1	.75	2.5	0	0
0	S_2	4 hr/day	0	.05	-.5	1	0
0	S_3	1.4 hr/day	0	.175	-.75	0	1
	Z_i	$32/day	8	6	20	0	0
	$C_i - Z_i$		0	0	-20	0	0

a. Is this an optimal solution?
b. Is there more than one optimal solution to this problem? If so, find another one.
c. What is the optimal objective value?

9-11 Solve the following problem using the simplex method:

Maximize: $D + 2F$

Subject to: $D + 3F \leqslant 50$
$6D + 9F \leqslant 150$
$3D + 8F \leqslant 120$
$D, F \geqslant 0$

What conclusions can you reach about this problem?

9-12 Consider the following linear programming problem:

Maximize: $5A + 6B$

Subject to: $2A - 3B \leqslant 12$

$A \qquad \leqslant 5$

$A, B \geqslant 0$

You can see by inspecting the constraints that the variable B can take on infinitely large values without violating the constraints. Attempt to solve the problem with the simplex method and take note of what happens.

9-13 Consider the following linear programming problem:

Maximize: $6X + 8Y$

Subject to: $2X + Y \geqslant 20$

$3X + 4Y \leqslant 10$

$X, Y \geqslant 0$

If you were to graph this problem, you would find that there are no nonnegative values for the variables X and Y which satisfy both of the constraints. Try to solve this problem with the simplex method and observe what happens to the artificial variable which you introduce into the $\geqslant$ constraint.

9-14 Use the simplex algorithm to find at least two optimal solutions to the following linear programming problem.

Minimize: $3X + 4Y$

Subject to: $3X - 2Y \leqslant 30$

$-X + 2Y \leqslant 40$

$6X + 8Y \geqslant 240$
$X, Y \geqslant 0$

9-15 Use the simplex algorithm to solve Exercise 8-1.

9-16 Use the simplex algorithm to solve Exercise 8-3.

9-17 Use the simplex algorithm to solve Exercise 8-6.

9-18 Use the simplex algorithm to solve Exercise 8-7.

9-19 Use the simplex algorithm to solve Exercise 8-10.

9-20 Use the simplex algorithm to solve Exercise 8-18.

9 Chapter concepts quiz

Fill in the
Blanks

9-1 If the value of a variable in the solution is zero, we say that we have a _____ solution. In such an instance, _____ of the simplex algorithm may result if successive pivots do not produce an improvement in the objective value of the problem.

9-2 If there are equality constraints or greater-than-or-equal-to constraints, it is necessary to add a(n) _____ variable to each such constraint to find an initial solution for the simplex method. In a maximization problem, these new variables are assigned arbitrarily _____ cost coefficients in the objective function.

9-3 In the simplex tableau, the _____ column contains the variables which are currently in the solution; the values of these variables can be read from the _____ column.

9-4 Because it is repeated over and over in a systematic fashion, the simplex algorithm is known as a(n) _____ process; each repetition is known as a(n) _____ and results in a(n) _____ solution.

9-5 The _____ contains the objective-function coefficients of the variables in the current solution; the _____ row indicates the net profit (or cost) resulting from adding one unit of the variable heading the column to the solution. The choice of the _____ column at each iteration depends on the values in this row.

9-6 The current value of the objective function for any simplex tableau is found in the _____ row and the _____ column.

9-7 When a new variable is introduced into the product-mix column of a simplex tableau, it is placed in the _____ row.

9-8 If an artificial variable is positive in the optimal simplex tableau, the original problem is _____.

9-9 Intersectional elements are found in the _____ column.

9-10 To go from one tableau to the next, the _____ row is determined by finding the _____ ratio of elements in the product-mix column divided by the corresponding positive elements in the _____ column. If there is a tie in finding this ratio, the next solution will be _____.

True-False

9-11 Each constraint, excluding nonnegativity constraints, in the mathematical formulation of a linear program generates one row in the simplex tableau.   **T F**

9-12 Every inequality constraint in a linear program adds exactly one variable to the problem.   **T F**

9-13 Every variable which does not appear in the product-mix column for a given simplex tableau has a value of zero in that solution.   **T F**

9-14 Every simplex iteration in a maximization problem replaces a variable **T F**
in the solution with another variable which has a larger unit profit as shown
in the C_j row.

9-15 Every feasible solution found by the simplex algorithm corresponds to **T F**
an extreme point of the feasible region of the graphic method.

9-16 The substitution rates in the body of the simplex tableau denote the **T F**
number of units of the quantity corresponding to that row which must be
sacrificed to add to the solution one unit of the quantity heading that column.

9-17 Since the Z_j row gives the loss of profit (in a maximization problem) **T F**
resulting from adding one unit of the column variable to the product mix,
we can select the best variable to add to our solution by choosing the most
negative Z_j value.

9-18 Artificial variables are added to a linear programming problem to aid **T F**
in finding an initial solution. All of the artificial variables are included in the
initial solution.

9-19 In the simplex method, optimality is signaled by the presence of all **T F**
negative values in the $C_j - Z_j$ row for a minimization problem and all positive
values in that row for a maximization problem.

9-20 All the rules and procedures of the simplex method are identical **T F**
whether solving a maximization or a minimization problem.

9-21 After slack, surplus, and artificial variables have been added to a linear **T F**
programming problem, if a constraint has the form

$$P + C + A_1 = 720$$

we know that the original constraint was a greater-than-or-equal-to inequality.

9-22 One difference between solving a maximization problem and a min- **T F**
imization problem is that the replaced row in the former is the row with the
smallest nonnegative quotient while in the latter, it is the row with the largest
nonnegative quotient.

9-23 Surplus, slack, and artificial variables are all included in the product- **T F**
mix column of the first simplex tableau.

9-24 The values for the replacing row must be computed before computing **T F**
the values for the remaining rows.

9-25 A linear programming problem is unbounded if there are any surplus **T F**
variables in the solution in the final simplex tableau.

9-26 If at optimality the slack variable S_R, corresponding to a less-than-or-equal-to   Multiple
inequality constraint for some resource R, is in the solution, then we know: Choice
    a. The problem was infeasible.
    b. All of resource R was not used up in the optimal solution.
    c. All of resource R was used in the optimal solution.
    d. A better solution could be achieved if resource R were increased.

9-27 Suppose that one of the substitution rates in a simplex tableau is negative. This
implies that:
    a. Adding one unit of the variable heading that column to the production mix
       would result in a possible increase in the number of units in the production
       mix for the variable corresponding to that row.

b. Adding one unit of the variable heading that column to the production mix would decrease the number of units in the production mix for the variable corresponding to that row.

c. The variable corresponding to that row will not leave the solution on this iteration.

d. Both (a) and (c).

9-28 How is the variable which will be replaced in the next simplex tableau determined?

a. By choosing the variable with the most positive $C_j - Z_j$ value in maximization problems.

b. By choosing the variable with the most negative $C_j - Z_j$ value in minimization problems.

c. By choosing the variable which yields the smallest nonnegative quotient when you divide quantity-column values by their corresponding optimal-column values.

d. Both (a) and (b).

9-29 When pivoting in the simplex algorithm, the intersectional elements are always found in the:

a. $C_j - Z_j$ row

b. Optimal column

c. Quantity column

d. None of the above

9-30 A possible increase in profits in a minimization problem is indicated by:

a. A negative value of $C_j - Z_j$ for a structural variable.

b. A negative value of $C_j - Z_j$ for a slack variable.

c. A positive value of $C_j - Z_j$ for a surplus variable.

d. All of the above.

e. (a) and (b), but not (c).

9-31 In any simplex tableau, the variables in the solution are found in the:

a. Quantity column

b. Product-mix column

c. Z_j row

d. $C_j - Z_j$ row

9-32 If an optimal solution is degenerate:

a. There are alternative optimal solutions.

b. The solution is useless to management.

c. The solution is not feasible.

d. None of the above.

9-33 In a maximization problem with all less-than-or-equal-to constraints, you would be correct in calling the solution in the first simplex tableau:

a. An all-slack solution.

b. A feasible solution.

c. A zero-profit solution.

d. All of the above.

9-34 The major difference between slack and artificial variables is that:

a. A slack variable should never be present in the product-mix column of an optimal solution.

b. An artificial variable should never be present in the product-mix column of an optimal solution.

c. An artificial variable can never be equal to zero.

d. A slack variable can never be equal to zero.

9-35 If the objective function coefficient in the C_j row above an artificial variable is $-M$, we know the problem must be:
 a. A maximization problem
 b. A minimization problem
 c. Infeasible
 d. Unbounded

9-36 If the $C_j - Z_j$ value for some nonbasic variable is zero in an optimal tableau, then the problem can:
 a. Be unbounded
 b. Have alternate optimal solutions
 c. Be infeasible
 d. (a) and (b), but not (c)

9-37 For a minimization problem, the objective function coefficient for an artificial variable is:
 a. Zero
 b. $+M$
 c. $-M$
 d. None of the above

9-38 If a negative number appears in the quantity column of a simplex tableau, we know that:
 a. The solution is optimal.
 b. A mistake has been made.
 c. The problem is unbounded.
 d. (b) or (c), but not (a).
 e. (a), (b), or (c).

9-39 For a maximization problem we would never pick a column with a negative $C_j - Z_j$ value as our optimal column because:
 a. It could result in an infeasible solution.
 b. It could cause the objective value to decrease in the next solution.
 c. It could cause the simplex algorithm to cycle.
 d. All of the above.

9-40 If you had a linear program with 100 constraints, and you examined the 100 substitution rates in the column for the variable x_5 (which was the first basic variable in the solution), then you should find that:
 a. The row 1 substitution rate is 1 and the other 99 are all 0.
 b. At least one substitution rate is positive and at least one is negative.
 c. All 100 substitution rates are 0.
 d. The row 1 substitution rate is 0 and the other 99 are all 1.

10 Real world MS/OR successes

▊ EXAMPLE: MAINTAINING THE BOXCAR FLEET IN THE CHESSIE RAILROAD SYSTEM

The Chessie System contains three major railroads, many small ones, and a fleet of 133,000 cars classified into 28 general types. To maintain this fleet, Chessie has its own car-building shop as well as a large repair operation. Cars are also replaced by purchases from other builders. In 1978, Chessie's   THE CHESSIE SYSTEM

Management Science team[1] (Lee C. Brosch, Richard J. Buck, William H. Sparrow, and James R. White) developed a linear programming model to recommend the timing and quantity of cars to be added or deleted from the fleet. The bottom line: a reduction in annual costs of $8 million.

The decision variables in the model are the numbers of cars, by type and by time period, that will be scrapped, built, repaired, and purchased. Coefficients for the variables are contributions (revenues less incremental operating costs), repair costs, scrap values, and replacement costs. The constraints include shop and manpower capacity for building and repairing cars, lead times for purchasing cars from other builders, the backlog of bad cars on hand, and projections of future needs. Two versions of the linear program are used at Chessie depending on the time horizon. A long-range planning model looks three years into the future, and has about 3,500

[1] Lee C. Brosch, Richard J. Buck, William H. Sparrow, and James R. White, "Boxcars, Linear Programming, and the Sleeping Kitten," *Interfaces,* vol. 10, no. 6, pp. 53–61, 1980.

STRUCTURE OF THE LP

variables and 1,000 constraints. A short-range model looks one quarter ahead and is much smaller. Both versions are solved with the simplex method.

The Chessie experience is perhaps the best example of how to implement a model in the MS/OR literature. Rather than overwhelm top management all at once with a complex model, the authors developed the model in stages. The first-stage model was small enough so that it was easy to explain to top management. The authors got top management interested by demonstrating the capability to answer "what-if" questions about company operations. The authors developed the rest of the model in the sequence that top management wanted. At the end of each stage of model-building, the authors reviewed the results with top management and fine-tuned the model accordingly. Today, linear programming is a routine tool for manpower planning, repair scheduling, purchasing, budgeting, and marketing decisions. Top management also uses the model for strategic planning. For example, the model revealed that Chessie had enough capacity to build and sell cars to other railroads. As a result, Chessie now makes more than $28 million in railroad car sales each year.

IMPLEMENTATION
BY STAGES

MANAGEMENT
DECISIONS

10

Wendy Matlock has a bright future with the Watertown Computer Company. At each weekly staff meeting, her boss is continually asking "What if?" questions: "What should we do if our competitors in Owego reduce the price of their 91497-based System/3 microcomputer?" "Nippon Instruments isn't sure that they'll be able to deliver 4000 of their 91497 microprocessor chips each week. How should we adjust our production if they can only deliver 3500?" Wendy always seems to have the answers to these questions at her fingertips.

Wendy's ability to respond accurately to such questions is partly a result of experience and keen observation of the company's daily operations. But equally important, much of her acuity results from the fact that she recognizes the power of sensitivity analysis. Sensitivity analysis addresses questions of the form, "How does the solution change as the data of the problem are modified?" It also provides information about the range of values over which single numbers in the input data can be changed and as a result produce proportional changes in the problem solution.

Sensitivity analysis provides important information—so important that many managers consider it to be more crucial to their operations than merely having the optimal solution. In this chapter, you will learn how the simplex algorithm and computer codes based on it can be used to obtain this valuable information. Your future in management can be as bright as Wendy's if you make an effort to find out what information is available, how to obtain it, and how to make effective use of it.

LINEAR PROGRAMMING III: BUILDING LP MODELS AND INTERPRETING SOLUTIONS

Problem Formulation, Duality, Sensitivity Analysis, Linear Programming Applications

CHAPTER OBJECTIVES

- SHOW HOW TO FORMULATE LINEAR PROGRAMMING MODELS.

- INTRODUCE THE CONCEPT OF DUALITY AND ITS ECONOMIC INTERPRETATION AND SIGNIFICANCE.

- SHOW HOW TO PERFORM SEVERAL KINDS OF SENSITIVITY ANALYSIS ON LINEAR PROGRAMMING "SOLUTIONS," INCLUDING RIGHT-HAND-SIDE AND OBJECTIVE RANGING AND PRICING OUT NEW VARIABLES.

- SHOW HOW TO USE THE OPTIMAL SIMPLEX TABLEAU TO PERFORM SENSITIVITY ANALYSES.

- DEMONSTRATE A RANGE OF LINEAR PROGRAMMING APPLICATIONS FROM THE AUTHORS' OWN INDUSTRIAL EXPERIENCES WITH THE TECHNIQUE.

In Chapter 8, we did not examine how you go about formulating problems as linear programs. Similarly, it simply was not possible in Chapters 8 and 9 to review the many economic and operational issues that are a part of successfully applying linear programming, nor to understand the managerial significance of the answers you get when you "crank the handle." Nor were we able to discuss problems that can be encountered in applying linear programming to "real-world" problems.

In this chapter we shall begin by looking at the process of problem formulation or "building linear programming models." Given a verbal description of some problem scenario, how do you go about setting up the mathematical expressions that describe the problem as a linear program?

Then we shall discuss the idea of "duality": for every linear programming problem, there is a second, related linear programming problem, called its *dual*. The dual problem provides significant additional economic information about the original problem, and turns out to be of great use to managers.

The interpretation of the information provided by the dual problem leads naturally into the area of *sensitivity analysis*. Sensitivity analysis is used to answer questions of the form, "If one of the input parameters (an objective function or right-hand-side coefficient) changes, how will that affect the optimal solution of the problem?" Since prices and costs change from time to time, since suppliers encounter production difficulties, and since the data used to set up problems often contain seat-of-the-pants "guesstimates," you can see why sensitivity analysis has great importance in managerial decision making. Of course, if you change an input parameter, that gives a different linear programming problem, which you could presumably solve by working the entire problem again from the beginning. However, it is frequently the case that the work of resolving the problem from scratch can be avoided. The information provided by the simplex algorithm's solution to the original problem and its dual problem can be used to answer many sensitivity analysis questions directly, *without resolving the modified problem from scratch.*

Our initial discussion of duality and sensitivity analysis will be based on the output from the LPSBA package which we introduced in Chapter 8. Section 6 will show you how to use the simplex algorithm to do this analysis.

Whenever you go from the textbook to the "real world," you encounter problems, and that is quite true of linear programming also. We have concluded this chapter with a section describing some interesting (and in some cases irksome) applications of linear programming which we have been involved with over the years. Perhaps you, too, will enjoy laughing at our mistakes!

1 Building models

Before you can set up and solve a linear programming problem, you must first start with a verbal description of the problem environment: an identification of the goal or objective you are trying to achieve, the resources which are available, the ways in which those resources can be put together, requirements which must be met, and all the relevant numerical data which quantify all aspects of the environment. The process of converting the verbal description and numerical data into mathematical expressions which capture the relevant relationships, goals, and restrictions is known as *modelling,* or *model building,* and the resulting mathematical description of the problem is called a *model.*

Modelling is not used only in linear programming. In fact, all of the techniques you have studied in the previous chapters of this book, as well as those you will study in the rest of the book, are mathematical modelling techniques. Just like Molière's would-be gentleman, M. Jordain, who had spoken prose all of his life without knowing that he was doing so, you have been building models for some time now (probability models, forecasting models, and inventory models), without having been told that you were doing so. And, you will continue to build models throughout the rest of the book (network, integer programming, queuing, simulation, and Markov chain models).

◼ THREE PARTS OF LP MODELS

All linear programming models are composed of three parts: *decision* (or *structural*) *variables, constraints,* and an *objective function.* To formalize what we did in Chapter 8, let's define these three parts in general and then identify them in the original Dimensions, Ltd., linear programming model.

Maximize:

$$8T + 6C$$

Subject to:

$$4T + 2C \leqslant 60$$
$$2T + 4C \leqslant 48$$
$$T,C \geqslant 0$$

1 *Decision variables* are quantities under the control of the decision maker (product mix, production schedules, personnel assignment, etc.) for which optimal values are to be determined.

Dimensions, Ltd., must decide how many tables (*T*) and chairs (*C*) to produce.

2 *Constraints* are restrictions on the process in question that limit the possible values the decision variables can take. There are two types of constraints: *structural constraints* such as contracts, resource availabilities, legal restraints, and so forth, and *nonnegativity constraints* that restrict the variables to take only zero and positive values.

Dimensions, Ltd., faces structural constraints imposed by the limited amounts of time available in the assembly and finishing departments.

3 The *objective function* is some function of the decision variables which, subject to satisfying the constraints, is to be maximized (for example, profits) or minimized (for example, costs).

Dimensions, Ltd., wants to set production levels in order to maximize profits.

THREE STEPS IN BUILDING LP MODELS

Let's now look at verbal descriptions of several problems and use them to formulate linear programming models. The procedure we'll follow has three steps, corresponding to the three parts of linear programming models that we have just discussed.

1 Choose the decision variables. This is often the key to a convenient formulation of the problem. There may be several different correct ways to formulate any given linear programming problem. However, some choices of variables may lead to a formulation which is clumsy. Even worse, an incorrect choice of the variables will make it impossible to complete building the model.

2 Express the constraints in terms of the variables. This is often conveniently broken down into two parts:

a. Express the constraints verbally. For example, in the Dimensions, Ltd., problem, the first constraint says

time used in assembly ≤ time available in assembly

Convert the verbal expression of the constraints into mathematical expressions in terms of the decision variables. Continuing our example:

$$\text{time used in assembly} = 4T + 2C, \text{ and}$$
$$\text{time available in assembly} = 60 \text{ hours,}$$

so the final constraint is

$$4T + 2C \leq 60$$

3 Express the objective function in terms of the variables. This, too, can be done in two parts:

a. Express the objective verbally:

Maximize profit

b. Convert the verbal expression of the objective function into a mathematical expression in terms of the decision variables:

$$\text{profit} = 8T + 6C,$$

so the final objective function is

$$\text{maximize } 8T + 6C$$

As you become more experienced in building linear programming models, you'll probably skip (a) and go directly to (b). However, if you encounter difficulty in any formulation, you might well find it helpful to go back to (a).

A FEED-MIXING PROBLEM

The Mittens Catfood Company is putting out a new line of cat food called Tuna-n-Stuff. It plans to list on the label that one ounce of Tuna-n-Stuff contains at least the following percentages of recommended daily allowances (RDA) as established by the National Feline Nutritional Council.

Nutrient	Protein	Thiamine	Niacin	Calcium	Iron
% RDA per ounce	2.6	13.7	14.3	5.7	4.3

Tuna-n-Stuff will be blended from the following ingredients

| Ingredient | % RDA per ounce | | | | | Cost ($/ounce) |
	Protein	Thiamine	Niacin	Calcium	Iron	
Albacore	20	0	0	6	5	.15
Bonito	12	0	0	5	3	.10
Supplement C	0	42	18	22	7	.20
Supplement D	0	36	40	8	9	.12
Filler	0	0	0	0	0	.02

Since the product name includes the word "tuna," government regulations specify that at least 40 percent of the ingredients should be albacore or bonito. How can Mittens Catfood blend Tuna-n-Stuff at the least possible cost? Let's build a linear programming model to solve this problem for them.

1 They must decide how much of each ingredient to use in the final product, so the decision variables are

A = ounces of albacore per ounce of product
B = ounces of bonito per ounce of product
C = ounces of supplement C per ounce of product
D = ounces of supplement D per ounce of product
F = ounces of filler per ounce of product

2 There are 5 constraints of the form "nutrient supplied $\geq$ nutrient RDA":

$$20A + 12B \qquad\qquad\qquad \geq\ 2.6 : \text{protein}$$
$$42C + 36D \geq 13.7 : \text{thiamine}$$
$$18C + 40D \geq 14.3 : \text{niacin}$$
$$6A + 5B + 22C + 8D \geq\ 5.7 : \text{calcium}$$
$$5A + 3B + 7C + 9D \geq\ 4.3 : \text{iron}$$

There is one constraint saying "tuna is at least 40 percent of the mix":

$$A + B \geq .4$$

We must also ensure that an ounce of ingredients is used:

$$A + B + C + D + F = 1$$

And, of course, there are the nonnegativity constraints:

$$A, B, C, D, F \geqslant 0$$

OBJECTIVE FUNCTION

3 The objective is to minimize cost per ounce of the product:

Minimize:

$$.15A + .10B + .20C + .12D + .02F$$

Putting it all together, we get the final linear programming model:

THE COMPLETE MODEL

Minimize:

$$.15A + .10B + .20C + .12D + .02F$$

Subject to:

$$
\begin{array}{rrrrrrl}
20A + & 12B & & & & & \geqslant 2.6 \\
 & & 42C + & 36D & & & \geqslant 13.7 \\
 & & 18C + & 40D & & & \geqslant 14.3 \\
6A + & 5B + & 22C + & 8D & & & \geqslant 5.7 \\
5A + & 3B + & 7C + & 9D & & & \geqslant 4.3 \\
A + & B & & & & & \geqslant .4 \\
A + & B + & C + & D + & F & = & 1 \\
 & & & A, B, C, D, & F & \geqslant & 0 \\
\end{array}
$$

▨ A PRODUCTION PLANNING PROBLEM

The Halston Farina Company markets its Hearts of Wheat cereal in three different sizes: large, giant, and jumbo. The company's plans call for production next month of 11,500 jumbo boxes, 15,400 giant boxes, and 2,000 large boxes. Actual production can vary from these target figures by no more than 10 percent in either direction. Toasted wheat, which is already on hand in unlimited quantities, is milled and then packaged as Hearts of Wheat. Milling and packaging times (in hours per box) are:

PROBLEM DATA

	Size of box		
	Large	**Giant**	**Jumbo**
Milling time	.009	.011	.012
Packaging time	.013	.017	.015

The firm has available 300 hours of milling time for the month. Packaging can be done on three units. Unit one is available for 80 hours per month, but can only package the giant and jumbo sizes. Unit two, which can package all three sizes, is available for 180 hours per month. Unit three can only package large- and giant-size boxes; it is available for 160 hours per month. Halston's profit margins are 20 cents on large boxes, 24 cents on giant boxes, and 30 cents on jumbo boxes. What production plan will maximize Halston's profits next month? Let's set up a linear program which will help them determine their optimal production plan.

1 At first glance, it appears that the decision variables should be how many boxes of each size to produce. However, looking ahead to the constraints, we see that we must keep track of how much time is scheduled on each of the three packaging units. This will require us to know how many boxes of each size are packaged on each unit, so the decision variables are:

DECISION VARIABLES

$L2$ and $L3$, the number of large boxes packaged on units 2 and 3 (there is no $L1$, because unit 1 can't package large boxes)
$G1$, $G2$, and $G3$, the number of giant boxes packaged on units 1, 2, and 3
$J1$ and $J2$, the number of jumbo boxes packaged on units 1 and 2 (there is no $J3$, because unit 3 can't package jumbo boxes).

2 There are six constraints relating quantities produced to the production targets and allowable deviations:

CONSTRAINTS

$$
\begin{aligned}
L2 + L3 &\leq 2{,}200 : \text{maximum number of large boxes} \\
G1 + G2 + G3 &\leq 16{,}940 : \text{maximum number of giant boxes} \\
J1 + J2 &\leq 12{,}650 : \text{maximum number of jumbo boxes} \\
L2 + L3 &\geq 1{,}800 : \text{minimum number of large boxes} \\
G1 + G2 + G3 &\geq 13{,}860 : \text{minimum number of giant boxes} \\
J1 + J2 &\geq 10{,}350 : \text{minimum number of jumbo boxes}
\end{aligned}
$$

There is one milling constraint saying "time used $\leq$ time available":

$$.009L2 + .009L3 + .011G1 + .011G2 + .011G3 + .012J1 + .012J2 \leq 300$$

There are 3 packaging constraints saying, "time used $\leq$ time available":

$$
\begin{aligned}
.017G1 + .015J1 &\leq 80 : \text{unit 1} \\
.013L2 + .017G2 + .015J2 &\leq 180 : \text{unit 2} \\
.013L3 + .017G3 \qquad\quad &\leq 160 : \text{unit 3}
\end{aligned}
$$

And, of course, all the variables must be nonnegative:

$$L2, L3, G1, G2, G3, J1, \text{ and } J2 \geq 0$$

3 The objective is to maximize Halston's profits in the next month:

OBJECTIVE FUNCTION

Maximize:

$$20L2 + 20L3 + 24G1 + 24G2 + 24G3 + 30J1 + 30J2$$

Putting it all together, we get the final linear programming model:

Maximize:

$$20L2 + 20L3 + 24G1 + 24G2 + 24G3 + 30J1 + 30J2$$

Subject to:

$$
\begin{array}{lllllllr}
L2 + & L3 & & & & & & \leq & 2{,}200 \\
& & G1 + & G2 + & G3 & & & \leq & 16{,}940 \\
& & & & & J1 + & J2 & \leq & 12{,}650 \\
L2 + & L3 & & & & & & \geq & 1{,}800 \\
& & G1 + & G2 + & G3 & & & \geq & 13{,}860 \\
& & & & & J1 + & J2 & \geq & 10{,}350 \\
.009L2 + & .009L3 + & .011G1 + & .011G2 + & .011G3 + & .012J1 + & .012J2 & \leq & 300 \\
& & .017G1 + & & & .015J1 & & \leq & 80 \\
.013L2 + & & & .017G2 + & & & .015J2 & \leq & 180 \\
& .013L3 + & & & .017G3 & & & \leq & 160 \\
\end{array}
$$

$$L2, L3, G1, G2, G3, J1, \text{ and } J2 \geq 0$$

◼ A PERSONNEL SCHEDULING PROBLEM

The San Antonio Fire & Casualty Company maintains a 24-hour telephone answering service. Personnel report at 4-hour intervals and work 8-hour shifts. An individual's wage per shift depends on the shift's starting time and is given in the table below, along with the minimum numbers of personnel that the company feels must be on duty to answer calls during the six daily 4-hour periods.

Period #	1	2	3	4	5	6
Hours	Midnight–4AM	4AM–8AM	8AM–noon	noon–4PM	4PM–8PM	8PM–midnight
# needed	4	7	20	12	30	15
Wage	$96.00	$88.00	$80.00	$84.00	$88.00	$94.00

The company would like to staff the answering service at the least possible labor cost. Let's see how to set up a linear programming model to accomplish this.

1 They need to know how many people should report at the beginning of each period, so the decision variables are $P1$, $P2$, $P3$, $P4$, $P5$, and $P6$.

2 The only structural constraints are the six minimum personnel constraints of the form "Number at work ≥ number needed." To express these in terms of the six decision variables, we need only note that an individual who starts working at the beginning of any period works during that period and the next period. (A worker who arrives at 8PM works until 4AM on the next day.) Hence the constraints are:

$$
\begin{aligned}
P1 + P2 &\qquad\geq \ 7 : \text{shift 2} \\
P2 + P3 &\qquad\geq 20 : \text{shift 3} \\
P3 + P4 &\qquad\geq 12 : \text{shift 4} \\
P4 + P5 &\qquad\geq 30 : \text{shift 5} \\
P5 + P6 &\geq 15 : \text{shift 6} \\
P1 + \qquad\qquad P6 &\geq \ 4 : \text{shift 1} \\
P1, P2, P3, P4, P5, \text{and } P6 &\geq \ 0
\end{aligned}
$$

3 The objective is to minimize SAF&C's total labor cost:

Minimize:

$$96P1 + 88P2 + 80P3 + 84P4 + 88P5 + 94P6$$

Putting it all together, the entire model is:

Minimize:

$$96P1 + 88P2 + 80P3 + 84P4 + 88P5 + 94P6$$

Subject to:

$$
\begin{aligned}
P1 + P2 &\qquad\qquad\qquad \geq \ 7 \\
P2 + P3 &\qquad\qquad\qquad \geq 20 \\
P3 + P4 &\qquad\qquad \geq 12 \\
P4 + P5 &\qquad \geq 30 \\
P5 + P6 &\geq 15 \\
P1 + \qquad\qquad P6 &\geq \ 4 \\
P1, P2, P3, P4, P5, \text{and } P6 &\geq \ 0
\end{aligned}
$$

The three examples we have considered in this section should begin to give you an idea of some of the sorts of problems that can be modelled as linear programming problems, as well as showing you how to go about building those models. In Section 7, Linear Programming Applications, we will show you some more LP models which we have encountered in our industrial consulting work.

2 The dual in linear programming

Associated with any linear programming problem is another linear programming problem, called its *dual*. Although the idea of *duality* is essentially mathematical, we shall see in this section that duality has important interpretations which can help managers answer questions about alternative courses of action and their relative values.

THE PRIMAL AND THE DUAL IN LINEAR PROGRAMMING

Each maximizing problem in linear programming has its corresponding dual, a minimizing problem; similarly, each minimizing problem in linear programming has *its* corresponding dual, a maximizing problem. As we shall see, it is an interesting feature of the simplex method that we can use it to solve either the original problem (called the *primal*) or the dual; whichever problem we start out to solve, it will also give us the solution to the other problem.

Let's consider an expanded version of the Dimensions, Ltd., problem discussed in Chapter 8, now with three departments (assembly, finishing, and packing) and with the capability to make three products: tables (T, at \$2/unit profit), chairs (C, at \$4/unit profit), and bookcases (B, at \$3/unit profit). The problem can be stated as

Maximize:

$$2T + 4C + 3B$$

Subject to:

$$3T + 4C + 2B \leq 60 \quad \text{assembly constraint}$$
$$2T + 1C + 2B \leq 40 \quad \text{finishing constraint}$$
$$1T + 3C + 2B \leq 80 \quad \text{packing constraint}$$
$$T, C, B \geq 0$$

FINDING THE DUAL AND INTERPRETING ITS MANAGERIAL SIGNIFICANCE

The *primal* was concerned with maximizing the contribution from the three products; the *dual* will be concerned with evaluating the time used in the three departments to produce the tables, chairs, and bookcases.

Jim Littlefield, the production manager of Dimensions, Ltd., recognizes that the productive capacity of the three departments is a valuable resource to the firm; he wonders whether it would be possible to place a monetary value on its worth. He soon comes to think in terms of how much he would receive from another furniture producer, a renter who wants to rent all the capacity in Jim's three departments. He reasons along the following lines.

Suppose the rental charges were \$$A$ per hour of assembly time, \$$F$ per hour of finishing time, and \$$P$ per hour of packing time. Then the cost to the renter of *all* the time would be

$$60A + 40F + 80P = \text{total rent paid}$$

And of course the renter would want to set the rental prices in such a way as to *minimize* the total rent he would have to pay; so the objective of the dual is

Minimize:

$$60A + 40F + 80P$$

Jim will not rent out his time unless the rent offered enables him to net as much as he would if he used the time to produce furniture for Dimensions, Ltd. This observation leads to the constraints of the dual.

433

LINEAR
PROGRAMMING III

DEVELOPING THE FIRST
CONSTRAINT FOR
THE DUAL

To make one table requires 3 assembly hours, 2 finishing hours, and 1 packing hour. The time that goes into making a table would be rented out for $3A + 2F + 1P$. If Jim used that time to make a table, he would earn \$2 in contribution to profit, and so he will not rent out the time unless

$$3A + 2F + 1P \geqslant 2$$

and this gives the first constraint in the dual. Similar reasoning with respect to chairs and bookcases gives the other two dual constraints,

$$4A + 1F + 3P \geqslant 4$$

and

$$2A + 2F + 2P \geqslant 3$$

and of course the rents must be nonnegative.

So the entire dual problem which determines for Jim the value of the productive resources of Dimensions, Ltd., (its plant hours) is

Minimize:

$$60A + 40F + 80P = \text{total rent paid}$$

Subject to:

$$3A + 2F + 1P \geqslant 2$$
$$4A + 1F + 3P \geqslant 4$$
$$2A + 2F + 2P \geqslant 3$$
$$A, F, P \geqslant 0$$

Notice that the dual problem has a structural variable for each structural constraint of the primal problem. In addition, the dual has one structural constraint for each structural variable of the primal problem. In this way, there is a natural correspondence between variables in one of the two problems and constraints in the other one. As we shall see, this correspondence will be associated with some very valuable economic information about the two problems.

Figure 10-1 shows the optimal solution to the primal problem, as obtained by LPSBA. We see there that the optimal solution is to produce 6.66667 chairs, 16.66667 bookcases, and no tables. The total contribution for this product mix is about \$76.67. We will shortly explain the meaning of the entries under the heading "Shadow prices for constraints," but for the moment note that the shadow price for the assembly constraint is .83333, the shadow price for the finishing constraint is .66667, and the shadow price for the packing constraint is 0.

Now look at the optimal solution to the dual problem, shown in Figure 10-2. The basic structural variables A and F have the values .83333 and .66667, respectively. The other structural variable, P, is nonbasic and hence

434

CHAPTER 10

THE SIMPLEX METHOD
SOLVES BOTH
PROBLEMS
SIMULTANEOUSLY

equals 0. Thus the worth to Dimensions, Ltd., of 1 productive hour in the assembly department is $0.83333, in the finishing department is $0.66667, and in the packing department is $0.00. Notice that these are precisely the shadow prices for the corresponding constraints that were reported in the primal solution. This is not a coincidence. **When the simplex algorithm is used to solve the primal problem,** *it also solves the dual problem at the same time.* **The values of the shadow prices in the optimal solution to the primal problem are always equal to the values of the structural variables in the optimal solution to the dual problem.**

Does solving the dual also give us the solution to the primal? Look at the shadow prices in the optimal dual solution in Figure 10-2. For the table, chair, and bookcase constraints, they are 0, 6.66667, and 16.66667, respectively, *precisely the values of the corresponding structural variables in the optimal primal solution.* From this we see that the result noted in the last paragraph is actually more general. **When the simplex algorithm is used to solve either member of a primal-dual pair of linear programming problems, it also solves the other problem at the same time. Furthermore, the optimal values of the structural variables in either problem are always equal to the values**

```
Optimal solution obtained after     2 pivots

Maximal objective function value:        76.66667

Basic structural variables          Basic slack and surplus variables
C        6.66667                     PACKING            26.66667     Slack
B       16.66667

Shadow prices for constraints       Reduced costs for nonbasic structural vars.
ASSEMBLY             .83333          T                    -1.83333
FINISHNG             .66667
PACKING              .00000
```

FIGURE 10-1
LPSBA solution to expanded Dimensions, Ltd., problem.

```
Optimal solution obtained after     4 pivots

Minimal objective function value:        76.66667

Basic structural variables          Basic slack and surplus variables
A                    .83333          TABLE              1.83333     Surplus
F                    .66667

Shadow prices for constraints       Reduced costs for nonbasic structural vars.
TABLE                .00000          P                    26.66667
CHAIR               6.66667
BOOKCASE           16.66667
```

FIGURE 10-2
LPSBA solution to expanded Dimensions, Ltd., dual problem.

of the shadow prices of the corresponding constraints in the optimal solution of the other problem in the primal-dual pair. The upshot of this observation is that all of the information that you can obtain from the dual problem will be available once you solve the primal.

We have seen that solving *either* the primal or the dual gets us the solution to *both* problems. Which one should we apply the simplex method to? Computational experience shows that the amount of work necessary to solve linear programs depends primarily on the *number of constraints* in the problem. Suppose we have a problem like Dimensions, Ltd., but with seven departments. The primal problem would have seven constraints, but the dual would have only three (three products). In this case it would be sensible to apply the simplex method to the dual.

CHOOSING WHICH
PROBLEM TO SOLVE,
THE PRIMAL OR
THE DUAL

FURTHER ECONOMIC INTERPRETATIONS OF DUALITY

Duality has several useful economic interpretations:

1 Suppose T, C, B is a feasible solution to the primal (that is, a level of output which can be achieved with the current resources) and A, F, P is a feasible solution to the dual (that is, a set of rents which would induce Jim to rent out the plant rather than use it himself). Then

ADDITIONAL
INTERPRETATIONS
OF THE DUAL

$$2T + 4C + 3B \leq 60A + 40F + 80P$$

In other words, in order to get Jim to rent rather than produce, the rents must total at least as much as he can get by producing.

2 Notice that the optimal objective value is the same in both problems ($76⅔). This is *always* the case. Whenever the primal has an optimal solution, so does the dual, and the optimal objective values are equal. How can we interpret this? It says that the value to Dimensions, Ltd., of all its productive resources is precisely equal to the profit the firm can make if it employs these resources in the best way possible. In this way, the profit made on the firm's output is used to derive *imputed values* of the inputs used to produce that output.

THE OBJECTIVE
FUNCTIONAL VALUE
FOR THE OPTIMAL
ANSWER IS THE SAME
IN BOTH PROBLEMS

3 Notice that the dual variable P was equal to 0 and that not all the packing time was used. This is entirely reasonable, since if Dimensions, Ltd., already has excess packing time, additional packing time cannot be profitably used and so is worthless. This is half of what is called the *principle of complementary slackness*.

COMPLEMENTARY
SLACKNESS

4 Notice that with $A = ⅚$, $F = ⅔$, and $P = 0$, $3A + 2F + 1P = 23⁄6$. This shows us that the value of the time needed to produce a table is $23⁄6. But a table only contributes a profit of $2. Since the time needed to produce a table is worth more than the return on a table, the optimal solution to the primal *does not* produce any tables for Dimensions, Ltd. This is the other half of the *principle of complementary slackness*.

3 Shadow prices and reduced costs

In the last section, we saw that the dual variables (and the shadow prices in the primal solution output) gave us the value of additional hours of productive time in several departments. In this section we continue our discussion of the rest of the information provided by LPSBA (and most other linear programming computer packages).

▊ SHADOW PRICES

Once again, look at Figure 10-1 on page 434. Each structural constraint has associated with it a *shadow price*. The shadow price tells how much the objective function will change if we increase the right-hand side of its associated constraint. More precisely, for any constraint we have

$$\text{shadow price} = \frac{\text{change in optimal objective function value}}{\text{unit increase in right-hand-side coefficient}}$$

Let's see what sort of things the shadow prices tell us about the expanded Dimensions, Ltd., problem:

The shadow price for the assembly department constraint is .83333. How

do we interpret this number? First of all, let's note that the units of a shadow price are objective function units per unit of the constraint right-hand side. In this particular case, then, the number .83333 is to be interpreted as $0.83333 (or about 83¢) per hour of assembly time. Thus, another hour of

assembly time could be used to make more chairs and bookcases and increase the total profit by 83¢.

Suppose an additional hour of assembly time could be acquired for 50¢. Should Jim Littlefield be interested in obtaining this additional hour? Yes, since by incurring a cost of 50¢ he can increase his profit contribution by 83¢, for a net gain of 33¢. What is the maximum amount he would pay to increase his assembly time by one hour? He will be willing to pay any amount up to 83¢.

If Jim could obtain unlimited additional assembly hours at a cost of 50¢ per hour, how many hours should he acquire? First of all, convince yourself that additional assembly hours can't always be worth 83¢ each. After all, since additional assembly hours enable Jim to make more chairs and bookcases, eventually he is going to use up the slack time in the packing department.

After that point, additional assembly time will be worthless, because he won't be able to pack any more chairs and bookcases even if he could assemble and finish them. In this way, you can see that a shadow price is only going to be valid over a limited range of changes in the right-hand-side coefficient. We shall see how to determine that range in the next section.

What happens if we decrease the right-hand-side coefficient of a constraint? In that case, the rate of change in the objective is given by the negative of the shadow price. One of the workers in the finishing department has called in sick. Jim figures that this will reduce the capacity of that department from 40 to 32 hours. How much will this reduce Dimensions, Ltd.'s profit? The shadow price for the finishing constraint is .66667, that is, about 67¢ per hour. Thus, losing 8 hours of finishing capacity will reduce the output of chairs and bookcases and thereby reduce the profit by $8 \times 67¢$, or approximately $2.67. How exactly will the optimal solution change? That question, too, will be answered in the next section.

There is one other set of entries on the LPSBA output of the optimal solution. It is headed "Reduced costs for nonbasic structural variables." Recall that the nonbasic variables have the value zero in the optimal solution. In the Dimensions, Ltd., problem, no tables are made ($T = 0$) because chairs and bookcases represent more profitable ways to use the company's productive resources.

There are two equivalent questions we could ask:

1 If Dimensions were forced to make one table (and adjust the production of chairs and bookcases to reflect the "loss" of the resources used in making that table), by how much would their profit decrease?

2 By how much would the contribution per table have to increase before Dimensions would produce any of them?

The answers to questions like these are given by reduced costs. More precisely, for any nonbasic structural variable we have

$$\begin{array}{c} \text{reduced cost of a} \\ \text{nonbasic variable} \end{array} = \dfrac{\text{change in optimal objective function value}}{\text{unit increase of that nonbasic variable}}$$

The units of a reduced cost are objective function units per unit of nonbasic variable. Once again, refer back to Figure 10-1 on page 434. The answer to our first question is that producing one table and then using the rest of their productive capacity optimally will *reduce* Dimensions, Ltd.'s profit by approximately $1.83 (since the reduced cost is -1.83333 and the objective function is measured in dollars).

UNITS IN WHICH
REDUCED COSTS ARE
MEASURED

The answer to our second question is that the contribution per table would have to increase by more than $1.83 (to offset the loss incurred by shifting resources from chairs and bookcases and to tables) before Dimensions, Ltd., would be willing to produce any tables. Suppose the contribution per table increased by $1.84. How many tables would they produce? That question is beyond the scope of the sensitivity analyses we will be discussing. Of course, you can always answer it by changing the problem data and resolving the new problem from scratch.

A COST MINIMIZATION PROBLEM

Let's see how to use shadow prices and reduced costs in a minimization problem. Recall the Mittens Catfood Company problem we formulated on pages 427–428. In Figure 10-3 we have LPSBA's printout of the problem and its solution:

The optimal solution is to blend .40000 ounce of bonito, with .04565 ounce of supplement C, .33696 ounce of supplement D, and .21739 ounce of filler to make each ounce of Tuna-n-Stuff. This will yield the minimum cost of $0.09391 per ounce of Tuna-n-Stuff. Consider the following sensitivity questions:

```
   7 Structural constraints      5 Structural variables
   0 (= Constraints      6 )= Constraints      1 = Constraints

Minimization problem

Objective

  Variable      A          B          C          D          F

Obj coeff     .150       .100       .200       .120       .020


Constraints

              A          B          C          D          F     Relation      RHS

  PROTEIN   20.000     12.000      .000       .000       .000      )=        2.600

  THIAMINE    .000       .000     42.000     36.000      .000      )=       13.700

  NIACIN      .000       .000     18.000     40.000      .000      )=       14.300

  CALCIUM    6.000      5.000     22.000      8.000      .000      )=        3.700

  IRON       5.000      3.000      7.000      9.000      .000      )=        4.300

  MIN-TUNA   1.000      1.000      .000       .000       .000      )=         .400

  TOTAL-WT   1.000      1.000      1.000      1.000      1.000      =        1.000


Optimal solution obtained after    8 pivots

Minimal objective function value:        .09391

Basic structural variables        Basic slack and surplus variables
B           .40000                THIAMINE        .34783    Surplus
C           .04565                PROTEIN        2.20000    Surplus
D           .33696                IRON            .25217    Surplus
F           .21739

Shadow prices for constraints     Reduced costs for nonbasic structural vars.
PROTEIN       .00000              A                .04266
THIAMINE      .00000
NIACIN        .00103
CALCIUM       .00734
IRON          .00000
MIN-TUNA      .04332
TOTAL-WT      .02000
```

FIGURE 10-3
LPSBA solution to Mittens Catfood Company problem.

1 How will the optimal cost change if the protein requirement is increased to 3.0 percent? Since the shadow price for the PROTEIN constraint is 0, and since the current mix already is 4.8 percent protein (note that the surplus variable in that constraint is 2.2), the optimal cost won't change if this change in the protein requirement is made.

2 How will the optimal cost change if the niacin requirement is increased to 14.8 percent? As we shall see in the next section, 14.8 percent is within the range of validity for the shadow price of the NIACIN constraint. Since that shadow price is .00103, the cost per ounce of Tuna-n-Stuff will increase by .00103(14.8 − 14.3) = .000565 if this change is made.

3 The U. S. Department of Agriculture is considering reducing to 32 percent the required percentage of tunafish in cat foods using the word "tuna" in their names. How will this affect the minimum cost of Tuna-n-Stuff? Once again, it turns out that 32 percent is within the range of validity for the shadow price of the MIN-TUNA constraint. Since the shadow price for the MIN-TUNA constraint is .04332, *reducing* the right-hand side of that constraint from .4 to .32 will *reduce* the optimal cost by .04332(.40 − .32) = 0.0034656, that is by approximately 0.35¢ per ounce.

4 By how much will the price of albacore have to fall before Mittens Catfood will consider using any of it in Tuna-n-Stuff? Since the reduced cost of *A* is .04266, the price of albacore will have to fall by at least $0.04266 per ounce for it to become economically attractive.

4 Right-hand-side and objective ranging

The shadow prices and reduced costs that we discussed in the last section give us some sensitivity information, but as we noted, there are some questions for which they don't provide the answers. In particular although they tell how the objective function changes in response to changes in right-hand-side coefficients, they don't tell how the optimal solution responds to these changes. Nor do they identify the ranges over which the shadow prices are valid. These questions are among those discussed in this section. In addition, we examine the effect on the optimal solution of changes in the objective function coefficients.

RIGHT-HAND-SIDE RANGING

As a right-hand-side coefficient is increased or decreased, the optimal solution changes in response. LPSBA provides *change vectors* which tells us exactly how the solution changes. The change vectors for the expanded Dimensions, Ltd., problem are given in Figure 10-4. Just as a shadow price gives us the change in the optimal objective function value per unit increase in a right-hand-side coefficient,

$$\text{change vector} = \frac{\text{changes in values of optimal basic variables}}{\text{unit increase in right-hand-side coefficient}}$$

In other words, a change vector tells us how *all* the basic variables change

Variable	C	B	PACKING
Value	6.667	16.667	26.667
Change vectors			
ASSEMBLY	.333	-.167	-.667
FINISHNG	-.333	.667	-.333
PACKING	.000	.000	1.000

when a right-hand-side coefficient changes. Let's look at an example of how this works.

Suppose the number of hours available in the assembly department were increased to 61. We compute the new solution as follows:

C	B	PACKING	
6.667	16.667	26.667	Old solution
.333	-.167	-.667	Change
7.000	16.500	26.000	New solution

Dimensions, Ltd., now makes 7 chairs and 16.5 bookcases, for a total profit of $4(7) + 3(16.5) = 77.5$ dollars, an increase in profit of $77.50 - 76.67 = 0.83$ dollars. (Recall that the shadow price for the assembly constraint was 83¢.)

What if the number of hours available in the assembly department were increased to 70? This would be an increase of 10 units in the right-hand-side of the assembly constraint. To get the new solution, we **multiply the ASSEMBLY change vector by 10 and add the result to the original solution:**

C	B	PACKING	
6.667	16.667	26.667	Old solution
3.333	-1.667	-6.667	Change
10.000	15.000	20.000	New solution

They now make 10 chairs and 15 bookcases, for a total profit of $4(10) + 3(15) = 85$ dollars, an increase of $85.00 - 76.67 = 8.33$ dollars over their original profit. Note that $8.33 is ten times the shadow price (83.3¢) of the ASSEMBLY constraint.

These constant rates of change in the objective function and the basic variables will continue so long as the basic variables remain nonnegative, that is, so long as the solution derived with the change vector remains feasible. How long will this remain true? Notice that as we add more hours in the assembly department, the optimal solution produces fewer bookcases and has less slack time left over in the packing department. Eventually one of these basic variables will be driven to zero. Which one will hit zero first? If we divide their original values by the rates at which they decrease as assembly time is increased, we find that B hits zero when we add a total of $16.667/.167$ = 100 hours, but that PACKING hits zero when we add a total of $26.667/.667$ = 40 hours. If we went any further, PACKING would become negative, and the solution would cease to be feasible. Since PACKING then blocks further increase in the assembly time, it is called the *blocking variable*. The shadow price and change vector for the ASSEMBLY constraint is valid up to an *upper bound* of 100 hours (= 60 + 40).

What if we *decrease* the number of hours available in the assembly department to 51, a decrease of 9 hours? To get the new solution, we **multiply the ASSEMBLY change vector by 9** and *subtract* the result from the original solution:

C	B	PACKING	
6.667	16.667	26.667	Old solution
−3.000	1.500	6.000	Change
3.667	18.167	32.667	New solution

They now make 3.667 chairs and 18.167 bookcases, for a total profit of $4(3.667) + 3(18.167) = 69.17$ dollars, a decrease of $76.67 - 69.17 = 7.50$ dollars from their original profit. Note that $7.50 is nine times the shadow price ($83.3¢$) of the ASSEMBLY constraint.

As we continue to take away assembly hours, C continues to decrease, so it will be the blocking variable at the lower end of the range of validity for the shadow price and change vector of the ASSEMBLY constraint. To find this lower bound, we divide the original value of C (6.667) by its rate of decrease as the right-hand-side of the ASSEMBLY constraint decreases ($-.333$, from the negative of the change vector) to get $6.667/(-.333)$ = -20. So the lower bound of the range is 40 hours (= 60 − 20).

The general rule for finding the new solution when a single right-hand-side coefficient is changed is: **Multiply the appropriate change vector by the number of units the right-hand side is being increased or decreased. (Always treat this increase or decrease as a positive number.) Then** *add* **the result to the original solution if the right-hand side is being** *increased;* **subtract the result from the original solution if the right-hand side is being** *decreased.* So long as this gives a feasible (that is, nonnegative) solution, this is the new optimal solution.

VALIDITY RANGES FOR SHADOW PRICES

The range of values of the right-hand side for which the change vector rule stated above produces a feasible solution is called the *validity range for the shadow price.* You can find the validity range as we did above by determining which of the basic variables (the *blocking variables*) are first driven to zero as the right-hand side is increased and decreased, and at what values of the right-hand side (the *upper bound* and *lower bound* of the range) the blocking variables are driven to zero. Alternatively, you can use the LPSBA output to determine the blocking variables and bounds of the validity ranges.

Figure 10-5 shows the next section of LPSBA's sensitivity analysis output. This section is headed, "Sensitivity analysis on right-hand-side coefficients." This output contains a row for each structural constraint in the problem. The three middle columns of the output identify the constraint's order in the problem (Row), its current right-hand-side coefficient, and its name. The second column from the right (Upper bound) gives the upper bound of the validity range for the constraint's shadow price; the second column from the left (Lower bound) gives the lower bound of the validity range. The leftmost and rightmost columns give the blocking variables at the lower and upper bounds, respectively.

Note that for the ASSEMBLY constraint, Figure 10-5 confirms that the validity range has a lower bound of 40 hours (with C as the blocking variable) and an upper bound of 100 hours (with PACKING as the blocking variable). What else does Figure 10-5 (together with Figures 10-3 and 10-4) tell us? Among other things, it says that Jim would be willing to spend up to 67¢ per hour (the shadow price for the FINISHNG constraint) for as many as 20 additional hours (60 − 40). If the number of hours available in the finishing department is decreased because of workers calling in sick, the first 25 such hours (40 − 15) will decrease profits by 67¢ per hour.

How do we interpret the fact that the PACKING constraint has no upper bound (or corresponding blocking variable)? Since there are 26.67 hours of packing time left over when the right-hand side of the constraint is 80, increasing the number of hours available does nothing more than increase the number of hours that will be left over. To verify this, note that the change vector for this constraint is

Variable	C	B	PACKING
PACKING	.000	.000	1.000

What if a right-hand side coefficient is changed to a value outside its validity range? In that case, you cannot use the change vector and shadow price to find the new optimal solution; you must change the data in your model and resolve the new problem from scratch.

```
Sensitivity analysis on right-hand-side coefficients

Blocking    Lower bound  Row    RHS Coeff   Name        Upper bound  Blocking
variable                                                              variable

C             40.000      1      60.000     ASSEMBLY     100.000     PACKING
B             15.000      2      40.000     FINISHNG      60.000     C
PACKING       53.333      3      80.000     PACKING        None
```

FIGURE 10-5
More LPSBA sensitivity analysis for expanded Dimensions, Ltd., problem.

The limits given by the validity ranges in Figure 10-5 can only be used when we are changing the right-hand side of a single constraint. However, the procedure used on pages 440–441 for finding the new solution can be used when several right-hand-side coefficients are changed simultaneously. **We just calculate the changes in the solution resulting from each of the right-hand-side changes and apply all of them. So long as the resulting solution remains feasible, it will be optimal. If some variable becomes negative, then the problem must be resolved from the beginning.**

Suppose Dimensions, Ltd., wishes to increase available assembly time to 80 hours and available finishing time to 70 hours (which is beyond the FINISHNG constraint single-change upper bound). We find the new solution by multiplying the ASSEMBLY change vector and shadow price by 20, multiplying the FINISHNG change vector and shadow price by 30, and adding both of these results to the old solution:

C	B	PACKING		Objective
6.667	16.667	26.667	Old solution	76.667
6.667	−3.333	−13.333	ASSEMBLY change	16.667
−10.000	20.000	−10.000	FINISHNG change	20.000
3.333	33.333	3.333	New solution	113.333

The new solution is to make 3.333 chairs and 33.333 bookcases, for a total profit of $4(3.333) + 3(33.333) = 113.333$ dollars, which is the same profit calculated above using the shadow prices.

OBJECTIVE RANGING

Having seen how the optimal solution is affected by changes in right-hand-side coefficients, we would now like to look at what happens when we change an objective function coefficient. Recall the graphic method of solution which we discussed on pages 344–356 in Chaper 8. Look at Figure 10-6, which is the same as Figure 8-10. Changing an objective function coefficient will change the slopes of the isoprofit lines. Since small changes in the coefficients will produce small changes in the slopes, it is geometrically obvious that the optimal solution to the problem will not change if we make small changes in an objective function coefficient. What is geometrically obvious in Figure 10-6 turns out to be true for linear programming problems in general.

For each objective function coefficient, there is a range of values, defined by a lower bound and an upper bound. As that coefficient varies within its range (while all other objective function coefficients are held at their original values), the optimal solution to the problem does not change. Of course, as an objective coefficient changes, the optimal objective function value and the shadow prices and reduced costs will change, even though the values of the optimal basic variables don't change.

What is the value of this information to Dimensions, Ltd.? Just this. The marketing manager now knows what pricing latitude he has (assuming that

OBJECTIVE FUNCTION
OPTIMALITY RANGES

MARKETING VALUE OF
OBJECTIVE FUNCTION
RANGING

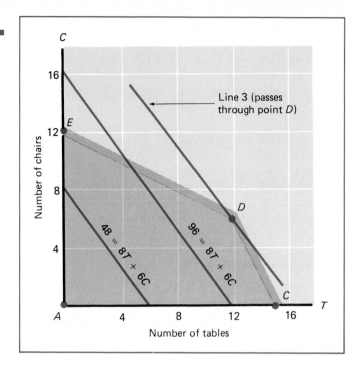

FIGURE 10-6
Three isoprofit
lines plotted.

costs stay the same); that is, in the face of competitive pressure or in the absence of any competition, the marketing manager knows just how much prices can be adjusted without interfering with the optimal solution.

LPSBA'S OBJECTIVE
FUNCTION SENSITIVITY
ANALYSIS

LPSBA and many other linear programming computer codes give these *objective function optimality ranges* as part of their output. Figure 10-7 gives the third section of LPSBA's sensitivity analysis output. It is headed, "Sensitivity analysis on objective coefficients." This output contains a row for each variable in the problem (structural, slack, or surplus). The three middle columns of the output identify the variable's order in the problem (Col), its current objective function coefficient, and its name. The second column from the

```
Sensitivity analysis on objective coefficients

Entering    Lower bound  Col   Obj coeff      Name    Upper bound  Entering
variable                                                           variable

            None         1     2.000   T                3.833      T
ASSEMBLY    1.500        2     4.000   C                6.000      FINISHNG
FINISHNG    2.000        3     3.000   B                5.000      ASSEMBLY
            None         4      .000   ASSEMBLY          .833      ASSEMBLY
            None         5      .000   FINISHNG          .667      FINISHNG
            None         6      .000   PACKING          1.100      T
```

FIGURE 10-7
More LPSBA sensitivity analysis for expanded Dimensions, Ltd., problem.

right (Upper bound) gives the upper bound of the optimality range for the objective coefficient; the second column from the left (Lower bound) gives the lower bound of the optimality range.

If we look at the row for the variable *C*, we see that the profit margin for chairs can vary from a lower bound of 1.5 dollars per chair to an upper bound of 6 dollars per chair without changing the optimal solution. What happens beyond these bounds?

ENTERING VARIABLES

As the profit margin on chairs decreases below 1.5 dollars per chair, chairs become relatively less attractive, so Dimensions, Ltd., will make fewer chairs. When they do so, they will use up less time in their operations, and in particular they will wind up having some time left over in the assembly department. This can be determined by looking at the leftmost column in Figure 10-7, which is headed "Entering variable." The slack variable for the ASSEMBLY constraint was nonbasic in the original optimal solution, so that solution used up all of the time available in the assembly department. Now, however, decreasing the profit margin on chairs to below $1.50 results in the ASSEMBLY slack entering the solution, that is, becoming basic in the new solution.

Similarly, as the profit margin for chairs increases above the upper bound of $6.00 per chair, chairs become even more attractive than they are now. Production will shift so that the number of chairs produced will increase. As a result of this production of bookcases will have to decrease, and Dimensions, Ltd., will wind up having some leftover time in the finishing department. This can be determined by looking at the "Entering variable" column corresponding to the upper bounds of the objective optimality ranges.

Let's see what happens if we change the profit margin of tables. The variable *T* has no lower bound to its objective optimality range. This should come as no surprise. After all, with its current objective coefficient of 2, *T* is nonbasic. Well, if tables aren't economically attractive when they contribute $2.00 each to Dimensions, Ltd.'s profit, they surely won't be attractive if their profit margins get any smaller! In the other direction, if we increase the profit margin on a table to an amount above $3.833, then tables become economically attractive and they enter the solution.

Although the objective function sensitivity analysis gives us some qualitative information about how the solution changes as we move past the bounds of the optimality ranges, it does not tell exactly what the new optimal solution will be. To obtain that, you will have to resolve the modified linear programming model.

A COST MINIMIZATION PROBLEM

Let's get some more practice answering sensitivity analysis questions by looking at Figure 10-8, the LPSBA sensitivity analysis for the Mittens Catfood Company cost minimization problem that we previously discussed in sections 1 and 3 of this chapter, on pages 427–428 and 437–439.

CHANGING THE NIACIN REQUIREMENT

1 What would be the minimum cost blend if the niacin requirement were increased to 15.6 percent from the current 14.3 percent; how would this change the cost of Tuna-n-Stuff?

Variable	B	C	D	THIAMINE	PROTEIN	IRON	F
Value	.400	.046	.337	.348	2.200	.252	.217

Change vectors

	B	C	D	THIAMINE	PROTEIN	IRON	F
PROTEIN	.000	.000	.000	.000	-1.000	.000	.000
THIAMINE	.000	.000	.000	-1.000	.000	.000	.000
NIACIN	.000	-.011	.030	.620	.000	.193	-.019
CALCIUM	.000	.054	-.024	1.402	.000	.160	-.030
IRON	.000	.000	.000	.000	.000	-1.000	.000
MIN-TUNA	1.000	-.272	.122	-7.011	12.000	2.198	-.851
TOTAL-WT	.000	.000	.000	.000	.000	.000	1.000

Sensitivity analysis on right-hand-side coefficients

Blocking variable	Lower bound	Row	RHS Coeff	Name	Upper bound	Blocking variable
	None	1	2.600	PROTEIN	4.800	PROTEIN
	None	2	13.700	THIAMINE	14.048	THIAMINE
THIAMINE	13.739	3	14.300	NIACIN	18.500	C
THIAMINE	5.452	4	5.700	CALCIUM	12.973	F
	None	5	4.300	IRON	4.552	IRON
IRON	.285	6	.400	MIN-TUNA	.450	THIAMINE
F	.783	7	1.000	TOTAL-WT	None	

Sensitivity analysis on objective coefficients

Entering variable	Lower bound	Col	Obj coeff	Name	Upper bound	Entering variable
A	.107	1	.150	A	None	
MIN-TUNA	.057	2	.100	B	.143	A
CALCIUM	.065	3	.200	C	.295	NIACIN
NIACIN	.085	4	.120	D	.420	CALCIUM
A	-1.407	5	.020	F	.071	MIN-TUNA
MIN-TUNA	-.004	6	.000	PROTEIN	None	
NIACIN	-.002	8	.000	THIAMINE	.006	MIN-TUNA
NIACIN	-.001	10	.000	NIACIN	None	
CALCIUM	-.007	12	.000	CALCIUM	None	
NIACIN	-.005	14	.000	IRON	None	
MIN-TUNA	-.043	16	.000	MIN-TUNA	None	

FIGURE 10-8

LPSBA sensitivity analysis for Mittens Catfood Company.

To solve this, we multiply the change vector and shadow price of the NIACIN constraint (.000, $-.011$, .030, .620, .000, .193, $-.019$, and .00103) by 1.3 ($= 15.6 - 14.3$) and add the result to the current solution:

B	C	D	THIAMINE	PROTEIN	IRON	F		Objective
.400	.046	.337	.348	2.200	.252	.217	Old solution	.09391
.000	$-.014$	.039	.806	.000	.251	$-.025$	Change	.00134
.400	.032	.376	1.154	2.200	.503	.182	New solution	.09525

They should increase the amount of supplement D in the mix to .376 ounce, decrease the supplement C and filler to .032 ounce and .182 ounce, respectively, and leave the bonito at .4 ounce. Doing so will increase the cost of Tuna-n-Stuff to $0.09525 per ounce.

2 How do the optimal blend and its cost change if the U.S. Department of Agriculture reduces the required percentage of tunafish to 32 percent; what if the reduction is to 25 percent?

CHANGING THE TUNA REQUIREMENT

Looking at the second question first, we see that the lower bound for the validity range of the MIN-TUNA change vector and shadow price is .285, corresponding to a tunafish content of 28.5 percent, so we would have to resolve the problem to answer this question. Since .32 is still within the validity range, we answer the first question by multiplying the MIN-TUNA change vector and shadow price (1.000, $-.272$, .122, -7.011, 12.000, 2.198, $-.851$, and .04332) by .08 ($= .40 - .32$) and subtract the result from the current solution:

B	C	D	THIAMINE	PROTEIN	IRON	F		Objective
.400	.046	.337	.348	2.200	.252	.217	Old solution	.09391
$-.080$	.022	$-.010$	.561	$-.960$	$-.176$	.068	Change	$-.00347$
.320	.068	.327	.909	1.240	.076	.285	New solution	.09044

They should decrease the amount of bonito in the mix to .320 ounce, increase the supplement C to .068 ounce, decrease the supplement D to .327 ounce, and increase the filler to .285 ounce. Doing so will decrease the cost of Tuna-n-Stuff to $0.09044 per ounce.

3 How much could the price of supplement C change (increase or decrease) without changing the optimal blend? If the price changes a bit more than this, how will the optimal blend change?

CHANGING THE PRICE OF SUPPLEMENT C

From the objective sensitivity analysis, we see that the price of supplement C could increase by 9.5¢ (to .295) or decrease by 3.5¢ (to .165) without changing the optimal blend. Above the upper bound, the entering variable is NIACIN, so they will use less supplement C and adjust the rest of the blend (presumably by using more supplement D) in such a way that there will be more niacin in the blend than the minimum amount required. Below the lower bound, the entering variable is CALCIUM, so they will use more supplement C and adjust the rest of the blend (presumably by using less supplement D) in such a way that there will be more calcium in the blend than the minimum amount required. To get the exact new solutions, the problem would have to be resolved.

5 Pricing out new variables

SHOULD DESKS
BE MADE?

The design department at Dimensions, Ltd., has just proposed that the company add desks to the tables, chairs, and bookcases that they currently produce. After looking over the design for the desk, Jim Littlefield, the production manager, has estimated that each desk will require 4 hours in the assembly department, 5 hours in the finishing department, and 2 hours in the packing department. He also estimates that at a selling price of $80 per desk, the profit contribution per desk will be $6. Should Dimensions, Ltd., change its previous production plan and begin to make some desks?

The problem outlined above is an example of another kind of linear programming sensitivity question, that of deciding whether the addition of a new decision variable will change the old optimal solution. When considering a new variable, two factors will be decisive: its costs and its benefits. A bit of reflection should convince you that if the costs exceed the benefits, then the new variable will not be economically attractive. Hence it will not enter the solution, and the old optimal solution will remain optimal. On the other hand, if the benefits exceed the costs, then the new variable will be economically attractive. In this case, there will be a new optimal solution which will include the new variable at a positive level.

COSTS AND BENEFITS
OF NEW VARIABLES

For Dimensions, Ltd., the benefits derived from making desks are the $6 that each desk contributes to the company's profits. What are the costs? In order to make a desk, productive resources in the three departments must be diverted from making tables, chairs, and bookcases. When these resources are diverted, the total profit contribution from tables, chairs, and bookcases will decrease. This decrease in profit is the cost of making a desk.

USING THE SHADOW
PRICES TO PRICE
OUT DESKS

You already know how to determine the values to Dimensions, Ltd., of an hour in each of the three departments. These values are precisely the shadow prices for the three departmental constraints. Referring back to Figure 10-1 on page 434, we see that an hour of assembly time is worth $0.83333, an hour of finishing time is worth $0.66667, and an hour of packing time is worth $0.00. Now let's combine these values with the quantities of the three resources in a process known as *pricing out* the new variable:

Resource	Number of hours needed	×	Value per hour	=	Total value
Assembly	5		.83333		4.16665
Finishing	4		.66667		2.66668
Packing	2		.00000		.00000
					6.83333

Since the resources needed to produce a desk are worth $6.83333 in profit when they are used to produce tables, chairs, and bookcases, and they are only worth $6 in profit when used to produce a desk, the cost of producing a desk exceeds its benefits. Dimensions, Ltd., should stick with the old optimal solution of 6.66667 chairs and 16.66667 bookcases. They should not produce any desks at a selling price of $80 per desk.

Assuming that each dollar increase in selling price gets translated directly into another dollar of profit and that prices are always set in whole dollars, what is the minimum price at which Dimensions, Ltd., will find it profitable to make desks? They won't make desks unless the profit margin exceeds $6.83333 per desk, so they will have to set a selling price of at least $81. If they do set a selling price of $81, we know that the optimal solution will now produce some desks, but in order to find the exact solution, you will have to resolve the problem.

THE GENERAL RULE

The technique we used above to price out desks for Dimensions, Ltd., works to evaluate any new variable in any linear programming problem, be it a maximization or minimization problem. The general procedure is:

1 Find the coefficients of the new variable in each of the structural constraints.

2 Multiply each of these coefficients by the shadow price of the corresponding constraint.

3 Sum up all of the products found in step 2.

4 The sum found in step 3 is the *cost* of the new variable in a *maximization* problem. It is the *benefit* of the new variable in a *minimization* problem.

A COST MINIMIZATION PROBLEM

The Mittens Catfood Company has just been informed that its supplier can provide them with skipjack, a third kind of tunafish. An ounce of skipjack supplies 15 percent, 0 percent, 0 percent, 7 percent and 4 percent, respectively, of the RDA's of protein, thiamine, niacin, calcium, and iron. What is the maximum amount that the company will be willing to pay for skipjack? Since this is a cost minimization problem, we use the general pricing out rule to determine the *benefits* of using skipjack in Tuna-n-Stuff. If we introduce a new variable, S, to represent the number of ounces of skipjack per ounce of Tuna-n-Stuff, then the coefficients of S in the first five constraints (the nutrient requirement constraints) are 15, 0, 0, 7, and 4. Since S is a variety of tunafish, its coefficient in the TUNA-MIN constraint is 1. Finally, the coefficient of S in the TOTAL-WT constraint is also 1. Using this information and the shadow prices from Figure 10-3 on page 438, we can now find the total benefit per ounce of using skipjack in the blend for Tuna-n-Stuff:

"Resource" (constraint)	Number of units needed (coefficient)	×	Benefit per unit (shadow price)	=	Total benefit
Protein	15		.00000		.00000
Thiamine	0		.00000		.00000
Niacin	0		.00103		.00000
Calcium	7		.00734		.05138
Iron	4		.00000		.00000
Min-Tuna	1		.04332		.04332
Total-Wt	1		.02000		.02000
					.11470

Since the total benefit per ounce of skipjack is .11470, that is, 11.47¢, the company will be willing to pay its supplier any amount less than 11.47¢ per ounce. If the market price for skipjack is $2.00 per pound (12.5¢ per ounce), the old optimal blend will still be optimal. However, if the market price for skipjack is only $1.50 per pound (9.375¢ per ounce), then the company will change its blend and include some skipjack. To find the exact new optimal blend, you will have to resolve the problem.

This concludes our discussion of linear programming sensitivity analysis. You have seen quite a bit of its ability to provide managers with important economic information about their current operations and how they can respond to changes and new opportunities in their decision-making environment. It has been said that, "The optimal solution to a linear programming problem is important because it solves today's problems, but sensitivity analysis is even more important because it provides information about tomorrow's problems and opportunities." We hope that our excursion through sensitivity analysis has convinced you of the truth of this assertion.

SOLVING TOMORROW'S PROBLEMS

6 Sensitivity analysis with the simplex algorithm

In Chapter 9, you learned how to do the simplex algorithm by hand to solve linear programming problems. The purpose of this section is to

1 Examine the optimal simplex tableau and show you where you can find all of the information necessary to perform the sensitivity analyses discussed in sections 9.3 through 9.5.

2 Show you how that information is used.

PRIMAL AND DUAL OPTIMAL TABLEAUS

Table 10-1 contains the optimal solution to the expanded Dimensions, Ltd., problem discussed on page 432. Compare it with the optimal solution from LPSBA, shown in Figure 10-1 on page 434.

SHADOW PRICES ARE IN THE Z_j ROW

Notice that the shadow prices (which LPSBA gave as .83333, .66667 , and .00000) can be found as the entries in the Z_j row and the columns for the

C_j	Product mix	Quantity	2 T	4 C	3 B	0 S_A	0 S_F	0 S_P
4	C	6⅔	⅓	1	0	⅓	-⅓	0
3	B	16⅔	⅚	0	1	-⅙	⅔	0
0	S_P	26⅔	-5/3	0	0	-⅔	-⅓	1
	Z_j	76⅔	23/6	4	3	⅚	⅔	0
	$C_j - Z_j$		-11/6	0	0	-⅚	-⅔	0

TABLE 10-1
Solution to the primal

slack variables. The reduced cost for the nonbasic structural variable T (which LPSBA gave as -1.83333) can be found as the entry of the $C_j - Z_j$ row and the column for T.

REDUCED COSTS ARE IN THE $C_j - Z_j$ ROW

Table 10-2 contains the optimal solution to the dual problem, which was discussed on pages 432–435. Compare it with the optimal solution from LPSBA, shown in Figure 10-2 on page 434.

Now the shadow prices (which LPSBA gave as .00000, 6.66667, and 16.66667) can be found as the entries in the Z_j row and the columns for the artificial variables. The reduced cost for the nonbasic structural variable P (which LPSBA gave as 26.66667) can be found as the entry of the $C_j - Z_j$ row and the column for P.

What are the general rules?

THE GENERAL RULES

1 The reduced cost for any nonbasic structural variable can always be found in the optimal tableau at the intersection of the $C_j - Z_j$ row and the column corresponding to that variable.

2 The shadow price for any constraint (which is also the corresponding dual variable) can always be found in the optimal tableau at the intersection of the Z_j row and
   a. the column containing the slack variable for the constraint, if it is a less-than-or-equal-to constraint, or
   b. the column containing the artificial variable for the constraint, if it is a greater-than-or-equal-to or an equal-to constraint.

TABLE 10-2
Solution to the dual

C_j	Product mix	Quantity	60 A	40 F	80 P	0 S_1	0 S_2	0 S_3	M A_1	M A_2	M A_3
60	A	⅚	1	0	⅔	0	-⅓	⅙	0	⅓	-⅙
0	S_1	1⅙	0	0	5/3	1	-⅓	-⅚	-1	⅓	⅚
40	F	⅔	0	1	⅓	0	⅓	-⅔	0	-⅓	⅔
	Z_j	76⅔	60	40	53⅓	0	-6⅔	-16⅔	0	6⅔	16⅔
	$C_j - Z_j$		0	0	26⅔	0	6⅔	16⅔	M	M - 6⅔	M - 16⅔

Since the values of the shadow prices for one member of the primal-dual pair of problems are the same as the values of the structural variables for the other member of the pair, we see again that using the simplex algorithm to solve either of the problems actually solves both of them simultaneously.

RIGHT-HAND-SIDE RANGING

In Table 10-3 we have repeated from Table 10-1 the final simplex tableau for the optimal solution to the expanded Dimensions, Ltd., problem. From our previous analysis of the dual, we can see from the $C_j - Z_j$ row of Table 10-3 that adding another hour of assembly time will increase profit $5/6, adding another hour of finishing time will increase profit $2/3, and adding another hour of packing time will leave profit unchanged. These three values ($5/6, $2/3, and $0) are the *shadow prices*. Our problem at this point is to determine how many hours of assembly or finishing time we can actually use to earn these potential increased profits, that is, *to determine the range over which the shadow prices will remain valid.*

OVER WHAT RANGE DOES THE SHADOW PRICE REMAIN VALID?

Obviously we can't add assembly hours forever or we will violate one of the other two constraints, and using the same logic, we can't add or subtract finishing hours forever or we will violate the assembly or packing constraints. Suppose you want to know the number of hours you can add to or remove from the assembly department and still have the shadow price of $5/6 remain valid. The process here is quite like finding the replaced row in the simplex method. To illustrate the process, we repeat the S_A column and the quantity column from Table 10-3 and perform the same division we did in the simplex method.

Quantity	S_A		
6⅔	⅓	(6⅔)/⅓ =	20
16⅔	−⅙	(16⅔)/−⅙ =	−100
26⅔	−⅔	(26⅔)/−⅔ =	−40

The least positive quotient (20) is the answer to how much the number of assembly hours can be decreased. The least negative quotient (40) is the answer to how much the number of assembly hours can be increased. Thus we have found that the shadow price for assembly ($5/6 per hour) is *valid*

TABLE 10-3
Final simplex tableau of expanded Dimensions, Ltd., problem

C_j	Product mix	Quantity	2 T	4 C	3 B	0 S_A	0 S_F	0 S_P
4	C	6⅔	⅓	1	0	⅓	−⅓	0
3	B	16⅔	5/6	0	1	−⅙	⅔	0
0	S_P	26⅔	−5/3	0	0	−⅔	−⅓	1
	Z_j	76⅔	23/6	4	3	5/6	⅔	0
	$C_j - Z_j$		−11/6	0	0	−5/6	−⅔	0

over a range from *reducing* the assembly hours by 20 to *increasing* them by 40. Since we started with 60 assembly hours, we would say that the right-hand-side range for assembly is 40 to 100, or $(60 - 20)$ to $(60 + 40)$. Applying the same method to the finishing department will demonstrate that the right-hand-side range there is 15 to 60 hours. Compare these results with those reported by LPSBA in Figure 10-5, on page 442.

Now what about the packing department? Things are different in this case because *all the packing hours have not been used* (S_P is in the final solution in Table 10-3). With $26\frac{2}{3}$ unused hours in packing still in the solution, we see that we can *reduce* the number of packing hours only by $26\frac{2}{3}$ before a shortage of packing time occurs; conversely, since we are not using all the packing hours now, we can *increase* them indefinitely without changing the solution to the problem. Thus the right-hand-side range for packing would be $53\frac{1}{3}$ to no limit, or $(80 - 26\frac{2}{3})$ to $(80 + \text{no limit})$. Most computer programs used to solve linear programming problems provide the right-hand-side ranges as a part of the output.

▨ OBJECTIVE RANGING

OVER WHAT RANGE OF
THE OBJECTIVE
FUNCTION COEFFICIENT
IS THE OPTIMAL
SOLUTION
UNCHANGED?

Variables that are not in the solution Look again at Table 10-3. T (tables) is *not* in the optimal solution. That means that T's C_j (its profitability, $2 a table) is *not* as great as its Z_j (the loss it would produce if it came into the solution, $2\frac{3}{6}$). This is the same as saying that its $C_j - Z_j$ is negative; $-1\frac{1}{6}$ in this case. To come into the solution, its profit, C_j, would have to exceed $2\frac{3}{6}$. This means its profit would have to increase $1\frac{1}{6}$ ($2\frac{3}{6} - 2$) before it would pay Dimensions, Ltd., to produce tables (in this expanded problem). In the case of a minimizing problem, a variable not in the solution would come in if its cost dropped *below* Z_j.

Variables that are already in the solution Suppose Dimensions, Ltd., wants to know how large or how small the profit for chairs (C) can become without changing the optimal solution. To do this, we repeat the C row and the $C_j - Z_j$ rows from the final simplex tableau, Table 10-3, and divide each $C_j - Z_j$ entry (for variables *not* in the solution) by its associated C entry.

| $C_j - Z_j$ | $-1\frac{1}{6}$ | 0 | 0 | $-\frac{5}{6}$ | $-\frac{2}{3}$ | 0 |
C	$\frac{1}{3}$	1	0	$\frac{1}{3}$	$-\frac{1}{3}$	0
$\dfrac{C_j - Z_j}{C}$	-5.50			(-2.50)	(2.00)	

The *smallest positive* quotient (2) is the answer to how much the profit per chair could *increase* without changing the solution. The *smallest negative* quotient (2.50) is how much the profit per chair could *decrease* without changing the solution. Therefore, the *range* of the profit for C is $1.50 to $6, or ($4 - $2.50) to ($4 + $2). Using the same method, the range for B is $2 to $8. Compare these results with those reported by LPSBA in Figure 10-7, on page 444.

7 Linear programming applications

LINEAR PROGRAMMING
IS THE FOURTH MOST
WIDELY USED
QUANTITATIVE
TECHNIQUE

In a recent study of MS/OR activities, linear programming was the fourth most widely used among all quantitative techniques.[1] It would be impossible to either list or show all the present or potential applications of this technique; however, to give you some idea of the scope of application of linear programming, we have included this section.

The number of applications we will present here makes it necessary that we use fairly small problems; it also makes it necessary to omit the actual solutions and concentrate on formulating the problem and setting it up in proper linear programming form. In each case, we shall describe the problem setting, define the variables, and illustrate how the objective function and constraints are written. Following through these applications will not only give you an appreciation of the potential areas of application but also develop further your skills in *formulating* linear programming applications; as is the case with most quantitative techniques, computer-assisted solutions are much easier to produce than correct problem formulations.

FORMULATING
PROBLEMS IS MUCH
MORE DIFFICULT THAN
SOLVING THEM

Finally, we should point out that in each instance, one or another of the authors has been involved in an active role in each of the applications chosen for inclusion here. We have had to simplify the formulation and reduce the number of variables and constraints, but the problem that remains comes directly from one that we have been involved in during the last 20 years. Although we cannot identify the organizations by name, we have indicated their type of business, their approximate size, and their general geographic location. We felt that this approach, rather than the all too common listing of contrived problems, would show you how effective and how simple some applications really are.

ALL THE PROBLEMS
HERE ARE REAL ONES

PRODUCTION SMOOTHING APPLICATION

MATCHING
PRODUCTION AND
DEMAND WITH LINEAR
PROGRAMMING

A large private-brand manufacturer of knitted products in Tennessee approached us some years ago looking for help in a situation where seasonal peaks in demand exceeded current production capacity. The manufacturer knew that to meet seasonal demand, earlier production of items would have to be scheduled and the items then stored; in addition, in this case, both regular time and overtime could be used for production of most items, at a higher labor cost for overtime. The fact that the manufacturer produced over 3,000 different items made this problem quite complex. Here is forecast demand (in plant hours) and available capacity (also in plant hours) for both

---

[1] Guisseppi A. Forgionne, "Corporate Management Science Activities: An Update," *Interfaces*, vol. 13, no. 3, pp. 20–23, 1983.

the *busy* season (last 6 months of the year) and the *slack* season (first 6 months of the year) for one product:

	Forecast demand, hours	Plant capacity, hours	
Time period		Regular time	Overtime
First quarter of year	24	28	12
Second quarter of year	29	28	12
Third quarter of year	34	28	14
Final quarter of year	48	28	14
	135	112	52

Since regular-time production and overtime production in any previous quarter could be sold in any later quarter of the year, we defined the variables in the problem this way:

		For sale			
An hour's production		1st quarter	2d quarter	3d quarter	4th quarter
First quarter:	Regular time	R_{11}	R_{12}	R_{13}	R_{14}
	Overtime	O_{11}	O_{12}	O_{13}	O_{14}
Second quarter:	Regular time		R_{22}	R_{23}	R_{24}
	Overtime		O_{22}	O_{23}	O_{24}
Third quarter:	Regular time			R_{33}	R_{34}
	Overtime			O_{33}	O_{34}
Fourth quarter:	Regular time				R_{44}
	Overtime				O_{44}

Although this notation may look cumbersome, it makes it easy to tell what each variable represents: R_{ij} and O_{ij} are the regular-time and overtime hours used in quarter i to produce knitwear sold in quarter j.

Taking into account (1) the $8 per-hour labor cost for regular time, (2) the $12 per-hour labor cost for overtime, and (3) the $1 per-quarter inventory holding cost for an hour's output of knitwear, the company's cost accountants came up with the following cost coefficients for the variables defined above:

R_{11} 8 R_{12} 9 R_{13} 10 R_{14} 11 O_{11} 12 O_{12} 13 O_{13} 14 O_{14} 15
R_{22} 8 R_{23} 9 R_{24} 10 O_{22} 12 O_{23} 13 O_{24} 14
R_{33} 8 R_{34} 9 O_{33} 12 O_{34} 13
R_{44} 8 O_{44} 12

The objective function and constraints for a linear programming solution to this problem are:

Formulation		Explanation
$8R_{11} + 9R_{12} + 10R_{13} + 11R_{14} + 12O_{11} +$ $13O_{12} + 14O_{13} + 15O_{14} + 8R_{22} + 9R_{23} +$ $10R_{24} + 12O_{22} + 13O_{23} + 14O_{24} + 8R_{33} +$ $9R_{34} + 12O_{33} + 13O_{34} + 8R_{44} + 12O_{44}$		Objective function (total cost, to be minimized)
$R_{11} + R_{12} + R_{13} + R_{14}$	≤ 28	Constraint on first-quarter regular-time hours available
$O_{11} + O_{12} + O_{13} + O_{14}$	≤ 12	Constraint on first-quarter overtime hours available
$R_{22} + R_{23} + R_{24}$	≤ 28	Constraint on second-quarter regular-time hours available
$O_{22} + O_{23} + O_{24}$	≤ 12	Constraint on second-quarter overtime hours available
$R_{33} + R_{34}$	≤ 28	Constraint on third-quarter regular-time hours available
$O_{33} + O_{34}$	≤ 14	Constraint on third-quarter overtime hours available
R_{44}	≤ 28	Constraint on fourth-quarter regular-time hours available
O_{44}	≤ 14	Constraint on fourth-quarter overtime hours available
$R_{11} + O_{11}$	$= 24$	Constraint on first-quarter demand
$R_{12} + O_{12} + R_{22} + O_{22}$	$= 29$	Constraint on second-quarter demand
$R_{13} + O_{13} + R_{23} + O_{23} + R_{33} + O_{33}$	$= 34$	Constraint on third-quarter demand
$R_{14} + O_{14} + R_{24} + O_{24} + R_{34} + O_{34} +$ $R_{44} + O_{44}$	$= 48$	Constraint on fourth-quarter demand

All variables ≥ 0

SOME PROBLEMS WE
HAD WITH THIS
SITUATION

Of course, it just was not that easy. Because there were more than 3,000 products, we didn't want to generate a set of constraints for each product, and so we grouped products into 17 homogeneous groups (one such group was children's knitted shirts, sizes 1 to 6X; another was men's thermal underwear, all sizes) and generated a set of constraints like those above for each of the 17 groups. Another problem we had with this formulation was storage. We had taken care of the storage *cost* in the objective function, but *storage space* was limited at this mill. We finally had to establish constraints on the slack variables representing quantities in excess of current demand (quantities stored). We then constrained these variables to an upper limit representing the practical capacity of the company's finished goods warehouse. After that point we got usable answers.

457

LINEAR
PROGRAMMING III

MAXIMIZING THE
RETURN ON A
PORTFOLIO OF
INVESTMENTS USING
LINEAR PROGRAMMING

PORTFOLIO SELECTION APPLICATION

The investment manager of a state employees' credit union came to a quantitative methods seminar at two of the authors' university and got excited about a linear programming application to his responsibilities. He, like all investment managers, was expected to make decisions regarding types of investment under constraints imposed on him by law, the policies of the credit union, and his own good common sense. In this particular situation, the need to minimize risk limited the investment portfolio to preferred stocks, public utility bonds, and U.S. government securities (Federal National Mortgage Association, Federal Intermediate Credit Banks, U.S. Treasury bills, U.S. Treasury notes, and so forth). Here is a condensed version of the investment opportunities which were open to our investment manager at the time (he had $250,000 to invest) and the constraints under which he was expected to invest to maximize the return on the credit union's portfolio:

Investment	Symbol	Projected rate of return, percent
Milwaukee Electric Company bonds	MIL	9.1
Florida Gas bonds	GAS	10.3
Federal Intermediate Credit bonds	FED	6.7
United Industries Preferred	UNI	8.7
Federal Home Loan Bank bonds	FHLB	5.9
Consumers Utility bonds	CON	8.8

(Variables are thousands of dollars invested.)

Government securities cannot be less than 25% of the investment.
Preferred stocks are limited to at most 20% of the investment.
Public utility bonds must account for at least 40% of the investment.
No one of the three investment possibilities (preferred stocks, utility bonds, or government securities) can account for more than half the investment.

The objective function and constraints required to solve the state employees' credit union investment problem are these:

Formulation	Explanation
$91MIL + 103GAS + 67FED + 87UNI + 59FHLB + 88CON$	Objective function (total return, to be maximized)
$MIL + GAS + FED + UNI + FHLB + CON = 250$	Constraint ensuring that all funds are invested
$FED + FHLB \geq 62.5$	Constraint on government securities (minimum)
$UNI \leq 50$	Constraint on preferred stocks
$MIL + GAS + CON \geq 100$	Constraint on public utility bonds (minimum)
$MIL + GAS + CON \leq 125$	Constraint on public utility bonds (maximum)
$FED + FHLB \leq 125$	Constraint on government securities (maximum)
All variables ≥ 0	

We have made some assumptions in the simplified version of the problem used here. First, we have eliminated a problem that could give you some trouble in the real case, that of maturity. No financial institution like this wants all its investments in either short-term securities or very long term securities; some balance must be reached. Therefore, we had to get a consensus from the union board about the maturities they wanted, specifically what percentage of their portfolio (or of additions to it) they wanted coming due in each future period. At the time, it looked like we were going to generate about a thousand new constraints, given the way the conversation was going, but we finally got the group to agree on nine different maturities (such as fewer than 6 months, 6 to 12 months, 1 to 2 years, and so forth).

Another simplifying assumption we have made here is that we have treated the new investment of $250,000 as if it were the whole portfolio; that is, we have subjected it to all the constraints the portfolio must meet. In fact, the size of this particular portfolio was over $100 million, and if a new investment or a reinvestment of $1 million were put entirely into preferred stocks, it would hardly violate our third constraint. What we finally did was to consider all funds which were to be invested or reinvested within a year—not any single investment or single day's investment—as having to meet the constraints. In that way, over time, the entire portfolio will take on the characteristics embodied in the constraints regardless of where you start from.

INGREDIENT MIX APPLICATION

For a number of years one of our universities offered a seminar for a state association of food processors. One participant ran a meat processing plant about 100 miles southeast of Chapel Hill. He got quite interested in whether linear programming could be applied to sausage mixing. We had seen similar applications in the journals for years but had never done one ourselves, so off we went to the sausage plant. This plant manufactured sausage and other meat products. The process involved the purchase of the required ingredients (meats of various kinds and qualities, spices, other additives, and packing material), the blending of these ingredients in specific proportions, and a mechanized packaging operation.

The company advertised several different sausage mixes—Super-Hot, Hot Special, Country Best, Superlean, and so forth—each representing a particular mix of eight very specifically described U.S. government grades of beef and pork with appropriate spices. These grades and their characteristics were:

Grade and symbol	Percent lean	Cost/pound
Imported beef, IB	95	$1.16
Boneless chuck beef, BCB	80	.99
Boneless carcass beef, BKB	65	.97
Boneless pork butts, BPB	85	.98
Boneless pork picnics, BPP	70	.91
Boneless pork trimmings (A quality), BPTA	50	.82
Boneless pork trimmings (B quality), BPTB	30	.61
Boneless pork fat, BPF	0	.12

The company asked us to figure out for it the least expensive way to mix up a batch (its standard batch of sausage was 1,000 pounds) of its Half-n-Half brand. The label on this brand guaranteed that it had a total lean content of 70 percent (that 70 percent of its total weight, exclusive of spices and additives, was either lean pork or lean beef). The label also promised that half the total weight, exclusive of spices and additives, was pork and the other half beef. The company generally always had several thousand pounds of each of the eight grades of meat on hand, and so constraints on raw materials were not necessary.

The objective function and constraints necessary to solve this sausage mix problem are:

Formulation		Explanation
1.16 IB + .99 BCB + .97 BKB + .98 BPB + .91 BPP + .82 BPTA + .61 BPTB + .12 BPF		Objective function (total cost, to be minimized)
IB + BCB + BKB + BPB + BPP + BPTA + BPTB + BPF	= 1,000	Constraint to ensure that we get 1,000 pounds of sausage in the solution
IB + BCB + BKB	= BPB + BPP + BPTA + BPTB + BPF	Constraint ensuring that mixture is half beef, half pork
.95 IB + .80 BCB + .65 BKB + .85 BPB + .70 BPP + .50 BPTA + .30 BPTB	≥ 700	Constraint ensuring that 70% of the mixture will be lean

WE ARE TOLD THE
OPTIMAL SOLUTION
WILL NOT WORK

The plant owner was more than mildly surprised to find that our average cost per pound was about 8 cents less than his historic cost. When he looked at the ingredients in our mix, he laughed and said something like, "It won't hold together." We were sort of mystified and asked him to explain. He pointed out that our mixture had too much BPF (boneless pork fat) to stay together as a mixture. We knew no constraint had been established on this ingredient and asked him to do exactly that. Back in it went; this time we were about 5 cents less than his historic cost, and this time he accepted the mixture as salable. Since we were competing with a man who had been mixing meat products for 30 years, we felt pretty good about the whole thing.

Subsequent work with this company produced some interesting situations. We encountered, for example, the issue of "texture"; that is, one of our optimal solutions didn't "look right" according to the packing plant owner. It turned out that too much BKB (boneless carcass beef) as opposed to chuck or imported beef produced a beef wiener which just had too many visible fat particles, and so once again we had to ask the company for another constraint to cover this rather nonmathematical situation.

One of the early experiences we had with linear programming concerned a company about 50 miles from one of our universities which produced cotton yarns used in clothing. Its financial vice-president attended an executive program in Chapel Hill, and the section on quantitative methods really caught his attention. His company had the typical problem of yarn producers called *mill balance*. In the manufacture of yarn, there are two primary operations, carding and spinning. Carding is a process which gets all the cotton fibers arranged in the same direction and spinning turns a loose mat of cotton into a strong yarn by simultaneously pulling and twisting it onto a spindle.

When our friend's mill was producing coarse yarns, the carding operation just could not keep up with spinning. (Each spindle put on so many pounds of coarse yarn per hour that the carding operation fell way behind. Unfortunately, in-process carding output is severely limiting.) Alternatively, when the mill was producing fine yarns, the amount of yarn put on per hour by a spindle was so small that the carding operation could supply enough cotton for spinning in only 2 hours a day and consequently was shut down a good part of the time. The situation was intolerable from labor's point of view because of irregular work hours and from management's point of view because it could never really determine what kinds of yarn to produce to maximize contribution. To make matters worse, the mill offered for sale six different thicknesses of yarn (called *counts*); each one of these put a different quantity of yarn per hour on a spindle and had its own profit contribution.

We asked our friend to supply us with (1) the maximum capacity of the carding room in pounds of cotton per shift, (2) the pounds per hour that the six different counts of yarn would put on a spindle, (3) the profit earned by each of the six counts of yarn, and (4) the number of spindles the company had in operation on its spinning machines (frames).

	Yarn count	Pounds/hour/spindle	Profit/pound
Coarse	3's $= X_3$	.78	$.08
	6's $= X_6$	.61	.11
	8's $= X_8$	.54	.12
	10's $= X_{10}$	.42	.14
	12's $= X_{12}$	.31	.15
Fine	16's $= X_{16}$	.22	.21

Maximum capacity of carding operation $=$ 20,000 pounds/8-hour shift
Current spindles in operation $=$ 15,000

The objective function and constraints necessary to solve this problem are:

Formulation		Explanation
$.08X_3 + .11X_6 + .12X_8 + .14X_{10}$ $+ .15X_{12} + .21X_{16}$		Objective function (total profit, to be maximized)
$X_3 + X_6 + X_8 + X_{10} + X_{12} + X_{16}$	$\leq 20{,}000$	Constraint necessary to ensure that yarn produced does not exceed carding capacity
$\dfrac{X_3}{.78} + \dfrac{X_6}{.61} + \dfrac{X_8}{.54} + \dfrac{X_{10}}{.42} + \dfrac{X_{12}}{.31} + \dfrac{X_{16}}{.22}$	$\leq (15{,}000)(8)$	Constraint necessary to ensure that yarn produced does not exceed spinning capacity in an 8-hour shift

When we presented our friend with the optimal solution to his problem, he was not surprised that it contained *two* counts of yarn; "After all," he said, "anyone who's worked in a cotton mill knows that you can't balance the mill with less than two counts." Our two counts, however, were just different enough from the two he had been using to increase contribution by over $1,100 a week.

USING LINEAR PROGRAMMING TO COPE WITH A RECESSION

But this isn't the whole story. Shortly after we had done this work, the textile industry, our friend included, suffered quite a recession. He asked us if linear programming had anything to say about running a cotton yarn mill in a recession. We took his question to mean, "What counts should I run to keep the mill running as long as possible without creating excessive inventory?" We used a variation of the objective function to maximize labor hours used, and of course the program indicated that he should run the finer counts (the spindles would work the same number of hours but put on less yarn and thus produce less finished goods inventory to carry). Again he didn't seem surprised; "Any fool knows you *fine up* when yarn isn't selling," he said. We were interested in the way in which good common sense, for years before linear programming, had found better ways to accomplish various goals.

ADDING OTHER CONSTRAINTS

Later applications of linear programming for this company saw us introduce marketing constraints into the program, both the kind that promise at least a given quantity to a customer and the kind that keep production of a low-selling yarn count to a minimum. Here too, we expanded the number of constraints to consider other manufacturing processes besides carding and spinning, including the way in which the yarn was packaged for sale (called *put up* in the industry), the processes of opening the cotton bales, plying yarns (putting two or more single yarns together to form a plied yarn), and blending synthetic fibers with the cotton to produce yarns like the now ubiquitous cotton-polyester blend.

8 Glossary

Blocking variable The basic variable which gets driven down to zero as a right-hand-side coefficient of a constraint is increased (decreased) from its initial value to the upper (lower) bound of the validity range of the shadow price for that constraint.

Change vector The changes in the basic variables per unit increase in the right-hand side of a constraint; how the solution changes when the right-hand side changes.

Dual Another linear programming problem associated with a given linear programming problem. The dual problem determines values of the resources corresponding to the constraints in the original, or primal, problem.

Entering variable The nonbasic variable which will enter the solution if an objective function coefficient of some variable is increased (decreased) to just above (below) the upper (lower) bound of its optimality range.

Lower bound The bottom of an objective function optimality range or of a shadow price validity range.

Model A set of mathematical expressions which captures the relevant relationships, goals, and restrictions of a decision-making problem.

Modelling The process of converting the verbal description and numerical data of a decision-making environment into a mathematical model of that problem.

Objective coefficient optimality range The set of values over which a variable's objective function coefficient can vary without changing the optimal solution of a linear programming problem.

Objective ranging Sensitivity analysis which determines and uses the objective coefficient optimality ranges of the variables in a linear programming problem.

Pricing out Using the shadow prices of the linear programming optimal solution to determine the cost (benefit) of a new variable in a maximization (minimization) problem. The new variable will enter into a new optimal solution if its cost (benefit) is less (more) than its objective function coefficient.

Primal Linear programming problems come in pairs, one called the primal, the other called the dual. Although either one can be identified as the primal, we usually refer to the model we build as the primal.

Principle of complementary slackness A rule that relates the optimal solutions of a primal-dual pair of linear programs: If a structural constraint in one of the problems is satisfied as a strict inequality, then the associated structural variable in the other problem is zero. In particular, if a resource is not completely used up, then the shadow price of its constraint is zero; and, if the resources needed to produce a unit of a structural variable are worth more than the resulting unit, then that variable is zero in the optimal solution.

Reduced cost The rate of change of the optimal objective function value per unit increase of a nonbasic variable.

Right-hand-side ranging Sensitivity analysis based on shadow prices and change vectors (1) which determines how the objective value and optimal solution change as right-hand-side coefficients are changed and (2) which finds the validity ranges for the shadow prices and change vectors.

Sensitivity analysis Techniques such as objective ranging, pricing out, and right-hand-side ranging which examine how the optimal solution to a linear programming problem changes as the problem data are modified.

Shadow price The rate of change of the optimal objective function value per unit increase in the right-hand-side coefficient of a constraint. The value of another unit of a scarce resource, sometimes called an *imputed* value.

Shadow price validity range The set of values over which a constraint's right-hand-side coefficient can vary, within which the shadow price and change vector give the rates of change of the objective function and optimal solution.

Upper bound The top of an objective function optimality range or of a shadow price validity range.

9 Exercises

10-1 Treasure Cove is a resort land development near Myrtle Beach, South Carolina. The primary market for lots is within 200 miles of Myrtle Beach, an area served by four radio stations. The developers have decided to limit their advertising campaign to radio spots, since television appears much too expensive for a venture this size. The William Carmichael Agency of Columbia, South Carolina, has been asked to put together a 1-month radio promotional campaign; the agency, in turn, has retained you as a consultant to help apportion the client's advertising budget—$5,000 in this case—among the four stations. Here are data on cost per spot, availability of spots, and the National Radio Association's listener count per station.

	Cost per 30-sec spot	Maximum no. of spots available next month	NRA listener count
WFRA (Columbia, SC)	$60	34	32,000
WSMB (Charleston, SC)	74	29	45,000
WKYT (Florence, SC)	46	44	14,000
WLAW (Myrtle Beach, SC)	52	30	20,000

The Carmichael Agency wants an allocation of the budget to achieve the highest possible listener count (defined as listeners per 30-second spot) for next month consistent with the client's budget. Set up the objective function and constraints to solve this problem.

10-2 Carolina Health Services, Inc., is a clinic specializing in four types of patient care: cosmetic surgery, dermatology, orthopedic surgery, and neurosurgery. It has been determined from past records that a patient in each of these specialties contributes to the profit of the clinic as follows: cosmetic, $200; dermatology, $150; orthopedic, $150; and neurosurgery, $250. The physicians are convinced that patients are not being processed in an optimal manner. The clinic has contracted with you to provide a weekly patient processing system. You have been able to determine the following time requirements and limitations:

Specialty	Hours required/patient				
	Lab	X-ray	Therapy	Surgery	Physicians
Cosmetic	5	2	1	4	10
Dermatology	5	8	10	8	14
Orthopedic	2	1	0	16	8
Neurosurgery	4	5	8	10	12
Total hours available per week with present staff and facilities	200	140	110	240	320

The physicians have access to as many of each type of patient as they wish. Additionally, they have limited their cosmetic and orthopedic practice to a combined total of no more than 120 hours a week. Set up the objective function and constraints to find the optimal patient mix on a weekly basis.

10-3 The Township Machine Company is planning to add a new product line and wishes to hire some experienced machinists. The local union hall has advised Township that machinists are categorized in one of three skill levels: expert, normal, and apprentice. An expert machinist has at least 10 years of experience and must exhibit a competence to produce 20 pieces a day in the job Township wants to fill. A normal machinist must have 6 years of experience and should produce 16 pieces a day. An apprentice machinist must have at least a year of experience and should produce 12 pieces a day. The Township Company's union contract calls for wage scales of $80, $60, and $40 per day for the three skill levels. Currently, there are at most 2 expert machinists, 7 normal machinists, and 9 apprentice machinists available for hire. Township has budgeted $4,000 a week (5-day week) for machinists' salaries for the manufacture of its new product. Township would like to hire a complement of new workers which will yield the highest output rate, but would like to keep both the union and present employees happy by ensuring that the total experience of the workers hired represents a seniority level of at least 60 worker-years. Formulate the linear programming objective function and constraints which will solve for the number of machinists of each category that Township should hire to maximize its expected output rate.

10-4 The Acme Company has budgeted $250,000 for the development of new products. The possible development plans, expected cost if adopted in the fall, expected yields, and degree of risk (rated from 0 to 10) are as follows:

Plan	Expected cost	Expected yield	Degree of risk
A	$100,000	.20	8
B	50,000	.10	4
C	50,000	.15	10
D	150,000	.10	0

Acme can accept an entire plan at its full cost, or it may accept a partial (fractional) plan and still expect a constant yield proportionate to the level of expenditure on the plan. However, the company has decided to limit its total weighted risk (degree of risk times budgeted amount) to 1 million units; that is, an adopted plan for a $10,000 expenditure with a degree of risk of 7 would be 70,000 risk units. Formulate the linear programming objective function and constraints which will allow Acme to determine the development plan which will net the highest yield.

 10-5 Sailcraft, Inc., is a builder of sailboats in New Bern, North Carolina. The company currently offers three models: the Adventurer (32 feet), the Explorer (42 feet), and the World Cruiser (50 feet). There is currently a large backlog of orders. The production process is in three steps; the number of worker-days required for each step for the three models is:

	Forming, fiberglass	Wood trim, hull and cabin	Outrigging, rigging and sails
Adventurer	60	100	80
Explorer	100	240	100
Cruiser	200	360	160

Past profits lead to these expectations of profit: Adventurer, $7,500; Explorer, $15,000; World Cruiser, $30,000. Sailcraft currently employs 15 persons in fiberglass forming, 30 in woodworking, and 15 in outfitting; the average worker is on the job 200 working days a year. With this capacity, determine Sailcraft's optimal product mix.

10-6 A producer of dolomitic limestone for agricultural use has three lime quarries which supply five regional warehouses. The inventory position of each of the quarries this week follows:

Quarry	Tons of lime on hand
1	200
2	100
3	150

Transportation costs per ton from each quarry to each of the regional warehouses are shown in the following table:

	Cost per ton to warehouse				
Quarry	1	2	3	4	5
1	$5	$1	$6	$3	$1
2	2	3	4	5	4
3	4	2	3	2	3

The warehouses need lime for next week in the following quantities:

Warehouse 1:   80 tons
Warehouse 2:   90 tons
Warehouse 3:   100 tons
Warehouse 4:   70 tons
Warehouse 5:   60 tons

Set up the objective function and constraints that will solve for the shipping schedule for next week to minimize the total cost of satisfying the requirements of each of the five warehouses.

10-7 Southland Petroleum operates a refinery in Galveston, Texas, which produces four petroleum products from crude. Refinery and crude oil data are as follows:

Source of crude	Cost per barrel*	Availability, barrels/day	Density, lb/gal	Sulfur content, oz/barrel
Texas	$16	12,000	6.1	.05
Pennsylvania	11	18,000	6.9	.03
Offshore	13	15,000	7.1	.04

* A barrel is 42 gallons.

Source of crude	Refinery yields, percent by volume				
	Gasoline	Diesel	Fuel oil	Kerosene	Residual
Texas	35	15	25	15	10
Pennsylvania	50	15	10	20	5
Offshore	20	25	30	15	10
Selling price	$.91/gal	$.88/gal	$.95/gal	$.83/gal	$.78/gal
Sulfur restriction (oz/gal)	.0009	.0010	.0008	.0009	.0008

You may assume that each gallon of refined output from a given source of crude has the same proportional sulfur content as the crude did. Refining costs are $4 a barrel, and the total capacity of the refinery is 150,000 gallons of crude a day. Formulate the objective function and constraints necessary to produce the optimal mix of the three crude sources. You may assume that there are no marketing constraints on the five refined finished products.

10-8 North Carolina State Bank is doing funds planning for next year. The bank has essentially five different funds uses, each with a different rate of return, as follows:

Signature loans (unsecured)	21%
Installment loans on vehicles (secured with a lien on the vehicle)	18%
Home improvement loans (secured with a second deed of trust)	16%
Miscellaneous installment loans (secured with liens)	16%
U.S. government securities	12%

State banking regulations impose these constraints on North Carolina State Bank's investments:

1 Signature loans may not exceed 10 percent of total loans.

2 Home improvement loans may not exceed 50 percent of total secured loans.

3 Signature loans may not exceed the amount invested in U.S. government securities.

4 Investment in U.S. government securities may not exceed 40 percent of total money invested.

State Bank has $25 million to invest next year and wishes to maximize the return on its investment portfolio consistent with banking regulations. Set up the objective function and constraints necessary to solve the problem.

10-9 The Friends of Africa have chartered an airplane to fly donated food to the Republic of Zanimez whose residents urgently need food because of severe droughts. The food is packaged in three different sized cartons. The type A cartons weigh 500 pounds and have a volume of 200 cubic feet. Type B cartons weigh 700 pounds and have a volume of 350 cubic feet. Type C cartons weigh 300 pounds and have a volume of 100 cubic feet. Currently, there are 30, 40, and 50 cartons of the three types ready to be shipped, but the airplane has limited capacity. The airplane's forward cargo area can hold up to 8,000 pounds with a volume limit of 3,000 cubic feet. The center cargo area can hold no more than 10,000 pounds or 4,000 cubic feet. The aft cargo area can hold up to 6,000 pounds or 2,500 cubic feet. In order to preserve the trim of the aircraft, the weight loaded into the three cargo areas must be in proportion to their load capacities. Formulate a linear programming problem to help the Friends of Africa determine how many of each type carton should be carried in each of the three cargo areas, so that the total weight carried is maximized.

10-10 U.S. Agricultural Products supplies fertilizers to Middle Carolinas Farmers' Exchange, a farmers' co-op serving the Piedmont area of North and South Carolina. The co-op has recently placed an order for 100,000 pounds of an all-purpose 10-13-10 fertilizer (that is, the fertilizer is to contain at least 10 percent nitrogen, 13 percent phosphorus, and 10 percent potash; the remainder of the fertilizer is inert filler). MCFE is willing to accept a final blend which exceeds any of the three minimum specifications by no more than 0.25 percent, but will not accept a blend which does not meet the minimum specifications. The 10-13-10 will be produced by blending four standard bulk fertilizers (whose exact chemical contents are given below) with inert filler to achieve MCFE's specifications. Use linear programming to determine how U.S. Agricultural can fill this order at minimum cost.

Ingredient	Cost (¢/lb.)	Availability (lbs.)
4-8-6	4	30,000
5-10-10	6	70,000
8-12-4	5	80,000
20-20-20	10	60,000
filler	0.4	unlimited

10-11 From a primal problem we know that one unit of X_1, which contributes $6, requires 2 hours in department A and 1 hour in department B. One unit of X_2 contributes $6 and requires 1 hour in department A and 3 hours in department B. Capacity operation for both departments is currently 40 hours. Set up a dual and indicate the worth to the company of another productive hour in each department.

10-12 From a primal problem we know that a single unit of product 1 contributing $7 requires 3 units of input 1 (an ingredient) and 2 hours of labor. A single unit of product 2, contributing $5, requires 1 unit of input 1 and 1 hour of labor. Capacity of input 1 is currently 48 units, and there are 40 hours of labor. Set up the dual to this problem and indicate the value to this firm of another unit of input 1 and another labor hour.

10-13 Find the dual of the linear program formulated in Exercise 10-1. What economic interpretations can you give to the dual variables?

10-14 Find the dual of the linear program formulated in Exercise 10-2. What economic interpretations can you give to the dual variables?

10-15 Find the dual of the linear program formulated in Exercise 10-4. What economic interpretations can you give to the dual variables?

10-16 Find the dual of the linear program formulated in Exercise 10-5. What economic interpretations can you give to the dual variables?

10-17 The Demming Florist Company is planning to make up floral arrangements for the upcoming Mother's Day weekend. The company has available the following supply of flowers at the costs shown.

Type	Number available	Cost per flower
Red roses	800	.20
White roses	920	.20
Yellow roses	420	.22
White gardenias	450	.25
Pink carnations	4,000	.15

These flowers can be used in any of the four popular arrangements whose makeup and selling prices are as follows:

	Requirements					
Arrangement	Red roses	White roses	Yellow roses	Gardenias	Carnations	Selling price
Economy	4	0	0	2	2	$ 6
Maytime	0	8	4	5	10	$ 8
Spring color	9	9	6	0	10	$10
Deluxe rose	12	12	12	0	0	$12

Formulate a linear programming problem which allows the florist company to determine how many of each arrangement should be made up in order to maximize profits assuming all arrangements can be sold. Determine also how many of each type of flower will not be used in making the arrangements.

10-18 Using whatever computer package is available to you, solve the Demming Florist Company problem given in Exercise 10-17. Find the optimal solution, shadow prices, reduced costs, change vectors, shadow price validity ranges, and objective coefficient optimality ranges. Using this information, answer the following questions:

 a. Assuming the cost of an Economy arrangement remains fixed, by how much can its selling price decrease before Demming will reduce the number of Economy arrangements produced? Below that point, what will Demming produce that they don't produce now?

 b. Assuming the cost of a Maytime arrangement remains fixed, by how much can its selling price increase before Demming will increase the number of Maytime arrangements produced? Above that point, what will Demming produce that they don't produce now?

 c. What would the selling price of the Deluxe rose arrangement have to be before it became an attractive arrangement to produce?

 d. Assume that another florist has excess red roses they would be willing to sell to Demming. What is the top price Demming would be willing to pay per red rose? How many red roses would they buy at that price? How would their optimal solution change?

 e. Demming has just discovered that 100 of its red roses are old and unusable. How will this affect the optimal solution and profit?

f. Demming has just realized that the local university will be holding its commencement exercises on Mother's Day, and has decided to offer a Graduation Special arrangement. This arrangement will contain 4 red roses, 4 yellow roses, 6 gardenias, and 6 carnations. If Demming wants to increase its previous optimal profit by at least $2.25 for each Graduation Special, what selling price should be set for this arrangement?

g. Assume that another florist wishes to buy 30 gardenias from Demming. What is the lowest price per gardenia that Demming would be willing to accept? If the other florist offers 10¢ more per gardenia than this minimum price, what will Demming's new optimal solution be? How will its total profit change? (Don't forget the revenue from the gardenias!)

10-19 The Benson Snack Company markets dry-roasted nut mixes. Ingredients in an 8-oz. bag of its 4 best-selling nut mixes, current selling prices of bags, purchase costs of the ingredients, and the available quantities of ingredients are as follows:

Mix	Selling price	Ingredients (oz per 8-oz bag)					
		Cashews	Peanuts	Brazils	Filberts	Pecans	Almonds
Cocktail Special	$3.00	2	2	1	1	1	1
Deluxe Mix	$3.50	3	0	2	0	2	1
Royal Mix	$4.00	3	0	0	2	3	0
Party Special	$3.50	0	4	0	0	4	0
Ingredient cost per pound		$2.56	$1.28	$2.08	$3.20	$3.52	$2.72
Availability (lbs)		300	unlimited	100	75	200	200

The company can't sell more than 20 bags of Royal Mix in the current period or more than 50 bags of Cocktail Special. Formulate a linear programming model whose solution will enable Benson to maximize their profit. How would your formulation change if Benson wanted to maximize the number of bags sold?

10-20 Using whatever computer package is available to you, solve the Benson Snack Company problem given in Exercise 10-19 (using the maximum profit objective). Find the optimal solution, shadow prices, reduced costs, change vectors, shadow price validity ranges, and objective coefficient optimality ranges. Using this information, answer the following questions:

a. By how much can the price of Cocktail Special mix drop before Benson will decrease the amount of Cocktail Special it produces? By how much can its price increase before the optimal solution changes? Explain why this is so.

b. A valuable customer wishes to purchase an additional bag of Royal mix. She is willing to pay as much as necessary to make it worthwhile for Benson to produce this 21st bag. What is the lowest price Benson could charge her without reducing their profits?

c. The Wilson Import Company has just received a shipment of pecans which they are willing to sell to Benson for $6.00 per pound. How many of these should Benson purchase; how will the optimal solution and optimal profit change?

d. Benson has discovered that some of the available 100 pounds of Brazil nuts are rotten and must be thrown away. What is the maximum weight of Brazil nuts that can be thrown away before Benson stops making one of the mixtures it is currently producing? How much do profits decrease per pound of discarded Brazil nuts? What is the new optimal solution if 50 pounds of Brazils must be discarded?

e. Benson would like to introduce a new mix, Snacker's Nosh. An 8-ounce bag of this mix will contain 2 ounces each of cashews, Brazils, filberts, and pecans. Benson is willing to sell the new mix at up to a 25¢ per bag loss of profit during the introductory period. What is the lowest price they can charge for Snacker's Nosh and still meet this restriction?

 10-21 Using whatever computer package is available to you, solve the Benson Snack Company problem given in Exercise 10-19 (using the maximum bags sold objective). Find the optimal solution, shadow prices, reduced costs, change vectors, shadow price validity ranges, and objective coefficient optimality ranges. Using this information, answer the following questions:

a. A valuable customer wishes to purchase an additional bag of Royal mix. She is willing to pay as much as necessary to make it worthwhile for Benson to produce this 21st bag. If Benson makes this additional bag, what will the new optimal solution be? How will the total number of bags produced change?

b. Benson has just decided to stop producing Cocktail Special. How can you incorporate this decision into the linear programming model by changing only a single number? What is the new optimal solution?

c. Benson would like to introduce a new mix, Snacker's Nosh. An 8-ounce bag of this mix will contain 2 ounces each of cashews, Brazils, filberts, and pecans. If they introduce Snacker's Nosh, will they be able to increase the total number of bags sold? Answer the same question for Nosher's Snack, an 8-ounce bag of which contains 2 ounces each of peanuts, cashews, Brazils, and almonds.

d. The Wilson Import Company has just informed Benson that they can supply up to 150 pounds of Brazil nuts, rather than the 100 pounds that Benson has been planning on. How will this affect the optimal solution?

10-22 Given below is some of the output from LPSBA for the Halston Farina problem discussed on pages 428–430. Use this output to answer the following questions:

```
Optimal solution obtained after      8 pivots

Maximal objective function value:     690599.98062

Basic structural variables           Basic slack and surplus variables
L2             1800.00000            LARGEMAX          400.00000    Slack
G3             9411.76419            GIANTMAX         3080.00000    Slack
J2            10440.00020            JUMBOMAX         1918.00065    Slack
G1             4448.23581            MILLING             2.55601    Slack
J1              291.99915            JUMBOMIN          381.99935    Surplus

Shadow prices for constraints        Reduced costs for nonbasic structural vars.
LARGEMAX           .00000            L3                    .00000
GIANTMAX           .00000            G2                    .00000
JUMBOMAX           .00000
LARGEMIN         -6.00000            Alternate optimal solution via L3
GIANTMIN        -10.00000            Alternate optimal solution via G2
JUMBOMIN           .00000
MILLING            .00000
UNIT1          2000.00004
UNIT2          2000.00004
UNIT3          2000.00004
```

Variable	LARGEMAX	GIANTMAX	JUMBOMAX	L2	G3	J2	MILLING	G1	JUMBOMIN	J1
Value	400.000	3080.000	1918.001	1800.000	9411.764	10440.000	2.556	4448.236	381.999	291.999

Change vectors

	LARGEMAX	GIANTMAX	JUMBOMAX	L2	G3	J2	MILLING	G1	JUMBOMIN	J1
LARGEMAX	1.000	.000	.000	.000	.000	.000	.000	.000	.000	.000
GIANTMAX	.000	1.000	.000	.000	.000	.000	.000	.000	.000	.000
JUMBOMAX	.000	.000	1.000	.000	.000	.000	.000	.000	.000	.000
LARGEMIN	-1.000	.000	.867	1.000	.000	-.867	.001	.000	-.867	.000
GIANTMIN	.000	-1.000	1.133	.000	.000	.000	.003	1.000	-1.133	-1.133
JUMBOMIN	.000	.000	.000	.000	.000	.000	.000	.000	-1.000	.000
MILLING	.000	.000	.000	.000	.000	.000	1.000	.000	.000	.000
UNIT1	.000	.000	-66.667	.000	.000	.000	-.800	.000	66.667	66.667
UNIT2	.000	.000	-66.667	.000	.000	66.667	-.800	.000	66.667	.000
UNIT3	.000	.000	-66.667	.000	58.824	.000	-.800	-58.824	66.667	66.667

Sensitivity analysis on right-hand-side coefficients

Blocking variable	Lower bound	Row	RHS Coeff	Name	Upper bound	Blocking variable
LARGEMAX	1800.000	1	2200.000	LARGEMAX	None	
GIANTMAX	13860.000	2	16940.000	GIANTMAX	None	
JUMBOMAX	10731.999	3	12650.000	JUMBOMAX	None	
L2	.000	4	1800.000	LARGEMIN	2200.000	LARGEMAX
MILLING	12876.920	5	13860.000	GIANTMIN	14117.646	J1
	None	6	10350.000	JUMBOMIN	10731.999	JUMBOMIN
MILLING	297.444	7	300.000	MILLING	None	
J1	75.620	8	80.000	UNIT1	83.195	MILLING
JUMBOMIN	174.270	9	180.000	UNIT2	183.195	MILLING
J1	155.620	10	160.000	UNIT3	163.195	MILLING

a. What is the optimal solution reported by LPSBA? How much milling time is left over? How much packaging time is left over on each of the three packaging machines? How much profit can Halston make?

b. The output indicates that there are alternate optimal solutions, which can be found by bringing either $L3$ or $G2$ into the solution. How does this relate to the fact that the reduced costs for these two variables are zero?

c. Suppose another hour of packaging time were available on unit 3. How much would this increase Halston's profit, and what would the new optimal solution be?

d. Suppose the target production figure for large boxes is increased to 2100 boxes. How does this change the problem formulation? Can you use the output from the original problem to find the new optimal solution? If so, do so; if not, explain why this can't be done.

e. Halston is considering introducing a "family-size" box of Hearts of Wheat. This box will require .010 hours of milling time and .016 hours of packaging time. What is the minimum profit margin that will induce Halston to produce any family-size boxes?

10-23 Given below is some of the output from LPSBA for the San Antonio Fire & Casualty Company problem discussed on pages 430–431. Use this output to answer the following questions:

a. What is the optimal solution reported by LPSBA? How many new operators report at each period? Are there ever any excess operators; when and how many? How much does it cost San Antonio Fire & Casualty to staff the answering service?

b. How much would the wage for an operator reporting to work in period 6 have to fall before SAF&C would want to have any operators report to work in that period?

c. A new analysis of calling patterns has revealed that 6 operators are needed in period 1, but only 5 are needed in period 2. Find the new optimal solution. How will SAF&C's minimal cost change?

d. SAF&C is considering allowing some operators who report in periods 1 or 2 to work 12-hour shifts. The operators' union is in favor of this, provided that SAF&C pays at least $160 to an operator starting a 12-hour shift at midnight and at least $130 to an operator starting a 12-hour shift at 4AM. Will SAF&C put any operators on either of these 12-hour shifts? Which one(s)?

e. How much could the wage paid to an operator reporting at 4AM be changed (increased or decreased) before the optimal solution would change? What qualitative things can you say about how the solution would change if the wage moved just past these bounds?

```
Optimal solution obtained after     6 pivots

Minimal objective function value:     4588.00000

Basic structural variables           Basic slack and surplus variables
P2                3.00000            PERIOD4           20.00000    Surplus
P3               17.00000
P4               15.00000
P5               15.00000
P1                4.00000

Shadow prices for constraints        Reduced costs for nonbasic structural vars.
PERIOD2           8.00000            P6                2.00000
PERIOD3          80.00000
PERIOD4            .00000
PERIOD5          84.00000
PERIOD6           4.00000
PERIOD1          88.00000
```

Variable	P2	PERIOD4	P3	P4	P5	P1
Value	3.000	20.000	17.000	15.000	15.000	4.000

Change vectors

	P2	PERIOD4	P3	P4	P5	P1
PERIOD2	1.000	-1.000	-1.000	.000	.000	.000
PERIOD3	.000	1.000	1.000	.000	.000	.000
PERIOD4	.000	-1.000	.000	.000	.000	.000
PERIOD5	.000	1.000	.000	1.000	.000	.000
PERIOD6	.000	-1.000	.000	-1.000	1.000	.000
PERIOD1	-1.000	1.000	1.000	.000	.000	1.000

Sensitivity analysis on right-hand-side coefficients

Blocking variable	Lower bound	Row	RHS Coeff	Name	Upper bound	Blocking variable
P2	4.000	1	7.000	PERIOD2	24.000	P3
P3	3.000	2	20.000	PERIOD3	None	
	None	3	12.000	PERIOD4	32.000	PERIOD4
P4	15.000	4	30.000	PERIOD5	None	
P5	.000	5	15.000	PERIOD6	30.000	P4
P1	.000	6	4.000	PERIOD1	7.000	P2

Sensitivity analysis on objective coefficients

Entering variable	Lower bound	Col	Obj coeff	Name	Upper bound	Entering variable
PERIOD1	8.000	1	96.000	P1	98.000	P6
P6	86.000	2	88.000	P2	176.000	PERIOD1
PERIOD3	.000	3	80.000	P3	82.000	P6
P6	82.000	4	84.000	P4	88.000	PERIOD6
PERIOD6	84.000	5	88.000	P5	90.000	P6
P6	92.000	6	94.000	P6	None	
PERIOD2	-8.000	7	.000	PERIOD2	None	
PERIOD3	-80.000	9	.000	PERIOD3	None	
PERIOD3	-80.000	11	.000	PERIOD4	4.000	PERIOD6
PERIOD5	-84.000	13	.000	PERIOD5	None	
PERIOD6	-4.000	15	.000	PERIOD6	None	
PERIOD1	-88.000	17	.000	PERIOD1	None	

10-24 Here are the objective function, the constraints, and the final simplex tableau for a linear programming product-mix problem:

Objective function: maximize $\quad 2X_1 + 5X_2 + 8X_3$

Constraints:

$$6X_1 + 8X_2 + 4X_3 \leq 96$$
$$2X_1 + 1X_2 + 2X_3 \leq 40$$
$$5X_1 + 3X_2 + 2X_3 \leq 60$$

$$X_1, X_2, X_3 \geq 0$$

C_j	Product mix	Quantity	2 X_1	5 X_2	8 X_3	0 S_1	0 S_2	0 S_3
5	X_2	$2\frac{2}{3}$	$\frac{1}{3}$	1	0	$\frac{1}{6}$	$-\frac{1}{3}$	0
8	X_3	$18\frac{2}{3}$	$\frac{5}{6}$	0	1	$-\frac{1}{12}$	$\frac{2}{3}$	0
0	S_3	$14\frac{2}{3}$	$\frac{7}{3}$	0	0	$-\frac{1}{3}$	$-\frac{1}{3}$	1
	Z_j	$162\frac{2}{3}$	$\frac{25}{3}$	5	8	$\frac{1}{6}$	$\frac{11}{3}$	0
	$C_j - Z_j$		$-\frac{19}{3}$	0	0	$-\frac{1}{6}$	$-\frac{11}{3}$	0

a. Comment on the value to the company of adding additional capacity in each of the three departments.
b. Determine the ranges over which the shadow prices are valid.
c. Determine the ranges over which the objective coefficients of X_2 and X_3 can vary without affecting the optimal solution.
d. What would the contribution per unit of X_1 have to be for it to be in the optimal solution?
e. What are the marketing implications of the answers you have found for parts c and d above?

10-25 Here are the objective function, constraints, and final simplex tableau for a linear programming product-mix problem involving four products and three departments:

Objective function: maximize $\quad 2X_1 + 4X_2 + X_3 + X_4$

Constraints:

$$X_1 + 3X_2 \quad\quad + X_4 \leq 4$$
$$2X_1 + X_2 \quad\quad\quad \leq 3$$
$$X_2 + 4X_3 + X_4 \leq 3$$
$$X_1, X_2, X_3, X_4 \geq 0$$

C_j	Product mix	Quantity	2 X_1	4 X_2	1 X_3	1 X_4	0 S_1	0 S_2	0 S_3
4	X_2	1	0	1	0	$\frac{2}{5}$	$\frac{2}{5}$	$-\frac{1}{5}$	0
2	X_1	1	1	0	0	$-\frac{1}{5}$	$-\frac{1}{5}$	$\frac{3}{5}$	0
1	X_3	$\frac{1}{2}$	0	0	1	$\frac{3}{20}$	$-\frac{1}{10}$	$\frac{1}{20}$	$\frac{1}{4}$
	Z_j	$6\frac{1}{2}$	2	4	1	$\frac{27}{20}$	$\frac{22}{20}$	$\frac{9}{20}$	$\frac{1}{4}$
	$C_j - Z_j$		0	0	0	$-\frac{7}{20}$	$-\frac{22}{20}$	$-\frac{9}{20}$	$-\frac{1}{4}$

a. Comment on the value to this company of adding additional capacity in each of its three departments.

b. Determine the ranges over which each of the shadow prices are valid.
c. Determine the ranges over which the objective coefficients of X_1, X_2, and X_3 can vary without affecting the optimal solution.
d. What would the contribution of X_4 have to be for it to be in the optimal solution?

10-26 We have a product-mix problem where we can produce product A and/or product B. We have two machines, L and P, which are both used in the production of A or B. Let us define.

$$X_1 = \text{number of units of A produced/month}$$
$$X_2 = \text{number of units of B produced/month}$$

The profit per unit of A is \$360, and the profit per unit of B is \$400.
With slack variables added, the problem is

Objective, maximize: $360X_1 + 400X_2 + 0S_1 + 0S_2$

Subject to:
$$5X_1 + 6X_2 + 1S_1 + 0S_2 = 260 \text{ hr/mo}$$
$$\text{machine L constraint}$$

$$3X_1 + 2X_2 + 0S_1 + 1S_2 = 300 \text{ hr/mo}$$
$$\text{machine P constraint}$$

The optimal tableau for this problem follows:

C_j	Product mix	Quantity	360 X_1	400 X_2	0 S_1	0 S_2
360	X_1	52	1	6/5	1/5	0
0	S_2	144	0	-8/5	-3/5	1
	Z_j	18,720	360	432	72	0
	$C_j - Z_j$		0	-32	-72	0

Assuming you produce at the optimal mix, answer the following:
a. How many of each product are produced per month, and what is the total monthly contribution?
b. Another manufacturer is in need of more capacity on machine P. He offers you \$10 per hour above the depreciation costs to rent machine P for 80 hours per month. Do you accept the offer?
c. One of your customers comes to you wishing to purchase 2 units of B next month. Upon discovering that you do not produce any B's at your maximum profit position, he offers to pay you enough for them so that your profit will not be reduced. How much increase in price will he be paying?
d. Assuming you agree to produce the 2 units of B next month, how many units of A must be deleted from next month's production schedule?
e. Management wishes to increase the availability of machine L as much as possible, provided each hour of additional time will yield an increase in profit of \$72 per hour. How much additional machine time can be justified?
f. Currently 52 units per month of product A are being produced for an optimal profit of \$18,720 per month. How large or small can the profit for product A become without causing a shift in the optimal production strategy?

10-27 The following is a tableau for a maximization problem:

C_j	Product mix	Quantity	8 X_1	6 X_2	0 S_1	0 S_2	0 S_3
8	X_1	4 units/day	1	.75	2.5	0	0
0	S_2	4 hr/day	0	.05	−.5	1	0
0	S_3	1.4 hr/day	0	.175	−.75	0	1
	Z_j	$32/day	8	6	20	0	0
	$C_j - Z_j$		0	0	−20	0	0

a. Is this an optimal solution?
b. Is there more than one optimal solution to this problem?
c. What is the optimal objective value?
d. If slack S_1 is associated with machine A, S_2 with machine B, and S_3 with machine C, how much profit do we lose tomorrow if machine B goes down for 2 hours of maintenance? How much profit do we lose if machine A goes down ½ hour for maintenance?
e. The shadow price for time on machine A is $20 per hour of machine time per day. Within what range of values may we increase or decrease the number of hours per day for machine A and still realize the $20 per hour change in profits?
f. How much may we increase or decrease the number of hours per day of available time on machines B or C without changing our profit?

10-28 Given below is the optimal tableau for the San Antonio Fire & Casualty Company problem discussed on pages 430–431. S_j is the surplus variable for the period j constraint, and A_j is the artificial variable for that constraint. Use this tableau to answer the questions posed in Exercise 10-23 on page 472.

C_j	Product mix	Quantity	96 P1	88 P2	80 P3	84 P4	88 P5	94 P6	0 S2	0 S3	0 S4	0 S5	0 S6	0 S1	M A2	M A3	M A4	M A5	M A6	M A1
88	P2	3	0	1	0	0	0	−1	−1	0	0	0	0	1	1	0	0	0	0	−1
0	S4	20	0	0	0	0	0	0	1	−1	1	−1	1	−1	−1	1	−1	1	−1	1
80	P3	17	0	0	1	0	0	1	1	−1	0	0	0	−1	−1	1	0	0	0	1
84	P4	15	0	0	0	1	0	−1	0	0	0	−1	1	0	0	0	0	1	−1	0
88	P5	15	0	0	0	0	1	1	0	0	0	0	−1	0	0	0	0	0	1	0
96	P1	4	1	0	0	0	0	1	0	0	0	0	0	−1	0	0	0	0	0	1
	Z_j	4588	96	88	80	84	88	92	−8	−80	0	−84	−4	−88	8	80	0	84	4	88
	$C_j - Z_j$		0	0	0	0	0	2	8	80	0	84	4	88	M−8	M−80	M	M−84	M−4	M−88

10-29 Given below is the optimal tableau for the Demming Florist Company problem discussed in Exercise 10-17 on page 468. Use this tableau to answer the questions posed in Exercise 10-18 on page 468.

C_j	Product mix	Quantity	4.40 ECONOMY	2.77 MAYTIME	3.58 SPRING	4.56 DELUXE	0.00 REDROSE	0.00 WHITROSE	0.00 YELLROSE	0.00 GARDENIA	0.00 CARNATN
4.40	ECONOMY	200	1.000	0.000	2.250	3.000	0.250	0.000	0.000	0.000	0.000
0.00	WHITROSE	840	0.000	0.000	16.200	21.600	0.800	1.000	0.000	−1.600	0.000
0.00	YELLROSE	380	0.000	0.000	9.600	16.800	0.400	0.000	1.000	−0.800	0.000
2.77	MAYTIME	10	0.000	1.000	−0.900	−1.200	−0.100	0.000	0.000	0.200	0.000
0.00	CARNATN	3500	0.000	0.000	14.500	6.000	0.500	0.000	0.000	−2.000	1.000
	Z_j	907.70	4.400	2.770	7.407	9.876	0.823	0.000	0.000	0.554	0.000
	$C_j - Z_j$		0.000	0.000	−4.827	−5.316	−0.823	0.000	0.000	−0.554	0.000

10-1 Associated with any linear programming problem is another linear program called the _____, which can be used to evaluate the resources in the original problem. If the original linear program, called the _____ is a maximization problem, then this associated problem is a _____ problem.

10-2 _____ analysis is the investigation of how the optimal solution to a linear program changes when the data of the problem are changed. One such technique is _____, which determines how much the right-hand-side coefficients of the problem constraints can vary without changing which variables are in the optimal solution.

10-3 The optimal structural variables for the dual problem, also known as _____, give the changes in the optimal value of the objective function per unit increase of the _____ of the corresponding constraints.

10-4 If a constraint in the primal problem has slack in the optimal solution, the corresponding dual variable will equal zero. This is part of a result known as the _____.

10-5 When the right-hand side of a constraint is either increased or decreased, the resulting changes in the values of the variables in the optimal solution can be obtained from the _____, so long as the new right-hand side is still within the _____ range of the _____ of that constraint.

10-6 If a primal problem has m structural variables and n structural constraints, then its dual will have _____ structural variables and _____ structural constraints.

10-7 The process called _____ uses the shadow prices to determine if the introduction of a new variable into a linear programming problem will change the optimal solution.

10-8 The variable which first gets driven down to zero when the right-hand side of a constraint is increased determines the _____ of the validity range of the shadow price for that constraint and is known as a _____ variable.

10-9 _____ variables are nonbasic variables which will enter the solution if an objective coefficient is changed to a value just beyond the bounds of its _____ range.

10-10 The process of _____ converts the verbal description and numerical data of a decision-making problem into a mathematical _____ of that problem.

10-11 The number of structural constraints in the primal is the same as the number of structural variables in the dual, and the number of structural variables in the primal is the same as the number of structural constraints in the dual.

T F

10-12 For a variable which is nonbasic at optimality in a maximization problem to enter the solution, its C_j value must be decreased by an amount slightly greater than the absolute value of its reduced cost.

T F

10-13 The change vectors included in the LPSBA sensitivity analysis output are useful in determining the effects on the optimal solution of changes in the C_j values.   **T F**

10-14 If a primal problem has an optimal solution, its optimal objective value is larger than the optimal objective value of the associated dual problem.   **T F**

10-15 Many linear programming computer packages print out only the values of the basic variables, because the nonbasic variables are equal to zero.   **T F**

10-16 According to the principle of complementary slackness, any two constraints which have slack in the optimal solution must have identical, non-zero shadow prices.   **T F**

10-17 Blocking variables are associated with the upper and lower bounds of the validity ranges of shadow prices.   **T F**

10-18 Reduced costs give the change in the optimal objective value per unit increase in constraint right-hand sides.   **T F**

10-19 In a minimization problem, pricing out a new variable determines the benefit gained from including a unit of that variable in the optimal solution.   **T F**

10-20 Whenever you build mathematical models, you are planning to use them in applications of linear programming.   **T F**

10-21 In building linear programming models, it is often useful to express the constraints and objective function verbally before converting them into mathematical expressions in terms of the decision variables.   **T F**

10-22 If the value of the resources (as measured by the optimal dual variables) used to produce one unit of a primal variable exceeds the contribution of that unit to the primal objective function, then that variable will not be in the primal optimal solution.   **T F**

10-23 A shadow price is measured in objective function units per unit of a nonbasic decision variable.   **T F**

10-24 The change in the optimal objective function value per unit decrease of a constraint right-hand side is given by the negative of the shadow price for that constraint.   **T F**

10-25 Change vectors can only be used to determine how the optimal solution changes as the right-hand side of a single constraint changes; if several right-hand sides change simultaneously, the problem must be resolved from scratch.   **T F**

Multiple
Choice

10-26 The validity range for a shadow price can have
    a. Finite upper and lower bounds.
    b. A finite upper bound and an infinite lower bound.
    c. A finite lower bound and an infinite upper bound.
    d. Any of the above possibilities can occur.

10-27 If we perform a ranging analysis on the right-hand side of some constraint, and the upper bound of that constraint is infinite, we can conclude that
    a. There is slack in the constraint.
    b. The constraint is redundant.
    c. The shadow price for that constraint is zero.
    d. None of the above.

10-28 If you changed the right-hand side of a constraint to another value within the validity range of the shadow price for that constraint and resolved the problem, the new optimal solution
a. Would have a higher objective value.
b. Would have the same set of variables in the solution.
c. Would have a different set of variables in the solution.
d. Would have the same optimal solution.

10-29 The right-hand-side coefficient of some constraint in a primal problem appears in the corresponding dual as
a. A coefficient in the objective function.
b. A right-hand-side coefficient.
c. A structural coefficient.
d. None of the above.

10-30 A shadow price tells how much a one unit increase in a right-hand-side coefficient will change the
a. Values of the basic variables in the optimal solution.
b. Optimal value of the objective function.
c. Optimality range of an objective function coefficient.
d. All of the above.

10-31 All linear programming models have
a. Constraints.
b. An objective function.
c. Decision variables.
d. All of the above.

10-32 Which of the following is not a kind of sensitivity analysis?
a. Right-hand-side ranging.
b. Model building.
c. Pricing out.
d. Objective ranging.

10-33 Which of the following is not a step in model building?
a. Choosing decision variables.
b. Expressing the constraints verbally.
c. Interpreting the optimal solution.
d. Expressing the objective as a mathematical expression in terms of the decision variables.

10-34 Which of the following statements about the simplex algorithm are true?
a. Solving the primal problem also solves the dual.
b. Solving the dual problem also solves the primal.
c. (a) and (b) are both true.
d. Neither (a) nor (b) is true.

10-35 The validity range of a shadow price determines bounds within which
a. A change vector is valid.
b. A shadow price is valid.
c. Changing a right-hand-side coefficient doesn't change the set of variables in the optimal solution.
d. All of the above.

10-36 If the slack variable for a less-than-or-equal-to constraint is positive in the optimal solution, then
a. Some of the resource measured by that constraint is left over.
b. The problem has alternate optimal solutions.

c. The dual variable associated with that constraint is zero.

d. (*a*) and (*c*), but not (*b*).

e. (*a*), (*b*), and (*c*).

10-37 Pricing out a new variable in a maximization problem yields a value of −16. Which of the following statements are true?

a. The new variable will be attractive even if its C_j is zero.

b. The old optimal solution will still be optimal.

c. The new variable will be attractive only if its C_j is greater than 16.

d. None of the above.

10-38 Since a shadow price gives the change in the optimal objective function per unit increase of a right-hand-side coefficient, the shadow price of a less-than-or-equal-to constraint in a minimization problem can be

a. Positive.

b. Negative.

c. Zero.

d. (*a*) or (*c*), but not (*b*).

e. (*b*) or (*c*), but not (*a*).

f. (*a*), (*b*), or (*c*).

10-39 If a variable is nonbasic in the optimal solution to a maximization problem, then

a. Its reduced cost is positive.

b. Its objective coefficient optimality range has no upper bound.

c. Its objective coefficient optimality range has no lower bound.

d. There is an alternate optimal solution in which it is basic.

10-40 After a model has been built and the optimal solution has been found, then you should

a. Go ahead and implement that solution.

b. Check to see if that solution violates some constraints that hadn't been included in the model.

c. Perform all of the sensitivity analyses discussed in the chapter.

d. All of the above.

11 Real world MS/OR successes

EXAMPLE: MANAGING FUEL AT NATIONAL AIRLINES

WHY THE AIRLINES ADOPTED LP

Times of business crisis often stimulate MS/OR studies. This was the case in the airline industry during the 1970s, when the cost of fuel increased rapidly and supplies became uncertain. In response, many airlines turned to linear programming to decide when to fuel each aircraft and which vendors to use. Today, such models are commonplace in the U.S. airline industry. Sensitivity analysis is an important part of these LP applications, since flight schedules and fueling needs change frequently. The first LP model for fueling decisions was developed in 1974 by D. Wayne Darnell and Carolyn Loflin[2] at National

[2] D. Wayne Darnell and Carolyn Loflin, "National Airlines Fuel Management and Allocation Model," *Interfaces*, vol. 7, no. 2, pp. 1–16, 1977. Also see the follow-up note on the savings from this application, "Fuel Management and Allocation Model," *Interfaces*, vol. 9, no. 2, pt. 2, pp. 64–65, 1979.

Airlines. The bottom line: cost savings of about $10 million in the first two years of implementation.

Each flight schedule in the National Airlines model was considered as a chain of flights or legs. Fuel could be bought at an aircraft's departure city or during any number of succeeding legs. The price of fuel (including base price, various taxes, into-plane charges, and quantity discounts) varied widely at potential fueling stations during a typical flight schedule. Another complication was that carrying more than the minimum amount of fuel added weight to an aircaft and increased fuel consumption.

To develop a fueling strategy, the decision variables were defined as the numbers of gallons of fuel purchased from each vendor during each leg of a flight schedule. Up to 15 legs were considered for each aircraft. The objective function was to minimize: (1) the cost of fuel plus (2) the increase in fuel consumption caused by carrying more than the minimum amount of fuel. Constraints took into account the minimum and maximum fuel loads that an aircraft had to carry, the distance between stations and alternate destinations, and fuel consumption as a function of fuel on board, projected load factors, flight altitude, weather, and speed. Different models were set up for different parts of the National Airlines system. A typical model had 2,400 variables and 800 constraints for a multiple-aircraft flight schedule of 350 legs and 50 vendor possibilities.

Computer reports of the optimal LP solutions provided thorough sensitivity information to help National's fuel management department deal quickly with unexpected problems in supply or changes in flight plans. For example, if fuel consumption increased above the plan, sensitivity analysis determined when to make up the shortfall during the remaining flight schedule and which vendors were to be used.

STRUCTURE OF THE LP

SENSITIVITY ANALYSIS

11

The chief dispatcher of the Bass Gravel Company has firm orders this week to deliver gravel to construction sites located in Greenville, Fountain, and Ayden. Each of these sites has its own demand requirements for the week. Greenville must receive delivery of 72 truckloads, Fountain needs 102 truckloads, and Ayden needs 41 truckloads. The gravel may be delivered from any of Bass' three gravel plants located in Kinston, Wilson, and Bethel. Each of these plants is capacity constrained. The most that can be delivered from Kinston this week is 58 truckloads, while Wilson and Bethel can supply as much as 82 and 77 truckloads, respectively. Bass' chief dispatcher would like to schedule delivery in such a way that the total transportation costs for the week are at a minimum. To solve his scheduling problem, the chief dispatcher can formulate it as a linear program and use the simplex method. However, there's an easier solution procedure he can use called the transportation method. The transportation method can't solve all types of linear programming problems as the simplex method can. However, many linear programming problems have a special structure to them, for which the transportation method can prove to be easier and less time consuming. In this chapter, you will learn how to solve problems of the type that the Bass Gravel Company faces in the coming week.

SPECIALLY STRUCTURED LINEAR PROGRAMS

Transportation and Assignment Problems

CHAPTER OBJECTIVES

■ INTRODUCE SOME OF THE SPECIAL-PURPOSE ALGORITHMS USED TO SOLVE PARTICULAR KINDS OF LINEAR PROGRAMS.

■ PROVIDE SPECIFIC INSTRUCTION IN THE USE OF THE TRANSPORTATION METHOD, INCLUDING BOTH BALANCED AND UNBALANCED CONDITIONS OF SUPPLY AND DEMAND.

■ INTRODUCE THE ASSIGNMENT METHOD FOR A SPECIAL CLASS OF TRANSPORTATION PROBLEMS AND DEMONSTRATE ITS USE.

■ SHOW HOW TO HANDLE DEGENERACY IN BOTH THE TRANSPORTATION AND ASSIGNMENT METHODS.

Some types of linear programming problems can be solved by using more efficient computational procedures than the simplex method. One of the most useful of these special-purpose algorithms is the *transportation method* examined in this chapter. The *assignment problem*, a special case of the more general transportation problem, will also be treated.

The *transportation problem* is concerned with selecting routes in a product-distribution network among manufacturing plants and distribution warehouses or among regional distribution warehouses and local distribution outlets. The *assignment* problem, on the other hand, involves assigning employees to tasks, salespersons to territories, contracts to bidders, or jobs to plants. In applying the transportation method and the assignment method, management is searching for a distribution route or an assignment which will optimize some objective; this can be the minimization of total transportation cost, the maximization of profit, or the minimization of total time involved.

Both the transportation and assignment problems are members of a large class of specially structured linear programming problems called *network flow problems*. Networks are composed of points (called *nodes*) and lines (called *arcs*) which join pairs of nodes. Physical examples of networks include cities and the roads joining them, water distribution networks (in which the arcs are pipes and the nodes are houses, pumping stations, and points where large pipes branch into smaller pipes), and our telephone network (what are the arcs and nodes here?). Sometimes a problem has a network structure even when there is no immediately apparent physical network involved. This is true in the project scheduling problems discussed in the next chapter. This chapter and the next show how to formulate and solve many different members of the very useful class of network flow models.

1 The transportation problem (demand equals supply)

As its name implies, the transportation method was first formulated as a special procedure for finding the minimum cost program for distributing homogeneous units of a product from several points of supply (*sources*) to a number of points of demand (*destinations*). Suppose a manufacturer has 5 plants (sources) and 20 warehouses (destinations), all located at different geographical points. For a specified time, each source has a given capacity and each destination has a given requirement, and the costs of shipping the product from each source to each destination are known. The objective is to schedule shipments from sources to destinations in such a way as to minimize the total transportation cost.

The earliest formulation of this basic transportation problem was stated by F. L. Hitchcock in 1941 and later expanded by T. C. Koopmans. The *linear programming* formulation was first given by G. B. Dantzig. In 1953, W. W. Cooper and A. Charnes developed the *stepping-stone* method, a special-purpose algorithm for solving the transportation problem. Subsequent improvements led to the computationally easier *modified distribution* (MODI) method in 1955.

Let us consider the case of the Bass Gravel Company, which has received a contract to supply gravel for three new road projects located in the towns of Greenville, Fountain, and Ayden. Construction engineers have estimated the amounts of gravel which will be needed at three road construction projects:

Project	Location	Weekly requirement, truckloads
A	Greenville	72
B	Fountain	102
C	Ayden	41
Total		215

The Bass Gravel Company has three gravel plants located in the towns of Kinston, Wilson, and Bethel. The gravel required for the construction projects can be supplied by these three plants. Bass's chief dispatcher has calculated the amounts of gravel which can be supplied by each plant:

Plant	Location	Amount available/week, truckloads
W	Kinston	56
X	Wilson	82
Y	Bethel	77
Total available		215

BALANCED CONDITION

At this point we see that the total amount available is exactly equal to the total amount required. When total supply is equal to total demand, a *balanced condition* is said to exist. Although the balanced case is very unlikely in actual practice, it will enable us to focus on the basic ideas underlying the transportation method. The *unbalanced case,* where supply and demand are unequal, will be discussed later in the chapter.

The company has computed the delivery costs from each plant to each project site. As in the linear programming problems discussed in previous chapters, we assume that the variables in the problem must be linearly related. In this case, total delivery costs between each plant and project site vary directly with the number of truckloads of gravel distributed. These costs are shown in Table 11-1.

In Figure 11-1, we have illustrated the underlying transportation network for this problem graphically. The circles represent the projects, and the rectangles represent the gravel plants. Delivery costs per truckload are shown on the arrows which connect each plant with each road construction project.

Given the amounts required at each project and the amounts available at each plant, the company's problem is to schedule shipments from each plant

From	Cost per truckload		
	To project A	To project B	To project C
Plant W	$ 4	$ 8	$ 8
Plant X	16	24	16
Plant Y	8	16	24

TABLE 11-1
Delivery costs

to each project in such a manner as to minimize the total transportation cost within the constraints imposed by plant capacities and project requirements. At this point we have all the information necessary to solve Bass's problem.

LINEAR PROGRAMMING FORMULATION

DECISION VARIABLES

Before we show how to use the transportation method to solve this problem, let's look at its linear programming formulation. The decision variables determine how much gravel to ship from each *origin* (gravel plant) to each *destination* (road project). Since there are three origins and three destinations, there will be nine (= 3 × 3) decision variables. Let's call them WA, WB, WC, XA, XB, XC, YA, YB, and YC; in each variable, the first letter of the name identifies the origin, and the second letter identifies the destination.

OBJECTIVE FUNCTION

The objective is to minimize the total transportation cost:

$$4WA + 8WB + 8WC + 16XA + 24XB + 16XC + 8YA + 16YB + 24YC$$

CONSTRAINTS

There are three "origin constraints," which say that Bass cannot ship out more gravel than they have:

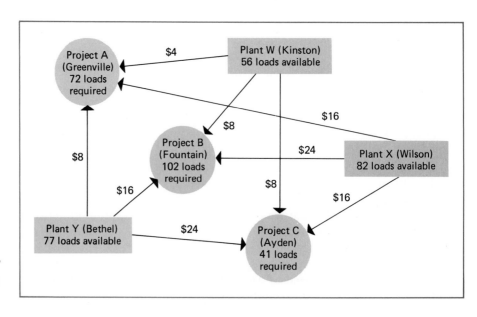

FIGURE 11-1
Gravel plants, road construction projects, and transportation costs for Bass Gravel Company.

$$WA + WB + WC \leq 56 : \text{Plant W}$$
$$XA + XB + XC \leq 82 : \text{Plant X}$$
$$YA + YB + YC \leq 77 : \text{Plant Y}$$

There are three "destination constraints," which say that each project must receive the gravel it requires:

$$WA + XA + YA \geq 72 : \text{Project A}$$
$$WB + XB + YB \geq 102 : \text{Project B}$$
$$WC + XC + YC \geq 41 : \text{Project C}$$

And of course all the variables must be non-negative.

Putting it all together, we get the final linear programming model: THE COMPLETE MODEL

minimize $4WA + 8WB + 8WC + 16XA + 24XB + 16XC + 8YA + 16YB + 24YC$
subject to

WA +	WB +	WC						≤ 56 : Plant W
			XA +	XB +	XC			≤ 82 : Plant X
						+ YA +	YB +	YC ≤ 77 : Plant Y
WA			+ XA			+ YA		≥ 72 : Project A
	WB			+ XB			+ YB	≥ 102 : Project B
		WC			+ XC			+ YC ≥ 41 : Project C

All variables ≥ 0

As you can easily see, this is a highly structured linear programming problem: each variable appears in exactly two of the constraints, once in an origin constraint and once in a destination constraint. Furthermore, the coefficients of the variables in the constraints are always $+1$. This special structure is characteristic of network flow problems. The transportation method is a way to take advantage of this structure, so that the more general (and more complex) simplex method need not be used.

Now that we've seen the linear programming formulation of this problem, let's see how it can be solved by the transportation method.

STEP 1: SET UP THE TRANSPORTATION TABLEAU

The transportation tableau serves the same basic purpose as the simplex tableau; it provides a framework for presenting all the relevant data in a concise manner and facilitates the search for progressively better solutions. In Figure 11-2 the standard format for the transportation tableau has been divided into *five* lettered sections—A, B, C, D, and E—each of which will be explained in detail. SETTING UP THE TRANSPORTATION TABLEAU

Section A In this part we list the sources of supply, plants W, X, and Y. Each row in the tableau represents a plant.

Section B The capacity for each plant is shown in section B. Thus we can think of the rows of the tableau as representing the capacity constraints. These are also referred to as the *rim requirements* for the rows. For example,

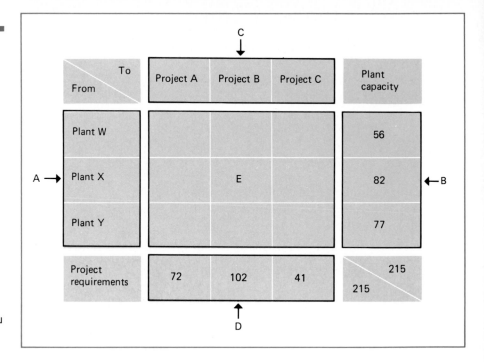

FIGURE 11-2
Transportation tableau for Bass Gravel Company problem.

the rim requirement in the first row means that plant W can supply no more than 56 truckloads per week.

Section C In this section are listed the destination points, road construction projects A, B, and C. Each column in the tableau represents a project.

Section D The requirements for each project are placed in this part. The columns, then, represent the demand constraints, or rim requirements, for the projects. For example, the rim requirement for column 1 signifies that project A requires exactly 72 truckloads per week. The total number of rim requirements in our problem is six, three for the rows and three for the columns.

Section E In this section are nine squares, or cells, representing the alternative source-to-destination assignments that could be made. For example, the 56 truckloads per week available at plant W may be used, in whole or in part, to fulfill the requirements of any of the three projects. Any combination of shipments from plant W is acceptable as long as the total equals exactly 56 truckloads. Similarly, the 72 truckloads required at project A may be met by any combination of shipments from the various plants as long as the total equals 72.

IDENTIFICATION SYMBOL AND DELIVERY COST

To complete the tableau, it will be helpful to add to each square of section E an identification symbol and a delivery cost figure. This has been done in Figure 11-3.

To From	Project A		Project B		Project C		Plant capacity
Plant W	WA X_1	4	WB X_2	8	WC X_3	8	56
Plant X	XA X_4	16	XB X_5	24	XC X_6	16	82
Plant Y	YA X_7	8	YB X_8	16	YC X_9	24	77
Project requirements	72		102		41		215 215

FIGURE 11-3
Transportation tableau with squares identified and delivery costs added.

Let us examine square WA located in the upper left-hand corner, repeated in Figure 11-4.

1 The WA in the upper-left-hand corner of the square is the identification symbol. This square represents the combination "plant W to project A" and therefore is identified as square WA.

2 The 4 in the upper-right-hand corner is the transportation cost per truckload between plant W and project A. The costs in each square were obtained from Table 11-1.

3 X_1 represents the number of truckloads shipped from Bass plant W to project A. In other words, all X's in Figure 11-3 denote the number of shipments between each plant and each project. The value of each X will be a positive whole number or zero. If in a particular solution the X value is missing for a square, this means that no quantity is shipped between the plant and project in question.

STEP 2: DEVELOP AN INITIAL SOLUTION

Now that the data have been arranged in tableau form, the next step is to find a solution to the problem in order to provide a starting point leading to

DEVELOPING AN INITIAL SOLUTION

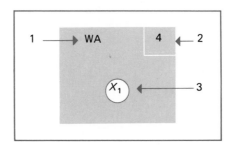

FIGURE 11-4
Square WA.

NORTHWEST
CORNER RULE

the procedure for developing improved solutions. Thus the initial solution in the transportation method serves the same purpose as the initial solution in the simplex method.

A systematic and logical procedure known as the *northwest corner rule* has been developed for setting up the initial solution. Although it does not *have* to be used, this rule offers the advantage of being systematic rather than trial and error. The northwest corner rule may be stated as follows:

1 Starting at the upper left-hand corner (the northwest corner) of the tableau, the supply available at each row must be exhausted before moving down to the next row, and the rim requirement of any column must be exhausted before moving to the right to the next column. If at any point before the end, a row supply and column demand are simultaneously satisfied, we have encountered a situation known as *degeneracy*. The procedure to use, should this occur, is given in section 3 of this chapter.

2 Check to see that *all* rim requirements have been satisfied.

The results of this procedure are shown in Figure 11-5.

An explanation of each assignment made in the initial solution shown in Figure 11-5 is given below:

INITIAL SOLUTION
ASSIGNMENT
EXPLAINED

Square WA Beginning in the upper left-hand corner, we compare the quantity available at plant W (56) with the quantity required at project A (72). Exhausting the supply at plant W, 56 truckloads are shipped to project A. This leaves project A short 16 truckloads. Move down to the second row in the same column to square XA.

Square XA Plant X has 82 truckloads available. Since project A is 16 short, Bass plant X will ship 16 of its 82 available truckloads to project A. The

FIGURE 11-5
The initial solution to the Bass Gravel Company problem.

requirements for project A have now been met. Since plant X has 66 truckloads remaining, we move to the next column to the right to square XB.

Square XB   Project B needs 102 truckloads. The remaining 66 truckloads from plant X will then be shipped to project B, leaving project B short 36 truckloads. As the amount available at plant X has been exhausted, we move vertically down to the next row to square YB.

Square YB   Plant Y has 77 truckloads available. Project B needs 36 more truckloads to fully satisfy its requirements. Hence plant Y will ship 36 of its 77 available truckloads to project B. We now move to the next column to the right to square YC.

Square YC   Plant Y has 41 truckloads remaining, which are shipped to project C, requiring 41 truckloads. The schedule of shipments is now complete.

The initial solution, then, includes the five source-destination combinations shown in Table 11-2. The squares in Figure 11-5 where no circled values appear are referred to as *unused squares;* that is, no quantity is shipped between the two points represented by an unused square. These squares therefore are not in the initial solution.

We must now determine the cost of this first solution for the Bass Gravel Company. To do this we multiply the quantities shipped between each source-destination combination in the solution by the respective unit cost. The results are shown in Table 11-3.

Before proceeding to the next step, several points should be made. The initial solution is a feasible one as all rim requirements have been met; that is, the sum of each row or column is equal to its rim requirement. Initial solutions obtained by using the northwest corner rule can always be recognized by their stairstep appearance, as shown by the path described in Figure 11-5.

Finally, for any solution, the number of used squares must be equal to the total number of rim requirements minus 1. In our first solution, there are 5 used squares, or source-destination combinations. The total rim requirements are 6, 1 for each plant (row) and each project (column). Thus

INITIAL SOLUTION
IS FEASIBLE

From plant	To project	Quantity, truckloads/week
W	A	56
X	A	16
X	B	66
Y	B	36
Y	C	41
Total		215

TABLE 11-2
Initial solution
illustrated

Source-destination combination	Quantity shipped	×	Unit cost	=	Total cost
WA	56		$ 4		$ 224
XA	16		16		256
XB	66		24		1,584
YB	36		16		576
YC	41		24		984
Total transportation cost					$3,624

TABLE 11-3
Total cost of
initial solution

INITIAL SOLUTION IS
NOT DEGENERATE

$$\text{Used squares} = \text{total rim requirements} - 1$$

$$5 = 6 - 1$$

When *any* solution does not conform to the above rule, *degeneracy* exists. The procedure for handling a degenerate solution will be discussed in a later section. The important point here is that each solution should be tested for degeneracy; that is, the number of used squares must be equal to the total rim requirements minus 1.

▌ STEP 3: TEST THE SOLUTION FOR IMPROVEMENT

TESTING THE INITIAL
SOLUTION FOR
IMPROVEMENT

Once a first solution to the Bass Gravel Company problem has been obtained, the next step is to determine whether this solution is the best, or least-cost, solution. The evaluation procedure involves the examination of each unused square in the tableau to see whether it is more desirable to move a shipment into one of them. The purpose of this evaluation is to determine whether a better schedule of shipments from plants to projects can be developed. Two alternative procedures for evaluating the unused squares will be presented, the *stepping-stone* and the *MODI* methods. The stepping-stone method (presented here) is the basis for the MODI method (presented later in the chapter) and provides a good introduction to it.

STEPPING-STONE
METHOD

STONE SQUARES

The used squares, those containing circled values, are said to be *in solution* and will be referred to as *stone squares*. In applying the stepping-stone method, we ask this question: What would happen if *one* truckload of gravel were tentatively shipped or assigned to an unused square? If this tentative assignment results in a favorable effect (reduces cost), the unused square evaluated then becomes a possible candidate for entering the next solution. This is analogous to the examination of the $C_j - Z_j$ row of the simplex tableau to determine which variable should be brought into the mix.

Let us now apply this reasoning to our present problem. In Figure 11-5 we note that the square WB is unused. Suppose that we assign 1 truckload to square WB, that is, ship 1 truckload from plant W to project B. In order to make this assignment and still satisfy the capacity restriction (rim requirement) for plant W, we must subtract from square WA 1 truckload so that the total shipments from plant W do not exceed 56. However, if we subtract 1 truckload from square WA, we must then add 1 truckload to square XA in order to meet the rim requirement for project A. Adding 1 truckload to square XA means that we must subtract 1 truckload from square XB in order to satisfy the rim requirement for that row (plant X). Finally, the truckload subtracted from square XB still enables project B requirements to total 102; one truckload has been tentatively added to square WB at the start of the evaluation. The evaluation is now back where it started. These changes in the shipping program can be much more readily seen in Figure 11-6.

Note that the net change for any row or column is zero; wherever 1 truckload was added to a square, another square was decreased by the same amount.

The question we now ask is: What effect will the assignment of 1 truckload to the unused square WB have on Bass's total cost? Looking at the path described in evaluating square WB (Figure 11-6), we see that shipping 1 truckload from plant W to project B results in an increase of $8 in distribution costs. The $8 cost per truckload between the two points is given in the upper right-hand corner of square WB. A similar increase from plant X to project A results in an additional cost of $16 (square XA). Likewise, the decrease of 1 truckload between plant W and project A reduces total costs by $4 (square WA). In addition, the decrease of 1 truckload between plant X and project B results in a reduction of $24 (square XB). The *net* change in costs, referred to as the *improvement index,* is computed as follows:

Addition to cost:	From plant W to project B	$ 8	
	From plant X to project A	16	$24
Reduction in cost:	From plant W to project A	$ 4	
	From plant X to project B	24	28
			− $4

From \ To	Project A		Project B		Project C		Plant capacity
Plant W	WA 56 −	4	WB +	8	WC	8	56
Plant X	XA 16 +	16	XB 66 −	24	XC	16	82
Plant Y	YA	8	YB 36	16	YC 41	24	77
Project requirements	72		102		41		215 / 215

FIGURE 11-6

Adjustment required in evaluating square WB.

The same answer can be obtained by following the path used directly and resorting to a sort of shorthand, as follows:

$$\text{Improvement index for square WB} = \text{WB} - \text{WA} + \text{XA} - \text{XB}$$

Now substituting the cost per truckload for each source-destination combination in the above equation, we have

$$\text{Improvement index for square WB} = \$8 - \$4 + \$16 - \$24 = -\$4$$

The $-\$4$ means that for every truckload shipped from plant W to project B, total transportation costs would be reduced by $4. Because this is true, it would be advantageous to use this route if this were the only choice available. However, the evaluation of other unused squares in our tableau might bring about an even greater reduction. The task remaining then is to evaluate all remaining unused squares.

Steps in evaluating any unused square

1 *Choose the unused square* to be evaluated.

2 Beginning with the selected unused square, *trace a closed path* (moving horizontally and vertically only) from this unused square via stone squares back to the original unused square. Only one closed path exists for each unused square in a given solution. Although the path may skip over stone or unused squares and may cross over itself, corners of the closed path may occur only at the stone squares and the unused square being evaluated.

3 *Assign plus* (+) *and minus* (−) *signs* alternately at each corner square of the closed path, beginning with a plus sign at the unused square. Assign these signs by starting in either a clockwise or a counterclockwise direction. The positive and negative signs represent the addition or subtraction of 1 unit (truckload in this case) to a square.

4 *Determine the net change in costs* as a result of the changes made in tracing the path. Summing the unit cost in each square with a plus sign will give the addition to cost. The decrease in cost is obtained by summing the unit cost in each square with a negative sign. Comparing the additions to cost with the decreases will give the improvement index. (The improvement index corresponds to the $C_j - Z_j$ value calculated by the simplex method.)

5 *Repeat the above steps* until an improvement index has been determined for each unused square.

If all the indices are greater than or equal to zero, an optimal solution has been found. Conversely, if any of the indices is negative, an improved (lower cost) solution is possible.

The above rules were used in tracing the path and determining the improvement index for square WB (Figure 11-6). Let us now evaluate the unused square WC. The traced path used in evaluating this square is shown in Figure 11-7.

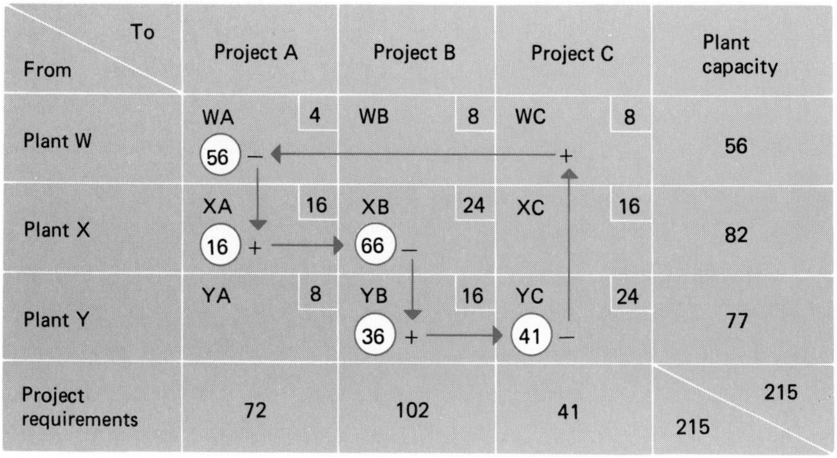
To
From
Project A
Project B
Project C
Plant capacity
Plant W
WA 4
56 −
WB 8
WC 8
+
56
Plant X
XA 16
16 +
XB 24
66 −
XC 16
82
Plant Y
YA 8
YB 16
36 +
YC 24
41 −
77
Project requirements
72
102
41
215
215

FIGURE 11-7
Path used in evaluating square WC.

The improvement index for unused square WC traced in Figure 11-7 is computed as follows:

$$\begin{aligned}\text{Improvement index for WC} &= \text{WC} - \text{WA} + \text{XA} - \text{XB} + \text{YB} - \text{YC}\\ &= \$8 - \$4 + \$16 - \$24 + \$16 - \$24\\ &= -\$12\end{aligned}$$

The closed paths and improvement indices for the remaining two unused squares are

$$\text{Path for square XC: } (+)\text{XC} \rightarrow (-)\text{XB} \rightarrow (+)\text{YB} \rightarrow (-)\text{YC}$$

$$\begin{aligned}\text{Improvement index for XC} &= \text{XC} - \text{XB} + \text{YB} - \text{YC}\\ &= \$16 - \$24 + \$16 - \$24\\ &= -\$16\end{aligned}$$

$$\text{Path for square YA: } (+)\text{YA} \rightarrow (-)\text{XA} \rightarrow (+)\text{XB} \rightarrow (-)\text{YB}$$

$$\begin{aligned}\text{Improvement index for YA} &= \text{YA} - \text{XA} + \text{XB} - \text{YB}\\ &= \$8 - \$16 + \$24 - \$16\\ &= \$0\end{aligned}$$

We have now completed the evaluation of all unused squares, each of which represents an alternative route that might be taken. The improvement index for each unused square is shown in Figure 11-8.

BRIEF SUMMARY OF STEPS TO THIS POINT

A brief summary might be helpful at this point. Step 3 called for testing the solution for improvement. In order to do this, the stepping-stone procedure was used to evaluate each unused square. The objective was to determine whether it would be profitable to use some other route, represented

From \ To	Project A		Project B		Project C		Plant capacity
Plant W	WA (56)	4	WB −4	8	WC −12	8	56
Plant X	XA (16)	16	XB (66)	24	XC −16	16	82
Plant Y	YA 0	8	YB (36)	16	YC (41)	24	77
Project requirements	72		102		41		215 / 215

FIGURE 11-8
All unused squares evaluated.

by some unused square. If any improvement index is *negative,* the best solution has not been obtained. Our evaluation resulted in three unused squares with negative improvement indices, and so we know that a better solution is possible. The next step, then, is to develop the new solution.

STEP 4: DEVELOP THE IMPROVED SOLUTION

DEVELOPING THE IMPROVED SOLUTION FOR THE BASS GRAVEL COMPANY PROBLEM

Each negative improvement index represents the amount by which Bass's total transportation costs could be reduced if 1 truckload were shipped by that source-destination combination. In this sense the improvement indices are analogous to the values in the $C_j - Z_j$ row of the simplex method. For example, the improvement index for square XC means that for every truckload shipped from plant X to project C, total transportation costs will be reduced by \$16. The question now is: Given three alternative routes with negative improvement indices (squares WB, WC, and XC), which one shall we choose in developing the improved solution? We shall select that route (unused square) with the *largest negative improvement index.* In our problem this is square XC, with a negative index of \$16.

SELECT THE ROUTE WITH THE LARGEST NEGATIVE IMPROVEMENT INDEX

Using this route will reduce costs. Bass must now decide how many truckloads to ship via this route, that is, from plant X to project C. To do this, we must reconstruct the closed path traced in evaluating unused square XC. This has been done in Figure 11-9, using only the relevant part of the tableau.

Now the maximum quantity which Bass can ship from plant X to project C is found by determining the smallest stone in a negative position on the closed path. The closed path for square XC has negative corners at squares XB and YC, and the smaller of these two stones is 41 truckloads per week. To obtain our new solution, we add 41 truckloads to all squares on the closed path with plus signs, and we subtract this quantity from all squares on the path assigned minus signs, as shown in Figure 11-10.

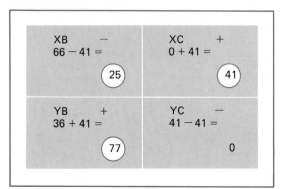

FIGURE 11-9
Closed path traced in
evaluating unused
square XC.

Why did we choose the smallest stone in a negative position on the closed path as the maximum number of truckloads that could be shipped from plant X to project C? Suppose we add 66 truckloads to square XC instead of 41. In order to satisfy our rim requirements, we would have to do the following: add 66 to XC, subtract 66 from XB, add 66 to YB, and subtract 66 from YC. The results are

XC:	$0 + 66 =$	66
XB:	$66 - 66 =$	0
YB:	$36 + 66 =$	102
YC:	$41 - 66 =$	-25

The computation for square YC shows that Bass Gravel Company plant Y would ship -25 truckloads to project C. This negative shipment is both meaningless in an actual problem and a violation of the requirement prohibiting the assignment of negative stone squares. As in the simplex method, all values in the solution must be greater than or equal to zero. Hence the maximum quantity which may be brought into a solution is found by determining the smallest stone in a negative position on the closed path of the square with the largest negative improvement index. This quantity is added to all squares on the closed path with plus signs and subtracted from

FIGURE 11-10
Forty-one loads added
and subtracted.

From \ To	Project A	Project B	Project C	Plant capacity
Plant W	WA 4 (56)	WB 8	WC 8	56
Plant X	XA 16 (16)	XB 24 (25)	XC 16 (41)	82
Plant Y	YA 8	YB 16 (77)	YC 24	77
Project requirements	72	102	41	215 / 215

FIGURE 11-11
The second solution.

all squares on the path with minus signs. The new, improved solution is shown in Figure 11-11.

Note that square YC, which was a stone square in the initial solution, is now an unused square. Square XC has entered the improved solution in place of square YC. As can be seen in Table 11-4, the total transportation cost for the new shipping assignments of our second solution is an improvement upon the cost of the first solution, $2,968 versus $3,624.

IS FURTHER IMPROVEMENT POSSIBLE?

We now go back to step 3 to determine whether further improvement is possible. Using the stepping-stone method described in that section, we calculate an improvement index for each unused square in the second solution. The closed paths and improvement indices for each unused square in Figure 11-11 are shown in Table 11-5.

SKIPPING OVER STONE SQUARES

As previously mentioned, in tracing a closed path, the resulting route may require *skipping* over stone squares as well as over unused squares. This occurs in tracing the path for square WC and is shown in Figure 11-12.

Looking at the improvement indices computed in Table 11-5, we find one negative index for unused square WB, indicating that further improvement is possible. For each truckload assigned to square WB, total costs will be

TABLE 11-4
Total cost of second solution

Shipping assignments	Quantity shipped	× Unit cost	= Total cost
WA	56	$ 4	$ 224
XA	16	16	256
XB	25	24	600
XC	41	16	656
YB	77	16	1,232
Total transportation cost			$2,968

Unused square	Closed path	Computation of improvement index
WB	+WB − WA + XA − XB	+ 8 − 4 + 16 − 24 = − 4
WC	+WC − WA + XA − XC	+ 8 − 4 + 16 − 16 = + 4
YA	+YA − XA + XB − YB	+ 8 − 16 + 24 − 16 = 0
YC	+YC − XC + XB − YB	+24 − 16 + 24 − 16 = +16

TABLE 11-5
Closed paths and
improvement indices
for unused squares of
Figure 11-11

reduced \$4. To determine the number of truckloads to be shipped, we select the smallest stone in a negative position on the closed path traced in evaluating square WB (step 4).

$$+ \text{WB} - \text{WA} + \text{XA} - \text{XB} + \longrightarrow - (56) \longrightarrow + (16) \longrightarrow - (25)$$

As seen above, the smallest stone in a negative position is 25. This quantity is added to all squares on the path with plus signs and subtracted from all squares on the path with minus signs, as shown in Figure 11-13.

The third improved solution is given in Figure 11-14, and the total cost of the third solution is shown in Table 11-6.

Again we go back to step 3 to determine if further improvement is possible. The closed paths and improvement indices for the unused squares in Figure 11-14 are given in Table 11-7. The negative improvement index for square YA indicates that the best solution has not been obtained. Now, following the same procedure discussed in step 4, we find that the maximum quantity to assign to square YA is 31 truckloads; the new solution is given in Figure 11-15. This is indeed the *optimal* solution. The improvement indices for Figure 11-15 are all greater than or equal to zero (see Table 11-8).

THIS IS THE OPTIMAL SOLUTION

The total cost for the optimal solution to the Bass Gravel Company problem is shown in Table 11-9. Bass might question the use of a somewhat tedious method for solving such a simple problem. Why not use a trial-and-error method? Why not begin by simply choosing the lowest-cost route and using it to the fullest extent? Then we might select the next lowest rate and use it to the fullest extent, and so on, until we have satisfied all the requirements

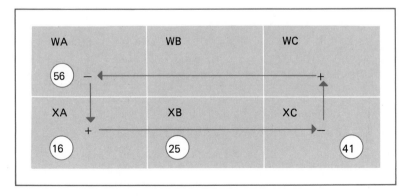

FIGURE 11-12
Tracing the path for
square WC.

FIGURE 11-13
Twenty-five loads
added and subtracted.

FIGURE 11-14
The third solution.

TABLE 11-6
Total cost of
third solution

Shipping assignments	Quantity shipped	×	Unit cost	=	Total cost
WA	31		$ 4		$ 124
WB	25		8		200
XA	41		16		656
XC	41		16		656
YB	77		16		1,232
Total transportation cost					$2,868

TABLE 11-7
Closed paths and improvement indices for Figure 11-14

Unused square	Closed path	Computation of improvement index
WC	+WC − WA + XA − XC	+ 8 − 4 + 16 − 16 = + 4
XB	+XB − WB + WA − XA	+24 − 8 + 4 − 16 = + 4
YA	+YA − WA + WB − YB	+ 8 − 4 + 8 − 16 = − 4
YC	+YC − YB + WB − WA + XA − XC	+24 − 16 + 8 − 4 + 16 − 16 = +12

From \ To	Project A		Project B		Project C		Plant capacity
Plant W	WA	4	WB (56)	8	WC	8	56
Plant X	XA (41)	16	XB	24	XC (41)	16	82
Plant Y	YA (31)	8	YB (46)	16	YC	24	77
Project requirements	72		102		41		215 / 215

FIGURE 11-15
The optimal solution to the Bass Gravel Company problem.

TABLE 11-8
Closed paths and improvement indices for Figure 11-15

Unused square	Closed path	Computation of improvement index
WA	+WA − YA + YB − WB	+ 4 − 8 + 16 − 8 = + 4
WC	+WC − XC + XA − YA + YB − WB	+8 − 16 + 16 − 8 + 16 − 8 = + 8
XB	+XB − YB + YA − XA	+24 − 16 + 8 − 16 = 0
YC	+YC − XC + XA − YA	+24 − 16 + 16 − 8 = +16

Shipping assignments	Quantity shipped	×	Unit cost	=	Total cost
WB	56		$ 8		$ 448
XA	41		16		656
XC	41		16		656
YA	31		8		248
YB	46		16		736
Total transportation cost					$2,744

TABLE 11-9

Total cost of optimal solution for Bass Gravel Company problem

for the project. The assumption underlying this thought is that making the best possible choice in each part of the scheduling program will automatically result in the best overall program. An examination of the final solution to our problem indicates that the assumption is not a valid one. Figure 11-15 shows that two of the least-cost routes, squares WA and WC, are *not* included in the optimal solution. Here we recognize the importance of a characteristic of MS/OR: a problem must be studied in terms of the *total system,* not merely the separate parts. The optimal source-destination combinations are often far from apparent, even in small problems like that of the Bass Gravel Company.

SOME LEAST-COST ROUTES MAY NOT BE IN THE OPTIMAL SOLUTION

ALTERNATIVE OPTIMAL SOLUTIONS

ARE THERE ANY OTHER SOLUTIONS WITH THE SAME COST?

Let us examine further the optimal solution to the Bass Gravel Company problem with particular attention to the improvement index of square XB computed in Table 11-8. The improvement index for square XB is zero. What does this signify? A zero improvement index for an unused square means that if this route were brought into the solution, *the shipping assignments would change, yet the total transportation cost would be the same.* Thus if we were to assign one truckload to unused square XB, the total cost figure would neither increase nor decrease. We can conclude, then, that in addition to our present optimal shipping schedule, another equally profitable schedule exists. To determine what *this* alternative optimal solution is, we follow the same procedure used for bringing any route into the solution (step 4). In this case the maximum number of truckloads that can be assigned to square XB is 41. The alternative solution and its total cost are given in Figure 11-16. The improvement indices are also included.

We see that the total cost is exactly the same as the total cost of the original optimal solution. Also, the improvement indices are positive except for square XA, which equals zero. This is to be expected, as square XA was the one replaced in the original optimal solution. From a practical viewpoint, the existence of alternative optimal solutions gives valuable flexibility to the management of the Bass Gravel Company.

THE MODI METHOD FOR COMPUTING IMPROVEMENT INDICES

The *modified distribution method,* referred to as the MODI method, is very similar to the stepping-stone method except that it provides a more efficient

From \ To	Project A		Project B		Project C		Plant capacity	Total cost
Plant W	WA +4	4	WB (56)	8	WC +8	8	56	56 × $ 8 = $ 448
Plant X	XA 0	16	XB (41)	24	XC (41)	16	82	41 × $24 = 948
Plant Y	YA (72)	8	YB (5)	16	YC +16	24	77	41 × $16 = 656
Project requirements	72		102		41		215 / 215	72 × $ 8 = 576

Total cost:
56 × $ 8 = $ 448
41 × $24 = 948
41 × $16 = 656
72 × $ 8 = 576
5 × $16 = 80
$2,744

FIGURE 11-16
Alternative solution and total cost.

means for computing the improvement indices for the unused squares. The major difference between these two methods concerns that step in the problem solution at which the closed paths are traced. In order to calculate the improvement indices for a particular solution, it was necessary in the stepping-stone method to trace a closed path for each unused square. The unused square with the most improvement potential (the largest negative value) was then selected to enter the next solution.

MODI AND STEPPING-STONE METHODS COMPARED

In the MODI method, however, the improvement indices can be calculated without drawing the closed paths. The MODI method, in fact, requires tracing only *one* closed path. This path is drawn after the unused square with the highest improvement index has been identified. As in the stepping-stone method, the purpose of this path is to determine the maximum quantity that can be assigned to the unused square entering the next solution.

Using the Bass problem, we shall illustrate the procedures used in applying the MODI method. Beginning with the same initial solution obtained by using the northwest corner rule, we first compute a value for each row and each column in the transportation tableau. These values depend on the particular solution and are used to compute the improvement indices for the unused squares. Assigning a number to each row and column requires a slight modification in the transportation tableau. This modification together with the initial solution is shown in Figure 11-17.

INITIAL SOLUTION OBTAINED BY THE NORTHWEST CORNER RULE

In this figure we let R and K represent the row and column values. We have attached a subscript to denote the specific row and column value. In our case, we have R_1, R_2, and R_3 to represent the rows and K_1, K_2, and K_3 to represent the columns. In general, then, we can say

R_i = value assigned to row i and K_j = value assigned to column j

R_i \\ K_j		K_1	K_2	K_3	
	From \\ To	Project A	Project B	Project C	Plant capacity
R_1	Plant W	WA 4 (56)	WB 8	WC 8	56
R_2	Plant X	XA 16 (16)	XB 24 (66)	XC 16	82
R_3	Plant Y	YA 8	YB 16 (36)	YC 24 (41)	77
	Project requirements	72	102	41	215 / 215

FIGURE 11-17
Transportation tableau using the MODI method.

The transportation cost, as in previous tableaus, is shown in the upper right-hand corner, or subsquare, of each large square.

For identification purposes, we can let

C_{ij} = cost in square ij (the square at the intersection of row i and column j)

COMPUTING VALUES FOR EACH ROW AND COLUMN

For example, C_{12} represents the cost in the square located at the intersection of row 1 and column 2. Now to compute the values for each row and column, we use the formula

$$\text{Cost at stone square } ij \qquad C_{ij} = R_i + K_j \qquad (11\text{-}1)$$

This formula is applied *only* to the stone squares in a particular solution. Because there are five stone squares in our problem, we must have *five* equations. For the stone square located at the intersection of row 1 and column 1 we write

$$R_1 + K_1 = C_{11}$$

and as there is a stone at the intersection of row 2 and column 1,

$$R_2 + K_1 = C_{21}$$

Similarly,

$$R_2 + K_2 = C_{22}$$
$$R_3 + K_2 = C_{32}$$
$$R_3 + K_3 = C_{33}$$

Because we are given the cost figure for each square in the table, we can substitute the appropriate value for each C_{ij} in our equations. The results are

$$R_1 + K_1 = 4$$
$$R_2 + K_1 = 16$$
$$R_2 + K_2 = 24$$
$$R_3 + K_2 = 16$$
$$R_3 + K_3 = 24$$

Notice that we have six unknowns and only five equations. Thus this system of equations has several solutions. In order to find a particular solution (a value for each R and K), we shall let $R_1 = 0$. We could have chosen any value for any row or column, but the usual procedure is to let row 1 (R_1) equal zero. This is legitimate since the entire process is a comparative one. In other words, the significance of the row and column values is not their absolute numerical value. We are interested only in comparing the figures, not in the figures themselves.

To solve the five equations, then, we proceed as follows. If $R_1 = 0$, then

SOLVING THE ROW AND
COLUMN EQUATIONS

$$R_1 + K_1 = 4$$
$$0 + K_1 = 4$$
$$K_1 = 4$$

Since $K_1 = 4$, then

$$R_2 + K_1 = 16$$
$$R_2 + 4 = 16$$
$$R_2 = 12$$

Since $R_2 = 12$, then

$$R_2 + K_2 = 24$$
$$12 + K_2 = 24$$
$$K_2 = 12$$

Since $K_2 = 12$, then

$$R_3 + K_2 = 16$$
$$R_3 + 12 = 16$$
$$R_3 = 4$$

Since $R_3 = 4$, then

$$R_3 + K_3 = 24$$
$$4 + K_3 = 24$$
$$K_3 = 20$$

The R and K values need not always be positive; indeed, they may be *positive, negative,* or *zero.* After some practice, computing the R and K values can usually be done mentally instead of writing out each equation as above.

R AND K MAY BE
POSITIVE, NEGATIVE,
OR ZERO

The transportation tableau with the R and K values included is shown in Figure 11-18.

With the row and column values computed, the next step in the MODI method is to evaluate each unused square in the present solution, that is, to compute the improvement indices. Computing the improvement index for any unused square is accomplished in the following manner: from the cost of an unused square subtract the corresponding row value and column value. Stating this rule as a general formula, we have

$$\text{Improvement index} = C_{ij} - R_i - K_j \qquad (11\text{-}2)$$

If the result is negative, further improvement is possible. When all indices are equal to or greater than zero, the optimal solution has been obtained.

Each unused square in the initial solution (Figure 11-18) can now be evaluated. For example, the route from plant W to project B at the intersection of row 1 and column 2 is one of the unused routes (unused squares) in our initial solution. Using our formula, we have

Unused square 12: $\quad C_{12} - R_1 - K_2 = $ improvement index
$$8 - 0 - 12 = -4$$

Similarly, for the other unused squares we have

Unused square	$C_{ij} - R_i - K_j$	Improvement index
13	$C_{13} - R_1 - K_3$ $8 - 0 - 20$	-12
23	$C_{23} - R_2 - K_3$ $16 - 12 - 20$	-16
31	$C_{31} - R_3 - K_1$ $8 - 4 - 4$	0

A comparison of these improvement indices with those obtained using the stepping-stone method (see Figure 11-8) shows them to be identical. From this point on, then, the procedure for developing a new, improved solution is identical to the one discussed in the previous sections.

Procedure for developing a new, improved solution

1 *Trace a closed path* for the cell having the largest negative improvement index.

2 *Place plus and minus signs* at alternate corners of the path, beginning with a plus sign at the unused square.

3 The smallest stone in a negative position on the closed path indicates the quantity that can be assigned to the unused square being entered into the

R_i \ K_j	From \ To	$K_1 = 4$ Project A	$K_2 = 12$ Project B	$K_3 = 20$ Project C	Plant capacity
$R_1 = 0$	Plant W	WA 4 (56)	WB 8	WC 8	56
$R_2 = 12$	Plant X	XA 16 (16)	XB 24 (66)	XC 16	82
$R_3 = 4$	Plant Y	YA 8	YB 16 (36)	YC 24 (41)	77
	Project requirements	72	102	41	215 / 215

FIGURE 11-18
Initial solution with R and K values for the Bass Gravel Company problem.

solution. *This quantity is added* to all squares on the closed path with plus signs *and subtracted* from those squares with minus signs.

4 Finally, the improvement indices for the new solution *are calculated.*

With this procedure, the second solution to the problem of the Bass Gravel Company is obtained (Figure 11-19). Notice that it is identical to our second

R_i \ K_j	From \ To	$K_1 = 4$ Project A	$K_2 = 12$ Project B	$K_3 = 4$ Project C	Plant capacity
$R_1 = 0$	Plant W	WA 4 (56)	WB 8	WC 8	56
$R_2 = 12$	Plant X	XA 16 (16)	XB 24 (25)	XC 16 (41)	82
$R_3 = 4$	Plant Y	YA 8	YB 16 (77)	YC 24	77
	Project requirements	72	102	41	215 / 215

FIGURE 11-19
Second solution to the Bass Gravel Company problem.

solution found by using the stepping-stone procedure (Figure 11-11). As we shall see in a moment, this holds true for all solutions.

To evaluate the unused squares of the second solution using the MODI method, we must calculate the R and K values. This must be done with every new solution. Again we begin by letting R_1 equal zero. Using the general formula $R_i + K_j = C_{ij}$ (the cost at stone square ij), the R and K values are computed as follows:

Stone square 11:

$$R_1 + K_1 = 4$$
$$0 + K_1 = 4$$
$$K_1 = 4$$

Stone square 21:

$$R_2 + K_1 = 16$$
$$R_2 + 4 = 16$$
$$R_2 = 12$$

COMPUTING R AND K VALUES

Stone square 22:

$$R_2 + K_2 = 24$$
$$12 + K_2 = 24$$
$$K_2 = 12$$

Stone square 23:

$$R_2 + K_3 = 16$$
$$12 + K_3 = 16$$
$$K_3 = 4$$

Stone square 32:

$$R_3 + K_2 = 16$$
$$R_3 + 12 = 16$$
$$R_3 = 4$$

These R and K values were included in Figure 11-19. In comparing our new R and K values with those obtained in the initial solution (Figure 11-18), we find that all R and K values are the same except for K_3, which is equal to 4 in the second tableau. Changing the solution changes some if not all of the R and K values. Hence, with every new solution, new values for R and K must be established in order to determine whether further improvement is possible, that is, to calculate the improvement indices.

The evaluation of each unused square of the second solution is shown in Table 11-10. The remaining improved solutions with their respective R and K values are given in Figures 11-20 and 11-21. The improvement indices are also included.

Unused square	$C_{ij} - R_i - K_j$	Improvement index
12	$C_{12} - R_1 - K_2$ $8 - 0 - 12$	-4
13	$C_{13} - R_1 - K_3$ $8 - 0 - 4$	$+4$
31	$C_{31} - R_3 - K_1$ $8 - 4 - 4$	0
33	$C_{33} - R_3 - K_3$ $24 - 4 - 4$	$+16$

TABLE 11-10
Evaluation of unused squares in second solution

The MODI method may be summarized by the following steps:

1 For each solution, *compute the R and K values* for the table using the formula

STEPS IN MODI METHOD

$$R_i + K_j = C_{ij} \text{ (the cost at } \textit{stone} \text{ square } ij\text{)}$$

Row 1 (R_1) is always set equal to zero.

2 *Calculate the improvement indices* for all unused squares using

$$C_{ij} \text{ (cost of } \textit{unused} \text{ square)} - R_i - K_j = \text{improvement index}$$

R_i \ K_j		To / From	$K_1 = 4$ Project A	$K_2 = 8$ Project B	$K_3 = 4$ Project C	Plant capacity
$R_1 = 0$	Plant W		WA 4 31	WB 8 25	WC 8 +4	56
$R_2 = 12$	Plant X		XA 16 41	XB 24 +4	XC 16 41	82
$R_3 = 8$	Plant Y		YA 8 −4	YB 16 77	YC 24 +12	77
	Project requirements		72	102	41	215 215

FIGURE 11-20
Third solution to the Bass Gravel Company problem.

R_i \ K_j		To / From	$K_1 = 0$ Project A		$K_2 = 8$ Project B		$K_3 = 0$ Project C		Plant capacity
$R_1 = 0$	Plant W		WA +4	4	WB (56)	8	WC +8	8	56
$R_2 = 16$	Plant X		XA (41)	16	XB 0	24	XC (41)	16	82
$R_3 = 8$	Plant Y		YA (31)	8	YB (46)	16	YC +16	24	77
	Project requirements		72		102		41		215 / 215

FIGURE 11-21
Optimal solution to the Bass Gravel Company problem.

3 *Select the unused square* with the largest negative index. (If all indices are equal to or greater than zero, the optimal solution has been obtained.)

4 *Trace the closed path* for the unused square having the largest negative index.

5 *Develop an improved solution* using the same procedure as outlined in the stepping-stone method.

6 *Repeat steps 1 to 5* until an optimal solution has been found.

2 The transportation problem (demand does not equal supply)

UNBALANCED FORM OF THE TRANSPORTATION PROBLEM

To this point the transportation method has required that supply and demand be equal: the rim requirements for the rows must equal the rim requirements for the columns. This is unlikely. Most real problems are of the so-called *unbalanced* type, where supply and demand are unequal. In such cases, there is a method for handling the inequality.

DEMAND LESS THAN SUPPLY

WHEN DEMAND IS LESS THAN SUPPLY

Considering the original Bass Gravel Company problem, suppose that plant W has a capacity of 76 truckloads per week rather than 56. The company would be able to supply 235 truckloads per week. However, the project requirements remain the same. Using the northwest corner rule to establish an initial solution, we get the program shown in Figure 11-22. Obviously the rim requirements for the rows and columns are not balanced. Plant Y still has 20 truckloads available for supply. The method employed to balance this type of problem is to create a fictitious destination or project requiring 20

From \ To	Project A	Project B	Project C	Plant capacity
Plant W	WA 4 (72)	WB 8 (4)	WC 8	76
Plant X	XA 16	XB 24 (82)	XC 16	82
Plant Y	YA 8	YB 16 (16)	YC 24 (41)	77
Project requirements	72	102	41	215 / 235

FIGURE 11-22
Unbalanced form when demand is less than supply.

truckloads per week. This fictitious project serves the same purpose as the *slack variable* in the simplex method. Since these truckloads will never be shipped, the transportation costs to this dummy project are equal to zero. An additional column is required to handle the dummy project in the transportation tableau. Again the northwest corner rule is used to determine the initial solution, as shown in Figure 11-23.

AN EQUIVALENT TO THE SLACK VARIABLE

The problem can now be solved using the steps discussed earlier. Let us look, however, at the final tableau, or optimal solution, to this problem

From \ To	Project A	Project B	Project C	Dummy D	Plant capacity
Plant W	4 (72)	8 (4)	8	0	76
Plant X	16	24 (82)	16	0	82
Plant Y	8	16 (16)	24 (41)	0 (20)	77
Project requirements	72	102	41	20	235 / 235

Total cost
```
72 × $4  = $  288
 4 × $8  =     32
82 × $24 =  1,968
16 × $16 =    256
20 × $0  =      0
41 × $24 =    948
              $3,528
```

FIGURE 11-23
Initial solution for unbalanced problem (demand less than supply).

(Figure 11-24). The optimal solution shows a shipment of 20 truckloads from plant X to the dummy project. This means that plant X will have an excess supply of 20 truckloads which will not really be shipped anywhere. With this information, the decision maker knows not only the optimal shipping program but also the plant which should not be utilized at full capacity.

DEMAND GREATER THAN SUPPLY

WHEN DEMAND IS GREATER THAN SUPPLY

Another type of unbalanced condition occurs when total demand is greater than total supply; that is, the customers (projects in our case) require more gravel than the Bass Gravel Company plants can supply. Again, referring to our sample problem, assume that project A will require 10 additional truckloads per week and that project C estimates additional requirements of 20 truckloads. The total project requirements now would be equal to 245 truckloads, as opposed to the 215 available from the plants. Similar to the previous type of unbalance, the key to solving this problem is to set up with balanced conditions. To accomplish this, we create a dummy plant having a capacity exactly equal to the additional demand (30 truckloads). The distribution costs from this plant are equal to zero, since no actual deliveries will be made from this dummy plant.

USE OF THE DUMMY SOURCE

As can be seen in the initial solution table (Figure 11-25), the inclusion of a dummy plant results in an additional row.

Having established the balanced condition, we solve the problem using exactly the same procedure as outlined in the previous sections. The optimal solution to this problem is given in Figure 11-26.

ASSUMPTIONS IN THIS SITUATION

This particular type of unbalanced problem implies that one or more of the projects will not have its requirements satisfied. In this case, the optimal solution indicates that project B will be short 30 truckloads per week, as it

To From	Project A	Project B	Project C	Dummy D	Plant capacity	Total cost
Plant W	4	8 (76)	8	0	76	76 × $8 = $ 608 21 × $24 = 504 41 × $16 = 656 20 × $0 = 0 72 × $8 = 576 5 × $16 = 80 $2,424
Plant X	16 (21)	24 (41)	16 (20)	0	82	
Plant Y	8 (72)	16 (5)	24	0	77	
Project requirements	72	102	41	20	235 / 235	

FIGURE 11-24
Optimal solution to unbalanced problem (demand less than supply).

To From	Project A	Project B	Project C	Plant capacity
Plant W	4 (56)	8	8	56
Plant X	16 (26)	24 (56)	16	82
Plant Y	8	16 (46)	24 (31)	77
Dummy	0	0	0 (30)	30
Project requirements	82	102	61	245 245

Total cost

$56 \times \$4 = \$\ \ 224$
$26 \times \$16 = \ \ \ 416$
$56 \times \$24 = 1{,}344$
$46 \times \$16 = \ \ \ 736$
$31 \times \$24 = \ \ \ 744$
$30 \times \$0 = \underline{\ \ \ \ \ \ \ 0}$
$\$3{,}464$

FIGURE 11-25
Initial solution for unbalanced problem (demand greater than supply).

To From	Project A	Project B	Project C	Plant capacity
Plant W	4	8 (56)	8	56
Plant X	16 (21)	24	16 (61)	82
Plant Y	8 (61)	16 (16)	24	77
Dummy	0	0 (30)	0	30
Project requirements	82	102	61	245 245

Total cost

$56 \times \$8 = \$\ \ 448$
$21 \times \$16 = \ \ \ 336$
$61 \times \$16 = \ \ \ 976$
$61 \times \$8 = \ \ \ 488$
$16 \times \$16 = \ \ \ 256$
$30 \times \$0 = \underline{\ \ \ \ \ \ \ 0}$
$\$2{,}504$

FIGURE 11-26
Optimal solution to the Bass Gravel Company unbalanced problem (demand greater than supply).

receives 30 from the dummy plant. This method, however, *does* distribute all available gravel at the lowest total transportation cost for the Bass Gravel Company.

3 Degeneracy

We have pointed out that the total number of stone squares in *any* solution must be equal to the number of rim requirements minus 1. An alternative way of stating this rule is that the number of stone squares in *any* solution must be equal to the number of rows plus the number of columns minus 1. When this rule is not met, the solution is degenerate.

Failure to meet the test for degeneracy in the transportation problem is indicated in *two* ways:

1 There may be an *excessive* number of stone squares in a solution; the number of stone squares is greater than the number of rim requirements minus 1. This type of degeneracy arises only in developing the initial solution and is caused by an improper assignment or an error in formulating the problem. In such cases, one must modify the initial solution so as to satisfy the rule of rim requirements minus 1.

2 There may be an *insufficient* number of stone squares in a solution. Degeneracy of this type may occur either in the initial solution or in subsequent solutions. It is this type of degeneracy which requires special procedures to resolve the degeneracy. With an insufficient number of stone squares in a solution, it would be impossible to trace a closed path for each unused square, and with the MODI method it would be impossible to compute the R and K values.

The procedures for handling degeneracy resulting from an insufficient number of stones will now be presented.

DEGENERACY IN ESTABLISHING AN INITIAL SOLUTION

Let us assume that the plant capacities and project requirements in the original Bass Gravel Company problem have been changed. Using the northwest corner rule, we obtain the initial solution in Figure 11-27.

In this solution we have four stone squares. According to our rule of rim requirements minus 1, we should have five stone squares. Hence the solution is degenerate. This particular case of degeneracy arises when, in using the northwest corner rule, both a column requirement and a row requirement are satisfied simultaneously, thus breaking the stairstep pattern. In our case, this occurs in square XB. Of course, the assignment of a value to the final stone square always satisfies the remaining row and column requirements simultaneously, but this will not result in a degenerate solution.

To resolve this degeneracy, we assign a zero stone to one of the unused squares. Although there is a great deal of flexibility in choosing the unused square for the zero stone, the general procedure, when using the northwest

To From	A		B		C		Plant capacity
W	WA (35)	4	WB (20)	8	WC	8	55
X	XA	16	XB (25)	24	XC	16	25
Y	YA	8	YB	16	YC (35)	24	35
Project requirements	35		45		35		115 / 115

FIGURE 11-27
Degenerate problem:
initial solution.

corner rule, is to assign it to a square in such a way that it maintains an unbroken chain of stone squares. Figure 11-28 shows the zero stone added to square XC, although it could have been assigned to square YB.

We now have five stone squares; this satisfies the degeneracy test. The problem can now be solved using the usual solution procedure with the zero stone square treated just like any other stone square in the solution. This zero stone square has no meaning in a problem; it is merely a computational device which permits the Bass Gravel Company to apply the regular solution method.

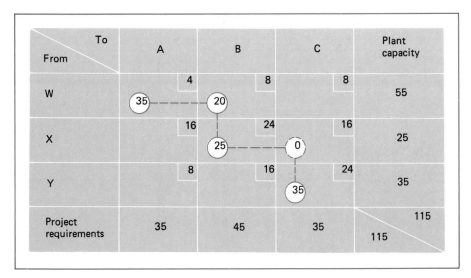

FIGURE 11-28
Degeneracy resolved.

From \ To	A		B		C		Plant capacity
W	WA (45)	4	WB (45)	8	WC +12	24	90
X	XA +8	8	XB (30)	4	XC (30)	8	60
Y	YA +8	16	YB −8	4	YC (30)	16	30
Project requirements	45		75		60		180 / 180

FIGURE 11-29
Degenerate problem:
initial solution.

▨ DEGENERACY DURING SUBSEQUENT SOLUTION STAGES

RESOLVING
DEGENERACY IN
SUBSEQUENT
SOLUTIONS

The initial solution to another problem is given in Figure 11-29. We observe that the initial solution is not degenerate. The improvement indices are shown in the unused squares and indicate that an improved solution may be obtained by introducing unused square YB into the next solution. Let us go through the procedure for developing the next solution to this problem and observe what happens. We first trace the closed path for unused square YB and then choose the smallest stone as the quantity to be assigned to unused square YB. This is shown in Figure 11-30. In this case all stones have a value of 30. The results of the assignment of 30 units to square YB are shown in Figure 11-31. When we added 30 units to square YB, the quantities shipped through squares XB and YC were *both* reduced to zero. This will always occur when a tie exists between two or more stone squares when these stones represent the smallest stones on the path in squares assigned a minus sign. Hence in our problem, adding an unused square resulted in the elimination of two

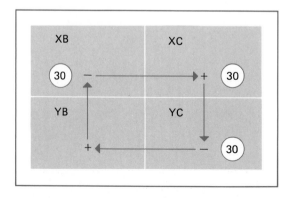

FIGURE 11-30
Tracing closed path
for square YB.

XB 30 − 30 = 0	XC 30 + 30 = (60)
YB 0 + 30 = (30)	YC 30 − 30 = 0

FIGURE 11-31
Thirty units assigned
to square YB.

stone squares from the previous solution, but in order to satisfy the rule that the number of stone squares equals the number of rim requirements minus 1, we will keep XB as a stone square and only eliminate square YC. We have placed the zero stone in square XB, as shown in Figure 11-32.

In some cases more than two stone squares may be reduced to zero. In such cases we eliminate only one of those squares, so that the number of stone squares in the solution still satisfies the rule of rim requirements minus 1. The Bass Gravel Company problem can now be solved using the standard procedure, which was discussed before.

4 The assignment problem

Another special-purpose algorithm used in linear programming is the *assignment method*. Like the transportation method, the assignment method is computationally more efficient than the simplex method for a special class of problems. We shall also show that the assignment problem is a special case

A SPECIAL CASE OF THE
TRANSPORTATION
PROBLEM: THE
ASSIGNMENT PROBLEM

From \ To		A		B		C		Plant capacity
W		WA (45)	4	WB (45)	8	WC	24	90
X		XA	8	XB (0)	4	XC (60)	8	60
Y		YA	16	YB (30)	4	YC	16	30
Project requirements		45		75		60		180 180

FIGURE 11-32
Degeneracy resolved:
subsequent solution
stage.

of the transportation problem. In other words, we can solve an assignment problem using the transportation method.

The Kellum Machine Shop does custom metalworking for a number of local plants. Kellum currently has three jobs to be done (let us symbolize them A, B, and C). Kellum also has three machines on which to do the work (X, Y, and Z). Any one of the jobs can be processed completely on any one of the machines. Furthermore, the cost of processing any job on any machine is known. The assignment of jobs to machines must be on a one-to-one basis; that is, each job must be assigned exclusively to one and only one machine. The objective is to assign the jobs to the machines so as to minimize total cost.

NUMBERS OF ROWS
EQUALS NUMBER OF
COLUMNS IN THE
ASSIGNMENT PROBLEM

The cost data are given in Table 11-11. The number of rows (jobs) equals the number of columns (machines). This is one characteristic of all assignment problems. Another characteristic is that in the optimal solution there will be one and only one assignment in a given row or column of the given assignment table. These characteristics are peculiar to the assignment problem. In the general transportation problem, for example, it is not necessary to have an equal number of sources and destinations; nor does the transportation method require that there be one assignment only in a given row or column of the optimal solution.

USING THE TRANSPORTATION METHOD
TO SOLVE THE ASSIGNMENT PROBLEM

Since each job must be assigned to one and only one machine, we can say that the job requirement for each job is 1 and that the machine capacity for each machine is also 1. This might be the case, for example, when the additional setup expenses are such as to prohibit the partial assignment of machines to more than one job. Given the cost data of Table 11-11, the job

USE THE NORTHWEST
CORNER RULE TO GET
THE INITIAL SOLUTION

requirements, and machine capacities, we can set up the transportation tableau given in Figure 11-33, showing the initial solution using the northwest corner rule.

There are three stone squares in this initial solution. However, according to the rule of rim requirements minus 1, we should have five stone squares. Hence we must add two zero stone squares to resolve the degeneracy. This has been done in Figure 11-34.

WHY THE
TRANSPORTATION
METHOD IS INEFFICIENT
FOR THE ASSIGNMENT
PROBLEM

The Kellum problem can now be solved in the usual manner. Because all the stone squares have a value of 1 or 0, a degenerate solution will result with each subsequent solution. The reason for this can be attributed to the

TABLE 11-11
Cost for each job-
machine assignment
for Kellum Machine
Shop problem

Job	Machine		
	X	**Y**	**Z**
A	$25	$31	$35
B	15	20	24
C	22	19	17

To / From	Machine X	Machine Y	Machine Z	Job requirements
Job A	25 ①(1)	31	35	1
Job B	15	20 ①(1)	24	1
Job C	22	19	17 ①(1)	1
Machine capacity	1	1	1	3 / 3

FIGURE 11-33
The Kellum
assignment problem
set up in the
transportation
tableau.

two special characteristics of the assignment problem mentioned in the previous section. Having to cope with the problem of degeneracy at each solution makes the transportation method computationally inefficient for solving an assignment problem.

USING THE ASSIGNMENT METHOD

The assignment method, also known as *Flood's technique* or the *Hungarian method of assignment*, provides a much more efficient method of solving assignment problems. There are basically three steps in the assignment method. We present the reasoning underlying each of these steps.

ASSIGNMENT METHOD
IS MORE EFFICIENT

To / From	X	Y	Z	Job requirements
A	25 ①(1)	31 ⓪(0)	35	1
B	15	20 ①(1)	24 ⓪(0)	1
C	22	19	17 ①(1)	1
Machine capacity	1	1	1	3 / 3

FIGURE 11-34
Degeneracy resolved.

520

CHAPTER 11

CONCEPT OF
OPPORTUNITY COST
AND OPPORTUNITY-
COST TABLE

Step 1: Determine the opportunity-cost table   Since the assignment method applies the concept of *opportunity costs*, a brief explanation of this concept may be helpful. The cost of any kind of action or decision consists of the opportunities that are sacrificed in taking that action. Many of us go through an opportunity-cost analysis without realizing it. For example, a friend who had been thinking of buying a new house drives by in a brand-new car. He promptly starts explaining how nice it is living in an apartment. This is an example of opportunity-cost analysis. If we do one thing, we cannot do another.

Let us now see how this concept plays an important part in the computational mechanics of the assignment method. For convenience, the cost data for the Kellum Machine Shop problem are repeated in Table 11-12.

Suppose we decide to assign job A to machine X. The table shows that the cost of this assignment is $25. Because machine X could just as well process job B for $15, it is clear that our assignment of job A to machine X is not the best decision. Therefore, when we arbitrarily assign job A to machine X, we are in effect sacrificing the opportunity to save $10 ($25 − $15). This sacrifice is more generally referred to as an opportunity cost. In other words, the decision to assign job A to machine X precludes the assignment of job B to machine X, given the restriction that one and only one job can be assigned to a machine. Thus we say that the opportunity cost of the assignment of job A to machine X is $10 with respect to the lowest-cost assignment for machine X (or column X). Similarly, a Kellum decision to assign job C to machine X would involve an opportunity cost of $7 ($22 − $15). Finally, since the assignment of job B to machine X is the best assignment, we can say that the opportunity cost of this assignment is zero ($15 − $15). More specifically

these costs can be called the *job-opportunity costs* with regard to machine X. If we were to subtract the lowest cost of column Y (machine Y) from all the costs in this column, we would have the job-opportunity costs with regard to machine Y. The same procedure in column Z would give the job-opportunity costs for machine Z.

In addition to these job-opportunity costs, there are *machine-opportunity costs*. We could, for example, assign job A to machine X, Y, or Z. If we assigned job A to machine Y, there would be an opportunity cost attached to this decision. The assignment of job A to machine Y costs $31, while the assignment of job A to machine X costs only $25. Therefore the opportunity cost of assigning job A to machine Y is $6 ($31 − $25). Similarly the assignment of job A to machine Z involves an opportunity cost of $10 ($35

TABLE 11-12
Cost of each job-
machine assignment
for the Kellum
Machine Shop
problem

	Machine		
Job	**X**	**Y**	**Z**
A	$25	$31	$35
B	15	20	24
C	22	19	17

	Machine			Computations		
Job	X	Y	Z	Column X	Column Y	Column Z
A	10	12	18	25 − 15 = 10	31 − 19 = 12	35 − 17 = 18
B	0	1	7	15 − 15 = 0	20 − 19 = 1	24 − 17 = 7
C	7	0	0	22 − 15 = 7	19 − 19 = 0	17 − 17 = 0

TABLE 11-13
Step 1, part *a:* job-opportunity table for Kellum Machine Shop problem

− $25). A zero opportunity cost is involved in the assignment of job A to machine X, since this is the best assignment for job A (row A). Hence we could compute the machine opportunity costs for each row (each job) by subtracting the lowest cost entry in each row from all cost entries in its row.

This discussion on opportunity costs should provide an understanding of the mechanics of the first step in the assignment method, which is to develop the total-opportunity-cost table. There are *two* parts to this first step. Part *a* is to subtract the lowest entry in each column of the original cost table from all entries in that column. The resulting new table with computations is given in Table 11-13.

Table 11-13 should be recognized as the job-opportunity table. Now the objective of this first step is to develop a total-opportunity-cost table. In other words, we want to consider the machine-opportunity costs also. Part *b* of step 1 accomplishes this, but not in exactly the same way as our intuitive analysis. The effect, however, is the same. Part *b* is to subtract the lowest entry in each row of the *table obtained in part a* from all numbers in that row. The new table and computations are shown in Table 11-14.

Step 2: Determine whether an optimal assignment can be made The objective is to assign the jobs to the machines so as to minimize total costs. With the total-opportunity-cost table, this objective will be achieved if we can assign the jobs to the machines in such a way as to obtain a total opportunity cost of zero. In other words, we want to make the three best possible assignments. *The best possible assignment of a job to a machine would involve an opportunity cost of zero.*

Looking at the total opportunity cost in Table 11-14, we find four squares with zeros, each indicating a zero opportunity cost for that square (assignment). Hence, we could assign job A to machine X and job C to machine Y or Z, all assignments having an opportunity cost of zero. If this were done, however,

TWO PARTS IN DETERMINING THE OPPORTUNITY-COST TABLE

PART *A*

PART *B*

CAN AN OPTIMAL ASSIGNMENT BE MADE?

THE BEST POSSIBLE ASSIGNMENT

TABLE 11-14
Step 1, part *b:* total-opportunity-cost table for Kellum Machine Shop problem

	Machine			Computations		
Job	X	Y	Z			
A	0	2	8	Row A: 10 − 10 = 0	12 − 10 = 2	18 − 10 = 8
B	0	1	7	Row B: 0 − 0 = 0	1 − 0 = 1	7 − 0 = 7
C	7	0	0	Row C: 7 − 0 = 7	0 − 0 = 0	0 − 0 = 0

we could not assign job B to any machine with a zero opportunity cost. The reason here is that the assignment of job A to machine X precludes the assignment of job B to machine X. If we had a zero in square BY, we could make an optimal assignment. In other words, to make an optimal assignment of the three jobs to the three machines, we must locate three zero squares in the table such that a complete assignment to these squares can be made with a total opportunity cost of zero.

There is a convenient method for determining whether an optimal assignment can be made. This method consists of drawing straight lines (vertically and horizontally) through the total-opportunity-cost table in such a manner as to minimize the numbers of lines necessary to cover all zero squares. If the number of lines equals the number of rows in the table, an optimal assignment can be made and the problem is solved. On the other hand, an optimal assignment cannot be made if the number of lines is less than the number of rows. In this case we must develop a new total-opportunity-cost table.

The test for optimal assignment has been applied to our present table and is shown in Table 11-15. It requires only two lines (row C and column X) to cover all the zero squares. Therefore, as there are three rows, an optimal assignment is not possible.

IF AN OPTIMAL
ASSIGNMENT CANNOT
BE MADE, MODIFY THE
OPPORTUNITY-COST
TABLE

Step 3: Revise the total opportunity-cost table   If an optimal assignment is not feasible, we must modify the total-opportunity-cost table by including some assignment not in the rows and columns covered by the lines. Of course, that assignment with the least opportunity cost is chosen; in our problem, this would be the assignment of job B to machine Y with an opportunity cost of 1. In other words we would like to change the opportunity cost for this assignment from 1 to zero.

The procedure for accomplishing this task is as follows: (*a*) select the smallest number in the table not covered by a straight line and subtract this number from all numbers not covered by a straight line; and (*b*) add this same lowest number to the numbers lying at the intersection of any two lines. The revised total-opportunity-cost table and computations of parts *a* and *b* of step 3 are shown in Table 11-16.

PARTS *A* AND *B* IN
MODIFYING THE
OPPORTUNITY-COST
TABLE

The test for optimal assignment described in step 2 is applied again to the revised table. This is shown in Table 11-17.

TABLE 11-15
Test for optimal
assignment for
Kellum Machine
Shop problem

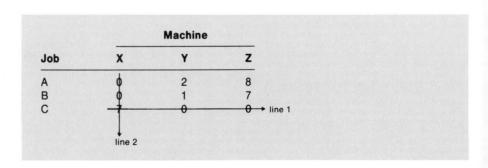

		Machine	
Job	**X**	**Y**	**Z**
A	0	2	8
B	0	1	7
C	7	0	0	→ line 1

line 2

TABLE 11-16
Revised opportunity-cost table for Kellum Machine Shop problem

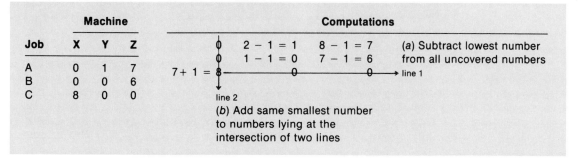

Job	Machine			Computations			
	X	Y	Z				
A	0	1	7	$7 + 1 = 8$	$2 - 1 = 1$ $1 - 1 = 0$	$8 - 1 = 7$ $7 - 1 = 6$	(a) Subtract lowest number from all uncovered numbers line 1
B	0	0	6				
C	8	0	0	line 2			

(b) Add same smallest number to numbers lying at the intersection of two lines

As the minimum number of lines necessary to cover all zeros is three, and as this number is equal to the number of rows, an optimal assignment can be made. In this case the optimal assignments are A to X, B to Y, and C to Z. In larger problems, however, the assignments may not be readily apparent and we must resort to a more systematic procedure. The first step is to select a row or column in which there is only one zero square. The first assignment is made to that zero square. Lines are then drawn through the column and row in which the zero square is located. From the remaining rows and columns we again select a row or column in which there is only one zero cell. Another assignment is made, and lines are drawn through the respective row and column. The procedure is repeated until a complete assignment has been made. The assignment sequence using this procedure in our problem is shown in Figure 11-35.

To calculate the total cost of these assignments for Kellum, we must go back to the original cost table. The computation of total cost is as follows:

Assignment	Cost
A to X	$25
B to Y	20
C to Z	17
Total	$62

Jobs	Machine		
	X	Y	Z
A	0	1	7
B	0	0	6 → line 2
C	0	0	0 → line 3

line 1

TABLE 11-17

Test for optimal assignment applied to revised opportunity-cost table

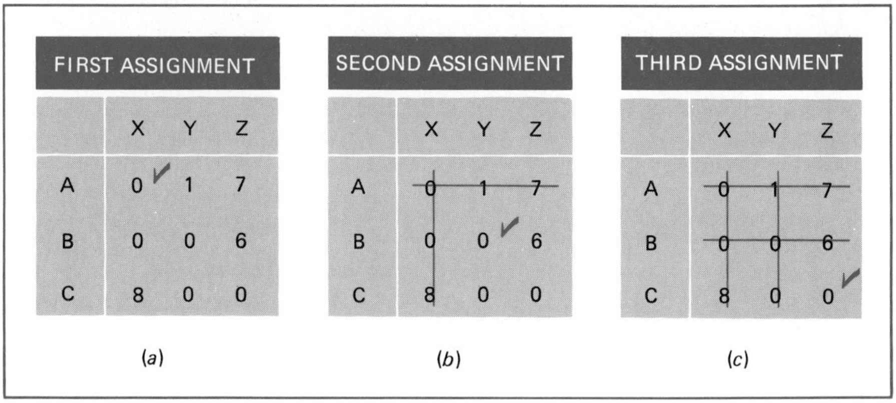

FIGURE 11-35
Assignment sequence.

SUMMARY OF THE ASSIGNMENT METHOD

SUMMARIZING THE ASSIGNMENT METHOD

1 *Determine the opportunity-cost table.*

a. Subtract the lowest entry in each column of the given cost table from all entries in that column.

b. Subtract the lowest entry in each row of the table obtained in part *a* from all numbers in that row.

2 *Determine whether an optimal assignment can be made.* The procedure is to draw straight lines (vertically and horizontally) through the total-opportunity-cost table in such a manner as to minimize the number of lines necessary to cover all zero squares. An optimal assignment can be made when the number of lines equals the number of rows. If the number of lines drawn is fewer than the number of rows, an optimal assignment cannot be made and the problem is not solved.

3 *Revise the total opportunity-cost table.*

a. Select the smallest number in the table not covered by a straight line and subtract this number from all numbers not covered by a straight line.

b. Add this same number to the numbers lying at the intersection of any two lines. Go back to step 2.

OTHER APPLICATIONS OF THE ASSIGNMENT METHOD

The assignment method has been applied successfully to a number of situations other than the Kellum job-machine problem we have used as an illustration here. This approach has produced optimal assignments of personnel to job situations requiring specialized talents. Included in successful applications of the assignment method are the assignments of selling personnel to territories, instructors to specialized learning situations, and auditors to client accounts. In order to apply this method successfully, management must be able to determine cost data or other effectiveness measures like the costs in Table 11-12.

5 Solving maximization problems with the transportation and assignment methods

Both the transportation and assignment methods are used to solve problems which exhibit certain characteristics. The term *transportation,* for example, implies a generic class of problems in which total supply equals total demand. However, this does not mean that a particular problem must literally be described as a transportation system having supplies and demands, nor does it imply that the objective must be to minimize total costs. In many cases, we might consider using either the transportation method or the assignment method to solve problems whose objective is to maximize some function such as total profit. The procedure used to solve a maximization problem is almost identical to that used for a minimization problem. You may recall that with the simplex method, the only difference between solving the two types of problems was the rule for deciding which variable should enter the solution at each iteration. If our objective is to maximize profit, we select the variable having the largest positive $C_j - Z_j$ value and continue to iterate in this fashion until all $C_j - Z_j$ values are either zero or negative. For minimization problems, we select the variable having the largest negative $C_j - Z_j$ value and continue iterating until all $C_j - Z_j$ values are either zero or positive. We will now describe the procedure for solving transportation and assignment type problems when our objective is maximization.

TRANSPORTATION METHOD FOR MAXIMIZATION PROBLEMS

Dave Danesh is Vice President for marketing with the Monarch Company. Monarch is planning to expand its sales of computer software into three new territories—Arizona, New Mexico, and Texas. It has been determined that 20, 15, and 30 salespersons will be required to service each of the three areas, respectively. The company recently hired 65 new salespersons to cover these areas, and based on their experience and prior sales performance, the new hires have been classified as Type A, B, or C salespersons. Depending upon the regions to which each of the three types are assigned, Monarch estimates the following annual revenues per salesperson:

Type	Number of salespersons available	Annual revenue by region		
		Arizona	New Mexico	Texas
A	24	$100,000	120,000	130,000
B	27	90,000	106,000	126,000
C	14	84,000	98,000	120,000

Dave wishes to determine how many salespersons of each type to assign to the three regions so that total annual revenues will be maximized.

FIGURE 11-36

Northwest corner initial solution and R_i and K_j values.

Let us begin by developing the northwest corner solution. This is shown in Figure 11-36. The first step of the MODI method, where all R_j and K_j values are computed, is identical for our maximization problem as it is for minimization problems. These computed R_i and K_j values are shown in Figure 11-36. Now we proceed to step 2 of the MODI method, where we compute improvement indices for all unused squares. This step is also identical to that for a minimization problem. Table 11-18 summarizes the step 2 calculations. Now we go to step 3 of the MODI procedure.

You may recall that when solving a minimization problem, we decided at step 3 to select the unused square having the largest negative improvement index. For our maximization problem, we do just the opposite and select the unused square having the largest positive improvement index. Since we are seeking the largest total revenue, by selecting either unused square 21 or 31 where improvement indices are both $+4$, revenues can *increase* by $4000 for

TABLE 11-18

Evaluation of unused squares in the initial solution

Unused square	$C_{ij} - R_i - K_j$	Improvement index
13	$C_{13} - R_1 - K_3$	
	$130 - 0 - 140$	-10
21	$C_{21} - R_2 - K_1$	
	$90 - (-14) - 100$	$+4$
31	$C_{31} - R_3 - K_1$	
	$84 - (-20) - 100$	$+4$
32	$C_{32} - R_3 - K_2$	
	$98 - (-20) - 120$	-2

K_j R_i	To From	$K_1 = 100$ Arizona	$K_2 = 120$ New Mexico	$K_3 = 136$ Texas	Salespersons available
$R_1 = 0$	A	100 ⑨	120 ⑮	130	24
$R_2 = -10$	B	90 ⑪	106	126 ⑯	27
$R_3 = -16$	C	84	98	120 ⑭	14
Salespersons required		20	15	30	65 / 65

FIGURE 11-37

Optimal solution to the Monarch Company problem.

each type B salesperson we assign to Arizona or for each type C salesperson we assign to Arizona. Let us arbitrarily select one of these unused squares, 21, and find the closest path into square 21 just as we did in solving a minimization problem. This path is square 21(+) to 11(−) to 12(+) to 22(−) and back to square 21, resulting in a shift of 11 salespersons into square 21, leaving 9 in square 11, 15 in square 12, and none in our new unused square 22. Our new solution is shown in Figure 11-37. The revised R_i and K_j values computed in step 1 of the MODI procedure are also shown in Figure 11-37.

The improvement indices for the unused squares in our new solution are summarized in Table 11-19. Upon inspection of Table 11-19, you should note that our new solution is optimal, because all the improvement indices are either zero or negative. The presence of a zero improvement index for unused square 31 indicates alternative optimal solutions. Two of these optimal solutions are summarized in Table 11-20.

TABLE 11-19

Evaluation of unused squares for the optimal solution

Unused square	$C_{ij} - R_i - K_j$	Improvement index
13	$C_{13} - R_1 - K_3$ $130 - 0 - 136$	−6
22	$C_{22} - R_2 - K_2$ $106 - (-10) - 120$	−4
31	$C_{31} - R_3 - K_1$ $84 - (-16) - 100$	0
32	$C_{32} - R_3 - K_2$ $98 - (-16) - 120$	−6

When Dave Danesh discovered there were alternative optimal solutions to his allocation problem, he was extremely pleased. Being an astute manager, he recognizes the benefits of locating his salespersons into territories where they have personal preferences. These benefits manifest themselves in the form of higher employee morale, higher retention of the sales staff, and improved job performance. Alternative solutions allow Dave much more flexibility in satisfying the preferences of his sales personnel while still meeting the sales objectives of the Monarch Company.

TABLE 11-20
Two optimal solutions for the Monarch Company problem

Salesperson type	Territory	Number assigned	Annual revenue
A	Arizona	9	$ 900,000
A	New Mexico	15	1,800,000
B	Arizona	11	990,000
B	Texas	16	2,016,000
C	Texas	14	1,680,000
		Total	$7,386,000

Salesperson type	Territory	Number assigned	Annual revenue
A	Arizona	9	$ 900,000
A	New Mexico	15	1,800,000
B	Texas	27	3,402,000
C	Arizona	11	924,000
C	Texas	3	360,000
		Total	$7,386,000

ASSIGNMENT METHOD FOR MAXIMIZATION PROBLEMS

Heidi Kurtz manages the Jamesville Car Rental Agency. This year, she plans to purchase five new automobiles to replace five older vehicles. The older vehicles are to be sold at auction. Heidi has solicited bids from five individuals, each of whom wishes to purchase only one vehicle but has agreed to make a sealed bid on each of the five. The bids are as follows:

| Buyer | Automobile | | | | |
	Ford	Dodge	Buick	Volkswagen	Toyota
Amy	$3,000	$2,500	$3,300	$2,600	$3,100
Bert	3,500	3,000	2,800	2,800	3,300
Carl	2,800	2,900	3,900	2,300	3,600
Dolly	3,300	3,100	3,400	2,900	3,500
Edgar	2,800	3,500	3,600	2,900	3,000

Heidi wishes to determine which bid to accept from each of the five bidders so that each of them can purchase one vehicle while the total of the five accepted bids is a maximum.

| Buyer | Automobile | | | | |
	Ford	Dodge	Buick	Volkswagen	Toyota
Amy	500	1000	600	300	500
Bert	0	500	1100	100	300
Carl	700	600	0	600	0
Dolly	200	400	500	0	100
Edgar	700	0	300	0	600

TABLE 11-21
Regret values for
automobile bids

Heidi's maximization problem is solved with the assignment method exactly the same way as a minimization problem, except for one important difference. We first need to convert each of the bids into a *regret value*. This is done in the same manner as we did in Chaper 4 with decision-making under uncertainty. Looking down the column for Ford, we see that the highest bid is $3,500 from Bert. We develop the regret values for the Ford column by subtracting each of the five bids in turn from $3,500. Following this same procedure for the other four vehicles, we develop the full set of regret values shown in Table 11-21. Our objective in maximizing the total of the accepted bids will now be met if we minimize the total regret. Consequently, we can solve the reformulated problem shown in Table 11-21 as a minimization problem using the assignment method. All the steps to the procedure are identical from this point on.

The optimal solution to the problem is shown in Figure 11-38. The calculations for the total bid returns to the Jamesville Car Rental Agency are summarized in Table 11-22.

6 Using the computer to solve assignment and transportation problems

The transportation and assignment problems are particularly easy to solve by hand since they don't require anything more complicated than addition and subtraction. However, even these methods become tedious if you have to solve a large problem by hand. Let's look at the output from some microcomputer implementations of these methods. The programs we used

| Buyer | Automobile | | | | |
	Ford	Dodge	Buick	Volkswagen	Toyota
Amy	200	700	200	(0)	100
Bert	(0)	500	1000	100	200
Carl	800	700	(0)	700	0
Dolly	200	400	400	0	(0)
Edgar	700	(0)	200	0	500

FIGURE 11-38
Optimal assignment
of bid awards.

Buyer	Bid accepted		Bid price
Amy	Volkswagen		$ 2,600
Bert	Ford		3,500
Carl	Buick		3,900
Dolly	Toyota		3,500
Edgar	Dodge		3,500
		Total	$17,000

TABLE 11-22

Optimal solution to the Jamesville Car Rental Agency problem

were written by Warren J. Erikson and Owen P. Hall, Jr.[1] The programs prompt the user for all the input data and are quite simple to use.

In Figure 11-39 we have the computer solution to the Kellum Machine Shop assignment problem. Of course, it's the same as the solution we got by hand on pages 520–523.

Figure 11-40 shows the solution to the Bass Gravel Company problem which we solved by hand on pages 487 to 510. Compare Figure 11-40 with the optimal solution we got in Figure 11-21.

[1] Warren J. Erikson and Owen P. Hall, Jr., *Computer Models for Management Science* (Reading, MA: Addison-Wesley Publishing Company, 1983).

```
******************************
*                            *
*    ASSIGNMENT   MODEL       *
*         ANALYSIS            *
*                            *
******************************
                                         ** RESULTS **
** INFORMATION ENTERED **
                                         ROW   ASSIGNMENTS

   NUMBER OF ROWS:   3
   NUMBER OF COLS:   3                     1    A    ----   ----

         PAYOFFS                           2    ----  A    ----

ROW 1      25    31    35                  3    ----  ----  A

ROW 2      15    20    24            MINIMUM TOTAL PAYOFF =   62

ROW 3      22    19    17                 ** END OF ANALYSIS **
```

FIGURE 11-39

Computer solution to Kellum Machine Shop assignment problem.

```
****************************
*                          *
* TRANSPORTATION ANALYSIS  *
*                          *
****************************

   ** INFORMATION ENTERED **

NUMBER OF SOURCE ROWS:   3
NUMBER OF DESTINATION COLUMNS:   3
PROBLEM TYPE: MINIMIZATION

PAYOFF PER UNIT                   UNITS
                                  AVAILABLE


   4      8      8                   56


  16     24     16                   82


   8     16     24                   77

UNITS NEEDED


  72    102     41
```

```
        ** RESULTS **

    OPTIMAL SHIPPING SCHEDULE


      0      56      0


     41       0     41


     31      46      0


    TOTAL PAYOFF:   2744

      ** END OF ANALYSIS **
```

FIGURE 11-40
Computer solution to Bass Gravel Company transportation problem.

7 Glossary

Assignment problem A special case of the transportation problem in which the number of columns equals the number of rows and in which in the optimal solution there will be one and only one assignment in a given row or column of the assignment table.

Balanced condition The condition when total demand is equal to total supply.

Degeneracy A condition in the transportation problem when the number of stone squares does not equal the number of rim requirements − 1.

Destination A point of demand in a transportation problem.

Flood's technique Another name given to the assignment method.

Hungarian method of assignment Another name given to the assignment method.

Improvement index The net change in cost occasioned by a one-unit change in the quantity shipped.

Job-opportunity costs Differences in cost between the best possible assignments of job to machine and the ones chosen (column differences).

Machine-opportunity costs Differences in cost between the best possible assignment of machines to jobs and the ones chosen (row differences).

Modified distribution method (MODI) A computationally efficient procedure for solving the transportation problem.

Northwest corner rule A systematic and logical procedure for setting up the initial solution to a transportation problem.

Opportunity cost The cost of the opportunities that are sacrificed in order to take a certain action.

Rim requirements Capacity constraints at sources and demand constraints at destinations in the transportation problem.

Source A point of supply in a transportation problem.

Stepping-stone method A special-purpose algorithm for solving the transportation problem.

Stone squares Used squares in the transportation problem containing circled values that are in solution.

Transportation problem A special linear program concerned with selecting optimal routes between sources and destinations.

Transportation tableau A tabular framework for solving the transportation problem.

Unbalanced case A condition in a transportation problem when supply and demand are unequal.

Unused squares Squares representing routes where no quantity is shipped between a source and a destination.

8 Review of equations

Page 504

$$C_{ij} = R_i + K_j \tag{11-1}$$

This equation is used to determine row and column values at stone squares in the MODI method of determining improvement indices.

Page 506

$$\text{Improvement index} = C_{ij} - R_i - K_j \tag{11-2}$$

This formulation is used to compute the improvement index. If the result is negative, further improvement is possible; when all indices are equal to or greater than zero, the optimal solution has been obtained.

9 Exercises

11-1 You are given the following transportation problem:

To From	Column 1	Column 2	Column 3	Supply
Row 1	7 15	9 4	3	19
Row 2	4 9	8 4	7	13
Row 3	2	5 7	9	7
Demand	15	13	11 39	39

a. Using the MODI method, assign $R_1 = 0$ and compute the other R_i and K_j values. Then compute the improvement indices for the unused squares.

b. Again using the MODI procedure, assign $R_1 = 50$, and compute the other R_i and K_j values. Then compute the improvement indices for the unused squares.

c. Now assign $K_3 = 0$ and compute all other R_i and K_j values as well as the improvement indices.

d. Compare your results from parts a, b, and c. Are the R_i and K_j values the same for the three cases? Are the improvement indices the same?

11-2 Using the northwest corner rule, develop an initial solution to the following transportation problem. You will find that degeneracy will occur when you do this.

To From	D	E	F	Supply
A	8	9	7	25
B	6	4	3	9
C	8	6	4	5
Demand	17	17	5 39	39

Which of the unused squares can be a zero stone square and which cannot? Of the ones which can be made a zero stone square, can you intuitively tell which one would be the preferred choice?

11-3 Central Construction Company moves materials between three plants and three projects. Project A requires 140 truckloads each week, project B requires 200, and project C requires 80. Plant W can supply 120 loads, plant X can supply 160, and plant Y can supply 140. Using the cost information given in the following table, compute the optimal transportation cost using the stepping-stone method.

COST INFORMATION

From	To project A	To project B	To project C
Plant W	$5	$4	$9
Plant X	4	3	5
Plant Y	7	4	2

11-4 T. C. Mellott trucking company has a contract to move 115 truckloads of sand per week between three sand-washing plants, W, X, and Y, and three destinations, A, B, and C. Cost and volume information is given below. Compute the optimal transportation cost using the stepping-stone method.

Project	Requirement per week, truckloads	Plant	Available per week, truckloads
A	45	W	35
B	50	X	40
C	20	Y	40

COST INFORMATION

From	To project A	To project B	To project C
Plant W	$ 5	$10	$10
Plant X	20	30	20
Plant Y	5	8	12

11-5 Sid Lane hauls oranges between Florida groves and citrus packing plants. His schedule this week calls for 520 boxes with locations and costs as follows:

Grove	Available per week	Packing plant	Requirement per week
A	170	W	130
B	250	X	200
C	100	Y	190

COST INFORMATION			
From	**To plant W**	**To plant X**	**To plant Y**
Grove A	$12	$ 8	$ 5
Grove B	11	15	10
Grove C	2	7	6

Use the MODI method to find the lowest transportation cost.

11-6 Jack Evans owns several trucks used to haul crushed stone to road projects in the county. The road contractor for whom Jack hauls, N. Teer, has given Jack this schedule for next week:

Project	**Requirement per week**	**Plant**	**Available per week**
A	50	W	45
B	75	X	60
C	50	Y	60

Jack figures his costs from the crushing plant to each of the road projects to be these:

COST INFORMATION			
From	**To project A**	**To project B**	**To project C**
Plant W	$4	$8	$3
Plant X	6	7	9
Plant Y	8	2	5

Using the MODI method, compute Jack's optimal hauling schedule for next week and his transportation cost.

11-7 The Advanced Company has three jobs to be done on three machines. Each job must be done on one and only one machine. The cost of each job on each machine is given in the following table:

COST INFORMATION			
Job	**X**	**Y**	**Z**
A	$4	$6	$8
B	2	3	4
C	4	8	5

Give the job assignments which will minimize cost.

11-8 Miles Del Balzo, Personnel Manager for the Brookeville Manufacturing Company, has recently hired 25 production workers, each of whom will be assigned to one of four positions—assembly, machining, packaging, and inspection. Fifteen of the hires are classified as apprentices while the other ten are experienced workers. The company has developed productivity measures for the workers as follows:

	Productivity per worker by position			
Class	Assembly	Machinery	Packaging	Inspection
Apprentice	58	62	76	29
Experienced	73	94	81	56

Seven workers are needed in each of the assembly, machining, and packaging departments, while four workers are to be located in the inspection department. Determine how many workers of each type to assign to each department so that the sum of the resulting productivity measures is maximized.

11-9 Coley's Machine Shop has four machines on which to do three jobs. Each job can be assigned to one and only one machine. The cost of each job on each machine is given in the following table:

	Machine			
Job	W	X	Y	Z
A	$18	$24	$28	$32
B	8	13	17	19
C	10	15	19	22

What are the job assignments which will minimize cost?

11-10 The Juarez Company has recently harvested 200 tons of bananas, 350 tons of avocados and 210 tons of oranges which they plan to export to Miami, Houston and/or New Orleans. They have estimated that profits in dollars per ton would be as follows:

	Port		
Commodity	Miami	Houston	New Orleans
Bananas	400	420	400
Avocados	900	860	850
Oranges	100	300	350

Trade agreements with Miami and Houston require that Juarez ship no more than 300 tons of produce to either city. However, any amount of produce may be shipped to New Orleans. Determine how many tons of each commodity should be shipped to each of the ports in order for Juarez to maximize total profits.

11-11 The Houston Aerospace Company has just been awarded a rocket engine development contract. The contract terms require that at least five other smaller companies be awarded subcontracts for a portion of the total work. So Houston requested bids from five small companies (A, B, C, D, and E) to do subcontract work in five areas (V, W, X, Y, and Z). The bids are as follows:

COST INFORMATION

Company	Subcontract bids				
	V	W	X	Y	Z
A	$45,000	$60,000	$75,000	$100,000	$30,000
B	50,000	55,000	40,000	100,000	45,000
C	60,000	70,000	80,000	110,000	40,000
D	30,000	20,000	60,000	55,000	25,000
E	60,000	25,000	65,000	185,000	35,000

Which bids should Houston accept in order to fulfill the contract terms at the least cost? What is the total cost of the subcontracts?

11-12 The town of Boulton is putting up for bids four used police vehicles. The town will allow individuals to make bids on all four vehicles but will accept only one bid per individual. Four individuals have made the following bids:

Individual	Vehicle			
	Chevrolet	Ford	Plymouth	AMC
Alice	$1,000	$ 900	$1,100	$ 900
Bruce	1,100	1,000	950	950
Charles	1,050	950	900	1,050
Dora	1,150	1,000	950	1,000

Which bids should be awarded in order to yield the town the maximum total sales revenue? What will the total revenue be?

11-13 You have begun a business of your own and have decided to produce one or more of products A, B, C, and D. You have approached four banks—W, X, Y, and Z—with your ideas on these projects in order to obtain the necessary financing. The following table reflects the level of financing required for each project, the interest rate each of the banks is willing to charge on loans for each of the projects, and the total line of credit each of the banks is willing to lend you.

Bank	Project (interest rate)				Max. credit
	A	B	C	D	
W	16%	18%	19%	17%	$20,000
X	15	17	20	16	10,000
Y	17	16	18	18	20,000
Z	18	19	19	18	30,000
Amount required	$40,000	$30,000	$20,000	$20,000	

As each project should be as attractive profitwise as any other, you have decided to undertake all or part of any number of projects you can at the lowest total interest cost. Which projects should you adopt and from which banks should you finance them?

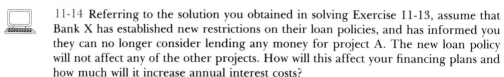

11-14 Referring to the solution you obtained in solving Exercise 11-13, assume that Bank X has established new restrictions on their loan policies, and has informed you they can no longer consider lending any money for project A. The new loan policy will not affect any of the other projects. How will this affect your financing plans and how much will it increase annual interest costs?

11-15 The purchasing agent of the Acme Plumbing Company wishes to purchase 3,000 feet of pipe A, 2,000 feet of pipe B, and 3,000 feet of pipe C. Three manufacturers (X, Y, and Z) are willing to provide the needed pipe at the costs given below (in dollars per 1,000 feet). Acme wants delivery within 1 month. Manufacturer X can produce up to 6,000 feet of pipe (total of types A, B, and C). Manufacturer Y can provide 5,000 feet, and Manufacturer Z can produce 3,000 feet.

Manufacturer	Type of pipe (cost $/1,000 ft) A	B	C	Available
X	$290	$300	$260	6,000
Y	310	280	290	5,000
Z	300	290	290	3,000
Amount required	3,000 ft	2,000 ft	3,000 ft	

Determine what Acme's least-cost purchasing plan for the pipe should be.

11-16 The Midtown Realty Company wishes to assign each of its six real-estate salespersons to one of six districts in Midtown. Based upon the demography of the six areas and the past performance of their six salespersons, the company estimates that sales of property, in houses per year, would be as follows:

Salesperson	Central	East	West	North	South	Lake
Adams	13	9	8	10	12	14
Benson	12	8	7	11	14	13
Cartright	10	9	6	9	12	12
Davis	12	11	9	9	10	11
Elmer	9	7	8	8	9	10
Francis	14	12	10	10	11	14

Determine to which area each of the six should be assigned in order to maximize total annual sales of houses.

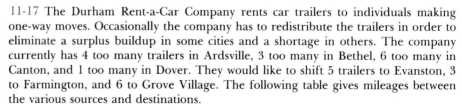

11-17 The Durham Rent-a-Car Company rents car trailers to individuals making one-way moves. Occasionally the company has to redistribute the trailers in order to eliminate a surplus buildup in some cities and a shortage in others. The company currently has 4 too many trailers in Ardsville, 3 too many in Bethel, 6 too many in Canton, and 1 too many in Dover. They would like to shift 5 trailers to Evanston, 3 to Farmington, and 6 to Grove Village. The following table gives mileages between the various sources and destinations.

Sources	Destinations			Total available
	Evanston	Farmington	Grove Village	
Ardsville	60 miles	50 miles	80 miles	4
Bethel	30	40	90	3
Canton	60	30	100	6
Dover	90	70	30	1
Total required	5	3	6	14

How should Durham redistribute the trailers so that total mileage traveled is minimized?

11-18 Ragsdale Textiles has four knitting plants located at Brevard, Flortown, Sillboro, and Siler City. They also own three finishing mills located at Adenton, Buford, and Silverville. The finishing mills have the following yardage requirements per week:

Adenton	1.5 million yards
Buford	.9 million yards
Silverville	2.1 million yards
Total	4.5 million yards

The four knitting mills project this output per week for the next few months:

Brevard	1.1 million yards
Flortown	1.4 million yards
Sillboro	1.2 million yards
Siler City	.8 million yards
Total	4.5 million yards

The delivery costs per 100,000 yards from knitting mill to finishing mills are:

From	Cost per 100,000 yards		
	To Adenton	To Buford	To Silverville
Brevard	$180	$210	$220
Flortown	180	250	240
Sillboro	220	220	210
Siler City	190	160	200

Given their information, schedule shipment from each knitting mill to each finishing mill to minimize total transportation cost. Use the transportation method.

11-19 Coach Bobby Daye is taking his Hoosier basketball team to New York to play the Redmen. Coach Daye always plays a man-to-man defense, assigning each of his players to defend one player on the opposing team. He estimates that if the Hoosier players were assigned to defend particular Redmen, the Redmen would score the number of points indicated on the next page.

	Redman Players				
Hoosier Players	**Jones**	**Kurtz**	**Layne**	**Manion**	**Nevers**
Allen	22	18	24	35	14
Berg	16	20	32	16	26
Carl	13	14	16	10	15
Daniels	33	24	18	19	23
Evers	28	20	18	23	20

Determine Coach Daye's optimal defensive strategy. How many points must the Hoosiers score in order to win the game?

 11-20 Ed Honey operates four used car lots: Mobile, Biloxi, Ocean Springs, and Pensacola. Ed has found it to be more efficient to operate two large "make ready" warehouses in Gulfport and Bay Minette and ship the prepared cars by truck to the four lots. The expected demand for cars at his four lots this month is:

Mobile	125 cars
Biloxi	110 cars
Ocean Springs	110 cars
Pensacola	165 cars

Each warehouse is expected to receive and make ready these cars during the month:

Gulfport	250 cars
Bay Minette	200 cars

Each of Ed's trucks will haul 5 cars; the cost of a load from each warehouse to each used car lot is:

	Cost per truckload			
From	**To Mobile**	**To Biloxi**	**To Ocean Springs**	**To Pensacola**
Gulfport	$75	$ 50	$ 50	$150
Bay Minette	90	120	140	75

By using the transportation method and the information given, devise a schedule which will minimize Ed's total transportation costs for the month.

 11-21 Mountain Furniture Company produces one product, a handcrafted cane-bottom rocking chair made of maple. From its three plants, Mountain projects this production over the next 2 months: Rock City, 7,250 units; Saluda, 10,150 units; Westphal, 4,350 units. Mountain wholesales these chairs to specialty stores in New York, Atlanta, Houston, and Los Angeles. Demand for the 2-month period in these four cities is

New York	8,700 chairs
Atlanta	5,800 chairs
Houston	2,900 chairs
Los Angeles	2,175 chairs

Each chair is packed in a separate box after being carefully wrapped with a special cover to prevent marring the finish. Transportation costs per chair from each plant to each distribution point are:

From	To New York	To Atlanta	To Houston	To Los Angeles
Rock City	$ 5.60	$12.00	$14.50	$11.00
Saluda	11.00	6.50	4.00	5.00
Westphal		9.00	5.50	

Mountain uses unionized labor at its Rock City and Saluda plants. The Westphal plant, however, is not unionized. For this reason, the specialty stores at New York and Los Angeles will not accept delivery of the Westphal products. Use the transportation method to find a shipping schedule that will minimize total transportation costs.

11-22 The purchasing agent for the Town of New Hope, Tennessee, wishes to purchase replacement tires for the town's service vehicles. She needs 300 E78 × 15, 300 D78 × 14, and 300 GR 78 × 15 tires. Three tire suppliers have bid at the prices given below; each says it will supply all or part of the order.

	E78 × 15	D78 × 14	GR78 × 15
Southern Tire Co.	$65	$80	$78
New Hope Tire Co.	66	78	79
Billy's Tire Service	60	79	79

The Town of New Hope has a policy of trying to involve as many local dealers as possible in the purchasing. Therefore, the purchasing agent would like to buy the tires in such a way that the entire requirement of each type is purchased from a single dealer, and all three dealers will be given a purchase order. Use the assignment method to determine the least-cost purchasing plan.

11-23 Linville Laboratories has just been notified that it has received three government research grants. The laboratory administrator must now assign research directors to each of these projects. There are four researchers available now who are relatively free from other duties. The time required to complete the required research activities will be a function of the experience and ability of the research director who is assigned to the project. The laboratory administrator has this estimate of project completion times (in weeks) for each director-grant combination:

Research directors	Grant		
	1	2	3
Louis Gump	80	90	54
Anne Aitken	54	108	30
Mary Albritton	46	104	48
Ned Powell	72	96	48

Since the three grants have about the same priority, the laboratory administrator would like to assign research directors in a way that would minimize the total time (in weeks) necessary to complete all three grant projects. What assignments should be made?

11-24 Charlie's Tuna Cannery produces tuna in two plants, Seattle and Anchorage. Seattle has a capacity of 20,000 cases monthly on regular time and another 5,000 cases by using overtime. Anchorage can produce 30,000 cases and 10,000 cases on regular time and overtime, respectively. Seattle's production costs are $6 a case on regular time and $9 a case on overtime. Anchorage has costs of $7 and $8, respectively. Tuna can be sold in the same month as canned or stored at a cost of $1 per case per month.

Charlie's two customers, Chicken of the Ocean and Moon-Kist, have the following monthly needs:

	Jan.	Feb.	Mar.
Chicken of the Ocean	20,000	30,000	40,000
Moon-Kist	20,000	40,000	30,000

Cost per case for shipping from the company's two canneries to the customers is:

From	To Chicken of the Ocean	To Moon-Kist
Seattle	$2	$3
Anchorage	2	1

Set up the transportation version of a solution to this problem that will minimize Charlie's total production, storage, and transportation costs for this period. Do not work the problem.

11-25 Frosty, Inc., manufactures picnic coolers in three sizes: party size, family size, and storage size. The major restriction on production is labor: party size takes 40 minutes a unit, family size an hour, and storage size 80 minutes a unit. Weekly demand for the coming 3 weeks has been estimated to be:

	Party	Family	Storage
Week 1	150	120	60
Week 2	150	240	120
Week 3	180	180	240

There are no storage costs associated with production which is not shipped, since the plant, for the present time, has considerable unused space. Labor rates are $8 an hour with time and a half for overtime. Labor availability for this production period is:

	Regular time	Overtime
Week 1	400 hours	160 hours
Week 2	400 hours	320 hours
Week 3	640 hours	400 hours

Using the transportation method, determine the optimal production schedule for

Frosty. (*Hint:* Convert demand from units to hours of production.) Use the transportation model to minimize the total labor cost for this period.

11-26 Refer to the optimal solution you obtained for Exercise 11-18 and answer the following:

   a. You have been informed that the road from Brevard to Buford has been washed out, and next week's shipment of 100,000 yards must be made from another knitting mill. What change in shipping plans will result in the least cost increase?

   b. You have been informed by your trucking supervisor that new shipping rates have been adopted, and the cost of shipping from Siler City to Silverville is now reduced to $160 per 100,000 yards. What change should you make to your shipping plans?

11-27 A job shop has received an order for six jobs, each of which requires processing on a lathe. The shop has six lathes of different levels of speed. The following table describes the time it would take (in hours) to process any of these jobs on any of the machines:

	Machine					
Job	1	2	3	4	5	6
A	7	6	2	8	5	5
B	6	8	4	5	4	6
C	9	9	8	12	10	6
D	1	3	1	2	1	1
E	16	18	10	14	19	12
F	12	14	12	18	20	24

Determine an assignment, one job to a machine, which will result in a minimum total processing time.

11-28 The Innovative Products Company is considering an expansion into five new sales districts. The company has been able to hire four new experienced salespersons. Upon analyzing the new salespersons' past experience in combination with a personality test which was given to them, the company assigned a rating to each of the salespersons for each of the districts. These ratings are as follows:

	District				
Salesperson	1	2	3	4	5
A	92	90	94	91	83
B	84	88	96	82	81
C	90	90	93	86	93
D	78	94	89	84	88

The company knows that with four salespersons, only four of the five potential districts can be covered. It would like to know which four districts the salespersons should be assigned to in order to maximize the total of the ratings.

Fill in the
Blanks

11-1 In the transportation problem, a rim requirement for a _____ is the capacity of a supplier, while a rim requirement for a _____ is the demand of a user.

11-2 The _____ method for solving the transportation problem calculates the improvement index for any unused square by adding up the positive and negative costs along a closed path; the _____ method computes the improvement index for used squares by solving a set of linear equations.

11-3 The net change in costs which results from transferring one unit of a transportation assignment from a stone to an unused square is called the _____; a closed path with a _____ improvement index indicates a possible improvement in the solution of a transportation problem.

11-4 The _____ problem is a special case of the balanced transportation problem where all rim requirements are equal to 1; this problem may be solved by the _____ method, which is also known as _____ technique.

11-5 In the assignment problem, the _____ cost is the difference between the best possible assignment of a job to a machine and the one chosen; the best possible assignment is an assignment with opportunity cost equal to _____.

11-6 Both the transportation and assignment problems are members of a large class of specially structured linear programming problems called _____.

11-7 The _____ serves the same purpose for the transportation method as the all-slack initial solution in the simplex method.

11-8 Networks are composed of points, called _____, and lines, called _____.

11-9 A solution to the cost minimization transportation problem is optimal when all unused squares have an improvement index which is _____.

11-10 In the transportation problem, squares which are in the solution because they have some value placed in them are called _____ squares, while those which do not are called _____ squares.

True-False

11-11 A transportation problem is said to be balanced if the same quantity is shipped from each plant to each project. **T F**

11-12 The northwest corner rule is a procedure used to find the best possible initial solution to a transportation problem. **T F**

11-13 The transportation problem is a special case of the assignment problem. **T F**

11-14 A particular solution of a transportation problem is feasible if all the rim requirements are exactly satisfied, that is, if all the circled values in a row sum to the row rim requirement and all the circled values in a column sum to the column rim requirement. **T F**

11-15 The test for degeneracy of a solution is to check if there are any unused squares with an improvement index equal to zero. If so, degeneracy exists. **T F**

11-16 The maximum quantity which can be shifted to an unused square **T F** with a negative improvement index is the smallest quantity in the closed path for that square which has a negative sign associated with it.

11-17 In the case of an unbalanced transportation problem, a new source **T F** or destination (whichever is needed) may be added to the problem, with transportation cost equal to zero, to form a balanced problem.

11-18 The advantage of the MODI method over the stepping-stone method **T F** of computing improvement indices for unused stones lies in its greater computational efficiency.

11-19 The results of a degenerate solution to the transportation problem **T F** are that it is impossible to trace a closed path for each unused square, and it is impossible to compute R_i and K_j values in the MODI method.

11-20 In the assignment problem, an optimal assignment requires that the **T F** maximum number of lines which can be drawn through squares with zero opportunity cost be equal to the number of rows.

11-21 Degeneracy occurs in the transportation problem whenever the num- **T F** ber of stone squares is less than the total number of rim requirements minus one.

11-22 When using the stepping-stone method for a non-degenerate trans- **T F** portation problem, only one closed path exists for evaluating the improvement index of an unused square.

11-23 When assigning plus and minus signs to the corner stone squares in **T F** the stepping-stone method, you always start by assigning a plus sign to the unused square whose improvement index is being evaluated.

11-24 When calculating the improvement indices for all unused squares **T F** using the MODI method, the values you compute are always the same as those you would have computed using the stepping-stone procedure.

11-25 Each iteration of the transportation method involves the elimination **T F** of one old stone square and the introduction of one new stone square. This is similar to a pivot in the simplex method.

11-26 A closed path has all the following characteristics except: Multiple
   a. It links an unused square with itself.   Choice
   b. Movements on the path may occur horizontally, vertically, or diagonally.
   c. The corners of the path must all be stones, except for the corner at the unused square being evaluated.
   d. The path may skip over unused squares or stones.

11-27 The maximum quantity which may be shipped via an unused stone with a negative improvement index is the value of the smallest stone with a negative sign in the closed path. Why?
   a. This ensures that some improvement in the total cost will occur.
   b. This ensures that no rim requirements are violated.
   c. This ensures that no negative quantities are shipped by any stone square.
   d. This ensures that the problem is not optimal.

11-28 A degeneracy may occur when:
   a. At optimality, the total cost is zero.
   b. In finding an initial solution, a row and a column rim requirement are simultaneously satisfied.

c. There are two or more stones with the same smallest negative value in a closed path for an incoming stone.

d. Both *b* and *c*.

11-29 Which of the following is true for the assignment problem?

a. The number of rows equals the number of columns.

b. All circled values in a stone are 1.

c. All rim requirements are 1.

d. All of the above.

11-30 The drawback to using the transportation problem method in solving an assignment problem is that:

a. A degeneracy results from every improvement in the total cost.

b. The assignment problem can't be formulated as a transportation problem.

c. The assignment problem is an unbalanced transportation problem.

d. Too many alternative optima result.

11-31 A stone square in the transportation method is analogous to:

a. A variable in the product mix column in the simplex method.

b. A $C_j - Z_j$ value in the simplex method.

c. A value in the quantity column in the simplex method.

d. A variable not in the product mix column in the simplex method.

11-32 An improvement index in the transportation method is analogous to:

a. A variable in the product mix column in the simplex method.

b. A $C_j - Z_j$ value in the simplex method.

c. A value in the quantity column in the simplex method.

d. A variable not in the product mix column in the simplex method.

11-33 A number placed in a stone square in the transportation method is analogous to:

a. A variable in the product mix column in the simplex method.

b. A $C_j - Z_j$ value in the simplex method.

c. A value in the quantity column in the simplex method.

d. A variable not in the product mix column in the simplex method.

11-34 An unused square in the transportation method is analogous to:

a. A variable in the product mix column in the simplex method.

b. A $C_j - Z_j$ value in the simplex method.

c. A value in the quantity column in the simplex method.

d. A variable not in the product mix column in the simplex method.

11-35 We have alternative optimal solutions to a minimization transportation problem whenever we find a solution where the improvement indices are:

a. All strictly positive and greater than zero.

b. All non-negative with at least one equal to zero.

c. All equal to zero.

d. All non-positive with at least one equal to zero.

11-36 When using the MODI method to compute an improvement index for all unused squares, we use the equation—improvement index $= C_{ij} - R_i - K_j$. If we were to use this equation to compute an improvement index for a stone square, we would find that:

a. It is always equal to zero.

b. It is always a negative number.

c. It is always a positive number.

d. None of the above. It could be any value.

11-37 If you were to solve a transportation problem with m rows (suppliers) and n columns (destination points) using the simplex method, you would have to formulate the problem with:
  a. m variables and n constraints.
  b. n variables and n constraints.
  c. $m \times n$ variables and $m + n$ constraints.
  d. $m + n$ variables and $m \times n$ constraints.

11-38 Suppose you had an assignment problem where 5 jobs are to be assigned to 5 people, but there are in fact 7 people available to do the 5 jobs. You could solve the problem in the same manner as an unbalanced transportation problem is solved by:
  a. Creating two dummy jobs with zero costs and solve a 7×7 problem.
  b. Arbitrarily eliminating two of the people and solve a 5×5 problem.
  c. Solving the assignment problem as a 5×7 problem.
  d. All of the above.

11-39 Using the stepping-stone method, you should always find exactly one closed path for a given unused square, thus allowing you to evaluate its improvement index. If you find more than one closed path, you should check for:
  a. Degeneracy—you have too few stone squares.
  b. A procedural error—you have too many stone squares.
  c. Infeasibility—the values placed in the rows or columns do not add up to their rim requirements.
  d. Both b and c are correct.

11-40 A dummy row or column is introduced in the transportation method in order to handle an unbalanced problem. This dummy serves the same purpose as a:
  a. Structural variable in the simplex method.
  b. Non-negativity constraint in the simplex method.
  c. Slack variable in the simplex method.
  d. None of the above is correct.

11 Real world MS/OR successes

EXAMPLE: MOVING SAND AT THE BRISBANE INTERNATIONAL AIRPORT

In 1982, developers of the Brisbane, Australia, International Airport faced a familiar problem in construction engineering: how to minimize the costs of moving sand from one location to another. In broad terms, more than 2,000,000 cubic meters of sand dredged from a nearby bay had to be moved by pipeline to various sites. The sand was needed because its weight would compress the swampy ground at the sites. Once the ground was compressed, the sand would be moved again to other places around the airport by truck or scraper. Chad Perry and Mike Iliff[2], consultants on the project, developed a transportation model to plan sand movement. The model was very similar to the Bass Gravel Company example in this chapter. The bottom line: savings of $400,000 compared to the original plans of the project engineers.

THE SAND MOVEMENT PROBLEM

[2] Chad Perry and Mike Iliff, "From the Shadows: Earthmoving on Construction Projects," *Interfaces*, vol. 13, no. 1, pp. 79–84, 1983.

When Perry and Iliff got involved in the project, sand had already been pumped from the bay to twenty initial sites. The problem was to move the sand by trucks to twenty destination sites. Although this was a relatively simple transportation problem, Perry and Iliff made it even simpler by grouping the sites into clusters. The initial sites were grouped into five clusters of nearby sites, while the destination sites were grouped into nine clusters. The result was a transportation model with five sources of supply and nine destination points, and with demand equal to supply (rim requirements for the rows equal to rim requirements for the columns). Basing the model on clusters rather than individual sites had little impact on total cost and it simplified the job of awarding contracts with trucking companies to move the sand.

Solution of the transportation model was straightforward using the methods in this chapter. To gain management acceptance of the model, Perry and Iliff computed shadow prices using the procedures in Chapter 10 to demonstrate how the original plans for moving sand increased total cost above the optimal solution.

Pioneer Audio is excited about their newly designed Response 1000 stereo speaker. Tests on the new speaker have demonstrated its superior performance, and Pioneer's management has good reason to be optimistic about future sales. Rollie Tillman, Pioneer's promotion and advertising director, has been assigned the responsibility of introducing the new product to the market. Rollie is eager to accept this challenge, because he recognizes that poor planning can lead to sales which fall well short of their potential, even for a product like the Response 1000 speaker. In order to get the job done right, Rollie must not only map out all the activities which need to be accomplished, but he must also exercise care to ensure that each activity is integrated with all other activities so that together they form an orderly progression of promotional effort. Rollie has decided to use a management tool known as Program Evaluation and Review Technique (PERT). This technique will enable him to identify the interrelationships among the activities; it will assist him in quickly isolating potential problem areas as they arise; and it will allow him to exercise better control of his budget.

In this chapter, you will learn how to use PERT to your advantage in managing large projects. You will learn of the many benefits the technique has to offer managers in controlling costs, schedules, and resources.

NETWORKS

PERT, CPM, PERT/Cost, Scheduling with Resource Limitations, Maximal-Flow Problem, Minimal-Spanning-Tree Problem, Shortest-Route Problem, Dynamic Programming

CHAPTER OBJECTIVES

■ INTRODUCE THE CONCEPT OF NETWORKS AND NETWORKING TECHNIQUES AS SOLUTION MODELS FOR COMPLEX PROJECT-SCHEDULING PROBLEMS.

■ REVIEW IN DETAIL THE CONCEPTS AND USE OF PERT AND PERT/COST TO PLAN AND CONTROL PROJECTS.

■ SHOW THE USE OF CPM IN THE PLANNING AND CONTROL OF PROJECTS.

■ EXAMINE SITUATIONS WHICH SUGGEST THE USE OF EACH TECHNIQUE.

■ DEMONSTRATE HOW TO SCHEDULE PROJECTS INVOLVING RESOURCE LIMITATIONS.

■ PROVIDE SPECIFIC INSTRUCTION IN THE TECHNIQUES USED TO SOLVE THE MAXIMAL-FLOW PROBLEM, AND THE MINIMAL-SPANNING-TREE PROBLEM.

■ INTRODUCE DYNAMIC PROGRAMMING AS A SOLUTION TECHNIQUE TO THE SHORTEST-ROUTE PROBLEM AND DEMONSTRATE ITS USE IN DECISION SITUATIONS INVOLVING OVERALL EFFECTIVENESS IN A SERIES OF RELATED DECISIONS OVER TIME.

The techniques to be introduced in this chapter have been applied successfully to a wide range of significant management problems. The Polaris missile project was planned with the aid of PERT (program evaluation and review technique), which we shall study in this chapter. CPM (critical path method) was successfully used by one of the authors to plan and coordinate the activities of two governments as they cooperated in an earthquake relief project in Turkey. Other uses of network models include planning the flow of traffic to minimize congestion in cities, determining the shortest pickup and delivery routes for package-handling companies like United Parcel Service, and even finding the best layout for the water system in a new residential subdivision.

1 PERT (program evaluation and review technique)

DEVELOPMENT OF PERT

PERT was developed by the Navy Special Projects Office in cooperation with Booz, Allen and Hamilton, a management consulting firm. It was specifically directed at planning and controlling the Polaris missile program, a massive project which had 250 prime contractors and over 9,000 subcontractors. Imagine the problems faced by the project director in attempting to keep track of hundreds of thousands of individual tasks on this project. The introduction of PERT into the Polaris project helped management answer questions like these:

QUESTIONS THAT PERT
HELPS ANSWER FOR
MANAGEMENT

1 When will the project be finished?

2 When is each individual part of the project scheduled to start and finish?

3 Of the hundreds of thousands of "parts" of the project, which ones must be finished on time to avoid making the entire project late?

4 Is it possible to shift resources to *critical* parts of the project (those that *must* be finished on time) from other *noncritical* parts of the project (parts which can be delayed) without affecting the overall completion time of the project?

5 Among all the hundreds of thousands of parts of the project, where should management concentrate its efforts at any one time?

PIONEER AUDIO EXAMPLE OF PERT

USING PERT TO PLAN
THE INTRODUCTION OF
A NEW HI-FI SPEAKER

Pioneer Audio has completed the design and testing of a new type of miniature speaker, the Response 1000, which Pioneer thinks can be produced and distributed at a price that will give it the strongest market position in the industry. Ken Vaughn, Pioneer's president, is quite concerned that this speaker get the best possible promotion, and he has had a number of meetings with Rollie Tillman, Pioneer's promotion and advertising director. Rollie plans an extensive promotion campaign involving specially prepared literature, training of the field sales force, media releases, and actual demonstrations in selected stores nationwide. Rollie knows that this involves a lot of cooperation and that a slipup will mean trouble not only for the Response 1000 speaker project but also for him.

An activity list   Rollie put together a careful list of all the different activities involved in the promotional campaign for the new Response 1000 speaker. This list is shown in Table 12-1. For each activity he identified, Rollie also identified its *immediate predecessors,* that is, the activities that must immediately precede a given activity. For example, in Table 12-1, Rollie noted that activity K, the training program, has as its immediate predecessors activities H and J; this simply indicates that the training program cannot be conducted without both the training material having been prepared and the participating store managers having been screened and selected. Similarly, activity L, the simultaneous in-store introduction of the Response 1000, cannot be accomplished without G (the in-store promotion materials), I (the preintroduction media campaign), and K (the training program) all having been completed.

PREPARING THE ACTIVITY LIST

PRECEDENCE RELATIONS AMONG ACTIVITIES

Drawing the network   With his list of activities carefully checked to make sure that all the activities were included and all the predecessors correctly identified, Rollie then drew the graph in Figure 12-1. This shows not only

DRAWING THE NETWORK TO DISPLAY PRECEDENCE RELATIONSHIPS GRAPHICALLY

TABLE 12-1
List of activities for the Response 1000 promotion campaign

Activity symbol	Activity description	Immediate predecessors
A	Develop the advertising plan (a detailed plan of projected radio, television, and newspaper advertising)	—
B	Develop the promotion and training materials plan (a detailed study of the materials that will be required for training the store managers and for the final in-store introduction)	—
C	Develop the training plan (the design of the training program that the store managers will undertake prior to the final in-store introduction)	—
D	Schedule the radio, television, and newspaper advertisements that will appear prior to the final introduction	A
E	Develop the advertising copy that will be required	A
F	A "dummy" activity (one that takes no time) which simply indicates activity I can't begin until activity E has been completed; explained on page 554	E
G	Prepare promotion materials which will be used during the in-store introduction	B
H	Prepare materials which will be used in the training program for the store managers	B
I	Conduct the preintroduction advertising campaign in the media	D, F
J	Screen and select the store managers who will undergo training	C
K	Conduct the training program	H, J
L	The final in-store introduction of the Response 1000	G, I, K

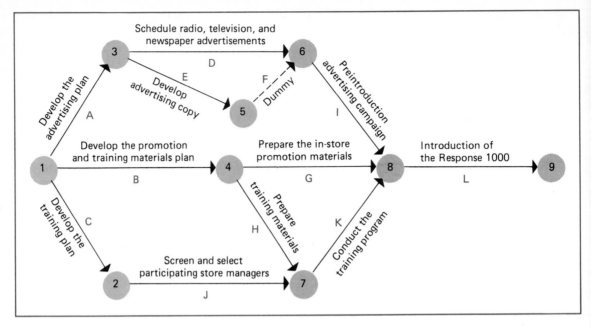

FIGURE 12-1
PERT network for the Response 1000 introduction.

all the activities in Table 12-1 but also all the predecessor relationships among the activities in the network.

From Figure 12-1 you can see that a PERT network is simply a network of numbered circles connected by arrows. In PERT, we call the circles *nodes* and the arrows *branches*. The arrows represent the activities in the project, and the nodes are the start and the finish of those activities. If all the activities leading to a node are finished, that node can be called an *event;* in the Response 1000 network, circle 8 (which we call node 8 in network language) can be called event 8 only when activities G, I, and K are complete.

Dummy activities in PERT Rollie showed one *dummy activity* in the network, activity F. What does this mean? Had he not used that format, it might have appeared that activities D and E had the *same* starting and ending nodes:

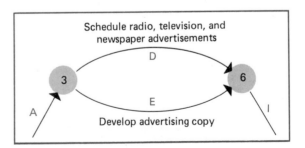

However, in PERT we avoid this by putting in a dummy activity F so that the same network can be drawn like this:

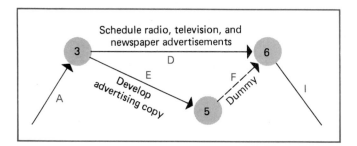

The dummy activity in PERT lets us draw networks with proper precedence relationships. The dummy activity F indicates that activity I *cannot* begin until *both* D and E are completed. These dummy activities exist solely for the purpose of establishing precedence relationships and are not assigned any time.

DUMMY ACTIVITIES TAKE NO TIME

Activity times in a PERT network   In PERT, *time* is often expressed in calendar weeks. The basic reason for not using smaller units is that most of the activities in a PERT network will take considerable time to accomplish. However, in some problems, time can be appropriately expressed in work days or even in hours.

EXPRESSING TIME IN PERT NETWORKS

To express the time required to complete an activity in the PERT system, we first estimate the number of working days required to do this work and then divide this by the number of working days per week. For example, if we have an activity that is expected to require 10 working days and our normal working week is 5 days, then we would say in the PERT system that this activity is expected to require 2 calendar weeks. Times are usually expressed to one decimal place.

Because of the uncertainty that is associated with projects which have never been done in the same way before, the estimated time for an activity is really better described by a probability distribution than by a single estimate.

The originators of PERT were faced with the problem of finding a particular kind of probability distribution; they wanted a distribution of activity times with the following four characteristics:

1 A small probability (1 in 100) of reaching the *optimistic time* (shortest time), symbolized *a*

CHARACTERISTICS OF THE DISTRIBUTION USED TO EXPRESS THE VARIATION IN TIME

2 A small probability (1 in 100) of reaching the *pessimistic time* (longest time), symbolized *b*

3 One and only one *most likely time,* symbolized *m,* which would be free to move between the two extremes mentioned in 1 and 2 above

4 The ability to measure *uncertainty* in the estimating

The *beta distribution* was picked because it has all four of these attributes.

THE BETA DISTRIBUTION

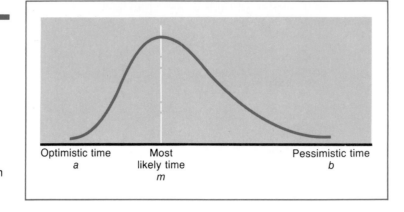

FIGURE 12-2
Beta distribution with
symbols for time
estimates.

Figure 12-2 illustrates a beta distribution with the time designations under the curve.

After these three time estimates have been made, they must be combined into a single workable time value. This is done algebraically, using a weighted average,

$$t = \frac{a + 4m + b}{6} \tag{12-1}$$

where t equals the expected time for the activity.

Studies have been made of the accuracy and validity of t computed by formula (12-1). One study showed that in most PERT situations, the error in t from calculating it with Eq. (12-1) was small enough to make the method quite satisfactory in most cases.[1]

To describe the variation or dispersion in the uncertain activity times in a PERT network, we use the standard deviation of the activity times. Because we have three time estimates for each activity, we can calculate a standard deviation for that activity. The difference between the a time and the b time represents the distance from the extreme left-hand end to the extreme right-hand end of a distribution of possible activity times. This distance is about ± 3 standard deviations; therefore $b - a = 6$ standard deviations. Thus

$$\text{Standard deviation of an activity} = \frac{b - a}{6} \tag{12-2}$$

CALCULATING
EXPECTED TIMES AND
STANDARD DEVIATIONS
OF THOSE TIMES FOR
THE PROJECT
ACTIVITIES
Activity times for the Response 1000 Rollie Tillman made his best guess of the *most likely time* for each of the 11 activities in the Response 1000 project; then he indicated how uncertain he was by providing the estimates of the *most pessimistic* and *most optimistic time* for each activity as well. These are shown in Table 12-2 along with the expected times, calculated using Eq. (12-1), and the standard deviation for each activity, calculated using Eq. (12-2).

Notice that in the case of activity L (the actual in-store introduction), there is no uncertainty about this time, since Rollie plans for a 4-week introduction.

---

[1] K. R. MacCrimmon and C. A. Ryavec, "An Analytical Study of the PERT Assumptions," Memo RM-3408-PR, RAND Corporation, Santa Monica, CA., December 1962.

Activity	a (most optimistic time)	m (most likely time)	b (most pessimistic time)	(a + 4m + b)/6 (expected time)	(b − a)/6 (activity std. dev.)
A	1	2	3	2	.33
B	1	2	3	2	.33
C	1	2	3	2	.33
D	1	2	9	3	1.33
E	2	3	10	4	1.33
F		(Dummy activity)		0	0
G	3	6	15	7	2.00
H	2	5	14	6	2.00
I	1	4	7	4	1.00
J	4	9	20	10	2.67
K	1	2	9	3	1.33
L	4	4	4	4	0

TABLE 12-2
Expected time and standard deviation for activities in the Response 1000 project

Notice also that Rollie's uncertainty is reflected in the standard deviation of the activity times; in the case of some activities—A, B, and C, for example— the standard deviation is quite small; in others, however (look at J), the standard deviation is quite large.

REFLECTING UNCERTAINTY IN THE NETWORK

Finding the critical path For Rollie to estimate how long the Response 1000 project will require, he will have to determine the *critical path* of this network. A path is defined as a sequence of connected activities that leads from the beginning of the project (node 1) to the end of the project (node 9). Since the work described by *all* the paths must be done before the project is considered complete, Rollie must find that path that requires the most work, the *longest* path through the network; this is called the *critical path*. If Rollie wants to *reduce* the time for the Response 1000 project, he will have to shorten the critical path; that is, he will have to reduce the time of one or more activities on that path—but first he has to *find* it.

DEFINING THE CRITICAL PATH

SIGNIFICANCE OF THE CRITICAL PATH

When the network is larger, it is very tedious, often impossible, to find the critical path by listing all the paths and picking the longest one. We need a more organized method. We start at node 1 with a starting time we define as zero; we then compute an *earliest start time* and an *earliest finish time* for each activity in the network. Look at activity A with an expected time of 2 weeks:

AN EFFICIENT WAY TO FIND THE CRITICAL PATH

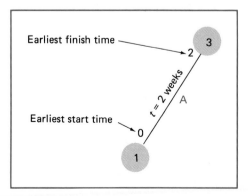

Earliest finish time

Earliest start time

$t = 2$ weeks

EARLIEST START AND EARLIEST FINISH TIMES

To find the earliest finish time for any activity, we use this formula:

Earliest finish time = earliest start time + expected time

$$EF = ES + t \qquad (12\text{-}3)$$

Now Rollie must find the ES time and the EF time for *all* the activities in the Response 1000 network.

The earliest-start-time rule Since no activity can begin until *all* its predecessor activities are complete, the earliest start time for an activity *leaving* any node is equal to the largest earliest finish time of all activities *entering* that same node. Look at the first few activities in the Response 1000 network:

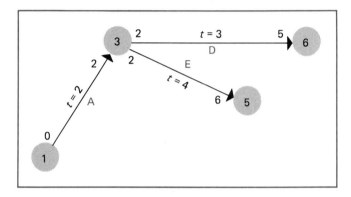

In this instance, the *earliest start time* for activities D and E is 2, the *earliest finish time* for activity A. Using this procedure we make what is called a *forward pass* through the network to get all the ES and EF times shown in Figure 12-3. Rollie can see right away from the earliest finish time for activity L that it is going to take 19 weeks to finish this project, and that is only if all the activities run on schedule.

The latest-finish-time rule The second step in finding the critical path is for Rollie to compute a *latest start time* and *latest finish time* for each activity.
This is done by using what is called a *backward pass;* that is, we begin at the completion point, node 9, and—using a latest finish time of 19 weeks for that activity (which we found in our forward pass method)—compute the *latest finish time* and *latest start time* for every activity. What is latest finish time? It is simply the latest time at which an activity can be completed without extending the completion time of the network. In the same sense, the latest start time is the latest time at which an activity can begin without extending the completion time on the project. In a more formal sense, the latest start time can be computed with Eq. (12-4):

Latest start time = latest finish time − expected time

$$LS = LF - t \qquad (12\text{-}4)$$

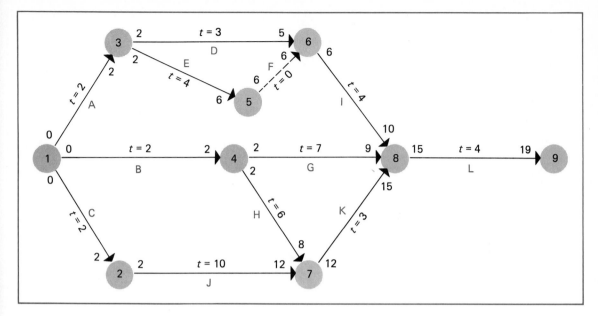

FIGURE 12-3

Response 1000 network with all earliest start (ES) and all earliest finish (EF) times.

For example, given the latest finish time for activity L of 19 weeks, then

$$\text{LS (for activity L)} = 19 - 4$$
$$= 15$$

In Figure 12-4 we have shown the LS and LF times for all the activities in the network.

A formal statement of the *latest-finish-time rule* would be that the latest finish time for an activity entering any node is equal to the smallest latest start time for all activities leaving that same node. Look at node 4 in Figure 12-4. The latest finish time for activity B entering that node is 6, the smallest start time for the two activities leaving node 4.

Now by comparing the *earliest start time* with the *latest start time* for any activity (that is, by looking at when it *can* be started compared with when it *must* be started), we see how much free time, or *slack*, that activity has. Slack is the length of time we can delay an activity without interfering with the project completion. We can also determine slack for any activity by comparing its *earliest finish time* with its *latest finish time*. Look at activity A on the network in Figures 12-3 and 12-4.

$$\text{LF} - \text{EF for activity A} = 7 - 2 = 5$$
$$\text{LS} - \text{ES for activity A} = 5 - 0 = 5$$

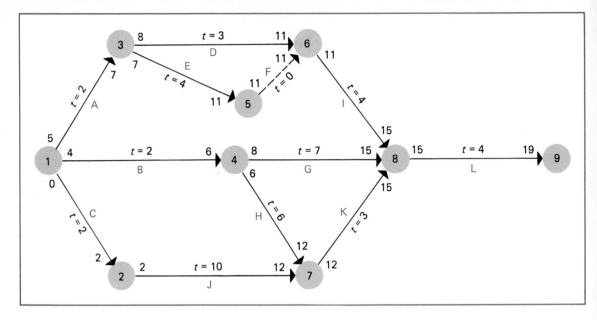

FIGURE 12-4
Response 1000 network with all latest start (LS) and all latest finish (LF) times.

The formal statement of these two methods is

$$\text{Slack} = \text{LF} - \text{EF} \quad \text{or} \quad \text{LS} - \text{ES} \qquad (12\text{-}5)$$

In Table 12-3, we have shown LF, EF, LS, ES, and slack for all the activities in the Response 1000 network. Those activities without any slack are C, J, K,

TABLE 12-3
Determination of
critical path for
Response 1000
project

Activity	Earliest start	Latest start	Earliest finish	Latest finish	Slack (LS − ES or LF − EF)	Activity on critical path
A	0	5	2	7	5	
B	0	4	2	6	4	
C	0	0	2	2	0	Yes
D	2	8	5	11	6	
E	2	7	6	11	5	
F			(Dummy activity)			
G	2	8	9	15	6	
H	2	6	8	12	4	
I	6	11	10	15	5	
J	2	2	12	12	0	Yes
K	12	12	15	15	0	Yes
L	15	15	19	19	0	Yes

and L. None of these can be delayed without delaying the whole project. The *critical path* for the Response 1000 project is C-J-K-L. Rollie will have to watch these four activities especially closely; delay in any one of them will cause a delay in the project completion. Delays in other activities (A, B, D, E, G, H, and I) will not affect on-time project completion (19 weeks) unless the delay is greater than the slack time an activity has. For example, it is all right for activity G (preparation of in-store promotion materials) to fall 6 weeks behind schedule because it has 6 weeks of slack; but if it falls *more* than 6 weeks behind schedule, it will delay completion of the Response 1000 project.

Probability estimates in PERT   So far, we have considered the activity times as fixed. Let's now examine the effect of uncertainty in Rollie's time-estimating process on completion dates. Rollie knows that the critical path is C-J-K-L, with an expected total time of 19 weeks. Look back at Table 12-2, where Rollie computed a standard deviation for each activity. If the activity times on the critical path are statistically independent, the standard deviation of the earliest finish time of the network is given by the following formula:

Standard deviation of the earliest finish time of a network with four activities on its critical path

$$= \sqrt{\left(\begin{array}{c}\text{std. dev.}\\ \text{for first}\\ \text{activity}\end{array}\right)^2 + \left(\begin{array}{c}\text{std. dev.}\\ \text{for second}\\ \text{activity}\end{array}\right)^2 + \left(\begin{array}{c}\text{std. dev.}\\ \text{for third}\\ \text{activity}\end{array}\right)^2 + \left(\begin{array}{c}\text{std. dev.}\\ \text{for fourth}\\ \text{activity}\end{array}\right)^2} \qquad (12\text{-}6)$$

$$= \sqrt{(.33)^2 + (2.67)^2 + (1.33)^2 + (0)^2}$$

$$= \sqrt{.1089 + 7.1289 + 1.7689 + 0}$$

$$= \sqrt{9.01}$$

$$= 3.00$$

Suppose Rollie wants to know the chances that he will be able to finish the project in 20 weeks. PERT assumes that the distribution of the total project completion time is normal; this permits us to draw the distribution in Figure 12-5, where we have shown the earliest finish time of the network (19 weeks) and the completion time Rollie has on his mind now (20 weeks). We know the standard deviation of the critical path is 3 weeks; thus the distance from the mean to 20 weeks is

$$\frac{20 - 19}{3} = .33 \text{ standard deviation}$$

If we look in Appendix Table 1 for the area under a normal curve from the left-hand tail to a point .33 standard deviation above the mean, we find the answer .62930. Thus there is better than a 60 percent chance that Rollie will finish in less than 20 weeks.

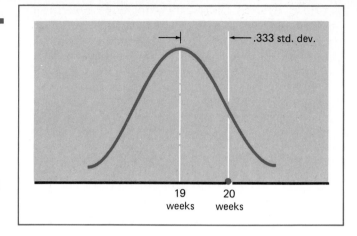

.333 std. dev.

19
weeks

20
weeks

FIGURE 12-5

Distribution of project
completion times for
the Response 1000
project.

What did Rollie find?   Use of PERT in this instance provides Rollie Tillman with some useful information about the Response 1000 project:

1 The expected project completion time is 19 weeks.

2 There is a better than 60 percent chance of finishing before 20 weeks. Rollie can also determine the chances of meeting any other deadline if he wishes.

INFORMATION
PROVIDED BY PERT

3 Activities C, J, K, and L are on the critical path; they must be watched more closely than the others, for if they fall behind, the whole project falls behind.

4 If extra effort is needed to finish the project on time, and if resources on one activity can possibly be used on another to reduce time, Rollie can *borrow* resources from any activity *not* on the critical path; these include A, B, D, E, G, H, and I.

5 Activities not on the critical path (A, B, D, E, G, H, and I) can fall behind by varying amounts (their slack times) without causing the project to be late.

6 The earliest starting and finishing times for all activities in the project are known from Figures 12-3 and 12-4.

NETWORK SCHEDULING WITH THE COMPUTER

Although it was easy to explain how to find the critical path by hand in solving Rollie Tillman's problem, for larger problems you would want to use a computer to find the critical path. In addition, computer software packages for network scheduling generate several kinds of reports which facilitate management's ability to understand and implement the resulting schedules.

Let's look at some of the network scheduling capabilities of the SAS® System,[2] developed by SAS Institute, Inc. The example used below was developed by one of the authors and Marc Cohen of SAS Institute and is used with the Institute's permission.

---

[2] SAS is a registered trademark of SAS Institute, Inc., Cary, NC.

A general contractor is building a house and has broken down this project into the list of activities given in Table 12-4. The times given in the table are the expected durations of each activity. The table also gives the number of workers (crew size) needed to do each activity. Figure 12-6 shows the project network for this job. You will notice that the format of this network is different from that of Rollie Tillman's network in Figure 12-1. That network was in a form called *activity-on arc*, whereas this one is in *activity-on-node* form. Both types of network are in common use and convey exactly the same information about the projects they represent.

Figure 12-7 gives the early start, early finish, late start, and late finish times for building the house. The column headed "T-FLOAT" gives the slack times for each activity. The start and finish times are not particularly useful in this form. The contractor would like to know the actual dates on which the individual activities will start and finish. In Figure 12-8, we show these dates under two different assumptions: first, if the house will be started on November 7, 1984, and second, if the house must be completed before December 1, 1984. The ability to see what the schedule will look like with various start and finish times for the entire project is one that users of PERT find to be very helpful.

TABLE 12-4

List of activities for building a house

Activity	Immediate predecessors	Duration, days	Crew size
A. Clear and prepare site	—	8	2
B. Footings and pillars	A	5	4
C. Crawl space plumbing	B	1	2
D. Furnace and air conditioner	B	1	1
E. Water heater	C	1	1
F. Storm drains	B	1	1
G. Frame and rough roofing	D, E	7	8
H. Rough plumbing	G	4	1
I. Rough wiring	G	3	2
J. Heating and AC ducts	G	3	3
K. Windows	G	2	2
L. Exterior siding	K	2	4
M. Wallboard	H, I, J	8	3
N. Finish roofing	L	5	3
P. Finish flooring	M	3	2
Q. Gutters and downspout	F, N	1	2
R. Kitchen and bathroom plumbing	P	1	2
S. Finish carpentry	K, P	2	3
T. Paint	R	3	4
U. Rugs and tile	S, T	2	2
V. Finish electrical and walls	T	1	1
W. Landscaping	Q	3	4
X. Finish	U, V, W	0	0

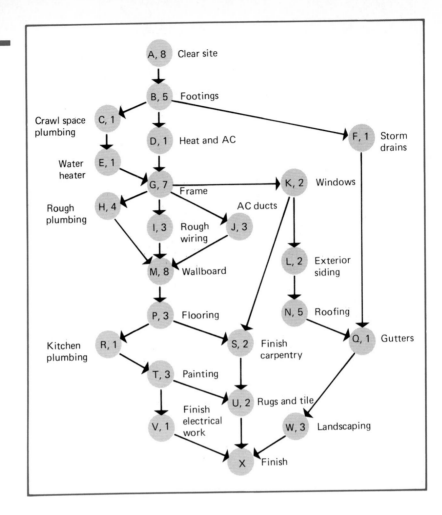

FIGURE 12-6
PERT network for
building a house
(activity-on-node
format).

The information contained in Figure 12-8 might be even more useful if displayed on a calendar. Figure 12-9 shows such a calendar produced by SAS software. The schedule given in Figure 12-9 is the early start schedule for completing the house by December 1.

The contractor wants to be able to schedule his workers and would like to know how many workers will be needed on each day. Figure 12-10 gives a bar chart with this information. The "FREQ" column tells how many different activities take place on each day, and the "WORKERS SUM" column tells how many workers are needed.

We have taken a brief look at just some of the capabilities of a typical software package for network scheduling. The SAS System can also produce calendars showing workers needed on each day, and it can schedule the project so that work is done only on weekdays. (In fact, it can also make sure that no work is done on Thanksgiving Day!) With such capabilities available,

ACTIVITY	E_START	E_FINISH	L_START	L_FINISH	T_FLOAT
		SAS			
	SCHEDULING A CONSTRUCTION PROJECT				
CLEAR & PREPARE SITE	0	8	0	8	0
FOOTINGS & PILLARS	8	13	8	13	0
CRAWL SPACE PLUMBING	13	14	13	14	0
FURNACE & AIR CONDITIONER	13	14	14	15	1
WATER HEATER	14	15	14	15	0
STORM DRAINS	13	14	38	39	25
FRAME & ROUGH ROOFING	15	22	15	22	0
ROUGH PLUMBING	22	26	22	26	0
ROUGH WIRING	22	25	23	26	1
HEATING & AC DUCTS	22	25	23	26	1
WINDOWS	22	24	30	32	8
EXTERIOR SIDING	24	26	32	34	8
WALLBOARD	26	34	26	34	0
FINISH ROOFING	26	31	34	39	8
FINISH FLOORING	34	37	34	37	0
GUTTERS & DOWNSPOUT	31	32	39	40	8
KITCHEN & BATHROOM PLUMBING	37	38	37	38	0
FINISH CARPENTRY	37	39	39	41	2
PAINT	38	41	38	41	0
RUGS & TILE	41	43	41	43	0
FINISH ELECTRICAL & WALLS	41	42	42	43	1
LANDSCAPING	32	35	40	43	8

FIGURE 12-7
Start and finish times for building a house.

the basic scheduling procedure discussed in this section becomes a very powerful tool for managerial planning and decision making.

NETWORK REPLANNING AND READJUSTMENT

PERT cannot be considered a sterile process of calculating times, drawing networks, and figuring slack time values; it is a dynamic process involved with change, with readjustment, with the formulation of new networks when there are changes in schedules, and with constant revision of plans to achieve better performance in the light of changing conditions. For this reason the process of readjusting and replanning a PERT network is of prime importance to us. Three methods are considered.

THREE METHODS OF REPLANNING AND READJUSTING A NETWORK

Interchanging resources When similar resources are employed on several different paths of a network, it is often possible *to switch resources from noncritical paths to the critical path* and thus effect a time savings in the overall network.

Relaxing the technical specifications A second method of reducing the time required to complete a certain project would be to *relax some of the technical specifications governing the project.* For instance, if one of our technical requirements for a certain project is that paint must be allowed to dry for .4

SCHEDULING A CONSTRUCTION PROJECT
START ON NOVEMBER 7 1984

ACTIVITY	E_START	E_FINISH	L_START	L_FINISH	T_FLOAT
CLEAR & PREPARE SITE	07NOV84	14NOV84	07NOV84	14NOV84	0
FOOTINGS & PILLARS	15NOV84	19NOV84	15NOV84	19NOV84	0
CRAWL SPACE PLUMBING	20NOV84	20NOV84	20NOV84	20NOV84	0
FURNACE & AIR CONDITIONER	20NOV84	20NOV84	21NOV84	21NOV84	1
WATER HEATER	21NOV84	21NOV84	21NOV84	21NOV84	0
STORM DRAINS	20NOV84	20NOV84	15DEC84	15DEC84	25
FRAME & ROUGH ROOFING	22NOV84	28NOV84	22NOV84	28NOV84	0
ROUGH PLUMBING	29NOV84	02DEC84	29NOV84	02DEC84	0
ROUGH WIRING	29NOV84	01DEC84	30NOV84	02DEC84	1
HEATING & AC DUCTS	29NOV84	01DEC84	30NOV84	02DEC84	1
WINDOWS	29NOV84	30NOV84	07DEC84	08DEC84	8
EXTERIOR SIDING	01DEC84	02DEC84	09DEC84	10DEC84	8
WALLBOARD	03DEC84	10DEC84	03DEC84	10DEC84	0
FINISH ROOFING	03DEC84	07DEC84	11DEC84	15DEC84	8
FINISH FLOORING	11DEC84	13DEC84	11DEC84	13DEC84	0
GUTTERS & DOWNSPOUT	08DEC84	08DEC84	16DEC84	16DEC84	8
KITCHEN & BATHROOM PLUMBING	14DEC84	14DEC84	14DEC84	14DEC84	0
FINISH CARPENTRY	14DEC84	15DEC84	16DEC84	17DEC84	2
PAINT	15DEC84	17DEC84	15DEC84	17DEC84	0
RUGS & TILE	18DEC84	19DEC84	18DEC84	19DEC84	0
FINISH ELECTRICAL & WALLS	18DEC84	18DEC84	19DEC84	19DEC84	1
LANDSCAPING	09DEC84	11DEC84	17DEC84	19DEC84	8

SCHEDULING A CONSTRUCTION PROJECT
FINISH BEFORE DECEMBER 1 1984

ACTIVITY	E_START	E_FINISH	L_START	L_FINISH	T_FLOAT
CLEAR & PREPARE SITE	19OCT84	26OCT84	19OCT84	26OCT84	0
FOOTINGS & PILLARS	27OCT84	31OCT84	27OCT84	31OCT84	0
CRAWL SPACE PLUMBING	01NOV84	01NOV84	01NOV84	01NOV84	0
FURNACE & AIR CONDITIONER	01NOV84	01NOV84	02NOV84	02NOV84	1
WATER HEATER	02NOV84	02NOV84	02NOV84	02NOV84	0
STORM DRAINS	01NOV84	01NOV84	26NOV84	26NOV84	25
FRAME & ROUGH ROOFING	03NOV84	09NOV84	03NOV84	09NOV84	0
ROUGH PLUMBING	10NOV84	13NOV84	10NOV84	13NOV84	0
ROUGH WIRING	10NOV84	12NOV84	11NOV84	13NOV84	1
HEATING & AC DUCTS	10NOV84	12NOV84	11NOV84	13NOV84	1
WINDOWS	10NOV84	11NOV84	18NOV84	19NOV84	8
EXTERIOR SIDING	12NOV84	13NOV84	20NOV84	21NOV84	8
WALLBOARD	14NOV84	21NOV84	14NOV84	21NOV84	0
FINISH ROOFING	14NOV84	18NOV84	22NOV84	26NOV84	8
FINISH FLOORING	22NOV84	24NOV84	22NOV84	24NOV84	0
GUTTERS & DOWNSPOUT	19NOV84	19NOV84	27NOV84	27NOV84	8
KITCHEN & BATHROOM PLUMBING	25NOV84	25NOV84	25NOV84	25NOV84	0
FINISH CARPENTRY	25NOV84	26NOV84	27NOV84	28NOV84	2
PAINT	26NOV84	28NOV84	26NOV84	28NOV84	0
RUGS & TILE	29NOV84	30NOV84	29NOV84	30NOV84	0
FINISH ELECTRICAL & WALLS	29NOV84	29NOV84	30NOV84	30NOV84	1
LANDSCAPING	20NOV84	22NOV84	28NOV84	30NOV84	8

FIGURE 12-8

Construction schedules relative to November 7 starting date or November 30 finishing date.

```
                              SAS
--------------------------------------------------------------------------
|                                                                        |
|                          OCTOBER   1984                                |
|                                                                        |
|------------+------------+-----------+-----------+---------+---------+---------|
|  SUNDAY    |  MONDAY    |  TUESDAY  | WEDNESDAY | THURSDAY |  FRIDAY  | SATURDAY |
|------------+------------+-----------+-----------+---------+---------+---------|
|            |     1      |     2     |     3     |    4     |    5     |    6     |
|            |            |           |           |          |          |          |
|            |            |           |           |          |          |          |
|            |            |           |           |          |          |          |
|------------+------------+-----------+-----------+---------+---------+---------|
|     7      |     8      |     9     |    10     |   11     |   12     |   13     |
|            |            |           |           |          |          |          |
|            |            |           |           |          |          |          |
|------------+------------+-----------+-----------+---------+---------+---------|
|    14      |    15      |    16     |    17     |   18     |   19     |   20     |
|            |            |           |           |          |          |          |
|            |            |           |           |          | +CLEAR & PREPARE SITE=> |
|------------+------------+-----------+-----------+---------+---------+---------|
|    21      |    22      |    23     |    24     |   25     |   26     |   27     |
|            |            |           |           |          |          |          |
|<=======================CLEAR & PREPARE SITE======================+|+FOOTINGS >|
|------------+------------+-----------+-----------+---------+---------+---------|
|    28      |    29      |    30     |    31     |          |          |          |
|            |            |           |           |          |          |          |
|<=============FOOTINGS & PILLARS=============+|          |          |          |
--------------------------------------------------------------------------
```

```
--------------------------------------------------------------------------
|                                                                        |
|                         NOVEMBER   1984                                |
|                                                                        |
|------------+------------+-----------+-----------+---------+---------+---------|
|  SUNDAY    |  MONDAY    |  TUESDAY  | WEDNESDAY | THURSDAY |  FRIDAY  | SATURDAY |
|------------+------------+-----------+-----------+---------+---------+---------|
|            |            |           |           |    1     |    2     |    3     |
|            |            |           |           |          |          |          |
|            |            |           |           |+STORM DRA+|          |          |
|            |            |           |           |+FURNACE &+|          |          |
|            |            |           |           |+CRAWL SPA+|+WATER HEA+|+FRAME & R>|
|------------+------------+-----------+-----------+---------+---------+---------|
|     4      |     5      |     6     |     7     |    8     |    9     |   10     |
|            |            |           |           |          |          |+=WINDOWS=>|
|            |            |           |           |          |          |+HEATING &>|
|            |            |           |           |          |          |+ROUGH WIR>|
|<========================FRAME & ROUGH ROOFING===================+|+ROUGH PLU>|
|------------+------------+-----------+-----------+---------+---------+---------|
|    11      |    12      |    13     |    14     |   15     |   16     |   17     |
|<=WINDOWS=+|+===EXTERIOR SIDING===+|           |          |          |          |
|<=HEATING & AC DUCTS==+|           |           |          |          |          |
|<====ROUGH WIRING=====+|           |+==============FINISH ROOFING==============>|
|<========ROUGH PLUMBING==========+|+==================WALLBOARD==================>|
|------------+------------+-----------+-----------+---------+---------+---------|
|    18      |    19      |    20     |    21     |   22     |   23     |   24     |
|            |            |           |           |          |          |          |
|<FINISH RO+|+GUTTERS &+|+==========LANDSCAPING===========+|          |          |
|<==================WALLBOARD==================+|+=========FINISH FLOORING=========+|
|------------+------------+-----------+-----------+---------+---------+---------|
|    25      |    26      |    27     |    28     |   29     |   30     |          |
|            |            |           |           |          |          |          |
|+==FINISH CARPENTRY===+|           |           |+FINISH EL+|          |          |
|+KITCHEN &+|+=============PAINT==============+|+=====RUGS & TILE=====+|          |
--------------------------------------------------------------------------
```

FIGURE 12-9

The early start
schedule for finishing
the house before
December 1.

```
                              SAS
                   SUMMARIZING PERSONNEL USE
                   THE EARLY START SCHEDULE

      DATE                                                FREQ     WORKERS
                                                                     SUM
            |
  19OCT84   |**********                                      1        2
  20OCT84   |**********                                      1        2
  21OCT84   |**********                                      1        2
  22OCT84   |**********                                      1        2
  23OCT84   |**********                                      1        2
  24OCT84   |**********                                      1        2
  25OCT84   |**********                                      1        2
  26OCT84   |**********                                      1        2
  27OCT84   |********************                            1        4
  28OCT84   |********************                            1        4
  29OCT84   |********************                            1        4
  30OCT84   |********************                            1        4
  31OCT84   |********************                            1        4
  01NOV84   |********************                            3        4
  02NOV84   |*****                                           1        1
  03NOV84   |****************************************         1        8
  04NOV84   |****************************************         1        8
  05NOV84   |****************************************         1        8
  06NOV84   |****************************************         1        8
  07NOV84   |****************************************         1        8
  08NOV84   |****************************************         1        8
  09NOV84   |****************************************         1        8
  10NOV84   |***********************************              4        7
  11NOV84   |***********************************              4        7
  12NOV84   |*********************************************    4        9
  13NOV84   |*************************                        2        5
  14NOV84   |******************************                   2        6
  15NOV84   |******************************                   2        6
  16NOV84   |******************************                   2        6
  17NOV84   |******************************                   2        6
  18NOV84   |******************************                   2        6
  19NOV84   |*************************                        2        5
  20NOV84   |***********************************              2        7
  21NOV84   |***********************************              2        7
  22NOV84   |******************************                   2        6
  23NOV84   |**********                                       1        2
  24NOV84   |**********                                       1        2
  25NOV84   |*************************                        2        5
  26NOV84   |***********************************              2        7
  27NOV84   |********************                             1        4
  28NOV84   |********************                             1        4
  29NOV84   |***************                                  2        3
  30NOV84   |**********                                       1        2
            -----+----+----+----+----+----+----+----+----+
                 1    2    3    4    5    6    7    8    9
                              WORKERS SUM
```

FIGURE 12-10
Bar chart of workers needed each day.

week between coats and we want to put two coats of paint on a certain building, our network might look something like this:

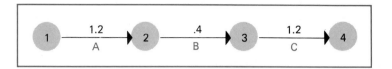

Activity A represents putting on the first coat, activity B represents the drying time, and activity C represents putting on the final coat. If we relax the technical specifications somewhat, perhaps to .3 week, or about 2 days, between coats, we can obviously reduce the time necessary to complete the work. The extent to which this can be done is severely restricted in many cases. Take, for instance, the process of pouring concrete. If the specifications call for concrete to cure (a process often called setup) for 5 days before a load is put on it and we arbitrarily reduce this specification to 2 days, we may experience disastrous results when the finished concrete is put under load.

Changing the arrangement of activities Suppose that a particular finished part must go through three machining operations before completion. If these parts were sent through the machine shop in batches of 100 and we wanted all pieces to travel along together, we would represent the process on a chart like this:

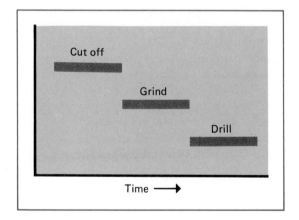

Activities which look like this are called *series-connected* in PERT terminology, meaning that one must be completed before the next can be begun. But when a few parts have gone through the cutoff process, what would be wrong with sending them along to the grinder instead of waiting for the entire batch of 100 to be processed at the cutoff station? When a few units have gone through the grinding process, what would be wrong with sending them along to the drill presses instead of waiting until the entire batch has been processed? The rearranged activities portrayed below reflect a considerable saving in time; however, we must realize that moving units through the processes in several batches may add to material handling cost.

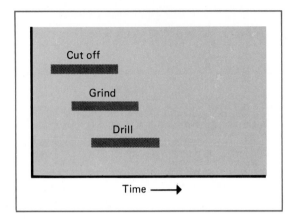

2 CPM (critical path method)

BACKGROUND OF CPM

Next to PERT, the critical path method (CPM) of planning and controlling projects has enjoyed the widest use among all the systems that follow the networking principle. CPM was developed by J. E. Kelly of Remington Rand and M. R. Walker of Du Pont to help schedule maintenance in chemical plants.

HOW CPM IS DIFFERENT FROM PERT

The fundamental departure of CPM from PERT is that CPM brings the concept of *cost* more prominently into the planning and control process. When time can be estimated rather well and when costs can be calculated rather accurately in advance (labor and materials for a construction project, for example), CPM may be superior to PERT. But when there is an extreme degree of uncertainty and when control over time outweighs control over costs (as in launching the spacelab, for example), PERT may well be the better choice. The networking principles involved in CPM are like those in the PERT system.

TIME ESTIMATING IN CPM

NORMAL AND CRASH TIME

Under the CPM system, *two* time and cost estimates are indicated for each activity in the network; these two are a *normal* estimate and a *crash* estimate. The *normal* estimate of time approximates the most likely time estimate in PERT. Normal cost is that associated with finishing the project in the normal time. The *crash* time estimate is the time that would be required if *no* costs were spared in reducing the project time. Crash cost is the cost associated with doing the job on a crash basis so as to minimize completion time.

Rob Teer is the project director for Nello Teer Company on the new Durham–Chapel Hill expressway. Rob has represented one segment of the project with the time-cost graph shown in Figure 12-11.

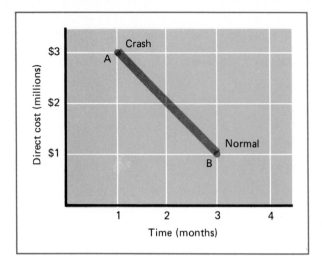

FIGURE 12-11
Crash time and cost compared with normal time and cost for one segment of the Durham–Chapel Hill expressway project.

The vertical axis represents the cost of completing one segment of the project, and the horizontal axis represents the time required for completion. Normal estimates call for 3 months and $1 million. Suppose a crash effort would complete the work in 1 month at a crash cost of $3 million. The line AB on Figure 12-11 is called a *time-cost curve*.

TIME-COST CURVE

CRASHING A PROJECT

To crash a project successfully, we examine the network, note its activities, and compare normal costs with crash costs for each activity. Our goal is to find those activities on the critical path where time can be cut substantially with minimum extra dollars spent. Our goal is the greatest reduction in project time for the least increase in project cost.

STEPS IN CRASHING A PROJECT

Figure 12-12 shows one of Rob Teer's networks for a small part of the Durham–Chapel Hill expressway project, a concrete catch basin to control runoff water at a busy intersection; all times are normal times. Table 12-5 contains the time-cost information for this small project.

CATCH BASIN CRASHING EXAMPLE

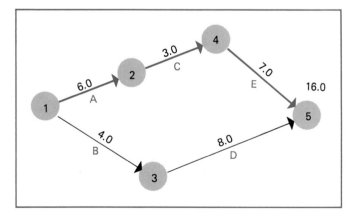

FIGURE 12-12
Catch basin network with all normal times.

	Time, weeks		Cost		Cost to reduce per week
Activity	Normal	Crash	Normal	Crash	
A	6.0	4.0	$10,000	$14,000	$2,000
B	4.0	3.0	5,000	8,000	3,000
C	3.0	2.0	4,000	5,000	1,000
D	8.0	6.0	9,000	12,000	1,500
E	7.0	4.0	7,000	8,000	333
		Total costs	$35,000	$47,000	

TABLE 12-5
Calculation of the cost of crashing the catch basin project

In Figure 12-12, path A-C-E is the critical path. The earliest finish time for the project is 16 weeks, and total costs with normal times are $35,000. Figure 12-13 shows the catch basin project with *all* crash times; now the earliest finish time is 10 weeks and the cost is $47,000. Rob wonders if the project time can be reduced to 10 weeks *without* increasing costs by $12,000 ($47,000 − $35,000).

CAN YOU REDUCE PROJECT TIME WITHOUT CRASHING ALL ACTIVITIES?

Figure 12-14 shows the network with activities E, C, D, and A crashed; activity B is the only activity not crashed. Table 12-6 recaps the crashing program. Notice that we began by crashing the least expensive activity, E; we then turned our attention to the next least expensive activity, C, and crashed that. At this point both paths through the network (A-C-E and B-D) require 12 weeks; thus further reduction of project time will require reducing activities on *both* paths. On path B-D the least expensive activity to crash is D; thus we crash that to 6 weeks. A similar 2-week reduction on the upper path (A-C-D) can be achieved by crashing activity A to 4 weeks. At this point all activities on the path A-C-E have been crashed to their minimum and further crashing on the lower path (B-D) will not produce any further benefit.

CRASHING THE LEAST EXPENSIVE ACTIVITY FIRST

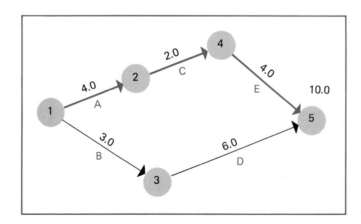

FIGURE 12-13
Catch basin project with crash times for all the activities.

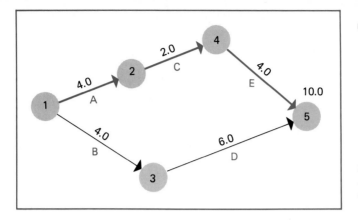

FIGURE 12-14
Activities E, C, D, and
A crashed on catch
basin project.

CRASHING A CPM NETWORK
WITH LINEAR PROGRAMMING

It is possible to find the best crash schedule for a CPM network by using linear programming. To illustrate this, we will use Rob Teer's project from Figure 12-12 and the project data in Table 12-5.

USING LINEAR
PROGRAMMING TO
CRASH A NETWORK

The first thing we do is define the variables; we let X = the time that an event will occur (measured in weeks after the project begins); in Rob's project we would define:

DEFINING THE
VARIABLES

$$X_1 = \text{the time event 1 will occur}$$
$$X_2 = \text{the time event 2 will occur}$$
$$X_3 = \text{the time event 3 will occur}$$
$$X_4 = \text{the time event 4 will occur}$$
$$X_5 = \text{the time event 5 will occur}$$

And we let Y = the number of weeks by which an activity is crashed, that is, the number of weeks we *reduce* that activity's normal time. So we have Y's like this:

$$Y_A = \text{number of weeks we } reduce \text{ the normal time of activity A}$$
$$Y_B = \text{number of weeks we } reduce \text{ the normal time of activity B}$$

TABLE 12-6
The network in Figure
12-12 and Table 12-5
after crashing

		Project duration	Total network cost
1.	Original network	16.0	$35,000
2.	Crash activity E to 4.0 weeks	13.0	36,000
3.	Crash activity C to 2.0 weeks	12.0	37,000
4.	Crash activity D to 6.0 weeks	12.0	40,000
5.	Crash activity A to 4.0 weeks	10.0	44,000

Y_C = number of weeks we *reduce* the normal time of activity C
Y_D = number of weeks we *reduce* the normal time of activity D
Y_E = number of weeks we *reduce* the normal time of activity E

Since we want to crash the project at minimum cost, the objective function, using the cost coefficients from Table 12-5, is

THE OBJECTIVE
FUNCTION

Minimize: $2,000 Y_A + $3,000 Y_B + $1,000 Y_C + $1,500 Y_D + $333 Y_E

Now what about the constraints? Look at event 2 in Figure 12-12. If event 1 began at time zero, then X_2 (the time for event 2) can be described this way:

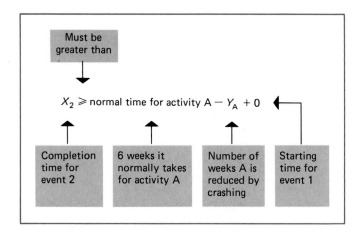

Putting in the normal time for activity A of 6 weeks, we have:

$$X_2 \geqslant 6 - Y_A + 0 \qquad (1)$$

And the constraint for event 3 is developed the same way:

$$X_3 \geqslant 4 - Y_B + 0 \qquad (2)$$

WRITING THE
CONSTRAINTS

Since activity C begins with event 2 (and not zero, as was the case with the two previous examples), we write the constraint for X_4 this way:

$$X_4 \geqslant 3 - Y_C + X_2 \qquad (3)$$

And since two activities lead into event 5, we shall need *two* constraints there:

$$X_5 \geqslant 7 - Y_E + X_4 \qquad (4)$$
$$X_5 \geqslant 8 - Y_D + X_3 \qquad (5)$$

So far we have five constraints. What about the maximum crashing that can be done? Activity times cannot be reduced forever. From Table 12-5, the maximum values for the Y variables is the difference between the normal and crash times:

$$Y_A \leq 2 \qquad (6)$$

$$Y_B \leq 1 \qquad (7)$$

$$Y_C \leq 1 \qquad (8)$$

$$Y_D \leq 2 \qquad (9)$$

$$Y_E \leq 3 \qquad (10)$$

And, of course, Rob wants to finish his project in 10 weeks, and so we need to write one more constraint on the project completion time:

$$X_5 \leq 10 \qquad (11)$$

If we minimize our objective function under these 11 constraints, we shall get the optimal Y values. (You should notice that the X values do not appear in the objective function because they merely indicate when an event occurs and do not themselves incur any costs; only the Y variables represent cost to Rob.)

If we add the constraint that all variables must be ≥ 0 and solve this linear programming problem (and it is a large one to be computed by hand, so we would use one of the canned computer programs to do it), the optimal answer turns out to be exactly the one we got using our original approach on page 572. The value of the objective function (the total crashing cost) is $9,000 ($44,000 − $35,000); Y_A is 2; Y_B is 0; Y_C is 1; Y_D is 2; and Y_E is 3.

OPTIMAL ANSWER TO ROB'S CRASHING PROBLEM

▮ INDIRECT AND UTILITY COSTS IN PROJECT CRASHING

Remember that in crashing this project to its lowest possible time at the minimum possible cost, we have taken into account only the *direct* costs associated with the project. Labor, materials, and such are essentially costs that vary directly with the time required to complete the work. Nothing has been said about (1) *indirect* costs (the overhead costs that go on throughout the entire project) or (2) costs sometimes referred to as *utility* costs (for example, penalties for being late and bonuses for finishing the project early). The behavior of these two types of costs can certainly influence the decision about the desirability of crashing a project.

OTHER KINDS OF COSTS RELEVANT IN CRASHING A NETWORK

Assume that a contracting firm in its original contract promised delivery in 12 weeks; assume further that the firm agreed to pay a penalty of $10,000 per week if delivery was made later than 12 weeks. Thus when the firm sees that the work cannot be finished before 16 weeks, it faces a possible total penalty of $40,000. No doubt the contractor would be glad to incur crashing costs that would reduce the time to 12 weeks as long as they were less than $40,000. On the other hand, there is no reason why additional money should be spent to reduce the project time to under 12 weeks unless the reduction in indirect costs were greater than the crashing costs.

3 PERT/Cost

When they were originally developed, PERT and CPM were both time-oriented; that is, they were designed to allow project planners to produce time schedules for the planning and monitoring of complex projects. In neither case was cost a major consideration, even though CPM did include the concepts of *direct cost, indirect cost,* and *utility cost,* each of which has been explained on page 575.

Earlier users of PERT and CPM noticed the need for these techniques to concern themselves with project cost control as well as time control; and in the early 1960s, after the publication of a U.S. government manual entitled *DOD and NASA Guide, PERT/Cost Systems Design,* most military and research contracts required the use of PERT/Cost on the part of the contractor. Today there are many different versions of this early project cost accounting technique; we shall illustrate one.

COSTING BY ACTIVITIES

WORK PACKAGES

The foundation of the PERT/Cost system is the measurement and control of costs by "work packages"; we would have called these *groups of activities* in our earlier discussion of networking. These activities generally represent parts of a project for which responsibility is easily determined; in the original *DOD and NASA Guide,* the lowest-level work package was limited to no more than $100,000 in cost and could not require more than 3 months' estimated completion time; subsequent variations of the PERT/Cost technique have been considerably more flexible in defining such limits.

ESTIMATING PROJECT COSTS BY ACTIVITY

HOW MUCH IS TO BE
SPENT ON EACH
ACTIVITY?

Managers should know the amounts of money that are to be expected for each activity over the planned duration of the project; one usually assumes that the expenditures for each activity are made at a constant rate during that activity, although with the use of computers this simplifying assumption can be dropped. To get an idea of how the project times and costs are set up, look at Figure 12-15. Here we have shown a project involving nine

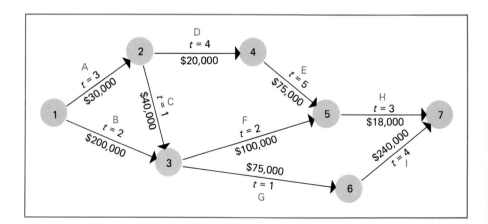

FIGURE 12-15
Nine-activity
project network.

activities; for each activity we have given its estimated duration (in months) and the total estimated cost of the activity. In Table 12-7, we show earliest start time, latest start time, duration (in months), total cost, and cost per month for all activities in the network.

PROJECT BUDGETING CHOICES

Now, from a technological point of view, the project director can choose when to begin each activity in this project; for example, the director could begin each activity at its *earliest start time.* Figure 12-16 illustrates the funds committed under this alternative; but the project director could wait to begin each activity until its *latest start time.* What is the difference? Figure 12-17 shows the cumulative amounts of money which would be spent during the project if every activity were to begin on a late start basis. One can see from this figure that beginning *all* the activities on a late start basis allows the project to continue on schedule but reduces the average commitment of funds spent on the project considerably. For example, at the end of 8 months, using the late start alternative would have committed only $65,000 to the project, as opposed to the $660,000 which would have been spent had the director begun all activities at their early start date. At any month, the difference between the cumulative totals in Figures 12-16 and 12-17 represents money which has not been committed to the project and is thus available for other purposes; in our example, this is a sizable sum. A quick calculation indicates that under the early start alternative, the *average funds committed* at any one time over the life of the project are $560,733; this may be compared with $269,066, which would be committed under the late start option. Figure 12-18 illustrates the general relationship between funds commitment under the early start option and that under the late start option.

CHOICES OPEN TO THE
PROJECT DIRECTOR

DIFFERENCES BETWEEN
COMMITTED FUNDS FOR
BOTH ALTERNATIVES

CONTROL OF PROJECT COSTS WITH PERT/COST

The use of PERT/Cost in project management allows one to go a bit beyond the traditional comparison of actual with budgeted costs. Since this technique deals with time and cost, one can compare, in addition, *scheduled* work with *completed* work. Generally costs are coded according to activity; at the time costs are gathered, estimates are made of the proportion of that activity that

COMPARISONS OF
COST IN PERT/COST

TABLE 12-7
Activity information
for nine-activity
project network

Activity	ES	LS	Duration, months	Total cost	Cost/month
A	0	0	3	$ 30,000	$ 10,000
B	0	8	2	200,000	100,000
C	3	9	1	40,000	40,000
D	3	3	4	20,000	5,000
E	7	7	5	75,000	15,000
F	4	10	2	100,000	50,000
G	4	10	1	75,000	75,000
H	12	12	3	18,000	6,000
I	5	11	4	240,000	60,000
			Total cost	$798,000	

FIGURE 12-16
Project cost with early starts (monthly and cumulative totals shown).

Activity	1	2	3	4	5	6	7	8	9	10	11	12	13	14	15
A	$10,000	$10,000	$10,000												
B	100,000	100,000													
C				$40,000											
D				5,000	$ 5,000	$ 5,000	$ 5,000								
E								$15,000	$15,000	$15,000	$15,000	$15,000			
F					50,000	50,000									
G					75,000										
H						60,000	60,000	60,000	60,000						
I													$ 6,000	$ 6,000	$ 6,000
Total	110,000	110,000	10,000	45,000	130,000	115,000	65,000	75,000	75,000	15,000	15,000	15,000	6,000	6,000	6,000
Cumulative	110,000	220,000	230,000	275,000	405,000	520,000	585,000	660,000	735,000	750,000	765,000	780,000	786,000	792,000	798,000

Month

Activity	1	2	3	4	5	6	7	8	9	10	11	12	13	14	15
A	$10,000	$10,000	$10,000												
B									$100,000	$100,000					
C										40,000					
D				$5,000	$5,000	$5,000	$5,000								
E								$15,000	15,000	15,000	$15,000	$15,000			
F											50,000	50,000			
G											75,000				
H												60,000			
I													$ 6,000	$ 6,000	$ 6,000
Total	10,000	10,000	10,000	5,000	5,000	5,000	5,000	15,000	115,000	155,000	140,000	125,000	66,000	66,000	66,000
Cumulative	10,000	20,000	30,000	35,000	40,000	45,000	50,000	65,000	180,000	335,000	475,000	600,000	666,000	732,000	798,000

Month

FIGURE 12-17

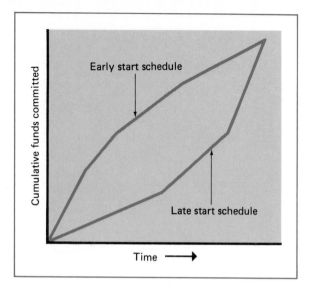

FIGURE 12-18
General relationship
between funds
commitment under
early start and late
start options.

has been completed. If our original assumption that cost and time are directly proportional is true, then comparison between cost incurred and work completed yields information vital to project control. Specifically, if an activity has incurred 75 percent of its budgeted cost but is only 55 percent completed, we have what is usually called a *budget overrun*. It is quite usual for project managers to receive reports which answer pertinent questions including:

1 What is the expected completion time?
2 Is the activity now on schedule?
3 What are the budget overruns on each activity?
4 Is the situation getting better or worse each reporting period?

TYPICAL QUESTIONS
ANSWERED BY PERT/
COST REPORTS

4 Network scheduling with resource limitations

Up to this point in our discussion of networking techniques, we have assumed that an activity can begin just as soon as all those activities which must precede it have been completed. This assumption is predicated on *there being sufficient resources available to perform all the work defined by the activities.* In our adjustment and replanning of PERT networks earlier in this chapter, we juggled starting times of activities; nonetheless, we still assumed there were resources sufficient to do all the work scheduled on a given day. In practice, this is often *not* the case.

WHAT HAPPENS WHEN
THERE ARE NOT
SUFFICIENT RESOURCES

PROBLEM WITH LIMITED RESOURCES

In Figure 12-19 we have illustrated a network with nine activities; the format of this network is different from the format of those we have presented previously in *two* ways:

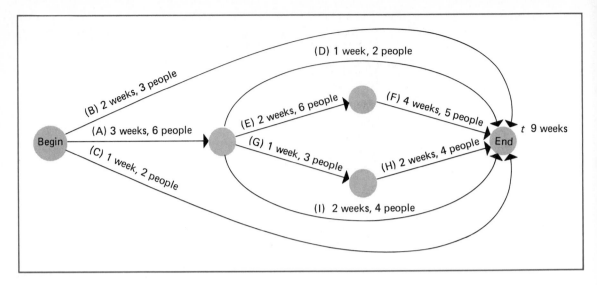

FIGURE 12-19
Network for problem with limited resources.

DIFFERENCES BETWEEN
THIS NETWORK AND
PREVIOUS ONES

1 It uses curved lines for activities; this eliminates the need for zero-time activities and thus simplifies our network.

2 Each activity is identified in three ways: *first* by an identification letter (A), (B), (C), and so forth, *then* by the estimated duration of that activity in weeks, and *finally* by the number of people we assumed would be available to work on that activity when we estimated its duration.

We can show our network in Figure 12-19 in another, perhaps more useful form by plotting each activity on a schedule graph with a horizontal time scale; this has been accomplished in Figure 12-20. There the duration of each activity is represented by the length of that activity's line; the description on each activity represents its letter designation and the number of people it is assumed will work on that activity at one time (crew size). The bottom row of Figure 12-20 is the total number of people scheduled to work in any one week. We can see from this total that we will require from 5 to 15 people, depending upon which week we are scheduling. But suppose the supply of workers is constrained—suppose we have only nine people available for work during this period; what alternatives are open to us?

▨ A METHOD FOR RESOURCE LEVELING

USE OF A PERSONNEL
LOADING CHART IN
RESOURCE LEVELING

Often a quick way to solve our personnel scheduling problem is to show it first in graphic form; if we plot the number of people working in any week against time, we produce the *personnel loading chart* illustrated in Figure 12-21. If we have just nine people available for work, we can see several things from this chart: first, we notice that we will be *short* of workers during the first, fourth, and fifth weeks; we also see that nine people are *exactly sufficient* to perform the work scheduled during the second and sixth weeks; finally,

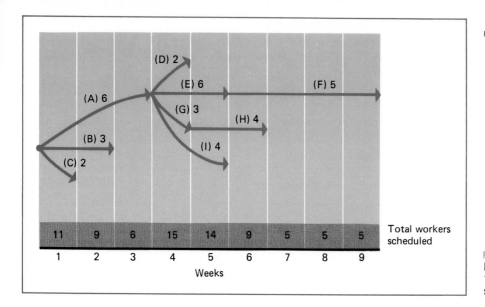

FIGURE 12-20
Network of Figure
12-19 plotted on
schedule graph.

we see that we have a *surplus* of workers for the work we have scheduled during the third, seventh, eighth, and ninth weeks. We can see that our task is to rearrange the schedule so that, insofar as possible, we even out the peaks and valleys without scheduling more work than nine people can do and without violating any of the precedence relationships in the network. It may not be possible to so rearrange the network and still finish in 9 weeks, but under the present circumstances we do not even have sufficient personnel for the *first* week's scheduled work.

A SURPLUS AND A
SHORTAGE OF
WORKERS AT
DIFFERENT TIMES

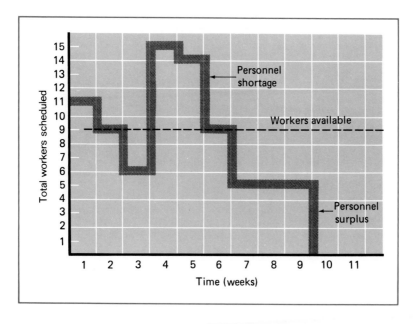

FIGURE 12-21
Personnel loading
chart for schedule
graph in Figure
12-20.

▌HEURISTIC PROGRAMMING AS A METHOD

Although the scheduling problem we are using as an illustration can be solved quite quickly by hand, when there are a large number of activities, it is generally impossible to enumerate all the answers (and thus find the optimal one) even with a large computer. For this reason, we typically use "rules of thumb" to solve these kinds of combinatorial problems. In Chapter 13 we'll go into the development and use of these rules of thumb (commonly called *heuristics*) in more detail. Quite a few such rules for leveling network schedules have been developed during the last few years. People have been using rules of thumb throughout recorded history, for example: get in the back of the shortest line; never try to leave town on Friday at 5 P.M.; and look after only the exceptional problems and leave all the others to your subordinates. Our approach to rescheduling in this sample problem is really nothing more complex than these simple examples.

Our approach generally looks first at the activities that have the most slack and attempts to delay them as long as possible without delaying the completion of the entire project. For example, if we delay the start of activity (C) (it has the greatest slack time), then activities (A) and (B) can begin simultaneously and yet not violate our personnel limit of nine workers. If we continue to apply this method, we can achieve the revised schedule graph illustrated in Figure 12-22. Notice that when an activity is delayed in order to achieve a better schedule, the time during which it is delayed is represented by a dotted line. Notice also that when we reached the end of the third week, we had a *choice* among delaying activities (D), (G), and (I); in this case we chose activity (I), even though it had somewhat less slack than the other two, because its personnel requirement of four workers would fit quite nicely with that of activity (F). The network we used for an example is a very simple one, and yet we are unable to come up with a perfectly balanced schedule with nine

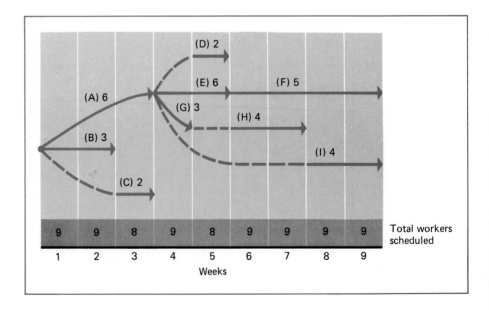

FIGURE 12-22
Revised schedule
graph.

people working all the time; we will perhaps have to be content with having too little work for our crew during the third and fifth weeks, but even this can be considered a very good balance. Generally, given the complexities of projects on which these types of techniques are used and considering the amount of time required to achieve balance among resources, most project managers would be happy with far less success than we had with our sample project.

5 The maximal-flow problem

In a network with one *source node* (point of entry) and one *output node* (point of exit), the maximal-flow problem seeks to find the maximal flow (whether it be cars, planes, fluids, or electricity) which can enter the network at the source node, flow through it, and exit at the output node in a given period of time. Let us use Durham, North Carolina, as our example of the maximal-flow problem. Normally, north-south traffic around Durham would use Interstate 85, but I-85 will be out of commission for extensive roadway repairs for 2 weeks, and the North Carolina Highway Commission engineers need to find out whether alternative routes (through the city) will safely handle the 6,000 cars an hour that normally use I-85 going south. Look at Figure 12-23, in which we have illustrated these north-south routes through the city. The numbers beside the nodes indicate the traffic capacity of the branches (streets in this case) in thousands of cars per hour. The 6 on branch 1-2 means that street has a capacity of 6,000 cars an hour heading toward node 2. The 0 on branch 1-2 means that the highway engineers do not want *any* cars going toward the source node, 1. Look at branch 3-5; 5,000 cars an hour can move in the direction of node 5, and 4,000 an hour can move along this branch in the direction of node 3. The zeros on branches 5-6 and 4-6 indicate that the highway engineers do not want traffic heading from node 6 toward either node 5 or node 4, or simply that these streets are one-way.

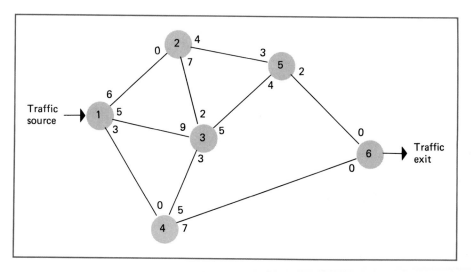

FIGURE 12-23
City street network for Durham, NC, with flow capacities.

HOW TO FIND THE
MAXIMAL FLOW IN
THE NETWORK

THE MAXIMAL-FLOW ALGORITHM

We can find the maximal flow by these steps:

1 Find a path from the source to the exit with flow capacity on *all* branches of that path (flow capacity would be designated by a positive number on the branch, next to the node you are moving from). If you can't find such a path, you already have the optimal solution.

2 Find the branch on your path with the smallest flow capacity (let us call this capacity C); increase the flow on this path by

    a *Decreasing* the capacity in the direction of flow of all branches on this path by C

    b *Increasing* the capacity in the reverse direction of all branches on this path by C

This procedure sounds much more difficult than it actually is, so let's get started with the Durham traffic flow network.

THREE STEPS IN THE
SOLUTION TO THE
DURHAM TRAFFIC
NETWORK

Step 1 Suppose we begin with path 1-2-5-6. (Actually it doesn't matter which path you choose, for you will eventually get the maximal flow regardless of this first choice.) Branch 5-6, with a flow capacity of 2, has the smallest flow capacity on this path. If we decrease the capacity in the direction of flow by 2 and increase it in the reverse direction by 2, we get the network in Figure 12-24.

Step 2 Now look at path 1-4-6; the smallest flow capacity on this path is branch 1-4, with flow capacity 3. When we decrease the flow capacity in the direction of flow by 3 and increase it in the reverse direction by 3, we get the network in Figure 12-25.

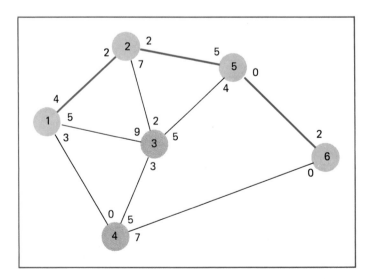

FIGURE 12-24
Step 1 in maximal-flow algorithm.

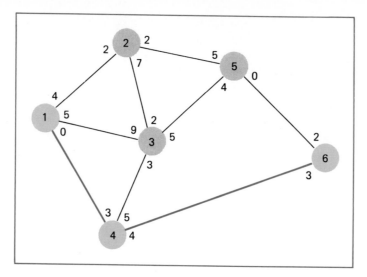

FIGURE 12-25
Step 2 in maximal-
flow algorithm.

Step 3 Can we find another path with positive flow capacity? Yes; path 1-3-4-6 has positive flow capacity, and the branch with the smallest capacity on this path is 3-4, with a flow capacity of 3. When we decrease the flow capacity in the direction of flow by 3 and increase it in the reverse direction by 3, we get the network in Figure 12-26. There is no path in Figure 12-26 with positive flow capacity on all its branches; therefore we have found the maximal flow for the network. Of course, it may be a bit difficult to recognize it from all the numbers in Figure 12-26, but in Table 12-8 we have shown you an easy way to see exactly where the flow of cars goes. This table indicates how much flow was assigned by each of the three steps it took us to get the maximal flow.

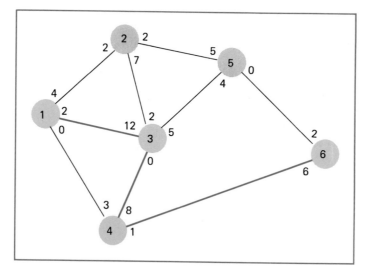

FIGURE 12-26
Step 3 in maximal-
flow algorithm.

TABLE 12-8
Flow assigned to each
branch by the
maximal-flow
algorithm

	Branches						
	1-2	1-3	1-4	3-4	2-5	4-6	5-6
Step 1 (C = 2)	2				2		2
Step 2 (C = 3)			3			3	
Step 3 (C = 3)		3		3		3	
Total flow assigned	2	3	3	3	2	6	2

Figure 12-27 shows the assigned flows from Table 12-8 on the network. It turns out, then, that the city street route has a maximal capacity of 8,000 cars per hour, which is well above the 6,000 an hour that the interstate normally carries. It should be feasible, then, to reroute the traffic through the city. Notice from Figure 12-27 that two branches (streets in our case) were assigned no traffic at all, and yet the network taken as a whole manages to produce the maximal traffic flow.

6 The minimal-spanning-tree problem

FOCUS OF THE
MINIMAL-SPANNING-
TREE PROBLEM

The minimal-spanning-tree problem is concerned with finding a way to reach *all* the nodes in a network from some particular node (a source) in such a way that the total length of all the branches used is minimal. There are two methods we can use. The algorithm developed by J. B. Kruskal is better for small hand-computed networks but inefficient for larger networks, so let us use R. C. Prim's method, which works on networks of all sizes.

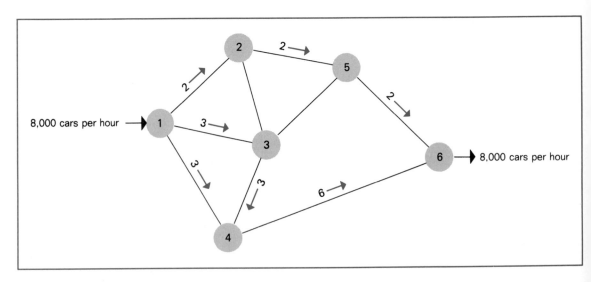

FIGURE 12-27
Assigned flows from Table 12-8.

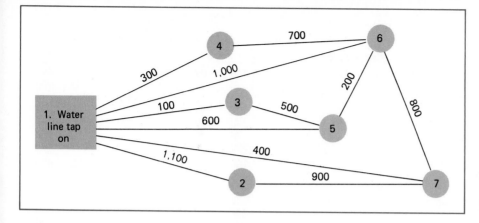

FIGURE 12-28
Alan Fine subdivision
showing distances for
possible water line
routes.

Suppose we introduce Prim's algorithm with the example of Alan Fine, a real estate developer who has just planned a small subdivision of rural homes, each quite some distance from the others. Alan is planning the water system for his development, and at this stage he is not obliged to lay the water lines beside the roads; in fact, after he eliminates routes which would cross streams and those which would involve considerable tunneling, the routes open to him for his water lines are those shown in Figure 12-28.

MINIMAL-SPANNING-TREE ALGORITHM

The minimal-spanning-tree algorithm operates by joining the nearest unconnected node to nodes that are already connected; of course, for this to happen, we must first connect two nodes to begin the process.

FIVE STEPS IN THE
MINIMAL-SPANNING-
TREE ALGORITHM

Step 1   Construct a table of distances between nodes. Alan made up the one illustrated as Table 12-9. Since some nodes cannot be connected to others, we show this by entering the letter M in the table. M here has the same meaning it did in linear programming—that is, a very large number.

Step 2   Select any node to begin the algorithm; indicate that this node is connected by some appropriate mark (we shall use an X) and delete the column headed by this node. (Now look at Table 12-10.)

TABLE 12-9
Distances between
nodes for Alan Fine
subdivision

From node	To node						
	1	**2**	**3**	**4**	**5**	**6**	**7**
1	0	1,100	100	300	600	1,000	400
2	1,100	0	M	M	M	M	900
3	100	M	0	M	500	M	M
4	300	M	M	0	M	700	M
5	600	M	500	M	0	200	M
6	1,000	M	M	700	200	0	800
7	400	900	M	M	M	800	0

TABLE 12-10

Solution to Alan Fine minimal-spanning-tree problem

	Connected		1	2	3	4	5	6	7
Step 2. Select node 1 to begin the algorithm; indicate with an X that it is connected and delete column 1. **Step 3.** Find the smallest number in the marked row (100) and circle it.	X	1		1,100	(100)	300	600	1,000	400
		2		0	M	M	M	M	900
		3		M	0	M	500	M	M
		4		M	M	M	M	700	M
		5		M	500	M	0	200	M
		6		M	M	700	200	0	800
		7		900	M	M	M	800	0
Step 4. Mark row 3 with an X and delete column 3. **Step 3.** Find the smallest number in all the marked rows (300) and circle it.	X	1		1,100		(300)	600	1,000	400
		2		0		M	M	M	900
	X	3		M		M	500	M	M
		4		M		M	M	700	M
		5		M		M	0	200	M
		6		M		700	200	0	800
		7		900		M	M	800	0
Step 4. Mark row 4 with an X and delete column 4. **Step 3.** Find the smallest number in all the marked rows (400) and circle it.	X	1		1,100			600	1,000	(400)
		2		0			M	M	900
	X	3		M			500	M	M
	X	4		M			M	700	M
		5		M			0	200	M
		6		M			200	0	800
		7		900			M	800	0
Step 4. Mark row 7 with an X and delete column 7. **Step 3.** Find the smallest number in all the marked rows (500) and circle it.	X	1		1,100			600	1,000	
		2		0			M	M	
	X	3		M			(500)	M	
	X	4		M			M	700	
		5		M			0	200	
		6		M			200	0	
	X	7		900			M	800	
Step 4. Mark row 5 with an X and delete column 5. **Step 3.** Find the smallest number in all the marked rows (200) and circle it.	X	1		1,100				1,000	
		2		0				M	
	X	3		M				M	
	X	4		M				700	
	X	5		M				(200)	
		6		M				0	
	X	7		900				800	
Step 4. Mark row 6 with an X and delete column 6. **Step 3.** Find the smallest number in all the marked rows (900) and circle it.	X	1		1,100					
		2		0					
	X	3		M					
	X	4		M					
	X	5		M					
	X	6		M					
	X	7		(900)					
Step 4. Mark row 2 with an X and delete column 2. All the nodes have been connected; the optimum answer has been found.	X	1							
	X	2							
	X	3							
	X	4							
	X	5							
	X	6							
	X	7							

Step 3 Find the smallest number in all the rows marked with an X and circle it. The column containing this circled number indicates the new connected node.

Step 4 Mark the newly connected node with an X and delete the column headed by this node.

Repeat steps 3 and 4 until all the nodes have been connected.

Figure 12-29 shows the optimal answer from Table 12-10. In the figure, the routes in the tree are those that were circled when we finished the final step in the table. The length of the minimal spanning tree is the sum of all the lengths of the circled values in Table 12-10; in this case 2,400 feet of water line will be required to connect all the homes in Alan's development.

OPTIMAL ANSWER

7 The shortest-route problem

In the shortest-route problem, we are trying to find the shortest route from a source to a destination through a connecting network; the destination may be any other node in the network. This is the problem faced by any organization that delivers or picks up material from a number of points. Take, for example, Eban Merritt, an operator of a fleet of trucks who has contracted to deliver a number of loads of lumber from Chapel Hill, North Carolina, to Toledo, Ohio. In Figure 12-30 we show the possible routes Eban's truck can take, along with the distances in miles between each node. Of course, with a problem this small it would be an easy matter to list all the possible routes and choose the shortest; but just as we found in PERT networks, when the problem becomes more complex, that kind of solution method becomes impractical.

EBAN MERRITT
SHORTEST-ROUTE
EXAMPLE

SHORTEST-ROUTE ALGORITHM

We begin by constructing a list for each node in the network of the branches leading out of that node. It is not necessary to include branches leading *into*

APPLYING THE
SHORTEST-ROUTE
ALGORITHM

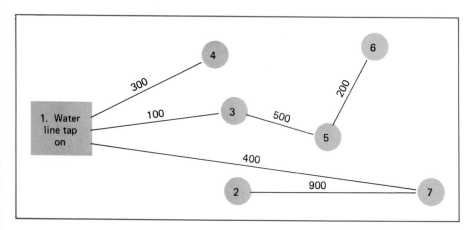

FIGURE 12-29
Minimal spanning tree for Alan Fine subdivision.

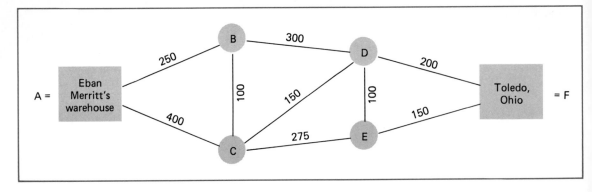

FIGURE 12-30

Network for Eban Merritt shortest-route problem. (The lengths of the branches are not proportional to the distances.)

IDENTIFYING
THE BRANCHES

Chapel Hill or *out of* Toledo. Each branch is identified by a two-letter symbol; the first letter is the node a branch leaves from, and the second letter is the node it goes to. Directly beside the symbol we indicate the length of that branch. These branches are arranged in ascending order of the branch lengths. In Table 12-11 we show such a list for Eban Merritt's route problem. The process we will use fans out from the origin (node A), identifying the shortest route to each of the nodes in the network in the ascending order of their distances from the origin. Let's begin by finding the nearest node to the origin.

Step 1 Only two branches lead away from the origin; branch AB is the shorter. Therefore node B is the nearest node to the origin. We indicate *above* node B that the shortest distance is 250 miles. Results of this step are

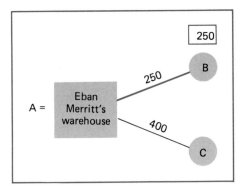

TABLE 12-11

Branches leading out of each node in shortest-route network

A	B	C	D	E	F
AB-250	BC-100	CB-100	DE-100	ED-100	
AC-400	BD-300	CD-150	DC-150	EF-150	
		CE-275	DF-200	EC-275	
			DB-300		

590

Step 2   The second-nearest nodes to the origin are those nearest A and B. These are C and D. D is 300 miles from B, and C is 100 miles from B. We choose C, and indicate below C that the shortest distance from the origin to C is 350 miles. This is shown as

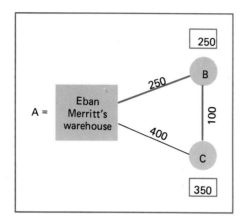

Step 3   The third-nearest nodes to the origin are those nearest B and C. These are D and E. There are two ways to get to D: from B and from C. B + 300 = 550, and C + 150 = 500; we pick branch CD. Now look at node E. E is C + 275 = 625. We conclude that node D is the nearest one to B or C, and we indicate that by entering 500 miles above node D like this:

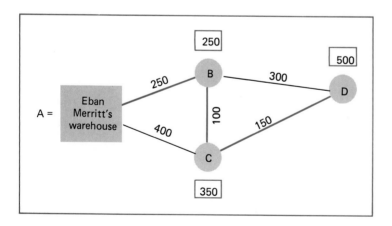

Step 4   The fourth-nearest nodes to the origin are those nearest C and D. These are E and F. There are two ways to get to E, from C and from D. C + 275 = 625, and D + 100 = 600; we pick branch DE. Now look at node F. F is D + 200 = 700. We conclude that node E is the nearest one to C and D, and we indicate this by entering 600 below node E. It is represented as

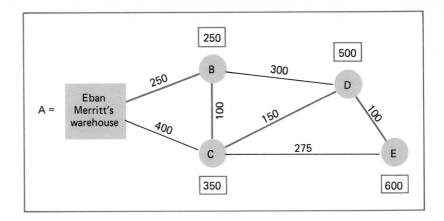

Step 5 The fifth-nearest nodes to the origin are those nearest D and E. Only one node, F, qualifies. We compare branch DF (500 + 200) and branch EF (600 + 150) and choose DF. We write 700 above node F, and we illustrate the completed shortest route like this:

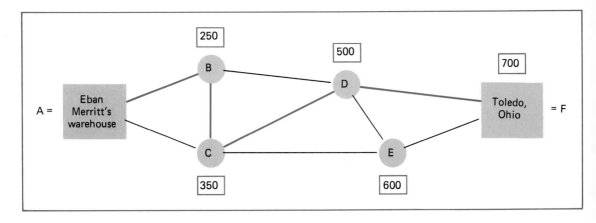

SHORTEST
ROUTE SHOWN

We see from this last network that the shortest route is A-B-C-D-F, with a total distance of 700 miles.

8 Dynamic programming

WHAT DYNAMIC
PROGRAMMING DOES

Dynamic programming is a quantitative technique used to make a series of *interrelated* decisions. It is concerned with finding a *combination* of decisions which will maximize overall effectiveness. For example, a company may wish to make a series of marketing decisions over time which will provide it with the highest possible sales volume. Another organization may wish to find that series of interrelated production decisions over time which will minimize production cost or minimize hiring and layoff to achieve some specified production goal.

In Chapter 5, we used decision trees to solve problems that involved probabilities. Dynamic programming can also be used to handle some probabilistic problems, but here we will only show its use in a deterministic problem. The dynamic programming approach divides the problem into a number of subproblems, or *stages*. The decision we make at each stage influences not only the next stage but also every stage to the end of the problem.

Dynamic programming starts with the last stage of the problem and works backward toward the first stage, making optimal decisions at each stage of the problem. In a three-stage problem, for example, the inputs for stage 3 are the outputs of stage 2, and the inputs for stage 2 are the outputs of stage 1. If, by working backward in this way, we can optimize at each stage, then the sequence of decisions we have made will optimize the whole problem.

Whereas linear programming has standard ways to formulate the problems and solve them, there is no such "standard approach" in dynamic programming. It is, instead, sort of a general way of solving large, complex problems by breaking them down into a series of smaller problems which are more easily solved. A good bit of ingenuity is necessary to know when a problem might be solved by using dynamic programming and how that solution should be approached. We think that if you work through the problem we will present in this section, you will have gone quite a way toward the development of those abilities.

DYNAMIC PROGRAMMING SOLUTION TO SHORTEST-ROUTE PROBLEM

John Kottas is the truck dispatcher for an Atlanta transportation company. His firm has been awarded a contract to pick up a number of loads of woven material in Atlanta and transport them to St. Louis. John has looked at a map of the alternative routes between these two points and constructed the highway network in Figure 12-31. The circles (or *nodes,* as they are commonly called) represent the origin (node 1 = Atlanta), the destination (node 10 = St. Louis), and other cities where routes intersect (nodes 2, 3, 4, 5, 6, 7, 8, and 9). The arrows (or *branches,* as they are called) represent highways between the nodes, each with its mileage indicated. John's problem is to find the shortest route from Atlanta to St. Louis.

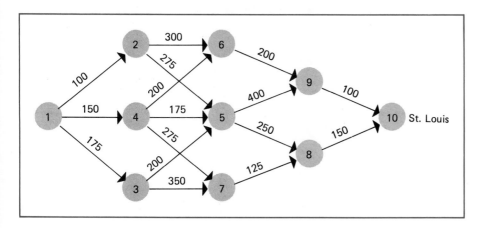

FIGURE 12-31
Highway network for John Kottas's shortest-route problem.

DYNAMIC PROGRAMMING ACTUALLY WORKS THE PROBLEM BACKWARD

THERE IS NO STANDARD APPROACH TO DYNAMIC PROGRAMMING

A SHORTEST-ROUTE PROBLEM SOLVED WITH DYNAMIC PROGRAMMING

Now look at Figure 12-32. Here we have broken John's problem into four smaller problems (stages). Each of these stages is described by its distance from St. Louis (measured in branches), and the input and output nodes for each stage are identified. At each of the four stages of John's problem, we need to determine the optimal branch to take to move from each input node to an output node. We begin the solution to John's problem with an examination of the stage 1 problem.

SOLVING THE
STAGE 1 PROBLEM

Stage 1   Look at node 8. Since there is only one route from node 8 to St. Louis (node 10), this is the shortest route; the distance is 150 miles. Look now at node 9. Here too there is only one route to node 10, which requires us to travel 100 miles. Thus we have found the optimal route from each input node (8 and 9) to an output node (10). Stage 1 results are

Input node	Output node	Route	Shortest distance to St. Louis
8	10	8-10	150
9	10	9-10	100

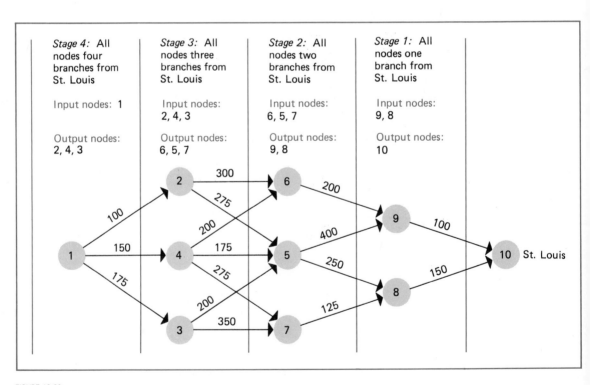

FIGURE 12-32
Highway network with problem stages, stage inputs, and stage outputs.

The solution to stage 1 is shown on the partial network in Figure 12-33 in two rectangular boxes above nodes 8 and 9. The solution is the shortest distance from each of the stage 1 input nodes to St. Louis.

Stage 2 The node we begin with at any stage is not important, so let's start with node 7. There is only one output node for node 7, and that is node 8. We already know (from stage 1) that the shortest distance from node 8 to St. Louis is 150 miles; therefore the shortest distance from node 7 to St. Louis is 275 miles (125 + 150). What about node 6? Again there is only one output node for node 6, and that is node 9. From stage 1 results we know that the shortest distance from node 9 to St. Louis is 100 miles; therefore the shortest distance from node 6 to St. Louis is 300 miles (200 + 100). Now look at node 5. There are *two* output nodes for node 5: 8 and 9. From stage 1 we *already* know the shortest route from nodes 8 and 9 to St. Louis, 150 and 100 miles, respectively. Therefore the choice of an optimal route between node 5 and St. Louis is either 500 miles (400 + 100) or 400 miles (250 + 150). Route 5-8-10 is the optimal one. Stage 2 results are

Input node	Output node	Route	Shortest distance to St. Louis
7	8	7-8	275
6	9	6-9	300
5	8	5-8	400

The partial network in Figure 12-34 shows the solution to the stage 2 problem.

Note that we solved the stage 2 problem by using the outputs from the stage 1 problem (the optimal distances 100 and 150 miles). We did *not* have to measure distances all the way from stage 2 nodes to St. Louis to find the shortest route, only those from stage 2 nodes to stage 1 nodes.

Stage 3 We choose to begin here with node 2. Using the optimal answers for nodes 6 and 5 from stage 2 (300 and 400, respectively), we evaluate routes 2-6 and 2-5 and choose 2-6 (300 + 300 is less than 275 + 400).

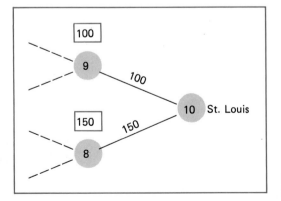

FIGURE 12-33
Solution to the stage 1 problem.

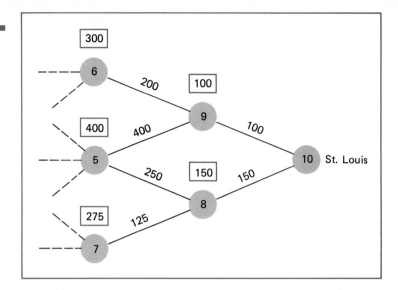

FIGURE 12-34
Solution to the
stage 2 problem.

Looking at node 4, we see we have three choices; we use the optimal answers for nodes 6, 5, and 7 from stage 2 (300, 400, and 275, respectively). We evaluate routes 4-6, 4-5, and 4-7 and choose 4-6 (500 is less than either 575 or 550). What about node 3? Here there are two choices, routes 3-5 and 3-7. Using the optimal answers for nodes 5 and 7 from stage 2 (400 and 275, respectively), we choose route 3-5 (600 is less than 625). Stage 3 results are

Input node	Output node	Route	Shortest distance to St. Louis
2	6	2-6	600
4	6	4-6	500
3	5	3-5	600

Figure 12-35 shows the solution to the stage 3 problem.

Notice here again that we solved the stage 3 problem by using the outputs from the stage 2 problem (the optimal distances 300, 400, and 275 miles). We did *not* have to measure distances all the way from stage 3 nodes to St. Louis to find the shortest route, only those from stage 3 nodes to stage 2 nodes.

SOLVING THE
STAGE 4 PROBLEM

Stage 4 There is only one input in stage 4, node 1, and so we have three choices (route 1-2, 1-4, or 1-3). Using the output of stage 3 (the optimal distances 600, 500, and 600 miles), we evaluate the three routes and choose 1-4 (650 is less than either 700 or 775). Stage 4 results are

Input node	Output node	Route	Shortest distance to St. Louis
1	4	1-4	650

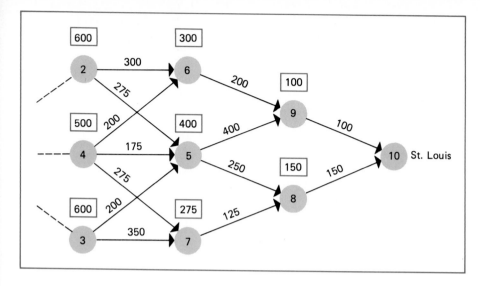

FIGURE 12-35
Solution to the
stage 3 problem.

Figure 12-36 shows the solution to stage 4 (together with the solutions to the
other stages).

THE SHORTEST ROUTE

Now that we have solved the four individual problems, let's go through the
network from stage 4 to stage 1 and pick the route at each stage which leads
us to the optimal decision. Table 12-12 illustrates this process. You can see

COMBINING ANSWERS
FROM THE FOUR
STAGES TO FIND THE
SHORTEST ROUTE

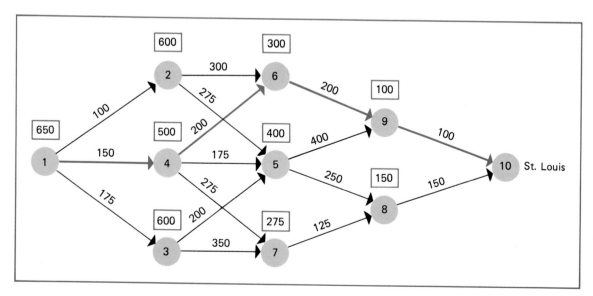

FIGURE 12-36
Solution to the stage 4 problem.

	Input node	Output node	Route	Shortest distance to St. Louis
Stage 4	①	④	1-4	650
Stage 3	2	6	2-6	600
	④	⑥	4-6	500
	3	5	3-5	600
Stage 2	7	8	7-8	275
	⑥	⑨	6-9	300
	5	8	5-8	400
Stage 1	8	10	8-10	150
	⑨	⑩	9-10	100

TABLE 12-12
Picking the best
decision at each stage

that the shortest route between Atlanta and St. Louis is 1-4-6-9-10, with a total distance of 650 miles.

COMPUTATIONAL
ADVANTAGE OF
DYNAMIC
PROGRAMMING

In using dynamic programming to get a solution to this problem, we did not have to enumerate all the possible paths through this network (and there are 10 of them). Whereas this would not have been such a terrible task for a network this size, think of the work that would be involved if the network had, say, 100 nodes. Once again, we should emphasize that when using dynamic programming, we did not have to evaluate *all* the paths at each stage as we moved from node 10 back to node 1; instead, we used the output from one stage as the input for a succeeding stage. That is how dynamic programming provides such consequential savings of computation time over other methods.

9 Glossary

Activity list A list of all the activities in a project.

Beta distribution A continuous distribution of a random variable which is used in time estimating in PERT.

Branches A term used to refer to the activities in a network.

Budget overrun The condition when an activity has expended a greater proportion of its estimated cost than its degree of completion would justify.

CPM (critical path method) A networking method developed in 1957 which adds the concept of cost to the PERT format.

Crash time The time required to finish an activity if special efforts are made to reduce the time to a minimum.

Crashing A method used to reduce the time in a network at the least cost.

Critical path The longest path through a network.

Direct costs Costs which vary directly with the time required to complete the work.

Dummy activity An activity which requires no time and which is used to establish a precedence relationship in a network.

Dynamic programming A quantitative technique useful in the solution to a problem where a number of interrelated decisions are to be made.

Earliest finish (EF) time The earliest time at which an activity can end.

Earliest start (ES) time The earliest time at which an activity can begin.

Event A node when all the activities leading to that node have been completed.

Expected time for an activity The time calculated by means of the weighted average $(a + 4m + b)/6$.

Flow Movement along a branch in a maximal-flow problem.

Forward pass A process moving from left to right in a network to define all the earliest start and finish times.

Immediate predecessor An activity that must immediately precede a given activity in a project.

Indirect costs Overhead costs which go on throughout the entire project.

Latest finish (LF) time The latest time at which an activity can be completed without extending the completion time of the network.

Latest start (LS) time The latest time at which an activity can begin without extending the completion time of the network.

Most likely time The time that the activity would most likely take if it were repeated time and time again, symbolized m.

Nodes The circles in a network representing the beginning and ending of activities.

Normal time The time required to finish an activity if it is done in the normal manner.

Optimistic time The shortest possible time in which an activity is likely to be completed, symbolized a.

Output node A point of exit in a maximal-flow problem.

Personnel loading chart A graph of available personnel plotted against time.

PERT (program evaluation and review technique) A networking system developed in the 1950s, useful in planning and controlling projects.

PERT/Cost A project management system developed by the U.S. government which measures and controls costs by use of work packages.

Pessimistic time The longest possible time in which an activity is likely to be completed, symbolized b.

Series-connected activities Activities related in such a way that one must be finished before another can begin.

Slack Free time in a network. Formally defined as LF − EF or LS − ES.

Source node A point of entry in a maximal-flow problem.

Stage One of the individual problems which, when taken together, make up a dynamic programming problem.

Utility costs Penalties for being late and bonuses for being early.

10 Review of equations

Page 556

$$t = \frac{a + 4m + b}{6} \tag{12-1}$$

With this formula, we can find the expected time for an activity in a PERT network by taking a weighted average of a (the most optimistic completion time), m (the most likely completion time), and b (the pessimistic completion time).

Page 556

$$\text{Standard deviation of an activity} = \frac{b - a}{6} \tag{12-2}$$

This calculates the standard deviation of the expected time for a PERT activity. The pessimistic time is b, and the optimistic time is a.

Page 558

$$\text{Earliest finish time} = \text{earliest start time} + \text{expected time} \tag{12-3}$$

If you add the expected time for an activity to that activity's earliest start time, you get the earliest time at which we could expect that activity to be completed (its earliest finish time).

Page 558

$$\text{Latest start time} = \text{latest finish time} - \text{expected time} \tag{12-4}$$

If you subtract the expected time for an activity from that activity's latest finish time, you get the latest start time for that activity, that is, the latest time at which the activity can begin without delaying completion of the network.

Page 560

$$\text{Slack} = \text{LF} - \text{EF} \quad \text{or} \quad \text{LS} - \text{ES} \tag{12-5}$$

Slack is equal to the difference between the latest finish time and the earliest finish time or—calculated another way—the difference between the latest start time and the earliest start time.

Page 561

Standard deviation of the earliest finish time of a network with four activities on its critical path

$$= \sqrt{\left(\begin{array}{c}\text{std. dev.}\\\text{for first}\\\text{activity}\end{array}\right)^2 + \left(\begin{array}{c}\text{std. dev.}\\\text{for second}\\\text{activity}\end{array}\right)^2 + \left(\begin{array}{c}\text{std. dev.}\\\text{for third}\\\text{activity}\end{array}\right)^2 + \left(\begin{array}{c}\text{std. dev.}\\\text{for fourth}\\\text{activity}\end{array}\right)^2} \tag{12-6}$$

The standard deviation of the earliest finish time of a network is found by taking the square root of the sum of the squared standard deviations of the individual activities on the critical path of that network.

12-1 Given the following project characteristics, construct a PERT network.

Activity	Predecessors
A	None
B	A
C	A
D	B, C
E	C
F	D
G	E, F

12-2 Construct a PERT network for the following project activities:

Activity	Predecessors
A	None
B	None
C	A, B
D	A, B
E	C
F	C, D
G	F

12-3 A project has the following characteristics:

Activity	Time	Predecessors
A	6	None
B	8	A
C	4	A
D	9	B
E	2	C
F	7	D

Construct a PERT network, and compute ES, LS, and slack time for each activity; find the critical path.

12-4 A project plan is as follows:

Activity	Time	Predecessors
A	4	None
B	9	None
C	3	A
D	8	B
E	7	B
F	2	D
G	5	E

Construct a PERT network, and compute ES, LS, and slack time for each activity; find the critical path.

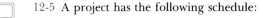

12-5 A project has the following schedule:

Activity	Predecessors	Time
A	None	8
B	None	2
C	A	1
D	B	9
E	B	4
F	C, D	5
G	E	6
H	E	3
I	G	3
J	H	5
K	I, J	2
L	F	3

Construct a PERT network, and compute ES, LS, and slack time for each activity; find the critical path.

12-6 Assume you are the project manager of the project whose schedule is described in Exercise 12-5. The project has progressed to the end of week 12. At this time activities A, B, C, D, E, G, and H are completed, and activities F, I, J can be started at the beginning of the following week. The project must be completed at the end of week 19. You have the choice of crashing certain activities. With the schedule as it now stands, what possible management actions might you take to hold the project completion at week 19?

12-7 A complex project has the following characteristics:

Activity	Predecessors	Time	Activity	Predecessors	Time
A	None	8	K	J, F	4
B	None	2	L	H, G, K	6
C	None	3	M	H, G, K	8
D	C	9	N	J, F	5
E	B, D	4	O	I, L	4
F	C	6	P	J, F	4
G	B, D	7	Q	I, L	3
H	A, E	1	R	O, M, N	2
I	A, E	2	S	O, M, N	1
J	B, D	3	T	Q, R	6

Construct a PERT network and compute the ES, LS, and slack time for all activities.

12-8 Assume you are project manager of the project whose schedule is described in Exercise 12-7. The project has progressed to the end of week 21 and the status is as follows:

Activities completed: A, B, C, D, E, F, H, I, J, K, P
Activities not started: L, M, O, Q, R, S, T

Activities in progress:

Activity	Weeks remaining before completion
G	2
N	3

What actions might you take to get the project back to a schedule that can be completed by the end of week 37?

12-9 The following list of activities must be accomplished in order to complete a construction project:

Activity	Time, weeks	Predecessors
A	3	None
B	8	None
C	4	A, B
D	2	B
E	1	A
F	7	C
G	5	E, F
H	6	D, F
I	8	G, H
J	9	I

Construct the PERT diagram for this project. *Note:* This diagram will require dummy activities. Compute the expected project completion time and the early start, late start, and slack time for each activity.

12-10 Assume you are the project manager of the project whose schedule is described in Exercise 12-9. The project has progressed to the end of week 10 and the status is as follows:

Activities completed: A, B, E
Activities not started: C, D, F, G, H, I, J

What actions might you take to get the project back to a schedule that can be completed by the end of week 42?

12-11 The activity-on-arc convention for constructing a PERT network uses arrows to designate activities and circles to designate events. The critical path method sometimes employs the activity-on-node convention where arrows represent precedence requirements and circles represent the activities. A network using this particular CPM convention would appear as:

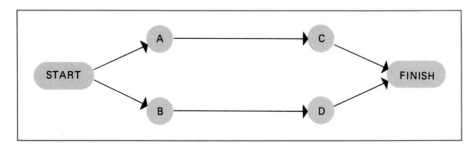

where:

CPM activity	Function or relationship to PERT
START	Dummy to indicate START (zero time)
A	Same as PERT activity
B	Same as PERT activity
C	Same as PERT activity
D	Same as PERT activity
FINISH	Dummy to indicate FINISH (zero time)

Draw the network diagram of Exercise 12-9 using this CPM convention.

 12-12 A project has the following characteristics:

Activity	Most optimistic time	Most likely time	Most pessimistic time	Predecessors
A	.5	1	2	None
B	1	2	3	A
C	1	3	5	A
D	3	4	5	B
E	2	3	4	C
F	3	5	7	C
G	4	5	6	D, E
H	6	7	8	F
I	2	4	6	G, H
J	5	6	8	G, H
K	1	2	3	I
L	3	5	7	J

Construct a PERT network and compute the probability that the project will be completed within 30 weeks. Round off the computed expected times and standard deviation values to the nearest tenth of a week.

 12-13 The Oshkosh Company is planning to design, develop, and market a new racing bicycle. The project is composed of the following activities:

Activity	Description	Predecessors	Time (weeks)
A	Design frame	none	4
B	Design wheels	none	3
C	Design gears	none	3
D	Design handlebars	C	2
E	Test steering	A, B, D	1
F	Test gears	A, B, D	2
G	Performance test	E, F	3
H	Manufacturing layout	A, B, D	3
I	Manufacture demonstrators	H	5
J	Prepare advertising	G	2
K	Prepare users' manuals	G	4
L	Distribute to dealers	I, J, K	2

Construct the PERT network, and determine the critical path and slack for each activity.

a. Oshkosh's management would like to get the new bicycle to their dealers in 15 weeks. Would it help if they:
1. Work overtime to get the frame designed in only 3 weeks?
2. Work overtime to get the wheels designed in only 2 weeks?
3. Assign more designers to gear design? If so, what activity should the designers be taken from?
4. Ship to dealers a week before the advertising is ready?
5. Ship to dealers a week before the users' manuals are ready?

b. Lenny Small is planning to race in the upcoming Reno to Las Vegas bicycle race. He is willing to use the new Oshkosh bicycle if a demonstrator model is ready within 12 weeks (completion of activity I). To do this would you:
1. Shorten the performance test to only 2 weeks?
2. Start laying out the manufacturing area a week before the handlebars are designed?
3. Cancel the performance test and let Lenny's race experience in week 13 satisfy the performance test requirement?

12-14 Refer to the resource leveling problem illustrated in Figure 12-19. Suppose the number of workers available during this period were increased to 11; what effect, if any, would this have on the total number of weeks required for completion of this project?

12-15 Refer again to the resource leveling problem illustrated in Figure 12-19. From Figure 12-20 we can see that we have an unbalanced work force (5 to 15 people working at different times). Suppose labor constraints prevented us from employing fewer than 7 or more than 8 people; what effect would these constraints have on the time required to complete this project?

12-16 Samantha (Sam) Stone is the plant manager for the Burlington Hosiery Mill, Inc. From time to time, Sam must send out information for controlling the production process to each work station supervisor for use by the employees at that station. Since delivery of the information involves quite a bit of walking, Sam is interested in installing microcomputers at all the work stations. Sam has drawn the following diagram showing distances in feet from her office to the work stations and indicating possible paths from one station to another. (Walls and stairs prevent direct connection of all work stations.) Using the minimal-spanning-tree algorithm, show Sam the most economical (shortest-length) cable to install.

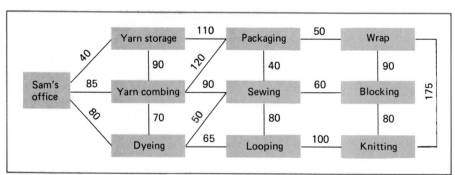

12-17 Ottawa Construction, Ltd., is preparing a PERT network for laying the foundation for a new art museum. They have the following activities to perform, with time estimates in weeks:

Activity	Description	Optimistic estimate	Pessimistic estimate	Most likely estimate	Immediate predecessors
A	Survey site	2	4	3	none
B	Excavation	9	15	12	A
C	Prepare drawings	4	7	6	none
D	Soil study	1	1	1	B
E	Prelim. report	1	3	2	C, D
F	Approve plans	1	1	1	E
G	Concrete forms	5	9	6	F
H	Procure steel	2	4	3	F
I	Order cement	1	1	1	F
J	Deliver gravel	2	5	3	G
K	Pour concrete	8	14	10	H, I, J
L	Cure concrete	2	2	2	K
M	Strength test	2	2	2	L

Construct the PERT network for the project and determine the critical path as well as the slack for each activity.

a. If Ottawa plans to include a completion date in their bid for this work, what completion time should they quote if it is their policy to ensure a 90 percent probability of being completed?

b. If the Canadian Ministry of Art desires to have the work completed within 41 weeks, determine the probability of meeting this objective.

c. The contract specifies a $10,000 per week penalty for each week the completion of the project extends past week 43. What is the probability Ottawa Construction will have to pay a $10,000 penalty? What is the probability they will have to pay a $20,000 penalty?

 12-18 Joe Ferner has just been caught by a surprise OSHA inspection, and one of the violations for which he was cited dealt with the absence of a sprinkler system in his electric-motor manufacturing plant. Business hasn't been too good lately, and Joe is caught between the prospect of a large fine or the cost of installing a sprinkler system. The factory has this floor plan:

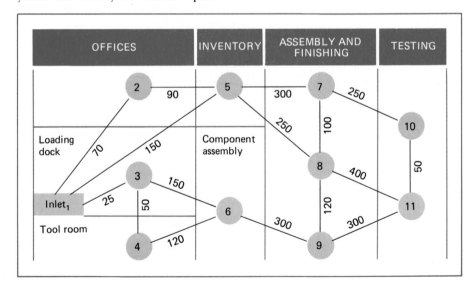

The circles indicate required sprinkler outlets in each area. In the interest of economy, Joe wants the least possible number of feet of piping. He has indicated the distances between sprinkler outlets in his sketch. Using the minimal-spanning-tree algorithm, determine which route will satisfy Joe's needs.

12-19 Lissette Edwards is an installer for the Burlington Telephone Company. She has been handed a service request for installation of a phone in an office building in the business district. When she arrives at the building, Lissette notices that the office which submitted the request is all the way across the building from the telephone junction box. In the interest of saving time and material, she calls you with a brief description of the situation and estimates of the distances involved. You sketch out the plan, and it looks something like the diagram below, where the black lines represent the existing conduit through which Lissette can pull a telephone line (distances are in feet). Using the shortest-route algorithm, advise Lissette which route to use.

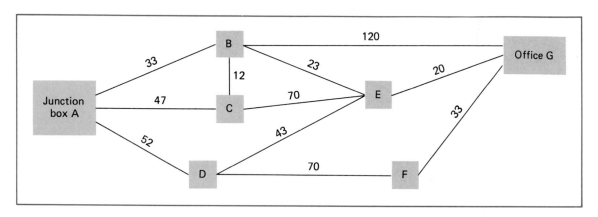

12-20 City Planning and Architectural Associates have been commissioned to design the new soccer stadium for the Miami Warhawks. Their design has the parking lot separated from the stadium with a single gate leading to the stadium (for security reasons). Within the gate, there are a number of possible routes through landscaped gardens to the single stadium entrance. The network through the gardens looks like this (numbers show capacity in thousands of persons per hour):

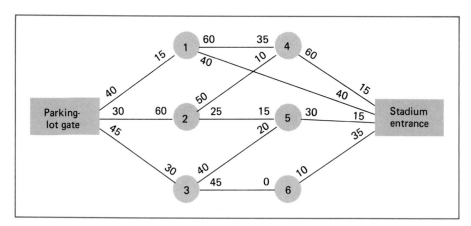

Using the maximal-flow algorithm, find the hourly capacity of the system to move spectators into the stadium. Charlie Willis, owner of the Warhawks, phoned to say that if the system couldn't accommodate 100,000 fans coming into the stadium during 1 hour, the architects should start redesigning. Will City Planning have to redesign?

12-21 Emily Schultz is project manager of the Weather-Watch satellite project. In the countdown before launch, she has 2 hours of available time to perform final systems tests, and she has only 4 technicians available to perform these tests. The activities to be performed are as follows:

Activity	Description	Time (minutes)	Number of technicians	Prede-cessors
A	Battery check	10	1	none
B	Circuit check	15	3	none
C	Computer test	12	1	none
D	Arm apogee rocket	4	2	A, B
E	Arm explosive bolts	8	2	B
F	Sequencer test	20	4	C, D, E
G	Camera test	30	2	F
H	Remove safety wires	15	1	F
I	Radio test	20	2	F
J	Command/Decoder test	18	3	I
K	Telemetry test	6	2	F
L	Final systems test	20	4	G, H, J, K

Develop a schedule of activities which will allow all tests to be completed in the available 2 hours.

12-22 General Carter Williams, Jr., is commander of the aggressor army in the current war games being conducted at Fort John McHenry. He wants to launch a sneak attack on the defender army but needs to be assured of enough troop movement capability to carry off the attack, since an unsuccessful venture here would spell defeat for his forces, not to mention a personal blow. His aides have drawn the following illustration of possible routes from the aggressor army headquarters to the defender headquarters, showing the troop capacity which each route will handle (troops per hour). General Carter feels that if he cannot move 22,000 troops an hour along the attack routes, his plan is not workable. Should he devise another plan?

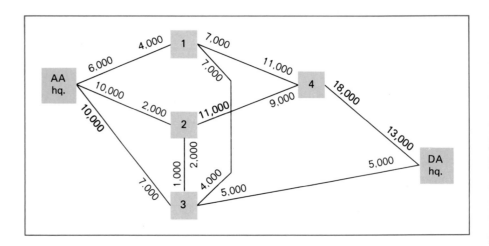

12-23 The First National Bank maintains a branch office in the Westvale Mall. Each day at 2 P.M. the Westvale branch collects all checks drawn on the bank's depositors and sends them by courier to the downtown office, where they are encoded and processed. It is important for the branch to transmit the checks in a timely fashion, because if they are delayed in arriving downtown, they may have to be processed on the next working day. This would deprive the bank of one day's interest earned on these funds, and over the long run, such losses would constitute a substantial amount. Lisa North, the Westvale branch manager, has studied this problem and has prepared a chart (see figure) showing the minutes of travel time along various legs of the possible routes from Westvale to downtown. Solve the problem using dynamic programming to determine if a route can be found which takes less than 10 minutes to deliver the checks.

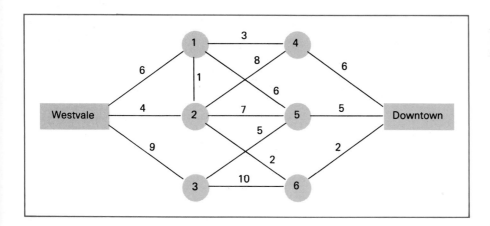

12-24 Bernard Richter is the president of a textile concern with mills in four southeastern states. He is currently in a mill which is the farthest one from his home office. He is traveling on the corporate jet. Since each state's mills are under the supervision of the same production officer, a visit to any one of them should give a typical picture of conditions in all the mills in that state. Bernard decides that on the way back to the home office he will visit one mill in each state for a surprise inspection. He wants to conserve fuel and intends to fly the absolute minimum number of air miles on this return trip. He gets out the sectional air chart and pencils in this sketch.

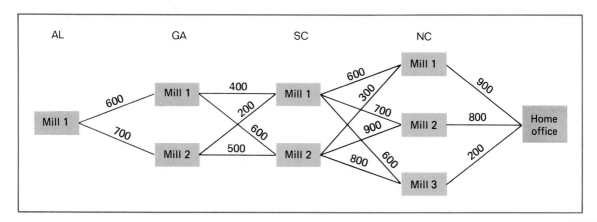

Using dynamic programming, help Bernard choose the shortest route which will meet his plan. The numbers on his sketch are in statute miles.

 12-25 For the following project, use the CPM method to crash the project to its minimum length at the lowest possible direct cost. (Assume there are no indirect or utility costs.)

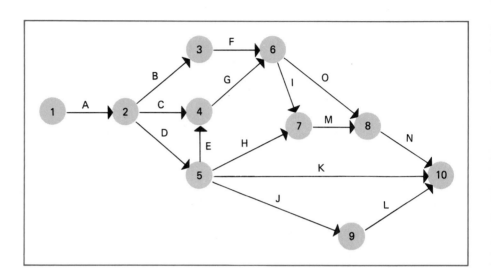

Activity	Normal time, weeks	Crash time, weeks	Normal cost	Crash cost
A	3.0	1.0	$11,000	$17,000
B	6.0	3.0	6,000	9,000
C	5.0	4.0	3,000	5,000
D	8.0	2.0	7,000	31,000
E	2.0	1.0	1,000	6,000
F	11.0	3.0	13,000	17,000
G	10.0	7.0	9,000	13,500
H	5.0	1.0	4,000	14,000
I	3.0	2.0	5,000	8,500
J	9.0	4.0	3,000	5,000
K	4.0	1.0	8,000	8,900
L	3.0	2.0	9,000	16,000
M	8.0	3.0	15,000	19,000
N	2.0	1.0	7,000	13,000
O	11.0	4.0	20,000	24,200

12-26 For the project given in Exercise 12-25, formulate the linear programming objective function and constraints which will enable the determination of least-cost crashing strategy to bring the project's completion down to 18 weeks. Solve the problem on a computer.

12-27 To the project in Exercise 12-25, add indirect costs of $2,000 per week and a utility cost (a penalty of $5,000 per week against the contractor for each week beyond 25 weeks required for completion). What is the least costly completion schedule the contractor should attempt to achieve on this project?

12-28 Jack Behrman is marketing manager for Computer Distributors. He wishes to assign each of his eight salespersons to one of three sales districts. Jack has estimated the probable profits (in thousands of dollars per year) that can be achieved with various numbers of salespersons assigned to the three districts as follows:

Number of persons assigned	Abbott County	Babson County	Clark County
0	$ 0	$ 0	$ 0
1	45	15	30
2	90	30	60
3	135	60	90
4	180	120	120
5	180	150	150
6 or more	180	150	180

Use dynamic programming to determine the most profitable assignment of personnel to sales districts.

12-29 One criticism of PERT's use of probability is that the probability of a project's completion on a given date is based upon the standard deviation of activities along the critical path. Yet the probability of completion by the same date along a noncritical path may be a lesser value. Consider, for example, the following project:

Activity	Most optimistic time	Most likely time	Most pessimistic time	Predecessors
A	3	6	9	None
B	2	5	8	None
C	2	4	6	A
D	2	3	10	B
E	1	3	11	B
F	4	6	8	C, D
G	1	5	15	E

First, find the critical path and its standard deviation. What is the probability that the activities on the critical path will be completed by 18 weeks? Then compute the standard deviation of path B-E-G. What is the probability that this noncritical path will be completed by 18 weeks?

12-30 For the project illustrated below, produce a schedule of funds that will be required each month and determine the lowest average commitment of funds during the project, using a late start approach to each activity. (Use a simple average, not a time-weighted average, in your calculations.)

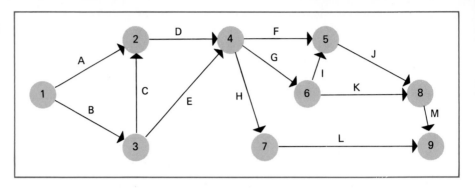

Activity	Duration, months	Total cost
A	3	$ 60,000
B	1	10,000
C	5	20,000
D	4	40,000
E	6	120,000
F	6	180,000
G	7	35,000
H	4	80,000
I	2	30,000
J	1	5,000
K	1	40,000
L	3	90,000
M	2	18,000

12-31 Dr. Clyde Carter, chief of emergency services at Orange General Hospital, is concerned about the length of time it takes the hematology labs to process blood samples in emergency situations. He has full authority to direct the route that blood samples take through the lab process to ensure the minimum total processing time possible. At Dr. Carter's request, the director of the hematology lab has provided the

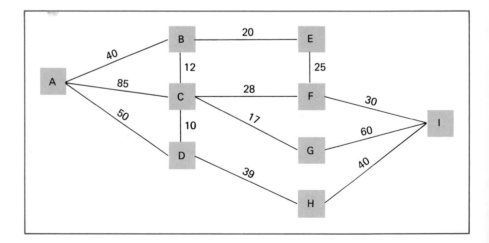

accompanying schematic of the possible routes; the numbers shown are the time in minutes from one work station to another. By using the shortest-route algorithm, calculate the minimum possible time for processing a blood sample through the lab. You may assume that any route will produce a comparable test; different routes simply indicate different test machines with different capacities.

12-32 Marsha Wendall is budget director for Westmoreland County. She has been asked to prepare a list of road repair projects for the following year's budget, with the restriction that a total of only $24 million can be allocated to the projects selected. She has identified the six most important repair projects as well as their cost and an importance factor (developed from a survey of county residents), shown below. Using dynamic programming, determine which projects should be included in the budget so that the total importance factor is maximized without exceeding the total budget level of $24 million.

Project	Cost, millions of dollars	Importance
Route 1	4	5
Route 2	7	6
Route 3	5	4
Route 4	6	7
Route 5	8	3 (least important)
Route 6	4	8 (most important)

12-33 Set up a linear program to find the earliest finish time for this project:

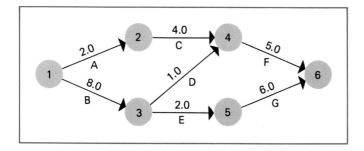

12-34 Given the following data for a project:

Activity	Predecessor	Time, wk Normal	Time, wk Crash	Cost Normal	Cost Crash	Cost to reduce/ wk
A	None	8	6	$ 8,000	$10,000	$1,000
B	None	7	5	6,000	8,400	1,200
C	A	5	4	7,000	8,500	1,500
D	B	4	3	3,000	3,800	800
E	A	3	2	2,000	2,600	600
F	D, E	5	3	5,000	6,600	800
G	C	4	3	6,000	7,000	1,000
		Total costs		$37,000	$46,900	

It is mandatory that this project be completed in 15 weeks. Determine the least-cost schedule for achieving this.

12-35 Set up the objective function and constraints which would allow Exercise 12-34 to be solved with linear programming.

12-36 The Wellington Electronics Company has been awarded a contract to develop radio components for the NASA spaceflight program. The PERT network is as follows:

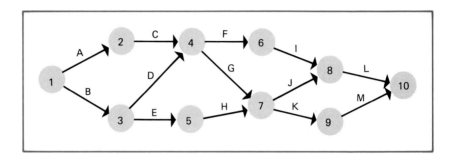

Wellington will be paid on a cost-plus-fixed-fee basis. NASA wants the project to be completed in 12 months and will pay Wellington one-fourth of the total cost at the end of each quarter. The fixed fee will be paid at the completion of the project. The following table gives the expected time to complete each activity as well as cost information for each of them:

Activity	Duration, months	Total cost	Cost/month
A	1	$ 10,000	$10,000
B	3	60,000	20,000
C	3	90,000	30,000
D	2	50,000	25,000
E	1	40,000	40,000
F	2	70,000	35,000
G	2	20,000	10,000
H	1	15,000	15,000
I	1	10,000	10,000
J	3	45,000	15,000
K	2	40,000	20,000
L	2	40,000	20,000
M	1	25,000	25,000
		Total cost $515,000	

Wellington would like to schedule each activity at its earliest start time, thus ensuring maintenance of each activity's slack. This will give the company maximum schedule flexibility to complete the project on time if unexpected delays are experienced after the project is underway. However, Wellington does not want the total cumulative costs incurred at the end of any quarter to exceed by more than $5,000 the total of all payments that it will have received at the end of the quarter. Develop a schedule that will meet these objectives.

12-37 The Burns Aircraft Company has received an order to deliver 18 of their LT-27 executive airplanes to the Benson Company. Four aircraft are to be delivered next month while 6 and 8 aircraft respectively are to be delivered in the two months following next month. Burns has the capacity to produce 5 aircraft per month on regular time at a cost of $100,000 each. They can produce 2 additional aircraft per month on overtime at a cost of $150,000 each. If an aircraft is produced in a given month, but is held for future delivery, a holding cost of $10,000 per month is incurred. Use dynamic programming to determine the least-cost production strategy which will allow them to deliver the 18 aircraft on schedule. Assume that the company has no LT-27 aircraft available at the beginning of the schedule period.

12-38 The Webster Construction Company is bidding on a contract to install a line of microwave towers. It has identified the following activities and their expected times, predecessor restrictions, and worker requirements:

Activity	Duration, weeks	Predecessors	Crew size, workers
A	4	None	4
B	7	None	2
C	3	A	2
D	3	A	4
E	2	B	6
F	2	B	3
G	2	D, E	3
H	3	F, G	4

The contract specifies that the project must be completed in 14 weeks. The Webster Company will assign a fixed number of workers to the project for its entire duration, and so it would like to ensure that the minimum number of workers is assigned and that the project will be completed in the 14 weeks. Find a schedule which will do this.

12 Chapter concepts quiz

12-1 In a PERT network, the manager must estimate three times for the completion of an activity: the earliest possible completion time, called the _____; the best estimate of completion time called the most _____; and the latest possible completion time, called the _____.

Fill in the Blanks

12-2 Activities which must be completed before another activity can begin are called _____ activities; those which must be completed just before a given activity can begin are called the _____ of that activity.

12-3 The _____ of a network is the path which contains the most work of any path in the network; the length of this path, measured in time units, is the expected _____ bound on the amount of time necessary to complete the project.

12-4 In a CPM network, the _____ time is the time required to finish an activity if no extraordinary measures are taken, while the _____ time is the shortest possible completion time and requires special efforts or resources.

The cost associated with the former is always _____ than the cost for the latter.

12-5 A dynamic programming problem consists of several smaller problems called _____ with interlocking decisions.

12-6 The _____ problem is concerned with finding the best way to reach all nodes in a network from some particular source node such that the total length of all branches used is a minimum.

12-7 The _____ problem is used to find the greatest volume of flow from some source node to some other sink node.

12-8 A _____ is a rule of thumb procedure for obtaining good but not necessarily optimal solutions for problems.

12-9 When combining three time estimates into a distribution of randomly distributed activity durations, we assume that the activities are _____ distributed.

12-10 When all activities leading into a node in the PERT network are completed, the node is referred to as a(n) _____.

True-False 12-11 A dummy activity is used to preserve precedence relationships in a network, in order to avoid having two activities with the same beginning and ending nodes, and is assigned a completion time of zero. **T F**

12-12 Reducing the completion time of any activity will always reduce the overall completion time of the project. **T F**

12-13 The slack in an activity is the difference between the late finish (LF) time and the early finish (EF) time for the activity. **T F**

12-14 If an activity is completed after its earliest finish (EF) time, then the project will necessarily be extended beyond its scheduled completion time. **T F**

12-15 All activities on a critical path have slack equal to zero. **T F**

12-16 CPM tends to emphasize controlling costs more than PERT does. **T F**

12-17 Regardless of the method of resource leveling used to satisfy resource limitations, we must always preserve precedence relationships in the network. **T F**

12-18 In a maximal-flow problem, it is necessary to designate the source node and the output node to solve the problem. **T F**

12-19 In a maximal-flow problem, if all the branches leading to the output node have zero capacity remaining, then the present solution is optimal. **T F**

12-20 Dynamic programming problems consist of a series of subproblems, each of which is independent of all the other subproblems. **T F**

12-21 PERT assumes that the distribution of completion times for a project is a normal distribution. **T F**

12-22 It is possible to use linear programming to analyze crashing strategies because crash costs are assumed to be a linear function of time. **T F**

12-23 Dynamic programming, like linear programming, is a systematic procedure that is general to a number of different problems. **T F**

12-24 Any activity which starts at its latest start time will have maximum slack. **T F**

12-25 A most likely time estimate is weighted four times as much as an optimistic time estimate in PERT. **T F**

12-26 Which of the following statements is true for PERT networks?
   a. The network is drawn so as to indicate precedence relationships.
   b. Each node represents the beginning or end of an activity, and each branch represents an activity.
   c. The activity times are described by a probability distribution which requires the specification of three time estimates to characterize it.
   d. All of the above.

12-27 In crashing a CPM network, which of the following is true?
   a. The first activity to be crashed is the least expensive activity on the critical path.
   b. All paths with the greatest length in the network must be reduced simultaneously.
   c. When the path or paths with the greatest length cannot be reduced further, no further reduction in project time is possible.
   d. All of the above.

12-28 Which of the following is true of a dynamic program?
   a. The problem is solved in stages, starting at the last stage and working backward to the initial stage.
   b. The decisions at each stage depend on decisions at other stages.
   c. There is no standard procedure to follow.
   d. All of the above.

12-29 Which of the following represents a method of readjusting a PERT network to achieve better project results?
   a. Shifting resources from the critical path to noncritical paths
   b. Reassessing the optimistic, pessimistic, and most likely times for all activities on the critical path
   c. Modifying the precedence relationships so that series-connected activities can be performed at the same time
   d. All of the above

12-30 In the shortest-route algorithm, the number placed above each node represents:
   a. The shortest distance from the origin to that node
   b. The shortest distance from that node to the closest of its immediate predecessors
   c. The shortest distance from the destination to that node
   d. The length of the most direct route from the origin to the node (that is, the route with the smallest number of nodes)

12-31 PERT assumes that the span of time between the optimistic and pessimistic time estimates of an activity is:
   a. 3 standard deviations
   b. 6 standard deviations
   c. 8 standard deviations
   d. 12 standard deviations

12-32 If a PERT activity has an optimistic time estimate which is identical to its pessimistic time estimate, the standard deviation of the activity will be equal to:
   a. Zero
   b. The most likely time
   c. One
   d. The square root of the pessimistic estimate

12-33 Every path in a PERT network would be critical if all activities:
   a. Were to start at their earliest finish times.
   b. Took as much time to accomplish as their pessimistic estimates.

617

   c. Have zero standard deviations.

   d. Were to start at their latest start times.

12-34 Another term commonly used for activity slack time is:
   a. Non-critical time
   b. Total float
   c. Activity-on-arc
   d. Resource idleness

12-35 A penalty cost for completing a project late is called:
   a. An indirect cost
   b. A direct cost
   c. A crash cost
   d. None of the above

12-36 The set of activities on the critical path are:
   a. Those having zero slack.
   b. Series-connected activities.
   c. Those whose earliest start times are equal to their latest start times.
   d. All of the above.

12-37 The advantage of scheduling a project with all activities starting at their latest start time is that:
   a. Non-critical activities will maintain maximum slack.
   b. Average commitment of funds is reduced.
   c. Resource requirements are more level.
   d. All of the above.

12-38 All nodes in the network must be considered in the:
   a. Maximal-flow problem
   b. Minimal-spanning tree problem
   c. Shortest-route problem
   d. All of the above

12-39 Dynamic programming is an approach which divides a problem into a number of subproblems called:
   a. Stages
   b. States
   c. Sub-networks
   d. Decision points

12-40 If activity X is an immediate predecessor to activity Y:
   a. Both X and Y are members of the critical path.
   b. Activity X's earliest finish time must equal activity Y's earliest start time.
   c. Both X and Y have the same slack.
   d. None of the above is correct.

13 Real world MS/OR successes

EXAMPLE: CUTTING TIMBER
WITH DYNAMIC PROGRAMMING

WEYERHAEUSER
OPERATIONS

The Weyerhaeuser Company is one of the largest forest products companies in the world. In 1986, sales exceeded $5 billion. The company handles a raw material flow of about one billion cubic feet each year—that's a volume of wood covering a football field and growing four miles high. Weyerhaeuser has an innovative operations research staff that has assisted management for more than twenty years. The payoff from operations research has been substantial. For example, two of the company's researchers, Mark Lembersky and Uli H. Chi,[3] used dynamic programming to develop decision rules for cutting tree stems into logs. The bottom line: more than \$100 million in increased profits over a nine-year period.

Each year, Weyerhaeuser cuts about 15 million trees. The value of a tree stem is the sum of the revenues from each individual log taken from the stem minus cutting and processing costs. Revenues depend on many factors: log length, curvature, diameter, taper, knot and quality characteristics, as well as the market or mill to which it is allocated. For example, a given log could be allocated to the production of various grades of lumber or plywood, or it might be used in paper production. Consequently, different decisions on cutting and allocating a tree stem to a market can result in very different profits.

WHY PROFITS DEPEND ON CUT/ALLOCATION DECISIONS

Lembersky and Chi formulated a dynamic program to find the optimal cut and allocation decisions for a tree stem. The program relies on a data base of stems and log values as a function of their physical attributes and potential markets. Like the shortest-route problem in this chapter, the solution algorithm proceeds in stages. In the first stage, the optimal cut is made considering the entire tree. In later stages, optimal cuts are made for remaining portions of the tree stem. Profit is determined by the size, characteristics, and market allocations of the logs. Again like the shortest route problem, it is unnecessary to evaluate all possible cutting decisions. Instead the output from one stage (the portion of the tree remaining) is used as the input for a succeeding stage.

DYNAMIC PROGRAMMING MODEL

SIMILARITY TO SHORTEST-ROUTE PROBLEM

In Weyerhaeuser operations, loggers in the field decide how to cut each tree stem. To persuade the loggers to accept the model, Lembersky and Chi developed a decision simulator called VISION, which operates like a video game. Working with a picture of a tree stem on-screen, the user tries to beat the dynamic program's cutting decisions. As a result, the user gains a better understanding of how to optimize the returns from each tree. VISION was a hit with the loggers. One logger told the authors that if they would install VISION in his favorite tavern, he would pay to play it. After the model gained credibility, the authors used VISION to develop a set of pocket-sized cutting instructions for field use.

IMPLEMENTATION: THE VISION GAME

IMPLEMENTATION: POCKET-SIZED INSTRUCTIONS

[3] Mark Lembersky and Uli H. Chi, "Weyerhaeuser Decision Simulator Improves Profits," *Interfaces*, vol. 16, no. 1, pp. 6–15, 1986.

Senator Millie Merritt is drafting new legislation for pollution control in New Hampshire. The new pollution controls will help keep the state's lakes clean—an important factor in maintaining out-of-state tourism as well as providing an attractive recreational environment for the state's residents. However, Millie also recognizes that if the pollution control regulations are too restrictive, many of the state's manufacturing plants might decide to curtail their plans for expansion. Some of them might even decide to relocate outside the state, where less stringent regulations allow them to operate at lower cost. If this should happen, the state could experience serious increases in its unemployment rate. Millie must, therefore, be very careful in drafting the new regulations: she must avoid optimizing one objective at the expense of another objective. One management tool Millie plans to use to help her solve this problem is goal programming. Goal programming is an extension of linear programming. It allows the problem to be formulated in such a way that multiple goals can be taken into account. In many applications, like Millie's problem, the goals conflict. The goal programming solution as well as its associated sensitivity analysis will provide Millie with a great deal of valuable information. It will help her to draft legislation that will have maximum overall benefit for her constituents. In this chapter, you will learn about this valuable management tool as well as several other important quantitative aids.

13

EXTENSIONS OF LINEAR PROGRAMMING

CHAPTER OBJECTIVES

- DEMONSTRATE WITH INTEGER PROGRAMMING HOW TO COMPUTE SOLUTIONS WHICH REQUIRE WHOLE NUMBER VALUES FOR THE VARIABLES.

- SHOW HOW TO APPLY THE BRANCH-AND-BOUND METHOD OF SEARCHING THE AREA OF FEASIBLE SOLUTIONS.

- INTRODUCE GOAL PROGRAMMING AS A METHOD FOR HANDLING DECISION ENVIRONMENTS WHERE MULTIPLE GOALS OR OBJECTIVES MUST BE SATISFIED.

- INTRODUCE HEURISTICS AND HEURISTIC PROGRAMMING, AND DEMONSTRATE ITS EFFECTIVENESS AS A SOLUTION TECHNIQUE IN SITUATIONS WHERE OTHER MORE FORMAL MS/OR TECHNIQUES WILL NOT WORK.

SOMETIMES
NONINTEGER ANSWERS
DON'T MAKE SENSE

ROUNDING OFF
NONINTEGER ANSWERS
IS NOT ALWAYS
FEASIBLE

1 Integer programming

In many real situations, solutions to linear programming problems make sense only if they have integer (whole number) values. Quantities like $16\frac{2}{3}$ chairs, $78\frac{1}{2}$ tables, or 3.46 railroad cars may be unrealistic. Simply rounding off the linear programming solution to the nearest whole numbers may not produce a feasible solution. Take, for example, the optimal linear programming solution to the expanded Dimensions, Ltd., problem introduced in Chapter 10. In the LPSBA output in Table 10-1 this was given as

$6\frac{2}{3}$ chairs
$16\frac{2}{3}$ bookcases

If you round off these quantities to the nearest integer values, 7 chairs and 17 bookcases, you will violate the time constraints in the assembly and finishing departments. In this chapter, we introduce a technique called *integer programming*. This will allow us to find the optimal *integer* solution to a problem without violating any of the constraints.

THE IDEA OF A CUT

ADDING A NEW
CONSTRAINT
CALLED A CUT

Integer programming is an extension of linear programming; that is, we begin by forgetting the integer requirement and solving the problem with the simplex method introduced in Chapter 9. If the solution we find has all integer values, we have found the optimal *integer* solution. If it does not, we continue by adding a new constraint to the problem. This new constraint, called a *cut*, permits the new feasible region to include *all* the feasible integer solutions for the original constraints, but it does not include the optimal noninteger solution originally found. Look at the expanded Dimensions, Ltd., answer above: $6\frac{2}{3}$ chairs and $16\frac{2}{3}$ bookcases. A cut would permit the new feasible region to include solutions like the three below:

1 6 chairs   16 bookcases
2 5 chairs   16 bookcases
3 6 chairs   15 bookcases

but it would exclude the noninteger solution originally found: $6\frac{2}{3}$ chairs and $16\frac{2}{3}$ bookcases.

WHAT TO DO AFTER
ADDING THE NEW
CONSTRAINT

Once we have added the cut, we solve the revised problem using the simplex method. If we get an integer solution this time, we are finished. If not, we add still another cut and continue until we find an integer solution. Since we never eliminate any feasible integer solutions from consideration, we hope to find the optimal integer solution to the problem sooner or later. There are many different kinds of cuts; we will discuss *Gomory's fractional cut*, which guarantees an optimal solution.

THE CUT SHOWN GRAPHICALLY

WHAT THE CUT LOOKS
LIKE IN THE GRAPHIC
SOLUTION

Look at the simple linear programming problem illustrated in Figure 13-1; there we show the one constraint in the problem, $3X_1 + 6X_2 \leq 16$. The

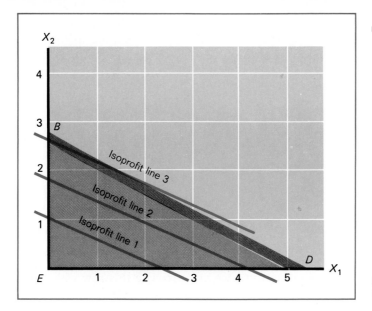

FIGURE 13-1
Original problem.

objective function, $2X_1 + 5X_2$, is such that point B ($X_1 = 0$, $X_2 = 2\frac{2}{3}$) is the optimal noninteger solution. Now look at Figure 13-2; here we have added the cut $X_2 \leq 2$ to the problem. None of the feasible solutions that this cut eliminated, those in the unshaded area ABC, is an integer solution. Therefore the new feasible region, the shaded area $EACD$, still contains *all* the possible integer solutions to the original problem. An examination of the feasible region, $EACD$, shows that the optimal integer solution is point F ($X_1 = 1$, $X_2 = 2$).

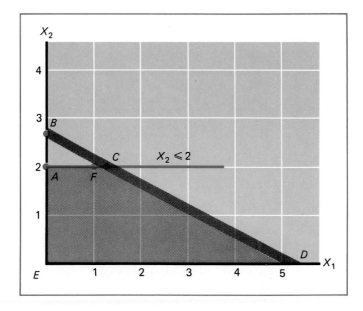

FIGURE 13-2
Cut ($X_2 \leq 2$) added.

THE INTEGER PROGRAMMING ALGORITHM

Let's demonstrate the integer programming algorithm by solving this new Dimensions, Ltd. problem, where the solution must be integer.

Maximize:

$$3T + 5C$$

Subject to:

$$T + 4C \leq 9$$
$$2T + 3C \leq 11$$

$$T, C \geq 0$$

EXPRESSING
NONINTEGER VALUES
AS THE SUM OF AN
INTEGER AND A
FRACTION

Table 13-1 shows the optimal noninteger solution to this problem.

To find the cut, we arbitrarily choose one of the noninteger variables in the optimal solution; we choose C. Look now at the row in the final tableau corresponding to C; we must rewrite this row with any noninteger value in it expressed as the sum of an integer and a nonnegative fraction less than 1. Look at these four examples of numbers similarly rewritten:

1	$\frac{4}{3} =$	$1 + \frac{1}{3}$
2	$\frac{5}{4} =$	$1 + \frac{1}{4}$
3	$\frac{2}{3} =$	$0 + \frac{2}{3}$
4	$-\frac{2}{3} =$	$-1 + \frac{1}{3}$

Repeating the C row, we have

Mix	Quantity	T	C	S_1	S_2
C	$\frac{7}{5}$	0	1	$\frac{2}{5}$	$-\frac{1}{5}$

DERIVATION
OF THE CUT

First we write these values in the C row $(1, \frac{2}{5}, -\frac{1}{5}, \frac{7}{5})$ as the sum of an integer and a nonnegative fraction less than 1:

$$(1 + 0)C + (0 + \tfrac{2}{5})S_1 + (-1 + \tfrac{4}{5})S_2 = (1 + \tfrac{2}{5})$$

TABLE 13-1
Optimal noninteger
solution

C_j			3	5	0	0
	Product mix	**Quantity**	**T**	**C**	**S_1**	**S_2**
5	C	$\frac{7}{5}$	0	1	$\frac{2}{5}$	$-\frac{1}{5}$
3	T	$\frac{17}{5}$	1	0	$-\frac{3}{5}$	$\frac{4}{5}$
	Z_j	$\frac{86}{5}$	3	5	$\frac{1}{5}$	$\frac{7}{5}$
	$C_j - Z_j$		0	0	$-\frac{1}{5}$	$-\frac{7}{5}$

Then we take all the integer coefficients to the right-hand side:

EXTENSIONS OF LINEAR
PROGRAMMING

$$\tfrac{2}{5}S_1 + \tfrac{4}{5}S_2 = \tfrac{2}{5} + (1 - 1C + 1S_2)$$

Now, think of this equation in a slightly different form:

$$\tfrac{2}{5}S_1 + \tfrac{4}{5}S_2 = \tfrac{2}{5} + \text{some integer}$$

If the left side is equal to $\tfrac{2}{5}$ *plus* some integer (0, 1, 2, and so forth), then the left side by itself must be greater than or equal to $\tfrac{2}{5}$. So we can rewrite

$$\tfrac{2}{5}S_1 + \tfrac{4}{5}S_2 \geqslant \tfrac{2}{5}$$

Now if we multiply this by -1, we avoid having to deal with subtracted slack variables (which require an artificial variable):

$$-\tfrac{2}{5}S_1 - \tfrac{4}{5}S_2 \leqslant -\tfrac{2}{5}$$

Adding a slack variable, we get

$$-\tfrac{2}{5}S_1 - \tfrac{4}{5}S_2 + S_3 = -\tfrac{2}{5}$$

This is the required cut. We add it to the simplex tableau in Table 13-1 and get the new simplex tableau shown in Table 13-2. We have a problem in trying to determine which variable to bring into the second solution in Table 13-2, since all $C_j - Z_j$ values are zero or negative. Just to get the solution started, divide the negative values in the S_3 row into the corresponding values in the $C_j - Z_j$ row and bring in that variable which has the smallest quotient:

$$S_3: \quad \frac{-\tfrac{1}{5}}{-\tfrac{2}{5}} = \boxed{\tfrac{1}{2}} \qquad \frac{-\tfrac{7}{5}}{-\tfrac{4}{5}} = \tfrac{7}{4} \qquad$$ (The S_1 column gives the smallest quotient; so S_1 comes in and S_3 goes out.)

From this point on, the procedure is the same as in the simplex method; in this particular problem, we will find the optimal *integer* solution in the next tableau, as shown in Table 13-3. In the Table 13-3 tableau, there are no more positive values in the $C_j - Z_j$ row, and so we know the optimal solution

COMPARING THE
INTEGER AND
NONINTEGER
SOLUTIONS

TABLE 13-2
Solution to the integer
problem (first tableau)

C_j	Product mix	Quantity	3 T	5 C	0 S_1	0 S_2	0 S_3
5	C	$\tfrac{7}{5}$	0	1	$\tfrac{2}{5}$	$-\tfrac{1}{5}$	0
3	T	$\tfrac{17}{5}$	1	0	$-\tfrac{3}{5}$	$\tfrac{4}{5}$	0
0	S_3	$-\tfrac{2}{5}$	0	0	$-\tfrac{2}{5}$	$-\tfrac{4}{5}$	1
	Z_j	$\tfrac{86}{5}$	3	5	$\tfrac{1}{5}$	$\tfrac{7}{5}$	0
	$C_j - Z_j$		0	0	$-\tfrac{1}{5}$	$-\tfrac{7}{5}$	0

C_j	Product mix	Quantity	3 T	5 C	0 S_1	0 S_2	0 S_3
5	C	1	0	1	0	−1	1
3	T	4	1	0	0	2	−3/2
0	S_1	1	0	0	1	2	−5/2
	Z_j	17	3	5	0	1	1/2
	$C_j - Z_j$		0	0	0	−1	−1/2

TABLE 13-3
Final tableau for integer solution

has been reached. It is to manufacture 4 tables and 1 chair; this uses all the hours available except for 1 hour in department 1, since S_1 has the value 1 in the final solution. The profit earned by this optimal integer solution is $17, which is only slightly lower than the $86/5 ($17.20) profit earned by the optimal noninteger solution in Table 13-1.

Although this simple example required only one cut and one simplex iteration to find the optimal integer solution, larger problems may require many cuts and iterations. The general procedure is as follows:

Step 1 Solve the original problem with the simplex algorithm.

Step 2 If the solution has all integer values, it is optimal for the integer program. If not, add a cut obtained from a row which has a noninteger variable in the solution.

Step 3 Pick any solution variable with a negative value to leave the solution. Select the incoming variable as we did in the example on page 625. Do a simplex iteration. If all variables in the new solution are zero or positive, go to step 2; if not, repeat step 3.

2 Branch-and-bound method

Consider the assignment problems we discussed in Chapter 11, where our objective was to assign one job to each machine. Because those have a finite number of possible solutions, it is possible to use *enumeration* as a solution method, that is, to list *all* the possible solutions and pick the one with, for example, the lowest cost. The availability of high-speed computers would lead one to believe that enumeration is a valid solution method even with large problems. However, when you look at the way in which the number of possible solutions increases relative to the size of the problem, you can see that enumeration quickly becomes impossible or at least economically impractical. For example, if there are only eight variables in the problem and each of these has only eight feasible (physically allowable) values, there can be *as many as* 8^8 (= 6,777,216) feasible solutions. Even in a case of this size, using a computer to enumerate all the feasible solutions would be excessively costly and time-consuming.

Jobs	Machines			
	1	2	3	4
A	$90	$ 5	$48	$73
B	69	14	83	86
C	57	93	2	79
D	7	77	75	23

TABLE 13-4
Cost for each job-
machine assignment

For this reason, we shall now introduce you to a technique known as *branch-and-bound*, which, although it uses enumeration, does it so efficiently that only a very small part of the total number of possible solutions need be examined individually. There is quite a large[1] body of literature on this subject and a rapidly increasing number of applications. Although we cannot go into all the nuances and variations of this technique, we can use an assignment problem of the type discussed in Chapter 11 to illustrate how it works.

BRANCH-AND-BOUND
ENUMERATES
EFFICIENTLY

Conceptually, you can think of branching-and-bounding as a method which keeps dividing up the feasible region into smaller and smaller parts until that single solution which either minimizes or maximizes some objective function is determined. (The concept of a feasible region was first developed in Chapter 8, in connection with graphic methods of linear programming.)

BRANCH-AND-BOUND SOLUTION TO AN ASSIGNMENT PROBLEM

In Table 13-4 we have illustrated a job-machine assignment problem like those in Chapter 11. Here we present four jobs that can each be done on any one of four machines together with the cost of doing each job on each machine. Our objective is to use the branch-and-bound technique to generate the least-cost assignment (that assignment which minimizes the total cost of doing all four jobs). We shall demonstrate the solution to the problem in Table 13-4 in four steps.

SOLVING A JOB-
MACHINE ASSIGNMENT
PROBLEM USING
BRANCH-AND-BOUND

Step 1   Out of the 24 possible solutions, first find a lower bound on the total cost of the assignment—that is, a cost point below which cost could never fall. The assignment which produces this lowest cost need not be a feasible one; there can be more than one job assigned to the same machine. The only purpose of this initial lower-bound calculation is to establish a "floor" below which cost cannot fall. In doing this, we are "bounding" cost on the lower side or setting a lower *bound* on total cost.

FIND A LOWER BOUND

The quickest way to establish the lowest possible cost is to add the smallest cost in each of the four columns; when we do this we get 7 + 5 + 2 + 23

---

[1] For a survey of branch-and-bound methods, the reader can see E. L. Lawler and J. D. Wood, "Branch-and-Bound Methods: A Survey," *Operations Research*, vol. 14, pp. 699–719, 1966.

Assignment	Lower bound on total cost
A done on machine 1	$90 + 14 + 2 + 23 = 129$ (feasible solution)
B done on machine 1	$69 + 5 + 2 + 23 = 99$ (feasible solution)
C done on machine 1	$57 + 5 + 48 + 23 = 133$
D done on machine 1	$7 + 5 + 2 + 73 = 87$

$= 37$. Because, in this particular assignment of jobs to machines, job D has been assigned to two machines (1 and 4), this assignment is not a feasible one; we must therefore proceed to find the least-cost feasible solution.

DIVIDING UP THE PROCESS OF LOOKING FOR SOLUTIONS

Step 2   Next, divide up the process of looking for solutions. Suppose we start by assigning each job in turn to machine 1 and observe the result in each of the four cases in Table 13-5. In each calculation in step 2, once we assigned each of the jobs to machine 1 in turn, we then added the smallest cost in each of the remaining three columns (as in step 1) without considering whether doing that would yield a feasible solution. Steps 1 and 2 are expressed in "tree" form in Figure 13-3. The circled value 37 represents the lowest-cost solution obtained in step 1; each of the four solutions obtained in step 2 is shown, and the smallest of these (87) is circled. Because 129 (the lowest-cost solution possible when job A is done on machine 1) is greater than 99, and as 99 is the cost of a known feasible solution, all the other solutions which could be computed when job A is assigned to machine 1 (which we denote by A = 1) are discarded without consideration, as none of them could be lower than 129. The same logic is applied when job C is assigned to machine 1 (denoted C = 1), and all possible solutions which could come from that branch of our tree are discarded. In this manner, the branch-and-bound method evaluates only a very small portion of the total possible alternatives but does not discard one which could be optimal. Specifically, in step 2 we have already avoided the evaluation of almost half the possible alternative assignments.

HALF THE POSSIBLE ASSIGNMENTS HAVE BEEN AVOIDED

Step 3   We next consider the lowest-cost branch on the tree in step 2, where job D is assigned to machine 1. (The fact that this cost of 87 does not represent

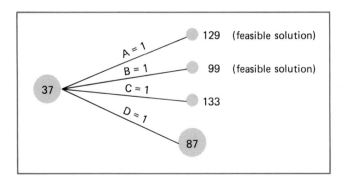

Assignment (when D = 1)	Lower bound on total cost
A done on machine 2	(7) + [5 + 2 + 79] = 93
B done on machine 2	(7) + [14 + 2 + 73] = 96 (feasible solution)
C done on machine 2	(7) + [93 + 48 + 73] = 221

TABLE 13-6
Assigning job D
to machine 1

a feasible assignment does not prevent us from searching for other lower-cost solutions on this branch which may be feasible.) In each calculation in this step (Table 13-6), once we had assigned job D to machine 1, we assigned each of the three remaining jobs to machine 2 in turn and added the smallest cost in each of the remaining two columns without considering whether a feasible solution would result. The one feasible assignment which results from this step and produces a total cost of 96 is D = 1, B = 2, C = 3, and A = 4.

In "tree" form, steps 1, 2, and 3 are shown in Figure 13-4. The circled value 93 represents the lowest-cost solution obtained in this step. Each of the other two solutions obtained in this step is also shown. As 221 (the lowest-cost solution possible when D = 1 and C = 2) is greater than 96 (a feasible solution), all the other solutions which could emanate from the D = 1, C = 2 branch of the tree are discarded without further evaluation. Here again, branch-and-bound illustrates how it evaluates only a portion of solutions yet *does not miss one* which might be optimal.

Step 4 We next consider the lowest-cost branch on the tree in step 3, the case where job D is assigned to machine 1 and job A to machine 2. The fact that the cost of 93 does not represent a feasible assignment does not prevent us from searching for *other* lower-cost solutions on this branch which *may* be feasible. The two possible alternative assignments when D = 1 and A = 2 are shown in Table 13-7.

THE FINAL STEP

In tree form, steps 1, 2, 3, and 4 are illustrated in Figure 13-5.

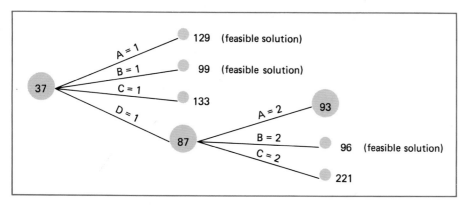

FIGURE 13-4
Steps 1, 2, and 3 of
branch-and-bound
solution.

Assignment, when D = 1 and A = 2	Lower bound on total cost
B done on machine 3; C done on machine 4	(12) + [83 + 79] = 174 (feasible solution)
B done on machine 4; C done on machine 3	(12) + [2 + 86] = 100 (feasible solution)

Because both feasible alternatives found in step 4 offer costs higher than 96 (the cost of a known feasible alternative found in step 3), both those solutions are discarded. The optimal answer to this assignment problem is the $96 feasible solution found in step 3, corresponding to the solution

$$
\begin{array}{rr}
D = 1 & \$\ 7 \\
B = 2 & 14 \\
C = 3 & 2 \\
A = 4 & \underline{73} \\
& \$96
\end{array}
$$

A short recapitulation of the four steps may be useful:

REVIEWING THE FOUR
STEPS IN THE
SOLUTION

Step 1 We established a lower bound on total cost of $37. (This was not a feasible solution, only a beginning point.)

Step 2 We established an upper bound on cost of $99 and a new lower bound of $87. The upper-bound cost of $99 represented a feasible solution, but the new lower bound of $87 did not.

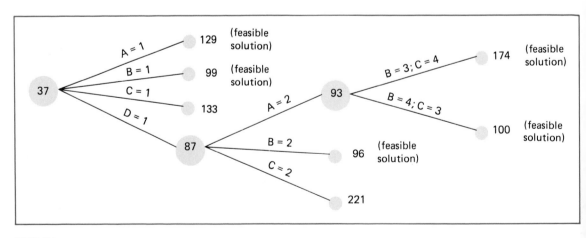

FIGURE 13-5
Steps 1, 2, 3, and 4 of branch-and-bound solution.

Step 3 We established a new upper bound on cost of $96 and a new lower bound of $93. The upper-bound cost of $96 represented a feasible solution, but the new lower bound of $93 did not.

Step 4 We evaluated the two possible solutions from the $93 lower bound in step 3 and found both to generate costs higher than the upper-bound cost of $96 established in step 3. Thus step 4 indicated to us that $96 was both the upper bound and the lower bound; that is, we had continued to partition our feasible region into smaller and smaller areas until only the $96 solution remained.

There are many computer programs which have been developed to apply the many variations of the branch-and-bound technique with considerable computational efficiency. With large computers, it is possible to evaluate quite large and complex problems in just a few minutes by using these programs.

3 Goal programming

Goal programming applies the linear programming model to situations which contain *multiple* goals or objectives. To begin this section, let's look back at the original Dimensions, Ltd., problem first introduced in Chapter 8. The linear programming simplex solution to this problem was presented in Chapter 9, Table 9-11. That solution is repeated here as Table 13-8 for reference. The optimal solution to that problem was to produce 12 tables and 6 chairs for a profit of $132. All hours in assembly and finishing were used.

SOME PROBLEMS HAVE
MULTIPLE GOALS

SHORTCOMINGS OF LINEAR PROGRAMMING

A problem with linear programming is that the objective function is measured in only *one dimension,* profit in this case. It is impossible in linear programming to have *multiple goals* in the objective function (say, profit, productivity, and cost). Organizations generally have *several* goals which usually conflict with each other. Suppose, for instance, that Dimensions, Ltd., has these goals:

SHORTCOMINGS OF
LINEAR PROGRAMMING

1 Maximize profit in dollars.
2 Maximize production of tables in units.
3 Maximize production of chairs in units.

TABLE 13-8
Optimal solution to
Dimensions, Ltd.,
problem

C_j	Product mix	Quantity	8	6	0	0
			T	C	S_A	S_F
8	T	12	1	0	$\frac{1}{3}$	$-\frac{1}{6}$
6	C	6	0	1	$-\frac{1}{6}$	$\frac{1}{3}$
	Z_j	132	8	6	$\frac{5}{3}$	$\frac{2}{3}$
	$C_j - Z_j$		0	0	$-\frac{5}{3}$	$-\frac{2}{3}$

In this case, deviating from the optimal solution of 12 tables and 6 chairs will *reduce* profit from the $132 optimum; thus we see that goals 2 and 3 conflict with goal 1.

MAKING TARGET ESTIMATES AND RANKING GOALS

SETTING TARGETS AND
PUTTING PRIORITIES
ON GOALS

Goal programming asks management to set some estimated targets for each of their goals and to put priorities on them—that is, to rank them in order of importance. Managers who want to use goal programming only have to say which goal they consider more important than another; they do not have to say *how much* more important they consider it.

WHAT GOAL
PROGRAMMING DOES

When this information is supplied by management, goal programming tries to minimize the deviations from the targets that were set. It begins with the most important goal and keeps on until the achievement of a less important goal would cause management to fail to achieve a more important one.

A SINGLE-GOAL MODEL

A SINGLE-GOAL
SITUATION

With only a single goal (say, profit), we could just as easily solve the Dimensions, Ltd., problem using linear programming, but a single-goal model is a good starting point for understanding goal programming. Suppose Dimensions, Ltd., sets its profit goal at $140 in this situation. If we let D_u equal the amount by which the goal is *underachieved* and D_o equal the amount by which the goal is overachieved, we can state the Dimensions, Ltd., problem as a goal programming problem:

Minimize:

$$D_u \qquad \text{Minimize underachievement of the profit target.}$$

OBJECTIVE FUNCTION
AND CONSTRAINTS IN A
SINGLE-GOAL PROBLEM

Subject to:

$$8T + 6C + D_u - D_o = 140$$

The profit obtained, $8T + 6C$, plus any underachievement minus any overachievement has to equal the target.

$$4T + 2C \leq 60 \qquad \text{Assembly constraint}$$
$$2T + 4C \leq 48 \qquad \text{Finishing constraint}$$
$$\text{All variables} \geq 0$$

With the addition of appropriate slack variables, this problem would be ready for solution by the simplex method. The actual answer turns out to be 12 tables and 6 chairs (the same as in the linear programming solution), but the value of the objective function is $8 (the amount by which we underachieved our $140 goal). Of course, we knew that $132 was the maximum profit earnable with these constraints, and so missing $140 by $8 was expected. Notice that in this formulation only D_u is in the objective function; therefore, only one entry will appear in the C_j row above the D_u column. This entry will be 1, representing a dollar of deviation.

EQUALLY RANKED MULTIPLE GOALS

Suppose Dimensions, Ltd., states two equally ranked goals, the first to reach a profit goal of $100, the second to produce to meet a table goal of 10. Since these goals are equally ranked, a $1 deviation from the profit target is just as important (in the goal programming model) as a deviation of 1 table. For this formulation, let's use the following notation:

A MULTIPLE-GOAL
PROBLEM WHERE
ALL GOALS ARE
EQUALLY DESIRED

D_{up} = amount by which the profit goal is underachieved
D_{op} = amount by which the profit goal is overachieved
D_{ut} = amount by which the table goal is underachieved
D_{ot} = amount by which the table goal is overachieved

The objective function and constraints for the solution to this goal programming problem are

Minimize:

$$D_{up} + D_{ut}$$

Subject to:

$$8T + 6C + D_{up} - D_{op} = 100 \quad \text{Profit goal}$$
$$T + D_{ut} - D_{ot} = 10 \quad \text{Tables goal}$$
$$4T + 2C \leq 60 \quad \text{Assembly constraint}$$
$$2T + 4C \leq 48 \quad \text{Finishing constraint}$$
$$\text{All variables} \geq 0$$

OBJECTIVE FUNCTION
AND CONSTRAINTS FOR
A PROBLEM WITH
MULTIPLE EQUALLY
RANKED GOALS

In Table 13-9, we show the initial solution and the optimal solution to this goal programming problem. We notice from the final tableau that our goal

INTERPRETING
THE ANSWER

TABLE 13-9
Initial solution and optimal solution to Dimensions, Ltd., problem with two equally ranked goals

C_j	Product mix	Quantity		0 T	0 C	0 S_A	0 S_F	1 D_{up}	0 D_{op}	1 D_{ut}	0 D_{ot}
1	D_{up}	100		8	6	0	0	1	−1	0	0
1	D_{ut}	10	initial	1	0	0	0	0	0	1	−1
0	S_A	60	solution	4	2	1	0	0	0	0	0
0	S_F	48		2	4	0	1	0	0	0	0
	Z_j	110		9	6	0	0	1	−1	1	−1
	$C_j - Z_j$			−9	−6	0	0	0	1	0	1
0	D_{ot}	2½		0	¾	0	0	⅛	−⅛	−1	1
0	T	12½	optimal	1	¾	0	0	⅛	−⅛	0	0
0	S_A	10	solution	0	−1	1	0	−½	½	0	0
0	S_F	23		0	2½	0	1	−¼	¼	0	0
	Z_j	0		0	0	0	0	0	0	0	0
	$C_j - Z_j$			0	0	0	0	1	0	1	0

633

of 10 tables was achieved and bettered ($12\frac{1}{2} - 10 = 2\frac{1}{2}$); $2\frac{1}{2}$ appears in the final solution as D_{ot} (overachievement of tables). Our profit goal of $100 was reached (both D_{up} and D_{op} are zero because they are not in the final solution, and so profit is exactly $100). Notice the alternative optimal solutions possible by bringing in C or D_{op}.

PRIORITY-RANKED MULTIPLE GOALS

In most cases, one goal is more important to management than another; goal programming can handle this situation too. Suppose Dimensions, Ltd., has established the following goals and has assigned them priorities (P_1, P_2, and P_3, where P_1 is most important) as follows:

Goal	Priority
1. Produce to meet a table goal of 13.	P_1
2. Reach a profit goal of $135.	P_2
3. Produce to meet a chair goal of 5.	P_3

For this formulation, let's use this notation:

D_{up} = amount by which the profit goal is underachieved
D_{op} = amount by which the profit goal is overachieved
D_{ut} = amount by which the table goal is underachieved
D_{ot} = amount by which the table goal is overachieved
D_{uc} = amount by which the chair goal is underachieved
D_{oc} = amount by which the chair goal is overachieved

The objective function and constraints for this version of the Dimensions, Ltd., goal programming problem are

Minimize:

$$P_1 D_{ut} + P_2 D_{up} + P_3 D_{uc}$$

The P's used here are called *preemptive priority factors*. In the goal programming algorithm which follows, we assume that the priority ranking is absolute; that is, P_1 goals are so much more important than P_2 goals that P_2 goals will never be achieved until P_1 goals are.

Subject to:

$$8T + 6C + D_{up} - D_{op} = 135 \quad \text{Profit goal}$$
$$T + D_{ut} - D_{ot} = 13 \quad \text{Tables goal}$$
$$C + D_{uc} - D_{oc} = 5 \quad \text{Chair goal}$$
$$4T + 2C \le 60 \quad \text{Assembly constraint}$$
$$2T + 4C \le 48 \quad \text{Finishing constraint}$$
$$\text{All variables} \ge 0$$

Table 13-10 presents the initial simplex tableau for this problem.

TABLE 13-10
Initial simplex tableau for priority-ranked Dimensions, Ltd., problem

C_j	Product mix	Quantity	0 T	0 C	0 S_A	0 S_F	P_2 D_{up}	0 D_{op}	P_1 D_{ut}	0 D_{ot}	P_3 D_{uc}	0 D_{oc}
P_2	D_{up}	135	8	6	0	0	1	−1	0	0	0	0
P_1	D_{ut}	13	1	0	0	0	0	0	1	−1	0	0
P_3	D_{uc}	5	0	1	0	0	0	0	0	0	1	−1
0	S_A	60	4	2	1	0	0	0	0	0	0	0
0	S_F	48	2	4	0	1	0	0	0	0	0	0
P_3	Z_j		0	1	0	0	0	0	0	0	1	−1
	$C_j - Z_j$		0	−1	0	0	0	0	0	0	0	1
P_2	Z_j		8	6	0	0	1	−1	0	0	0	0
	$C_j - Z_j$		−8	−6	0	0	0	1	0	0	0	0
P_1	Z_j		1	0	0	0	0	0	1	−1	0	0
	$C_j - Z_j$		−1	0	0	0	0	0	0	1	0	0

$\uparrow_{In}$

There are a number of characteristics of this tableau we should explain.

SPECIAL CHARACTERISTICS OF THE GOAL PROGRAMMING TABLEAU WITH RANKED GOALS

1 Notice that there is a separate Z_j and $C_j - Z_j$ row for *each of the* P_1, P_2, and P_3 priorities. Since we do not add deviations from the chair goal, for example, to those from the profit goal (the priorities are different), we need these separate priority rows to keep track of things. It is common practice to illustrate the P rows from *bottom to top* in order of priority.

2 The $C_j - Z_j$ value for any *column* is shown in the priority rows at the bottom of the tableau; for example, the $C_j - Z_j$ value for the T column is contained in the P_2 and P_1 rows at the bottom and is read $-8P_2 - 1P_1$; similarly, the $C_j - Z_j$ value for the C column is read $-1P_3 - 6P_2$.

3 In selecting the variable to enter the mix (T in this case), we start with the most important priority, P_1, and pick the most negative $C_j - Z_j$ value in that row; if there had *not* been a negative $C_j - Z_j$ value in that row, we would have moved up to the next most important priority, P_2, and looked in that row.

4 To determine the variable that is replaced, we use the same procedure we have always used; in this instance, 13/1 is the smallest positive value; therefore the D_{ut} row will be replaced in the next tableau.

5 If we find a negative $C_j - Z_j$ value that has a *positive* $C_j - Z_j$ value in one of the P rows *underneath* it, we disregard it. Such a positive value would mean that deviations from the lower (and more important) goal would be *increased* if we brought in that variable, and this is avoided since it won't lead us to a better solution.

635

636

CHAPTER 13

PROCEEDING TOWARD
THE OPTIMAL
SOLUTION

INTERPRETING THE
FINAL SOLUTION

Once the initial simplex tableau is set up, we proceed just as we have done in the simplex method, keeping in mind the five characteristics just discussed. The final simplex tableau for this problem is shown in Table 13-11. Notice there that we will have negative $C_j - Z_j$ values in both the P_2 and P_3 rows (-4 and -2, respectively). However, in both cases there is a positive value in the P_1 row beneath them (1), and so we disregard both of them.

We notice from the final solution in Table 13-11 that the goals have been met to different extents. Our most important goal (produce 13 tables) was achieved. Our second most important goal (reach $135 profit) was missed (we generated only $128 profit); the deviation, however, was slight, something on the order of 5 percent (notice that this deviation shows up as D_{up} in the final solution). Our lowest-ranked goal (produce 5 chairs) was missed by 1 chair; however, this represents a 20 percent deviation. Notice here too that the deviation shows up in the final solution as D_{uc} with a value of 1. Finally, notice that there are 6 hours unused in finishing. Whereas it might seem that these should have been used, remember that to manufacture another chair, for example, would also have required time in assembly, where all the time has been used.

4 Heuristics

Heuristic programming is a technique used to find *quick and dirty* solutions to problems. Heuristics are also used in conjunction with other techniques such as linear programming and branch-and-bound methods in order to speed up the process of finding an optimal solution. A heuristic is nothing more than a decision rule based upon either your intuition or some empirical evidence which leads you to believe that some particular decision generally is a good one to follow. In contrast to an algorithm such as the simplex

TABLE 13-11
Final solution for priority-ranked Dimensions, Ltd., problem

C_j	Product mix	Quantity	0 T	0 C	0 S_A	0 S_F	P_2 D_{up}	0 D_{op}	P_1 D_{ut}	0 D_{ot}	P_3 D_{uc}	0 D_{oc}
P_2	D_{up}	7	0	0	-3	0	1	-1	4	-4	0	0
0	T	13	1	0	0	0	0	0	1	-1	0	0
P_3	D_{uc}	1	0	0	$-\frac{1}{2}$	0	0	0	2	-2	1	-1
0	C	4	0	1	$\frac{1}{2}$	0	0	0	-2	2	0	0
0	S_F	6	0	0	-2	1	0	0	6	-6	0	0
P_3	Z_j		0	0	$-\frac{1}{2}$	0	0	0	2	-2	1	-1
	$C_j - Z_j$		0	0	$\frac{1}{2}$	0	0	0	⟨-2⟩	2	0	1
P_2	Z_j		0	0	-3	0	1	-1	4	-4	0	0
	$C_j - Z_j$		0	0	3	0	0	1	⟨-4⟩	4	0	0
P_1	Z_j		0	0	0	0	0	0	0	0	0	0
	$C_j - Z_j$		0	0	0	0	0	0	⟨1⟩	0	0	0

method, which produces an optimal, or *exact*, solution, heuristic programming
cannot guarantee optimality. Good heuristics often do yield optimal solutions,
but in some cases the best we can hope for is a solution that is just close to
being optimal. Consequently, heuristic solutions are called *approximate* or *near-
optimal*.

Heuristics are used extensively in practice to develop solutions to management problems. It may seem strange to you that managers are satisfied with
a near-optimal solution when they could, with more effort, get the best
solution possible by using an exact algorithm. There are many reasons for
this. First, heuristics require substantially less time to solve either by computer
or by hand. Second, in many cases the problem to be solved is not well-
defined. Cost and profit inputs may not be known with certainty. Similarly,
the constraints to the problem may be considered only estimates. Within such
an environment, the manager can easily view a heuristic solution as being
more cost-effective. The third reason for using heuristics is that they tend to
be more flexible than exact algorithms, which are fairly restrictive in terms
of both their assumptions and the types of constraints they can handle. Many
constraints are matters of organizational policy, union agreements, or other
factors both internal and external. Such constraints may be difficult, or
perhaps impossible, to quantify. The fourth, and perhaps most important,
reason for using heuristics is that they can be more responsive to change.
Managers function within a dynamic environment. New orders for finished
goods are continuously being placed while some existing orders are canceled.
Prices, costs, and interest rates change; machines break down; workers call
in sick; shipments of raw materials are delayed. Exact algorithms, because of
their static nature, lose some of their effectiveness within such an environment.
Heuristics, on the other hand, can often be formulated to adapt more easily
to these changes.

FOUR REASONS FOR
USING HEURISTICS

▐ USES OF HEURISTICS IN CONJUNCTION
WITH EXACT ALGORITHMS

Heuristics are used quite extensively to enable exact algorithms to work more
efficiently. Consider, for example, the simplex algorithm of linear programming. As you recall, that algorithm uses an iterative scheme in which each
iteration involves the introduction of one new variable into the product mix
while one old one is removed. If you recall the simplex step that is followed
in order to decide which new variable is brought into the mix (described in
Chapter 9), you will remember that step 1 of the simplex procedure tells you
that you should select this new variable according to which of them adds the
most profit per unit for a maximization problem (largest $C_j - Z_j$ value). For
a problem whose objective function is to minimize cost, step 1 tells you to
select the variable that reduces cost per unit by the largest amount; this is
identified by the largest negative value in the $C_j - Z_j$ row. We further defined
the column associated with this largest value in the $C_j - Z_j$ row as being the
optimal column.

HEURISTICS CAN
IMPROVE OTHER
ALGORITHMS

USE OF HEURISTICS
IN THE SIMPLEX
PROCEDURE

The term *optimal column* is somewhat deceptive because ideally we would
like to pick new variables in such a way that we could arrive at the optimal
solution in the least number of iterations. The simplex method does guarantee

A GREEDY HEURISTIC

that we will eventually arrive at an optimal solution, but unfortunately it makes no guarantee that we can do so using the least number of iterations. It is not unusual for the simplex method to introduce a new variable into the product mix at some iteration and then later on replace it by yet another new variable. Consequently, step 1 of the simplex procedure is really a heuristic, and more specifically, since it always picks the largest $C_j - Z_j$ value, it is commonly called a *greedy heuristic*.

Greedy heuristics are relatively popular in practical applications because they are simple to use. Sometimes they are quite effective in producing solutions which are consistently near-optimal. In many applications, however, they are inconsistent, and other more effective heuristics may be applied. Let us now consider the use of some heuristics in solving a transportation problem.

USING HEURISTICS IN SOLVING THE TRANSPORTATION PROBLEM

Let's assume we have the transportation problem given in Figure 13-6 for Ajax Shipping. The optimal solution to this problem is shown in Figure 13-7, and its cost is given in Table 13-12. When we learned how to solve a transportation problem using the techniques given in Chapter 11, we started out by developing an initial solution using the northwest corner rule. The northwest corner rule is a heuristic; its major advantage is that it is systematic and very easy to apply. Its disadvantage, however, is that it is not sensitive to costs.

CAN HEURISTICS DO BETTER THAN THE NORTHWEST CORNER SOLUTION?

If you take a minute to examine the optimal solution in Figure 13-7, you will readily see that since our objective is to minimize total cost, there is a tendency to avoid shipping from W to A, or Y to C, where the per unit costs are quite high, $9 per unit. Similarly, the routes W to B, and X to B, which also are relatively high ($8 per unit), are avoided. Now compare the optimal solution in Figure 13-7 with the northwest corner solution given in Figure

From \ To	A	B	C	Plant capacity
W	9	8	5	25
X	6	8	4	35
Y	7	6	9	40
Project requirements	30	25	45	100 / 100

FIGURE 13-6
Transportation tableau for Ajax Shipping.

From / To	A	B	C	Plant capacity
W	9	8	5 25	25
X	6 15	8	4 20	35
Y	7 15	6 25	9	40
Project requirements	30	25	45	100 / 100

FIGURE 13-7
Optimal solution
for Ajax Shipping.

13-8. The corresponding costs of these two solutions are given in Tables 13-12 and 13-13.

Suppose we start with our northwest corner solution, and using either the stepping-stone method or MODI, we solve for the optimum. We will find that it is necessary to develop four additional tableaus before finding the optimum. Perhaps if we used some heuristic other than the northwest corner rule, we could start out with a lower-total-cost initial solution and thus reduce the number of tableaus required to find the optimal solution. Let's try a greedy heuristic and see what happens.

A FIRST SOLUTION

With the greedy heuristic we begin by identifying the square with the lowest possible cost per unit, and we assign as many units to it as we can. The lowest cost of $4 per unit is in square XC, and we can assign at most 35 units, which is all plant X can supply. Figure 13-9 illustrates our first allocation of 35 units to square XC. The row for plant X is shaded in order to remind us that plant X now has its entire capacity of 35 units already allocated.

TABLE 13-12
Total cost of
optimal solution

Shipping asignments	Quantity shipped	×	Unit cost	=	Total cost
WC	25		5		$125
XA	15		6		90
XC	20		4		80
YA	15		7		105
YB	25		6		150
		Total transportation cost			$550

From \ To	A	B	C	Plant capacity
W	9 25	8	5	25
X	6 5	8 25	4 5	35
Y	7	6	9 40	40
Project requirements	30	25	45 100	100

FIGURE 13-8
Northwest corner solution for Ajax Shipping.

TABLE 13-13
Total cost of northwest corner solution

Shipping assignments	Quantity shipped	×	Unit cost	=	Total cost
WA	25		9		$225
XA	5		6		30
XB	25		8		200
XC	5		4		20
YC	40		9		360
			Total transportation cost		$835

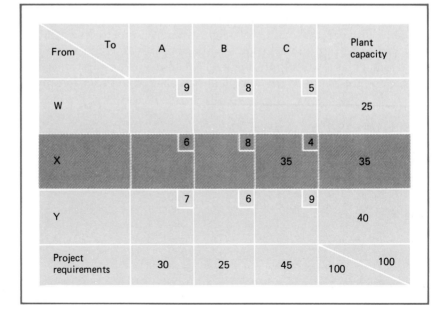

FIGURE 13-9
First allocation using the greedy heuristic.

From \ To	A	B	C	Plant capacity
W	9	8	5 / 10	25
X	6	8	4 / 35	35
Y	7	6	9	40
Project requirements	30	25	45	100 / 100

FIGURE 13-10
Second allocation using the greedy heuristic.

Therefore, we will ignore any shaded square as we look for the square with the next-lowest cost per unit. We find that square WC, with a cost of $5 per unit, is now the lowest, and since C is already receiving 35 units from X, the most we can ship from W to C is 10 units, thus fulfilling C's requirements.

We are now at the partial solution given in Figure 13-10, where we find that the unshaded square with the lowest cost is square YB, with a cost of $6 per unit. After allocating the maximum of 25 units to YB, we now find ourselves at the partial solution given in Figure 13-11. As you can see, we

From \ To	A	B	C	Plant capacity
W	9	8	5 / 10	25
X	6	8	4 / 35	35
Y	7	6 / 25	9	40
Project requirements	30	25	45	100 / 100

FIGURE 13-11
Third allocation using the greedy heuristic.

To From	A	B	C	Plant capacity
W	9 15	8	5 10	25
X	6	8	4 35	35
Y	7 15	6 25	9	40
Project requirements	30	25	45	100 100

FIGURE 13-12
Final allocation using
the greedy heuristic.

are effectively finished developing our greedy solution. The only squares left unshaded are WA and YA, and in order to satisfy the rim requirements, we must allocate 15 units to WA and 15 units to YA. Our completed greedy solution is shown in Figure 13-12, and its associated cost is given in Table 13-14.

COMPARING OUR GREEDY HEURISTIC WITH THE NORTHWEST CORNER SOLUTION

In comparing the greedy solution of $580 with the $835 obtained by the northwest corner rule, we find a substantial improvement in cost. Consequently, if we use the greedy solution as an initial tableau and proceed to solve for the optimum, we expect to use fewer iterations to find the optimum. Indeed, this is the case for our sample problem; the optimum is only one iteration removed from the greedy solution, whereas we needed to develop four iterations when we used the northwest corner solution as our starting point.

SHORTCOMING OF THE GREEDY HEURISTIC

The major shortcoming of a greedy heuristic is that it is myopic; it is unable to look beyond a single target. We can get around this deficiency to some extent by using another heuristic that responds to more cost information.

TABLE 13-14
Total cost of the
greedy solution

Shipping assignments	Quantity shipped	×	Unit cost	=	Total cost
WA	15		9		$135
WC	10		5		50
XC	35		4		140
YA	15		7		105
YB	25		6		150
			Total transportation cost		$580

This heuristic, known as the Vogel approximation method, or VAM, is based upon the concept of minimizing *opportunity costs*. For our transportation problem, the opportunity cost for a given supply row or demand column is defined as the *difference* between the lowest-cost and second-lowest-cost alternative. In other words, if we fail for some reason to achieve the lowest cost, by how much will costs increase if we take the second-best alternative? The steps to the VAM are as follows:

Step 1 For each row and column select the lowest- and second-lowest-cost alternatives from among those not already allocated. The difference between these two costs will be the opportunity cost for the row or column.

Step 2 Scan these opportunity-cost figures, and identify the row or column with the *largest* opportunity cost.

Step 3 Allocate as many units as possible to this row or column in the square having the *least* cost.

Let's illustrate VAM by developing a solution to the Ajax Shipping problem given in Figure 13-6. The calculations for step 1 are shown in Table 13-15. We observe from that table that the largest opportunity cost is associated with plant W. In other words, we would like to ship from W as many units as we can to its lowest-cost project, project C, at only $5 per unit. If for some reason, we do not ship to C, the next-best alternative is to ship to project B at $8 per unit, thus incurring an increase in cost of $3 per unit. Since plant W's opportunity cost is higher than that of any other row or column, we will in step 2 select plant W for our first allocation. According to step 3, this allocation will be to W's least-cost alternative, which is $5 per unit in column C. This allocation is shown in Figure 13-13, where we allocate 25 units to square WC.

As we return again to step 1 of VAM for the second allocation, keep in mind that plant W's capacity has now been reached, so when we recompute opportunity costs, we will ignore any cost in row W. Table 13-16 shows the opportunity-cost calculations for the second allocation. Here we find that the largest opportunity cost is now with project C, at $5 per unit. Therefore the second allocation will be in the lowest-cost available square in column C, which is square XC at $4 per unit. The maximum allocation to XC is 20 units, as shown in Figure 13-14.

TABLE 13-15
Opportunity costs for the first allocation

Row or column	Second-lowest cost	_	Lowest cost	=	Opportunity cost
Row W	8		5		3 ← Largest
Row X	6		4		2
Row Y	7		6		1
Column A	7		6		1
Column B	8		6		2
Column C	5		4		1

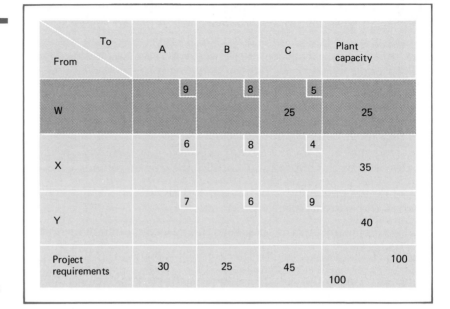

FIGURE 13-13
First allocation using
the VAM heuristic.

TABLE 13-16
Opportunity costs for
the second allocation

Row or column	Second-lowest cost	−	Lowest cost	=	Opportunity cost
Row X	6		4		2
Row Y	7		6		1
Column A	7		6		1
Column B	8		6		2
Column C	9		4		5 ← Largest

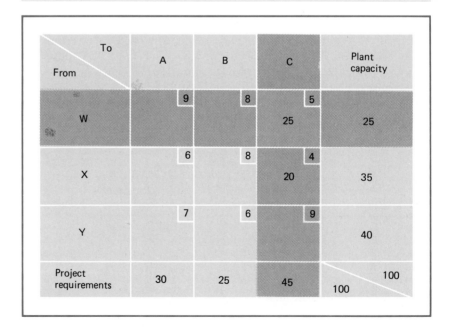

FIGURE 13-14
Second allocation
using the VAM
heuristic.

Row or Column	Second-lowest cost	−	Lowest cost	=	Opportunity cost
Row X	8		6		2 ← Largest
Row Y	7		6		1
Column A	7		6		1
Column B	8		6		2 ← Largest

TABLE 13-17
Opportunity costs for
the third allocation

THE THIRD ALLOCATION

The opportunity-cost calculations for the third allocation are shown in Table 13-17. We now find that we have a tie for largest opportunity cost between row X and column B, both at $2 per unit. Ordinarily we would break the tie by selecting the one having the lesser cost in the lowest-cost column of Table 13-17. But since X's lowest cost of $6 per unit is still tied with B's lowest cost, also $6, we must seek another way to break the tie. Let's attempt to do this by identifying which of the two—row X or column B—can allocate the larger number of units. If we were to select row X for allocation, we would allocate to its least-cost column, which is column A, a total of 15 units. On the other hand, if we were to select column B for allocation, we would allocate to its least-cost row, which is row Y, a total of 25 units. Let's be greedy and bias our choice to column B, thus allocating 25 units to square YB. Figure 13-15 shows this as the third allocation. We now find that we have only one project whose requirements are not fully allocated. This is project A. So we allocate to column A the remaining capacity of plant X, 15 units, and the remaining capacity of plant Y, also 15 units. The completed VAM solution is identical to the solution we originally identified as being optimal and is shown in Figure 13-7 on page 639 and Table 13-12 on page

THE COMPLETED
VAM SOLUTION

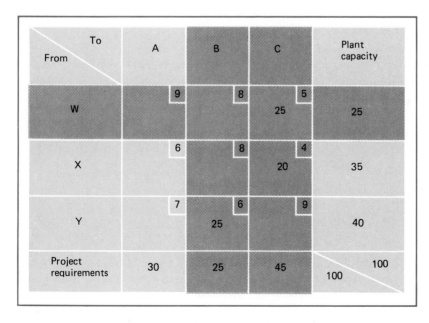

FIGURE 13-15
Third allocation using
the VAM heuristic.

639. The VAM heuristic, of course, does not always produce an optimal solution, but it does consistently find a starting solution that is close to the optimum.

■ USE OF HEURISTIC PROGRAMMING AS AN INDEPENDENT SOLUTION METHODOLOGY

As we previously mentioned, managers often make decisions based upon information that is developed exclusively by heuristics. These heuristic procedures are an integral part of the software included in many decision support systems in use today. In many cases involving day-to-day routine activities, the heuristics are used to issue directives such as the sequence for producing finished products and the quantities to be produced. Heuristics are used to develop daily machine and personnel work schedules, and they are used to track raw material and finished goods inventory levels. When new raw materials need to be ordered, heuristics are used to project future requirements and to place orders for sufficient quantities to satisfy the manufacturing schedules. One of the major advantages of these heuristics is that they are not limited to any standardized approach. They may be formulated according to the specific needs of the organization using them, and they are limited only by the imagination and intuition of its management.

Another interesting example of heuristics, one involving office layout, is given in Chapter 15.

5 Glossary

Branch-and-bound An efficient enumeration method for finding the optimal solution to certain types of combinatorial problems.

Cut A new constraint added to a linear programming problem as a step in producing the optimal integer solution.

Goal programming A variation of the simplex algorithm which permits the decision maker to specify multiple objectives and to target goals in order of their priorities.

Heuristic A rule of thumb that works.

Heuristic program A set of heuristics which together solve a problem.

Integer programming A mathematical programming method which generates optimal integer answers to a linear program.

VAM (Vogel approximation method) A heuristic which produces very good starting solutions for the transportation problem.

6 Exercises

13-1 Table 13-1 gives an optimal solution to a linear programming problem in which the basic variables C and T are both nonintegers. We illustrated the procedure for making a cut to produce an integer solution by arbitrarily choosing the noninteger variable C. Perform the same steps, but instead of choosing C, choose T, and develop the new cut constraint equation. Compare your results with those obtained when the cut constraint was based on the selection of C.

13-2 Table 13-9 presents an optimal solution to a goal programming problem with two equally ranked goals—achieve a $100 profit and produce 10 tables. The optimal tableau indicates that both goals are met or exceeded, but neither of the two constraints is used to full capacity. $S_A = 10$ indicates 10 unused hours in the assembly constraint, and $S_F = 23$ indicates 23 unused hours in the finishing constraint. This might suggest that an alternative optimal solution to the one given in Table 13-9 might be something to consider. Introduce the variable D_{op} and pivot to the alternative optimal solution where the profit goal is exceeded. Interpret your results.

13-3 Develop heuristic solutions to the assignment problem given in Exercise 11-11. Use both the greedy heuristic and the VAM heuristic to develop the solutions. Compare these solutions to the optimal solution you obtained using the assignment method.

13-4 The Electric Car Company, Inc., manufactures three vehicles, the Scooter, the Metro, and the Delivery Special. The contributions to profit are $270, $300, and $450, respectively. The battery requirements for each vehicle are as follows: Scooter, 1; Metro, 3; Delivery Special, 4. The charging generators installed on the vehicle are needed in these quantities: Scooter, 2; Metro, 3; Delivery Special, 5. If the Electric Car Company has 100 batteries and 127 generators on hand and no chance to get any more this week, what should the integer product mix be to maximize profit?

13-5 Park Lane, Ltd., is a custom coachbuilder specializing in two types of coachwork: limousine conversion L and hearses H. The contribution to profit from each of the two products is $6,000 and $4,000, respectively. The limitations on Park Lane are strictly labor, since each product is essentially handmade. The production manager has offered these constraints representing time allocations and labor hours available during the next production scheduling period (13 weeks):

$$40L + 42H \leq 105,300 \qquad \text{Bodywork}$$
$$26L + 32H \leq 92,400 \qquad \text{Interior}$$
$$L, H \geq 0$$

Find the integer solution which will maximize Park Lane's profit for the next scheduling period.

13-6 Curt McLaughlin is an electrical contractor who has just landed the wiring contract for the new Durham Public Library. He has to decide shortly whether to hire one or more apprentice electricians (for 8 hours a day each) or to hire one or more part-time journeyman electricians (for 5 hours a day each). Apprentices can be hired for $8 an hour, while part-time journeyman electricians earn a union scale of $18 an hour. Curt wants to limit his extra payroll to $500 a day and to use no more than 16 hours of extra time a day because of limited supervision. He estimates that an apprentice will generate an extra $5 a day in profits, and a part-time journeyman electrician $9 a day. Formulate an integer programming problem to help Curt select the optimal number of apprentices and part-time journeymen. Solve the problem using cuts.

13-7 Imperial Clocks, Inc., is a subcontractor making clock faces for a clock manufacturer. The amount of brass required, the storage space used (to protect the delicate handworked face), the production rates for each face, and the contribution to profit from each clock face are as follows:

	Grandfather	Mantle	Wall	Chime
Pounds of brass per face	5	5	3.75	6.25
Square feet of storage per face	5	6.25	5	3.75
Faces per hour	3.75	7.5	2.5	3.75
Profit per face (dollars)	5.00	6.50	5.00	5.50

Imperial gets a daily allocation of 300 pounds of brass. The company has a total square footage of storage space of 375 for faces, and the plant operates 8 hours a day. All faces produced each day are shipped at the end of the day; this means storage space, material, and production time are shared by all faces. If Imperial must produce integer quantities of faces, find the optimal mix.

13-8 Here is the final simplex tableau for a product-mix maximizing problem:

c_j	Product mix	Quantity	6 X_1	14 X_2	0 S_1	0 S_2
0	S_1	10	2	0	1	$-2/3$
14	X_2	3.5	$1/2$	1	0	$1/12$
	Z_j	49	7	14	0	$7/6$
	$C_j - Z_j$		-1	0	0	$-7/6$

Find the integer programming solution to this problem.

13-9 Below is the final simplex tableau for a product-mix maximizing program:

c_j	Product mix	Quantity	1 X_1	1 X_2	0 S_1	0 S_2
1	X_1	$6^1/_3$	1	$4/_3$	$1/_6$	0
0	S_2	5	0	4	-1	1
	Z_j	$6^1/_3$	1	$4/_3$	$1/_6$	1
	$C_j - Z_j$		0	$-1/_3$	$-1/_6$	0

Find the integer programming solution to this problem.

13-10 Here is a schedule of annual shipping costs for a group of marble quarries and associated monument plants in Tennessee, all owned by the same corporation. Each quarry must supply one plant. Your task is to find an assignment of quarries to plants which will minimize the total shipping cost per year. Use branch-and-bound.

Plants	Quarries (cost in thousands of dollars)			
	Linwood	Sherrard	Johnsonville	Arlington
Tammerville	11	35	44	24
Kingstown	27	20	55	66
Carrboro	43	35	59	32
Roseboro	27	32	44	41

13-11 William Sherrard's Auto-Quick does repairs on foreign cars. William has five mechanics, each of whom specializes in two makes of car but all of whom can work on many makes. When he came in this morning, William saw five cars in the service line with repair orders written up. Interestingly, all five were in the shop today for a valve-grinding job. William thought a minute about the respective abilities of his mechanics on each make and wrote down these figures:

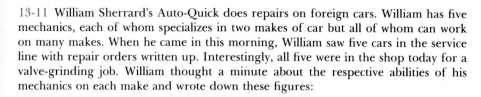

	Ham	Lacy	Bill	Art	Tuller
Volvo	8	7	6	9	11
Mazda	6	9	9	10	9
Fiat	5	7	6	8	6
Saab	8	9	11	6	7
Datsun	9	8	5	5	10

Use the branch-and-bound method to help William assign the five cars to the five mechanics so that the total time for all valve jobs is minimized.

13-12 Fallwell Manufacturing has firm orders to deliver 1,000 of its model X-79 electric motors and 1,500 model X-85 electric motors in the following month. Each X-79 motor requires 6 worker-hours of manufacturing time, while an X-85 motor requires 7.5 worker-hours of manufacturing time. In the coming month, the company has available 12,000 worker-hours of manufacturing time if the work is scheduled on regular time. If overtime is scheduled, another 3,000 worker-hours of time can be made available. Other options to the company are subcontracting, or hiring temporary labor. If these options are selected, inexperienced personnel are used, and 7.5 and 9.5 worker-hours, respectively, are required to produce the two products. The company estimates that at most 2,500 worker-hours of temporary labor can be made available, while there is no limit to the availability of subcontracting worker-hours. The company will incur loss of goodwill if the demands are not met, whereas overproduction could result in inventory holding costs. They would like to solve this problem using goal programming. Their goals are as follows:

1 Avoiding loss of goodwill (twice as important as the other goals).

2 Avoiding overproduction.

3 Maintaining a target manufacturing cost of $250,000.

The costs for the various alternatives are:

	Regular time	Overtime	Temporary	Sub-contracting
Cost per worker-hour	$15	$23	$14	$22

Formulate the problem as a goal programming problem so the company can determine its best manufacturing strategy.

13-13 Harold Coleman has been allocated four locations at the Iowa State Fair. He plans to use the locations for his four game and concession stands—ring toss, basketball shooting, target shooting, and cotton candy. In recent years, he has rotated the location of these stands and has received average profits (in thousands of dollars) as follows:

	Location			
Stand	**East**	**West**	**North**	**South**
Ring toss	9	6	12	9
Basketball	8	8	11	9
Target	10	12	14	12
Cotton Candy	11	10	12	11

Use the branch-and-bound method to determine which of the four game/concession stands to locate in each area so that his profits will be maximized. In a maximization problem, the roles of the upper and lower bounds are reversed from those of a minimization problem.

13-14 Sentimental Lighting, Inc., produces three styles of old-fashioned but currently popular lamps: a desk lamp, a bedside lamp, and a floor lamp. The lamps are all solid brass and are produced in two distinct steps: turning and finishing. The schedule for labor and material inputs and availability for each style is as follows:

	Desk lamp	Bedside lamp	Floor lamp	Availability
Turning labor	1 hr	3 hr	1.5 hr	2,000/mo
Finishing labor	1.5 hr	1.5 hr	4 hr	1,000/mo
Brass	4 lb	3 lb	6 lb	3,000/mo

Contribution to profit for the styles is $35, $40, and $65, respectively. Sentimental has two equally desirable goals: minimizing the idle time in finishing and making a monthly profit of $20,000. Set up the problem as a goal program, and if you have access to a computer, solve it using linear programming.

13-15 Develop heuristic solutions for the transportation problem given in Exercise 11-5. Use the greedy heuristic for one solution and the Vogel approximation method for another. Compare your heuristic solutions with the optimal solution you obtained for this problem.

13-16 Frances Sutton is planning a bus tour for the Detroit Senior Citizens Club. She can schedule stops at any of the following locations on the tour, which are listed along with their overnight costs:

Stop	Cost
Allenwood	$3600
Bristol	3400
Cedarwood	3800
Dryden	4000
Eustis	3200
Farnsworth	3900
Gardenville	4100
Harrow	3900

In planning the tour, she has established the following goals listed in order of priority from highest to lowest.

1 Stop at 5 or more locations.

2 Keep total cost at or below $19,000.

3 Include Dryden on the tour.

Formulate the goal programming problem and set up the initial tableau.

13-17 For the assignment problem given in Exercise 13-11, develop a heuristic solution using the Vogel approximation method. Compare your heuristic solution with the optimal solution which you obtained using the branch-and-bound method.

13-18 Marcel Robbins is a contractor who currently has five homes under construction in Orange County. Marcel's usual practice is to visit every jobsite once or twice a day to check the progress of the work. He finds himself driving a longer distance than he thinks he should and, over a cup of coffee, has put down these mileages from job to job:

	Marcel's office	Jones job	Whitney job	Parrish job	Hamlin job	Stuart job
Marcel's office	0	4	3	6	2	1
Jones job	2	0	7	3	8	3
Whitney job	5	2	0	1	3	1
Parrish job	3	6	2	0	4	5
Hamlin job	8	6	3	2	0	4
Stuart job	6	2	2	2	5	0

Using the branch-and-bound method, can you find the shortest way for Marcel to leave his office, visit each job, and finish up at his office?

13-19 Use the VAM heuristic to find an initial solution for the maximization transportation problem given in Exercise 11-10. Compare your solution to the optimal solution.

13-20 Pat Penland has just purchased the boat building firm of Elliot and Smith from the families who had run it for 70 years. She got quite a deal on the sale (low price, high leverage, and so forth) but had to agree to these conditions: (1) she has to manufacture a total of at least four boats this year, (2) she has to use up the stock of lumber that is on hand, (3) she has to keep the boat finishing crew busy at least half the time, and (4) she must show a profit of at least $10,000 in a year or the families will foreclose. The Elliot and Smith families insist that Pat achieve these goals in the order they appear here: 1, 2, 3, 4. Here is a table of the boats she can make, with lumber requirements, contribution, and resource availability:

	28-ft Sport Fisherman	36-ft Twin Cabin Cruiser	42-ft Flying Bridge	Availability
Assembly labor	1,800 hr	2,300 hr	3,000 hr	8,000 hr
Finishing labor	900 hr	1,150 hr	1,300 hr	4,000 hr
Lumber	5,000 bd ft	8,000 bd ft	9,500 bd ft	19,000 bd ft
Profit	$3,000	$5,000	$6,000	

Set up the initial goal programming tableau to solve this problem.

13-21 Using a greedy heuristic, develop six heuristic solutions to the problem given in Exercise 13-18. For the first solution, start at Marcel's office and travel to the closest job. Then go to the next-closest unvisited job. Continue this until all jobs are visited, and then return to Marcel's office. Repeat this procedure for five other solutions; in each case start the procedure at a different jobsite and complete the tour back to that site. Compare your solutions with the optimal branch-and-bound solution.

13-22 Management for the Progressive Company have established their goals for the production of art prints. Their goals, in order of importance, are as follows:

1 Achieving a profit of $300,000 per month.

2 Producing at least 1,500 Degas prints per month.

3 Utilizing their labor force to the fullest extent possible.

There are 60,000 worker-hours of labor available per month to produce the company's three products: Monet, Renoir, and Degas prints. The profits per print as well as the worker-hours of labor required for each are as follows:

Print	Profit, $/unit	Labor, worker-hr/unit
Monet	26	6.1
Renoir	22	5.2
Degas	28	5.3

Formulate this problem as a goal programming problem, and set up the initial tableau.

13-23 Use the VAM heuristic to find an initial solution to the maximization assignment problem given in Exercise 11-16. Compare your solution to the optimal solution.

13-24 The Northern Bank of Brazil was formed by the Brazilian government to promote agricultural development in the northeast region. The government owns 51 percent of the bank, and private investors own the other 49 percent. The private investors have put up their money with the agreement that the bank will strive to distribute earnings of 1 million cruzeiros to them annually. The combined level of available lending by government and private sources totals 300 million cruzeiros annually. Loans may be made for agricultural development. These loans result in a loss of 2 percent of the amount loaned per year. The bank can also make commercial loans which produce earnings of 8 percent of the amount loaned per year. In addition to the goal of distributing annual earnings to the private owners, the bank hopes to lend out at least 150 million cruzeiros per year in agricultural loans. These two goals have equal priority. Using goal programming, determine if these goals can both be satisfied.

13-25 The Pittsfield Paint Company produces blue, white, red, and black paint in batches using a large vat to mix all the necessary ingredients and pigments. The paint is produced in continuous cycles. One such cycle might be blue, white, red, black, and then back to blue again. Another cycle might be blue, black, red, white, and blue. When going from one color to another in the cycle, the vat must be cleaned, but the time it takes to do the cleaning for a given color depends on which color paint preceded it. The following table gives the required cleaning times in hours.

Predecessor	Follower			
	Blue	**White**	**Red**	**Black**
Blue	—	9	6	3
White	1	—	1	1
Red	3	10	—	2
Black	4	14	6	—

Use the branch-and-bound method to determine the sequence of colors in a cycle such that total cleaning time is minimized. You may start with blue and then find the optimal ordering of colors returning back to blue.

13-26 The Danbury Company has 2 flexible machines on which they need to schedule a total of 6 jobs starting tomorrow. Each of the machines will be configured, prior to the start of production, with certain tool fixtures so that it can process, at most, only 3 of the jobs. Consequently, 3 of the 6 jobs will be scheduled on one machine while the other 3 jobs will be processed on the other. The company plans to start production at 8:00 A.M. and wants all 6 jobs to be completed as soon thereafter as possible so they can all be shipped together to the Lincoln Construction Company. The required process times for the 6 jobs on either machine, in hours, are as follows:

Machine	Jobs					
	1	**2**	**3**	**4**	**5**	**6**
A	12	13	15	10	16	17
B	9	8	10	9	10	19

Solve the problem using the branch-and-bound method.

7 Chapter Concepts Quiz

13-1 _____ programming is an extension of linear programming in which feasible solutions must have variables in the product mix which have integer values; _____ programming is an extension of linear programming in which multiple goals ranked according to priorities may be included in the formulation.

13-2 A new constraint added to a linear programming problem which eliminates some noninteger solutions is called a _____.

13-3 The _____ method is a modified enumeration procedure which eliminates nonoptimal solutions along the way.

13-4 In goal programming, two new variables are added to the formulation for each goal considered. One represents how much the goal is _____; the other, how much the goal is _____.

*Fill in the
Blanks*

13-5 A _____ programming approach may be used to find good, but not always optimal, solutions to complex problems.

13-6 If all possible solutions to a problem are evaluated in order to find the best one, we call this _____.

13-7 In a goal programming problem with prioritized goals, the coefficients of the underachievement variables in the objective function are called _____.

13-8 The major shortcoming of a greedy heuristic is that it is _____.

13-9 The Vogel approximation method is based on the concept of minimizing _____.

13-10 In goal programming, we attempt to minimize _____.

True-False

13-11 Integer programs always require more iterations of the simplex method **T F** than their accompanying linear programs, formed by relaxing the integer constraint on the variables in the product mix.

13-12 To find a cut, we choose a row in the optimal tableau which corresponds **T F** to a noninteger variable and generate a new constraint from it.

13-13 When a new cut constraint is added to a noninteger optimal simplex **T F** tableau, the new tableau represents an infeasible solution because of the negative value in the quantity column of the new constraint.

13-14 When the branch-and-bound method is applied to a minimization **T F** problem, the current upper bound is always the feasible solution with the lowest cost encountered up to this point.

13-15 The branch-and-bound method terminates when we reach the point **T F** where the upper and lower bounds are identical, and the solution is that single value.

13-16 The main advantage of goal programming over linear programming **T F** is its ability to solve problems which have multiple constraints.

13-17 In a goal programming formulation, each goal generates a new **T F** constraint and adds at least one new variable to the objective function.

13-18 At optimality, the value of the objective function reflects by how much **T F** we have overachieved the goals in our goal programming problem.

13-19 The Vogel approximation method is a heuristic which is sensitive to **T F** opportunity costs.

13-20 The branch-and-bound method examines individually the total num- **T F** ber of possible solutions, but it does so very efficiently.

13-21 If the optimal solution to a linear programming problem has all **T F** integer values, it is also an optimal integer solution.

13-22 Managers who use goal programming have to specify the relative **T F** importance of the goals as well as how much more important one is with respect to another.

13-23 In branch-and-bound, a lower bound for a minimization problem **T F** fulfills the same role as an upper bound for a maximization problem.

13-24 In contrast to exact algorithms, heuristics do not always develop **T F** optimal solutions.

13-25 In developing a starting solution to the transportation problem, the **T F**

Vogel approximation method usually gives a better solution than a greedy
heuristic.

13-26 Adding a new cut constraint to an optimal simplex tableau has which of the
following effects?
  a. It adds a new variable to the tableau.
  b. It makes the previous optimal solution infeasible by eliminating that part of
     the region of feasibility of the problem which contained the previous optimal
     solution.
  c. It eliminates only noninteger solutions from the region of feasibility.
  d. All of the above.

13-27 The branch-and-bound method is a modified form of enumeration. In a
minimization problem, the modification is that:
  a. All solutions which will result in costs greater than the current upper bound
     are not evaluated.
  b. All solutions resulting in costs lower than the current upper bound, which are
     infeasible, are ignored.
  c. All infeasible solutions are not evaluated.
  d. Only feasible solutions with costs lower than the lower bound of the problem
     are evaluated.

13-28 Which of the following conditions indicates that a goal has been exactly satisfied
at optimality in a goal program?
  a. The variable which measures underachievement of that goal is in the product
     mix with a negative value.
  b. The variables which measure underachievement and overachievement of that
     goal are both in the product mix at optimality.
  c. The variables which measure overachievement and underachievement are
     both absent from the product mix at optimality.
  d. None of the above.

13-29 In goal programming problems, priorities are established for each goal such
that:
  a. No goal of higher priority is ever sacrificed to achieve a goal of lower priority.
  b. A goal of lower priority may be achieved over a goal of higher priority if the
     decrease in the objective function makes such a move favorable.
  c. Goals may not have equal priority.
  d. Goals of greatest importance are given lowest priority.

13-30 A heuristic solution may be used to enhance the performance of a minimizing
problem solved by the branch-and-bound method when it is used as:
  a. An initial lower bound
  b. An initial upper bound
  c. A check for feasibility
  d. All of the above

13-31 In goal programming, if there are two or more Z_j and $C_j - Z_j$ rows, the
problem has:
  a. Equal priority goals.
  b. Prioritized goals.

c. Unattainable goals.

d. Profit goals only.

13-32 In integer programming, each fractional cut that is made requires the addition of a:

a. $\leq$ constraint

b. $\geq$ constraint

c. $=$ constraint

d. Artificial variable

13-33 In integer programming, we can pick any noninteger variable in the solution to:

a. Leave the solution.

b. Enter the solution.

c. Obtain the cut constraint.

d. None of the above.

13-34 In goal programming, a goal constraint having underachievement and over-achievement variables is expressed as:

a. An equality constraint.

b. A $\leq$ constraint.

c. A $\geq$ constraint.

d. All of the above.

13-35 The initial tableau of a goal programming problem should never have a variable in the product mix which is:

a. An overachievement variable

b. An underachievement variable

c. A slack variable

d. An artificial variable

13-36 Branch-and-bound divides the feasible region into smaller parts through the process of:

a. Branching

b. Bounding

c. Enumerating

d. All of the above

13-37 Heuristics may be used in conjunction with:

a. Goal programming

b. Branch-and-bound

c. Integer programming

d. All of the above

13-38 In integer programming, the part of the feasible region eliminated by a cut contains:

a. Only noninteger solutions.

b. Only integer solutions.

c. Only slack in one or more constraints.

d. The optimal integer solution.

13-39 As you proceed along the tree of a branch-and-bound minimization problem, the lower bounds:

a. Do not decrease in value.

b. Do not increase in value.

c. Remain constant.

d. None of the above is correct.

13-40 Alternative optimal solutions are never encountered with:
   a. Branch-and-bound
   b. Goal programming
   c. Integer programming
   d. None of the above

8 Real world MS/OR successes

EXAMPLE: PLANNING REAL ESTATE STRATEGY
AT HOMART DEVELOPMENT COMPANY

Homart Development Company, a subsidiary of Sears, Roebuck, and Company, is one of the largest commercial land developers in the United States. In 1986, the firm owned 31 regional shopping centers, 18 major office buildings, and was involved in land development of properties totaling more than 1,000 acres. As development projects mature, Homart executives review the properties involved to determine whether they should be retained or sold (divested). James C. Bean, Charles E. Noon, and Gary J. Salton[2] designed an integer programming model to analyze Homart's divestiture strategy. The bottom line: the first run of the model yielded additional profit of $40 million.

HOMART LAND
DEVELOPMENT
OPERATIONS

Choosing properties to sell and scheduling the sales are complex decisions. The goal is to maximize net present value over a 5–10 year planning horizon. There are many different combinations of properties that must be considered for sale each year. Homart can't be short-sighted and solve the problem one year at a time, since profits typically depend on how long a property is held. A major complication is that Homart's financial reports are consolidated with other Sears divisions. Sears is concerned that wide fluctuations in earnings could hurt its stock price. Therefore, Sears imposes a lower bound on the return on equity that Homart must achieve each year. This policy often forces Homart to sell a property to boost short-term earnings even though net present value would be increased if the property were retained.

GOAL: MAXIMIZE NET
PRESENT VALUE

RETURN-ON-EQUITY
CONSTRAINT IMPOSED
BY SEARS

The complexity of the planning effort is best illustrated by Homart's traditional methods of analysis. An initial divestitute schedule was constructed and evaluated for return on equity. It if did not meet the requirement in any year, an asset sale would be moved to cover that year. If changes of this type did not produce a feasible schedule, assets would be moved around, not to meet the requirement, but to free up other assets for testing against the requirement. It is unlikely that an optimal decision would be reached in this manner. Due to the large sums of money involved, the cost of deviation from optimality easily runs into tens of millions of dollars.

TRADITIONAL ANALYSIS
DONE BY TRIAL-AND-
ERROR

The researchers developed a "multiple-choice" integer programming model to solve this problem. In this type of model, all decision variables are zero or one. The variables are defined as follows: let $X_{is} = 1$ if asset i is sold in year

THE MULTIPLE-CHOICE
INTEGER PROGRAM

[2] James C. Bean, Charles E. Noon, and Gary J. Salton, "Asset Divestiture at Homart Development Company," *Interfaces*, vol. 17, no. 1, pp. 48–64, 1987.

658

CHAPTER 13

SOLUTION METHOD:
BRANCH-AND-BOUND

SALES AT A LOSS
MAKE SENSE

s and 0 otherwise. Each decision variable has a coefficient c_{is}, the net present value profit from asset i if sold in year s. The objective function maximizes the sum of $c_{is}X_{is}$ subject to constraints requiring that any feasible solution assign the value one to exactly one variable for each asset. Other constraints require that the return-on-equity goal be achieved throughout the planning horizon. The model is solved with a specialized version of the branch-and-bound method for multiple-choice models.

The first run of the model made major changes in Homart's divestiture plans. For example, Homart had always operated under a policy that properties should never be sold at a loss. The model showed that this policy did not make sense. A conservative estimate of the present value cost of the policy was $14 million over the next 10 years.

The success of this initial effort in integer programming led Homart to consider other applications. At the time their article appeared, the authors were developing integer programs to determine the optimal mix of merchants for shopping malls and to determine the optimal size of office buildings.

OTHER REAL ESTATE
APPLICATIONS

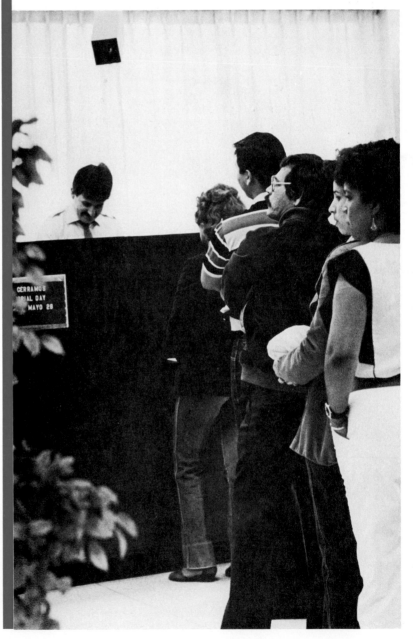

14

Donna Thibideau is manager of the Skowhegan branch of the Western Maine Trust and Banking Company. She is concerned about staffing and scheduling her tellers. During peak hours at the bank, customers often encounter long waits, especially when they are in line behind business people who have lengthy transactions. Donna is considering the possibility of changing the queue discipline so that all customers wait in a single queue leading to the next available teller. She is also contemplating the hiring of additional tellers. More tellers, of course, will significantly reduce waiting times, but at increased payroll cost. In analyzing the problem, Donna plans to use waiting line models. These models will provide her with information about average waiting time, average queue length, average time spent in the bank, and the percent of time her tellers are busy. She can determine how much these performance measures are affected by each possible decision she might take in staffing the teller windows.

This kind of information will greatly assist Donna in making her most cost effective decisions. In this chapter, you will become familiar with waiting line models. You will also learn how to use information provided by these models to analyze the cost tradeoffs involved with such queuing systems.

WAITING LINES

CHAPTER OBJECTIVES

- EXAMINE SITUATIONS THAT GENERATE QUEUING PROBLEMS.
- INTRODUCE THE VARIOUS OBJECTIVES THAT MAY BE SET FOR THE OPERATION OF A WAITING LINE.
- EXAMINE COSTS ASSOCIATED WITH QUEUING SITUATIONS.
- INTRODUCE STANDARD QUEUING LANGUAGE AND SYMBOLS.
- SHOW HOW TO SOLVE QUEUING PROBLEMS USING STANDARD QUEUING EQUATIONS IN BOTH THE SINGLE-CHANNEL AND MULTIPLE-CHANNEL CASE.
- DEMONSTRATE A SIMULATION SOLUTION FOR A QUEUING PROBLEM.

1 Introductory queuing ideas

In almost every organization there are examples of processes which generate *waiting lines*, referred to as *queues*. Such waiting lines occur when some employee, part, machine, or unit must wait for service because the servicing facility, operating at capacity, is temporarily unable to provide that service.

If you travel by airline, you have firsthand experience with several types of waiting lines. To buy your ticket, you may have to stand in line at the travel agent's office. When you arrive at the airport, you stand in line to check your bags; then you may stand in line again to get a seat assignment. You line up once more for a security check and then again in the boarding lounge before entering the airplane. When you are inside the plane, you wait for those ahead of you to take their seats. When the plane leaves the gate, it may wait in line for takeoff clearance; when it arrives at its destination, it may circle for some time waiting for landing clearance. And finally, when a gate is assigned and you disembark, you may wait for your baggage to arrive and then for ground transportation. It is possible to be a member of at least 10 queues on one such trip.

And consider for a moment the *airline's* queuing experience for that same trip. The plane you ride in has to "wait in line" for fueling, inspection, a particular gate, a specific flight route, an assigned crew, food loading, verified passenger count, and taxi takeoff and landing clearance for each trip; no wonder airlines are also concerned with queuing, for poorly managed waiting lines result in underutilized equipment and dissatisfied customers.

The pioneering work in the field of queuing theory was done by A. K. Erlang, a Danish engineer associated with the telephone industry. Early in this century Erlang was doing experiments involving the fluctuating demand for telephone facilities and its effect upon automatic dialing equipment. It was not until the end of World War II that this early work was extended to other more general problems involving queues or waiting lines.

You see the operation of a simple queue at the single checkout counter of your neighborhood convenience store when you drop by on the way home to pick up a barbecued chicken. Figure 14-1 illustrates the operation of the checkout counter. In this simple situation, if the convenience store operator wants to minimize the length of the waiting line that would normally form at the single checkout counter, another cash register and another checker can be added. If the queues that form are still too long, more counters can

FIGURE 14-1
A queuing system.

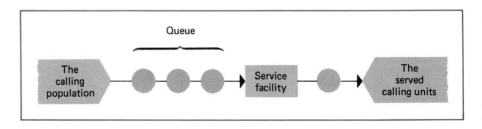

be added. Each addition, of course, adds to expense, but at the same time, each further reduces the time customers have to wait for service. The manager tries to hit a happy medium where waiting lines are short enough to minimize customer ill will, but it is clearly not practical to provide such extensive service facilities that no waiting line, or queue, can ever develop. In effect, our manager *balances* the increased cost of additional facilities against the customer ill will which increases as the average length of the queue increases.

There are many industrial applications of queuing theory in which the cost of time lost by the personnel in the waiting line *and* the cost of additional facilities can be determined accurately. In many of these problems, we can arrive at a solution which provides the lowest total cost of (1) the lost time of persons waiting for service plus (2) the wages of persons who provide the service. Let us look at such a situation.

In the typical machine shop, the expensive cutting tools required in the machining processes are kept in a central location often referred to as a *tool crib*. This crib is staffed by one or more persons who check out the tools required by the machinists in the shop. The machinist who requires a certain tool proceeds to the tool crib, presents a tool authorization to the attendant, and is issued the required tool. The machinist then goes back to work, does the job, and finally goes back to the tool crib and checks in the tool; if required, the machinist then draws another for the next job to be performed. Because some of the tools involved in work of this kind are very expensive, this procedure is necessary to ensure adequate control of the tool inventory.

During the time machinists wait in line at the tool crib for service, they are idle; a loss is incurred by the company. This type of loss is measurable because it is simply the amount of time workers are required to wait multiplied by the wages they receive per hour. By the same token, when the employees who staff the tool crib are idle because no machinist is requiring service, their wages represent a loss to the company.

One way to reduce the waiting time of the machinists is to provide sufficient tool crib attendants so that no queue is allowed to form. Since the machinists may arrive in bunches from time to time, this will take quite a few attendants. During the time when no machinists arrive for service, the entire combined wages of this large group of attendants are a loss, unless there are other duties they can perform in the interim. What we need is a workable solution which takes into account all the factors in the problem *and* determines the ratio of tool crib attendants to machinists which will yield the lowest total cost. This type of situation can best be illustrated by using the figures in Table 14-1, collected by observing the operation over an extended period of time under several different staffing alternatives.

From Table 14-1 it seems that *two* crib attendants will minimize the total cost of (1) the machinists' lost time plus (2) the crib attendants' wages. Having fewer *or* more than two attendants will raise this total cost.

In a real industrial situation, of course, no one wants to observe the operation for the extended period of time necessary to acquire these figures. That would be an unnecessary waste of time and money when the same solution to the problem can be obtained using some quantitative techniques associated with queuing theory. These we shall develop and discuss later.

	Number of attendants			
	1	2	3	4
Number of arrivals of machinists during 8-hr shift	100	100	100	100
Average time each machinist spends waiting for service (minutes)	10	6	4	2
Total time lost by machinists during 8-hr shift (minutes)	1,000	600	400	200
Machinists' average pay (hourly)	$12	$12	$12	$12
Value of machinists' lost time	$200	$120	$80	$40
Tool crib attendants' average pay (hourly)	$6	$6	$6	$6
Total pay of tool crib attendants for 8-hr shift	$48	$96	$144	$192
Machinists' lost time plus tool crib attendants' pay	$248	$216	$224	$232

Optimal no. of tool crib attendants = 2

TABLE 14-1

Tool crib system under several alternatives

The problem of the tool crib attendants and the machinists represents, of course, only one application of queuing theory. Consider the illustrations in Table 14-2, which lists cases where application of this useful technique can provide optimal solutions to common managerial problems. These are just a few of the many opportunities for the application of the theory of queues, or waiting lines.

TABLE 14-2

Examples of queues

Situation	Arrivals	Queue	Service facility
Airport	Airplanes	Planes stacked up	Runway
Restaurant	Customers	Customers waiting to eat	Tables/waiters
Class registration	Students	Students waiting to register	Registrars
Hospital	Patients	Patients waiting to use facility	Rooms/physicians
Post Office	Letters	Letters waiting for distribution	Sorting system
Telephone exchange	Incoming calls	Persons making calls	Switching system
Gasoline station	Motorists	Motorists waiting for gasoline	Pumps/personnel
Job interview	Applicants	Applicants waiting to see interviewer	Interviewer
Court system	Cases	Untried cases	Judge/courtroom
Intersection	Motorists	Cars backed up	Traffic light/ highway capacity

2 Queuing objectives and cost behavior

In the tool crib example illustrated in Table 14-1, our objective was to minimize the *total* cost of (1) time lost by the arrivals waiting for service *and* (2) providing that service. We observed from the example that as we provided more attendants, the average time each machinist spent waiting for service decreased. This reduction in waiting time and its associated cost was achieved, however, by increasing the cost of service (the wages paid to the added attendants).

The basic relationships between and among the elements involved in queuing problems can be illustrated graphically. In Figure 14-2, we show the relationship between the level of service provided and the cost of *waiting time*. We observe that as the level of service is increased (as more attendants are provided in our tool crib, for example), the cost of time spent waiting by the machinists decreases. In Figure 14-3, we illustrate graphically the relationship between the level of service and the cost of *providing that service.* In this case,

we observe that as the level of service increases, so does the cost of providing that increased service; in our tool crib example, each additional tool crib attendant was paid $48 a day in wages. Combining these two input costs with the queuing decision has been accomplished in Figure 14-4. Here the cost of the time spent waiting by the arrivals has been added to the cost of providing service to establish a *total expected cost* for the operation of the facility. From

Figure 14-4 we see that the total expected cost is minimized at a level of service which we have denoted with the symbol H. Thus the objective of the techniques which we explain in the remainder of this chapter is really to determine that particular level of service which minimizes the total cost of providing service *and* waiting for that service. Although conceptually this may appear to be a simple notion, the various possible ways in which arrivals can appear and be serviced, the many possible ways in which arrivals can be selected for service, and the multitude of possible physical layouts of service

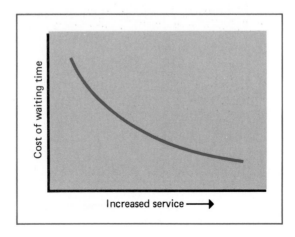

FIGURE 14-2
Relationship between level of service and cost of waiting time.

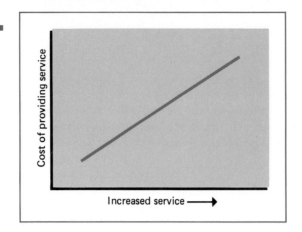

FIGURE 14-3

Relationship between level of service and cost of providing service.

facilities make the problem a difficult one. Let us turn now to an understanding of some of the terms used in the study of waiting lines.

3 Standard language and definitions for waiting lines

POPULATION, QUEUE, AND SERVICE FACILITY

We will be dealing in some detail with three parts of queuing systems: (1) the calling population (you were a part of this population when you entered the convenience store we used as an example earlier); (2) the queue, or waiting line, itself (you became a part of this when you selected your purchase and walked to the checkout counter); and (3) the service facility (in our example, this was the single checkout counter). Each of these three parts has characteristics described in specific language.

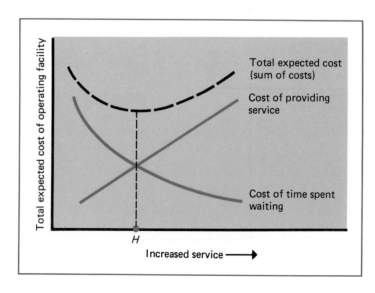

FIGURE 14-4

Total cost of operating service facility.

CHARACTERISTICS OF THE CALLING POPULATION

This part of a queuing system has three characteristics we shall deal with:

THE CALLING POPULATION

1 Size of the calling population
2 Arrival characteristics of the calling population
3 Behavior of the calling population

Let's look at each of these in turn.

Size of the calling population   Calling populations can be either *infinite* or *finite*. Examples of practically *infinite* calling populations include cars arriving at toll booths, patients arriving at the emergency room of a large hospital, and 20,000 students lined up on registration day. These are actually finite populations, but they are very large, and for mathematical convenience we treat them as infinite. When calling populations are infinite, it is much easier to apply quantitative techniques to their analysis. *Finite* calling populations, on the other hand, would be represented by a group of three looms in a weaving mill that require operator service from time to time, or a small taxi fleet of four cars which visit a repair facility from time to time. How to tell the difference between finite and infinite calling populations? Generally, if the probability of an arrival is greatly changed when one member of the calling population is receiving service, we consider the calling population to be *finite*. After all, if one of the four taxis is already in the shop, chances that another will arrive while it is being repaired are substantially reduced.

FINITE AND INFINITE CALLING POPULATIONS

Arrival characteristics of the calling population   Members of the calling population arrive at the service facility either in some organized pattern or in random order. When arrivals are random, we have to know the probability distribution describing arrivals, specifically the *time between arrivals*. MS/OR analysts have demonstrated that random arrivals are often well described by the Poisson distribution, which we discussed in some detail in Chapter 2. Of course, arrivals are not always Poisson-distributed, and we need to be sure the distribution is appropriate before we use it. Whether the Poisson distribution is correct can be checked by comparing samples of actual arrivals with expected arrivals using the Poisson formula, Eq. (2-10).

ORGANIZED OR RANDOM ARRIVALS

Behavior of the calling population   Calling populations and their individual members have different attitudes about "getting into line." Most of us routinely skip a gas station when we see most of the pumps busy, and yet we may willingly wait in line for several hours to get tickets to a special event. Whether you would support it or not, many queuing models assume that the calling population is rather patient and willing to wait.

ATTITUDES ABOUT GETTING INTO A WAITING LINE

There are three terms which are commonly used in queuing to describe the behavior of the calling population: *Reneging* refers to the situation when someone joins a queue and then leaves. *Balking* means not joining. And *jockeying* refers to the condition in multiple queue situations when someone moves back and forth among queues.

RENEGING, BALKING, AND JOCKEYING

CHARACTERISTICS OF THE QUEUE (WAITING LINE)

LIMITED OR
UNLIMITED LENGTH

It is common practice to describe queue characteristics in terms of the maximum length to which the queue can grow. This length is classified as either *limited* or *unlimited*. Limited queue lengths are usually due to lack of space (on a very cold night, the waiting line for a restaurant may be limited to the number of people who can crowd into the entrance hall) or to the attitude of the members of the calling population (some folks just don't like to wait in lines). When we can assume the queue can grow to *infinite* length, life is much simpler for the MS/OR analyst.

CHARACTERISTICS OF THE SERVICE FACILITY

In examining the characteristics of a service facility, we are interested in three things:

LAYOUT, QUEUE
DISCIPLINE, AND
DISTRIBUTION OF
SERVICE TIME

1 The physical layout of the queuing system

2 The queue discipline

3 The appropriate probability distribution describing service times

A few words about each of these is in order.

CHANNEL AND SERVER

The physical layout of the queuing system   The physical layout of a queuing system is described by the number of *channels,* also called the number of *servers.* As shown in Figure 14-5, a *single-channel* system has one server. A multichannel system has two or more servers which operate in parallel. If you stop at a gas station which has one pump, that is a single-channel system. If it has more than one pump, that is a multichannel system. Our discussion will be limited to single and multichannel systems where there is only one queue. If customers are allowed to form more than one queue, the system is much more difficult to analyze because of the jockeying that almost invariably occurs and thus beyond the scope of this book.

PRIORITY QUEUE
DISCIPLINE

The queue discipline   Here we are referring to which unit in the calling population receives service. Two classifications are used: *priority* and *first come, first served.* In priority disciplines, there are two subclassifications: *preemptive* and *nonpreemptive.* Preemptive discipline permits members of the calling population to interrupt members already receiving service. If the president of your company dashes into the company cafeteria, and asks if you would mind stepping out of line so he or she can make an important meeting, and you do so, you understand preemptive priority discipline. Nonpreemptive queue discipline arranges the queue so that the member with the highest priority gets the first *open* service facility.

FIRST-COME, FIRST-
SERVED QUEUE
DISCIPLINE

First-come, first-served queue discipline does not assign priorities and serves the queue member who got there first. Combinations of these queue disciplines are very much in evidence. Consider the express line at the supermarket for shoppers with fewer than 10 items. It is operated on a queue discipline of first come, first served *once you get in the line;* however, this express line does provide a high-priority channel for those shoppers with few items.

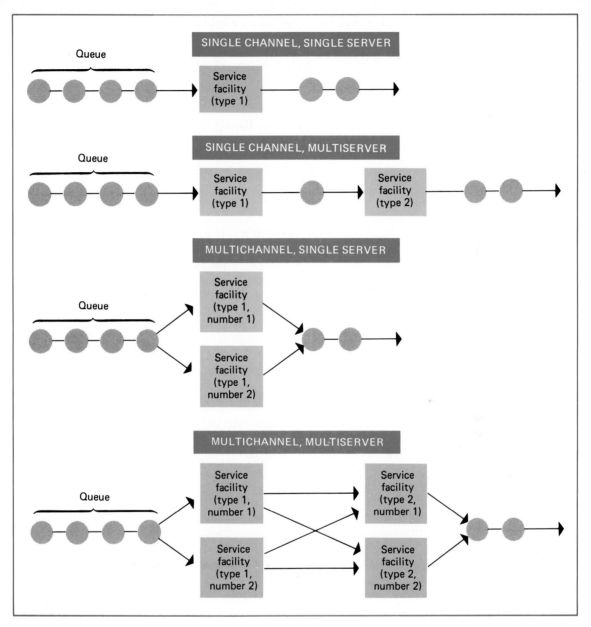

FIGURE 14-5
Physical layouts of queuing systems described by channel and server.

The appropriate probability distribution describing service times It is possible for service times to be constant (each member of the queue requires the same time to be serviced) or random. If service times are randomly distributed, we have to find out what probability distribution best describes their behavior. In many cases where service times are random, MS/OR analysts

DISTRIBUTIONS OF
SERVICE TIME

669

have found that they are well described by the *exponential probability distribution* discussed in Chapter 2. Again we need to check whether the exponential distribution is correct. This can be done by comparing samples of actual service times with expected times using the exponential formula, Eq. (2-11).

4 Elementary queuing system: constant arrival and service times

The case in which *both* the arrival rate and the servicing rate are constant can be illustrated with the following examples:

EXAMPLE 1: NO QUEUE, IDLE TIME

Assume that arrivals occur at the constant rate of 10 per hour, 10 arrivals each hour and every hour, occurring precisely every 6 minutes. Assume also that services can be performed at a constant rate of 12 per hour every hour. With this situation, a queue will not form because the servicing facility can handle with ease the entire arrival workload. In fact, we can easily calculate that the servicing facility will be idle $\frac{2}{12}$, or 16.67 percent, of the time because arrivals need only $\frac{10}{12}$, or 83.33 percent of servicing capacity.

EXAMPLE 2: NO QUEUE, NO IDLE TIME

Assume now that arrivals occur at a constant rate of 10 per hour, 10 arrivals each hour and every hour, occurring at 6-minute intervals during that hour. Assume also that services can be and are performed at a constant rate of 10 per hour every hour. With this situation, a queue cannot form because arrivals are serviced at the same rate at which they arrive. Also in this situation, there will be no idle time in the servicing facility because it must operate at full capacity to handle the arrivals.

EXAMPLE 3: QUEUE FORMS, NO IDLE TIME

Assume that arrivals occur at a constant rate of 10 per hour, occurring every 6 minutes during that hour. Assume also that services are performed at a constant rate of 8 per hour every hour. With this situation, a queue will form and grow because the input rate is higher than the ability of the servicing facility to handle it. The queue of unserviced arrivals builds up at the rate of 2 units per hour, the excess of arrivals over serviced items. At the end of 8 hours, for instance, we would normally expect to see 16 units in the queue.

Thus the assumption of *constant* arrival and service times makes quite easy the calculation of whether a queue will form and what its length will be after any period of time. If, however, we move to the more usual case in which both arrivals and services are not constant, in which they happen at other than precise intervals, the problem and the calculations become more difficult. For instance, if we allow arrivals and services to be randomly distributed, even though the servicing facility has a capacity greater than the average arrivals, a group of items arriving at the same time for service may form a temporary queue. And, of course, by the same token, a temporary reduction in arrivals may enable the service facility to catch up, to remove a queue that has previously formed. The next few sections are devoted to models which permit us to analyze queuing systems more complex than these three examples.

5 Single-channel queuing model: Poisson-distributed arrivals and exponentially distributed service times

The queuing model we are about to present fits situations where these conditions are satisfied:

1 The number of arrivals per unit of time is described by a Poisson distribution.

2 Service times are described by an exponential distribution.

3 Queue discipline is first come, first served.

4 The calling population is infinite.

5 There is *one* channel.

6 The mean arrival rate is less than the mean service rate (on page 673, we shall demonstrate why this is important).

7 The waiting space available for customers in the queue is infinite.

If these seven conditions are met, it is possible to analyze a queuing system with a series of equations which MS/OR analysts have derived. These equations make use of the following symbols:

λ = mean arrival rate per unit of time (say, an hour)
μ = mean service rate per unit of time
L_q = mean number in queue
L_s = mean number in system (number in queue plus number being served)
W_q = mean time in queue
W_s = mean time in system (time in queue plus service time)
P_w = probability the service facility is busy (utilization factor)

▓ EQUATIONS FOR SINGLE-CHANNEL MODEL

The equations for the single-channel model satisfying the seven conditions given above are

$$L_q = \text{mean number in the queue}$$

$$= \frac{\lambda^2}{\mu(\mu - \lambda)} \tag{14-1}$$

$$L_s = \text{mean number in the system}$$

$$= \frac{\lambda}{\mu - \lambda} \tag{14-2}$$

$$W_q = \text{mean time in the queue}$$

$$= \frac{\lambda}{\mu(\mu - \lambda)} \tag{14-3}$$

W_s = mean time in the system

$$= \frac{1}{\mu - \lambda} \tag{14-4}$$

P_w = probability the service facility is busy (utilization factor)

$$= \frac{\lambda}{\mu} \tag{14-5}$$

▓ APPLICATION OF THE MODEL

METROLEASE EXAMPLE
OF SINGLE-CHANNEL
QUEUING SYSTEM

Let's consider the case of Metrolease Furniture Rental in Raleigh, North Carolina, with one warehouse serving its four stores in the area. The warehouse has only one loading dock staffed by a three-person crew. President Jerry Fox has observed that at certain times several of his trucks are waiting in the yard to be loaded; yet at other times the three-person crew is idle. Jerry has done some preliminary analysis and feels sure the warehouse loading system fits the seven conditions on page 671. His records indicate that the average arrival rate λ is 4 trucks per hour, and the average service rate μ is 6 trucks per hour. What can we tell Jerry about the appropriateness of adding another crew, or even two more crews, to increase the service rate at his single loading dock?

If Jerry adds one or more crews, the loading dock will still be a single-channel system, because only one customer (truck) can be in service at any one time. If he uses two crews, μ will be 12. If he uses three crews, μ will be 18.

ECONOMIC
INTERPRETATION OF
METROLEASE RESULTS

In Table 14-3, we have used Eqs. (14-1) to (14-5) to calculate the effect of increased numbers of crews on the warehouse operation. On Jerry's advice, we have assumed that work capacity is proportional to the number of crews. From Table 14-3, it is clear that adding additional crews reduces both the number of trucks waiting and the time they wait. But this has been accomplished only by assuming that additional crews were available. What of the economics of this situation? Jerry says his trucks cost $20 an hour to operate, and he pays the members of his loading crew $6 an hour each. In Table 14-4, we have shown the cost of idle truck time and of warehouse crew wages for the three alternatives we are examining.

In interpreting the *times* in Table 14-3, remember they are stated as fractions of an hour, which is the time unit in which the arrival and service rates are given.

TABLE 14-3
Effect of number of
crews on warehouse
operation

		1 crew	2 crews	3 crews
Mean number of trucks in the queue	(L_q)	1.333	.167	.063
Mean number of trucks in the system	(L_s)	2.000	.500	.286
Mean time in the queue by a truck	(W_q)	.333	.042	.016
Mean time in the system by a truck	(W_s)	.500	.125	.071
Probability service facility is busy	(P_w)	.667	.333	.222

	Truck cost/day	Crew cost/day	Total cost/day
1 crew	2 × 8 hr × $20 = $320	3 × $6 × 8 hr = $144	$464
2 crews	.5 × 8 hr × $20 = $80	6 × $6 × 8 hr = $288	$368
3 crews	.286 × 8 hr × $20 = $46	9 × $6 × 8 hr = $432	$478

TABLE 14-4
Total system cost per
day under three
alternatives

Jerry ought to add a second crew to the warehouse operation. It not only will reduce cost by $464 − $368, or $96, a day but will reduce the utilization factor to .333; this means that Jerry's crews will have, on average, 5⅓ hours every 8-hour day to spend on other productive work.

RESULTS OF
METROLEASE QUEUING
ANALYSIS

AN INTERESTING CHARACTERISTIC OF WAITING LINES

Look back for a moment at Eqs. (14-1) through (14-4). All of them have the term $\mu - \lambda$ in the denominator. Therefore, if the service rate equals the arrival rate (if $\mu = \lambda$), then $\mu - \lambda = 0$ in all those equations, and the queue lengths and waiting times are all infinitely long. How can this be? In slack periods, the service facility can't store up service time, although the waiting line does in fact "store up" arrivals in its slack periods. Ultimately a rush period does occur (heavy arrivals) and the service facility falls behind. Whenever there is a heavy arrival period, the service facility falls further behind, and thus the infinitely long queues build up over time.

6 Single-channel queuing model: Poisson-distributed arrivals and any service-time distribution

There are many practical problems in which the service times do not fit an exponential distribution. However, the single-channel model can be modified to use any service-time distribution provided that

1 The service times are independent of each other (the length of service for any customer does not affect the service for any other customer).

CONDITIONS FOR USE
OF THIS MODEL

2 The same distribution of service times applies to all customers.

3 The mean service time ($1/\mu$) and the variance of the service time (σ^2) are known.

The other conditions are the same as the previous model with exponential service times.

EQUATIONS FOR SINGLE-CHANNEL, ANY SERVICE-DISTRIBUTION MODEL

The equations for this model are

$$L_q = \text{mean number in the queue}$$

$$= \frac{\lambda^2\sigma^2 + (\lambda/\mu)^2}{2(1 - \lambda/\mu)} \tag{14-6}$$

L_s = mean number in the system

$$= L_q + \frac{\lambda}{\mu} \tag{14-7}$$

W_q = mean time in the queue

$$= \frac{L_q}{\lambda} \tag{14-8}$$

W_s = mean time in the system

$$= W_q + \frac{1}{\mu} \tag{14-9}$$

P_w = probability the server is busy (utilization factor)

$$= \frac{\lambda}{\mu} \tag{14-10}$$

To apply these equations, L_q must be computed first. The equations for L_s, W_q, and W_s all depend on the answer for L_q.

If the service-time distribution is exponential, its variance is $\sigma^2 = 1/\mu^2$. If this variance is substituted into the formulas above, the solutions are the same as those of the single-server model with exponential service times.

▌ APPLICATION OF THE MODEL

THE CCNB UNIVERSITY-
OFFICE PROBLEM

To demonstrate this model, let's take a look at a small branch office operated by CCNB Bank on the campus of Pennsylvania State University. The branch, located in the student union, has one teller and is open from noon to 4 P.M. on weekdays. Chris McKenna, CCNB's vice president for the University Park area, has received complaints from students about two things: the limited operating hours and the waiting time at the branch on Fridays. Chris looked into the problem and found that the arrival rate averaged 8 students per hour on Monday through Thursday. On Fridays, however, arrivals averaged 34 per hour, Poisson distributed.

On Monday through Thursday, the banch processed a variety of different types of transactions at the average rate of 24 per hour. On Fridays, the type of business changed—more than 90 percent of the transactions were either cashing of personal checks or withdrawals from savings accounts. The service rate went up to 40 per hour, with the times exponentially distributed.

Chris is reluctant to increase the operating hours of the branch because of the low utilization factor ($^8/_{24} = .33$) on Monday through Thursday. He is also reluctant to hire an additional teller just for the peak Friday business. He decides to investigate replacing the teller with a 24-hour banking machine. The lease cost of the machine is $250 per week, considerably more than the cost of the teller at $180 per week. However, the machine will take care of the complaints about operating hours.

		Teller	Banking machine
Mean number of students in the queue	(L_q)	4.817	2.428
Mean number of students in the system	(L_s)	5.667	3.278
Mean time in the queue by a student	(W_s)	.142	.071
Mean time in the system by a student	(W_q)	.167	.096
Probability the service facility is busy	(P_w)	.850	.850

TABLE 14-5
Performance comparison of teller and 24-hour banking machine

Chris is willing to pay the increased cost if the banking machine will reduce waiting time on Friday afternoons. Although Chris is uncertain about what will happen to waiting time, he believes it will be reduced. One of the advantages of a banking machine is that service times are less variable than those of a teller. Operations are standardized, and the customer is forced to be better prepared for the transaction. Stopwatch studies of CCNB's machines at other locations show that the service time for cash withdrawals is normally distributed, with a mean of 90 seconds and a standard deviation of 8 seconds. Thus the service rate μ is $(60 \times 60)/90 = 40$ per hour, the same as that of the teller. To use the variance in Eq. (14-6), we must state it as a fraction of an hour. The standard deviation σ is $8/(60 \times 60) = .002222$. The variance σ^2 is thus $(.002222)^2 = .000005$.

We can help Chris evaluate whether the banking machine will reduce waiting time as follows. First we use the basic single-server model in Section 5 to compute the teller's performance characteristics. Next we use the model for any service distribution to compute the banking machine's performance characteristics. The results of the comparison are shown in Table 14-5. The machine makes a big dent in waiting time. With the teller, waiting time is $.142 \times 60 = 8.52$ minutes. With the machine, waiting time is reduced by about half: $.071 \times 60 = 4.26$ minutes. Chris will very likely order the banking machine.

HOW THE TWO SINGLE-SERVER MODELS ARE COMPARED

7 Single-channel queuing model: Poisson-distributed arrivals, exponentially distributed service times, and finite waiting capacity

Another important variation of the single-channel model is the case where some maximum number of customers can be in the system at one time. This maximum is M, a number which includes those waiting as well as those in service. If a customer arrives when there are M or more in the system, the customer leaves immediately and does not return. This type of model is often a reasonable approximation to the queuing problems faced by service businesses. Consider a restaurant with limited parking capacity. If a customer arrives and cannot find a place to park, he or she may have no choice but to go somewhere else. Except for the limit on the number in the system the

CONDITIONS FOR USE OF THIS MODEL

assumptions underlying this model are the same as those of the basic single-server model in Section 5.

◼ EQUATIONS FOR THE SINGLE-CHANNEL, FINITE-WAITING-CAPACITY MODEL

The equations for this model are

P_0 = probability of zero in the system

$$= \frac{1 - (\lambda/\mu)}{1 - (\lambda/\mu)^{M+1}} \qquad (14\text{-}11)$$

P_w = probability the service facility is busy

$$= 1 - P_0 \qquad (14\text{-}12)$$

P_M = proportion of customers lost because system is "full"

$$= \left(\frac{\lambda}{\mu}\right)^{M} P_0 \qquad (14\text{-}13)$$

L_s = mean number in the system

$$= \frac{P_w - M(\lambda/\mu)P_M}{1 - (\lambda/\mu)} \qquad (14\text{-}14)$$

L_q = mean number in the queue

$$= L_s - \frac{\lambda(1 - P_M)}{\mu} \qquad (14\text{-}15)$$

W_s = mean time in the system

$$= \frac{L_s}{\lambda(1 - P_M)} \qquad (14\text{-}16)$$

W_q = mean time in the queue

$$= W_s - \frac{1}{\mu} \qquad (14\text{-}17)$$

Again the equations must be computed in the order given. They have been arranged to simplify the arithmetic as much as possible. The first job is to compute P_0, which is the probability the system is idle (there are no customers in the queue or being served). Next P_w is 1 minus P_0. P_0 is also used to get P_M, the proportion of customers lost because the system is full. Next we compute L_s which is needed for the remainder of the equations. If we increase

M, at some point the value of P_M will become very small and this model will give the same answers as the basic model in Section 5 with an unlimited waiting capacity.

APPLICATION OF THE MODEL

CCNB has another capacity problem at a drive-in branch in the suburbs of University Park. Chris McKenna is wondering whether the limited space for cars waiting in line should be expanded. The drive-in branch has one teller window and space for 3 cars, 1 being served and 2 waiting in line. The branch is located on a busy street. When the system is full ($M = 3$), customers are reluctant to wait on the street. During Chris's last visit to the branch, the teller told him that numerous cars slow down near the branch entrance and then drive on when the system is full.

Chris would like to know if he really has a problem. What is the proportion of customers who do not stop because the system is full? He would also like to know the effects on system performance if the number of spaces for cars is expanded to $M = 4$ or 5. There is enough room on the property to expand the driveway to hold $M = 4$. It would be possible to expand to $M = 5$, but the teller's booth would have to be moved. The peak arrival rate at the branch is 14 per hour, Poisson distributed. The mix of transactions at the branch results in service at the rate of 20 per hour with the times exponentially distributed.

Comparisons using the finite-waiting-capacity model for $M = 3$, 4, and 5 are shown in Table 14-6. The teller is right—CCNB is either losing or inconveniencing many customers because of the limited waiting capacity. With $M = 3$, about 13.5 percent of the customers cannot get into the driveway during peak periods. If 1 extra space is added, this can be reduced to 8.7 percent. If 2 spaces are added, the proportion of customers who leave is 5.7 percent.

It is interesting that all performance measures except the proportion of customers who leave get worse as M gets larger. This always happens. The reason is that making M larger is a way of increasing the effective arrival rate. What we are doing is giving the teller more customers to serve.

		System capacity (M)		
		3	4	5
Probability the service facility is idle	(P_0)	.395	.361	.340
Probability the service facility is busy	(P_w)	.605	.639	.660
Proportion of customers who drive away because the system is full	(P_M)	.135	.087	.057
Mean number of cars in the system	(L_s)	1.070	1.320	1.532
Mean number of cars in the queue	(L_q)	.465	.681	.872
Mean time in the system by a car	(W_s)	.088	.103	.116
Mean time in the queue by a car	(W_q)	.038	.053	.066

TABLE 14-6
Performance comparisons for the CCNB drive-in branch with different driveway capacities

What should Chris do? The costs of losing customer goodwill are hard to measure. Chris has to ask himself if the costs of expanding the branch driveway are less than his subjective estimate of the costs of losing goodwill. Customers may come back later or go to some other CCNB branch; but they may eventually change banks. Here, as in many complex situations, quantitative analysis does not provide the manager with a prescription of what to do. However, the analysis does give insights which Chris can combine with his subjective cost estimates to reach a final decision.

8 Multiple-channel queuing model: Poisson-distributed arrivals and exponentially distributed service times

CONDITIONS FOR THE
USE OF THIS MODEL

Many queuing situations are *not* limited to one channel but involve situations where two or more channels are available and where members of the calling population form a single queue and wait for any *one* of the channels to become available for service. Banks and airline counters that ask customers to wait in a single line and then assign them to the first open teller or ticket agent are common examples of this situation. The multiple-channel queuing model we will now introduce fits situations where the mean arrival rate is less than the *aggregate service rate,* which is defined as the mean service rate per channel times the number of channels. The other conditions are the same as the basic single-server model in Section 5.

EQUATIONS FOR MULTIPLE-CHANNEL MODEL

The equations for this model depend on P_0, the probability all channels (servers) are idle. Appendix 5 allows you to look up P_0 for different values of the ratio $\lambda/k\mu$, where k is the number of channels, and

EQUATIONS FOR USE
IN THE MULTIPLE-
CHANNEL QUEUING
MODEL

$P_w =$ probability all channels are simultaneously busy (utilization factor)

$$= \frac{1}{k!}\left(\frac{\lambda}{\mu}\right)^k \frac{k\mu}{k\mu - \lambda} P_0 \qquad (14\text{-}18)$$

$L_s =$ mean number in the system $= \dfrac{\lambda\mu(\lambda/\mu)^k}{(k-1)!(k\mu - \lambda)^2} P_0 + \dfrac{\lambda}{\mu}$ $\quad(14\text{-}19)$

$L_q =$ mean number in the queue $= L_s - \dfrac{\lambda}{\mu}$ $\qquad (14\text{-}20)$

$W_s =$ mean time in the system $= \dfrac{L_s}{\lambda}$ $\qquad (14\text{-}21)$

$W_q =$ mean time in the queue $= \dfrac{L_q}{\lambda}$ $\qquad (14\text{-}22)$

Remember that in these equations μ is the service rate *per channel.*

		2 cashiers	3 cashiers
Probability all cashiers are idle	(P_0)	.111	.190
Probability all cashiers are busy	(P_w)	.710	.278
Mean number of customers in the system	(L_s)	4.442	1.918
Mean number of customers in the queue	(L_q)	2.842	.318
Mean time in the system by a customer	(W_s)	.555	.240
Mean time in the queue by a customer	(W_q)	.355	.040

TABLE 14-7
Effect on payment system of number of cashiers

APPLICATION OF THE MODEL

METROLEASE EXAMPLE OF MULTIPLE-CHANNEL QUEUING SYSTEM

Let's take another look at Jerry Fox's furniture leasing operation. At his Durham showroom, Jerry has two rental "windows"; these are cashier stations where his customers arrange for payment after they have chosen their furniture. Jerry notices that most of the time customers have to wait in front of these windows; he cannot put a cost on their waiting time, but he says he is willing to consider opening another cashier's window (which will cost him $40 per day) if this will reduce the average time a customer spends in the payment system by about half. He figures the present customer load at 8 per hour, and each cashier can service 5 customers an hour. What help can we give him now?

In Table 14-7, we use the multiple-channel formulas, Eqs. (14-18) through (14-22), to calculate the effect of increasing the number of cashier windows in Jerry's showroom from two to three. In using the multiple-channel formulas, we remember that μ (5 in Jerry's case) is the service rate for *each* channel.

ECONOMIC INTERPRETATION OF METROLEASE RESULTS

From Table 14-7 we can see that adding a third cashier reduced a customer's time in the system from .555 hours to .240 hours. This is more than a 50 percent reduction in the time spent in the system, which was the condition under which Jerry would spend another $40 per day for the third cashier. We also see that with three cashiers, customers spend most of their time being waited on and very little (.040 hour) waiting in line. In this problem, as in many managerial situations, Jerry was *not* able to put a precise cost on customer waiting time, but by stating the conditions under which he would add another cashier, he in effect is saying "Reduction by half of the time an average customer spends in the system is worth $40 a day to me in goodwill." Having made this subjective determination, he was able to make use of this particular queuing model.

9 The limitations of queuing theory

MORE COMPLEX QUEUING MODELS DEPEND ON STRINGENT ASSUMPTIONS

The models we have introduced are the most useful in practice but represent only a few of the queuing models developed by MS/OR analysts. Models are available for more complex situations, for example, problems in which the population of customers served is finite; the queue discipline is not first come, first served; the service rate depends on the number in the queue; and the arrival rate is something other than Poisson. In general these models depend on stringent assumptions that are rarely realistic in practice.

Even when the model assumptions are realistic, there is another limitation of queuing theory that is often overlooked. Queuing models give steady-state solutions; that is, the models tell you what will happen after the queuing system has been in operation long enough to eliminate the effects of starting with an empty queue at the beginning of each business day. In some applications, the queuing system never reaches a steady state, so the model solutions are of little value.

The authors encountered the steady-state problem in a queuing study of a military disbursing (payroll) office. At first glance the office seemed to be a perfect example of a multichannel model like the one discussed in this chapter. But the model solutions were quite different from what actually happened in the office. A close examination of arrival patterns showed that mean rates changed at least four times during the day. The changes were drastic and never allowed the system to reach a steady state. It was necessary to simulate the disbursing office in order to get realistic solutions that could be used by management.

Simulation is an expensive alternative to queuing models but may be the only alternative when (1) the system never reaches a steady state or (2) a model with realistic assumptions does not exist. In the next section, we shall introduce a *hand-computed* simulation of a waiting-line situation. In practice, simulating a complex queuing system by hand would be nearly impossible, and we would turn to a computer to perform the simulation; however, some experience with a fairly simple queuing simulation will be a useful introduction to the material to be covered in detail in Chapter 15.

10 Simulation of a queuing system

The Valdese Machine Tool Company operates an inventory warehouse which issues raw material to supervisors. Currently, two persons are assigned to operate the system. The number of supervisors who use the warehouse is 10. Beth James, a senior member of the operations department, believes that the line of supervisors which develops at the warehouse every day is inefficient. She realizes from her knowledge of queuing models that the number of supervisors is probably too small to be represented by an infinite population; she also has come to the conclusion that the distribution of the number of arrivals per unit of time is not Poisson; neither is the distribution of service times exponential. She realizes that with a multiple-channel queuing situation which doesn't meet those conditions, finding an analytical model is almost impossible. Therefore she decides to simulate the system.

OBSERVATION

Beth observed the operation of the warehouse for 1-hour periods spread over a month. These 1-hour periods were scheduled at random during the day in order to get a reasonable cross section of activity. She gathered the following data during her observations:

Length of service time, minutes	Number
8	15
9	30
10	45
11	60
Total requests	150

Average time between requests: 5 minutes

In addition to recording the above data, Beth divided her observation time into 5-minute intervals and recorded the number of shop supervisors who arrived during each interval. The mean was one arrival within each 5-minute period.

At the completion of the observation period, Beth tabulated the results of her observations as follows:

Percentage distribution of service times:

$$^{15}/_{150} = 10\% \quad (\ 8 \text{ min})$$
$$^{30}/_{150} = 20\% \quad (\ 9 \text{ min})$$
$$^{45}/_{150} = 30\% \quad (10 \text{ min})$$
$$^{60}/_{150} = 40\% \quad (11 \text{ min})$$

Weighted average of service times:

$10\% \times 8$ min =	0.8 min
$20\% \times 9$ min =	1.8 min
$30\% \times 10$ min =	3.0 min
$40\% \times 11$ min =	4.4 min
Average service time:	10.0 min

With this information, Beth is ready to simulate the operation of the materials warehouse using a table of random digits, Appendix 6.

SIMULATING ARRIVALS

Beth first considers the task of simulating the arrivals of shop supervisors at the materials warehouse. She knows that supervisors arrive randomly, although the mean arrival rate is about 1 every 5 minutes. Because she is dealing with 10 digits (0, 1, 2, 3, 4, 5, 6, 7, 8, 9), she selects one of these (7) and lets it represent an arrival.

If she breaks the simulation down into a number of 5-minute periods of operation and goes through a different list of random 10-digit numbers for each simulated period, the number of 7s she finds in each 10-digit random number will represent the number of arrivals during that period.

Beth simulates arrivals at the materials warehouse for a total of 24 five-minute periods. This is certainly not an optimal length of simulation, but the

Period number	Number of arrivals	Period number	Number of arrivals
1	0	13	0
2	2	14	0
3	0	15	1
4	1	16	4
5	2	17	1
6	0	18	1
7	2	19	1
8	0	20	0
9	3	21	0
10	1	22	1
11	2	23	0
12	1	24	2

TABLE 14-8
Simulated arrivals
for 24 periods

procedure is identical whether the number of periods is 10, 20, or even 100. In practice we would simulate many more periods to be sure that we really knew how the system behaved.

To illustrate the procedure of simulating arrivals, let's reproduce the first 12 ten-digit numbers from Appendix 6 and note the number of 7s appearing in each. Beth reads from left to right *across* the five columns of random digits.

1581922396	None	4637567488	2	7055508767	3
2068577984	2	0928105582	None	6472382934	1
8262130892	None	7295088579	2	4112077556	2
8374856049	1	9586111652	None	3440672486	1

Using the number of arrivals she has just computed for the first 12 five-minute periods and using the same technique to compute the number of arrivals during the *next* 12 five-minute periods, Beth simulates the arrival of shop supervisors at the warehouse. Results for all 24 periods of simulation are shown in Table 14-8.

SIMULATING SERVICE TIMES

USING RANDOM
NUMBERS TO SIMULATE
SERVICING

Having simulated the arrivals at the warehouse, she now turns her attention to a simulation of the service times that would be required by each of the above arrivals. Beth recalls the distribution of service times she originally observed:

Minutes	Percent
8	10
9	20
10	30
11	40

Because she is still working with the same random digits (0, 1, 2, 3, 4, 5, 6, 7, 8, 9), she could divide them up in this sequence:

Let 0 represent the arrival of a supervisor requiring a service time of 8 minutes.

Let 1 and 2 represent the arrival of a supervisor requiring a service time of 9 minutes.

Let 3, 4, and 5 represent the arrival of a supervisor requiring a service time of 10 minutes.

Let 6, 7, 8, and 9 represent the arrival of a supervisor requiring a service time of 11 minutes.

Because Beth has 1 chance in 10 of getting a 0, it represents a .1 probability. Because she has 2 chances in 10 of getting either a 1 or a 2, they represent together a .2 probability. Because she has 3 chances in 10 of getting 3, 4, or 5, they represent together a .3 probability. Because she has 4 chances in 10 of getting a 6, 7, 8, or 9, they represent together a .4 probability. In this manner Beth is able to simulate the behavior of randomly distributed service times using a table of random numbers.

To illustrate this procedure, let's go back to the first 5-minute period of simulation in Table 14-8 and look at the arrivals. There were no arrivals during the first 5-minute period.

SIMULATING ARRIVALS FOR ALL 24 OBSERVATION PERIODS

Looking at the second 5-minute period of simulated activity, Beth sees that there were 2 arrivals. To simulate their service times, she turns to the table of random digits. For service time simulation, Beth elects to use the random digits beginning at the left-hand side of the fourth-from-bottom row of the table. The first two random digits on this row are 9 and 8. According to the procedure described above for simulating service times, the first 2 arrivals require 11 minutes each for servicing.

To repeat this process for clarity: Beth turns to the third 5-minute period and sees from Table 14-8 that there were no arrivals during this time; so she goes on to the fourth period, when there was 1 arrival. The third random digit in the row Beth is using is 4, signifying that this particular arrival required 10 minutes for servicing. If there are no arrivals, Beth does *not* skip a number in the random numbers table. She completes Table 14-9 by working through the above process for all 24 periods of simulation. Each arrival has been assigned a circled number.

SIMULATING THE OPERATION

Now that Beth has simulated both the arrivals at the warehouse and the service time required for each arrival, she is ready to simulate the entire operation of the warehouse. She wants to determine the optimal number of attendants in the warehouse in order to minimize the total cost of warehouse operation *plus* time lost by waiting on the part of the supervisors.

She uses as her queue discipline the first come, first served rule: the supervisors are served as they arrive. The best method to illustrate the overall operation is to use a time scale covering the entire period of simulation. Since

FIRST COME, FIRST SERVED QUEUE DISCIPLINE

ILLUSTRATION OF
ARRIVALS AND THEIR
SERVICE TIMES

Period number	Number of arrivals	Service time of each
1	0	
2	2	① ② 11 min, 11 min
3	0	
4	1	③ 10 min
5	2	④ ⑤ 11 min, 10 min
6	0	
7	2	⑥ ⑦ 9 min, 10 min
8	0	
9	3	⑧ ⑨ ⑩ 10 min, 10 min, 11 min
10	1	⑪ 11 min
11	2	⑫ ⑬ 10 min, 8 min
12	1	⑭ 11 min
13	0	
14	0	
15	1	⑮ 11 min
16	4	⑯ ⑰ ⑱ ⑲ 10 min, 11 min, 11 min, 11 min
17	1	⑳ 9 min
18	1	㉑ 8 min
19	1	㉒ 11 min
20	0	
21	0	
22	1	㉓ 11 min
23	0	
24	2	㉔ ㉕ 9 min, 11 min

TABLE 14-9
Simulated service
times for 24 periods

FORMAT OF THE
SIMULATION

the 24 simulated 5-minute periods are so long as to require a pull-out page if placed end to end, we shall get around this by using time scales placed under each other on a single page, each unit or segment representing 15 minutes; eight such representative scales will be required. Beth begins the simulation at, say, 9 A.M. To make it easier to refer to arrivals, she uses the circled numbers assigned to them in Table 14-9. Directly below each circled arrival is its service time.

To establish a routine for arrivals within each 5-minute period of simulation, Beth makes these assumptions:

1 If there is 1 arrival, it will be assumed to occur at the beginning of the 5-minute period.

2 If there are 2 arrivals, one will be assumed to arrive at the beginning of the period, and the other at the beginning of the third minute during the period.

3 If there are 3 arrivals, one will be assumed to arrive at the beginning of the period, the second at the beginning of the third minute, and the third at the beginning of the fifth minute.

4 If there are 4 arrivals, they will be assumed to arrive at the beginning of the second, third, fourth, and fifth minutes.

To avoid dealing with fractional minutes, Beth elects to set up the pattern assumed above. She knows that the power of simulation lies in its ability to treat situations and events as they actually happen—to avoid forcing them into arbitrary distribution or behavior patterns. Ideally, she knows that the distribution of arrivals within the 5-minute period should be based on *observed* patterns of behavior; however, this information was not recorded, so she must make some assumptions, and she chooses the ones above.

Figure 14-6 illustrates the arrival of all the supervisors who used the service facility during the 2-hour period of simulated activity. Beth first tries to operate the warehouse with two attendants.

To illustrate the actual behavior of the system, Beth uses a diagram in which each minute of time is represented in the left-hand margin. Beside each minute she shows each arrival, the time it begins service, its service time, and the time it waits if waiting is necessary. This diagram is shown in Figure 14-7. Because there are two attendants in the warehouse, they can serve two supervisors simultaneously. You will notice from Figure 14-7 that only *two* solid lines may appear at any one time, since only two attendants are in the warehouse.

DETERMINING THE OPTIMAL
NUMBER OF ATTENDANTS

Beth gathers her results. If she counts the total length (in minutes) of all the waiting time, she sees that it totals 213 minutes, or an average waiting time per arrival of 213/25 = 8.52 minutes. To convert her findings into dollars, she assigns a wage rate to both the warehouse staff and the supervisors:

Hourly wage rate for warehouse attendants = $7

Hourly wage rate for supervisors = $12

Now, if the average time between arrivals was 5 minutes (page 681), the supervisors must make 96 trips to the warehouse daily (8 hours per day × 12 trips per hour). And if the average waiting time is 8.52 minutes per trip,

EXACT TIME ASSIGNED
TO ARRIVALS IN THE
SIMULATED PERIOD

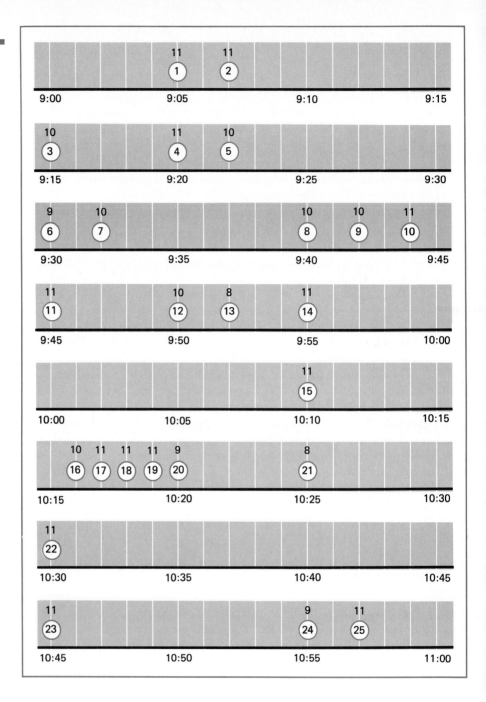

FIGURE 14-6
Arrivals.

total waiting time is $8.52 \times 96 = 817.9$ minutes, or 13.63 hours of lost time daily.

The supervisors' time costs \$12 per hour; therefore, the daily cost of lost time is 13.63 hours $\times$ \$12 = \$163.56. Adding to this the cost of the two warehouse attendants (8 hours $\times$ \$7 per hour $\times$ 2 people = \$112), Beth gets the total cost of operating the warehouse in this manner:

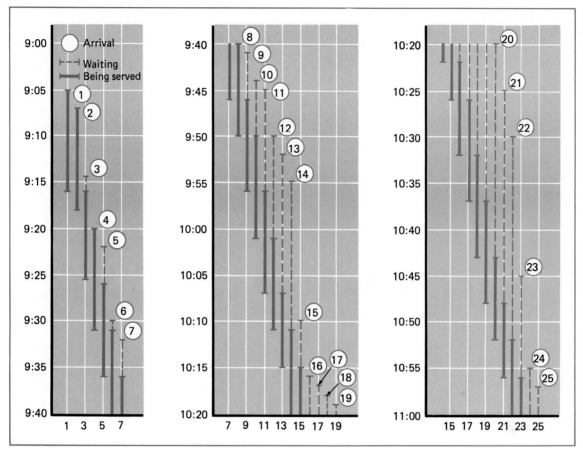

FIGURE 14-7
Warehouse operation with two attendants.

Cost of lost time of supervisors		$163.56
Wages of attendants		112.00
Total daily cost		$275.56

Is two, then, the optimal number of attendants to assign to the warehouse? There is only one way Beth can be sure, and that is to simulate the system with *three* attendants.

Beth has done this in Figure 14-8 in exactly the same manner as before, except that now she has allowed three solid lines to exist simultaneously because three supervisors can now be served at the same time.

Again she counts the total number of minutes of lost waiting time, which in this case totals 47 minutes. This is equivalent to 47/25, or 1.88 minutes lost per arrival. With 96 arrivals per day, the total time lost is 96 × 1.88, or 180.48 minutes, which equals approximately 3 hours per day.

ECONOMIC CONSEQUENCES OF THREE-PERSON STAFFING

Cost of lost time of supervisors	3 × $12	= $ 36
Wages of attendants	8 × $ 7 × 3 =	168
Total daily cost		$204

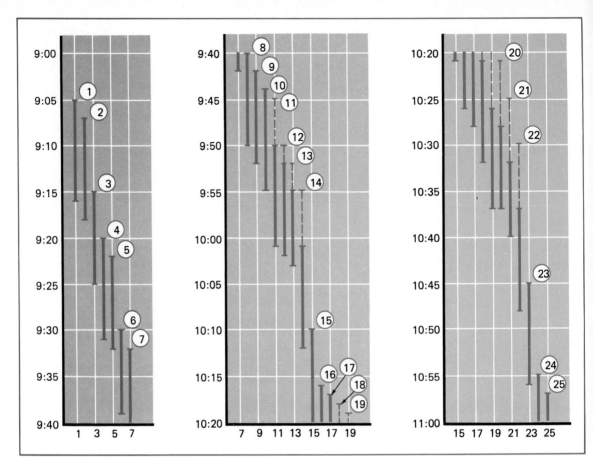

FIGURE 14-8
Warehouse operation with three attendants.

CONSIDERATION OF FOUR-PERSON STAFFING

This is lower than that incurred with two attendants; thus it is the better alternative. But what about the possibility that using four attendants would lower costs still more? Should Beth simulate this too?

Suppose that four attendants did somehow manage to remove *all* waiting time on the part of the supervisors. If this were the case, costs would be as follows:

Cost of lost time of supervisors	$0 \times \$12$	$= \$ \quad 0$
Wages of attendants	$8 \times \$ 7 \times 4 =$	$\underline{224}$
Total daily cost		$\$224$

This clearly results in an alternative that is less attractive financially than having three attendants. Thus, in this problem, Beth finds from her simulation of the queuing system that the best warehouse staffing is three attendants.

11 Comparing the simulation solution with a formula solution

It may be interesting to compare Beth's simulated solution with a "formula" solution using Eq. (14-22) (this formula yields the mean time in the queue for the multichannel case). To solve for the mean waiting time using Eq. (14-22), we see that we first need to solve Eq. (14-20) for the value of L_q. And we further see that to solve for L_q, we first need to solve Eq. (14-19) for L_s. Here are the appropriate calculations for the three-attendant case:

$$L_s = \frac{\lambda\mu(\lambda/\mu)^k}{(k-1)!\,(k\mu - \lambda)^2} P_0 + \frac{\lambda}{\mu} \qquad (14\text{-}19)$$

$$= \frac{12 \times 6(12/6)^3}{(3-1)!\,(3 \times 6 - 12)^2}(.11435) + \frac{12}{6}$$

$$= 2.915$$

$$L_q = L_s - \frac{\lambda}{\mu} \qquad (14\text{-}20)$$

$$= 2.915 - \frac{12}{6}$$

$$= .915$$

$$W_q = \frac{L_q}{\lambda} \qquad (14\text{-}22)$$

$$= \frac{.915}{12}$$

$$= .076 \text{ hour}$$

WHY THE NEW DIFFERENCE?

Now, .076 hour is about 4.5 minutes, which is about twice the answer (1.88 minutes) Beth got with her simulation. What happened? Well, as Beth knew, her arrival distribution was not Poisson, and her service distribution was not exponential. And we ran her simulation for just a few hours, hardly time for the queue to really begin to build up. Finally, we used $\lambda/k\mu = .66$ when the true value is $\frac{2}{3}$. Interpolation in the table would have yielded $P_0 = .11116$. Nevertheless, even with this short, "nonconforming" simulation, we can legitimately speculate that running it additional hours would likely increase the waiting time beyond the nearly 2 minutes Beth found with her simulation. Just out of curiosity, one of the authors programmed a very simple simulation and ran it for a simulated 12 hours; the waiting time seemed to stabilize at nearly 2.63 minutes per arrival, an answer not very different from Beth's.

In situations where we cannot handle the mathematical complexities inherent in a queuing problem, we have no choice other than to use simulation as an approach to solving the problem.

12 Glossary

Aggregate service rate In a multiple-channel queuing system, the mean service rate per channel times the number of channels.

Calling population The population from which the queue forms.

Finite calling population A calling population where the probability of an arrival is changed when one member of the population is receiving service.

Finite queue length A situation where the number in the system is restricted to some maximum (M).

First-come, first-served queue discipline A system in which the queue member who arrived first is served first.

Infinite calling population A calling population where the probability of an arrival is not changed when one member of the population is receiving service.

Multichannel system A queuing system with more than one parallel service facility.

Multiserver system A queuing system where service must be received from more than one station in order.

Priority queue discipline A system in which members of the calling population may have different priorities entitling them to service on either a *preemptive* basis (when they can interrupt members already receiving service) or a *nonpreemptive* basis (where they hold a priority over other members of the calling population but cannot interrupt a member already receiving service).

Service facility The facility which provides service to the waiting line.

Single-channel system A queuing system where there is one service facility.

Unlimited queue length A situation where there are no restrictions on the maximum number in the system.

Waiting line, or queue A group of arrivals waiting for service.
Waiting time The time spent in the queue or in the queue plus being served.

13 Review of equations

Equations (14-1) through (14-5) compute performance measures for the basic single-channel model with these assumptions: Poisson-distributed arrivals; exponentially distributed service times; infinite waiting capacity for customers; an infinite calling population; first-come, first-served queue discipline; and a mean arrival rate λ less than the mean service rate μ.

Page 671

$$L_q = \text{mean number in the queue} = \frac{\lambda^2}{\mu(\mu - \lambda)} \tag{14-1}$$

Page 671

$$L_s = \text{mean number in the system} = \frac{\lambda}{\mu - \lambda} \tag{14-2}$$

W_q = mean time in the queue = $\dfrac{\lambda}{\mu(\mu - \lambda)}$ (14-3)

Page 672

W_s = mean time in the system = $\dfrac{1}{\mu - \lambda}$ (14-4)

Page 672

P_w = probability the service facility is busy (utilization factor) = $\dfrac{\lambda}{\mu}$ (14-5)

Equations (14-6) through (14-10) compute performance measures for the single-channel model with any service distribution (not just the exponential), provided the service times are independent, the same distribution applies to all customers served, and the mean service time ($1/\mu$) and the variance of the service time (σ^2) are known. Other assumptions needed to use these equations are exactly the same as for Eqs. (14-1) through (14-5).

Page 673

L_q = mean number in the queue = $\dfrac{\lambda^2\sigma^2 + (\lambda/\mu)^2}{2(1 - \lambda/\mu)}$ (14-6)

Page 674

L_s = mean number in the system = $L_q + \dfrac{\lambda}{\mu}$ (14-7)

Page 674

W_q = mean time in the queue = $\dfrac{L_q}{\lambda}$ (14-8)

Page 674

W_s = mean time in the system = $W_q + \dfrac{1}{\mu}$ (14-9)

Page 674

P_w = probability the service facility is busy (utilization factor) = $\dfrac{\lambda}{\mu}$ (14-10)

Equations (14-11) through (14-17) compute performance measures for the single-channel model with finite waiting capacity. The capacity is M, the maximum number which can be in the system at one time. M includes those waiting as well as those in service. If a customer arrives when M are already in the system, the customer is lost forever. Other assumptions needed to use these equations are the same as for Eqs. (14-1) through (14-5).

Page 676

$$P_0 = \text{probability of zero in the system} = \frac{1 - (\lambda/\mu)}{1 - (\lambda/\mu)^{M+1}} \tag{14-11}$$

Page 676

$$P_w = \text{probability the service facility is busy (utilization factor)} = 1 - P_0 \tag{14-12}$$

Page 676

$$P_M = \begin{array}{l}\text{proportion of customers} \\ \text{lost because system is full}\end{array} = \left(\frac{\lambda}{\mu}\right)^M P_0 \tag{14-13}$$

Page 676

$$L_s = \begin{array}{l}\text{mean number in} \\ \text{the system}\end{array} = \frac{P_w - M(\lambda/\mu)P_M}{1 - (\lambda/\mu)} \tag{14-14}$$

Page 676

$$L_q = \text{mean number in the queue} = L_s - \frac{\lambda(1 - P_M)}{\mu} \tag{14-15}$$

Page 676

$$W_s = \text{mean time in the system} = \frac{L_s}{\lambda(1 - P_M)} \tag{14-16}$$

Page 676

$$W_q = \text{mean time in the queue} = W_s - \frac{1}{\mu} \tag{14-17}$$

Equations (14-18) through (14-22) compute performance measures for the multiple-channel queuing model. The assumptions are the same as for equations (14-1) through (14-5) except the mean arrival rate must be less than the number of channels (k) times the mean service rate per channel. P_0 is obtained from Appendix 5.

Page 678

$$P_w = \begin{array}{l}\text{probability all channels} \\ \text{are simultaneously busy} \\ \text{(utilization factor)}\end{array} = \frac{1}{k!}\left(\frac{\lambda}{\mu}\right)^k \frac{k\mu}{k\mu - \lambda}P_0 \tag{14-18}$$

Page 678

$$L_s = \text{mean number in the system} = \frac{\lambda\mu(\lambda/\mu)^k}{(k - 1)!(k\mu - \lambda)^2}P_0 + \frac{\lambda}{\mu} \tag{14-19}$$

Page 678

$$L_q = \text{mean number in the queue} = L_s - \frac{\lambda}{\mu} \tag{14-20}$$

$$W_s = \text{mean time in the system} = \frac{L_s}{\lambda} \qquad (14\text{-}21)$$

$$W_q = \text{mean time in the queue} = \frac{L_q}{\lambda} \qquad (14\text{-}22)$$

14 Exercises

14-1 In Exercise 15-5, you will simulate a drive-in facility of a single-channel bank. Using the data given in that problem, compute the mean arrival rate (where arrival rate is the reciprocal of interarrival time) and mean service time. Using these means, compute the mean time waiting in the queue using Eq. (14-3).

14-2 Ernie's Super Service has a special bay in the service station which is set up to perform state inspection on customer's cars. The state inspection law requires all cars to be inspected during the month of January if their owners are to avoid paying a late fee. The cars arrive at Ernie's at an average rate of 3 an hour in a pattern which can be described by a Poisson distribution. The attendant in the inspection bay can inspect an average of 6 cars an hour. Inspection times are exponentially distributed. Ernie was overheard to make this statement: "If I could reduce the average time a customer has to wait by a third, I would open another inspection bay." Would opening a second bay achieve Ernie's goal?

14-3 Trucks arrive at a facility to be unloaded in a pattern which can be characterized by the Poisson distribution. The average rate of arrivals is 30 per hour, and the service times are normally distributed with a mean service time of 1.5 minutes and a standard deviation of .2 minutes. The drivers make $12 each hour and do not unload the trucks. How much expense, on the average, is incurred by the trucking company for idle time on the part of each driver for each visit to the facility?

14-4 The arrival of employees at a tool crib can be described by a Poisson distribution. Service times are exponentially distributed. The rate of arrivals averages 45 machinists each hour, while an attendant can serve an average of 50 employees each hour. The machinists are paid $15 per hour, while the attendants are paid $10 per hour. Find the optimal number of attendants to place in the crib.

14-5 The registrar at Western University is making plans for fall registration. The final step in the registration process is the bursar's office, which determines the fees owed by each student. Students arrive at the bursar's office in a pattern which is well-described by a Poisson distribution at an average rate of 500 an hour. A single clerk in the office can perform the necessary check at a mean rate of 60 an hour where the service times are exponentially distributed. If the registrar thinks that, on average, students should not have to wait longer than 30 minutes to be served, how many clerks should she schedule for registration?

14-6 Charlotte's lunch break is only 30 minutes. Her favorite restaurant is the Carolina Coffee Shop, but it is also the favorite of many other people and there is often a line at the door. Charlotte knows that she can wait in line no more than 5 minutes if she is to get back to work on time. If persons arrive at the Carolina Coffee Shop at an average rate of 30 an hour in a manner that can be described by a Poisson distribution and if the restaurant can serve 40 customers an hour with service times that are exponentially distributed, will Charlotte be able to eat there and still get back to work on time?

14-7 Jackie Marsh works at the Talmage Insurance Company processing claims. The claims arrive at her desk according to a Poisson distribution with a mean of 10 claims per day. She processes the claims according to a uniform distribution with a mean of 11 claims per day and a standard deviation of 2 hours per claim during each 8-hour day. What is the average time taken before a newly arrived claim is processed?

14-8 Frank Filipiak plans to open a Dairy Queen restaurant in Mt. Holly Springs, Pennsylvania. The restaurant will have a drive-in window, although Frank is uncertain about the number of spaces to allow for cars. During peak business hours, Frank estimates that cars will arrive at the drive-in window at the rate of 20 per hour, Poisson distributed. He estimates that the average service time per car will be 2.5 minutes, exponentially distributed. There are a number of fast-food restaurants with drive-in windows in the area, so Frank believes that any customer who arrives when the line is full will be lost. Frank wants to keep the proportion of lost customers to less than 5 percent. How many spaces should the drive-in line have?

14-9 Harmon White is manager of inventory at East Bloomington Appliance Repair. His current policy is to maintain open bins of parts and electrical components. The repair personnel have free access to these bins. A major problem he experiences with this policy is that many of the repair personnel pilfer parts and components as a source of supply for their off-duty hobby activities as well as unauthorized repairs they perform on a moonlighting basis. He estimates that the company experiences losses of about $160 per day due to pilferage. In order to correct this problem, he is considering the adoption of a new policy where the repair personnel would be required to go to a service desk where they would receive the parts and components. All parts and components would then be identified and charged against authorized work orders, thus eliminating the pilferage loss. He has decided to adopt the new policy if the total cost of staffing the service desk and of lost time due to waiting on the part of repair personnel is less than his current pilferage costs. He would have to pay the service desk employee $70 per day. He estimates that the repair personnel would arrive at the desk for parts according to a Poisson distribution with a mean of 40 arrivals per day. The service desk employee could handle these arrivals according to an exponential distribution with a mean service rate of 90 requests per day. Repair personnel are paid $90 per day. Can Harmon justify the new policy on the basis of cost?

14-10 Charlie Gearing's U-Fill-Em and Quicki-Wash gives a free car wash with each fill-up of gasoline. After paying for the gas, customers get in line to be cycled through either of two car washers. The response to this promotional idea has been so great that the car-wash line is interfering with the operation of the gas pumps, causing problems for Charlie. Charlie notes that arrivals for the car wash average 30 an hour and can be described by a Poisson distribution; he also notes that each car wash can service 20 cars an hour with exponentially distributed service times. Charlie is willing to increase the number of car washers until he has decreased the mean length of the waiting line by half. How many car washers does Charlie need to meet this goal?

14-11 Carol Franklin schedules conference rooms for the Desmond Company. She receives requests for conference rooms according to a Poisson distribution with a mean of 12 requests per day. She processes the requests manually and follows up her work by distributing memoranda and daily room scheduling announcements. She can schedule an average of 16 conference rooms per day, using the manual method. She is uncertain about how her service time is distributed. She is contemplating the use of a computerized scheduling system. With such a system, her scheduling time would be greatly reduced, because personnel who request the rooms can access the schedule from their own terminals and this will make it unnecessary to issue confirmation memoranda and daily room schedules. Carol feels that with the computerized system she could process 26 requests per day. She would like to determine how much more time in an 8-hour day she could free up to do other productive work if she adopts the computerized system.

14-12 The Orange County Community Health Center is responsible for administering polio vaccine to school-age children. The center is set up in such a way that parents, with their children, form a single line from which they are served at a mean exponential rate of 40 an hour, by any one of several nurses on duty. The service is offered once a week, and on that day the mean Poisson arrival rate is 60 an hour. The director of the center knows that most of the parents are employed and have taken time off from work to bring the children for shots. The director wishes to limit the average time for receiving the shots to 15 minutes. How many nurses are needed to meet that goal?

14-13 The Henson Airlines office in Richmond, Virginia, has one agent and four telephone lines. If the agent is talking to a customer on one line, up to three calls can be put on hold. If all four telephone lines are busy, a potential customer gets a busy signal. Calls arrive at the rate of 30 per hour, Poisson distributed. The average length of a call is 1.5 minutes, exponentially distributed. Assuming that anyone who gets a busy signal calls another airline (the customer is lost), compute:
   a. The probability that a caller will get to talk to the agent immediately
   b. The probability that a caller will be put on hold
   c. The average time a caller will spend on hold
   d. The average number of customers lost in an 8-hour business day

14-14 The Mastercraft Machine Company operates a warehouse that serves its mechanics. An observer has determined that the mechanics arrive at the warehouse at the random arrival rate of 12 per hour. The one warehouse attendant currently assigned is able to serve these arrivals at the uniform rate of 8 per hour. The observer has also recorded data which indicate that on the average there are 2 arrivals during any 10-minute period. The attendant is paid $5 per hour, and each mechanic is paid $8 per hour. Use the simulation method to determine the optimal number of attendants to assign to the warehouse to minimize total cost.

14-15 The personnel manager of the Acme Machine Shop needs to hire a mechanic to fix a certain type of lathe when in need of repair. Breakdowns on the lathes are Poisson-distributed and occur on the average of 3 per hour. Any lathe out of service, either being repaired or waiting to be repaired, costs the company $80 per hour. The personnel manager can consider hiring either one of two applicants. The first applicant is a very speedy worker who can repair these types of lathes at an average rate of 5 per hour (exponentially distributed) and expects to be paid $18 per hour. The second applicant is somewhat slower, performing on the average 4 repairs per hour (also with exponentially distributed service times) and he expects a wage of $10 per hour. Should the company hire either or both workers in order to minimize total cost? Assume that if both are hired, they would work as a team with mean service rate equal to the sum of the two individual service rates.

14-16 Motorists arrive at Tony's Filling Station for state auto inspection at a mean rate of 10 cars per hour, Poisson distributed. Tony is able to perform 12 inspections per hour on average and his inspection time is exponentially distributed. He only has room at his filling station to accommodate 6 cars waiting in line for inspections. What percentage of the time is Tony working on inspections, and what is the percentage of potential customers who go elsewhere for inspections because his waiting area is full?

14-17 The owner of the Crow's Nose frozen pea factory is considering the layout of processing equipment to package and freeze a grade of peas for consumers. Each day a quantity of peas is harvested and sent to "vineries," where the peas are removed from the pods. From there, they are trucked to the frozen pea factory. Arrivals at the factory are Poisson-distributed with a mean arrival rate of 7 trucks per hour. The owner of the factory knows that peas are quite perishable and should not be left on the loading dock for too long before they are processed. He figures that if the waiting time before processing can be kept below 4 hours on the average, then the peas will have an adequate level of freshness for processing. Assuming that the processing and freezing times of peas are exponentially distributed, determine the minimum average service rate (in truckloads per hour) that the factory must be designed to accommodate.

14-18 Dr. Wilma McFall, a dentist, schedules her patients for half-hour visits; she can, on the average, finish work on her patients in the half hour allocated. Her process time per patient is variable, however, and approximates a normal distribution (1 standard deviation = 10 minutes). The patients sometimes come early or late, and occasionally they do not show up at all. Dr. McFall figures the probability that a given patient will not show up is .10. The probability of the patient being on time is .60. The probability of arrivals half an hour early or half an hour late is .15 for each individual. Simulate Dr. McFall's schedule for an 8-hour day (16 scheduled patients). Assume Dr. McFall takes patients on a first-come, first-served basis, except that when two or more arrive at the same time, she takes the one with the earlier scheduled appointment.

14-19 At the Custom Machine Shop, Martha Wilson works all jobs requiring a numerically controlled lathe operation. Her process time is normally distributed with a mean of 30 minutes and a standard deviation of 10 minutes. She is kept busy 80 percent of the time. Determine the average time a newly arriving job spends at Martha's work station before it has been completed.

14-20 Fast-Foto is a rapid film processor with drive-up depositories scattered around metropolitan Minneapolis. Jerry Dana, the owner, guarantees 24-hour delivery on processing. Film is picked up at each depository frequently and delivered to the processing center. Arrivals at the processing center are described by a Poisson distribution with a mean of 500 rolls an hour. Jerry has a single processing machine which has a capacity of 600 rolls of film an hour and on which the service times are exponentially distributed. Jerry is thinking of changing his guarantee to 4-hour delivery. He has space to add up to two more processing machines. He charges an average of $5 a roll for processing and estimates his total costs at $4 a roll. He thinks his current business would increase by 50 percent if he could advertise 4-hour delivery. Additional costs incurred by this guarantee (increased pickups and maintenance, for example) would raise his costs per roll by 20 cents with each new machine brought online. For example, adding a second machine would raise the cost to $4.20. Should Jerry add machines to meet his new guarantee if he requires that his total profits must remain at least as high as before?

14-21 Gwin Lumber Company has a logging operation near Crossville, Tennessee. Cut logs are skidded from the cut site to a logging road where a crew loads log trucks. Gwin has sufficient log trucks to ensure that there is always at least one empty truck available for loading. Load skidders arrive at the truck loading area at an average rate of 3 per hour in a manner that follows a Poisson distribution. A crew of 5 can take care of 4 skidders an hour with service times that are exponentially distributed. Gwin wants a less costly way to load, since it costs $60 an hour to operate a skidder, loaded or empty. There is a hydraulic off-loader on the market which can service 7 skidders an hour, with normally distributed service times, with a standard deviation of 2 minutes per skidder. It will cost twice as much as the manual crew, each of whose 5 members gets $8.50 an hour. A second alternative for Gwin is to add another crew who could service as many skidders as the original crew. However, this will also call for the addition of a supervisor at $14 an hour. Which of these alternatives is the less costly for Gwin?

14-22 Penny Jones is an investment broker who has recently rented an office in the Merrill Building. She is interested in having a rotary telephone system installed, but cannot decide how many phone lines are needed. If a call comes in while Penny is talking on another line, her secretary can answer the call and put the client on hold. However, if a call comes in while all lines are tied up, Penny is afraid the caller will go to another broker. How many phone lines should Penny have installed if she wishes 5 percent or less lost calls? She estimates that calls arrive according to a Poisson distribution with a mean of 15 calls per hour. She also estimates that the time she spends on a call is exponentially distributed with a mean service rate of 20 calls per hour.

14-23 The Big Value Market has 13 counters. The average time spent per customer by each clerk is 5 minutes. Average arrivals per hour during three types of activity periods have been calculated, and customers have been surveyed to determine how long they are willing to wait during each type of period.

Type of period	Arrivals per hour	Store's average waiting time target
Peak	110	15
Normal	60	10
Low	30	5

Determine how many counters should be open during each type of period. What assumptions must be made in calculating your answers?

14-24 The Downtown Photographic Studio has taken some proofs of a number of schoolchildren and has scheduled the parents to come into the studio to view the proofs. After viewing the proofs, the parents decide whether or not to buy prints. If they decide to buy, a representative of the studio spends a certain amount of time going over the various types of photos available, their costs, and so forth, and takes the order. Each set of parents makes its purchasing decision independently of all other parents, with a .5 probability that they will buy. The studio has decided to schedule six sets of parents to come into the studio every hour for an 8-hour period. The distribution of times spent serving parents who buy the prints is as follows:

Time spent	Probability of occurrence
10 min	.10
15 min	.20
20 min	.50
25 min	.10
30 min	.10

Assume that the parents are taken first come, first served and that a given set of parents who would normally buy prints becomes discouraged if the line of those waiting to see a representative is three or more. Simulate the system for the 8-hour period when there are two service representatives. Simulate the system with one server. If servers are paid $40 a day, and profit from an average customer is $20, which of the two options (one or two servers) is better?

14-25 The State University medical clinic has four full-time physicians on hand to care for its large student population. A student who visits the clinic checks in at the reception desk and then waits on a first-come, first-served basis until one of the four physicians is available. Arrival of the students is Poisson-distributed with a mean arrival rate of 20 students per hour. The physicians' service time is exponentially distributed with a mean rate of 7 students per hour per physician. Determine:
  a. The time an average student spends in the clinic
  b. The average number of students in the waiting room
  c. The utilization factor for the clinic

14-26 The Liverpool Machine Shop keeps a large number of machines in operation. The machine operators are paid $14 per hour. Often the machine operators must go to the tool crib to check out a special tool. They wait at the tool crib on a first-come first-served basis until they are served by one of the two tool crib attendants. Machine operator arrivals at the crib are Poisson distributed with a mean rate of 40 machinists per hour. The time it takes for each tool crib clerk to locate a tool is exponentially distributed, with a mean service rate per attendant of 24 machinists per hour. If Liverpool pays its tool crib clerks $10 per hour, would it be worthwhile to hire more clerks? If so, how many should the company employ?

14-27 After fall registration at State University, there was an unusual amount of grumbling among the freshmen. It seems that everyone in the freshman class had to stand in line to register for English 101, and only a single faculty member was there to serve them all. Frieda asked her brother, Sam, what she could do about this, and Sam suggested she write a letter to the campus paper. "You can say in the letter that the English department has implied through its actions that your time isn't worth very much," suggested Sam. "In fact, if you can find out how much the average faculty member is paid per hour, and also find out the average number of persons in the English 101 queue, I can compute for you the approximate value the department places on an hour of your time." Frieda was impressed with her brother's ability with numbers, and so she got for him the following data:

Average faculty pay = $8/hr

Average length of queue = 55 students

In order to compute the approximate value, Sam had to get an indication of how long the queue would have been if two faculty members had been available at the English 101 registration desk. After a little investigation, he found that approximately the same number of students had registered for History 101, where two faculty members were on duty. The average queue length there was only 10 students. What approximate value can Frieda say the English department places on a freshman's time?

14-28 Sam Benson is a physical therapist who works with people who have had knee operations. His clients arrive during the afternoons according to a Poisson distribution with a mean of 8 arrivals per hour. Sam's service time is exponentially distributed with a mean service rate of 9 clients per hour. In the morning hours, he is not kept at all busy, because most of the clients prefer to come in the afternoon. He feels that if a client arrives in the afternoon when there are 3 persons waiting, then the arriving client will go to another therapist for treatment. As a means of inducing some of his clients to come in the morning hours, he plans to offer coupons for a free brunch at the Burger Delight. With this plan, he estimates the afternoon arrivals will drop to only 5 arrivals per hour on average. If a lost customer results in a $20 loss in potential profit, what is the most he would be willing to spend on each breakfast coupon each day if his morning and afternoon hours are each 4 hours in length?

14-29 Beth Athers is a junior member in the law firm Jones, Bailey, Fischer, and Athers. The firm maintains a pool of typists who have been unable to keep up with the workload. Beth has been asked to hire three more typists, each of whom will cost the firm $6 per hour in pay and benefits. In checking up on the situation, Beth has discovered that the typists spend a good deal of unproductive time standing in line while waiting to use the firm's duplicating machine. She has developed the following estimates of the duplicating machine's usage:

$$\text{Mean arrival rate} = 25 \text{ typists/hr}$$

$$\text{Mean service rate} = 2 \text{ min/usage}$$

The firm pays $8 per day in rental costs for the duplicating machine. Upon checking with a representative of the machine-rental company, Beth finds that instead of the present machine, she can rent another model, which is twice as fast, for $60 per day. The firm has only enough space to accommodate one duplicating machine. What decisions should Beth make regarding the rental of the new machine and/or the hiring of new typists?

14-30 Mary Jenkins has been placed in charge of a countywide program to immunize high-risk persons against the dreaded H-strain flu. It has been estimated that people will arrive at the immunization center at a mean rate of 400 people per hour. They will form a single queue and be serviced by a number of medical technicians using "shot guns." An individual technician, using one of these guns, can service 100 people per hour. Mary recognizes that many of these high-risk people are elderly and feels that an average time greater than 1 hour spent at the immunization center would be unacceptable. What minimum number of medical technicians should Mary plan for?

15 Chapter concepts quiz

14-1 Queue lengths will be infinite unless the mean service rate is greater than the _____.

14-2 The quantities W_s and W_q differ in that _____ includes time spent in the queue and being serviced.

14-3 In the single-channel model for any service distribution, the service times must be _____ of each other.

14-4 In the finite-waiting-capacity model, the proportion of customers lost increases as the capacity M _____.

14-5 In the multiple-channel model, the mean _____ must be less than the mean service rate times the number of channels.

14-6 Calling populations may be either _____ or _____.

Fill in the Blanks

14-7 Arrivals at many queuing systems have been found in practice to be well described by a _____ distribution.

14-8 A situation where persons join a queue and then later leave it before being served is called _____. If they decide not to enter the queue at all, this is called _____.

14-9 Two classifications for queue discipline are _____ and _____.

14-10 The probability that the service facility is busy is called the _____.

True-False

14-11 In general, the cost of waiting decreases with increased service, and the cost of providing service increases with increased service. **T F**

14-12 The main objective of the analysis of waiting lines is to minimize the cost of operating service facilities to serve customers. **T F**

14-13 The calling population is considered to be infinite if the average length of service time for the next customer is independent of the service time for the preceding customer. **T F**

14-14 The most important arrival characteristic of the calling population is the distribution of the time between arrivals. **T F**

14-15 All the queuing models we considered are assumed to have a non-preemptive priority queuing discipline. **T F**

14-16 In the multiple-channel model, P_0 refers to the probability any one of the servers is busy when a customer arrives. **T F**

14-17 In the single-channel model for any service time, the mean number in the queue decreases as the variance of service time increases. **T F**

14-18 If the mean arrival rate changes during the course of the business day, this may prevent the queuing system from reaching a steady state. **T F**

14-19 In the finite-waiting-capacity model, the probability an arriving customer will join the queue depends on the mean service rate. **T F**

14-20 If both arrival and service rates are constant, a queue cannot form. **T F**

14-21 In the single-channel model, if $\mu = \lambda$, infinite queues would build up. **T F**

14-22 In a single-channel queuing model with a finite capacity, M, the value M is the maximum number of persons the queue can hold. **T F**

14-23 One limitation of queuing models is that they assume the system is in steady state. **T F**

14-24 Because of sheer numbers, an infinite calling population is a much more complex queuing problem to handle than one with a finite population. **T F**

14-25 If more capacity is added to a finite-waiting-capacity queuing system, this will reduce the average time waiting. **T F**

Multiple Choice

14-26 Which of the following is not an assumption of the single-channel queuing model with Poisson arrivals and exponential service times?
   a. The queue discipline is first come, first served.
   b. The calling population is finite.
   c. There is a single-service facility.
   d. The mean arrival rate is less than the mean service rate.

14-27 From the equations for the results of the single-channel model with Poisson arrivals and exponential service times, we get:

a. $L_s < L_q$
b. $W_s < W_q$
c. $W_q < W_s$
d. $L_s = (\lambda/\mu) \times L_q$

701
WAITING LINES

14-28 Which of the following is not an assumption of the multichannel queuing model with Poisson arrivals and exponential service times?
a. Queue discipline is first come, first served.
b. The calling population is infinite.
c. There is more than one channel.
d. The mean arrival rate is less than the mean service rate for each channel.

14-29 Which of the following is necessary if simulation is to be used to analyze a queuing system?
a. A distribution for arrival times and service times, whether assumed or empirical
b. Infinite calling population
c. First-come, first-served queuing discipline
d. All of the above

14-30 In the finite-waiting-capacity model, the mean arrival rate:
a. Decreases with the number in the queue
b. Increases with the number in the queue
c. Is not affected by the number in the queue
d. None of the above

14-31 Another term for "channels" in a queuing system is:
a. Queue discipline
b. Servers
c. Arrivals
d. Queue length

14-32 A priority queue discipline may be classified as:
a. Preemptive or nonpreemptive
b. Finite or infinite
c. Limited or unlimited
d. All of the above

14-33 In a queuing system where the elapsed time between consecutive customer arrivals is 12 minutes on average, the mean arrival rate, λ, is:
a. 12 arrivals per hour
b. 12 arrivals per minute
c. 5 arrivals per minute
d. 5 arrivals per hour

14-34 The term used to describe the situation where customers move from one queue to another in a multiple channel situation is:
a. Balking
b. Reneging
c. Alternating
d. Jockeying

14-35 The physical layout of a waiting line system is described by the:
a. Queue discipline
b. Number of channels
c. Server utilization
d. All of the above

14-36 If a person with priority arrives at a waiting line system and goes to the front of the queue but does not interrupt people who are currently being served, this is called a:

    a. Preemptive queue discipline

    b. Nonpreemptive queue discipline

    c. Limited queue discipline

    d. Unlimited queue discipline

14-37 If a service system is characterized by no person ever having to wait for service, this could possibly be a result of the fact:

    a. The arrival rate exceeds the service rate.

    b. There are multiple channels.

    c. Service time is distributed by something other than exponential.

    d. Arrivals come at scheduled times.

14-38 A characteristic of the exponential distribution is that:

    a. Its variance equals the square of its mean.

    b. Its variance equals its mean.

    c. Its mean can be negative.

    d. None of the above.

14-39 For the multiple channel queuing model the mean number in the queue depends on:

    a. The probability all channels are idle.

    b. The mean arrival rate.

    c. The mean service rate.

    d. All of the above.

14-40 The cost of providing service in a queuing system increases with:

    a. Increased mean time in the queue.

    b. Increased arrival rate.

    c. Decreased arrival rate.

    d. None of the above.

16 Real world MS/OR successes

EXAMPLE: TELLER STAFFING AT BANKERS TRUST COMPANY

QUEUING THEORY COMMON IN BANKING

Since the late 1970s, queuing theory has been widely used in the banking industry as a tool for determining teller staffing requirements. The Banker's Trust Company of New York was one of the pioneers in applying queuing theory. In 1976, Banker's Trust used the multiple-channel model in Section 8 to determine the number of tellers needed at 104 branch banks. The bottom line: annual savings in labor costs of $1 million per year.

STAFF PLANNING SYSTEM

The multiple-channel model is part of a staff planning system developed by Howard Deutsch and Vincent A. Mabert.[1] This system is used periodically to update teller requirements and has three functions: data collection, data

DATA COLLECTION

analysis, and staff determination. Data is collected at each branch over a two-week period. During 15-minute sampling periods, an observer records the

[1] Howard Deutsch and Vincent A. Mabert, "Queuing Theory and Teller Staffing: A Successful Application," *Interfaces,* vol. 10, no. 5, pp. 63–66, 1980.

number of customers arriving, the queue length, and the number of tellers serving customers. The average customer service time for the branch is determined by timing a large number of customers. A minimum of 1,000 customers is usually timed—a sample large enough to ensure that the mean customer service time is statistically reliable. Although arrival rates and customer service times vary considerably by branch, data analysis has consistently shown that they fit the standard queuing assumptions. That is, arrival rates are Poisson-distributed, while service times are exponential.

ARRIVAL RATES ARE POISSON AND SERVICE TIMES ARE EXPONENTIAL

To determine staff requirements, equations (14-18) to (14-22) are solved for a range of values of k, the number of channels or teller windows that are manned. The minimum k is selected that meets management's goal for mean time in the queue. Goals are set by considering the profitability of the branch and the proximity to competing banks. At most branches, a queue time of less than three minutes is the established goal. Since arrival rates at each branch vary considerably during the business week, separate solutions for k are computed by hour of the day and by day of the week. Thus the multiple-channel model is solved many times to develop staff requirements for a branch. To simplify the solution procedure for branch managers, Deutsch and Mabert prepared a set of tables to look up the value of k for a range of typical values of arrival rate, service time, and mean time in the queue.

SOLVING THE QUEUING EQUATIONS

QUEUE TIME GOAL

LOOK-UP TABLES FOR NUMBER OF CHANNELS

The final step in developing a staffing plan is to break down staff requirements for each time period into a detailed schedule showing the number of full- and part-time employees that will be on duty. When this system was implemented, Banker's Trust discovered that numerous full-time tellers were idle much of the day. Therefore, part-time work was emphasized in recruiting and full-time tellers were offered the opportunity to convert to part time. An average of one full-time teller was eliminated at each of the 104 branch banks.

PREPARING DETAILED SCHEDULES

IMPLEMENTATION

15

John Bruse is president of a firm engaged in the distribution of petroleum products to residential consumers. John has a number of trucks available to deliver these products, and for most of the year, these trucks can easily handle demand. However, in the winter months, especially during extended cold snaps, the trucks cannot keep up with demand. John would like to investigate his delivery problem using a quantitative model, but none of the models which analytically produce optimal solutions seem to be adequate for his particular problem. They all have limitations requiring that he make assumptions he feels to be unrealistic. Fortunately, there is a technique John can use—computer simulation. This technique can be used to analyze virtually any problem; it is limited only by the amount of time and money one wishes to spend. Simulation does not, in general, find optimal answers; instead it provides comparative information relating to the performance of some system when different parameters are changed. In John's case, simulation analysis is appropriate because he has been able to identify several alternative courses of action he might take to solve his problem. Each of the alternatives can then be simulated, and John can adopt the alternative that results in least cost.

Simulation, in spite of its inability to provide optimal solutions, is one of the most widely used quantitative techniques in use today. Many managers, like John, find simulation analysis to be of significant value in a wide variety of applications. In this chapter you will learn how simulations are designed, how they are used, and how their results are interpreted.

SIMULATION

CHAPTER OBJECTIVES

■ EXAMINE SITUATIONS IN WHICH
SIMULATION *MUST* BE USED IN PLACE OF
ANALYTICAL SOLUTIONS.

■ REVIEW THE REASONS WHY SIMULATION
MAY BE *PREFERABLE* TO OTHER
DECISION MODELS.

■ DEFINE THE STEPS IN THE
SIMULATION PROCESS.

■ REVIEW SEVERAL SITUATIONS WHERE
SIMULATION PROVIDED USABLE
SOLUTIONS TO COMPLEX PROBLEMS
INVOLVING THE AUTHORS.

■ DEVELOP A HAND-COMPUTED SIMULATION
SOLUTION FOR A PROBLEM.

■ DEVELOP COMPUTER SIMULATIONS FOR
THREE COMPLEX PROBLEMS.

■ REVIEW THE CAVEATS ON THE USE OF
SIMULATION AS A DECISION TECHNIQUE.

1 Introduction

Simulation is a quantitative procedure which describes a process by developing a model of that process and then conducts a series of organized trial-and-error experiments to predict the behavior of the process over time. Observing the experiments is very much like observing the process in operation. To find out how the real process would react to certain changes, we can produce these changes in our model and simulate the reaction of the real process to them.

For instance, in designing an airplane, the designer can solve various equations describing the aerodynamics of the plane. Or if those equations are too difficult to solve, a scale model can be built, and its behavior can be observed in a wind tunnel. In simulation, we build mathematical models which we cannot solve analytically and run them on trial data to simulate the behavior of the system.

ANALYTICAL SOLUTIONS VERSUS SIMULATION

In the case of a number of problems, we have been able to find an analytical solution. We found the economic order quantity in Chapter 6, the simplex solution to a linear programming problem in Chapter 9, and a branch-and-bound solution in Chapter 13. However, in each of these cases the problem was simplified by certain assumptions so that the appropriate analytical techniques could be employed. It is not difficult to think of managerial situations so complex that analytical solution is impossible given the current state of the art in mathematics. In these cases, simulation offers a reasonable alternative.

If we insist that all managerial problems have to be solved analytically, we may find ourselves *simplifying* the situation so that it *can* be solved; sacrificing realism to solve the problem can get us in trouble. Whereas the assumption of normality in dealing with a distribution of inventory demand may be reasonable, the assumption of linearity in order to apply linear programming in a specific environment may be totally unrealistic.

In many cases, the solutions which result from simplifying assumptions are suitable for the decision maker; in other cases, they simply are not. Simulation is an appropriate substitute for analytical solution of a model in many situations. Although it too involves assumptions, they are manageable. The use of simulation enables us to provide insights into certain management problems where analytical solution of a model is not possible.

USE OF SIMULATION

Some mathematicians insist that simulation should be used only as a "last ditch" approach, that is, when nothing else seems to work. Despite attitudes like this, it turns out that simulation is one of the most widely used MS/OR techniques. A survey of quantitative techniques used in the corporate planning processes of the 1,000 largest companies in the United States indicated that simulation was the most widely used method; some 29 percent of the respondents indicated that they employed simulation studies in their corporate planning. Compare this, for example, with 21 percent who said they used linear programming and only 12 percent who reported using inventory theory in the same process.[1] Another study of the nonacademic members of the Operations Research Society of America showed that, to practicing MS/OR analysts, simulation had the third-highest value of all the quantitative techniques in use.[2] It seems clear, therefore, that simulation, despite its lack of mathematical elegance, is one of the most widely used quantitative techniques employed by management.

SIMULATION

REASONS FOR USING SIMULATION

Among the reasons why MS/OR analysts would consider using simulation to solve management problems are these:

WHY WE USE SIMULATION

1 Simulation is the only method available because the actual environment is difficult to observe. (In spaceflight or the charting of satellite trajectories, it is widely used.)

2 It is not possible to develop an analytical solution.

3 Actual observation of a system is too expensive. (The operation of a large computer center under a number of different operating alternatives might be too expensive to be feasible.)

4 There is not sufficient time to allow the system to operate extensively. (If we were studying long-run trends in world population, for instance, we simply could not wait the required number of years to see results.)

5 Actual operation and observation of a system is too disruptive. (If you are comparing two ways of providing food service in a hospital, the confusion that would result from operating two different systems long enough to get valid observations might be too great.)

SHORTCOMINGS OF SIMULATION

Use of simulation in place of other techniques, like everything else, involves a trade-off, and we should be mindful of the disadvantages involved in the simulation approach. These include:

DISADVANTAGES OF USING SIMULATION

1 Simulation is not precise. It is *not* an optimization process and does not yield an *answer* but merely provides a set of the system's responses to different operating conditions. In many cases, this *lack* of precision is difficult to measure.

2 A good simulation model may be very expensive. Often it takes years to develop a usable corporate planning model.

---

[1] F. C. Weston, "O.R. Techniques Relevant to Corporate Planning Function Practices, an Investigative Look," *Operations Research Bulletin,* vol. 19, suppl. 2, Spring 1971.
[2] R. E. Shannon and W. E. Biles, "The Utility of Certain Curriculum Topics to Operations Research Practitioners," *Operations Research,* vol. 18, no. 4, 1970. (For another excellent study of corporate use of simulation in planning, see Thomas H. Naylor and Horst Schauland, "A Survey of Users of Corporate Planning Models," *Management Science,* vol. 22, no. 9, pp. 927–937, 1977.)

3 Not all situations can be evaluated using simulation. Only situations involving uncertainty are candidates, and without a random component, all simulated experiments would produce the same answer.

4 Simulation generates a way of evaluating solutions but does not generate the solution techniques. Managers must still generate the solution approaches they want to test.

STEPS IN THE SIMULATION PROCESS

EIGHT STEPS IN
USING SIMULATION

All effective simulations require a great deal of planning and organization. Although simulations vary in complexity from situation to situation, in general you would have to go through these steps:

1 Define the problem or system you intend to simulate.

2 Formulate the model you intend to use.

3 Identify and collect the data needed to test the model.

4 Test the model; compare its behavior with the behavior of the actual problem environment.

5 Run the simulation.

6 Analyze the results of the simulation, and, if desired, change the solution you are evaluating.

7 Rerun the simulation to test the new solution.

8 Validate the simulation; that is, increase the chances that any inferences you draw about the real situation from running the simulation will be valid.

2 Simulation in practice

THREE ACTUAL
PROBLEMS SOLVED
WITH SIMULATION

The problems to which simulation has been applied successfully are far too numerous to list here. It is useful at this point, however, to give you some idea of the variety of managerial situations in which this technique has been able to aid the decision process. Each of the situations which we will now describe represents an actual problem in which the authors have been involved.

THE HOME-HEATING-OIL SIMULATION

SIMULATING A
DISTRIBUTION SYSTEM

John Bruse, the president of a petroleum products distribution firm in eastern North Carolina, attended a university seminar in quantitative techniques. John became interested in the possibility of using simulation to test the relative effectiveness of several alternative methods of dispatching his eight home-heating-oil delivery trucks. He served over 3,000 residential customers in his marketing area; these residences had oil tanks ranging in capacity from 55 to 1,000 gallons. John's trucks ranged in size from 1,000 to 3,000 gallons, and his bulk plant (the terminal where he stored his heating oil) had a tank capacity of 150,000 gallons. John had one transport truck (used to haul heating oil from the port of Wilmington) but could lease others if necesssary.

John was well aware that periods of low temperature put a strain on his whole delivery system. His eight trucks could not keep up with residential usage; there was confusion and inefficiency around the bulk plant, and additional transport trucks had to be leased at unfavorable short-term rates. There seemed to be three alternatives.

Alternative 1 Increase truck and bulk-plant equipment and personnel so that capacity would be equal to the maximum cold-weather demand. John knew this would be quite expensive, and he had already calculated the additional investment in equipment alone to be near $140,000.

Alternative 2 Deliver heating oil to residences more frequently, that is, keep customers' tanks more nearly full, so that demand during low-temperature periods would be lessened.

Alternative 3 Replace all tanks of the 55-gallon size (at company expense) to increase significantly the efficiency of the delivery trucks (fewer stops each day and more gallons per stop would significantly increase the capacity of the present delivery fleet).

John also realized that combinations of alternatives were another possibility. It seemed clear to us that solving this problem analytically was impossible (or at least beyond our mathematical abilities). Therefore we developed a simulation model of John's system which included these elements:

1 The bulk plant

2 The customers

3 Varying residential tank sizes

4 Local delivery trucks

5 Transport trucks (owned and leased)

6 Employees

7 Heating-oil consumption based on temperature

THE ELEMENTS IN THE SIMULATION MODEL

We simulated several alternative delivery systems over a wide range of demand conditions. The results persuaded us that John should adopt a combination of alternatives 2 (more frequent delivery) and 3 (replacement of 55-gallon tanks). By replacing about 450 small tanks at a cost near $70,000 and by increasing the frequency of deliveries to the point that the average customer's tank was 45 percent full, we were able to *reduce* the number of local delivery trucks by two and effect a comparable saving in personnel as well. Our simulation indicated that even with this reduced delivery capacity, John's system could withstand a prolonged drop in temperatures. In three winters (one of which was the most severe on record), John's new system has operated quite effectively.

WHAT THE SIMULATION INDICATED

THE CARPET-CUTTING APPLICATION

The production vice president of a regional carpet manufacturing company attended our Executive Program. One day he asked if we had ever done any work with "carpet cutting." Soon after that we were in the mill observing the

USING SIMULATION TO REDUCE WASTE

operation. Carpet was manufactured in 175-foot rolls, all 12 feet wide. This company stocked over 200 styles and colors of carpet; usually there were multiple rolls or pieces of rolls of each style and color on hand in the warehouse. Incoming orders for carpet called for lengths ranging from about 3 feet all the way up to an entire roll (175 feet). Incoming orders were delivered to the cutting room, where cutting-machine operators attempted to match existing rolls with incoming orders in such a way that the unusable piece left at the end of the roll (the remnant) would be as small as possible. You can get an idea of the significance of unusable remnants if you consider that the average price per lineal foot of the carpet was about $18 and that any remnant under 3 feet was worth only about 10% of the regular price; remnants between 3 feet and 6 feet were sold for about a third of the regular price. The cost of unusable remnants was amounting to almost $250,000 a year.

TOO MANY WAYS
TO CUT CARPETS

The cutting-machine operators pointed out to us that there were hundreds of ways you could fill an order for a piece of carpet: (1) cut it from the longest roll of the required style and color; (2) cut it from the roll which would leave the shortest piece left over; (3) find two orders which would use up an entire roll or piece of a roll; and so on. To complicate matters, the vice president also wanted us to find out whether it would be economical to collect carpet orders for more than 1 day (2 days, 3 days, etc.) before cutting them, his idea being that the more orders you had, the better match of orders and rolls you could make. Of course, you would have to be willing to risk the wrath of those customers who would be kept waiting longer.

We studied the operation at some length and constructed a simulation model of the system. The components of this model included:

COMPONENTS OF THE
CARPET-CUTTING
MODEL

1 The production operation (the manner in which carpets were delivered to the cutting operation, frequency, etc.)

2 The distribution of incoming orders (size, color, style)

3 The inventory (rolls in sizes, colors, styles)

4 The cutting process (time, employees)

5 The prices of sold carpet and remnants

We simulated the cutting operation under a wide number of different possible "cutting rules"; each simulation run was for 1,000 days, a period deemed long enough to represent a typical order and production pattern. Each time we ran another simulation, we kept track of the effect on inventory, remnants, labor cost, and revenues from sold carpets and remnants. For each different set of cutting rules we evaluated, we allowed carpet orders to accumulate for 1, 2, and 3 days, the last being the maximum that management was willing to try for fear of antagonizing customers.

WHAT THE
SIMULATION SHOWED

Our results showed that the accumulation of orders beyond 2 days had no appreciable effect on reducing remnants, a fact that pleased the customer service manager greatly. We did find a set of seven cutting rules which appeared to be superior to any other set we simulated; application of these rules reduced remnants by 21 percent. Although this may not seem much of a victory, you must remember that (1) the carpet-cutting operation was staffed by intelligent people who had tried different cutting rules for the last 50 years, and (2) a 21 percent reduction in remnants amounted to a saving of over $50,000 annually.

THE PUBLIC SCHOOL PLANNING APPLICATION

One of the authors taught an MS/OR course for the senior administrators of a large metropolitan school system in the northeast. One day the superintendent (a participant in the course) indicated how difficult it was to deal with his school board on certain long-range planning issues and asked whether simulation had anything to offer in such a situation. It seemed that the board was always asking questions like, "What would happen if enrollments began to grow at 9 percent a year instead of 6 percent a year?" Or, "How many years do you think it will be before the population shifts enough to warrant making this elementary school into an adult education center?" There was a whole series of these "how," "when," and "what if" questions.

It was not long before work was under way on a large simulation model of the public school system. With it, the superintendent hoped to be able to do a better job of long-range planning in his very complex environment. The model had to accommodate variables like these:

1   Enrollments (by grade, kindergarten through grade 12)
2   Teacher/pupil ratios
3   Classroom capacities
4   Salaries
5   District population
6   Number of schools (including capacities)
7   Number of teachers by subject, function, or grade
8   Construction cost
9   Transportation equipment
10 Warehousing and repair facilities
11 Administrative personnel by grade and function
12 Service personnel (maintenance, custodial, and so forth)

Over a year of work went into this model; the variables (like the 12 above) had to be related in it. The model had to be able to accept demographic data and, with them, forecast the effects on the school system of future changes in the environment. And the superintendent insisted that the simulation model be in a form that would allow it to be run during school board meetings to test the effect of alternative assumptions about the future.

One evening two very interesting decisions were made as a result of this simulation. A school board member wanted to know why building costs for a proposed elementary school were so high; she was rather impatient while the superintendent explained that a school had to last for about 20 years and that costly construction was necessary to achieve that goal. "But," she said,

PLANNING FOR A SCHOOL SYSTEM WITH SIMULATION

DIFFICULT QUESTIONS

VARIABLES IN THE SIMULATION MODEL

ANSWERING TWO INTERESTING QUESTIONS WITH SIMULATION

"are there going to be any kids in that neighborhood in 20 years?" The superintendent asked us to run the model, making some projections about school-age populations from present demographic data and the trends that were a part of the model. It took only a few minutes to make a run and bring the results back to the board room. "It turns out," the superintendent announced, "that our simulator (as he called it) projects fewer than .1 school-age child per household for that district within 20 years." In the ensuing discussion, the board decided to provide for the enrollment in that district with temporary classroom buildings.

In a later discussion of the Coleman report (a study of effects of sociological variables on learning), the board questioned the cost of altering the teacher/ pupil ratio. Now that sounds like a simple question, but when you consider that to answer it you have to begin with a change in class size and then calculate the effects of that change on teachers, classrooms, buildings, equipment, salaries, administrative personnel, transportation, and benefits— to name only a few of the variables affected—you can see what a task is involved in answering that question. The "simulator" was able to estimate within a few minutes that the cost of decreasing the size of elementary school classes by *one* pupil would be approximately $7.3 million per year, a disclosure which quickly ended further discussion.

3 A hand-computed simulation

DEVELOPING A
HAND-COMPUTED
SIMULATION OF AN
OPERATING ROOM

In this section, we shall introduce you to simulation by using an example which can be simulated manually, that is, done without using a computer. This example concerns the scheduling of patients in a hospital operating room. In the next section, we shall introduce three more simulations which are too complex to be done by hand and therefore require a computer.

WAKE MEMORIAL HOSPITAL SIMULATION

THE WAKE MEMORIAL
SIMULATION
DESCRIBED

Wednesday's schedule for operating room number 3 at Wake Memorial Hospital is as shown in Table 15-1. From looking at this schedule, the head operating room nurse concludes that it may not be possible to finish with the

TABLE 15-1
Wednesday operating
schedule, room no. 3

Time	Activity	Expected time
8:00 A.M.	Appendectomy	40 min
8:40	Cleanup	20 min
9:00	Laminectomy	90 min
10:30	Cleanup	20 min
10:50	Kidney removal	120 min
12:50 P.M.	Cleanup	20 min
1:10	Hysterectomy	60 min
2:10	Cleanup	20 min
2:30	Colostomy	100 min
4:10	Cleanup	20 min
4:30	Lesion removal	10 min
4:40	Cleanup	20 min

Patient arrives on time	.50 probability
Patient arrives 5 minutes early	.10 probability
Patient arrives 10 minutes early	.05 probability
Patient arrives 5 minutes late	.20 probability
Patient arrives 10 minutes late	.15 probability

TABLE 15-2
Arrival expectations

operating and cleanup schedule by 5 P.M., the time at which this operating room must be available for emergency night service.

The hospital management analyst, Margaret Sheeran, suggests that simulation might indicate whether the schedule for Wednesday is workable and, if not, what changes could be made in it. Margaret reviews the operating room records for the past few months and finds that patients do not always arrive at the operating room at the scheduled time. They often have to wait for preoperative medication to be administered, sometimes operating room transportation personnel are late, and from time to time physicians forget to order the patient moved from the floor to the operating room. Margaret's investigation of the operating room log indicates that arrival expectations are about as shown in Table 15-2. Margaret finds that operating times also vary according to surgical difficulties encountered, differences in surgical skills, and the effectiveness of the surgical team in general. An analysis of operations scheduled over the past few months produces the results shown in Table 15-3, which gives a good indication of this variation. Margaret also recognizes that any variation in the expected cleanup time will affect the schedule, and she checks the records once again. Here she finds that about half the time the cleanup crew finishes in 10 minutes. The rest of the time, it takes them 30 minutes. With her data collected, she is ready to begin the simulation.

VARIATION IN THE
PATIENT ARRIVAL
SCHEDULE

VARIATION IN
OPERATING TIMES

VARIATION IN
CLEANUP TIME

GENERATING THE VARIABLES IN THE SYSTEM
(PROCESS GENERATORS)

Margaret needs a way to generate arrival times, operating times, and cleanup times. The methods she uses to do this are called *process generators*. She decides to use a *random number table,* Appendix 6. A random number table is the output we would expect to get from sampling a *uniformly distributed random variable,* a random variable all of whose values (digits from 0 through 9 in this case) are equally likely.

PROCESS GENERATORS
FOR THE SIMULATION

Generating arrival times   Margaret decides to use the *first two* digits of each 10-digit number in Appendix 6 as her process generator for arrival times.

PROCESS GENERATOR
FOR ARRIVAL TIMES

Operation is completed in the expected time	.45 probability
Operation is completed in 90% of the expected time	.15 probability
Operation is completed in 80% of the expected time	.05 probability
Operation is completed in 110% of the expected time	.25 probability
Operation is completed in 120% of the expected time	.10 probability

TABLE 15-3
Operation time
expectations

Since there are 100 possible two-digit numbers from 00 through 99, she relates these two-digit numbers to arrival variation like this:

Random numbers	Arrival	
00–49	On time	(.50 probability)
50–59	5 min early	(.10 probability)
60–64	10 min early	(.05 probability)
65–84	5 min late	(.20 probability)
85–99	10 min late	(.15 probability)

PROCESS GENERATOR FOR OPERATING TIMES

Generating operating times   Now Margaret decides to use the *last two* digits of each 10-digit number in Appendix 6 as her process generator for operating times. She relates these two-digit numbers to operating times in this way:

Random numbers	Operating times	
00–44	On-time completion	(.45 probability)
45–59	Completion in 90% of expected time	(.15 probability)
60–64	Completion in 80% of expected time	(.05 probability)
65–89	Completion in 110% of expected time	(.25 probability)
90–99	Completion in 120% of expected time	(.10 probability)

PROCESS GENERATOR FOR CLEANUP TIMES

Generating cleanup times   Since the random variable takes on only *two* values here, Margaret decides to use a single digit, the *fourth* digit of each 10-digit number in Appendix 6 as her process generator. If it is an odd number, she will let that represent a 10-minute cleanup; an even number will represent a 30-minute cleanup.

THE SIMULATION

Margaret proceeds with the simulation. First she generates an arrival-time deviation for the first patient; then she generates an operating-time deviation for the first operation; finally she generates a cleanup time for that operation. She continues with this process until the last operation has been performed and the operating room cleaned up for the final time that day. The results of her simulation are shown in Table 15-4.

INTERPRETING THE RESULTS

From Margaret's simulation, it appears that the scheduled operations can be completed and the room vacated by 5 P.M. In fact, her simulation indicates that the day's schedule ends at 4:55 P.M., a few minutes early.

ASSUMPTIONS AND CAVEATS

TAKING CARE WITH ASSUMPTIONS

Margaret simulated the day's operation only once, and it is very dangerous for us to draw general conclusions from such a short simulation. If she had repeated the day's simulation several times using different random numbers, then we could feel better about generalizing from her results. Margaret also assumed that the variables in this simulation (arrival deviation, operating

TABLE 15-4

Results of simulation of activity in operating room no. 3

Random number	First two digits	Last two digits	Fourth digit	Meaning	Outcome
15	X			On-time arrival of appendectomy patient	Appendectomy begun at 8 A.M.
96		X		Appendectomy completed in 120% of expected time (48 min)	Appendectomy completed at 8:48 A.M.
1			X	Cleanup done in 10 min	Room ready for second operation at 8:58 A.M.
09	X			On-time arrival of laminectomy patient (9 A.M.)	Laminectomy begun at 9 A.M.
82		X		Laminectomy completed in 110% of expected time (99 min)	Laminectomy completed at 10:39 A.M.
8			X	Cleanup done in 30 min	Room ready for third operation at 11:09 A.M.
41	X			On-time arrival of kidney patient (10:50 A.M.)	Kidney removal begun at 11:09 A.M.
56		X		Kidney removal completed in 90% of expected time (108 min)	Kidney removal completed at 12:57 P.M.
2			X	Cleanup done in 30 min	Room ready for fourth operation at 1:27 P.M.
74	X			Hysterectomy patient arrives 5 min late (1:15 P.M.)	Hysterectomy begun at 1:27 P.M.
68		X		Hysterectomy completed in 110% of expected time (66 min)	Hysterectomy completed at 2:33 P.M.
7			X	Cleanup done in 10 min	Room ready for fifth operation at 2:43 P.M.
00	X			On-time arrival of colostomy patient (2:30 P.M.)	Colostomy begun at 2:43 P.M.
58		X		Colostomy completed in 90% of expected time (90 min)	Colostomy completed at 4:13 P.M.
9			X	Cleanup done in 10 min	Room ready for sixth operation at 4:23 P.M.
72	X			Lesion patient arrives 5 min late (4:35 P.M.)	Lesion operation begun at 4:35 P.M.
40		X		On-time completion of lesion operation (10 min)	Lesion operation completed at 4:45 P.M.
5			X	Cleanup done in 10 min	Operating room schedule for Wednesday completed at 4:55 P.M.

time deviation, and cleanup deviation) were independent of each other. If this is not the case, her simulation is not valid. Finally, Margaret used *discrete* distributions of the three variables. In actual practice, were computation time not such a problem, continuously distributed random variables would be appropriate.

4 Computer simulation

It is difficult, if not impossible, to perform simulations without a computer. Imagine what work would be involved in Margaret's simulation if she simulated that one operating room for a month or simulated the entire suite of 12 operating rooms at Wake Memorial Hospital for a month's time. Because hand-computed simulations are so expensive and so tedious, real simulations are done by computer.

One of the most efficient computer simulation languages is GPSS (General Purpose Simulation System) developed by IBM. We have used GPSS in the three computer simulations which follow. GPSS has these characteristics, which are found in almost every simulation situation:

1 *Transactions.* Transactions are the units of traffic or flow that move through the system. In the example of the operating room, these would be the patients. Transactions in the three simulations to come will be inventory items, ships, and airplanes.

2 *Facilities and storages.* Transactions move from point to point in a system; these points at which units stop or move along are called *facilities* and *storages*. In the hospital simulation, the operating room is a facility. In the airport simulation in this section, a runway is a facility. In the ship simulation we will present, the harbor is a storage, because it can be occupied by a number of units.

3 *Waiting lines.* Because a facility is occupied by only one unit at a time, a waiting line generally develops. Patients waiting for an operating room form a waiting line.

4 *Time.* Time measures the progress of units through the system.

In each case, we begin by first describing the situation we are simulating; then we present a flowchart (a graphic illustration of the flow of units through the system). Finally we show the results of the simulation and discuss the implications of the simulation output.

FLOWCHARTS

Flowcharts are commonly used in simulation. They are nothing more than graphic aids which help us think logically and keep track of the entire process being simulated. Flowchart construction uses a set of standard symbols illustrated in Figure 15-1. You will encounter these again in the three

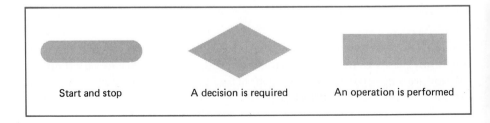

FIGURE 15-1
Standard simulation
flowchart symbols.

Start and stop   A decision is required   An operation is performed computer simulations which follow, so take a minute now and become familiar with these symbolic representations.

COMPUTER LANGUAGES FOR SIMULATION

The authors have used any number of programming languages to do simulations, including what may be the simplest language, BASIC. The problem with using common languages like BASIC, FORTRAN, and COBOL for simulations is that they are often not able to generate random variables in the best way, they require quite a bit of programming to handle simple simulation requirements like tables, and being general-purpose languages, they are considerably less efficient than special-purpose simulation languages.

For these and other reasons, persons who perform quite a bit of simulation or who get involved in very complex simulations generally use one of the special-purpose simulation languages like GPSS, or SIMSCRIPT, or GASP. Although these simulation languages take a bit of learning, they are so much more efficient (of both human and machine time) than the general-purpose ones that the investment is generally well worthwhile.[3]

INVENTORY CONTROL SIMULATION

Bill Perrault, a new MS/OR analyst for the Conner Wholesaling Corporation, is investigating the inventory situation of his company's 24-inch self-propelled rotary mower. The mean and standard deviation of the normally distributed demand for this product are 20 and 5 units a day, respectively. Lead time on reorders is normally distributed, with mean and standard deviation in working days being 6 and 1, respectively. Reorder quantities are in multiples of 100, since the manufacturer ships this mower only in truck lots.

A SIMULATION OF VARIOUS COMBINATIONS OF INVENTORY POLICIES

Bill wants to estimate the number of units of lost sales per week and the average inventory on hand which would result from reorder points of 120, 140, and 160 mowers, *each* combined with reorder quantities of 100 and 200 units. The structure of Bill's simulation model to estimate these statistics is shown in Figure 15-2.

WHAT WOULD LOSSES AND INVENTORY LEVELS BE UNDER VARIOUS COMBINATIONS?

After initializing the stock on hand (setting up a beginning inventory) at the beginning of the simulation, the program cycles through a common series of steps for each business day. First a random number is selected to determine the day's demand value. If demand can be filled in its entirety, it is subtracted from stock on hand. Otherwise lost sales are recorded and stock is set equal to zero. Next, any orders due in during the day are added to stock before recording the stock on hand at the end of the day. To keep track of when orders are due, the program maintains an "event" file, which is simply a list of order due dates. When the "clock" (a counter) is incremented to a value equal to the due date of an order, that order is added to stock. In the reorder division block, stock on hand is compared with the reorder point. If a reorder is necessary, a random number is used to draw a lead time and the due date is posted to the event file. This cycle repeats until the specified number of days elapse.

DESCRIPTION OF THE INVENTORY SIMULATION

[3] For additional references on simulation languages, you can see A. M. Law and C. S. Larmey, *An Introduction to Simulation Using SIMSCRIPT II.5* (La Jolla, CA: CACI, Inc., 1984).

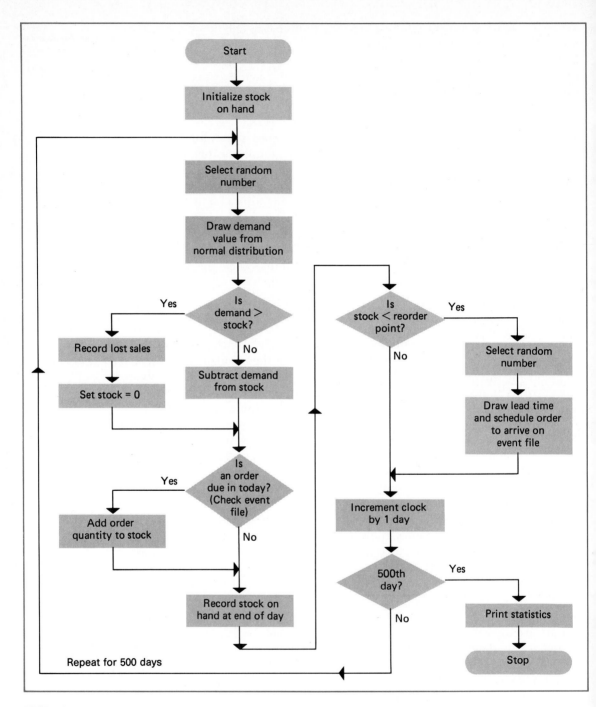

FIGURE 15-2
Flowchart for Bill Perrault's inventory control simulation.

718

Note that two assumptions are implicit in Bill's simulation. When sales are lost, they are lost entirely and do not reappear when stock becomes available later. Also, orders are received and reorder decisions made only at the *end* of each day. Both these assumptions are a matter of convenience and can easily be modified to reflect other conditions.

The problem was programmed in GPSS-V and run with these results:

BILL MAKES TWO IMPORTANT ASSUMPTIONS

Reorder point	Reorder quantity	Average weekly lost sales in units	Average on-hand stock in units
120	100	10.375	44.455
140	100	7.565	50.033
160	100	6.055	56.583
120	200	3.285	97.439
140	200	.765	119.673
160	200	.015	138.439

SIMULATION RESULTS

Runs were made for 500 business days for each reorder point–reorder quantity combination. The same series of random numbers was used in each run to ensure comparability of results. Each run started with the stock on hand equal to the reorder point and with no orders due in.

When Bill checked the results, he saw that higher reorder points, higher reorder quantities, or both generate fewer lost sales, and that lost sales seem to be inversely related to on-hand stocks; of course, he knew all this before he ran the simulation. Since Bill knows the cost of being out of stock and the cost of carrying inventory, he can use the simulation results to find a least-cost combination of reorder point and quantity.

INTERPRETATION OF THE RESULTS

▌ HARBOR SIMULATION

Seth Adams is a U.S. Navy MS/OR analyst assigned to the analysis section of a large harbor installation. He wants to study the waiting-time distribution for ships using this harbor. Seth spends some time analyzing past harbor records and comes up with these figures:

A SIMULATION OF A HARBOR INSTALLATION

Interarrival time in hours (time between arriving ships)	Cumulative frequency with which these times occur
0–6	.1
6.1–12	.2
12.1–18	.9
18.1–24	1.0

Seth notices that arriving ships move into an unloading complex which can handle only one ship at a time. Unloading time is variable because of the different cargoes involved; it ranges over a period of 12 to 16 hours, uniformly distributed.

UNLOADING TIME

SIMULATION CLOCK
AND EVENT FILE

SETH'S SIMULATION
DESCRIBED

RESULTS OF SETH'S
SIMULATION

SUMMARY STATISTICS

Figure 15-3 shows the flowchart Seth made for the simulation he has decided to use to study the harbor operation. He plans to simulate the waiting time experienced by a sample of 500 ships. Here again, Seth uses a simulation clock and an event file (Figure 15-3). The clock is simply a counter that is incremented by the number of time units between consecutive arrivals. The event file is a list of the times at which the two types of events in the simulation (arrivals and unloadings) will occur.

To initialize the simulation, the event file is loaded with two events. In order to operate the program, the first ship arrival and the first unloading completion must be scheduled and placed on the event file. Then the clock is advanced to the first event (which is the arrival).

If an arrival event is "due," the program schedules the next future arrival before processing the current arrival. This procedure keeps the simulation moving. The next step is to check to see whether the unloading complex is free. If so, an unloading completion event is placed on the event file. If the complex is *not* free, an entry is made in a waiting-line file in order to record the time at which waiting begins.

When an unloading completion event is due, the program first records the unloading time in a "service" file to keep the unloading times separate from the waiting times. If the completion is the 500th, the simulation stops. Otherwise the waiting-line file is checked to see whether another ship is waiting to unload. If so, a random number is used to schedule an unloading completion on the event file. The waiting time of the ship is compiled in the waiting-line file by posting the unloading start time to that file (unloading start time minus arrival time in the waiting line equals waiting time). The program then returns to process the next event.

This program was written in GPSS-V and first run for 100 ship completions to "warm up" the model—that is, to wash out the effects of starting the simulation with no ships in line or being unloaded. After the warmup period, statistics were collected for the next 500 ship completions. The results are shown below.

The program printed out some summary statistics which indicated that the mean of the waiting time was 20 hours with a standard deviation of 18.65

Upper limit (hours) of waiting time	Observed frequency	Percent of total	Cumulative percentage
6	150	30.0	30.0
12	74	14.8	44.8
18	53	10.6	55.4
24	52	10.4	65.8
30	41	8.2	74.0
36	33	6.6	80.6
42	19	3.8	84.4
48	17	3.4	87.8
54	23	4.6	92.4
60	21	4.2	96.6
66	8	1.6	98.2
72	5	1.0	99.2
78	4	0.8	100.0

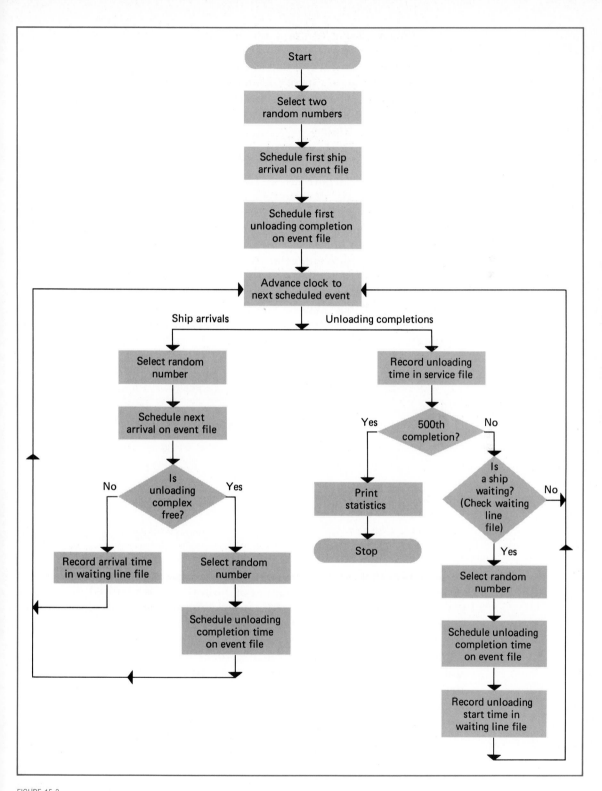

FIGURE 15-3
Flowchart for Seth Adams' harbor simulation.

721

hours. The unloading complex was in use 97.5 percent of the time, and unloading time averaged 14 hours per ship. A maximum of 6 ships were waiting to unload at any one time. Seth reported to his commanding officer that the high utilization rate of the unloading complex coupled with the high waiting time seemed to indicate the need for increasing the capacity of the facility. He asked for some additional cost data and authorization to do further simulation studies.

▌EAST MUNICIPAL AIRPORT SIMULATION

SIMULATION OF
AIRPORT TRAFFIC

The East Municipal airport has two runways available. During the rush period from 8 to 10:05 A.M., 12 takeoffs and 12 landings must be scheduled. Joy Klompmaker, an MS/OR analyst, wants to evaluate the following proposed scheme: takeoffs will be scheduled every 10 minutes beginning at 8 A.M. and landings every 10 minutes beginning at 8:05 A.M. These are the times when planes are scheduled to enter the active runway (for takeoff) or to announce that they are on final landing approach. Planes may be late in arriving at the runway for takeoff because of maintenance, passenger-loading delays, or taxi clearance delays; they may be late landing because of weather, air-traffic-control delays, or late departure. Joy has been able to gather these probability distributions of lateness:

Takeoffs		Landings	
Number of minutes late	**Probability**	**Number of minutes late**	**Probability**
0	.40	0	.30
1–5	.30	1–5	.20
6–10	.20	6–10	.20
11–20	.05	11–20	.20
21–30	.05	21–30	.05
>30	0	31–40	.05
		>40	0

Joy notices that once a plane arrives at the runway for either a takeoff or a landing, an average of 10 minutes of runway time is required to complete the takeoff or landing and free the runway for another plane. Runway time is variable and uniformly distributed from 8 to 12 minutes.

Joy has been told that the schedule that management is proposing is tentative; before it is released, management wants to estimate the runway utilization and the delays encountered by both takeoffs and landings. Joy develops the simulation flowchart in Figure 15-4 and plans to evaluate 25 days of operation under the proposed schedule. Her program starts by loading all scheduled takeoffs and landings and the simulation stop time (10:05 A.M.) to the event file. Thereafter, one of four events can occur: (1) a scheduled takeoff or landing, (2) a "ready" for takeoff or landing, (3) a completion of a takeoff or landing, or (4) the arrival of the simulation stop time. After these events are processed for a given day, the program is reset

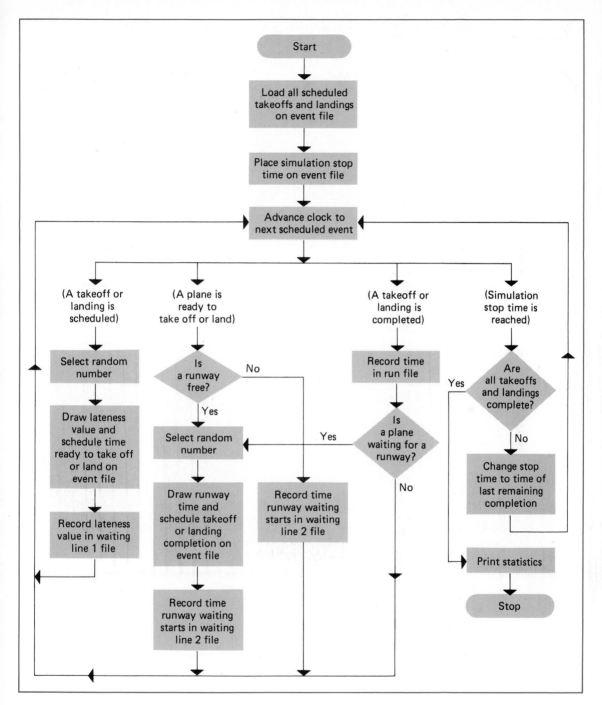

FIGURE 15-4
Flowchart for Joy Klompmaker's airport simulation.

The flowchart contains the following elements:

Start

Load all scheduled takeoffs and landings on event file

Place simulation stop time on event file

Advance clock to next scheduled event

(A takeoff or landing is scheduled)

Select random number

Draw lateness value and schedule time ready to take off or land on event file

Record lateness value in waiting line 1 file

(A plane is ready to take off or land)

Is a runway free?

No → Record time runway waiting starts in waiting line 2 file

Yes → Select random number

Draw runway time and schedule takeoff or landing completion on event file

Record time runway waiting starts in waiting line 2 file

(A takeoff or landing is completed)

Record time in run file

Is a plane waiting for a runway?

Yes → Select random number

No

(Simulation stop time is reached)

Are all takeoffs and landings complete?

Yes → Print statistics

No → Change stop time to time of last remaining completion

Print statistics

Stop

for the next day. Notice from the flowchart that the simulation does not always stop at 10:05 A.M. If planes are still waiting for a runway or are late in getting ready to use a runway, the program finishes such processing before stopping the day's run.

These were Joy's results for 25 days:

Day	Runway utilization	Takeoffs		Landings	
		Minutes late arriving at runway	Minutes late waiting till runway free	Minutes late arriving at runway	Minutes late waiting till runway free
1	.837	2.4	3.4	8.0	2.7
2	.875	1.3	3.8	8.6	4.6
3	.834	4.7	8.1	8.2	10.2
4	.796	1.9	2.6	9.3	4.4
5	.876	1.8	4.0	8.7	4.2
6	.776	2.4	6.0	14.9	5.0
7	.794	1.3	1.8	7.4	2.5
8	.854	4.7	3.8	9.7	5.2
9	.796	4.6	2.1	9.2	4.1
10	.844	4.5	4.1	11.6	2.7
11	.927	2.9	3.0	4.5	2.3
12	.860	4.1	3.3	5.3	1.3
13	.773	5.4	2.4	4.2	2.6
14	.856	6.3	1.3	4.9	2.6
15	.778	5.5	.8	11.5	1.8
16	.828	3.4	2.0	11.8	2.5
17	.847	6.1	4.8	5.8	5.9
18	.849	5.6	6.3	7.6	5.8
19	.835	1.2	2.2	4.3	2.6
20	.799	3.1	2.3	8.2	2.2
21	.834	5.3	6.2	7.4	5.0
22	.840	3.1	5.7	8.9	8.0
23	.872	3.7	5.3	3.6	4.8
24	.891	2.2	2.8	6.1	2.3
25	.888	1.3	1.2	5.2	2.6

INTERPRETING THE RESULTS

Joy observed that the average number of minutes spent waiting for takeoff once a plane reached the runway was 3.57, a figure well within the tolerance of airlines during rush periods. She also noticed that the time spent circling, waiting for a runway to land on, was 3.82 minutes during the rush period; this latter figure was also well within the expectations of the airlines. Joy reported to the airport authority that it looked as though the proposed schedule would operate satisfactorily.

5 Using heuristics in simulation

ANOTHER USE OF HEURISTICS

In Chapter 13, we introduced heuristics, rules of thumb that work. They can often be used in conjunction with simulation techniques to solve a variety of problems. To illustrate this, let's consider an office layout problem.

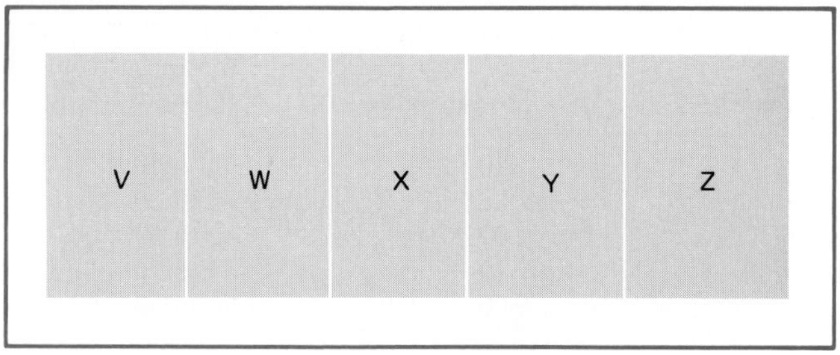

FIGURE 15-5
Department
spaces available.

Stacey Randall is manager of the Beneficial Insurance Company. The company is planning to relocate to a new office building, and Stacey feels that the manner in which she allocates work space can significantly contribute to office productivity. She supervises five functions—accounting (A), billing (B), claims/adjustments (C), new policies (N), and sales (S). Each of these functions will be located in one of the departments shown in Figure 15-5. Since the departments are of equal area, we can simplify the problem by assuming that any two adjacent departments are one unit of distance apart. In other words, V is one distance unit from W, while X and Y are two and three units, respectively, from V. Stacey recognizes that if her office layout is to be efficient, she should locate two functions close to each other if the traffic between them is relatively high, whereas two functions sharing a low volume of traffic may be a greater distance apart. Therefore, she has estimated the traffic between all functions in terms of client files per day. These estimates are shown in Figure 15-6. From that figure we see that the highest traffic is between accounting and billing, where an average of 150 client files are transferred each day. The lowest traffic is between the claims/adjustment and new-policies functions, which only exchange an average of 10 client files per day. Stacey feels that the most productive office layout is one that minimizes the total cost in terms of traffic times distance over all the functions.

ALLOCATING
WORK SPACE

ESTIMATING TRAFFIC
BETWEEN FUNCTIONS

OBJECTIVE OF
THE SIMULATION

Although heuristic programming procedures sometimes produce only a single solution to a given problem, there are occasions when the manager may desire several heuristic solutions, thus providing a number of good alternatives upon which to base decisions. A heuristic procedure known as *random sampling* is used to produce multiple solutions for a wide variety of problems. Random sampling may strike you as being a simple but somewhat

	A	B	C	N	S
A		150	60	50	80
B			90	100	70
C				10	20
N					140
S					

FIGURE 15-6
Traffic between
functions (files
per day).

Function	Probability	Range of random numbers
A	.20	00 to 19
B	.20	20 to 39
C	.20	40 to 59
N	.20	60 to 79
S	.20	80 to 99

crude methodology, because it relies upon the speed of the computer to randomly generate thousands of solutions. The effectiveness of this technique is based upon its ability to isolate several very good solutions when there are so many of them available to choose from.

PRODUCING SEVERAL HEURISTIC SOLUTIONS

Using random sampling to solve Stacey's problem, we first assign one of the five functions randomly to department V. Since each of the five has an equal chance of being selected, we give each of them a probability of 1/5 or .20. These probabilities are then converted into an equivalent range of random numbers such that each function is assigned exactly one-fifth of the total set, ranging from 00 to 99. These calculations are shown in Table 15-5. The first 20 random numbers, ranging from 00 to 19, are assigned to accounting, and the second set of 20 numbers, ranging from 20 to 39, are assigned to billing. Similarly, each of the other three functions is assigned exactly 20 of the random numbers. Now we draw a pair of random digits from the table in Appendix 6. Let us make these draws by picking the first two digits reading downward in the leftmost column of the table. Our first draw is 15, which we find lies in the range from 00 to 19 assigned to function A as shown in Table 15-5. Consequently, function A is assigned to department V.

ASSIGNING PROBABILITIES

RANDOMLY SELECTING A FUNCTION FOR DEPARTMENT W

Next we wish to randomly select a function to be located in department W. With function A already assigned, the four remaining functions are each given probabilities of .25. Note that in giving equal probabilities to the four functions, we are using no bias. A *biased* sampling approach would involve the use of unequal probabilities. For example, we might give function B a higher probability than function N, because A has a relatively higher amount of traffic with B—150 files per day—than with N—only 50 files per day. Table 15-6 shows the random number ranges now assigned for selecting without bias a function to be located in department W. Our second draw from the random numbers table of Appendix 6 is 09, which lies in the range

Function	Probability	Range of random numbers
B	.25	00 to 24
C	.25	25 to 49
N	.25	50 to 74
S	.25	75 to 99

from 00 to 24 assigned to function B. Therefore function B is located in department W.

Our third selection is to department X. Table 15-7 gives the range of numbers now assigned to the three remaining functions which can be selected. (If we draw the number 99 from the table, we just skip it and draw again.) After making the draw of 41 from Appendix 6, we find that function N is to be located in department X.

Table 15-8 contains the random number ranges assigned to the last two remaining functions to be randomly located in department Y. Our final draw from the random numbers table is 74, which lies in the range 50 to 99 assigned to function S. After locating function S in department Y, the last remaining function, C, must then be located in department Z. The cost of our solution is shown in Table 15-9.

TWO FUNCTIONS FOR
DEPARTMENT Y

You may be somewhat skeptical about this procedure. After all, there are only 5! = 120 possible ways to assign the 5 functions to the 5 departments, and surely we can evaluate all 120 possible layouts without much difficulty and then choose the best one. But suppose we had 10 functions and 10

Function	Probability	Range of random numbers
C	.33	00 to 32
N	.33	33 to 65
S	.33	66 to 98

TABLE 15-7
Random number ranges to locate a function in department X

Function	Probability	Range of random numbers
C	.50	00 to 49
S	.50	50 to 99

TABLE 15-8
Random number ranges to locate a function in department Y

Function or department	Function or department	Traffic, files/day	× Distance	=	Cost
A in V	B in W	150	× 1	=	150
A in V	C in Z	60	× 4	=	240
A in V	N in X	50	× 2	=	100
A in V	S in Y	80	× 3	=	240
B in W	C in Z	90	× 3	=	270
B in W	N in X	100	× 1	=	100
B in W	S in Y	70	× 2	=	140
C in Z	N in X	10	× 2	=	20
C in Z	S in Y	20	× 1	=	20
N in X	S in Y	140	× 1	=	140
Total cost					1,420

TABLE 15-9
Cost of the random solution measured in total traffic times distance

departments. Then there would be 10! = 3,628,800 possible layouts, and even with a computer it would be difficult to evaluate all of them. However, if we were to repeat the above procedure several thousand times on the computer, saving only our three or four best solutions, we would have a very good likelihood of producing layouts of minimum cost. We might further introduce a bias into the random selections in order to improve our chances of producing good solutions. Even for problems with many functions and departments, the amount of computer time required is surprisingly small.

6 Glossary

Clock In a simulation, a counting device which indicates the passage of time.

Event file In a simulation, a computer file which indicates when certain events are to take place.

GPSS General Purpose Simulation System. A computer language developed by IBM Corporation.

Process generator A method used to generate a distribution which is used in a simulation.

Random number table A table of numbers that simulates the output that one would get from sampling a uniformly distributed random variable.

Simulation A quantitative procedure which conducts a series of organized trial-and-error experiments on a model of a process to predict the behavior of that process over time.

Transaction A unit of traffic or flow in a GPSS simulation.

7 Exercises

15-1 Betsy Walker is project manager of the Guilford Construction Company. The company has been awarded three contracts to perform repair work on three bridges. She feels that the probability of completing a contract on time is .7, and she further feels that the on-time completion of any contract is independent of the completion of the other projects. If Betsy wishes to conduct a simulation of the on-time performance for the three contracts, what assignments of random numbers should she make for the eight possible different outcomes?

15-2 Suppose you are planning to simulate a system where the number of arrivals to the system follows a Poisson probability distribution. The mean of the distribution is 4 arrivals per hour. Make an assignment of random numbers appropriate to the various possible number of arrivals per hour. Use the first four random numbers reading down the first column in Appendix 6 and determine the number of arrivals for each hour of a simulated 4-hour period.

15-3 John Pringle is director of finance for Iowa Farm Cooperative. He is concerned about the yields per acre he can expect from this year's corn crop. This is the probability distribution John estimates for yields, given current weather conditions:

Yield in bushels/acre	Probability
120	.18
140	.26
160	.44
180	.12

The expected value of the yield is 150 bushels per acre. However, John would like to see a simulation of the yields he might expect over the next 10 years for weather conditions similar to those he is now experiencing. Use random numbers to simulate the yield John might expect.

15-4 John Pringle (from Exercise 15-3) is also interested in the effect of market-price fluctuations on the cooperative's farm revenue. He makes this estimate of per-bushel prices for corn:

Price/bushel	Probability
$2.00	.05
2.10	.15
2.20	.30
2.30	.25
2.40	.15
2.50	.10

Using random numbers, simulate both the yield and the price John might expect to observe over the next 10 years, and combine these two into the revenue per acre. You may assume that prices are independent of yields (at least for one cooperative).

15-5 Sam Douglas, branch administrator of People's Bank and Trust Company, is thinking of operating a drive-in facility in a suburban location in Wallace, Virginia. A market research study has projected these interarrival times at the branch:

Time between arrivals, minutes	Probability
1	.17
2	.25
3	.25
4	.20
5	.13

The bank plans call for one teller's window at this branch. The teller can service customers at this rate:

Service time, minutes	Probability
1	.10
2	.30
3	.40
4 (maximum)	.20

Before signing the contract for construction, Sam would like to know how much space to allow for waiting cars. He is also concerned about the mean waiting time for arriving customers. Simulate operation of the facility for an arriving sample of 20 cars, and indicate to Sam how many spaces he should plan for. Suppose the location has space for only three cars; how many customers would be turned away because of lack of space? What is the mean waiting time in your sample? Compare your result with the one you obtained when you worked Exercise 14-1.

15-6 An assembly line at Triem Electric Motor has three work stations. The time required for each station to complete its operation on the motor is as follows:

Time, minutes	Probabilities		
	Station 1	Station 2	Station 3
4	.25	.10	.05
5	.25	.30	.25
6	.25	.40	.25
7	.25	.20	.45

The times given are the only values the operation times take on. Simulate the flow of 10 motors through the assembly line. Make the assumption that if a unit is completed, for example, at station 1 while station 2 is busy, the operator at station 1 will be forced to wait. When station 2 is free to work on the output from station 1, then station 1 can proceed to work on the next unit. This is called *blocking*, and for the simulation assume that blocking can occur to either station 1 or station 2. What is the average output rate of the line?

15-7 Bob Headen's company plans to introduce a new device for automobiles to warn the driver of the proximity of the car in front. Bob can follow two different engineering strategies to develop the product. These two strategies have different probability distributions for development time, as follows:

Development time, months	Strategy	
	1	2
6	.2	.4
9	.3	.4
12	.5	.2

Strategy 1 will require a $600,000 investment and will result in a variable cost per unit of $7.50. Strategy 2 will require a $1,500,000 investment and will result in a variable cost per unit of $6.75. The product will sell for $10. Bob believes that the sales volume of the product depends on the development time, since the industry is highly competitive. Bob has formulated the table below, which gives estimated sales volumes for the life of the product and the probability distributions.

Unit sales volume	Development time, months		
	6	9	12
1,000,000	.2	.4	.5
1,500,000	.8	.6	.5

Simulate 10 trials for introducing the new product for each engineering strategy. What is Bob's expected profit for each strategy? Compare your results with the expected value of profit for the new strategies.

15-8 The Atwood Construction Company will incur a penalty of $10,000 a day for every day it is late completing a road construction project. The project is due to be completed in 15 more days. The remaining four activities to be completed are arranged like this:

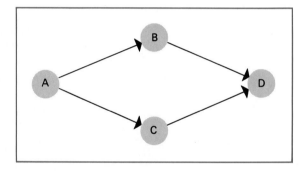

Activities B and C can begin as soon as activity A is completed. Activity D can begin as soon as both B and C are completed.

The activity times (in days) for the four remaining parts of the project are estimated as follows:

Activity A		Activity B		Activity C		Activity D	
Time	Proba-bility	Time	Proba-bility	Time	Proba-bility	Time	Proba-bility
6	.4	5	.2	4	.3	1	.1
7	.1	6	.5	5	.5	2	.1
8	.1	7	.3	6	.2	3	.2
9	.1					4	.3
10	.1					5	.1
11	.1					6	.1
12	.1					7	.1

Simulate three completions of the project. Determine the penalty that Atwood will pay for each simulation.

15-9 Stephanie Thau is Manager of Advertising for the Nutri-Food Company. She has recently contracted for two advertising slots each on three television shows giving her a total of six weekly slots. She plans to advertise one of six food products on each of these slots. Based upon an analysis of the type of audience which views the show, Stephanie estimates that sales of the products would increase as follows:

Food Product	Revenue increase (thousands of dollars) by show		
	Nature hour	Whodunit?	Guess my name
Bran Cereal	50	40	60
Fruit Snack	70	80	75
Nut Bar	75	70	65
Fresh Fibre	60	45	50
Happy Mix	30	65	75
Camper Delight	85	40	30

Assign each of the six products so that two of the six are advertised on each of the three shows. Develop two heuristic solutions using random sampling. Draw your random numbers from the first four digits of column 4 in Appendix 6. Determine the increased revenue for each of your solutions.

15-10 Using the data given in Exercise 15-9, develop a heuristic solution using biased random sampling. Draw your random numbers from the first four digits of column 4 in Appendix 6.

15-11 Refer to the inventory control problem on page 717. Simulate the following inventory policy for 20 days. Order 100 units when the stock on hand reaches 180 units. Do not place another order until the previous order has been received. Compute the average weekly lost sales in units (use 5-day working weeks), and compute the average inventory on hand. Start your simulation with 180 units on hand and no

Areas under the normal curve to the left of z							
z	Area	z	Area	z	Area	z	Area
−3.0	.0013	−1.4	.0808	.1	.5398	1.6	.9452
−2.9	.0019	−1.3	.0968	.2	.5793	1.7	.9554
−2.8	.0026	−1.2	.1151	.3	.6179	1.8	.9641
−2.7	.0035	−1.1	.1357	.4	.6554	1.9	.9713
−2.6	.0047	−1.0	.1587	.5	.6915	2.0	.9772
−2.5	.0062	− .9	.1841	.6	.7257	2.1	.9821
−2.4	.0082	− .8	.2119	.7	.7580	2.2	.9861
−2.3	.0107	− .7	.2420	.8	.7881	2.3	.9893
−2.2	.0139	− .6	.2743	.9	.8159	2.4	.9918
−2.1	.0179	− .5	.3085	1.0	.8413	2.5	.9938
−2.0	.0228	− .4	.3446	1.1	.8643	2.6	.9953
−1.9	.0287	− .3	.3821	1.2	.8849	2.7	.9965
−1.8	.0359	− .2	.4207	1.3	.9032	2.8	.9974
−1.7	.0446	− .1	.4602	1.4	.9192	2.9	.9981
−1.6	.0548	0	.5000	1.5	.9332	3.0	.9987
−1.5	.0668						

order due in. Use the table at the bottom of page 732 in your simulation. To use the table, draw a four-digit random number. Put a decimal point in front of that number, and use the resulting number to enter the area column of the table. Find the closest value of z. Multiply the value of z by the standard deviation of either sales or lead time, and add the result to the mean of either sales or lead time to get a simulated value. (For example, assume you drew 0806. That corresponds to -1.4 standard deviations. For the problem, we saw that the standard deviation of sales was 5 units, so $-1.4 \times 5 = -7$ units. And $20 - 7 = 13$. So we take 13 units as the sampled sales value.)

In your calculations, if the simulated value of demand or lead time comes out to be a fraction, round to the nearest whole number before recording the result. Round after the deviation has been added to the mean.

15-12 Repeat Exercise 15-11, but this time use a new reordering rule. Order 100 units when the stock on hand *plus* the stock on order reaches 180 units. More than one order may thus be outstanding at one time. Use the same random numbers for this problem as for Exercise 15-11. Did the new rule reduce lost sales or average on-hand stock? What would you expect to happen?

15-13 The Western National Bank has agreed to finance the working capital needs of Hi-Fi Ltd., a stereo wholesaler, for the next month. To complete the loan agreement, Hi-Fi Ltd. must estimate the maximum loan required. Daily receipts are normally distributed with a mean of $50,000 and a standard deviation of $12,000. Disbursements are also normally distributed, with a mean and standard deviation of $48,000 and $3,000, respectively. Simulate the cash flow of Hi-Fi Ltd. for 15 working days. What is the maximum loan required? Assume that any beginning cash balance will not be available to meet disbursements and that Hi-Fi Ltd. must rely on daily operations to pay its bills. Use the normal distribution introduced in Exercise 15-11.

15-14 The main cargo hoist engine on the Fruit Carrier, a ship which runs between Guatemala City and Fort Lauderdale, Florida, has two bearings that fail periodically. The life of the first bearing is normally distributed, with a mean and standard deviation of 80 and 12 operating hours, respectively. The life of the second bearing is also normally distributed, with a mean and standard deviation of 100 and 20 operating hours, respectively. The first bearing costs $60, and the second $50. When either bearing fails, it costs the Fruit Carrier owners $90 in labor charges to install a new one. If both bearings were installed at once, the labor charge would be only $110. Simulate 1,000 hours of the operation of the hoist on the Fruit Carrier. Compare replacing only one bearing at a time with replacing both bearings whenever one fails. Which policy involves the least cost in your sample? Use the normal distribution discussed in Exercise 15-11 to draw your samples.

15-15 Lt. Jerry Abrams needs to schedule six military personnel for overseas assignment. Each of the six will be processed first at Station 1 where their personnel records will be checked and brought up to date. Then they will proceed to Station 2 where their medical records, immunizations, and passports will be checked and brought up to date. He estimates the following time requirements in minutes.

	Person					
Station	**Ames**	**Booth**	**Casey**	**Danvers**	**Edgars**	**Flutie**
1	35	40	20	30	25	50
2	40	45	25	60	35	30

He would like to schedule the six people in such a way that processing for all six will take the least total time. Using random sampling, determine the ordering of the six people and compute the completion time of the last person to finish processing. Assume there is unlimited waiting capacity between the two stations. Assume also that each station can only process one person at a time. Draw your random numbers from column 5 of Appendix 6 using the first four digits.

15-16 Develop a heuristic solution to the problem given in Exercise 15-15, using a bias. Assign higher probabilities of selecting personnel who have shortest expected process times at the first station. Use weights of 6, 5, 4, 3, 2 and 1 for the first selection as follows:

Ranking of Station 1 process time	Person	Probability of selection
20	Casey	6/21 = .2857
25	Edgars	5/21 = .2381
30	Danvers	4/21 = .1905
35	Ames	3/21 = .1429
40	Booth	2/21 = .0952
50	Flutie	1/21 = .0476

After making the first selection, use weights of 5, 4, 3, 2 and 1 for the second selection and 4, 3, 2, 1 for the third, and so on. Draw your random numbers, using four digits, from column 5 of Appendix 6.

15-17 Refer to the harbor simulation on page 719 of the text. Simulate the first 10 unloading completions at the harbor. Assume that there is one ship in service at the start of your simulation, with completion scheduled for 7 hours from the start of your simulation. Assume that your next ship will arrive in 3 hours from the start of your simulation. When using the frequency distribution given in the text for the harbor problem, interpolate between the class limits of the times.

For example, suppose you use the random numbers 00 to 09 to represent interarrival times of 0 to 6 hours. If you draw the random number 04, that represents an interarrival time of 2.7 hours for the next ship. That is, when a ship arrives and you draw 04, the next ship is scheduled to arrive at 2.7 hours from the current arrival. This interpolation formula may be useful:

$$Y - Y_1 = \frac{Y_2 - Y_1}{X_2 - X_1}(X - X_1)$$

where X = the random number chosen
Y = the number of hours we wish to find
Y_1 = the lower limit of the interval of hours in which Y is included
Y_2 = the upper limit of the interval of hours in which Y is included
X_1 = the lower limit of the interval of random numbers in which X is included
X_2 = the upper limit of the interval of random numbers in which X is included

In this example,

$X = 04$
Y = an unknown number of hours between 0 and 6
$Y_1 = 0$
$Y_2 = 6$
$X_1 = 00$
$X_2 = 09$

and

$$Y - Y_1 = \frac{Y_2 - Y_1}{X_2 - X_1}(X - X_1)$$

$$Y - 0 = \frac{6 - 0}{9 - 0}(4 - 0)$$

$$= 2.67 \text{ hours}$$

In this problem, rounding to the next tenth of an hour is acceptable; hence we would schedule the next ship arrival at 2.7 hours.

For the service times, you can interpolate between 12 and 16 hours. When the tenth ship is complete, compute for Seth Adams the mean and standard deviation of the waiting time. How do they compare with those found on page 720 of the text?

15-18 A traffic signal operates in the east-west direction in the following intervals during the rush hour: green for 60 seconds, yellow for 5 seconds, red for 30 seconds, green for 60 seconds, and so forth. Cars arrive with these interarrival times:

Direction from	Mean time between arrivals, seconds
N	.9
S	.7
E	.3
W	.3

Draw a flowchart similar to that for the airport simulation on page 722 to fit this situation. Use the "event file" concept and include two files to collect maximum line length during yellow and red lights. Assume that the first car to arrive after a yellow light flashes on drives through the light. All others stop. Avoid excessive detail and concentrate on the logical checks the flowchart must allow for to record statistics properly.

15-19 Beth Komeau works alone in her beauty shop. She has studied the arrival pattern of her customers and has put together the following distribution of interarrival times:

Time between arrivals, min	Probability
0	.15
5	.10
10	.12
15	.14
20	.17
30	.26
40	.06

Beth has also determined that the distribution of her service time (the time it takes for her to cut and set a customer's hair) is as follows:

Service time, min	Probability
14	.05
16	.50
18	.20
20	.20
22	.05

Assume that if a customer arrives and two people are already waiting, the customer leaves and goes to another shop. Simulate the system, beginning at 8 A.M., for 15 customers. Be sure to record the idle time Beth experiences and the number of customers lost. Draw the random number for arrivals from column 1 and for service times from column 2 of Appendix 6.

15-20 The Village Machine Shop has three special machines. Each of these machines demands the full time of a machinist-repairer, because the machines are subject to frequent breakdown. The machinist-repairers operate their respective machines until a breakdown occurs. They then go to the tool crib and check out a special repair tool (if one is available) and proceed to repair the machine. After repairing the machine the machinist-repairers return the tool and commence their normal work operation. Since the repair tool is very expensive, the company can afford to keep only one of them on hand. Therefore, if a machine breaks down while the tool is in use at another machine, the machine must sit idle, along with its operator, until the tool is available to effect the necessary repairs. The company wishes to simulate this system in order to determine if it would be cost-effective to maintain more than one of the repair tools. It has found that the distribution of times-to-failure (elapsed normal operating time between the completion of a repair and the next breakdown) is as follows:

Time-to-failure, min	Probability
180	.20
190	.30
200	.25
210	.12
220	.08
230	.05

The distribution of times to make a repair is as follows:

Repair time, min	Probability
50	.50
60	.36
70	.08
80	.04
90	.02

Simulate the system for 700 minutes, drawing the simulated times-to-failure for machines A, B, and C from the first, second, and third columns, respectively, of Appendix 6. Draw the tool usage times from column 4. Be sure to record the time lost while a worker is waiting for the repair tool. Assume that machines A and B have just been repaired and that machine C is just starting repair at the initiation of the simulation.

15-21 Use the random sampling heuristic with no bias to develop five heuristic solutions to the integer programming problem given in Exercise 13-6. Use the random numbers reading down the first column of Appendix 6, and add either an apprentice electrician or a journeyman electrician (equal probability) with each random-number draw. Continue this process until a constraint is reached. Compare your heuristic solutions with the optimal solution you obtained using integer programming.

15-22 Use the random sampling heuristic method with bias to develop a heuristic solution for the dynamic programming problem given in Exercise 12-32. Use the random numbers reading down the second column of Appendix 6, and sequentially add projects according to the random numbers drawn. Bias your selections in such a way that the probability of selecting a project is equal to its importance level divided by the sum of the importance levels of all unselected projects. For example, in the first selection from among the six projects (total importance is $5 + 6 + 4 + 7 + 3 + 8 = 33$), the probability of selecting route 1 is $\frac{5}{33}$, while the probability of selecting route 2 is $\frac{6}{33}$.

15-23 Judge Marcia Withers is concerned about the time it takes to process cases for juvenile offenders. She has asked her assistant for an analysis of cases considered during the preceding five years, and her assistant has provided her with the following:

Process	Time (Days)	Prob- ability	Next Step			
			Process	Prob	Process	Prob
Parent consultation	1 2 3	.2 .5 .3	Case Worker	.75	Dismissal of charges	.25
Case Worker	9 10 11 12	.2 .2 .3 .3	Psychologist	.40	Judicial Review	.60
Psychologist	12 13 14	.4 .5 .1	Judicial Review	.80	Dismissal of charges	.20
Judicial Review	15 16 17	.3 .3 .4	Pretrial Hearing	.90	Dismissal of charges	.10
Pretrial Hearing	2 3	.5 .5	Plea Bargaining	.30	District attorney	.70
Plea Bargaining	3 4 5	.2 .4 .4	Sentencing Case Closed	1.00		
District Attorney	30 35 40	.3 .4 .3	Trial	.90	Dismissal of charges	.10
Trial	8 9 10	.5 .4 .1	Sentencing	.80	Acquittal	.20

As the above table indicates, all cases initially require a parent consultation which takes 1 to 3 days. After this process, 75 percent of the cases are forwarded to a case worker while the remaining 25 percent of the cases are dismissed. A case which is forwarded to a case worker requires 9 to 12 days' time. Once the case worker finishes, the case is either sent along to a psychologist or to judicial review with 40 percent and 60 percent probabilities, respectively. All other processes and case dispositions are interpreted in a similar fashion. Draw a simulation flow chart for this problem.

15-24 Simulate three cases coming to Judge Wither's court using the data given in Exercise 15-23. Assume there is no waiting time (that is, each process is a storage with unlimited capacity). Consequently, in the simulation, you can take a case and process it from start to finish before starting the following case. Use the first two digits of the random numbers in column 1 of Appendix 6. Use these random numbers as you require them for deciding either a simulated process time or a simulated disposition decision. Determine the average time to process a case in the system.

15-25 Marty Barrows is in charge of investments for the Benson Company. He estimates from past price fluctuations in the gold market that the probabilities of price changes on a given day are dependent upon the price change during the preceding day. If gold prices increase or remain constant on a certain day, the following distribution represents the probabilities of change in dollars per ounce for the day to follow:

Price change ($)	Probability
−4.00	.05
−2.00	.10
no change	.20
+2.00	.25
+4.00	.30
+6.00	.10

On the other hand, if the gold price decreases on a given day, the following day's distribution of price change in dollars per ounce is:

Price change ($)	Probability
−6.00	.10
−4.00	.30
−2.00	.25
no change	.15
+2.00	.20

Simulate the prices of gold for twenty days, using the first two digits of the random numbers reading down column 3 of Appendix 6. Test the policy of buying 100 ounces when prices drop for the preceding 3 consecutive days and selling 100 ounces when prices rise for the previous 3 consecutive days. Assume at the start that Marty has 1000 ounces of gold in his portfolio for which he paid $300 per ounce. Determine how much gold he will own at the end of the 20 days, as well as his net profit/loss position during this period. Assume at the start that gold is selling for $300 per ounce and that during the day before the start of the simulation, gold prices rose.

15-1 In a simulation, a process generator is a way of generating the _____ of an item of interest which is considered to be a random variable; the particular values for the random variable produced in this way are known as _____

15-2 A _____is a graphic aid which helps illustrate the logical relationships and time sequences involved in a computer simulation program; in this instance, a diamond-shaped symbol signifies where a _____is made.

15-3 Units of flow in a simulation are known as _____and move through the simulated system to and from points which are either _____ or _____ .

15-4 In every simulation, there is a device called a _____which keeps track of the passage of simulated time.

15-5 A(n) _____is required in a simulation to keep track of when certain events are to occur; the times when events are to occur are usually produced by a _____which generates these random times.

15-6 The elapsed time between consecutive arrivals in a simulation is called _____ .

15-7 A heuristic procedure which produces multiple randomly generated solutions to a problem is called _____ .

15-8 Simulation uses a model of some process and predicts the behavior of that process by conducting _____ .

15-9 A random variable that can take on any value within a given range with equal probability is called _____ .

15-10 In order to obtain statistical output which represents a steady state system, the transient effects of the beginning of the simulation must be discarded. This simulated time period is called _____ .

15-11 Simulation is an especially valuable tool in a situation where the mathematics needed to describe a system realistically is too complex to yield analytical solutions.　**T F**

15-12 Waiting lines can form in front of facilities, which can only service one transaction at a time; however, waiting lines do not exist in front of storages, which can service multiple transactions simultaneously.　**T F**

15-13 When validating a simulation, you are in effect increasing your confidence regarding any inference you draw from its results.　**T F**

15-14 Simulations can be developed quickly and run inexpensively so long as all distributions in the simulation are discrete and all random quantities are independent.　**T F**

15-15 Simulations are normally run on computers because they are often long and involve tedious calculations and because repetition of a simulation with different system parameters is often beneficial.　**T F**

15-16 It is necessary to include a waiting line for each storage unit in a simulation because only one unit at a time can occupy a storage unit.　**T F**

15-17 The use of an event file in a simulation greatly increases the speed of the simulation because it allows simulated time to skip from one event to the time of the next scheduled event, ignoring the intervening time. **T F**

15-18 Optimal policies can often be estimated from the output of a simulation by computing costs associated with system statistics generated by the simulation and finding the set of parameters which resulted in the minimal cost. **T F**

15-19 One drawback to the use of simulation is that it is only applicable in situations where all quantities are deterministic. **T F**

15-20 Because of the random nature of the systems modeled by simulations, and because simulations are just models of more complex phenomena, we would not ever expect to see simulation results duplicated in nature. **T F**

15-21 In drawing random digits from a table of random digits, it is acceptable to follow any pattern as long as it is consistent and unbiased. **T F**

15-22 The clock in a simulation is a counter that advances one unit of time with each advance it makes. **T F**

15-23 Simulations are used to study only systems where waiting lines can form. They are not appropriate to study other types of systems. **T F**

15-24 Random sampling is a heuristic procedure which capitalizes on the speed of the computer to generate many solutions to a problem randomly. **T F**

15-25 One advantage of using a special-purpose simulation language is that random number generators are an integral part of these simulation packages. **T F**

Multiple
Choice

15-26 One of the disadvantages of simulation is that:
   a. Simulation models may be very expensive and require much time to develop.
   b. Simulations do not generate optimal policies by themselves.
   c. Simulations are applicable only in cases where there is an element of randomness in a system.
   d. All of the above.

15-27 With the absence of any random components, all simulations of a given process would produce:
   a. Invalid results
   b. The same answers
   c. Long waiting lines
   d. None of the above

15-28 In order to ensure consistency when comparing different sets of system parameters in a simulation, it is necessary to:
   a. Run the simulation several times, each time using the mean of the parameters to be compared.
   b. Run the simulation several times with the same set of parameters and different random numbers.
   c. Run the simulation several times, each time with a different set of system parameters and the same random numbers.
   d. Run the simulation several times, each time with different parameters and different random numbers.

15-29 The purpose of "warming up" the system by running the simulation for a while before collecting statistics is to:
   a. Make sure that the computer is performing at peak efficiency.
   b. Allow the system to reach a steady state in which the effects of choosing an arbitrary initial state are overshadowed.

c. Make sure that a run of sufficient length is produced to generate valid random variables.

d. All of the above.

15-30 The advantages of simulation over analytical methods include the following:

a. No actual observations of a system need be made.

b. Information about the distribution of random quantities in the system is unnecessary.

c. Results of simulations are always more precise than those using analytical methods.

d. Any system can be analyzed effectively by means of a simulation.

15-31 Which of the following is not a special-purpose simulation language?

a. BASIC

b. GPSS

c. SIMSCRIPT

d. GASP

15-32 You can increase the probability that the results of a simulation are not erroneous by:

a. Changing the input parameters.

b. Using discrete probability distributions instead of continuous ones.

c. Validating the simulation.

d. All of the above.

15-33 Biased random sampling differs from pure random sampling because each decision in the former technique is made from among alternatives which have:

a. Equal probabilities.

b. Unequal probabilities.

c. A set of probabilities which do not sum to 1.

d. A set of probabilities which are randomly assigned.

15-34 Random numbers generated by a computer are often called pseudo-random numbers, because they repeat themselves in cycles. This would be considered acceptable for practical simulation studies if:

a. The length of the cycle is very long.

b. The length of the cycle is very short.

c. A small random number is always followed by a large one.

d. No digit follows itself in a stream of digits.

15-35 The clock in a simulation advances in units of:

a. Seconds

b. Minutes

c. Days

d. Anything the programmer defines it to be.

15-36 Because random numbers are drawn from a uniform distribution, it is not possible to simulate events which are:

a. Normally distributed

b. Uniformly distributed

c. Exponentially distributed

d. None of the above

15-37 Simulations often involve replication, where a system is simulated a number of times using different streams of random numbers. This procedure may help establish the validity of the simulation if:

a. The output is consistent among the various replications.

b. The behavior of the system is consistent among the various replications.

c. The simulated system itself is not changed in any of the replications.

d. All of the above.

15-38 In a simulation, a transaction is:
   a. Either a facility or a storage.
   b. A waiting line.
   c. A unit of flow.
   d. All of the above.

15-39 In a given simulation, there may be a number of transactions moving through the system simultaneously even though the simulation software package is really only physically moving one of them at any given time. This is an entirely acceptable procedure as long as:
   a. The simulation is allowed to warm up.
   b. The clock is not advanced until all transactions have been moved.
   c. All transactions are moving to the same place.
   d. There is a waiting line.

15-40 When a transaction is due to arrive in a simulated system, it is not moved through the system until:
   a. The next transaction following the one currently arriving is assigned a scheduled arrival time.
   b. A check is made to see if there is room in the waiting line.
   c. The transaction just ahead of the one currently arriving has completed service.
   d. None of the above.

9 Real world MS/OR successes

EXAMPLE: SIMULATING A BURGER KING RESTAURANT

SIMULATION COMMON IN FAST-FOOD INDUSTRY

The major fast-food chains use simulation models of their restaurants to study ways to improve productivity and customer service. Burger King's experiences are a good example of the results. Two operations researchers on the Burger King headquarters staff, William Swart and Luca Donno,[4] developed a general-purpose simulation model used to study existing operations as well as design new restaurants. The bottom line: the model generated new ideas worth at least $50 million per year in cash flow.

GPSS MODEL

The model, programmed in GPSS, contains three related systems to simulate customers, production, and delivery. In the customer system, arrival rates

CUSTOMER SYSTEM

vary tremendously, sometimes as much as 1000 percent within a 30-minute period. Order processing time depends on staffing, the products ordered, and how the order is placed (in-store or drive-thru). Orders are transmitted via CRT to the kitchen where up to four production areas (drinks, fryers,

PRODUCTION SYSTEM

main sandwich line, and specialty sandwich line) may respond. Production action may replenish stocks of a standard product or prepare a custom product. Simultaneously, in-process inventories of various items (drinks, preassembled sandwiches, mayonnaise, and so on) are checked to see if replenishment is required. Inventory decisions are critical since most products

DELIVERY SYSTEM

have a shelf life of only 10 minutes. Concurrent with production, the delivery

---

[4] William Swart and Luca Donno, "Simulation Modeling Improves Operations, Planning, and Productivity of Fast Food Restaurants," *Interfaces*, vol. 11, no. 6, pp. 35–47, 1981.

system is active in dealing with the customer, making change, and assembling the order.

Swart and Donno went to great lengths to validate their model and gain management acceptance of the model's predictions. For example, top managers and franchisees were invited to witness a live test in which a complete restaurant was assembled in a warehouse and staffed with crew members from nearby Burger Kings. For two days, this facility was subjected to a variety of customer arrival patterns, with each pattern serviced by a variety of manning levels. Customer service, production, and delivery operations were videotaped for comparison with actual operations. The simulation model gave very accurate predictions of line lengths, waiting time, service time, inventory levels, and many other indicators of performance. Today, virtually no operational decision is made without a model analysis. On average, the model is run 300 times per month to fine-tune Burger King operations.

Here are a few examples of how management has used the simulation model to improve operations: New labor standards were developed that save more than $32 million annually. Several efficient kitchen layouts for different ranges of sales volume were designed. Productivity improvements over old designs save more than $3.4 million annually. Many improvements were made in drive-thru window operations. For example, the model showed that the "stack," the distance between order station and pick-up window, should be lengthened to serve more customers during peak hours. During the lunch hour alone, longer stacks generate an additional $15 million in annual sales capacity.

VALIDATING
THE MODEL

MODEL ACCURACY

FREQUENCY OF
MODEL USE

EXAMPLES OF
IMPROVED OPERATIONS

16

Jerry Abbot, owner of Abbot's Dairy, is concerned about his sales of dairy products in West Lynn, Alabama. Jerry has only two competitors, Branch Dairy Products and Carter Milk Products. Customers of dairy products in West Lynn tend to switch from one dairy to another over a period of time because of advertising, dissatisfaction with service or product, and other reasons. From one month to the next, Jerry has noted that most of his customers remain loyal to his products. However, some customers switch to one of the other dairies, while others, who previously bought his competitors' products, have switched to him. Jerry has maintained fairly accurate records of this type of behavior in the past, and he would like to use the information to forecast his future sales. He also feels the information may be of some value to him in evaluating his advertising effectiveness and service performance. In making these forecasts and evaluations, Jerry plans to use Markov analysis. Since the population in West Lynn, as well as the brand-switching behavior of its residents, is fairly stable, Markov analysis can provide Jerry with valuable planning and evaluation information. Through your study of Markov analysis in this chapter, you will learn how this important tool can be used to solve a variety of problems of the type Jerry faces.

MARKOV ANALYSIS

CHAPTER OBJECTIVES

- INTRODUCE MARKOV ANALYSIS AS A DECISION METHOD FOR PREDICTING THE RESULTS OF "SWITCHING BEHAVIOR" OVER TIME.

- DEMONSTRATE THE ELEMENTS OF MATRIX MULTIPLICATION AS THE SOLUTION TECHNIQUE IN MARKOV ANALYSIS.

- DERIVE AND USE THE MATRIX OF TRANSITION PROBABILITIES TO SOLVE A BRAND-SWITCHING PROBLEM.

- DETERMINE EQUILIBRIUM FOR A MARKOV PROCESS AND EXAMINE HOW MARKETING STRATEGIES AFFECT THAT OUTCOME.

- SHOW HOW MARKOV ANALYSIS IS USEFUL IN THE SOLUTION OF A WIDE RANGE OF MANAGERIAL PROBLEMS.

Markov analysis is a method of analyzing the *current* behavior of some variable in an effort to predict the *future* behavior of that same variable. This procedure was developed by the Russian mathematician Andrei A. Markov early in this century. He first used it to describe and predict the behavior of particles of gas in a closed container. As a management tool, Markov analysis has been successfully applied to a wide variety of decision situations. Perhaps its widest

use is in examining and predicting the behavior of consumers in terms of their brand loyalty and their switching from one brand to another. Another interesting application of Markov analysis has been to the study of the life of newspaper subscriptions. A more recent application of this technique has been to the study of accounts receivable behavior, that is, to the study of customers as they change from "current account," through "30 days overdue," to "60 days overdue," and then to "bad debt." In each of these applications, management is interested in predicting what the future will bring (number of bad debts, for example, in the accounts receivable application) by analyzing what the current behavior is (propensity of customers to move from current account to various past due categories).

1 Introduction to brand-switching analysis

The basics of Markov analysis are best demonstrated with a brand-switching problem. There are three dairies in a community which supply all the milk consumed: Abbot's Dairy, Branch Dairy Products Company, and Carter Milk Products, Inc. For simplicity, let's refer to them hereafter as A, B, and C.

Each of the dairies knows that consumers switch from dairy to dairy over time because of advertising, dissatisfaction with service, and other reasons. If all three dairies maintain records of the number of their customers *and* the dairy from which they obtained each new customer, we have all the ingredients necessary for the application of this management tool.

Let us further suppose that Table 16-1 illustrates the movement of customers from one dairy to another over an observation period of 1 month. To further simplify the mathematics necessary, we shall assume that no new customers enter and no old customers leave the market during this period.

Casual observation may suggest that a total of 20 customers switched during the month: 10 from B to A and 10 from C to A. However, more detailed inspection may not support this initial inference. Suppose, for instance, that Table 16-2 is the true explanation of the exchange of customers among the

TABLE 16-1
Net changes
in customers

Dairy	Number of customers	
	June 1	July 1
A	200	220
B	500	490
C	300	290

| Dairy | June 1 customers | Changes during June | | July 1 customers |
		Gain	Loss	
A	200	60	40	220
B	500	40	50	490
C	300	35	45	290

TABLE 16-2

Actual exchanges of customers

three dairies. From it we see that 20 customers were gained by dairy A in a somewhat complex movement of customers involving all three dairies, a movement sometimes referred to in marketing as *brand switching*.

Each dairy needs details about brand switching if it is to do the best marketing job possible. If dairy B, for example, designs a promotional campaign under the impression that it is the only dairy losing customers *and* that it is losing them only to dairy A, B is operating under a false assumption. In fact, dairy B is not just losing 10 customers per month; rather, each month it is *gaining 40* new customers from the other two dairies and *losing 50* old customers to the other two dairies.

Similarly, suppose that dairy A, noticing that it is gaining 20 customers each month, concentrates solely on efforts to lure additional customers away from its competitors. What dairy A has overlooked is its own losses of 40 customers per month. Perhaps some attempt to reduce this loss of 40 customers per month would be as effective dollarwise as efforts to capture additional customers from B and C.

The upshot of this whole matter is that simple analysis in terms of net gain or net loss of customers is inadequate for intelligent management. What management needs is a more detailed analysis concerning the rate of gains from and losses to *all competitors*. With such data, management can make an effort to:

1 Predict the share of market that sellers will have at some future time

2 Predict the rate at which sellers will gain or lose their shares of market in the future

3 Predict whether or not some market equilibrium (constant or level market shares) will obtain in the future

4 Analyze a seller's promotion efforts in terms of exactly what effects they are having on gain and loss of market share

Markov analysis offers us just such a tool for marketing analysis. By employing this tool of management, we are able to draw more accurate conclusions about our marketing position, both present and future. Without it, we tend to be in the position of dairy A when A knew that 20 customers per month were being gained but did not know that this gain was the net result of an interchange among all three dairies.

To move beyond this simple analysis and into the use of Markov analysis, we will have to compute *transition probabilities* for all three of our dairies. Transition probabilities are nothing more than the probabilities that a certain seller (a dairy, in this instance) will retain, gain, and lose customers. In other words, dairy B observes from Table 16-3 that it loses 50 customers this month; this is the same as saying that it has a probability of .9 of retaining customers; similarly, dairy A has a probability of .8 of retaining its customers; dairy C has a probability of .85 of retaining its customers. These transition probabilities for the retention of customers are calculated in Table 16-3.

At this point, we have some measure of the proportion of old customers each dairy retains each month, but we have not said anything about the rates at which the three dairies gain new customers each month. Calculation of a complete set of these transition probabilities would require data on the flow of customers among all the dairies. Data of this sort demand good record keeping and take the form of Table 16-4.

At this point, all the basic data are grouped in one table. We are able to observe not only the net gain or loss for any of the three dairies but also the interrelationship between the gains and losses of customers by each of the dairies. For instance, it is now quite clear that dairy A gains the majority of its new customers from B. We can reason more intelligently from Table 16-4 concerning these interrelationships than we could when we knew only the net gain or loss by each of the dairies.

2 A matrix algebra primer

The next step in the application of Markov analysis is to convert Table 16-4 into a more concise form where all the gains and losses are converted into transition probabilities. Transition probabilities are displayed in a pattern called a *matrix;* therefore it is necessary at this point to introduce some material on *matrix algebra* which will allow you to proceed with the Markov analysis material which follows.

MATRICES

A *matrix* can be defined as an array of numbers arranged into rows and columns. A matrix, taken as a whole, *has no numerical value.* The numbers in

TABLE 16-3
Transition
probabilities for
retention of
customers

Dairy	June 1 customers	Number lost	Number retained	Probability of retention
A	200	40	160	$160/200 = .8$
B	500	50	450	$450/500 = .9$
C	300	45	255	$255/300 = .85$

		Gains			Losses			
Dairy	June 1 customers	From A	From B	From C	To A	To B	To C	July 1 customers
A	200	0	35	25	0	20	20	220
B	500	20	0	20	35	0	15	490
C	300	20	15	0	25	20	0	290

TABLE 16-4
Flow of customers

a matrix, however, may represent useful business data. When seen as an entire unit, such data may be of considerable help in the solution to certain problems. Here is a matrix with two rows and three columns:

$$\begin{bmatrix} 1 & 2 & 4 \\ 3 & 5 & 6 \end{bmatrix} \quad \downarrow \text{Columns}$$

Rows
→

It would be referred to as a 2×3 matrix. (The number of rows always precedes the number of columns when describing the dimensions of a matrix.)

ROWS AND COLUMNS

To illustrate a management use of matrices, let us assume a simple condition in international trade; that is, countries X and Y import steel from countries A, B, and C. Country X receives 100 tons annually from A, 200 tons annually from B, and 400 tons annually from C. Y receives 300 tons annually from A, 500 tons annually from B, and 700 tons annually from C. In this written form, it is difficult to visualize the flow of steel from suppliers to users, but if the conditions are expressed in matrix form, the flows of steel are easily indicated as follows:

PRESENTING DATA
WITH A MATRIX

$$\text{Users} \begin{array}{cc} & \begin{array}{ccc} \text{Suppliers} & & \\ A & B & C \end{array} \\ \begin{array}{c} X \\ Y \end{array} & \begin{bmatrix} 100 & 200 & 400 \\ 300 & 500 & 700 \end{bmatrix} \end{array}$$

The first column in the matrix indicates the total shipments from country A to both users. The second column indicates the total shipments from country B, and the third column indicates the total shipments from country C. The first row indicates the total sources of country X's requirements, and the second row indicates the total sources of country Y's requirements. In this matrix form, the conditions are more easily visualized; the entire situation can be represented briefly, and the relationships are quite evident. Although this is not the *only* use we can make of matrices, further uses will have to wait until we have had some practice in understanding and dealing with matrices.

MATRICES OF
DIFFERENT SIZES

Here are several different matrices with size indicated beside each.

$$\begin{bmatrix} 2 & 1 \\ 4 & 6 \end{bmatrix} \qquad 2 \times 2$$

$$\begin{bmatrix} 1 \\ 6 \end{bmatrix} \qquad 2 \times 1$$

$$[1 \quad 2 \quad 6] \qquad 1 \times 3$$

$$\begin{bmatrix} -1 & 4 & 6 & 2 \\ 7 & 0 & -3 & 8 \end{bmatrix} \qquad 2 \times 4$$

$$\begin{bmatrix} 1 \\ -4 \\ 8 \end{bmatrix} \qquad 3 \times 1$$

The location of an individual element within any matrix can be described by indicating the row and column (in that order) in which the element appears. Below, the location of each element in the matrix is described by its row and column location.

INDIVIDUAL ELEMENTS
IN A MATRIX

				Row	Column
			$1 =$ element 1, 1	1	1
			$-1 =$ element 2, 1	2	1
			$3 =$ element 3, 1	3	1
1	2	7	$2 =$ element 1, 2	1	2
-1	4	6	$4 =$ element 2, 2	2	2
3	5	8	$5 =$ element 3, 2	3	2
			$7 =$ element 1, 3	1	3
			$6 =$ element 2, 3	2	3
			$8 =$ element 3, 3	3	3

▮ MATRIX MULTIPLICATION

MULTIPLYING
TWO MATRICES

Two matrices can be multiplied together if the *number of columns* in the first matrix equals the *number of rows* in the second matrix. If this condition is not met, multiplication is impossible. Here are two matrices, **A** and **B**, with their dimensions (the number of rows and columns) indicated directly beneath each of them:

$$\underset{\text{Matrix } \mathbf{A}}{\begin{bmatrix} 2 & 1 \\ 4 & 3 \end{bmatrix}} \times \underset{\text{Matrix } \mathbf{B}}{\begin{bmatrix} 3 & 3 \\ 2 & 1 \end{bmatrix}}$$

$$2 \times \textcircled{2} \leftarrow = \rightarrow \textcircled{2} \times 2$$

If the two circled numbers (the number of columns in matrix **A** and the number of rows in matrix **B**) are equal, multiplication *is* possible. This rule is a basic requirement in matrix algebra. Its logic will become obvious later in the exposition when you attempt to multiply matrices which do not conform to the rule. This rule will *always* be satisfied when the two matrices to be multiplied are square and both of the same size.

Below are several pairs of matrices. The number of columns in the first matrix in each case is compared with the number of rows in the second matrix, and a decision is made as to whether they can be multiplied:

$$\begin{bmatrix} 1 & 2 & 6 \\ 3 & 1 & 4 \end{bmatrix} \times \begin{bmatrix} 1 \\ 2 \\ 6 \end{bmatrix} \qquad \textit{can} \text{ be multiplied}$$

$$2 \times ③ \leftarrow = \rightarrow ③ \times 1$$

$$\begin{bmatrix} 1 & 3 & 6 \end{bmatrix} \times \begin{bmatrix} 1 \\ 7 \\ -2 \end{bmatrix} \qquad \textit{can} \text{ be multiplied}$$

$$1 \times ③ \leftarrow = \rightarrow ③ \times 1$$

$$\begin{bmatrix} 1 & 2 & 3 \\ 1 & 2 & 6 \end{bmatrix} \times \begin{bmatrix} 1 & 2 \\ 3 & 1 \end{bmatrix} \qquad \textit{cannot} \text{ be multiplied}$$

$$2 \times ③ \leftarrow \neq \rightarrow ② \times 2$$

$$\begin{bmatrix} 2 & 1 & 3 \\ 3 & 4 & 4 \\ 2 & 1 & 6 \end{bmatrix} \times \begin{bmatrix} 1 \\ 2 \\ 6 \\ 3 \end{bmatrix} \qquad \textit{cannot} \text{ be multiplied}$$

$$3 \times ③ \leftarrow \neq \rightarrow ④ \times 1$$

Here are two matrices, **A** and **B**. The number of *columns* in matrix **A** equals the number of *rows* in matrix **B**; thus they can be multiplied:

Matrix **A**   Matrix **B**

$$\begin{bmatrix} 5 \\ 6 \end{bmatrix} \times \begin{bmatrix} 4 & 3 \end{bmatrix}$$

$$2 \times ① \leftarrow = \rightarrow ① \times 2$$
$$\text{Columns} \qquad\qquad \text{Rows}$$

If we compare the *outer two* numbers of their dimensions, we get some useful information. The outer two numbers of the dimensions indicate the size of the matrix which we shall get as an answer; in the last example the answer will be a 2 × 2 matrix. Here are the same two matrices with their outer dimensions circled:

$$\text{Matrix } \mathbf{A} \quad\quad \text{Matrix } \mathbf{B}$$

$$\begin{bmatrix} 5 \\ 6 \end{bmatrix} \times [4 \quad 3]$$

$$\textcircled{2} \times 1 \quad 1 \times \textcircled{2}$$

Rows   Cols.

The outer dimension of matrix **A** indicates the number of rows in the answer. The outer dimension of matrix **B** indicates the number of columns in the answer.

DOING THE MULTIPLICATION

The actual multiplication is quite simple now that we know the size of the answer. If a 2 × 2 matrix will result, it must contain four elements. Let's show (first in symbolic form, then by numbers) how the multiplication is carried out. To obtain any element in the answer, first determine the *row* and *column* location of that element in the answer. For example, here's how the element *24* was computed in the answer. This element is in the *second row* and the *first column*. To compute it, we simply multiplied the *second row of matrix* **A** by the *first column of matrix* **B**; that is, 6 × 4 = 24.

$$\text{Matrix } \mathbf{A} \quad\quad \text{Matrix } \mathbf{B} \quad\quad\quad\quad \text{Matrix } \mathbf{C}$$

$$\begin{bmatrix} a \\ b \end{bmatrix} \times [c \quad d] = \begin{bmatrix} a \times c & a \times d \\ b \times c & b \times d \end{bmatrix}$$

$$\begin{bmatrix} 5 \\ 6 \end{bmatrix} \times [4 \quad 3] = \begin{bmatrix} 20 & 15 \\ 24 & 18 \end{bmatrix}$$

Matrix **A**	Matrix **B**	Calculations	Location of figure in answer
Row 1 (5) × col. 1 (4)		5 × 4 = 20	Row 1, col. 1
Row 1 (5) × col. 2 (3)		5 × 3 = 15	Row 1, col. 2
Row 2 (6) × col. 1 (4)		6 × 4 = 24	Row 2, col. 1
Row 2 (6) × col. 2 (3)		6 × 3 = 18	Row 2, col. 2

MORE EXAMPLES

Here are three more examples of matrix multiplication:

Example 1

$$\text{Matrix } \mathbf{A} \quad\quad \text{Matrix } \mathbf{B} \quad\quad \text{Matrix } \mathbf{C}$$

$$\begin{bmatrix} 2 & 3 \\ -1 & 4 \end{bmatrix} \times \begin{bmatrix} 5 & 6 \\ 7 & -2 \end{bmatrix} = \begin{bmatrix} 31 & 6 \\ 23 & -14 \end{bmatrix}$$

Matrix **A**	Matrix **B**	Calculations	Location of figure in answer
Row 1 [2 3] × col. 1 $\begin{bmatrix} 5 \\ 7 \end{bmatrix}$		2(5) + 3(7) = 31	Row 1, col. 1
Row 1 [2 3] × col. 2 $\begin{bmatrix} 6 \\ -2 \end{bmatrix}$		2(6) + 3(-2) = 6	Row 1, col. 2

Row 2 $[-1 \quad 4]$ × col. 1 $\begin{bmatrix} 5 \\ 7 \end{bmatrix}$ $\quad -1(5) + 4(7) = 23 \quad$ Row 2, col. 1

Row 2 $[-1 \quad 4]$ × col. 2 $\begin{bmatrix} 6 \\ -2 \end{bmatrix}$ $\quad -1(6) + 4(-2) = -14 \quad$ Row 2, col. 2

Example 2

Matrix **A** Matrix **B** Matrix **C**

$$\begin{bmatrix} 2 & 1 & -6 \\ -1 & 4 & 3 \\ 6 & 1 & -5 \end{bmatrix} \times \begin{bmatrix} 3 \\ -5 \\ 7 \end{bmatrix} = \begin{bmatrix} -41 \\ -2 \\ -22 \end{bmatrix}$$

Matrix **A**	Matrix **B**	Calculations	Location of figure in answer
Row 1 $[\ 2 \quad 1 \quad -6]$ × col. 1	$\begin{bmatrix} 3 \\ -5 \\ 7 \end{bmatrix}$	$2(3) + 1(-5) + (-6)(7) = -41$	Row 1, col. 1
Row 2 $[-1 \quad 4 \quad 3]$ × col. 1	$\begin{bmatrix} 3 \\ -5 \\ 7 \end{bmatrix}$	$(-1)(3) + 4(-5) + 3(7) = -2$	Row 2, col. 1
Row 3 $[6 \quad 1 \quad -5]$ × col. 1	$\begin{bmatrix} 3 \\ -5 \\ 7 \end{bmatrix}$	$6(3) + 1(-5) + (-5)(7) = -22$	Row 3, col. 1

Example 3

Matrix **A** Matrix **B** Matrix **C**

$$\begin{bmatrix} 1 & 4 & -2 \\ 3 & 2 & 0 \\ 6 & 5 & 7 \end{bmatrix} \times \begin{bmatrix} -3 & 8 & -5 \\ 0 & 9 & -4 \\ -1 & 10 & 11 \end{bmatrix} = \begin{bmatrix} -1 & 24 & -43 \\ -9 & 42 & -23 \\ -25 & 163 & 27 \end{bmatrix}$$

Matrix **A**	Matrix **B**	Calculations	Location of figure in answer
Row 1 $[1 \quad 4 \ -2]$ × col. 1	$\begin{bmatrix} -3 \\ 0 \\ -1 \end{bmatrix}$	$1(-3) + 4(0) + (-2)(-1) = -1$	Row 1, col. 1
Row 1 $[1 \quad 4 \ -2]$ × col. 2	$\begin{bmatrix} 8 \\ 9 \\ 10 \end{bmatrix}$	$1(8) + 4(9) + (-2)(10) = 24$	Row 1, col. 2
Row 1 $[1 \quad 4 \ -2]$ × col. 3	$\begin{bmatrix} -5 \\ -4 \\ 11 \end{bmatrix}$	$1(-5) + 4(-4) + (-2)(11) = -43$	Row 1, col. 3

Matrix **A**		Matrix **B**	Calculations	Location of figure in answer
Row 2 [3 2 0] × col. 1		$\begin{bmatrix} -3 \\ 0 \\ -1 \end{bmatrix}$	$3(-3) + 2(0)$ $+ 0(-1) = -9$	Row 2, col. 1
Row 2 [3 2 0] × col. 2		$\begin{bmatrix} 8 \\ 9 \\ 10 \end{bmatrix}$	$3(8) + 2(9)$ $+ 0(10) = 42$	Row 2, col. 2
Row 2 [3 2 0] × col. 3		$\begin{bmatrix} -5 \\ -4 \\ 11 \end{bmatrix}$	$3(-5) + 2(-4)$ $+ 0(11) = -23$	Row 2, col. 3
Row 3 [6 5 7] × col. 1		$\begin{bmatrix} -3 \\ 0 \\ -1 \end{bmatrix}$	$6(-3) + 5(0)$ $+ 7(-1) = -25$	Row 3, col. 1
Row 3 [6 5 7] × col. 2		$\begin{bmatrix} 8 \\ 9 \\ 10 \end{bmatrix}$	$6(8) + 5(9)$ $+ 7(10) = 163$	Row 3, col. 2
Row 3 [6 5 7] × col. 3		$\begin{bmatrix} -5 \\ -4 \\ 11 \end{bmatrix}$	$6(-5) + 5(-4)$ $+ 7(11) = 27$	Row 3, col. 3

3 Prediction of market shares for future periods

STANDARD FORM FOR ILLUSTRATING THE MATRIX OF TRANSITION PROBABILITIES

STANDARD FORM FOR BRAND-SWITCHING PROBLEMS

Now that we have completed our very brief introduction to matrices and matrix multiplication, let us return to the brand-switching example first introduced on page 746. In the matrix of transition probabilities below, we have included for each dairy the retention probability *and* the probability of its loss of customers to its two competitors. The rows in this matrix show the retention of customers and the loss of customers; the columns represent the retention of customers and the gain of customers. These probabilities have been calculated to three decimal places.

Retention and loss →

	A	B	C	
A	.800	.100	.100	Retention and gain
B	.070	.900	.030	
C	.083	.067	.850	

Below is a matrix of the same dimensions as the one above, illustrating exactly how each probability was determined:

$$\begin{array}{c} & A & B & C \\ \begin{matrix} A \\ B \\ C \end{matrix} & \begin{bmatrix} {}^{160}/_{200} = .800 & {}^{20}/_{200} = .100 & {}^{20}/_{200} = .100 \\ {}^{35}/_{500} = .070 & {}^{450}/_{500} = .900 & {}^{15}/_{500} = .030 \\ {}^{25}/_{300} = .083 & {}^{20}/_{300} = .067 & {}^{255}/_{300} = .850 \end{bmatrix} \end{array}$$

The *rows* of the matrix of transition probabilities can be read as follows:

INTERPRETING THE ROWS

Row 1 indicates that dairy A retains .8 of its customers (160), loses .1 of its customers (20) to dairy B, and loses .1 of its customers (20) to dairy C.

Row 2 indicates that dairy B retains .9 of its customers (450), loses .07 of its customers (35) to dairy A, and loses .03 of its customers (15) to dairy C.

Row 3 indicates that dairy C retains .85 of its customers (255), loses .083 of its customers (25) to dairy A, and loses .067 of its customers (20) to dairy B.

Reading the *columns* yields the following information:

INTERPRETING THE COLUMNS

Column 1 indicates that dairy A retains .8 of its customers (160), gains .07 of B's customers (35), and gains .083 of C's customers (25).

Column 2 indicates that dairy B retains .9 of its customers (450), gains .1 of A's customers (20), and gains .067 of C's customers (20).

Column 3 indicates that dairy C retains .85 of its customers (255), gains .1 of A's customers (20), and gains .03 of B's customers (15).

With the information in this form, basic relationships can more easily be observed. In addition, through the use of matrix algebra we will be able to accomplish the four management objectives listed on page 747.

STABILITY OF THE MATRIX OF TRANSITION PROBABILITIES

Markov analysis is concerned with the *patronage* decisions of consumers; it involves how many consumers are buying from which dairies. A basic assumption is that consumers do not shift their patronage from dairy to dairy at random; instead, we assume that choices of dairies to buy from in the future reflect choices made in the past.

ASSUMPTIONS ABOUT BRAND SWITCHING

A *first-order* Markov process is based on the assumption that the probability of the next event (customers' choices of vendors *next* month, in this case) depends upon the outcomes of the last event (customers' choices *this* month) and not at all on any earlier buying behavior. A *second-order* Markov process assumes that customers' choices next month may depend upon their choices during the immediate past 2 months (or other buying period, if months are not used). In turn, *a third-order* process is based upon the assumption that customers' behavior is best predicted by observing and taking into account their behavior during the past 3 months (or other appropriate buying periods).

The mathematics of first-order Markov processes is not difficult. In second- and third-order processes, however, the computations become more cumbersome and difficult. Studies suggest that using first-order assumptions for prediction purposes is not invalid, particularly if data appear to indicate that customer choices follow a fairly stable pattern, that is, if the matrix of transition probabilities remains stable. Because they have proved to be reliable predictors of future behavior, we shall limit our treatment to processes of the first order.

USING MATRIX ALGEBRA TO DO THE CALCULATIONS

Let us return to our three dairies and assume that the matrix of transition probabilities remains fairly stable and that the July 1 market shares are these: A = 22 percent, B = 49 percent, C = 29 percent. Managers of the three dairies would benefit, of course, from knowing the market shares that would occur in some future period.

To calculate the probable share of the total market likely to be held by each of the dairies on August 1 (the month is our basic data-gathering period), we would simply set up the July 1 market shares as a matrix and multiply this matrix by the matrix of transition probabilities as follows:

$$[.22 \quad .49 \quad .29] \times \begin{bmatrix} .800 & .100 & .100 \\ .070 & .900 & .030 \\ .083 & .067 & .850 \end{bmatrix} = [.234 \quad .483 \quad .283]$$

July 1 market shares — Total = 1.00

Transition probabilities

Probable August 1 market shares — Total = 1.000

The matrix multiplication is explained in detail below.

Row 1 × column 1:

A's share of market × A's propensity to retain its customers $= .22 \times .800 = .176$

B's share of market × A's propensity to attract B's customers $= .49 \times .070 = .034$

C's share of market × A's propensity to attract C's customers $= .29 \times .083 = \underline{.024}$

A's share of market on August 1 $= .234$

Row 1 × column 2:

A's share of market × B's propensity to attract A's customers $= .22 \times .100 = .022$

B's share of market × B's propensity to retain its customers $= .49 \times .900 = .441$

C's share of market × B's propensity to attract C's customers $= .29 \times .067 = \underline{.020}$

B's share of market on August 1 $= .483$

Row 1 × column 3:

A's share		C's propensity to
of market	×	attract A's customers = .22 × .100 = .022

B's share	×	C's propensity to
of market		attract B's customers = .49 × .030 = .015

C's share		C's propensity to
of market	×	retain its customers = .29 × .850 = .246

C's share of market on August 1 = .283

The probable market share on September 1 can also be calculated by squaring the matrix of transition probabilities and multiplying the squared matrix by the July 1 market shares:

PREDICTING SHARES TWO PERIODS IN THE FUTURE; TWO DIFFERENT METHODS

$$\textbf{Method 1:} \quad [.22 \quad .49 \quad .29] \quad \times \quad \begin{bmatrix} .800 & .100 & .100 \\ .070 & .900 & .030 \\ .083 & .067 & .850 \end{bmatrix}^2$$

$$= \begin{array}{l} \text{probable Sept. 1} \\ \text{market shares} \end{array}$$

or by multiplying the matrix of transition probabilities by the market shares on August 1:

$$\textbf{Method 2:} \quad [.234 \quad .483 \quad .283] \quad \times \quad \begin{bmatrix} .800 & .100 & .100 \\ .070 & .900 & .030 \\ .083 & .067 & .850 \end{bmatrix}$$

$$= \begin{array}{l} \text{probable Sept. 1} \\ \text{market shares} \end{array}$$

METHOD 1

We can explain the logic behind method 1 this way. By squaring the original matrix of transition probabilities, we have in fact calculated the probabilities of retention, gain, and loss which can be multiplied by the original market shares (22, 49, and 29 percent) to yield the market shares which will obtain on September 1. To obtain, for example, the column 1–row 1 term X in the product, we multiply row 1 by column 1:

FIRST METHOD EXPLAINED

$$\begin{bmatrix} .800 & .100 & .100 \end{bmatrix} \quad \times \quad \begin{bmatrix} .800 \\ .070 \\ .083 \end{bmatrix} \quad = \quad \begin{bmatrix} X \end{bmatrix}$$

Row 1 × column 1:

A's propensity to retain its own customers times A's propensity to retain its own customers equals that proportion of its original customers it holds for both periods

.8 × .8 = .64

DETAILS OF SQUARING THE MATRIX OF TRANSITION PROBABILITIES

+

B's propensity to gain customers from A times A's propensity to gain customers from B equals A's regain of its own customers from B $\quad .1 \times .07 = .007$

$+$

C's propensity to gain customers from A times A's propensity to gain customers from C equals A's regain of its own customers from C $\quad .1 \times .083 = .0083$

We get the X term in the product by adding together the results of the three calculations:

.6400
.0070
.0083
.6553 = portion of A's original customers A retains on September 1

In similar fashion, the other eight terms in the square of the matrix can be explained and calculated. The resulting matrix for use in method 1 is

$$\begin{bmatrix} .6553 & .1767 & .1680 \\ .1215 & .8190 & .0595 \\ .1416 & .1256 & .7328 \end{bmatrix}$$

COMPLETING METHOD 1

To complete method 1, we multiply the squared matrix by the July 1 market shares:

$$[.22 \quad .49 \quad .29] \times \begin{bmatrix} .6553 & .1767 & .1680 \\ .1215 & .8190 & .0595 \\ .1416 & .1256 & .7328 \end{bmatrix}$$

with the result

A	.245	
B	.477	← Probable market shares on September 1
C	.278	
Total	1.000	

For clarity, we shall explain the multiplication of the first row by the first column in detail:

$$[.22 \quad .49 \quad .29] \quad \times \quad \begin{bmatrix} .6553 \\ .1215 \\ .1416 \end{bmatrix} = [.245]$$

MATRIX DETAILS OF
COMPLETING METHOD 1

A's original market share times A's propensity to retain its own customers after two periods equals A's share of its original customers on September 1
$\quad .22 \times .6553 = .144$

$+$

B's original market share times A's propensity to gain B's original customers after two periods equals A's share of B's original customers on September 1

$$.49 \times .1215 = .060$$

$$+$$

C's original market share times A's propensity to gain C's original customers after two periods equals A's share of C's original customers on September 1

$$.29 \times .1416 = .041$$

Adding the results of the three calculations, we get

$$
\begin{array}{l}
.144 \\
.060 \\
\underline{.041} \\
.245 \ = \ \text{A's probable market share on September 1}
\end{array}
$$

METHOD 2

SECOND METHOD OF COMPUTING MARKET SHARES TWO PERIODS IN THE FUTURE

Multiplication of the *original* matrix of transition probabilities by the August 1 market shares yields the same result as method 1. We shall reproduce the two matrices and explain one of the multiplications, as follows:

$$
[.234 \quad .483 \quad .283] \ \times \
\begin{bmatrix}
.800 & .100 & .100 \\
.070 & .900 & .030 \\
.083 & .067 & .850
\end{bmatrix}
$$

Row 1 × column 1:

MATRIX DETAILS OF SECOND METHOD

A's share of market on August 1 times A's propensity to retain its own customers equals A's retained share of its own customers it had on August 1

$$.234 \times .800 = .187$$

$$+$$

B's share of market on August 1 times A's propensity to gain customers from B equals A's gain of the customers B had on August 1 $.483 \times .070 = .034$

$$+$$

C's share of market on August 1 times A's propensity to gain customers from C equals A's gain of the customers C had on August 1 $.283 \times .083 = .024$

$$
\begin{array}{l}
.187 \\
.034 \\
\underline{.024} \\
.245 \ = \ \text{A's probable share of market on September 1}
\end{array}
$$

Method 1 has some advantages over method 2. If we want to go from the initial period to the third period, for instance, we do *not* have to go through the intermediate steps if we use method 1. We simply proceed as follows:

ADVANTAGE OF METHOD 1

Market shares after three periods:

July 1
market shares

Matrix of transition
probabilities cubed

$$[.22 \quad .49 \quad .29] \quad \times \quad \begin{bmatrix} .800 & .100 & .100 \\ .070 & .900 & .030 \\ .083 & .067 & .850 \end{bmatrix}^3 = \begin{matrix} \text{probable market shares} \\ \text{on October 1} \end{matrix}$$

And, of course, if we want the market shares which will occur after six periods, we set up the problem as follows:

Market shares after six periods:

July 1
market shares

Matrix of transition
probabilities to the
sixth power

$$[.22 \quad .49 \quad .29] \quad \times \quad \begin{bmatrix} .800 & .100 & .100 \\ .070 & .900 & .030 \\ .083 & .067 & .850 \end{bmatrix}^6 = \begin{matrix} \text{probable market shares} \\ \text{on January 1} \end{matrix}$$

Of course, raising a matrix to the sixth or an even higher power is no easy job if you must do the calculations by hand. Computer programs are available, however, which will perform this otherwise onerous task in a few seconds.

In Figure 16-1 is some output from a microcomputer program written by Paul A. Jensen.[1] We used this program to estimate market shares of the three dairies for the next 20 months. The probabilities given for each period are those at the end of the period, that is, at the beginning of the next period.

ADVANTAGE OF METHOD 2

To summarize the uses of the two alternative methods of computing market shares for future periods, we would obviously employ method 1 if we simply wanted the market shares for the specified future period, while we would choose method 2 if we wanted to observe the changes which were occurring in the market shares during all the intervening periods.

4 Equilibrium conditions

EQUILIBRIUM DEFINED

It is quite reasonable to assume in our dairy problems that in the future a state of equilibrium might be approached regarding market shares; that is, the exchange of customers under equilibrium would be such as to continue— to freeze—the three market shares which obtained at the moment equilibrium was reached. Of course, equilibrium could result *only* if no dairy took action which altered the matrix of transition probabilities. From a marketing point of view, we would want the answer to this question: What would the three final, or equilibrium, shares of the market be?

---

[1] Paul A. Jensen, *Microsolve/Operations Research* (San Francisco: Holden-Day, Inc., 1983).

	ABBOT	BRANC	CARTR
PER 1	.23437	.48243	.2832
PER 2	.244771	.476598	.278629
PER 3	.252305	.472083	.275610
PER 4	.257766	.468572	.273662
PER 5	.261726	.465826	.272446
PER 6	.264602	.463670	.271727
PER 7	.266692	.461969	.271338
PER 8	.268212	.460621	.271165
PER 9	.269320	.459548	.271130
PER 10	.270128	.458691	.271179
PER 11	.270719	.458004	.271276
PER 12	.271151	.457451	.271397
PER 13	.271468	.457004	.271526
PER 14	.271702	.456643	.271654
PER 15	.271874	.456350	.271775
PER 16	.272001	.456111	.271887
PER 17	.272095	.455916	.271987
PER 18	.272165	.455757	.272076
PER 19	.272217	.455627	.272154
PER 20	.272256	.455521	.272221

FIGURE 16-1
Market shares for the next 20 months.

A ONE-DAIRY EQUILIBRIUM

To illustrate equilibrium, assume a new matrix of transition probabilities:

Retention and loss →

$$\begin{array}{c} A \\ B \\ C \end{array} \begin{bmatrix} .85 & .10 & .05 \\ .15 & .75 & .10 \\ 0 & 0 & 1.0 \end{bmatrix} \begin{array}{l} \text{Retention} \\ \text{and gain} \end{array} \downarrow$$

Because C never loses any customers and because both other dairies *do* lose customers to C, it is only a question of time until C has all the customers. In Markov terminology this would be called a *sink,* or *basin,* of one state, meaning that one of our dairies (C) eventually gets all the customers. C is also called an *absorbing state.*

ONE DAIRY GETS ALL THE CUSTOMERS

A TWO-DAIRY EQUILIBRIUM

A second type of equilibrium could occur. To illustrate this, here is a new matrix of transition probabilities:

$$\begin{array}{c} A \\ B \\ C \end{array} \begin{bmatrix} .90 & .05 & .05 \\ 0 & .50 & .50 \\ 0 & .50 & .50 \end{bmatrix}$$

One can easily see that, in time, dairy B and dairy C capture *all* A's customers. Why is this true? Because A loses .05 of its customers to B and .05 to C and does not regain any new customers from either B or C. As B and C both have the same probability of retaining customers (.50), they must eventually

TWO DAIRIES GET ALL THE CUSTOMERS

divide up the market. This would be referred to as a sink, or basin, of two states. That is, two dairies, B and C, eventually share all the customers in the whole market.

◼ A THREE-DAIRY EQUILIBRIUM

We could, of course, have a type of equilibrium where no sink, or basin, exists. Here no one dairy gets *all* the customers—no two dairies capture the entire market. But some final, or equilibrium, condition develops and continues in which the market shares will not change *so long as the matrix of transition probabilities remains the same.* Our original three-dairy problem illustrates this third type of equilibrium. To find out what the final, or equilibrium, shares of the market will be with our original problem, let us proceed as follows:

$$
\begin{array}{c}
\quad\quad A \quad\quad B \quad\quad C \\
\begin{array}{c} A \\ B \\ C \end{array}
\begin{bmatrix}
.800 & .100 & .100 \\
.070 & .900 & .030 \\
.083 & .067 & .850
\end{bmatrix}
\end{array}
=
\begin{array}{l}
\text{original matrix of} \\
\text{transition probabilities}
\end{array}
$$

Now, A's share of the market in the equilibrium period [let us label this unspecified future period the *eq period* and the period immediately preceding equilibrium the *(eq − 1) period*] equals

.800 times the share A had in the (eq. − 1) period

\+ .070 times the share B had in the (eq. − 1) period

\+ .083 times the share C had in the (eq. − 1) period

We can write this relationship as an equation:

$$A_{eq} = .800A_{eq-1} + .070B_{eq-1} + .083C_{eq-1}$$

And, of course, we can write two more equations illustrating the shares of market B and C will have in the equilibrium period:

$$B_{eq} = .100A_{eq-1} + .900B_{eq-1} + .067C_{eq-1}$$

$$C_{eq} = .100A_{eq-1} + .030B_{eq-1} + .850C_{eq-1}$$

In the early periods, the gains and losses from dairy to dairy are usually of fairly high magnitude. But as equilibrium is approached, the gains and losses become smaller and smaller, until just before equilibrium they are infinitesimally small. This concept is not a unique one; many phenomena behave in this manner. If you are skeptical, try dividing a number in half again and again and watch how the changes you produce become smaller and smaller. In the case of our Markov process, the changes in market shares between the equilibrium period and the period just preceding it are so slight that they may for mathematical purposes be treated as equal; that is, $A_{eq} = A_{eq-1}$. This allows us to rewrite our three equations as follows:

$$A = .800A + .070B + .083C \qquad \text{①}$$

$$B = .100A + .900B + .067C \qquad \text{②}$$

$$C = .100A + .030B + .850C \qquad \text{③}$$

Because the sum of the three market shares equals 1.0, we can add another equation:

$$1 = A + B + C \qquad \text{④}$$

In Eqs. ① to ③ we have similar terms on both sides of the equality sign, so that we can reduce these equations to

$$0 = -.200A + .070B + .083C \qquad \text{①}$$

$$0 = .100A - .100B + .067C \qquad \text{②}$$

$$0 = .100A + .030B - .150C \qquad \text{③}$$

$$1 = A + B + C \qquad \text{④}$$

As we have four equations and only three unknowns, we can drop any one of the first three equations (we drop Eq. ③) and solve the remaining three equations simultaneously for the equilibrium market shares.

$$0 = -.200A + .070B + .083C \qquad \text{①}$$

$$0 = .100A - .100B + .067C \qquad \text{②}$$

$$1 = A + B + C \qquad \text{③}$$

Step 1 Multiply Eq. ② by .7 and add it to Eq. ①.

$$0 = -.200A + .070B + .083C \qquad \text{①}$$
$$\underline{0 = .070A - .070B + .047C} \qquad \text{②} \times .7$$
$$0 = -.130A + .130C$$

$$.130A = .130C$$

$$A = C$$

Step 2 Multiply Eq. ② by 2 and add it to Eq. ①.

$$0 = -.200A + .070B + .083C \qquad \text{①}$$
$$\underline{0 = .200A - .200B + .134C} \qquad \text{②} \times 2$$
$$0 = - .130B + .217C$$

$$.130B = .217C$$

$$B = 1.67C$$

Step 3 Repeat Eq. $\boxed{4}$.

$$1 = A + B + C$$

Because $A = C$, then

$$1 = C + B + C$$

and because $B = 1.67C$,

$$1 = C + 1.67C + C$$
$$1 = 3.67C$$
$$C = .273 = C\text{'s equilibrium market share}$$

Because $A = C$,

$$A = .273 = A\text{'s equilibrium market share}$$

and because $1 = A + B + C$,

$$1 = .273 + B + .273$$
$$1 = B + .546$$
$$B = .454 = B\text{'s equilibrium market share}$$

CHECKING THAT
EQUILIBRIUM HAS
BEEN REACHED

Are you skeptical that an equilibrium has actually been reached? If so, let's prove it. Multiply the equilibrium market share (A, .273; B, .454; C, .273) by the matrix of transition probabilities:

$$[.273 \quad .454 \quad .273] \times \begin{bmatrix} .800 & .100 & .100 \\ .070 & .900 & .030 \\ .083 & .067 & .850 \end{bmatrix} = [.273 \quad .454 \quad .273]$$

Although the idea of equilibrium is a long-range concept, it is interesting to ask how quickly the equilibrium market shares are approached. If you look back at Figure 16-1 on page 761, you will see that after 20 months the three dairies will be essentially at their equilibrium shares, and that even after only 10 months they will already be quite close to the equilibrium.

ASSUMPTIONS ABOUT
EQUILIBRIUM

Just a word about the equilibrium market shares we have calculated. They are based upon the assumption that the matrix of transition probabilities remains *fixed*, that the propensities of all three dairies to retain, gain, and lose customers do not change over time. In many cases this may be somewhat invalid, but no harm is done even so. For the period during which the transition probabilities *are* stable, we can calculate an equilibrium which will result. Then if we have good reason to believe that the transition probabilities

are indeed changing because of some action by management, we can use the
new transition probabilities and calculate the equilibrium market shares which
will result. In that manner, we are essentially using Markov analysis as a
short- or intermediate-run tool.

RELATIONSHIP OF MARKET SHARES AND EQUILIBRIUM

An interesting fact about Markov analysis is that the final equilibrium will be
the same (provided the transition probabilities remain fixed) *regardless* of the
initial market shares held by various producers or suppliers. That is to say,
we will always end with the same final proportion of customers no matter
what the original shares were. For example, if three suppliers have as their
current shares of market

$$A = 30\%$$
$$B = 60\%$$
$$C = 10\%$$

and the matrix of transition probabilities is

$$
\begin{array}{c c}
 & \begin{array}{ccc} A & B & C \end{array} \\
\begin{array}{c} A \\ B \\ C \end{array} &
\left[\begin{array}{ccc}
.90 & .10 & 0 \\
.05 & .80 & .15 \\
.20 & .20 & .60
\end{array} \right]
\end{array}
$$

then by using the technique for determining the equilibrium market shares
discussed in the previous section, we can determine that the equilibrium
market shares would be A, .476; B, .381; C, .143.

   If, on the other hand, the initial market shares were

$$A = 20\%$$
$$B = 45\%$$
$$C = 35\%$$

the equilibrium market shares for the three firms would still be the same (A,
.476; B, .381; C, .143) as long as the matrix of transition probabilities did
not change. You can satisfy yourself that this is true by noting that the market
shares were *not* used in explaining the equilibrium process; only the matrix
of transition probabilities enters into the determination of equilibrium.

   Of course, the nearer the initial market shares happen to be to the final
or equilibrium market shares, the faster equilibrium will be approached. If
the beginning shares for three firms are

$$A = 35\%$$
$$B = 40\%$$
$$C = 25\%$$

and the final or equilibrium shares will be

$$A = 30\%$$
$$B = 35\%$$
$$C = 35\%$$

SPEED WITH WHICH
AN EQUILIBRIUM IS
APPROACHED

we can see that the process will approach equilibrium much faster than if the initial market shares are

$$A = 10\%$$
$$B = 75\%$$
$$C = 15\%$$

simply because in the former case, less change needs to occur to get close to the final equilibrium. In the latter case, for instance, firm A needs to acquire sufficient net customers to bring its market share from 10 percent to its equilibrium share of 30 percent, whereas in the former case, A moves only from 35 to 30 percent before equilibrium is approached.

If this concept that the initial market shares have no bearing on the final equilibrium shares still appears a bit difficult to accept, consider the following example:

$$
\begin{array}{c}
\quad\; A \quad\; B \quad\; C \\
\begin{array}{c} A \\ B \\ C \end{array}
\left[
\begin{array}{ccc}
1.0 & 0 & 0 \\
.3 & .6 & .1 \\
.1 & .2 & .7
\end{array}
\right]
\end{array}
$$

One can immediately see that *regardless of the initial market shares held by these three firms,* firm A will eventually get all the customers: A does not lose any of the customers gained from B and C. Thus although beginning with only 5 percent of the customers, A will eventually have 100 percent of the customers. Of course, the higher the initial percentage of customers held by firm A, the faster equilibrium will be approached.

5 Use of Markov analysis in marketing strategy

EVALUATING ALTERNATIVE STRATEGIES

A PROBLEM IN THE USE
OF MARKOV ANALYSIS

To illustrate how Markov analysis is helpful in determining marketing strategy, consider the following situation. For three competing sellers, the matrix of transition probabilities is as follows:

Retention
and loss →

$$
\begin{array}{c}
\quad\; A \quad\; B \quad\; C \\
\begin{array}{c} A \\ B \\ C \end{array}
\left[
\begin{array}{ccc}
.2 & .6 & .2 \\
.1 & .5 & .4 \\
.2 & .3 & .5
\end{array}
\right]
\end{array}
$$

Retention
and gain

If the marketing strategies of these three firms do not change so as to affect the matrix of transition probabilities, we could reasonably expect equilibrium market shares of A, .156; B, .434; and C, .410.

In an effort to better a rather poor showing, seller A might consider two new marketing strategies.

Strategy 1 Seller A might try to retain more of its own customers. Assume that strategy 1 increases retention from 20 to 40 percent, and assume that this change consists of A's reducing its loss of customers to seller B.

The new matrix of transition probabilities is

$$
\begin{array}{c c}
 & \begin{array}{c c c} A & B & C \end{array} \\
\begin{array}{c} A \\ B \\ C \end{array} &
\left[\begin{array}{c c c}
.4 & .4 & .2 \\
.1 & .5 & .4 \\
.2 & .3 & .5
\end{array} \right]
\end{array}
$$

The new equilibrium market shares work out to be A, .2; B, .4; and C, .4. A's showing now is better; but even though A's campaign was specifically directed against B, note that firm C suffered somewhat. Why? C gains new customers from A and B but more from B than from A. Now that B gets fewer of A's customers as a result of A's strategy, C's gain from B (.4) will represent a smaller number. We should not be too surprised that C's fortunes are not more drastically affected as a result of A's action; C does get back from A some of the customers A takes from B.

Strategy 2 As an alternative, seller A might direct its marketing efforts at capturing a greater share of the buyers who switch from C. Suppose that A's campaign is designed to induce .4 of those who switch from C to move to A, instead of the .2 who now do.

The matrix of transition probabilities now becomes

$$
\begin{array}{c c}
 & \begin{array}{c c c} A & B & C \end{array} \\
\begin{array}{c} A \\ B \\ C \end{array} &
\left[\begin{array}{c c c}
.2 & .6 & .2 \\
.1 & .5 & .4 \\
.4 & .1 & .5
\end{array} \right]
\end{array}
$$

If we calculate the equilibrium market shares which would result from this type of strategy, we find them to be A, .233; B, .391; and C, .376.

We infer from this example that if the costs of the two programs are the same, clearly strategy 2 is the better one. Again in the case of strategy 2, notice that even though A's encroachment efforts were not directed against B at all, B suffers loss of customers as a result of A's marketing program directed against C. Why? B used to get .3 of C's customers each month. Now that A's efforts have been successful in getting .4 of C's customers, B's share of switchers is reduced to .1. Again, we should not be too surprised at seeing that B's share does not shrink drastically; B will eventually get back from A some of the new customers A was successful in taking away from C.

ASSUMPTIONS WE HAVE MADE

In setting up our dairy problem at the beginning of this chapter, we assumed, in order to simplify the mathematics, that no old customers *leave* the market and no new customers *enter* the market during the time period involved. We know that this is seldom the case. What, then, about the more realistic experience, in which new customers do move in and begin patronizing dairies and old customers do disappear from or drop out of the market? In these circumstances, the effects of the additions and the losses on (1) the market shares obtaining in immediately future periods and (2) the market shares at equilibrium, depend on three variables:

1 The dairy from which each newcomer begins to buy

2 The dairy from which each consumer was buying at the moment he or she ceased to be a customer

3 The extent to which the brand loyalty of each newcomer differs from the brand loyalty pattern obtaining at the time of his or her entry into the market as a customer

SOURCE OF INFORMATION

Perhaps you have been wondering how the firms we have been referring to can get the data needed for the application of Markov analysis to their marketing problems. One solution is for a firm to buy the services of a market research organization. Some of these organizations collect information about brand loyalty and brand switching for clients. For example, the Market Research Corporation of America has established a sample of U.S. families who record and report all purchases of certain branded products to MRCA. Because the buying units constituting this consumer panel reveal which brands they buy, MRCA data can be used in Markov analysis. Some individual sellers are in a position to collect the information on brand preference they would need in order to make use of Markov analysis. Other market-research firms like A. C. Nielsen provide information appropriate for use with Markov analysis.

6 Other uses of Markov analysis

Our discussion of Markov analysis has been limited to its use in brand-share analysis and prediction. Granted, this *is* a leading use of the technique; there are, however, other areas in which the application of Markov analysis has produced significant contributions. We shall examine several of these in the following sections.

EQUIPMENT REPAIR APPLICATION
OF MARKOV ANALYSIS

Karen Rand is the Coca-Cola dealer in Hillsborough, Virginia. Her warehouse manager inspects her soft drink crates (these are the wooden crates that hold 24 bottles) each week and classifies them as "just rebuilt this week," "in good working condition," "in fair condition," or "damaged beyond use." If a crate is damaged beyond use, it is sent to the repair area, where it is usually out of use for a week. Karen's warehouse records indicate that this is the appropriate matrix of transition probabilities for her soft drink crates:

	Rebuilt	Good	Fair	Damaged
Rebuilt	0	.8	.2	0
Good	0	.6	.4	0
Fair	0	0	.5	.5
Damaged	1.0	0	0	0

TRANSITION PROBABILITIES FOR CRATES, ALTERNATIVE 1

Karen's accountant tells her that it costs $2.50 to rebuild a crate and that the company incurs a loss of $1.85 in production efficiency each time a crate is found to be damaged beyond use. This efficiency is lost because broken crates slow down the truck-loading process.

COSTS

To calculate the expected weekly cost of both rebuilding *and* loss of production efficiency, we need the equilibrium probabilities of Karen's matrix. Using the method previously illustrated, we find them to be as follows: rebuilt, $\frac{1}{6}$; good, $\frac{1}{3}$; fair, $\frac{1}{3}$; and damaged, $\frac{1}{6}$. The average weekly cost of rebuilding and loss of production efficiency is then

EQUILIBRIUM PROBABILITIES

$$
\underset{\substack{\text{Rebuilding} \\ \text{cost}}}{\frac{1}{6} \times \$2.50} + \underset{\substack{\text{Damage} \\ \text{(out of use)} \\ \text{loss}}}{\frac{1}{6} \times \$1.85} = \$.725 \text{ per crate per week}
$$

COSTS UNDER FIRST ALTERNATIVE

Suppose now that Karen wants to consider rebuilding crates whenever they are inspected and found to be in *fair* shape. This eliminates the possibility of a crate being damaged. In this instance, the new matrix of transition probabilities is

	Rebuilt	Good	Fair
Rebuilt	0	.8	.2
Good	0	.6	.4
Fair	1.0	0	0

TRANSITION PROBABILITIES FOR CRATES, ALTERNATIVE 2

The equilibrium probabilities for this matrix have been found to be as follows: rebuilt, $\frac{1}{4}$; good, $\frac{1}{2}$; and fair, $\frac{1}{4}$. The average weekly cost of rebuilding and loss of production efficiency under these circumstances is

EQUILIBRIUM PROBABILITIES

$$
\underset{\substack{\text{Rebuilding} \\ \text{cost}}}{\frac{1}{4} \times \$2.50} + \underset{\substack{\text{Damage} \\ \text{(out of use)} \\ \text{loss}}}{0} = \$.625 \text{ per crate per week}
$$

COSTS UNDER SECOND ALTERNATIVE

Rebuilding crates as soon as they are found to be in "fair" shape will save Karen a little over 10 cents per crate per week in this case. Since Karen owns over 6,000 crates, this is a substantial saving for her. You have probably already recognized that we used Markov analysis here to solve a "replacement type" of problem; in Chapter 5, we solved a similar problem (filter replacement) by the use of a less elegant method.

▊ EMPLOYEE PRODUCTIVITY APPLICATION OF MARKOV ANALYSIS

United Industries, a manufacturer of women's sleepwear, classifies its sewing operators into four categories depending upon their productivity during the preceding month; 1 is the lowest category and 4 the highest. Historically, the sewing work force has been distributed across the four categories as follows: 1 = 30 percent, 2 = 35 percent, 3 = 25 percent, 4 = 10 percent. Seven months ago, United introduced a new organizational system into its Mt. Gilead plant, one of its largest units, with 450 operators. The new system groups the operators into voluntary work units which not only elect their own supervisors but also determine their own work schedules. Production records kept since the new plan was adopted have enabled Bill Haywood, plant manager, to construct this matrix of transition probabilities illustrating month-to-month changes in employee productivity:

<table>
<tr><td></td><td></td><td colspan="1">Lowest</td><td></td><td></td><td colspan="1">Highest</td></tr>
<tr><td></td><td></td><td>1</td><td>2</td><td>3</td><td>4</td></tr>
<tr><td>Lowest</td><td>1</td><td>.5</td><td>.3</td><td>.2</td><td>0</td></tr>
<tr><td></td><td>2</td><td>.3</td><td>.4</td><td>.3</td><td>0</td></tr>
<tr><td></td><td>3</td><td>.1</td><td>.2</td><td>.2</td><td>.5</td></tr>
<tr><td>Highest</td><td>4</td><td>.1</td><td>.1</td><td>.1</td><td>.7</td></tr>
</table>

Bill would like to know what to expect in the way of productivity distribution of the work force as a result of the new organizational system. Further, he would like to know the long-run benefit per month of this system considering that operators earn an average of $700 a month and productivity losses for the four categories of employee are 40 percent, 25 percent, 15 percent, and 5 percent, respectively, for categories 1, 2, 3, and 4.

Using the method we first introduced on pages 762–764, we can determine that the equilibrium probabilities of Bill Haywood's matrix are

Lowest	1	.247
	2	.241
	3	.192
Highest	4	.320

Bill now sets up Table 16-5 to calculate the monthly productivity losses under the new and the previous system; it appears that the new organizational system has the potential to save United over $14,000 per month in productivity losses in its Mt. Gilead plant.

▊ ACCOUNTS RECEIVABLE APPLICATION OF MARKOV ANALYSIS

Markov analysis has been successfully applied to accounts receivable analysis, specifically to the estimation of that portion of the accounts receivable which will eventually become uncollectible (become bad debts). We can illustrate this application by considering Milton's Clothing Cupboard, a clothing store

	Employee category	Percent of employees		Productivity loss		
Old organizational system	1	30	×	40%	=	12.00%
	2	35	×	25	=	8.75
	3	25	×	15	=	3.75
	4	10	×	5	=	.50
						25.00%

25% × $700/mo × 450 employees = $78,750

	Employee category	Percent of employees		Productivity loss		
New organizational system	1	24.7	×	40%	=	9.88%
	2	24.1	×	25	=	6.03
	3	19.2	×	15	=	2.88
	4	32.0	×	5	=	1.60
						20.39%

20.39% × $700/mo × 450 employees = $64,229

TABLE 16-5
Cost comparison
of old and new
organizational system

catering to college students. Milton divides his accounts receivable into two classifications: 0 to 60 days old and 61 to 180 days old. Accounts which are more than 180 days old are written off by Milton (considered bad debts). Milton follows the general practice of classifying a customer's account receivable according to the oldest unpaid bill in the account (this is referred to in accounting as the *total balance* method of aging accounts because the customer's total balance is classified in the aging category of that customer's oldest unpaid bill). This method of aging accounts receivable permits an account which is *now* in the 61- to 180-day category to appear next month in the 0- to 60-day category if the customer pays an older bill during the month. Milton currently has $6,500 in accounts receivable; from analysis of his past records, he has been able to provide us with this matrix of transition probabilities (the matrix can be thought of in terms of what happens to *one dollar* of accounts receivable):

$$
\begin{array}{l}
\quad\quad\quad\quad \text{Paid} \quad \text{Bad debt} \quad \text{0–60 days} \quad \text{61–180 days} \\
\begin{array}{l}
\text{Paid} \\
\text{Bad debt} \\
\text{0–60 days} \\
\text{61–180 days}
\end{array}
\left[
\begin{array}{cccc}
1 & 0 & 0 & 0 \\
0 & 1 & 0 & 0 \\
.5 & 0 & .3 & .2 \\
.4 & .3 & .2 & .1
\end{array}
\right]
\end{array}
$$

Three features of this matrix of transition probabilities need to be discussed. First, notice the black circled element, 0. This indicates that $1 in the 0- to 60-day category cannot become a bad debt in 1 month's time. Now look at the two color-circled elements; each of these is 1, indicating that, in time, *all* the accounts receivable dollars will either be paid or become bad debts. But in our previous discussions of equilibrium conditions in Markov analysis, we never computed equilibrium probabilities when any *retention* probability was equal to 1, because we knew the process would end up with that company or category having all of the market (or in this case all the dollars). It is true that eventually *all* the dollars *do* wind up as either paid or bad debts, but Milton *would* benefit from knowing the probability that a dollar of 0- to 60-day or 61- to 180-day receivables would eventually find its way into *either* paid bills *or* bad debts. Determining these four probabilities of interest to Milton is done in four steps:

Step 1 First we partition Milton's original matrix of transition probabilities into four matrices, each identified by a letter:

$$\begin{bmatrix} 1 & 0 & 0 & 0 \\ 0 & 1 & 0 & 0 \\ .5 & 0 & .3 & .2 \\ .4 & .3 & .2 & .1 \end{bmatrix} \qquad \mathbf{I} = \begin{bmatrix} 1 & 0 \\ 0 & 1 \end{bmatrix} \qquad \mathbf{O} = \begin{bmatrix} 0 & 0 \\ 0 & 0 \end{bmatrix}$$

$$\mathbf{R} = \begin{bmatrix} .5 & 0 \\ .4 & .3 \end{bmatrix} \qquad \mathbf{Q} = \begin{bmatrix} .3 & .2 \\ .2 & .1 \end{bmatrix}$$

Step 2 We subtract matrix **Q** from an *identity matrix* of the same size, to get a new matrix we have called **N**. (An identity matrix is a square matrix whose diagonal is composed entirely of 1s and in which the remainder of the terms are 0s.) Matrices with the same dimensions (the same number of rows and columns) can be subtracted from each other by subtracting elements which appear in the same location in each matrix. In this case the subtraction is

Identity	Q	N

$$\begin{bmatrix} 1 & 0 \\ 0 & 1 \end{bmatrix} \quad \begin{bmatrix} .3 & .2 \\ .2 & .1 \end{bmatrix} \quad \begin{bmatrix} .7 & -.2 \\ -.2 & .9 \end{bmatrix}$$

Step 3. We find the *inverse* of matrix **N**. The function of an inverse and the process for obtaining it can be illustrated by multiplying the matrix $[1 \quad 2]$ by the matrix $\begin{bmatrix} 2 & 3 \\ 4 & 5 \end{bmatrix}$ to produce a new matrix. This is accomplished below using the multiplication method illustrated earlier in the chapter:

$$[1 \quad 2] \quad \begin{bmatrix} 2 & 3 \\ 4 & 5 \end{bmatrix} = [10 \quad 13]$$

Multiplying the *inverse* of the 2 × 2 matrix (steps in computing the inverse follow in just a moment) by the new matrix $[10 \quad 13]$ will return us to the original matrix $[1 \quad 2]$.

An inverse is formed by performing certain procedures on the original matrix. There are three of these procedures, each involving the rows of the matrix:

1 One *row* can be *interchanged* with another *row*.

2 A *row* can be *multiplied* by a *constant*.

3 A *multiple of a row* can be *added* to or *subtracted* from another *row*.

To invert a matrix, we first place beside it an identity matrix of the same size. Row procedures are then performed on both matrices *simultaneously.* When the original matrix has been altered by these procedures so that it becomes an identity matrix, the identity matrix which was originally placed there is the inverse. In short, then, the object is to convert the original matrix into an identity matrix by performing the row procedures upon it. Let's now illustrate the inversion of a 2×2 matrix.

Original matrix	Identity matrix	Steps performed
$\begin{bmatrix} 2 & 3 \\ 4 & 5 \end{bmatrix}$	$\begin{bmatrix} 1 & 0 \\ 0 & 1 \end{bmatrix}$	1. Place identity matrix next to original matrix.
$\begin{bmatrix} 1 & 3/2 \\ 4 & 5 \end{bmatrix}$	$\begin{bmatrix} 1/2 & 0 \\ 0 & 1 \end{bmatrix}$	2. Multiply row 1 by ½ (procedure 2).
$\begin{bmatrix} 1 & 3/2 \\ 0 & -1 \end{bmatrix}$	$\begin{bmatrix} 1/2 & 0 \\ -2 & 1 \end{bmatrix}$	3. Multiply row 1 by 4 and subtract it from row 2 (procedure 3).
$\begin{bmatrix} 1 & 3/2 \\ 0 & 1 \end{bmatrix}$	$\begin{bmatrix} 1/2 & 0 \\ 2 & -1 \end{bmatrix}$	4. Multiply row 2 by (-1) (procedure 2).
$\begin{bmatrix} 1 & 0 \\ 0 & 1 \end{bmatrix}$	$\begin{bmatrix} -5/2 & 3/2 \\ 2 & -1 \end{bmatrix}$	5. Subtract ³⁄₂ row 2 from row 1 (procedure 3).

FINDING THE INVERSE

Since the original matrix is now an identity matrix, we know our process is complete. Thus the inverse of the original matrix is

$$\begin{bmatrix} -5/2 & 3/2 \\ 2 & -1 \end{bmatrix}$$

We can check our calculations by multiplying the inverse by the matrix $[10 \quad 13]$ to see if the multiplication will produce the original matrix, $[1 \quad 2]$:

CHECKING THE INVERSE

$$[10 \quad 13] \times \begin{bmatrix} -5/2 & 3/2 \\ 2 & -1 \end{bmatrix} = [1 \quad 2]$$

Using the procedure we have just illustrated, we find the inverse of matrix

$$\mathbf{N} \begin{bmatrix} .7 & -.2 \\ -.2 & .9 \end{bmatrix} \text{ to be } \begin{bmatrix} 1.5254 & .3390 \\ .3390 & 1.1864 \end{bmatrix}.$$

Step 4 We multiply this inverse by matrix $\mathbf{R}$ from step 1. This multiplication is

STEP 4: MULTIPLY THE INVERSE OF MATRIX N BY MATRIX R

$$\begin{bmatrix} 1.5254 & .3390 \\ .3390 & 1.1864 \end{bmatrix} \begin{bmatrix} .5 & 0 \\ .4 & .3 \end{bmatrix} = \begin{bmatrix} .8983 & .1017 \\ .6441 & .3559 \end{bmatrix}$$

Let's now interpret the answer from step 4 for Milton. The top row in the answer is the probability that $1 of this accounts receivable in the 0- to 60-day category will end up in the "paid" and "bad debt" categories. Specifically, there is a .8983 probability that $1 currently in the 0- to 60-day category will be paid and a .1017 probability that it will eventually become a bad debt. Now the second row. These two entries represent the probability that $1 now in the 61- to 180-day category will end up in the "paid" and "bad debt" categories. We can see from this row that there is a .6441 probability that $1 currently in the 61- to 180-day category will be paid and a .3559 probability that it will eventually become a bad debt.

If Milton wants to forecast the future of his $6,500 of accounts receivable, he first determines how much of the total is in each category, 0- to 60-days and 61- to 180-days. In this instance his accountant tells him that $4,500 is in the 0- to 60-day category and $2,000 is in the 61- to 180-day category. Milton then sets up this matrix multiplication:

$$[\$4,500 \quad \$2,000] \begin{bmatrix} .8983 & .1017 \\ .6441 & .3559 \end{bmatrix} = [\$5,330.55 \quad \$1,169.45]$$

Milton should interpret this answer to mean that $5,330.55 of his current accounts receivable is likely to wind up being paid and $1,169.45 is likely to become bad debts. If he follows the standard practice of setting up a reserve for "doubtful" accounts, his accountant will set up approximately $1,170 as the best estimate for this category.

7 Glossary

Brand switching The movement of customers from one supplier to another.

Equilibrium A position that a Markov process reaches in the long run, after which no further net change occurs.

First-order Markov process A Markov process in which the probability of occurrence of the next event depends only upon the outcome of the last event.

Markov analysis A method of analyzing the current behavior of some variable to predict the future behavior of that variable.

Matrix An array of numbers arranged into rows and columns.

MRCA Market Research Corporation of America, an organization which supplies market share data to industry.

Second-order Markov process A Markov process in which the probability of occurrence of the next event depends upon the outcomes of the last two events.

Sink, basin, or absorbing state A state in a Markov process which is never left once it is entered.

Third-order Markov process A Markov process in which the probability of occurrence of the next event depends upon the outcomes of the last three events.

Transition probabilities Probabilities that suppliers will retain customers, gain customers, and lose customers from one period to another.

16-1 Given:

$$A = \begin{bmatrix} 3 & 2 \\ 9 & 4 \end{bmatrix} \quad \text{and} \quad B = \begin{bmatrix} 9 & -3 \\ -4 & 0 \end{bmatrix}$$

a. Compute $A - B$.
b. Compute A^2.
c. Compute $A \times B$.
d. Compute $B \times A$.

16-2 Given:

$$A = \begin{bmatrix} 9 & 3 & -7 \\ 4 & 6 & 2 \end{bmatrix} \quad \text{and} \quad B = \begin{bmatrix} 3 & 7 \\ 0 & 3 \\ -2 & -6 \end{bmatrix}$$

a. Compute $A \times B$.
b. Compute $B \times A$.

16-3 Find the inverse of the matrix:

$$\begin{bmatrix} 3 & -2 \\ 4 & -3 \end{bmatrix}$$

16-4 Ancient Times Distillery is one of the two largest bourbon distilleries in the eastern United States. Its market analysts are currently investigating the brand loyalty of Ancient Times in relation to the loyalty of their major competitor, Jack Donalds, and to all other bourbons considered as a single group. A questionnaire filled out by 1,000 bourbon drinkers indicates the following marketing patterns. In a typical month, Ancient Times retains 80 percent of its customers while losing 8 percent to Jack Donalds and 12 percent to all other bourbons. Jack Donalds retains 85 percent of its customers while losing 6 percent to Ancient Times and 9 percent to all other bourbons. All the other bourbons, taken as a group, retain 86 percent while losing 7 percent each to Ancient Times and Jack Donalds. What can Ancient Times plan on as an equilibrium share of market?

16-5 Assume that runproof pantyhose were introduced on the market simultaneously by three companies. The three firms, F, B, and C, launched their respective brands in January. At the start, each company had approximately one-third of the market. During the year, these developments took place:

Company F retained 80 percent of its customers; it lost 16 percent to B and 4 percent to C.

Company B retained 76 percent of its customers; it lost 18 percent to F and 6 percent to C.

Company C retained 84 percent of its customers; it lost 12 percent to F and 4 percent to B.

Assume that the market does not expand.
  a. What share of the total market was held by each company at the end of the year?
  b. Predict what the long-run market shares will be at the equilibrium state if buying habits do not change.

16-6 A large department store has secured a breakdown on the transition among three categories of accounts receivable by its customers, as follows:

	Jan. 1	From pay on time	From delinquent	From bad debt	Feb. 1
Pay on time	300	285	20	10	315
Delinquent	750	10	700	50	760
Bad debts	450	5	30	390	425

What percentage of credit customers will be classified in each category on April 1? Assume that no new credit customers are included.

16-7 The Peoria Fitness Center competes with two other health clubs—Exercise Unlimited and Slim-Yourself. Currently, the matrix of transition probabilities for the three clubs describing year-to-year changes in membership is as follows:

$$
\begin{array}{c@{\quad}ccc}
 & \textbf{P} & \textbf{E} & \textbf{S} \\
\textbf{P} & .80 & .10 & .10 \\
\textbf{E} & .05 & .80 & .15 \\
\textbf{S} & .08 & .12 & .80
\end{array}
$$

Peoria currently has 2,500 members while Exercise Unlimited and Slim-Yourself have 3,000 and 3,500 members, respectively. Peoria's annual fixed costs are $250,000; variable costs are $50 per member. Peoria's management is considering construction of a swimming pool facility which will cost one million dollars; they feel the venture will be worthwhile if annual profits can be increased by $100,000 per year. Based upon a survey of Peoria residents who are fitness club members, they feel the addition of a pool facility would result in the following changes in membership, assuming total membership over the three clubs does not change:

$$
\begin{array}{c@{\quad}ccc}
 & \textbf{P} & \textbf{E} & \textbf{S} \\
\textbf{P} & .90 & .03 & .07 \\
\textbf{E} & .15 & .75 & .10 \\
\textbf{S} & .20 & .10 & .70
\end{array}
$$

Determine next year's projected membership with both the current trends as well as expected trends using the pool facility. How much added profit can be realized over the next year if the pool is built? Annual membership fees at Peoria Fitness are $300 per year per member.

16-8 An organization dependent upon volunteer help is divided into three divisions and allows free movement of personnel between any two. Between June and September, personnel movement was as indicated in this table.

		Gains			
Div.	June	From 1	From 2	From 3	Sept.
1	30	27	3	4	34
2	60	2	57	4	63
3	40	1	0	32	33

What percentage of the volunteers will be working for each division in December?

16-9 Assume that radial tires were introduced on the market by three companies at the same time. When the tires were introduced, each firm had an equal share of the market, but during the first year, the following changes in market share took place:

Company A retained 80 percent of its customers; it lost 5 percent to B and 15 percent to C.

Company B retained 90 percent of its customers; it lost 10 percent to A and none to C.

Company C retained 60 percent of its customers; it lost 20 percent to A and 20 percent to B.

Assume that the market will not expand and that buying habits will not change.
   a. What total share of the market is likely to be held by each company at the end of the second year?
   b. Predict what the equilibrium market shares will be.

16-10 Three radio stations (call them A, B, and C) compete for advertising shares of market. At the end of last year, A had 20 percent of the market. Its competitors, stations B and C, each had 40 percent of the market. During last year, total sales for the three stations were $100 million, and station A had a net income of 5 percent on its sales. Both these figures are expected to remain the same for next year. Station A's manager suggests that if during next year A would spend an additional $100,000 on selling, A would retain 85 percent of its customers while gaining 8 percent of B's customers and 7 percent of C's. Company B is expected to retain 85 percent of its customers while gaining 10 percent from A and 3 percent from C. Company C is expected to retain 90 percent of its customers while gaining 5 percent from A and 7 percent from B. Should company A make the additional expenditure for selling?

16-11 Faith Burton has reviewed the historical trends of accounts receivable at the Savannah Medical Supply Company. She has developed the following month to month transition of these accounts:

Beginning of the month	End of the month			
	Paid	Current	Late	Bad Debt
Paid	1.0	0	0	0
Current	.7	.2	.1	0
Late	.4	.3	.1	.2
Bad Debt	0	0	0	1.0

The company at the present time has $68,000 of current receivables and $26,000 of late receivables. How much of the total debt can Faith forecast to be paid off, and how much should she forecast to be written off as bad debt?

16-12 The Over-the-Road Trucking Company periodically inspects the bearings on its trucks and categorizes them in one of four states: (1) new bearings, (2) lightly worn bearings, (3) moderately worn bearings, and (4) worn-out bearings. If the company replaces a set of bearings during inspection, it costs $50. If, however, a truck in service develops bad bearings, the company estimates the cost to be $250. On the basis of past experience, it has been found that a set of bearings which is new at a given inspection has a .9 probability of being in state 2 and a .1 probability of being in state 3 by the next inspection. A set of bearings classified as state 2 has a .6 probability of remaining in state 2, a .3 probability of going to state 3, and a .1 probability of wearing out by the next inspection date. A set of bearings classified as state 3 has a .7 probability of remaining in state 3 and a .3 probability of wearing out by the next inspection. The company has decided to either (1) replace all bearings in state 2 or worse at each inspection or (2) replace all bearings in state 3 or worse at each inspection. Which policy will result in lower cost?

16-13 In the town of Ramsville, a life insurance salesperson has computed the following statistics:

There are 100 births and deaths each year.

A newborn child has a .95 probability of reaching age 20.

A 20-year-old has a .85 probability of reaching age 40.

A 40-year-old has a .75 probability of reaching age 60.

A 60-year-old has a .40 probability of reaching age 80.

An 80-year-old has a .04 probability of reaching age 100.

No one lives to age 120.

After a long period of time, what will be the population of Ramsville, and what percentage of the population will be in each of the age brackets?

16-14 A university study of population mobility in the midwest has revealed the following yearly trends among urban, suburban, and rural families. Of those families in urban locations at the beginning of the year, 60 percent will remain there, 30 percent will move to suburban locations during the year, and 10 percent will move to rural locations. Of those families in suburban locations, 70 percent will remain there, 15 percent will move to urban locations, and 15 percent will move to rural locations. Of rural families, 70 percent will remain there, 20 percent will move to urban locations, and 10 percent will move to suburban locations. If the population distribution is currently 50 percent urban, 40 percent suburban, and 10 percent rural, what will the distribution look like in 2 years?

16-15 The Sunshine Tennis Camp provides free tennis instruction to young, aspiring athletes with the stipulation that the athletes pay the camp 10 percent of their winnings if they later turn professional. The camp rates the players as novice, intermediate, advanced, or professional. Currently, there are 60 athletes affiliated with the camp, and for each athlete who either drops out of camp or retires from professional status, one new novice athlete is admitted. Based on past experience, the matrix of transition probabilities reflecting state changes over a year's period is as follows (where state R indicates a dropout or retirement from professional status):

	N	I	A	P	R
N	.3	.2	0	0	.5
I	0	.4	.3	0	.3
A	0	.1	.8	.1	0
P	0	0	.3	.3	.4
R	1	0	0	0	0

If an average professional player wins $200,000 per year, determine the annual forecasted revenue for the tennis camp at equilibrium. Since all players who go to state R result in a new novice player being admitted to the camp, you can combine states R and N into a single state, N, when performing your calculations.

16-16 The Tarheel Telephone Company, a small private system which serves a university community, is well known for the unreliable nature of its equipment on rainy days. This Father's Day began with a downpour in the area served by TTC. A graduate student in business who was working part-time for TTC quickly formulated this matrix showing the likelihood of the trunk lines being "open," "busy," or "down" from one minute to the next. Because of the loss of customer goodwill if the phones are out of order on a day like Father's Day, when many calls are made, the manager of TTC wants to know what the equilibrium state of the system will be.

	Open	Busy	Down
Open	.5	.3	.2
Busy	.2	.6	.2
Down	.3	.2	.5

Can you provide her with this information?

16-17 In January, Major Motors, the nation's largest auto manufacturer, was warned by the FTC that if its share of the automobile market went above 65 percent, antitrust action would be initiated against the company. At that time Major Motors had 50 percent of the market. Its chief competitors, Ferd Motors and Kisler, had 25 percent and 10 percent, respectively, with the rest being divided among other manufacturers, primarily foreign. Market analysts at Major Motors were able to devise this transition matrix of market shares for yearly changes:

	MM	Ferd	Kisler	Others
MM	.6	.1	.05	.25
Ferd	.1	.7	.0	.2
Kisler	.15	.1	.6	.15
Others	.2	.1	.1	.6

Will Major Motors face antitrust action? If so, when?

16-18 In the years prior to 1986, the Devlon Company experienced an erosion in their share of the market for tennis balls in California. Devlon's major competitors in this market are Williams Sportsgear and Bounceright, Inc. The year-to-year matrix of transition probabilities describing their market erosion at that time was as follows:

$$
\begin{array}{c c c c}
 & \mathbf{D} & \mathbf{W} & \mathbf{B} \\
\mathbf{D} & \begin{bmatrix} .70 & .15 & .15 \\ .03 & .85 & .12 \\ .04 & .06 & .90 \end{bmatrix}
\end{array}
$$

In an effort to correct the situation, Devlon launched an aggressive advertising campaign which was primarily focused toward increasing sales in the middle-age, middle-income groups. During 1987, Devlon noticed the following trend in tennis ball sales in the California market.

$$
\begin{array}{c c c c}
 & \mathbf{D} & \mathbf{W} & \mathbf{B} \\
\mathbf{D} & \begin{bmatrix} .75 & .10 & .15 \\ .05 & .80 & .15 \\ .05 & .07 & .88 \end{bmatrix}
\end{array}
$$

Based upon these facts, what conclusions can you reach concerning the effectiveness of Devlon's advertising strategy?

16-19 Semiconductor Research Corporation has divided its accounts receivable into four classes based on the size of the average purchase made by the account and the length of time the account has been a customer. SRC labels the accounts as new accounts, regular accounts, preferred accounts, and priority accounts, ranging from smallest and newest to largest and oldest. Over time, accounts are moved through the four classes. Currently there are 190 new accounts, 130 regular accounts, 120 preferred accounts, and 75 priority accounts. Historical evidence shows that each year 20 percent of the new accounts become inactive for one reason or another. Similarly, 15 percent of the regular accounts, 10 percent of the preferred accounts, and 30 percent of the priority accounts also become inactive. SRC has a goal of moving 15 percent of each class of account into the next-highest class by the end of the year. Assuming that for each account that becomes inactive, SRC finds a new account to replace it, how many of each class of account will SRC have at the end of the year if it reaches its goal?

16-20 Pedal Power, Inc., sells bicycles in competition with two other shops in a university community. Reports from the local chamber of commerce indicate that Pedal Power has about 25 percent of the local market, while its two competitors, The Bicycle Shop, and Wheels, Unlimited, have about 40 percent and 35 percent, respectively. Pedal Power had a profit last year of 6 percent of its sales in a total market of approximately $1 million sales. An M.B.A. class in marketing at the local university offered Pedal Power its advice as a part of a project. The class feels that $1,500 invested in more well-directed advertising by Pedal Power would create this matrix of transition probabilities:

	Pedal Power	Bicycle Shop	Wheels
Pedal Power	.80	.15	.05
Bicycle Shop	.15	.80	.05
Wheels	.05	.05	.90

If Pedal Power wants to get a 20 percent return on the $1,500 within a year, should it take the students' advice?

16-21 Ridgefield Hospital specializes in heart patients and serves an area in which there is zero population growth (a Markov process with deaths can have a change-of-state system where for each death there is also a birth). From past history, it is known that each month about .001 of the population of 100,000 served by the hospital have heart attacks and are admitted to the hospital. By the end of the first month after being admitted, a patient has a 60 percent probability of being released from the hospital, a 20 percent probability of staying in the hospital another month, and a 20 percent probability of dying during the month. For those who stay the second month, there is a 90 percent probability of their being released by the end of the second month and a 10 percent probability of their dying during the second month. Solve for the equilibrium values, showing the number of patients in the hospital who have had heart attacks within 1 month, the number of patients in their second month of recovery, and the number of patients who die each month from heart attacks.

16-22 Hank's Electronics employs 20 inspectors in their stereo assembly operations. The inspectors are classified as apprentice, journeyman, and master inspectors and are paid $48, $56, and $74 per day, respectively. All the inspectors work at an intermediate point in the assembly line where they remove defective units before these units proceed down the line. Any defective units which pass the inspection point undetected later undergo costly operations, and this costs the company $100 per defective unit. Mary Hanks, the Operations Manager, is concerned about the high turnover rate among the inspectors, because for each inspector who leaves the company, one new apprentice inspector is hired, and inexperienced inspectors are less competent in detecting defective units. An apprentice inspector can detect 3 defective units per day, while journeymen inspectors average 5 defects per day, and master inspectors can remove 8 defective units from the line per day. Mary has observed the following matrix of year-to-year transition probabilities describing both the advancement of inspectors to a more experienced status as well as resignation of the employees (that is, change of state from one of the three classes back to the apprentice state).

$$
\begin{array}{c} & \begin{array}{ccc} \mathbf{A} & \mathbf{J} & \mathbf{M} \end{array} \\ \begin{array}{c} \mathbf{A} \\ \mathbf{J} \\ \mathbf{M} \end{array} & \left[\begin{array}{ccc} .70 & .30 & 0 \\ .40 & .40 & .20 \\ .30 & 0 & .70 \end{array} \right] \end{array}
$$

Mary feels she can make a strong case for raising the pay scale for her inspectors if she can convince her Uncle Will, owner of the company, that this would result in an overall cost savings to the company. She has studied the pay scales and employee retention history of companies similar to hers, and has estimated that if the employees were paid $60, $78, and $98 per day for the three classes, the year-to-year transition probabilities would be as follows:

$$
\begin{array}{c} & \begin{array}{ccc} \mathbf{A} & \mathbf{J} & \mathbf{M} \end{array} \\ \begin{array}{c} \mathbf{A} \\ \mathbf{J} \\ \mathbf{M} \end{array} & \left[\begin{array}{ccc} .60 & .40 & 0 \\ .20 & .50 & .30 \\ .20 & 0 & .80 \end{array} \right] \end{array}
$$

Does Mary have a good argument for raising the pay scales?

16-23 The Better-Made Company employs four classes of machine operators (A, B, C, and D); all new employees are hired as class D and, through a system of promotion, may work up to a higher class. Currently there are 200 class D, 150 class C, 100 class B, and 50 class A employees. The company has signed an agreement with the union specifying that 20 percent of all employees in each class are to be promoted one class in each year. Statistics show that each year 25 percent of the class D employees are separated from the company by retirement, resignation, death, and so forth. Similarly, 15 percent of class C, 10 percent of class B, and 5 percent of class A employees are also separated. After the union agreement has been in effect for 1 year, how many of each class of employees should the company expect to have in its employ? (Assume that for each employee lost, the company will hire a new class D employee.)

16-24 Centerville Hospital has a policy of keeping 200 pints of blood in inventory. If not used within four time periods, the blood is thrown away. In the past, there has been no set policy on the use of blood, and each pint was taken randomly from the inventory when needed. The hospital found that there was a .30 probability of any pint of blood being used in a given period and a .70 probability of its remaining in inventory into the next period. Lately, the hospital has become concerned about the shortage of blood donors. It is considering the adoption of a policy which requires that all blood drawn from inventory be the oldest (FIFO). If the hospital adopts the new policy, how many fewer donations per period will be required to maintain the 200-pint inventory level if every donor gives 1 pint?

 16-25 Northeast Electrical is a company specializing in appliances. Many of Northeast's sales are on the installment basis; as a result, much of the firm's working capital is tied up in accounts receivable. Although most of the firm's customers make their payments on time, a certain percentage of the accounts are always overdue, and some few customers never pay, thereby becoming bad debts. Northeast Electrical's experience is that when a customer is two or more payments behind, the account will generally turn into a bad debt. In these cases, Northeast discontinues credit to the customer and writes the account off as a bad debt. At the beginning of each month, the accounts receivable manager reviews each account and classifies it as paid, current (being paid on time), overdue (one payment behind), or bad debt. The accounts receivable manager has provided this transition matrix from the last month's data and this month's data:

| | | State of a dollar this month | | | |
		Paid	Current	Overdue	Bad debt
State of a dollar last month	Paid	1.0	0	0	0
	Current	.4	.3	.3	0
	Overdue	.5	.2	.2	.1
	Bad debt	0	0	0	1.0

If Northeast now has $20,000 in the current category and $14,000 in the overdue classification, how much will eventually be paid and how much should it plan to write off as bad debts?

16-26 Upstate Hospital uses Markov analysis to determine weekly staffing requirements for nurses. Its matrix of transition probabilities reflecting week-to-week changes in patient status is quite stable as follows (where C is critical, P is poor, F is fair, G is good, and S is source population):

Retention and loss →

$$
\begin{array}{c c c c c c}
 & \mathbf{C} & \mathbf{P} & \mathbf{F} & \mathbf{G} & \mathbf{S} \\
\mathbf{C} & .05 & .60 & .15 & 0 & .20 \\
\mathbf{P} & .20 & .20 & .30 & .30 & 0 \\
\mathbf{F} & 0 & .10 & .10 & .80 & 0 \\
\mathbf{G} & 0 & 0 & .10 & 0 & .90 \\
\mathbf{S} & .001 & .001 & .003 & 0 & .995
\end{array}
$$

Retention and gain ↓

A patient in good condition at the beginning of a given week who remains in good condition at the end of the week is released. Upstate serves a zero-growth population, and so for each death there is one birth. The flow represented by the above transition matrix is shown by the figure on page 783.

At the beginning of the first week in June, the state of the population of the community and hospital is as follows:

S	99,500	
C	30	
P	70	
F	100	
G	300	
Total	100,000	people served by the hospital

Determine the projected number of people in the hospital in the following week as well as their health condition, so that the hospital administrators may plan for adequate nurse staffing schedules.

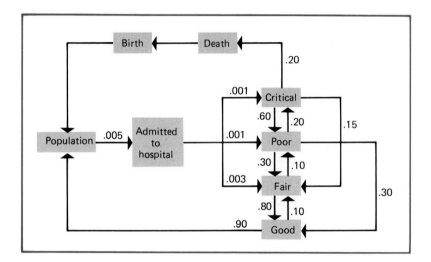

16-27 The Move-Yourself Truck Rental Company operates over a network of four cities: Allenville, Bakertown, Charlesburg, and Delta City. Most of its rentals are for one-way hauls, and so periodically the number of rental units in one or more of the cities drops to a level where the trucks must be redistributed. It is company policy to keep at least 135 vehicles on hand at the beginning of each month in each of the cities. During June the following movements were recorded:

	To			
From	**A**	**B**	**C**	**D**
A	5	40	80	60
B	30	10	50	40
C	60	60	6	10
D	50	50	20	2

At the beginning of July the number of vehicles on hand at each of the cities is as follows:

Allenville	150
Bakertown	160
Charlesburg	160
Delta City	150
Total	620 vehicles on hand

Determine if the inventory of vehicles at each city is above the minimum level on August 1 and September 1.

16-28 The Northeast Central Railroad brings in each of its locomotives twice each year for a diesel engine inspection. During this inspection, the piston rings are checked and classified for wear according to the four state conditions:

State 1: New rings

State 2: Lightly worn rings

State 3: Moderately worn rings

State 4: Worn-out rings

If the railroad changes a piston ring during the inspection, it incurs a cost of $100 per ring. If a locomotive is brought in for ring replacement during some other time, however, this tends to affect the schedule of the freight-handling operations and costs the company $800 per ring replaced. The company has studied the problem of piston ring wear and has established that during a 6-month period a new ring has a .8 probability of moving to state 2 and a .2 probability of moving to state 3. A piston ring classified in state 2 in a given inspection has a .5 probability of remaining in state 2, a .4 probability of being in state 3, and a .1 probability of wearing out by the next inspection. Rings classified in state 3 have a .8 probability of remaining in state 3 and a .2 probability of becoming worn out before the next inspection. Would it be more cost-effective for the company to systematically replace all rings classified as state 3 or worse during an inspection, or to replace all rings classified as state 2 or worse?

16-29 A European automobile company has been experimenting with a job-enrichment program in which small groups of workers are allowed to work independently as a team. At the end of each month, the workers in these groups are asked which of four job functions, which we classify as A, B, C, and D, they wish to perform in the coming month. The company has determined the following matrix of transition probabilities reflecting job preferences:

Retention and loss →

	A	B	C	D	
A	.50	.20	.20	.10	
B	.20	.40	.20	.20	Retention
C	.10	.20	.60	.10	and gain
D	.10	.20	.20	.50	↓

In other words, a worker performing job A last month has a .50 probability of asking for job A in the coming month and has .20, .20, and .10 probabilities of asking for jobs B, C, and D, respectively. The company is interested to find out in the long run what percentage of the workers would be in each of the four jobs if they worked on any job they wished each month.

16-30 Lt. Jenkins of the Memphis Police Department is concerned about planning the retirement fund for the 30 new police officers who recently joined the police force. He has defined the states of the officers as follows:

R = retirement for 20 years service or for disability
Q = quit the police force
F = first 10 years of service
S = second 10 years of service

Past experience has shown the following transition matrix for Memphis police officers:

	R	Q	F	S
R	1	0	0	0
Q	0	1	0	0
F	.2	.4	0	.4
S	.9	.1	0	0

Determine the expected number of new officers from this group of 30 who will eventually retire.

9 Chapter concepts quiz

16-1 _____ is a form of forecasting which attempts to predict the future behavior of some variable by observing its current behavior.

16-2 A set of _____ arranged in matrix form displays the probabilities of going from any one state to any other state in one period (where a state is a variable of interest).

16-3 A(n) _____ is a tabular representation of numbers in which each element of the table is uniquely identified by two numbers: a(n) _____ number and a(n) _____ number.

16-4 When a Markov process has reached the point where there are no net changes in the variables representing the states of the system, we say we have reached a state of _____ ; when the transition probabilities are assumed to remain constant for all time, we can find the values of these states by solving a set of equations known as the _____.

16-5 The movement of customers from one supplier to another is known as _____.

16-6 In a matrix of transition probabilities, the probability values across the rows represent _____ while the probability values down the columns represent _____.

16-7 A(n) _____ matrix has the same number of rows as it has number of columns.

16-8 A(n) _____ matrix is a square matrix whose diagonal is composed of 1s while all remaining elements are 0s.

16-9 A particular state which is never left once it is entered is called a(n) _____ state.

16-10 A(n) _____ Markov process is one in which the outcome in the next period depends only on the outcome in the current period, and not on any results from past periods.

True-False	16-11 In the brand-switching example, knowledge of the net gains and losses of customers for each dairy was not enough to make intelligent decisions. It was also necessary to know the transition probabilities in order to know what proportion of customers was gained and lost between any two dairies.	**T F**

16-12 A crucial assumption used in Markov analysis is that the transition probabilities remain the same over time. **T F**

16-13 The equilibrium condition of a Markov process depends upon the transition probabilities remaining fixed over time and upon the initial state of the system. **T F**

16-14 The number of periods required to reach an equilibrium condition is the same regardless of the initial state of the system. **T F**

16-15 If an $i \times j$ matrix is multiplied by a $k \times j$ matrix, the resulting matrix has size $i \times k$. **T F**

16-16 In the brand-switching example, a column in the matrix of transition probabilities corresponds to the probabilities that customers will switch from the other dairies to the dairy corresponding to that column. **T F**

16-17 Under the assumptions of a first-order Markov process, we can determine the state of the system (for example, the market share of each dairy in the brand-switching example) n periods after the first period by multiplying the matrix corresponding to the initial period by the nth power of the matrix of transition probabilities. **T F**

16-18 If two matrices can be multiplied, then the resulting matrix will have the same number of rows as the second matrix and the same number of columns as the first matrix. **T F**

16-19 A matrix, taken as a whole, has no single numerical value. **T F**

16-20 Even if there are absorbing states in our problem, Markov analysis can be of use by determining the probabilities of ending up in any of the absorbing states, having started in any of the nonabsorbing states. **T F**

16-21 Any matrix regardless of its size may be multiplied by itself. **T F**

16-22 A matrix may be added or subtracted from another matrix provided they both have the same number of rows and columns. **T F**

16-23 Another name for an absorbing state is a sink. **T F**

16-24 Any two square matrices may be multiplied provided they are both the same size. **T F**

16-25 The steps used to get the inverse of a matrix are identical to the steps used to make a pivot in the simplex procedure. **T F**

Multiple Choice

16-26 A state which is a sink can be identified from the matrix of transition probabilities. If a state is a sink, then:
   a. The sum of the probabilities in the row corresponding to that state is 1.
   b. The probability of a transition from that state back to that state is 1.
   c. The probability of a transition from that state back to that state is 0.
   d. The transition probabilities for that state remain constant over time.

16-27 Which of the following are questions which can be answered by the use of Markov analysis?
    a. What will be the state of the system at some future time?
    b. Will the system attain an equilibrium condition?
    c. What will be the transition probabilities at some future time?
    d. All of the above.

16-28 Markov analysis can be used to evaluate different marketing strategies by:
    a. Comparing the initial conditions for each strategy.
    b. Comparing the equilibrium conditions which result from the different transition probability matrices associated with different strategies.
    c. Determining how quickly each strategy will lead to a predetermined equilibrium condition.
    d. All of the above.

16-29 Which of the following is an assumption of the Markov analysis of the brand-switching example?
    a. The probabilities of retaining customers and gaining and losing customers remain fairly stable over time.
    b. No new customers enter the problem, and no customers leave the problem.
    c. Careful records of the changes in brand loyalty are kept.
    d. All of the above.

16-30 Which of the following is an example of a row operation?
    a. One row can be multiplied by another row.
    b. A row can be multiplied by a constant.
    c. A row can be rewritten in reverse order.
    d. None of the above.

16-31 In a matrix of transition probabilities, the probability values should add up to 1 in each:
    a. Row
    b. Column
    c. Diagonal
    d. All of the above

16-32 In a matrix of transition probabilities the element in row i, column j, where $i = j$, is a:
    a. Gain
    b. Loss
    c. Retention
    d. None of the above

16-33 A, B, and C are three matrices, with $A \times B = C$. If C has 5 rows and 8 columns, then:
    a. A has 8 rows.
    b. B has 5 columns.
    c. A has 5 columns and B has 8 rows.
    d. None of the above.

16-34 In finding the equilibrium market shares from a matrix of transition probabilities having n rows and n columns, the number of equilibrium equations would be:
    a. n
    b. $n - 1$
    c. $n + 1$
    d. n times m

16-35 If matrix A contains the initial values for some set of state variables, matrix B

is the matrix of transition probabilities, and A × B = C, where C is identical to A, then we know:
   a. At least one state is an absorbing state.
   b. The system is at equilibrium.
   c. The system is not yet at equilibrium.
   d. The system can never reach equilibrium.

16-36 In order to solve for equilibrium in a Markov process, we assume the values for each state variable in the equilibrium period are equal to those:
   a. In the period prior to the equilibrum period.
   b. In all periods leading to the equilibrium period.
   c. In the matrix of transition probabilities.
   d. In the initial state.

16-37 In an accounts-receivable application of Markov analysis:
   a. There are two absorbing states.
   b. There is one absorbing state.
   c. There are no absorbing states.
   d. The matrix of transitional probabilities is partitioned into two smaller matrices.

16-38 Given the following matrix of transition probabilities for three competing companies in a restricted market:

	A	B	C
A	.80	.18	.02
B	.05	.90	.05
C	.10	.05	.95

Assume that Company A wishes to improve its market share, which of the following strategies should prove most effective?
   a. Try to reduce its losses to Company B.
   b. Try to reduce its losses to Company C.
   c. Try to reduce B's losses to Company C.
   d. Try to reduce C's losses to Company B.

16-39 Matrices A and B are multiplied to obtain matrix C as A × B = C. If A is a 3 × 4 matrix and B is a 4 × 9 matrix, then C is:
   a. A 9 × 3 matrix.
   b. A 9 × 4 matrix.
   c. A 3 × 9 matrix.
   d. None of the above.

16-40 Matrices A and B are multiplied to obtain C as A × B = C. If C is an 8 × 12 matrix, you can conclude:
   a. A has 12 columns.
   b. A has 8 columns.
   c. B has 12 rows.
   d. None of the above.

10 Real world MS/OR successes

EXAMPLE: MAINTAINING ROADS IN ARIZONA

A pavement maintenance system based on Markov analysis was developed by Kamal Golabi, Ram Kulkarni, and George B. Way[2] for the state of Arizona.

[2] Kamal Golabi, Ram B. Kulkarni, and George B. Way, "A Statewide Pavement Management System," *Interfaces*, vol. 12, no. 6, pp. 5–21, 1982.

The system decides how far a road should be allowed to deteriorate before it is repaired and which of many possible repair and maintenance alternatives should be used. The bottom line: a conservative estimate of first-year savings of $14 million, almost ⅓ of Arizona's preservation budget, with further savings of $101 million projected over the next four years. At the time this article appeared, the authors were developing similar systems for other states, so total savings for this use of Markov analysis should be spectacular.

Two problems prompted the Arizona Department of Transportation to contract for the development of a decision model for pavement management. First, maintenance decisions were subjective and made by seven different district engineers. The result was that road conditions varied widely throughout the state. Second, budget cuts were predicted and a model was needed to evaluate alternative preservation policies. The authors formulated a decision model that gives the least-cost maintenance policy, while achieving minimum standards for road conditions. The model has two parts: a Markov analysis to predict the effects of maintenance actions, and a linear program to minimize costs.

In the Markov analysis, transition probabilities link a set of current road states (conditions) and maintenance actions to future road states. A transition probability $P_{ij}^{(a)}$ specifies the likelihood that one mile of road will move from state i to state j in one year, if repair action (a) is taken. To obtain transition probabilities, records of past road states and maintenance actions taken were analyzed. The statewide network was divided into nine road categories based on average traffic density and climatic conditions. Within each category, 120 condition states were defined. Next, a master list of 17 alternate maintenance actions was prepared. At this point, a huge transition matrix was available. The authors cut the problem down to size by determining that an average of only six maintenance actions were feasible for each state. They also found that a pavement in a given state could go to only three or four new states. In the final transition matrix, the number of nonzero $P_{ij}^{(a)}$ values is about 2,600 for each road category or slightly more than 1 per cent.

Maintenance actions for each road state are determined by two related linear-programming models. A long-term model determines the steady-state optimal policy. A short-term model is used to deal with budgets that do not allow an optimal long-term policy. In both models, the objective function minimizes the total cost of repair actions subject to constraints on the proportion of roads that the Markov model predicts will be in desirable states. The models demonstrate that past policies allowed roads to deteriorate much too far before taking action. New policies save money in the long run by emphasizing preventive maintenance. Another important benefit is that the system gives the Arizona Department of Transportation a solid basis for defending its budgets and dealing with legislative oversight committees.

17

MS/OR: PAST, PRESENT, AND FUTURE

CHAPTER OBJECTIVES

■ A GREAT DEAL OF CHANGE HAS OCCURRED IN MANAGEMENT SCIENCE DURING THE LAST QUARTER CENTURY. FROM THE HUMBLE BEGINNINGS DESCRIBED IN CHAPTER 1, MS/OR HAS ENJOYED SIGNIFICANT GROWTH, ESPECIALLY DURING THE LAST 25 YEARS. THE LITERATURE, APPLICATIONS, NUMBER OF PRACTITIONERS, SUCCESSES, *AND* FAILURES HAVE ALL INCREASED SIGNIFICANTLY. IN THIS FINAL CHAPTER, WE SHALL BRIEFLY CONSIDER WHERE WE HAVE BEEN, WHAT THINGS LOOK LIKE TODAY, AND WHERE WE SEEM TO BE GOING.

1 Phases of growth

THE 1940s AND 1950s

It is possible to find some roots of MS/OR in the early part of this century; however, in the form in which we study and use it today, the discipline probably emerged formally during World War II. The needs of the war resulted in the first operational research group in Great Britain, followed by other well-documented military uses. John Magee,[1] referring to this early phase, noted that the problem solvers were interested in practical operational problems. He characterized these problems as well-defined and capable of being handled by the smaller, less sophisticated computers available then. People who worked in the field tended to come from other disciplines: chemistry, statistics, mathematics, and physics.

By the mid-1950s MS/OR was in the process of developing into a separate professional field, and the theoretical foundations of the discipline developed rapidly. The academic community and private research organizations channeled significant resources into the development of new techniques. It was in this phase that researchers and practitioners first realized that continued effectiveness in applications would depend on their ability to perform extensive computations effectively; the linear programming applications of this period demonstrate the emerging relationship between MS/OR and the computer.

THE 1960s

This period saw the emergence of Ph.D.s trained in MS/OR, as well as more applications, more publications, and more problems, too. Magee called this the *academic phase* and noted that in the early 1960s, the number of universities offering programs in operations research grew over 500 percent. Magee pointed out that in this phase, people with some operations research experience began to be found at the higher corporate levels in private enterprise. The increasing speed and availability of computers were of great help during this time. Magee noted that research during the 1960s tended to be academic; that is, it was more concerned with developing theory than with finding workable applications. From the practitioner's point of view, however, it was during this time that the limitations of operations research and the organizational problems of introducing new ideas became evident.[2] It was during this phase that significant advances were made in optimization related to production, distribution, and marketing. The 1960s also saw the computer focus begin to change from data processing to management information systems.

THE 1970s

Magee described this phase as the *maturing phase*, a time when balance between theory and practice was obtained. He suggested that even though evidence

---

[1] J. F. Magee, "Progress in the Management Sciences," *TIMS Interfaces*, vol. 3, February 1973.
[2] Ibid.

of such concerns was noted years ago, the real thrust toward *practice* and *applications* did not come until the 1970s. Magee said he felt that in the maturing phase there had been

1 More realistic understanding by both managers and management scientists of what the management sciences can and cannot accomplish.

2 More attention paid to getting the facts . . . compared with development of abstract techniques.

3 Less attention to finding optimal answers, more to developing processes and evolving successively better answers adapted to evolving circumstances.

4 Better integration of behavioral, functional, and quantitative analysis . . . .[3]

It can be said of this period that the applications and publications in MS/OR tended to be extensions of work done rather than pioneering applications or discoveries. In many instances, the formal MS/OR groups of the 1960s were decentralized into functional staff groups with less focus on broad strategic problems and more focus on operating savings.

2 Extent of use of quantitative methods in organizations, 1970s and 1980s

Surveys are always being conducted to determine what kinds of quantitative techniques are being used and who is using them. Let's take a minute to review some of the work in this area.

WHAT IS BEING USED
AND WHO IS USING IT

THE TURBAN STUDY (OPERATIONS RESEARCH AT THE CORPORATE LEVEL)

One of the earliest broad surveys of the use of quantitative methods was that of Efraim Turban.[4] Questionnaires were sent to 475 of *Fortune*'s list of the top 500 companies. His survey presented statistics on

1 Name of OR department and to whom it reports

SCOPE OF
TURBAN STUDY

2 Degree of acceptance of the OR department by other organizational segments

3 Self-appraisal of the OR department

4 OR department makeup (that is, size, educational level, age, turnover, salary, etc.)

5 Costs and benefits of OR activities

6 Breakdown of activities by project—past, present, and future

7 Use of OR tools and techniques

8 Implementation of the OR projects

In Table 17-1 we show some of the results of Turban's study.

[3] Ibid.
[4] Efraim Turban, "A Sample Survey of Operations-Research Activities at the Corporate Level," *Operations Research*, vol. 20, no. 3, May–June 1972.

Techniques	Number of projects	Percentage
Statistical analysis (probability theory, regression, exponential smoothing, sampling, hypothesis testing)	63	29
Simulation	54	25
Linear programming	41	19
Inventory theory	13	6
PERT/CPM	13	6
Dynamic programming	9	4
Nonlinear programming	7	3
Queuing theory	2	1
Heuristic programming	2	1
Other	13	6

TABLE 17-1
Use of quantitative methods in current activities (study by Turban)

CONCLUSIONS OF TURBAN STUDY

Turban concluded from his study that operations research activities had made an impressive gain at the corporate level in the United States. Fewer than 5 percent of U.S. corporations had a special OR unit at their headquarters at the end of the 1950s, and he forecast that about two-thirds of the U.S. corporations would have a unit by the mid-1970s. OR projects that were under way were quite diversified; there was a trend to move from simple projects on lower organizational levels to more sophisticated projects involving higher levels of the organization as well as environmental factors. The techniques most often used were statistical analysis, simulation, and linear programming. Projects lasted about 10 months on the average and involved about 2.5 researchers.

THE LEDBETTER AND COX STUDY

INVENTORY THEORY FOUND TO BE PRIMARY AREA OF APPLICATION

A half dozen years after the pioneering Turban study, Ledbetter and Cox undertook a survey of the use of quantitative methods in companies.[5] Their findings supported the earlier rankings found in the Turban study. In Table 17-2 we illustrate the rankings found by Ledbetter and Cox. The Ledbetter and Cox survey also indicated that inventory theory (while not ranked in Table 17-2) was a primary area of application of quantitative techniques along with such other well-known areas as production scheduling, project planning, and plant location.

GENERAL CONCLUSIONS OF STUDIES

Although there are differences among these studies (and among all the usage studies that have been done over the last 20 years), what emerges is a clear pattern of fairly consequential use of techniques such as linear programming, simulation, PERT/CPM, inventory theory, and statistical analysis, with significantly lower use of the remaining techniques. The Ledbetter and Cox study seems to confirm stability of this pattern with the possible exception of queuing theory.

[5] W. Ledbetter and J. F. Cox, "Are O.R. Techniques Being Used?" *Journal of Industrial Engineering*, vol. 9, pp. 19–21, February 1977.

TABLE 17-2
Ranking in order of use of quantitative techniques (Ledbetter and Cox study)

Regression analysis
Linear programming
Simulation
PERT/CPM
Queuing theory
Dynamic programming
Game theory

THE FORGIONNE STUDY IN LARGE
AMERICAN-OPERATED CORPORATIONS

Five years after the Ledbetter and Cox study, Guisseppi A. Forgionne of the
California State Polytechnic University conducted a comprehensive study
dealing with corporate use of MS/OR techniques. He collected information
on (1) user characteristics, (2) techniques being utilized and the extent of
utilization, (3) areas and degree of application, and (4) perceived effectiveness,
benefits, and implementation problems. Table 17-3 illustrates user characteristics, Table 17-4 covers the frequency of use Forgionne found, and Table
17-5 shows areas and frequency of application. Over two-thirds of the firms
responding (125) gave "good" or "excellent" effectiveness ratings to MS/OR
research, with over 16 percent in the "excellent" category. No respondents
said that MS/OR methodologies were poor, and slightly more than 30 percent
said the performance was fair. Over 82 percent said the major benefit was
the generation of useful data; about 74 percent said MS/OR helped them
define the problem; over 61 percent said it helped identify relevant policies;
and almost 52 percent said MS/OR provided a useful test laboratory. Most

TABLE 17-3
Respondent
characteristics

Characteristic	Percentage of respondents
Type of organization:	
Industrial	40.3
Service sector	59.7
Name of project team:	
Operational sciences	40.3
Corporate planning	33.9
Operations planning	11.3
No such group	14.5
Size of analysis group:	
Less than 5	35.5
5 to 15	37.1
Over 15	27.4
Immediate supervisor:	
Presidential planning	46.8
Accounting and finance	38.7
Research director	14.5

Methodology	Frequency of use (% of respondents)		
	Never	**Moderate**	**Frequent**
Statistical analysis	1.6	38.7	59.7
Computer simulation	12.9	53.2	33.9
PERT/CPM	25.8	53.2	21.0
Linear programming	25.8	59.7	14.5
Queuing theory	40.3	50.0	9.7
Nonlinear programming	53.2	38.7	8.1
Dynamic programming	61.3	33.9	4.8
Game theory	69.4	27.4	3.2

TABLE 17-4
The utilization of MS/OR methodologies

Area	Frequency of application (% of respondents)		
	Never	**Moderate**	**Frequent**
Project planning	33.9	45.2	21
Capital budgeting	40.3	41.9	17.7
Production planning	43.5	27.4	29
Inventory analysis	48.4	30.6	21
Accounting	50	33.9	16.1
Marketing planning	53.2	35.5	11.3
Quality control	58.1	25.8	16.1
Plant location	59.7	35.5	4.8
Maintenance policy	61.3	30.6	8.1
Personnel management	67.7	25.8	6.5

TABLE 17-5
Areas where MS/OR methodologies are applied

of the respondents (87.1 percent) thought the benefits were greater than the costs.[6]

3 Some interesting international MS/OR applications

MS/OR IN CHINA

Cheng Kan of the Institute of Applied Mathematics, Academia Sinica, reports on four classes of MS/OR applications in China:[7]

Mathematical programming

Queuing theory and Markov processes

Reliability theory

Simulation

[6] Guisseppi A. Forgionne "Corporate Management Science Activities: An Update," *Interfaces,* vol. 13, no. 3, pp. 20–23, 1983.
[7] Cheng Kan, "Applications of O.R. in China," *Operations Research,* vol. 37, no. 2, pp. 181–185, 1986.

The mathematical programming application involved the dozen major oil fields of China that together produce about 100 million tons of petroleum. The linear programming formulation involved these two stages of the production process:

Distribution of crude oil from oil fields to various refineries

Distribution of petroleum products from refineries to customers

The mathematical programming solution bettered the previous one by 6 percent.

The Chinese also used a mathematical model in the design of a 15,000 ton ship. Here the objective was to design an optimal ship under constraints of speed, freight charges, and capacity. Improvements were able to be realized over traditional design approaches.

Linear programming was used in Shandong province to maximize total profitability over two years under such constraints as required contribution of grains to the state, demands of grain from people in the country, and available water supply.

Under the queuing theory heading, the author reports successful design of a data processing center, optimal design of buffer storage capacity of an assembly line, and optimal release of water for an electric power dam.

Application of reliability theory enabled the Chinese government to evaluate the reliability of some complex systems. In addition, successful results were obtained from this technique in safety analysis of nuclear power stations, and in papermaking and chemical engineering installations.

Finally, simulation produced interesting and improved results in the Chinese mining industry, in the design of a city bus system, and in managing a harbor transportation system. The author suggests that the gap between theory and practice must be removed and that further efforts are needed in promoting the discipline, two arguments that we have seen before in this chapter in the U.S. context.

▌ MS/OR IN NIGERIA

A most interesting application of MS/OR was conducted in Nigeria; it was called the Root Crops Project.[8] Tubers and root crops are a major source of food in Nigeria; the two main crops are yams and cassava. The objective of this particular project was to study the indigenous methods of processing these two crops with a view to easing the seasonal imbalance in supply, reducing crop losses, and contributing to the development of the regions through improved processing technologies, storage, and marketing methods.

4 Improving the long-run success of MS/OR

Let's examine the views of several writers in the field of quantitative methods on these issues: (1) what they see as the principal roadblocks to improved

FINDING WHAT IS
WRONG AND FIXING IT

[8] F. G. Foster, "Experiences with Developing Management Sciences/Operational Research in Nigeria," *Operations Research*, vol. 37, no. 2, pp. 217–221, 1986.

success in quantitative applications, and (2) methods which they deem appropriate for removing some of these impediments.

SERIOUS PROBLEMS IN IMPLEMENTING MS/OR

Forgionne's 1983 study on management science activities reported that over 61 percent of the respondents believed that inadequate data was a barrier to successful implementation. Of the 125 respondents, slightly over 58 percent believed that poor communication between analyst and manager interfered with successful results, almost 55 percent thought inadequate resources were a problem, and 37 percent felt that the length of time it took to complete MS/OR projects was a deterrent to success. Forgionne's study came to similar conclusions as earlier studies by Gaither[9] and Thomas and DaCosta.[10]

AN ENLIGHTENING AND HUMOROUS NONSCIENTIFIC FINDING

In their delightful 1983 TIMS article "Growing MS/OR Groups for Fun and Profit," Professors Wilson Price and Christian Bernard begin by asserting that they make no claim to scientific results and that they have not contacted a representative sample of professionals.[11] Rather, their hypotheses are based on observations, conversations, and a small number of in-depth interviews. Nevertheless, their six "findings" are entertaining as well as enlightening and are worthy of further discussion; they are summarized here:

1 *Working on projects is better than working on techniques.* MS/OR groups that were technique-oriented felt that their environment was an unhappy place to work and saw themselves as the "pocket calculator" of the organization. Groups that were able to work on projects, however, felt more like a "general contractor" and had more success.

2 *Generalists do better than specialists.* MS/OR groups in which each group member was able to work on a wide range of problems and use a wide range of techniques were more successful than groups in which each member was highly specialized in one technique. The most successful groups were those in which specialists were prepared to undertake work outside their specialty and to take the time to become knowledgeable about the operations of the entire organization in which they worked.

3 *Accountability is important.* In an organization that has an internal billing and cost-recovery system, the MS/OR group is not likely to spend much time contemplating its navel, and this will certainly contribute to its success. In an organization which has an internal billing system, everyone must be much more cost-conscious, and functional managers have more of an incentive to call on the MS/OR group for help.

4 *MS/OR does better in high-technology industries.* MS/OR groups seem to have more opportunity for success when they have some affinity with the managers

---

[9] N. Gaither, "The Adoption of Operations Research Techniques by Manufacturing Organizations," *Decision Sciences*, vol. 6, no. 4, pp. 797–813, October 1975.

[10] G. Thomas and J. DaCosta, "A Sample Survey of Corporate Operations Research," *Interfaces*, vol. 9, no. 4, pp. 102–111, 1979.

[11] Wilson Price and Christian Bernard, "Growing MS/OR Groups for Fun and Profit," *Interfaces*, vol. 13, no. 3, pp. 39–43, 1983.

of other divisions in the organization. Having managers with some technical training seems to be an advantage. Many social scientists neither like nor trust numbers, and when persons of this background are in management positions, the MS/OR group is not held in the highest esteem.

5 *Some career patterns are better than others.* Some organizations are structured so that MS/OR itself is a major portion of an individual's career. On the other hand, there are organizations which move people in and out of the MS/OR function. By doing so, these latter firms increase the analysts' knowledge of the organization.

6 *There is safety in numbers.* The availability of "numbers," that is, *data*, is important to the growth and success of the MS/OR function. One of the main tasks of MS/OR is the conversion of *data* into *information* for decision making. MS/OR is more likely to flourish in an information-rich environment, filled with the trappings of the computer age, than in an information-poor environment.

5 The future of MS/OR

SOME CONCERNS OF MS/OR ORGANIZATION MEMBERSHIPS

MS/OR is a very healthy activity today and continues to make significant contributions to industry. But as in any activity, there are changes in the MS/OR environment which require changes in MS/OR strategy. Let's look at a few articles published very recently that capture the concern of the researchers and professionals in this field.

At a recent TIMS/ORSA conference, about 25 academic and business MS/OR practitioners assembled to discuss problems with MS/OR.[12] They agreed that MS/OR needs to have a clearer definition of exactly what it is and what it can do, that it must better educate top managers to recognize what MS/OR is and does, and that practitioners in the field confuse the tools they use with the problems they solve. The group suggested that—whereas managers in the messy real world wanted solutions that were simple, certain, immediate, and concrete—MS/OR practitioners tended to provide ones which were complex, probabilistic, abstract, and too far in the future. Even given the significant number of successful public and private sector MS/OR applications, there was skepticism about whether MS/OR was having any impact on management strategy and whether top managers would miss MS/OR if it weren't here. It was pointed out that MS/OR groups were being replaced by decision sciences groups, often with the same membership, and that MS/OR people were being placed in functional areas of the firm to work on key problems. Too, MS/OR groups in university business schools were being merged into functional departments (production, marketing, finance). It was the conclusion of the group that these problems had two causes: (1) losing touch with the roots of MS/OR (real world problem-solving) and (2) insufficient publicity (MS/OR doesn't get credit for many of its successes). Avoiding elegant solutions to abstract problems and doing a better job of educating

---

[12] Gary L. Lilien, "MS/OR: A Mid-Life Crisis," *Interfaces*, vol. 17, no. 2, pp. 35–38, 1987.

management about the real potential of MS/OR were offered as solutions. The article reporting these concerns reinforces many of the author's feelings expressed two years earlier in the same journal.

Continuing this same theme of concern, George A. Tingley, an MS/OR employee of Swissair in Zurich, shared his concern that MS/OR was being overtaken by newer decision aids like decision support systems and expert systems, and that MS/OR had not received credit for its real contributions.[13] His suggestions to solve this problem included:

1 taking full advantage of computer hardware and software

2 emphasizing prototyping, modeling, and heuristics (rules of thumb that work) in addition to analytic methods of optimization

3 promoting MS/OR accomplishments in trade and management magazines, not just in academic journals

And finally, an article by two ORSA members in late 1987 reported results of a study of the ORSA membership begun in 1984.[14] Results showed that membership had been shrinking since 1970, and would be even lower except for efforts to attract many student members. The article noted that about half of ORSA's members worked in applications, one-sixth in management, another sixth in research, and the final sixth in teaching. The authors conclude that ORSA is struggling to maintain membership, despite low society dues and employer-paid trips to national meetings. One problem appears to be the journal *Operations Research*, which reportedly does not meet the demand of the membership for MS/OR applications. This finding corroborates several of the findings of the two previously cited studies.

A CAVEAT

John Gratwick of the Canadian National Railways provides us with some concluding food for thought in his address to the Canadian Operational Research Society meeting in May 1982. Gratwick asserts that OR has become much less respected today, and that as a manager he is distressed by the significant mismatch between what he needs and what is offered by OR.

Gratwick says that managers today are not seeking sophisticated algorithms that maximize a hypothetical and unnaturally tidy situation, but rather, they are grasping for a survival kit that will give them a fighting chance to cope with their world of ill-defined pressures and constraints. He says that managers' problems are never resolvable in single-formula terms, but rather have economic, political, social, organizational, environmental, cultural, and linguistic dimensions.

What managers find *most* incomprehensible is a so-called solution that ignores all the intractable pieces of the problem, because the MS/OR analyst cannot accommodate them within the mathematical formulation he or she

---

[13] George A. Tingley, "Can MS/OR Sell Itself Well Enough?," *Interfaces*, vol. 17, no. 4, pp. 41–52, 1987.

[14] Stephen J. Balut and R. A. Armacost, "ORSA As Viewed By Its Members," *Operations Research*, vol. 34, no. 6, pp. 940–953, 1987.

has constructed. Gratwick sagely cautions us as MS/OR practitioners that mathematics is not enough; what we need is a feeling for numbers and words *together* with the structures and relationships that link them. MS/OR practitioners should always be aware that none of the quantitative tools they are able to fashion, buy, or borrow can replace their own intrinsic skills.[15]

CONCLUSION

MS/OR has proven itself in business and government to the point where there can no longer be any excuse for a student graduating from a university program in business or public administration without being conversant with both the *techniques* and the *constraints* on its effective use.

The problems that private and public organizations face are mind-boggling in scope. Much new managerial technology must be brought to bear on these problems before they will yield solutions which can be implemented in a practical manner.

It is no longer possible for organizations to avoid researching the potential usefulness of the techniques presented in this book to their policy and operating problems. Past successes indicate a large potential for further application of MS/OR.

Despite the negative impression you may have gotten from this section and from Section 4 of this chapter, there have been some very impressive successful applications of MS/OR techniques. We have been sharing some of these with you in the "Real world MS/OR successes" sections at the end of the previous chapters. Those MS/OR analysts who know both the capabilities and the limitations of their science, and who take care to understand the viewpoints of managers and to communicate with them, can make significant contributions to the organizations they serve.

Every year, the TIMS College on the Practice of Management Science (CPMS) awards a prize for the best application of MS/OR that year. One of the criteria for choosing the best application is how much money the firm saved by using the analysts' results. In 1984, this award was won by a team of analysts who helped Blue Bell, Inc. (a manufacturer of blue jeans and other apparel) reduce the amount of fabric they wasted and improve their inventory management. The savings? Millions of dollars in annual operating costs and a one-time reduction in inventory of over $100 million.[16]

Each year, one issue (usually the December issue) of *Interfaces* is devoted to the best five or six entries in the CPMS competition for the previous year. We encourage you to examine some of these articles, the better to appreciate the value of the MS/OR techniques we have presented in this volume.

Managers at all levels in organizations require additional education in this field, and students entering organizations from university curricula in administration must have a working knowledge of the ideas presented herein if they are to contribute effectively to the solution of organizational problems; to that end this book was written.

---

[15] John Gratwick, "The Importance of Being Trivial," *Interfaces*, vol. 13, no. 3, pp. 59–61, 1983.
[16] Jerry R. Edwards, Harvey M. Wagner, and William P. Wood, "Blue Bell Trims Its Inventory," *Interfaces*, vol. 15, no. 1, pp. 34–52, 1985.

APPENDIX ONE   The Standard Normal Probability Distribution

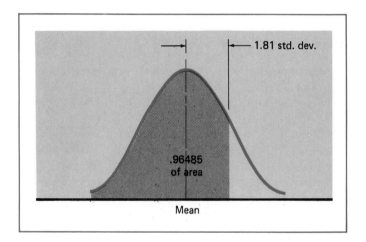

Directions: To find the area under the normal curve between the left-hand end and any point, determine how many standard deviations that point is to the right of the mean, and then read the area directly from the body of the table. *Example:* The area under the curve from the left-hand end to a point 1.81 standard deviations to the right of the mean is .96485 of the total area under the curve.

	.00	.01	.02	.03	.04	.05	.06	.07	.08	.09
0.0	.50000	.50399	.50798	.51197	.51595	.51994	.52392	.52790	.53188	.53586
0.1	.53983	.54380	.54776	.55172	.55567	.55962	.56356	.56749	.57142	.57535
0.2	.57926	.58317	.58706	.59095	.59483	.59871	.60257	.60642	.61026	.61409
0.3	.61791	.62172	.62552	.62930	.63307	.63683	.64058	.64431	.64803	.65173
0.4	.65542	.65910	.66276	.66640	.67003	.67364	.67724	.68082	.68439	.68793
0.5	.69146	.69497	.69847	.70194	.70540	.70884	.71226	.71566	.71904	.72240
0.6	.72575	.72907	.73237	.73536	.73891	.74215	.74537	.74857	.75175	.75490
0.7	.75804	.76115	.76424	.76730	.77035	.77337	.77637	.77935	.78230	.78524
0.8	.78814	.79103	.79389	.79673	.79955	.80234	.80511	.80785	.81057	.81327
0.9	.81594	.81859	.82121	.82381	.82639	.82894	.83147	.83398	.83646	.83891
1.0	.84134	.84375	.84614	.84849	.85083	.85314	.85543	.85769	.85993	.86214
1.1	.86433	.86650	.86864	.87076	.87286	.87493	.87698	.87900	.88100	.88298
1.2	.88493	.88686	.88877	.89065	.89251	.89435	.89617	.89796	.89973	.90147
1.3	.90320	.90490	.90658	.90824	.90988	.91149	.91309	.91466	.91621	.91774
1.4	.91924	.92073	.92220	.92364	.92507	.92647	.92785	.92922	.93056	.93189
1.5	.93319	.93448	.93574	.93699	.93822	.93943	.94062	.94179	.94295	.94408
1.6	.94520	.94630	.94738	.94845	.94950	.95053	.95154	.95254	.95352	.95449
1.7	.95543	.95637	.95728	.95818	.95907	.95994	.96080	.96164	.96246	.96327
1.8	.96407	.96485	.96562	.96638	.96712	.96784	.96856	.96926	.96995	.97062
1.9	.97128	.97193	.97257	.97320	.97381	.97441	.97500	.97558	.97615	.97670
2.0	.97725	.97784	.97831	.97882	.97932	.97982	.98030	.98077	.98124	.98169
2.1	.98214	.98257	.98300	.98341	.98382	.98422	.98461	.98500	.98537	.98574
2.2	.98610	.98645	.98679	.98713	.98745	.98778	.98809	.98840	.98870	.98899
2.3	.98928	.98956	.98983	.99010	.99036	.99061	.99086	.99111	.99134	.99158
2.4	.99180	.99202	.99224	.99245	.99266	.99286	.99305	.99324	.99343	.99361
2.5	.99379	.99396	.99413	.99430	.99446	.99461	.99477	.99492	.99506	.99520
2.6	.99534	.99547	.99560	.99573	.99585	.99598	.99609	.99621	.99632	.99643
2.7	.99653	.99664	.99674	.99683	.99693	.99702	.99711	.99720	.99728	.99736
2.8	.99744	.99752	.99760	.99767	.99774	.99781	.99788	.99795	.99801	.99807
2.9	.99813	.99819	.99825	.99831	.99836	.99841	.99846	.99851	.99856	.99861
3.0	.99865	.99869	.99874	.99878	.99882	.99886	.99899	.99893	.99896	.99900
3.1	.99903	.99906	.99910	.99913	.99916	.99918	.99921	.99924	.99926	.99929
3.2	.99931	.99934	.99936	.99938	.99940	.99942	.99944	.99946	.99948	.99950
3.3	.99952	.99953	.99955	.99957	.99958	.99960	.99961	.99962	.99964	.99965
3.4	.99966	.99968	.99969	.99970	.99971	.99972	.99973	.99974	.99975	.99976
3.5	.99977	.99978	.99978	.99979	.99980	.99981	.99981	.99982	.99983	.99983
3.6	.99984	.99985	.99985	.99986	.99986	.99987	.99987	.99988	.99988	.99989
3.7	.99989	.99990	.99990	.99990	.99991	.99991	.99992	.99992	.99992	.99992
3.8	.99993	.99993	.99993	.99994	.99994	.99994	.99994	.99995	.99995	.99995
3.9	.99995	.99995	.99996	.99996	.99996	.99996	.99996	.99996	.99997	.99997

APPENDIX TWO

The Cumulative Binomial Distribution

The following tables describe the cumulative binomial distribution; a sample problem will illustrate how they are to be used.

Problem

What is the probability that an inspector will find *8 or more* defects in inspecting a lot of 15 pieces when the probability that any one piece is defective is .30?

Steps

1 In binomial distribution notation, the elements in this problem can be represented as follows:

$$n = 15 \quad \text{number of pieces to be inspected}$$
$$p = .30 \quad \text{probability that any one piece will be defective}$$
$$r = 8 \quad \text{number of defects in question}$$

2 Since the problem involves 15 trials or inspections, first find the table corresponding to $n = 15$.

3 The probability of a defect in any one piece is .30; thus we must look through the $n = 15$ table until we find the column where $p = 30$.

4 We then move down the $p = 30$ column until we are opposite the $r = 8$ row.

5 The answer there is found to be 0500; this is interpreted as being a probability value of .0500.

Notes

The problem asked for the probability of *8 or more* defects; had it asked for the probability of *more than 8* defects, we would have looked up the probability of *9 or more* defects.

This table only goes up to $p = .50$. When p is *larger* than .50, q $(1 - p)$ is *less* than .50. Therefore the problem is worked in terms of q and the number of good pieces $(n - r)$ rather than in terms of p and r (the number of defects). For example, suppose $p = .60$ and $n = 15$. What is the probability of more than 12 defects? More than 12 defects (13, 14, or 15 defects) is the same as 2 or fewer good pieces. The probability of 2 or fewer good pieces is 1 minus the probability of 3 or more good pieces. We look in the $n = 15$ table for the $p = 40$ column and the $r = 3$ row. There we see the number 9729, which we interpret as a probability of .9729; so the answer is $1 - .9729$, or .0271.

Cumulative binomial distribution

$$n = 1$$

P R	01	02	03	04	05	06	07	08	09	10
1	0100	0200	0300	0400	0500	0600	0700	0800	0900	1000

P R	11	12	13	14	15	16	17	18	19	20
1	1100	1200	1300	1400	1500	1600	1700	1800	1900	2000

P R	21	22	23	24	25	26	27	28	29	30
1	2100	2200	2300	2400	2500	2600	2700	2800	2900	3000

P R	31	32	33	34	35	36	37	38	39	40
1	3100	3200	3300	3400	3500	3600	3700	3800	3900	4000

P R	41	42	43	44	45	46	47	48	49	50
1	4100	4200	4300	4400	4500	4600	4700	4800	4900	5000

$$n = 2$$

P R	01	02	03	04	05	06	07	08	09	10
1	0199	0396	0591	0784	0975	1164	1351	1536	1719	1900
2	0001	0004	0009	0016	0025	0036	0049	0064	0081	0100

P R	11	12	13	14	15	16	17	18	19	20
1	2079	2256	2431	2604	2775	2944	3111	3276	3439	3600
2	0121	0144	0169	0196	0225	0256	0289	0324	0361	0400

P R	21	22	23	24	25	26	27	28	29	30
1	3759	3916	4071	4224	4375	4524	4671	4816	4959	5100
2	0441	0484	0529	0576	0625	0676	0729	0784	0841	0900

P R	31	32	33	34	35	36	37	38	39	40
1	5239	5376	5511	5644	5775	5904	6031	6156	6279	6400
2	0961	1024	1089	1156	1225	1296	1369	1444	1521	1600

P R	41	42	43	44	45	46	47	48	49	50
1	6519	6636	6751	6864	6975	7084	7191	7296	7399	7500
2	1681	1764	1849	1936	2025	2116	2209	2304	2401	2500

$$n = 3$$

P R	01	02	03	04	05	06	07	08	09	10
1	0297	0588	0873	1153	1426	1694	1956	2213	2464	2710
2	0003	0012	0026	0047	0073	0104	0140	0182	0228	0280
3				0001	0001	0002	0003	0005	0007	0010

P R	11	12	13	14	15	16	17	18	19	20
1	2950	3185	3415	3639	3859	4073	4282	4486	4686	4880
2	0336	0397	0463	0533	0608	0686	0769	0855	0946	1040
3	0013	0017	0022	0027	0034	0041	0049	0058	0069	0080

P R	21	22	23	24	25	26	27	28	29	30
1	5070	5254	5435	5610	5781	5948	6110	6268	6421	6570
2	1138	1239	1344	1452	1563	1676	1793	1913	2035	2160
3	0093	0106	0122	0138	0156	0176	0197	0220	0244	0270

P	31	32	33	34	35	36	37	38	39	40
R										
1	6715	6856	6992	7125	7254	7379	7500	7617	7730	7840
2	2287	2417	2548	2682	2818	2955	3094	3235	3377	3520
3	0298	0328	0359	0393	0429	0467	0507	0549	0593	0640

P	41	42	43	44	45	46	47	48	49	50
R										
1	7946	8049	8148	8244	8336	8425	8511	8594	8673	8750
2	3665	3810	3957	4104	4253	4401	4551	4700	4850	5000
3	0689	0741	0795	0852	0911	0973	1038	1106	1176	1250

$$n = 4$$

P	01	02	03	04	05	06	07	08	09	10
R										
1	0394	0776	1147	1507	1855	2193	2519	2836	3143	3439
2	0006	0023	0052	0091	0140	0199	0267	0344	0430	0523
3			0001	0002	0005	0008	0013	0019	0027	0037
4									0001	0001

P	11	12	13	14	15	16	17	18	19	20
R										
1	3726	4003	4271	4530	4780	5021	5254	5479	5695	5904
2	0624	0732	0847	0968	1095	1228	1366	1509	1656	1808
3	0049	0063	0079	0098	0120	0144	0171	0202	0235	0272
4	0001	0002	0003	0004	0005	0007	0008	0010	0013	0016

P	21	22	23	24	25	26	27	28	29	30
R										
1	6105	6298	6485	6664	6836	7001	7160	7313	7459	7599
2	1963	2122	2285	2450	2617	2787	2959	3132	3307	3483
3	0312	0356	0403	0453	0508	0566	0628	0694	0763	0837
4	0019	0023	0028	0033	0039	0046	0053	0061	0071	0081

P	31	32	33	34	35	36	37	38	39	40
R										
1	7733	7862	7985	8103	8215	8322	8425	8522	8615	8704
2	3660	3837	4015	4193	4370	4547	4724	4900	5075	5248
3	0915	0996	1082	1171	1265	1362	1464	1569	1679	1792
4	0092	0105	0119	0134	0150	0168	0187	0209	0231	0256

P	41	42	43	44	45	46	47	48	49	50
R										
1	8788	8868	8944	9017	9085	9150	9211	9269	9323	9375
2	5420	5590	5759	5926	6090	6252	6412	6569	6724	6875
3	1909	2030	2155	2283	2415	2550	2689	2831	2977	3125
4	0283	0311	0342	0375	0410	0448	0488	0531	0576	0625

$$n = 5$$

P	01	02	03	04	05	06	07	08	09	10
R										
1	0490	0961	1413	1846	2262	2661	3043	3409	3760	4095
2	0010	0038	0085	0148	0226	0319	0425	0544	0674	0815
3		0001	0003	0006	0012	0020	0031	0045	0063	0086
4						0001	0001	0002	0003	0005

P	11	12	13	14	15	16	17	18	19	20
R										
1	4416	4723	5016	5296	5563	5818	6061	6293	6513	6723
2	0965	1125	1292	1467	1648	1835	2027	2224	2424	2627
3	0112	0143	0179	0220	0266	0318	0375	0437	0505	0579
4	0007	0009	0013	0017	0022	0029	0036	0045	0055	0067
5				0001	0001	0001	0001	0002	0002	0003

P	21	22	23	24	25	26	27	28	29	30
R										
1	6923	7113	7293	7464	7627	7781	7927	8065	8196	8319
2	2833	3041	3251	3461	3672	3883	4093	4303	4511	4718
3	0659	0744	0836	0933	1035	1143	1257	1376	1501	1631
4	0081	0097	0114	0134	0156	0181	0208	0238	0272	0308
5	0004	0005	0006	0008	0010	0012	0014	0017	0021	0024

Cumulative binomial distribution (*continued*)

P R	31	32	33	34	35	36	37	38	39	40
1	8436	8546	8650	8748	8840	8926	9008	9084	9155	9222
2	4923	5125	5325	5522	5716	5906	6093	6276	6455	6630
3	1766	1905	2050	2199	2352	2509	2670	2835	3003	3174
4	0347	0390	0436	0486	0540	0598	0660	0726	0796	0870
5	0029	0034	0039	0045	0053	0060	0069	0079	0090	0102

P R	41	42	43	44	45	46	47	48	49	50
1	9285	9344	9398	9449	9497	9541	9582	9620	9655	9688
2	6801	6967	7129	7286	7438	7585	7728	7865	7998	8125
3	3349	3525	3705	3886	4069	4253	4439	4625	4813	5000
4	0949	1033	1121	1214	1312	1415	1522	1635	1753	1875
5	0116	0131	0147	0165	0185	0206	0229	0255	0282	0313

$$n = 6$$

P R	01	02	03	04	05	06	07	08	09	10
1	0585	1142	1670	2172	2649	3101	3530	3936	4321	4686
2	0015	0057	0125	0216	0328	0459	0608	0773	0952	1143
3		0002	0005	0012	0022	0038	0058	0085	0118	0159
4					0001	0002	0003	0005	0008	0013
5										0001

P R	11	12	13	14	15	16	17	18	19	20
1	5030	5356	5664	5954	6229	6487	6731	6960	7176	7379
2	1345	1556	1776	2003	2235	2472	2713	2956	3201	3446
3	0206	0261	0324	0395	0473	0560	0655	0759	0870	0989
4	0018	0025	0034	0045	0059	0075	0094	0116	0141	0170
5	0001	0001	0002	0003	0004	0005	0007	0010	0013	0016
6										0001

P R	21	22	23	24	25	26	27	28	29	30
1	7569	7748	7916	8073	8220	8358	8487	8607	8719	8824
2	3692	3937	4180	4422	4661	4896	5128	5356	5580	5798
3	1115	1250	1391	1539	1694	1856	2023	2196	2374	2557
4	0202	0239	0280	0326	0376	0431	0492	0557	0628	0705
5	0020	0025	0031	0038	0046	0056	0067	0079	0093	0109
6	0001	0001	0001	0002	0002	0003	0004	0005	0006	0007

P R	31	32	33	34	35	36	37	38	39	40
1	8921	9011	9095	9173	9246	9313	9375	9432	9485	9533
2	6012	6220	6422	6619	6809	6994	7172	7343	7508	7667
3	2744	2936	3130	3328	3529	3732	3937	4143	4350	4557
4	0787	0875	0969	1069	1174	1286	1404	1527	1657	1792
5	0127	0148	0170	0195	0223	0254	0288	0325	0365	0410
6	0009	0011	0013	0015	0018	0022	0026	0030	0035	0041

P R	41	42	43	44	45	46	47	48	49	50
1	9578	9619	9657	9692	9723	9752	9778	9802	9824	9844
2	7819	7965	8105	8238	8364	8485	8599	8707	8810	8906
3	4764	4971	5177	5382	5585	5786	5985	6180	6373	6563
4	1933	2080	2232	2390	2553	2721	2893	3070	3252	3438
5	0458	0510	0566	0627	0692	0762	0837	0917	1003	1094
6	0048	0055	0063	0073	0083	0095	0108	0122	0138	0156

$$n = 7$$

P R	01	02	03	04	05	06	07	08	09	10
1	0679	1319	1920	2486	3017	3515	3983	4422	4832	5217
2	0020	0079	0171	0294	0444	0618	0813	1026	1255	1497
3		0003	0009	0020	0038	0063	0097	0140	0193	0257
4				0001	0002	0004	0007	0012	0018	0027
5								0001	0001	0002

P	11	12	13	14	15	16	17	18	19	20
R
1	5577	5913	6227	6521	6794	7049	7286	7507	7712	7903
2	1750	2012	2281	2556	2834	3115	3396	3677	3956	4233
3	0331	0416	0513	0620	0738	0866	1005	1154	1313	1480
4	0039	0054	0072	0094	0121	0153	0189	0231	0279	0333
5	0003	0004	0006	0009	0012	0017	0022	0029	0037	0047
6					0001	0001	0001	0002	0003	0004

P	21	22	23	24	25	26	27	28	29	30
R
1	8080	8243	8395	8535	8665	8785	8895	8997	9090	9176
2	4506	4775	5040	5298	5551	5796	6035	6266	6490	6706
3	1657	1841	2033	2231	2436	2646	2861	3081	3304	3529
4	0394	0461	0536	0617	0706	0802	0905	1016	1134	1260
5	0058	0072	0088	0107	0129	0153	0181	0213	0248	0288
6	0005	0006	0008	0011	0013	0017	0021	0026	0031	0038
7					0001	0001	0001	0001	0002	0002

P	31	32	33	34	35	36	37	38	39	40
R
1	9255	9328	9394	9454	9510	9560	9606	9648	9686	9720
2	6914	7113	7304	7487	7662	7828	7987	8137	8279	8414
3	3757	3987	4217	4447	4677	4906	5134	5359	5581	5801
4	1394	1534	1682	1837	1998	2167	2341	2521	2707	2898
5	0332	0380	0434	0492	0556	0625	0701	0782	0869	0963
6	0046	0055	0065	0077	0090	0105	0123	0142	0164	0188
7	0003	0003	0004	0005	0006	0008	0009	0011	0014	0016

P	41	42	43	44	45	46	47	48	49	50
R
1	9751	9779	9805	9827	9848	9866	9883	9897	9910	9922
2	8541	8660	8772	8877	8976	9068	9153	9233	9307	9375
3	6017	6229	6436	6638	6836	7027	7213	7393	7567	7734
4	3094	3294	3498	3706	3917	4131	4346	4563	4781	5000
5	1063	1169	1282	1402	1529	1663	1803	1951	2105	2266
6	0216	0246	0279	0316	0357	0402	0451	0504	0562	0625
7	0019	0023	0027	0032	0037	0044	0051	0059	0068	0078

$$n = 8$$

P	01	02	03	04	05	06	07	08	09	10
R
1	0773	1492	2163	2786	3366	3904	4404	4868	5297	5695
2	0027	0103	0223	0381	0572	0792	1035	1298	1577	1869
3	0001	0004	0013	0031	0058	0096	0147	0211	0289	0381
4			0001	0002	0004	0007	0013	0022	0034	0050
5							0001	0001	0003	0004

P	11	12	13	14	15	16	17	18	19	20
R
1	6063	6404	6718	7008	7275	7521	7748	7956	8147	8322
2	2171	2480	2794	3111	3428	3744	4057	4366	4670	4967
3	0487	0608	0743	0891	1052	1226	1412	1608	1815	2031
4	0071	0097	0129	0168	0214	0267	0328	0397	0476	0563
5	0007	0010	0015	0021	0029	0038	0050	0065	0083	0104
6		0001	0001	0002	0002	0003	0005	0007	0009	0012
7									0001	0001

P	21	22	23	24	25	26	27	28	29	30
R
1	8483	8630	8764	8887	8999	9101	9194	9278	9354	9424
2	5257	5538	5811	6075	6329	6573	6807	7031	7244	7447
3	2255	2486	2724	2967	3215	3465	3718	3973	4228	4482
4	0659	0765	0880	1004	1138	1281	1433	1594	1763	1941
5	0129	0158	0191	0230	0273	0322	0377	0438	0505	0580
6	0016	0021	0027	0034	0042	0052	0064	0078	0094	0113
7	0001	0002	0002	0003	0004	0005	0006	0008	0010	0013
8									0001	0001

Cumulative binomial distribution (*continued*)

P	31	32	33	34	35	36	37	38	39	40
R
1	9486	9543	9594	9640	9681	9719	9752	9782	9808	9832
2	7640	7822	7994	8156	8309	8452	8586	8711	8828	8936
3	4736	4987	5236	5481	5722	5958	6189	6415	6634	6846
4	2126	2319	2519	2724	2936	3153	3374	3599	3828	4059
5	0661	0750	0846	0949	1061	1180	1307	1443	1586	1737
6	0134	0159	0187	0218	0253	0293	0336	0385	0439	0498
7	0016	0020	0024	0030	0036	0043	0051	0061	0072	0085
8	0001	0001	0001	0002	0002	0003	0004	0004	0005	0007

P	41	42	43	44	45	46	47	48	49	50
R
1	9853	9872	9889	9903	9916	9928	9938	9947	9954	9961
2	9037	9130	9216	9295	9368	9435	9496	9552	9602	9648
3	7052	7250	7440	7624	7799	7966	8125	8276	8419	8555
4	4292	4527	4762	4996	5230	5463	5694	5922	6146	6367
5	1895	2062	2235	2416	2604	2798	2999	3205	3416	3633
6	0563	0634	0711	0794	0885	0982	1086	1198	1318	1445
7	0100	0117	0136	0157	0181	0208	0239	0272	0310	0352
8	0008	0010	0012	0014	0017	0020	0024	0028	0033	0039

$$n = 9$$

P	01	02	03	04	05	06	07	08	09	10
R
1	0865	1663	2398	3075	3698	4270	4796	5278	5721	6126
2	0034	0131	0282	0478	0712	0978	1271	1583	1912	2252
3	0001	0006	0020	0045	0084	0138	0209	0298	0405	0530
4			0001	0003	0006	0013	0023	0037	0057	0083
5						0001	0002	0003	0005	0009
6										0001

P	11	12	13	14	15	16	17	18	19	20
R
1	6496	6835	7145	7427	7684	7918	8131	8324	8499	8658
2	2599	2951	3304	3657	4005	4348	4685	5012	5330	5638
3	0672	0833	1009	1202	1409	1629	1861	2105	2357	2618
4	0117	0158	0209	0269	0339	0420	0512	0615	0730	0856
5	0014	0021	0030	0041	0056	0075	0098	0125	0158	0196
6	0001	0002	0003	0004	0006	0009	0013	0017	0023	0031
7							0001	0001	0002	0002	0003

P	21	22	23	24	25	26	27	28	29	30
R
1	8801	8931	9048	9154	9249	9335	9411	9480	9542	9596
2	5934	6218	6491	6750	6997	7230	7452	7660	7856	8040
3	2885	3158	3434	3713	3993	4273	4552	4829	5102	5372
4	0994	1144	1304	1475	1657	1849	2050	2260	2478	2703
5	0240	0291	0350	0416	0489	0571	0662	0762	0870	0988
6	0040	0051	0065	0081	0100	0122	0149	0179	0213	0253
7	0004	0006	0008	0010	0013	0017	0022	0028	0035	0043
8			0001	0001	0001	0001	0002	0003	0003	0004

P	31	32	33	34	35	36	37	38	39	40
R
1	9645	9689	9728	9762	9793	9820	9844	9865	9883	9899
2	8212	8372	8522	8661	8789	8908	9017	9118	9210	9295
3	5636	5894	6146	6390	6627	6856	7076	7287	7489	7682
4	2935	3173	3415	3662	3911	4163	4416	4669	4922	5174
5	1115	1252	1398	1553	1717	1890	2072	2262	2460	2666
6	0298	0348	0404	0467	0536	0612	0696	0787	0886	0994
7	0053	0064	0078	0094	0112	0133	0157	0184	0215	0250
8	0006	0007	0009	0011	0014	0017	0021	0026	0031	0038
9				0001	0001	0001	0001	0001	0002	0002	0003

P	41	42	43	44	45	46	47	48	49	50
R
1	9913	9926	9936	9946	9954	9961	9967	9972	9977	9980
2	9372	9442	9505	9563	9615	9662	9704	9741	9775	9805
3	7866	8039	8204	8359	8505	8642	8769	8889	8999	9102
4	5424	5670	5913	6152	6386	6614	6836	7052	7260	7461
5	2878	3097	3322	3551	3786	4024	4265	4509	4754	5000
6	1109	1233	1366	1508	1658	1817	1985	2161	2346	2539
7	0290	0334	0383	0437	0498	0564	0637	0717	0804	0898
8	0046	0055	0065	0077	0091	0107	0125	0145	0169	0195
9	0003	0004	0005	0006	0008	0009	0011	0014	0016	0020

$n = 10$

R	01	02	03	04	05	06	07	08	09	10
1	0956	1829	2626	3352	4013	4614	5160	5656	6106	6513
2	0043	0162	0345	0582	0861	1176	1517	1879	2254	2639
3	0001	0009	0028	0062	0115	0188	0283	0401	0540	0702
4			0001	0004	0010	0020	0036	0058	0088	0128
5					0001	0002	0003	0006	0010	0016
6									0001	0001

R	11	12	13	14	15	16	17	18	19	20
1	6882	7215	7516	7787	8031	8251	8448	8626	8784	8926
2	3028	3417	3804	4184	4557	4920	5270	5608	5932	6242
3	0884	1087	1308	1545	1798	2064	2341	2628	2922	3222
4	0178	0239	0313	0400	0500	0614	0741	0883	1039	1209
5	0025	0037	0053	0073	0099	0130	0168	0213	0266	0328
6	0003	0004	0006	0010	0014	0020	0027	0037	0049	0064
7			0001	0001	0001	0002	0003	0004	0006	0009
8									0001	0001

R	21	22	23	24	25	26	27	28	29	30
1	9053	9166	9267	9357	9437	9508	9570	9626	9674	9718
2	6536	6815	7079	7327	7560	7778	7981	8170	8345	8507
3	3526	3831	4137	4442	4744	5042	5335	5622	5901	6172
4	1391	1587	1794	2012	2241	2479	2726	2979	3239	3504
5	0399	0479	0569	0670	0781	0904	1037	1181	1337	1503
6	0082	0104	0130	0161	0197	0239	0287	0342	0404	0473
7	0012	0016	0021	0027	0035	0045	0056	0070	0087	0106
8	0001	0002	0002	0003	0004	0006	0007	0010	0012	0016
9							0001	0001	0001	0001

R	31	32	33	34	35	36	37	38	39	40
1	9755	9789	9818	9843	9865	9885	9902	9916	9929	9940
2	8656	8794	8920	9035	9140	9236	9323	9402	9473	9536
3	6434	6687	6930	7162	7384	7595	7794	7983	8160	8327
4	3772	4044	4316	4589	4862	5132	5400	5664	5923	6177
5	1679	1867	2064	2270	2485	2708	2939	3177	3420	3669
6	0551	0637	0732	0836	0949	1072	1205	1348	1500	1662
7	0129	0155	0185	0220	0260	0305	0356	0413	0477	0548
8	0020	0025	0032	0039	0048	0059	0071	0086	0103	0123
9	0002	0003	0003	0004	0005	0007	0009	0011	0014	0017
10								0001	0001	0001

R	41	42	43	44	45	46	47	48	49	50
1	9949	9957	9964	9970	9975	9979	9983	9986	9988	9990
2	9594	9645	9691	9731	9767	9799	9827	9852	9874	9893
3	8483	8628	8764	8889	9004	9111	9209	9298	9379	9453
4	6425	6665	6898	7123	7340	7547	7745	7933	8112	8281
5	3922	4178	4436	4696	4956	5216	5474	5730	5982	6230
6	1834	2016	2207	2407	2616	2832	3057	3288	3526	3770
7	0626	0712	0806	0908	1020	1141	1271	1410	1560	1719
8	0146	0172	0202	0236	0274	0317	0366	0420	0480	0547
9	0021	0025	0031	0037	0045	0054	0065	0077	0091	0107
10	0001	0002	0002	0003	0003	0004	0005	0006	0008	0010

$n = 11$

R	01	02	03	04	05	06	07	08	09	10
1	1047	1993	2847	3618	4312	4937	5499	6004	6456	6862
2	0052	0195	0413	0692	1019	1382	1772	2181	2601	3026
3	0002	0012	0037	0083	0152	0248	0370	0519	0695	0896
4			0002	0007	0016	0030	0053	0085	0129	0185
5					0001	0003	0005	0010	0017	0028
6								0001	0002	0003

Cumulative binomial distribution (*continued*)

P	11	12	13	14	15	16	17	18	19	20
R										
1	7225	7549	7839	8097	8327	8531	8712	8873	9015	9141
2	3452	3873	4286	4689	5078	5453	5811	6151	6474	6779
3	1120	1366	1632	1915	2212	2521	2839	3164	3494	3826
4	0256	0341	0442	0560	0694	0846	1013	1197	1397	1611
5	0042	0061	0087	0119	0159	0207	0266	0334	0413	0504
6	0005	0008	0012	0018	0027	0037	0051	0068	0090	0117
7		0001	0001	0002	0003	0005	0007	0010	0014	0020
8							0001	0001	0002	0002

P	21	22	23	24	25	26	27	28	29	30
R										
1	9252	9350	9436	9511	9578	9636	9686	9730	9769	9802
2	7065	7333	7582	7814	8029	8227	8410	8577	8730	8870
3	4158	4488	4814	5134	5448	5753	6049	6335	6610	6873
4	1840	2081	2333	2596	2867	3146	3430	3719	4011	4304
5	0607	0723	0851	0992	1146	1313	1493	1685	1888	2103
6	0148	0186	0231	0283	0343	0412	0490	0577	0674	0782
7	0027	0035	0046	0059	0076	0095	0119	0146	0179	0216
8	0003	0005	0007	0009	0012	0016	0021	0027	0034	0043
9			0001	0001	0001	0002	0002	0003	0004	0006

P	31	32	33	34	35	36	37	38	39	40
R										
1	9831	9856	9878	9896	9912	9926	9938	9948	9956	9964
2	8997	9112	9216	9310	9394	9470	9537	9597	9650	9698
3	7123	7361	7587	7799	7999	8186	8360	8522	8672	8811
4	4598	4890	5179	5464	5744	6019	6286	6545	6796	7037
5	2328	2563	2807	3059	3317	3581	3850	4122	4397	4672
6	0901	1031	1171	1324	1487	1661	1847	2043	2249	2465
7	0260	0309	0366	0430	0501	0581	0670	0768	0876	0994
8	0054	0067	0082	0101	0122	0148	0177	0210	0249	0293
9	0008	0010	0013	0016	0020	0026	0032	0039	0048	0059
10	0001	0001	0001	0002	0002	0003	0004	0005	0006	0007

P	41	42	43	44	45	46	47	48	49	50
R										
1	9970	9975	9979	9983	9986	9989	9991	9992	9994	9995
2	9739	9776	9808	9836	9861	9882	9900	9916	9930	9941
3	8938	9055	9162	9260	9348	9428	9499	9564	9622	9673
4	7269	7490	7700	7900	8089	8266	8433	8588	8733	8867
5	4948	5223	5495	5764	6029	6288	6541	6787	7026	7256
6	2690	2924	3166	3414	3669	3929	4193	4460	4729	5000
7	1121	1260	1408	1568	1738	1919	2110	2312	2523	2744
8	0343	0399	0461	0532	0610	0696	0791	0895	1009	1133
9	0072	0087	0104	0125	0148	0175	0206	0241	0282	0327
10	0009	0012	0014	0018	0022	0027	0033	0040	0049	0059
11	0001	0001	0001	0001	0002	0002	0002	0003	0004	0005

$$n = 12$$

P	01	02	03	04	05	06	07	08	09	10
R										
1	1136	2153	3062	3873	4596	5241	5814	6323	6775	7176
2	0062	0231	0486	0809	1184	1595	2033	2487	2948	3410
3	0002	0015	0048	0107	0196	0316	0468	0652	0866	1109
4		0001	0003	0010	0022	0043	0075	0120	0180	0256
5				0001	0002	0004	0009	0016	0027	0043
6							0001	0002	0003	0005
7										0001

P	11	12	13	14	15	16	17	18	19	20
R										
1	7530	7843	8120	8363	8578	8766	8931	9076	9202	9313
2	3867	4314	4748	5166	5565	5945	6304	6641	6957	7251
3	1377	1667	1977	2303	2642	2990	3344	3702	4060	4417
4	0351	0464	0597	0750	0922	1114	1324	1552	1795	2054
5	0065	0095	0133	0181	0239	0310	0393	0489	0600	0726
6	0009	0014	0022	0033	0046	0065	0088	0116	0151	0194
7	0001	0002	0003	0004	0007	0010	0015	0021	0029	0039
8					0001	0001	0002	0003	0004	0006
9										0001

P	21	22	23	24	25	26	27	28	29	30
R										
1	9409	9493	9566	9629	9683	9730	9771	9806	9836	9862
2	7524	7776	8009	8222	8416	8594	8755	8900	9032	9150
3	4768	5114	5450	5778	6093	6397	6687	6963	7225	7472
4	2326	2610	2904	3205	3512	3824	4137	4452	4765	5075
5	0866	1021	1192	1377	1576	1790	2016	2254	2504	2763
6	0245	0304	0374	0453	0544	0646	0760	0887	1026	1178
7	0052	0068	0089	0113	0143	0178	0219	0267	0322	0386
8	0008	0011	0016	0021	0028	0036	0047	0060	0076	0095
9	0001	0001	0002	0003	0004	0005	0007	0010	0013	0017
10						0001	0001	0001	0002	0002

P	31	32	33	34	35	36	37	38	39	40
R										
1	9884	9902	9918	9932	9943	9953	9961	9968	9973	9978
2	9256	9350	9435	9509	9576	9634	9685	9730	9770	9804
3	7704	7922	8124	8313	8487	8648	8795	8931	9054	9166
4	5381	5681	5973	6258	6533	6799	7053	7296	7528	7747
5	3032	3308	3590	3876	4167	4459	4751	5043	5332	5618
6	1343	1521	1711	1913	2127	2352	2588	2833	3087	3348
7	0458	0540	0632	0734	0846	0970	1106	1253	1411	1582
8	0118	0144	0176	0213	0255	0304	0359	0422	0493	0573
9	0022	0028	0036	0045	0056	0070	0086	0104	0127	0153
10	0003	0004	0005	0007	0008	0011	0014	0018	0022	0028
11				0001	0001	0001	0001	0002	0002	0003

P	41	42	43	44	45	46	47	48	49	50
R										
1	9982	9986	9988	9990	9992	9994	9995	9996	9997	9998
2	9834	9860	9882	9901	9917	9931	9943	9953	9961	9968
3	9267	9358	9440	9513	9579	9637	9688	9733	9773	9807
4	7953	8147	8329	8498	8655	8801	8934	9057	9168	9270
5	5899	6175	6443	6704	6956	7198	7430	7652	7862	8062
6	3616	3889	4167	4448	4731	5014	5297	5577	5855	6128
7	1765	1959	2164	2380	2607	2843	3089	3343	3604	3872
8	0662	0760	0869	0988	1117	1258	1411	1575	1751	1938
9	0183	0218	0258	0304	0356	0415	0481	0555	0638	0730
10	0035	0043	0053	0065	0079	0095	0114	0137	0163	0193
11	0004	0005	0007	0009	0011	0014	0017	0021	0026	0032
12				0001	0001	0001	0001	0001	0002	0002

$$n = 13$$

P	01	02	03	04	05	06	07	08	09	10
R										
1	1225	2310	3270	4118	4867	5526	6107	6617	7065	7458
2	0072	0270	0564	0932	1354	1814	2298	2794	3293	3787
3	0003	0020	0062	0135	0245	0392	0578	0799	1054	1339
4		0001	0005	0014	0031	0060	0103	0163	0242	0342
5				0001	0003	0007	0013	0024	0041	0065
6						0001	0001	0003	0005	0009
7									0001	0001

P	11	12	13	14	15	16	17	18	19	20
R										
1	7802	8102	8364	8592	8791	8963	9113	9242	9354	9450
2	4270	4738	5186	5614	6017	6396	6751	7080	7384	7664
3	1651	1985	2337	2704	3080	3463	3848	4231	4611	4983
4	0464	0609	0776	0967	1180	1414	1667	1939	2226	2527
5	0097	0139	0193	0260	0342	0438	0551	0681	0827	0991
6	0015	0024	0036	0053	0075	0104	0139	0183	0237	0300
7	0002	0003	0005	0008	0013	0019	0027	0038	0052	0070
8			0001	0001	0002	0003	0004	0006	0009	0012
9								0001	0001	0002

Cumulative binomial distribution (*continued*)

P	21	22	23	24	25	26	27	28	29	30
R										
1	9533	9604	9666	9718	9762	9800	9833	9860	9883	9903
2	7920	8154	8367	8559	8733	8889	9029	9154	9265	9363
3	5347	5699	6039	6364	6674	6968	7245	7505	7749	7975
4	2839	3161	3489	3822	4157	4493	4826	5155	5478	5794
5	1173	1371	1585	1816	2060	2319	2589	2870	3160	3457
6	0375	0462	0562	0675	0802	0944	1099	1270	1455	1654
7	0093	0120	0154	0195	0243	0299	0365	0440	0527	0624
8	0017	0024	0032	0043	0056	0073	0093	0118	0147	0182
9	0002	0004	0005	0007	0010	0013	0018	0024	0031	0040
10			0001	0001	0001	0002	0003	0004	0005	0007
11									0001	0001

P	31	32	33	34	35	36	37	38	39	40
R										
1	9920	9934	9945	9955	9963	9970	9975	9980	9984	9987
2	9450	9527	9594	9653	9704	9749	9787	9821	9849	9874
3	8185	8379	8557	8720	8868	9003	9125	9235	9333	9421
4	6101	6398	6683	6957	7217	7464	7698	7917	8123	8314
5	3760	4067	4376	4686	4995	5301	5603	5899	6188	6470
6	1867	2093	2331	2581	2841	3111	3388	3673	3962	4256
7	0733	0854	0988	1135	1295	1468	1654	1853	2065	2288
8	0223	0271	0326	0390	0462	0544	0635	0738	0851	0977
9	0052	0065	0082	0102	0126	0154	0187	0225	0270	0321
10	0009	0012	0015	0020	0025	0032	0040	0051	0063	0078
11	0001	0001	0002	0003	0003	0005	0006	0008	0010	0013
12							0001	0001	0001	0001

P	41	42	43	44	45	46	47	48	49	50
R										
1	9990	9992	9993	9995	9996	9997	9997	9998	9998	9999
2	9895	9912	9928	9940	9951	9960	9967	9974	9979	9983
3	9499	9569	9630	9684	9731	9772	9808	9838	9865	9888
4	8492	8656	8807	8945	9071	9185	9288	9381	9464	9539
5	6742	7003	7254	7493	7721	7935	8137	8326	8502	8666
6	4552	4849	5146	5441	5732	6019	6299	6573	6838	7095
7	2524	2770	3025	3290	3563	3842	4127	4415	4707	5000
8	1114	1264	1426	1600	1788	1988	2200	2424	2659	2905
9	0379	0446	0520	0605	0698	0803	0918	1045	1183	1334
10	0096	0117	0141	0170	0203	0242	0287	0338	0396	0461
11	0017	0021	0027	0033	0041	0051	0063	0077	0093	0112
12	0002	0002	0003	0004	0005	0007	0009	0011	0014	0017
13							0001	0001	0001	0001

$$n = 14$$

P	01	02	03	04	05	06	07	08	09	10
R										
1	1313	2464	3472	4353	5123	5795	6380	6888	7330	7712
2	0084	0310	0645	1059	1530	2037	2564	3100	3632	4154
3	0003	0025	0077	0167	0301	0478	0698	0958	1255	1584
4		0001	0006	0019	0042	0080	0136	0214	0315	0441
5				0002	0004	0010	0020	0035	0059	0092
6						0001	0002	0004	0008	0015
7									0001	0002

P	11	12	13	14	15	16	17	18	19	20
R										
1	8044	8330	8577	8789	8972	9129	9264	9379	9477	9560
2	4658	5141	5599	6031	6433	6807	7152	7469	7758	8021
3	1939	2315	2708	3111	3521	3932	4341	4744	5138	5519
4	0594	0774	0979	1210	1465	1742	2038	2351	2679	3018
5	0137	0196	0269	0359	0467	0594	0741	0907	1093	1298
6	0024	0038	0057	0082	0115	0157	0209	0273	0349	0439
7	0003	0006	0009	0015	0022	0032	0046	0064	0087	0116
8		0001	0001	0002	0003	0005	0008	0012	0017	0024
9						0001	0001	0002	0003	0004

P	21	22	23	24	25	26	27	28	29	30
R										
1	9631	9691	9742	9786	9822	9852	9878	9899	9917	9932
2	8259	8473	8665	8837	8990	9126	9246	9352	9444	9525
3	5887	6239	6574	6891	7189	7467	7727	7967	8188	8392
4	3366	3719	4076	4432	4787	5136	5479	5813	6137	6448
5	1523	1765	2023	2297	2585	2884	3193	3509	3832	4158
6	0543	0662	0797	0949	1117	1301	1502	1718	1949	2195
7	0152	0196	0248	0310	0383	0467	0563	0673	0796	0933
8	0033	0045	0060	0079	0103	0132	0167	0208	0257	0315
9	0006	0008	0011	0016	0022	0029	0038	0050	0065	0083
10	0001	0001	0002	0002	0003	0005	0007	0009	0012	0017
11						0001	0001	0001	0002	0002

P	31	32	33	34	35	36	37	38	39	40
R										
1	9945	9955	9963	9970	9976	9981	9984	9988	9990	9992
2	9596	9657	9710	9756	9795	9828	9857	9881	9902	9919
3	8577	8746	8899	9037	9161	9271	9370	9457	9534	9602
4	6747	7032	7301	7556	7795	8018	8226	8418	8595	8757
5	4486	4813	5138	5458	5773	6080	6378	6666	6943	7207
6	2454	2724	3006	3297	3595	3899	4208	4519	4831	5141
7	1084	1250	1431	1626	1836	2059	2296	2545	2805	3075
8	0381	0458	0545	0643	0753	0876	1012	1162	1325	1501
9	0105	0131	0163	0200	0243	0294	0353	0420	0497	0583
10	0022	0029	0037	0048	0060	0076	0095	0117	0144	0175
11	0003	0005	0006	0008	0011	0014	0019	0024	0031	0039
12		0001	0001	0001	0001	0002	0003	0003	0005	0006
13										0001

P	41	42	43	44	45	46	47	48	49	50
R										
1	9994	9995	9996	9997	9998	9998	9999	9999	9999	9999
2	9934	9946	9956	9964	9971	9977	9981	9985	9988	9991
3	9661	9713	9758	9797	9830	9858	9883	9903	9921	9935
4	8905	9039	9161	9270	9368	9455	9532	9601	9661	9713
5	7459	7697	7922	8132	8328	8510	8678	8833	8974	9102
6	5450	5754	6052	6344	6627	6900	7163	7415	7654	7880
7	3355	3643	3937	4236	4539	4843	5148	5451	5751	6047
8	1692	1896	2113	2344	2586	2840	3105	3380	3663	3953
9	0680	0789	0910	1043	1189	1348	1520	1707	1906	2120
10	0212	0255	0304	0361	0426	0500	0583	0677	0782	0898
11	0049	0061	0076	0093	0114	0139	0168	0202	0241	0287
12	0008	0010	0013	0017	0022	0027	0034	0042	0053	0065
13	0001	0001	0001	0002	0003	0003	0004	0006	0007	0009
14										0001

$$n = 15$$

P	01	02	03	04	05	06	07	08	09	10
R										
1	1399	2614	3667	4579	5367	6047	6633	7137	7570	7941
2	0096	0353	0730	1191	1710	2262	2832	3403	3965	4510
3	0004	0030	0094	0203	0362	0571	0829	1130	1469	1841
4		0002	0008	0024	0055	0104	0175	0273	0399	0556
5			0001	0002	00·06	0014	0028	0050	0082	0127
6					0001	0001	0003	0007	0013	0022
7							0001	0002	0003

P	11	12	13	14	15	16	17	18	19	20
R										
1	8259	8530	8762	8959	9126	9269	9389	9490	9576	9648
2	5031	5524	5987	6417	6814	7179	7511	7813	8085	8329
3	2238	2654	3084	3520	3958	4392	4819	5234	5635	6020
4	0742	0959	1204	1476	1773	2092	2429	2782	3146	3518
5	0187	0265	0361	0478	0617	0778	0961	1167	1394	1642
6	0037	0057	0084	0121	0168	0227	0300	0387	0490	0611
7	0006	0010	0015	0024	0036	0052	0074	0102	0137	0181
8	0001	0001	0002	0004	0006	0010	0014	0021	0030	0042
9					0001	0001	0002	0003	0005	0008
10									0001	0001

Cumulative binomial distribution (*continued*)

P / R	21	22	23	24	25	26	27	28	29	30
1	9709	9759	9802	9837	9866	9891	9911	9928	9941	9953
2	8547	8741	8913	9065	9198	9315	9417	9505	9581	9647
3	6385	6731	7055	7358	7639	7899	8137	8355	8553	8732
4	3895	4274	4650	5022	5387	5742	6086	6416	6732	7031
5	1910	2195	2495	2810	3135	3469	3810	4154	4500	4845
6	0748	0905	1079	1272	1484	1713	1958	2220	2495	2784
7	0234	0298	0374	0463	0566	0684	0817	0965	1130	1311
8	0058	0078	0104	0135	0173	0219	0274	0338	0413	0500
9	0011	0016	0023	0031	0042	0056	0073	0094	0121	0152
10	0002	0003	0004	0006	0008	0011	0015	0021	0028	0037
11			0001	0001	0001	0002	0002	0003	0005	0007
12									0001	0001

P / R	31	32	33	34	35	36	37	38	39	40
1	9962	9969	9975	9980	9984	9988	9990	9992	9994	9995
2	9704	9752	9794	9829	9858	9883	9904	9922	9936	9948
3	8893	9038	9167	9281	9383	9472	9550	9618	9678	9729
4	7314	7580	7829	8060	8273	8469	8649	8813	8961	9095
5	5187	5523	5852	6171	6481	6778	7062	7332	7587	7827
6	3084	3393	3709	4032	4357	4684	5011	5335	5654	5968
7	1509	1722	1951	2194	2452	2722	3003	3295	3595	3902
8	0599	0711	0837	0977	1132	1302	1487	1687	1902	2131
9	0190	0236	0289	0351	0422	0504	0597	0702	0820	0950
10	0048	0062	0079	0099	0124	0154	0190	0232	0281	0338
11	0009	0012	0016	0022	0028	0037	0047	0059	0075	0093
12	0001	0002	C003	0004	0005	0006	0009	0011	0015	0019
13				0001	0001	0001	0002	0002	0003	

P / R	41	42	43	44	45	46	47	48	49	50
1	9996	9997	9998	9998	9999	9999	9999	9999	10000	10000
2	9958	9966	9973	9979	9983	9987	9990	9992	9994	9995
3	9773	9811	9843	9870	9893	9913	9929	9943	9954	9963
4	9215	9322	9417	9502	9576	9641	9697	9746	9788	9824
5	8052	8261	8454	8633	8796	8945	9080	9201	9310	9408
6	6274	6570	6856	7131	7392	7641	7875	8095	8301	8491
7	4214	4530	4847	5164	5478	5789	6095	6394	6684	6964
8	2374	2630	2898	3176	3465	3762	4065	4374	4686	5000
9	1095	1254	1427	1615	1818	2034	2265	2510	2767	3036
10	0404	0479	0565	0661	0769	0890	1024	1171	1333	1509
11	0116	0143	0174	0211	0255	0305	0363	0430	0506	0592
12	0025	0032	0040	0051	0063	0079	0097	0119	0145	0176
13	0004	0005	0007	0009	0011	0014	0018	0023	0029	0037
14			0001	0001	0001	0002	0002	0003	0004	0005

$$n = 16$$

P / R	01	02	03	04	05	06	07	08	09	10
1	1485	2762	3857	4796	5599	6284	6869	7366	7789	8147
2	0109	0399	0818	1327	1892	2489	3098	3701	4289	4853
3	0005	0037	0113	0242	0429	0673	0969	1311	1694	2108
4		0002	0011	0032	0070	0132	0221	0342	0496	0684
5			0001	0003	0009	0019	0038	0068	0111	0170
6					0001	0002	0005	0010	0019	0033
7							0001	0001	0003	0005
8										0001

P / R	11	12	13	14	15	16	17	18	19	20
1	8450	8707	8923	9105	9257	9386	9493	9582	9657	9719
2	5386	5885	6347	6773	7161	7513	7830	8115	8368	8593
3	2545	2999	3461	3926	4386	4838	5277	5698	6101	6482
4	09C7	1162	1448	1763	2101	2460	2836	3223	3619	4019
5	0248	0348	0471	0618	0791	0988	1211	1458	1727	2018
6	0053	0082	0120	0171	0235	0315	0412	0527	0662	0817
7	0009	0015	0024	0038	0056	0080	0112	0153	0204	0267
8	0001	0002	0004	0007	0011	0016	0024	0036	0051	0070
9			0001	0001	0002	0003	0004	0007	0010	0015
10							0001	0001	0002	0002

P	21	22	23	24	25	26	27	28	29	30
R										
1	9770	9812	9847	9876	9900	9919	9935	9948	9958	9967
2	8791	8965	9117	9250	9365	9465	9550	9623	9686	9739
3	6839	7173	7483	7768	8029	8267	8482	8677	8851	9006
4	4418	4814	5203	5583	5950	6303	6640	6959	7260	7541
5	2327	2652	2991	3341	3698	4060	4425	4788	5147	5501
6	0992	1188	1405	1641	1897	2169	2458	2761	3077	3402
7	0342	0432	0536	0657	0796	0951	1125	1317	1526	1753
8	0095	0127	0166	0214	0271	0340	0420	0514	0621	0744
9	0021	0030	0041	0056	0075	0098	0127	0163	0206	0257
10	0004	0006	0008	0012	0016	0023	0031	0041	0055	0071
11	0001	0001	0001	0002	0003	0004	0006	0008	0011	0016
12						0001	0001	0001	0002	0003

P	31	32	33	34	35	36	37	38	39	40
R										
1	9974	9979	9984	9987	9990	9992	9994	9995	9996	9997
2	9784	9822	9854	9880	9902	9921	9936	9948	9959	9967
3	9144	9266	9374	9467	9549	9620	9681	9734	9778	9817
4	7804	8047	8270	8475	8661	8830	8982	9119	9241	9349
5	5846	6181	6504	6813	7108	7387	7649	7895	8123	8334
6	3736	4074	4416	4759	5100	5438	5770	6094	6408	6712
7	1997	2257	2531	2819	3119	3428	3746	4070	4398	4728
8	0881	1035	1205	1391	1594	1813	2048	2298	2562	2839
9	0317	0388	0470	0564	0671	0791	0926	1076	1242	1423
10	0092	0117	0148	0185	0229	0280	0341	0411	0491	0583
11	0021	0028	0037	0048	0062	0079	0100	0125	0155	0191
12	0004	0005	0007	0010	0013	0017	0023	0030	0038	0049
13		0001	0001	0001	0002	0003	0004	0005	0007	0009
14								0001	0001	0001

P	41	42	43	44	45	46	47	48	49	50
R										
1	9998	9998	9999	9999	9999	9999	10000	10000	10000	10000
2	9974	9979	9984	9987	9990	9994	9994	9995	9997	9997
3	9849	9876	9899	9918	9934	9947	9958	9966	9973	9979
4	9444	9527	9600	9664	9719	9766	9806	9840	9869	9894
5	8529	8707	8869	9015	9147	9265	9370	9463	9544	9616
6	7003	7280	7543	7792	8024	8241	8441	8626	8795	8949
7	5058	5387	5711	6029	6340	6641	6932	7210	7476	7728
8	3128	3428	3736	4051	4371	4694	5019	5343	5665	5982
9	1619	1832	2060	2302	2559	2829	3111	3405	3707	4018
10	0687	0805	0936	1081	1241	1416	1607	1814	2036	2272
11	0234	0284	0342	0409	0486	0574	0674	0786	0911	1051
12	0062	0078	0098	0121	0149	0183	0222	0268	0322	0384
13	0012	0016	0021	0027	0035	0044	0055	0069	0086	0106
14	0002	0002	0003	0004	0006	0007	0010	0013	0016	0021
15					0001	0001	0001	0001	0002	0003

$$n = 17$$

P	01	02	03	04	05	06	07	08	09	10
R										
1	1571	2907	4042	5004	5819	6507	7088	7577	7988	8332
2	0123	0446	0909	1465	2078	2717	3362	3995	4604	5182
3	0006	0044	0134	0286	0503	0782	1118	1503	1927	2382
4		0003	0014	0040	0088	0164	0273	0419	0603	0826
5			0001	0004	0012	0026	0051	0089	0145	0221
6					0001	0003	0007	0015	0027	0047
7							0001	0002	0004	0008
8										0001

P	11	12	13	14	15	16	17	18	19	20
R										
1	8621	8862	9063	9230	9369	9484	9579	9657	9722	9775
2	5723	6223	6682	7099	7475	7813	8113	8379	8613	8818
3	2858	3345	3836	4324	4802	5266	5711	6133	6532	6904
4	1087	1383	1710	2065	2444	2841	3251	3669	4091	4511
5	0321	0446	0598	0778	0987	1224	1487	1775	2087	2418
6	0075	0114	0166	0234	0319	0423	0548	0695	0864	1057
7	0014	0023	0037	0056	0083	0118	0163	0220	0291	0377
8	0002	0004	0007	0011	0017	0027	0039	0057	0080	0109
9		0001	0001	0002	0003	0005	0008	0012	0018	0026
10						0001	0001	0002	0003	0005
11										0001

Cumulative binomial distribution (*continued*)

P	21	22	23	24	25	26	27	28	29	30
R										
1	9818	9854	9882	9906	9925	9940	9953	9962	9970	9977
2	8996	9152	9285	9400	9499	9583	9654	9714	9765	9807
3	7249	7567	7859	8123	8363	8578	8771	8942	9093	9226
4	4927	5333	5728	6107	6470	6814	7137	7440	7721	7981
5	2766	3128	3500	3879	4261	4643	5023	5396	5760	6113
6	1273	1510	1770	2049	2347	2661	2989	3329	3677	4032
7	0479	0598	0736	0894	1071	1268	1485	1721	1976	2248
8	0147	0194	0251	0320	0402	0499	0611	0739	0884	1046
9	0037	0051	0070	0094	0124	0161	0206	0261	0326	0403
10	0007	0011	0016	0022	0031	0042	0057	0075	0098	0127
11	0001	0002	0003	0004	0006	0009	0013	0018	0024	0032
12				0001	0001	0002	0002	0003	0005	0007
13									0001	0001

P	31	32	33	34	35	36	37	38	39	40
R										
1	9982	9986	9989	9991	9993	9995	9996	9997	9998	9998
2	9843	9872	9896	9917	9933	9946	9957	9966	9973	9979
3	9343	9444	9532	9608	9673	9728	9775	9815	9849	9877
4	8219	8437	8634	8812	8972	9115	9241	9353	9450	9536
5	6453	6778	7087	7378	7652	7906	8142	8360	8559	8740
6	4390	4749	5105	5458	5803	6139	6465	6778	7077	7361
7	2536	2838	3153	3479	3812	4152	4495	4839	5182	5522
8	1227	1426	1642	1877	2128	2395	2676	2971	3278	3595
9	0492	0595	0712	0845	0994	1159	1341	1541	1757	1989
10	0162	0204	0254	0314	0383	0464	0557	0664	0784	0919
11	0043	0057	0074	0095	0120	0151	0189	0234	0286	0348
12	0009	0013	0017	0023	0030	0040	0051	0066	0084	0106
13	0002	0002	0003	0004	0006	0008	0011	0015	0019	0025
14				0001	0001	0001	0002	0002	0003	0005
15										0001

P	41	42	43	44	45	46	47	48	49	50
R										
1	9999	9999	9999	9999	10000	10000	10000	10000	10000	10000
2	9984	9987	9990	9992	9994	9996	9997	9998	9998	9999
3	9900	9920	9935	9948	9959	9968	9975	9980	9985	9988
4	9610	9674	9729	9776	9816	9849	9877	9901	9920	9936
5	8904	9051	9183	9301	9404	9495	9575	9644	9704	9755
6	7628	7879	8113	8330	8529	8712	8878	9028	9162	9283
7	5856	6182	6499	6805	7098	7377	7641	7890	8122	8338
8	3920	4250	4585	4921	5257	5590	5918	6239	6552	6855
9	2238	2502	2780	3072	3374	3687	4008	4335	4667	5000
10	1070	1236	1419	1618	1834	2066	2314	2577	2855	3145
11	0480	0503	0597	0705	0826	0962	1112	1279	1462	1662
12	0133	0165	0203	0248	0301	0363	0434	0517	0611	0717
13	0033	0042	0054	0069	0086	0108	0134	0165	0202	0245
14	0006	0008	0011	0014	0019	0024	0031	0040	0050	0064
15	0001	0001	0002	0002	0003	0004	0005	0007	0009	0012
16							0001	0001	0001	0001

$$n = 18$$

P	01	02	03	04	05	06	07	08	09	10
R										
1	1655	3049	4220	5204	6028	6717	7292	7771	8169	8499
2	0138	0495	1003	1607	2265	2945	3622	4281	4909	5497
3	0007	0052	0157	0333	0581	0898	1275	1702	2168	2662
4		0004	0018	0050	0109	0201	0333	0506	0723	0982
5			0002	0006	0015	0034	0067	0116	0186	0282
6				0001	0002	0005	0010	0021	0038	0064
7							0001	0003	0006	0012
8									0001	0002

P	11	12	13	14	15	16	17	18	19	20
R										
1	8773	8998	9185	9338	9464	9566	9651	9719	9775	9820
2	6042	6540	6992	7398	7759	8080	8362	8609	8824	9009
3	3173	3690	4206	4713	5203	5673	6119	6538	6927	7287
4	1282	1618	1986	2382	2798	3229	3669	4112	4554	4990
5	0405	0558	0743	0959	1206	1482	1787	2116	2467	2836

P	11	12	13	14	15	16	17	18	19	20
R										
6	0102	0154	0222	0310	0419	0551	0708	0889	1097	1329
7	0021	0034	0054	0081	0118	0167	0229	0306	0400	0513
8	0003	0006	0011	0017	0027	0041	0060	0086	0120	0163
9		0001	0002	0003	0005	0008	0013	0020	0029	0043
10					0001	0001	0002	0004	0006	0009
11								0001	0001	0002

P	21	22	23	24	25	26	27	28	29	30
R										
1	9856	9886	9909	9928	9944	9956	9965	9973	9979	9984
2	9169	9306	9423	9522	9605	9676	9735	9784	9824	9858
3	7616	7916	8187	8430	8647	8839	9009	9158	9288	9400
4	5414	5825	6218	6591	6943	7272	7578	7860	8119	8354
5	3220	3613	4012	4414	4813	5208	5594	5968	6329	6673
6	1586	1866	2168	2488	2825	3176	3538	3907	4281	4656
7	0645	0799	0974	1171	1390	1630	1891	2171	2469	2783
8	0217	0283	0363	0458	0569	0699	0847	1014	1200	1407
9	0060	0083	0112	0148	0193	0249	0316	0395	0488	0596
10	0014	0020	0028	0039	0054	0073	0097	0127	0164	0210
11	0003	0004	0006	0009	0012	0018	0025	0034	0046	0061
12		0001	0001	0002	0002	0003	0005	0007	0010	0014
13					0001	0001	0001	0002	0003

P	31	32	33	34	35	36	37	38	39	40
R										
1	9987	9990	9993	9994	9996	9997	9998	9998	9999	9999
2	9886	9908	9927	9942	9954	9964	9972	9978	9983	9987
3	9498	9581	9652	9713	9764	9807	9843	9873	9897	9918
4	8568	8759	8931	9083	9217	9335	9439	9528	9606	9672
5	7001	7309	7598	7866	8114	8341	8549	8737	8907	9058
6	5029	5398	5759	6111	6450	6776	7086	7379	7655	7912
7	3111	3450	3797	4151	4509	4867	5224	5576	5921	6257
8	1633	1878	2141	2421	2717	3027	3349	3681	4021	4366
9	0720	0861	1019	1196	1391	1604	1835	2084	2350	2632
10	0264	0329	0405	0494	0597	0714	0847	0997	1163	1347
11	0080	0104	0133	0169	0212	0264	0325	0397	0480	0576
12	0020	0027	0036	0047	0062	0080	0102	0130	0163	0203
13	0004	0005	0008	0011	0014	0019	0026	0034	0044	0058
14	0001	0001	0001	0002	0003	0004	0005	0007	0010	0013
15					0001	0001	0001	0002	0002

P	41	42	43	44	45	46	47	48	49	50
R										
1	9999	9999	10000	10000	10000	10000	10000	10000	10000	10000
2	9990	9992	9994	9996	9997	9998	9998	9999	9999	9999
3	9934	9948	9959	9968	9975	9981	9985	9989	9991	9993
4	9729	9777	9818	9852	9880	9904	9923	9939	9952	9962
5	9193	9313	9418	9510	9589	9658	9717	9767	9810	9846
6	8151	8372	8573	8757	8923	9072	9205	9324	9428	9519
7	6582	6895	7193	7476	7742	7991	8222	8436	8632	8811
8	4713	5062	5408	5750	6085	6412	6728	7032	7322	7597
9	2928	3236	3556	3885	4222	4562	4906	5249	5591	5927
10	1549	1768	2004	2258	2527	2812	3110	3421	3742	4073
11	0686	0811	0951	1107	1280	1470	1677	1902	2144	2403
12	0250	0307	0372	0449	0537	0638	0753	0883	1028	1189
13	0074	0094	0118	0147	0183	0225	0275	0334	0402	0481
14	0017	0022	0029	0038	0049	0063	0079	0100	0125	0154
15	0003	0004	0006	0007	0010	0013	0017	0023	0029	0038
16		0001	0001	0001	0001	0002	0003	0004	0005	0007
17									0001	0001

$$n = 19$$

P	01	02	03	04	05	06	07	08	09	10
R										
1	1738	3188	4394	5396	6226	6914	7481	7949	8334	8649
2	0153	0546	1100	1751	2453	3171	3879	4560	5202	5797
3	0009	0061	0183	0384	0665	1021	1439	1908	2415	2946
4		0005	0022	0061	0132	0243	0398	0602	0853	1150
5			0002	0007	0020	0044	0085	0147	0235	0352
6				0001	0002	0006	0014	0029	0051	0086
7						0001	0002	0004	0009	0017
8								0001	0001	0003

Cumulative binomial distribution (*continued*)

P	11	12	13	14	15	16	17	18	19	20
R										
1	8908	9119	9291	9431	9544	9636	9710	9770	9818	9856
2	6342	6835	7277	7669	8015	8318	8581	8809	9004	9171
3	3488	4032	4568	5089	5587	6059	6500	6910	7287	7631
4	1490	1867	2275	2708	3159	3620	4085	4549	5005	5449
5	0502	0685	0904	1158	1444	1762	2107	2476	2864	3267
6	0135	0202	0290	0401	0537	0700	0891	1110	1357	1631
7	0030	0048	0076	0113	0163	0228	0310	0411	0532	0676
8	0005	0009	0016	0026	0041	0061	0089	0126	0173	0233
9	0001	0002	0003	0005	0008	0014	0021	0032	0047	0067
10				0001	0001	0002	0004	0007	0010	0016
11							0001	0001	0002	0003

P	21	22	23	24	25	26	27	28	29	30
R										
1	9887	9911	9930	9946	9958	9967	9975	9981	9985	9989
2	9313	9434	9535	9619	9690	9749	9797	9837	9869	9896
3	7942	8222	8471	8692	8887	9057	9205	9333	9443	9538
4	5877	6285	6671	7032	7369	7680	7965	8224	8458	8668
5	3681	4100	4520	4936	5346	5744	6129	6498	6848	7178
6	1929	2251	2592	2950	3322	3705	4093	4484	4875	5261
7	0843	1034	1248	1487	1749	2032	2336	2657	2995	3345
8	0307	0396	0503	0629	0775	0941	1129	1338	1568	1820
9	0093	0127	0169	0222	0287	0366	0459	0568	0694	0839
10	0023	0034	0047	0066	0089	0119	0156	0202	0258	0326
11	0005	0007	0011	0016	0023	0032	0044	0060	0080	0105
12	0001	0001	0002	0003	0005	0007	0010	0015	0021	0028
13				0001	0001	0001	0002	0003	0004	0006
14									0001	0001

P	31	32	33	34	35	36	37	38	39	40
R										
1	9991	9993	9995	9996	9997	9998	9998	9999	9999	9999
2	9917	9935	9949	9960	9969	9976	9981	9986	9989	9992
3	9618	9686	9743	9791	9830	9863	9890	9913	9931	9945
4	8856	9028	9169	9297	9409	9505	9588	9659	9719	9770
5	7486	7773	8037	8280	8500	8699	8878	9038	9179	9304
6	5641	6010	6366	6707	7032	7339	7627	7895	8143	8371
7	3705	4073	4445	4818	5188	5554	5913	6261	6597	6919
8	2091	2381	2688	3010	3344	3690	4043	4401	4762	5122
9	1003	1186	1389	1612	1855	2116	2395	2691	3002	3325
10	0405	0499	0608	0733	0875	1035	1213	1410	1626	1861
11	0137	0176	0223	0280	0347	0426	0518	0625	0747	0885
12	0038	0051	0068	0089	0114	0146	0185	0231	0287	0352
13	0009	0012	0017	0023	0031	0041	0054	0070	0091	0116
14	0002	0002	0003	0005	0007	0009	0013	0017	0023	0031
15			0001	0001	0001	0002	0002	0003	0005	0006
16									0001	0001

P	41	42	43	44	45	46	47	48	49	50
R										
1	10000	10000	10000	10000	10000	10000	10000	10000	10000	10000
2	9994	9995	9996	9997	9998	9999	9999	9999	9999	10000
3	9957	9967	9974	9980	9985	9988	9991	9993	9995	9996
4	9813	9849	9878	9903	9923	9939	9952	9963	9971	9978
5	9413	9508	9590	9660	9720	9771	9814	9850	9879	9904
6	8579	8767	8937	9088	9223	9342	9446	9537	9615	9682
7	7226	7515	7787	8039	8273	8488	8684	8862	9022	9165
8	5480	5832	6176	6509	6831	7138	7430	7706	7964	8204
9	3660	4003	4353	4706	5060	5413	5762	6105	6439	6762
10	2114	2385	2672	2974	3290	3617	3954	4299	4648	5000
11	1040	1213	1404	1613	1841	2087	2351	2631	2928	3238
12	0429	0518	0621	0738	0871	1021	1187	1372	1575	1796
13	0146	0183	0227	0280	0342	0415	0500	0597	0709	0835
14	0040	0052	0067	0086	0109	0137	0171	0212	0261	0318
15	0009	0012	0016	0021	0028	0036	0046	0060	0076	0096
16	0001	0002	0003	0004	0005	0007	0010	0013	0017	0022
17				0001	0001	0001	0001	0002	0003	0004

$$n = 20$$

P	01	02	03	04	05	06	07	08	09	10
R										
1	1821	3324	4562	5580	6415	7099	7658	8113	8484	8784
2	0169	0599	1198	1897	2642	3395	4131	4831	5484	6083
3	0010	0071	0210	0439	0755	1150	1610	2121	2666	3231
4		0006	0027	0074	0159	0290	0471	0706	0993	1330
5			0003	0010	0026	0056	0107	0183	0290	0432
6				0001	0003	0009	0019	0038	0068	0113
7						0001	0003	0006	0013	0024
8								0001	0002	0004
9										0001

P	11	12	13	14	15	16	17	18	19	20
R										
1	9028	9224	9383	9510	9612	9694	9759	9811	9852	9885
2	6624	7109	7539	7916	8244	8529	8773	8982	9159	9308
3	3802	4369	4920	5450	5951	6420	6854	7252	7614	7939
4	1710	2127	2573	3041	3523	4010	4496	4974	5439	5886
5	0610	0827	1083	1375	1702	2059	2443	2849	3271	3704
6	0175	0260	0370	0507	0673	0870	1098	1356	1643	1958
7	0041	0067	0103	0153	0219	0304	0409	0537	0689	0867
8	0008	0014	0024	0038	0059	0088	0127	0177	0241	0321
9	0001	0002	0005	0008	0013	0021	0033	0049	0071	0100
10			0001	0001	0002	0004	0007	0011	0017	0026
11						0001	0001	0002	0004	0006
12									0001	0001

P	21	22	23	24	25	26	27	28	29	30
R										
1	9910	9931	9946	9959	9968	9976	9982	9986	9989	9992
2	9434	9539	9626	9698	9757	9805	9845	9877	9903	9924
3	8230	8488	8716	8915	9087	9237	9365	9474	9567	9645
4	6310	6711	7085	7431	7748	8038	8300	8534	8744	8929
5	4142	4580	5014	5439	5852	6248	6625	6981	7315	7625
6	2297	2657	3035	3427	3828	4235	4643	5048	5447	5836
7	1071	1301	1557	1838	2142	2467	2810	3169	3540	3920
8	0419	0536	0675	0835	1018	1225	1455	1707	1982	2277
9	0138	0186	0246	0320	0409	0515	0640	0784	0948	1133
10	0038	0054	0075	0103	0139	0183	0238	0305	0385	0480
11	0009	0013	0019	0028	0039	0055	0074	0100	0132	0171
12	0002	0003	0004	0006	0009	0014	0019	0027	0038	0051
13			0001	0001	0002	0003	0004	0006	0009	0013
14							0001	0001	0002	0003

P	31	32	33	34	35	36	37	38	39	40
R										
1	9994	9996	9997	9998	9998	9999	9999	9999	9999	10000
2	9940	9953	9964	9972	9979	9984	9988	9991	9993	9995
3	9711	9765	9811	9848	9879	9904	9924	9940	9953	9964
4	9092	9235	9358	9465	9556	9634	9700	9755	9802	9840
5	7911	8173	8411	8626	8818	8989	9141	9274	9390	9490
6	6213	6574	6917	7242	7546	7829	8090	8329	8547	8744
7	4305	4693	5079	5460	5834	6197	6547	6882	7200	7500
8	2591	2922	3268	3624	3990	4361	4735	5108	5478	5841
9	1340	1568	1818	2087	2376	2683	3005	3341	3688	4044
10	0591	0719	0866	1032	1218	1424	1650	1897	2163	2447
11	0220	0279	0350	0434	0532	0645	0775	0923	1090	1275
12	0069	0091	0119	0154	0196	0247	0308	0381	0466	0565
13	0018	0025	0034	0045	0060	0079	0102	0132	0167	0210
14	0004	0006	0008	0011	0015	0021	0028	0037	0049	0065
15	0001	0001	0001	0002	0003	0004	0006	0009	0012	0016
16						0001	0001	0002	0002	0003

P	41	42	43	44	45	46	47	48	49	50
R										
1	10000	10000	10000	10000	10000	10000	10000	10000	10000	10000
2	9996	9997	9998	9998	9999	9999	9999	10000	10000	10000
3	9972	9979	9984	9988	9991	9993	9995	9996	9997	9998
4	9872	9898	9920	9937	9951	9962	9971	9977	9983	9987
5	9577	9651	9714	9767	9811	9848	9879	9904	9924	9941
R										
6	8921	9078	9217	9340	9447	9539	9619	9687	9745	9793
7	7780	8041	8281	8501	8701	8881	9042	9186	9312	9423
8	6196	6539	6868	7183	7480	7759	8020	8261	8482	8684
9	4406	4771	5136	5499	5857	6207	6546	6873	7186	7483
10	2748	3064	3394	3736	4086	4443	4804	5166	5525	5881
11	1480	1705	1949	2212	2493	2791	3104	3432	3771	4119
12	0679	0810	0958	1123	1308	1511	1734	1977	2238	2517
13	0262	0324	0397	0482	0580	0694	0823	0969	1133	1316
14	0084	0107	0136	0172	0214	0265	0326	0397	0480	0577
15	0022	0029	0038	0050	0064	0083	0105	0133	0166	0207
16	0004	0006	0008	0011	0015	0020	0027	0035	0046	0059
17	0001	0001	0001	0002	0003	0004	0005	0007	0010	0013
18						0001	0001	0001	0001	0002

APPENDIX THREE

Unit Normal Loss Integral

The following table presents the unit normal loss integral. In the example below, to determine the expected loss from point Q to the left-hand tail of the distribution when the loss per unit is C and the standard deviation of the distribution is σ,

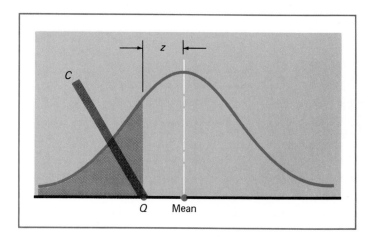

1 Determine distance z (the distance between point Q and the mean expressed in standard deviations).

2 Look up the value corresponding to z standard deviations in the unit normal loss integral table in this appendix (call this value *UNLI*).

3 Multiply together: $C \times \sigma \times UNLI$.

4 If the loss line crosses the mean, then the loss is $C \times \sigma \times (UNLI + z)$.

z	.00	.01	.02	.03	.04	.05	.06	.07	.08	.09
.0	.3989	.3940	.3890	.3841	.3793	.3744	.3697	.3649	.3602	.3556
.1	.3509	.3464	.3418	.3373	.3328	.3284	.3240	.3197	.3154	.3111
.2	.3069	.3027	.2986	.2944	.2904	.2863	.2824	.2784	.2745	.2706
.3	.2668	.2630	.2592	.2555	.2518	.2481	.2445	.2409	.2374	.2339
.4	.2304	.2270	.2236	.2203	.2169	.2137	.2104	.2072	.2040	.2009
.5	.1978	.1947	.1917	.1887	.1857	.1828	.1799	.1771	.1742	.1714
.6	.1687	.1659	.1633	.1606	.1580	.1554	.1528	.1503	.1478	.1453
.7	.1429	.1405	.1381	.1358	.1334	.1312	.1289	.1267	.1245	.1223
.8	.1202	.1181	.1160	.1140	.1120	.1100	.1080	.1061	.1042	.1023
.9	.1004	.09860	.09680	.09503	.09328	.09156	.08986	.08819	.08654	.08491
1.0	.08332	.08174	.08019	.07866	.07716	.07568	.07422	.07279	.07138	.06999
1.1	.06862	.06727	.06595	.06465	.06336	.06210	.06086	.05964	.05844	.05726
1.2	.05610	.05496	.05384	.05274	.05165	.05059	.04954	.04851	.04750	.04650
1.3	.04553	.04457	.04363	.04270	.04179	.04090	.04002	.03916	.03831	.03748
1.4	.03667	.03587	.03508	.03431	.03356	.03281	.03208	.03137	.03067	.02998
1.5	.02931	.02865	.02800	.02736	.02674	.02612	.02552	.02494	.02436	.02380
1.6	.02324	.02270	.02217	.02165	.02114	.02064	.02015	.01967	.01920	.01874
1.7	.01829	.01785	.01742	.01699	.01658	.01617	.01578	.01539	.01501	.01464
1.8	.01428	.01392	.01357	.01323	.01290	.01257	.01226	.01195	.01164	.01134
1.9	.01105	.01077	.01049	.01022	$.0^2$9957	$.0^2$9698	$.0^2$9445	$.0^2$9198	$.0^2$8957	$.0^2$8721
2.0	$.0^2$8491	$.0^2$8266	$.0^2$8046	$.0^2$7832	$.0^2$7623	$.0^2$7418	$.0^2$7219	$.0^2$7024	$.0^2$6835	$.0^2$6649
2.1	$.0^2$6468	$.0^2$6292	$.0^2$6120	$.0^2$5952	$.0^2$5788	$.0^2$5628	$.0^2$5472	$.0^2$5320	$.0^2$5172	$.0^2$5028
2.2	$.0^2$4887	$.0^2$4750	$.0^2$4616	$.0^2$4486	$.0^2$4358	$.0^2$4235	$.0^2$4114	$.0^2$3996	$.0^2$3882	$.0^2$3770
2.3	$.0^2$3662	$.0^2$3556	$.0^2$3453	$.0^2$3352	$.0^2$3255	$.0^2$3159	$.0^2$3067	$.0^2$2977	$.0^2$2889	$.0^2$2804
2.4	$.0^2$2720	$.0^2$2640	$.0^2$2561	$.0^2$2484	$.0^2$2410	$.0^2$2337	$.0^2$2267	$.0^2$2199	$.0^2$2132	$.0^2$2067
2.5	$.0^2$2004	$.0^2$1943	$.0^2$1883	$.0^2$1826	$.0^2$1769	$.0^2$1715	$.0^2$1662	$.0^2$1610	$.0^2$1560	$.0^2$1511
2.6	$.0^2$1464	$.0^2$1418	$.0^2$1373	$.0^2$1330	$.0^2$1288	$.0^2$1247	$.0^2$1207	$.0^2$1169	$.0^2$1132	$.0^2$1095
2.7	$.0^2$1060	$.0^2$1026	$.0^3$9928	$.0^3$9607	$.0^3$9295	$.0^3$8992	$.0^3$8699	$.0^3$8414	$.0^3$8138	$.0^3$7870
2.8	$.0^3$7611	$.0^3$7359	$.0^3$7115	$.0^3$6879	$.0^3$6650	$.0^3$6428	$.0^3$6213	$.0^3$6004	$.0^3$5802	$.0^3$5606
2.9	$.0^3$5417	$.0^3$5233	$.0^3$5055	$.0^3$4883	$.0^3$4716	$.0^3$4555	$.0^3$4398	$.0^3$4247	$.0^3$4101	$.0^3$3959
3.0	$.0^3$3822	$.0^3$3689	$.0^3$3560	$.0^3$3436	$.0^3$3316	$.0^3$3199	$.0^3$3087	$.0^3$2978	$.0^3$2873	$.0^3$2771
3.1	$.0^3$2673	$.0^3$2577	$.0^3$2485	$.0^3$2396	$.0^3$2311	$.0^3$2227	$.0^3$2147	$.0^3$2070	$.0^3$1995	$.0^3$1922
3.2	$.0^3$1852	$.0^3$1785	$.0^3$1720	$.0^3$1657	$.0^3$1596	$.0^3$1537	$.0^3$1480	$.0^3$1426	$.0^3$1373	$.0^3$1322
3.3	$.0^3$1273	$.0^3$1225	$.0^3$1179	$.0^3$1135	$.0^3$1093	$.0^3$1051	$.0^3$1012	$.0^4$9734	$.0^4$9365	$.0^4$9009
3.4	$.0^4$8666	$.0^4$8335	$.0^4$8016	$.0^4$7709	$.0^4$7413	$.0^4$7127	$.0^4$6852	$.0^4$6587	$.0^4$6331	$.0^4$6085
3.5	$.0^4$5848	$.0^4$5620	$.0^4$5400	$.0^4$5188	$.0^4$4984	$.0^4$4788	$.0^4$4599	$.0^4$4417	$.0^4$4242	$.0^4$4073
3.6	$.0^4$3911	$.0^4$3755	$.0^4$3605	$.0^4$3460	$.0^4$3321	$.0^4$3188	$.0^4$3059	$.0^4$2935	$.0^4$2816	$.0^4$2702
3.7	$.0^4$2592	$.0^4$2486	$.0^4$2385	$.0^4$2287	$.0^4$2193	$.0^4$2103	$.0^4$2016	$.0^4$1933	$.0^4$1853	$.0^4$1776
3.8	$.0^4$1702	$.0^4$1632	$.0^4$1563	$.0^4$1498	$.0^4$1435	$.0^4$1375	$.0^4$1317	$.0^4$1262	$.0^4$1208	$.0^4$1157
3.9	$.0^4$1108	$.0^4$1061	$.0^4$1016	$.0^5$9723	$.0^5$9307	$.0^5$8908	$.0^5$8525	$.0^5$8158	$.0^5$7806	$.0^5$7469
4.0	$.0^5$7145	$.0^5$6835	$.0^5$6538	$.0^5$6253	$.0^5$5980	$.0^5$5718	$.0^5$5468	$.0^5$5227	$.0^5$4997	$.0^5$4777
4.1	$.0^5$4566	$.0^5$4364	$.0^5$4170	$.0^5$3985	$.0^5$3807	$.0^5$3637	$.0^5$3475	$.0^5$3319	$.0^5$3170	$.0^5$3027
4.2	$.0^5$2891	$.0^5$2760	$.0^5$2635	$.0^5$2516	$.0^5$2402	$.0^5$2292	$.0^5$2188	$.0^5$2088	$.0^5$1992	$.0^5$1901
4.3	$.0^5$1814	$.0^5$1730	$.0^5$1650	$.0^5$1574	$.0^5$1501	$.0^5$1431	$.0^5$1365	$.0^5$1301	$.0^5$1241	$.0^5$1183
4.4	$.0^5$1127	$.0^5$1074	$.0^5$1024	$.0^6$9756	$.0^6$9296	$.0^6$8857	$.0^6$8437	$.0^6$8037	$.0^6$7655	$.0^6$7290
4.5	$.0^6$6942	$.0^6$6610	$.0^6$6294	$.0^6$5992	$.0^6$5704	$.0^6$5429	$.0^6$5167	$.0^6$4917	$.0^6$4679	$.0^6$4452
4.6	$.0^6$4236	$.0^6$4029	$.0^6$3833	$.0^6$3645	$.0^6$3467	$.0^6$3297	$.0^6$3135	$.0^6$2981	$.0^6$2834	$.0^6$2694
4.7	$.0^6$2560	$.0^6$2433	$.0^6$2313	$.0^6$2197	$.0^6$2088	$.0^6$1984	$.0^6$1884	$.0^6$1790	$.0^6$1700	$.0^6$1615
4.8	$.0^6$1533	$.0^6$1456	$.0^6$1382	$.0^6$1312	$.0^6$1246	$.0^6$1182	$.0^6$1122	$.0^6$1065	$.0^6$1011	$.0^7$9588
4.9	$.0^7$9096	$.0^7$8629	$.0^7$8185	$.0^7$7763	$.0^7$7362	$.0^7$6982	$.0^7$6620	$.0^7$6276	$.0^7$5950	$.0^7$5640

Example of table notation: $.0^4$5848 = .00005848.

Source: Robert O. Schlaifer, *"Introduction to Statistics for Business Decisions"* (New York: McGraw-Hill Book Company, 1961).

APPENDIX FOUR

Values of $e^{-\lambda}$ for Computing Poisson Probabilities

λ	$e^{-\lambda}$	λ	$e^{-\lambda}$	λ	$e^{-\lambda}$	λ	$e^{-\lambda}$
0.1	0.90484	2.6	0.07427	5.1	0.00610	7.6	0.00050
0.2	0.81873	2.7	0.06721	5.2	0.00552	7.7	0.00045
0.3	0.74082	2.8	0.06081	5.3	0.00499	7.8	0.00041
0.4	0.67032	2.9	0.05502	5.4	0.00452	7.9	0.00037
0.5	0.60653	3.0	0.04979	5.5	0.00409	8.0	0.00034
0.6	0.54881	3.1	0.04505	5.6	0.00370	8.1	0.00030
0.7	0.49659	3.2	0.04076	5.7	0.00335	8.2	0.00027
0.8	0.44933	3.3	0.03688	5.8	0.00303	8.3	0.00025
0.9	0.40657	3.4	0.03337	5.9	0.00274	8.4	0.00022
1.0	0.36788	3.5	0.03020	6.0	0.00248	8.5	0.00020
1.1	0.33287	3.6	0.02732	6.1	0.00224	8.6	0.00018
1.2	0.30119	3.7	0.02472	6.2	0.00203	8.7	0.00017
1.3	0.27253	3.8	0.02237	6.3	0.00184	8.8	0.00015
1.4	0.24660	3.9	0.02024	6.4	0.00166	8.9	0.00014
1.5	0.22313	4.0	0.01832	6.5	0.00150	9.0	0.00012
1.6	0.20190	4.1	0.01657	6.6	0.00136	9.1	0.00011
1.7	0.18268	4.2	0.01500	6.7	0.00123	9.2	0.00010
1.8	0.16530	4.3	0.01357	6.8	0.00111	9.3	0.00009
1.9	0.14957	4.4	0.01228	6.9	0.00101	9.4	0.00008
2.0	0.13534	4.5	0.01111	7.0	0.00091	9.5	0.00007
2.1	0.12246	4.6	0.01005	7.1	0.00083	9.6	0.00007
2.2	0.11080	4.7	0.00910	7.2	0.00075	9.7	0.00006
2.3	0.10026	4.8	0.00823	7.3	0.00068	9.8	0.00006
2.4	0.09072	4.9	0.00745	7.4	0.00061	9.9	0.00005
2.5	0.08208	5.0	0.00674	7.5	0.00055	10.0	0.00005

APPENDIX FIVE   Values of P_0

Probability of zero units in the system (P_0)

$\dfrac{\lambda}{k\mu}$	Number of Channels (k)									
	1	2	3	4	5	6	7	8	9	10
.02	.98000	.96078	.94176	.92312	.90484	.88692	.86936	.85214	.83527	.81873
.04	.96000	.92308	.88692	.85214	.81873	.78663	.75578	.72615	.69768	.67032
.06	.94000	.88679	.83526	.78663	.74082	.69768	.65705	.61878	.58275	.54881
.08	.92000	.85185	.78659	.72614	.67032	.61878	.57121	.52729	.48675	.44933
.10	.90000	.81818	.74074	.67031	.60653	.54881	.49659	.44933	.40657	.36788
.12	.88000	.78571	.69753	.61876	.54881	.48675	.43171	.38289	.33960	.30119
.14	.86000	.75439	.65679	.57116	.49657	.43171	.37531	.32628	.28365	.24660
.16	.84000	.72414	.61837	.52720	.44931	.38289	.32628	.27804	.23693	.20190
.18	.82000	.69492	.58214	.48660	.40653	.33959	.28365	.23693	.19790	.16530
.20	.80000	.66667	.54795	.44910	.36782	.30118	.24659	.20189	.16530	.13534
.22	.78000	.63934	.51567	.41445	.33277	.26711	.21437	.17204	.13807	.11080
.24	.76000	.61290	.48519	.38244	.30105	.23688	.18636	.14660	.11532	.09072
.26	.74000	.58730	.45640	.35284	.27233	.21007	.16200	.12492	.09632	.07427
.28	.72000	.56250	.42918	.32548	.24633	.18628	.14082	.10645	.08045	.06081
.30	.70000	.53846	.40346	.30017	.22277	.16517	.12241	.09070	.06720	.04978
.32	.68000	.51515	.37913	.27676	.20144	.14644	.10639	.07728	.05612	.04076
.34	.66000	.49254	.35610	.25510	.18211	.12981	.09247	.06584	.04687	.03337
.36	.64000	.47059	.33431	.23505	.16460	.11505	.08035	.05609	.03915	.02732
.38	.62000	.44928	.31367	.21649	.14872	.10195	.06981	.04778	.03269	.02236
.40	.60000	.42857	.29412	.19929	.13433	.09032	.06064	.04069	.02729	.01830
.42	.58000	.40845	.27559	.18336	.12128	.07998	.05267	.03465	.02279	.01498
.44	.56000	.38889	.25802	.16860	.10944	.07080	.04573	.02950	.01902	.01226
.46	.54000	.36986	.24135	.15491	.09870	.06265	.03968	.02511	.01587	.01003
.48	.52000	.35135	.22554	.14221	.08895	.05540	.03442	.02136	.01324	.00820
.50	.50000	.33333	.21053	.13043	.08010	.04896	.02984	.01816	.01104	.00671

Probability of zero units in the system (P_0) (continued)

$\dfrac{\lambda}{k\mu}$	Number of Channels (k)									
	1	2	3	4	5	6	7	8	9	10
.52	.48000	.31579	.19627	.11951	.07207	.04323	.02586	.01544	.00920	.00548
.54	.46000	.29870	.18273	.10936	.06477	.03814	.02239	.01311	.00767	.00448
.56	.44000	.28205	.16986	.09994	.05814	.03362	.01936	.01113	.00638	.00366
.58	.42000	.26582	.15762	.09119	.05212	.02959	.01673	.00943	.00531	.00298
.60	.40000	.25000	.14599	.08306	.04665	.02601	.01443	.00799	.00441	.00243
.62	.38000	.23457	.13491	.07750	.04167	.02282	.01243	.00675	.00366	.00198
.64	.36000	.21951	.12438	.06847	.03715	.01999	.01069	.00570	.00303	.00161
.66	.34000	.20482	.11435	.06194	.03304	.01746	.00918	.00480	.00251	.00131
.68	.32000	.19048	.10479	.05587	.02930	.01522	.00786	.00404	.00207	.00106
.70	.30000	.17647	.09569	.05021	.02590	.01322	.00670	.00338	.00170	.00085
.72	.28000	.16279	.08702	.04495	.02280	.01144	.00570	.00283	.00140	.00069
.74	.26000	.14943	.07875	.04006	.01999	.00986	.00483	.00235	.00114	.00055
.76	.24000	.13636	.07087	.03550	.01743	.00846	.00407	.00195	.00093	.00044
.78	.22000	.12360	.06335	.03125	.01510	.00721	.00341	.00160	.00075	.00035
.80	.20000	.11111	.05618	.02730	.01299	.00610	.00284	.00131	.00060	.00028
.82	.18000	.09890	.04933	.02362	.01106	.00511	.00234	.00106	.00048	.00022
.84	.16000	.08696	.04280	.02019	.00931	.00423	.00190	.00085	.00038	.00017
.86	.14000	.07527	.03656	.01700	.00772	.00345	.00153	.00067	.00029	.00013
.88	.12000	.06383	.03060	.01403	.00627	.00276	.00120	.00052	.00022	.00010
.90	.10000	.05263	.02491	.01126	.00496	.00215	.00092	.00039	.00017	.00007
.92	.08000	.04167	.01947	.00867	.00377	.00161	.00068	.00028	.00012	.00005
.94	.06000	.03093	.01427	.00627	.00268	.00113	.00047	.00019	.00008	.00003
.96	.04000	.02041	.00930	.00403	.00170	.00070	.00029	.00012	.00005	.00002
.98	.02000	.01010	.00454	.00194	.00081	.00033	.00013	.00005	.00002	.00001

APPENDIX SIX

Random Numbers Table (2500 Random Digits)

2500 Random digits

1581922396	2068577984	8262130892	8374856049	4637567488
0928105582	7295088579	9586111652	7055508767	6472382934
4112077556	3440672486	1882412963	0684012006	0933147914
7457477468	5435810788	9670852913	1291265730	4890031305
0099520858	3090908872	2039593181	5973470495	9776135501
7245174840	2275698645	8416549348	4676463101	2229367983
6749420382	4832630032	5670984959	5432114610	2966095680
5503161011	7413686599	1198757695	0414294470	0140121598
7164238934	7666127259	5263097712	5133648980	4011966963
3593969525	0272759769	0385998136	9999089966	7544056852
4192054466	0700014629	5169439659	8408705169	1074373131
9697426117	6488888550	4031652526	8123543276	0927534537
2007950579	9564268448	3457416988	1531027886	7016633739
4584768758	2389278610	3859431781	3643768456	4141314518
3840145867	9120831830	7228567652	1267173884	4020651657
0190453442	4800088084	1165628559	5407921254	3768932478
6766554338	5585265145	5089052204	9780623691	2195448096
6315116284	9172824179	5544814339	0016943666	3828538786
3908771938	4035554324	0840126299	4942059208	1475623997
5570024586	9324732596	1186563397	4425143189	3216653251
2999997185	0135968938	7678931194	1351031403	6002561840
7864375912	8383232768	1892857070	2323673751	3188881718
7065492027	6349104233	3382569662	4579426926	1513082455
0654683246	4765104877	8149224168	5468631609	6474393896
7830555058	5255147182	3519287786	2481675649	8907598697
7626984369	4725370390	9641916289	5049082870	7463807244
4785048453	3646121751	8436077768	2928794356	9956043516
4627791048	5765558107	8762592043	6185670830	6363845920
9376470693	0441608934	8749472723	2202271078	5897002653
1227991661	7936797054	9527542791	4711871173	8300978148
5582095589	5535798279	4764439855	6279247618	4446895088
4959397698	1056981450	8416606706	8234013222	6426813469
1824779358	1333750468	9434074212	5273692238	5902177065
7041092295	5726289716	3420847871	1820481234	0318831723
3555104281	0903099163	6827824899	6383872737	5901682626

2500 Random digits (*continued*)

9717595534	1634107293	8521057472	1471300754	3044151557
5571564123	7344613447	1129117244	3208461091	1699403490
4674262892	2809456764	5806554509	8224980942	5738031833
8461228715	0746980892	9285305274	6331989646	8764467686
1838538678	3049068967	6955157269	5482964330	2161984904
1834182305	6203476893	5937802079	3445280195	3694915658
1884227732	2923727501	8044389132	4611203081	6072112445
6791857341	6696243386	2219599137	3193884236	8224729718
3007929946	4031562749	5570757297	6273785046	1455349704
6085440624	2875556938	5496629750	4841817356	1443167141
7005051056	3496332071	5054070890	7303867953	6255181190
9846413446	8306646692	0661684251	8875127201	6251533454
0625457703	4229164694	7321363715	7051128285	1108468072
5457593922	9751489574	1799906380	1989141062	5595364247
4076486653	8950826528	4934582003	4071187742	1456207629

Source: Dudley J. Cowden and Mercedes S. Cowden, *Practical Problems in Business Statistics,* 2d ed., © 1963, by permission of Prentice-Hall, Inc., Englewood Cliffs, N.J.

APPENDIX SEVEN

Derivation of EOQ Formulas

 Chapter 6

Page 257

Total cost:

$$TC = N_0 P + \frac{AC}{2N_0}$$

$$\frac{dTC}{dN_0} = P - \frac{AC}{2N_0{}^2}$$

Setting the first derivative equal to zero and solving for N_0,

$$P - \frac{AC}{2N_0{}^2} = 0$$

$$P = \frac{AC}{2N_0{}^2}$$

$$2N_0{}^2 P = AC$$

$$N_0{}^2 = \frac{AC}{2P}$$

$$N_0 = \sqrt{\frac{AC}{2P}} \qquad\qquad (6\text{-}1)$$

Total cost:
$$TC = \frac{UP}{N_u} + \frac{RCN_u}{2}\left(1 - \frac{y}{x}\right)$$

$$\frac{dTC}{dN_u} = \frac{-UP}{N_u{}^2} + \frac{RC}{2}\left(1 - \frac{y}{x}\right)$$

Setting the first derivative equal to zero and solving for N_u,

$$\frac{-UP}{N_u{}^2} + \frac{RC}{2}\left(1 - \frac{y}{x}\right) = 0$$

$$\frac{RC}{2}\left(1 - \frac{y}{x}\right) = \frac{UP}{N_u{}^2}$$

$$\frac{N_u{}^2 RC}{2}\left(1 - \frac{y}{x}\right) = UP$$

$$N_u{}^2 = \frac{2UP}{RC(1 - y/x)}$$

$$N_u = \sqrt{\frac{2UP}{RC(1 - y/x)}} \tag{6-5}$$

APPENDIX EIGHT

Functional List of Text Exercises

This appendix lists all the exercises in the text according to the functional area of the organization to which they apply (e.g., accounting, finance, marketing, organizational behavior, production, etc.). Problems which apply to not-for-profit organizations (e.g., education, government, and public and social services) are also arranged under those categories.

To find a linear programming application in marketing, for example, look in the marketing category for problem numbers beginning with the chapter number 8 (Linear Programming I), 9 (Linear Programming II), or 10 (Linear Programming III).

Similarly, to find a not-for-profit example of the use of waiting lines, look under the not-for-profit headings for problems beginning with the chapter number 14 (Waiting Lines). Where appropriate, exercises have been cross-listed.

An annotated list of chapter titles for those chapters which have exercises follows:

2 A Review of Probability Concepts Introduction to probability; basic probability concepts; three types of probabilities; probability rules; probabilities under statistical independence; probabilities under statistical dependence; revising prior estimates of probabilities (Bayes' theorem); the concept of probability distributions; random variables; the binomial distribution; the Poisson distribution; the exponential distribution; the normal distribution.

3 Forecasting Introduction; judgmental forecasting; time-series patterns; evaluating forecast accuracy; moving averages; simple exponential smoothing; time-series regression; smoothing linear trends; smoothing nonlinear trends; decomposition of seasonal data; forecasting with the PC.

4 Decision Making Using Probabilities I Introduction to decision making; steps in decision making; different environments in which decisions are made; criteria for decision making under uncertainty; decision making under conditions of risk; using the expected value criterion with continuously distributed random variables; supplying the numbers; combining experience and numbers; utility as a decision criterion.

5 Decision Making Using Probabilities II The normal probability distribution and cost-volume-profit analysis; combining unit monetary values and probability distributions; replacement analysis (items which fail over time); decision trees; decision making with an active opponent.

6 Inventory I: Order Quantity Models What functions does inventory perform; inventory decisions; selective approach to managing inventory; economic order quantity; how to eliminate the instantaneous receipt assumption in EOQ models; using EOQ models when annual demand cannot be forecast; using EOQ models when cost information is not available; applying the EOQ model to production processes; some conclusions about EOQ models.

7 Inventory II: Reordering, Backorders, Discounts, Material Requirements Planning Deciding when to buy; how to determine the optimal level of safety stock when out-of-stock costs are known; setting safety stock levels when out-of-stock costs are not known; joint ordering; reordering with planned stockouts; how to evaluate quantity discounts offered by suppliers; material requirements planning (MRP).

8 Linear Programming I: Solution Methods Introduction to linear programming; graphic method to solve linear programs; some technical issues in linear programming; using the computer to solve linear programs.

9 Linear Programming II: The Simplex Method Setting up the initial solution; developing the second solution; developing the third solution; justification and significance of all elements in the simplex tableau; minimization problems and equal-to and greater-than-or-equal-to constraints; some technical issues in the simplex method.

10 Linear Programming III: Building LP Models and Interpreting Solutions Building models; the dual in linear programming; shadow prices and reduced costs; right-hand-side and objective ranging; pricing out new variables; sensitivity analysis with the simplex algorithm; linear programming applications.

11 Specially Structured Linear Programs: Transportation and Assignment Problems The transportation problem (demand equals supply); the transportation problem (demand does not equal supply); degeneracy; the assignment problem; solving maximization problems with the transportation and assignment methods.

12 Networks PERT (program evaluation and review technique); CPM (critical path method); PERT/Cost; network scheduling with resource limitations; the maximal-flow problem; the minimal-spanning-tree problem; the shortest-route problem; dynamic programming.

13 Integer Programming, Branch-And-Bound Method, Goal Programming, Heuristics Integer programming; branch-and-bound method; goal programming; heuristics.

14 Waiting Lines Introductory queuing ideas; queuing objectives and cost behavior; standard language and definitions for waiting lines; elementary queuing system: constant arrival and service times; single-channel queuing model: Poisson distributed arrivals and exponentially distributed service times; single-channel queuing model: Poisson distributed arrivals and any service time distribution; single-channel queuing model: Poisson distributed arrivals, exponentially distributed service times, and finite waiting capacity; multiple-channel queuing model: Poisson distributed arrivals and exponentially distributed service times; the limitations of queuing theory; simulation of a queuing system; comparing the simulation solution with a formula solution.

15 Simulation Introduction; simulation in practice; a hand-computed simulation; computer simulation; using heuristics in simulation.

16 Markov Analysis Introduction to brand-switching analysis; a matrix algebra primer; prediction of market shares for future periods; equilibrium conditions; use of Markov analysis in marketing strategy; other uses of Markov analysis.

ANSWERS TO THE CHAPTER CONCEPTS QUIZZES

Chapter 1

1-1 **F**	1-11 **T**	1-21 **c**
1-2 **F**	1-12 **F**	1-22 **b**
1-3 **T**	1-13 **F**	1-23 **d**
1-4 **F**	1-14 **T**	1-24 **b**
1-5 **F**	1-15 **T**	1-25 **a**
1-6 **F**	1-16 **d**	1-26 **d**
1-7 **T**	1-17 **e**	1-27 **a**
1-8 **F**	1-18 **d**	1-28 **d**
1-9 **F**	1-19 **a, b, d, g**	1-29 **d**
1-10 **F**	1-20 **c**	1-30 **c**

1-31 **a** batch processing **b** real-time processing **c** online processing **d** timesharing

1-32 **a** imagination **b** flexibility **c** memory **d** inconsistency

1-33 **a** cannot learn deductively **b** react consistently **c** never forget **d** does only what its programmers tell it to do

1-34 **a** report generators **b** what-if systems

1-35 **a** They integrate the decision maker, the data base, the quantitative models being used. **b** Require a very comprehensive data base together with the ability to manage that data base.

1-36 **a** The problem is complex. **b** The problem is repetitive. **c** A solution cannot be developed without using quantitative tools. **d** They don't know what to do and are attracted by new tools they don't understand.

1-37 **a** problem knowledge **b** a definition of the problem **c** a model **d** appropriate inputs **e** a solution **f** an accepted solution

1-38 **a** qualitative **b** quantitative

1-39 **a** purchasing inventory **b** carrying inventory **c** stocking out

1-40 **a** medical diagnosis **b** bidding strategy **c** personnel assignment **d** transportation scheduling **e** determination of interest rates **f** product mix **g** purchasing **h** vendor selection

Chapter 2

2-1 the sample space; events
2-2 dependent; $P(A|B)$
2-3 posterior; $P(A|B)$; prior
2-4 probability distribution
2-5 expected value; mean
2-6 subjective; relative frequency
2-7 marginal; both/and
2-8 discrete; continuous
2-9 standard deviation
2-10 successes; Bernoulli process

2-11 **T**	2-21 **T**	2-31 **c**
2-12 **F**	2-22 **F**	2-32 **a**
2-13 **T**	2-23 **T**	2-33 **d**
2-14 **T**	2-24 **F**	2-34 **b**
2-15 **F**	2-25 **F**	2-35 **c**
2-16 **F**	2-26 **c**	2-36 **a**
2-17 **T**	2-27 **d**	2-37 **b**
2-18 **T**	2-28 **a**	2-38 **c**
2-19 **T**	2-29 **d**	2-39 **d**
2-20 **T**	2-30 **d**	2-40 **a**

Chapter 3

3-1	naive	3-11	F	3-21	T	3-31	b
3-2	conservatism	3-12	T	3-22	F	3-32	d
3-3	number; periods; weights	3-13	F	3-23	T	3-33	a
3-4	intercept	3-14	F	3-24	F	3-34	c
3-5	$N-7$	3-15	T	3-25	T	3-35	d
3-6	extrapolation, causal, judgmental	3-16	F	3-26	d	3-36	a
3-7	time series methods	3-17	F	3-27	b	3-37	d
3-8	trend line analysis	3-18	T	3-28	c	3-38	a
3-9	forecast profiles	3-19	F	3-29	d	3-39	d
3-10	mean absolute deviation, mean absolute percentage error, mean square error	3-20	F	3-30	a	3-40	c

Chapter 4

4-1	payoff table; profit; loss	4-11	F	4-21	F	4-31	b
4-2	opportunity losses	4-12	T	4-22	T	4-32	a
4-3	optimistic; largest	4-13	F	4-23	T	4-33	d
4-4	expected profit; expected loss	4-14	T	4-24	T	4-34	d
4-5	rationality; $1/n$	4-15	F	4-25	F	4-35	a
4-6	states of nature	4-16	T	4-26	b	4-36	c
4-7	risk	4-17	T	4-27	d	4-37	d
4-8	expected value of perfect information	4-18	T	4-28	d	4-38	b
4-8	expected marginal profit	4-19	F	4-29	a	4-39	a
4-10	utility	4-20	T	4-30	c	4-40	d

Chapter 5

5-1	fixed; variable	5-11	F	5-21	F	5-31	b
5-2	breakeven point	5-12	F	5-22	T	5-32	d
5-3	state of nature; decision	5-13	T	5-23	F	5-33	a
5-4	rollback or feedback	5-14	F	5-24	T	5-34	d
5-5	pure; mixed	5-15	T	5-25	F	5-35	a
5-6	value of the game	5-16	T	5-26	c	5-36	d
5-7	dominance	5-17	T	5-27	c	5-37	b
5-8	replacement analysis	5-18	T	5-28	d	5-38	b
5-9	expected value of sample information	5-19	T	5-29	a	5-39	a
5-10	unit normal loss integral	5-20	F	5-30	a	5-40	d

Chapter 6

6-1	type A; type C	6-11	F	6-21	T	6-31	d
6-2	carrying; ordering	6-12	F	6-22	F	6-32	a
6-3	order quantity; total annual	6-13	T	6-23	F	6-33	a
6-4	A; N_0; dollars	6-14	T	6-24	T	6-34	d
6-5	setup; production lot size	6-15	T	6-25	F	6-35	c
6-6	holding	6-16	F	6-26	d	6-36	a
6-7	annual ordering costs	6-17	T	6-27	c	6-37	d
6-8	setup	6-18	F	6-28	d	6-38	b
6-9	the square root of X	6-19	T	6-29	d	6-39	b
6-10	half the maximum level	6-20	T	6-30	b	6-40	d

Chapter 7

7-1	lead time; lead time demand	7-11	T	7-21	F	7-31	b
7-2	external; internal	7-12	T	7-22	F	7-32	a
7-3	fixed review interval; fixed reorder point	7-13	F	7-23	F	7-33	d
7-4	service level	7-14	F	7-24	F	7-34	c
7-5	trigger; line item	7-15	T	7-25	T	7-35	c
7-6	reorder point	7-16	F	7-26	d	7-36	a
7-7	safety stock	7-17	F	7-27	a	7-37	d
7-8	header; line items	7-18	F	7-28	b	7-38	b
7-9	backorder	7-19	F	7-29	d	7-39	d
7-10	Material Requirements Planning	7-20	T	7-30	d	7-40	a

Chapter 8

8-1	limited resources; objective	8-11	T	8-21	T	8-31	c
8-2	objective function; constraints	8-12	T	8-22	T	8-32	d
8-3	feasible region; infeasible	8-13	F	8-23	F	8-33	d
8-4	non-negativity; structural	8-14	T	8-24	T	8-34	b
8-5	redundant; does not	8-15	F	8-25	T	8-35	c
8-6	linearly	8-16	F	8-26	c	8-36	d
8-7	equation; inequality	8-17	T	8-27	d	8-37	b
8-8	parallel	8-18	F	8-28	a	8-38	a
8-9	an extreme point (or corner)	8-19	T	8-29	b	8-39	d
8-10	contribution	8-20	F	8-30	a	8-40	d

Chapter 9

9-1	degenerate; cycling	9-11	T	9-21	F	9-31	a
9-2	artificial; large negative	9-12	F	9-22	F	9-32	d
9-3	product mix; quantity	9-13	T	9-23	F	9-33	d
9-4	iterative; iteration; improved	9-14	F	9-24	T	9-34	b
9-5	C_j; $C_j - Z_j$; optimal	9-15	T	9-25	F	9-35	a
9-6	Z_j; quantity	9-16	T	9-26	b	9-36	b
9-7	replaced	9-17	F	9-27	a	9-37	b
9-8	infeasible	9-18	T	9-28	c	9-38	b
9-9	optimal	9-19	F	9-29	b	9-39	b
9-10	replaced; smallest; optimal; degenerate	9-20	F	9-30	e	9-40	a

Chapter 10

10-1	dual; primal; minimization	10-11	T	10-21	T	10-31	d
10-2	sensitivity; right-hand-side ranging	10-12	F	10-22	T	10-32	b
10-3	shadow prices; right-hand sides	10-13	F	10-23	F	10-33	c
10-4	principle of complementary slackness	10-14	F	10-24	T	10-34	c
10-5	change vectors; validity range; shadow price	10-15	T	10-25	F	10-35	d
		10-16	F	10-26	d	10-36	d
10-6	n; m	10-17	T	10-27	d	10-37	a
10-7	pricing out	10-18	F	10-28	b	10-38	e
10-8	upper boundary; blocking	10-19	T	10-29	a	10-39	c
10-9	entering; optimality	10-20	F	10-30	b	10-40	b
10-10	modelling (or model building); model						

Chapter 11

11-1	row; column	11-11	F	11-21	T	11-31	a
11-2	stepping stone; MODI	11-12	F	11-22	T	11-32	b
11-3	improvement index; negative	11-13	F	11-23	T	11-33	c
11-4	assignment; Hungarian; Flood's	11-14	T	11-24	T	11-34	d
11-5	job opportunity; 0	11-15	F	11-25	T	11-35	b
11-6	network flow problems	11-16	T	11-26	b	11-36	a
11-7	northwest corner rule	11-17	T	11-27	c	11-37	c
11-8	nodes; arcs	11-18	T	11-28	d	11-38	a
11-9	non-negative	11-19	T	11-29	d	11-39	b
11-10	stone; unused	11-20	F	11-30	a	11-40	c

Chapter 12

12-1	optimistic time; likely time; pessimistic time	12-11	T	12-21	T	12-31	b
12-2	predecessor; immediate predecessors	12-12	F	12-22	T	12-32	a
12-3	critical path; lower	12-13	T	12-23	F	12-33	d
12-4	normal; crash; less	12-14	F	12-24	F	12-34	b
12-5	stages	12-15	T	12-25	T	12-35	d
12-6	minimal-spanning tree	12-16	T	12-26	d	12-36	d
12-7	maximal-flow	12-17	T	12-27	d	12-37	b
12-8	heuristic	12-18	T	12-28	d	12-38	b
12-9	beta	12-19	T	12-29	c	12-39	a
12-10	event	12-20	F	12-30	a	12-40	d

Chapter 13

13-1	Integer; goal	13-11	F	13-21	T	13-31	b
13-2	cut	13-12	T	13-22	F	13-32	a
13-3	branch-and-bound	13-13	T	13-23	T	13-33	c
13-4	underachieved; overachieved	13-14	T	13-24	T	13-34	a
13-5	heuristic	13-15	T	13-25	T	13-35	a
13-6	enumeration	13-16	F	13-26	d	13-36	a
13-7	preemptive priority factors	13-17	T	13-27	a	13-37	d
13-8	myopic	13-18	F	13-28	c	13-38	a
13-9	opportunity costs	13-19	T	13-29	a	13-39	b
13-10	deviations from targets	13-20	F	13-30	b	13-40	d

Chapter 14

14-1	mean arrival rate	14-11	T	14-21	T	14-31	b
14-2	W_s	14-12	T	14-22	F	14-32	a
14-3	independent	14-13	F	14-23	T	14-33	d
14-4	decreases	14-14	T	14-24	F	14-34	d
14-5	arrival rate	14-15	F	14-25	F	14-35	b
14-6	infinite or finite	14-16	F	14-26	b	14-36	b
14-7	Poisson	14-17	F	14-27	c	14-37	d
14-8	reneging; balking	14-18	T	14-28	d	14-38	a
14-9	priority; first-come, first-served	14-19	T	14-29	a	14-39	d
14-10	utilization factor	14-20	F	14-30	c	14-40	d

Chapter 15

Chapter 16

BIBLIOGRAPHY

INTRODUCTION TO MS/OR

ALTER, STEVEN, *Decision Support Systems: Current Practices and Continuing Challenges* (Reading, MA: Addison-Wesley, 1980).

HILLIER, F., and G. J. LIEBERMAN, *Introduction to Operations Research*, 4th ed. (San Francisco: Holden-Day, 1986).

KEEN, PETER F., and MICHAEL S. SCOTT-MORTON, *Decision Support Systems: An Organizational Perspective* (Reading, MA: Addison-Wesley, 1978).

MARKLAND, ROBERT E., *Topics in Management Science* (New York: John Wiley and Sons, 1983).

TRUEMAN, RICHARD E., *An Introduction to Quantitative Methods for Decision Making* (New York: Holt, Rinehart and Winston, 1981).

PROBABILITY REVIEW

LEVIN, RICHARD I., *Statistics For Management*, 4th ed. (Englewood Cliffs, NJ: Prentice-Hall, 1987).

LEVIN, RICHARD I., and D. S. RUBIN, *A Short Course in Business Statistics* (Englewood Cliffs, NJ: Prentice-Hall, 1982).

FORECASTING

ABRAHAM, B., and J. LEDOLTER, *Statistical Methods for Forecasting* (New York: John Wiley and Sons, 1983).

ARMSTRONG, J., *Long Range Forecasting*, rev. ed. (New York: John Wiley and Sons, 1985).

GARDNER, E. S., "Exponential Smoothing: The State of the Art," *Journal of Forecasting*, vol. 4. no. 1 (1985).

MAKRIDAKIS, S., S. WHEELWRIGHT, and V. McGEE, *Forecasting: Methods and Applications*, 2d ed. (New York: John Wiley and Sons, 1983).

MENTZER, J. T., and J. E. COX, "Familiarity, Application, and Performance of Sales Forecasting Techniques," *Journal of Forecasting*, vol. 3 (1984).

THOMOPOULOS, N. T., *Applied Forecasting Methods* (Englewood Cliffs, NJ: Prentice-Hall, Inc., 1980).

DECISION MAKING USING PROBABILITIES

BEHN, R. D., and J. W. VAUPEL, *Quick Analysis for Decision Makers* (New York: Basic Books, Inc., 1982).

BUNN, D., *Applied Decision Analysis* (New York: McGraw-Hill, 1984).

SAATY, T. L., *The Analytic Hierarchy Process* (New York: McGraw-Hill, 1980).

SAATY, T. L., *Decision Making for Leaders* (Belmont, California: Basic Books, Inc., 1982).

▮ INVENTORY

BROWN, R. C., *Decision Rules for Inventory Management* (New York: Holt, Rinehart and Winston, 1970).

HADLEY, G., and T. M. WHITIN, *Analysis of Inventory Systems* (Englewood Cliffs, NJ: Prentice-Hall, 1963).

PETERSON, REIN, and EDWARD A. SILVER, *Decision Systems for Inventory Management and Production Planning*, 2nd ed. (New York: John Wiley and Sons, 1985).

TERSINE, RICHARD J., *Principles of Inventory and Materials Management*, 2nd ed. (New York: North Holland, 1982).

▮ LINEAR PROGRAMMING AND ALLIED TOPICS

CHVATAL, V., *Linear Programming* (San Francisco: Freeman, 1983).

HILLIER, F., and G. J. LIEBERMAN, *Introduction To Operations Research*, 4th ed. (San Francisco: Holden Day, 1986).

IGNIZIO, J. P., *Goal Programming and Extensions* (Lexington, MA: Lexington Books, 1976).

SALKIN, HARVEY M., *Integer Programming* (Reading, MA: Addison-Wesley, 1975).

SCHRAGE, LINUS E., *Linear, Integer, and Quadratic Programming with LINDO*, (Palo Alto, CA: Scientific Press, 1984).

▮ TRANSPORTATION, ASSIGNMENT, AND OTHER NETWORK PROBLEMS

ELMAGHRABY, S. E., *Activity Networks: Project Planning and Control by Network Methods* (New York: John Wiley and Sons, 1977).

HAX, A., and D. CANDEA, *Production and Inventory Management* (Englewood Cliffs, NJ: Prentice-Hall, 1984).

MODER, JOSEPH J., CECIL R. PHILLIPS, and E. DAVIS, *Project Management with CPM, PERT, and Precedence Diagramming* (New York: Van Nostrand, 1983).

WIEST, J., and F. LEVY, *Management Guide to PERT-CPM*, 2nd ed. (Englewood Cliffs, NJ: Prentice-Hall, 1977).

▮ SIMULATION

CHRISTY, D. P., and H. J. WATSON, "The Application of Simulation: A Survey of Industrial Practice," *Interfaces*, October 1983.

FISHMAN, GEORGE S., *Principles of Discrete Event Simulation* (New York: John Wiley and Sons, 1978).

LAW, AVERILL M., and W. DAVID KELTON, *Simulation Modelling and Analysis* (New York: McGraw-Hill, 1982).

RUBENSTEIN, R. Y., *Simulation and the Monte Carlo Method* (New York: John Wiley and Sons, 1981).

WATSON, H. J., *Computer Simulation in Business* (New York: John Wiley and Sons, 1981).

WAITING LINES

COOPER, R., *Introduction to Queuing Theory*, 2nd ed. (New York: North Holland, 1981).

HEYMAN, D., and M. SOBEL, *Stochastic Models in Operations Research*, vol. 1 (New York: McGraw-Hill, 1984).

HILLIER, F., and O. YU, *Queuing Tables and Graphs* (New York: North Holland, 1981).

SAATY, T., *Elements of Queuing Theory with Applications* (New York: Dover, 1983).

MARKOV ANALYSIS

BHAT, N., *Elements of Applied Stochastic Processes*, 2nd ed. (New York: John Wiley and Sons, 1985).

BESSENT, W., and A. BESSENT, "Student Education Flow in a University Department: Results of a Markov Analysis," *Interfaces*, 1980.

ISAACSON, D., and R. MADSEN, *Markov Chains, Theory and Applications* (New York: John Wiley and Sons, 1976).

FLAMHOLTS, E., G. GEIS, and R. PERLE, "A Markovian Model for the Evaluation of Human Assets Acquired by an Organizational Purchase," *Interfaces*, 1984.

MS/OR: PAST, PRESENT, FUTURE

Individual references are provided in that chapter.

INDEX